This book is dedicated to several very special people:

Above all, to Barbara;

To Dan, Mike, and Susan;

To my mother, father, and Mom.

September, 1994

AGE DISCRIMINATION

SECOND EDITION

Volume 1
Chapters 1-6

Howard C. Eglit
Professor
Illinois Institute of Technology/
Chicago-Kent College of Law

Shepard's/McGraw-Hill, Inc.
P.O. Box 35300
Colorado Springs, Colorado 80935-3530

*The **McGraw-Hill** Companies*
New York • St. Louis • San Francisco • Auckland • Bogotá • Caracas
Colorado Springs • Hamburg • Lisbon • London • Madrid • Mexico
Milan • Montreal • New Delhi • Panama • Paris • San Juan
São Paulo • Singapore • Sydney • Tokyo • Toronto

July, 1995

Information has been obtained by Shepard's/McGraw-Hill, Inc. from sources believed to be reliable. However, because of the possibility of human or mechanical error by our sources, Shepard's/McGraw-Hill, Inc., or others. Shepard's/McGraw-Hill, Inc. does not guarantee the accuracy, adequacy, or completeness of any information and is not responsible for any errors or omissions or for the results obtained from use of such information.

Library of Congress Cataloging-in-Publication Data

Eglit, Howard C.

Age discrimination / Howard C. Eglit —
2nd. ed. p. cm. — (Individual rights series)

Includes index.
ISBN 0-07-172387-0
1. Age discrimination in employment—Law and legislation—United States. I. Series.

KF3465.E38 1994
344.73'01398—dc20
[347.3041398] 94-19880
ISBN: 0-07-172387-0 CIP
Supplement ISBN: 0-07-172393-5

5848/8653

Acknowledgments

I want to thank Lisa Danna Fanella, Marjorie Herceg, Cheryl Sellers, and Tammara Lovett, each of whom is, or was, a student at Chicago-Kent College of Law, and each of whom performed some research and/or technical work on the second edition of *Age Discrimination.* I also appreciate the secretarial work done by Sharon Smith.

I want to note the work of those students who worked on the first edition (and who were specifically identified in the previous edition), and I want to express my appreciation to my colleague, Professor Martin Malin, for his contributions to the first edition. Obviously, without the earlier efforts of these individuals, the production of this new edition would have been considerably more difficult. I appreciate, also, the support provided by the Marshall Ewell Research Fund of Chicago-Kent College of Law.

Finally, I want to thank Keith Angle, the Shepard's/McGraw-Hill senior editor who has suffered through this experience along with me, for his support.

Howard Eglit
Professor of Law
July 15, 1994

Introduction

The Age Discrimination in Employment Act (ADEA), 29 USC §§621-634, is a complicated, convoluted statute, replete with prohibitions, exceptions, definitions, and provisos. That it is not a simple statute to interpret or to apply is hardly surprising, given its subject matter. Discrimination in the workplace of any kind is an issue of complexity and subtlety. Economic factors, moral issues, and concerns involving justice and fairness all come into play. Pragmatism and politics also are involved in determining how decisions are made and actions implemented in the workplace. This complexity is particularly acute in the instance of age bias, since age is a characteristic that all of us possess, and so any one of us may have occasion at one time or another to conclude that our own ages, or the ages of our competitors, colleagues, subordinates, or superiors, have been improperly taken into account in the work setting.

My fundamental conclusion insofar as the ADEA is concerned is that many of the issues that arise in construing and applying its terms do not lend themselves to any manifestly correct readings. There are no clearly discernible legal touchstones, in other words, for ascertaining the *right* answer as to whether an objective or a subjective test ought to be used in constructive discharge settings; or whether claims that are initially addressed in the arbitral forum ought to be susceptible to relitigation in the courtroom; or whether compensatory damages ought to be available under the ADEA or should be barred. Rather, to be pragmatic (or cynical) about all this, it seems to me that the *right* answer turns out to be very much a matter of perspective.

An advocate for employers is going to take a different view of the correct interpretation of a given provision of the ADEA than is an advocate for employees. There is nothing wrong with this; that's the way our adversarial system of justice works, and that's the way our political system works. People have different interests and as long as they pursue them within the bounds of acceptable practice, their efforts are certainly to be condoned and often even encouraged.

What this all means for me is that I am generally reluctant to state, "This is the right interpretation, that is the wrong construction." I am not, nor do I care to be in the context of this book, an advocate either for employees or employers. My goal is not to be didactic but to be informative. To this end, this book sets out (not uniformly, but in most instances) what the law is, rather than what the law ought to be. I hope that it succeeds in my goal of fair exposition. I hope, also, that it is of use to its readers, whatever their perspectives.

One more point. The production of a book such as this takes a tremendous amount of time to produce. The consequence is that there is a considerable lag time between a book's being finished and its appearing in print. Insofar as cases decided by the Supreme Court are concerned, this book is current through August, 1994. The same holds true for any relevant statutory and regulatory changes or additions. Insofar as lower court decisions are concerned, the book is current through June 1, 1993.

Contents

Detailed

Volume 1

3 The Age Discrimination in Employment Act—Who is Protected and Which Entities Must Comply with Its Requirements

Identifying Those Who May Invoke the ADEA's Protection

4 The Age Discrimination in Employment Act—Prohibitions and Requirements

5 The Age Discrimination in Employment Act—Statutory Affirmative Defenses, Regulatory Exemptions, and Waivers of Liability

Employee Benefits and Employee Benefit Plans

Volume 2

7 The ADEA in the Judicial and Arbitral Forums: the Grievant's, Respondent's, and Decision-Maker's Roles

8 The Age Discrimination in Employment Act—Remedies, Fees, and Costs

9 The Age Discrimination in Employment Act: Federal Employees and Job Applicants

Volume 3

10 Employment Discrimination: Constitutional and Other Nonstatutory Parameters at the Federal and State Levels

11 Other Bars to Age Discrimination in Employment: Federal and State Statutes, Executive Orders, and Regulations

Potential Federal Limitations on Employment Discrimination

State Statutes

Appendix A

Appendix B

Appendix C

Appendix D

Appendix E

Equal Employment Opportunity Commission Regulations re Federal Employees, 29 CFR pt 1614 (1993)

Appendix F

29 CFR pt 1613 Appendix A (1993) Policy Statement on Remedies and Relief for Individual Cases of Unlawful Discrimination

Appendix G

Equal Employment Opportunity Commission Interpretations, 29 CFR pt 1625 (1993)

Appendix H

29 CFR §§521.1-521.3 (1993)

Appendix I

29 CFR §541.1 (1993)

Appendix J

Equal Employment Opportunity Commission Regulations, 29 CFR pt 1626 (1993)

Appendix Q

Appendix R

Appendix S

Appendix T

Appendix EE

Appendix FF

Appendix GG

Appendix HH

Age in American Society and in the American Workplace

1

§1.01 The Roles of Age in Structuring Society

However else individuals may differ, we all confront—and inevitably succumb to—the implacable force of time. Each of us, if we elude an early death, will move from childhood to young adulthood, onward to middle age, and thence to the status of being old.

While this universally shared phenomenon of aging can be studied and remarked upon, the ultimate fact is that each facet of the life cycle can only be completely understood by its actually being lived. Thus, a young adult can observe, but cannot fully *know*—in an immediate, personal way—what it is to be middle aged. The 25-year-old and the 45-year-old speak across a chronological chasm that, for the former, will be bridged only by the passage of time. (Of course, by the time the 25-year-old is 20 years older, his or her predecessor likewise will have moved on to a new state of knowledge, forged through experience.)

Malcolm Cowley, the literary critic, wrote of the culmination of this journey into old age in *The View From 80:* "To enter the country of age is a new experience, different from what you supposed it to be. Nobody, man or woman, knows the country until he has lived in it and has taken out his citizenship papers."[1] Simone de Beauvoir, the noted French essayist and social critic, wrote of how ill-prepared each of us is to confront on a personal level being old, notwithstanding that intellectually each of us knows—even when not yet old—what lies ahead:

> Die early or grow old: there is no other alternative. And yet, as Goethe said, 'Age takes hold of us by surprise.' For himself each man is the sole, unique subject, and we are often astonished when the common fate becomes our own. . . . [W]e accept fortuitous accidents readily enough, making them part of our history, because they affect us as unique beings: but old age is the general fact, and when it seizes upon our own personal life we are dumbfounded.[2]

Of course, one does not have to actually experience old, or even middle, age first hand to comprehend in important ways that age is a powerful force not only at the personal, individual level, but that it is so in the context of society at large, as well. "Every known society," it has been observed, "has a named social category of people who are old—chronologically, physiologically, or generationally."[3] And the same authors further note that "[i]n every case these people have different rights, duties, privileges, and burdens from those enjoyed or suffered by their juniors."[4] The American experience reveals no departure from this universal cultural phenomenon: in a number of respects older people in the United States are treated as a distinct subset

---

[1] M. Cowley, The View From 80, at 2-3 (1980) (Penguin Books 1982).

[2] S. de Beauvoir, The Coming of Age 419 (Warner Paperback 1975).

[3] P. Amoss & S. Harrell, *Introduction: An Anthropological Perspective on Aging, in* Other Ways of Growing Old 3 (P. Amoss & S. Harrell eds 1981). *See also* Neugarten, *Age Discrimination and Their Social Functions,* 57 Chi-Kent L Rev 809 (1981); 3 M.W. Riley, M. Johnson & A. Foner, Aging and Society—A Sociology of Age Stratification 402 (1972).

[4] P. Amoss & S. Harrell, *supra* note 3, at 3.

of the population,[5] and age-based differentiations accordingly are utilized in a variety of contexts. Age is used, sometimes in statutory or regulatory provisions, sometimes in private sector entities' policies and rules, and sometimes more informally, for allocating public and private resources, for extending or denying public benefits, for imposing or relaxing legal responsibilities, and for distributing or restricting various types of opportunities.

While old, or older, age often is the fulcrum for decision making, it should be understood that the use of age as a linchpin

---

[5] At the margin, there certainly is ambiguity as to just when one enters the ranks of the *aged*, the *old*, the *elderly*, or whatever other term is used. One of the leading experts in gerontology, Dr. Bernice Neugarten, constructed what is now a generally accepted distinction between the *young-old* and the *old-old*. In an analysis published some years after she first started to articulate this distinction, she wrote (with a co-author) as follows:

> The old distinctions between life periods are blurring in today's society. The clearest evidence for this is the appearance of the young-old. It is a new historical phenomenon that a very large group of retirees and their spouses are healthy and vigorous, relatively well-off financially, well integrated into the lives of their families and communities, and politically active. The term "young-old" has become part of everyday parlance, and it needs little elaboration here other than to point out that the concept was originally based, not on chronological age, but on health and social characteristics. The term represents the social reality that the line between middle age and old age is no longer clear. What was once considered old age is now recognized to be pertinent only to that minority of persons who are the old-old, that particularly vulnerable group in need of special care.

Neugarten & Neugarten, *Changing Meanings of Age in the Aging Society, in* Our Aging Society 33, 35 (A. Pifer & L. Bronte eds 1986).

From the perspective of the largest and most powerful organization claiming to represent the interests of older persons, i.e., the American Association of Retired Persons (AARP), one becomes eligible for membership and for the perquisites of AARP membership upon attainment of age 50. From the perspective of the federal government, one becomes too old to function as a federal law enforcement officer at age 57. 5 USC §8335(b). Also from the perspective of the federal government, one becomes too old to function as a pilot of a commercially operated air carrier at age 60. 14 CFR §121.383(c) (1994). On the other hand, the age at which one becomes old for purposes of full Social Security benefits is slowly inching up towards age 67. 42 USC §416(l)(1). Insofar as the Age Discrimination in Employment Act (ADEA), 29 USC §§621-634, is concerned, one is never too old (with a couple of exceptions) to be deprived of legal protection from age-based decisions and actions by employers. See **ch 3.**

for social and political decisions is not reserved just for the elderly. Age, generally, is a pervasive determinant. Accordingly, statutes, regulations, and policies often single out the young, particularly children, for differential treatment. And while they typically are the "forgotten" majority, those in the middle, i.e., those who are neither children nor are old, are through default likewise accorded age-defined treatment.[6] For example, a pension program that expressly defines those who are 55 and older as the group eligible to receive benefits necessarily excludes those under 55.[7]

Examples of the uses of age abound.

Definitions of crime and the imposition of imprisonment as a penalty for criminality can turn on the perpetrator's age.[8] The victim's lack of years may be a factor in defining crimes, e.g., statutory rape entails sexual relations with a female under a certain age, and there also is the occasional statute that is geared to the victim's being older.[9] Social insurance programs often are keyed to age, the most notable examples being the chronological benchmarks used for eligibility for Social Security benefits[10] and for coverage by Medicare.[11] Age-based employment restrictions may be utilized: there are laws, for example, barring the hiring of inexperienced police officers and firefighters over a certain

---

[6] Of course, those in the middle are not always ignored: the Age Discrimination in Employment Act (ADEA), 29 USC §§621-634, protects individuals from age 40 on. See **ch 3.**

[7] As to the legality under the Age Discrimination in Employment Act (ADEA), 29 USC §§621-634, of pension plans that exclude individuals for being too young, see **ch 5.**

[8] *See, e.g.*, Ill Ann Stat ch 38, ¶12-4.3(A) (Smith-Hurd Supp 1992). For an interesting article concerning old age as a defense in criminal cases, see Cohen, *Old Age as a Criminal Defense*, 212 Crim L Bull 5 (1985).

[9] *See* Ill Ann Stat ch 38, ¶12-4(b)(10) (Smith-Hurd Supp 1992) (aggravated battery exists when person committing battery knows the victim is 60 years of age or older).

[10] See *supra* note 5.

[11] 42 USC §1395o(2).

age, often 35 or 36,[12] and requiring retirement for law enforcement personnel those who attain some set older age, 55 or 57 for example.[13] Public educational institutions exclude those too young (the 3-year-old from kindergarten[14]) and, on occasion have barred those supposedly too old as well.[15] Older drivers may be subject to special re-licensure requirements, with age being the trigger for these demands coming into play.[16] And, of course, attainment of a certain age, typically age 16, is a common predicate to initial driver licensure.[17] Zoning ordinances and rulings have been used to create exclusive precincts for the middle aged and the elderly[18] (although increasingly statutes have been enacted limiting the freedom of housing developments and landlords to distinguish either on the basis of age generally[19] or, at least, to exclude families with children.[20])

Other, less overt, forms of age-based distinctions also may occur. For example, one now-dated study reported that as a mat-

---

[12] *See, e.g.*, Ill Ann Stat ch 24, ¶10-2.1-14 (Smith-Hurd 1990).

[13] *See, e.g.*, 5 USC §8335(b). For the most part, mandatory retirement is barred by the Age Discrimination in Employment Act (ADEA), 29 USC §§621-634. See **ch 4.** But the ADEA does not apply to all employers, see **ch 3,** and even those to which it applies may be able to invoke a statutory exception or defense as the legal basis for imposing age-based involuntary retirement on employees. See **ch 5.**

[14] *See, e.g.*, Hammond v Marx, 406 F Supp 853 (D Me 1975).

[15] *See, e.g.*, Purdie v University of Utah, 584 P2d 831 (Utah 1978). Some years ago the United States Civil Rights Commission reported that a number of medical schools in the past excluded applicants over 30 or 35. United States Commn on Civil Rights, The Age Discrimination Study 76 (1977).

[16] *See, e.g.*, Ill Ann Stat ch 95½, ¶6-109(b), (c) (Smith-Hurd Supp 1992).

[17] *See* State *ex rel* Oleson v Graunke, 119 Neb 440, 229 NW 329 (1930); Berberian v Petit, 118 RI 448, 374 A2d 791 (1977). *See generally* W.F. Foster, Annotation, *Validity, Construction and Application of Age Requirements for Licensing of Motor Vehicle Operators,* 86 ALR3d 475 (1978).

[18] *See generally* H. Eglit, Age Discrimination ch 13 (1st ed 1981, 1982, 1986 & annual supps).

[19] *See, e.g.*, Conn Gen Stat §46a-64c (West Supp 1993); Iowa Code Ann §216.8.4 (West Supp 1993); Mont Code Ann §49-2-305 (1993).

[20] *See, e.g.*, 36 USC §3601 *et seq;* Ill Ann Stat ch 68 ¶3-102 (Smith-Hurd Supp 1992); NC Gen Stat §41A-1 *et seq* (Michie 1992). *See generally* Morales, *Creating New Housing Opportunities for Families with Children: The Fair Housing Amendments Act of 1988,* 22 Clearinghouse Rev 744 (1988).

ter of practice (rather than written policy) hospital emergency room services were denied to the aged in favor of younger patients when medical personnel and supplies were scarce.[21] In a completely different context, the Court of Appeals for the First Circuit has pointed out that the judically fashioned scope of First Amendment protection afforded a schoolteacher will vary, with the age of his or her students being one of the factors taken into account in gauging the extent of his or her free speech rights in the classroom.[22]

Specific uses of age aside, it is beyond peradventure that age-based conceptions and misconceptions pervade American culture, particularly insofar as those who have accumulated a goodly portion of years are concerned. The aged, indeed even those in their fifties and sixties, are the objects of an array of generalizations regarding their abilities,[23] their attitudes,[24] their

---

[21] *See* Sudnow, *Dead on Arrival, in* Sociological Realities 225, 227 (I.L. Horowitz & M.S. Strong eds 1971). There is, however, later contrary data. *See* Schroeder, *A Comparison of Western European and US University Hospitals,* 252 JAMA 240 (July 13, 1984) (concluding that there is a virtual absence of rationing of health care on the basis of age in American university hospitals, in contrast to European hospitals where older patients are denied intensive medical services).

The question of allocation of health resources based on age is increasingly being addressed. *See generally* H.J. Aaron & W. Schwartz, The Painful Prescription: Rationing Hospital Care (1984); Avorn, *Benefit and Cost Analysis in Geriatric Care,* 310 New Eng J Med 1294 (May 17, 1984); D. Callahan, Setting Limits—Medical Goals in an Aging Society (1987); Eglit, *Health Care Allocation for the Elderly: Age Discrimination by Another Name?,* 26 Hous L Rev 813 (1989).

[22] *See* Ward v Hickey, 996 F2d 447, 453 (1st Cir 1993).

[23] See **§1.04.**

[24] For example, it is thought that older people vote as a bloc, dedicated to pursuing some notion of particularized age-defined special interests. This is a misperception, however:

> As the data from recent presidential and congressional elections should make clear, election exit polls have shown repeatedly that the votes of older persons distribute among candidates in about the same proportions as the votes of other age groupings of citizens. Although men and women can be seen to have distributed their votes in patterns, persons in the differing age categories of thirty to forty-four, forty-five to fifty-nine, and sixty and older who cast their ballots in these elections did not. . . .
>
> These data should not be surprising since there is no sound reason to expect that a cohort of persons would suddenly become homogenized

economic status,[25] and so on. While such generalizations are sometimes apt, given that they typically are grounded on *some* verifiable facts, there always is the risk that those who use them will slide over into engaging in inaccurate stereotyping. That is where the misuse of age, *discrimination* in the common parlance, comes to the fore.

§1.02 The Uses and Abuses of Age Distinctions

Unreflective habit no doubt accounts for some of the uses of age distinctions—uses affecting the young, the old, and those in between—that are seen in a broad variety of federal, state, and local laws and regulations in the United States.[26] But given

---

> in its political behavior when it reached the "old age" category. Diversity among older persons may be at least as great with respect to political attitudes and behavior as it is in relation to economic, social, and other characteristics. . . .

Binstock, *Aging, Politics, and Public Policy, in* Growing Old in America 325, 331 (B.B. Hess & E.W. Markson eds 1991).

[25] Routinely, the elderly are portrayed as a comparatively affluent group whose economic problems have faded away to the vanishing point, and who simply do not deserve the nation's attention at a time when many other problems merit higher priority. . . .
The facts are very different. Poverty *is* a daily fact of life for several million elderly Americans. It threatens millions more.

On the Other Side of Easy Street 5 (1987) (a report of the now-defunct Villers Foundation). *See also* K.K. Scholl & M. Moon, Dispelling the Myth of the "Undeserving Rich" (1988) (monograph published by the Public Policy Institute of the American Assn of Retired Persons).

[26] A classic example of the lack of thought that can accompany the injecting of age distinctions into our statutes is provided by the recollections of Wilbur Cohen, who was one of the chief legislative aides involved in the drafting of the landmark Social Security Act of 1935 (and who years later served as head of the federal government's then-Department of Health, Education and Welfare). He wrote as follows:

> The simple fact is that at no time in 1934 did the staff or members of the Committee on Economic Security deem feasible any other age than 65 as the eligible age for the receipt of old age insurance benefits. There is, therefore, very little material available to analyze the economic, social, gerontological, or other reasons for the selection of this particular age. . . . The Committee made no detailed studies of alternative ways

the attention to age that permeates our general social attitudes and concerns, and, more importantly here, given the common use of age distinctions in formal enactments, age differentiations must be seen as more than merely the sloppy products of ignorant legislators and administrators. Rather, at least some uses of age distinctions in legislative and regulatory language properly can be understood as constituting purposive responses to what are perceived to be valid (if not always wise or informed) social, economic, political, and cultural needs and/or demands. Thus, for example, enormous amounts of government funds are channeled through statutorily devised programs that employ older age as the basis for eligibility[27] because the beneficiaries

---

> or of any proposals for voluntary retirement or of any flexible retirement program in relation to the disability of any individual.
>
> It was understood that a reduction in the age below 65 would substantially increase costs, and, therefore, might impair the possibility of . . . acceptance of the plan by Congress. A higher retirement age, of say 68 or 70, was never considered because of the belief that public and congressional opposition would develop against such a provision in view of the widespread unemployment that existed.

W. Cohen, Retirement Policies Under Social Security 17-18 (1957) (footnotes omitted). *See also* Withers, *Some Irrational Beliefs About Retirement in the United States,* 1 Indus Gerontology 23, 24 (Winter 1974) (New Series).

Age 65 as an important touchstone had apparently first risen to the level of government consciousness in the late nineteenth century, in Bismarck's Germany, when the first national social welfare program was devised and that age was utilized as the trigger for eligibility. The Social Security Act's utilization of this age line, little analyzed as it was, succeeded in making age 65 a demarcation of considerable significance throughout our society. *See* Rose, *The Subculture of the Aging: A Topic for Sociological Research, in* Middle Age and Aging 29, 32 (B. Neugarten ed 1968). Today, age 65 is in very large measure no longer a legally acceptable age for mandatory retirement imposed by employers with 20 or more employees for 20 or more weeks of the current or preceding calendar year, by virtue of the Age Discrimination in Employment Act, 29 USC §§621-634. See **ch 3.**

[27] Since 1960, the share of the Federal budget spent on programs serving the elderly has nearly doubled. In 1960, less than 15 percent of the Federal budget was spent on the elderly. In fiscal year 1991, however, programs benefiting the elderly will account for just over 30 percent of the Federal budget. . . .

Senate Special Comm on Aging, American Assn of Retired Persons, Federal Council on the Aging, and Administration on Aging, Aging America—Trends and Projections, 1991 Edition, at 238. Additional figures detail the extent of

of these programs, older Americans, are seen as being both deserving, and in need, of such support (and they have the political strength to assure, in considerable measure, the satisfaction of their needs and demands.[28])

Apart from economic and other tangible advantages accruing to those who are the age-defined beneficiaries of government programs, gains of a less concrete dimension—both of an individual and an institutional nature—also may be derived from the use of age distinctions. An administrator of an age-defined program can avoid engaging in a time consuming and perhaps financially burdensome effort to determine a given applicant's satisfaction of a need-based program's terms. Instead, the bureaucrat can simply rely on a readily ascertainable, and typi-

---

resources directed to older Americans, usually in the context of programs that are age defined:

> In fiscal year 1991, an estimated $387.3 billion of federal spending will directly benefit older Americans. Of every dollar to be spent on the elderly through the federal budget in that year, 54 cents will go to Social Security and 31 cents to Medicare and Medicaid. . . .
>
> The federal government also provides pensions and compensation in exchange for services provided by citizens to the government. It provides disability compensation and pension benefits to veterans of military service, and retirement and health benefits to its own former employees and their survivors 65+. About 10 cents of every federal dollar spent on the elderly in fiscal year 1991 will support these programs.
>
> A third area of federal involvement with the elderly is in providing means-tested benefits to elderly poor people who are unable, despite the existence of a universal social insurance system, to meet basic subsistence needs. Eight cents of every dollar spent on the elderly in fiscal year 1991 is expected to provide Medicaid benefits (4.4 percent), Supplemental Security Income (SSI) benefits (1.4 percent), housing (1.6 percent), food stamps (0.4 percent), energy assistance (0.1 percent), and social services to low-income individuals (0.2 percent).
>
> The fourth area of federal spending on the elderly includes programs of general benefit to the elderly such as social, nutrition, and employment services provided through the Older Americans Act; research conducted through the National Institute on Aging; and volunteer services through the ACTION agency. Less than 1 percent of the elderly's share of the federal budget is spent on these programs.

Id 240.

[28] See note 34.

cally indisputable, fact: the age of the person involved.[29] Thereby, presumably at least some individual program participants benefit, by virtue of being insulated from potential abuses of bureaucratic discretion. Moreover, they further enjoy the benefit of eligibility determinations that likely are more speedily made than otherwise would be the case. From the institutional perspective, efficiency is obtained, both because the initial decisions are rendered more quickly and because there are reduced opportunities for extensive and expensive appeals by disappointed individuals, given the inarguable, objective factor of age serving as the predicate for the decisions below.

The use of age as a basis for decision making may also produce societal benefits of a larger dimension. So long as a system operates consistently by dispassionately relying on the objective factor of age as the determinant for decision making, both the appearance of impartiality and perhaps even actual justice, to some extent, are obtained. These are not inconsiderable gains, given the general distrust of government that afflicts (and protects) the American body politic today (as well as in the past, for that matter).

There are of course significant arguments that go in the other direction, identifying at least some uses of age distinctions as invidious *ageism*.[30] When someone is labeled old (or "young,"

---

[29] The Age Discrimination Act, 42 USC §§6101-6107, ostensibly sets limits on the uses of age by programs receiving federal financial assistance. In fact, the statute's prohibition is so laden with caveats and so confined by limiting language that it is of very little practical effect. *See generally* H. Eglit, 1 Age Discrimination chs 5-6 (1st ed 1981, 1982, 1986 & annual supps); Eglit, *The Age Discrimination Act of 1975, as Amended: Genesis and Selected Problems Areas,* 57 Chi-Kent L Rev 915 (1981); Schuck, *The Graying of Civil Rights Law: The Age Discrimination Act of 1975,* 89 Yale LJ 27 (1979).

[30] The term *ageism* denotes the use of age-based perceptions and distinctions to impose negative consequences on their targets. Some ascribe the coining of the term to Dr. Robert Butler. *See, e.g.,* R.N. Butler, Why Survive? Being Old in America 11 (1975). However, he confined the term to prejudice and stereotyping directed against the old. Ageism, as addressed in this book, is a vice that has broader sway, being a form of stereotypical thinking that singles out any age-defined group or individual for adverse treatment because of age. This is an understanding that has been expressed by others, as well. *See* G.M. Barrow & P.A. Smith, Aging, Ageism and Society 8 (1979).

or "middle aged," for that matter) he or she is thereby set at psychological arm's length by virtue of that designation: "you are not one of *us,* you are one of *them.*" This distancing of those who are so defined in turn can facilitate the use of stereotypes, generally negative ones,[31] in lieu of judgments based on individual characteristics. And the treating of individuals in terms of generalizations ultimately can redound to the detriment of some who, if considered on their own merits and in terms of their own needs, clearly would fare better. For example, in the past age-based mandatory retirement policies were implacably applied to force numerous men and women out of their jobs. Yet, some of these people no doubt would have been able, if addressed in terms of their individual abilities, to demonstrate their capacities and willingness to continue as productive and able workers. Unrefined uses of age lines also can generate other costs that more finely tuned systems could avert: reduced mass transit fares, for example, are made available to persons over 60, whether or not they are actually needy,[32] while younger people who suffer from genuine financial distress are denied such subsidies solely because they are not old enough to qualify.

On a more general level, it can be argued that age distinctions undermine basic values of egalitarianism and respect for individ-

---

[31] Numerous studies suggest that society in general stereotypes aging and the aged with negative evaluations. The stereotype reflects the expectations that old age is a time characterized by a decreasingly active role in life, economic insecurity, loneliness, resistance to change, poor health, and failing mental and physical powers. In short, old age is not seen as conducive to feelings of adequacy, adjustment, usefulness, and security.

Peters, *Self-Conceptions of the Aged, Age Identification, and Aging,* 11 Gerontologist pt II, at 69, 72-73 (Winter 1971) (citations omitted).

There is a whole array of terms and phrases that have been utilized to identify, isolate, and thereby directly or implicitly stigmatize the elderly for being different, in negative ways: words such as *bag, codger, coot, crone, dirty old man, fogy, fuddy-duddy, gaffer, geezer, goat,* and *over the hill. See generally* Nuessel, *The Language of Ageism,* 22 Gerontologist 243 (1982).

[32] Reduced fares are required to be extended by recipients of federal financial assistance under the Urban Mass Transit Act, 49 USC §1604(m). Similarly, Amtrak is required to provide reduced fares for seniors. Amtrak Reorganization Act of 1979, 45 USC §545(c).

uals. Age, like race and gender, is a characteristic that a person has neither chosen nor has the power to change. Thus, when harmful age distinctions are embedded in laws and regulations, they run afoul of a fundamental societal value: "[l]egal burdens," the Supreme Court has said in another context, "should bear some relationship to individual responsibility or wrongdoing."[33]

In any event, whatever one's conclusions about the benefits and detriments of age categorization, as a practical, political reality the day when one could simply accept age-infused institutions and practices in a matter-of-fact manner is behind us. Political and social sensitivities have been triggered both by increasingly aggressive interest groups, most significantly those representing seniors[34] but also including organizations advocating on behalf of children, and by arguable similarities between the readily condemned evils of racism and sexism, on the one hand, and ageism on the other.[35] These sensitivities are reflected in a broad array of federal and state statutes regulating or prohibiting age discrimination in areas ranging from credit[36] to

---

[33] Weber v Aetna Casualty & Sur Co, 406 US 164, 175 (1972).

[34] As to the political activism of seniors' groups generally, see H.J. Pratt, The Gray Lobby (1976). *See also* Binstock, *Aging, Politics, and Public Policy, in* Growing Old In America 325-340 (B.B. Hess & E.W. Markson eds 4th ed 1991). As to an historical analysis of the defining of the needs of the elderly, and of the federal government's responses to these perceived needs, see W. A. Achenbaum, Shades of Gray—Old Age, American Values, and Federal Policies Since 1920 (1983).

There has been a growing litany of accusations and complaints that the elderly indeed have too much power, and that they have used that power to selfish ends. *See, e.g.,* Carpenter, *The New Anti-Youth Movement,* 240 Nation 40 (Jan 19, 1985); Chakravarty & Weisman, *Consuming Our Children?,* 142 Forbes 222 (Nov 14, 1988); Christenson, *Gray-haired Greed,* 4 Experience 8 (Fall 1993); Fairlie, *Talkin' 'Bout My Generation,* 198 New Republic 19 (Mar 28, 1988); P. Longman, Born to Pay (1987); Schurenberg & Luciano, *The Empire Called AARP,* 17 Money 128 (Oct 1988). *See also* Eglit, *Health Care Allocation for the Elderly: Age Discrimination by Another Name?,* 26 Hous L Rev 814, 823-34 (1989).

[35] See **ch 10.**

[36] *See, e.g.,* the Equal Credit Opportunity Act, 15 USC §§1691-1691f. *See generally* H. Eglit, 2 Age Discrimination ch 12 (1st ed 1981, 1982, 1986 & annual supps). There are states that have enacted laws barring, or at least restricting, the use of age in credit transactions. *See, e.g.,* Iowa Code Ann §216.10 (West

public accommodations[37] to governmental assistance.[38] Correlatively, there are growing bodies of case law generated by at least some statutes, most particularly those addressing age discrimination in employment,[39] and by the alleged dictates of the Constitution.[40]

§1.03 Age Demographics and the Labor Force

In colonial times half the United States population was under age 16. Even at the beginning of this century people under age 18 constituted 40 per cent of the populace; fewer than 1 in 10 Americans was over the age of 55, and only 4 per cent of the population was over age 65. By 1990, however, less than 25 per cent of Americans were under age 16, while half were 33 or older. In 1990 1 in 5 Americans was at least 55. And 1 in 8 was 65 or older in that year—more than 31 million people, 7 million of whom were 80 or older.[41] "By the year 2030, there will be proportionately more elderly than young people in the population: 22 percent of the population will be 65+, and 21 percent will be under age 18. . . ."[42]

There are a variety of other figures illustrating the changing demographics of the United States:

Supp 1993); Mont Code Ann §49-2-306 (1993); Va Code Ann §59.1-21.19 *et seq* (Michie 1992). *See generally* H. Eglit, *supra.*

37 *See, e.g.*, Ill Ann Stat ch 68, ¶¶5-101 to -103 (Smith-Hurd 1989); Md Ann Code art 49B, §5 (Michie 1991 & Supp 1993); Mich Comp Laws Ann §§37.2301 *et seq* (West 1985 & Supp 1993-1994), 750.146 (West 1991). *See generally* H. Eglit, *supra* note 36, at ch 11.

38 See note 29.

39 See **chs 2, 9 & 11.**

40 See **ch 3.**

41 The foregoing data is set forth in United States Dept of Commerce, Bureau of the Census, Profiles of America's Elderly (nd).

42 United States Senate Special Comm on Aging, American Assn of Retired Persons, Federal Council on the Aging, US Administration on Aging, Aging America—Trends and Projections, 1991 Edition, at xix.

—The projected growth in the older population is expected to raise the median age of the U.S. population to 36 by the year 2000, to 42 by the year 2030, and to 43 by the year 2040.
—Between 1989 and 2030, the 65+ population is expected to more than double. . . .
—In 1900, there were about 7 elderly people for every 100 people of working age. As of 1990, the ratio was about 20 for every 100. By 2020, the ratio will have risen to about 29 per 100, after which it will rise rapidly to 38 per 100 by 2030.[43]

These statistics leave no doubt that the United States is "graying."[44]

There also have been major changes in the composition of the American work force. Between 1950 and 1990 the number of workers, i.e., those people actually working and those actively seeking work, increased from 62.2 million to 124.8 million.[45] While it is the so-called baby boomers, the 77 million people born between 1946 and 1964, who have accounted in large measure for the massive growth in the labor force in the last 25 or so years, the number today of older workers, all of whom were born before the baby boom years, still is very considerable: in 1989 there were about 6.8 million men and 5.1 million women ages 55 to 64 in the work force,[46] and there were about 2 million men and 1.4 women ages 65 and over.[47] Moreover, there is going to be an increase in the absolute number of older workers: "Bureau of Labor Statistics projections indicate that by the year 2000, 9.8 million men and 7.6 million women age 55+ will be

---

[43] *Id.*

[44] This term, certainly an apt one, is not of the author's devise. It has been used before by others. *See, e.g.,* H.L. Sheppard & S.E. Rix, The Graying of Working America (1977).

[45] Fullerton, *New Labor Force Projections, Spanning 1988 to 2000,* 112 Monthly Lab Rev 3 (Nov, 1989).

[46] Aging America, Trends and Projections, 1991 Edition, *supra* note 42, at xxii.

[47] *Id* 93.

in the labor force—an overall increase of 1 million older men and 1.3 million older women participants since 1988."[48]

Absolute numbers tell a story of growth; but a different story is that in percentage terms there has been a steady decline in the twentieth century of work force participation by older workers:

> In 1950, almost half (46 percent) of all men 65+ were in the labor force. . . . This figure had dropped to 33 percent by 1960 and to 27 percent by 1970. By 1989, only 17 percent of older men were in the labor force. . . . The decrease in male labor force participation extends even to men in their 50s. By 1989, the labor force participation rate among men age 55 to 59 had dropped to 79.5 percent from almost 92 percent in 1960.[49]

Working against this trend is the factor of women having entered the paid work force in increasing numbers in recent years, the result being that one does not yet see the same striking decline in labor force participation for women:

> Labor force participation of older women . . . has varied only slightly. In 1950, 9.7 percent of women age 65+ were in the labor force, but in 1989, their participation fell to 8.4 percent. Over the same period, women in the 55 to 64 age group joined the work force in growing numbers. In 1950, only 27 percent of women in this age category were in the labor force, but by 1970, their participation had risen to 43 percent. The labor force participation rate for these women has been relatively constant since then, and by 1989, it was 45 percent).[50]

While the percentage decrease in older male workers is clear, the explanations are diffuse. In any event, this decrease cannot readily be attributed just, or even significantly, to employer bias:

---

[48] *Id* xxii.

[49] *Id* 94.

[50] *Id.*

> Studies indicate that people retire for a variety of reasons, including health, the availability of Social Security or private pension benefits, the retirement of a spouse, and the opportunity to participate in leisure and volunteer pursuits. Downturns in the economy and corporate mergers and bankruptcies can also induce unanticipated early retirement. Above all, however, most workers retire when they feel they can afford to do so. Thus, people without pensions or sizable personal savings, including home ownership, are likely to remain in the labor force longer than people who have such resources.[51]

Even though there are a number of explanations for the departure of older men from employment, the fact is that there still are millions of older workers (those 55 and over) in the American labor force, and the projections predict an increase in their absolute numbers. Given that the leading edge of the vast number of baby boomers, i.e., those born in the 1940s and 1950s, are moving into middle age,[52] and given further that it typically is at this point that age starts to emerge as a factor (covert or overt) in at least some work settings,[53] the likely prospect is for more, rather than less, focus on the phenomenon of an aging work force[54] and, correlatively, on the uses and misuses of age as a factor involved in workplace decisions.

---

[51] *Id* 90. For a useful review of a number of issues involving older workers, see The Older Worker (M.E. Borus, H.S. Parnes, S.H. Sandell & B. Seidman eds 1988). *See also* B. Rosen & T.H. Jerdee, Older Employees: New Roles for Valued Resources (1985).

[52] In 1990 28.7% of the work force was 45 and older. By 2000 it is predicted that 34.2% of the work force will fall into this age grouping. Rix, *America's Aging Workforce* 2 (Public Policy Inst of AARP Mar 1991).

[53] See **ch 2,** describing the typical complainant under the Age Discrimination in Employment Act, 29 USC §§621-634.

[54] *See generally* The Aging of the American Work Force (I. Bluestone, R.J.V. Montgomery, & J. Owen eds 1990).

§1.04 Age in the Workplace

Decisions are made daily and actions are daily taken in thousands of workplaces, in a myriad of employment contexts, by employers, employment agencies, and labor organizations operating in the federal, state, local government, and private sectors. Inevitably, some of these decisions and actions visit adversity on some employees and job applicants: workers are fired or demoted; job seekers are rejected; union members are mistreated by their own labor organizations; and so on.

It is only human nature for an individual who is on the receiving end of a harmful decision or action to search for a rationale that absolves him or her of any blame or inadequacy. Thus, the employee who is fired will often seek to explain his or her plight (as may the decision maker) by attributing the adverse decision to global issues over which the individual and the employer have no control: the poor economy; a decline in demand for the employer's product; a change in the employer's business emphasis; and so on. Sometimes, the disappointed employee or job applicant may narrow his or her focus and conclude that it is some deficiency of the decision maker—a misguided policy, a wrongheaded evaluation, stupidity, cupidity, venality, or bias—that is responsible for inflicting the harm in question.

Often, of course, the aggrieved individual's assessment of his or her own competence and, conversely, the unfairness of the employer's decision or action, will be ill-founded. Sometimes, on the other hand, that discharged former employee or that rejected job applicant will be very much on the mark in concluding that he or she was mistreated. In either instance the pursuit of legal redress, whether based on a well-founded or an ill-supported belief that a wrong rising to the level of illegality has been perpetrated, may ensue. A terminated or demoted employee, a worker who feels his or her salary to be unjustifiably less than that of his or her co-workers, a disappointed applicant for a job or a promotion, or any other aggrieved individual may seek a variety of forms of relief: monetary recompense; restoration to the job from which he or she was terminated or demoted; a court order directing that he or she be given the desired job, promotion or perquisite that had been unsuccessfully sought; and so on. This redress may be pursued through administrative, judicial, and/or alternative dispute resolution forums in which grievants may invoke federal or state constitutional provisions, state common law theories, and federal and/or state statutory guarantees.

Often, the grievant will fail. Sometimes, however, he or she will secure an advantageous settlement at some point in the process, or a favorable ruling from an arbitrator or a judge, or a favorable verdict from a jury. At least in the latter two instances[55] one can conclude (even accepting that sometimes erroneous decisions are made) that age bias indeed played a determinative role in the decision or action that generated the victim's claim. More generally, the empirical data, i.e., the reported cases rendered every year in which plaintiffs prevail,[56] support the

---

[55] A settlement favorable to a complainant actually may be a reflection of the employer's assessment that its economically most beneficial course is to avoid litigation, rather than an indicator of the substantive merit of the grievant's claim.

[56] One might conclude that there is a significant amount of age bias in the workplace if one simply looks, without a critical eye, at the statistics regarding administrative filings under the leading statute addressing age discrimination in employment, the Age Discrimination in Employment Act (ADEA), 29 USC §§621-634. For the first six months of fiscal year 1993, i.e., October 1, 1992 through March 31, 1993, there were 41,455 administrative charges of discrimination filed with the ADEA enforcement agency, the Equal Employment Opportunity Commission (EEOC), which also is responsible for enforcing Title VII of the Civil Rights Act of 1964, 42 USC §§2000e through 2000e-17, which addresses employment discrimination based on race, color, national origin, religion, and sex; the Equal Pay Act, 29 USC §206(d), which addresses gender-based compensation discrimination; and the Americans with Disabilities Act, 42 USC §12101 *et seq*, which addresses employment discrimination based on handicap. Of these 41,455 filings, 37.5% charged race discrimination, 27.8% made claims of gender discrimination, and 23.7% involved age—an impressive percentage in its own right and one that is even more impressive, perhaps, for being so close to the percentage of gender-based claims. Fair Employment Practices 55 (BNA) (May 24, 1993).

The fact is, however, that an administrative charge can easily be filed pro se by a grievant. Moreover, almost none of these charges result in any affirmative response from the EEOC. Given that charges, both meritorious and nonmeritorious, can readily be filed, and given that the very large majority of these charges do not ever result in any determination, either at the administrative

broader conclusion that age discrimination in employment has been and continues to be an issue of significant dimension in the American workplace. On the other hand, the fact that there are many cases reported each year in which plaintiffs fail on substantive, as opposed to procedural, grounds confirms that claims of discrimination often are misplaced.[57]

Putting to the side the significance or insignificance of the cases, there also are research findings indicating that age bias, conscious or otherwise, continues to exist in the workplace:

> Stereotypical views depict older workers as potentially less employable than younger persons, particularly for managerial positions. Research findings suggest that older persons are seen as less capable of responding creatively, enthusiastically, or efficiently to job demands. Moreover, age stereotypes depict older employees as less interested in change and less capable of coping with future challenges. To the extent that these stereotypes [which are not borne out by the research as being empirically correct] influence managerial decisions, there are potentially serious consequences for older employees, including lowered motivation, career stagnation, and eventual career obsolescence.[58]

Few would argue that either misdirected stereotypes or outright ageist bias have any redeeming value, or that they should

---

or judicial levels, of a substantive violation, statistics regarding charge filings cannot really support any useful conclusions as to the merits of the claims asserted. Of course, given the EEOC's strained budgets and consequently overworked staff, it cannot be concluded that the EEOC's failure to find more actual violations is necessarily a function of the lack of merit of all these charges; insufficient personnel to engage in adequate investigations may also play a role here).

[57] Undoubtedly, factfinders sometimes err, and so genuine victims of wrongdoing will from time to time fail to prevail. Hopefully, however, the civil justice system more often produces correct decisions than incorrect ones.

[58] B. Rosen & T.H. Jerdee, Older Employees: New Roles for Valued Resources 35-36 (1985).

be tolerated either in the workplace or any other setting.[59] Condemnation of tainted decision making does not mean, however, that employment agencies should be held to a duty of assisting unqualified job seekers; or that unions should be expected to refer incompetent workers to employers; or that employers should be expected to hire, promote, or retain individuals who cannot do the job. The tasks, then, that are set by informed social policy, by statutes in some instances, and by the courts in some cases, are two fold. First, in making their decisions, employers, union and employment agencies are to be free to exercise legitimate discretion. Second, and at the same time, these entities are to be foreclosed from relying on improper (and often illegal) bias. The ensuing chapters of this book address the ways in which legislatures, grievants, those accused of wrongdoing, courts, and arbitrators have engaged in pursuing and accomplishing these tasks.

---

[59] *But see* R.A. Epstein, Forbidden Grounds 441-79 (1992).

The Age Discrimination in Employment Act—Introduction

2

§2.01 The Age Discrimination in Employment Act: An Overview

The goals of the Age Discrimination in Employment Act (ADEA)[1] are "to promote employment of older persons based on their ability rather than age; to prohibit arbitrary age discrimination in employment; [and] to help employers and workers find ways of meeting problems arising from the impact of age on employment."[2] Age discrimination is condemned across a broad range of actions and decisions, and in a variety of contexts: hiring and discharge decisions made by employers; determinations by employers regarding compensation, terms, conditions, and

---

[1] 29 USC §§621-634.

[2] §2(b), 29 USC §621(b).

privileges of employment; job referrals by employment agencies; exclusions by labor organizations of over-age individuals from membership; discriminatory advertising; and retaliation against employees and other individuals who assist in the enforcement of the ADEA.[3]

The statute protects—with only a few relatively minor exceptions—persons who are age 40 or older.[4] Federal employees are covered, albeit pursuant to a separate statutory scheme set forth in §15 of the ADEA.[5] State and local government employees also come within the Act's purview.[6] Employers, employment agencies, and labor organizations must abide by the Act's demands, provided they meet the prescribed qualifying criteria—such as the requirement that an employer must have at least 20 employees for 20 or more weeks of the current or preceding calendar year.[7]

Notwithstanding the breadth of the ADEA, reaching as it does employment decisions ranging from hiring to retiring, the statute does not outlaw all consideration of age and age-related criteria. Quite the contrary. The legislative language condemns only discrimination that is arbitrary.[8] Moreover, several exceptions and defenses set forth in the statute or infused into it by judicial decisions,[9] as well as a statutory defense incorporated into the Act from another statute,[10] legitimize uses of age in some

---

[3] §4(a)-(c), 29 USC §623(a)-(c).

[4] See **ch 3.**

[5] 29 USC §633a. See **chs 3** and **9.**

[6] §11(b), 29 USC §630(b). See **ch 3.**

[7] See **ch 3.**

[8] §2(b), 29 USC §621(b). Arbitrariness is referred to no less than three times in the Act's Statement of Findings and Purposes. ADEA §2(a)(2), (a)(4), (b), 29 USC §621(a)(2), (a)(4), (b).

[9] See chs **3, 5, 7** and **8.**

[10] §7(e), 29 USC §626(e), incorporates §10 of the Portal-to-Portal Act of 1947, 29 USC §259, which creates a statutory defense whereby an employer can escape liability by proving that its alleged wrongful conduct was done in good-faith conformity with, and in reliance on, a written administrative regulation, order, ruling, approval, or interpretation of the Equal Employment Opportunity Commission (EEOC), or an administrative practice or enforcement policy of the agency. See **ch 5.**

contexts that, otherwise would run afoul of the Act's proscriptions. These provisions thus make clear that in some circumstances age distinctions indeed are legally tolerable.[11]

The Typical Plaintiff

While the primary motivating force for adoption of the ADEA was the problem of older workers not being able to secure employment,[12] it has turned out that the large majority of ADEA cases concern alleged illegal discharges. For the most part, males are the plaintiffs in ADEA lawsuits. Indeed, the authors of a study done some years ago reported that the large majority of ADEA cases—about 80 per cent—were filed by men.[13] To add another element to this profile, the typical ADEA plaintiff is a middle-level manager or professional.[14] The authors of the aforementioned study further noted that 55 per cent of the actions analyzed were filed by employees between the ages of 50 and 59.[15]

---

[11] Throughout age discrimination law—whether the legal lever for analysis is the Equal Protection Clause of the Fourteenth Amendment, US Const amend XIV; the Age Discrimination Act of 1975 (ADA), 42 USC §§6101-6107; the Equal Credit Opportunity Act (ECOA), 15 USC §§1691-1691f, or other legal texts or cases—there is the persistently troubling task of distinguishing between acceptable age distinctions and unacceptable age discrimination. *See generally* Eglit, *Age and the Law, in* Handbook of Aging and the Social Sciences 528 (R. Binstock & E. Shanas 2d ed 1985). As to constitutional analysis, see **ch 10.** *See also* Eglit, *Of Age and the Constitution,* 57 Chi-Kent L Rev 859 (1981). As to the ADA, see 1 H. Eglit, Age Discrimination chs 5-6 (Shepard's/McGraw-Hill 1st ed 1981 & annual supps); Eglit, *The Age Discrimination Act of 1975, as Amended: Genesis and Selected Problem Areas,* 57 Chi-Kent L Rev 915 (1981); Schuck, *The Graying of Civil Rights Law: The Age Discrimination Act of 1975,* 89 Yale LJ 27 (1979). As to the ECOA, see 1 H. Eglit, Age Discrimination ch 12 (Shepard's/McGraw-Hill 1st ed 1981 & annual supps).

[12] See **§2.02.**

[13] Schuster & Miller, *An Empirical Assessment of the Age Discrimination in Employment Act,* 38 Indus & Lab Rel Rev 64, 68 (1984). While this study was of limited scope, inasmuch as it only reviewed 153 cases, the gender profile it revealed is corroborated by a wider-ranging review of the case law.

[14] *Id* 68.

[15] *Id* 69.

One can only speculate as to what accounts for this profile of litigants.[16] Several interconnected explanations appear reasonable. For one, the fact is that males (at least white males) continue to occupy those positions in the American workplace that are most rewarding in terms of dollars and prestige. Thus, they have a greater incentive to fight when they lose such positions than do individuals whose jobs are less attractive. Moreover, because of the salaries they have been earning, they may be more financially able to litigate than are individuals who over the years have occupied lower-level, lesser-paying jobs.

In addition, the likelihood of an individual who is discharged from a middle-management position—finally secured after years of moving up the proverbial corporate ladder—to secure a comparable job is perhaps slimmer than is the case in the instance of a 45-year-old factory worker who, having lost one job, can at least identify, if not necessarily obtain, a number of comparable, fungible jobs. (Actually, this last observation perhaps is less perspicacious than it might have been 10 or 15 years ago, given the continuing disappearance from the labor market over these past years of well-paying blue-collar positions.) In other words, the middle-level manager has a greater practical (as well as ego-driven) need to fight for his or her job, since it likely represents

---

[16] The case law only records, efforts by those people who have been both motivated and able to fight in court. No doubt, some people who may have valid age discrimination claims never even realize that age bias may have been a factor in whatever decisions or actions were taken regarding them. Even if a given individual may suspect that his or her age was a relevant aspect of the decision or action, he or she may not be aware that legal recourse is an option. Or, if he or she is cognizant of the ADEA, there may be a lack of willingness or ability, for psychological, political, financial, or other reasons, to pursue legal redress. Even if a charge of unlawful discrimination is filed with the ADEA enforcement agency, the EEOC, a settlement may be negotiated at some point prior to suit being filed or, if a lawsuit ensues, prior to judgment. Typically, the settlement agreements will include confidentiality clauses, thereby foreclosing any reliable means of obtaining data as to the numbers and kinds of claims settled before trial. In sum, disputes that wind up being recorded in reported judicial opinions hardly reflect the actual incidence of age discrimination in settings covered by the ADEA.

On the other hand, it should come as no surprise to realize that some entirely appropriate decisions made, and actions taken, by covered entities evoke meritless legal challenges.

a career peak that, once lost, is unlikely to be replaced.[17] Still another potential explanation for the skewing of the case law in the direction of management-level plaintiffs has been suggested by the authors of the 153-case study earlier noted. They reasoned that lower-ranking grievants likely would have union protection and the remedies available under collective bargaining contracts, whereas managerial employees would not have this alternative to the ADEA.[18]

Enforcement Statistics

The ADEA authorizes enforcement both by individual plaintiffs and the Equal Employment Opportunity Commission (EEOC). The agency also has enforcement responsibility for Title VII of the Civil Rights Act of 1964,[19] the Equal Pay Act,[20] and the American with Disabilities Act (ADA).[21] A necessary precursor to private suits, which form the great majority of ADEA cases, and the standard—but not required—precursor to EEOC suits enforcing the age discrimination statute, is the filing of a charge of unlawful discrimination with the agency by the

---

[17] *See* Schuster & Miller, *supra* note 13, at 69. Another less persuasive explanation that has been offered for the high percentage of males making up ADEA plaintiffs was ventured by the same authors: they attributed the disproportionate number of male grievants to the likelihood that there simply was no other legal recourse available for these individuals, in contrast to the option likely available to aggrieved women employees of looking to Title VII of the Civil Rights Act of 1964, 42 USC §§2000e through 2000e-17—which proscribes employment discrimination based on gender—as an alternative source of protection. This explanation seems unpersuasive because there is nothing to preclude a woman who is asserting a claim under Title VII from also suing under the ADEA. Thus, the availability of the Title VII route does not really explain the relatively small number of women suing under the age statute.

[18] Schuster & Miller, *supra* note 13, at 68-69.

[19] 42 USC §§2000e through 2000e-17.

[20] 29 USC §206(d).

[21] 42 USC §12101 *et seq.* The ADA became effective on July 27, 1992 for employees with 25 or more employees for 20 or more weeks of the current or preceding calendar year, and it became effective on July 27, 1994 for employees with 15 or more employees for 20 or more weeks of the current or preceding calendar year.

aggrieved individual.[22] Fiscal year 1980 was the first full year for which the EEOC had ADEA enforcement authority.[23] In that fiscal year there were 59,328 charges filed with the EEOC; of these, 11,076—18.6 per cent—were ADEA charges. In fiscal year 1986 the total number of charges had risen to 68,822; 25.3 per cent—17,443—were filed under the ADEA.[24] By fiscal year 1991 the number of ADEA filings had reached 17,449, out of a total of 62,806.[25] And in fiscal year 1992 the number of filings with the EEOC amounted to 70,339, of which 19,253 were age discrimination charges.[26] The following fiscal year there was a surge in filings—up to almost 88,000—which was attributable to persons making claims under the ADA. Of the total, age discrimination charges constituted 22.6 per cent.[27]

For years, the number of reported decisions litigated annually by private individuals has been in the hundreds, most of which are discussed, or at least cited, in AGE DISCRIMINATION. As for EEOC litigation, in fiscal year 1990 the EEOC filed 138 ADEA suits,[28] and 102 suits were filed in fiscal year 1991.[29] Only 84 EEOC suits were filed in fiscal year 1992, however.[30] In the next fiscal year, however, the filings increased to 114.[31]

---

[22] See **ch 6.**

[23] See **§2.02.**

[24] *Twenty Years of the Age Discrimination in Employment Act: Success or Failure?, Hearing Before the Senate Special Committee on Aging,* 100th Cong, 1st Sess 85 (1987) (Testimony of Clarence Thomas, Chairman, and R. Gaull Silberman, Vice Chairman, Equal Employment Opportunity Commission).

[25] Fair Employment Practices, Summary of Latest Developments 2 (BNA May 1992).

[26] United States General Accounting Office, EEOC'S Expanding Workload—Increases in Age Discrimination and Other Charges Call for New Approach 10 (GAO/HEHS-94-32 Feb 9, 1994).

[27] EEOC Compliance Manual, News and Developments 3 (Jan 31, 1994).

[28] Fair Employment Practices, *supra* note 25, at 29 (Mar 18, 1991).

[29] *Id* 4 (May 1992).

[30] EEOC Compliance Manual, News and Developments 3 (Dec 27, 1993). In addition, there were 19 suits filed concurrently under Title VII of the Civil Rights Act of 1964, 42 USC §§2000e through 2000e-17, and the ADEA or the Equal Pay Act, 29 USC §206(d).

[31] EEOC Compliance Manual, *supra* note 27, at 3.

§2.02 The ADEA's Legislative History

Prior to the enactment in 1967 of the Age Discrimination in Employment Act (ADEA)[32] there had been only sporadic and ineffectual attention addressed at the federal level to the issue of age bias in the workplace.[33] During consideration of the Civil Rights Act of 1964[34] proposals were made to include age in the list of prohibited criteria set forth in that Act's employment provision. While Congress rejected these efforts,[35] the 1964 Act did direct the Secretary of Labor to undertake a study to ascertain the nature and extent of age discrimination in employment and to make recommendations for dealing with the problem, if it existed.[36]

In 1965 the Secretary reported to Congress that ageism in the workplace indeed was a significant problem, and that federal remedial legislation was needed to combat it.[37] He reported that

---

32 29 USC §§621-634.

33 Efforts to prohibit arbitrary age discrimination by federal statute went back as far as the 1950s. *See Age Discrimination in Employment: Hearings Before the Subcomm on Labor, Senate Comm on Labor and Public Welfare,* 90th Cong, 1st Sess 23 (1967) (statement of Sen. Javits). On February 12, 1964, President Johnson issued Exec Order No 11141, 3 CFR §§117-118 (1964), *reprinted in* 5 USC §3301 app at 401-02 (entitled *Discrimination on the Basis of Age*). This order, which was supplanted by a later, broader executive order that addresses employment discrimination but that omits mention of age, ostensibly proscribed age discrimination in employment by government contractors. However, the order provided for no enforcement mechanism, and the regulations that have been issued pursuant to the order, 48 CFR §§22.901-.902 (1993), do not remedy this. Moreover, in Kodish v United Air Lines, 628 F2d 1301, 1303 (10th Cir 1980), it was held that a private right of action could not be implied from the executive order. See **ch 11**.

34 42 USC §§2000a through 2000h-6.

35 An amendment offered by Representative Dowdy was rejected by a 123 to 94 vote. 110 Cong Rec 2596-99 (1964). An amendment offered by Senator Smathers likewise was rejected, by a 63 to 28 vote. 110 Cong Rec 9911-13 (1964); 110 Cong Rec 13490-92 (1964).

36 Civil Rights Act of 1964, Pub L No 88-352, §715, 78 Stat 287, 316 (superseded by the Equal Employment Opportunity Act of 1972, Pub L No 92-261, §10, 86 Stat 111, 132).

37 *The Older American Worker—Age Discrimination in Employment,* Report of the Secretary of Labor to the Congress under Section 715 of the Civil Rights Act of 1964 (1965).

the major problem confronting older workers was the refusal of employers to hire them.[38] (In fact, while discriminatory refusals to hire have generated some case law, the large majority of cases that have been litigated over the years have not dealt with hiring, but rather with the discharge of older workers—an issue that was not identified in the 1965 report as being of significance.) In light of this report, the Fair Labor Standards Amendments of 1966[39] directed the Secretary to submit specific legislative recommendations. A draft bill was submitted to Congress in early 1967 and in that same year the ADEA was considered, passed, and signed into law[40] (although it did not go into effect until June 12, 1968).[41]

The ADEA has since been amended on a number of occasions. In 1974 the Act's coverage was extended, *inter alia,* to the federal government.[42] It also was extended at that time to state and local government employers.[43] In 1978 the statute was amended in a number of respects.[44] Most notably, the amendments (1) raised the age cap, i.e., the age ceiling at which the Act's protection ceased, from 65 to 70 for most nonfederal employees;[45] (2) removed the age cap entirely for federal employees;[46] (3) established a statutory guarantee of jury trials;[47] (4) changed the nomenclature regarding filings with the ADEA enforcement

---

[38] *Id* 5.

[39] Pub L No 89-601, §606, 80 Stat 830, 845.

[40] Age Discrimination in Employment Act of 1967, Pub L No 90-202, 81 Stat 602.

[41] Pursuant to *id* §15, 81 Stat 602, 606-07, the Act became effective 180 days after enactment. The Act was signed into law on December 15, 1967; inasmuch as 1968 was a leap year, the effective date was June 12, 1968. *See* Hodgson v First Fed Sav & Loan, 455 F2d 818, 821 (5th Cir 1972).

[42] Fair Labor Standards Amendments of 1974, Pub L No 93-259, §28, 88 Stat 55, 74-75 (codified as amended at 29 USC §633a).

[43] *Id* §28, 88 Stat 55, 74 (codified as amended at 29 USC §630(b)).

[44] Age Discrimination in Employment Act Amendments of 1978, Pub L No 95-256, 92 Stat 189.

[45] See **ch 3.**

[46] *Id.*

[47] See **ch 6.**

agency;[48] and (5) barred involuntary retirement prior to age 70, even if an employer sought to justify such retirement under the ADEA's bona fide benefit plan exception set forth in §4(f)(2) of the Act.[49]

In 1982 the Act was amended to add a §4(g)[50] regarding employers' obligations to extend health benefits to employees between 65 and 69.[51] In 1984 the Act was amended so as to extend coverage in some instances to employees working abroad.[52] In the same year §4(g) was amended so as to extend health insurance coverage to the spouses of employees between the ages of 65 and 69.[53] In 1985 §4(g) was amended once again so as to impose upon employers the obligation to extend health insurance coverage plans to employees and spouses ages 70 and over.[54]

In 1986 the age ceiling for employees in the private sector was removed, subject to only a couple of exceptions.[55] In addition, the ADEA was amended in the same year to assure that, as of January 1, 1988 (or later in the case of some plans maintained pursuant to collective bargaining contracts), employers would be barred from following the previously approved practice of stopping contributions to pension plans and the accrual of pension benefits at normal retirement age (usually deemed to be age 65).[56] Also, §4(g) was reenacted in 1986.[57]

---

[48] *Id.*

[49] 29 USC §623(f)(2). As to this exception, see **ch 5.**

[50] 29 USC §623(g) (repealed). See **ch 5.**

[51] Tax Equity and Fiscal Responsibility Act of 1982, Pub L No 97-248, §116(a), 96 Stat 324, 353 (codified at 29 USC §623(g) (repealed). See **ch 5.**

[52] Older Americans Act Amendments of 1984, Pub L No 98-459, §802, 98 Stat 1767, 1792 (codified at 29 USC §§623(f)(1), (h) & 630(f)). **See ch 3.**

[53] Deficit Reduction Act of 1984, Pub L No 98-369, §2301(b)(1), 98 Stat 494, 1063. See **ch 5.**

[54] Consolidated Omnibus Budget Reconciliation Act of 1985, Pub L No 99-272, §9201(b)(1), 100 Stat 82, 171; see **ch 5.**

[55] Age Discrimination in Employment Amendments of 1986, Pub L No 99-592, §2(c), 100 Stat 3342; see **ch 3.**

[56] Omnibus Budget Reconciliation Act of 1986, Pub L No 99-509, §9201, 100 Stat 1874, 1973-75; see **ch 5.**

In 1988 the statute of limitations for filing suit was extended for certain individuals by the Age Discrimination Claims Assistance Act of 1988.[58] Section 4(g) was deleted from the Act in 1989.[59] The statute of limitations for filing suit again was extended for certain individuals in 1990.[60] Major changes were made in the same year by the Older Workers Benefit Protection Act.[61] These modifications focused on the ADEA's defenses concerning bona fide employee benefit plans[62] and seniority systems,[63] on the legitimizing of voluntary retirement plans,[64] and on the requirements for valid releases of liability executed by ADEA claimants.[65] In 1991 the ADEA was amended once again, although in a much more minor respect: the Civil Rights Act of 1991[66] changed the statute of limitations relevant to the filing of ADEA lawsuits.[67]

§2.03 Interpretive Tools: Interpretations, Regulations, and Title VII Case Law

As originally enacted, the Age Discrimination in Employment Act (ADEA)[68] designated the Department of Labor (DOL) as the agency charged with the Act's administration and enforcement. During its tenure in this role DOL issued what it entitled an

---

[57] Age Discrimination in Employment Amendments of 1986, Pub L No 99-592, §2(b), 100 Stat 3342.

[58] Pub L No 100-283, 102 Stat 78. See **ch 6.**

[59] Omnibus Reconciliation Act of 1989, Pub L No 101-239, Title VI, §6202(b)(3)(C)(i), 103 Stat 2106, 2233 (1989). See **ch 5.**

[60] Age Discrimination Claims Assistance Amendments of 1990, Pub L No 101-504, 104 Stat 1298. See **ch 6.**

[61] Pub L No 101-433, 104 Stat 978, *as amended by* Pub L No 101-521, 104 Stat 2278 (1990).

[62] See **ch 5.**

[63] *Id.*

[64] See **chs 4, 5.**

[65] See **ch 5.**

[66] Pub L No 101-166, §115, 105 Stat 1071, 1079.

[67] See **ch 6.**

[68] 29 USC §§621-634.

Interpretative Bulletin.[69] The Bulletin "indicate[d] the construction of the law which the Department . . . [believed] to be correct and which . . . [would] guide it in the performance of its . . . duties."[70] In 1978 President Carter issued an order transferring administrative and enforcement authority to the Equal Employment Opportunity Commission (EEOC) as of July 1, 1979.[71] While the transfer generated a number of constitutional challenges,[72] the transfer's legitimacy was upheld by a majority of the courts[73] and ultimately was ensured by specific legislation authorizing EEOC enforcement of the ADEA.[74]

---

[69] 29 CFR pt 860 (1986) (effectively rescinded, 46 Fed Reg 47724 (Sept 29, 1981), and ordered removed from the CFR, 52 Fed Reg 23812 (June 25, 1987)).

[70] 29 CFR §860.1 (1986).

[71] Reorganization Plan No 1 of 1978, 92 Stat 3781, 43 Fed Reg 19807 (May 9, 1979), *reprinted at* 5 USC app.

[72] In Immigration & Naturalization Serv v Chadha, 462 US 919 (1983), the Court held unconstitutional the legislative veto provision contained in the Immigration and Nationality Act, 8 USC §1254(c)(2). Since the transfer of enforcement authority to the EEOC was effectuated by an executive order issued pursuant to another federal statute containing a legislative veto provision, i.e., the Reorganization Act of 1977, 5 USC §§901-912, *Chadha* was looked to as the analogical basis for disputing the constitutionality of that transfer.

[73] The very large majority of courts upheld the constitutionality of the transfer on various grounds—both in the context of challenges concerning ADEA enforcement authority, as well as challenges concerning EEOC enforcement authority regarding the Equal Pay Act, 29 USC §206(d), responsibility for which also was transferred pursuant to the same Reorganization Plan No 1. The highest courts to so hold were those deciding Muller Optical Co v Equal Employment Opportunity Commn, 743 F2d 380 (6th Cir 1984), and Equal Employment Opportunity Commn v Hernando Bank, 724 F2d 1188 (5th Cir 1984). A few courts, however, held the transfer to be unconstitutional. Equal Employment Opportunity Commn v CBS, Inc, 743 F2d 969 (2d Cir 1984); Equal Employment Opportunity Commn v Martin Indus, 581 F Supp 1029 (ND Ala), *appeal dismissed,* 469 US 806 (1984); Equal Employment Opportunity Commn v Westinghouse Elec Corp, 33 FEP Cas (BNA) 1232 (WD Pa), *appeal dismissed,* 469 US 806 (1984), *vacated,* 765 F2d 389 (3d Cir 1985). (Other negative decisions were overridden by the decisions in *Muller Optical* and *Hernando Bank*).

[74] Ratification of Reorganization Plans as a Matter of Law, Pub L No 98-532, 98 Stat 2705 (1984) (codified at 5 USC §901 *et seq*). While the enactment itself did not resolve the issue of whether this new law should be applied retroac-

The EEOC soon issued its own regulations[75] dealing with procedural and record-keeping issues, as well as interpretations regarding substantive issues.[76] In so doing, the agency effectively rescinded most of DOL's Interpretative Bulletin,[77] although the Bulletin continued to appear in the annual issuances of the Code of Federal Regulations (CFR) through 1986. In 1987 the EEOC formally transferred the one still viable portion of the Interpretative Bulletin to its own section of the CFR.[78] Almost simultaneously, the DOL ordered the removal of the Bulletin[79] from the CFR.

Agency regulations, whether of the EEOC or other agencies, are legally binding. Although not having the force of law, since it was not promulgated pursuant to the rulemaking procedures of the Administrative Procedure Act,[80] the Interpretative Bulletin was cited often in early ADEA cases, as have the EEOC interpretations, or guidelines, often been cited by later courts. The usual judicial respect accorded these interpretations is understandable: as the Court said in *Griggs v Duke Power Co*,[81] a case

---

tively, several courts ruled that it should be. Equal Employment Opportunity Commn v Westinghouse Elec Corp, 765 F2d 389 (3d Cir 1985) (case arising under Equal Pay Act, 29 USC §206(d)); Equal Employment Opportunity Commn v Merrill Lynch, Pierce, Fenner & Smith, 677 F Supp 918 (ND Ill), *appeal dismissed,* 44 Empl Prac Dec (CCH) ¶37,666 (7th Cir 1987) (*id*); Equal Employment Opportunity Commn v KDM School Bus Co, 612 F Supp 369, 371 n4 (SDNY 1985); Meckes v Reynolds Metals Co, 604 F Supp 598, 603 (ND Ala), *affd without opinion,* 770 F2d 1055 (11th Cir 1985).

[75] 29 CFR pts 1626, 1627 (1993). The EEOC's authority to issue substantive regulations flows from 29 USC §628. (Insofar as Title VII of the Civil Rights Act of 1964, 42 USC §§2000e through 2000e-17, is concerned, the rulemaking power of the EEOC, which also is responsible for enforcement of that statute, is restricted to procedural rules. 42 USC §2000e-12(a).)

[76] 29 CFR pt 1625 (1953).

[77] The EEOC so asserted when it issued interpretations in 1981. 46 Fed Reg 47724 (Sept 29, 1981).

[78] 52 Fed Reg 23811 (June 25, 1987).

[79] *Id* 23812.

[80] 5 USC §553.

[81] 401 US 424 (1971).

arising under Title VII of the Civil Rights Act of 1964[82] in which the Court referred to comparable guidelines issued by the EEOC regarding that statute: "The administrative interpretation[s] of the Act by the enforcing agency . . . [are] entitled to great deference."[83] (Still, *Griggs* notwithstanding, EEOC guidelines are less authoritative than regulations.)[84]

The EEOC also issues policy statements and other directives that provide guidance to Commission staff, as well as to attorneys outside the Commission and the general public, regarding the administration of the laws that the EEOC enforces. Unlike the regulations, but like the interpretations, these do not have the force of law. But like the interpretations, these directives may evoke judicial deference or respect, as explained in the course of the Court's assessment of comparable policy statements issued by the EEOC regarding Title VII in *Equal Employment Opportunity Commission v Arabian American Oil Co.*[85] The Court wrote as follows:

> [T]he level of deference afforded " 'will depend upon the thoroughness evident in its consideration, the validity of its reasoning, its consistency with earlier and later pronouncements, and all those factors which give it power to persuade.' "[86]

Also in the Title VII context, and also analogically relevant to the ADEA, the Court in *Equal Employment Opportunity*

---

82 42 USC §§2000e through 2000e-17.

83 401 US at 434. *See also* Orzel v City of Wauwatosa Fire Dept, 697 F2d 743, 748 (7th Cir), *cert denied,* 464 US 992 (1983). An interpretive guideline's weight, upon judicial review, "will depend upon the thoroughness evident in its consideration, the validity of its reasoning, the consistency with earlier and later pronouncements, and all those factors which give it power to persuade, if lacking power to control." Skidmore v Swift Co, 323 US 134, 140 (1944); *accord* Quinn v New York State Elec & Gas Corp, 569 F Supp 655, 660 (NDNY 1983).

84 *Cf* Ansonia Board of Educ v Philbrook, 479 US 60, 69 n6 (1986) (case arising under Title VII).

85 499 US 244 (1991).

86 *Id* 257 (quoting General Elec Co v Gilbert, 429 US 125, 142 (1976) (quoting Skidmore v Swift & Co, 323 US 134, 140 (1944)).

Commission v Commercial Office Products Co[87] asserted (albeit in the context of addressing an argument made by the agency before the Court, rather than in terms of parsing an agency issuance) that "the EEOC's interpretation of ambiguous language need only be reasonable to be entitled to deference."[88]

Another source of guidance is opinion letters—although they are in fact very few in number—that the EEOC may issue.[89]

Apart from EEOC issuances, case law developed under Title VII has played a particularly important role in the development of the ADEA. Courts interpreting the age discrimination statute regularly have looked to Title VII authority for analogical guidance.[90] This reliance has been grounded on several factors. First, the two statutes share a common goal, i.e., eradication of discrimination in the workplace. In addition, the ADEA was an outgrowth, in some sense, of Congress's consideration of Title VII.[91] Finally, in significant respects the ADEA is modeled after the earlier statute, resulting in a comparability of terms and prohibitions that has been noted by numerous courts,[92] including the Supreme Court.[93] (It must be recognized, however, that the two statutes certainly are not identical. First, the ADEA contains exceptions not present in Title VII. Second, the age statute's enforcement mechanisms are derived from the Fair Labor Standards Act,[94] rather than Title VII. Third, the ADEA is directed to a problem—ageism—that is in some respects different than

---

[87] 486 US 107 (1988).

[88] *Id* 115.

[89] The ADEA opinion letters are discussed in the text in those sections where they are relevant. They also are reproduced in the Appendix, at the end of the last volume of this text.

[90] With lesser frequency Title VII courts have looked to ADEA rulings for guidance. Lower courts addressing Title VII claims have looked to an ADEA ruling, Gilmer v Interstate/Johnon Lane Corp, 500 US 20 (1991) (which concerns the arbitrability of claims arising under the ADEA), for instruction. See **ch 7.**

[91] See **§2.02.**

[92] *See, e.g.*, Loeb v Textron, Inc, 600 F2d 1003 (1st Cir 1979).

[93] Oscar Mayer & Co v Evans, 441 US 750, 755-58 (1978).

[94] 29 USC §§200-219.

the evils which are the focus of Title VII, i.e., discrimination based on race, sex, religion, color, and national origin. Thus, Title VII case law cannot thoughtlessly be infused into the ADEA.)

Finally, there is one more general element to note regarding the interpretation and application of the ADEA. This is a remedial statute, and so the often asserted canon that remedial statutes are to be liberally construed in favor of their beneficiaries[95] is applicable.[96] Thus, the court deciding *MacDonald v Wyoming Mental Health Center*[97] observed as follows: " 'The ADEA is remedial and humanitarian legislation and should be liberally construed to effectuate the congressional purpose of ending age discrimination in employment.' "[98] In the same vein, the Court of Appeals for the Sixth Circuit, confronted with the issue of whether the plaintiff was an employee for purposes of the ADEA, stated that "[t]he term 'employee' is to be given a broad construction in order to effectuate the remedial purposes of the" age discrimination statute.[99]

§2.04 Exclusivity of the ADEA as a Remedy for Age Discrimination in Employment

Other Bases for Redress at the Federal Level

While the Age Discrimination in Employment Act (ADEA)[100] is the preeminent federal mechanism for dealing with age bias in the workplace, it is not the exclusive source of potential

---

95 *See, e.g.*, Oscar Mayer & Co v Evans, 441 US 750, 765 (1979) (Blackmun, J., concurring).

96 As a practical matter, of course, this canon offers nothing of analytical substance; it usually (but not always) is used for nothing more than a rhetorical flourish to justify a conclusion already reached on other bases.

97 941 F2d 1115 (10th Cir 1991).

98 *Id* 1118 (quoting Dartt v Shell Oil Co, 539 F2d 1256, 1260 (10th Cir 1976), *affd*, 434 US 99 (1977)).

99 Lilley v BTM Corp, 958 F2d 746, 750 (6th Cir), *cert denied*, 113 S Ct 376 (1992).

100 29 USC §§621-634.

redress. For one, the federal Constitution is a potential basis of vindication for victims of discrimination,[101] although it is rarely invoked successfully and it is in any event inherently limited in its reach because it only extends to governmental actions and so does not govern the conduct of private employers. There are a few federal statutes in addition to the ADEA that explicitly regulate discrimination in employment,[102] as well as more general provisions that one might argue are relevant.[103] There also are some federal regulations of some relevance.[104] And collective bargaining agreements, growing out of a federal statutory base, may afford protection for union members.[105]

While a number of alternative or additional avenues of attack thus may be open to some individuals, it is nonetheless true that in many instances these will be of limited or no value. For example for most federal employees, constitutional attacks are foreclosed: several courts have held that insofar as such employees are covered by the ADEA, they are confined to this remedy.[106]

---

[101] See **ch 9.**

[102] See **ch 11.**

[103] *See, e.g.*, 42 USC §§1983, 1985(3). See **ch 11.**

[104] See **ch 11.**

[105] See **ch 7.**

[106] *See, e.g.*, Chennareddy v Bowsher, 935 F2d 315, 318 (DC Cir 1991); Purtill v Harris, 658 F2d 134 (3d Cir 1981), *cert denied*, 462 US 1131 (1983); Paterson v Weinberger, 644 F2d 521 (5th Cir 1981); Attwell v Granger, 748 F Supp 866, 870 (ND Ga 1990); Thorne v Cavazos, 744 F Supp 348, 352 (DDC 1990); Rattner v Bennett, 701 F Supp 7 (DDC 1988); Coleman v Nolan, 693 F Supp 1544, 1546 n1 (SDNY 1988); Dodson v United States Army & Accounting Ctr, 636 F Supp 894 (SD Ind 1986); Wilkins v Walters, 571 F Supp 474, 477 (ND Ohio 1983); Favors v Ruckelshaus, 569 F Supp 363, 367 (ND Ga 1983); Davis v Devine, 554 F Supp 1165, 1170 (WD Mich 1983), *affd on other grounds*, 736 F2d 1108 (6th Cir), *cert denied*, 469 US 1020 (1984); Krodel v Young, 33 FEP Cas (BNA) 649 (DDC 1981), *affd on other grounds*, 748 F2d 701 (DC Cir 1984), *cert denied*, 474 US 817 (1985); Nelson v Williams, 25 FEP Cas (BNA) 1214 (DDC 1981); Christie v Marston, 451 F Supp 1142 (ND Ill 1978). The same has been held as to common-law claims. Rattner v Bennett, 701 F Supp 7 (DDC 1988); Dolan v United States, 31 FEP Cas (BNA) 548 (DDC 1983); *cf* Brown v General Servs Admin, 425 US 820 (1976) (establishing exclusivity of Title VII of the Civil Rights Act of 1964, 42 USC §§2000e through 2000e-17). See generally **ch 3.** *But see* Mang v Blumenthal, 26 FEP Cas (BNA) 1353 (WD Pa 1981).

But for the under-40 federal employee or job applicant seeking federal employment the ADEA is not available, and so the Constitution can be looked to.[107] Similarly, certain federal jobs may be exempt from the ADEA's coverage,[108] and thus constitutionally based recourse for federal employees and applicants would accordingly not be foreclosed. (The case law, however, almost uniformly rejects claims grounded in the Constitution, whether the defendant is a federal entity, a state, or a local governmental body.)[109]

If a plaintiff wishes to invoke a federal statute or regulation other than the ADEA that in some measure expressly attacks age discrimination, or if a defendant argues that one of these statutes displaces the age statute, the question necessarily arises as to whether the ADEA supersedes, or is superseded by, that other enactment. Certainly, on its face the ADEA does not expressly displace other federal laws. Nor does the Act's legislative history support reading the ADEA as repealing other federal remedies. Likewise, these other statutes evidence no explicit congressional intent to be subordinated to the ADEA.[110] Arguably, the ADEA repeals these statutes by implication or, conversely, one or more of these other laws does the same to the ADEA. These arguments, however, are not persuasive, given the rigorous standards that must be met for a court to imply a repeal.[111] Moreover,

---

107 *See, e.g.*, Christie v Marston, 451 F Supp 1142 (ND Ill 1978).

108 See generally **ch 3**.

109 See **ch 10**.

110 See **ch 11**.

111 In Radzanower v Touche Ross & Co, 426 US 148 (1976), the Court addressed a conflict between two venue statutes, the later enacted of which was broader than the earlier provision. The Court concluded that the later statute—which said nothing about the earlier law—did not repeal by implication its predecessor. In so holding the Court outlined the standards applicable to repeals by implication:

> It is a basic principle of statutory construction that a statute dealing with a narrow, precise, and specific subject is not submerged by a later enacted statute covering a more generalized spectrum. "Where there is no clear intention otherwise, a specific statute will not be controlled or nullified by a general one, regardless of the priority of enactment." *Morton v Mancari,* 417 U.S. 535, 550-551.

the ADEA was enacted prior to these other provisions, and this chronology accordingly prevents reading into the ADEA an implied repeal of statutes that did not even exist at the time of the ADEA's adoption.

The case law does establish, however, that a specific federal statute—such as the statute setting a mandatory retirement age for federal law enforcement personnel[112]—can prevail over the ADEA's more general prohibition of age-based employment decisions.[113] More general federal statutes dealing with employment issues will not supersede the ADEA, however. Thus, in deciding *Britt v Grocers Supply Co, Inc,*[114] the Court of Appeals for the Fifth Circuit held that the ADEA is the exclusive federal remedy for age discrimination in employment, and so it is not sup-

---

Id 153.

The Court went on to iterate the " 'cardinal principle of statutory construction that repeals by implication are not favored.' " *Id* 154 (quoting United States v United Continental Tuna Corp, 425 US 164, 168 (1976)). It then set forth the two well-settled categories of repeals by implication:

> (1)Where provisions in the two acts are in irreconcilable conflict, the later act to the extent of the conflict constitutes an implied repeal of the earlier one; and (2) if the later act covers the whole subject of the earlier one and is clearly intended as a substitute, it will operate similarly as a repeal of the earlier act. But, in either case, the intention of the legislature to repeal must be clear and manifest. . . . *Posadas v National City Bank,* 296 U.S. 497, 503 [1936].

Id 154.

[112] 5 USC §8335(b).

[113] *See, e.g.,* Bowman v United States Dept of Justice, 510 F Supp 1183 (ED Va 1981), *affd without opinion,* 679 F2d 876 (4th Cir), *cert denied,* 459 US 1072 (1982). It also has been held that the ADEA does not effectuate a repeal of 5 USC §3323(b), pursuant to which civil service annuitants who earlier retired may be rehired, but only on an at-will basis. Davis v Devine, 836 F2d 1108 (6th Cir), *cert denied,* 469 US 1020 (1984). And it has been held that the ADEA does not repeal 5 USC §5595, which addresses severence pay. Dinerslein v Frank, 58 FEP Cas (BNA) 1544 (SDNY 1991). Conversely, the Employee Retirement Income Security Act (ERISA), 29 USC §1001 *et seq,* does not displace, or supersede, the ADEA. International Assn of Machinists & Aerospace Workers, Local Lodge No 967 v General Elec Co, 713 F Supp 547, 558 (NDNY 1989).

[114] 978 F2d 1441 (5th Cir 1992), *cert denied,* 113 S Ct 2929 (1993).

planted, or preempted, by the National Labor Relations Act.[115] This ruling is paralleled by the judicial treatment of age discrimination claims advanced under 42 USC §1983, discussed *infra.* (The *Britt* court further "decline[d] to hold that the courts under the ADEA and the NLRB have concurrent jurisdiction" over age discrimination claims.)[116]

Federal statutes not dealing with age discrimination specifically, or employment issues generally, that arguably can be invoked in the age discrimination context are 42 USC §§1981, 1982, 1983, and 1985(3). Case law, however, establishes that §§1981[117] and 1982[118] are confined to racial discrimination.[119] Section 1983[120] in theory could be an appropriate statute to

---

[115] 29 USC §§151-187.

[116] 978 F2d at 1447 n10.

[117] 42 USC §1981 provides as follows:

> All persons within the jurisdiction of the United States shall have the same right in every State and Territory to make and enforce contracts, to sue, be parties, give evidence, and to the full and equal benefit of all laws and proceedings for the security of persons and property as is enjoyed by white citizens, and shall be subject to like punishment, pains, penalties, taxes, licenses, and exactions of every kind, and to no other.

[118] 42 USC §1982 provides as follows: "All citizens of the United States shall have the same right, in every State and Territory, as is enjoyed by white citizens thereof to inherit, purchase, lease, sell, hold, and convey real and personal property."

[119] Cases rejecting age discrimination claims under §1981 include Kodish v United Air Lines, Inc, 628 F2d 1301 (10th Cir 1980); Wilkins v Walter, 571 F Supp 474, 477 (ND Ohio 1983); Seidel v Chicago Sav & Loan Assn, 544 F Supp 508 (ND Ill 1982); Vuksta v Bethlehem Steel Corp, 540 F Supp 1276 (ED Pa 1982), *affd without opinion,* 707 F2d 1405 (3d Cir), *cert denied,* 464 US 835 (1983); Barkley v Carraux, 533 F Supp 242 (SD Tex 1982); Giles v Equal Employment Opportunity Commn, 520 F Supp 1198 (ED Mo 1981). See generally **ch 11.**

An age claim under §1982 was rejected in Barkley v Carraux, 533 F Supp 242 (SD Tex 1982). See generally **ch 11.**

[120] 42 USC §1983 provides as follows:

> Every person who, under color of any statute, ordinance, regulation, custom, or usage, of any State or Territory or the District of Columbia, subjects, or causes to be subjected, any citizen of the United States or other person within the jurisdiction thereof to the deprivation of any rights, privileges, or immunities secured by the Constitution and laws, shall be

invoke, although its reach is confined to persons acting under color of state law and thus it cannot be utilized either by federal employees or by individuals in the private sector.[121] Section 1983, however, creates no substantive rights; rather, it provides a cause of action for violations of constitutional rights or rights secured under other federal statutes. Insofar as §1983 is used to make a constitutional claim, it is available to an age discrimination plaintiff[122] (although the likelihood of success in making a constitutionally based argument is minimal).[123] Insofar as §1983 is relied upon to vindicate rights under the ADEA, a different conclusion follows. The Supreme Court has limited utilization of §1983 to situations where the other federal statute allegedly violated does not itself afford an exclusive remedy.[124] It has been held that the ADEA indeed does do so, and so §1983 cannot be used as a mechanism for securing redress for a violation of the ADEA.[125]

Case law, while in some disagreement, establishes that §1985(3)[126] possibly may be utilized with regard to both govern-

---

> liable to the person injured in an action at law, suit in equity, or other proper proceeding for redress.

[121] As to §1983 generally, see S. Nahmod, Civil Rights And Civil Liberties Litigation (Shepard's/McGraw-Hill 3d ed 1991).

[122] *See, e.g.*, Alford v City of Lubbock, 664 F2d 1263 (5th Cir), *cert denied*, 456 US 975 (1982); Equal Employment Opportunity Commn v City of Janesville, 630 F2d 1254 (7th Cir 1980); Arritt v Grissell, 567 F2d 1267 (4th Cir 1977).

[123] As to the likelihood of success in making a constitutionally based argument see **ch 10.**

[124] *See, e.g.*, Middlesex County Sewerage Auth v National Sea Clammers Assn, 453 US 1 (1981). See generally **ch 11.**

[125] McCroan v Bailey, 543 F Supp 1201, 1208-10 (SD Ga 1982); Bleakley v Jekyll Island—State Park Auth, 536 F Supp 236, 242 (SD Ga 1982). See generally **ch 11.**

[126] 42 USC §1985(3) provides as follows:

> If two or more persons in any State or Territory conspire or go in disguise on the highway or on the premises of another, for the purpose of depriving, either directly or indirectly, any person or class of persons of the equal protection of the laws, or of equal privileges and immunities under the laws, . . . the party so injured or deprived may have an action

Conspiracy

ment officials and private employers, but only to the extent that the ADEA is itself not available to a grievant.[127]

State Vehicles for Redress

There also are possible avenues of attack at the state level for individuals who believe themselves to be victims of wrongful age discrimination. The ADEA does not automatically preempt state statutes,[128] and so it is conceivable that a plaintiff may be able to pursue a claim based on a state constitutional[129] or statutory provision[130] or on a state common-law theory[131] affording more protection than is provided by the federal Act.[132] (However, a defendant will not be able to successfully invoke as a defense reliance upon a state law that affords less protection to employees and job applicants than does the ADEA.)[133]

---

for the recovery of damages occasioned by such injury or deprivation, against any one or more of the conspirators.

[127] *Compare* Pavlo v Stiefel Labs, Inc, 22 FEP Cas (BNA) 489 (SDNY 1979) (§1985(3) is available to some grievants) *with* White v Frank, 718 F Supp 592, 598 (WD Tex 1989), *affd on other grounds,* 895 F2d 243 (5th Cir), *cert denied,* 498 US 890 (1990); Wippel v Prudential Ins Co, 33 FEP Cas (BNA) 412 (D Md 1982); Seidel v Chicago Sav & Loan Assn, 544 F Supp 508 (ND Ill 1982); Smith v Walsh, 519 F Supp 853 (D Conn 1981); Platt v Burroughs Corp, 424 F Supp 1329 (ED Pa 1976) (§1985(3) not available). *See also* Boddorff v Publicker Indus, Inc, 488 F Supp 1107 (ED Pa 1980), in which the court, while explicitly declining to decide whether age discrimination claims are cognizable under §1985(3), dismissed the plaintiff's claim because of insufficient specificity; *see also* Abbott v Moore Business Forms, Inc, 439 F Supp 643, 649-50 (DNH 1977); Hines v Norfolk Naval Base, 17 Empl Prac Dec (CCH) ¶8387 (ED Va 1977). For a discussion of these cases, see generally **ch 11.**

[128] See **§2.05.**

[129] See **ch 11.**

[130] *Id.*

[131] See **ch 10.**

[132] As to jointly pursuing in one federal lawsuit claims under both the ADEA and these state bases for relief, see the sections regarding supplemental, or pendent, jurisdiction in **ch 6.**

[133] *See, e.g.,* Equal Employment Opportunity Commn v County of Allegheny, 519 F Supp 1328, 1335 n19 (WD Pa 1981), *affd,* 705 F2d 769 (3d Cir 1983).

Conclusion

In sum, from the grievant's perspective it would be unwise to focus only on the ADEA in fashioning a legal attack on age discrimination in employment. From the perspective of a potential defendant, it would be equally unwise to ignore the potential liability that may ensue as a result of failure to heed any strictures but those of the ADEA.

§2.05 —Preemption of State Provisions by the ADEA

Most states have enacted statutes barring, or at least limiting, age discrimination in employment.[134] Some of these statutes may afford greater protection than does the Age Discrimination in Employment Act (ADEA).[135] For example, a given state law may protect workers from age 18 on, whereas the ADEA's coverage does not extend to individuals under age 40.[136]

The ADEA clearly recognizes the existence of state antidiscrimination laws: the Act requires grievants to avail themselves of such laws as a predicate to seeking relief under the federal statute.[137] It is clear, then, that the ADEA is not as a matter of course preemptive.[138] Indeed, the ADEA's very language rebuts any contention that the Act automatically preempts state legislation; §14(a)[139] provides: "Nothing in this chapter shall affect the jurisdiction of any agency of any State performing like functions with regard to discriminatory employment practices on account of age except that upon commencement of action under this chapter such action shall supersede any State action."

---

[134] See **ch 11.**

[135] 29 USC §§621-634.

[136] See **ch 3.**

[137] §14, 29 USC §633(b). See **ch 6.**

[138] *See, e.g.*, Moody v Pepsi-Cola Metropolitan Bottling Co, Inc, 915 F2d 201, 210 (6th Cir 1990); Payne v Rozendaal, 147 Vt 488, 520 A2d 586, 589 (1986); Hillman v Consumers Power Co, 90 Mich App 627, 282 NW2d 422 (1979); *see also* Mason v Midwestern Fidelity Corp, 589 F Supp 751 (SD Ohio 1984).

[139] 29 USC §633(a).

Legislative history, committee commentary, case law, and agency guidelines confirm the nonpreemptive nature of the ADEA. In 1977 an effort was made on the floor of the House of Representatives to amend the Act by providing for preemption of any inconsistent state law. Representative Erlenborn offered the amendment to a bill then being considered that made other changes in the Act; he justified it as a measure to reduce the complexity ensuing from multistate companies having to comply both with differing state laws and with the federal law.[140] The amendment was rejected,[141] and this action confirms the nonpreemptive nature of the ADEA.[142] Additionally, it was stated in the Senate committee report accompanying 1978 amendments[143] that were adopted that "the ADEA does not preempt State laws," the language of §14(a) being pointed to as the basis for this statement.[144]

There also is relevant case law confirmation. In *Simpson v Alaska State Commission for Human Rights*[145] a district court addressed the argument that the ADEA—which at that time only protected persons up to age 65—preempted an Alaska statute that contained no such age ceiling. The court rejected the argument. It construed the ADEA as only setting minimum standards, pointing to legislative history in support of this conclusion,[146] and thus "the fact that Alaska . . . [had] gone beyond the federal government in enacting a complementary

---

140 123 Cong Rec 30559 (Sept 23, 1977).

141 *Id* 30567.

142 *Cf* Youngstown Sheet & Tube Co v United States, 343 US 579 (1952) (rejection by Congress of amendment to Taft-Hartley Act that would have given President authority to seize private property during labor strikes helped to establish lack of President's authority to do so pursuant to his claimed constitutional (as opposed to statutory) authority).

143 See **§2.02.**

144 Senate Comm on Human Resources, Amending the Age Discrimination in Employment Act Amendments of 1977, S Rep No 493, 95th Cong, 1st Sess 5 (1977).

145 423 F Supp 552 (D Alaska 1976), *affd,* 608 F2d 1171 (9th Cir 1979).

146 *Id* 556.

scheme in this area . . . [did] not make the Alaska law void."[147] Subsequently, the Court of Appeals for the Ninth Circuit, in affirming, adopted the district court's opinion.[148] Likewise, in *Fisher v Quaker Oats Co*[149] it was held that the ADEA did not preempt the New Jersey antidiscrimination law, under which a grievant was afforded a longer period of time within which to file suit than is provided by the ADEA.[150] The ADEA also does not preempt nonconflicting state common-law remedies.[151]

Of course, if the ADEA conflicts with a state statute, the employer may not rely upon that state law as a defense to an ADEA claim[152] or otherwise follow with impunity the state law. Rather, the state statute will be deemed to be invalidated by the federal statute.[153] Likewise, a state constitutional provision that

---

[147] *Id; accord* Crawford v ITT Consumer Fin Corp, 653 F Supp 1184 (SD Ohio 1986); Bailey v Container Corp of Am, 594 F Supp 629 (SD Ohio 1984); Hulme v Barrett, 449 NW2d 629 (Iowa 1989) (claim under state antidiscrimination law of plaintiff who was under 40 not preempted); Maine Human Rights Commn v Kennebec Water Power Co, 468 A2d 307 (Me 1983).

[148] Simpson v Alaska State Commn for Human Rights, 608 F2d 1171 (9th Cir 1979).

[149] 233 NJ Super 319, 559 A2d 1 (App Div), *cert denied,* 117 NJ 628, 569 A2d 1331 (1989).

[150] *Accord* Moody v Pepsi-Cola Bottling Co, 915 F2d 201 (6th Cir 1990) (state law allowing recovery of damages for emotional distress not preempted by the ADEA, which does not authorize such damages); Secretary of State v Mikusch, 181 Ill App 3d 431, 536 NE2d 1237 (1989), *revd,* 138 Ill 2d 242, 562 NE2d 168 (1990).

[151] Bernstein v Aetna Life & Casualty, 843 F2d 359 (9th Cir 1988); Torre v Figgie Intl, Inc, 50 FEP Cas (BNA) 1143, 1143 (ED Mo 1987). *But see* Howard v Daiichiya-Love's Bakery, Inc, 714 F Supp 1108, 1113 (D Haw 1989).

[152] *See, e.g.,* Equal Employment Opportunity Commn v County of Allegheny, 519 F Supp 1328, 1335 n19 (WD Pa 1981), *affd,* 705 F2d 679 (3d Cir 1983).

[153] *See, e.g.,* Equal Employment Opportunity Commn v Massachusetts, 987 F2d 64 (1st Cir 1993); Equal Employment Opportunity Commn v City of Altoona, 723 F2d 4 (3d Cir 1983), *cert denied,* 467 US 1204 (1984); United States Equal Employment Opportunity Commn v County of Calumet, 686 F2d 1249, 1257 n6 (7th Cir 1982); Equal Employment Opportunity Commn v County of Santa Barbara, 666 F2d 373, 378 (9th Cir 1982); Schlitz v Commonwealth of Va, 681 F Supp 330 (ED Va), *revd & remanded on other grounds,* 854 F2d 43 (4th Cir 1988); Betts v Hamilton County Bd of Mental Retardation, 631 F Supp 1198, 1206 (SD Ohio 1986), *affd,* 848 F2d 692 (6th Cir 1988), *revd on other grounds,* 492 US 158 (1989); Smith v Alum Rock Union Elementary Sch Dist,

conflicts with the ADEA will be preempted.[154] So, too, will be state common law that conflicts with the ADEA.[155]

(Given the foregoing discussion, several lower court rulings are at least questionable. In a series of decisions, an Ohio district court held that a plaintiff could not recover both liquidated dam-

---

6 Cal App 4th 1651, 8 Cal Rptr 2d 399 (1992); *accord* 29 CFR §1625.6(c) (1993). *Contra* Adams v Leatherbury, 388 So 2d 510 (Ala 1980).

In Nolan v Otis Elevator Co, 102 NJ 30, 505 A2d 580, *cert denied,* 479 US 820 (1986), a portion of the state law conflicted with the Employee Retirement Income Security Act (ERISA), 29 USC §1001 *et seq,* which provides that it is preemptive except where the preemption of a state law would impair a federal law. The question for the court was whether the state law's preemption by ERISA would impair the ADEA. The court misread the ADEA as requiring that suit must be filed within 300 days following the alleged unlawful practice, or within 30 days after the termination of a state law-based administrative proceeding. (As to the filing requirements, see **ch 6**). Thus, as the court misunderstood the matter, a grievant had more time under the New Jersey antidiscrimination law to pursue his or rights than was available under the ADEA. The court concluded that the availability of a state remedy, even after the federal ADEA remedy was no longer available, did not further the federal program, and so the preemption of the state law would not harm the ADEA scheme. *Accord* Warren v Oil, Chem & Atomic Workers, Union-Indus Pension Fund, 729 F Supp 563, 567 (ED Mich 1989). In Franke v Department of Indus, Labor & Human Relations, 45 FEP Cas (BNA) 72 (Wis 1987), the court held that ERISA preempted the state antidiscrimination statute insofar as the state law dealt with benefit plans covered by ERISA. *Accord* Lucas v Wheeler Machinery Co, 53 FEP Cas (BNA) 1729 (D Utah 1989); *see also* Babcock & Wilcox v Department of Human Rights, 189 Ill App 3d 827, 545 NE2d 799 (1989), *cert denied,* 479 US 1004 (1990). (State common-law wrongful discharge claims, based on the alleged wrongful administration of benefit plans, also are preempted by ERISA. *See, e.g.,* Pratt v Delta Air Lines, Inc, 675 F Supp 991 (D Md 1987); Cahall v Westinghouse Elec Corp, 644 F Supp 806 (ED Pa 1986).) ERISA, however, does not preempt state antidiscrimination laws insofar as those laws address matters such as unrelated plans not covered by ERISA, hiring, promotion, salary, and similar issues. Shaw v Delta Air Lines, Inc, 463 US 85, 97 (1983); Lane v Goren, 743 F2d 1337 (9th Cir 1984); *see also* Bernard v Browning-Ferris Indus, 57 FEP Cas (BNA) 924 (SD Tex 1990). *See generally* Mackey v Lanier Collections Agency & Serv, Inc, 486 US 825 (1988); T. B. Jovanovic, Annotation, *Pre-Emption of State Fair Employment Laws Under Provisions of §514 of Employee Retirement Income Security Act (29 USCS §1144),* 72 ALR Fed 489 (1985).

[154] Gregory v Ashcroft, 898 F2d 598, 600 (8th Cir 1990), *revd on other grounds,* 111 S Ct 2395 (1991).

[155] Rand v CF Indus, Inc, 797 F Supp 643 (ND Ill 1992).

ages under the ADEA and punitive damages under state law. In brief, the court vetoed what it perceived would be a duplicative recovery.[156] Another court erroneously reasoned, in declining to exercise supplemental, or pendent, jurisdiction over a state common-law claim,[157] that it had no jurisdiction to rule on the plaintiff's ADEA and state claims since they arose out of the same incident.[158] These courts, then, seemed to be of the erroneous view that a state remedy could not co-exist with the ADEA, even if the two were not in conflict. Other courts addressing pendent jurisdiction claims have not found concurrent state and federal claims to be incompatible.[159]

---

[156] *See* Merkel v Scovill, Inc, 573 F Supp 1055 (SD Ohio 1983), *affd in part & revd in part on other grounds,* 787 F2d 174 (6th Cir), *cert denied,* 479 US 990 (1986); Merkel v Scovill, Inc, 570 F Supp 141 (SD Ohio 1983); Merkel v Scovill, Inc, 570 F Supp 133 (SD Ohio 1983).

[157] As to such jurisdiction, see **ch 6.**

[158] Lettich v Kenway, 590 F Supp 1225 (D Mass 1984).

[159] As to such contrary rulings, see **ch 6.**

3

The Age Discrimination in Employment Act—Who is Protected and Which Entities Must Comply with Its Requirements

Identifying Those Who May Invoke the ADEA's Protection

§3.01 Age as a Benchmark for Protection: Generally

The protection afforded by the Age Discrimination in Employment Act (ADEA),[1] as originally enacted, extended only to persons between the ages of 40 and 65.[2] In 1978 the statute was amended to change the age-defined protection afforded by the Act in two major respects. First, the age cap for federal employees was removed entirely; second, the cap for employees in the

---

[1] 29 USC §§621-634.

[2] Pub L No 90-202, §12, 81 Stat 602, 607 (1967).

nonfederal sector was raised to age 70.[3] In 1986 the Act was amended once again to accord to most nonfederal employees the same treatment given their federal counterparts: the age 70 cap was removed entirely from the ADEA.[4] Thus, for the most part all individuals are now protected by the ADEA upon attainment of age 40.

There are some exceptions that limit the reach of the Act, however. For one, a federal statute may impose age-based mandatory retirement on certain federal employees, the ADEA notwithstanding.[5] In addition, certain high-level executives and policy makers likewise may be subjected to mandatory retirement once they attain age 65.[6] Moreover, the 1986 amendments provided for special treatment, now repealed, regarding law enforcement officers,[7] firefighters,[8] and tenured university employees.[9]

---

[3] The Age Discrimination in Employment Act Amendments of 1978, Pub L No 95-256, 92 Stat 189, amended §12 of the Act (codified at 29 USC §631).

[4] Age Discrimination in Employment Amendments of 1986, Pub L No 99-592, §2(c), 100 Stat 3342. While the amendment was, by its terms, effective as of January 1, 1987, it was held in Aledo-Garcia v Puerto Rico Natl Guard Fund, Inc, 887 F2d 354 (1st Cir 1989), that its protection extended retroactively to a 70-year-old plaintiff who had been discharged after its enactment (which occurred on October 31, 1986), but prior to January 1, 1987.

Clear statutory language notwithstanding, courts continue to misstate the statute's reach. A number of them have mistakenly asserted, years after the removal in 1986 of the age 70 ceiling from the Act, that the ADEA's protection ceases upon attainment of that age. *See, e.g.*, Equal Employment Opportunity Commn v Century Broadcasting Corp, 957 F2d 1446, 1451 (7th Cir 1992); Ware v Howard Univ, 816 F Supp 737, 750 (DDC 1993); Conroy v Anchor Sav Bank, FSB, 810 F Supp 42, 46 (EDNY 1993); Morton v Associated Dry Goods Corp, 792 F Supp 1136, 1142 (SD Ind 1992). Even more amazing, in Breiding v Garrett, 816 F Supp 708 (MD Fla 1993), the court described the protected class under the ADEA as being individuals ages 40 through 64. *Id* 711. That description was 15 years out of date, given the 1978 amending of the Act.

[5] *See* 5 USC §8335(b) (imposing mandatory retirement at age 55 on certain federal law officers and firefighters). See generally **§3.09.**

[6] See **§3.12.**

[7] See **§3.11.**

[8] *Id.*

[9] See **§3.10.**

Much of the case law deals with alleged violations arising from the victimization of persons under age 65 or age 70—the age limits in effect at the time the wrongs addressed in those particular cases occurred. Notwithstanding their being dated in this one respect, these rulings can be used to glean or support general propositions that remain valid and pertinent. These older cases therefore are of enduring interest and significance.

§3.02 —Grievants Who Are Under Age 40

Given the language of the Age Discrimination in Employment Act (ADEA),[10] which explicitly provides that its prohibitions are limited to individuals at least 40 years of age,[11] it is clear that in most instances persons under the age of 40 are unprotected. Thus, several courts have expressly ruled that persons under 40 cannot sue under the ADEA. Alternatively, some courts have reached the same result by holding that such individuals do not have standing to sue.[12] Numerous other courts have asserted in passing that in order for a plaintiff to establish a prima facie case, he or she must first establish membership in the protected class—i.e., persons 40 and over—at the time of the alleged wrong.[13] There are a handful of decisions, however—including, arguably, even a ruling of the Supreme Court—that go in the other direction.

---

[10] 29 USC §§621-634.

[11] §12(a), 29 USC §631(a) (addressing nonfederal employees); §12(b), 29 USC §631(b) (addressing federal employees).

[12] *See, e.g.*, Spain v Ball, 928 F2d 61 (2d Cir 1991); Hahn v City of Buffalo, 770 F2d 12, 14 (2d Cir 1985); Arnold v Postmaster Gen, 46 FEP Cas (BNA) 481 (DDC 1988), *cert denied*, 493 US 846 (1989); Settino v City of Chicago, 642 F Supp 755 (ND Ill 1986); Crane v Schneider, 635 F Supp 1430, 1434 (EDNY 1986); Klotsche v City of New York, 621 F Supp 1113, 1119 (SDNY 1985); Allen v Henifin, 26 FEP Cas (BNA) 581 (DDC 1980); Kodish v United Airlines, Inc, 463 F Supp 1245, 1249 (D Colo 1979), *affd on other grounds*, 628 F2d 1301 (10th Cir 1980); Bishop v Jelleff Assocs, Inc, 7 FEP Cas (BNA) 510 (DDC 1974); *see also* Thomas v United States Postal Inspection Serv, 647 F2d 1035, 1036 (10th Cir 1981).

[13] See **ch 7.**

Under-Age Claimants Who Turn 40 During the Pendency of Litigation

Three rulings constitute only minor departures from the statutorily set age 40 standard. In *Hahn v City of Buffalo,*[14] a case involving a challenge to a state statute barring anyone over 29 from being hired for a certain job, the court allowed individuals who were under 40 at the time the suit commenced to maintain their ADEA claims since they had attained 40 during the pendency of the suit. In *Pears v Spang*[15] the plaintiff was permitted to pursue his ADEA claim since, although he was under 40 at the time he was laid off, his formal termination occurred after his 40th birthday. The court reasoned that "[u]ntil termination was actually effected, the . . . [defendant] at least had the option of recalling plaintiff."[16] Similarly, in *Arnold v Postmaster General*[17] the federal employee plaintiff, who was 39 when the transfer about which he complained occurred, was allowed to maintain his suit since the transfer continued to affect him after he turned 40.

The Supreme Court's *Johnson* Decision

The general rigidity of the courts (save for those that issued the *Hahn, Pears,* and *Arnold* opinions) arguably is unwarranted insofar as they inflexibly exclude persons under age 40 from seeking relief under the ADEA. This argument follows from the decision of the Supreme Court in *Johnson v Mayor of Baltimore.*[18] The *Johnson* litigation began with six plaintiffs challenging a city ordinance requiring the retirement of firefighters at the age of 55 or 60. One of the six, Porter, was 30 at the time suit was filed in 1979. As to the five plaintiffs other than Porter, the trial court ruled that the provision that required their retirement at age 60

---

[14] 596 F Supp 939, 954 (WDNY 1984), *affd on other grounds,* 770 F2d 12 (2d Cir 1985).

[15] 718 F Supp 441 (WD Pa 1989).

[16] *Id* 444.

[17] 667 F Supp 6 (DDC 1987), *revd on other grounds,* 863 F2d 994 (DC Cir 1988), *cert denied,* 493 US 846 (1989).

[18] 472 US 353 (1985).

was illegal under the ADEA. With respect to Porter, another provision of the ordinance at issue came into play: since he was hired after July 1, 1962, he eventually would be required to retire at age 55. The district court held that Porter had standing to sue, reasoning that if he survived and was still employed by the fire department when he attained age 55, he would then be able to invoke the ADEA's protection.

In response to the defendant's argument that Porter's claim was not ripe, the court first stated that "since this Court has found that the provisions . . . which mandate retirement at age sixty violate the ADEA, a fortiori the provisions of the legislation which mandate that plaintiff Porter must retire at age fifty-five are likewise invalid."[19] The court then addressed directly the ripeness issue as follows:

> The provisions of the law applying to . . . [the] two separate groups [i.e., those hired before July 1, 1962, and those hired thereafter] are hardly severable. . . . The principle of statutory severability plays a special role when a court is presented with questions of ripeness. . . . Severability . . . may make ripe issues that otherwise would be better deferred. . . .
>
> Under the particular circumstances of this case, considerations of judicial economy lead this Court to the conclusion that plaintiff Porter's claim is ripe for determination at this time. It would make little sense . . . to defer consideration of Porter's claim until a later date.[20]

The Court of Appeals for the Fourth Circuit reversed the ruling for the plaintiffs. It did so on grounds totally unrelated to the question of Porter's age. Clearly, however, the court was aware that Porter was a plaintiff: it explicitly noted (without

---

[19] Johnson v Mayor of Baltimore, 515 F Supp 1287, 1301-02 (D Md 1981), *revd on other grounds,* 731 F2d 209 (4th Cir 1984), *revd,* 472 US 353 (1985).

[20] *Id* 1301-02.

expressly approving) the trial court's holding that this under-age-40 plaintiff had standing to sue.[21]

Subsequently, the Supreme Court reversed the Fourth Circuit's reversal. Again, the reversal—which reinstated the original ruling for the plaintiffs—did not directly address the standing question. Again, however, it was clear that this Court also was aware that there were six plaintiffs: the Court explicitly so noted.[22] (Absent Porter, there would have been only five). Thus, the Court upheld a ruling holding a city ordinance violative of the ADEA, which ruling was rendered vis-a-vis an under-age-40 plaintiff. What makes this particularly noteworthy is that it is standard doctrine that jurisdiction cannot be conferred on a federal court by the parties. Indeed, the court itself must raise and dispose of jurisdictional issues, even if the parties do not.[23] Thus, even if the defendant had not argued Porter's lack of standing before the Supreme Court or the court of appeals, those courts still would have had to have addressed the matter—and to have dismissed Porter as a party plaintiff—if indeed he lacked standing. That the Supreme Court did not do so therefore can be read as approbation by the Court of the trial court's initial determination regarding Porter's standing.

In brief, then, the Supreme Court approved an ADEA claim being pursued by an under-age-40 plaintiff. However, it is true that the *Johnson* litigation's significance arguably is limited by the particular facts, i.e., an ordinance with two closely related parts, one of which affected over-age-40 plaintiffs and the other that affected a plaintiff under the age of 40. Moreover, the case already included plaintiffs who did fall within the ADEA's pro-

---

[21] Johnson v Mayor of Baltimore, 731 F2d 209, 210 (4th Cir 1984), *revd,* 472 US 353 (1985). The dissenting judge read the majority opinion as holding that Porter had standing to sue, and he further noted that he agreed with that much of the majority's ruling. *Id* 216 n1 (Winter, C.J., dissenting).

[22] 472 US at 357.

[23] *See, e.g.,* Sumner v Mata, 449 US 539, 547 n2 (1981); Louisville & Nashville RR Co v Mottley, 211 US 149, 152 (1908).

ADEA,[28] which authorizes "[a]ny person aggrieved" to bring "a the reach of *Johnson.*[24] Finally, it may be significant that the under-age plaintiff involved in *Johnson* would not have secured relief by virtue of a ruling for his five co-plaintiffs had only they been allowed to pursue redress. Were it the case that a judgment for them would at the same time have benefited their younger colleague, the *Johnson* courts might have been less willing to hold that the under-age-40 plaintiff had standing. (Indeed, this perhaps explains why the court in *Hahn v City of Buffalo*[25] was unwilling to hold that the under-age-40 plaintiffs in that case had standing.[26])

Decisions Clearly Allowing ADEA Claims By Under-Age-40 Plaintiffs

Two decisions clearly demonstrate judicial approval of suits by under-age-40 plaintiffs. Neither of them can be distinguished, like *Johnson,* by virtue of a peculiar procedural or factual situation. Likewise, neither involved plaintiffs about to turn 40 as their claims, or the harm of which they complained, came to fruition, as in *Hahn, Pears,* and *Arnold.*

The first of these rulings is *Allen v American Home Products, Inc,*[27] which involved 51 plaintiffs who argued that the defendant in part based its decision to close the plant in which they had worked on the fact that older workers predominated at the facility. Some of the plaintiffs, i.e., individuals who had been terminated as a result of the plant closing, were under age 40, and so the defendant moved to dismiss them. The court, however, reasoned that these younger plaintiffs indeed had suffered an injury, i.e., the loss of their jobs, and that this injury was due to the allegedly unlawful plant closure. Thus, these under-age-40 plaintiffs fit within the language of §7(c)(1) of the

---

[24] *See* Settino v City of Chicago, 642 F Supp 755, 759 n6 (ND Ill 1986).

[25] 770 F2d 12 (2d Cir 1985).

[26] *Id* 14 n2.

[27] 644 F Supp 1553 (ND Ind 1986).

[28] 29 USC §626(c)(1).

tected class. This, too, may be seen as a significant factor limiting civil action . . . for . . . legal or equitable relief[.]"[29]

The second decision that clearly allowed suit to be brought by a plaintiff less than 40 years of age is *Anderson v Phillips Petroleum Co,*[30] which involved a 32-year-old union president who filed a charge of age discrimination on behalf of those union members who were over age 40. Subsequently, he was discharged. He then filed suit under the ADEA, claiming that he was the victim of unlawful discrimination. The defendant argued that Anderson, being under age 40, could not invoke the ADEA's protection. The court disagreed, setting forth several bases for concluding that an individual under age 40 who either participates in or files an age discrimination charge can maintain a cause of action based on retaliation.[31]

First, the court noted, analogical support for its ruling was afforded by case law developed under Title VII of the Civil Rights Act of 1964.[32] Second, the court looked to the language

---

[29] The *any person aggrieved* language has been used in other federal statutes, in the context of which the phrase has been given a very broad reading. It has been read as evincing Congress' intent to extend standing to individuals as broadly as is compatible with the constitutional requisites set by Article III of the United States Constitution. US Const art III. *See* Trafficante v Metropolitan Life Ins Co, 409 US 205 (1972) (construing the federal Fair Housing Act, 42 USC §3601 *et seq*). Even more relevant is the fact that Title VII of the Civil Rights Act of 1964, 42 USC §§2000e through 2000e-17, contains virtually identical language. *Id* §2000e-5(b), (f)(1). That language has been read liberally so as to allow individuals to maintain suit even though they themselves are not members of the protected class, so long as they are harmed by virtue of wrongs done to persons in the protected class. *See, e.g.,* Stewart v Hannon, 675 F2d 846 (7th Cir 1982); Waters v Heublein, Inc, 547 F2d 466 (9th Cir 1976), *cert denied,* 433 US 915 (1977) (white woman could maintain suit based on discrimination against blacks and Hispanics). Since Title VII case law is looked to by ADEA courts for guidance, see **ch 2,** these cases afford analogical support for a broad reading of the *any person aggrieved* language of §7(c)(1) so as to allow an under-age-40 individual to sue where injury inflicted on an ADEA-protected individual also harms the younger person. In fact, *Allen* presents just such a scenario.

[30] 722 F Supp 668 (D Kan 1989).

[31] As to retaliation generally, see **ch 4.**

[32] 42 USC §§2000e through 2000e-17.

of the retaliation ban set forth in §4(d) of the ADEA,[33] which provides that it is unlawful for an employer "to discriminate against any individual." The court emphasized the word "any", and concluded from the use of the word in §4(d) that the age limitation set forth in §12(a)[34] of the Act was inapplicable to retaliation claims. The court wrote as follows:

> Section 12(a) limits the "prohibitions" of age discrimination set out in section 4 to individuals at least 40 years of age. The court finds that section 4(d) was enacted to aid the enforcement of those prohibitions on age discrimination. The court does not believe that congress [sic] intended for section 12(a) to abrogate the clear protection provided in section 4(d) for "any individual who has made a charge, testified or assisted or participated in the investigation or proceeding."[35]

Third, the court noted that the Equal Employment Opportunity Commission (EEOC) takes the position in its compliance manual, which affords guidance to EEOC staff, "that it is not necessary for the charging party to allege that he was treated differently because of his age to make an allegation based on Section 4(d)[.]"[36] Finally, the court reasoned that "age related animus is not a required element for a claim of retaliation."[37] This being so, "it would be ridiculous to require plaintiff to show that he is in the protected age class to state a claim of retaliation."[38]

---

[33] 29 USC §623(d).

[34] *Id* §631(a).

[35] 722 F Supp at 672.

[36] *Id.*

[37] *Id.*

[38] *Id.*

§3.03 —Age 40-and-Over Plaintiffs Who Complain of Better Treatment Accorded Other Persons Over Age 40

The handful of decisions involving plaintiffs who were under age 40 at some point during the course of their litigation, and yet managed to pursue their claims under the Age Discrimination in Employment Act (ADEA),[39] comprises a unique group of rulings. All the thousands of other ADEA cases involve complainants who, by virtue of their ages, clearly fit within the ADEA's protected class. The great majority of these cases involve individuals who complained that they had been treated less favorably than younger persons.

When an older individual complains of being treated less favorably than a younger person, there has been—and remains—a question as to whether that younger person must be someone who is under age 40. The answer of the ADEA enforcement agency, the Equal Employment Opportunity Commission (EEOC), in an interpretive guideline is a negative one: discrimination can occur even when the favored individual is himself or herself within the ADEA's protected class.[40] According to the EEOC, "if two people apply for the same position, and one is 42 and the other 52, the employer may not lawfully turn down either one on the basis of age[.]"[41] The case law in large measure supports this position, allowing a plaintiff to establish a prima facie case and ultimately to prevail under the ADEA even if the favored person to whom he or she points is, while younger, not under age 40.[42] There has been some disagreement among the courts, however, regarding this proposition—a disagreement that is manifested primarily in judicial formulations of what constitutes a prima facie case.[43]

---

[39] 29 USC §§621-634.

[40] 29 CFR §1625.2(a) (1993). Such guidelines do not have the force of law, but the courts generally accord them considerable deference. See **ch 2**.

[41] 29 CFR §1625.2(a) (1993).

[42] See **ch 7**.

[43] *Id.*

There are a few cases dealing with grievants who claim they are the victims of discrimination notwithstanding that people even older than themselves are the alleged recipients of discriminatory favorable treatment. This issue also has been dealt with primarily in the context of decisions focusing on whether the plaintiff has succeeded in establishing a prima facie case.[44] The issue also may come to the fore in the context of retirement plans for which some minimum age—let us say, age 55—is a condition of eligibility, with the consequence that under-55 employees are excluded and they accordingly complain about the beneficial treatment accorded older workers.[45] As for the EEOC, it approves some preferential treatment of older workers.[46]

Section 9 of the ADEA[47] authorizes the EEOC to make reasonable exceptions from the Act's coverage, and this authority in fact has been exercised to exclude certain individuals who otherwise would be protected by the Act.[48]

§3.04 Status as a Benchmark for Protection: Generally

Even though an individual satisfies the generally accepted (but not universally required) minimum age hurdle imposed by the Age Discrimination in Employment Act (ADEA)[49]—i.e., the necessity of being at least age 40—it does not follow necessarily that he or she may invoke the Act's protection. A variety of issues can arise related to the status of those who may, and those who may not, look to the ADEA for redress.

---

[44] *Id.*

[45] See **chs 4, 5.**

[46] *See* 29 CFR §1625.2(b) (1993). See generally **ch 4.**

[47] 29 USC §628.

[48] See **ch 4.**

[49] 29 USC §§621-634.

§3.05 —Job Applicants, Employees, and Former Employees

The Age Discrimination in Employment Act (ADEA)[50] speaks to discrimination in the workplace. Thus, the Act obviously protects people who are employees. It also protects, although the literal terms of the Act do not make this clear, other actors on the employment scene such as individuals who are not employees per se. To be more specific, the ADEA is understood to ban discrimination against job applicants. It also extends to former employees, i.e., people who have been discharged, or have otherwise left their jobs, and believe they have some legal claim based either on the manner in which they departed the workplace or on events occurring subsequent to their departure.

Employees

Most of the prohibitions of the ADEA purport to protect *any individual.*[51] Thus, for example, §4(a)[52] provides as follows:

> It shall be unlawful for an employer—
>
> (1) to fail or refuse to hire or to discharge any individual or otherwise discriminate against any individual with respect to his compensation, terms, conditions, or privileges of employment, because of such individual's age[.]

Likewise, the Act provides that it shall be unlawful for "an employment agency to fail or refuse to refer for employment, or otherwise discriminate against, any individual because of such individual's age[.]"[53] The common use of the word "individual" notwithstanding, there are some provisions of the Act that use

[50] 29 USC §§621-634.

[51] *Id* §623(a)(1), (b), (c)(1), (3).

[52] *Id* §623(a).

[53] §4(b), 29 USC §623(b).

the word *employee.*[54] For example, §4(d)[55] makes it unlawful "for an employer to discriminate against any of his employees or applicants for employment" by retaliating against such persons for participating in efforts to enforce the ADEA. And the provision authorizing civil enforcement of the Act appears to equate "person" "aggrieved" with "employee."[56]

The ADEA itself offers nothing by way of explication of these various terms. In a totally circular effort, the Act simply defines "employee" as an individual employed by an employer.[57] The ADEA administrative interpretations shed little additional light on the meaning of the term: an Equal Employment Opportunity Commission (EEOC) guideline simply refers to the statutory definition.[58] It would seem proper to conclude, the lack of statutory exposition notwithstanding, that common-law agency doctrine provides the guide for determining employee status.[59] The Supreme Court's analysis in *Nationwide Mutual Insurance Co v Darden,*[60] a ruling addressing the term *employee* as it appears in §3(6)[61] of the Employee Retirement Income Security Act of 1974 (ERISA),[62] is the legal touchstone for this conclusion.[63] *Darden*

---

[54] *Id* §623(a)(2), (3), (d).

[55] *Id* §623(d).

[56] Section 7(c), 29 USC §26(c)(1), provides: "Any *person aggrieved* may bring a civil action . . . provided, that the right of *any person* to bring such action shall terminate upon the commencement of an action by the Secretary to enforce the right of such *employee.*" (Emphasis added.)

[57] 29 USC §630(f).

[58] 29 CFR §1625.1 (1993).

[59] Frankel v Bally, Inc, 987 F2d 86 (2d Cir 1993).

[60] 112 S Ct 1344 (1992).

[61] 29 USC §1002(6).

[62] *Id* §1001 *et seq.*

[63] *Darden* was followed in Frankel v Bally, Inc, 987 F2d 86 (2d Cir 1993). In Levine v Fairleigh Dickinson Univ, 646 F2d 825 (3d Cir 1981), the Court of Appeals for the Third Circuit had deemed the essence of the employment relationship to be an exchange of services for pay. *Id* 829. The court concluded that Levine, a professor at Fairleigh Dickinson who had retired and relinquished his tenure and who then was reappointed to a one-year nontenured professorship, was an employee despite his emeritus status. The relationship between the plaintiff and the university had, in the court's view, the characteris-

is relevant because the definition at issue there, i.e., an employee is "any individual employed by an employer," parallels that appearing in the ADEA.

The *Darden* Court pointed out that the definition of *employee* in ERISA is "completely circular and explains nothing"[64]—a characterization equally applicable to the ADEA definition. The Court further observed that it did "not find . . . any provision either giving specific guidance concerning the term's meaning or suggesting that construing it according to traditional agency law principles would thwart the congressional design or lead to absurd results."[65] (Again, this is an observation equally apposite in the case of the ADEA.) Accordingly, the Supreme Court adopted a common-law test for determining who qualifies under ERISA (and, analogically, under the ADEA as well) as an employee:

> "In determining whether a hired party is an employee under the general common law of agency, we consider the hiring party's right to control the manner and means by which the product is accomplished. Among the other factors relevant to this inquiry are the skill required; the source of the instrumentalities and tools; the location of the work; the duration of the relationship between the parties; whether the hiring party has the right to assign additional projects to the hired party; the extent of the hired party's discretion over when and how long to work; the method of payment; the hired party's role in hiring and paying assistants; whether the work is part of the regular business of the hiring party; whether the hiring party is in business; the provision of employee benefits; and the tax treatment of the hired party."[66]

---

tic features of employment, including a letter agreement obligating Levine to perform specified services for which he was to be paid. *Id* 828.

[64] 112 S Ct at 1348.

[65] *Id.*

[66] *Id* (quoting Community for Creative Non-Violence v Reid, 490 US 730, 751-52 (1989) (footnotes omitted)). The ADEA is in part modeled on the Fair

As indicated by the foregoing discussion, a number of questions can arise as to whether a given individual is an employee for the purposes of the ADEA. These issues are discussed further below, as well as in succeeding sections. For the most part, it is correct to conclude that if a grievant is neither a job applicant nor an employee (or a former employee, as discussed below), suit may not be maintained.[67] However, there is some case law establishing (in contexts other than job application situations)

Labor Standards Act (FLSA), 29 USC §§200-219, and so the Court's rejection of the plaintiff's effort to analogize the ERISA definition of *employee* to that set forth in the FLSA is also pertinent here. *Employee* is defined in the FLSA, as in the ADEA and ERISA, to include "any individual employed by an employer." 29 USC §203(e)(1). However, the verb *employ* is further defined in the FLSA to mean "suffer or permit to work," *id* §203(g), an additional definition absent both from ERISA and the ADEA. From these facts the Court in *Darden* drew the conclusion that the analogy to the FLSA, whose definition of *employee* had been more broadly construed in Rutherford Food Corp v McComb, 331 US 722 (1947), than it had been in the case relied upon by the *Darden* Court, i.e., *Reid,* was inappropriate:

> The . . . definition [of *employ* to mean "suffer or permit to work"] . . . stretches the meaning of "employee" to cover some parties who might not qualify as such under a strict application of traditional agency law principles. ERISA lacks any such provision, however, and the textual asymmetry between the two statutes precludes reliance on FLSA cases when construing ERISA's concept of "employee."

112 S Ct at 1350. This analysis is equally apt with regard to rejecting an FLSA-ADEA analogy.

[67] Thus, for example, in Asklar v Honeywell, Inc, 95 FRD 419 (D Conn 1982), the plaintiff—the surviving spouse of a deceased employee—was barred from suing where she claimed that the defendant had retaliated against her, in violation of the ADEA, by withholding pension benefits. While the Act outlaws retaliation, see **ch 4,** it applies only to employees, in the *Asklar* court's view—a category into which the spouse of the former employee clearly did not fit. In fact, §4(d), 29 USC §623(d), which is the section concerning retaliation, on its face explicitly also refers to "applicants for employment." In any event, the *Asklar* court's analysis arguably was too narrow; the policy ends of the ADEA would have been served, it would seem, had the plaintiff been allowed to pursue her claim. At the same time, no violence would have been done to the literal terms of the ADEA inasmuch as the surviving spouse could have been seen as being a surrogate for the decedent, who clearly had been an employee.

that an employment relationship—present or past—is not invariably a predicate to invoking the protection of the ADEA.[68]

Job Applicants

Clearly, the ADEA protects not only employees, but job applicants as well. Section §4(a)(1)[69] makes it unlawful for an employer "to fail or refuse to hire . . . any individual . . . because of such individual's age[.]" Section 4(b),[70] dealing with employment agencies, makes it unlawful for an employment agency "to fail or refuse to refer for employment . . . any individual because of such individual's age, or to classify or refer for employment any individual on the basis of such individual's age." Obviously, it is job applicants (albeit not applicants for jobs with the employment agencies themselves) who are those seeking to be referred. Furthermore, §4(c)[71] expressly refers to job applicants:

> It shall be unlawful for a labor organization—
>
> . . . .
>
> (2) to limit, segregate, or classify its membership, or to classify or fail to refuse to refer for employment any individual, in any way which would deprive or tend to deprive any individual of employment opportunities, or would limit such employment opportunities or otherwise adversely affect his status as an employee or as an applicant for employment, because of such individual's age[.]

Section 4(d),[72] which prohibits retaliation against individuals who oppose practices that are violative of the ADEA, or who assist in the enforcement of the Act, also expressly refers to "applicants for employment[.]"

---

[68] See **§3.15.**

[69] 29 USC §623(a)(1).

[70] *Id* §623(b).

[71] *Id* §623(c).

[72] *Id* §623(d).

Former Employees

The majority of ADEA cases involve the claims of people who have alleged that they were wrongfully discharged. Obviously, such individuals are no longer involved in an employment relationship at the point they are pursuing claims under the ADEA. Of course, while it is correct to note that there is, at the time the legal process begins, no longer an employment relationship between the parties, there at least was such a relationship at the time the alleged wrong occurred. But inasmuch as the ADEA's prohibitory language regarding the actions of employers, employment agencies, and labor organizations speaks, as pointed out earlier, to barring discrimination against "individual[s],"[73] there appears to be no need to rely upon that factual nicety.[74] On the other hand, the alleged discrimination generally must be tied to a relationship that at least existed at some point. In other words, as stated by the Court of Appeals for the Fifth Circuit in *Equal Employment Opportunity Commission v Cosmair, Inc,*[75] "[t]he term 'employee' . . . includes a former employee as long as the alleged discrimination is related to or arises out of the employment relationship."[76]

Even discrimination that occurs following the end of the employment relationship falls within the ADEA's ambit. In other words, former employees can sue even when they are the victims of postemployment wrongdoing. Thus, for example, a plaintiff

---

[73] §4(a), (b), (c), 29 USC §623(a), (b), (c).

[74] Section 4(d), 29 USC §623(d), which concerns retaliation, only addresses an "employer [that] . . . discriminate[s] against any of his employees or applicants for employment[.]" In contrast, the same section applies to "an employment agency . . . [that] discriminate[s] against any individual[.]" This difference in language arguably supports the argument that only employees, and therefore not former employees, can raise claims of retaliation against employers. As noted in the text, however, the case law refutes this conclusion. Moreover, further language in §4(d) negates this narrow reading: the section goes on to provide that the discrimination that is proscribed is that which arises out of "such *individual* . . . [having] opposed any practice made unlawful . . . or . . . such *individual*" having assisted in an enforcement action. (Emphasis added.)

[75] 821 F2d 1085 (5th Cir 1987).

[76] *Id* 1088; *see also* Caudill v Farmland Indus, Inc, 698 F Supp 1476, 1485 (WD Mo 1988), *affd,* 919 F2d 83 (8th Cir 1990).

was allowed to maintain a claim based on retaliation that occurred after he left his position with the defendant employer.[77] In this same case the Court of Appeals for the District of Columbia also made the following observation with regard to other, common instances of postemployment termination discrimination:

> [I]t is well established that efforts by an employer to scuttle a former employee's search for a new job, such as by withholding a letter of recommendation or by providing negative information to a prospective employer, can constitute illegal retaliation within the meaning of ADEA and parallel anti-retaliation provisions.[78]

In *Helwig v Suburban Chevrolet, Inc,*[79] a district court took a somewhat more cautious stance. While the court rejected the argument that a former employee could not maintain a suit based on alleged postemployment retaliation perpetrated by his former employers, it was careful to state that it did not "interpret the term 'employee' . . . to always include a former employee."[80] The court continued: "It simply may be that a retaliatory act which comes close on the heels of an employee's termination is of such a nature to be fairly includable as a cause of action."[81] And so, at the preliminary stage at which the litigation then stood, the court refused to dismiss the plaintiff's claim.

Discovery Regarding the Status of Individuals

The EEOC, in the course of investigating an entity, may subpoena documents to determine whether persons designated as partners (and therefore employers) actually are employees.[82]

---

77 Passer v American Chem Socy, 935 F2d 322, 330-31 (DC Cir 1991).

78 *Id* 331.

79 33 FEP Cas (BNA) 1261 (D Md 1983).

80 *Id* 1264.

81 *Id.*

82 Equal Employment Opportunity Commn v Peat, Marwick, Mitchell & Co, 775 F2d 928 (8th Cir 1985), *cert denied,* 475 US 1046 (1986).

Who Determines Employment Status and Who Bears the Burden of Proof

According to the Court of Appeals for the Sixth Circuit, "[t]he term 'employee' is to be given a broad construction in order to effectuate the remedial purposes of the ADEA."[83] In responding to (and finding no fault with) the fact that a jury had made the determination of whether the plaintiff was an employee, the appellate court also addressed the question of who decides the issue of whether an individual is an employee:

> The determination of employment status is a mixed question of law and fact. Normally, a judge will be able to make this determination as a matter of law. However, where there is a genuine issue of fact or conflicting inferences can be drawn from the undisputed facts . . . the question is to be resolved by the finder of fact in accordance with the appropriate rules of law.[84]

In a similar vein, the court deciding *Kennel v Dover Garage, Inc,*[85] followed the earlier discussed Supreme Court *Darden* decision. In looking to the same factors that the *Darden* Court had set forth, as quoted above, the *Kennel* court opined that "[t]he existence and degree of each factor is a question of fact, while the legal conclusion to be drawn from these facts is a question of law."[86] In *Martin v United Way of Erie County*[87] the Court of Appeals for the Second Circuit asserted that the question of status as an employee is a jury issue. The district court that decided *Golden v AP Orleans, Inc,*[88] took a contrary position, however.

---

[83] Lilley v BTM Corp, 958 F2d 746, 750 (6th Cir), *cert denied,* 113 S Ct 376 (1992).

[84] *Id* 750 n1; *accord* Cox v Master Lock Co, 815 F Supp 844, 845 (ED Pa), *affd without opinion,* 14 F3d 46 (3d Cir 1993).

[85] 816 F Supp 178 (EDNY 1993), *affd without opinion,* 9 F3d 1536 (2d Cir 1993).

[86] *Id* 184.

[87] 829 F2d 445, 451 (2d Cir 1987).

[88] 681 F Supp 1100, 1102 n2 (ED Pa 1988).

It is the plaintiff who bears the burden of proving his or her employment status, by a preponderance of the evidence.[89]

§3.06 —Independent Contractors

The Age Discrimination in Employment Act (ADEA)[90] does not extend its protection against discrimination in the workplace to independent contractors.[91] That much is clear. What typically generates a dispute is the question of whether, in a given case, the individual making a claim of discriminatory treatment is an employee, and thus protected under the ADEA, or is an unprotected independent contractor. Three tests are relevant in making this determination.[92]

Under the economic realities test, which typically is used in cases arising under the Fair Labor Standards Act (FLSA),[93] persons are considered employees if " 'as a matter of economic reality, [they] are dependent upon the business to which they render service.' "[94] As the Court of Appeals for the Tenth Circuit put it in *Oestman v National Farmers Union Insurance Co,*[95] "the central question becomes: Is this worker, as a matter of economic fact,

---

[89] Lilley v BTM Corp, 958 F2d 746, 751 (6th Cir), *cert denied,* 113 S Ct 376 (1992).

[90] 29 USC §§621-634.

[91] *See, e.g.,* Cobb v Sun Papers, 673 F2d 337 (11th Cir), *cert denied,* 459 US 874 (1982).

[92] In Frishberg v Esprit de Corp, Inc, 778 F Supp 793 (SDNY 1991), *affd without opinion,* 969 F2d 1042 (2d Cir 1992), the plaintiff urged the court to use the *single employer* doctrine. The court responded by pointing out that this doctrine actually is used to determine whether two entities are so interrelated that they both can be held responsible for the acts of the immediate employer, see **§3.28,** and it is not apposite regarding the question of whether an individual is an employee, rather than an independent contractor. 778 F Supp at 800.

[93] 29 USC §§200-219.

[94] Hickey v Arkla Indus, Inc, 699 F2d 748, 751 (5th Cir 1983) (quoting Mednick v Albert Enters, Inc, 508 F2d 297, 299 (5th Cir 1975), in turn quoting Bartels v Birmingham, 332 US 126, 130 (1947)).

[95] 958 F2d 303 (10th Cir 1992).

in business for himself?"[96] This approach, while utilized in the past by a minority of ADEA courts, no longer seems viable in light of a Supreme Court 1992 ruling, *Nationwide Mutual Insurance Co v Darden,*[97] which addressed the Employee Retirement Income Security Act (ERISA)[98] and is relevant by way of analogy.

The second tack, which is consistent with *Darden,* is a hybrid approach that looks to the economic realities of the situation to assess the degree of economic dependence of the alleged employee on the business with which he or she is connected, while focusing on the employer's right to control the " 'means and manner' of the worker's performance"[99] as the most important factor in determining employee status.

The Hybrid Approach

The Courts of Appeals for the Second, Third, Fourth, Fifth, and Tenth Circuits have endorsed the hybrid approach. In *Equal Employment Opportunity Commission v Zippo Manufacturing Co*[100] the Court of Appeals for the Third Circuit acknowledged both that the more protective economic realities test is utilized in FLSA cases, and that the ADEA incorporates the remedies provisions of the FLSA. However, the court reasoned that the ADEA's substantive provisions are derived from Title VII of the Civil Rights Act of 1964,[101] and thus the scope of the ADEA's substantive provisions is to be determined by Title VII standards. In other words, the determination of employee status is a question involving the substantive prohibitions of the ADEA and not merely its remedies. The court observed that Title VII courts regularly have refrained from using the economic realities test,

---

[96] *Id* 305.

[97] 112 S Ct 1344 (1992).

[98] 29 USC §1001 *et seq.*

[99] Oestman v National Farmers Union Ins Co, 958 F2d 303, 305 (10th Cir 1992) (quoting Spirides v Reinhardt, 613 F2d 826, 831 (DC Cir 1979)).

[100] 713 F2d 32 (3d Cir 1983).

[101] 42 USC §§2000e through 2000e-17.

but rather have utilized the hybrid approach. Thus, it is this approach that should apply to the ADEA as well, the court concluded.[102]

The Court of Appeals for the Fifth Circuit, which earlier had avoided taking a firm position in *Hickey v Arkla Industries, Inc,*[103] also opted for the hybrid approach in *Fields v Hallsville Independent School District.*[104] The Court of Appeals for the Second Circuit initially did likewise in *Martin v United Way.*[105] The Court of Appeals for the Fourth Circuit in *Garrett v Phillips Mills, Inc,*[106] and the Court of Appeals for the Tenth Circuit in *Oestman v National Farmers Union Insurance Co,*[107] also have adopted the hybrid approach. Some district courts outside these circuits also have endorsed this analysis.[108]

While under the hybrid approach control is the most important factor to consider, there are other important considerations. In *Darden* the Supreme Court set forth a nonexclusive listing of factors that clearly are now to be taken into account in determin-

---

[102] For a detailed application of *Zippo* to the particular facts presented to the court, see Carney v Dexter Shoe Co, 701 F Supp 1093 (DNJ 1988).

[103] 699 F2d 748 (5th Cir 1983); *accord* Ehret v Louisiana, 58 FEP Cas (BNA) 658 (ED La 1992). The *Hickey* court viewed the FLSA economic realities test as the most liberal, concluded that even under that test the plaintiff would not qualify as an employee, and thus reserved opinion as to whether one or the other of the tests should be used. In reviewing the FLSA test, the court identified five considerations involved in assessing the alleged employee's degree of dependence on the business: "degree of control; opportunities for profit or loss; investment in facilities; permanency of relationship; and skill required." 699 F2d at 752; *see also* Weber v George Cook, Ltd, 563 F Supp 598 (SDNY 1983).

[104] 906 F2d 1017 (5th Cir 1990), *cert denied,* 498 US 1026 (1991).

[105] 829 F2d 445 (2d Cir 1987); *accord* Frishberg v Esprit de Corp, Inc, 778 F Supp 793 (SDNY 1991), *affd without opinion,* 969 F2d 1042 (2d Cir 1992); Frank v Capital Cities Communications, Inc, 48 FEP Cas (BNA) 551 (SDNY 1983). The Court of Appeals for the Second Circuit later discarded the hybrid approach, and embraced common-law agency principles for determining employee status, in Frankel v Bally, Inc, 987 F2d 86 (2d Cir 1993).

[106] 721 F2d 979 (4th Cir 1983).

[107] 958 F2d 303, 305 (10th Cir 1992).

[108] Gordon v The Birmingham News, 53 Empl Prac Dec (CCH) ¶39,978 (ND Ala 1989); Dake v Mutual of Omaha Ins Co, 600 F Supp 63 (ND Ohio 1984).

ing employee status. Many of the factors pointed to in *Darden,* which are quoted below, were also set forth in *Spirides v Reinhardt,*[109] a Title VII ruling that was cited in *Zippo, Fields,*[110] *Garrett,*[111] and *Oestman:*[112]

> (1) the kind of occupation, with reference to whether the work usually is done under the direction of a supervisor or is done by a specialist without supervision; (2) the skill required in the particular occupation; (3) whether the "employer" or the individual in question furnishes the equipment used and the place of work; (4) the length of time during which the individual has worked; (5) the method of payment, whether by time or by the job; (6) the manner in which the work relationship is terminated; i.e., by one or both parties, with or without notice and explanation; (7) whether annual leave is afforded; (8) whether the work is an integral part of the business of the "employer;" (9) whether the worker accumulates retirement benefits; (10) whether the "employer" pays social security taxes; and (11) the intention of the parties.[113]

The Economic Realities Test

The economic realities test was endorsed by the Court of Appeals for the Sixth Circuit in *Lilley v BTM Corp.*[114] Pointing

---

[109] 613 F2d 826, 832 (DC Cir 1979).

[110] 906 F2d at 1020.

[111] 721 F2d at 982.

[112] 958 F2d at 305.

[113] *Garrett,* 721 F2d at 982 (*quoting* Spirides v Reinhardt, 613 F2d at 832); *accord* Golden v AP Orleans, Inc, 681 F Supp 1100 (ED Pa 1988); Frank v Capital Cities Communications, 48 FEP Cas (BNA) 1381, 1382 (SDNY 1984).

[114] 958 F2d 746 (6th Cir), *cert denied,* 113 S Ct 376 (1992); *cf* Vakharia v Swedish Covenant Hosp, 765 F Supp 461, 466-68 (ND Ill 1991) (case arising under Title VII. In Clancey v American Management Assn, Inc, 781 F Supp 286 (SDNY 1992), the court, in embracing the economic realities test for ADEA purposes, took its cue from the fact that the Court of Appeals for the Second Circuit had adopted this standard in Brock v Superior Care, Inc, 840 F2d 1054, 1059 (2d Cir 1988), a case arising under the FLSA. The *Clancey* court later seemed to assert that the court of appeals had itself established the economic

out that "[t]his test is a loose formulation, leaving the determination of employment status to case-by-case resolution based on the totality of the circumstances,"[115] the court reviewed the facts involving the plaintiff and concluded that the jury's determination that he was an employee was sustainable.[116] In *Equal Employment Opportunity Commission v Century Broadcasting Corp*[117] the district court identified six key factors to take account of: (1) the nature and degree of control by the alleged employer; (2) "the alleged employee's opportunity for profit or loss depending upon his managerial skill"; (3) the alleged employee's capital investment; (4) the degree of skill required; (5) "the degree of permanency and duration of the working relationship"; and (6) "the extent to which the service rendered is an integral part of the alleged employer's business."[118] The court explicitly disclaimed consideration of the method of payment, i.e., "whether by time or by the job," as a factor to be considered in the evaluation.[119] In *Clancey v American Management Association,*

---

realities approach as being applicable to the ADEA, stating: "The Third Circuit['s hybrid approach] . . . is not binding on this Court especially in this case where the Second Circuit's test for determining worker status is different." 781 F Supp at 289. In fact, the Second Circuit does not now utilize the economic realities test. See note 105 and accompanying text.

[115] 958 F2d at 750.

[116] With regard to a jury having made this determination, the court observed as follows:

> The determination of employment status is a mixed question of law and fact. Normally, a judge will be able to make this determination as a matter of law. However, where there is a genuine issue of fact or conflicting inferences can be drawn from the undisputed facts, as here, the question is to be resolved by the finder of fact in accordance with the appropriate rules of law.

Id 750 n1. In Martin v United Way, 829 F2d 445, 451 (2d Cir 1987), also, the court ruled that employment status was a jury question. *Contra* Golden v Opal Orleans, Inc, 681 F Supp 1100, 1102 n2 (ED Pa 1988).

[117] 53 FEP Cas (BNA) 250 (ND Ill 1990), *affd in part & revd in part on other grounds,* 957 F2d 1446 (7th Cir 1992).

[118] *Id* 252; *accord* Clancey v American Management Assn, Inc, 781 F Supp 286, 288 (SDNY 1992).

[119] 53 FEP Cas (BNA) at 254.

Inc,[120] the court asserted that the employer's ability to control the individual's job is the most important factor.[121]

The analysis by the *Lilley* court in concluding that there was sufficient evidence to raise a question for the jury as to the plaintiff's employment status, and that the district court had properly denied BTM's motion for judgment notwithstanding the verdict, illustrates the application of the economic realities approach:

> BTM [the defendant] exercised control over Lilley. Although Lilley set his own hours and vacation schedule, such flexibility is not sufficient to negate control. . . . BTM had the authority to remove Lilley from particular sales. In at least one instance, BTM exercised this authority. . . . In addition, BTM required Lilley to obtain its approval before he could quote a price to a potential buyer.
>
> Although he paid some of his own expenses, Lilley did not make an investment in the business. BTM supplied Lilley with an office, secretarial services, business cards and stationery bearing BTM's name, brochures and stickers advertising BTM's products, and telephone privileges.
>
> In addition, Lilley was integrated into BTM's normal business operations. After BTM approved a price quotation, Lilley was authorized to sign for and bind BTM. He also attended weekly meetings of BTM's sales staff, whose members are undisputedly employees. Lilley went on "trouble-shooting" trips, involving the resolution of problems that customers had with BTM's products *after* purchase. Finally, BTM invited its customers to visit its facility and offered that "our people will give you all the help you need. . . ." Lilley was listed among BTM's "people."
>
> It is also significant that Lilley sold only BTM's products. Although this is by no means determinative, it provides support for the existence of an employment relationship, par-

---

[120] 781 F Supp 286 (SDNY 1992).

[121] *Id* 288.

ticularly when viewed within the totality of the facts of this case.[122]

The *Darden* Ruling

The definition of *employee* in the ADEA[123] is the same as that used in ERISA:[124] an "individual employed by an employer." As discussed in **§3.05,** the *Darden* Court adopted, for ERISA purposes, the common-law agency test for determining who qualifies as an employee under that statute. The same rationale that led to this approach regarding ERISA applies vis-a-vis the ADEA.[125] Accordingly, the factors deemed relevant in *Darden* in determining whether a person is an employee apply by way of analogy here.[126] These are as follows: " . . . [W]e consider the hiring party's right to control the manner and means by which the product is accomplished. Among the other factors relevant to this inquiry are the skill required; the sources of the instrumentalities and tools; the location of the work; the duration of the relationship between the parties; whether the hiring party has the right to assign additional projects to the hired party; the extent of the hired party's discretion over when and how long to work; the method of payment; the hired party's role in hiring and paying assistants; whether the work is part of the regular business of the hiring party; whether the hiring party is in business; the provision of employee benefits; and the tax treatment of the hired party.". . . .[127]

The Court of Appeals for the Second Circuit, which had subscribed to the hybrid test prior to *Darden,* embraced the *Darden*

---

[122] 958 F2d at 750.

[123] §11(f), 29 USC §630(f). As to the definition of employee, see **§3.05.**

[124] 29 USC §1002(6).

[125] See **§3.05.**

[126] Bally v Frankel, Inc, 987 F2d 861 (2d Cir 1993).

[127] Nationwide Mut Ins Co v Darden, 112 S Ct 1344, 1348 (1992), *quoting* Community for Creative Non-Violence v Reid, 490 US 730, 751-52 (1989).

common-law analysis in *Frankel v Bally, Inc.*[128] So, too, have district courts.[129]

While the economic realities test is not all that different from the hybrid approach, the latter better correlates with the common-law agency test embraced in *Darden.* Thus, it would appear that decisions such as *Lilley* notwithstanding, the economic realities test no longer provides a viable analysis.[130] And to the extent that there is some distinction between the hybrid test and the common-law approach, the former likewise is supplanted by the latter.

Burdens of Proof and Evidentiary Standards

In the Sixth Circuit the "[e]stablishment of an independent contractor relationship . . . require[s] a convincing accumulation of . . . evidence.' "[131] It is the plaintiff who bears the burden of proof of employment status by a preponderance of the evidence.[132]

§3.07 —Corporation Directors, and Shareholders in Professional Corporations

Directors

In *Equal Employment Opportunity Commission v First Catholic Slovak Ladies Association,*[133] the Court of Appeals for the Sixth Circuit looked beyond labels to the functions actually performed by the individuals in question in order to determine whether they were employees. The defendant, a nonprofit society, required that its officers also be members of its board of directors, and limited

---

[128] 987 F2d 86 (2d Cir 1993).

[129] *See* Kennel v Dover Garage, Inc, 816 F Supp 178, 184 (EDNY), *affd without opinion,* 9 F2d 1536 (2d Cir 1933); Cox v Master Lock Co, 815 F Supp 844, 846 (ED Pa), *affd without opinion,* 14 F3d 46 (3d Cir 1993).

[130] Frankel v Bally, Inc, 987 F2d 86, 90 (2d Cir 1993).

[131] Lilley v BTM Corp, 958 F2d 746, 751 (6th Cir), *cert denied,* 113 S Ct 376 (1992) (quoting Falls v Sporting News Publishing Co, 834 F2d 611, 614 (6th Cir 1987)).

[132] *Lilley,* 958 F2d at 751.

[133] 694 F2d 1068 (6th Cir 1982), *cert denied,* 464 US 819 (1983).

eligibility for the board to persons under age 67. The defendant argued that inasmuch as the officers—who were paid salaries—were also directors, they were not employees but rather employers. The court disagreed:

> [The] determination should not center on the label which the organization has chosen to give to the position. . . . These individuals performed traditional employee duties: maintaining records, preparing financial statements, managing the office. They were responsible for their work to the governing body of the organization and they drew salaries as employees. Their participation on the policy-making Board of Directors does not detract from their primary role as employees.[134]

In *Zimmerman v North American Signal Co*[135] the question directly before the court was whether the defendant satisfied the definition of *employer* contained in §11(b)[136] of the Age Discrimination in Employment Act (ADEA),[137] i.e., an entity having 20 or more employees for each working day in each of 20 or more weeks in the current or preceding calendar year.[138] In concluding that the defendant did not fit within this definition and that the plaintiff accordingly could not maintain his suit, the court rejected the argument that two unpaid officers and directors of the corporation were employees: "We do not believe Congress intended the word 'employee' to include persons who are no more than directors of a corporation or unpaid, inactive officers."[139] In a footnote, however, the court uttered a cautionary note echoing the court's analysis in *First Catholic Slovak Ladies Association:* "[E]mployers cannot avoid having employees counted toward the jurisdictional threshold by denominating them as directors,

---

[134] *Id* 1070.

[135] 704 F2d 347 (7th Cir 1983).

[136] 29 USC §630(b).

[137] *Id* §§621-624.

[138] See **§3.19.**

[139] 704 F2d at 352.

independent contractors, or other designations besides 'employee.' The issue is whether an employer-employee relationship exists, not what title a worker holds."[140] In *McGraw v Warren County Oil Co*[141] the Court of Appeals for the Eighth Circuit cited *Zimmerman* in affirming the district court's holding that directors of the defendant corporation were not employees.[142]

Partners, and Shareholders in Professional Corporations

Like the court that decided *First Catholic Slovak Ladies Association,* the Court of Appeals for the Eleventh Circuit refused to be bound by labels in addressing the status of an accountant in *Fountain v Metcalf, Zima & Co, PA.*[143] Rather, it endorsed an "economic reality" analysis[144] in determining the correct characterization of a shareholder of a professional corporation. The court concluded that the plaintiff could not be deemed to be an employee:

> [U]nlike the firm's employees, . . . [the plaintiff]: shared in the firm's profits, losses, and expenses; was compensated on the basis of a share in the firm's profits; was liable for certain debts, obligations, and liabilities of the firm; and had a right to vote his thirty-one percent ownership on member/shareholders' amendments to the agreement, on termination of relationship with member/shareholders, on draws, and on distribution of profits and income. Those fact[or]s are virtually a textbook listing of the management, control and ownership factors that establish . . . [the plaintiff's] role as that of partner, not employee.[145]

---

[140] *Id.*

[141] 707 F2d 990 (8th Cir 1983).

[142] *Accord* Schoenbaum v Orange County Ctr for the Performing Arts, Inc, 677 F Supp 1036 (CD Cal 1987).

[143] 925 F2d 1398 (11th Cir 1991).

[144] *Id* 1401.

[145] *Id.*

The court's conclusion was not shaken by the facts that the label *employee* was used in two firm documents to refer to the accountant in question, and that the president and co-managing director exercised autocratic control over the firm's affairs.

The district court that decided *Caruso v Peat, Marwick, Mitchell & Co*[146] similarly held that the designation of an individual as a partner in an accounting firm does not preclude the individual from being deemed an employee if his or her duties "more closely . . . [resemble] those of a typical salaried worker, with little role in corporate decisionmaking[.]"[147] The court, in concluding that the plaintiff indeed was an employee, focused on three primary considerations:

> (1) The extent of the individual's ability to control and operate his business; (2) The extent to which an individual's compensation is calculated as a percentage of business profits; and (3) The extent of the individual's employment security.[148]

Partners, the court observed, typically participate in the control and operation of the business; they receive their income by way of profit sharing, rather than by way of a wage; and they are permanent employees. Applying these factors, the court concluded that Caruso was in fact an employee.[149]

In *Jones v Baskin, Flaherty, Elliot & Mannino, PC,*[150] the Court of Appeals for the Third Circuit applied the hybrid test used in *Equal Employment Opportunity Commission v Zippo Manufacturing Co,*[151] and concluded that a shareholder in a professional corpo-

---

146 664 F Supp 144 (SDNY 1987).

147 *Id* 148.

148 *Id* 149.

149 *See also* Caruso v Peat, Marwick, Mitchell & Co, 717 F Supp 218 (SDNY 1989).

150 670 F Supp 597 (WD Pa 1987).

151 713 F2d 32 (3d Cir 1983). Under this approach the courts look to the economic realities of the relationship between the parties, while focusing on employer control as the most important factor in determining whether the individual involved is or is not an employee.

ration could be—and in this case indeed was—an employee. The Court of Appeals for the Tenth Circuit took a different tack, however, in *Wheeler v Main Hurdman.*[152] In that case the court engaged in an extensive analysis and discussion leading up to its ultimate conclusion that "bona fide general partners are not employees" under the ADEA.[153] In summarizing its analysis the court explained as follows:

> There may be many aspects of a partner's work environment in a partnership which are indistinguishable from that of a corporate employee. But in general the total bundle of partnership characteristics sufficiently differentiates between the two to remove general partners from the statutory term "employee." . . . Wheeler's circumstances as a partner are portrayed as indistinguishable from her prior employee status. Yet they are distinguishable, and substantially so. Her participation in profits and losses, exposure to liability, investment in the firm, partial ownership of firm assets, and her voting rights—plus her position under the partnership agreement and partnership laws—clearly placed her in a different economic and legal category.[154]

From this analysis followed the court's refusal to apply either the common-law right of control test or the economic realities test used in determining whether individuals are independent contractors,[155] as had been urged by the plaintiff and by the Equal Employment Opportunity Commission (EEOC). The court reasoned that "[S]uch tests ignore or unacceptably diminish the essential attributes of partnership, as well as being inca-

---

[152] 825 F2d 257 (10th Cir), *cert denied,* 484 US 986 (1987).

[153] *Id* 277.

[154] *Id* 276. In Holland v Ernst & Whinney, 44 FEP Cas (BNA) 474 (ND Ala 1984), the court—without any of the analysis articulated in *Wheeler*—reached essentially the same conclusion. It dismissed a suit brought by a former partner because, in its view, a partner is an employer, not an employee.

[155] See **§3.06.**

pable of rational application."[156] (In contrast, the *Fountain* court applied and obviously considered an "economic reality" approach to be workable, since that is what it used, as discussed above).

In most of the foregoing cases—*First Catholic Slovak Ladies Association* and *Fountain,* for example—the courts resisted arguments that they should be oblivious to actual relationships and rather should rely just on the label assigned to the plaintiff, such as *partner* or *director,* to determine whether the individuals were in fact employees. In contrast, the Court of Appeals for the Second Circuit, in deciding *Hyland v New Haven Radiology Associates,*[157] did adopt the rigid position of looking just at the label. However, it did so with the result—as in the other decisions—of producing a ruling protective of the plaintiff's interests. The physician defendants argued that notwithstanding that they had formed a professional corporation, the court should look at the reality of their relationship and hold that they really were partners. Were the court to do so, it would follow that the plaintiff, who was a shareholder in the corporation and was denominated (as were the other shareholders) an employee, would be deemed a partner, and not an employee. The court responded: "[T]he use of the corporate form precludes any examination to determine whether the entity is in fact a partnership."[158] Thus, "where the individual involved is a corporate employee, . . . such employee is 'covered' for purposes of the ADEA and . . . any inquiry respecting partnership status would be irrelevant."[159] (*Hyland's* continuing viability is in doubt, however, in light of a later ruling of the Court of Appeals for the Second Circuit, i.e., *Frankel v Bally, Inc.*)[160]

---

[156] 825 F2d at 276.

[157] 794 F2d 793 (2d Cir 1986).

[158] *Id* 798.

[159] *Id; accord* Gorman v North Pittsburgh Oral Surgery Assocs, 664 F Supp 212 (WD Pa 1987). *Contra* Equal Employment Opportunity Commn v Dowd & Dowd, Ltd, 736 F2d 1177 (1984) (arising under Title VII of the Civil Rights Act of 1964, 42 USC §§2000e through 2000e-17).

[160] 987 F2d 86 (2d Cir 1993).

Organizational Members

The members of a nonprofit unincorporated association are not employees of that association.[161]

§3.08 —Nonfederal Public Officials, Their Appointees and Personal Staff, and State Employees

Section 11(f)[162] of the Age Discrimination in Employment Act (ADEA)[163] excludes from the definition of *employee* a person who is "elected to public office in any State or political subdivision of any State . . . , or any person chosen by such officer to be on such officer's personal staff, or an appointee on the policy-making level or an immediate adviser with respect to the exercise of the constitutional or legal powers of the office."[164] Thus, there are two broad categories of persons excluded from the ADEA's protection: elected officials, and some appointees of elected officials. A number of courts have been called upon to flesh out this provision;[165] the typical case concerns the question of whether a given public individual occupies a position that, by its nature, takes him or her beyond the reach of the ADEA.

It should be noted that even if it is determined that a given individual fits within one or the other of the foregoing exceptions to the ADEA, it does not follow that he or she is left unprotected from age discrimination. Title III of the Civil Rights Act

---

[161] Allen v McEntee, 61 FEP Cas (BNA) 867 (DDC 1993).

[162] 29 USC §630(f).

[163] *Id* §§621-634.

[164] The next sentence of §11(f) provides that the quoted exemptions "shall not include employees subject to the civil service laws of a State government, governmental agency, or political subdivision."

[165] In Sabo v Casey, 757 F Supp 587 (ED Pa), *revd in part & dismissed in part without opinion,* 968 F2d 14 (3d Cir 1991), the court rejected the argument that it was unconstitutional to exclude from the ADEA's coverage elected officials and their appointees who are at the policymaking level.

of 1991,[166] entitled the Government Employee Rights Act of 1991,[167] extends the protection afforded by the prohibitions of the ADEA to persons chosen or selected by state and local elected public officials to be members of the officials' personal staffs, or to serve the elected officials on the policymaking level; and to persons who serve these elected officials as "immediate advisor[s] with respect to the exercise of the constitutional or legal powers of the office."[168] These individuals have rights independent of the ADEA by virtue of the separate enforcement scheme that has been established by the 1991 Act.[169]

Policymakers

The Court of Appeals for the Second Circuit concluded in *Tranello v Frey*[170] that if a nonelected policymaking individual is not an appointee of an elected official, he or she by definition does not fit within the ADEA exception notwithstanding the fact that he or she engages in policymaking functions.[171] While the court acknowledged that the wording of §11(f) does not explicitly require that an appointee on the policy-making level must be appointed by an elected official, it read the structure of §11(f) as nonetheless requiring that conclusion, stating: "[T]he placement of [the clause dealing with appointees] . . . in the middle of a statute primarily exempting elected officials from ADEA coverage strongly indicates that this provision must be read to require appointment by an elected official."[172] The court further looked to the legislative history of a like provision in Title VII of the Civil Rights Act of 1964[173] to buttress its conclusion.[174]

---

[166] Pub L No 102-166, 105 Stat 1071, 1088-89.

[167] 2 USC §1201 *et seq.*

[168] *Id* §1220(a). See **ch 11.**

[169] See **ch 11.**

[170] 962 F2d 244 (2d Cir), *cert denied,* 113 S Ct 813 (1992).

[171] *Accord* Mareno v County of Westchester, 58 FEP Cas (BNA) 1361 (SDNY 1991).

[172] 962 F2d at 249; *accord* Wanner v Kansas, 766 F Supp 1005 (D Kan 1991).

[173] 42 USC §§2000e through 2000e-17.

[174] 962 F2d at 249-50.

The defendant in *Tranello* had argued that the plaintiff, a deputy county attorney, fit within the §11(f) exclusion because his appointment by the County Attorney (who was admittedly not an elected official) had to be approved by the County Executive (who was elected). The court rejected this contention, however, reasoning that the language of §11(f) speaks only to policymakers working closely with elected public officials. It went on to reason as follows:

> The mere fact that the County Executive must approve the County Attorney's appointee does not convince us that the appointee would be a "policymaker working closely with the elected official," and does not compel the conclusion that the Deputy County Attorney is an appointee of the County Executive. We refuse to stretch the language and purpose of the exception to reach so broadly, lest the exception swallow the rule and defeat the statutory purpose.[175]

In *Lee v Wojnarowski*[176] a federal district court held that the plaintiff had occupied a policymaking position and so was unprotected by the ADEA. The court looked to the office itself, rather than to what the occupant of that position in fact did:

> The terms of the ADEA require examination of the statutory powers of the . . . [office in question] to determine whether the post is a policymaking one. The performance or lack of performance by any given officeholder of policymaking functions is irrelevant to that determination.[177]

This same tack was espoused by the Supreme Court in *Gregory v*

[175] *Id* 250 (quoting Equal Employment Opportunity Commn v Vermont, 904 F2d 794, 798 (2d Cir 1990) (state judges not within ADEA policymaking exception because they do not work closely with the elected official, i.e., the governor, who appoints them)).

[176] 751 F Supp 58 (WD Pa 1990).

[177] *Id* 60.

Ashcroft,[178] —a decision addressing the issue of whether appointed judges fit within the §11(f) exclusion, as discussed below.

In *Equal Employment Opportunity Commission v Board of Trustees*[179] the court held that the exclusionary language set forth in §11(b) was applicable to the president of a county community college district—a political subdivision of the state—who was appointed by the board of trustees to his position. In *Stillians v Iowa*[180] it was the director of the state arts council who was deemed to occupy a policymaking position exempting the individual from the ADEA's coverage. And in *Heck v City of Freeport*[181] an official whose responsibilities involved supervising the city's five garbage collectors and the city dump failed to convince the court that the policymaker exception was inapplicable to him. In contrast, the applicant for an assistant county attorney position in *Mareno v County of Westchester*[182] was not deemed to be seeking a policy-making job.

Judges—The Pre-*Gregory v Ashcroft* Case Law

The status of judges in terms of their protection or exclusion by reason of §11(f) has generated a major body of case law interpreting this provision. The courts have addressed both claims made on behalf of elected judges and on behalf of those appointed to their offices. Prior to the Supreme Court's addressing the applicability of the ADEA to judges in *Gregory v Ashcroft* the lower courts were split.

With regard to appointed judges, the Court of Appeals for the Second Circuit reasoned in *Equal Employment Opportunity Commission v Vermont,*[183] which concerned a state constitution's a mandatory retirement provision applicable to judges, that the policy-maker exception to the ADEA's coverage of employees

---

178 111 S Ct 2395 (1991).

179 723 F2d 509 (6th Cir 1983).

180 843 F2d 276 (8th Cir 1988).

181 985 F2d 305 (7th Cir 1993).

182 58 FEP Cas (BNA) 1361 (SDNY 1991).

183 904 F2d 794 (2d Cir 1990).

applies only to policymakers who work closely with elected officials. Appointed judges did not fit within this definition, in the court's view. Thus, such judges could invoke the ADEA's protection.[184] However, several other courts, including the Court of Appeals for the First Circuit,[185] took a contrary position, holding that appointed state court judges were not protected under the Act by virtue of the §11(f) policymaker exclusion.[186]

Elected judges mounting age discrimination claims in the years prior to *Gregory v Ashcroft* met with unvarying defeat, given that §11(f) excludes from the protection of the ADEA elected officials.[187] There were factual variations in some cases, but these produced no different results. In *Diamond v Cuomo,*[188] for example, the court, while acknowledging that pursuant to a state administrative interpretation of the ADEA appointed judges could not be mandatorily retired at age 70, went on to reject a constitutional challenge by elected judges to their forced retirement since they were elected officials and so were exempted from coverage under the ADEA. In *Dolan v Secretary of State*[189] the court addressed the claim of a man who wanted to seek election to a municipal court judgeship, but who would

---

184 In an opinion letter issued by the Equal Employment Opportunity Commission (EEOC) in 1987 the Commission also asserted that appointed state and local court judges were employees for purposes of the ADEA, and so could invoke the Act's protection. EEOC OL-7 (Apr 7, 1987). (This letter is reproduced at the end of the last volume in **app L**.)

185 Equal Employment Opportunity Commn v Massachusetts, 858 F2d 52 (1st Cir 1988).

186 Sabo v Casey, 757 F Supp 587 (ED Pa), *revd in part & dismissed in part without opinion,* 968 F2d 14 (3d Cir 1991); United States Equal Employment Opportunity Commn v Illinois, 721 F Supp 156 (ND Ill 1989); Apkin v Treasurer & Receiver Gen, 401 Mass 427, 517 NE2d 141 (1988); *In re* Stout, 521 Pa 571, 559 A2d 489 (1989).

187 *See* Sabo v Casey, 757 F Supp 587 (ED Pa), *revd in part & dismissed in part without opinion,* 968 F2d 14 (3d Cir 1991); Equal Employment Opportunity Commn v New York, 907 F2d 316 (2d Cir 1990); Gondelman v Commonwealth, 120 Pa Commw 625, 550 A2d 814 (1988), *dismissed,* 520 Pa 451, 554 A2d 896, *cert denied,* 493 US 849 (1989).

188 70 NY2d 338, 514 NE2d 1356, 520 NYS2d 732 (1987), *appeal dismissed,* 486 US 1028 (1988).

189 55 Ohio App 3d 157, 563 NE2d 745 (1988).

have been 70 by the date he would be sworn in. His problem was that, even if he won election, the Ohio Constitution barred judges from being elected or appointed after attaining age 70. The court conceded that a reasonable argument could be made that the plaintiff candidate could invoke the ADEA with regard to his candidacy, but observed that §11(f) would come into play in any event once he was elected and would deprive him of the ADEA's protection. The court concluded, therefore, that "it would be a vain and senseless act to permit a candidate to be placed upon the ballot if he was ineligible to assume the office to which he aspires,"[190] and thus ruled against him.

In *Schlitz v Virginia*[191] the Court of Appeals for the Fourth Circuit dealt with yet another scenario. In that case the court held that the plaintiff's challenge to the state legislature's refusal to reelect him to the position of circuit judge could not be attacked under the ADEA because of the doctrine of legislative immunity.

Gregory v Ashcroft: Judges Specifically, and the Policymaker Exception Generally

In *Gregory v Ashcroft* the Court addressed a mandatory retirement provision contained in a state constitution that required judges to retire at age 70. The judges who sought relief initially had been appointed to office by the governor; subsequently, each won a retention election. The Court expended much effort in addressing its uneasiness relating to federal intervention into matters primarily of state interest, as well as its specific concern regarding federal regulation of state judicial office holding. Thus, the Court wrote as follows:

> The present case concerns a state constitutional provision through which the people of Missouri establish a qualification for those who sit as their judges. This provision . . . [expresses] a decision of the most fundamental sort for a sovereign entity. Through the structure of its government,

[190] 563 NE2d at 748.

[191] 854 F2d 43 (4th Cir 1988).

> and the character of those who exercise government authority, a state defines itself as a sovereign. . . .
>
> Congressional interference with the decision of the people of Missouri, defining their constitutional offices, would upset the usual constitutional balance of federal and state powers.[192]

In order to properly reflect its concerns regarding the federal-state balance, the Court adopted a *plain statement* rule, i.e., the requirement of a clear statement on Congress's part that it had " 'in fact faced, and intended to bring into issue, the critical matters involved in the judicial decision.' "[193]

In applying this rule the Court focused on the language of §11(f) that excludes from the Act's protection "appointee[s] on the policymaking level." The proponent of exclusion, i.e., the Missouri governor, contended that state judges make policy, inasmuch as they fashion and apply the common law. Moreover, he argued, the higher state courts exercise supervisory authority over inferior courts, pursuant to the Missouri Constitution. The judges challenging the Missouri provision argued to the contrary, asserting that they "merely resolve[d] factual disputes and decide[d] questions of law; they . . . [did] not make policy."[194]

The Court did not resolve the dispute as to the policymaking role of judges, but it did react to these arguments with reasoning that provides fodder for argumentation in future cases involving not only judges, but appointees to other government positions, as well:

> [I]t is far from plain that the statutory exception requires that judges actually make policy. The statute refers to appointees "on the policymaking level," not to appointees "who make policy." It may be sufficient that the appointee

---

192 111 S Ct at 2400-01.

193 *Id* 2401 (quoting United States v Bass, 404 US 336, 349 (1971)).

194 111 S Ct at 2403.

> is in a position requiring the exercise of discretion concerning issues of public importance.[195]

In any event, the Court ultimately resolved the case in favor of the state by applying its plain statement rule, holding:

> "[A]ppointee at the policy making level," . . . is an odd way for Congress to exclude judges; a plain statement that judges are not "employees" would seem the most efficient phrasing. But in this case we are not looking for a plain statement that judges are excluded. We will not read the ADEA to cover state judges unless Congress has made it clear that judges are *included.* This does not mean the Act must mention judges explicitly, though it does not. . . . Rather, it must be plain to anyone reading the Act that it covers judges. In the context of a statute that plainly excludes most important state public officials, "appointee on the policy-making level" is sufficiently broad that we cannot conclude that the statute plainly covers appointed state judges. Therefore, it does not.[196]

In light of this holding, the Court did not choose to resolve the further argument made in support of the state court judges not being protected by the ADEA, to wit, that because they were subject to retention elections the judges were "elected to public office" and so, by virtue of the language of §11(f), were not to be deemed employees covered by the statute.[197]

Elected Officials' Personal Staff Members

Section 11(f) excludes from the term *employee* persons on an elected official's personal staff. In *Equal Employment Opportunity*

---

[195] *Id* 2404. (This same tack—i.e., looking to the office, rather than what the office holder does in it—was taken in Lee v Wojnarowski, 751 F Supp 58, 60 (WD Pa 1990).)

[196] 111 S Ct at 2404 (emphasis in original).

[197] *Id.*

Commission v Reno[198] the Court of Appeals for the Eleventh Circuit held that assistant state's attorneys, who were appointed to their positions by the defendant state's attorney, were personal staff. In reaching that conclusion the court expressed the view that an employee's status for purposes of the exemption is a matter of federal, not state, law.[199] Likewise, in *Monce v City of San Diego,*[200] a ruling by the Court of Appeals for the Ninth Circuit, a deputy city attorney was held to be a member of the elected City Attorney's personal staff.

In determining whether an individual fits within the statutory exception to coverage, common law legislative immunity cases decided under state law are inapposite; the exception at issue here is narrower in scope, its contours defined by the statutory language.[201] Several factors are relevant in determining whether an individual fits within the *personal staff* exemption:

> (1) whether the elected official has plenary powers of appointment and removal,
> (2) whether the person in the position at issue is personally accountable to only that elected official,
> (3) whether the person in the position at issue represents the elected official in the eyes of the public,
> (4) whether the elected official exercises a considerable amount of control over the position,
> (5) the level of the position within the organization's chain of command, and

---

198 758 F2d 581 (11th Cir 1985).

199 *Id* 584; *accord* Ingram v Dallas County, 688 F Supp 1146, 1160 (ND Tex 1988).

200 895 F2d 560 (9th Cir 1990).

201 Bostick v Rappleyea, 629 F Supp 1328 (NDNY 1985); *cf* Teneyuca v Bexar County, 767 F2d 148 (5th Cir 1985) (construing a comparable *personal staff* exemption contained in Title VII of the Civil Rights Act of 1964, 42 USC §§2000e through 2000e-17); Goodwin v Circuit Court, 729 F2d 541 (8th Cir 1984) (*id*); Ramirez v San Mateo County, 639 F2d 509 (9th Cir 1981) (*id*); Owens v Rush, 654 F2d 1370 (10th Cir 1981) (*id*).

(6) the actual intimacy of the working relationship between the elected official and the person filling the position.[202]

State Employees

As a general matter, state employees who do not fit with the foregoing exceptions to coverage are protected under the ADEA.[203] In *Frey v California*[204] the Court of Appeals for the Ninth Circuit addressed an unusual situation, however. The plaintiff had been a commissioned officer in the California National Guard until he was forced to retire in 1991 at age 60, pursuant to a state statute requiring such an age-based dismissal. Previously, in 1985, the plaintiff, having attained 30 years of commissioned service, had lost what is known as *federal recognition,*[205] the result being that he was deprived of his status as a member of the National Guard of the United States.[206] Thus, decisions establishing that members of the federal military establishment are not protected by the ADEA[207] were not deemed to be dispositive as to his forced retirement in 1991.

The court concluded, nonetheless, that Frey could not invoke the ADEA's protection. The court explained that it "[h]istorically . . . [had] restricted its review of military decision making out of deference 'to the special function of the military in our constitutional structure and in the system of national defense.' "[208] Accordingly, the court held as follows:

---

[202] Ingram v Dallas County, 688 F Supp 1146, 1160 (ND Tex 1988). In setting forth these factors, the court relied upon a ruling by the Court of Appeals for the Fifth Circuit in Teneyuca v Bexar County, 767 F2d 148 (5th Cir 1985), construing the comparable *personal staff* exemption contained in Title VII of the Civil Rights Act of 1964, 42 USC §§2000e through 2000e-17.

[203] As to the ADEA's coverage of state and local government employers, see **§3.20.**

[204] 982 F2d 399 (9th Cir), *cert denied,* 113 S Ct 3000 (1993).

[205] The concept of federal recognition is explained in the decision. *See id* 400 n 3.

[206] The court explained this scenario as follows: "The National Guard of the several states and the National Guard of the United States are overlapping entities." *Id* 400 n2.

[207] See **§3.21.**

[208] 982 F2d at 402.

> The policy considerations that preclude us from applying the ADEA to the federal military in the absence of a clear congressional directive similarly preclude the application of the ADEA to the state militia based solely upon the loss of federal recognition, when Congress has not expressly so directed.[209]

§3.09 —Job Applicants, Employees, and Former Employees in the Federal Sector

Pursuant to §15(a)[210] of the Age Discrimination in Employment Act (ADEA),[211] individuals who apply for jobs in the competitive services of the executive and judicial branches of the federal government, as well as employees and former employees in the competitive services of these branches, clearly may invoke the Act's protection. What they may not do, however, is utilize the enforcement mechanisms set forth in the Act for nonfederal grievants. Rather, §15[212] establishes a separate enforcement scheme that involves some substantive differences, such as the exclusion of the *reasonable factors other than age* exception;[213] different enforcement procedures;[214] and some differences in the relief available to prevailing plaintiffs.[215]

Inasmuch as §15 applies only to persons in the competitive service, presidential appointees are not protected under this section. However, §320[216] of the Government Employee Rights Act

---

[209] *Id* 404.

[210] 29 USC §633a(a).

[211] *Id* §§621-634. The ADEA's coverage was extended to federal employees by a 1974 amendment. Fair Labor Standards Amendments of 1974, Pub L No 93-259, §28, 88 Stat 55, 74-75.

[212] 29 USC §633a.

[213] See **ch 5.**

[214] See **ch 9.**

[215] *Id.*

[216] 2 USC §1219.

of 1991 (GERA)[217] extends the protection established in §15 of the ADEA to these individuals. Presidential appointees differ, however, from other federal employees in terms of the procedures applicable to pursuing age discrimination claims—a separate enforcement scheme is established by §320.

Employees of the legislative branch of the federal government likewise are not expressly covered by §15 of the ADEA. However, §302[218] of GERA extends the protection offered by §15 to Senate employees, former employees, and applicants for employment (including employees of the Architect of the Capitol assigned to the Senate restaurants or to the Superintendent of the Senate Office Buildings).[219] Again, a separate enforcement scheme is established by the 1991 Act to address the claims of these individuals.[220]

The ADEA does not apply to members of the armed forces; it does cover civilian employees of the military, however.[221]

---

[217] Civil Rights Act of 1991, Pub L No 102-166, Tit III, 105 Stat 1071, 1088-99 (codified at 2 USC §1201 *et seq*). See **ch 11.**

[218] 2 USC §1201.

[219] *Id* §1201(c)(B).

[220] See **ch 11.**

[221] House Comm on Education and Labor, Age Discrimination in Employment Act Amendments of 1977, HR Rep No 527, 95th Cong, 1st Sess 11 (1977). As to noncoverage of uniformed military personnel, see Spain v Ball, 928 F2d 61 (2d Cir 1991); Kawitt v United States, 842 F2d 951 (7th Cir 1988); Costner v Oklahoma Natl Guard, 833 F2d 905 (10th Cir 1987) (National Guard member); Helm v California, 722 F2d 507 (9th Cir 1983); Lear v Schlesinger, 17 FEP Cas (BNA) 337 (WD Mo 1978); Simpson v United States, 467 F Supp 1122 (SDNY 1979). *See also* Sylvestre v United States, 771 F Supp 515 (D Conn 1990) (upholding statute requiring retirement at age 60 of individuals in United States Army Reserve, without any mention being made of the ADEA). The termination of a civilian employee of the military gives rise to a nonjusticiable military matter, not subject to scrutiny under the ADEA, when his or her termination from the civilian position is a consequence of being mandatorily retired from a military position with which the civilian job is linked. Ridgeway v Aldrige, 709 F Supp 265 (D Mass 1989).

§3.10 —The Former Exception for Tenured University Employees

The Age Discrimination in Employment Act (ADEA)[222] first specifically addressed tenured university employees in 1978. In that year the Act was amended so as to raise the age ceiling from age 65 to 70 for nonfederal employees.[223] There was an exception to this expansion of statutory protection, however: institutions of higher education were permitted to compel the retirement of tenured employees once they attained age 65.[224] This amendment had a built-in termination date, however, it was to expire on July 1, 1982.[225] Thus, tenured university employees had to wait several years to benefit from the 1978 expansion of protection to persons ages 65 to 69.[226]

In 1986 the ADEA again was amended, this time to the end of completely removing any age cap from the Act.[227] Again, however, an exception—very similar to the prior one—accompanied this action: an institution of higher education[228] was allowed to impose compulsory retirement upon a tenured employee upon

---

[222] 29 USC §§621-634.

[223] Age Discrimination in Employment Act Amendments of 1978, Pub L No 95-256, §3(a), 92 Stat 189.

[224] *Id* §3(a), 92 Stat at 189-90 (codified at §12(d), 29 USC §631(d) (repealed)).

[225] *Id* §3(b), 92 Stat at 190.

[226] A constitutional attack on this differing treatment was rejected in McAloon v Bryant College of Business Admin, 520 F Supp 103 (DNH 1981); *cf* Lamb v Scripps College, 627 F2d 1015 (9th Cir 1980) (reaching same result with regard to a similar provision of a California statute). The justifications for this special treatment of tenured employees of colleges and universities were set forth in the Senate report on the 1978 amendments (there was no comparable provision in the House version of the bill). Senate Comm on Human Resources, Amending the Age Discrimination in Employment Act Amendments of 1977, S Rep No 493, 95th Cong, 1st Sess 8-9 (1977).

[227] Age Discrimination in Employment Amendments of 1986, Pub L No 99-592, §2(c), 100 Stat 3342.

[228] The term *institution of higher education* is defined by §1201(a) of the Higher Education Act of 1965, 20 USC §1141, which definition was incorporated into the ADEA by §12(d), 29 USC §631(d) (repealed).

the employee's attainment of age 70.[229] And again, there was a sunset provision: the exception was to terminate automatically as of December 31, 1993.[230]

The 1986 amendment, codified at §12(d) of the ADEA,[231] went into effect on January 1, 1987, except with regard to employees subject to some collective bargaining agreements, in which case the new section could have become effective as late as January 1, 1990.[232] Causes of action in existence prior to January 1, 1987 were not affected.[233]

The 1986 amendment directed the Equal Employment Opportunity Commission (EEOC) to enter into an agreement with the National Academy of Sciences to conduct a study analyzing the potential consequences of the elimination of mandatory

---

[229] Age Discrimination in Employment Amendments of 1986, Pub L No 99-592, §6(a), 100 Stat 3342, 3344, amending §12 of the ADEA, 29 USC §631 to add a new §12(d) (repealed). The seven-year exemption for tenured employees was not contained in the legislation initially passed by the House. Rather, it was contained in the bill that was first passed in the Senate and then sent to the House, which adopted it as well. The discussion during Senate consideration was only slightly enlightening. The manager of the bill noted that "[s]pecial concerns about the . . . tenure system at colleges and universities . . . [had] been raised." 133 Cong Rec S16852 (daily ed Oct 16, 1986) (statement of Sen Heinz). Only Senator Moynihan addressed this provision in any more than a cursory manner. He identified the provision's purpose as being to help ensure the movement of younger people into academia, which would include, for the rest of the 20th century, a large number of older faculty members. *Id* S16856 (statement of Sen Moynihan).

[230] Age Discrimination in Employment Amendments of 1986, Pub L No 99-592, §6(b), 100 Stat 3342, 3344. The exception for tenured university employees, as well as the broader issue of mandatory retirement of such individuals, generated a number of articles in the legal literature. *See, e.g.*, Finkin, *Commentary—Tenure After an Uncapped ADEA: A Different View*, 15 JC & UL 43 (1988); Ruebhausen, *Commentary—The Age Discrimination in Employment Act Amendments of 1986: Implications for Tenure and Retirement*, 14 JC & UL 561 (1988); Note, *Questioning Age-Old Wisdom: The Legality of Mandatory Retirement of Tenured Faculty Under the ADEA*, 105 Harv L Rev 889 (1992).

[231] 29 USC §631(d) (repealed).

[232] Age Discrimination in Employment Amendments of 1986, Pub L No 99-592, §7(a), 100 Stat 3342, 3344-45.

[233] *Id* §7(b), 100 Stat at 3345.

retirement for institutions of higher education.[234] Eight of the nine members to be included in the study panel were specified by employment background, and their selection could be made only after consultation with designated national organizations.[235] The results of the study were to be reported, with recommendations, to the President and Congress no later than five years after enactment of the amendment.[236] The Committee on Mandatory Retirement, which was created by the National Research Council in response to the statutory directive, issued its report in May 1991. The Committee arrived at two key conclusions:

1. At most colleges and universities, few tenured faculty would continue working past age 70 if mandatory retirement were eliminated.
2. At some research universities, a high proportion of faculty would choose to work past age 70 if mandatory retirement were eliminated.[237]

After making several recommendations, the Committee concluded with the recommendation "that the ADEA exemption permitting the mandatory retirement of tenured faculty be allowed to expire at the end of 1993."[238]

Congress in fact did not act to fashion a new version of the exception, and so on January 1, 1994, tenured university employees gained the full protection of the ADEA. Thereby the common practice of imposing mandatory retirement at age 70 became illegal.[239] (Other forms of age discrimination that might affect these individuals already were illegal, for §12(d) only legit-

---

[234] *Id* §6(c), 100 Stat at 3344.

[235] *Id.*

[236] *Id.*

[237] Ending Mandatory Retirement for Tenured Faculty (P. Hammond & H. Morgan eds 1991).

[238] *Id* 5.

[239] Agency interpretations concerning the tenured university employee exception had been promulgated by the EEOC, 29 CFR §1625.11 (1993), but these became moot by virtue of the demise of the exception.

imized compulsory retirement; it did not allow any other form of age-based disadvantage.)

§3.11 —The Former Exceptions for Firefighters and Law Enforcement Officers

As originally enacted, the Age Discrimination in Employment Act (ADEA)[240] extended its protection only to persons aged 40 to 65. In 1978 the Act was amended to raise the age ceiling for nonfederal employees to 70,[241] and in 1986 the Act was amended once again—this time to remove the age cap entirely.[242] However, with regard to firefighters[243] and law enforcement officers,[244] exceptions were made to the abolition of the age ceiling on ADEA protection. As to these employees, §4(i) of the Act[245] provided as follows:

> (i) It shall not be unlawful for an employer which is a state, a political subdivision of a state, or an interstate agency to fail or refuse to hire or to discharge any individual because of such individual's age if such action is taken—(1) with respect to the employment of an individual as a firefighter or as a law enforcement officer and the individual has attained the age of hiring or retirement in effect under applicable state or local law on March 3, 1983, and (2) pursuant to a bona fide hiring or retirement plan that is not a subterfuge to evade the purposes of this Act.[246]

---

[240] 29 USC §§621-634.

[241] Age Discrimination in Employment Act Amendments of 1978, Pub L No 95-256, §2(c), 92 Stat 189.

[242] Age Discrimination in Employment Amendments of 1986, Pub L No 99-592, §2(c) 100 Stat 3342.

[243] *Firefighter* is defined in §11(j), 29 USC §630(j).

[244] *Law enforcement officer* is defined in §11(k), 29 USC §630(k).

[245] 29 USC §623(i).

[246] The Omnibus Budget Reconciliation Act of 1986, Pub L No 99-592, §9201, 100 Stat 1874, 1973-75, also added a §4(i) to the ADEA. The confusion created by labelling two sections as "§4(i)" was rectified by a technical amendment in 1990. Whereby the second subsection (i) was redesignated as subsection

Section 4(i) went into effect on January 1, 1987, except for employees subject to some collective bargaining agreements, in which case it could have been as late as January 1, 1990 before the new section took effect.[247] Causes of action in existence prior to January 1, 1987 were not affected by the changes.[248] However, §4(i)—by its terms—was scheduled for automatic repeal as of December 31, 1993.[249]

Prior to §4(i)'s scheduled expiration, the Secretary of Labor and the Equal Employment Opportunity Commission (EEOC)—in accordance with statutory mandate—conducted a study: (1) to determine whether physical and mental fitness were valid measures of the ability and competency of police officers and firefighters; (2) to determine if these factors were valid measures, and if so, which tests were most effective; and (3) to recommend specific standards that such tests and their administration should satisfy.[250] A report, including the results of the study and recommendations, was to be submitted to the two houses of Congress. That report, submitted in 1992, called for allowing the exception regarding firefighters and law enforcement officers to expire on schedule.[251] The authors of the report concluded that "age is a poor predictor of individual capacity and limitation," and that "public safety is seldom at substantial risk from ineffective performance of the single public

---

(j) by the Older Workers Benefit Protection Act, Pub L No 101-433, §103, 104 Stat 978, 979, *as amended by* Pub L No 101-521, 104 Stat 2287 (1990).

[247] Age Discrimination in Employment Amendments of 1986, Pub L No 99-952, §7(a), 100 Stat 3342, 3344-45.

[248] *Id* §7(b), 100 Stat at 3345. Not later than five years after enactment of the foregoing provisions, the EEOC was to propose guidelines for the administration and use of physical and mental fitness tests. Age Discrimination in Employment Amendments of 1986, Pub L No 99-952, §5(c), 100 Stat 3342, 3343. The agency in fact never issued such guidelines.

[249] Age Discrimination in Employment Amendments of 1986, Pub L No 99-592, §3(b), 100 Stat 3342.

[250] *Id* §5(a), 100 Stat at 3343.

[251] F.J. Landy, Alternatives to Chronological Age in Determining Standards of Suitability for Public Safety Jobs (1992).

safety officer."[252] Accordingly, the authors asserted that they could not "recommend the retention of chronological age as a criterion for mandatory retirement decisions."[253]

The exception regarding law enforcement of officers and firefighters indeed did expire as scheduled, but as of mid 1994, proposed legislation was moving through the Congress in an effort to resurrect it.

Legislative History

Section 4(i) did not originate in committee, but rather resulted from a substitute bill that originated in the Senate, following passage of a different bill, not containing §4(i), in the House. As a result, there was no committee report concerning §4(i). As explained during Senate consideration of the legislation, however, "special concerns about the public safety . . . [h]ad been raised,"[254] and the temporary, seven-year exemption for firefighters and police officers was the result of a compromise. Senator Ford—a prime proponent of the exemption—explained the justification for it as follows:

> It is important to note that it was not the intention of those negotiating this provision that . . . a plan [allowing a firefighting department or a law enforcement agency to refuse to hire, or to involuntarily retire, individuals over a certain age] be either a specific legislative enactment or a detailed written plan, but that it be a bona fide hiring or retirement plan which was established for legitimate governmental reasons and not merely as a way to evade the purposes of the ADEA.
>
> A further component of this compromise establishes a floor for the hiring and retirement requirements which a State or local government can set. The hiring and retirement age requirements of a plan in effect as of March 3,

---

[252] F.J. Landy, Alternatives to Chronological Age in Determining Standards of Suitability for Public Safety Jobs, *Executive Summary* 13 (1992).

[253] *Id.*

[254] 133 Cong Rec S16852 (daily ed Oct 16, 1986) (remarks of Sen Heinz).

1983 become the floor for allowable plans. This is the date that the EEOC versus Wyoming case [*Equal Employment Opportunity Commission v Wyoming,* 460 US 226 (1983), see **3.20**] was decided. If jurisdictions have raised or eliminated mandatory retirement ages after this date, they have the choice of either moving back to the plan requirements in effect on March 3, 1983, or remaining where they are. However, State and local governments would not be able to lower retirement age requirements below what was in effect as of March 3, 1983. The purpose of this provision is to provide relief to those jurisdictions which were forced to respond to the Wyoming case, while at the same time ensuring that no lesser discrimination protection will be provided for these workers than what was in effect at the time the Wyoming case was decided.[255]

Case Law

The effect of §4(i) was to circumvent those decisions construing the ADEA's bona fide occupational qualification (BFOQ) exception[256] in which courts had struck down mandatory retirement and minimum hiring age requirements imposed on law enforcement officers and firefighters.[257] However, if an age-based hiring standard was not in effect as of March 3, 1983—the critical date set forth in §4(i)—the BFOQ provision's requirements, and the BFOQ case law, still would apply to refusals to hire job applicants and to forced retirements of employees deemed too old.[258] Dispute conceivably could arise, as evidenced

---

[255] 133 Cong Rec S16853-854 (daily ed Oct 16, 1986) (remarks of Sen. Ford); *see also id* S16854 (remarks of Sen Bradley).

[256] §4(f)(1), 29 USC §623(f)(1).

[257] See **ch 5.**

[258] *See* Gately v Massachusetts, 2 F3d 1221 (1st Cir 1993). In Chicago, the mandatory retirement age of 63 that had existed in 1983 for members of its police force was reinstituted in 1988 by enactment of a municipal ordinance. This was deemed to be consistent with the ADEA in McCann v City of Chicago, 968 F2d 635 (7th Cir), *cert denied,* 113 S Ct 495 (1992).

by *Petrelli v City of Mount Vernon,*[259] as to whether a law was in effect as of the critical date. Moreover, the enactment of §4(i) also left room for dispute as to whether a given individual, or group of individuals, fit within the definitions of the terms *firefighter*[260] or *law enforcement officer*[261] in given situations. For example, at issue in *Equal Employment Opportunity Commission v Michigan*[262] was the question whether high-ranking supervisory law enforcement officers who were not involved primarily and directly in apprehending criminals were to be deemed law enforcement officers for the purposes of the statutory exclusion. Their ability to invoke the protection of the ADEA in order to fend off involuntary retirement hung in the balance.[263]

Even though the *Michigan* court was unwilling to narrowly construe *law enforcement officer* so as to protect the individuals on whose behalf the EEOC was suing from the exclusionary language of the exception, the court saw the 1986 amendment as still leaving employers with a heavy task of justification if they sought to impose age-based retirement. The court held that even though the age-based retirement requirement did not have to be justified in terms of the BFOQ exception, the employer still had to establish that the retirement requirement was part of a bona fide retirement plan that was not a subterfuge to evade the purposes of the ADEA. In other words, the employer had

---

[259] 9 F3d 250 (2d Cir 1993).

[260] High-ranking supervisory firefighters not involved primarily and directly in firefighting activities, as well as firefighters working on the "line," have been held to fit within this definition and so are not protected under the ADEA. Boylan v State, 116 NJ 236, 561 A2d 552 (1989), *cert denied,* 494 US 1061 (1990).

[261] *See* Equal Employment Opportunity Commn v Illinois, 986 F2d 187 (7th Cir 1993); Equal Employment Opportunity Commn v Massachusetts, 864 F2d 933 (1st Cir 1988); Burke v Margolis, 738 F Supp 1201 (CD Ill 1990); Schulze v Illinois State Police, 736 F Supp 193 (ND Ill), *vacated & dismissed,* 764 F Supp 495 (ND Ill 1990).

[262] 51 FEP Cas (BNA) 294 (ED Mich 1988).

[263] The court determined that these individuals indeed were law enforcement officers for the purpose of §4(i).

the burden of proving an affirmative defense under the then-extant §4(f)(2)[264]—the bona fide benefit plan exception.

The ADEA exception allowing firefighters to be forced to retire on the basis of age, whereas most other workers would not be, withstood constitutional attacks made on equal protection grounds in both *Michigan* and *Boylan v New Jersey*.[265]

(There also is an exception to the ADEA created by 5 USC §3307(d), whereby Congress is authorized to set minimum and maximum age limitations for federal law enforcement officers. This exception has been recognized and applied in several decisions.)[266]

§3.12 —The Bona Fide Executive and High Policymaker Exceptions

The Age Discrimination in Employment Act (ADEA)[267] permits an employer to compel the retirement at age 65 or later of any employee who for the two years preceding retirement has held a bona fide executive or high policymaking position and is entitled to an immediate annual, nonforfeitable retirement benefit of at least $44,000.[268] Thus, an employer may choose to remove an individual who fits within one of these exceptions from his or her position. Of course, rather than fully dispensing with the services of the retiree, an employer may choose to retain that person in a different position.[269] In the latter instance, it should be understood that the bona fide executive and high policymaker exceptions only authorize the involuntary retirement

---

[264] 29 USC §623(f)(2). See **ch 5**.

[265] 116 NJ 236, 561 A2d 552 (1989), *cert denied*, 494 US 1061 (1990).

[266] *See* Benford v Frank, 943 F2d 609 (6th Cir 1991); Patterson v United States Postal Serv, 901 F2d 927 (11th Cir 1990); Stewart v Smith, 673 F2d 485 (DC Cir 1982); Francke v United States Dept of the Treasury, 721 F Supp 47 (SDNY 1989).

[267] 29 USC §§621-634.

[268] §12(c)(1), 29 USC §631(c)(1).

[269] Koprowski v Wistar Inst of Anatomy & Biology, 819 F Supp 410 (1992); *accord* 29 CFR §1625.12(c) (1993).

of an individual age 65 or older. Once retirement i.e., removal from the executive or high policymaking position, has occurred, these exceptions afford no defense to an employer for subsequent acts of discrimination that occur in the course of the employee's occupying his or her new position. In other words, the exceptions do not authorize any other kinds of less favorable treatment based on age.[270]

The burden of proof is on the employer to establish the applicability of these exceptions to the ADEA's general ban on age-based treatment, including mandatory retirement, of individuals over age 39.[271]

Legislative History

The bona fide executive and high policymaker exceptions originated in the Senate in 1978, as part of a package of proposed amendments to the ADEA. The Senate bill permitted mandatory retirement at age 65 of "a select group of management or highly compensated employees" entitled to immediate annual retirement benefits of at least $20,000,[272] with the Secretary of Labor being directed to adjust annually the $20,000 amount to account for changes in the cost of living.[273] The Senate proposal was aimed at enabling employers to replace key employees and thereby keep promotion channels open for younger employees.[274]

In the conference committee convened to iron out the differences between the House and Senate bills (the House bill, while addressed to other issues, did not contain a comparable provision), the exception was narrowed. Only those employees who

---

270 29 CFR §1625.12(c) (1993).

271 Equal Employment Opportunity Commn v Liggett & Meyers, Inc, 29 FEP Cas (BNA) 1611, 1643 (MDNC 1982) (dictum); *accord* 29 CFR §1625.12(b) (1993); *see also* Zises v Prudential Ins Co, 30 FEP Cas (BNA) 1218 (D Mass 1982).

272 Senate Comm on Human Resources, Amending the Age Discrimination in Employment Act Amendments of 1977, S Rep No 493, 95th Cong, 1st Sess 28 (1977).

273 *Id.*

274 *Id* 7.

had been employed for at least two years before mandatory retirement in bona fide executive or high policymaking positions were to be affected. This two-year requirement was added to prevent employers from circumventing the ADEA's general prohibition on age-based decisions and practices by appointing employees to executive positions and then quickly ousting them.[275] The limitation of the exceptions to bona fide executives and high policymakers resulted from conference committee fears that the Senate provision would permit the forced retirement of low level managers, supervisors, and blue collar workers.[276] The conference version of the bill also raised the minimum annual retirement benefit to $27,000 and eliminated the provision requiring annual adjustments to the income threshold by the Secretary of Labor.[277] (In 1984 the provision was amended so as to delete the $27,000 figure and substitute in lieu of it a benchmark of $44,000.)[278]

Defining Who Fits Within the Bona Fide Executive and High Policymaker Exemptions

The conference committee report explaining the 1978 legislation[279] endorsed as a guideline the definition of *bona fide executive* that was utilized with regard to a provision of the Fair Labor Standards Act (FLSA).[280] Additional criteria were included, however, in response to concerns regarding expansive interpretations. The conference committee report thus expressed the view that "[t]ypically the head of a significant and substantial local or regional operation of a corporation, such as a major produc-

---

275 Conference Comm, Age Discrimination in Employment Act Amendments of 1978, HR Rep No 950, 95th Cong, 2d Sess 9 (1978) [hereinafter Conference Committee Report].

276 *Id.*

277 *Id.*

278 Older Americans Act Amendments of 1984, Pub L No 98-459, §802(c)(1), 98 Stat 1767, 1792. It was further provided, in §802(c)(2), that this change would not apply to any employee who retired, or was compelled to retire, before October 9, 1984.

279 Conference Committee Report, *supra* note 275, at 9.

280 29 USC §§200-219.

tion facility or retail establishment, but not the head of a minor branch, warehouse or retail store, would be covered by the term 'bona fide executive.' "[281] Persons serving as heads of departments or divisions at corporate headquarters (central or regional) also were identified in the committee report as bona fide executives, and thus were subject to mandatory retirement or other differential treatment upon attaining age 65.[282] Subordinates of division heads likewise could fit within the exemption if their authority or responsibility was comparable to that possessed by the head of a significant and substantial local operation.[283]

According to the conference committee, a policymaking individual was one who exercised "little or no line authority but whose position and responsibility are such that . . . [he or she] play[s] a significant role in the development of corporate policy and effectively recommend[s] its implementation."[284] However, "the support personnel of a 'high policymaking' employee would not be subject to the exemption even if they supervise the development, and draft the recommendation, of various policies submitted by their supervisors."[285]

The committee further indicated that the exemption was not to be applicable to federal employees.[286]

Guidelines issued by the Equal Employment Opportunity Commission (EEOC) provide some further elucidation.[287] The

---

[281] Conference Committee Report, *supra* note 275, at 9; *see* Zises v Prudential Ins Co, 30 FEP Cas (BNA) 1218 (D Mass 1982). The Conference Committee Report added that "[i]ndividuals at higher levels in the corporate organizational structure who possess comparable or greater levels of responsibility and authority as measured by established and recognized criteria would also be covered." Conference Committee Report, *supra* note 275, at 9.

[282] Conference Committee Report, *supra* note 275, at 9.

[283] *Id* 9-10.

[284] *Id* 10.

[285] *Id.*

[286] *Id* 9. As to the separate treatment of federal employees under the ADEA, see generally **ch 9.**

[287] 29 CFR §1625.12(d) (1993). Such guidelines do not have the force of law, but they do command considerable judicial deference. See **ch 2.**

EEOC definition requires that, in order for an employee to qualify as a bona fide executive, he or she must meet every requirement of the Labor Department's regulations[288] interpreting the term *bona fide executive,* as used in the FLSA.[289] The EEOC guidelines further require that the executive meet the other criteria set forth in the conference report discussed above. They also specify that the exemption does not cover middle-level manag-

---

[288] These regulations provide as follows:

The term "employee employed in a bona fide executive . . . capacity" . . . shall mean any employee:

(a) Whose primary duty consists of the management of the enterprise in which he is employed or of a customarily recognized department or subdivision thereof; and

(b) Who customarily and regularly directs the work of two or more other employees therein; and

(c) Who has the authority to hire or fire other employees or whose suggestions and recommendations as to the hiring or firing and as to the advancement and promotion or any other change of status of other employees will be given particular weight; and

(d) Who customarily and regularly exercises discretionary powers; and

(e) Who does not devote more than 20 percent, or, in the case of an employee of a retail or service establishment who does not devote as much as 40 percent, of his hours of work in the workweek to activities which are not directly and closely related to the performance of the work described in paragraphs (a) through (d) of this section: *Provided,* That this paragraph shall not apply in the case of an employee who is in sole charge of an independent establishment or a physically separated branch establishment, or who owns at least a 20-percent interest in the enterprise in which he is employed; and

(f) Who is compensated for his services on a salary basis at a rate of not less than $155 per week (or $130 per week, if employed by other than the Federal Government in Puerto Rico, the Virgin Islands, or American Samoa) exclusive of board, lodging, or other facilities: *Provided,* That an employee who is compensated on a salary basis at a rate of not less than $250 per week (or $200 per week, if employed by other than the Federal Government in Puerto Rico, the Virgin Islands, or American Samoa), exclusive of board, lodging, or other facilities, and whose primary duty consists of the management of the enterprise in which the employee is employed or of a customarily recognized department or subdivision thereof, and includes the customary and regular direction of the work of two or more other employees therein, shall be deemed to meet all the requirements of this section.

29 CFR §541.1 (1993).

[289] *Id* §1625.12(d)(1).

ers, "no matter how great their retirement income."[290] Rather, the exemption applies "only to a very few top level employees who exercise substantial executive authority over a significant number of employees and a large volume of business."[291] The guidelines adopt the conference report definition of *high policymaker.*[292]

Case Law Addressing the Exceptions

The opinion in *Whittlesey v Union Carbide Corp*[293] constituted the first judicial analysis of the bona fide executive and high policymaker exceptions. In the main, the decision did not afford much guidance since the court's analysis was very much geared to matching the plaintiff's activities and functions in the particular job at issue against the standards set forth in the EEOC's guidelines. However, some aspects of the case are more generally instructive.

One argument made by the defendant was that the exceptions were satisfied by virtue of the fact that the plaintiff received a high salary: in excess of $100,000. The court rejected any per se rule, however. It stated: "High pay . . . is not determinative as to whether a position comes within the bona fide executive or high policymaker exemption. The test is one of function, not of pay."[294] In so reasoning, the court relied on the legislative history of the exceptions, observing that while the proposed Senate version of the exemptions used the phrase "select group of management or highly compensated employees," this language was deleted in the House-Senate conference committee.[295] This was not to say, however, that the level of pay was an irrelevant factor. The court further noted that "high or low pay can be relevant,

---

290 *Id* §1625.12(d)(2).

291 *Id.*

292 *Id* §1625.12(e).

293 567 F Supp 1320 (SDNY 1983), *affd,* 742 F2d 724 (2d Cir 1984).

294 *Id* 1326.

295 *Id* 1326 n4.

and often compelling evidence, as to an employee's executive or policymaking importance."[296]

Another argument advanced by the defendant-employer in *Whittlesey* was that the court had no power to review its decisions as to which of its employees occupied exempted positions. This argument also was rejected by the court in the following unequivocal passage: "There is no indication that the statute or the regulations intended to give management unreviewable discretion to decide whom it could retire at age 65 and whom it could not."[297] The district court's decision was affirmed without any additional analysis by the appellate court.[298]

The court that decided *Yoder v Carnegie Institution*[299] approvingly quoted the EEOC commentary that accompanied issuance of the EEOC guidelines: "An EEOC interpretation has made clear . . . that 'the . . . [bona fide executive] exemption does not require the employer to offer an employee a job with reduced status in lieu of mandatory retirement.' "[300] In *Koprowski v Wistar Institute of Anatomy & Biology*[301] the court rejected the argument that in order for the bona fide executive exception to be relied upon by an employer to justify retiring a specific individual, the employer must have a mandatory retirement program for all bona fide executives.

The exemption also has been addressed in a few other instances.[302] In the main, however, generalizations are difficult

---

[296] *Id* 1326.

[297] *Id* 1328.

[298] Whittlesey v Union Carbide Corp, 742 F2d 724 (2d Cir 1984).

[299] 47 Empl Prac Dec (CCH) ¶38,151 (DDC 1988).

[300] *Id* at 52,933 n5 (citing 44 Fed Reg 66791, 66976 (Nov 21, 1979)).

[301] 819 F Supp 410 (ED Pa 1992).

[302] *See* Passer v American Chem Socy, 935 F2d 322 (DC Cir 1991); Hysell v Mercantile Stores Co, Inc, 49 FEP Cas (BNA) 770 (SDNY 1989); Colby v Graniteville Co, 635 F Supp 381 (SDNY 1986).

In an opinion letter issued in 1987 the EEOC opined that, as a general matter, the exemption is not applicable to appointed state and local court judges, although the Commission conceded that, if the facts warranted, a given judge could fit within the exemption. EEOC OL-7 (Apr 7, 1987). (This letter is reproduced at the end of the last volume as a part of **app L.**) However, the status of appointed judges has since otherwise been resolved in decisions holding

to extract from the case law because of the fact-oriented nature of the inquiry in each case. For example, in *Priester v Amoco Corp, Inc*,[303] the court engaged in an extensive review of the duties performed by the plaintiff, who was the second-in-command of a company division. It then compared his activities to those performed by other employees who, being heads of significant local operations, clearly fit within the bona fide executive provision.[304] The court concluded that the defendant had failed to provide sufficient information regarding the functions of similar employees and concluded that there was significant question as to whether the plaintiff's position was comparable to that of the other individuals pointed to by the defendant. Accordingly, it denied the defendant's motion for summary judgment.

In *Breckenridge v Bristol-Meyers Co*[305] the court went through an extended analysis of the FLSA regulations regarding bona fide executives as they applied to the facts of the case before it. The court further examined the high policymaking position aspect of the statutory exceptions, and concluded—as it had regarding the bona fide executive issue—that the plaintiff fit within the provision and so could not invoke the ADEA's protection.

§3.13 —Determining the $44,000 Minimum Retirement Benefit

Section 12(c)(2)[306] of the Age Discrimination in Employment

---

them to be unprotected under the ADEA by virtue of another exception to the Act's coverage. See **§3.08.**

[303] 60 FEP Cas (BNA) 1083 (ND Ill 1990).

[304] This inquiry was prompted by the EEOC guidelines, which, as noted, adopt the conference committee standards, which in turn provide, as discussed above, that immediate subordinates of heads of divisions in large corporations fall within the exemption if they possess responsibility comparable to that of the heads of significant and substantial local operations.

[305] 43 FEP Cas (BNA) 1011 (SD Ind 1987).

[306] 29 USC §631(c)(2).

Act (ADEA)[307] provides that in determining whether a bona fide executive or high policymaker is entitled to a $44,000 minimum annual retirement benefit (and so is unprotected by the ADEA upon attainment of age 65), the benefit shall be adjusted—if it is in a "form other than a straight life annuity (with no ancillary benefits), or if employees contribute to any such plan or make rollover contributions"—so that "the benefit is the equivalent of a straight life annuity (with no ancillary benefits) under a plan to which employees do not contribute and under which no rollover contributions are made." The guidelines issued by the Equal Employment Opportunity Commission (EEOC) provide further guidance concerning this provision.

The existence of the $44,000 minimum benefit is established (1) if the individual in question is entitled to receive an annual payment of at least this amount or periodic payments during a year that total at least $44,000,[308] or (2) he or she is entitled to a lump sum with which it is possible to purchase a single life annuity of at least $44,000 per year.[309] The requisite minimum benefit also is established "where the employee is entitled to receive, upon retirement, benefits whose aggregate value, as of the date of . . . retirement, with respect to those payments which are scheduled to be made within the period of [the employee's] life expectancy . . . is $44,000 per year as adjusted."[310]

In *Passer v American Chemical Society*[311] the plaintiff, who unsuccessfully sought to elude classification as a bona fide executive, was receiving after his involuntary retirement a monthly retirement benefit of $2,783 from an annuity plan that guaranteed 180 payments. The court noted that §12(c)(2)[312] "permits the

---

[307] *Id* §§621-634.

[308] 29 CFR §1627.17(c)(1) (1993).

[309] *Id* §1627.17(c)(2).

[310] *Id* §1627.17(c)(3).

[311] 749 F Supp 277 (DDC 1990), *affd in part, revd in part & remanded on other grounds,* 935 F2d 322 (DC Cir 1991).

[312] 29 USC §631(c)(2).

actuarially equivalent calculation,"[313] and while on an annual basis Passer's monthly payments totaled $33,394, this amount was actuarially equivalent to a $44,690 straight-life annuity. (The determination of the value of the benefits that may be counted towards making up the $44,000 minimum "must be made on the basis of reasonable actuarial assumptions with respect to mortality and interest.")[314]

The EEOC guidelines provide that the benefit must be "immediately available," i.e., it must be available no later than 60 days after the effective date of retirement to an employee who is forced to retire.[315] While the $44,000 minimum annual retirement benefit may consist of the aggregate of sums derived from more than one source, "the only benefits which may be counted are those authorized by and provided under the terms of a pension, profit-sharing, savings, or deferred compensation plan."[316] It is explained that "[s]uch plans include, but are not limited to, stock bonus, thrift and simplified employee pensions."[317] Amounts derived from Social Security benefits, employee contributions, and rollover contributions must be excluded,[318] and benefits such as life and health insurance also are not to be included.[319] Lump-sum payments made by an employer are not to be counted in determining whether the requisite $44,000 minimum annual retirement benefit exists, according to the Court of Appeals for the District of Columbia:[320]

---

313 749 F Supp at 286.

314 29 CFR §1627.17(c)(5) (1993).

315 *Id* §1625.12(i). In Zises v Prudential Ins Co, 30 FEP Cas (BNA) 1218 (D Mass 1982), the court held that the annuitized value of past benefits was not to be taken into account in establishing the dollar minimum because the exemption depends according to the language of §12(c)(1), 29 USC §631(c)(1), on an "immediate" benefit.

316 29 CFR §1625.12(j)(2) (1993).

317 *Id* §1627.17(d).

318 *Id* §1627.17(e); *see* Passer v American Chem Socy, 935 F2d 322, 329 (DC Cir 1991).

319 29 CFR §1627.17(d) (1993).

320 Passer v American Chem Socy, 935 F2d 322 (DC Cir 1991).

> It could not be plainer that the . . . [annual total payment] received by the exempted retiree must be due under the terms of the applicable retirement plan; the language of the statute squarely refutes the . . . [defendant's] contention that Congress meant to require only that the employer unconditionally promise to pay a certain annual sum, as a sort of "golden parachute" by which it might purchase the right to discriminate on the basis of age.[321]

Contributions made by prior employers likewise must be excluded.[322] Insofar as such contributions are concerned, if the current employer maintains or contributes to a benefit plan that is distinct from the plans maintained by prior employers, there should be no difficulty in identifying the amount of the employee's benefits that are attributable to prior employers. There will be instances, however, where the present employer has contributed to the same plan as that to which prior employers had contributed. In such instance, the EEOC guidelines provide as follows:

> The benefit attributable to the current employer shall be the total benefit received by the employee, reduced by the benefit that the employee would have received from the plan if he or she had never worked for the current employer. For purposes of this calculation, it shall be assumed that all benefits have always been vested, even if benefits

---

[321] *Id* 329.

[322] The applicable guidelines provide as follows:

> ["][A] prior employer is every previous employer of the employee except those previous employers which are members of a 'controlled group of corporations' with, or 'under common control' with, the employer which forces the employee to retire, as those terms are used in sections 414 (b) and 414(c) of the Internal Revenue Code, as modified by section 414(h) (26 U.S.C. (b), (c), and (h)).

29 CFR §1627.17(e)(3)(i) (1993); *see* Zises v Prudential Ins Co, 30 FEP Cas (BNA) 1218 (D Mass 1982) (holding that a prior employer of the plaintiff was not under the control of the defendant employer, and thus benefits attributable to having worked for the prior employer were not includable).

accrued as a result of service with a prior employer had not in fact been vested.[323]

The EEOC guidelines provide specific rules for calculating the value of a pension, profit-sharing, savings, or deferred compensation plan, or any combination thereof. Amounts attributable to employee contributions must be excluded.[324] Different calculations apply, depending upon whether the retirement income plan is a defined contribution plan[325] or a defined benefit plan.[326] The calculations set forth in the guidelines address both the situation of a defined contribution plan where a separate account is maintained and where it is not maintained.[327] Likewise, in the case of defined benefit plans, the guidelines speak to both situations.[328]

"The annual retirement benefit must be nonforfeitable."[329] Thus, the bona fide *executive* and high policymaker exemptions will not come into play if a benefit plan authorizes either the ces-

---

[323] 29 CFR §1627.17(e)(3)(ii) (1993).

[324] *Id* §1627.17(e)(2).

[325]

> Defined contribution plans (also referred to as individual account plans) generally provide that each participant has an individual account and the participant's benefits are based solely on the account balance. No set benefit is promised in defined contribution plans, and the final amount is a result not only of the actual contributions, but also of other factors, such as investment gains and losses.

Id.

[326]

> Any retirement income plan which is not an individual account plan is a defined benefit plan. Defined benefit plans generally provide a definitely determinable benefit, by specifying either a flat monthly payment or a schedule of payments based on a formula (frequently involving salary and years of service), and they are funded according to actuarial principles over the employee's period of participation.

Id.

[327] *Id* §1627.17(e)(2)(i)(A), (B).

[328] *Id* §1627.17(e)(2)(ii)(A), (B).

[329] *Id* §1625.12(k)(1).

sation of benefits or their reduction to less than $44,000.[330] For example, if a plan calls for, or allows, the suspension of benefits if the employee competes with or litigates against the employer, the retirement benefit will be deemed to be forfeitable.[331] A retirement benefit will not be considered to be forfeitable, however, if it is discontinued or suspended for reasons permitted under §411(a)(3) of the Internal Revenue Code.[332] Furthermore, a retirement benefit will not be deemed forfeitable "merely because the minimum statutory benefit level is not guaranteed against the possibility of bankruptcy or is subject to benefit restrictions in the event of early termination of the plan in accordance with [the relevant Department of Treasury regulation(s)]." This is true so long as there was a reasonable expectation, as of the effective date of the retirement in question, that the plan would meet its obligations.[333]

§3.14 —Other Status Issues: Testers, Priests, Nuns, Bankruptcy Trustees, Prison Inmates, In-House Counsel, and Others

Testers

The deployment by public and private agencies of persons not actually seeking housing, but only pretending to do so, has for years been a prominent means for uncovering discrimination in violation of the federal Fair Housing Act, i.e., Title VIII of the Civil Rights Act of 1968.[334] These individuals, known as *testers,* have been defined as "individuals who, without an intent to rent or purchase a home or apartment, pose as renters or purchasers for the purpose of collecting evidence of unlawful . . . prac-

---

330 *Id.*

331 *Id.*

332 *Id* (citing 26 USC §411(a)(3)).

333 29 CFR §1625.12(k)(2) (1993).

334 42 USC §3601 *et seq.*

tices."[335] The Supreme Court has confirmed that these testers have standing under Title VIII to complain of racial discrimination in violation of that Act: in *Havens Realty Co v Coleman*[336] the Court ruled that a tester who was given inaccurate or incomplete information regarding housing was an aggrieved person within the meaning of 42 USC §3610(a), which authorizes any "person aggrieved" under the Act to file a complaint with the Secretary of the federal Department of Housing and Urban Development.

The Equal Employment Opportunity Commission (EEOC) in 1990 began to promote the idea of using testers to ferret out employment discrimination in violation of Title VII of the Civil Rights Act of 1964.[337] In an EEOC policy issuance the agency supported the position that testers have standing to bring actions both under Title VII and, of direct relevance here, the Age Discrimination in Employment Act (ADEA),[338] as well.[339] The agency pointed out that §706(b) of Title VII[340] authorizes the Commission to accept a charge of employment discrimination "filed by or on behalf of a person claiming to be aggrieved." And it further reasoned as follows:

> Title VII and Title VIII are "functionally identical" in purpose and structure. Testers in both the housing and employment areas serve essentially the same function. It is well established that testers in the housing area have standing to challenge prohibited discriminatory practices by landlords/realtors. There is no reason to distinguish

---

335 Havens Realty Co v Coleman, 455 US 363, 373 (1982).

336 455 US 363 (1982).

337 42 USC §§2000e through 2000e-17.

338 29 USC §§621-634.

339 EEOC Policy Guide No N-915-062: Whether "Testers" Have Standing to File Charges of Employment Discrimination Against Employers, Employment Agencies, and/or Labor Organizations Which Have Discriminated Against Them Because of Their Race, Color, Religion, Sex, or National Origin (Nov 20, 1990).

340 42 USC §2000e-5(b).

between the standing of testers in the housing area and testers in the employment context.[341]

Priests and Nuns

In an opinion letter issued in 1984 the EEOC opined that, for the purposes of the ADEA, priests who are serving their dioceses, pursuant to their religious obligations are not employees.[342] The EEOC took a similar position regarding nuns serving in parish schools.[343]

Conjugal Partnerships

In *Paredes Figueroa v International Air Services of Puerto Rico, Inc,*[344] the court refused to allow suit by a conjugal partnership—an entity created by statute in Puerto Rico.[345]

Prison Inmates

It has been held that a federal prison inmate is not an employee of the Federal Bureau of Prisons, even though the relationship with the Bureau may include some elements of an employment relationship.[346]

Bankruptcy Trustees and Persons Who Have Declared Bankruptcy

The district court that decided *Kuchan v Heston*[347] held that an individual who is, or seeks appointment as, a private bankruptcy trustee pursuant to 28 USC §586 is not an employee for purposes of the ADEA.

---

[341] EEOC Policy Guide No N-915-062, at 12.

[342] EEOC OL-5 (Nov 9, 1984). (This letter is reproduced at the end of the last volume as part of **app L.**)

[343] *Id* OL-4 (Nov 9, 1984). (This letter is reproduced at the end of the last volume as part of **app L.**)

[344] 662 F Supp 1202 (DPR 1987).

[345] *Accord* Zavala v GD Searle & Co, 56 FEP Cas (BNA) 1197 (DPR 1991).

[346] Williams v Meese, 926 F2d 994, 997 (10th Cir 1991).

[347] 59 FEP Cas (BNA) 891 (WD Wash 1992).

When an individual files a bankruptcy petition under Chapter 7 of the Bankruptcy Code,[348] he or she is required to include with the petition a schedule of assets and liabilities. This schedule must list the petitioner's legal and equitable interests, which are deemed to include causes of action existing at the time of the commencement of the bankruptcy. It is the Chapter 7 trustee who is the sole representative of the estate. He or she is the individual who "has the capacity to sue and be sued."[349] Accordingly, after the trustee's appointment a Chapter 7 debtor no longer has standing to pursue any cause of action that existed at the time the bankruptcy petition was filed.[350] Rather, an ADEA cause of action becomes a part of a Chapter 7 petitioner's estate upon the filing of the petition, and it is only the trustee in bankruptcy—and not the grievant—who has standing to sue.[351]

In-House Counsel

In-house counsel who have attempted to challenge their retaliatory discharges under common-law principles have not fared particularly well. For example, in *Balla v Gambro, Inc,*[352] the Supreme Court of Illinois rejected the claim of the plaintiff attorney, reasoning as follows:

> We believe that if in-house counsel are granted the right to sue their employers for retaliatory discharge, employers might be less willing to turn to their in-house counsel for advice regarding potentially questionable corporate conduct knowing that their in-house counsel could use this information in a retaliatory discharge suit.[353]

---

348 11 USC §§701-766.

349 *Id* §323(b).

350 Harris v St Louis Univ, 52 FEP Cas (BNA) 643 (ED Mo 1990).

351 *Id.*

352 145 Ill 2d 492, 584 NE2d 104 (1991).

353 145 Ill 2d at 503, 584 NE2d at 109.

In *Rand v CF Industries, Inc,*[354] however, the district court rejected an analogy to cases such as *Balla* and held that the ADEA "pre-empted defendants' rights under state law to discharge their in-house attorney/employees for any reason."[355] The court justified this conclusion with the observation that "[t]he issues involved in an age discrimination action brought by a discharged member of a corporate in-house legal staff are less likely to touch on matters sensitive to the attorney-client relationship than are issues arising in a retaliatory discharge suit."[356]

Employees of National Banks

Pursuant to federal statute, a national banking association has the power to "dismiss officers . . . at pleasure."[357] In *Mueller v First National Bank*[358] the court held that the "at pleasure" language did not remove national bank executives from the coverage of the ADEA.

Medical Interns and Residents

In a 1988 administrative ruling[359] the EEOC ruled that medical interns and residents are employees for purposes of Title VII of the Civil Rights Act of 1964.[360] In a footnote the agency noted that its position would be the same were the ADEA at issue.[361]

---

[354] 797 F Supp 643 (ND Ill 1992).
[355] *Id* 647.
[356] *Id.*
[357] 12 USC §24 (Fifth).
[358] 797 F Supp 656 (CD Ill 1992).
[359] EEOC Decision 86-1 (June 27, 1988).
[360] 42 USC §§2000e through 2000e-17.
[361] EEOC Decision 86-1 at 8 n16.

§3.15 —Persons Claiming Injury by Entities That Interfere with Relationships with Third Parties

The Age Discrimination in Employment Act (ADEA)[362] in the main covers only two-party relationships that are expressly (or implicitly, in the case of former employees) identified: employee-employer; job applicant-employer; member-labor organization; applicant-labor organization; and job-seeker-employment agency. In other words, the ADEA primarily addresses wrongs perpetrated in the context of a direct relationship between an individual grievant and the covered entity.

In some instances, however, the ADEA has a broader reach. The statute specifically proscribes discrimination that arises by virtue of a labor organization taking actions vis-a-vis an employer that redound to the detriment of a third party, i.e., the protected job applicant, employee, or former employee.[363] In addition, discrimination by employment agencies typically involves a three-party scenario involving the agency, the employer, and the job-seeker. There are, moreover, a few cases confirming the proposition that a cause of action may exist against an entity, usually an employer, for interfering with the relationship of an individual with a third party, even where the culpable entity was not itself involved in an employment relationship with the plaintiff.[364]

---

[362] 29 USC §§621-634.

[363] *Id* §623(c)(3) provides that "[i]t shall be unlawful for a labor organization . . . (3) to cause or attempt to cause an employer to discriminate against an individual in violation of this section."

[364] There are cases establishing that it may constitute illegal retaliation for a former employer to provides a negative reference to a prospective employer regarding an individual. See **ch 4.** In a policy statement issued by the Equal Employment Opportunity Commission (EEOC) for use by its personnel in determining the substantive merit of claims, the agency agreed that liability should be imposed on the retaliating employer in such a situation. EEOC Policy Statement on Control by Third Parties Over the Employment Relationship Between an Individual and His/Her Employer 3 (May 20, 1987). The EEOC further stated that "a sufficient nexus [between the third party's action and the plaintiff's employment status] will exist where the third party has the ability

ADEA Case Law

Equal Employment Opportunity Commission v KDM School Bus Co[365] involved a plaintiff who was forced by his employer, a private bus company, to retire at age 65, pursuant to a provision contained in the contract that the company had with a school district to provide transportation services for the district's students. The involuntarily retired former driver filed suit, naming the district as a defendant. The school district argued that no employee-employer relationship existed between it and the plaintiff, but the court denied the district's motion to dismiss, stating as follows: "Statutory employers 'who are neither actual or potential direct employers of particular complainants, but who control access to such employment and who deny such access by reference to invidious criteria,' may be held liable for violations of the ADEA."[366] Similarly in *Vakharia v Swedish Covenant Hospital*,[367]

---

to thwart the creation or continuance of a direct employment relationship or where it has the ability to affect the terms, conditions, or privileges of employment." *Id* 7. (This policy statement was scheduled to expire as of November 8, 1987. *Id* 1.) The EEOC issued another policy statement in 1986 in which it articulated the same view. EEOC Policy Statement N-915: Work Release Programs (May 30, 1986). This policy statement concerned the question of whether work release programs administered by penal institutions are covered by Title VII of the Civil Rights Act of 1964, 42 USC §§2000e through 2000e-17, for purposes of scrutinizing their placement of inmates with employers. The agency set forth an affirmative response, and in so doing stated that the discussion in the policy statement was applicable to the ADEA. *Id* 2 n1. The agency reasoned as follows:

> Although "there must be some connection with an employment relationship for Title VII's protections to apply, (t)he connection with employment need not necessarily be direct." *Lutcher v. Musicians Union Local 47.* 633 F.2d 880, 883 (9th Cir, 1980). The courts have interpreted the language of §703(a) [of Title VII] (1) to encompass situations where a third party, who is . . . [an] employer, has the ability to control or interfere with the employment opportunities of another employer and its employee.

Id 4. (Such policy issuances are not legally binding, but they may be accorded some deference by the courts. See **ch 2**.)

[365] 612 F Supp 369 (SDNY 1985).

[366] *Id* 372-73.

[367] 765 F Supp 461 (ND Ill 1991).

in which the plaintiff made claims both under the ADEA and under the ADEA's analogue, Title VII of the Civil Rights Act,[368] the court was willing to find liability arising out of an entity's interference with an individual's employment relationship with a third party.

Grossman v Suffolk County District Attorney's Office[369] also fits within this category of decisions. Here, the New York State Employee's Retirement System had informed the plaintiff, who was an employee of the Suffolk County District Attorney's Office, that he would either have to change his pension plan or lose his job—a choice that was not forced upon individuals under the age of 62. The court quoted a decision interpreting Title VII for the proposition that " 'the term 'employer,' . . . is sufficiently broad to encompass any party who significantly affects access of any individual to employment opportunities, regardless of whether that party may technically be described as an 'employer' of an aggrieved individual as that term has generally been defined at common law.' "[370]

The district court's analysis in *Frankel v Bally, Inc,*[371] contrasted with the foregoing decisions. The court quoted a decision by the Court of Appeals for the Second Circuit, *Hyland v New Haven Radiology Associates, PC,*[372] in which the appellate court stated:

> A plain reading of the Act indicates that its protection extends only to those individuals who are in a direct employment relationship with an employer, and that a claim under its provisions lies solely in favor of a person who is an employee at the time of termination.[373]

---

[368] 42 USC §§2000e through 2000e-17.

[369] 777 F Supp 1101 (EDNY 1991).

[370] *Id* 1104 (quoting Spirt v Teachers Ins & Annuity Assn, 691 F2d 1054, 1063 (2d Cir 1982), *vacated & remanded on other grounds,* 463 US 1223 (1983) (which in turn was quoting Vanguard Justice Socy, Inc v Hughes, 471 F Supp 670, 696 (D Md 1979))).

[371] 59 FEP Cas (BNA) 593 (SDNY 1992), *vacated & remanded,* 987 F2d 86 (2d Cir 1993).

[372] 794 F2d 793 (2d Cir 1986).

[373] *Id* 796.

The *Frankel* court read this requirement of a "direct employment relationship" as meaning that the plaintiff "must show that 'he is an employee of the defendant.' "[374] Accordingly, the district court stated, "*Hyland's* requirement of a direct employment relationship, distinguishes ADEA from Title VII, as to which cases hold that there does not need to be a direct employment relationship with the defendant."[375] Thus, the plaintiff—who was both the sole shareholder and the sole employee of a corporation that had a contract with the defendant—was held to be unable to maintain a suit against the defendant for having terminated the contract with the corporation and thereby having effectively deprived the plaintiff of employment, inasmuch as the plaintiff was deemed to not be in a direct employment relationship with the defendant.

The Court of Appeals for the Second Circuit vacated the ruling and remanded the case for reconsideration.[376] It reasoned that the lower court's reading of *Hyland* did not reflect developments in the case law since the date of that ruling, and it prescribed the following analytical framework for consideration of the case on remand:

> We agree . . . that Frankel's establishment of . . . [the corporation], and . . . [the corporation's] payment of salary and benefits to Frankel are important factors to be weighed in an analysis under the common law agency test [prescribed by the Court in *Nationwide Mutual Insurance Co v Darden,*[377] a case analogically relevant here]. However, the corporate form under which a plaintiff does business is not dispositive in a determination of whether an individual is an employee or an independent contractor[.][378]

---

[374] 59 FEP Cas at 595 (quoting Frishberg v Esprit De Corp, 778 F Supp 793, 798 (SDNY 1991), *affd without opinion,* 969 F2d 1042 (2d Cir 1992)).

[375] 59 FEP Cas at 595, n3.

[376] Frankel v Bally, Inc, 987 F2d 86 (2d Cir 1993).

[377] 112 S Ct 1344 (1992). See **§3.05.**

[378] 987 F2d at 91.

Title VII Case Law

Much of the initial case law in this area arose under Title VII.[379] The seminal decision, *Sibley Memorial Hospital v Wilson,*[380] involved a hospital that helped to place private nurses with patients in need of their services. The hospital maintained a registry with which the nurses signed up to indicate their availability. Patient requests were referred to the registry, which matched the requests with available nurses. The plaintiff alleged that the hospital had rejected him as a private nurse for female patients because he was a male, while it accepted referrals of female nurses for male patients. The Court of Appeals for the District of Columbia ruled that the hospital was the plaintiff's employer, even though no direct employment relationship existed between them. The court noted that by providing for Title VII's applicability to labor unions and employment agencies, Congress had intended the statute to address interference with direct employment relationships by "institutions which have . . . a highly visible nexus with the creation and continuance of direct employment relationships between third parties."[381]

The Nature of the Interfering Entity, and the Nature of the Relationship of the Grievant to It

Two key issues emerge from an examination of the case law. First, there is the question of whether the entity charged with engaging in unlawful interference must itself be an *employer,* as

---

379 *See, e.g.,* Shrock v Altru Nurses Registry, 810 F2d 658 (7th Cir 1987); Naismith v Professional Golfers Assn, 85 FRD 552, 559-60 (ND Ga 1979); Smith v Dutra Trucking Co, 410 F Supp 513, 518 (ND Cal 1976), *affd without opinion,* 580 F2d 1054 (9th Cir 1978), *cert denied,* 439 US 1076 (1979); Mathis v Standard Brands Chem Indus, 10 FEP Cas (BNA) 295, 297 n2 (ND Ga 1975).

380 488 F2d 1338 (DC Cir 1973).

381 *Id* 1340; *accord* Curran v Portland Superintending Sch Comm, 435 F Supp 1063, 1073 (Me 1977) (Title VII case); Puntolillo v New Hampshire Racing Commn, 375 F Supp 1089 (DNH 1974) (*id*).

that term is defined by the ADEA.[382] The court that decided *Ehret v Louisiana*[383] answered this question in the affirmative. The Equal Employment Opportunity Commission (EEOC), however, took the contrary position in a policy statement issued in 1987.[384]

The second question is whether there must be an employment relationship between the grievant and the employer that is charged with the unlawful interference. The ADEA rulings discussed earlier—*KDM School Bus Co, Grossman,* and the Court of Appeals ruling in *Frankel,* as well as *Ehret*—support the conclusion that there need not be any such relationship between the alleged wrongdoer and the plaintiff. The Title VII case law is in accord. For example, in *Doe v St Joseph's Hospital*[385] the defendant hospital's motion to dismiss was denied in a suit by a doctor who claimed that disciplinary action taken by the hospital in restricting her staff privileges interfered with her employment by her patients. The fact that the doctor was not an employee of the hospital did not preclude her pursuing the claim, in the court's view.

Similarly, other Title VII courts have taken a broad view, not requiring an employment relationship between the plaintiff and the defendant. Rather, they have found to be within the reach of the statute "any party who significantly affects access of any individual to employment opportunities, regardless [of] whether that party may technically be described as an 'employer' of an

---

[382] See **§§3.18-3.19.**

[383] 58 FEP Cas (BNA) 658, 662 (ED La 1992).

[384] In the agency's view, in order for the complainant to maintain an action against this third party the complainant's direct employer need not satisfy the statutory definition of *employer.* EEOC Policy Statement on Control by Third Parties Over the Employment Relationship Between an Individual and His/Her Employer 6 (May 20, 1987). (This policy statement was scheduled to expire on November 8, 1987). *Id* 1. (Such issuances do not have the force of law, but they may elicit some degree of judicial deference. See **ch 2.** As to the definition of *employer,* see **§ 3.18.**)

[385] 788 F2d 411 (7th Cir 1986).

aggrieved individual as that term has generally been defined at common law."[386]

In *Vakharia v Swedish Covenant Hospital,*[387] which arose under both Title VII and the ADEA, the court stressed the need for an employment relationship between the plaintiff and the third party,[388] with which relationship the defendant allegedly had interfered. The court did not require an employment relationship between the plaintiff and the defendant, however.

§3.16 —Persons Complaining of Discrimination by Employment Agencies and Labor Organizations

Section 4(b)[389] of the Age Discrimination in Employment Act (ADEA)[390] proscribes discrimination by employment agencies in terms of their refusing or failing to refer for employment, classifying or referring for employment, or otherwise discriminating against any "individual" because of age. Obviously, an employment relationship—either with the agency itself, or with an employer—is not necessary for §4(b) to come into play.

Section 4(c)[391] speaks to discrimination by labor organizations. It is violative of the Act for such an organization "to exclude or to expel from its membership, or otherwise to discriminate

---

[386] Spirt v Teachers Ins & Annuity Assn, 691 F2d 1054, 1063 (2d Cir 1982), *vacated & remanded on other grounds,* 463 US 1223 (1983); *see also* Gomez v Alexian Bros Hosp, 698 F2d 1019 (9th Cir 1983); Livingston v Ewing, 601 F2d 1110, 1114 (10th Cir), *cert denied,* 444 US 879 (1979); Pao v Holy Redeemer Hosp, 547 F Supp 484 (ED Pa 1982).

[387] 765 F Supp 461 (ND Ill 1991).

[388] *Accord* Diggs v Harris Hospital-Methodist, Inc, 847 F2d 270, 273 (5th Cir), *cert denied,* 488 US 956 (1989); Smith v Dutra Trucking Co, 410 F Supp 513, 518 & n11 (ND Cal 1976), *affd,* 580 F2d 1054 (9th Cir 1978), *cert denied,* 439 US 1076 (1979); Beverly v Douglas, 591 F Supp 1321 (SDNY 1984).

[389] 29 USC §623(b).

[390] *Id* §§621-634.

[391] *Id* §623(c).

against, any individual because of his age."[392] The other subsections of §4(c) also extend their protection to "individual[s]". Clearly, then, there is no requirement that persons who complain of labor organization practices be members of the organization. However, in some situations membership will be a prerequisite to invoking the ADEA provision. For example, as earlier noted, §4(c)(1)[393] makes it unlawful for a labor organization "to exclude or expel from its membership . . . any individual because of his age." Obviously, this language requires that one be, or have been, a member in order to complain of discriminatory expulsion.

§3.17 —Persons Complaining of Discriminatory Advertising

Section 4(e)[394] of the Age Discrimination in Employment Act (ADEA)[395] makes it unlawful for an "employer, labor organization, or employment agency to print or publish, or cause to be printed or published," discriminatory advertisements. There are only a few cases arising under this provision, and they all involve lawsuits brought by the ADEA enforcement agency.[396] Presumably, an aggrieved individual could sue, provided he or she were able to establish sufficient injury to satisfy standing requirements.

---

392 §4(c)(1), 29 USC §623(c)(1).

393 29 USC §623(c)(1).

394 29 USC §623(e).

395 *Id* §§621-634.

396 See **ch 4**.

The Entities that are Required to Comply with the ADEA

§3.18 *Employer* Defined: Generally

Employer is defined in §11(b)[397] of the Age Discrimination in Employment Act (ADEA)[398] as a "person engaged in an industry affecting commerce who has twenty or more employees for each working day in each of twenty or more calendar weeks in the current or preceding calendar year." *Person* is in turn defined in §11(a)[399] to mean "one or more individuals, partnerships, associations, labor organizations, corporations, business trusts, legal representatives, or any organized groups of persons."

According to the district court that decided *Wanamaker v Columbia Rope Co,*[400] "the term 'employer' is to be liberally interpreted."[401] The court further observed that *employer* " 'has been construed in a functional sense to encompass persons who are not employers in conventional terms, but who nevertheless control some aspect of an individual's compensation, terms, conditions, or privileges of employment.' "[402] In *Betts v Hamilton County Board of Mental Retardation*[403] a state entity—the Public Employees Retirement System (PERS)—was held to be an employer vis-a-vis the plaintiff, even though the plaintiff actually had worked for the Hamilton County Board. The court reasoned that PERS, which was vested with responsibility for the general administration and management of the retirement system and which had

---

397 29 USC §630(b).

398 *Id* §§621-634.

399 *Id* §630(a).

400 740 F Supp 127 (NDNY 1990).

401 *Id* 134.

402 *Id* (quoting Bostick v Rappleyea, 629 F Supp 1328, 1334 (NDNY 1985) quoting Spirt v Teachers Ins & Annuity Assoc, 475 F Supp 1298, 1308 (SDNY 1979), *affd in part & revd in part on other grounds,* 691 F2d 1054 (2d Cir 1982), *vacated & remanded on other grounds,* 463 US 1223 (1983)). This position is supported by the cases discussed in **§3.15.**

403 631 F Supp 1198 (ND Ohio), *affd,* 848 F2d 692 (6th Cir 1988), *revd on other grounds,* 492 US 158 (1989).

denied the plaintiff's application for disability benefits, was an employer "because it controls some aspects of plaintiff's compensation, terms, conditions, and privileges of employment."[404]

In *Equal Employment Opportunity Commission v Argent Industries, Inc,*[405] the district court opined "that the definition of employer . . . is more properly addressed as a jurisdictional element—that is, the ADEA simply does not confer jurisdiction over claims of age discrimination in employment against persons who are not 'employers' under the Act—rather [than] as an element of Plaintiff's claim."[406] Thus, in the view of the *Argent* court and courts of like perspective, the proper way to deal with the question, at the pretrial stage of the litigation, of whether a given entity is an employer is by way of a motion to dismiss for lack of subject-matter jurisdiction under Rule 12(b)(1),[407] rather than pursuant to a Rule 12(b)(6)[408] motion to dismiss for failure to state a claim upon which relief may be granted.[409]

The *Industry* and *Industry Affecting Commerce* Requirements

In *Walling v Jacksonville Paper Co*[410] the Supreme Court expressed the view that the appropriate language for Congress to use when it intends to utilize its full authority under the Commerce Clause[411] is "in any industry affecting commerce".[412] That phraseology of course is used in the ADEA's definition of *employer,* and so it is fair to infer that Congress intended, by enacting the age discrimination statute, to use the full range of its

---

404 631 F Supp at 1206.

405 58 FEP Cas (BNA) 844 (SD Ohio 1989).

406 *Id* 846.

407 Fed R Civ 12(b)(1).

408 Fed R Civ 12(b)(6).

409 58 FEP Cas at 845-47.

410 317 US 564 (1943).

411 US Const art I, §8.

412 317 US at 570.

commerce power.[413] The meaning of the term *industry* "affecting commerce" was addressed in *Martin v United Way of Erie County,*[414] in which the court ruled that the word "industry" encompassed both for-profit enterprises and those "operated for non-profit or charitable purposes."[415] In assessing the meaning of "affecting commerce" the court enunciated a very broad interpretation, holding that only a very minor economic activity was necessary to establish the requisite affect. The court deciding *Usery v Manchester East Catholic Regional School Board*[416] was in accord in deeming a local school to be an "industry affecting commerce."[417]

The *State Instrumentality* and *Interstate Agency* Language

Section 11(b) includes within the term *employer* "(1) any agent of such a person, and (2) a State or political subdivision of a State and any agency or instrumentality of a State or a political subdivision of a State, and any interstate agency." The term "any interstate agency" was explained in *Schaefer v Transportation Media, Inc*:[418] it refers to "the sort of multi-state agency formed by interstate compact," and not to an entity "having something to do with interstate transportation of commerce."[419] The *Schaefer* court also addressed the question of how one determines whether an entity is an instrumentality of a state or a political subdivision of a state. Key, the court concluded, is the presence of control over the ostensible instrumentality.[420]

---

413 *See* Usery v Manchester East Catholic Regional Sch Bd, 430 F Supp 188, 189 (DNH 1977).

414 829 F2d 445 (3d Cir 1987).

415 *Id* 448.

416 430 F Supp 188 (DNH 1977).

417 *Id* 490.

418 859 F2d 1251 (7th Cir 1988).

419 *Id* 1255 n5.

420 *Id* 1255.

Other Issues

While §11(b) excludes from the definition of employer the United States and corporations wholly owned by the United States,[421] these entities are in any event brought within the reach of the ADEA by §15 of the Act.[422]

A licensor-licensee relationship will not suffice to make the licensor an employer.[423] On the other hand, given the language of §11(a),[424] it is no surprise that case law confirms that a partnership may be an employer.[425]

Most commonly, the question of whether an employer-employee relationship exists will be determined by assessing the status of the putative employee to determine whether he or she is indeed an employee within the meaning of the statutory language.[426] Status, insofar as employers are concerned, has been a less controversial matter: the broad definition of *employer* brings within its sweep almost every entity, and thus little room has been left for questioning whether a given company or government agency performs functions that make it an employer for statutory purposes. This is not to say there are not disputes, however. Indeed, there are, and these are addressed in the succeeding sections.

---

[421] §11(b), 29 USC §630(b).

[422] 29 USC §633a. See **§3.21.** The Equal Employment Opportunity Commission has taken the position that Federal Reserve banks are private sector employers, rather than federal sector executive agencies covered by §15. EEOC Enforcement Guide No N-915-002: Coverage of Federal Reserve Banks (Oct 20, 1993). This issuance is reproduced in the appendix at the end of the final volume. Such issuances are not legally binding, but they generally elicit considerable judicial deference. See **ch 2.**

[423] Ehret v Louisiana, 58 FEP Cas (BNA) 658, 662 (ED La 1992); Equal Employment Opportunity Commn v Waterfront Commn, 665 F Supp 197 (SDNY 1987); Miles v Pennsylvania Pub Util Commn, 73 Pa Commw 53, 457 A2d 221 (1983).

[424] 29 USC §630(a). This subsection defines *person* to include "one or more individuals, partnerships, associations . . . or any organized groups of persons."

[425] *See, e.g.*, Lettich v Kenway, 41 Empl Prac Dec (CCH) ¶36,543 (D Mass 1986).

[426] See **§§3.05-3.14.**

§3.19 The Numerosity Requirement of 20 or More Employees

Section 11(b)[427] of the Age Discrimination in Employment Act (ADEA)[428] defines *employer* as any person engaged in an industry affecting interstate commerce "who has twenty or more employees for each working day in each of twenty or more calendar weeks in the current or preceding calendar year."[429] In *McGraw v Warren County Oil Co*[430] the Court of Appeals for the Eighth Circuit affirmed the district court's holding that the words "calendar years" in §11(b) mean the period January 1 through December 31, rather than any other period of 12 consecutive calendar months. The trigger for determining what constitutes the "current or preceding calendar years" is the date on which the alleged discriminatory conduct occurred.[431] Thus, if a lawsuit is filed in January of 1994, but the alleged discrimination occurred in 1993, the years to be used in determining whether the employer had the requisite number of employees are 1993, the *current* year, and 1992, the year *preceding* the current year.

Defining a *Week*

Section 11(b) defines *employer* by reference to the number of weeks an entity has, or does not have, the requisite number of employees. There is no ADEA case law that directly focuses on defining what constitutes a work week per se, although the statutory language does speak to "calendar weeks". In *Wright v Kosci-*

---

[427] 29 USC §630(b).

[428] *Id* §§621-634.

[429] This definition differs from that contained in Title VII of the Civil Rights Act of 1964, 42 USC §§2000e through 2000e-17, on which the ADEA is modeled, see **ch 2,** only in the minimum number of employees: Title VII sets the figure at 15. 42 USC §2000e(b).

[430] 707 F2d 990 (8th Cir 1983).

[431] Wright v Kosciusko Medical Clinic, Inc, 791 F Supp 1327, 1329 (ND Ind 1992); Lord v Casco Bay Weekly, Inc, 789 F Supp 32, 34 (D Me 1992).

usko Medical Clinic, Inc,[432] which involved an employer that was open six days a week, the court pointed to the defendant's reduced Saturday hours in reasoning that "Saturday . . . was not a 'working day' in the same sense" as were Monday through Friday.[433] To supplement this conclusion, the court further noted that there was a "substantially diminished staffing on Saturday, compared to the other five days, . . . [and this suggested] that the normal range of patient services and officer operations . . . are not performed on that day."[434] The court therefore concluded that "for purposes of determining the scope of protection afforded by Title VII [of the Civil Rights Act of 1964[435] which was one of the two statutory bases for the plaintiff's suit, the other being the ADEA], a day on which the employer does not conduct normal, full operations is not be treated as a 'working day.' "[436] It offered the following policy justification for this reading:

> Treating diminished days of operations as "working days" would have anomalous, and potentially absurd, results: a 200-employee factory, running three shifts from Monday through Saturday, could be placed beyond the reach of Title VII by sending a lone telephone operator to work on Sunday. While the court does not suggest that the . . . [defendant here] has so structured its operations to circumvent Title VII, a determination of the statute's reach must be objective, rather than dependent on some corporate state of mind.[437]

---

[432] 791 F Supp 1327 (ND Ind 1992).

[433] *Id* 1333. In reaching this conclusion, the court noted that, although the defendant's clinic was open six days a week, it was open for only 5 hours on Saturday versus 12½ hours on Monday through Thursday and 8½ hours on Friday.

[434] *Id.*

[435] 42 USC §§2000e through 2000e-17.

[436] 791 F Supp at 1333.

[437] *Id.*

The *Wright* court addressed an easy factual scenario, since the sixth day of operations clearly entailed diminished activity. It did not address the harder situation, i.e., the status of an entity that operates for more than five days a week, during none of which days operations are diminished. Arguably a calendar week for such an entity would be the entire six- or seven-day week it is open and doing business. And arguably, then, any individual who works less than the full six or seven days should not be counted as an employee for purposes of the 20-employee requirement. Another variation on this theme would involve individuals who work 10-hour shifts, with some working Monday through Thursday, and others Tuesday through Saturday. In that situation one could reason that 40 hours of work, even though performed over a period of just four days, constitutes a week for the purposes of §11(b). Alternatively, one could argue that only the customary modern-day five days of work would equal a "calendar week".

There is no readily apparent guideline for deciding whether only days worked—as opposed to hours worked—should determine what constitutes a week. Nor is there any readily apparent guideline for determining whether one should abide by a particular entity's or industry's definition of a week, which definition might mean a four-, six- or seven-day week, or whether one should utilize the customary five-day week standard. (Of course, even if the latter benchmark were used, there is no guideline for determining whether the five-day standard should include Monday through Friday, rather than, let us say, Tuesday through Saturday.)

Ordinarily, the standard Monday through Friday five-day week should be the applicable standard. But if there is a different industry standard or community standard that is generally followed, that standard should be deemed controlling. Or, if a particular defendant's typical practice is to utilize some departure from the norm, such as extended shifts of 10 hours per day for four days or a Tuesday through Sunday work week, that defendant's variation on the normal Monday through Friday work week should be deemed to be the standard for determining whether it is an employer for ADEA purposes. Clearly, it is the plaintiff's burden to establish that the defendant is an employer for the purposes of §11(b), and so it should be the plaintiff's task in a given case to prove which standard for establishing the requisite number of weeks is to apply.

Work Force That Varies in Size During the Year

If the size of an employer's work force fluctuates throughout the year, it is not readily apparent whether the employer is covered for the entire year or only for the weeks that it has at least 20 employees. The legislative history of the ADEA is silent on this point; the legislative history of the comparable numerosity provision[438] contained in Title VII, the judicial interpretations of which are often looked to for guidance by ADEA courts,[439] is ambiguous.[440] The court that decided *Slack v Havens,*[441] a Title VII ruling, addressed this issue, however. The plaintiff was discharged in February 1968; inasmuch as only four weeks of the year had elapsed at that point, the defendant did not yet have the minimum number of employees for 20 weeks of the calendar year. Moreover, the defendant had only had the minimum number of employees for 11 or 12 weeks of the preceding year, Eventually, the defendant met the statutory requirement for 1968. The court rejected the defendant's argument that it was not covered at the time of the discharge, holding that if the statutory minimum number of employees was met for *any* 20 weeks of a calendar year, coverage would thereby be established for actions occurring any time during that year. This reasoning is both on target and applicable—by way of analogy—to the ADEA.

---

[438] See note 429.

[439] See **ch 2.**

[440] During the Senate debates on Title VII, one senator declared that coverage would not be year round, while another later said that it would be. *See* 110 Cong Rec 6996 (1964) (remarks of Sen Clark); *id* 12296 (remarks of Sen Humphrey). *See generally* Benevitz, *Coverage Under Title VII,* 17 Lab LJ 285, 287 (1966).

[441] 17 FEP Cas (BNA) 885 (SD Cal 1973), *affd in part & remanded in part,* 522 F2d 1091 (9th Cir 1975).

Counting Part-Time Employees

The administrative interpretations and legislative history of the ADEA are silent concerning the treatment of part-time employees. In *Zimmerman v North American Signal Corp*[442] the court was called upon to address this issue. In dispute was the method of determining the number of the defendant's employees for each week. Under the employer's method, hourly workers were counted as employees only on days when they were actually at work and on days of paid leave. Thus, an hourly paid worker who worked Monday through Thursday was not counted as an employee on Friday, regardless of the number of hours he or she had worked the other four days of that week and regardless of whether he or she was a permanent employee who would be expected to return to work the next week. Pursuant to this methodology, the defendant in *Zimmerman* would count its employees for each day of each week; then, for each week, it would determine whether there were 20 or more employees for each day. If the number of employees fell below 20 on any day of a week, that week would not be counted towards the ADEA's requisite of 20 weeks. The plaintiff, on the other hand, argued that all hourly paid workers who worked or were on paid leave during the week should be counted, the total being derived simply by counting the total number of workers who were on the payroll for each work week.

Thus, from the defendant's perspective, even if there were 20 or more employees on four days of the week, that week would be disregarded if on any one day of the week the total fell below 20. From the plaintiff's perspective, the week would count even if on no day there were 20 or more employees, so long as the total of names on the payroll for the week as a whole equaled 20 or more.

The Court of Appeals for the Seventh Circuit subscribed to the defendant's method; it looked to the explicit language of §11(b) that defines employer as an entity having "twenty or more employees for each working day in each of twenty or more

---

[442] 704 F2d 347 (7th Cir 1983).

calendar weeks," and it read this language as precluding the plaintiff's approach. In brief, the *Zimmerman* court's position is that the only part-time workers who may be counted when determining whether a given week is to be included in the 20-week calculation are those workers who worked each day of the work week in question. The Court of Appeals for the Eighth Circuit is in agreement with this approach,[443] as are various district courts both within the Seventh Circuit[444] and outside it.[445]

There are a couple of ADEA rulings,[446] as well as several Title VII decisions[447] that support the contrary position. These rulings endorse the view that it is the number of workers on the payroll in a given week, rather than the number at work each day, that determines coverage. The Equal Employment Opportunity Commission (EEOC) likewise rejects *Zimmerman.* "The Commission's position," the agency asserted in a 1990 policy issuance, "is that all part-time employees are counted whether they work

---

443 Equal Employment Opportunity Commn v Garden & Assocs, Ltd, 956 F2d 842 (8th Cir 1992); McGraw v Warren County Oil Co, 707 F2d 990 (8th Cir 1983).

444 Wright v Kosciusko Medical Clinic, Inc, 791 F Supp 1327 (ND Ind 1992).

445 Lord v Casco Bay Weekly, 789 F Supp 32 (D Me 1992); Equal Employment Opportunity Commn v Argent Indus, Inc, 746 F Supp 705, 708-09 (SD Ohio 1989).

446 Cohen v SUPA, Inc, 814 F Supp 251, 254-55 (NDNY 1993); Gorman v Surgery Assocs, Ltd, 664 F Supp 212 (WD Pa 1987).

447 *See, e.g.,* Thurber v Jack Reilly's, Inc, 717 F2d 633 (1st Cir 1983), *cert denied,* 466 US 904 (1984); Petreyra v Cornell Prescription Pharmacies, Inc, 465 F Supp 936 (D Colo 1979); Pascutoi v Washburn-McReavy Mortuary, Inc, 11 FEP Cas (BNA) 1325 (D Minn 1975). However, according to one Title VII court, an employee who merely fills in for a short period of time may be so casual or transient as not to be counted. *See* Takeall v WERD, Inc, 23 FEP Cas (BNA) 947 (MD Fla 1979). In a policy guide issued by the EEOC, the Commission expressed the view that the position taken by the *Takeall* court is erroneous. EEOC Policy Guide No N-915:052: Whether Part-Time Employees are Employees Within the Meaning of §701(b) of Title VII and §11(b) of the ADEA 3 n4 (Apr 20, 1990). This policy guide is reproduced in the Appendix at the end of the last volume. As to the legal significance of such policy issuances, see note 448.

part of each day or part of each week, as long as they are on the payroll."[448]

If one takes to heart the common refrain that the ADEA is to be liberally construed,[449] it would appear that the *Zimmerman* court's reading of the language of §11(b) is inconsistent with the notion of interpreting the Act so as to diminish age discrimination in the workplace. While it is true that the statutory language arguably could be seen as compelling the result arrived at in *Zimmerman,* one could also legitimately reason as the court did in *Wright v Kosciusko Medical Clinic, Inc:*[450]

> The opposite result, . . ., and one that seems equally consistent with the statutory language, could be reached by focusing . . . on the requirement that the "employer *have* twenty . . . or more employees". It is certainly not inconsistent . . . to conclude that an employer "has" an employee on a working day, even if that employee is not physically present on that day—especially if he or she was there the day before and is expected to show up for work on the next day. *Zimmerman* gave some recognition to that fact, by allowing inclusion of workers on vacation or sick leave in the total. It is not obvious why those categories of absent present workers should be counted, but one who works four or five days a week, instead of seven, should not be counted on those other days.[451]

---

[448] EEOC Policy Guide No N-915:052: Whether Part-Time Employees Are Employees within the meaning of §701(b) of Title VII and §11(b) of the ADEA 3 (Apr 20, 1990). Such internal EEOC issuances are designed to give guidance to agency staff. They clearly do not have any legal force and thus are not binding on the courts. Nonetheless, they can be looked to and given considerable credence, if a court is so inclined. *Cf* Albemarle Paper Co v Moody, 422 US 405, 431 (1975) (considering statements issued by EEOC under Title VII of Civil Rights Act of 1964, 42 USC §§2000e through 2000e-17). See generally **ch 2.**

[449] See **ch 2.**

[450] 791 F Supp 1327 (ND Ind 1992).

[451] *Id* 1331-32. While the *Wright* court disagreed with *Zimmerman,* it felt bound to follow the precedent set for its circuit by the *Zimmerman* decision. *Id.*

The Numerosity Requirement as Applied to Government Entities

In *Kelly v Wauconda Park District*[452] the Court of Appeals for the Seventh Circuit rejected the argument that the 20-employee requirement was inapplicable to governmental agencies.[453] This position has been echoed by the Court of Appeals for the Sixth Circuit.[454] In another Seventh Circuit Court of Appeals ruling, *Schaefer v Transportation Media, Inc,*[455] the appellate court was willing to afford some flexibility on the issue: it held that an agency or instrumentality of a state or political subdivision need not meet the numerosity requirement so long as the larger government body with which it is associated does.[456]

Procedure

It is the plaintiff's task to establish that the employer has a sufficient number of employees to meet the ADEA's numerosity requirement.[457] If this burden is not satisfied, the court will not have jurisdiction to entertain the plaintiff's claim.[458]

According to the court that decided *Equal Employment Opportunity Commission v Argent Industries, Inc,*[459] the issue of whether an employer has a number of employees sufficient for it to qualify as an employer for the purposes of the ADEA is more properly

---

[452] 801 F2d 269 (7th Cir 1986), *cert denied,* 480 US 940 (1987).

[453] *Accord* Smith v Wythe-Grayson Regional Library Bd, 657 F Supp 1216 (WD Va 1987).

[454] Equal Employment Opportunity Commn v Monclova Township, 920 F2d 360 (6th Cir 1990). This decision thereby effectively overruled an earlier district court ruling in which the 20-employee requirement was rejected as being applicable to government entities. Equal Employment Opportunity Commn v Hudson Township, 40 FEP Cas (BNA) 691 (ND Ohio 1986).

[455] 859 F2d 1251 (7th Cir 1988).

[456] *Id* 1254. The court abjured deciding whether joinder of the larger entity was necessary. *Id* 1255 n4.

[457] Lord v Casco Bay Weekly, Inc, 789 F Supp 32, 33 (D Me 1992).

[458] *Id* 33.

[459] 746 F Supp 705 (SD Ohio 1989).

dealt with pursuant to a §12(b)[460] motion to dismiss for lack of subject-matter jurisdiction rather than by either: (1) a §12(b)(6)[461] motion to dismiss for failure to state a claim upon which relief can be granted; or (2) a motion for summary judgment.

§3.20 State and Local Governments

As originally enacted,[462] the Age Discrimination in Employment Act (ADEA)[463] did not apply to state and local governments. A 1974 amendment modified §11(b)[464] of the act so as to extend coverage to these entities.[465] However, §11(f)[466] of the Act, which was also amended at that time, exempts several categories of individuals:

—elected officials,
—the personal staff and policymaking appointees of such elected officials, and
—individuals who are immediate advisers to such officials with respect to the exercise of the constitutional or legal powers of office, if such individuals are not subject to civil service laws.[467]

(Notwithstanding the fact that the foregoing individuals are not

---

[460] Fed R Civ P 12(b)(1).

[461] Fed R Civ P 12(b)(6).

[462] Pub L No 90-202, 81 Stat 605 (1967).

[463] 29 USC §§621-634.

[464] *Id* §630(b).

[465] Fair Labor Standards Amendments of 1974, Pub L No 93-259, §28, 88 Stat 55, 74. The added language does not refer to the 20-employee requirement, which is clearly applicable to private employers. See **§3.19.** Nonetheless, this numerosity requirement has been deemed applicable by some courts to state and local governmental entities. See **§3.19.**

[466] 29 USC §630(f).

[467] *Id.* See **§3.08.**

directly protected by the terms of the ADEA itself, §321[468] of the Government Employee Rights Act of 1991[469] extended the Act's protection to them. There is, however, a separate enforcement scheme erected by the 1991 Act.)[470]

Until the Supreme Court laid the matter to rest in 1983 in *Equal Employment Opportunity Commission v Wyoming*,[471] there were frequent challenges by state and local governments to the 1974 amendment insofar as it brought these entities within the ADEA's ambit. In the large majority of cases, these challenges were unsuccessful.

The Development of the Case Law

In 1976 the Court held, in *National League of Cities v Usery*,[472] that the extension of the Fair Labor Standards Act's (FLSA)[473] minimum wage and maximum hour provisions to state and local governments was unconstitutional. It reasoned that these provisions exceeded congressional power under the Commerce Clause[474] by invading the powers reserved to the states under the Tenth Amendment.[475] Compliance with the FLSA was seen as directly impairing the ability of state governments to structure integral operations in areas of traditional governmental functions.[476]

---

[468] 2 USC §1220.

[469] Pub L No 102-166, 105 Stat 1071, 1088-99, codified at 2 USC §1201 *et seq*.

[470] See **ch 11**.

[471] 460 US 226 (1983).

[472] 426 US 833 (1976).

[473] 29 USC §§200-219.

[474] US Const art I, §8.

[475] *Id* amend X.

[476] 426 US at 852. The Court subsequently interpreted *National League of Cities* as requiring three elements to invalidate congressional commerce power legislation under the Tenth Amendment:

1. The legislation must regulate the states as states
2. It must address matters that are indisputably attributes of state sovereignty

The Court earlier had rejected the argument advanced in *Fitzpatrick v Bitzer*[477] that the extension to state governments of Title VII of the Civil Rights Act of 1964,[478] which also regulates employment, violated the Eleventh Amendment.[479] The *Fitzpatrick* Court reasoned that Congress had acted pursuant to §5 of the Fourteenth Amendment,[480] which empowers Congress to enforce the amendment by appropriate legislation and thereby necessarily limits state sovereignty.

In the years immediately following *Usery*, judicial responses to litigants' claims that the ADEA's coverage of state and local governments was unconstitutional turned, in the first instance, on whether Congress was understood as having acted pursuant to the Fourteenth Amendment or the Commerce Clause. If the former was seen as the source of congressional authority, it followed that the ADEA's extension to state and local governmental entities passed constitutional muster, given the breadth of Congress's authority under §5 of the Fourteenth Amendment and given *Fitzpatrick*. The large majority of lower courts indeed did look to §5 and they concluded that the ADEA amendment was an appropriate exercise of Congress's authority under that constitutional provision.[481]

---

3. Compliance must directly impair a state's ability to structure integral operations in areas of traditional functions.

United Transp Union v Long Island RR, 455 US 678 (1982).

[477] 427 US 445 (1976).

[478] 42 USC §§2000e through 2000e-17.

[479] US Const amend XI.

[480] *Id* amend XIV, §5.

[481] *See, e.g.*, Ramirez v Puerto Rico Fire Serv, 715 F2d 694 (1st Cir 1983); Arritt v Grisell, 567 F2d 1267 (4th Cir 1977); Coffin v South Carolina Dept of Social Servs, 562 F Supp 579 (DSC 1983); United States Equal Employment Opportunity Commn v City of Minnespolis, 537 F Supp 750 (D Minn 1982); Equal Employment Opportunity Commn v County of Los Angeles, 526 F Supp 1135 (CD Cal 1981), *affd on other grounds*, 706 F2d 1039 (9th Cir 1983), *cert denied*, 464 US 1073 (1984); Adams v James, 526 F Supp 80 (MD Ala 1981); Carpenter v Commonwealth of Pa Liquor Control Bd, 508 F Supp 148 (ED Pa 1981); Equal Employment Opportunity Commn v City of Allen Park, 30 FEP Cas (BNA) 162 (ED Mich 1981); Marshall v Delaware River & Bay Auth, 471 F Supp 886 (D Del 1979); Equal Employment Opportunity Commn v Florissant Valley Fire Protection Dist, 21 FEP Cas (BNA) 973 (ED Mo 1979);

Some lower courts, however, concluded that Congress had acted under the Commerce Clause, as it had when it passed the FLSA provisions at issue in *Usery.* Among these courts there was a more significant split, with some upholding the constitutionality of the amended §11(b)[482] and other courts finding it unconstitutional.[483]

In 1983 the Supreme Court addressed the constitutionality of the application of the ADEA to state employers. By a 5-4 vote the Court upheld the law as a valid exercise of Congress's commerce power in *Equal Employment Opportunity Commission v Wyoming.*[484] The Court harmonized its holding with *Usery* by reasoning that one of the requirements necessary for a state to successfully invoke the Tenth Amendment protection afforded by that case was a finding that the federal statute directly impaired the state's ability to structure integral operations in areas of traditional governmental functions. The ADEA, in the *Wyoming* Court's view, does not do that. In any event, any questions concerning the *Wyoming* Court's juxtaposing of the *Usery* standard with the ADEA were mooted when the Court overruled

---

Remmick v Barnes County, 435 F Supp 914 (DND 1977); Aaron v Davis, 424 F Supp 1238 (ED Ark 1976); Usery v Board of Educ, 421 F Supp 718 (D Utah 1976).

[482] *See, e.g.,* Equal Employment Opportunity Commn v City of Altoona, 723 F2d 4 (3d Cir 1983), *cert denied,* 467 US 1204 (1984); Equal Employment Opportunity Commn v County of Los Angeles, 706 F2d 1039 (9th Cir 1983), *cert denied,* 464 US 1073 (1984); United States Equal Employment Opportunity Commn v Elrod, 674 F2d 601 (7th Cir 1982).

[483] *See, e.g.,* Black v Goodman, 736 F Supp 1042 (D Mont 1990); Morgan v Department of Offender Rehabilitation, 30 FEP Cas (BNA) 160 (ND Ga 1982); Campbell v Connelie, 542 F Supp 275 (NDNY 1982); Taylor v Department of Fish & Game, 523 F Supp 514 (D Mont 1981); Equal Employment Opportunity Commn v Wyoming, 514 F Supp 595 (D Wyo 1981), *revd,* 460 US 226 (1983). In Farkas v New York State Dept of Health, 554 F Supp 24 (NDNY 1982), *affd without opinion,* 767 F2d 907 (2d Cir), *cert denied,* 474 US 1033 (1985), the court was of the view that *Usery* would not preclude all applications of the ADEA to the states, but inasmuch as the ADEA was only an exercise of Congress's commerce power, the federal statute was inadequate, in the court's analysis of the matter, to override the state's immunity under the Eleventh Amendment as to monetary liability for past wrongdoing. *Id* 28.

[484] 460 US 226 (1983).

Usery in *Garcia v San Antonio Metropolitan Transit Authority.*[485] Thus, the question of whether in a given situation the ADEA's application to a state or local governmental activity would impair that body's ability to structure integral operations in areas of traditional governmental concern became irrelevant.

The *Wyoming* majority refrained from determining whether the statute was also a valid exercise of Congress's power under §5 of the Fourteenth Amendment.[486] But while eschewing a ruling on that issue, the majority did assert that one basis for the ruling of the lower court—which had held that the Act could not be upheld under §5—was misplaced. The district court had erred, the Court stated, in reading *Pennhurst State School v Halderman*[487] as holding that congressional action could not be upheld on the basis of §5 unless Congress expressly articulated its intent to legislate under that provision. The majority stated as follows in this regard:

> It is in the nature of our review of congressional legislation defended on the basis of Congress' power under §5 of the Fourteenth Amendment that we be able to discern some legislative purpose or factual predicate that supports the exercise of that power. That does not mean, however, that Congress need anywhere recite the words "section 5" or "Fourteenth Amendment" or "equal protection,"[.][488]

While at first blush it might appear that it does not matter whether §5 of the Fourteenth Amendment or the Commerce Clause is the basis for upholding the application of the ADEA to state and local governmental bodies, this in fact is not the case. As *Fitzpatrick* establishes, a statute passed pursuant to Congress' §5 power will override a state's Eleventh Amendment immunity

---

[485] 469 US 528 (1985).

[486] In contrast, the four dissenters did address the issue. They asserted that the extension of the ADEA to state and local governmental bodies was not a valid expression of §5 power.

[487] 451 US 1 (1981) (*Pennhurst* I).

[488] 460 US at 243 n18.

from suit in federal court.[489] In contrast, a statute passed pursuant to Congress's commerce power may not necessarily be read in the same way.[490]

Wyoming of course left intact those decisions in which lower courts had ruled that §5 of the Fourteenth Amendment was the source of Congress's authority for passing the ADEA. Since *Wyoming* there have been additional lower courts decisions that have set forth the same position.[491] For example, in deciding *Hurd v Pittsburg State University*[492] the court held that Congress had acted pursuant to §5 and, further, that in doing so Congress had expressed the unequivocal intent to abrogate Eleventh Amendment immunity that the *Hurd* court understood is required by *Pennhurst State School and Hospital v Halderman.*[493] The court reasoned that this intent, while not literally articulated in the statute or the legislative history, followed from the fact that the ADEA expressly authorizes suit against state employers.[494] On the other hand, the Court of Appeals for the Fourth Circuit, which in

---

[489] The Eleventh Amendment provides that "[t]he Judicial power of the United States shall not be construed to extend to any suit in law or equity, commenced or prosecuted against one of the United States by Citizens of another State." US Const amend XI. It is erroneous to view the amendment as only conferring protection from liability; rather, the amendment bars the federal courts from even exercising jurisdiction in the first instance. Puerto Rico Aqueduct & Sewer Auth v Metcalf & Eddy, Inc, 112 S Ct 684, 689 (1993).

[490] As to how the liability of states for monetary relief has been resolved in light of the Eleventh Amendment issue, see **ch 8.**

[491] *See, e.g.,* Davidson v Board of Governors of State Colleges & Universities for W Ill Univ, 920 F2d 441 (7th Cir 1990); Heiar v Crawford County, 746 F2d 1190 (7th Cir 1984), *cert denied,* 472 US 1027 (1985); Grossman v Suffolk County Dist Attorney's Office, 777 F Supp 1101, 1104 (EDNY 1991); Swanson v Department of Health, State of Colo, 773 F Supp 255, 257 (D Colo 1991); Schloesser v Kansas Dept of Health & Environment, 766 F Supp 984, 990 (D Kan 1991), *revd without opinion,* 991 F2d 806 (10th Cir), *cert denied,* 114 S Ct 307 (1993); Equal Employment Opportunity Commn v KDM Sch Bus Co, 612 F Supp 369, 372 (SDNY 1985); Barrett v Suffolk Transp Servs, Inc, 600 F Supp 81 (EDNY 1984); *see also* Bell v Trustees of Purdue Univ, 975 F2d 422, 425 n5 (7th Cir 1992).

[492] 821 F Supp 1410 (D Kan 1993).

[493] 465 US 89 (1984) (*Pennhurst II*).

[494] 821 F Supp at 1413.

Johnson v Mayor of Baltimore[495] addressed—but ultimately avoided deciding—the §5 issue expressed doubt as to whether the extension of the ADEA to state and local governments could be upheld under §5.[496]

Immunities

The Court of Appeals for the Fourth Circuit on two occasions has applied the doctrine of legislative immunity in assessing whether an ADEA claim could proceed.[497] The underlying rationale of the doctrine, as it has developed in that circuit, has been articulated as being " 'to prevent legislators from having to testify regarding matters of legislative conduct, whether or not they are testifying to defend themselves.' "[498] This rationale has been employed to block several claims.

In *Baker v Mayor of Baltimore,*[499] for example, the court reasoned in a suit that involving the elimination of certain positions, thereby causing the loss of the two plaintiffs' jobs, that the plaintiffs, "[t]o prevail on their ADEA claims, . . . would have to show that age was a determining factor in their termination."[500] And were the plaintiffs able to establish a prima facie case by showing that age was such a factor, the court was "unable to conceive [of] a viable defense which would not include testimony from the Board's members [i.e., the members of the City Board of

---

495 731 F2d 209 (4th Cir 1984), *revd,* 472 US 353 (1985).

496 Without identifying either Congress's commerce power or its power under §5 of the Fourteenth Amendment as the grounding for its decision, the Court of Appeals for the Second Circuit held in Equal Employment Opportunity Commn v Vermont, 904 F2d 794 (2d Cir 1990), that the Tenth Amendment did not bar reading the ADEA as protecting appointed state court judges from age-based mandatory retirement. Subsequently, however, the Supreme Court ruled in Gregory v Ashcroft, 111 S Ct 2395 (1991), that appointed judges were not protected under the ADEA because the term *employee* is defined in §11(b), 29 USC §630(b), to exclude policymakers who are appointees of elected officials. See **§3.08.**

497 Baker v Mayor of Baltimore, 894 F2d 679 (4th Cir), *cert denied,* 498 US 815 (1990); Schlitz v Virginia, 854 F2d 43 (4th Cir 1988).

498 Schlitz v Commonwealth of Va, 854 F2d 43, 46 (4th Cir 1988).

499 894 F2d 679 (4th Cir), *cert denied,* 498 US 815 (1990).

500 *Id* 682.

Estimate, which acts in a legislative capacity] to the effect that they were not motivated by the plaintiffs' ages."[501] Accordingly, the court affirmed the trial court's dismissal of the suit and its granting of summary judgment in favor of the defendants.[502]

The legislative immunity doctrine, as applied in the Fourth Circuit both in discriminatory intent[503] and discriminatory impact[504] situations, has the potential to virtually eliminate the possibility of suits against state and local governmental bodies. This is an untoward consequence at odds with the language of the ADEA and Congress' intent to eliminate age discrimination in the public sector.

The issue of the immunity of state employees also has been addressed by the courts.[505] *Harlow v Fitzgerald*[506] set the legal framework for the qualified immunity of such individuals. The Supreme Court established that "government officials performing discretionary functions generally are shielded from liability for civil damages insofar as their conduct does not violate clearly established statutory or constitutional rights of which a reasonable person would have known."[507] In *Lewis v City of Fort Collins,*[508] which involved claims arising under the ADEA as well as other

---

[501] *Id.*

[502] *See also* Schlitz v Commonwealth of Va, 854 F2d 43 (4th Cir 1988); Nuchims v West Va, 724 F Supp 1219 (SD W Va 1989), *revd without opinion,* 914 F2d 248 (4th Cir 1990); Drayton v Mayor of Rockville, 699 F Supp 1155 (D Md 1988), *affd without opinion,* 855 F2d 864 (4th Cir 1989); *cf* Meek v Rideoutte, 56 FEP Cas (BNA) 879 (DSC 1990) (in challenge to state statute requiring retirement of state police officers, legislators could not be deposed as to their motives for voting for or against the statute).

[503] *See* Baker v Mayor of Baltimore, 894 F2d 679 (4th Cir), *cert denied,* 498 US 815 (1990).

[504] *See* Nuchims v West Va, 724 F Supp 1219 (SD W Va 1989), *revd without opinion,* 914 F2d 248 (4th Cir 1990).

[505] In those jurisdictions which have held that the ADEA should be interpreted as preventing individual governmental employees from being held liable, see **§3.27,** the question of whether judicially created immunity can protect an individual from liability is of course beside the point.

[506] 457 US 800 (1982).

[507] *Id* 818.

[508] 903 F2d 752 (10th Cir 1990).

statutory and constitutional provisions, the defendant city officials invoked the qualified immunity defense. Applying *Harlow,* the *Lewis* court concluded that the defendant's demotion of the plaintiff was objectively reasonable. Accordingly, the court held that the defendant's motion for summary judgment could be denied only if the plaintiff produced evidence that the defendant's actions were discriminatorily motivated. This the plaintiff failed to do.

In *Van Arsdel v Indiana Utility Regulatory Commission*[509] the individual defendants, who were employees of the Commission, also invoked the qualified immunity defense both as to the plaintiff's ADEA claim and her constitutionally based equal protection argument. As interpreted by the *Van Arsdel* court, *Harlow* requires a court "to conduct a two-part analysis: (1) does the alleged conduct set out a constitutional violation? and (2) were the constitutional standards clearly established at the time in question."[510] The court concluded (even though it couched this two-part test only in constitutional terms) that the defendants could not successfully establish their claim to immunity because, during the years in question (1984 to 1986) "it was well known that an employer could face liability for age discrimination under the ADEA."[511]

Other Case Law

A disingenuous argument that the defendant agencies were not employers was rejected in *Coffin v South Carolina Department of Social Services.*[512] The court also rejected the argument that supervisory agency employees who were sued in their official capacities were not employers for the purposes of the ADEA.[513] The court did the same with regard to the argument that such

---

509 54 Empl Prac Dec (CCH) ¶40,081 (SD Ind 1989).

510 *Id* ¶63,309.

511 *Id.*

512 562 F Supp 579 (DSC 1983).

513 See generally **§3.27.**

employees, when sued in their individual capacities, were not employers within the meaning of the Act.[514]

§3.21 The Federal Government

The definition of *employer* contained in the Age Discrimination in Employment Act (ADEA)[515] specifically excludes the federal government.[516] But a separate section of the ADEA, §15,[517] protects applicants for federal employment and federal employees in the competitive services of the executive and judicial branches who are at least 40 years old.[518] Prior to 1978 federal employees were required to retire at age 70. Mandatory retirement of federal employees was eliminated by a 1978 amendment,[519] except for certain employees whose retirement is authorized or required by statute.[520]

---

[514] *Accord* House v Cannon Mills Co, 713 F Supp 159, 159-62 (MDNC 1988); Goodman v Board of Trustees, 498 F Supp 1329, 1335-36 (ND Ill 1980).

[515] 29 USC §§621-634.

[516] *Id* §630(b). In Ralis v Radio Free Europe/Radio Liberty, Inc, 34 FEP Cas (BNA) 400 (DDC 1984), *affd,* 770 F2d 1121 (DC Cir 1985), it was held that Radio Free Europe/Radio Liberty is not a government-controlled corporation; therefore, its employees are not government employees.

[517] §15, 29 USC §633a. See generally **ch 9.**

[518] As to other general nondiscrimination provisions regarding federal employees, see 5 USC §§2301, 2302; as to protection of Foreign Service officers, see 22 USC §3905(b), (e); as to protection of employees of the General Accounting Office, see 31 USC §52-2(g). The Equal Employment Opportunity Commission has taken the position the Federal Reserve Banks are private sector employers, rather than federal sector executive agencies covered by §15 of the ADEA. EEOC Enforcement Guide No N-915.002: Coverage of Federal Reserve Banks (Oct 20, 1993). This issuance is reproduced in the appendix at the end of the final volume. Such issuances are not legally binding, but they generally elicit considerable judicial deference. See **ch 2.**

[519] Age Discrimination in Employment Act Amendments of 1978, Pub L No 90-256, §5(a), 92 Stat 189, 191.

[520] Air traffic controllers are required to retire at age 56, law enforcement officers and firefighters at age 55, and employees of the Alaska Railroad and the Panama Canal Company at age 62. 5 USC §8335(a)-(c). These provisions were not disturbed by the 1978 amendment. *See* Bowman v United States Dept of Justice, 510 F Supp 1183 (ED Va 1981), *affd without opinion,* 679 F2d 876 (4th Cir), *cert denied,* 459 US 1072 (1982). It has been held that the ADEA did

The ADEA does not cover job applicants and employees not in the competitive services, i.e., presidential appointees. However, §320[521] of the Government Employee Rights Act of 1991 (GERA)[522] exposes the federal government to liability vis-a-vis these individuals insofar as they are victims of discrimination within the meaning of §15. A separate enforcement scheme is established by the 1991 Act.[523]

Heads of federal law enforcement agencies are authorized by a specific statute to fix minimum and maximum age limits for those serving as law enforcement officers.[524] In *Stewart v Smith*[525] the plaintiff challenged the Federal Bureau of Prisons' policy of refusing to consider applicants over 34 years of age for jobs within federal prisons. The plaintiff argued that the Bureau's authority to set a maximum age qualification was limited by the ADEA. The court rejected this contention, concluding that Congress intended to provide federal law enforcement agencies with the flexibility to use maximum entry age rules to secure a young and vigorous law enforcement work force.[526] The court thus read the statute involved, 5 USC §3307(d), as creating an exception to the ADEA for the appointment of federal law enforcement personnel.[527]

Another federal statute claimed to be in conflict with the ADEA was at issue in *Muller v Lujan.*[528] The Federal Employees Salary Act, 5 USC §5595, provides that severance pay is not

---

not repeal 5 USC §3323(b), pursuant to which civil service annuitants who earlier retired may be rehired, but only on an at-will basis. Davis v Devine, 736 F2d 1108 (6th Cir), *cert denied,* 469 US 1020 (1984).

521 2 USC §1219.

522 This Act was enacted as Title III of the Civil Rights Act of 1991, Pub L No 102-166, 105 Stat 1071, 1088-99.

523 See **ch 11.**

524 5 USC §3307(d).

525 673 F2d 485 (DC Cir 1982).

526 *Id* 492.

527 *Accord* Benford v Frank, 943 F2d 609 (6th Cir 1991); Patterson v United States Postal Serv, 901 F2d 927 (11th Cir 1990); Francke v United States Dept of the Treasury, 721 F Supp 47 (SDNY 1989).

528 928 F2d 207 (6th Cir 1991).

available for involuntarily terminated federal employees who are eligible to receive pensions. The court held that this statute was not repealed by implication by the ADEA.

It is also to be noted that individual federal employees who are sued may be able to invoke a qualified immunity defense. In *Harlow v Fitzgerald*[529] the Court established that "government officials performing discretionary functions generally are shielded from liability for civil damages insofar as their conduct does not violate clearly established statutory or constitutional rights of which a reasonable person should have known."[530]

Job applicants for positions in, and employees and former employees of, the United States Senate are protected by virtue of §302[531] of GERA. So, too, are employees of the Architect of the Capitol who are assigned to the Senate restaurants or to the Superintendent of the Senate Office Buildings.[532] As is the case regarding presidential appointees covered by GERA, a separate enforcement scheme is established by the 1991 Act for these individuals.[533]

§3.22 Religious Institutions

The Age Discrimination in Employment Act (ADEA)[534] is silent as to whether or not it covers religious institutions that act as employers. In contrast, Title VII of the Civil Rights Act of 1964[535] contains a specific limited exemption for religious

---

529 457 US 800 (1982).

530 *Id* 818. *Harlow* was applied in an ADEA case involving state employees, Van Arsdel v Indiana Utility Regulatory Commn, 54 Empl Prac Dec (CCH) ¶40,081 (SD Ind 1990), and in another case involving city employees. Lewis v City of Fort Collins, 903 F2d 752 (10th Cir 1990). See **§3.20.**

531 2 USC §1202.

532 *Id* §1201(c)(B).

533 See **ch 11.**

534 29 USC §§621-634.

535 42 USC §§2000e through 2000e-17.

institutions.[536] Even though the ADEA, unlike Title VII, does not exclude from its reach religious institutions, its failure to exempt religious institutions does not, in and of itself, preclude reading the ADEA as being inapplicable to them. As it turns out, the courts are split. Still, despite the constitutional problems that arguably may arise as a result of application of the ADEA to such institutions, the majority of appellate courts that have addressed discrimination claims have held the statute to be applicable to these entities.

A Supreme Court decision interpreting the coverage of the National Labor Relations Act (NLRA)[537] is generally read by the courts as setting the analytical backdrop. In *NLRB v Catholic Bishop*[538] the Court held that the NLRA does not extend to church-operated schools. This conclusion flowed from the Court's concern that the assertion of jurisdiction by the National Labor Relation Board (NLRB) could entangle the Board with the schools' religious practices, and could intrude into the religious aspects of the school-teacher relationship. To avoid the First Amendment issues that would ensue, the Court held that the NLRA would apply to church-operated schools only if the "affirmative intention of Congress [was] clearly expressed."[539]

ADEA Rulings Establishing the Act's Applicability

Several appellate courts have concluded that the ADEA may be applied to religious institutions, at least under some circumstances. In *Ritter v Mount St Mary's College*[540] the district court examined the legislative history of the ADEA and found it to be silent regarding religious institutions. Relying on *Catholic Bishop,* the court held that the ADEA was inapplicable to the

---

536 *Id* §2000(e)-1.

537 29 USC §§141-144, 151-167.

538 440 US 490 (1979).

539 *Id* 501. No such intention was found to exist here because congressional attention, the Court concluded, had been focused on private industry; no consideration had been accorded church-operated schools. *Id* 504.

540 495 F Supp 724 (D Md 1980), *affd in part & revd in part without opinion,* 738 F2d 431 (4th Cir 1984).

defendant, a church-affiliated college. Subsequently, the Court of Appeals for the Fourth Circuit reversed the ruling with an unpublished opinion. In a later decision rendered in the course of the same litigation the appellate court explained that the earlier reversal was due to its determination that an ADEA suit did "not present a significant risk of infringement upon the First Amendment rights of" a church-sponsored college.[541]

The Court of Appeals for the Second Circuit also has held that the ADEA is properly applicable to religious institutions. In deciding *DeMarco v Holy Cross High School*[542] the court addressed the claim of a lay teacher who taught in a Catholic parochial school and whose duties included leading his students in prayer and taking them to Mass. The court rejected concerns regarding the possibility that application of the Act would result in excessive government entanglement with the institution, in violation of the First Amendement's Establishment Clause.[543] Responding to the conjecture that courts would be called upon to inquire as to the value or truthfulness of church doctrine in the guise of examining the persuasiveness of a religious institution's explanation for the complained-of action or decision, the court reasoned as follows:

> The pretext inquiry . . . [as to whether the defendant's explanation is pretextual, i.e., a disguise for discrimination] normally focuses upon factual questions such as whether the asserted reason for the challenged action comports with the defendant's policies and rules, whether the rule applied to the plaintiff has been applied uniformly, and whether the putative non-discriminatory reason was stated only after the allegation of discrimination. . . . Thus, in those cases where a defendant proffers a religious purpose for its allegedly discriminatory employment action, a plaintiff will usu-

541 Ritter v Mount St Mary's College, 814 F2d 986, 988 n1 (4th Cir), *cert denied,* 484 US 913 (1987).

542 4 F3d 166 (2d Cir 1993).

543 US Const amend I.

> ally be able to challenge as pretextual the employer's justification without calling into question the value or truthfulness of religious doctrine.[544]

Still, the court recognized that a plaintiff might argue that the defendant religious institution's explanation was implausible, absurd, or unwise, and he or she thereby could bring to the fore constitutional problems. The court's response was "to conclude that ADEA plaintiffs may not challenge the plausibility of putative religious purposes.[545] Accordingly, "[a] fact-finder will necessarily have to presume that an asserted religious motive is plausible in the sense that it is reasonably or validly held.[546]

The *DeMarco* court further confined its ruling by pointing out that it was only addressing the claims of a secular teacher, rather than a dispute involving "the pervasive religious relationship between a member of the clergy and his religious employer."[547] Even as to lay employees, however, the court was willing to concede that there could be instances in which the employment relationship "is so pervasively religious that it is impossible to engage in an age-discrimination inquiry without serious risk of offending the Establishment Clause."[548] DeMarco, himself, did not present such a situation.

Finally, the court articulated the view that Congress had implicitly expressed an intention that the ADEA apply to religious institutions:

> Given that Congress intended to apply Title VII to religious institutions [insofar as discrimination based on race, color, national origin, and sex are concerned,] and that Congress modelled the ADEA's coverage upon that of Title VII, we

---

544 4 F3d at 171.

545 *Id.*

546 *Id.*

547 *Id.*

548 *Id* 172.

> are convinced that they also intended to apply the ADEA to such institutions.[549]

The Court of Appeals for the Third Circuit, in deciding *Geary v Visitation of the Blessed Virgin Mary Parish School,*[550] also held that the lay faculty of religious schools could invoke the ADEA. Like the *DeMarco* court,[551] the *Geary* court reasoned that an ADEA suit only involves limited inquiry, as opposed to ongoing supervision, regarding the activities of a religious entity, and so there is not a significant risk of government entanglement with the institution's religious functions. Moreover, the court reasoned that inasmuch as the Catholic religion does not mandate age discrimination, there was no direct conflict between religious tenets and application of the statute to the defendant school.

The *Geary* court did recognize that First Amendment problems could arise, since the plaintiff had sought in the trial court to prove that the defendant's religion-based explanation for the firing—i.e., that the plaintiff had entered into a canonically condemned marriage with a divorced man—was pretextual. But the court still did not see an insurmountable barrier to the plaintiff's reliance on the ADEA:

> So long as Geary does not challenge the validity of the religious doctrine (and she does not), this . . . argument does not raise entanglement concerns. . . . At most, Geary asks the court to determine whether the religious reason stated by Visitation School actually motivated the dismissal.[552]

Even if one might argue that a determination of pretext implied an attentuated rejection of a religious organization's good faith regarding its proffered rationale, this determination still would not, in the court's view, generate the kind of entanglement concerns that preoccupied the *Catholic Bishop* court:

---

549 *Id* 173.

550 7 F3d 324 (3d Cir 1993).

551 4 F3d at 169-70.

552 7 F3d at 329.

> *Catholic Bishop* concerned a legislative scheme in which a government body could, sua sponte, challenge *any* religious doctrine or practice and then directly inquire into the good faith of the religious reason for it. In an ADEA case, the inquiry is far more limited and any determination of pretext would implicate good faith only indirectly in the context of litigation.[553]

Despite its viewing the application of the ADEA with sanguinity, the *Geary* court did insist on a limitation. Parelling (but expanding) on the restriction on litigants imposed in *DeMarco,* the court asserted that "the First Amendment dictates that . . . [an ADEA] plaintiff may not challenge the validity, existence, or 'plausibility' of a proffered religious doctrine . . . "[554] Insofar as the matter of Congress' expression of an affirmative intention to have the ADEA apply was concerned, the court reasoned that since application of the statute did not in the first instance present a significant risk of entanglement, there was no need for such intention to have been expressed. But, in any event, it reasoned that such intention could be inferred, inasmuch as the ADEA is modelled on Title VII, and Title VII does not exempt religious institutions from its reach.

As for the merits, the *Geary* court concluded that the plaintiff had failed to submit any affidavits in response to the defendant's motion for summary judgment on her discrimination claim, and so the defendant's motion was granted. Contrarily, the court denied the defendant's motion with regard to the plaintiff's retaliation claim.

A few district courts are in agreement that application of the ADEA to religious institutions is constitutionally permissible.[555]

---

553 *Id* 330.

554 *Id.*

555 *See, e.g.*, Soriano v Xavier Univ Corp, 687 F Supp 1188 (SD Ohio 1988). In Russell v Belmont College, 554 F Supp 667 (MD Tenn 1982), the court held that the Equal Pay Act, 29 USC §206(d), applies to religious institutions. While that Act is obviously a different statute than the ADEA, and it therefore has a different history, the two are similar in that they both utilize the enforcement provisions of the Fair Labor Standards Act, 29 USC §§200-219.

In *Lukaszewski v Nazareth Hospital,*[556] the court held that the application of the ADEA to a religiously affiliated hospital did not violate either the Free Exercise or Establishment Clauses of the First Amendment. The court reasoned that the "case-by-case inquiry [by the Equal Employment Opportunity Commission (EEOC)] into employee complaints of age discrimination is not administrative entanglement barred by the Establishment Clause."[557] In addition, the court viewed an Establishment Clause violation as unlikely on the facts because the defendant was a hospital employing more than 1,400 people: "[r]eligious doctrine is a much less important factor in most hospital personnel decisions than it is in religious school decisions to hire and fire teachers."[558] The court distinguished *Minker v Baltimore Annual Conference of United Methodist Church,*[559] discussed *infra,* as involving a clergyman. Here, in contrast, the plaintiff "was a secular employee; his responsibilities did not include church administration or religious matters."[560] The legislative history of the ADEA further suggested, in the *Lukaszewski* court's view, a congressional intent to have the ADEA extend to religious institutions. This conclusion satisfied the requirement of *Catholic Bishop.*

As for the Free Exercise Clause claim, the *Lukaszewski* court deemed it to be precluded by *Employment Division, Department of Human Resources v Smith,*[561] in which the Supreme Court held that neutral statutes of general applicability are not unconstitutional so long as they are not specifically directed at religious practices.

Usery v Manchester East Catholic Regional Sch Bd, 430 F Supp 188 (DNH 1977), involved a suit against a religious school. While the court denied the defendant's motion to dismiss, no mention was made of the fact that the defendant was a religious institution. Rather, the school urged that it was not covered by the ADEA because it was a school and it was therefore not engaged in an industry affecting commerce; the court rejected that argument.

556 764 F Supp 57 (ED Pa 1991).

557 *Id* 60.

558 *Id.*

559 894 F2d 354 (DC Cir), *cert denied,* 484 US 913 (1990).

560 764 F Supp at 60.

561 494 US 872 (1990).

Here, the ADEA was deemed to be a such a statute since "it . . . [did] not target or discriminate against religious organizations in any way."[562]

ADEA Cases Establishing the Act's Inapplicability

The Court of Appeals for the District of Columbia Circuit held in *Minker,* which was referred to earlier in the course of discussion of the *Lukaszewski* decision, that the First Amendment's Free Exercise Clause would be violated if the claimant, a pastor complaining of a discriminatory denial of a promotion, were allowed to maintain his ADEA suit. The court refrained from addressing the claimant's Establishment Clause argument. In *Scharon v St Luke's Episcopal Presbyterian Hospital*[563] the Court of Appeals for the Eighth Circuit, also looked to the Free Exercise Clause, and held that it "prohibits the courts from deciding cases" involving personnel decisions by church-affiliated institutions that affect clergy.[564] Unlike the *Minker* court, the *Scharon* court also relied on the Establishment Clause, holding that a review of the decision of the defendant to discharge the plaintiff, an ordained minister, would entail excessive government entanglement.[565] The court narrowed its holdings by explicitly "leaving for another day the question of whether the ADEA definitively applies to such employees in . . . contexts" other than "an employment decision by a church-affiliated hospital concerning a chaplain-employee."[566]

In deciding *Cochran v St Louis Preparatory Seminary*[567] the court ruled that the ADEA was inapplicable to the defendant, although it did not explicitly hold that either the Establishment Clause or the Free Exercise Clause would be violated.

---

[562] 764 F Supp at 61.

[563] 929 F2d 360 (8th Cir 1991).

[564] *Id* 363.

[565] *Id* 362.

[566] *Id* 362 n2.

[567] 717 F Supp 1413 (ED Mo 1989).

The EEOC's Position

In an opinion letter issued in 1984, the Equal Employment Opportunity Commission (EEOC) expressed its view that priests who are serving in their dioceses are not employees for purposes of the ADEA.[568] The EEOC asserted a like view regarding nuns serving in their parish schools pursuant to their religious obligations, in another opinion letter issued that same year.[569]

§3.23 Labor Organizations

The activities of labor organizations are governed by the Age Discrimination in Employment Act (ADEA).[570] The term *labor organization* is broadly defined as any organization, agency, employee representation committee, group, association, or plan that is engaged in an industry affecting commerce and that exists for the purpose of dealing with employers concerning grievances, labor disputes, wages, hours, or terms and conditions of employment.[571] The definition includes bodies such as conferences, general committees, system boards, and joint councils that are subordinate to national or international labor organizations.[572] Thus, labor organizations must meet two general requirements: they must have the purpose of dealing with employers, and they must be engaged in industries affecting commerce.

Dealing with employers is a term that is clearly broader than collective bargaining. However, there must be some interaction between the organization and an employer. Thus, union pension or other benefit funds are not labor organizations because they

---

568 EEOC OL-5 (Nov 9, 1984). (This letter is reproduced at the end of the last volume as a part of **app L.**)

569 EEOC OL-4 (Nov 9, 1984). (This letter is reproduced at the end of the last volume as a part of **app. L.**)

570 29 USC §§621-634.

571 *Id* §630(d).

572 *Id.*

do not deal with employers.[573] Moreover, the purported labor organization must deal with an *employer,* which is defined in the ADEA to mean an entity having "twenty or more employees for each working day in each of twenty or more calendar weeks in the current or preceding calendar year."[574] Thus, if no employer with whom the labor organization deals meets this standard, the labor organization is not covered by the ADEA.[575]

The ADEA specifies several ways in which a labor organization can be deemed to be engaged in an industry affecting commerce. These include operating a hiring hall, having at least 25 members and being a certified representative under the National Labor Relations Act[576] or the Railway Labor Act,[577] serving as a representative of employees of a covered employer, having chartered or having been chartered by such a representative, or being a subordinate body of a covered national or international union.[578] A local union that does not have the required minimum number of members may still be covered if there is a substantial connection between it and a sister local so as to render them indistinguishable, and if the two combined have the requisite minimum number of members.[579]

Under certain circumstances a successor union can be held liable for the acts of its predecessor.[580]

---

573 *See, e.g.,* De Loraine v MEBA Pension Trust, 355 F Supp 89, 91-92 (SDNY 1973), *affd on other grounds,* 499 F2d 49 (2d Cir), *cert denied,* 419 US 1009 (1974).

574 29 USC §630(b). See generally **§§3.18-.19.**

575 *Cf* Renfro v Office & Professional Employers Intl, Local 277, 545 F2d 509 (5th Cir 1977) case arising under Title VII of the Civil Rights Act of 1964, 42 USC §§2000e through 2000e-17.

576 29 USC §§141-144, 151-167.

577 45 USC §§151-188.

578 29 USC §630(e).

579 *Cf* International Alliance of Theatrical State Employees Local 293 v International Alliance of Theatrical State Employees Local 293A, 526 F2d 316 (5th Cir 1976) (case arising under Title VII of the Civil Rights Act of 1964, 42 USC §§2000e through 2000e-17).

580 Boieru v Cuyahoga County Library Union, 46 Empl Prac Dec (CCH) ¶38,059 (ND Ohio 1988).

§3.24 Employment Agencies

An employment agency is, for the purposes of the Age Discrimination in Employment Act (ADEA),[581] an entity that regularly undertakes, with or without compensation, to procure employees for a covered employer.[582] Thus, an entity that procures independent contractors for other entities will not qualify as an employment agency, since it is not securing employees for those entities.[583]

There is one decision expressing the view that if an employment agency performs services for at least one entity that satisfies the definition of *employer* under the ADEA, i.e., an entity having 20 or more employees for each working day in each of 20 or more calendar weeks of the current or preceding calendar year,[584] then all of the agency's activities will fall within the ambit of the ADEA.[585] Thereby, those services performed for entities that do not meet the statutory definition of employer come within the ADEA's reach. The Equal Employment Opportunity Commission (EEOC) has interpreted the provision in the same way.[586]

The EEOC also interprets the ADEA as being applicable to the actions of a covered employment agency vis-a-vis its own employees, whether or not the agency itself has 20 or more employees.[587] This interpretation is based on the Act's language, which makes it unlawful for an employment agency to "otherwise discriminate against any individual."[588] However, in

---

581 29 USC §§621-634.

582 *Id* §630(c). The agent of an employment agency is included within the term *employment agency. Id.*

583 Ehret v Louisiana, 58 FEP Cas (BNA) 658 (ED La 1992).

584 §11(b), 29 USC §630(b). See **§§ 3.18-.19.**

585 Brennan v Aldert Root, 16 FEP Cas (BNA) 1643 (EDNC 1974).

586 29 CFR §1625.3(a) (1993).

587 *Id* §1625.3(b).

588 *Id,* citing 29 USC §623(b).

Brennan v Paragon Employment Agency, Inc,[589] the court, in rejecting this analysis, ruled that an employment agency seeking employees for itself acts as an employer and accordingly only will be bound to abide by the requirements of the ADEA if it meets the *20-employees-for-20-weeks* standard.

There can be uncertainty as to whether a given entity is in fact an employment agency if its chief function is not the procurement of employees for employers, but it does engage in some employment referral activities. The plaintiff in *Cannon v University of Chicago*[590] challenged the university's refusal to admit her to its medical school, claiming that the university was an employment agency because of the placement functions which it performed on behalf of its students. The court was willing to assume that the school's placement office might be an employment agency,[591] but held that in any event the university's refusal to admit the plaintiff could not violate the ADEA because it did not amount to a discriminatory refusal to refer for employment.[592]

Some courts addressing claims arising under Title VII of the Civil Rights Act of 1964,[593] the ADEA's analogue, have endorsed the proposition that newspapers that carry "help wanted" advertisements thereby serve only as conduits of employment information and thus are not employment agencies.[594] In contrast,

---

589 356 F Supp 286 (SDNY 1973), *affd without opinion,* 489 F2d 752 (2d Cir 1974).

590 559 F2d 1063 (7th Cir 1976), *revd on other grounds,* 441 US 677 (1979).

591 *See* Kaplowitz v University of Chicago, 387 F Supp 42 (ND Ill 1974), where the court, after finding no violation of Title VII of the Civil Rights Act of 1964, 42 USC §§2000e through 2000e-17, in dicta reasoned that the University of Chicago Law School's placement office was an employment agency because: (a) it was the primary source through which employers hired University of Chicago law students and recent graduates; (b) the vast majority of students found their jobs through the placement office; and (c) the assistant dean spent 25% of his time on placement activities.

592 559 F2d at 1076.

593 42 USC §§2000e through 2000e-17.

594 *See, e.g.,* Greenfield v Field Enters, Inc, 4 FEP Cas (BNA) 548 (ND Ill 1972); Brush v San Francisco Newspaper Printing Co, 315 F Supp 577 (ND Cal 1970), *affd,* 469 F2d 89 (9th Cir 1972), *cert denied,* 410 US 943 (1973).

however, there is support for the view that if a newspaper reserves editorial authority to classify copy, it can be seen as having thereby become actively involved in the referral process and it will therefore be covered by Title VII (and, analogically, by the ADEA).[595]

§3.25 Foreign Employers

The Age Discrimination in Employment Act (ADEA)[596] is made applicable to United States citizens who work abroad for United States companies or their subsidiaries by §§4(h)[597] and 11(f)[598] of the Act. Insofar as United States citizens employed abroad by foreign employers are concerned, the ADEA is inapplicable.[599] The issue of the applicability of the Act is a more complicated one in the case of employees—of whom there are many[600]—who work in the United States for foreign-owned companies.

Generally, a foreign employer in the United States is required to abide by United States law. However, in some circumstances there may be some basis for concluding that United States law does not apply. "[T]he existence of a treaty may demand that a court not enforce the ADEA[.]"[601] In *MacNamara v Korean Air Lines*[602] the district court held that a bilateral friendship, commerce, and navigation (FCN) treaty with Korea prevailed over the ADEA. The employer—Korean Air Lines—was thus allowed

---

595 Morrow v Mississippi Publishers Corp, 5 FEP Cas (BNA) 287 (SD Miss 1972) (Title VII case). As to the propriety of looking to Title VII decisions for analogical guidance, see **ch 2.**

596 29 USC §§621-634.

597 *Id* §623(h). *See* **§3.26.**

598 *Id* §630(f). *See* **§3.26.**

599 See **§3.26.**

600 "[O]ver 1,700 foreign-owned companies employ more than 2.5 million Americans." Street, *Application of U.S. Fair Employment Laws in the United States and Abroad,* 19 NYU J Intl L & Pol 357, 358 (1987) [hereinafter Street].

601 Street, *supra* note 600, at 374.

602 45 FEP Cas (BNA) 384 (ED Pa 1987), *revd & remanded,* 863 F2d 1135 (3d Cir 1988), *cert denied,* 493 US 944 (1989).

to discriminate in ways which, but for the treaty, could be violative of the age statute, as well as of Title VII of the Civil Rights Act of 1964.[603] On appeal, however, the court of appeals held that the specific language of the treaty at issue did not afford the employer immunity from complying with the ADEA.[604] The court further concluded that there was no inherent conflict between the ADEA and the management rights accorded by the treaty to Korean companies.

Another appellate court relied, in a Title VII case, on *Sumitomo Shoji American, Inc v Avagliano*[605] in reaching the contrasting conclusion that the employer did have "a narrow privilege to discriminate" regarding positions covered by the FCN treaty there at issue.[606] In *Starett v Iberia Airlines*[607] the court ruled that "a corporation owned by a foreign government operating under an 'of their choice' clause [in an FCN treaty] . . . [was permitted to discriminate, but only to the extent of] favor[ing] nationals of that particular country."[608]

Multilateral treaties to which the United States is a party also may immunize some entities from ADEA coverage.[609]

The Equal Employment Opportunity Commission (EEOC) has issued a policy guide which replicates the foregoing discussion.[610]

---

603 42 USC §§2000e through 2000e-17.

604 MacNamara v Korean Air Lines, 863 F2d 1135 (3d Cir 1988), *cert denied,* 494 US 944 (1989). *But see* Spiess v C Stoh & Co (America), 643 F2d 353 (5th Cir 1981), *vacated on other grounds,* 457 US 1128 (1982) (Title VII case).

605 457 US 176 (1982). In *Sumitomo Shoji American* the Supreme Court was presented with the question of whether a bilateral FCN treaty with Japan exempted a United States company that was a subsidiary of a Japanese company from having to comply with Title VII. Ultimately, the Court did not provide an answer.

606 Wickes v Olympic Airways, 745 F2d 363 (6th Cir 1984).

607 756 F Supp 292 (SD Tex 1989).

608 *Id* 295.

609 *See generally* Street, *supra* note 600.

610 EEOC Policy Guide No N-915.039: Application of the Age Discrimination in Employment Act of 1967 (ADEA) and the Equal Pay Act of 1963 (EPA) to American Firms Overseas, Their Overseas Subsidiaries, and Foreign Firms

Instrumentalities of Foreign Governments

In *Gazder v Air India*[611] it was held that instrumentalities of foreign governments that engage in commercial activities within the United States are employers for the purposes of the ADEA.[612] However, when an agency or instrumentality of a foreign state is sued, a jury trial is not allowed.[613]

Native American Tribes

In *Equal Employment Opportunity Commission v The Cherokee Nation*[614] the Court of Appeals for the Tenth Circuit held that when a treaty between the United States and a Native American tribe clearly and unequivocally recognizes the right to tribal self-government, the ADEA is not applicable because its enforcement would interfere with this treaty-protected right. The Court of Appeals for the Eighth Circuit is in accord.[615] *Cherokee Nation* was distinguished in *Myrick v Devils Lake Sioux Manufacturing Corp,*[616] which involved an ADEA suit by a Native American employee of a corporation, 51 per cent of which was owned by an Indian tribe. The court, while reading *Cherokee Nation* as establishing that the ADEA is inapplicable to such entities, reasoned that it was not controlling in the case of "non-tribal reservation employees."[617]

(Mar 3, 1989). (This issuance is reproduced in the Appendix at the end of the final volume.)

611 574 F Supp 134 (SDNY 1983).

612 *Accord* Starrett v Iberia Airlines, 756 F Supp 292 (SD Tex 1989); Helm v South African Airways, 44 FEP Cas (BNA) 261 (SDNY 1987).

613 Kraikeman v Sabena Belgian World Airlines, 674 F Supp 136 (SDNY 1987); Carponcy v Air France, 38 FEP Cas (BNA) 1518 (SDNY 1985).

614 871 F2d 937 (10th Cir 1989).

615 Equal Employment Opportunity Commn v Fond du Lac Heavy Equip & Constr Co, Inc, 986 F2d 246 (8th Cir 1993).

616 718 F Supp 753 (DND 1989).

617 *Id* 754 n1.

§3.26 Employers in Other Countries

In a number of cases[618] in the 1980s employees who worked in foreign countries for American-owned companies, or job applicants who—if hired—would have worked abroad for these companies, sought to invoke the protections afforded by the Age Discrimination in Employment Act (ADEA).[619] Such efforts proved unsuccessful; the courts uniformly rejected the argument that the ADEA applied extraterritorially.[620]

In 1984 Congress amended the statute so as to give it extraterritorial reach,[621] thereby extending the ADEA's protection to United States citizens employed in foreign workplaces by United

---

[618] Lopez v Pan Am World Servs, Inc, 813 F2d 1118 (11th Cir 1987); Zahourek v Arthur Young & Co, 750 F2d 827 (10th Cir 1984); Thomas v Brown & Root, Inc, 745 F2d 279 (4th Cir 1984); Cleary v United States Lines, 728 F2d 607 (3d Cir 1984); Belanger v Keydril Co, 596 F Supp 823 (ED La 1984), *affd without opinion,* 772 F2d 902 (5th Cir 1985); Ralis v Radio Free Europe/Radio Liberty, Inc, 34 FEP Cas (BNA) 400 (DDC 1984), *affd,* 770 F2d 1121 (DC Cir 1985); *see also* Osborne v United Technologies Corp, 16 FEP Cas (BNA) 586 (D Conn 1977).

[619] 29 USC §§621-634.

[620] So, too, did the ADEA's original enforcement agency, the Department of Labor. 29 CFR §860.20 (1986) (effectively rescinded, 46 Fed Reg 47724 (Sept 24, 1981), and ordered removed from the Code of Federal Regulations, 52 Fed Reg 23812 (June 25, 1987)) provided that the prohibitions set forth in the Act "were considered to apply only to performance of the described discriminatory acts in places over which the United States has sovereignty, territorial jurisdiction, or legislative control."

[621] The effective date of the amendments was October 9, 1984. Older Americans Act Amendments of 1984, Pub L No 98-459, §803, 98 Stat 1767, 1793. They did not apply retroactively, however. DeYoreo v Bell Helicopter Textron, Inc, 785 F2d 1282 (5th Cir 1986); Ralis v Radio Free Europe/Radio Liberty, Inc, 770 F2d 1121 (DC Cir 1985); Pfeiffer v William Wrigley Jr Co, 775 F2d 554, 559 (7th Cir 1985); Helm v South African Airways, 44 FEP Cas (BNA) 261 (SDNY 1987). The prohibition against retroactive application was held to apply even where the ADEA claim was not initiated until after enactment of the amendments, so long as the cause of action arose prior to the enactment. Wolf v JI Case Co, 617 F Supp 858 (ED Wis 1985).

For a useful assessment of some of the problems associated with the extension of the ADEA extraterritorially, see Street, *Application of U.S. Fair Employment Laws to Transnational Employers in the United States and Abroad,* 19 NYU J Intl L & Pol 357 (1987).

States corporations and/or their subsidiaries.[622] The legislative history makes clear, however, that the intent of the Senate committee in which the legislation originated was that the statute not be applied if compliance with its prohibitions would place a company or its subsidiary in violation of the laws of the host country.[623] This caveat, taking the form of an affirmative defense, is set forth in §4(f).[624]

By virtue of the amending of §11(f),[625] *employee* is defined to include "an employee who is a citizen of the United States employed by an employer in a workplace in a foreign country." Thereby, as an initial matter, workers abroad are protected—so long as they are United States citizens. However, such individuals are not protected if they are employed by foreign companies, unless such companies are controlled by United States firms. The criteria for determining whether a foreign company is or is not controlled by an American firm are set forth in §4(h),[626] which provides in part as follows:

> (2) The prohibitions of this section shall not apply where the employer is a foreign person not controlled by an American employer.

---

[622] This change was made pursuant to §802 of the Older Americans Act Amendments of 1984, Pub L No 98-459, 98 Stat 1767, 1792, whereby §11(f), 29 USC §630, and §4(f)(1), 29 USC §623(f)(1), were amended, and a subsection (g) was added to §4, 29 USC §623. (Actually, §4 already included a subsection (g); the consequence of Congress's error in designation was to create two subsection (g)'s. This error was rectified in 1985. The Comprehensive Omnibus Budget Reconciliation Act of 1985, Pub L No 99-272, §9201(b)(3), 100 Stat 82, 171, redesignated the subsection as subsection (h).)

[623] Senate Comm on Labor and Human Resources, Older Americans Act Amendments of 1984, S Rep No 467, 98th Cong, 2d Sess 28 (1984).

[624] 29 USC §623(f). The affirmative defense created by §4(f)(1) allows an overseas employer to justify acts which would otherwise violate subsections (a), (b), (c), or (e) of §4, 29 USC §623, of the Act. This is the case only "where such practices involve an employee in a workplace in a foreign country, and compliance with such subsections would cause such employer, or a corporation controlled by such employer, to violate the laws of the country in which such workplace is located[.]" See **ch 5** as to affirmative defenses.

[625] 29 USC §630(f).

[626] 29 USC §623(h).

(3) For the purpose of this subsection the determination of whether an employer controls a corporation shall be based upon the—

(A) interrelation of operations,

(B) common management,

(C) centralized control of labor relations, and

(D) common ownership or financial control, of the employer and the corporation.

The Equal Employment Opportunity Commission has issued a policy guide that includes the foregoing criteria.[627]

(In *Kovalic v DEC International, Inc,*[628] a state court addressed a question concerning the appropriate time for filing a charge of discrimination against an employer based in Wisconsin, but employing—and allegedly discriminating against—an employee working abroad for the employer's British subsidiary).[629]

§3.27 Agents of the Employer

The definition of *employer* set forth in §11(b)[630] of the Age Discrimination in Employment Act (ADEA)[631] includes the employer's agents:

> The term "employer" means a person engaged in an industry affecting commerce who has twenty or more employees for each working day in each of twenty or more calendar

---

627 EEOC Policy Guide No N-915.039: Application of the Age Discrimination Act of 1967 (ADEA) and the Equal Pay Act of 1963 (EPA) to American Firms Overseas, Their Overseas Subsidiaries, and Foreign Firms (Mar 3, 1989). (This policy guide is reproduced in the Appendix at the end of the final volume.) Such policy issuances are not legally binding, but they can receive considerable deference from the courts nonetheless. See **ch 2.**

628 161 Wis 2d 863, 469 NW2d 224 (1991).

629 As to filing issues generally, see **ch 6.**

630 29 USC §630(b). The definition of *employment agency* also includes agents. *Id* §630(c).

631 *Id* §§621-634.

> weeks in the current or preceding calendar year. . . . The term also means (1) any agent of such a person[.]

The determination of whether an individual is an agent focuses, according to one court, on whether the individual's position constitutes "an integral part of the employer unit."[632] Another court asserted that "[a] person is an agent of an employer ' " if he participated in the decision making process that forms the basis of the discrimination." ' "[633] More generally, "the term 'agent' has been construed [albeit not by all courts, as noted below] as including supervisory or managerial employees to whom some employment decisions have been delegated."[634]

Individuals have been found to be agents if they have been given specific authority to recommend who shall be hired,[635] or if they have substantial ownership interests in the employing entity and actively carry out the employer's decisions.[636] Thus, general partners of a law firm have been deemed to be agents of the defendant partnership.[637] The term "agent" does not include, however, an association to which an employer belongs.[638] Nor will an employer/union trust fund, which must be administered by trustees consistent with traditional fiduciary obligations to the fund's beneficiaries, be deemed to be an agent

---

[632] Marshall v Arlene Knitwear, Inc, 454 F Supp 715, 721 (EDNY 1978), *affd in part & revd in part without opinion,* 608 F2d 1369 (2d Cir 1979).

[633] Wanamaker v Columbian Rope Co, 740 F Supp 127, 134 (NDNY 1990) (quoting Bostick v Rappleyea, 629 F Supp 1328, 1334 (NDNY 1985)) (quoting Jones v Metropolitan Denver Sewage Disposal Dist No 1, 537 F Supp 966, 970 (D Colo 1981)).

[634] House v Cannon Mills, 713 F Supp 159, 161 (MDNC 1988); *accord* Moore v Reese, 817 F Supp 1290, 1296 (CD Md 1993).

[635] *See, e.g.,* Goodman v Board of Trustees of Community College, 498 F Supp 1329 (ND Ill 1980); *see also* Barkley v Carraux, 533 F Supp 242 (SD Tex 1982) (department managers found to be agents of employer).

[636] *See, e.g.,* Marshall v Arlene Knitwear, Inc, 454 F Supp 715, 721 (EDNY 1978), *affd in part & revd in part without opinion,* 608 F2d 1369 (2d Cir 1979).

[637] Lettich v Kenway, 590 F Supp 1225 (D Mass 1984).

[638] York v Tennessee Crushed Stone Assn, 684 F2d 360 (6th Cir 1982).

of the persons or organizations responsible for appointing the trustees.[639]

There is support for the conclusion that a supervisory employee, who informed the employee of the employer's adverse employment decision, is not an agent.[640] However, there is contrary case law, as already noted, in which courts have held that a supervisor can be deemed to be an agent—at least where he or she has been delegated some responsibility regarding employment decisions.[641] At least one ruling supports the narrower proposition that a supervisor can be held accountable as an agent if he or she participated in the alleged discriminatory decision.[642] Indeed, according to this court, even if a supervisory employee did not actually supervise the plaintiff, he or she still can be held accountable as an agent if he or she participated in the alleged discriminatory decision.[643] Under these rulings allowing a supervisor to be considered an agent "a substantial ownership interest is not necessary to create an agency relationship[.]"[644]

Bankruptcy Trustees

In *Barnett v Meyers*[645] the plaintiff argued that the defendant, a trustee in bankruptcy who supervised the progress of Chapter 13 bankruptcy cases and who employed fewer than 20 people, was an agent of creditors in bankruptcy, which creditors had the

---

639 Yares v Great Cleveland Pipefitting Training Fund, 782 F Supp 68, 70 (ND Ohio 1990), *affd without opinion,* 929 F2d 702 (6th Cir 1991).

640 *See* Friend v Union Dime Sav Bank, 24 Empl Prac Dec (CCH) ¶31,209 (SDNY 1980); Patrowich v Chemical Bank, 63 NY2d 541, 473 NE2d 11, 483 NYS2d 659 (1984).

641 Elias v Sitomer, 60 FEP Cas (BNA) 758 (SDNY 1992); House v Cannon Mills Co, 713 F Supp 159 (MDNC 1988); *cf* Harvey v Blake, 913 F2d 226, 227 (5th Cir 1990) (case arising under Title VII of the Civil Rights Act of 1964, 42 USC §§2000e through 2000e-17, where court said that "immediate supervisors are Employers when delegated the employer's traditional rights, such as hiring and firing").

642 Koppman v South Cent Bell Tel Co, 59 FEP Cas (BNA) 345, 349 (ED La 1992).

643 *Id.*

644 Elias v Sitomer, 60 FEP Cas (BNA) 758, 761 (SDNY 1992).

645 59 FEP Cas (BNA) 1559 (D Or 1992).

requisite number of employees. The court rejected this argument:

> According to the Restatement, "[a]gency is the fiduciary relation which results from the manifestation of consent by one person to another that the other shall act on his behalf and subject to his control, and consent by the other so to act." Restatement (Second) of Agency §(1) (1958). However, "[a] person appointed by a court to manage the affairs of others is not an agent of the others." *Id.* at §14F. . . . [Here, the defendant] has been appointed by the bankruptcy court to supervise the progress of Chapter 13 cases filed in the bankruptcy court. He is not an agent of either the debtors or the creditors.[646]

State Government Employees as Agents

Several courts have held that the statutory inclusion of agents in the definition of *employer* does not apply to agents of state governments.[647] In *Hurd v Pittsburg State University,*[648] as in other cases, the court looked to the ADEA's language to reach this result:

> The term "employer" under the ADEA is a "person engaged in an industry affecting commerce who has twenty or more employees. . . . The term also means (1) any agent

---

[646] *Id* 1560.

[647] Kizer v Curators of Univ of Mo, 816 F Supp 548, 551 (ED Mo 1993); Kauffman v Kent State Univ, 815 F Supp 1077, 1082 (ND Ohio 1993); Swanson v Department of Health, 773 F Supp 255 (D Colo 1991); Wanner v Kansas, 766 F Supp 1005, 1006-07 (D Kan 1991); Schloesser v Kansas Dept of Health & Envt, 766 F Supp 984, 989 (D Kan 1991), *revd without opinion,* 991 F2d 806 (10th Cir), *cert denied,* 114 S Ct 307 (1993); Court v Administrative Office of the Third Judicial Dist Court, 764 F Supp 168 (D Utah 1991); Tranello v Frey, 758 F Supp 841 (WDNY 1991), *affd,* 962 F2d 244 (2d Cir 1991), *cert denied sub nom* County of Monroe v Tranello, 113 S Ct 813 (1992); Sagarino v Town of Danvers, 750 F Supp 51 (D Mass 1990); Young v Sedgwick County, 660 F Supp 918 (D Kan 1987); Price v County of Erie, 654 F Supp 1206 (WDNY 1987); Ditch v Board of County Commissioners, 650 F Supp 1245 (D Kan 1986), *amended,* 669 F Supp 1553 (D Kan 1987); McCroan v Bailey, 543 F Supp 1201 (SD Ga 1982).

[648] 60 FEP Cas (BNA) 669 (D Kan 1992).

> of such person, and (1) a state or political subdivision of a state . . . " . . . The structure of the statute makes it clear that an individual who is an agent of an employer may only be an employer in his or her individual capacity if that individual is an agent of a "person." The statutory definition of "person" in the ADEA does not include a state. . . . Therefore, an agent of an agency or instrumentality of a state is not an employer for the purposes of the ADEA.[649]

There are a couple of rulings to the contrary—i.e., decisions in which governmental employees were deemed to be agents.[650] Moreover, the analysis and reasoning of the Court of Appeals for the Seventh Circuit in *Kelly v Wauconda Park District*[651] supports this minority position, even though the court did not directly address the agency issue. *Kelly* concerned the question of whether the 20-employee requirement set forth in the definition of employer in §11(b)[652] applies to governmental employers. The court answered in the affirmative, reasoning that the ADEA's legislative history supports the conclusion that Congress did not intend to treat governmental employers differently from private employers. It arguably follows from this analysis that agents of the former should be treated in the same manner as agents of the latter.

Liability of the Employer for the Acts of its Agent

The question of employer responsibility for the discriminatory acts of its employees—typically, although not necessarily, those in supervisory positions—against other employees, i.e.,

---

[649] *Id* 670. The ADEA definition of *person* is "one or more individuals, partnerships, associations, labor organizations, corporations, business trusts, legal representatives or any organized groups of persons." 29 USC §630(a).

[650] *See* Coffin v South Carolina Dept of Social Servs, 562 F Supp 579 (DSC 1983); Goodman v Board of Trustees of Community College, 498 F Supp 1329 (ND Ill 1980). A governmental employee who is sued may be able to invoke a qualified immunity defense. See **§3.20.**

[651] 801 F2d 269 (7th Cir 1986), *cert denied,* 480 US 940 (1987).

[652] 29 USC §630(b). See **§3.19.**

the plaintiffs in ADEA suits, has been only infrequently addressed. The paucity of discussion notwithstanding, the fact is that in almost every case the defendant is not an individual, but rather is an entity, e.g., a corporation, government agency, partnership, etc. Accordingly, while the courts and commentators speak of ADEA defendants having acted with discriminatory animus (or not having so acted), the fact is that such entities of course are not sentient bodies that are themselves capable of entertaining animus or of acting. These entities, in other words, formulate intent and pursue actions through individuals, i.e., their supervisory employees, agents, officers, and so on. And so when a court speaks of a defendant corporation having violated or not violated the ADEA, what it really is stating (albeit *sub silentio*) is that that defendant's employees, i.e., supervisors, etc., acted, or did not act, in violation of the Act. In brief, the courts regularly and without pause, in case after case, ascribe the intent and actions of employees to the entities by whom these individuals are employed.[653]

Shager v Upjohn Co is the rare ruling in which the issue of employer liability for the acts of insubordination was addressed.[654] In attempting to set forth a prima facie discrimination claim, and in further responding to a motion for summary judgment, the plaintiff adduced evidence of the hostility of his young supervisor toward older workers generally, and toward him in particular. The court queried whether the supervisor's hostility could be imputed to the defendant company, which was the supervisor's employer and the discharged plaintiff's former employer. "The common law rule," the court observed, "is that an employer is liable for intentional torts of its employees com-

---

[653] *See* Meritor Savings Bank, FSB v Vinson, 477 US 57, 74-76 (1986) (Marshall, J., joined by Brennan, Blackmun, and Stevens, J.J., concurring) (case arising under Title VII of the Civil Rights Act of 1964, 42 USC §§2000e through 2000e-17.) See generally **ch 7** as to the role of intent in establishing a defendant's liability under the ADEA.

[654] 913 F2d 398 (7th Cir 1990).

mitted in furtherance of their employment."[655] This rule, the court further noted, "usually is carried over to statutory torts."[656] Despite the fact that *employer* is defined in §11(b) to include agents, the court rejected the conclusion that this definition necessarily led to the conclusion that an employer is responsible for the acts of its employees: "The statutory language could mean nothing more than that . . . the agent [i.e., the supervisor here], is liable along with . . . [the employer company]."[657] Accordingly, the court reasoned that given "this [possible] understanding, the statute is silent on the issue of derivative liability and it is thus left to the courts as a matter of federal common law whether to apply the doctrine of respondeat superior in age discrimination cases."[658]

In devising a solution, the court took into account the "considerable complication"[659] generated by the Supreme Court's decision in *Meritor Savings Bank v Vinson.*[660] The *Meritor* Court construed Title VII of the Civil Rights Act of 1964,[661] which is the model for the ADEA and in fact contains the same definition of *employee.* In that case, which involved a claim of sexual harassment, the Court rejected automatically ascribing an employee's misconduct—at least misconduct involving sexual harassment—to his or her employer. The *Shager* court assessed *Meritor's* significance as follows:

> The rule that falls out of *Meritor* . . . is . . . a recognition of the unrealism of expecting an employer to be able to purge every trace of sexual harassment from the workplace; so strict liability would add nothing to liability based on fault. Concern with the futility of derivative liability is absent where the challenged action is not harassment,

---

[655] *Id* 404.

[656] *Id.*

[657] *Id.*

[658] *Id.*

[659] *Id.*

[660] 477 US 57 (1986).

[661] 42 USC §§2000e through 2000e-17.

> whether on sexual or other grounds, by a fellow employee but discharge by a supervisory employee. The deliberate act of an employee acting within the scope of his authority is the act of the employer, for an employer, at least where it is a corporation, acts only through agents. . . . This much derivative liability . . . surely survives . . . *Meritor.*[662]

In resolving the possible tension between *Meritor* and the proposition that an employer is liable for the acts of its supervisors in nonsexual harassment situations, the *Shager* court reasoned as follows:

> Discrimination is an intentional tort and . . . an employer is liable for the intentional torts of an employee only if they are in furtherance (though possibly misguided) of the employer's business, implying some relation between the tort and the business. If one low-level employee makes sexual advances to another, his conduct is so unrelated to the employer's business that the employer will ordinarily be excused from liability under the doctrine of respondeat superior. . . . But a supervisory employee who fires a subordinate is doing the kind of thing he is authorized to do, and the wrongful intent with which he does it does not carry his behavior so far beyond the orbit of his responsibilities as to excuse the employer.[663]

The foregoing analysis endorsing respondeat superior applies, the *Shager* court concluded, even vis-a-vis the issue of willfulness, which is a prerequisite to the imposition of liability for liquidated damages.[664] Unless there was an intervening, independent decision-maker who made the challenged decision without relying upon the discriminatory supervisory employee, the defendant company, the court wrote, would be "responsible

---

[662] 913 F2d at 404; *accord* Wanner v Kansas, 766 F Supp 1005, 1010-11 (D Kan 1991); *see also* North v Madison Area Assn of Retarded Citizens, 844 F2d 401, 407 (7th Cir 1988).

[663] 913 F2d at 405.

[664] See **ch 8.**

for . . . [its supervisory employee's] misconduct [vis-a-vis the plaintiff], itself a violation of the Act by virtue of . . . [the supervisory employee's] status as an agent acting within the scope of his authority, even though . . . [the supervisory employee's] conduct was willful and unauthorized."[665]

Hamm v Dresser Industries[666] involved a company, Dresser, that had sold its plant facilities to McWane, Inc. Three Dresser employees—who had been offered jobs with McWane once it took over—helped a McWane employee in deciding which other Dresser employees should be hired by McWane. Under these circumstances, the court ruled Dresser could not be held liable by those of its employees who were not hired by McWane. In other words, even though the three Dresser employees participated in the allegedly discriminatory decisions, Dresser—although it was paying their salaries at the time—really had no control over these employees in the decision–making process that they performed on behalf of McWane.

Liability of Individual Employees

The courts have focused little attention on the question of whether employees may, given their roles as agents of the employer, be held individually liable under the ADEA. The Courts of Appeals for the Fifth[667] and Ninth Circuits[668] have opined that the Act provides no basis for relief to be awarded against them. For a court that is unwilling to hold individual employees liable under the ADEA, §11(b)'s numerosity requirement pertaining to defining *employer* is a relevant factor in supporting that view. Thus, the Court of Appeals for the Ninth

---

665 913 F2d at 406.

666 41 Empl Prac Dec (CCH) ¶36,653 (ND Ala 1986).

667 Slaughter v Allstate Ins Co, 803 F2d 857, 859 (5th Cir 1986); *accord* Koppman v South Cent Bell Tel Co, 59 FEP Cas (BNA) 345, 352-53 (ED La 1992); Ditch v Board of County Commrs, 650 F Supp 1245 (D Kan 1986), *amended,* 669 F Supp 1553 (D Kan 1987).

668 Miller v Maxwell's Intl, Inc, 991 F2d 583 (9th Cir 1993), *cert denied sub nom* Miller v LaRosa, 114 S Ct 1049 (1994).

Circuit reasoned as follows in deciding *Miller v Maxwell's International, Inc*:[669]

> The statutory scheme itself indicates that Congress did not intend to impose individual liability. . . . [T]he ADEA limits liability to employers with twenty or more employees . . . in part because Congress did not want to burden small entities with the costs associated with litigating discrimination claims. If Congress decided to protect small entities with limited resources from liability, it is inconceivable that Congress intended to allow civil liability to run against individual employees.[670]

The district court that decided *Low v Hasbro, Inc*[671] agreed that employees generally cannot be held liable, but it added some cautionary notes:

> The legislative history indicates that by incorporating the term "any agent" into the definition of "employer" Congress intended only to make an employer liable for the acts of his agent and did not intend to treat supervisory employees as "employers.". . .
>
> Of course, there may be circumstances where a supervisory employee may be deemed an "employer" because he or she has an ownership interest in the enterprise . . . Similarly, there may be occasions where a supervisory employee may be individually liable because he or she engages in discriminatory practices that are clearly unrelated to performance of the supervisory employee's duties. . . .[672]

---

[669] 991 F2d 583 (9th Cir 1993), *cert denied sub nom* Miller v LaRosa, 114 S Ct 1049 (1994).

[670] *Id* 587. *But see* Owens v Rush, 636 F2d 383 (10th Cir 1980) (case arising under Title VII of the Civil Rights Act of 1964, 42 USC §§2000e through 2000e-17).

[671] 817 F Supp 249 (DRI 1993).

[672] *Id* 250.

In contrast to the foregoing decisions, several courts have held that employees can be held liable.[673] For example, the court that decided *Wanamaker v Columbian Rope Co*[674] ruled that "corporate officers and directors may be individually liable for violations of the ADEA if they exercise control over an employee."[675] In *Wanamaker* the plaintiff alleged that the individual defendants, who were officers and directors (as well as one who was an employee) of the employer company, took part in the initial decision to discharge him. This was sufficient for the court to deny the defendants' motion to dismiss. In other cases the courts, without directly addressing the issue, have assumed that suit may be maintained against individual defendants.[676]

In *Elias v Sitomer*[677] the defendant company president argued that the company should be joined as a defendant because it was possible that he otherwise could be held responsible for liability that actually should be imposed on the company. The court rejected the argument, asserting that "under the ADEA there

---

[673] Moore v Reese, 817 F Supp 1290 (D Md 1993); Elias v Sitomer, 60 FEP Cas (BNA) 758 (SDNY 1992); House v Cannon Mills Co, 713 F Supp 159–62 (MDNC 1988); Smith v Sentry Ins, 674 F Supp 1459, 1466 (ND Ga 1987); Smith v Sentry Ins, 41 FEP Cas (BNA) 1569 (ND Ga 1986). In two decisions, state employees who were deemed to be agents of their employers were deemed to be subject to personal liability. Coffin v South Carolina Dept of Social Servs, 562 F Supp 579 (DSC 1983); Goodman v Board of Trustees of Community College, 498 F Supp 1329 (ND Ill 1980).

The district court that decided Shostak v United States Postal Serv, 655 F Supp 764 (D Me 1987), upheld a suit against four individual supervisors. The court rejected the argument that only the Postal Service could be sued; it relied on the language of §15(d), 29 USC §633a(d), which is a component of the ADEA section that erects a separate scheme of liability and enforcement for the federal government, and which refers to "all persons named . . . as prospective defendants[.]" Inasmuch as this same language appears in §7(d), 29 USC §626(d), which provides for ADEA enfocement in the nonfederal government context, *Shostak* is relevant to nonfederal employers.

[674] 740 F Supp 127 (NDNY 1990).

[675] *Id* 135.

[676] *See, e.g.*, Haag v Board of Educ, 655 F Supp 1267, 1273 (ND Ill 1987); Weber v LDC/Milton Roy, 42 FEP Cas (BNA) 1507 (DNJ 1986).

[677] 60 FEP Cas (BNA) 758 (SDNY 1992).

is no reason to believe that Congress did not intend joint tortfeasors to be liable jointly and severally."[678]

§3.28 Related Entities

When a plaintiff's direct employer does not employ a sufficient number of workers to satisfy the numerosity requirement of §11(b)[679] of the Age Discrimination in Employment Act (ADEA),[680] the plaintiff may seek to combine the direct employer's work force with that of a parent or sister corporation to reach the requisite minimum of 20 employees. What is more, even where the number of employees employed by the claimant's direct employer is not at issue, the grievant still may have reason to seek to hold related corporations liable for the alleged ADEA violation.

In and of itself, the mere fact that Entity A is related to Entity B will not necessarily result in B being considered the employer of A's employees.[681] More is needed. Three approaches have been utilized by the courts in assessing the status of workers vis-a-vis related entities. In all of them, the party seeking to establish a connection between two or more entities bears the burden of proving the nexus between them by a preponderance of the evidence.[682]

Under the first approach, two (or more) entities may be so closely related that in reality they are a single integrated enterprise.[683] Four criteria are considered in making this assessment:

---

[678] *Id* 760.

[679] 29 USC §630(b). See **§3.19.**

[680] 29 USC §§621-634.

[681] *See, e.g.,* Bumpers v International Mill Servs, Inc, 595 F Supp 166 (ED Pa 1984); Sobelman v Commerce Bancshares, Inc, 444 F Supp 84 (ED Mo 1977); *see also* York v Tennessee Crushed Stone Assn, 684 F2d 360 (6th Cir 1982).

[682] Equal Employment Opportunity Commn v Argent Indus, Inc, 58 FEP (Cas (BNA) 842, 843 (SD Ohio 1988).

[683] *See, e.g.,* Linskey v Heidelberg E, Inc, 470 F Supp 1181 (EDNY 1979); Marshall v Arlene Knitwear, Inc, 454 F Supp 715 (EDNY 1978), *affd in part & revd in part without opinion,* 608 F2d 1369 (2d Cir 1979).

(1) the interrelation of the operations, (2) commonality of management, (3) the existence of centralized control of labor relations, and (4) common ownership or financial control.[684] If these four criteria are not satisfied, the actions of the one entity cannot be deemed to be the actions of the other.[685] An example of a court reviewing these factors in terms of considering the *integrated enterprise* approach's applicability to specific facts is provided by *Bruce v S & H Riggers & Erectors, Inc.*[686] The court asserted, as have other courts, that the third factor is the most important.[687]

Under the second, *mere instrumentality* approach, control is the key: two corporations will be considered a single employer such that the parent will be held liable, if the following factors are present:

> [The parent] controls the subsidiary to such a degree that the subsidiary is its instrumentality, (2) it is perpetrating a wrong, e.g., violating a statute, through its subsidiary, and (3) an unjust loss would result if the parent is allowed to be shielded by its separate corporation.[688]

---

684 *See, e.g.*, York v Tennessee Crushed Stone Assn, 684 F2d 360 (6th Cir 1982); Cohen v SUPA, Inc, 814 F Supp 251, 256 (NDNY 1993); Ames v Whitman's Chocolates, 57 FEP Cas (BNA) 1301, 1305-06 (ED Pa 1991); Yares v Great Cleveland Pipefitting Training Fund, 782 F Supp 68 (ND Ohio 1990), *affd without opinion*, 929 F2d 702 (6th Cir 1991); Bruce v S&H Riggers & Erectors, Inc, 732 F Supp 1172 (ND Ga 1990); Byer v Gordos Ark, Inc, 712 F Supp 149, 152 (WD Ark 1989); United States Equal Employment Opportunity Commn v KWMT, Inc, 718 F Supp 1425, 1427 (ND Iowa 1988); Beckwith v International Servs, Inc, 617 F Supp 187 (ED Pa 1985); Lang v El Paso Natural Gas Co, 35 FEP Cas (BNA) 1161 (WD Tex 1984); Hague v Spencer Trubine Co, 28 FEP Cas (BNA) 450 (MDNC 1982); Marshall v Arlene Knitwear, Inc, 454 F Supp 715, 719 (EDNY 1978), *affd in part & revd in part without opinion*, 608 F2d 1369 (2d Cir 1979); Zieger v Manhattan Coffee Co, 112 Ill App 3d 518, 445 NE2d 844 (1983).

685 *See, e.g.*, Allen v Mc Entee, 61 FEP Cas (BNA) 867 (DDC 1993).

686 732 F Supp 1172 (ND Ga 1990).

687 *Id* 1176.

688 Ames v Whitman's Chocolates, 57 FEP Cas (BNA) 1301, 1305 (ED Pa 1991); *see also* Wood v Southern Bell T&T Co, 724 F Supp 1244 (ND Ga 1989); Hague v Spencer Turbine Co, 28 FEP Cas (BNA) 450 (MDNC 1982); Linskey v Heidelberg E, Inc, 470 F Supp 1181 (EDNY 1979); Friedman v KFC Corp,

Thus, in a case in which the facts revealed that (a) a parent retailer exercised considerable control over its subsidiary's personnel matters, (b) the parent employed a district manager who supervised stores owned by the parent and those owned by the subsidiary, and (c) all of the stores within the district were operated as an integrated unit, the parent was held liable for the discriminatory practices of its subsidiary.[689]

Under the third approach a court may disregard a parent corporation's separate existence where one company is the *alter ego* of the other[690] and such disregard will " 'prevent fraud, illegality, or injustice, or when recognition of the corporate entity would defeat public policy or shield someone from liability of a crime.' "[691]

---

21 FEP Cas (BNA) 338 (WD Ky 1978); Seider v Canada Dry Corp, 18 FEP Cas (BNA) 1786 (SDNY 1978); Woodford v Kinney Shoe Corp, 369 F Supp 911 (ND Ga 1973).

[689] Woodford v Kinney Shoe Corp, 369 F Supp 911 (ND Ga 1973). In Brenimer v Great W Sugar Co, 567 F Supp 218 (D Colo 1983), the court considered both the *integrated enterprise* and the *mere instrumentality* approaches, but ultimately concluded—given that it was ruling on a motion for summary judgment by the defendant parent corporation—that it did not have to follow either approach, since there was a genuine issue of fact as to the defendant's status as an employer and therefore, at that point in the suit, the motion was inappropriate.

[690] Generally, the separate corporate status of subsidiaries or related corporations is disregarded where: their transactions, property, or records have been intermingled; the formalities of maintaining district corporate procedures have been disregarded; one entity has been inadequately capitalized; the companies are held out to the public as one; or the policies of one corporation are directed to serve the interests of the other corporation rather than its own interests. *See* H. Henn, Handbook of the Law of Corporations 2158-59 (2d ed 1970).

[691] Kamens v Summit Stainless, Inc, 586 F Supp 324, 327 (ED Pa 1984) (quoting Publicker Indus v Roman Ceramics, 603 F2d 1065, 1069 (3d Cir 1979)). For failed efforts by plaintiffs under the *alter ego* theory, see Sandlin v Corporate Interiors, Inc, 972 F2d 1212 (10th Cir 1992). *see also* Spence v Maryland Casualty Co, 803 F Supp 649, 663-64 (WDNY 1992), *affd on other grounds,* 995 F2d 1147 (2d Cir 1993); Ames v Whitman's Chocolates, 57 FEP Cas (BNA) 1301 (ED Pa 1991). In Zinaman v USTS NY, Inc, 798 F Supp 128, 132 (SDNY 1992), the court, taking its cue from New York law, asserted that two elements must be established under the *alter ego* approach: the parent must have exercised complete discretion, and this domination was used to commit fraud or wrong against the plaintiff.

In *Johnson v Flowers Industries, Inc,*[692] the Court of Appeals for the Fourth Circuit described the integrated enterprise approach as simply expressing relevant inquiries regarding the ultimate issue, which is whether the parent corporation dominates the subsidiary.[693] This is, of course, the issue which is paramount in the other approaches, as well. *Riley v County of Pike*[694] dealt with the issue of whether a county and the county state's attorney's office should be deemed to be a single employer. The court answered this question in the negative. While it approvingly looked to the four criteria used in the integrated enterprise approach, the court concluded that ultimately "the criteria that determine who should be considered an employer should focus on who has control over the employee."[695]

The district court that decided *Odriozola v Superior Cosmetic Distributors, Inc,*[696] examined the three approaches and concluded that, regardless of the method used, the basic inquiry is always whether a certain corporate entity is to be regarded as an employer. Accordingly, the court reasoned, the factual analysis should focus on the interrelation of the corporations in matters related to employment.[697] The court believed that it did not need to totally disregard the separate status of the two corporations; it needed only to find an employment nexus between them.[698] *Odriozola* involved a plaintiff who sued two corporations that were subsidiaries of a third. One subsidiary corporation was the plaintiff's immediate employer; the second subsidiary shared common officers and directors with the first. It also provided marketing strategies and programs, promotions, and sales training to the first at no cost. Furthermore, the second corporation possessed the authority to discharge employees of the first, and

---

692 814 F2d 978 (4th Cir 1987).

693 *Id* 981 n*.

694 761 F Supp 74 (CD Ill 1991).

695 *Id* 77.

696 531 F Supp 1070 (DPR 1982).

697 *Id* 1075.

698 *Id* 1074-75. Much the same analysis was put forth in Berkowitz v Allied Stores of Penn-Ohio, Inc, 541 F Supp 1209 (ED Pa 1982).

it both had supervised and fired the plaintiff. The court concluded that these factors indicated that the first corporation was treated as a special subdivision of the second, and accordingly denied the second corporation's motion for summary judgment.

Another way of formulating the foregoing argument is to contend that one corporation is the agent of the other, so that the actions of the first can be imputed to the second, to the end of holding the second entity liable as an employer. This argument flows from the language of §11(b), which defines the term *employer* to include "any agent of" an employer. In *Ames v Whitman's Chocolates*[699] the court concluded that the facts did not support deeming the chocolate company to be an agent of the parent since the former was not "*totally* under the control and domination" of the parent."[700]

While plaintiffs may seek to consolidate two separate entities into a single employer, the defendant may seek to subdivide one entity into several separate employers. In *Brennan v Ace Hardware Corp*[701] the employer sought to avoid ADEA liability by claiming that its Lincoln, Nebraska, branch was sufficiently autonomous to be deemed a separate employer. The branch was one of four warehouse distribution centers it operated across the country. Although labor relations were controlled locally, information and advice were obtained from the main office in Chicago. The central office also handled the branch's ordering, payment, and accounting records and supplied the general manager and traffic manager when the branch was opened. The court concluded, given these facts, that the branch was not a separate employer.

Successor Entities

A variation on the inquiry as to whether there is a sufficient nexus between two or more existing entities to justify treating them as one employer arises when one entity takes over another.

---

[699] 57 FEP Cas (BNA) 1301 (ED Pa 1991).

[700] *Id* 1306 (quoting Beckwith v International Mill Servs, 617 F Supp 187, 189 (ED Pa 1985) (emphasis added by *Ames* court).

[701] 362 F Supp 1156 (D Neb 1973), *affd on other grounds,* 495 F2d 368 (8th Cir 1974).

The question then is whether an individual who had a grievance against the original corporation can maintain an action against the successor. In the labor law context the Supreme Court has addressed this issue of a successor corporation's liability for the practices, contracts, and labor relationships of the predecessor, and has prescribed a balancing approach that takes into account the interests of the employer, the employee, and labor law policy generally.[702] In this regard, the Court asserted in *Howard Johnson, Inc v Detroit Local Joint Executive Board*[703] that "[t]here is, and can be, no single definition of 'successor' which is applicable in every legal context. A new employer . . . may be a successor for some purposes and not for others."[704]

The labor law rulings have been deemed relevant in a number of cases arising under the ADEA and the ADEA's analogue—Title VII of the Civil Rights Act of 1964.[705] Accordingly, in *Equal Employment Opportunity Commission v Puerto Rico Job Corps*[706] the court utilized the balancing test—which focuses on the particular facts in a given case—that has been prescribed in the labor law context.[707] The Court of Appeals for the Sixth Circuit articulated a number of factors to be taken into account in this balancing process in *Equal Employment Opportunity Commission v MacMillan Bloedel Containers, Inc,*[708] a Title VII ruling, and these have been approvingly noted by other courts:

> 1) whether the successor company had notice of the charge, 2) the ability of the predecessor to provide relief, 3) whether there has been a substantial continuity of business operations, 4) whether the new employer uses the

---

[702] *See, e.g.*, Howard Johnson Co, Inc v Detroit Local Joint Executive Bd, 417 US 249 (1974); Golden State Bottling Co, Inc v NLRB, 414 US 168 (1973).

[703] 417 US 249 (1974).

[704] *Id* 262 n9.

[705] 42 USC §§2000e through 2000e-17.

[706] 729 F Supp 208 (DPR 1990).

[707] In Shannon v Potter Distilleries, Inc, 678 F Supp 239 (D Or 1987), the court upheld the legitimacy of a claim asserted against a successor corporation without offering any analysis as to how it had arrived at this result.

[708] 503 F2d 1086 (6th Cir 1974).

> same plant, 5) whether he uses the same or substantially the same work force, 6) whether he uses the same or substantially the same supervisory personnel, 7) whether the same jobs exist under substantially the same working conditions, 8) whether he uses the same machinery, equipment and methods of production and 9) whether he produces the same product.[709]

However, in *Wiggins v Spector Freight System, Inc,*[710] the same court added the following caveat to *MacMillan*: if no charge of discrimination had been filed with the Equal Employment Opportunity Commission (EEOC) at or before the time of acquisition, and the successor had no notice of contingent charges of discrimination at or before the time of acquisition, successor liability will not attach, and so application in the Sixth Circuit of the *MacMillan* balancing factors will be inapplicable.

In *Brown v Delaware & Hudson Railway Co*[711] the defendant's motion for summary judgment was denied, based on the fact that while it had not been the plaintiff's employer, it had acquired substantially all of the plaintiff's employer's assets and operations. Moreover, the closing documents had expressly disclosed that there were age discrimination claims (including that of the plaintiff) pending against the acquired company, and the successor had "expressly assumed any and all liabilities associated with those claims."[712]

Joint Employers

It should be understood that the question of whether two purportedly separate entities can be deemed to be one is to be dis-

---

[709] *Id* 1094; *see also In re* National Airlines, Inc, 700 F2d 695, 698 (11th Cir), *cert denied,* 464 US 933 (1983); Trujillo v Longhorn Mfg Co, Inc, 694 F2d 221, 224-25 (10th Cir 1982); Dominguez v Hotel, Motel, Restaurant & Miscellaneous Bartenders Union, Local 64, 674 F2d 732 (8th Cir 1982); Spence v Maryland Cas Co, 803 F Supp 649, 663 (WDNY 1992), *affd on other grounds,* 995 F2d 1147 (2d Cir 1993).

[710] 583 F2d 882 (6th Cir 1978).

[711] 60 FEP Cas (BNA) 345 (ED Pa 1992).

[712] *Id* 349.

tinguished from the question of whether two separate entities can be deemed to be the joint employers of a given individual or group of individuals. "The 'joint employer' concept recognizes that the business entities involved are in fact separate but that they share or co-determine . . . conditions of employment."[713] While under the *integrated enterprise* approach discussed above several factors—i.e., interrelation of operations, commonality of management, centralized control of labor relations, and common ownership—typically are addressed, in the joint employer context these factors are not relevant. "The joint employer inquiry . . . 'is a matter of determining which of two, or whether both, . . . [entities] control, in the capacity of employer the labor relations of a given group of workers.' "[714] In making this determination, a number of factors have been deemed relevant by non-ADEA courts. For example, in *G Heileman Brewery Co, Inc v NLRB*[715] the court looked to " 'the supervision of the employees' day to day activities, authority to hire or fire employees, promulgation of work rules and conditions of employment, work assignments, and issuance of operating instructions.' "[716]

---

[713] NLRB v Browning-Ferris Indus, Inc, 691 F2d 1117, 1123 (3d Cir 1982).

[714] Rivas v Federacion de Asociaciones Pecuaria de Puerto Rico, 929 F2d 814, 820 (1st Cir 1991) (quoting NLRB v Browning-Ferris Indus, Inc, 691 F2d 1117, 1122-23 (3d Cir 1982)).

[715] 879 F2d 1526 (7th Cir 1989).

[716] *Id* 1531 (quoting Rivas v Federacion de Asociaciones Pecuaria de Puerto Rico, 929 F2d 814, 820-21 (1st Cir 1991)).

The Age Discrimination in Employment Act—Prohibitions and Requirements

4

Posting and Record-Keeping Requirements

§4.01 Prohibited Practices: Generally

This chapter reviews the multiplicity of ways in which actions and decisions may be thought to violate, and sometimes may be established as violating, the Age Discrimination in Employment Act (ADEA).[1] This effort is not an exhaustive one. Indeed, it hardly could be: relations between employers and job applicants, employees, and former employees; labor organizations and their members; and employment agencies and their clients are all very much fact-bound and can be exceedingly complex. The purpose of this chapter simply is to provide a sampling of cases and issues in order to illustrate that a whole host of decisions and actions can give rise to claims of discrimination. (Of course, discrimination in the abstract is legally meaningless. For a violation of the ADEA to exist, there must be some sort of perceptible adverse consequence experienced by the grievant.[2])

Some practices are peculiar to a given covered entity. For example, while discharges certainly can give rise to claims of discrimination, it generally is only employers that will engage in the actual acts of terminating people.[3] Thus, an employment agency, when acting in its role as such (as opposed to acting as an employer vis-a-vis its own employees) is simply not going to be in a position to discharge those individuals with whom it is in active contact, i.e., its clients. Other practices—retaliation, for example, or the use of proxies for age—can be engaged in by any covered entity, i.e., an employer, a labor organization, or

---

[1] 29 USC §§621-634.

[2] *See, e.g.*, Crady v Liberty Natl Bank, 993 F2d 132 (7th Cir 1993); Spring v Sheboygan Area Sch Dist, 865 F2d 883, 885 (7th Cir 1989); Cherry v Thermo Electron Corp, 800 F Supp 508, 511 (ED Mich 1992); Haimovitz v United States Dept of Justice, 720 F Supp 516, 526-27 (WD Pa 1989), *affd without opinion*, 902 F2d 1560 (3d Cir 1990); Equal Employment Opportunity Commn v Firestone Tire & Rubber Co, 650 F Supp 1561, 1569 (WD Tenn 1987).

[3] A union, however, can be held liable for influencing an employer's decisions. More specifically, §4(b), 29 USC §623(b), bars a labor organization from causing or attempting to cause "an employer to discriminate against an individual in violation of" the ADEA.

an employment agency. The organization of this chapter reflects this distinction between entity-specific practices and general practices in which all can engage.[4]

One final matter. Section 15[5] of the ADEA establishes a separate regulatory scheme for the federal government and federal employees, whereby "[a]ll personnel actions affecting employees or applicants for employment who are at least 40 years of age . . . shall be made free from any discrimination based on age."[6] Although this language is not as detailed as that set forth in the ADEA's prohibitory provisions dealing with individuals in the nonfederal sector, §15 clearly brings within its scope many of the various kinds of actions and decisions discussed in the following sections of this chapter.

§4.02 Prohibited Employer Practices: Generally

The Age Discrimination in Employment Act (ADEA)[7] prohibits employers from refusing to hire, from discharging, and from otherwise discriminating against individuals with respect to compensation, terms, conditions, or privileges of employment

---

[4] There can be decisions and actions that implicate age but that are beyond the reach of the ADEA. For one, decisions regarding individuals who are not within the protected class, which is made up persons ages 40 and over, are generally (but not completely) beyond the reach of the statute. See **ch 3.** Employers with less than 20 employees do not have to comply with the ADEA. See **ch 3.** Other limits also exist. See **ch 3.**

In Egnatz v Medical Protective Co, 581 NE2d 438 (Ind Ct App 1991), the 71-year-old plaintiff doctor sued as a result of the defendant company's refusal to renew his malpractice insurance policy, the consequence being that the plaintiff was effectively forced to sell his practice and retire. The company acknowledged that age was one of the factors it took into account. The court rejected the plaintiff's argument that the public policy evidenced by the ADEA should be extended to his situation: "Neither federal, state, or common law impose a duty to renew upon a medical liability insurance company. Extending an age discrimination statute to cover cases such as this is the legislature's prerogative, not the judiciary's." *Id* 442.

[5] 29 USC §633a. See generally **Ch 9.**

[6] §15(a), 29 USC §633a(a).

[7] 29 USC §§621-634.

because of age.[8] The Act further outlaws employers' classifications that deprive or tend to deprive individuals of employment opportunities or that otherwise adversely affect them because of age.[9] The reduction of an employee's wages so as to bring an employer into compliance with the Act also is banned.[10]

Discrimination can occur in a variety of ways. The largest number of ADEA cases involve discharges.[11] Smaller, but still sizeable, categories of cases entail either refusals to hire, refusals to promote, or demotions. There also are more complex ways in which discrimination may be manifested. For example, the facts addressed by the court deciding *Bruno v Western Electric Co,*[12] as described subsequently in *Glass v IDS Financial Services, Inc,*[13] are illustrative of a multifaceted discriminatory situation:

> In *Bruno,* the plaintiff alleged that his employer engaged in a series of related acts as a part of its overall plan to force him into voluntary or involuntary retirement, including the employer's refusal to promote or transfer him, his transfer to a position for which he was not qualified "to build a record that would justify his voluntary dismissal", offers of early retirement, a demotion and decrease in salary, harass-

---

[8] §4(a)(1), 29 USC §623(a)(1).

[9] §4(a)(2), 29 USC §623(a)(2).

[10] §4(a)(3), 29 USC §623(a)(3).

[11] *See, e.g.,* EEOC Compliance Manual, News and Developments 3 (Jan 31, 1994). The once common practice of age-based mandatory retirement, i.e., discharge based on nothing more than attainment of a certain age, is in most instances now illegal. However, there are some exceptions: mandatory retirement may be legitimized in a given instance by virtue of an employer's successful invocation of the bona fide occupational defense, see **ch 5;** or by application of one of the specific exemptions in the Act, see **ch 3;** or—in the instance of federal employees—by a specific federal statute authorizing the forced retirement of certain employees. See **ch 3.** Involuntary retirement cannot, however, be justified by claiming that it was imposed pursuant to an employee benefit plan. See **ch 5.**

[12] 829 F2d 957 (10th Cir 1987).

[13] 778 F Supp 1029 (D Minn 1991).

ment on the basis of his age and various other adverse working conditions.[14]

Other cases illustrate discrimination, alleged and/or proven, occurring in less typical manifestations than discharges, demotions, denials of hire, and denials of promotion.[15] In *Winslow v FERC*[16] the wrongdoing consisted in part of the defendant's placing the plaintiff in an untenable job setting and subjecting him to uniquely rigorous conditions—treatment different than that accorded younger employees. The discrimination addressed in *Coates v National Cash Register Co*[17] arose out of the employer's assignment of only younger employees for special training, with the older workers' lack of training then being used as the basis for discharging them. In a similar vein, it has been held that a wrongful denial to promote to a position that in turn would have afforded the requisite experience for the next move upwards cannot be used as the basis for a refusal to promote to that latter position[18] The court deciding *Sharpe v Philadelphia Housing Authority*,[19] in reversing a dismissal by the trial court, held that the plaintiff had made a timely allegation regarding discriminatory treatment, which allegedly was manifested by the defendant's treating the plaintiff's in-house administrative appeal differently than the appeal of a younger employee. In *Mellor v*

---

[14] *Id* 1055.

[15] As to an employer's ability to hold liable an insurance company from which it purchased a policy that allegedly discriminated against its employees, see Germann v Pekow, 531 F Supp 355 (ND Ill 1981).

[16] 43 FEP Cas (BNA) 1311 (DDC 1987).

[17] 433 F Supp 655 (WD Va 1977); *see also* Acrey v American Sheep Indus Assn, 981 F2d 1569, 1572-73 (10th Cir 1992); Brooks v Monroe Sys for Business, Inc, 873 F2d 202 (8th Cir), *cert denied,* 493 US 853 (1989); Uffelman v Lone Star Steel Co, 863 F2d 404, 408 (5th Cir), *cert denied,* 490 US 1098 (1989); James v Capital City Press, 742 F Supp 347 (MD La 1990); Hall v Central Medical Pavilion, 654 F Supp 1156 (WD Pa 1987). *See also* Hamilton v Komatsu Dresser Indus, Inc, 964 F2d 600 (7th Cir), *cert denied,* 113 S Ct 324 (1992)

[18] *See* Kirschner v Office of the Controller of NY, 973 F2d 88, 94 (2d Cir 1992).

[19] 693 F2d 24 (3d Cir 1982).

Shell Oil Co[20] the plaintiff's claim (albeit an unpersuasive one) was that the inclusion of claim-release clauses in ostensibly voluntary termination agreements constituted a per se violation of the ADEA.

Still another less common factual situation was addressed in *Miller v General Electric Co,*[21] where the plaintiff argued that there was unlawful age discrimination involved in the employer's alleged frustration of the plaintiff's efforts to obtain other employment.[22] While the plaintiff failed with his claim, this failure was on the merits; the court did not deem such a claim to be per se invalid under the Act. In *Fink v Western Electric Co*[23] the plaintiff unsuccessfully argued that the defendant had favored younger employees by assisting them in finding new jobs. In *Colizza v United States Steel Corp,*[24] the plaintiffs failed to establish a prima facie violation based on their theory that their layoffs were unlawful by virtue of the defendant having contracted out work to outside companies that employed younger workers.

§4.03 —Recruiting and Hiring Practices

The practices utilized, and the decisions made, by employers in seeking out potential employees,[25] as well as regarding the hiring of individuals, clearly can implicate the proscriptions of the Age Discrimination in Employment Act (ADEA).[26]

---

[20] 30 Empl Prac Dec (CCH) ¶33,180 (SD Tex 1982).

[21] 562 F Supp 610 (ED Pa 1983).

[22] A former employer's actions vis-a-vis a former employee may, in some circumstances, be attacked as constituting unlawful retaliation. See **§4.16.**

[23] 708 F2d 909 (4th Cir 1983).

[24] 49 FEP Cas (BNA) 779 (WD Pa 1989).

[25] Since the Age Discrimination in Employment Act (ADEA), 29 USC §§621-634, "spells out criteria for job advertisements and employment referrals," see **§4.13** as to advertisements, it follows that "the topic of recruitment is covered under ADEA." Equal Employment Opportunity Commn v Arizona, 824 F Supp 898 (D Ariz 1991).

[26] 29 USC §§621-634.

In the context of addressing a claim arising under Title VII of the Civil Rights Act of 1964,[27] to which ADEA courts commonly look for analogical guidance given the similarities in language of the two statutes,[28] the Court of Appeals for the Fifth Circuit criticized an employer that limited its chief recruitment efforts to predominantly white institutions.[29] The district court deciding *Mistretta v Sandia Corp,*[30] an ADEA case, took a different tack in a similar situation: it approved an employer's concentrating its recruiting efforts for entry-level positions on college campuses, despite the fact that the likelihood of finding any but young applicants in that setting presumably would be slim.

The *Mistretta* court also addressed the use by the employer of guidelines for its college recruiters requiring especially careful screening of bachelor's degree recipients older than 23, master's degree recipients older than 25-26, and Ph.D. awardees older than 30. The proffered rationale supporting these guidelines was the perception that an applicant's being older than typical degree recipients possibly indicated that he or she had taken a light course load, thereby rendering suspect the applicant's high grade-point average. Ultimately, the court concluded that the recruiting guidelines were not violative of the ADEA inasmuch as no one in the protected age group had in fact been denied employment because of their use.

An obvious question that arises is whether an employer may inquire as to an applicant's age. One decision articulates an affirmative conclusion; in other words, it is not illegal per se to make inquiry as to a job applicant's age.[31] However, the Court of Appeals for the Seventh Circuit, in deciding *Herman v National*

---

[27] 42 USC §§2000e through 2000e-17.

[28] See **ch 2.**

[29] *See, e.g.,* United States v Georgia Power Co, 474 F2d 906, 926 (5th Cir 1973).

[30] 15 FEP Cas (BNA) 1690 (DNM 1977), *affd,* 639 F2d 600 (10th Cir 1980).

[31] Landau v Bolger, 47 Empl Prac Dec (CCH) ¶38,236 (EDNY 1988), at p 53,376.

Broadcasting Co,[32] relied on the defendant's collection of birth date data as partial basis for its conclusion that a prima facie case of age discrimination had been established.[33] Similarly, in *Reed v Signode Corp*[34] the court—in denying the defendant's motion for summary judgment—observed that the plaintiff's attempt to establish as pretextual the defendant's excuse for not hiring him was buttressed by the fact that the employer had made notations regarding the age of each applicant.[35]

The Equal Employment Opportunity Commission (EEOC)—the enforcement agency for the ADEA—takes the position that inquiries as to age are not per se illegal.[36] However, the EEOC further has cautioned that "because the request that an applicant state his age may tend to deter older applicants or otherwise indicate discrimination based on age, employment application forms which request . . . information [as to date of birth or age] will be closely scrutinized."[37] (The agency also suggests that a reference to the ADEA be set forth on the face of any employment application.)[38]

§4.04 —Compensation

Differentials in pay can run afoul of the Age Discrimination

---

[32] 744 F2d 604 (7th Cir 1984), *cert denied,* 470 US 1028 (1985).

[33] In deciding Fink v Western Elec Co, 708 F2d 909 (4th Cir 1983), the court rejected any inference of discriminatory motive as properly being drawn from the fact that the defendant, in seeking to assist the plaintiff in finding other employment, submitted a resume for the plaintiff that specified his age. *Id* 917.

[34] 652 F Supp 129 (D Conn 1986).

[35] *Id* 135.

[36] 29 CFR §1625.5 (1993).

[37] *Id.* The term *employment applications* is defined in the EEOC interpretation. *Id.*

[38] *Id.* The EEOC interpretation sets forth recommended language: "The Age Discrimination in Employment Act of 1967 prohibits discrimination on the basis of age with respect to individuals who are at least 40 years of age." *Id.*

in Employment Act's (ADEA)[39] proscription against discrimination "with respect to . . . compensation."[40] Generally, whatever the form remuneration for work takes, it will be deemed to be compensation. (However, it was held that a state law terminating workers' compensation benefits at age 65 did not violate the ADEA because such benefits were not deemed to constitute compensation.)[41] Most fringe benefit issues arising under the ADEA are resolved in terms of the statutory exception regarding bona fide employee benefit plans;[42] issues involving wages do not fall within this exception, however.[43]

One aspect of the ADEA's impact on compensation schemes is very clear: the reduction of an employee's wages so as to bring an employer into compliance with the Act is prohibited.[44] The proper treatment of other facets of compensation systems and practices can be more problematic.

It is possible that an employer may pay a higher salary to younger employees than to older ones, even though both are performing the same tasks. Such a situation gave rise to an ADEA claim in *Hamilton v 1st Source Bank.*[45] However, such differentials may well not violate the ADEA. One explanation for this involves the fact that increases in salaries—at least in the early years of

---

[39] 29 USC §§621-634.

[40] §4(a)(1), 29 USC §623(a)(1).

[41] O'Neil v Department of Transp, 10 Fla 157, 468 So 2d 904, *cert denied,* 474 US 861 (1985); *see also* Brown v Goodyear Tire & Rubber Co, 3 Kan App 2d 648, 599 P2d 1031 (1979), *affd,* 227 Kan 645, 608 P2d 1356, *appeal dismissed,* 449 US 914 (1980).

[42] §4(f)(2), 29 USC §623(f)(2). See **ch 5.** Not all fringe benefit issues are dealt with under the bona fide benefit plan caveat, however: in Equal Employment Opportunity Commn v Minneapolis Police Relief Assn, 645 F Supp 367 (D Minn 1986), the discontinuance of pension benefits for two employees who chose to work past age 65 was deemed to be per se illegal; the employer did not even invoke the bona fide benefit plan exception.

[43] It has been stated that the failure to adopt a pension plan does not constitute a violation of the ADEA. Rothenberger v Douglas County, 586 F Supp 210, 211 (DSD 1983), *affd,* 736 F2d 1240 (8th Cir 1984), *cert denied,* 469 US 1213 (1985).

[44] §4(a)(3), 29 USC §623(a)(3).

[45] 895 F2d 159 (4th Cir), *vacated in part on other grounds,* 928 F2d 86 (4th Cir 1990) (en banc).

an employee's tenure with an employer—often are based on the notion that the employee becomes increasingly valuable with experience and maturity. Periodically, the employee's compensation will be enhanced to reflect his or her increased value to the employer. Because the typical individual employee will usually demonstrate more marked increases in performance at the outset of his or her career than will be seen once the individual has become an expert in his or her particular field, merit increases may be larger for younger employees in a given workplace than they will be for older workers. One court has ruled that the ADEA is not violated when a larger merit increase given to a younger employee merely reflects the differing rates of increase in experience and expertise as between him or her and other, older workers.[46] Presumably, the same logic could be applied to justify pay raises being given with less frequency (as opposed to less dollars) to older workers.

Another nondiscriminatory justification for according higher salary increases to younger employees, as contrasted to the pay raises given to older workers, may be the fact that younger employees start off with considerably lower base salaries, and so an employer may have to engage in a more aggressive game of "catch-up." Thus, the court deciding *D'Aquino v Citicorp/Diner's Club, Inc,*[47] rejected the discrimination claim of an older, highly paid employee who complained that his annual salary increases were lower, in percentage terms, than those of younger workers. The court concluded that there was no age animus here; rather, the differentials in salary increases were consistent with, and pursuant to, a company policy entailing larger salary increases being given to workers with lower base salaries.

Notwithstanding there being room, legally, for an employer to give a younger employee a larger pay raise than it gives to

---

[46] Smith v Flax, 618 F2d 1062 (4th Cir 1980).

[47] 755 F Supp 218 (ND Ill 1991).

an older employee, the employer in *Mistretta v Sandia Corp*[48] went beyond legal bounds. It adopted a policy that employees' salaries would not be increased unless a minimum standard, determined by a combination of the employees' ages and the time that had elapsed since their last raises, was achieved, with the result being that older employees had to qualify for much larger raises than younger employees before any raises at all would be given them. The way that this system worked, a 29-year-old who had last received a pay raise a year earlier would receive a raise provided he or she qualified for at least a 5 per cent increase. However, no pay raise would be due a similarly situated 46-year-old employee unless he or she qualified for at least a 12.5 per cent increase. The *Mistretta* court deemed this system violative of the ADEA because by virtue of the linkage between the minimum raise percentage and the employee's age, the employee's movement upwards in the salary structure was impeded because of his or her age. In brief, the system did not merely reflect increases in experience and expertise, such that the pay raises were larger in early years simply because of the faster rise in these factors at the outset of an employee's career.

The Court of Appeals for the Seventh Circuit addressed a different facet of compensation differentials in *Davidson v Board of Governors*[49] *of State Colleges & Universities for Western Illinois University.* The plaintiff's claim arose out of a collectively bargained salary scheme pursuant to which a new hire could be paid whatever salary he or she negotiated with the employer, whereas an existing employee would not secure more than a standard, across-the-board salary increase unless it could be established that he or she had received an offer from another employer of a job paying the higher amount. Moreover, even in such instance the enhanced salary increase to be secured from the defendant could not exceed that offered by the other employer. The plaintiff argued that this compensation plan had, or would have, a discriminatory impact on older employees inasmuch as existing

---

48 15 FEP Cas (BNA) 1690 (DNM 1977), *affd,* 639 F2d 588 (10th Cir), 639 F2d 600 (10th Cir 1980).

49 920 F2d 441 (7th Cir 1990).

employees were likely, on average, to be older than newly hired individuals:

> As . . . [the plaintiff] sees it, his university's compensation scheme set in motion a chain of events certain to result eventually in his receiving a lower salary than some younger faculty members of no greater experience or ability. He can get raises only by producing offers from other employers, while new and presumably younger employees can sign on at any salary that the university is generous enough to offer them.[50]

The *Davidson* court ruled against the plaintiff, using market-based economic analysis in holding that he had failed to state a claim under the ADEA:

> Western Illinois University bases salary on the market. It will not give a salary member a raise that raises him above the salary of his peers unless he provides proof of his market value, in the form of a bona fide written offer from another employer. The university does not apply this policy to new employees, since it could not hope to hire someone . . . away from that person's existing employer without paying more than his present salary. Because of the psychic and pecuniary costs of relocation, an existing employee can usually be retained if his offer from another employer is matched. This assumption cannot be made with a new employee. He is unlikely to leave his present job if his new employer offers him merely the same salary that he is getting in that job.
>
> If disparate impact is a permissible theory . . . , then a practice innocent on its face, as . . . [this] compensation scheme is, could be shown to be discriminatory by considering its effect and the justifications offered for it. But not just by showing that one or two younger faculty members have been hired at higher salaries than the plaintiff, an existing employee. For that is inevitable. Employees who

---

[50] *Id* 444.

> stay longest, are on average [,] though of course not in every case, those who have the fewest offers to go elsewhere. Their market alternatives are therefore relatively poor and they fare relatively badly under any market-based compensation scheme, irrespective of age. Employees newly hired must, as we have said, have been lured away from other jobs or job opportunities. Some of these employees will have high market value and therefore command a high initial salary under . . . [the defendant's] method of fixing starting salaries. The limited disparate impact that is all that . . . [the plaintiff] has offered to show does not come close to demonstrating a taint of age discrimination.[51]

In *Britt v Grocers Supply Co, Inc,*[52] the court addressed a claim arising out of the employer's switching from a flat-rate system, i.e., an hourly wage, to a system based on employee productivity. The argument was made that the new pay scheme would favor younger workers because it would require harder work (which, the assumption seemed to be, they would be better able to perform than would older workers). The court responded as follows: "[A]ssuming that to be true, it does not violate the act to require all workers to increase output, hours, or other burdens."[53]

In *Miller v General Electric Co*[54] the plaintiff was unsuccessful in proving that his age was a factor in the employer's alleged wrongful failure to give him salary increases and to adequately compensate him for overtime. In *Fong v Beggs*[55] the plaintiffs failed to prevail on their claim, which arose out of alleged differentials in the granting of salary increases. Likewise, the plaintiff

---

[51] *Id* 460; *see also* MacPherson v University of Montevallo, 922 F2d 766 (11th Cir 1991). As to disparate impact analysis generally, see **ch 7.**

[52] 760 F Supp 606 (SD Tex 1991), *affd on other grounds,* 978 F2d 1441 (5th Cir 1992), *cert denied,* 113 S Ct 2929 (1993).

[53] *Id* 608.

[54] 562 F Supp 610 (ED Pa 1983).

[55] 620 F Supp 847 (DDC 1985).

failed in *Hickerson v Armour Food Co,*[56] where it turned out that the differential between her salary and that of a younger hire was due to the latter's better credentials.

Dorsch v LB Foster Co[57] involved an allegedly discriminatory retirement plan whereby employees who retired early were paid $600 per month until age 62, provided the employee's age at retirement, when combined with years of service, equaled at least 75 years. The consequence was that younger employees received greater total payments than did employees close to age 62—the cutoff point for the program. In other words, an employee age 55, with 20 years of service, would receive $600 monthly for seven years, whereas a 61-year-old employee with 20 years of service would only receive payments for one year. The *Dorsch* court rejected the argument that the plan constituted a discriminatory form of compensation. The court, in a cryptic presentation, saw no problem with the payment of equal monthly payments—regardless of age—rather than equal total payments.

The question of whether the denial of severance pay to retirees can, or should, be deemed to constitute a manifestation of age discrimination has generated a number of judicial decisions. Most of these have arisen in the context of consideration of the bona fide employee benefit plan exception noted earlier.[58]

§4.05 —Harassment

Ranging from the Supreme Court on down, the courts have established beyond any doubt that a cause of action may be based on the plaintiff's alleged subjection to race or gender-based harassment, with this victimization being manifested by

---

[56] 59 FEP Cas (BNA) 1615 (WD Ky 1992).

[57] 782 F2d 1412 (7th Cir 1986).

[58] See **Ch 5.** *See also* Geltman v Verity, 716 F Supp 491 (D Colo 1980) (federal statute whereby terminated federal employee who was eligible to receive a retirement annuity was rendered ineligible to receive severance pay was deemed not violative of §15, 29 USC §633a, of ADEA).

a hostile work environment.[59] In contrast, harassment per se has received very little attention in cases arising under the Age Discrimination in Employment Act (ADEA).[60] However, this is not necessarily because age-based harassment is absent from the workplace. Rather, what has happened is that employees complaining of what otherwise might be termed harassment have brought suits alleging they were constructively discharged—i.e., they were subjected to work situations so intolerable that they felt that they had to resign.[61] (Actually, in the areas of race, gender, and other discrimination, the line between constructive discharge and unlawful harassment also often is blurred.)

A rare decision in which an ADEA court recognized in and of itself age-based harassment as a cognizable legal wrong is *Young v Will County Department of Public Aid.*[62] The Court of Appeals for the Seventh Circuit concluded in *Young,* however, that the facts did not support the plaintiff's claim, which arose out of a series of valid criticisms of her work performance: "The withholding of a salary increase, unfavorable work evaluations and . . . [her supervisor's] referring older employees to the [agency] manual for answers . . . do not in combination rise to . . . [a discriminatory] level of harassment[.]"[63]

The district court deciding *Spence v Maryland Casualty Co*[64] also readily embraced the proposition that hostile environment harassment theory applies in the age setting:

---

59 *See, e.g.,* Meritor Sav Bank, FSB v Vinson, 477 US 57, 65-66 (1986) (case concerning gender-based harassment arising under Title VII of the Civil Rights Act of 1964, 42 USC §§2000e through 2000e-17).

60 29 USC §§621-634. The Equal Employment Opportunity Commission published a proposed guideline, 29 CFR pt 1609 (proposed), covering harassment based on race, color, religion, gender, national origin, age, and disability on October 1, 1993. 58 Fed Reg 51266 (Oct 1, 1993.) As of June 10, 1994, no final guideline had been issued. Such guidelines are not legally binding, but they generally are accorded considerable judicial deference. See **Ch 2.**

61 *See, e.g.,* Lewis v Federal Prison Indus, Inc, 953 F2d 1277 (11th Cir 1992). As to constructive discharge generally, see **ch 7.**

62 882 F2d 290 (7th Cir 1989).

63 *Id* 294.

64 803 F Supp 649 (WDNY 1992), *affd on other grounds,* 995 F2d 1147 (2d Cir 1993).

> A hostile work environment theory requires that the plaintiff show that 1) he was a member of a protected class, 2) he was subject to unwelcome harassment, 3) the harassment was prompted solely because of his age, 4) the harassment affected a term, condition or privilege of his employment, and 5) the existence of respondeat superior liability.[65]

The court further pointed out that the burden imposed upon the plaintiff is not a particularly easy one although the court—while acknowledging that the plaintiff "bears a stronger burden here"[66]—further noted "that the burden of proving a prima facie case of discrimination is not onerous."[67] The court, in detailing this "stronger burden," wrote as follows:

> [U]nder a hostile work environment analysis, courts have required [in non-ADEA cases] a stronger showing of offensive employer conduct. For example, the conduct must be "pervasive," or "continuous and concerted," or "occur[ring] either in concert or with a regularity that that [sic] can be reasonably termed pervasive," considering such factors as the offensiveness of the complained against behavior.[68]

The court concluded that the plaintiff had alleged facts sufficient to establish the existence of harassment: "Plaintiff herein asserts that his employer . . . discriminated against him in the conditions and privileges of his employment, by consistently intimidating and harassing him in several incidents, meetings, and reviews."[69] The plaintiff failed, however, to establish respondeat superior liability. The court pointed out that the "Second Circuit has required that in order to show that the

---

[65] *Id* 671.

[66] *Id.*

[67] *Id.*

[68] *Id* (quoting Trotta v Mobil Oil Corp, 788 F Supp 1336, 1349-50 (SDNY 1992)).

[69] 803 F Supp at 666.

employer is responsible for the hostile environment, the 'plaintiff must prove that the employer either provided no reasonable avenue for complaint or knew of the harassment but did nothing about it.' "[70]

In *Drez v ER Squibb & Sons, Inc,*[71] the court also recognized the existence of a hostile environment claim.[72] The *Drez* court quoted from *Meritor Savings Bank, FSB v Vinson,*[73] the seminal sexual harassment decision by the Supreme Court arising under Title VII of the Civil Rights Act of 1964:[74]

> "In concluding that so-called 'hostile environment' (i.e., non quid pro quo) harassment violates Title VII, the EEOC [Equal Employment Opportunity Commission] drew upon a substantial body of judicial decisions and EEOC precedent holding that Title VII affords employees the right to work in an environment free from discriminatory intimidation, ridicule, and insult."[75]

The *Drez* court reasoned that "[t]here is no sound reason this court should interpret identical statutory language [, i.e., language in the ADEA regarding prohibitions of discrimination that is identical to that in Title VII,] in the context of age discrimination any differently."[76] Relying again on *Meritor,* and echoing requirements articulated also by the *Spence* court (which itself relied on case law derivative of *Meritor*), the *Drez* court further asserted: "Of course, the harassment must be sufficiently severe or pervasive to alter the employee's employment and create an

---

[70] *Id* 671 (quoting Kotcher v Rosa & Sullivan Appliance Ctr, Inc, 957 F2d 59, 63 (2d Cir 1992)).

[71] 674 F Supp 1432 (D Kan 1987).

[72] *See also* Blake v JC Penney Co, Inc, 894 F2d 274, 278 (8th Cir 1990).

[73] 477 US 57 (1986).

[74] 42 USC §§2000e through 2000e-17.

[75] 674 F Supp at 1436 (quoting *Meritor,* 477 US at 65).

[76] 674 F Supp at 1436.

abusive working environment.''[77] Looking to the facts before it, the court concluded that the plaintiff's evidence was sufficient for the jury to have found the existence of unlawful harassment. (The court did not discuss that evidence, however).

The fact that in *Drez* the court looked to Title VII precedent for guidance is not surprising; this is a tack typically pursued by ADEA courts.[78] Of course, in the harassment context, the body of case law that is developing regarding sexual harassment is not entirely apposite: harassment flowing from the gender of the victim is considerably different in kind and motivation than that directed towards people because of their ages. Thus, one must approach the Title VII case law with some caution. Still, *Harris v Forklift Systems, Inc,*[79] another Supreme Court sexual harassment case, is—like *Meritor*—intructive.

In *Harris* the Court ruled that the alleged victim of sexual harassment need not establish that he or she suffered concrete psychological harm in order to establish wrongdoing on the defendant's part. The Court went on to provide some general admonitions regarding what will constitute evidence of harassment:

> [W]hether an environment is "hostile" or "abusive" can be determined only by looking at all the circumstances. These may include the frequency of the discriminatory conduct; its severity; whether it is physically threatening or humiliating, or a mere offensive utterance; and whether it unreasonably interferes with an employee's work performance. The effect on the employee's psychological well-being is, of course, relevant to determining whether the plaintiff actually found the environment abusive. But while psychological harm, like any other relevant factor, may be taken into account, no single factor is required.[80]

---

77 *Id* 1437.
78 See **ch 2.**
79 114 S Ct 367 (1993).
80 *Id* 371.

§4.06 —Transfers and Refusals to Transfer

Both transfers and refusals to transfer can generate age discrimination claims under the Age Discrimination in Employment Act (ADEA).[81]

Undesired Transfers

A number of courts have dealt with unwelcome transfers.[82] In *Hoefelman v Conservation Commission,*[83] for example, the plaintiff challenged his transfer from the position of chief pilot to equipment supervisor. The defendants contended that no unlawful discrimination was involved, inasmuch as the plaintiff continued to receive the same salary and benefits. The court, however, viewed the transfer as being discriminatory, given that the new job was less pleasant, less satisfying, and less rewarding in other nonmonetary ways.[84] (Ultimately, the defendants prevailed through invocation of the bona fide occupational qualification defense.)[85]

In contrast to *Hoefelman, Haimovitz v United States Department of Justice*[86] revealed a more constricted judicial view of what constitutes an actionable claim arising out of an undesired transfer. The plaintiff, a federal employee in Pittsburgh, Pennsylvania, faced a transfer to Harlingen, Texas, as a result of the reorganization of his agency and the abolition of the Pittsburgh position.

---

[81] 29 USC §§621-634.

[82] *See, e.g.,* Darnell v Campbell County Fiscal Court, 731 F Supp 1309 (ED Ky 1990), *affd without opinion,* 924 F2d 1057 (6th Cir 1991); Bruno v Western Elec Co, 829 F2d 957 (10th Cir 1987); Arnold v Postmaster Gen, 667 F Supp 6 (DDC 1987), *revd,* 863 F2d 994 (DC Cir 1988), *cert denied,* 493 US 846 (1989) (federal employee suit); Stover v Chairman, Equal Employment Opportunity Commn, 673 F Supp 522 (DDC 1987) (*id*); Rotert v Jefferson Fed Sav & Loan Assn, 623 F Supp 1114 (D Conn 1985); Doscherholmen v Walters, 575 F Supp 1552 (D Minn), *affd without opinion,* 754 F2d 377 (8th Cir 1984) (federal employee suit).

[83] 541 F Supp 272 (WD Mo 1982), *affd,* 718 F2d 281 (8th Cir 1983).

[84] *Id* 274 n2.

[85] As to this defense, see **ch 5.**

[86] 720 F Supp 516 (WD Pa 1989), *affd without opinion,* 902 F2d 1560 (3d Cir 1990).

The court reasoned that the ADEA only protects individuals from adverse employment decisions, and it concluded that no adverseness existed here since the plaintiff "was offered a job" and he "was to be relocated at the cost of the defendant."[87] The court responded unsympathetically to the fact that the plaintiff strongly opposed being moved to a city, distant from family and friends, in which he had no desire to live:

> Although plaintiff may have concluded that such a relocation would adversely affect his personal life, the ADEA *only addresses those business decisions which adversely affect one's business opportunities.* Furthermore, while it may be that Harlingen is not the Garden of Eden, no objective evidence of its undesirability was presented at trial . . . except for . . . [the plaintiff's and his fellow potential transferee's] subjective and conclusory antipathy toward a reassignment there. For these reasons, we find that the plaintiff has failed to establish . . . a prima facie case[.][88]

Here, the plaintiff's pay and benefits would have remained the same had he accepted the transfer, and he had not shown that the transfer constituted a demotion or was—despite his resistance to moving—otherwise adverse.[89]

In deciding *Crady v Liberty National Bank*[90] the Court of Appeals for the Seventh Circuit likewise concluded that the undesired transfer of the plaintiff did not involve a "materially adverse" change in the terms and conditions of employment[91] and it accordingly affirmed the district court's grant of the defendant's motion for summary judgment. The court made the following observations:

---

[87] *Id* 526.

[88] *Id* 526-27 (emphasis added).

[89] *See also* Cherry v Thermon Electron Corp, 800 F Supp 508, 511 (ED Mich 1992).

[90] 993 F2d 132 (7th Cir 1993).

[91] *Id* 136 (quoting Spring v Sheboygan Area Sch Dist, 865 F2d 884, 886 (7th Cir 1989)).

> Crady would have maintained a management-level position at the same salary and benefits he was already receiving. Although his responsibilities changed, he does not show that they were less significant than the responsibilities he previously enjoyed . . . [at the branch of the bank from which he was to be transferred]. Assuming that Crady was an assistant vice president [AVP] . . . [at the branch from which he was transferred] and that the collections officer position [to which he was to be transferred] did not carry the AVP designation, this alone is not enough to constitute a materially adverse employment action.[92]

The analysis of the court deciding *Kauffman v Kent State University*[93] more or less paralleled the analysis of the *Haimovitz* and *Crady* courts. The plaintiff complained of having been forced into an intradepartmental transfer that involved less work to keep her busy and that further entailed diminished opportunities for promotion and for filling in for the office manager when that person was on leave. The changed position, however, involved no diminution either in pay or in benefits. The court rejected the argument that a discriminatory transfer had been effectuated:

> "[T]he ADEA is not intended to prevent employers from changing the job responsibilities of their . . . employees. Neither is the Act intended to give . . . employees the right to walk out and sue their employer because they dislike their changed job responsibilities."[94]

The court concluded that a transfer that involved neither a loss in pay nor benefits could not constitute a materially adverse action unless it amounted to a constructive discharge. The court further concluded that the plaintiff's problems with the position into which she was transferred, i.e., less work and less opportuni-

---

[92] *Id* 136.

[93] 815 F Supp 1077 (ND Ohio 1993).

[94] *Id* 1084 (quoting Spring v Sheboygan Area Sch Dist, 865 F2d 883, 885 (7th Cir 1989).

ties for advancement, did not constitute conditions that would have been objectively intolerable to a reasonable person—the standard applicable (in most jurisdictions) to determining whether the requisite elements of a constructive discharge have been established.[95] (In fact, the plaintiff had acknowledged in the course of being deposed that she enjoyed the new job.) Thus, the transfer did not constitute an adverse employment action.

The court deciding *Adams v West Publishing Co*[96] reasoned somewhat differently. While agreeing that the plaintiff had to establish that her interdepartmental transfer effectuated a materially adverse change in her employment, the court did not deem dispositive, for purposes of a motion for summary judgment, the fact that the plaintiff had suffered no diminution in salary as a result of her transfer. The record indicated that the plaintiff's "opportunities for raises, better benefits and promotions were reduced because of her transfer . . . [and] a transfer that results in a loss of promotional opportunities or benefits constitutes an adverse employment action."[97]

The court deciding *Medwid v Baker*[98] also took a more solicitous view of the the plaintiff's position, looking at facts similar to those in *Haimovitz* but arriving a different conclusion (although that conclusion was only articulated at a preliminary stage of the litigation). The plaintiff's claim arose out of an undesired transfer from New York to Los Angeles. Denying the defendant's motion for summary judgment, the court reasoned as follows: "[A] transfer to a distant region after twenty-four years of service with the same agency in the same locale on one month's notice could be a 'materially adverse' job action."[99]

---

95 See **ch 7**.

96 812 F Supp 925 (D Minn 1993).

97 *Id* 930.

98 752 F Supp 125 (SDNY 1990).

99 *Id* 138.

Refusals to Transfer or to Allow Transfers

Refusals to transfer can trigger liability.[100] Or at least a refusal to transfer may be probative of discrimination.[101]

Concededly, the case law is clear that an employer that reduces its work force for economic reasons has no obligation to transfer a discharged employee to another position.[102] However, "when there are *vacant* positions similar to the position from which an older employee is terminated, an employer cannot consider age in deciding which employee should be transferred to fill the vacancy."[103]

Prohibitions against downbidding, e.g., the movement downwards into a lower position by an employee who is displaced from his or her present position, have been particularly common in the airline industry. Because a Federal Aviation Administration (FAA) regulation for years has barred individuals over age 60 from working for commercial airlines as pilots or first officers,[104] older individuals employed in these positions regularly

---

100 *See, e.g.,* Curto v Sears, Roebuck & Co, 38 FEP Cas (BNA) 547 (ND Ill 1984); O'Donnell v Georgia Osteopathic Hosp, 574 F Supp 214 (ND Ga 1983), *affd in part & revd in part,* 748 F2d 1543 (11th Cir 1984); *see also* Tyler v Bethlehem Steel Corp, 958 F2d 1176 (2d Cir), *cert denied,* 113 S Ct 82 (1992).

101 *See* Bruno v Western Elec Co, 829 F2d 957, 963 (10th Cir 1987).

102 Rose v Wells Fargo & Co, 902 F2d 1417, 1422 (9th Cir 1990); Barnes v Gencorp, Inc, 56 FEP Cas (BNA) 1203, 1213 (6th Cir 1990); Simpson v Midland-Ross Corp, 823 F2d 937, 942 n6 (6th Cir 1987); Haynes v Alumax Recycling Group, Inc, 719 F Supp 707, 714 (ND Ill 1989), *affd without opinion,* 899 F2d 16 (7th Cir 1990); *see also* Just v River, II, Inc, 784 F Supp 1145, 1151 (D Del 1992).

103 Walther v Lone Star Gas Co, 952 F2d 119, 123 (5th Cir 1992).

104 14 CFR §121.383(c) (1993). This rule has withstood legal challenge on a number of occasions. *See* Starr v Federal Aviation Admin, 589 F2d 307 (7th Cir 1978); O'Donnell v Shaffer, 491 F2d 59 (DC Cir 1974); Air Line Pilots Assn Intl v Quesada, 276 F2d 892 (2d Cir 1960), *cert denied,* 366 US 962 (1961); *see also* Rombough v Federal Aviation Admin, 594 F2d 839 (2d Cir 1979). The 1981 Report of the National Institute on Aging Panel on the Experienced Pilots Study concluded that changes related to aging adversely affect capacities critical to pilot performance, and that there is no assessment procedure for determining accurately which individuals are less affected by this aging process. In Aman v Federal Aviation Admin, 856 F2d 946 (7th Cir 1988), the court held inadequate the FAA's findings and explanations with regard to the effort of a number of pilots to circumvent the so-called Age 60 Rule through a petition

have sought to downbid, or transfer, into second officer positions, which are not subject to the so-called Age 60 Rule. In *Criswell v Western Air Lines*[105] the court held that the defendant violated the ADEA by refusing to allow captains and first officers to avoid mandatory retirement at age 60 by downbidding. The court found that Western had allowed downbids under many circumstances by younger pilots, and concluded as follows:

> It is clear from the above evidence that Western's downbidding policy is not one of allowing downbids in only a few exceptional circumstances, but has sanctioned hundreds of downbids in a wide variety of circumstances, including downbids and downgrades for reasons of health and unilateral downbids not approved by ALPA [Air Line Pilots Association] or the Pilot Agreement. This downbid policy was administered in such a way as to have a disparate impact on pilots nearing their sixtieth birthday.[106]

Other challenges to restrictions on downbidding also have been successful.[107] In contrast, the plaintiffs failed in *Aldendifer v*

---

for exemptions from the rule. Accordingly, the court vacated the denial of the exemptions and remanded to the FAA for further proceedings. Ultimately, however, the pilots failed in their effort.

Courts construing the ADEA have not uniformly accepted the Age 60 Rule as justification for barring over-age-60 pilots in noncommercial pilot situations. *See, e.g.,* Tuohy v Ford Motor Co, 675 F2d 842 (6th Cir 1982).

There is one statute that specifically goes to the issue of employment discrimination by airlines. 49 USC §1552(d)(1) imposes on airlines an affirmative duty to hire employees suffering dislocation as a result of deregulation of the airline industry "regardless of age." *See* Robinson v American Airlines, Inc, 908 F2d 1020 (DC Cir 1990).

[105] 514 F Supp 384 (CD Cal 1981), *affd,* 709 F2d 544 (9th Cir 1983), *affd,* 472 US 400 (1985).

[106] *Id* 392.

[107] *See, e.g.,* Air Line Pilots Assn Intl v Trans World Airlines, Inc, 713 F2d 940 (2d Cir 1983), *affd in part & revd in part on other grounds sub nom* Trans World Airlines, Inc v Thurston, 469 US 111 (1985); *see also* Equal Employment Opportunity Commn v Northwest Airlines, Inc, 51 FEP Cas (BNA) 1317 (WD Wash 1989); Monroe v United Air Lines, Inc, 32 FEP Cas (BNA) 1139 (ND Ill 1981) (summary judgment denied where evidence indicated airline's policy against downbids had a disparate impact on older pilots).

Continental Air Lines, Inc,[108] which concerned a policy requiring all qualified second officers to be promoted to first officers and all qualified first officers to be promoted to captains whenever their seniority would entitle them to promotion. If an employee was unable to advance, he or she was to be discharged. The airline did not allow downbidding, and—unlike the situation in *Criswell*—this policy had been applied consistently, with only a one-time exception for five captains who had flown DC-9s and who were allowed to switch to Boeing 747s when the latter aircraft was first introduced. Pointing out that flight safety required the smooth, cooperative, and unquestioned flow of commands from captain to crew, the court reasoned that this flow would be disrupted if former captains were allowed to serve as second officers, thereby placing them in situations where they would have to obey orders from individuals who had previously been their subordinates. Accordingly, the court ruled that the rejection of the downbids did not constitute a violation of the ADEA.

An unsuccessful challenge to a refusal to transfer also was made in *Nicholson v Western Electric Co.*[109] In contrast, in *Jackson v Shell Oil Co*[110] the defendant was held liable after first refusing to transfer the plaintiff—a 43-year-old excellent employee—while agreeing to transfer a 30-year-old with an indifferent performance record, and then later discharging the 43-year-old. In another refusal-to-transfer case, the plaintiffs lost because they had failed, in the first instance, to apply for transfers.[111]

In *Stover v Thomas*[112] the plaintiff was discharged as the result of a reduction in force. He argued that his employer had earlier

---

108 18 Empl Prac Dec (CCH) ¶8874 (CD Cal 1978), *affd,* 650 F2d 171 (9th Cir 1981).

109 555 F Supp 3 (MDNC 1982), *affd without opinion,* 701 F2d 167 (4th Cir 1983).

110 702 F2d 197 (9th Cir 1983).

111 Glismann v AT&T Technologies, Inc, 827 F2d 262 (8th Cir 1987).

112 48 Empl Prac Dec (CCH) ¶38,435 (DDC 1988) (federal employee suit).

purposefully transferred him into a division that subsequently was abolished as a result of the force reduction, knowing that that division's demise was in the works and that, therefore, the transfer would ultimately lead to the discharge. As it turned out, however, the evidence did not support this theory.[113]

§4.07 —Practices Involving Promotions

Sometimes a claim of discrimination in violation of the Age Discrimination in Employment Act (ADEA)[114] will arise out of a refusal to promote the aggrieved individual.[115] As the court pointed out in *Kauffman v Kent State University,*[116] "it is quite clear that a failure to promote someone because of their [sic] age is considered an adverse employment action under the ADEA."[117] In *Kirschner v Office of the Comptroller of City of New York*[118] the court reversed a grant of judgment as a matter of law for the defendants. In so doing, the court reasoned that an initial discriminatory denial of promotion that resulted in the plaintiffs not gaining the requisite experience for the second move upwards could not be relied upon to legitimize the later refusal to promote into that second position.[119]

---

[113] For somewhat similar factual scenarios, see McCoy v WGN Continental Broadcasting Co, 957 F2d 368 (7th Cir 1992); Morton v Associated Dry Goods Corp, 792 F Supp 1136 (SD Ind 1992); *see also* Cherry v Thermo Electron Corp, 800 F Supp 508, 513 (ED Mich 1992).

[114] 29 USC §§621-634.

[115] *See, e.g.*, Lindsey v Prive Corp, 987 F2d 324 (5th Cir 1993).

[116] 815 F Supp 1077 (ND Ohio 1993).

[117] *Id* 1086.

[118] 973 F2d 88 (2d Cir 1992).

[119] *Id* 94; *see also* Hamilton v Komatsu Dresser Indus, Inc, 964 F2d 600 (7th Cir), *cert denied,* 113 S Ct 324 (1992).

§4.08 —Other Terms, Conditions, and Privileges of Employment

The Age Discrimination in Employment Act (ADEA)[120] prohibits discrimination with regard to "compensation, terms, conditions, or privileges of employment[.]"[121] Thus, employer decisions involving work assignments, benefits, and a host of other matters come within the Act's reach.

Focusing here specifically on privileges of employment, it should be noted that in *Trans World Airlines, Inc v Thurston*[122] the Court deemed the ability of retiring pilots to bump less senior flight engineers to be a privilege of employment, and in *Potenze v New York Shipping Association, Inc,*[123] a special type of pay that was provided even if the recipients did not work and which was the product of collective bargaining was designated as a privilege of employment.

Harrington v Aetna-Bearing Co[124] involved a contract geared to the contracting employee's age. The original contract provided for employment of the plaintiff until January 1, 1991. After the ADEA was amended in 1978 to protect individuals ages 65 through 69,[125] the contract was modified to extend its expiration date until Harrington "reaches age 70."[126] Some months before his 70th birthday, Harrington asked that the contract be extended, but Aetna in 1988 refused to assent to his request. By this time the ADEA had been amended so as to protect individuals 70 and over, thereby barring age-based terminations, i.e., mandatory retirement, at any age.[127] Even though the contract itself was not extended, Harrington was kept on after his

---

120 29 USC §§621-634.

121 §4(a)(1), 29 USC §623(a)(1).

122 469 US 111 (1985).

123 39 Empl Prac Dec (CCH) ¶35,974 (SDNY), *revd on other grounds,* 804 F2d 235 (2d Cir 1986), *cert denied,* 481 US 1029 (1987).

124 921 F2d 717 (7th Cir), *cert denied,* 111 S Ct 1685 (1991).

125 See **ch 3.**

126 921 F2d at 718.

127 See **ch 3.**

70th birthday, although since he no longer had a contract he now was merely an employee-at-will.

Six months after his 70th birthday, Harrington was terminated by the company that had purchased Aetna. Harrington filed suit, contending that the age-based contract termination violated the ADEA. The underlying injury was alleged to flow from the facts that under the contract Harrington could have been fired only for cause and that he had had a guaranteed salary, whereas once the contract ended he no longer enjoyed either of these employment rights. Harrington lost in the district court, and lost again on appeal. The court of appeals saw an unacceptable implication flowing from Harrington's claim:

> An employer does not by signing a term contract with an employee commit itself to employ him forever just because when the term is up he will be 40 or older.
>
> The only thing that makes Harrington's claim plausible is that age is mentioned in the contract. But we cannot see a practical difference between fixing a term of years and fixing the date at which the contract expires, and we see no magic in the fact that the date here was a birthday, and a seventieth one at that.[128]

In the court's view, all that was involved was a contract expiration following from the fact that "the contract had a definite term and the term had ended."[129] Still, the court perhaps felt some discomfort about its attempt to portray as entirely innocuous Harrington's age-generated move from the status of a contractually protected employee to an unprotected employee-at-will, since the court both (1) seemed to indirectly acknowledge that unlawful age discrimination perhaps had earlier occurred, and (2) stressed that the legal flaw in the plaintiff's efforts lay in his not having challenged that earlier discrimination:

---

[128] 921 F2d at 720.

[129] *Id.*

> The decision in 1988 not to extend the contract before it expired may have been motivated by age discrimination . . . , but if so the statute of limitations has probably run; in any event Harrington has not challenged that decision. All that he is challenging is an event—the expiration of his employment contract—that occurred not by virtue of a contemporaneous judgment by the company but as the consequence of decisions *that he does not challenge* taken in previous years—the decision to extend the contract to age 70 in the first place and the decision not to extend the contract in 1988, before it expired.[130]

The court reiterated the point about Harrington's having failed to timely challenge the real discrimination perpetrated here, and in so doing left room for the conclusion that a timely challenge to an age-geared contractual provision that results in a diminution of an employee's rights could succeed. The court did this with the following hypothetical:

> We hope that we shall not be misunderstood as suggesting that the withdrawal of a benefit cannot violate the age discrimination law. If an employer says to an employee that [“]when you reach the age of 70 I am cutting your salary in half[”], it is no defense that the new salary may be twice as high as the salary of an average worker. But Aetna made no judgment, on August 7, 1988, when Harrington's contract expired, that Harrington was too old to be entitled to the protections of the contract. Any such decision was made earlier and, to repeat the tiresome but essential refrain of the opinion, is not challenged.[131]

There was another factor relevant here, as well, in the court's view: Harrington was not injured as a result of the contract's expiring upon his attaining age 70.

---

130 *Id* (emphasis in original).

131 *Id* 721 (emphasis added).

> It is not discrimination to offer . . . a contract that lasts ten years, or until the year 2000, or until . . . [the plaintiff's] seventieth birthday, provided that at the end of the contractual period you do not fire the person, or subject him to other adverse personnel action, because of his age. The expiration of a contract is not an act of age discrimination.[132]

The court that decided *Equal Employment Opportunity Commission v School Board of Pinellas County, Florida*[133] addressed what was, in contrast to the situation in *Harrington,* a timely challenge to an age-geared contractual provision terminating the plaintiff's protected employment status. Here, the court held (and thereby disagreed with the *Harrington* court) that the termination of tenure at age 70 did violate the ADEA. The *Pinellas County* case was generated by the school board's compliance with a Florida statute terminating the continued employment of teachers upon their attaining age 70, but allowing an individual to continue as an at-will employee on an annual basis thereafter upon the recommendation of his or her school district's superintendent. The court condemned the change in contractual status of tenured teachers at age 70 as discriminatory:

> [S]uch a change is discriminatory . . . because it changes the terms, conditions and privileges of an instructor's employment. Upon turning seventy, an instructor is deprived of that privilege often most coveted by those in the education field—tenure. . . . The contract change from continuing to annual dramatically affects the conditions of an instructor's employment because he now, simply because of his age and not because of any alleged incompetency, has no expectation of employment for the next year, an expectation that he enjoyed only one year previously.[134]

---

[132] *Id.*

[133] 742 F Supp 622 (MD Fla 1990).

[134] *Id* 624. As to attacks on changes in status based on the impairment of contract prohibition set forth in the Constitution, US Const art I, §10, or on a common-law breach of contract theory, see **ch 10.**

(The court rejected the defendant's effort to rely on the Florida statute: "Case law demonstrates that reliance on a discriminatory statute is not considered a reasonable factor other than age.")[135]

In *Massie v Indiana Gas Co*[136] the plaintiff argued that different policies for absenteeism, whereby pregnant women were treated better than other medically disabled employees, constituted age discrimination. The plaintiff failed, however, to produce evidence in support of this theory. In *Holzman v Jaymar-Ruby, Inc,*[137] a discrimination claim arose out of a differing disciplinary standard imposed on the plaintiff, a 64-year-old, as contrasted with the treatment accorded his younger colleagues.[138]

An evaluation system may be conducted in a discriminatory manner.[139] And restricted access to training programs likewise may generate claims of discrimination.[140]

§4.09 —Demotions and Discharges

The large majority of cases arising under the Age Discrimination in Employment Act (ADEA)[141] concern discharges.[142]

---

[135] *Id.* The Florida statute terminating tenure status upon attainment of age 70 was also at issue in a case litigated under the state antidiscrimination statute. The Florida Supreme Court, without addressing the validity of tenure termination per se, ruled that the plaintiff had been illegally discriminated against because of age by virtue of his not being rehired following his age-based loss of tenure. Morrow v Duval County Sch Bd, 514 So 2d 1086 (Fla 1987), *disapproving* Duval County Sch Bd v Florida, Dept of Admin, 500 So 2d 158 (Fla Dist Ct App 1986).

[136] 752 F Supp 261 (SD Ind 1990).

[137] 916 F2d 1298 (7th Cir 1990).

[138] *Accord* Tennes v Massachusetts Dept of Revenue, 944 F2d 372, 379 (7th Cir 1991).

[139] *See* Colgan v Fisher Scientific Co, 935 F2d 1407 (3d Cir), *cert denied,* 112 S Ct 379 (1991) (an untimely claim of this nature was made); *see also* Fallis v Kerr-McGee Corp, 944 F2d 743, 745 (10th Cir 1991).

[140] *See* **§4.02.**

[141] 29 USC §§621-634.

[142] See **ch 2.**

Employee terminations—as well as demotions—may be focused on a specific individual or on an age-defined group of which the employee is a member. A discharge or demotion may result from a single act of discriminatory treatment inflicted by an employer on a particular individual[143] or from a pattern or practice of discrimination pursued over time and on numerous occasions.[144] Or a discharge or demotion may be the consequence of the application of an ostensibly neutral policy or practice that has a disproportionately adverse impact[145] on those who fit within the ADEA's protections, i.e., persons 40 and over.[146] A discharge may be effectuated by a specific notice of termination provided by the employer, or an employee may be subjected (or feel that he or she is being subjected) to conditions that leave him or her no alternative save resignation. This latter situation gives rise to a claim of constructive discharge.[147]

Because the cases involving discharges form the bulk of ADEA decisions and they therefore generate a variety of procedural and substantive issues, they are discussed throughout the succeeding chapters.

§4.10 —Retirement

Mandatory retirement on the basis of age generally is prohibited by the Age Discrimination in Employment Act (ADEA).[148] This does not mean such retirement is always impossible: it may be legitimized in a given instance by virtue of an employer's successful invocation of the bona fide occupational qualification defense;[149] by application of one of the specific exemptions in the Act;[150] or—in the instance of federal employees—by a

---

143 As to discriminatory treatment analysis, see **ch 7.**

144 As to pattern and practice suits, see **ch 7.**

145 As to discriminatory impact analysis, see **ch 7.**

146 See **ch 3.**

147 See **ch 7.**

148 29 USC §§621-634.

149 §4(f)(1), 29 USC §623(f)(1). See **ch 5.**

150 See **ch 3.**

specific federal statute authorizing retirement for certain employees.[151]

Forced retirement aside, an employer that wishes to secure the departure of employees may seek to induce their voluntary retirement. Indeed, it has become increasingly common for employers to offer incentives to employees to retire early.[152] The legitimacy of this tack, which was supported by the case law, was further confirmed in 1990 when the ADEA was amended by the Older Workers Benefit Protection Act (OWBPA)[153] so as to expressly approve, in §4(f)(2)(B)(ii),[154] voluntary retirement incentive plans. More specifically, an employer, employment agency, or labor organization may make decisions and take actions that otherwise would violate the ADEA, provided the entity is able to prove that in so acting or deciding it "observe[d]

---

151 *Id.*

152 *See generally* E.L. Meier, Early Retirement Incentive Programs: Trends and Implications (1986). The findings of a United States General Accounting Office (GAO) study of age-specific provisions in company incentive programs were published in 1990. The GAO, which focused on the practices of Fortune 100 companies between 1979 and 1988, "found very few instances where exit incentive programs used age-specific provisions for eligibility." United States Gen Accounting Office, Age Discrimination—Use of Age-Specific Provisions in Company Exit Incentive Programs 12 (Feb 1990). However, a majority of the programs offered age-specific enhanced benefits to workers who were eligible. "In these programs certain enhanced benefits were provided exclusively to younger eligible workers." *Id* 13. These entailed one or more of the following:

> *Liberalized early retirement benefits.* This provision lessens or eliminates the actuarial reduction factor usually applied to early retirement benefits. It does not apply to workers who have reached normal retirement age.
>
> *Age Credits.* This provision credits additional years to workers' actual ages to make them eligible for retirement benefits, or to liberalize early retirement benefits, or both. . . .
>
> *Retirement supplements until a specified age.* This provision gives workers below the specified age a benefit not available to older workers.
>
> *Health or life insurance coverage until a specified age.* This provision provides benefit coverage for workers below the age limit but not above it.

Id.

153 Pub L No 101-433, 104 Stat 978, *as amended by* Pub L No 101-521, 104 Stat 2287 (1990).

154 29 USC §623(f)(2)(B)(ii).

the terms of a bona fide employee benefit plan that is a voluntary early retirement incentive plan consistent with the relevant purposes of" the Act.[155]

A number of reasons may motivate employers to extend offers of early retirement: the desire to achieve enhanced efficiency;[156] an effort to save the costs associated with older, generally higher-paid employees;[157] the desire to encourage the departure of an unsatisfactory employee;[158] or a desire to create opportunities for advancement for younger workers.[159] Generally, the courts approved early retirement plans even prior to their being accorded the statutory seal of approval, so to speak, by the 1990 amendment to the ADEA. In *Sutton v Atlantic Richfield Co,*[160] for example, the court addressed the claim of a plaintiff who had generated considerable dissatisfaction on the part of his superiors. Because of their displeasure, they offered him an enhanced benefits retirement package, conditioned upon his actual retirement by a certain date. Sutton reluctantly acceded to the retirement, and then filed suit. The appellate court, in affirming the dismissal of the suit, wrote as follows:

> Sutton . . . argues that age necessarily played a factor in that Sutton's age prompted ARCO to offer the plan as a "carrot" with the "stick" being the negative evaluation of his future with the company. We do not agree. An employer's extension of extra-contractual benefits to an employee—whose termination the employer has, on neutral principles, decided to seek—is not violative of the ADEA.[161]

---

[155] *Id.* As to this provision, see **ch 5.**

[156] *See* Ackerman v Diamond Shamrock Corp, 670 F2d 66 (6th Cir 1982).

[157] *See* Coburn v Pan Am World Airways, Inc, 711 F2d 339, 344 (DC Cir), *cert denied,* 464 US 994 (1983).

[158] *See* Cannon v McWane, Inc, 40 FEP Cas (BNA) 1230 (D Utah 1986).

[159] *See* Patterson v Independent Sch Dist No 709, 742 F2d 465 (8th Cir 1984).

[160] 646 F2d 407 (9th Cir 1981).

[161] *Id* 410 n4; *accord* Gustovich v AT&T Communications, Inc, 972 F2d 845, 851 (7th Cir 1992); Sorosky v Burroughs Corp, 37 FEP Cas (BNA) 1510, 1519 (CD Cal 1985), *affd in part & revd in part on other grounds,* 826 F2d 794 (9th Cir 1987); *see also* de Loraine v MEBA Pension Trust, 499 F2d 49 (2d Cir), *cert*

Likewise, in *Gray v New England Telephone & Telegraph Co*[162] the court observed—more or less in passing—that voluntary early retirement plans did not violate the Act.

Prior to the 1990 amendment case law had established that an offer of an early retirement incentive or just an early retirement option would "not indicate a policy of age discrimination[.]"[163] In other words, "the mere offer of an early retirement program . . . [would] not support an inference of discrimination[.]"[164] And, as a general matter, the mere query to an employee by an employer as to his or her interest in early retirement would not constitute evidence of discrimination.[165] What is more, even an employer's urging an employee to retire would not necessarily in and of itself establish discriminatory intent[166] Certainly, these propositions are unimpeachable now that the ADEA expressly approves early retirement plans by virtue of the 1990 modification of the statute.

On the other hand, discussion of retirement plans, or[167] an offer of early retirement may, in a given factual context, be probative of discriminatory intent.[168] Indeed, an offer of an early

---

denied, 419 US 1009 (1974). The availability of early retirement benefits cannot, however, be "a basis or factor for a discharge decision." McCorstin v United States Steel Corp, 621 F2d 749, 755 (5th Cir 1980); *see also* Hannan v Chrysler Motors Corp, 443 F Supp 802 (ED Mich 1978).

162 792 F2d 251 (1st Cir 1986).

163 Wilson v Firestone Tire & Rubber Co, 932 F2d 510, 514 (6th Cir 1991); *accord* D'Aquino v Citicorp/Diner's Club, Inc, 755 F Supp 218, 222-23 (ND Ill 1991).

164 Colgan v Fisher Scientific Co, 935 F2d 1407, 1422 (3d Cir), *cert denied,* 112 S Ct 379 (1991); *accord* Gray v York Newspapers, Inc, 957 F2d 1070, 1081 (3d Cir 1992); Lasley v Veterans Admin, 789 F Supp 1468, 1475 (ED Mo 1992).

165 *See* Wingfield v United Technologies Corp, 678 F Supp 973, 981 (D Conn 1988).

166 *See* Young v General Foods Corp, 840 F2d 825, 831 (11th Cir 1988), *cert denied,* 488 US 1004 (1989).

167 Sever v Department of Commerce, 818 F Supp 382, 387 (DDC 1993). (federal employee suit)

168 *See* Bruno v Western Elec Co, 829 F2d 957 (10th Cir 1987); Walker v Mountain States Tel & Tel Co, 686 F Supp 269 (D Colo 1988); *cf* Harris v Mallinckrodt, Inc, 886 F2d 170, 172 (8th Cir 1989) (trial court should have admitted evidence regarding plaintiff having been urged to take early retire-

retirement option may, in a given factual context, amount to a constructive discharge.[169]

A number of legal problems can arise. Challenges to plans may be made by people who feel they have been wrongfully excluded from the retirement option, or whose participation in a plan is viewed as being less advantageous than that afforded other employees. These issues typically are addressed—although not always properly so—in the context of the bona fide employee benefit plan exception set forth in §4(f)(2)[170] of the Act.[171] Another common question is whether a given employee's retirement was voluntary. This issue also intersects with the exception.[172]

Typically, in accepting an early retirement incentive, an employee will be required to execute a release, or waiver, of present and future, actual and possible, claims of discrimination. A number of legal issues are raised by such releases, which also were addressed by the OWBPA, which added §7(f)[173] to the ADEA.[174]

§4.11 Prohibited Labor Organization Practices

Section 4(c)[175] of the Age Discrimination in Employment Act (ADEA)[176] imposes several proscriptions on labor organizations; it is unlawful under the Act to do any of the following:

---

ment, but error was not reversible here, given "overwhelming evidence that . . . [defendant] had sufficient nondiscriminatory reasons for" discharging plaintiff).

[169] As to constructive discharges, see **ch 7.**

[170] 29 USC §623(f)(2). *See generally* McMorrow, *Retirement and Worker Choice: Incentives to Retire and the Age Discrimination in Employment Act,* 29 BC L Rev 347 (1988).

[171] See **ch 5.**

[172] *Id.*

[173] 29 USC §626(f).

[174] See **ch 5.**

[175] 29 USC §623(c).

[176] *Id* §§621-634.

> (1) . . . exclude or . . . expel from membership, or otherwise . . . discriminate against, any individual because of his age;
>
> (2) . . . limit, segregate, or classify . . . membership, or . . . classify or fail or refuse to refer for employment any individual, in any way which would deprive or tend to deprive any individual of employment opportunities, or would limit such employment opportunities or otherwise adversely affect his status as an employee or an applicant for employment, because of such individual's age;
>
> (3) . . . cause or attempt to cause an employer to discriminate against an individual in violation of . . . [the ADEA].[177]

In *Equal Employment Opportunity Commission v Local 350, Plumbers & Pipefitters*[178] the Equal Employment Opportunity Commission (EEOC) successfully challenged a union policy providing that members who were retired and receiving a pension could not use the hiring hall to obtain work unless they first gave up their retirement benefits. The Court of Appeals for the Ninth Circuit reasoned that the union policy violated §4(c)(2)[179] because the union refused to "refer certain employees for work on the basis of a factor [, i.e., the status of being retired,] very closely related to age."[180]

There are a few other rulings involving prohibited practices, but they reveal no common theme. A discriminatory policy is not immune from challenge by virtue of its incorporation in a collective bargaining agreement.[181] Nor may a "collective bargaining agreement . . . provide that grievances will proceed to arbitration only if the employee refrains from participating in

---

[177] *Id* §623(c).

[178] 982 F2d 1305 (9th Cir 1992), *revg* 741 F Supp 199 (D Nev 1990).

[179] 29 USC §623(c)(2).

[180] 982 F2d at 1310.

[181] *See, e.g.*, Levine v Fairleigh Dickinson Univ, 646 F2d 825, 832 (3d Cir 1981); Quinn v New York State Elec & Gas Corp, 569 F Supp 655, 658 (NDNY 1983); Equal Employment Opportunity Commn v Air Line Pilots Assn, 489 F Supp 1003 (D Minn 1980), *revd on other grounds*, 661 F2d 90 (8th Cir 1981).

protected activity under the ADEA."[182] A union may not waive an individual's rights under the ADEA.[183] In *Bartman v Allis-Chalmers Corp*,[184] the Court of Appeals for the Seventh Circuit stated: "[W]e may assume (without deciding) that plaintiffs could state an ADEA claim against . . . [a union] based on failure to bargain with sufficient vigor [with the consequence being that union members are subjected to discriminatory acts by the employer]."[185] The plaintiffs, however, failed to establish that the union defendant indeed had failed to adequately attempt to protect their interests. In a related vein, in *Goodman v Lukens Steel Co*[186] the Supreme Court addressed the question of union liability under Title VII of the Civil Rights Act of 1964,[187] the judicial interpretations of which often are looked to by ADEA courts.[188] The Court ruled as follows:

> [Title VII does] not permit a union to refuse to file any and all grievances presented by a black person on the ground that the employer looks with disfavor on and resents such grievances. It is no less violative of these laws for a union to pursue a policy of rejecting disparate-treatment grievances presented by blacks solely because the claims assert racial bias and would be very troublesome to process.[189]

---

[182] Equal Employment Opportunity Commn v Board of Governors of State Colleges & Univs, 957 F2d 424 (7th Cir), *cert denied*, 113 S Ct 299 (1992). See §§4.15-.18 regarding retaliation.

[183] Equal Employment Opportunity Commn v Board of Governors of State Colleges & Univs, 957 F2d 424, 431 (7th Cir), *cert denied*, 113 S Ct 299 (1992); Bartman v Allis-Chalmers Corp, 799 F2d 311, 315 (7th Cir 1986), *cert denied*, 479 US 1092 (1987); Equal Employment Opportunity Commn v County of Calumet, 686 F2d 1249, 1256 (7th Cir 1982); Westfall v City of Cohoes, 683 F Supp 888, 897 n14 (NDNY 1988); Potenze v New York Shipping Assn, Inc, 39 Empl Prac Dec (CCH) ¶35,974, (SDNY), at p 41,623, *revd on other grounds*, 804 F2d 235 (2d Cir 1986), *cert denied*, 481 US 1029 (1987).

[184] 799 F2d 311 (7th Cir 1986), *cert denied*, 479 US 1092 (1987).

[185] *Id* 315.

[186] 482 US 656 (1987).

[187] 42 USC §§2000e through 2000e-17.

[188] See **ch 2.**

[189] 482 US at 669.

There is no reason to think that *Goodman* should not apply, by way of analogy, to the ADEA and a union's duty to pursue the grievances of older members.

The court deciding *Hart v United Steelworkers of America*[190] ruled that age cannot be used as a basis for restricting eligibility for election as union officials because running for union office is an "employment opportunity."[191] And, of course, when a union acts as an employer, it falls within the proscriptions of the Act that concern the employee-employer relationship.

§4.12 Prohibited Employment Agency Practices

Section 4(b)[192] of the Age Discrimination in Employment Act (ADEA)[193] imposes specific prohibitions on employment agencies with regard to discriminating in job referrals and in classifying individuals, as well as a general prohibition as to otherwise discriminating against individuals on the basis of age. *Employment*

---

[190] 350 F Supp 294 (WD Pa 1972), *vacated as moot,* 482 F2d 282 (3d Cir 1973).

[191] *Id* 296. The court also ruled that a provision in the union's constitution making members ineligible for nomination if they turned 65 before the end of the nominating period did not discriminate against members within the protected age group. (This case was decided before adoption of the 1986 amendment extending the protection of the ADEA to almost all persons age 40 and over without any age cap or ceiling, see **ch 3,** and thus this portion of the ruling would no longer be valid, even if the decision had not been vacated on mootness grounds.)

Dole v American Fedn of State, County & Mun Employees, AFL-CIO, 715 F Supp 1119 (DDC 1989), also involved a union's age restriction on eligibility for election to union office. Rather than the ADEA being looked to as the basis for the cause of action, it was §401(e) of the Labor-Management Reporting and Disclosure Act (LMRDA), 29 USC §481(e), on which the challenge to the age-65 limitation was grounded. Section 401(e) allows reasonable qualifications to be set for union offices; however, an implementing regulation—29 CFR §452.46 (1993)—provides that a labor organization may not "establish a compulsory retirement age or comparable age restriction on candidacy since this would be inconsistent with the" ADEA. The court held that the union restriction was violative of the LMRDA "due to the inadequate fit between [the] goal of preventing entrenched, corrupt leadership and excluding those over 65 from running for office." 715 F Supp at 1121.

[192] 29 USC §623(b).

[193] *Id* §§621-634.

agency is defined in §11(c)[194] as a "person regularly undertaking with or without compensation to procure *employees* for an employer."[195] Thus, an entity that interacts with independent contractors, one of whom complains of discrimination at the hands of that agency, cannot be liable under the ADEA inasmuch as the alleged wrongdoing does not involve the procuring of an employee.[196]

The Equal Employment Opportunity Commission (EEOC) takes the position that if an employment agency regularly procures employees for at least one entity meeting the statutory definition of *employer,* i.e., an entity having 20 or more employees for each working day in each of 20 or more calendar weeks of the current or preceding calendar year,[197] then all of the activities of the employment agency—including those on behalf of entities not qualifying as employers under the ADEA's particular definition of the term—will come within the reach of the ADEA.[198] There is one district court ruling in accord with this view.[199]

Given the proscriptions set forth in §4(b), an employment agency may not accept an age specification in an employer's job order.[200] The Act is not violated, however, by the maintenance by an agency of internal records of the ages of individual job

---

[194] *Id* §630(c).

[195] Emphasis added.

[196] Ehret v Louisiana, 58 FEP Cas (BNA) 658, 663 (ED La 1992). As to who are protected employees, see generally **ch 3.**

[197] See **ch 3.**

[198] 29 CFR §1625.3(a) (1993).

[199] Brennan v Aldert Root, 16 FEP Cas (BNA) 1643, 1644 (EDNC 1974).

[200] *See, e.g.,* Brennan v Hughes Personnel, Inc, 8 Empl Prac Dec (CCH) ¶9571 (WD Ky), *amended,* 8 Empl Prac Dec (CCH) ¶9679 (WD Ky 1974). According to an opinion letter issued by the Department of Labor when it was responsible for enforcing the ADEA, an agency may not specify, in the lists of personnel that it sends to employers, the ages of individuals. W&H Opinion Letter WH-139 (June 29, 1971). *But see* W&H Opinion Letter WH-116 (Jan 19, 1971) (special exemption granted to nonprofit temporary help service agency working exclusively with persons older than 55). As of July 1, 1979, the EEOC assumed responsibility for enforcement of the Act. See **ch 2.** While the opinion letters are relics of history, the positions they articulate retain, it would seem, continuing merit.

seekers.[201] Most employment agency cases (of which there are few in number) involve the use of discriminatory advertisements, discussed in the next section.

§4.13 Discriminatory Advertising by Covered Entities

Section 4(e)[202] of the Age Discrimination in Employment Act (ADEA)[203] prohibits employers, employment agencies, and labor organizations from indicating any "preference, limitation, specification, or discrimination, based on age" when advertising job opportunities.[204] The Equal Employment Opportunity Commission (EEOC), the agency responsible for enforcing the ADEA, takes the position that job notices using the phrases " 'age 40 to 50,' 'age over 65,' 'retired person,' or 'supplement your pension' " are prohibited because they discriminate against other individuals within the protected age group.[205] The EEOC is not averse, however, to age-neutral advertising aimed at members of the protected class, i.e., persons over age 39. This is confirmed by a policy guide issued in 1989 by the commission in which the EEOC approvingly hypothesized a help-wanted advertisement stating as follows:

---

201 *See* Brennan v Hughes Personnel, Inc, 8 Empl Prac Dec (CCH) ¶9571 (WD Ky), *amended,* 8 Empl Prac Dec (CCH) ¶9679 (WD Ky 1974).

202 29 USC §623(e).

203 *Id* §§621-634.

204 Early on, the Department of Labor (DOL)—the original ADEA enforcement agency—asserted that age limits could not be used in job advertisements even if most older individuals would not in any event qualify for the positions advertised. W&H Opinion Letter (July 26, 1968). While the Equal Employment Opportunity Commission took over enforcement responsibility for the Act in 1979, see ch 2, this interpretation of the ADEA advertising provision still seems the correct one. The Labor Department also asserted that advertisements specifying a preference for persons ages 40 and over were lawful because they only discriminated against individuals outside the protected group. W&H Opinion Letter (Jan 7, 1969). This position also continues to be correct.

205 29 CFR §1625.4(a) (1993). Such interpretations do not have the force of law, but they do ordinarily evoke considerable judicial deference. See **ch 2.**

> WANTED: Individuals of all ages. Day and evening hours available. Full and part-time positions. All inquiries welcomed. Excellent secondary source of income for retirees.[206]

With regard to this language, the EEOC stated: "[T]he Commission would be unlikely to find a violation in situations where an age-neutral advertisement encourages individuals within the protected age group to actively seek the position(s) available."[207]

The EEOC further interprets the ADEA's advertising provision as prohibiting the use of such terms as " 'age 25 to 35,' 'young,' 'college student,' 'recent college graduate,' 'boy,' 'girl,' " and other similar terms because these tend to deter the employment of older individuals.[208] This interpretation, which was preceded by a like issuance[209] articulated by the Department of Labor (DOL) when it was responsible for enforcing the Act,[210] has met with mixed judicial reaction. Several early rulings expressed agreement with the DOL (and by inference the later EEOC) position.[211] However, the district

---

206 EEOC Policy Guide N-915.043: Job Advertising and Pre-Employment Inquiries Under the Age Discrimination in Employment Act (ADEA) 6 (July 1989). (This policy guide is reproduced in the Appendix at the end of the last volume. Such policy guides may elicit some degree of judicial deference, but they clearly are not legally binding. See **ch 2.**

207 EEOC Policy Guide, *supra* note 206, at 5-6.

208 29 CFR §1625.4(a) (1993). The EEOC also has investigated whether advertisements by law firms seeking to hire associates may be discriminatory insofar as the ads make reference to maximum years of experience, i.e., three years, for example, or to the years of potential applicants' graduation. Both of these factors, it is suggested, can correlate with age: an older individual is likely to have more years of experience and to have graduated longer ago than a younger individual. The EEOC has taken no official position on such ads, however. *See Firms React to Charges of Age Bias in Ads,* Natl Law J, Mar 7, 1994, at 22.

209 29 CFR §860.92(b) (1986) (effectively rescinded, 46 Fed Reg 47724 (Sept 29, 1981), and ordered removed from the CFR, 52 Fed Reg 23812 (June 25, 1987)).

210 See **ch 2** as to DOL enforcement.

211 *See, e.g.,* Brennan v Hughes Personnel, Inc, 8 Empl Prac Dec (CCH) ¶9571 (WD Ky), *amended,* 8 Empl Prac Dec (CCH) ¶9679 (WD Ky 1974); Brennan v C/M Mobile, Inc, 8 Empl Prac Dec (CCH) ¶9532 (SD Ala 1974); Hodgson v Western Textile Co, 7 Empl Prac Dec (CCH) ¶9383 (ND Ill 1974); Hodgson v

court that decided *Brennan v Paragon Employment Agency*[212] deemed the DOL's interpretation "wholly lacking in reasonableness"[213] and held that the use of the terms *college students, girls, boys,* and *June graduates* was a lawful means of encouraging young persons to work.[214]

In deciding *Hodgson v Approved Personnel Service, Inc,*[215] the Court of Appeals for the Fourth Circuit refused to adopt a per se rule concerning the illegality of such terms as *recent grads, boys, girls,* and *returning veterans.* Rather, the court held that such terms had to be examined in context.[216] Terms, such as *junior executive,* that described the nature and scope of job duties and responsibilities were deemed lawful by the court.[217] The court also approved general appeals by an employment agency to *recent graduates, returning veterans,* and *laid-off auto workers* to use the agency's services in light of the facts that such individuals were frequently inexperienced in job hunting, and that such information would serve to acquaint these inexperienced individuals with the agency's services.[218] However, the court did conclude that terms having some correlation with age, when utilized in connection with specific jobs, constituted unlawful deterrents for older job seekers.[219] In the earlier-noted policy guide issued by the EEOC in 1989, the Commission expressly disagreed with this exception erected in *Hodgson* legitimizing the use of age-correlated terms to acquaint inexperienced job hunters with the agency's services, and the agency went on to state its enforcement policy vis-a-vis such advertising:

Career Counsellors Intl, Inc, 5 FEP Cas (BNA) 129 (ND Ill 1972) (relying on expert testimony that use of term *girl* showed a preference for younger females).

212 356 F Supp 286 (SDNY 1973), *affd without opinion,* 489 F2d 752 (2d Cir 1974).

213 *Id* 289.

214 *Id* 288-89.

215 529 F2d 760 (4th Cir 1975).

216 *Id* 765.

217 *Id* 765-66.

218 *Id* 765.

219 *Id.*

> As a general enforcement principle, the Commission will closely scrutinize all ads that use words and phrases that would deter older persons from applying, including those used by employment agencies to inform the public of their services. An employment agency could as easily advertise generally for persons looking for employment by including in the advertisement language making it clear that both young and older applicants are wanted.[220]

The Department of Labor took the position that it was permissible to specify educational requirements in a job notice;[221] the EEOC has not spoken to this issue.

The EEOC has addressed the matter of requesting job applicants to state their ages, and it has taken the position that such requests are not unlawful.[222] Application forms that call for information as to age will be closely scrutinized by the agency, however.[223] In addition, such application forms should be accompanied, according to the agency, by assurances against age discrimination.[224]

Because these agency interpretations involve government regulation of speech, there is reason for taking account of the fact that the Supreme Court has established that commercial speech is protected under the First Amendment to a significant extent.[225] However, speech that is related to unlawful activity is not protected.[226] In this latter regard, *Pittsburgh Press Co v Pitts-*

---

[220] EEOC Policy Guide N-915.043, *supra* note 206, at 6-7.

[221] 29 CFR §860.92(c) (1986) (effectively rescinded, 46 Fed Reg 47724 (Sept 29, 1981), and ordered removed from the CFR, 52 Fed Reg 23812 (June 25, 1987)).

[222] 29 CFR §1625.4(b) (1993).

[223] *Id.*

[224] *Id.* While, as earlier noted in note 205, such agency interpretations do not have binding legal force, they do ordinarily evoke considerable judicial deference. See **ch 2.**

[225] Virginia State Bd of Pharmacy v Virginia Citizens Consumer Council, Inc, 425 US 748 (1976).

[226] Central Hudson Gas Co v Public Serv Commn, 447 US 557, 564 (1980).

burgh Commission on Human Rights[227] is particularly apposite. Decided prior to the Court's establishing commercial speech as protected communication under the First Amendment, *Pittsburgh Press* involved a municipal ban on advertisements that classified on the basis of sex. The Court upheld the ban, reasoning that the underlying action that the advertisements would abet—sex discrimination—would be unlawful. Despite the enhanced constitutional status of commercial speech that was subsequently articulated by the Court, *Pittsburgh Press* should still apply in assessing whether any given EEOC restriction as to advertising, whether by way of regulation, interpretation, or policy statement,[228] transgresses the First Amendment.[229]

§4.14 Preferences for Older Individuals by Covered Entities

The Age Discrimination in Employment Act (ADEA)[230] was enacted in response to the perceived employment problems of older workers, particularly their difficulties in competing with younger individuals for jobs.[231] Not surprisingly, the great majority of cases arising under the ADEA concern claims by older plaintiffs of victimization due to their being too old. Still, despite the primary thrust of the ADEA and of the case law, it can happen that an individual will claim that he or she was discriminated against because older—not younger—workers were favored over him or her.

While actual holdings as to ultimate liability are rare, several courts have ruled with regard to the establishment of a prima facie violation (which, of course, is not equivalent to establishing

---

[227] 413 US 376 (1973).

[228] As to the various ways in which the EEOC expresses its views as to the proper interpretation of the statute, see **ch 2**.

[229] A precise parsing of each element of the present restrictions to determine each one's validity for First Amendment purposes is beyond the scope of this chapter.

[230] 29 USC §§621-634.

[231] See **ch 2**.

the ultimate fact of a violation of the Act), that, the fact that a discharged plaintiff's replacement was older than him or her need not be fatal to his or her case.[232] An interpretive guideline issued by the ADEA's enforcement agency, the Equal Employment Opportunity Commission (EEOC), echoes this view at least in part: the agency condemns preferences in terms of hiring, discharge decisions, etc. for older workers over younger workers who also fit within the ADEA-protected class, i.e., individuals age 40 and over.[233]

Most courts, however, have taken the position that not even a prima facie violation (not to mention an ultimate finding of liability) can be established under the ADEA unless the discharged individual can establish that a younger person replaced him or her.[234] A particularly emphatic, and even broader-ranging rejection of the proposition that younger individuals can complain of adverse treatment by virtue of older individuals being preferred in some way—not only in a discharge situation, but in any context—was articulated by the Court of Appeals for the Seventh Circuit in *Hamilton v Caterpillar, Inc.*[235] The court asserted that "[t]he ADEA does not provide a remedy for reverse age discrimination."[236] All that was actually at issue in *Hamilton* was a claim that an early retirement incentive plan was discriminatory because it excluded younger employees, i.e., those under age 50, from eligibility for early retirement benefits. The court went beyond the facts, however, in offering the observation, in dictum, that younger individuals could not as a general matter

---

[232] *See, e.g.*, Haskell v Kaman Corp, 743 F2d 113, 122 (2d Cir 1984); Douglas v Anderson, 656 F2d 528, 533 (9th Cir 1981); Loeb v Textron, Inc, 600 F2d 1003 (1st Cir 1979); Obitko v Ohio Barge Line, Inc, 628 F Supp 62 (WD Pa 1986); Smith v World Book-Childcraft Intl, Inc, 502 F Supp 96 (ND Ill 1980). See generally **ch 7.**

[233] 29 CFR §1625.2(a) (1993). Such interpretations are not legally binding, but they do evoke considerable judicial deference. See **ch 2.**

[234] See **ch 7.**

[235] 966 F2d 1226 (7th Cir 1992).

[236] *Id* 1228.

maintain reverse discrimination suits arising out of any type of preference, be it in terms of eligibility for a benefit plan or in terms of an older worker being hired instead of a younger one.[237]

Benefit Plans

As *Hamilton* illustrates, a common requirement of benefit plans is that some minimum age must be attained as a condition precedent for participation in a given program, with the consequence being that younger employees who are under that age, i.e., who are too young, are foreclosed from benefits available to older workers. Other courts have lined up with the *Hamilton* court in rejecting challenges by younger workers to such exclusions.[238] And the EEOC has issued an interpretive guideline that also supports to some extent the legality of enhanced benefits for older individuals.

> The extension of additional benefits, such as increased severance pay, to older employees within the protected age bracket may be lawful if an employer has a reasonable basis to conclude that those benefits will counteract problems related to age discrimination.[239]

---

[237] There are no reported cases dealing either with court-imposed or voluntary affirmative action efforts on behalf of older workers. The literature is almost as sparse: there is one article—Note, *Preferential Hiring Policies for Older Workers Under the Age Discrimination in Employment Act,* 56 S Cal L Rev 825 (1983).

[238] *See* Mason v Lister, 562 F2d 343 (5th Cir 1977); Wehrly v American Motors Sales Corp, 678 F Supp 1366 (ND Ind 1988); *see also* Brown v M&M/Mars, 883 F2d 505, 511 n3 (7th Cir 1989) ("[I]t is not age discrimination to offer a voluntary separation plan that is more attractive to older workers than younger workers, even if done to induce older workers to leave, unless the plan is not truly voluntary"); Schuler v Polaroid Corp, 848 F2d 276, 278 (1st Cir 1988) (the ADEA "does not forbid treating older persons *more* generously than others" (emphasis in original)); Karlen v City Colleges, 837 F2d 314, 318 (7th Cir), *cert denied,* 486 US 1044 (1988) ("an early retirement plan that treats you better the older you are is not suspect under the [ADEA]"); Cronin v ITT Corp, 737 F Supp 224, 229 n6 (SDNY), *affd without opinion,* 916 F2d 709 (2d Cir 1990).

[239] 29 CFR §1625.2(b) (1993). The EEOC also issued an opinion letter in 1985 asserting that an amendment to a benefit plan that erected a provision giving preference to older workers comported with the ADEA. EEOC OL-6 (July 2, 1985). In so doing, the agency cited the foregoing interpretation. (In

In a policy guide issued in June 1988, the EEOC set forth general criteria that in its view would indicate that the extension of additional benefits to an older individual is not violative of the ADEA.[240] Legitimate additional benefits are those that do the following:

> 1) Promote the employment of older persons, e.g., encourage older employees to continue employment; and/or
>
> 2) Reasonably counteract problems related to age discrimination, e.g., increased severance pay because the employer reasonably concluded that, due to myths about aging, persons 60 and older would encounter greater difficulty finding employment; and/or
>
> 3) Are offered in good faith to meet problems arising from the impact of age on employment.[241]

The EEOC went on to assert in the same policy guide that the burden of demonstrating that the favorable treatment of older workers is legal is on the employer, whether its defense is based on good-faith reliance on an administrative ruling,[242] or is asserted as a general exception to the ADEA.[243]

Rationale for Distinguishing Between Legal and Wrongful Preferences

The earlier quoted EEOC interpretive guideline embodies a distinction whereby preferences for older workers that take the

---

addition, the EEOC in the same opinion letter concluded that the particular preference at issue could be justified under the then-extant employee benefit plan defense set forth in §4(f)(2), 29 USC §623(f)(2), of the Act. See generally **ch 5.**) (This letter is reproduced at the end of last volume as a part of **app L.**)

[240] EEOC Policy Guide No N-915.029: Cases Involving the Extension of Additional Benefits to Older Workers (June 30, 1988). (This policy guide is reproduced in the Appendix at the end of the last volume.)

[241] *Id* 5.

[242] See **ch 5.**

[243] Policy Statement Guide, *supra* note 240, at 5.

form of enhanced benefits are approved, while other types of preferences for older individuals are condemned. The case law is only partially in accord, however. Most courts require that for a violation of the ADEA to be established, the plaintiff must prove that his or replacement (in a discharge situation) or the person who actually secured the sought-after job (in a denial-of-hire situation) was younger.[244] Thereby, the courts, in contrast to the EEOC, have implicitly approved—by immunizing from successful attack—situations where an older individual is preferred over a younger one. On the other hand, the case law, as already noted, does support the EEOC's position as to enhanced benefits for older individuals not being violative of the Act (although actually the Agency's stance is somewhat narrower than that set forth in the case law, inasmuch as the EEOC only approves enhanced benefits if they are aimed at counteracting the effects of discrimination.)[245]

There is no explanation in the history of the EEOC guideline for the distinction it makes. The provision urging a ban on adverse treatment in personnel actions (as opposed to distinctions in terms of benefit plan participation) as between two individuals who both fit within the ADEA's protected class, i.e., persons over age 39, descends from the original interpretation published by the initial ADEA enforcement agency—the Department of Labor (DOL).[246] However, the DOL issuance did not contain any language regarding the legitimacy of additional benefits for older workers. The language expressing approval of the extension of such benefits only first appeared in final form (in conjunction with the provision dealing with hiring and other personnel actions) in 1981, when the EEOC—which had assumed responsibility for enforcement of the ADEA on July 1,

---

244 See **ch 7**.

245 See also **ch 5**.

246 This was codified at 29 CFR §860.91 (1986) (effectively rescinded, 46 Fed Reg 47724 (Sept 29, 1981), and ordered removed from the CFR, 52 Fed Reg 23812 (June 25, 1987)).

1979[247]—published its final interpretations. In the supporting material explaining these interpretations, the EEOC relied upon what it asserted to be a proposition already established in opinion letters issued by the DOL's Wage-Hour Administrator:

> The basis for both opinion letters was that an employer can take measures to counteract discrimination which is more prevalent against older members of the protected group. The former letter . . . [, issued in 1976], recognized that an older employee (55 and over) may be a more frequent target of age discrimination and the latter opinion . . . [, issued in 1978], recognized that same principle in the context of job relocation. In both instances, the opinions were based on tacit recognition of the fact that age discrimination is frequently more prevalent and more severe against older workers in the protected age group.[248]

While this explanation justifies preferences taking the form of enhanced benefits, it does not explain the rejection of preferences for older workers over younger, but still ADEA-protected, individuals in the context of hiring, etc. After all, a 60-year-old seeking employment is more likely to confront ageist animus than a 42-year-old is and so, using the same rationale that is set forth in the above-quoted language, one could justify giving preference to older job applicants.

There is, however, a logic that can explain (although not necessarily justify) the distinction. Concededly, this logic is not articulated in the EEOC explanatory material. (Conversely, it also is not rejected.) This explanation goes as follows:

> When an older employee receives an added benefit from an employer, the younger employee, it can be argued, is not harmed: he or she is no worse off than he or she otherwise would have been, since the resource—the funds for

---

[247] See **ch 2.**

[248] EEOC, Final Interpretations: Age Discrimination in Employment Act, 46 Fed Reg 47724 (1981).

> the benefit—does not come out of his or her pocket, but rather is provided by the employer. In contrast, if an employer gives preference in hiring to an older worker over a younger one (albeit one who still falls within the class protected by the ADEA), the younger applicant does suffer a direct harm—denial of the job for which she applied. Likewise, a younger employee experiences direct and immediate injury when he or she is discharged so that an older employee may be retained. There is, then, a difference between a preference whose burden is borne by a third party, i.e., the employer, which is outside the universe of those protected by the ADEA from discrimination, and a preference that imposes the burden on someone who does fit within the Act's ambit, i.e., an employee or job applicant age forty or older.[249]

Whatever the logical persuasiveness of this explanation, the fact is—as noted earlier—that only a few courts have been willing to envision a younger plaintiff prevailing where he or she has complained that an older individual fared better, whether in terms of benefits or any other kind of employment-related perquisite or decision.

Preferences as Being Required

While preferences may be extended to older individuals, at least so long as they do not violate the ADEA, it is clear that the Act does not require that older workers be accorded preferential treatment.[250] Certainly, for example, the ADEA does not require that younger employees be fired to make room for older

---

[249] Eglit, *Health Care Allocation for the Elderly: Age Discrimination by Another Name?*, 26 Hous L Rev 813, 864 (1989).

[250] *See, e.g.*, Equal Employment Opportunity Commn v Sperry Corp, 852 F2d 503, 509 (10th Cir 1989); Tice v Lampert Yards, Inc, 761 F2d 1210, 1217 (7th Cir 1985); Parcinski v Outlet Co, 673 F2d 34, 37 (2d Cir 1982), *cert denied*, 459 US 1103 (1983); Williams v General Motors Corp, 656 F2d 120, 129 (5th Cir 1981), *cert denied*, 455 US 943 (1982); Crews v Memorex Corp, 677 F Supp 63 (D Mass 1987); *see also* Just v James River, II, Inc, 784 F Supp 1145 (D Del 1992).

job applicants,[251] or that younger employees be discharged so that older workers caught up in a reduction in force may be retained.[252] Nor does the ADEA impose an obligation on an employer to hire "older and more experienced . . . [workers] at a higher wage than other young or old applicants."[253] The Act does not even require an employer to seek "to place in another position an employee whose age brings him or her under the ADEA's protective shield when that employee is being terminated for nondiscriminatory reasons.[254]

In sum, older employees are not—simply because they are older—entitled as a matter of law to preferences.[255] Thus, "in the absence of a preponderance of evidence that age is a determinative factor, an employer who is forced to choose between equally qualified candidates cannot be liable for age discrimination [just because it chooses the younger candidate]."[256]

§4.15 Retaliation by Covered Entities

Section 4(d)[257] of the Age Discrimination in Employment Act (ADEA)[258] prohibits retaliation by employers, employment agencies, and labor organizations:

---

[251] Earley v Champion Intl Corp, 907 F2d 1077, 1083 (11th Cir 1990); Berlett v Cargill, Inc, 780 F Supp 560, 566 (ND Ill 1991); Zick v Verson Press Co, 644 F Supp 906, 913 (ND Ill 1986), *affd without opinion,* 819 F2d 1143 (7th Cir 1987).

[252] *See, e.g.,* Walther v Lone Star Gas Co, 952 F2d 119, 123 (5th Cir 1992); Bibby v Drummond Co, 818 F Supp 325, 329 (ND Ala 1993).

[253] Rivas v Federacion de Asociaciones Pecuaria de Puerto Rico, 929 F2d 814, 822 (1st Cir 1991).

[254] Stacey v Allied Stores Corp, 768 F2d 402, 409 (DC Cir 1985).

[255] *See* Haimovitz v United States Dept of Justice, 720 F Supp 516, 528 (WD Pa 1989), *affd without opinion,* 902 F2d 1560 (3d Cir 1990) (federal employee suit).

[256] *Id* 528.

[257] 29 USC §623(d).

[258] *Id* §§621-634.

> It shall be unlawful for an employer to discriminate against any of his employees or applicants for employment, for an employment agency to discriminate against any individual, or for a labor organization to discriminate against any member thereof or applicant for membership, because such individual, member or applicant for membership has opposed any practice made unlawful by . . . [the ADEA], or . . . has made a charge, testified, assisted, or participated in any manner in an investigation, proceeding, or litigation under [the ADEA].

Who is Protected

Clearly, by the very terms of §4(d), a number of individuals are protected from retaliation: employees, job applicants, labor organization members and applicants for membership, and individuals with whom employment agencies deal (although this latter group is particularly ill-defined insofar as both the statutory language and the case law is concerned). Former employees also are covered by the retaliation prohibition "as long as the alleged discrimination is related to or arises out of the employment relationship."[259]

One court has taken the plaintiff-generous position, predicated on extensive analysis of the purpose and language of the ADEA, that a cause of action for retaliation even may be maintained by one who is not himself or herself within the ADEA's protected class; in other words, the plaintiff need not be 40 or older.[260] In contrast, another court, in deciding *Asklar v Honeywell, Inc,*[261] utilized an unduly narrow analysis to rule that §4(d) only applies to persons who have been in some direct actual or potential employment relationship with the defendant employer, i.e.,

---

259 Equal Employment Opportunity Commn v Cosmair, Inc, 821 F2d 1085, 1088-89 (5th Cir 1987); *accord* Passer v American Chem Socy, 935 F2d 322, 330-31 (DC Cir 1991); Connell v Bank of Boston, 924 F2d 1169, 1179 (1st Cir), *cert denied,* 111 S Ct 2828 (1991); Caudill v Farmland Indus, Inc, 698 F Supp 1476, 1485 (WD Mo 1988), *affd,* 919 F2d 83 (8th Cir 1990).

260 *See* Anderson v Phillips Petroleum Co, 722 F Supp 668 (D Kan 1989).

261 95 FRD 419 (D Conn 1982).

employees and job applicants. (The court did not, however, expressly exclude former employees, nor was it addressing retaliation by a labor organization or an employment agency.) The case involved a widow who claimed that the defendant company's withholding of pension benefits constituted retaliation against her in response to the filing of a suit against it by her late husband, who had worked for the company prior to his death. The court equated the word "individual" in §4(d) with *employee* and concluded, notwithstanding that the provision states that "[i]t shall be unlawful for an employer . . . to discriminate against *any* individual,"[262] that the spouse could not maintain the action.

Procedural Predicates

Because it constitutes a distinct cause of action in and of itself, a retaliation claim ordinarily must be preceded by the filing of a charge of unlawful discrimination, to wit, retaliation, with the Equal Employment Opportunity Commission (EEOC), as well as with the appropriate state antidiscrimination agency.[263] While conciliation efforts by the EEOC regarding the prior substantive charge of discrimination that triggered the alleged retaliation may have been unavailing, that fact will not relieve a complainant of the requirement of first resorting to administrative remedies.[264] However, a timely charge of age discrimination filed with the EEOC as to the initial substantive claim of wrongdoing may be deemed to be sufficient—according to a number of courts (but not all)—to cover instances of retaliation that occur subse-

---

[262] Emphasis added.

[263] As to the required filing of a charge of unlawful discrimination, see **ch 6.**

[264] *See, e.g.*, Platt v Burroughs Corp, 424 F Supp 1329, 1334 (ED Pa 1976). *But see* McCarthy v Cortland County Community Action Program, Inc, 487 F Supp 333 (NDNY 1980) (case arising under 42 USC §2000e-3(a), the antiretaliation provision of Title VII of the Civil Rights Act of 1964, *id.* §§2000e through 2000e-6), and cases cited therein for authority reaching a contrary result under Title VII.

quent to the filing of the charge, thereby relieving the grievant of the need to file a new charge addressed to the retaliation claim.[265]

It would seem that inasmuch as a retaliation claim constitutes a separate cause of action, should be maintainable even if the original alleged instance of age bias cannot be pursued because the grievant failed to file the required charge of unlawful discrimination with the EEOC as to that prior claim,[266] or he or she failed to timely file that charge. However, there is case law to the contrary.[267] On the other hand, there is case law support for the proposition that the running of the statute of limitations for suing, thereby barring a complainant's pursuing his or her underlying discrimination substantive ADEA claim will not bar a timely retaliation lawsuit.[268] Similarly, a retaliation claim, made by an overseas employee of an American company is not barred, even if a substantive ADEA claim is precluded by virtue of the ADEA's inapplicability, under the circumstances, outside the United States.[269]

Federal Employees

Section 4(d) is inapplicable to federal employees, who are covered by a separate section, i.e., §15,[270] of the Act. While §15 does not expressly outlaw retaliation, the court deciding *Haxton v Regan,*[271] without identifying the authority for its position, entertained a federal employee's retaliation claim. So, too, did the

---

265 *See, e.g.,* Kristufek v Hussmann Foodservice Co, 985 F2d 364 (7th Cir 1993). For a full review of this issue and the case law, see generally **ch 6.**

266 As to the filing of charges, see **ch 6.**

267 *See* Barrow v General Longshore Workers Local Union No 3000, 58 FEP Cas (BNA) 847, 848 (ED La 1992).

268 *See, e.g.,* Tonka v American Tel & Tel Co, 35 FEP Cas (BNA) 1208 (ND Ga 1980), *affd without opinion,* 679 F2d 251 (11th Cir 1982). As to the statute of limitations under the ADEA, see **ch 6.**

269 Wolf v JI Case Co, 617 F Supp 858 (ED Wis 1985). As to the extraterritorial application of the ADEA, see **ch 3.**

270 29 USC §633a(f). See **ch 9.**

271 33 FEP Cas (BNA) 675 (MD Fla 1983).

court in *Thorne v Alexander.*[272] And in deciding *Bornholdt v Brady*[273] the court, while ultimately asserting that it did not actually have to decide the issue, observed that "it may be inferred that the breadth of the language of . . . [§15], requiring that federal government employment decisions affecting covered personnel be 'free from any discrimination based on age' . . . , is sufficiently broad to prohibit age-based retaliation[.]"[274] In any event, an EEOC regulation regarding, in part, the ADEA, outlaws retaliation against federal employees.[275]

§4.16 —The Scope of the Retaliation Prohibition

The Age Discrimination in Employment Act's (ADEA)[276] ban on retaliation, set forth in §4(d)[277] of the Act, brings within its compass a wide range of actions, including (but not limited to) the following:

---

[272] 782 F Supp 677 (DDC 1992); *accord* Sever v Department of Commerce, 61 FEP Cas (BNA) 955, 960 (DDC 1993).

[273] 869 F2d 57 (2d Cir 1989).

[274] *Id* 62. The Court did not actually decide the issue, however, because it read 5 USC §2302(b)(9) as outlawing reprisals against federal employees. It was argued by the dissenting judge in Siegel v Kreps, 654 F2d 773, 782 n43 (DC Cir 1981) (Robinson, J., dissenting on other grounds), that retaliation for filing a complaint of age discrimination or for otherwise opposing age discrimination itself constitutes discrimination on the basis of age, which clearly is barred by the federal employee provision.

While retaliation against federal employees arguably might violate their due process rights under the Fifth Amendment, US Const amend V, the ADEA has been held to be the exclusive remedy for federal employees, and so a cause of action under the Constitution may not be maintained. *See, e.g.*, Purtill v Harris, 658 F2d 134 (3d Cir 1981), *cert denied,* 462 US 1131 (1983). See generally **ch 3.**

[275] *See* 29 CFR §1614.101(b), .103(a) (1993).

[276] 29 USC §§621-634.

[277] *Id* §623(d).

—the discharge of an employee who asserts his or her own rights under the ADEA;[278]
—the discharge of an employee who assists a colleague who is the target of age discrimination;[279]
—the termination of health benefits;[280]
—the refusal of an employer to place an employee in a position he or she desires;[281]
—the reevaluation of job qualification ratings;[282]
—the refusal to provide work instructions;[283]
—the denial of an employee's requested transfer;[284]
—a transfer to an undesirable position;[285] and
—the discontinuation of severance pay in response to a former employee's filing suit.[286]

---

[278] *See, e.g.*, Shirley v Chrysler First, Inc, 970 F2d 39 (5th Cir 1992); Dominic v Consolidated Edison Co, 822 F2d 1249 (2d Cir 1987); Kentroti v Frontier Airlines, Inc, 585 F2d 967 (10th Cir 1978); Oshiver v Court of Common Pleas, 469 F Supp 645 (ED Pa 1979); Mead v United States Fidelity Guar Co, 442 F Supp 114 (D Minn 1977); Magruder v Selling Areas Mktg, Inc, 439 F Supp 1155 (ND Ill 1977).

[279] Kristufek v Hussman, 985 F2d 364 (7th Cir 1993).

[280] Cohen v SUPA, Inc, 814 F Supp 251 (NDNY 1993).

[281] *See* Malarkey v Texaco, Inc, 983 F2d 1204 (2d Cir 1993).

[282] *See, e.g.*, Schmid v Frosch, 515 F Supp 1260 (DDC 1981), *revd on other grounds*, 680 F2d 248 (DC Cir 1982).

[283] *See, e.g.*, Robinson v Middendorf, 13 Empl Prac Dec (CCH) ¶11,415 (DDC 1976).

[284] *See, e.g.*, Olsen v Southern Pac Transp Co, 480 F Supp 773 (ND Cal 1979), *affd without opinion*, 654 F2d 733 (9th Cir 1981).

[285] *See, e.g.*, Hatton v Ford Motor Co, 508 F Supp 620 (ED Mich 1981); Brown v Colman-Cocker Co, 10 Empl Prac Dec (CCH) ¶10,492 (WDNC 1975).

[286] Equal Employment Opportunity Commn v Cosmair, Inc, 821 F2d 1085, 1089 (5th Cir 1987). Notwithstanding this wide range of actions deemed to run afoul of the antiretaliation prohibition, the court deciding Hickerson v Armour Food Co, 59 FEP Cas (BNA) 1615 (WD Ky 1992), articulated a narrow (unduly so) view of §4(d)'s scope. The plaintiff argued that several different actions each constituted retaliation, i.e., the employer's failure to deliver telephone messages to her; the employer's refusal to give her a raise; the indefinite suspension imposed on her as contrasted with the treatment accorded to two other workers, who were not suspended; and general harassment. The court was willing, for the purposes of discussion, to deem these to be adverse employment actions, but it noted that "[g]enerally, adverse employment action refers to discharges, pay cuts, and similar actions." *Id* 1620 n11.

It also has been held by the Court of Appeals for the Seventh Circuit that it constitutes retaliatory conduct for an employer to foreclose a union member from being able to seek arbitration of a dispute once he or she has filed an ADEA action, even if that foreclosure is authorized by the terms of the contract arrived at by collective bargaining with the employee's union.[287]

In *Mellor v Shell Oil Co*[288] the employer for the first time imposed a claim-release provision as a condition of its severance plan. The court stated that (1) the finding of retaliation by the jury "undoubtedly depended heavily on the timing of Shell's decision to include a claim-release provision in its voluntary severance plan and its awareness of Mellor's lawsuit;"[289] (2) such clauses are now routinely included in such plans; and (3) accordingly, the inclusion of such claim-release clauses did not constitute a per se violation of the Act.[290]

Even where an employer offers evidence of the employee's poor work performance to justify a discharge, the justification will be considered pretextual where the evidence was gathered for the specific purpose of retaliating against the employee.[291] On a different note, in deciding *Connell v Bank of Boston*[292] the Court of Appeals for the First Circuit ruled that the employer's acceleration of the plaintiff's date of discharge, unattended by any loss of benefits or salary, did not constitute an adverse employment action.

While one ADEA court has expressed some doubt as to

---

287 Equal Employment Opportunity Commn v Board of Governors of State Colleges & Universities, 957 F2d 424 (7th Cir), *cert denied,* 113 S Ct 299 (1992).

288 30 Empl Prac Dec (CCH) ¶33,180 (SD Tex 1982).

289 *Id* at p 27,661.

290 *Id.*

291 *See* Powell v Rockwell Intl Corp, 788 F2d 279, 283 (5th Cir 1986); *cf* Mead v United States Fidelity & Guar Co, 442 F Supp 114 (D Minn 1977) (case arising under Title VII of the Civil Rights Act of 1964, 42 USC §§2000e through 2000e-17).

292 924 F2d 1169 (1st Cir), *cert denied,* 112 S Ct 2828 (1991).

whether a defendant's counterclaim can constitute retaliation,[293] there is a decision construing Title VII of the Civil Rights Act of 1964[294] that supports an affirmative view as to the issue.[295] Indeed, much of the case law regarding discriminatory retaliation by employers has been developed under Title VII. Inasmuch as the ADEA is modeled on that statute and ADEA courts accordingly regularly look to judicial interpretations of Title VII for guidance in construing the age statute,[296] Title VII case law is very much apposite in construing §4(d).

There is Title VII case law recognizing unlawful retaliation in the guise of a number of situations in addition to those already noted as having arisen in the ADEA context:

—a suspension;[297]
—a demotion;[298]
—a refusal to promote;[299]
—a refusal to hire or rehire;[300] and
—an extension of an employee's probationary period.[301]

Title VII case law establishes that an employer, labor organization, or employment agency may not rely on an individual's participation in a civil rights enforcement proceeding as providing a legitimate nondiscriminatory reason for its alleged wrongdoing. For example, an employer may not refuse to hire an

---

293 Glass v IDS Fin Servs, Inc, 778 F Supp 1029, 1061 n53 (D Minn 1991).

294 42 USC §§2000e through 2000e-17.

295 *See* Cooper v Pic-Walsh Freight Co, 27 FEP Cas (BNA) 344 (ED Mo 1976).

296 See **ch 2.**

297 Hearth v Metropolitan Transit Commn, 436 F Supp 685 (D Minn 1977).

298 Cohen v Fred Meyer, Inc, 686 F2d 793 (9th Cir 1982).

299 Berio v Equal Employment Opportunity Commn, 18 FEP Cas (BNA) 1213 (DDC 1979); Hackley v Cleland, 13 Empl Prac Dec (CCH) ¶11,585 (DDC 1977).

300 East v Romine, Inc, 518 F2d 332 (5th Cir 1975); Barela v United Nuclear Corp, 462 F2d 149 (10th Cir 1972); *see also* DeMedina v Reinhardt, 444 F Supp 573 (DDC 1978) (refusal to rehire spouse).

301 Sherkow v Wisconsin Dept of Pub Instruction, 17 Empl Prac Dec (CCH) ¶8553 (ED Wis 1978), *affd in part, revd in part as to remedy,* 630 F2d 498 (7th Cir 1980).

employee who has filed several civil rights charges on the ground that the employee is litigious.[302] An employer that paid its supervisors for time spent testifying in court on the employer's behalf violated Title VII by refusing to pay other employees who took time off from work to testify for a plaintiff.[303]

Retaliatory Actions Expressed Through Actions Vis-a-Vis Third Parties

A retaliation claim may arise out of action taken by an employer that jeopardizes or undermines either an individual's ability to obtain new employment or his or her ability to retain a position obtained following departure from the defendant's employ. The Court of Appeals for the District of Columbia approvingly observed in *Passer v American Chemical Society* that[304] "it is well established that efforts by an employer to scuttle a former employee's search for a new job, such as by withholding a letter of recommendation or by providing negative information to a prospective employer, can constitute illegal retaliation within the meaning of ADEA and parallel anti-retaliation provisions."[305]

A former employer may exert pressure on a grievant's later employer to discharge him or her, thereby engaging in unlawful retaliation.[306] In a related vein, a Title VII ruling established that an employer's informing an individual's potential future employer that the applicant had filed charges with the Equal

---

302 East v Romine, Inc, 518 F2d 332 (5th Cir 1975).

303 Kyraizi v Western Elec Co, 469 F Supp 672 (DNJ 1979), *affd*, 647 F2d 388 (3d Cir 1981).

304 935 F2d 322 (DC Cir 1991).

305 *Id* 331; *accord* Kittredge v Parker Hannifin Corp, 597 F Supp 605 (WD Mich 1984).

306 *See* Caudill v Farmland Indus, Inc, 698 F Supp 1476, 1484-85 (WD Mo 1988), *affd on other grounds*, 919 F2d 87 (8th Cir 1990). The district court had directed a verdict for the defendant. The appellate court, which affirmed, did not reject the notion that a viable retaliation claim could result under the circumstances described, but rather focused on the lack of evidence to establish that the plaintiff's discharge indeed was caused by the defendant.

Employment Opportunity Commission (EEOC) also could constitute unlawful retaliation.[307]

In *Espenshade v Pennsylvania State University*[308] the court rejected the defendant's argument, made in support of a motion for summary judgment, that the alleged wrongful acts fell outside the scope of the retaliation ban. The plaintiff had taught a class from which a number of students withdrew, and he argued that these withdrawals were in retaliation for his having filed an ADEA action against the university. The court stated as follows:

> We believe retaliation against an employee can occur when individuals are encouraged to exercise a right, [i.e., the right to withdraw from a class,] that they would not have exercised but for the actions of an employer. Likewise retaliation may exist when an employer cooperates in actions taken against an employee when such actions could not occur without the employer's assent.[309]

Retaliatory Actions Not Affecting Employment Opportunities or Conditions of Current Employment

In *Passer v American Chemical Society*[310] the court addressed the plaintiff's contention that the cancellation by Passer's former employer of a post-retirement symposium that was to have been held in honor of the plaintiff, an unwilling retiree who was pursuing redress to bar his retirement under the ADEA, constituted actionable retaliation. The court agreed with the plaintiff. What matters, legally, is whether " '*the employer . . . engaged in conduct having an adverse impact on the plaintiff*[.]' "[311] Here, the American Chemical Society's "action in aborting a 'rare and prestigious,'

---

307 *See, e.g.,* Rutherford v American Bank of Commerce, 565 F2d 1162 (10th Cir 1977).

308 563 F Supp 1172 (MD Pa 1983).

309 *Id* 1176.

310 935 F2d 322 (DC Cir 1991).

311 *Id* 331 (quoting Berger v Iron Workers Reinforced Rodmen Local 201, 843 F2d 1395, 1423 (DC Cir), *supplemented on other grounds on rehg,* 852 F2d 619 (DC Cir 1988), *cert denied,* 490 US 1105 (1989)) (emphasis added by court).

and highly public honor for an employee on the eve of its occurrence simply . . . [could not] be dismissed . . . as the inconsequential withdrawal of a mere gratuity.' "[312]

While, as *Passer* and other decisions illustrate, there need not be a present employment relationship between the plaintiff and defendant, the court deciding *Patel v Lutheran Medical Center, Inc,*[313] reasoned that unlawful retaliation must bear on the plaintiff's ability to continue in his or her current employment, or on the plaintiff's ability to procure employment. In *Patel* the plaintiff unsuccessfully maintained that the defendant's allegedly having lured away one Dr. Kumar, an employee of Patel, from his business relationship with Patel, constituted illegal retaliation in reaction to Patel's having filed a charge of discrimination against the defendant during his earlier period of employment with the defendant. Patel claimed that this luring away of his employee constituted tortious interference with a contract and that a claim of retaliation under the ADEA could be pursued as a mechanism for establishing liability as to this alleged wrong. The *Patel* court concluded that the plaintiff's claim should be dismissed because the defendant's alleged action "impacted the relationship of Dr. Kumar with plaintiff," rather than "impact[ing] on the plaintiff's ability to continue or procure employment."[314]

Passer suggests a different reading of the proscription on retaliation. The *Passer* court of appeals expressed no explicit concern as to whether the cancellation of the symposium for the plaintiff would have detrimental consequences for his employment prospects. What is more, the court reversed the district court, which—in denying Passer's claims—had asserted that retaliation within the ambit of the ADEA had not been alleged because "the symposium was not part of plaintiff's past or future relationship with the defendant, *nor did the cancellation affect his relationship with*

---

[312] 935 F2d at 331.

[313] 753 F Supp 1070 (EDNY 1990).

[314] *Id* 1075.

potential employers."[315] The court deciding *Cohen v SUPA, Inc*[316] also disagreed with *Patel,* in the context of denying the defendant's motion for summary judgment in a case arising out of the defendant's allegedly retaliatory termination of the plaintiff's health benefits.

Retaliation by Labor Organizations

Section 4(d) by its terms is not confined just to retaliation by employers. Denials of work referrals by unions,[317] as well as the administration of membership dues and suspension policies[318] in a retaliatory manner, will run afoul of the provision.

Good Faith as a Defense

In *Equal Employment Opportunity Commission v Board of Governors of State Colleges & Universities*[319] the Court of Appeals for the Seventh Circuit addressed a board policy providing that an employee's initiation of a claim in an administrative or judicial forum would foreclose his or her right to pursue contractual grievance rights, i.e., arbitration, etc., under the extant collective bargaining agreement. The court ruled that this policy constituted unlawful retaliation within the meaning of §4(d). In so doing, moreover, the court asserted that intent is irrelevant insofar as employer culpability is concerned, and thus the employer's claimed good faith in having adopted this policy was not a viable defense. The court stated as follows:

> When an employee's participation in statutorily protected activity is the determining factor in an employer's

---

315 Passer v American Chem Socy, 701 F Supp 1, 3 (DDC 1988), *revd,* 935 F2d 322 (DC Cir 1991) (emphasis added).

316 814 F Supp 251 (NDNY 1993).

317 *Cf* Grant v Bethlehem Steel Corp, 622 F2d 43 (2d Cir 1980) (Title VII case); Equal Employment Opportunity Commn v Operating Engrs Locals 14 & 15, 438 F Supp 876 (SDNY 1977) (*id*).

318 *See, e.g.,* Equal Employment Opportunity Commn v Operating Engrs Locals 14 & 15, 438 F Supp 876 (SDNY 1977) (Title VII case).

319 957 F2d 424 (7th Cir), *cert denied,* 113 S Ct 299 (1992).

> decision to take adverse employment action, that action is invalid regardless of the employer's intent. If the employer's differential treatment of its employees is impermissible, the policy which provides for its differential treatment is invalid regardless of the employer's motivation for adopting or invoking the policy. Hence, the Board's asserted good faith in discriminating against employees who file claims in administrative and judicial forums is irrelevant.[320]

In brief, "a retaliatory policy constitutes a *per se* violation of Section 4(d)[.]"[321]

§4.17 —Protected Conduct: Participation

Section 4(d)[322] of the Age Discrimination in Employment Act (ADEA)[323] speaks to two kinds of prohibited conduct: retaliation against an individual who has participated in a proceeding under the ADEA, and retaliation against an individual who expresses opposition—by word or deed—to practices outlawed by the ADEA. *Participation* has been broadly construed, both in ADEA cases and in cases arising under the analogous antiretaliation ban contained in Title VII of the Civil Rights Act of 1964.[324]

The retaining of an attorney is a protected activity.[325] The filing of a charge with the Equal Employment Opportunity Com-

---

320 *Id* 428. The court recognized that its analysis did not entirely square with an earlier ruling, i.e., Rose v Hearst Magazines Div, Hearst Corp, 814 F2d 491 (7th Cir 1987), and in addition to its attempting to distinguish the case on its facts, the court further stated that it "decline[d] to extend . . . [*Rose's*] rationale [, which arose in the context of an individual disparate treatment case,] to this case which concerns a discriminatory policy." 957 F2d at 429.

321 *Id.*

322 29 USC §623(d).

323 *Id* §§621-634.

324 42 USC §§2000e through 2000e-17.

325 Connell v Bank of Boston, 924 F2d 1169, 1179 (1st Cir), *cert denied,* 111 S Ct 2828 (1991); *cf* Equal Employment Opportunity Commn v Kallir, Philips, Ross, Inc, 401 F Supp 66 (SDNY 1975), *affd without opinion,* 559 F2d 1203 (2d Cir), *cert denied,* 434 US 920 (1977) (Title VII case).

mission (EEOC) and the giving of testimony to the agency both clearly constitute protected participation. The filing of charges with state and local agencies also is protected, given that the use of these agencies is contemplated by the ADEA statutory enforcement scheme.[326] A policy whereby a grievant who files a charge with the EEOC or who files suit will be barred from pursuing his contractual rights under a collective bargaining agreement also will be deemed to constitute unlawful retaliation.[327]

Section 4(d)'s protection extends not only to an employee who files a charge of discrimination regarding himself or herself, but also to an employee who files a charge on behalf of others, i.e., his or her co-workers.[328] An ADEA retaliation claim can be based on an employee's discharge arising out of his or her involvement in an investigation by a state agency of a possible violation of state law.[329] It has been held under Title VII that the refusal to testify in favor of a party also constitutes protected activity.[330] Assistance provided to an individual in filing a charge cannot be the basis for retaliation against the person providing the assistance.[331] And efforts to interfere with the gathering of evidence or testimony will constitute forbidden retaliation.[332]

---

326 *Cf* Kralowec v Prince George's County, 503 F Supp 985 (D Md 1980), *affd without opinion,* 679 F2d 883 (4th Cir), *cert denied,* 459 US 872 (1982) (Title VII Case); Hayden v Chrysler Corp, 486 F Supp 557 (ED Mich 1980) (*id*); Dunlop v Hanover Shoe Farms, Inc, 441 F Supp 385 (MD Pa 1976) (construing similar antiretaliation provision of the Occupational Safety and Health Act of 1970, 29 USC §§651-678). As to deferral to state agencies, see **ch 6.**

327 Equal Employment Opportunity Commn v Board of Governors of State Colleges & Univs, 957 F2d 424 (7th Cir), *cert denied,* 113 S Ct 299 (1992).

328 *See* Anderson v Phillips Petroleum Co, 722 F Supp 668 (D Kan 1989).

329 Merkel v Scovill, Inc, 787 F2d 174, 179 n2 (6th Cir), *cert denied,* 479 US 990 (1986).

330 Smith v Columbus Metro Hous Auth, 443 F Supp 61 (SD Ohio 1977) (refusal to execute affidavit favorable to employer).

331 *See* Merkel v Scovill, Inc, 573 F Supp 1055 (SD Ohio 1983), *revd on other grounds,* 787 F2d 174 (6th Cir), *cert denied,* 479 US 990 (1986).

332 *Cf* United States v City of Milwaukee, 390 F Supp 1126 (ED Wis 1975) (Title VII case concerning police department's rule forbidding officers from discussing department business with persons outside the department; rule

Equal Employment Opportunity Commission v United States Steel Corp[333] illustrates some of the foregoing propositions. The case involved a release whereby an employee who wanted to receive an enhanced pension upon voluntary retirement had to agree not to counsel or assist in the prosecution of claims under the ADEA on his or her own behalf or on behalf of others. The court concluded that this *counsel or assist* provision constituted unlawful retaliation and enjoined its further use, as well as the enforcement of the release by US Steel as to individuals who already had signed it.

Because the retaliation proscription set forth in §4(d) outlaws retaliation taken against an employee who acts affirmatively by participating in an ADEA matter, it could be argued that an employee who does not act, that is, who refuses to participate, cannot invoke the protection of §4(d). Indeed, this argument was made in *Merkel v Scovill, Inc.*[334] Merkel refused to sign an affidavit that was prepared pursuant to an investigation and that was sought pursuant to the directive of the state antidiscrimination agency which was investigating the state age discrimination claims of Merkel's former co-workers. Merkel was then fired. The court was unwilling to agree that refusal to participate could never be the basis for a retaliation claim. Here, however, the facts did not support the validity of the claim.

Even false or malicious charges that are filed with the EEOC are protected, and so they cannot be the basis for adverse action against the charge filer. The leading decision is *Pettway v American Cast Iron Pipe Co,*[335] a Title VII ruling involving an individual who had filed a charge with the EEOC alleging that the two-week disciplinary suspension that had been imposed on him had been racially motivated. Finding that no reasonable cause existed for believing that a violation of Title VII actually had occurred, the EEOC dismissed the charge. In a letter he wrote to the EEOC

---

could not be used to prohibit employees from cooperating with federal civil rights investigators).

[333] 671 F Supp 351 (WD Pa 1987).

[334] 787 F2d 174 (6th Cir), *cert denied,* 479 US 990 (1986).

[335] 411 F2d 998 (5th Cir 1969).

seeking reconsideration of the dismissal, the grievant made statements that the employer claimed were false and malicious and the statements were used as the basis for firing him. Ultimately, this termination was deemed to constitute unlawful retaliation.

In the court's view, there was a strong need to protect employees filing charges since such charges were essential to the enforcement process.[336] This need outweighed the employer's interest in being able to use the penalty of discharge as a mechanism for protecting itself from libelous statements. In any event, the court reasoned, the employer's interests were protected by Title VII's requirements regarding the confidentiality of EEOC investigative material.[337] Thus, the court concluded that the charge filed with the EEOC could not be used as the basis for discharge, its malicious character notwithstanding.[338]

In sum, a participant in an ADEA proceeding is absolutely protected from retaliation. This is so whether or not the employee is found to have acted unlawfully.[339] The employer's good faith

---

[336] *Id* 1005.

[337] *Id* 1007. While one might conjecture that this factor could serve as a basis for distinguishing *Pettway* in the ADEA context, there is no comparable provision in the age statute imposing a bar on public disclosure of investigatory files. On the other hand, and the silence of the ADEA notwithstanding, the EEOC in fact treats all open ADEA case files as exempt from disclosure under the Freedom of Information Act. 29 CFR §1610.17(g) (1993). See generally **ch 6**.

[338] Although the court left open the possibility that an employee could be held liable in a state tort action, 411 F2d at 1007 n22, some later Title VII courts have read the statutory ban on retaliation as barring such actions. *See, e.g.*, Equal Employment Opportunity Commn v Levi Strauss & Co, 515 F Supp 640 (ND Ill 1981); Equal Employment Opportunity Commn v Virginia Carolina Veneer Corp, 495 F Supp 775 (WD Va 1980), *appeal dismissed,* 652 F2d 380 (4th Cir 1981) (defamation); Cooper v Pic-Walsh Freight Co, 19 Empl Prac Dec (CCH) ¶8994 (ED Mo 1976) (malicious prosecution). *But see* Noel v McCain, 538 F2d 633, 636 (4th Cir 1976); Bartulica v Paculdo, 411 F Supp 392 (WD Mo 1976) (defamation action may not be removed from state to federal court on basis that allegedly defamatory statement was protected by Title VII's antiretaliation procedure).

[339] *See, e.g.*, Wolf v JI Case Co, 617 F Supp 858, 868 (ED Wis 1985) (dictum); *cf* Parker v Baltimore & Ohio RR Co, 652 F2d 1012, 1019 (DC Cir 1981) (Title VII case). *But see* Marshall v Pyramid Life Ins Co, 52 FEP Cas (BNA) 1398,

will be irrelevant, at least insofar as a retaliatory policy (as opposed to an instance of individualized retaliation) is concerned.[340]

§4.18 —Protected Conduct: Opposition

Section 4(d)[341] of the Age Discrimination in Employment Act (ADEA)[342] prohibits retaliation against individuals who oppose illegal discriminatory practices. This opposition need only be based on a reasonable good-faith belief that discrimination exists.[343] Moreover, most courts have taken the position that so long as the individual acted reasonably and in good faith, it will not matter that the practices he or she opposed ultimately proved to be legal.[344]

For opposition to fit within the reach of §4(d), it must be directed against (1) the discriminatory practices or policies of

---

1401 n4 (D Kan 1990) (employee must "have had a reasonable belief that an unlawful employment practice was occurring").

[340] Equal Employment Opportunity Commn v Board of Governors of State Colleges & Univs, 957 F2d 424, 428 (7th Cir), *cert denied,* 113 S Ct 299 (1992).

[341] 29 USC §623(d).

[342] *Id* §§621-634.

[343] *See, e.g.,* Grant v Hazelett Strip-Casting Corp, 880 F2d 1564, 1569 (2d Cir 1989); Wentz v Maryland Casualty Co, 869 F2d 1153, 1155 (8th Cir 1989); Mellor v Shell Oil Co, 30 Empl Prac Dec (CCH) ¶33,180, at p 27,659 (SD Tex 1982) (omitting requirement that the belief be a good-faith one).

[344] *See, e.g.,* Mesnick v General Elec Co, 950 F2d 816, 827 (1st Cir 1991), *cert denied,* 112 S Ct 2965 (1992); Wentz v Maryland Casualty Co, 869 F2d 1155 (8th Cir 1989); *cf* Love v RE/MAX of Am, Inc, 738 F2d 383, 385 (10th Cir 1984) (case arising under the comparable antiretaliation provision of Title VII of the Civil Rights Act of 1964, 42 USC §§2000e through 2000e-17); Gifford v Atchison, Topeka & Santa Fe Ry, 685 F2d 1149 (9th Cir 1982) (*id*); De Anda v St Joseph Hosp, 671 F2d 850 (5th Cir 1982) (*id*); Rucker v Higher Educ Aids Bd, 669 F2d 1179 (7th Cir 1982) (*id*); Parker v Baltimore & Ohio RR Co, 652 F2d 1012 (DC Cir 1981) (*id*); Monteiro v Poole Silver Co, 615 F2d 4, 8 (1st Cir 1980) (*id*). *Contra* Whitten v Farmland Indus, Inc, 759 F Supp 1522, 1538 n16 (D Kan 1991) (employee need only have "a reasonable belief that an unlawful employment practice was occurring"); Equal Employment Opportunity Commn v C&D Sportswear Corp, 398 F Supp 300 (MD Ga 1975); *cf* Silver v KCA, Inc, 586 F2d 138 (9th Cir 1978) (Title VII case).

(2) a covered entity, i.e., an employer, labor organization, or employment agency.

Insofar as the first requirement is concerned, *Kauffman v Kent State University*[345] is illustrative. The plaintiff had complained about having to do her supervisor's personal work. Subsequently, she was transferred and it was this transfer that gave rise, in part, to her ADEA suit. While noting a decision in which it had been asserted that " '[i]n retaliation cases, the courts are more willing to redress transfers involving changes of working conditions, with no loss of pay or benefits,' "[346] the court nonetheless rejected the proposition that unlawful retaliation existed here, asserting as follows: "Such a complaint, of course, would not give rise to a retaliation claim because such complaints [regarding personal disputes with supervisors about work assignments] are not a protected activity."[347]

The second aspect of opposition case law, i.e., that the activity which is to be protected under §4(d) must have been directed against a covered entity, has resulted in conflicting case law as to whether an individual's opposition to the discriminatory actions of his or her co-workers is protected. The Court of Appeals for the Ninth Circuit, in deciding *Equal Employment Opportunity Commission v Crown Zellerbach Corp*,[348] reasoned that the employee who had engaged in the alleged bigotry at issue was an agent of the employer and was directly responsible for employment practices, and so the plaintiff's opposition to his conduct constituted protected activity. It was this agency relationship that distinguished the situation, in the court's view, from that at issue in *Silver v KCA, Inc*,[349] in which the court held that an employer did not violate the comparable antiretaliation

---

345 815 F Supp 1077 (ND Ohio 1993).

346 *Id* 1084 n3 (quoting Darnell v Campbell County Fiscal Court, 731 F Supp 1309, 1313 n2 (ED Ky 1990), *affd*, 924 F2d 1057 (6th Cir 1991)).

347 815 F Supp at 1084-85 n3.

348 32 FEP Cas (BNA) 809 (9th Cir 1983).

349 586 F2d 138 (9th Cir 1978).

provision contained in Title VII of the Civil Rights Act of 1964[350] when it fired an employee who had forced a co-worker to apologize to an African-American for having uttered a racial slur. The court reasoned that racial slurs by individuals in isolated incidents unrelated to the practices of the employer were not the sort of conduct Title VII was aimed at prohibiting.[351]

Examples of Protected Opposition

The activities that will fit within §4(d)'s protection can take a variety of forms (some of which are illustrated by way of rulings construing the antiretaliation provision of Title VII, the judicial interpretations of which often are looked to for analogical guidance by ADEA courts).[352] Protected opposition includes an employee's statements to his or her employer pointing out or protesting discriminatory conduct.[353] An employee who refuses to obey his or her employer's order to violate the Act will be protected.[354] And an individual who alerts a government agency with which the employer deals to the employer's discrimination is also protected against retaliation.[355] An employee's request for an explanation of his or her termination also can constitute protected activity under the opposition clause of the antiretaliation provision.[356]

Limits as to the Form Opposition May Take

There are limits, of course, to what will constitute protected opposition, as *Silver v KCA, Inc,*[357] illustrates. The form of the opposition must be assessed in light of the peculiarities of the

---

[350] 42 USC §§2000e through 2000e-17.

[351] 586 F2d at 141.

[352] See **ch 2.**

[353] *See* Berg v LaCrosse Cooler Co, 612 F2d 1041 (7th Cir 1980) (Title VII case).

[354] *See* Tidwell v American Oil Co, 332 F Supp 424 (D Utah 1971).

[355] *Cf* Sias v City Demonstration Agency, 588 F2d 692 (9th Cir 1978) (Title VII case); Hicks v ABT Assocs, Inc, 572 F2d 960 (3d Cir 1978) (*id*).

[356] *See* Whitten v Farmland Indus, Inc, 759 F Supp 1522, 1539 (D Kan 1991).

[357] 586 F2d 138 (9th Cir 1978) (Title VII case).

job involved and all of the surrounding circumstances in the workplace.[358] The method chosen for opposing discrimination must be "reasonable in light of the employer's interest in maintaining a harmonious and efficient operation,"[359] and it must be lawful.[360] But the Court of Appeals for the Second Circuit has cautioned that in assessing a plaintiff's actions to determine whether they exceed the bounds of acceptable opposition activity, one must take care not to deter " 'legitimate activism by employees asserting [their] civil rights[.]' "[361] Obviously, reasonableness must be determined on a case-by-case basis. In *O'Day v McDonnell Douglas Helicopter Co*[362] the court concluded that "no reasonable jury would find that O'Day's conduct, surreptitiously removing confidential management files from his supervisor's desk, photocopying them, and showing the file to a co-worker, was reasonable in light of the circumstances."[363] *Racich v National Railroad Passenger Corp*[364] concerned a personnel supervisor who had assisted other employees. The defendant contended that the

---

358 *See, e.g.*, Grant v Hazelett Strip-Casting Corp, 880 F2d 1564, 1570 (2d Cir 1989).

359 O'Day v McDonnell Douglas Helicopter Co, 784 F Supp 1466, 1469-70 (D Ariz 1992); *cf* Hochstadt v Worcester Foundation for Experimental Biology, 545 F2d 222 (1st Cir 1976) (Title VII case; no protection for employee who constantly complained to colleagues about her salary, spread untrue rumors that the employer's federal grant money was about to be lost because of its discriminatory practices, and told one administrator that he would have to choose sides in her dispute with another administrator).

360 O'Day v McDonnell Douglas Helicopter Co, 784 F Supp 1466, 1469-70 (D Ariz 1992); *cf* Jefferies v Harris County Community Action Assn, 615 F2d 1025 (5th Cir 1980) (Title VII case; copying and transmitting of employer's confidential documents not protected); Green v McDonnell Douglas Corp, 463 F2d 337 (8th Cir), *vacated on other grounds*, 411 US 792 (1973) (Title VII case; illegal *stall-in* unprotected); King v Illinois Bell Tel Co, 476 F Supp 495 (ND Ill 1978) (strike in breach of no-strike clause in collective bargaining agreement unprotected).

361 Grant v Hazelett Strip-Casting Corp, 880 F2d 1564, 1570 (2d Cir 1989) (quoting Wrighten v Metropolitan Hosps, Inc, 726 F2d 1346, 1355 (9th Cir 1984)).

362 784 F Supp 1466 (D Ariz 1992).

363 *Id* 1470.

364 47 FEP Cas (BNA) 146 (ND Ill 1988).

plaintiff's stated intent to testify at an Equal Employment Opportunity Commission (EEOC) conference on behalf of a fellow employee, who had a sex discrimination charge pending against the defendant, did not constitute protected activity. The court concluded that the defendant had failed to adduce evidence in support of the applicable legal standard, which was "whether 'the employee's conduct in protest of an unlawful employment practice so interferes with the performance of his job that it renders him ineffective in [his] position[.]' "[365]

Reduced Protection for Certain Employees

There is Title VII case law to the effect that some employees—specifically, equal employment opportunity counselors and employees of unions—may enjoy a lesser degree of protection from retaliation. One court ruled that if a manager of an employer's equal employment opportunity program filed complaints, and solicited employees to file complaints, with federal civil rights agencies, he or she could be fired without the employer running afoul of Title VII's antiretaliation provision. The rationale was that the manager's activities incapacitated him or her from performing the job, which entailed representing the employer's interests in dealing with those very agencies.[366] On the other hand, another Title VII court ruled that it was unlawful for an employer to retaliate against an equal employment opportunity manager who worked internally to eliminate discriminatory practices.[367]

Insofar as union employees are concerned, another Title VII court upheld the firing, on grounds of political disloyalty, of a dues posting clerk whose effort to be elected to the office of secretary-treasurer was aimed at expressing her opposition to what

---

[365] *Id* 151 n4 (quoting Jones v Flagship Intl, 793 F2d 714, 728 (5th Cir 1986), *cert denied,* 479 US 1065 (1987)).

[366] *See* Smith v Singer Co, 650 F2d 214 (9th Cir 1981); *see also* Pendleton v Rumsfeld, 628 F2d 102 (DC Cir 1980) (Title VII federal employee case).

[367] Berg v LaCrosse Cooler Co, 612 F2d 1041 (7th Cir 1980).

she believed to be discriminatory practices.[368] Similarly, a district court ruled that Title VII's antiretaliation provision was not violated by the firing of a union representative who had told African-American workers that some unions did not respond to African-Americans' needs, that historically the union movement had been insensitive to their needs, and that certain union leaders lacked social awareness. The court reasoned that the union was entitled to expect loyalty from its field representatives, and that the lack of loyalty here justified termination.[369]

§4.19 The Use of Proxies for Age

There are a number of scenarios that can occur whereby an employer, labor organization, or employment agency may rely on a factor other than age as a basis for making decisions that is so closely related to, or correlated with, age as to constitute a proxy for age, itself. Sometimes, this issue will be addressed in the context of considering whether the proxy can be justified as fitting within the Age Discrimination in Employment Act's (ADEA)[370] reasonable factors other than age (RFOA) exception, set forth in §4(f)(2).[371] Sometimes this issue will be addressed in terms of assessing a claimant's disparate impact theory of liability.[372] Typically, the courts have been willing to recognize and to condemn such proxies. However, as discussed below, the reasoning and result in *Hazen Paper Co v Biggins,*[373] a 1993 decision of the Supreme Court, requires reassessment of the legal status of such proxies.

---

368 Rosser v Laborers' Local 438, 616 F2d 221 (5th Cir), *cert denied,* 449 US 886 (1980). *See generally* Rose, *Going Too Far or Just Doing Their Job: The Double Bind Facing EEO and AA Officers,* 6 Lab LJ 439 (1990).

369 Doe v AFL-CIO, 405 F Supp 389 (ND Ga 1975), *affd without opinion,* 537 F2d 1141 (5th Cir 1976), *cert denied,* 429 US 1102 (1977).

370 29 USC §§621-634.

371 *Id* §623(f)(2). For a discussion of the RFOA exception, see **ch 5.**

372 As to disparate impact analysis, theory of liability, see **ch 7.**

373 113 S Ct 1701 (1993).

Retirement Status, Eligibility for Retirement, and Abbreviated Future Work Life

In *Equal Employment Opportunity Commission v Local 350*[374] the Court of Appeals for the Ninth Circuit addressed a union policy that barred retired members from seeking work through the union hiring hall unless they agreed to cease receiving their pensions. In holding this policy to be violative of the ADEA, the court pointed to the close correlation between age and retirement status:

> On its face . . . [the policy] discriminates only against retired employees; however, only employees 55 or older are eligible to retire. There is thus a very close connection between age and the factor on which discrimination is based. . . .
>
> Thus, Local 350's policy violates . . . [the ADEA] because it refuses to refer certain employees for work on the basis of a factor very closely related to age.[375]

Similarly, the Courts of Appeals for the Third[376] and Ninth[377] Circuits have held that an employer's utilization of eligibility for early retirement as a basis for dealing with employees constitutes reliance on a factor so closely linked to age that this is tantamount to reliance on age, itself.[378]

While one cannot predict with specificity the duration of any specific individual's future work life, it is safe to conclude that, as a general matter, an older worker has fewer future work years ahead of him or her than does a younger worker. Future work expectancy, then, arguably can be a fairly workable, albeit not

---

[374] 982 F2d 1305 (9th Cir 1992).

[375] *Id* 1310.

[376] *See* Equal Employment Opportunity Commn v Westinghouse Elec Corp, 725 F2d 211, 222 (3d Cir 1983), *cert denied,* 469 US 820 (1984).

[377] *See* Equal Employment Opportunity Commn v Borden's, Inc, 724 F2d 1390, 1393 (9th Cir 1984).

[378] See generally ch 5 regarding the *reasonable factors other than age* exception.

completely exact, proxy for age. However, "[a]n 'expectation of longer service' by a younger, retained employee, has been held an impermissible reason to discharge the older employer."[379]

High Salaries

Older employees are likely to be better paid than their younger colleagues.[380] An employer that seeks to reduce costs by singling out its more highly compensated employees for termination likely will wind up discharging mainly (or possibly even exclusively) older workers. The Court of Appeals for the Seventh Circuit has been quite emphatic in adhering to the proposition "that wage discrimination can be a proxy for age discrimination, so that lopping off high salaried workers can violate the ADEA—although the circumstances under which this holds true remain to be determined."[381] Other courts also have been sensitive to the age/cost equation, and accordingly have deemed cost-based decisions to be suspect, at the least, and in most instances unlawful.[382]

There is no per se rule of illegality here, however. If an individual contends that because of his or her high salary he or she was the victim of intentional discriminatory treatment in violation of the ADEA, the plaintiff will have to prove—as in any discrimi-

---

379 Wolf v Ferro Corp, 772 F Supp 139, 142 (WDNY 1991) (quoting Marshall v Arlene Knitwear, Inc, 454 F Supp 715, 728 (EDNY 1978), *affd in part & revd in part without opinion,* 608 F2d 1369 (2d Cir 1979)).

380 This will not always be so, however. *See* Nelson v Kennicott Bros Co, Inc, 58 FEP Cas (BNA) 187 (ED Wis 1990).

381 Gustovich v AT&T Communications, Inc, 972 F2d 845, 851 (7th Cir 1992); *see also* Finnegan v Trans World Airlines, Inc, 967 F2d 1161 (7th Cir 1992); Metz v Transit Mix, Inc, 828 F2d 1201 (7th Cir 1987).

382 *See, e.g.,* Metz v Transit-Mix, Inc, 828 F2d 1201 (7th Cir 1987); Leftwich v Harris-Stowe State College, 702 F2d 686 (8th Cir 1983); Geller v Markham, 635 F2d 1027 (2d Cir), *cert denied,* 451 US 945 (1981); Equal Employment Opportunity Commn v Francis W Parker Sch, 61 FEP Cas (BNA) 967 (ND Ill 1993). *But see* Equal Employment Opportunity Commn v Atlantic Community Sch Dist, 879 F2d 434 (8th Cir 1989). With regard to the RFOA *reasonable factors other than age* exception and its application to the age/cost correlation see generally **ch 5.** With regard to the application of disparate impact analysis to that correlation, see **Ch 7.**

natory treatment case[383]—that the defendant indeed was motivated by the plaintiff's age, since it is only discrimination based on age that the ADEA proscribes.[384] And if a plaintiff argues that the defendant's reliance on cost has an adverse disparate impact on older employees—a theory that does not entail proof of discriminatory intent or motivation—the plaintiff will have to carry the burden of proving his or her case in this context, as well.[385] In brief, even a court sympathetic to the age/cost equation will not endorse, without more, an automatic equation between cost and age bias such that the plaintiff will be relieved of having to prove his or her claim.[386]

Seniority, Tenure, and Pension Eligibility

Sometimes an employer will utilize the factor of seniority as the basis for making a decision regarding an employee.[387] Likewise, tenure status in a higher education setting may be relied upon by an employer.[388] No per se rule of liability has been embraced here, either. While it has been acknowledged that "[t]here may well be cases in which seniority is a code word for discrimination,"[389] there is also resistance to unblinkingly accepting an age/seniority equation.[390] This reluctance to too readily read seniority as a proxy for age is seen in the reasoning of the Court of Appeals for the Third Circuit in *Gray v York News-*

---

[383] See **ch 7.**

[384] *See* Gustovich v AT&T Communications, Inc, 972 F2d 845, 851 (7th Cir 1992).

[385] *See* Equal Employment Opportunity Commn v Francis W Parker Sch, 61 FEP Cas (BNA) 967, 975 (ND Ill 1993). In regard to disparate impact analysis, see generally **ch 7.**

[386] Cost can be a legitimate basis for justifying some differential treatment, so long as that treatment follows from observance of a bona fide employee benefit plan. See **ch 5.**

[387] See generally the discussion of the RFOA exception, in **ch 5.**

[388] *See* Leftwich v Harris-Stowe State College, 702 F2d 686 (8th Cir 1983).

[389] Arnold v United States Postal Serv, 863 F2d 994, 1000 (DC Cir 1988), *cert denied,* 493 US 846 (1989); *accord* Equal Employment Opportunity Commn v Clay Printing Co, 955 F2d 936, 942 (4th Cir 1992).

[390] See ch 5 regarding the *reasonable factors other than age* exception.

papers, Inc,[391] in which one of the plaintiffs argued that although his replacement was less than a year younger than him in chronological terms, the replacement's " 'age with the company was twenty-three years younger,' "[392] and so the replacement was much cheaper for the defendant to employ because of his lesser entitlement to paid vacation and to other benefits associated with seniority. The court found the plaintiff's argument unpersuasive:

> [The plaintiff] cites no support for his proposition that the ADEA protects an employee from an adverse employment decision based on *seniority* even if it cannot be demonstrated that chronological age was a factor. Indeed, it has been recognized that "seniority and age discrimination are unrelated. The ADEA targets discrimination against employees who fall within a protected age category, not employees who have attained a given seniority status." *Williams v General Motors Corp.,* 656 F.2d 120, 130 n. 17 (5th Cir. 1981), *cert. denied,* 455 U.S. 943 . . . (1982).[393]

Pension eligibility may serve as a basis for making decisions regarding employees.[394] Courts addressing ADEA claims have perceived such a close relationship between this factor and age that they have equated the two.[395] The actual availability of a pension (as opposed to imminent eligibility for a pension) also may constitute a proxy for age, although "the use of pensions as a

---

391 957 F2d 1070 (3d Cir 1992).

392 *Id* 1087.

393 *Id.*

394 *See, e.g.,* Equal Employment Opportunity Commn v City of Altoona, 723 F2d 4, 6 (3d Cir 1983), *cert denied,* 467 US 1264 (1984). See generally ch 5 regarding the *reasonable factors other than age* exception.

395 *See, e.g.,* Equal Employment Opportunity Commn v City of Altoona, 723 F2d 4, 6 (3d Cir 1983), *cert denied,* 467 US 1264 (1984); Equal Employment Opportunity Commn v Babcock & Wilcox Co, 43 FEP Cas (BNA) 736 (EDNC 1987).

proxy for age should be examined on a case by case basis.''[396] Those lower court rulings standing for the proposition that it is a violation of the ADEA to fire an employee to prevent the vesting of his or her pension[397] are no longer valid in light of *Hazen Paper Co v Biggins,* discussed *infra.*[398] (A discharge allegedly motivated by the employer's desire to avoid the vesting of a pension, or its desire to prevent the further accrual of benefits by the employee, can be attacked, however, under §510 of the Employee Retirement Income Security Act.)[399]

Hazen Paper Co v Biggins

Biggins involved a 62-year-old plaintiff who had been fired just weeks before his pension would have vested pursuant to the terms of the company plan, which provided for vesting once an employee had worked for the employer for 10 years. The court of appeals had sustained the jury verdict in his favor, reasoning as follows:

> The jury . . . could also have reasonably found that age was inextricably intertwined with the decision to fire . . . [Biggins]. If it were not for . . . [his] age, sixty-two, his pension rights would not have been within a hairbreadth of vesting. . . . [He] was fifty-two years old when he was hired; his pension rights vested in ten years.[400]

---

[396] Wheeldon v Monon Corp, 946 F2d 533, 536 (7th Cir 1991).

[397] *See e.g.,* Tuck v Henkel Corp, 973 F2d 371, 376 (4th Cir 1992), *cert denied,* 113 S Ct 1276 (1993); Reichman v Bonsignore, Brignati & Mazzotta, PC, 818 F2d 278 (2d Cir 1987); Pirone v Home Ins Co, 507 F Supp 1281 (SDNY 1981); Marshall v Arlene Knitwear, Inc, 454 F Supp 715 (EDNY 1978), *affd in part & revd in part without opinion,* 608 F2d 1369 (2d Cir 1979); Bishop v Jelleff Assocs, Inc, 398 F Supp 579 (DDC 1974); *see also* Castleman v Acme Boot Co, 959 F2d 1417, 1421 (7th Cir 1992) (''evidence of timing [of discharge] in relation to the vesting of pension benefits can be evidence of age discrimination.''). *But see* Greanias v Sears, Roebuck & Co, 774 F Supp 462, 472 (ND Ill 1991).

[398] 113 S Ct 1701 (1993).

[399] 29 USC §1140.

[400] Biggins v Hazen Paper Co, 953 F2d 1405, 1412 (1st Cir 1992), *revd,* 113 S Ct 1701 (1993).

The Supreme Court, noting the case law discussed *supra* concerning situations where an employer utilizes "a factor, such as an employee's pension status or seniority, that is empirically correlated with age,"[401] unreservedly stated as follows: "We now clarify that there is no disparate treatment under the ADEA when the factor motivating the employer is some feature other than the employee's age."[402] The court went on to point out that "[w]hatever the employer's decisionmaking process, a disparate treatment claim cannot succeed unless the employee's protected trait [, i.e., age,] actually played a role in that process and had a determinative influence on the outcome."[403] The Court then explained why it is that the mere correlation between age and some factor other than age cannot suffice to establish that the employer was in fact motivated by the employee's age:

> When the employer's decision is wholly motivated by factors other than age, the problem of inaccurate and stigmatizing stereotypes disappears. This is true even if the motivating factor is correlated with age, as pension status typically is. . . . On average, an older employee has had more years in the work force than a younger employee, and thus may well have accumulated more years of service [a factor which is typically correlated with pension eligibility] with a particular employer. Yet an employee's age is analytically distinct from his years of service. An employee who is younger than 40, and therefore outside the class of older workers as defined by the ADEA, . . . may have worked for a particular employer his entire career, while an older worker may have been newly hired. Because age and years of service are analytically distinct, an employer can take account of one while ignoring the other, and thus it is incorrect to say that a decision based on years of service is necessarily "age-based."[404]

---

401 113 S Ct at 1705.

402 *Id.*

403 *Id* 1706.

404 *Id* 1706-07.

In sum, the Court rejected an unthinking equation whereby an employer's utilization of an age-correlated factor can be deemed to constitute a violation of the ADEA. In so doing the Court did not do anything that really flew in the face of the lower court case law discussed *supra.* (save for the case law specifically condemning discharges resulting from imminent pension vesting as being violative of the ADEA). Nor did it do anything that marked a departure from pre-existing doctrine: it has always been required of a plaintiff in a discriminatory treatment case that he or she prove that age animus motivated the defendant's challenged decision or action, such that the plaintiff's age played a determinative, or but-for role, in the defendant's decision-making process.[405] Thus, the foregoing case law in very large measure survives (although in light of *Hazen Paper* a court will have to carefully ensure that it was the grievant's age that actually was determinative in motivating the defendant to utilize the proxy). Indeed, the Court itself went on to make clear that an analysis taking into account a defendant's reliance upon an age-correlated factor remains viable:

> We do not preclude the possibility that an employer who targets employees with a particular pension status on the assumption that these employees are likely to be older thereby engages in age discrimination. Pension status may be a proxy for age, not in the sense that the ADEA makes the two factors equivalent, cf. *Metz* [*v Transit Mix, Inc*], 828 F.2d [1202,] at 1208 [7th Cir 1987] . . . (using "proxy" to mean statutory equivalence), but in the sense that the employer may suppose a correlation between the two factors and act accordingly. . . . Our holding is simply that an employer does not violate the ADEA just by interfering with an older employee's pension benefits that would have vested by virtue of the employee's years of service.[406]

---

[405] In regard to discriminatory treatment case law, see **ch 7.**

[406] 113 S Ct at 1707-08. The Court also pointed out that it was not addressing "the special case where an employee is about to vest in pension benefits as a result of his *age,* rather than years of service . . . and the employer fires the employee in order to prevent vesting." *Id* 1707 (Court's emphasis).

The *Hazen Paper* opinion, which was unanimous, did not address disparate impact analysis other than to note, in a general review of ADEA case law, that the Court had "never decided whether a disparate impact theory of liability is available under the ADEA . . . and we need not do so here."[407] It was able to avoid discussion of the issue because the plaintiff had not pursued an impact theory; he claimed "only that he received disparate treatment."[408] Justice Kennedy concurred, in an opinion joined by the Chief Justice and Justice Thomas. He pointed out, as had Justice O'Connor in her opinion for the Court, that the plaintiff had not argued disparate impact, and he then proceeded to stress that the applicability of that theory in the ADEA context was not being addressed here. Having made these points, he nonetheless went on to suggest that impact analysis was of questionable validity vis-a-vis the ADEA: "[T]here are substantial arguments that it is improper to carry over disparate impact analysis from Title VII [of the Civil Rights Act of 1964[409]] to the ADEA."[410]

It would seem reasonable to conclude that the case law condemning the use of age-related proxies survives in the discriminatory treatment context—albeit with a need for careful insistence by the courts that a plaintiff prove intent to unlawfully discriminate. In other words, when a factor correlated with age is relied upon by an employer, the plaintiff who seeks to establish an intentional discrimination claim has the task of proving that the employer, by relying on that factor, intended to discriminate on the basis of age. The possibility of successfully attacking proxies for age on discriminatory impact grounds also likely survives *Hazen Paper.*

(It might be reasoned that if the discharge at issue in *Hazen Paper* had been invalid on discriminatory impact grounds, the Court could have affirmed the lower court's ruling for the plain-

---

[407] *Id* 1706.

[408] *Id.*

[409] 42 USC §§2000e through 2000e-17.

[410] 113 S Ct at 1710 (Kennedy, J., concurring, joined by Rehnquist, C.J., and Thomas, J.).

tiff, even though the plaintiff had not pursued an impact theory. Since the Court did not affirm, one might conjecture that its doing so in some way cast a pall over the relevance of disparate impact analysis to age-related proxies. However, such conjectural analysis would be inapt, because the Court on numerous occasions has asserted that it will not address issues not raised below.[411] Thus, the plaintiff's failure to pursue an impact claim below naturally would lead to the Court's not addressing impact analysis, without any adverse conclusions to be drawn from the Court's silence.

What *Hazen Paper* probably actually signals, insofar as disparate impact analysis is concerned, is the fact that the Court is divided on the applicability of such analysis to the ADEA. For a long time, Chief Justice Rehnquist had stood alone in suggesting that such analysis was inapplicable;[412] the *Hazen Paper* concurrence suggests that he had secured, by 1993, two allies. But the majority of the Court, unwilling to tackle the issue, was able to use the excuse of the plaintiff's not having argued disparate impact analysis in *Hazen Paper* to avoid resolving the Court's internal conflict, thereby leaving the matter for another day.

Posting and Record-Keeping Requirements

§4.20 Notice Requirements

Those entities that are required to comply with the requirements of the Age Discrimination in Employment Act (ADEA),[413] i.e., entities that qualify as employers,[414] employment agencies,[415]

---

[411] *See, e.g.*, Youakim v Miller, 425 US 231, 234 (1976); California v Taylor, 353 US 553, 557 n2 (1957).

[412] *See* Markham v Geller, 451 US 945 (1981) (Rehnquist, J., dissenting from denial of certiorari). See **ch 7.**

[413] 29 USC §§621-634.

[414] See **ch 3.**

[415] *Id.*

and labor organizations,[416] must post notices as to the rights afforded by the ADEA. The notice either must be prepared by, or approved by, the Equal Employment Opportunity Commission (EEOC).[417] It must be posted in a prominent and accessible place where it readily can be seen by individuals who are protected, or may be protected, under the Act.[418] A covered entity's failure to post such a notice will provide a sufficient basis for a court to excuse a late-filing grievant—i.e., an individual who had not timely filed a charge of unlawful discrimination with the EEOC—from what would otherwise be the adverse consequences of that late filing.[419]

§4.21 Record-Keeping Requirements

The Equal Employment Opportunity Commission (EEOC) is the enforcement agency for the Age Discrimination in Employment Act (ADEA).[420] The Act empowers the agency to issue regulations requiring the keeping of records,[421] and the EEOC has exercised that authority. Covered employers are required to retain for three years each employee's name, address, date of birth, occupation, rate of pay, and weekly compensation.[422] Additionally, employers must retain for one year records relating to job applications, resumés, employment inquiries, promotions, demotions, transfers, selections for training, layoffs, recalls, discharges, job orders submitted to employment agencies, applicant test papers, results of physical exams, and advertisements.[423] Employers also must keep copies of employee

---

[416] *Id.*

[417] 29 USC §627.

[418] 29 CFR §1627.10 (1993).

[419] See **ch 6.**

[420] 29 USC §§621-634.

[421] *Id* §626(a).

[422] 29 CFR §1627.3(a) (1993).

[423] *Id* §1627.3(b)(1).

benefit plans and merit or seniority systems for the periods during which they are in force, and for one year after their termination.[424]

Records must be retained for one year by employment agencies regarding placements, referrals, job orders, job applications, resumés, employment inquiries, test papers, and advertisements.[425] Labor organizations are required to maintain current records of the names, addresses, and dates of birth of their members.[426] These organizations also are required to keep for one year the names, addresses, and ages of any persons "seeking membership," a term of art defined in the regulations.[427]

When an enforcement action is pending, a covered entity may be required by the EEOC to keep its records until the action is concluded.[428]

Covered entities are not required to use any special forms for record keeping.[429] "If the information required is available in records kept for other purposes, or can be obtained readily by recomputing or extending data recorded in some other form, no further records are required to be made or kept on a routine basis."[430] An entity that is required to maintain records can petition the EEOC for an exemption from a record-keeping requirement if the exemption will not interfere with enforcement of the Act.[431]

---

[424] *Id* §1627.3(b)(2). "If the plan or system is not in writing, a memorandum fully outlining the terms of such plan or system and the manner in which it has been communicated to the affected employees, together with notations relating to any changes or revisions thereto, shall be kept on file for a like period." *Id.*

[425] *Id* §1627.4(a)(1).

[426] *Id* §1627.5(a).

[427] *Id* §1627.5(b).

[428] *Id* §§1627.3(b)(3) (employers), 1627.4(a)(2) (employment agencies), 1627.5(c) (labor organizations).

[429] *Id* §1627.2.

[430] *Id.*

[431] *Id* §1627.11.

The records that are maintained pursuant to the regulations are to be kept in a safe and accessible place at "the place of business or employment at which the individual to whom they relate is employed or has applied for employment or membership, or at one or more established central recordkeeping offices."[432] These records must be available for inspection and transcription by authorized representatives of the EEOC during the business hours observed by the office at which they are located or in the community generally.[433] Covered entities must make such extensions, recomputations, or transcriptions of records, and must submit such reports concerning actions taken and limitations and classifications of individuals set forth in its records, as the EEOC or its authorized representative may request in writing.[434]

---

[432] *Id* §1627.6(a).

[433] *Id* §1627.6(b). "Where records are maintained at a central recordkeeping office . . ., such records shall be made available at the office at which they would otherwise be required to be kept within 72 hours following request from the Commission or its authorized representative." *Id.*

[434] *Id* §1627.7.

5 The Age Discrimination in Employment Act—Statutory Affirmative Defenses, Regulatory Exemptions, and Waivers of Liability

Releases from, or Waivers of, Liability

Administrative Exemptions

§5.01 Introduction

In several instances the Age Discrimination in Employment Act (ADEA)[1] carves out exceptions to its various prohibitions on discrimination in the work place. In some instances these exceptions are definitional in nature. For example, the ADEA requires that for an employer to be covered by the Act, i.e., for it to be required to comply with the statute, it must have at least 20 employees for each working day in 20 or more weeks of the

---

[1] 29 USC §§621-634.

current or preceding calendar year.[2] Or, to use another example, while the act extends protection to individuals from age 40 on, it at the same time excludes certain executives and high-level policy makers upon their turning 65. These exceptions, i.e., provisions that go to defining who may and who may not invoke the protection of the ADEA and that go to defining what entities must comply with the Act, are addressed in Chapter 3.

The ADEA sets forth statutory provisions that constitute, either clearly or arguably, affirmative defenses. These provisions carve out exceptions to the Act's prohibitions, such that an entity that makes a decision or takes an action that would otherwise violate the statute will be deemed to have acted lawfully, or at least be insulated from liability, by virtue of its proving that one of these statutory defenses is applicable. This chapter addresses these statutorily enunciated affirmative defenses, of which there are several:

—the §4(f)(2)[3] bona fide occupational qualification defense;
—the §4(f)(2) reasonable factors other than age exception, which arguably constitutes an affirmative defense;
—the §4(f)(3)[4] good cause exception, which only barely arguably is an affirmative defense;
—the §4(f)(2) bona fide employee benefit plan defense;
—the various benefit-related defenses set forth in §4(l);[5]
—the §4(f)(2)(B)(ii)[6] defense regarding voluntary retirement plans;
—the §7(f)[7] defense regarding waivers, or releases, of liability;

---

[2] §11(b), 29 USC §630(b).

[3] 29 USC §623(f)(2).

[4] *Id* §623(f)(3).

[5] *Id* §623(1).

[6] *Id* §623(f)(2)(B)(ii).

[7] *Id* §626(f).

[8] *Id* §623(f)(1).

—the §4(f)(1)[8] foreign laws defense; and
—the §7(e)[9] good-faith reliance defense.

There also are affirmative defenses that have been devised by the courts. In the context of disparate impact litigation the defendant as to which a prima facie case has been proven bears the burden of proving the business necessity defense.[10] In the context of discriminatory intent cases, the defendant as to which a prima facie case has been proven on the basis of direct evidence bears the burden—according to some courts—of proving that it would have made the same decision even had it not taken the forbidden factor of age into account.[11] The *same decision* defense also applies in the context of discriminatory intent mixed motives cases.[12] And it may even apply, as well, in less discretely identifiable situations. In the context of damages, the defendant bears the burden of proving the applicability of set-offs, i.e., amounts to be set off against the monetary award due a prevailing plaintiff.[13] The defendant that seeks to reduce its exposure to liability for back pay relief has the burden of proving that the plaintiff failed to mitigate damages.[14] Of course, issues involving defects in the plaintiff's pursuit of his or her claim, such as the untimeliness of the filing of a charge of unlawful discrimination,[15] must be raised and proven by the defendant.[16]

This chapter also addresses the administrative exemptions that have been made to the Act's prohibitions by the ADEA enforcement agency, the Equal Employment Opportunity Commission (EEOC), pursuant to the authority vested in it by §9.[17]

---

9 *Id* §626(e).

10 See **ch 7.**

11 *Id.*

12 *Id.*

13 *See* Tyler v Bethlehem Steel Corp, 958 F2d 1176 (2d Cir 1992). See **ch 7.**

14 See **ch 8.**

15 See **ch 6.**

16 *Id.*

17 *Id* §628.

The Bona Fide Occupational Qualification Defense

§5.02 The Bona Fide Occupational Qualification Defense: Generally

The bona fide occupational qualification defense (BFOQ) set forth in §4(f)(1)[18] of the Age Discrimination in Employment Act (ADEA)[19] is one of the key affirmative defenses created by the statute. Section 4(f)(1), which has generated a considerable amount of litigation—including three Supreme Court rulings[20] —provides as follows:

> It shall not be unlawful for an employer, employment agency, or labor organization—
>
> (1) to take any action otherwise prohibited under subsections (a), (b), (c), or (e) of this section where age is a bona fide occupational qualification reasonably necessary to the normal operation of the particular business[.][21]

A defendant that invokes this provision in effect admits that it engaged in an action, or made a decision, that ordinarily would constitute unlawful age discrimination. But the BFOQ defense contention, if successfully invoked, will insulate the defendant

---

[18] 29 USC §623(f)(1).

[19] *Id* §§621-634.

[20] Johnson v Mayor & City Council of Baltimore, 472 US 353 (1985); Western Air Lines, Inc v Criswell, 472 US 400 (1985); Trans World Air Lines, Inc v Thurston, 469 US 111 (1985).

[21] This provision is not applicable to federal employees. As to them, the Act provides that BFOQs may be established by the Equal Employment Opportunity Commission (EEOC). §15(b), 29 USC §633a(b). See generally **ch 9.** In 1986 the Act was amended to allow employers to impose age limitations for the hiring and retirement of firefighters and law enforcement officers without the obligation to justify such requirements in terms of the BFOQ defense. See **ch 3.** This amendment had a limited life span, however, and thus the ability of entities to impose such age limitations expired on December 31, 1993. See **ch 3.**

from liability.[22] Of course, since the BFOQ exception constitutes an affirmative defense, as the defendant bears the burden of proof which burden entails a preponderance of the evidence standard.[23]

In the great majority of BFOQ cases it will be some particular age that is the disputed qualification. For example, an employer will contend that the status of being under age 60 is a bona fide occupational qualification for the job of test pilot, or the employer will maintain that the status of not being over age 45 is a bona fide requirement for being hired as a bus driver. The typical scenerio notwithstanding, it is conceivable that in some instances age per se will not be the claimed BFOQ. For example, *Johnson v American Airlines, Inc*[24] concerned a policy whereby all crew members who were ineligible for promotion to captain—the highest cockpit position—were fired. Since there was a federal regulation (not challenged in the case) that required the retirement of captains, or pilots, at age 60, it followed that lower-ranking officers who attained 59 would be discharged since by virtue of their ages they would not be eligible to rise to captaincies. The airline's up-or-out policy further effectively precluded

---

[22] A cause of action may not be maintained to force an employer to assert a BFOQ defense. Air Line Pilots Assn, Intl v Trans World Airlines, Inc, 713 F2d 940, 950-51 (2d Cir 1983), *affd in part & revd in part on other grounds,* 469 US 111 (1985).

[23] *See, e.g.,* Heiar v Crawford County, 746 F2d 1190, 1198 (7th Cir 1984), *cert denied,* 472 US 1027 (1985); Hoefelman v Conservation Commn, 718 F2d 281, 283 (8th Cir 1983); Equal Employment Opportunity Commn v University of Tex Health Science Ctr, 710 F2d 1091, 1093 (5th Cir 1983). In Mang v Blumenthal, 26 FEP Cas (BNA) 1353 (WD Pa 1981), the court presented a confused amalgamation of the BFOQ analysis with the burdens imposed when this affirmative defense is not invoked. See **ch 7.** It stated that the burden was on the defendant only to produce a legitimate nondiscriminatory reason for its refusal to hire the plaintiff; proceeded to conclude that the defendant had failed to establish what appeared to be a BFOQ defense; and thus held that the defendant had failed to produce a legitimate, nondiscriminatory reason. While the court was correct in concluding that a BFOQ defense was not sufficiently proven, the defendant indeed had satisfied the minimal burden of production that the court erroneously stated was all that applied. Thus, the court erred in both the standard it set forth and in its application of that erroneous standard.

[24] 745 F2d 988 (5th Cir 1984), *cert denied,* 472 US 1027 (1985).

captains who reached 60 from transferring to lower-level flight officer positions; it also barred other 59-and-over individuals from being hired in the first instance as flight officers. American contended that it was eligibility for promotion, rather than any particular age, that was a BFOQ. The court was persuaded by this contention: it concluded that the policy could qualify as a valid BFOQ.[25]

The agencies that have been charged with responsibility for administration and enforcement of the ADEA consistently have interpreted the BFOQ defense as a very narrow one. The Secretary of Labor, who initially had enforcement authority, issued an interpretation which declared that the BFOQ provision had only "limited scope and application" and had to "be construed narrowly."[26] The Equal Employment Opportunity Commission (EEOC), to which enforcement authority was transferred as of July 1, 1979,[27] takes a similar position: "It is anticipated that this concept of a bona fide occupational qualification will have limited scope and application. Further, as this is an exception to the Act it must be narrowly construed."[28] The Supreme Court placed its stamp of approval on these readings of the BFOQ defense in *Western Air Lines, Inc v Criswell*:[29]

> The restrictive language of the statute, and the consistent interpretation of the administrative agencies charged with

---

[25] *See also* Murnane v American Airlines, Inc, 667 F2d 98 (DC Cir 1981), *cert denied,* 456 US 915 (1982). *But see* Smallwood v United Air Lines, Inc, 661 F2d 303, 308 (4th Cir 1981), *cert denied,* 456 US 1007 (1982). In Iervolino v Delta Air Lines, Inc, 796 F2d 1408 (11th Cir 1986), *cert denied,* 479 US 1090 (1987), the court adverted to, but did not resolve, the question of whether non-age factors may be considered in determining the validity of a job criterion defended as a BFOQ. *Id* 1418 & 1418 n11. Almost all courts reject taking into consideration economic concerns as a factor buttressing, excusing, or otherwise supporting an age-based job criterion as a BFOQ. See **§5.09**.

[26] 29 CFR §860.102(b) (1986) (effectively rescinded, 46 Fed Reg 47724 (Sept 29, 1981), and ordered removed from the CFR, 52 Fed Reg 23812 (June 25, 1987)).

[27] See **ch 2**.

[28] 29 CFR §1625.6 (1993). Such interpretations do not have the force of law, but they are accorded considerable deference by the courts. See **ch 2**.

[29] 472 US 400 (1985).

> enforcing the statute convince us that, like its . . . counterpart [in Title VII of the Civil Rights Act of 1964,[30]] the BFOQ exception "was in fact meant to be an extremely narrow exception to the general prohibition" of age discrimination contained in the ADEA.[31]

Title VII's BFOQ provision—the language of which is identical to that of the ADEA—was addressed in *International Union v Johnson Controls, Inc,*[32] which concerned a fetal protection policy requiring the exclusion of fertile women from jobs involving exposure to lead. The employer argued that its policy was justifiable as a BFOQ because it served to protect fetuses from potential harm. The problem for the employer, as a legal matter, was that the policy had nothing to do with the question of job performance. In holding that the policy could not survive attack under Title VII, the court focused on the language of the BFOQ defense and articulated an analysis clearly applicable, by way of analogy,[33] to the identical language of the ADEA BFOQ provision:

> The concurrence defines "occupational" as meaning related to a job. . . . According to the concurrence, any discriminatory treatment imposed by an employer is "job-related" simply because the employer has chosen to make the requirement a condition of employment. . . . This reading of "occupational" renders the word mere surplusage. "Qualification" by itself would encompass an employer's idiosyncratic requirements. By modifying "qualification"

---

30 42 USC §§2000e through 2000e-17. The ADEA is in part modeled on Title VII. See **ch 2.** Indeed, the *Criswell* Court noted that the ADEA's BFOQ exception specifically was derived from Title VII. 472 US at 412-13.

31 472 US at 412 (quoting Dothard v Rawlinson, 433 US 321, 334 (1977)).

32 499 US 187 (1991).

33 ADEA courts regularly look to Title VII rulings for analogical guidance, given the similar ends, i.e., eradication of discrimination in the workplace, and the similar prohibitory language of the two statutes. See **ch 2.**

> with "occupational," Congress narrowed the term to qualifications that affect an employee's ability to do the job.[34]

The Supreme Court has enunciated a formulation of the burden that a defendant invoking the BFOQ defense must satisfy.[35] The actual application of that test can only be understood on a case-by-case basis, however.[36] Thus, generalizations inevitably must be tempered with the cautionary note that specific cases should be examined. In this vein, the district court aptly observed as follows in *Equal Employment Opportunity Commission v New Jersey*:[37]

> The decisions are, in a phrase, "all over the lot" with little consistency seen even between cases in which the "essence of the business" appears to be identical. In large measure, of course, this result emanates from the fact-dependent nature of each case.[38]

§5.03 The BFOQ Defense's Legislative History

The legislative history of the Age Discrimination in Employment Act's (ADEA)[39] bona fide occupational qualification (BFOQ) exception,[40] which has been a part of the statute since its enactment in 1967, is not illuminating. Of tangential relevance is a reference in the report accompanying the House version of the original legislation to the fact that the House Committee on Education and Labor had rejected a suggestion

---

[34] 499 US at 201 (emphasis added).

[35] See **§5.05.**

[36] The EEOC interpretation states as follows:

> (a) Whether occupational qualifications will be deemed to be "bona fide" to a specific job and "reasonably necessary to the normal operation of the particular business," will be determined on the basis of all the pertinent facts surrounding each particular situation.

29 CFR §1625.6(a) (1993).

[37] 620 F Supp 977 (DNJ 1985).

[38] *Id* 982.

[39] 29 USC §§621-634.

[40] §4(f)(1), 29 USC §623(f)(1).

that the bill being considered—which bill ultimately was enacted as the ADEA—be amended to specifically allow bona fide management training programs to constitute exceptions to the bill's proscriptions. The report then went on as follows: "The committee recognizes . . . that bona fide age requirements do exist for some positions designed to give employees knowledge and experience which can reasonably be expected to aid in developing capabilities required for future advancement to executive, administrative, or professional positions.[41] At best, this statement was not directly linked to the BFOQ exception that was contained in the bill and that ultimately was enacted into law as the §4(f)(1)[42] BFOQ provision. Moreover, the Committee commentary in any event offered little by way of substance.

As for the actual BFOQ provision embodied in §4(f)(1), the Committee made no direct mention of it. On a more general note, however, the Committee observed as follows:

> The case-by-case basis should serve as the underlying rule in the administration of the legislation. Too many different types of situations in employment occur for the strict application of general prohibitions and provisions. It is enough that the bill outlines a national policy against discrimination in employment on account of age . . . and establishes broad guidelines for its implementation.[43]

The Senate Committee report on its version of the legislation was even less informative.[44]

The debates in the House and Senate added nothing. The chairman of the Senate Committee, acting as manager of the legislation on the Senate floor, simply stated that the bill contained four exceptions, one of which was the BFOQ provision. He further observed: "The example is often given—although I do not

---

[41] Committee on Educ & Labor, Age Discrimination in Employment Act of 1967, HR Rep No 805, 90th Cong, 1st Sess 4-5 (1967).

[42] 29 USC §623(f)(1).

[43] HR Rep No 805, *supra* note 41, at 7.

[44] Committee on Labor & Pub Welfare, Age Discrimination in Employment Act of 1967, S Rep No 723, 90th Cong, 1st Sess (1967).

know at what age this limit would apply—of a jet pilot who flies a plane at many hundreds of miles an hour."[45] In the House, several Representatives made reference to the forced retirement at age 32 or 35 of airline stewardesses by airlines. Representative Mink in particular condemned this practice; she also reported it was justified by the airlines as constituting a BFOQ.[46] No specific action was taken, however, regarding this practice; rather, the legislation contained a section requiring the Secretary of Labor to conduct a study regarding age barriers such as that imposed vis-a-vis the stewardesses.[47]

---

[45] 113 Cong Rec 31253 (Nov 6, 1967) (statement of Sen. Yarborough).

[46] Rep. Mink stated as follows:

> I submit, Mr. Speaker, that it seems to me perfectly legitimate to set very high standards of physical ability, even, if the airlines think it absolutely necessary, of appearance, for the job of stewardess. But these criteria should be objective criteria. They should not be reinforced by the apparent assumption that a stewardess becomes senile, incapable of assisting passengers and generally so repulsive as to drive customers out of the air simply because they have reached the age of 32.

113 Cong Rec 34743 (Dec 4, 1967).

[47] In 1978 the Act was amended in several respects. One of these changes involved raising the age ceiling for protection from age 65 to 70. See **ch 3.** The Senate bill proposed to amend the BFOQ provision so as to assure that, notwithstanding this increase in the ceiling, mandatory retirement at a lesser age still could be imposed where age was a BFOQ. This latter provision ultimately was rejected by the conference committee that met to work out differences between the Senate and House versions of the 1978 legislation. The basis for this rejection was the conclusion that "the [proposed BFOQ] amendment neither added to nor worked any change upon present law." Conference Comm, Age Discrimination in Employment Act Amendments of 1978, HR Rep No 950, 95th Cong, 2d Sess 6 (1978). In other words, the Senate provision was unnecessary.

In 1986 the Act was amended by the Age Discrimination in Employment Amendments of 1986, Pub L No 99-592, 100 Stat 3342, to allow employers to impose age limitations for the hiring and retirement of firefighters and of law enforcement officers without obliging the employers to justify such requirements in terms of the BFOQ defense, so long as the ages used were in existence on March 3, 1983, and so long as these requirements were not subterfuges to avoid the purposes of the Act. §4(i), 29 USC §623(i). See **ch 3.** This amendment had a limited lifespan: it automatically expired on December 31, 1993. Age Discrimination in Employment Amendments of 1986, Pub L No 99-592, §3(b), 100 Stat 3342. See **ch 3.**

§5.04 Agency Interpretations

The Department of Labor was the agency initially charged with administration and enforcement of the Age Discrimination in Employment Act (ADEA),[48] and in pursuance of this role the Department issued what it termed an Interpretative Bulletin that set forth interpretations regarding the Act.[49] Since July 1, 1979, the Equal Employment Opportunity Commission (EEOC) has administered the ADEA.[50] It, too, has issued interpretations; these supplanted the Department of Labor's Bulletin, which subsequently was rescinded.[51] While such interpretations—both those of the Labor Department during its tenure as the enforcement agency and those of the EEOC—do not have the force of law, they do command considerable judicial respect, given that they are the expressed views of the agency charged with the responsibility of enforcing the ADEA.[52]

In its interpretation the Labor Department set forth illustrations of possible bona fide occupational qualifications (BFOQs).[53] The EEOC, however, has abjured articulating examples of valid BFOQs in order to avoid being perceived as expressing approbation for any specific age-based policies.[54] However, the EEOC interpretation, after asserting the position

---

[48] 29 USC §§621-634.

[49] 29 CFR pt 860 (1986) (effectively rescinded, 46 Fed Reg 47724 (Sept 29, 1981), and ordered removed from the CFR, 52 Fed Reg 23812 (June 25, 1987)).

[50] As to the transfer of authority to the EEOC, see **ch 2.**

[51] 29 CFR §1625.6 (1993). Even before the removal by the Labor Department of the Bulletin from the Code of Federal Regulations, 52 Fed Reg 23812 (June 25, 1987), the EEOC had pointed out that its issuance of interpretations effectively rescinded the Bulletin. 46 Fed Reg 47724 (Sept 29, 1981).

[52] As to the significance accorded by the courts to agency interpretations, see generally **ch 2.**

[53] 29 CFR §860.102(d), (e) (1986) (effectively rescinded, 46 Fed Reg 47724 (Sept 29, 1981), and ordered removed from the CFR, 52 Fed Reg 23812 (June 25, 1987)).

[54] 46 Fed Reg 47725 (Sept 29, 1981).

that the BFOQ exception is to be narrowly construed[55] and that the validity of a claimed BFOQ should be determined on a case-by-case basis,[56] does set forth the test that, in the agency's view, must be met by an entity that invokes the BFOQ defense. The Commission's formulation, which closely parallels that enunciated in 1985 by the Supreme Court in *Western Air Lines, Inc v Criswell,*[57] provides as follows:

> An employer asserting a BFOQ defense has the burden of proving that (1) the age limit is reasonably necessary to the essence of the business, and either (2) that all or substantially all individuals excluded from the job involved are in fact disqualified, or (3) that some of the individuals so excluded possess a disqualifying trait that cannot be ascertained except by reference to age.[58]

In addition, the EEOC interpretation adds a twist that the *Criswell* Court did not adopt: "If the employer's objective in asserting a BFOQ is the goal of public safety, the employer must prove that the challenged practice does indeed effectuate that goal and that there is no acceptable alternative which would better advance or equally advance it with less discriminatory impact."[59] In its interpretation the agency further asserts that state and local laws and/or regulations that conflict with the BFOQ exception by extending lesser protection to employees than does the BFOQ provision will be deemed to be superseded by the ADEA.[60]

---

55 29 CFR §1625.6(a) (1993).

56 *Id.*

57 472 US 400 (1985).

58 29 CFR §1625.6(b) (1993). The EEOC test differs from the *Criswell*-approved formulation in that, insofar as the second part of the test—as articulated by the agency—is concerned, a defendant does not appear to be required to have a factual basis for believing the proposition set forth in the second clause. *Criswell* does require such a basis. See **§5.05.** Of course, to the extent that the EEOC standard differs from the standard embraced by the Supreme Court, the agency language is invalid.

59 29 CFR §1625.6(b) (1993).

60 *Id* §1625.6(c). As to preemption generally, see **ch 2.**

The EEOC also has issued a policy guide for the processing of claims by the agency, wherein the EEOC takes the position that "an employee disqualified from one job or position because of an age-based BFOQ or other age-based statutory provision must be afforded the same employment options as other employees disqualified for non-age related reasons."[61]

§5.05 Case Law Defining the BFOQ Test

In *Western Air Lines, Inc v Criswell*[62] the Supreme Court embraced a two-part formula that a number of courts of appeals,[63] as well as federal district and state courts,[64] had been

---

[61] EEOC Policy Guide No N-915.045: Cases Involving Charging Parties who Have Been Disqualified by Bona Fide Occupation Qualification or Other Age-Based Statutory Provisions and not Given the Same Options Afforded Employees Disqualified for Reasons Unrelated to Age 2 (Dec 5, 1989). (This policy guide is reproduced in the Appendix at the end of the last volume.

[62] 472 US 400 (1985).

[63] By the time *Criswell* was decided the following circuits already had adopted the test embraced in the Supreme Court ruling: **First:** Mahoney v Trabucco, 738 F2d 35 (1st Cir), *cert denied,* 469 US 1036 (1984); **Fourth:** Smallwood v United Air Lines, Inc, 661 F2d 303 (4th Cir 1981), *cert denied,* 456 US 1007 (1982); **Fifth:** Usery v Tamiami Trail Tours, Inc, 531 F2d 224 (5th Cir 1976); **Sixth:** Tuohy v Ford Motor Co, 675 F2d 842 (6th Cir 1982); **Seventh:** Orzel v City of Wauwatosa Fire Dept, 697 F2d 743 (7th Cir), *cert denied,* 464 US 992 (1983); **Eighth:** Equal Employment Opportunity Commn v City of St Paul, 671 F2d 1162 (8th Cir 1982); **Ninth:** Criswell v Western Airlines, Inc, 709 F2d 544 (9th Cir 1983), *affd,* 472 US 400 (1985). The *Orzel* court effectively overruled an earlier Seventh Circuit ruling—Hodgson v Greyhound Lines, Inc, 499 F2d 859 (7th Cir 1974), *cert denied,* 419 US 1122 (1975)—in which the court had imposed a milder burden on the defendant. (The *Orzel* court unconvincingly sought to harmonize its ruling with the earlier *Greyhound* decision, but the conflict between the two was obvious. Ultimately, the *Criswell* court observed that *Orzel* had repudiated *Greyhound.* 472 US at 417 n26.) The District of Columbia Circuit subscribed to that milder test in Murnane v American Airlines, Inc, 667 F2d 98 (DC Cir 1981), *cert denied,* 456 US 915 (1982). Given *Criswell,* however, *Murnane* is no longer good law.

[64] *See, e.g.,* Hahn v City of Buffalo, 596 F Supp 939 (WDNY 1984), *affd,* 770 F2d 12 (2d Cir 1985); Maki v Commissioner of Educ, 568 F Supp 252 (NDNY 1983), *affd & dismissed without opinion,* 742 F2d 1437 (2d Cir 1984); Adams v James, 526 F Supp 80 (MD Ala 1981); Beck v Borough of Manheim, 505 F Supp 923 (ED Pa 1981); Rodriguez v Taylor, 428 F Supp 1118 (ED Pa 1976),

using already in determining whether the §4(f)(1) bona fide occupational qualification (BFOQ) defense[65] contained in the Age Discrimination in Employment Act (ADEA)[66] was satisfied. The initial version of this two-part test, which understandably devolves from the statutory language, was first articulated by an ADEA court in *Usery v Tamiami Trail Tours, Inc,*[67] and it was in the context of approvingly discussing *Tamiami* that the *Criswell* Court explained the factors involved in evaluating the merits of a BFOQ defense to a claim of age discrimination.

Tamiami had a policy of refusing to hire persons over age 40 as intercity bus drivers; it based this policy on safety considerations, i.e., the need to employ persons who had a low risk of accidents. The *Tamiami* court asserted, as quoted with approval in *Criswell,* the following:

> "[T]he job qualifications which the employer invokes to justify his discrimination must be *reasonably necessary* to the essence of his business—here, the *safe* transportation of bus passengers from one point to another. The greater the safety factor, measured by the likelihood of harm and the probable severity of that harm in case of an accident, the more stringent may be the job qualifications designed to insure safe driving." 531 F2d at 236.[68]

The *Criswell* Court went on to observe that age qualifications must "be something more than 'convenient' or 'reasonable'; they must be 'reasonably necessary . . . to the particular business,' and this is only so when the employer is compelled to rely on age as a proxy for the safety-related job qualifications validated in the first inquiry."[69]

---

affd on other grounds, 569 F2d 1231 (3d Cir 1977), *cert denied,* 436 US 913 (1978); Poteet v Palestine, 620 SW2d 181 (Tex Civ App 1981).

65 29 USC §623(f)(1).

66 *Id* §§621-634.

67 531 F2d 224 (5th Cir 1976).

68 472 US at 413 (*Tamiami* court's emphasis).

69 *Id.*

There are two ways in which the employer can establish that it is "compelled"—to use the *Criswell* Court's term—to rely on age:

> The employer could establish that it " 'had reasonable cause to believe, that is, a factual basis for believing, that all or substantially all [persons over the age qualification at issue] would be unable to perform safely and efficiently the duties of the job involved.' " . . .
>
> Alternatively, the employer could establish that age was a legitimate proxy for the safety-related job qualifications by proving that it is " 'impossible or highly impractical' " to deal with the older employees on an individualized basis. "One method by which the employer can carry this burden is to establish that some members of the discriminated-against class possess a trait precluding safe and efficient job performance that cannot be ascertained by means other than knowledge of the applicant's membership in the class."[70]

The *Criswell* Court, in the foregoing excerpt from its opinion, spoke of the employer "proving" the impracticality of individualized assessments.[71] More generally, all elements of the BFOQ test must be proven by the defendant, by a preponderance of

---

[70] *Id* 414 (quoting Usery v Tamiami Trail Tours, Inc, 531 F2d 224, 235 (5th Cir 1976), which in turn was quoting from Weeks v Southern Bell Tel & Tel Co, 408 F2d 228 (5th Cir 1969)).

[71] The court in Williams v Hughes Helicopters, Inc, 806 F2d 1387 (9th Cir 1986), put forth an unduly weak formulation when it said that "an employer need only show that individualized testing of job fitness is impossible or highly impracticable." *Id* 1391. Other courts also have been somewhat too loose (in light of *Criswell*) in their formulations. *See* Equal Employment Opportunity Commn v Mississippi State Tax Commn, 873 F2d 97, 98 (5th Cir 1989) ("employer must show"); Equal Employment Opportunity Commn v City of E Providence, 798 F2d 524, 528 (1st Cir 1986) (employer must "demonstrate" impracticality of individualized assessments); Equal Employment Opportunity Commn v Mississippi, 837 F2d 1398, 1401 (5th Cir 1988) (employer must "show"); Equal Employment Opportunity Commn v Pennsylvania, 829 F2d 392, 395 (3d Cir 1987), *cert denied,* 485 US 935 (1988) (employer must "show").

the evidence.[72] In satisfying this burden, the defendant that invokes the BFOQ defense must do two things, to restate *Criswell.* First, it must identify, i.e., prove, the essence, or essential operation, of its business. Second, it must prove that the age-based job qualification at issue is reasonably necessary to this essential operation.[73] In satisfying the latter task, the defendant has open to it two courses. It can seek to prove that it has reasonable cause to believe, that is, a factual basis for believing, that all or substantially all persons over the prescribed age cannot perform, and so no individualized assessment of abilities need be undertaken. Alternatively, the invoker of the BFOQ can seek to prove that it is impossible or highly impractical to deal on an individualized basis with persons who have attained, or exceed the prescribed age. (As to this latter tack, the "reasonable cause to believe," or "factual basis for believing" element is absent.)[74] As to the *impracticality/impossibility* facet of this stan-

---

[72] *See, e.g.,* Heiar v Crawford County, 746 F2d 1190, 1198 (7th Cir 1984), *cert denied,* 472 US 1027 (1985); Hoefelman v Conservation Commn, 718 F2d 281, 283 (8th Cir 1983); Equal Employment Opportunity Commn v University of Tex Health Science Ctr, 710 F2d 1091, 1093 (5th Cir 1983).

[73] *Cf* International Union v Johnson Controls, Inc, 499 US 187, 205-06 (1991) (construing BFOQ provision of Title VII of Civil Rights Act of 1964, 42 USC §§2000e through 2000e-17).

[74] In Equal Employment Opportunity Commn v University of Tex Health Science Ctr, 710 F2d 1091 (5th Cir 1983), the court misstated the *Tamiami* test. (This presumably was unintentional, since the court, immediately after its misstatement, cited the *Tamiami* decision as support for its erroneous formulation of the BFOQ test. Moreover, the court at no time suggested that it intended to modify *Tamiami.* In any event, unintentional or not, the formulation in the *Texas Health Science Center* case does not survive *Criswell.*) The court stated the test as being that, first, the classification must be reasonably necessary to the essence of the employer's business, and second:

> [T]he employer must have reasonable cause, that is, a factual basis, for believing *either* that all or substantially all persons within the excluded class would be unable to perform safely and efficiently the duties of the job or that it is impossible or impractical to deal with persons over the age limit on an individualized basis.

Id 1093 (court's emphasis). Thus, the court applied the reasonable-cause-to-believe predicate to both possibilities available to the defendant. However, in *Tamiami* the court only applied the "reasonable-cause-to-believe" language to the first possibility, i.e., the inability to perform safely and efficiently. As to the second, i.e., establishing that it is impossible or impractical to deal with

dard, it will be of no avail to a plaintiff to show that he or she was performing the job safely and efficiently if the employer establishes the impracticability of individualized assessments generally.[75]

The *Criswell* court stressed that the language of §4(f)(1) requiring that an age qualification be "reasonably necessary" in order to qualify as a BFOQ precludes a defendant-protective mere reasonableness test.[76] This rejection of a reasonableness standard occurred at two points. First, the Court deemed unpersuasive the defendant's argument that the challenged job qualification—i.e., a requirement that flight engineers be under age 60—should have been upheld as long as it was reasonable in light of the safety risks.[77] Second, the Court rejected the argument that an employer only need establish a rational basis in fact for its belief that all or substantially all persons over the prescribed age can-

---

persons over 40 on an individualized basis, that introductory plaintiff-protective (in that it increases the rigor of the defendant's task) phrase is omitted. Iervolino v Delta Air Lines, Inc, 796 F2d 1408, 1417 (11th Cir 1986), *cert denied,* 479 US 1090 (1987); Usery v Tamiami Trail Tours, Inc, 531 F2d 224, 236 (5th Cir 1976). In a subsequent ruling the same court engaged in the same infusion of the "reasonable cause to believe" language into the second option available to defendants, i.e., proving that it is impossible or highly impractical to deal on an individualized basis with the individuals in question. Johnson v American Airlines, Inc, 745 F2d 988 (5th Cir 1984), *cert denied,* 472 US 1027 (1985); *accord* Equal Employment Opportunity Commn v Pennsylvania, 596 F Supp 1333, 1337-38 (MD Pa 1984), *vacated & remanded on other grounds,* 768 F2d 514 (3d Cir 1985). And the court in Equal Employment Opportunity Commn v Pennsylvania, 645 F Supp 1545, 1546 (MD Pa 1986), *vacated & remanded on other grounds,* 829 F2d 352 (3d Cir 1987), *cert denied,* 488 US 935 (1988), construed an earlier ruling of the Court of Appeals for the Third Circuit as affirming this approach. Other courts have not engaged in this erroneous merger of the language of the BFOQ defense standard.

[75] Williams v Hughes Helicopters, Inc, 806 F2d 1387, 1391 (9th Cir 1986).

[76] Consequently, and as observed in Gately v Massachusetts, 811 F Supp 26, 29 (D Mass 1992), *affd on other grounds,* 2 F3d 1221 (1st Cir 1993), decisions utilizing a reasonableness standard, such as Mahoney v Trabucco, 738 F2d 35, 37 (1st Cir), *cert denied,* 469 US 1036 (1984), and Orzel v City of Wauwatosa Fire Dept, 697 F2d 743, 753 (7th Cir), *cert denied,* 464 US 992 (1983), were effectively overruled.

[77] 472 US at 419-20.

not perform. Rather, the defendant must prove by a preponderance of the evidence that it has "a substantial basis" for its belief.[78]

As the foregoing discussion reveals, the *Criswell* Court continuously couched its discussion in terms of a BFOQ invoked on the grounds of safety. Since both *Criswell* and the ruling on which it relied, *Tamiami*, involved safety issues, it is not surprising that the *Criswell* Court wrote as it did. Actually, safety concerns typically are invoked by defendants in BFOQ cases.[79] More than that, the case law discloses that such concerns constitute the most compelling bases for judicial tolerance of what otherwise would be unlawful discrimination; the greatest degree of leeway is afforded defendants where these concerns legitimately and persuasively are presented.[80] (Indeed, this assessment is confirmed by the extract from *Tamiami* relied upon in *Criswell* and quoted *supra*.) The point to be made here is that it is arguable that a different test might apply in nonsafety BFOQ cases. This inference can be drawn from the *Criswell* Court's phraseology, particularly its concluding sentence in the section of the opinion discussing the test, wherein the *Court* focused on the safety issue: "[W]e conclude that this two-part inquiry properly identifies the relevant considerations for resolving a BFOQ defense to an age-based qualification purportedly justified by considerations of safety."[81] Inasmuch as judicial willingness to tolerate age-based policies and practices will be at its height where legitimate safety issues are involved, it follows logically that *Criswell* and like rulings set the outer boundary for such judicial deference. In nonsafety cases, entailing less compelling justifications for overriding the ADEA's proscriptions, more rigorous applications of the BFOQ test's elements arguably should be in order.

---

78 *Id* 422. In the context of several mandatory retirement cases there has developed a split among the circuits as to whether an employer—in order to succeed in proving that an age-based mandatory policy is reasonably necessary—must develop and apply minimum standards of health and fitness for all of its employees. See **§5.11.**

79 See **§5.10.**

80 *Id.*

81 472 US at 416-17.

In *Johnson v Mayor of Baltimore*[82] the Court focused on the question of the judicial deference due administrative and legislative determinations regarding age restrictions.[83] In the course of its opinion the Court asserted that employers are required to make a "particularized factual showing" regarding each element of the BFOQ defense.[84] In *Equal Employment Opportunity Commission v Pennsylvania*[85] the Court of Appeals for the Third Circuit focused on this language. The district court apparently had assumed that good health and physical strength were job qualifications reasonably necessary to the essence of the state police agency business. But, as the appellate court read the lower court ruling, the trial court had made no particularized findings to that effect, and so the judgment was vacated.[86]

It has been reasoned that where there are exceptions to a policy of an employer whose use of an age requirement purportedly can be justified as a BFOQ, the employer will not be able to establish the BFOQ defense, since the exceptions belie the claimed need for using that requirement.[87] It also is possible that a BFOQ may be valid at one point in time, and then lose its validity by virtue of changed circumstances, such as advances in medical science.[88] In such a situation liability would be appropriately limited just to that period of time following cessation of the BFOQ's validity.[89]

---

[82] 472 US 353 (1985).

[83] See **§5.08.**

[84] 472 US at 362.

[85] 768 F2d 514 (3d Cir 1985).

[86] In contrast, such a finding was made in Equal Employment Opportunity Commn v New Jersey, 620 F Supp 977 (DNJ 1985).

[87] Equal Employment Opportunity Commn v Pan Am World Airways, Inc, 52 FEP Cas (BNA) 920, 925 (ND Cal 1987). See also **§5.11.**

[88] *See* Monroe v United Air Lines, Inc, 736 F2d 394 (7th Cir 1984), *cert denied*, 470 US 1004 (1985).

[89] *Id* 405.

§5.06 The "Particular Business" Requirement

Section 4(f)(1)[90] of the Age Discrimination in Employment Act (ADEA),[91] setting forth the Act's bona fide occupational qualification (BFOQ) exception, provides that "[i]t shall not be unlawful . . . to take any action otherwise prohibited . . . where age is a bona fide occupational qualification reasonably necessary to the normal operation of the particular business[.]"[92] Thus, one of the elements that a defendant invoking the BFOQ defense must satisfy is that its age-based discrimination relate to a particular business.

In *Trans World Airlines, Inc v Thurston*[93] the Supreme Court addressed the airline's policies regarding the transfer of pilots, or captains, to flight engineer positions. If a captain became disqualified from serving in his or her position for reasons other than age, he or she automatically was able to transfer to the position of flight engineer, even if that meant displacing a senior flight engineer. In contrast, if a captain became disqualified because of age—and there was a requirement, not challenged in the case, that pilots leave their positions at age 60[94]—then he or she would not be afforded the same *bumping* privilege. Instead, the captain would be forced to bid for a flight engineer position and, if there were no vacancy prior to his or her 60th birthday, the pilot would have to retire.

The airline contended that its transfer policy, which differentiated on the basis of age regarding who could automatically transfer, was lawful because age was a valid BFOQ for the position of pilot, or captain. The Court rejected the argument, observing with approbation that "[e]very court to consider the issue has assumed that the 'particular business' to which the statute refers

---

[90] 29 USC §623(f)(1).

[91] *Id* §§621-634.

[92] *Id* §623(f)(1).

[93] 469 US 111 (1985).

[94] This requirement was, and continues to be, imposed by 14 CFR §121.383(c) (1993).

is the job from which the protected individual is excluded."[95] In applying this general rule to the facts before it the Court stated as follows: "TWA's discriminatory transfer policy is not permissible under §4(f)(1) because age is not a BFOQ for the 'particular' position of flight engineer."[96]

The *Thurston* ruling offers some insight, but does not completely resolve the issue of whether, in asserting a BFOQ defense, the defendant can point to the job requirements of the generic work setting generally, or rather must direct its defense to the particular job occupied by the aggrieved employee or sought by the applicant in the defendant's business. Several courts of appeals have considered this issue, and it would appear likely that at least the ruling of the Court of Appeals for the Seventh Circuit in *Equal Employment Opportunity Commission v City of Janesville*[97] cannot be squared with *Thurston.*

In *Janesville* the court addressed a mandatory retirement policy that applied to what were termed *protective service* employees. This policy had been applied so as to require the chief of police to retire at age 55. The city argued that the particular business involved was the police department as a whole. The district court rejected this contention, looking rather to the activities of the particular job at issue.[98] Thus, the district court construed "particular business" as being synonymous with particular occupation. The court of appeals reversed. Focusing on the phrase "particular business" in §4(f)(1), the court reasoned that Congress could have used the word *occupation,* instead of "business," had it wanted to. The court concluded that the city only "had the burden of establishing that its mandatory retirement program, as applied to the *generic class* of law enforcement personnel employed by the City to operate the 'business' of its police

---

[95] 469 US at 122.

[96] *Id.*

[97] 630 F2d 1254 (7th Cir 1980).

[98] Equal Employment Opportunity Commn v City of Janesville, 480 F Supp 1375 (WD Wis 1979), *revd,* 630 F2d 1254 (7th Cir 1980).

department, falls within the terms of the BFOQ exception."[99]

Were the *Janesville* logic persuasive, presumably the airline would have prevailed in *Thurston,* because it could have maintained that the age-60 retirement requirement—valid as to pilots—was good for its entire business, i.e., flying, and all the occupations involved in that business. That such logic was not articulated by the *Thurston* Court leads to the conclusion that *Janesville,* while not explicitly overruled in *Thurston,* stands on very shaky ground today.

Janesville was explicitly rejected by the Court of Appeals for the Eighth Circuit in *Equal Employment Opportunity Commission v City of St Paul.*[100] At issue was an age-65 mandatory retirement requirement applicable to firefighters. The question was whether this requirement could be applied to all personnel, and the court held that it could not. The court approved of the trial court's tack of considering different subclasses of firefighting personnel, and it affirmed the lower court's conclusion that age was not a BFOQ for the city's fire chief. In the view of the *St Paul* court, the plain meaning of the phrase "bona fide occupational qualification reasonably necessary to the . . . particular business" did not preclude consideration of a particular occupation within a particular business. In support of its reading of the BFOQ provision the *St Paul* court looked to the intent underlying the ADEA and reasoned that the statute's goals would be frustrated if employment decisions were based on a generic class as a whole, rather than on separate consideration being given to different occupations within a business. Accordingly, the court concluded as follows: "We cannot believe that the ADEA was intended to allow a city to retire a police dispatcher because that person is too old to serve on a SWAT team."[101]

---

99 630 F2d at 1258 (emphasis added); *accord* Popkins v Zagel, 611 F Supp 809 (CD Ill 1985).

100 671 F2d 1162 (8th Cir 1982); *accord* Equal Employment Opportunity Commn v City of Minneapolis, 537 F Supp 750 (D Minn 1982).

101 671 F2d at 1166. Equal Employment Opportunity Commn v El Paso Natural Gas Co, 626 F Supp 182 (WD Tex 1985), *appeal dismissed,* 40 Empl Prac Dec (CCH) ¶36,339 (5th Cir 1986), is in accord with this approach.

The Courts of Appeals for the First and Third Circuits have taken a middle position. *Mahoney v Trabucco,*[102] the ruling by the former, involved an age-50 retirement requirement imposed by statute on state troopers. The court accepted the idea that within a particular business there could exist specific occupations requiring separate training, career progressions, and age limitations. Thus, it rejected the *Janesville* approach. The court was concerned, however, that the *St Paul* approach would be unworkable, at least in the context of a paramilitary organization, i.e., the state troopers. The court feared that "a particularistic analysis of the actual duties performed to overcome an otherwise justified BFOQ for similarly classified employees, would raise immeasurable problems of morale, administration, litigation, and adjudication."[103] The position the *Mahoney* court opted for was the conclusion that " 'occupational qualification' means more of a recognized and discrete vocation."[104] Its approach, "recognizing the need to focus not only on the 'particular business' but also on genuine and well recognized occupations within such businesses,"[105] thus prevents sweeping employees of distinct vocations and occupations into generic classes. At the same time, it avoids the crafting of nice distinctions between different jobs, a course which could result from the *St Paul* approach.

The Court of Appeals for the Third Circuit endorsed the *Mahoney* analysis in *Equal Employment Opportunity Commission v Pennsylvania.*[106] In applying this approach to the particular facts before it, the court reasoned that the defendant state police agency was a paramilitary organization, all of whose officers—regardless of whether they were normally assigned to desk or field jobs—were required to carry guns and to respond in emergency situations. Accordingly, it was inappropriate in the court's view, to single out for scrutiny just the jobs filled by the plaintiffs,

---

[102] 738 F2d 35 (1st Cir), *cert denied,* 469 US 1036 (1984).

[103] *Id* 39.

[104] *Id.*

[105] *Id* 42.

[106] 768 F2d 514 (3d Cir 1985).

i.e., sedentary administrative assignments, and then determine whether an age-60 retirement requirement was a legitimate BFOQ for those particular occupations.[107]

§5.07 Establishing a Particular Age

It is obvious that as far as age is concerned, people only grow in one way: older. Along with increased years, there typically are some declines in physical capability that come to manifest themselves with the passage of time.[108] It is clear, however, that there are numerous misconceptions of a negative nature about the aging process, as well as stereotypical images of physical decrepitude, gross intellectual decline, and other untoward characteristics associated with old people.[109] There also is a general failure to recognize this, even given that there are of course changes associated with aging, the fact is that people age differently. Two woman who are both age 55 are equal chronologically, but they almost certainly will be quite different in terms of their individual physical, intellectual, and judgmental capacities.

Because the decrements associated with aging occur at different times and in varying degrees for different individuals, and because pejorative stereotyping commonly is applied to people in the upper reaches of age, as well as even those who are in their 50s and 60s, the two-part test for assessing the merits of a defense asserted under the bona fide occupational qualification (BFOQ) provision set forth in §4(f)(1)[110] of the Age Discrimination in Employment Act (ADEA)[111] will not be satisfied by the mere assertion of the problematic truism (some would say

---

107 *Accord* Equal Employment Opportunity Commn v New Jersey, 620 F Supp 977 (DNJ 1985). In Adams v James, 526 F Supp 80 (MD Ala 1981), the court did not resolve the question discussed in the text. *See also* Aaron v Davis, 414 F Supp 453 (ED Ark 1976).

108 *See* D. Tomb, Growing Old 15-40 (1984).

109 *See* Arluke & Levin, *Second Childhood: Old Age in Popular Culture,* in Growing Old in America 151-53 (B.B. Hess & E.W. Markson eds 1985).

110 29 USC §623(f)(1).

111 *Id* §§621-634.

canard) that all people deteriorate with age.[112] Nor will it be acceptable to rely upon subjective opinions by hiring officials that older persons cannot handle the jobs in question.[113] "Instead, the defendant must demonstrate a specific, objective, or factual basis for its . . . qualifications based on age."[114]

In deciding *Orzel v City of Wauwatosa Fire Department*[115] the court stressed the need on the part of the defendant to justify the particular age chosen. The district court that decided *Gately v Massachusetts*[116] also was particularly insistent as to this. The latter court, which addressed an age-55 mandatory retirement requirement imposed on law enforcement officers, pointed out that "the most thorough and authoritative evidence presented states unequivocally that currently available tests are more effective than age in identifying officers who may be unable to perform the law enforcement and public safety tasks required of them."[117]

---

[112] Equal Employment Opportunity Commn v University of Tex Health Science Ctr, 710 F2d 1091, 1094 (5th Cir 1983); Equal Employment Opportunity Commn v Pennsylvania, 596 F Supp 1333, 1338 (MD Pa 1984), *vacated & remanded on other grounds,* 768 F2d 514 (3d Cir 1985); Equal Employment Opportunity Commn v Pennsylvania Liquor Control Bd, 565 F Supp 520, 522 (ED Pa 1983).

[113] Equal Employment Opportunity Commn v University of Tex Health Science Ctr, 710 F2d 1091, 1094 (5th Cir 1983).

[114] *Id; accord* Equal Employment Opportunity Commn v Pennsylvania Liquor Control Bd, 565 F Supp 520, 522 (ED Pa 1983). Actually, there is some case law establishing that age per se does not have to be involved in a policy for that policy to qualify as a BFOQ. *See* Johnson v American Airlines, Inc, 745 F2d 988 (5th Cir 1984), *cert denied,* 472 US 1027 (1985); Murnane v American Airlines, Inc, 667 F2d 98 (DC Cir 1981), *cert denied,* 456 US 915 (1982). See **§5.02.**

[115] 697 F2d 743 (7th Cir), *cert denied,* 464 US 992 (1983); *accord* Equal Employment Opportunity Commn v Pennsylvania Liquor Control Bd, 565 F Supp 520, 522 (ED Pa 1983).

[116] 811 F Supp 26 (D Mass 1992), *affd on other grounds,* 2 F3d 1221 (1st Cir 1993).

[117] *Id* 31 (citing F. Landy, Alternatives to Chronological Age in Determining Standards of Suitability for Public Safety Jobs, Executive Summary 17-18

Accordingly, there had to be "particularized factual findings" justifying the mandatory retirement age "on its own facts."[118] In contrast, in *Equal Employment Opportunity Commission v Pennsylvania*[119] the court rejected the argument of the Commission that the state had to justify the specific age of 60, which was the mandatory retirement age at issue in the case. However, the ruling was vacated because of the trial court's failure to apply the BFOQ defense in other respects with sufficient stringency (insofar as the defendant was concerned). While the appellate court did not address the issue of whether a particular age had to be justified, its general condemnation of the trial court's insufficiently rigorous analysis makes suspect the trial court's decision on the *particular age* issue. In any event, even if a defendant is not put to the test of justifying the specific age it uses as a job requirement, it still must prove[120] that there is a factual basis for believing that all, or substantially all, persons bearing the characteristic in question—being over age 45, for example—are unqualified to perform, or that dealing with persons on an individualized basis is impossible or highly impractical.[121] Thus, insofar as the impossibility *impracticality* aspect of the BFOQ defense test is concerned, it has been observed that "[t]he BFOQ . . . cannot be established without proof relating to the inability of medical science to 'predict, on an individual basis, the likelihood that a pilot who has reached age 60 will become incapacitated during flight.' "[122]

(1992)). (The Landy study is addressed in **ch 3** with regard to the treatment of law enforcement officers and firefighters.)

[118] 811 F Supp at 31.

[119] 596 F Supp 1333, 1347 (MD Pa 1984), *vacated on other grounds*, 768 F2d 514 (3d Cir 1985).

[120] Equal Employment Opportunity Commn v Pennsylvania, 768 F2d 514 (3d Cir 1985).

[121] See **§5.05.**

[122] Airline Pilots Assn, Intl v Trans World Airlines, Inc, 713 F2d 940, 951 (2d Cir 1983), *affd in part & revd in part on other grounds*, 469 US 992 (1985) (quoting Tuohy v Ford Motor Co, 675 F2d 842, 846 (6th Cir 1982)); *accord* Monroe v United Air Lines, Inc, 736 F2d 394, 402 (7th Cir 1984), *cert denied*, 470 US 1004 (1985).

§5.08 Deference to Administrative and Legislative Determinations

The bona fide occupational qualification (BFOQ) defense set forth in §4(f)(1)[123] of the Age Discrimination in Employment Act (ADEA)[124] typically is invoked in cases involving public safety. Because courts sometimes are hesitant about evaluating experts' testimony when safety is at issue,[125] there is a temptation for them to defer to the administrative or legislative determinations that are embodied in, or which underlie, age-based restrictions.

The lower courts have demonstrated a polarity in their positions. *Equal Employment Opportunity Commission v City of Janesville,*[126] a decision of the Court of Appeals for the Seventh Circuit, is illustrative of one position, (although it later was effectively rejected in *Orzel v City of Wauwatosa Fire Department.*)[127] The *Janesville* court demonstrated an extremely deferential position regarding the age-55 mandatory retirement law before it, stating that "the wisdom of a legislative act is not subject to judicial scrutiny."[128] The court concluded that in light of evidence that the state legislature was "acting on a good faith belief that the public safety required early retirement of all protective service employees,"[129] it was likely that the city would prevail on the merits of its BFOQ defense.[130] A few other courts also have demonstrated

---

[123] 29 USC §623(f)(1).

[124] *Id* §§621-634.

[125] See **§5.10.**

[126] 630 F2d 1254 (7th Cir 1980).

[127] 697 F2d 743 (7th Cir), *cert denied,* 464 US 992 (1983). See note 130.

[128] 630 F2d at 1259.

[129] *Id* 1258.

[130] The defendant in Orzel v City of Wauwatosa Fire Dept, 697 F2d 743 (7th Cir), *cert denied,* 464 US 992 (1983), argued that insufficient deference had been accorded the state law, which set age 55 as the normal retirement age for protective service employees and on which the city based its retirement. The court, while not in so many words overruling *Janesville,* stated as follows:

> It is true that, as a general matter, state legislative judgments are entitled to considerable deference. *EEOC v Janesville.* . . . We do not believe, however, that in situations where a state or local government's forced retire-

particular deference to legislative or administrative determinations.[131]

In contrast to *Janesville,* the Court of Appeals for the Sixth Circuit rejected the defendant's effort to justify its forced retirement of private pilot employees at age 60 on the ground that there was a federal regulation imposing retirement at that age that was applicable to commercial airline pilots.[132] Most other lower courts that have addressed the question of deferring to an administrative or legislative determination likewise have rejected the type of deference seen in *Janesville.*[133] Thus, for example, in deciding *Equal Employment Opportunity Commission v City of St Paul,*[134] the Court of Appeals for the Eighth Circuit reasoned that applying a presumption of correctness to legislative determinations would effectively and unwarrantedly shift the burden of proof in BFOQ cases to the plaintiff.

The issue ultimately reached the Supreme Court in *Johnson v Mayor & City Council of Baltimore.*[135] The case involved a manda-

---

ment of older employees is being challenged under the ADEA, state mandatory retirement schemes are automatically to be presumed valid. *Id* 751. Of course, *Janesville* had in effect subscribed to the very presumption that *Orzel* disavowed. *See also* Heiar v Crawford County, 746 F2d 1190 (7th Cir 1984), *cert denied,* 472 US 1027 (1985).

131 *See, e.g.,* Johnson v Mayor & City Council of Baltimore, 731 F2d 209 (4th Cir 1984), *revd & remanded,* 472 US 353 (1985); Gathercole v Global Assocs, 727 F2d 1485 (9th Cir), *amended,* 34 Empl Prac Dec (CCH) ¶34,563 (9th Cir), *cert denied,* 469 US 1087 (1984); Adams v Leatherbury, 388 So 2d 510 (Ala 1980).

132 Tuohy v Ford Motor Co, 675 F2d 842 (6th Cir 1982).

133 *See, e.g.,* Heiar v Crawford County, 746 F2d 1190 (7th Cir 1984), *cert denied,* 472 US 1027 (1985); Air Line Pilots Assn, Intl v Trans World Airlines, Inc, 713 F2d 940 (2d Cir 1983), *affd in part & revd in part on other grounds,* 469 US 111 (1985); Orzel v City of Wauwatosa Fire Dept, 697 F2d 743, 752 (7th Cir), *cert denied,* 464 US 992 (1984); Equal Employment Opportunity Commn v Commonwealth of Pa, 596 F Supp 1333, 1338-40 (MD Pa 1984), *vacated & remanded on other grounds,* 768 F2d 514 (3d Cir 1985); Galvin v Vermont, 598 F Supp 144 (D Vt 1984); Equal Employment Opportunity Commn v City of Minneapolis, 537 F Supp 750 (D Minn 1982).

134 671 F2d 1162 (8th Cir 1982).

135 472 US 353 (1985).

tory retirement ordinance that required some of the plaintiff firefighters to retire at age 60 and the remaining plaintiffs to retire at age 55. The city asserted that age was a BFOQ for the position. The trial court ruled for the plaintiffs, but the Court of Appeals for the Fourth Circuit reversed, holding that the city was entitled to the BFOQ defense as a matter of law.[136] In so doing, it relied on *Equal Employment Opportunity Commission v Wyoming*,[137] in which the Supreme Court had upheld as constitutional the extension of the ADEA to state and local governments. In *Wyoming* the Court had observed that the ADEA tests a state's discretion to impose a mandatory retirement age "against a reasonable federal standard."[138] Taking this reference out of context, the *Johnson* Court of Appeals had undertaken a search for a reasonable federal standard by which to test the BFOQ before it, and it had found that standard in a federal statute that generally requires federal firefighters to retire at age 55. The court of appeals held that because Congress had selected age 55 as the retirement age for most federal firefighters, as a matter of law the same age constituted a BFOQ for all state and local firefighters. Thus, the city was not required to make any factual showing at trial as to its need for the mandatory retirement age.

The Supreme Court reversed. It reviewed the legislative history of the federal statute dealing with firefighters and concluded that at no time had Congress indicated that the retirement age set in that statute was a BFOQ within the meaning of the ADEA. Therefore, it had been error for the court of appeals to have given any weight at all to the federal retirement provision. The Court further suggested, however, that if there were evidence that Congress, in determining that a class of federal employees must retire early, had based its position on the same considerations that supported a finding of a BFOQ under the ADEA, it would follow that "the federal . . . exemption might be relevant to an appropriate employer when deciding whether

---

[136] Johnson v Mayor & City Council of Baltimore, 731 F2d 209 (4th Cir 1984), *revd & remanded* 472 US 353 (1985).

[137] 460 US 226 (1983).

[138] *Id* 240.

to impose a mandatory retirement age, and to a district court engaged in reviewing an employer's BFOQ defense."[139] The Court continued: "The evidence Congress has considered, and the conclusions it has drawn therefrom, might be admissible as evidence in judicial proceedings to determine the existence of a BFOQ for nonfederal employees."[140] In assessing the probative value of that evidence, a court would have to consider the "actual tasks of the nonfederal employees and the circumstances of employment, in order to determine the extent to which congressional conclusions about federal employees in fact are relevant."[141]

In *Western Air Lines, Inc v Criswell*[142] the Court discussed *Johnson.* At issue in *Criswell* was a policy of the airline whereby flight engineers over the age of 59 were barred from employment. The airline, in invoking the BFOQ defense, pointed to a federal regulation requiring the retirement of commercial pilots at age 60, even though there was no comparable regulation applicable to flight engineers. The *Criswell* Court acknowledged that the "FAA's rule for pilots, adopted for safety reasons, is relevant evidence in the airline's BFOQ defense, [but] it is not to be accorded conclusive weight."[143] Rather, the Court asserted, "[t]he extent to which the rule is probative varies with the weight of the evidence supporting its safety rationale and 'the congruity between the . . . occupations at issue.' "[144]

---

139 472 US at 371.

140 *Id.*

141 *Id.*

142 472 US 400 (1985).

143 *Id* 418.

144 *Id* (quoting *Johnson,* 472 US at 371). Taking its cue from *Johnson* and *Criswell,* the court deciding Equal Employment Opportunity Commn v El Paso Natural Gas Co, 626 F Supp 182 (WD Tex 1985), *appeal dismissed,* 40 Empl Prac Dec (CCH) ¶36,339 (5th Cir 1986), looked to the same federal regulation and upheld the defendant's age-60 retirement policy for pilots of its fleet of company planes. *Accord* Rasberg v Nationwide Life Ins Co, 671 F Supp 494 (SD Ohio 1987).

The *Criswell* court said that the Federal Aviation Administration (FAA) Commercial pilot's rule was not to be accorded conclusive weight in a case involving flight engineers. Because the district court accorded that rule exclusive weight

It seems safe to conclude that no matter how broadly or narrowly *Johnson* and *Criswell* are read, determinations external to the ADEA will not be actually binding on an ADEA court considering a BFOQ defense. And it certainly is the case that while legislative and administrative determinations, whether made at the federal or nonfederal level, will vary in terms of their probative value, nothing in either *Johnson* or *Criswell* suggests that the extreme deference expressed in *Janesville* is appropriate.

(Both *Johnson* and *Criswell* dealt with the question of judicial deference to federal standards external to the ADEA; in both cases the Court was willing to regard evidence regarding these standards as being relevant, albeit not dispositive. It is understandable that the Court might deem it appropriate for a court addressing a suit under a federal statute to give credence to federal standards. Arguably, however, equivalent federal court deference to legislative or administrative determinations made by state and local governmental bodies is less appropriate because they do not constitute findings or conclusions by federal entities.[145] Assuming this distinction to be a credible one, the question arises as to whether at least some deference should be accorded such local determinations. It seems correct to conclude that, at the least, state and local governmental legislative and/or administrative determinations should be admissible, as long as they are colorably relevant. Their probative value of course will vary with the facts. But certainly the probative value of such determinations would not be greater than would be that accorded to federal legislative and administrative determinations.)

---

in a case involving noncommercial pilots, the appellate court reversed the grant of the defendant's summary judgment motion in Equal Employment Opportunity Commn v Boeing Co, 843 F2d 1213 (9th Cir), *cert denied,* 488 US 889 (1988), *revg* 40 FEP Cas (BNA) 292 (WD Wash 1986). However, the FAA rule could be introduced in the court's view, as relevant evidence regarding the legitimacy of Boeing's policy. *See also* Williams v Hughes Helicopters, Inc, 806 F2d 1387 (9th Cir 1986).

[145] As to the general issue of preemption of state laws and local ordinances by the ADEA, see **ch 2.**

§5.09 The Relevance of Employers' Costs and Motives

The costs of doing business of course are an ever present concern for employers. The Age Discrimination in Employment Act's (ADEA)[146] §4(f)(2)[147] exception, dealing with employee benefit plans, allows such costs to be taken into account as a basis for differential treatment of older employees. But the §4(f)(1)[148] bona fide occupational qualification (BFOQ) exception to the prohibitions of the ADEA does not do so, notwithstanding some reference in the hearings on the original legislation to the contrary.[149] The courts—with but one exception[150]—have asserted that economic factors cannot be the basis for a BFOQ.[151]

The employer's motives have been deemed to be irrelevant to the merits of a BFOQ defense. *Equal Employment Opportunity Commission v University of Texas Health Science Center*[152] illustrates this proposition. The Equal Employment Opportunity Commis-

---

146 29 USC §§621-634.

147 *Id* §623(f)(2). See **§5.32.**

148 29 USC §623(f)(1).

149 *See Age Discrimination in Employment, Hearings Before the General Subcomm on Labor, Comm on Labor and Public Welfare, US Senate,* 90th Cong, 1st Sess 49 (1967) (testimony of Secretary of Labor Wirtz).

150 Johnson v American Airlines, Inc, 745 F2d 988, 993 n3 (5th Cir 1984), *cert denied,* 472 US 1027 (1985).

151 *See, e.g.,* Monroe v United Air Lines, Inc, 736 F2d 394, 407 (7th Cir 1984), *cert denied,* 470 US 1004 (1985); Air Line Pilots Assn, Intl v Trans World Airlines, Inc, 713 F2d 940, 951 (2d Cir 1983), *affd in part & revd in part on other grounds,* 469 US 111 (1985); Smallwood v United Airlines, Inc, 661 F2d 303, 307 (4th Cir 1981), *cert denied,* 456 US 1007 (1982); Gathercole v Global Assocs, 545 F Supp 1280, 1282 (ND Cal 1982), *later proceeding,* 560 F Supp 642 (ND Cal 1983), *revd on other grounds,* 727 F2d 1485 (9th Cir), *amended,* 34 Empl Prac Dec (CCH) ¶34,563 (9th Cir), *cert denied,* 469 US 1087 (1984); Equal Employment Opportunity Commn v County of Los Angeles, 526 F Supp 1135, 1140-41 (CD Cal 1981), *affd,* 706 F2d 1039 (9th Cir 1983), *cert denied,* 464 US 1073 (1984); Adams v James, 526 F Supp 80 (MD Ala 1981). In Galvin v Vermont, 598 F Supp 144 (D Vt 1984), the court carried this proposition a step further, stating that the defendant bore the burden of proving that its age restriction was not motivated by economic considerations. *Id* 149. The court cited *Smallwood* for this assertion, but actually *Smallwood* does not support it.

152 710 F2d 1091 (5th Cir 1983).

sion (EEOC) argued that the defendant's adoption of an age-45 hiring maximum was arbitrarily chosen for reasons having nothing to do with ability to do the job. In response the court stated as follows:

> [W]e are extremely indisposed to read an intent requirement into the *Tamiami* test. While the wording of previous cases can be read in different ways, we think it wiser to interpret the text as requiring the defendant to demonstrate *at trial,* with *objective* evidence, that the age qualification is justified, rather than looking to the subjective motivation originally behind the qualification. . . . [This is because,] [t]ypically, intent requirements disfavor plaintiffs because they are extraordinarily hard to meet.[153]

The Court of Appeals for the Seventh Circuit also addressed the issue of motive in *Monroe v United Air Lines, Inc.*[154] The court ruled that if the defendant established a BFOQ defense in support of its mandatory retirement policy, it was entitled to impose involuntary retirement on its employees, regardless of evidence of ageist animus indicating the defendant would have forced their retirement even absent the BFOQ justification. In brief, "animus toward older workers becomes irrelevant"[155] once the BFOQ's requirements are satisfied by the employer.

While both *University of Texas* and *Monroe* were decided prior to the Supreme Court's articulation of the appropriate BFOQ test in *Western Air Lines, Inc v Criswell,*[156] there is nothing in the *Criswell* opinion that would suggest that the foregoing assertions are invalid.

---

[153] *Id* 1096; *accord* Equal Employment Opportunity Commn v Commonwealth of Pa, 596 F Supp 1333, 1344 (MD Pa 1984), *vacated & remanded on other grounds,* 768 F2d 514 (3d Cir 1985). As to the *Tamiami* test referred to in the quotation, see **§5.05.**

[154] 736 F2d 394 (7th Cir 1984), *cert denied,* 470 US 1004 (1985).

[155] *Id* 404.

[156] 472 US 400 (1985). See **§5.05.**

§5.10 Safety Considerations

Age-based restrictions commonly are imposed, both for hiring and retirement, with regard to occupations that implicate public safety concerns, such as policing, firefighting, and bus driving. Such restrictions—when challenged—often prompt invocation on the defendant's part of the bona fide occupational qualification (BFOQ) defense set forth in §4(f)(1)[157] of the Age Discrimination in Employment Act (ADEA).[158] Not surprisingly, courts are leery of too aggressively second-guessing the public safety needs asserted by the expert witnesses who typically are called upon by defendants to testify in these cases. This is understandable, since if a court "were to prohibit the plaintiff from terminating the defendant, and if it then turned out that the defendant's experts had been right, many people might lose their lives."[159]

The established BFOQ test, enunciated in *Western Air Lines, Inc v Criswell,*[160] clearly takes account of the safety issue: safety is both relevant to determining the essence of an employer's business and to determining whether the age distinction at issue is reasonably necessary to that essence. In *Usery v Tamiami Trail Tours, Inc,*[161] in which the test subsequently espoused by the *Criswell* Court was set forth, and which involved a hiring-age maximum for bus drivers, the Court of Appeals for the Fifth Circuit deemed the essence of the defendant's business to be the safe transportation of passengers. The *Tamiami* court asserted, in assessing whether the age limit was reasonably necessary to this

---

157 29 USC §623(f)(1).

158 *Id* §§621-634.

159 Tuohy v Ford Motor Co, 490 F Supp 258, 262 (ED Mich 1980), *revd,* 675 F2d 842 (6th Cir 1982). In the first appellate court ruling to address a BFOQ justified in safety terms, the Court of Appeals for the Seventh Circuit—in Hodgson v Greyhound Lines, Inc, 499 F2d 859, 863 (7th Cir 1974), *cert denied,* 419 US 1122 (1975)—imposed a very relaxed burden of justification on the defendant. This decision was effectively overruled, however, in Orzel v City of Wauwatosa Fire Dept, 697 F2d 743 (7th Cir), *cert denied,* 464 US 992 (1983).

160 472 US 400 (1985). See **§5.05.**

161 531 F2d 224 (5th Cir 1976).

essential operation, that "[t]he greater the safety factor, measured by the likelihood of harm and the probable severity of that harm in case of an accident, the more stringent may be the job qualifications designed to insure safe driving."[162] This language subsequently was quoted with approval in *Criswell.*[163]

The *Criswell/Tamiami* test thus allows for safety to be fully considered in assessing the merits of a BFOQ defense. The *Criswell* Court's ruling makes clear, however, that safety cannot be regarded as such a sacrosanct concern that its mere invocation will effectively decide the matter. In *Criswell* the airline argued that because it was engaged in the transportation of airline passengers, the jury should have been instructed to defer to the airline's selection of job qualifications—in this instance, a requirement that flight engineers not be over age 59—so long as such requirements were reasonable in light of the safety risks. In rejecting that argument, the Court balanced safety concerns and the thrust of the ADEA:

> This proposal is plainly at odds with Congress' decision, in adopting the ADEA, to subject such management decisions to a test of objective justification in a court of law. The BFOQ standard adopted in the statute is one of "reasonable necessity," not reasonableness.
>
> In adopting that standard, Congress did not ignore the public interest in safety. That interest is adequately reflected in instructions that track the language of the statute. When an employer establishes that a job qualification has been carefully formulated to respond to documented concerns for public safety, it will not be overly burdensome to persuade a trier of fact that the qualification is "reasonably necessary" to safe operation of the business. The uncertainty implicit in the concept of managing safety risks always makes it "reasonably necessary" to err on the side of caution in a close case. The employer cannot be expected to establish the risk of an airline accident "to a certainty,

---

[162] *Id.* 236.

[163] 472 US at 413.

> for certainty would require running the risk until a tragic accident would prove that the judgment was sound. . . ." When the employer's argument has a credible basis in the record, it is difficult to believe that a jury of lay persons . . . would not defer in a close case to the airline's judgment.[164]

In a footnote the *Criswell* court, noting that several courts of appeals had recognized that safety considerations were relevant in making or reviewing findings of fact, stressed that such considerations are only relevant "at the margin of a close case, and do not relieve the employer from its burden of establishing the BFOQ by the preponderance of credible evidence."[165] This latter cautionary note should be read as reining in the willingness of some courts to afford great leeway to defendants that invoke the shibboleth of public safety[166] this judicial deference being premised on the courts' concerns that they lack sufficient expertise to evaluate the employers' judgments.[167]

The Court again addressed BFOQ language in *International*

---

[164] *Id* 419-20 (quoting Usery v Tamiami Trail Tours, Inc, 531 F2d 224, 238 (5th Cir 1976)) (footnote omitted).

[165] *Id.* 419 n29.

[166] *See, e.g.,* Murnane v American Airlines, Inc, 667 F2d 98 (DC Cir 1981), *cert denied,* 456 US 915 (1982); Maki v Commissioner of Educ, 568 F Supp 252 (NDNY 1983), *aff'd & dismissed without opinion,* 742 F2d 1437 (2d Cir 1984); Beck v Borough of Manheim, 505 F Supp 923 (ED Pa 1981); Tuohy v Ford Motor Co, 490 F Supp 258 (ED Mich 1980), *revd,* 675 F2d 842 (6th Cir 1982); Monroe v United Air Lines, 32 FEP Cas (BNA) 1117, 1124 (ND Ill 1979).

[167] *See, e.g.,* Murnane v American Airlines, Inc, 667 F2d 98, 101 (DC Cir 1981), *cert denied,* 456 US 915 (1982); Tuohy v Ford Motor Co, 490 F Supp 258, 262 (ED Mich 1980), *revd,* 675 F2d 842 (6th Cir 1982). Some courts, however, have demonstrated a ready willingness to evaluate conflicting medical evidence. *See, e.g.,* Equal Employment Opportunity Commn v Missouri State Highway Patrol, 748 F2d 447 (8th Cir 1984), *cert denied,* 474 US 828 (1985); Monroe v United Air Lines, Inc, 736 F2d 394 (7th Cir 1984), *cert denied,* 470 US 1004 (1985); Equal Employment Opportunity Commn v University of Tex Health Science Ctr, 710 F2d 1091 (5th Cir 1983); Equal Employment Opportunity Commn v Florida Dept of Highway Safety & Motor Vehicles, 660 F Supp 1104 (ND Fla 1986); Equal Employment Opportunity Commn v New Jersey, 631 F Supp 1506 (DNJ 1986), *affd without opinion,* 815 F2d 694 (3d Cir 1987).

Union v Johnson Controls, Inc,[168] a decision involving the identical BFOQ provision contained in Title VII of the Civil Rights Act of 1964.[169] The case dealt with the legality of an employer-imposed fetal protection policy requiring the exclusion of all women, other than those medically documented as being infertile, from jobs involving actual or potential exposure to lead. To the company's argument that its policy was grounded on safety concerns and thus fell within a "so-called safety exception to the BFOQ,"[170] the Court responded by first asserting that "[o]ur cases have stressed that discrimination on the basis of sex because of safety concerns is allowed only in narrow circumstances."[171] Addressing *Criswell,* the *Johnson* Court described that decision as one in which the Court's "safety concerns were not independent of the individual's ability to perform the assigned tasks."[172] Moreover, "although . . . [the Court] considered the safety of third parties [, i.e., airline passengers,] in . . . *Criswell,* those third parties were indispensable to the particular business at issue."[173] Reiterating this observation, the Court asserted as follows: "Third-party safety considerations properly entered into the BFOQ analysis in . . . *Criswell* because they went to the core of the employee's job performance. Moreover, that performance involved the central purpose of the enterprise."[174] Thus, the Court concluded: "Our case law . . . makes clear that the safety exception is limited to instances in which sex or pregnancy actually interferes with the employee's ability to perform the job."[175] This is an observation that necessarily applies to the ADEA BFOQ, as well, given the Court's reliance on *Criswell.*

The Equal Employment Opportunity Commission (EEOC) takes a particularly tough stance vis-a-vis public safety argu-

---

168 499 US 187 (1991).

169 42 USC §§2000e through 2000e-17.

170 499 US at 202.

171 *Id.*

172 *Id* 203.

173 *Id.*

174 *Id.*

175 *Id* 204.

ments. In its interpretation of the BFOQ defense the EEOC asserts that "if the employer's objective in asserting a BFOQ is the goal of public safety, the employer must prove that the challenged practice does indeed effectuate that goal and that there is no acceptable alternative which would better advance or equally advance it with less discriminatory impact."[176] Agency support notwithstanding, this *least restrictive alternative* position never has generated significant judicial support,[177] and the *Criswell* Court's failure to assert a similar position—while perhaps not precluding lower courts from doing so—likely signifies that it never will garner widespread approbation. However, in one narrow context it has had some play: it has been established that where the alternative of testing could have been used, but was not, the defendant's invocation of the BFOQ defense will fail.[178]

Understandably, the safety concern arises particularly in cases involving law enforcement officers and firefighters. Decisions involving the BFOQ defense's applicability to law enforcement personnel form a very considerable portion of the BFOQ case law. However, the continuing development of this case law was effectively brought to a halt for a time by virtue of a 1986 amendment to the ADEA that allowed state and local governmental agencies to utilize hiring and retirement ages without having to justify them as BFOQs, provided two conditions were satisfied. The age criteria had to have been in place under state or local law as of March 3, 1983, and these requirements had to have been imposed pursuant to bona fide hiring or retirement plans

---

176 29 CFR §1625.6(b) (1993).

177 However, particular reliance was placed on this provision in Equal Employment Opportunity Commn v Pennsylvania Liquor Control Bd, 565 F Supp 520 (ED Pa 1983); *accord* Equal Employment Opportunity Commn v City of Linton, 623 F Supp 724, 726 (SD Ind 1985) (erroneously reading an earlier decision of the Court of Appeals for the Seventh Circuit as supporting such position); *see also* Equal Employment Opportunity Commn v Mississippi, 654 F Supp 1168, 1183 (SD Miss 1987), *affd on other grounds,* 837 F2d 1398 (5th Cir 1988).

178 Heiar v Crawford County, 746 F2d 1190 (7th Cir 1984), *cert denied,* 472 US 1027 (1985); *accord* Equal Employment Opportunity Commn v Mississippi, 654 F Supp 1168, 1183 (SD Miss 1987), *affd on other grounds,* 837 F2d 1398 (5th Cir 1988).

that were not subterfuges to evade the purposes of the ADEA.[179] This exception to the BFOQ's otherwise narrow scope expired on December 31, 1993, by virtue of a self-executing termination, or sunset, provision contained in the 1986 legislation.[180]

§5.11 Age Limits as BFOQs Justifying Involuntary Retirement

The Age Discrimination in Employment Act (ADEA)[181] protects workers and job applicants from age 40 on, with only a few exceptions.[182] Absent one of these exceptions being applicable, an employer that imposes involuntary age-based retirement can look only to the bona fide occupational qualification (BFOQ) defense, set forth in §4(f)(1)[183] of the Act, as the arguable basis for avoiding liability for violating the statute. On numerous occasions, the courts have addressed BFOQ defenses raised in support of mandatory retirement policies.[184]

---

[179] §4(i), 29 USC §623(i). See **ch 3.**

[180] Age Discrimination in Employment Amendments of 1986, Pub L No 99-592, §3(b), 100 Stat 3342, 3342.

[181] 29 USC §§621-634.

[182] As to these exceptions, see **ch 3.**

[183] 29 USC §623(f)(1).

[184] *See, e.g.,* Johnson v Mayor & City Council of Baltimore, 472 US 353 (1985); Williams v Hughes Helicopters, Inc, 806 F2d 1387 (9th Cir 1986); Equal Employment Opportunity Commn v City of E Providence, 798 F2d 524 (1st Cir 1986); Equal Employment Opportunity Commn v Pennsylvania, 768 F2d 514 (3d Cir 1985); Equal Employment Opportunity Commn v Missouri State Highway Patrol, 748 F2d 447 (8th Cir 1984), *cert denied,* 474 US 828 (1985); Heiar v Crawford County, 746 F2d 1190 (7th Cir 1984), *cert denied,* 472 US 1027 (1985); Monroe v United Air Lines, Inc, 736 F2d 394 (7th Cir 1984), *cert denied,* 470 US 1004 (1985); Air Line Pilots Assn, Intl v Trans World Air Lines, Inc, 713 F2d 940 (2d Cir 1983), *affd in part & revd in part,* 469 US 111 (1985); Equal Employment Opportunity Commn v County of Allegheny, 705 F2d 679 (3d Cir 1983); Orzel v City of Wauwatosa Fire Dept, 697 F2d 743 (7th Cir 1983), *cert denied,* 464 US 992 (1984); Tuohy v Ford Motor Co, 675 F2d 842 (6th Cir 1982); Equal Employment Opportunity Commn v City of St Paul, 671 F2d 1162 (8th Cir 1982); Equal Employment Opportunity Commn v County of Santa Barbara, 666 F2d 373 (9th Cir 1982); Houghton v McDonnell Douglas Corp, 553 F2d 561 (8th Cir), *cert denied,* 434 US 966 (1977).

(In 1986 the Act was amended to allow state and local governmental employers to use age as a basis for imposing retirement on law enforcement officers and firefighters, provided that the age in question was applicable pursuant to a law or ordinance that was in effect on March 3, 1983, and provided further that the age was utilized pursuant to a bona fide retirement plan that was not a subterfuge to avoid the purposes of the ADEA.[185] This amendment effectively negated the requirement that a mandatory retirement policy could only withstand scrutiny under the ADEA if it was justified as a BFOQ.[186] Thus, a number of the BFOQ cases concerning mandatory retirement were relegated to the status of historical curiosities, given that these rulings dealt with the forced retirement of law enforcement officers. However, the section of the ADEA enabling employers to avoid having to justify their policies in terms of the BFOQ defense expired on December 31, 1993.[187] The demise of this provision, taking the statutory scenerio back to where it had been prior to the provision's enactment, resulted in the resurrection of the pre-amendment BFOQ case law as relevant authority.)

As has often been observed, the contours of the BFOQ exception can only be discerned on a case-by-case basis.[188] Thus, the success of an employer in asserting a BFOQ defense in support of its retirement policy will depend upon the nature of the job and the evidence adduced. Even where essentially the same job is involved, different jurisdictions may set different retirement ages: in *Equal Employment Opportunity Commission v New Jersey*[189] the court noted that several BFOQ cases regarding mandatory

---

[185] §4(i), 29 USC §623(i). See **ch 3.**

[186] In Equal Employment Opportunity Commn v Kentucky State Police Dept, 43 FEP Cas (BNA) 1045 (ED Ky 1986), *revd on other grounds,* 860 F2d 665 (6th Cir 1988), *cert denied,* 490 US 1066 (1989), the court relied heavily on the 1986 amendment "as being reflective of pre-existing legislative intent to regard mandatory retirement for police officers as [a] BFOQ until more returns [i.e., further data] are in." *Id* 1048.

[187] Age Discrimination in Employment Amendments of 1986, Pub L No 99-592, §3(b), 100 Stat 3342, 3342. See **ch 3.**

[188] *See, e.g.,* 29 CFR §1625.6(a) (1993).

[189] 620 F Supp 977 (DNJ 1985).

retirement requirements imposed on state police had been litigated in which retirement ages ranged from 50 to 60.[190] Depending on the persuasiveness of the evidence, the skill of the advocates, and the disposition of the factfinder, an age-55 retirement requirement might survive attack in one jurisdiction, while an age-62 retirement requirement might fall in another.

There are two, related arguments that typically are advanced by employers for their early retirement policies. First, it often is contended that the rigors of the particular job are such that older workers are unable to perform adequately and safely. Second, it is further regularly argued that accurate individualized assessments to determine which particular employees are capable of continuing to perform and which are not, are unattainable. From these arguments flows the conclusion that a retirement policy using age alone as the basis for determining who may continue to work is appropriate.

Hoefelman v Conservation Commission[191] is an example of a BFOQ case involving mandatory retirement. The trial court upheld an age-60 retirement requirement imposed on pilots, concluding that it was not possible to determine other than by age which pilots could fly safely and which could not. Likewise, in *Maki v Commissioner of Education*[192] the court, addressing a policy requiring the retirement of school bus drivers at age 65, concluded that it was impossible to reliably test for the psychological and physiological changes that occur due to age after age 65. And in a third case of the same ilk, the Court of Appeals for the Eighth Circuit reversed the trial court, which had rejected the defendant's BFOQ argument in support of an age-60 retirement requirement for state troopers. The appellate court, in *Equal Employment Opportunity Commission v Missouri State Highway*

---

[190] *Id* 983 n5.

[191] 541 F Supp 272 (WD Mo 1982), *affd,* 718 F2d 281 (8th Cir 1983).

[192] 568 F Supp 252 (NDNY 1983), *affd & dismissed without opinion,* 742 F2d 1437 (2d Cir 1984).

Patrol,[193] engaged in an extensive review of the activities in which the police engaged and concluded as follows:

> [T]he Patrol has clearly established that physical ability and ability to withstand stress are job qualifications which are reasonably necessary to the performance of its functions, and that in these terms there is a correlation between the mandatory retirement age of sixty and the safe and efficient performance of the Patrol's functions.[194]

The court next reviewed the medical evidence:

> [T]he Patrol has established that there is a factual basis for believing that substantially all Patrol members over the age of sixty lack sufficient aerobic capacity to perform their duties safely and efficiently. The Patrol also has established the inefficacy of testing, as an alternative to age, as a means of distinguishing among individuals over sixty.[195]

Other plaintiffs have fared better. For example, in *Equal Employment Opportunity Commission v City of Bowling Green*[196] the court reasoned that individualized testing of police officers was both feasible and affordable, and so it preliminarily enjoined the forced retirement of the plaintiff. In *Equal Employment Opportunity*

---

[193] 748 F2d 447 (8th Cir 1984), *cert denied,* 474 US 828 (1985), *revg* 555 F Supp 97 (WD Mo 1982).

[194] *Id* 451.

[195] *Id* 455; *see also* Equal Employment Opportunity Commn v Pennsylvania, 645 F Supp 1545 (MD Pa 1986), *vacated & remanded,* 829 F2d 392 (3d Cir 1987), *cert denied,* 485 US 935 (1988); Equal Employment Opportunity Commn v New Jersey, 631 F Supp 1506 (DNJ 1986), *affd without opinion,* 815 F2d 694 (3d Cir 1987); Equal Employment Opportunity Commn v New Jersey, 620 F Supp 977 (DNJ 1985). Actually, the *Missouri State Highway Patrol* opinion stands on shaky grounds in terms of legal—as opposed to factual—analysis. The court imposed on the defendant the burden of proving, as quoted, "a factual basis." This falls short of what is now required in light of Western Air Lines, Inc v Criswell, 472 US 400 (1985). See **§5.05.**

[196] 607 F Supp 524 (WD Ky 1985).

Commission v City of St Paul[197] the issue was whether forced ouster at age 65 could be justified for district fire chiefs. The traits to which the defendant pointed as precluding safe and efficient job performance were susceptibility to heart attacks and loss of strength and stamina. The evidence, however, failed to support the defendant's position:

> [D]efendant . . . could not point to a single incident where the lives and safety of the St. Paul firefighters or the public were jeopardized because of the performance of older District Chiefs. Moreover, evidence presented at trial indicates that District Chiefs over the age of 64 are no more likely than other District Chiefs to experience injuries at fire scenes, that District Chiefs over the age of 60 are less prone than younger District Chiefs to sudden death due to heart attacks and strokes, and that District Chiefs over the age of 64 retain sufficient strength and endurance to adequately perform their duties.[198]

The court further observed that "susceptibility to heart attack and possession of the muscle strength and endurance required by District Chiefs may be ascertained with greater accuracy by individual testing them [sic] on the basis of age."[199]

The argument has been made that if an employer fails to ensure that its employees who are under the mandatory retirement age meet the physical fitness standards that are utilized to justify the employer's mandatory retirement requirement, that requirement by definition could not be reasonably necessary to the employer's business. In other words, if physical fitness really were reasonably necessary, then assurances of fitness would be required during the entire duration of employees' careers, rather than just at the closing phase. This argument was rejected by the Court of Appeals for the First Circuit in *Equal*

---

[197] 500 F Supp 1135 (D Minn 1980), *affd*, 671 F2d 1162 (8th Cir 1982).

[198] *Id* 1145.

[199] *Id* 1146; *see also* Equal Employment Opportunity Commn v Florida Dept of Highway Safety & Motor Vehicles, 660 F Supp 1104 (ND Fla 1986).

Employment Opportunity Commission v City of East Providence.[200] On the other hand, the Court of Appeals for the Third Circuit, in deciding *Equal Employment Opportunity Commission v Pennsylvania,*[201] rejected *City of East Providence.* The *Pennsylvania* court reasoned that since no minimum standards regarding health and physical fitness had been set by the state police agency, it was error for the trial court to have held that good health and physical fitness were BFOQs that justified retiring officers at age 60. The Courts of Appeals for the Fifth[202] and Sixth Circuits[203] are in agreement with the Court of Appeals for the Third Circuit.[204]

---

200 798 F2d 524, 528-29 (1st Cir 1986); *see also* Williams v Hughes Helicopters, Inc, 806 F2d 1387, 1391 (9th Cir 1986).

201 829 F2d 392 (3d Cir 1987), *cert denied,* 485 US 935 (1988).

202 Equal Employment Opportunity Commn v Mississippi State Tax Commn, 848 F2d 526 (5th Cir 1988), *vacated & remanded,* 873 F2d 97 (5th Cir 1989) (en banc); Equal Employment Opportunity Commn v Mississippi, 837 F2d 1398 (5th Cir 1988). In the vacated *Mississippi Tax Commission* ruling the court concluded that the defendant indeed did not have standards in place and operative. The court was particularly struck by the fact that after the initial hiring, the defendant conducted no fitness or health programs or tests to determine whether an officer remained competent to serve. The court commented: "However stringent the qualifications for admission[,] . . . the [defendant] would be hard pressed to justify a mandatory retirement age without showing that it continues, somehow, to monitor the health and fitness of its employees [after their initial hiring]." 848 F2d at 533. The en banc *Mississippi State Tax Commission* court rejected what it saw as a virtual per se rule adopted by the three-judge panel in the case. The en banc court stated as follows:

> We do not disagree with the panel . . . in stressing the weight of standards of health and fitness in the fact determination; we only say that physical fitness may be a job qualification despite the lack of formal standards. The weight to be given the existence or absence of formal standards is for the fact finder to decide.

873 F2d at 99.

203 Equal Employment Opportunity Commn v Kentucky State Police Dept, 860 F2d 665 (6th Cir 1988), *cert denied,* 490 US 1066 (1989); Equal Employment Opportunity Commn v Tennessee Wildlife Resources Agency, 859 F2d 24 (6th Cir 1988), *cert denied,* 489 US 1066 (1989).

204 *See also* Heiar v Crawford County, Wis, 746 F2d 1190 (7th Cir 1984), *cert denied,* 472 US 1027 (1985); Equal Employment Opportunity Commn v Florida Dept of Highway Safety & Motor Vehicles, 660 F Supp 1104, 1110 (ND Fla 1986).

The presence of employees who are over the mandatory retirement age, yet who have not been forced out, will not undercut the employer's argument that the physical fitness qualifications claimed to justify a mandatory retirement age are reasonably necessary—at least so long as the over-age employees are employed in limited capacities only.[205] On the other hand, the presence of full-time employees over the mandatory retirement age in jobs for which there is no retirement requirement, and which are comparable to jobs for which the employer has imposed a mandatory retirement requirement, can be very damning for the employer.[206] Similarly, evidence that comparable businesses in the same industry do not utilize a mandatory retirement policy can be significant.[207]

Some courts have sought guidance from analogous legislative or administrative determinations.[208] Some have been particularly reluctant to parse public safety arguments.[209]

---

[205] Equal Employment Opportunity Commn v City of E Providence, 798 F2d 524, 531 (1st Cir 1986).

[206] *See* Equal Employment Opportunity Commn v Tennessee Wildlife Resources Agency, 859 F2d 24, 26 (6th Cir 1988), *cert denied,* 489 US 1066 (1989); Equal Employment Opportunity Commn v Mississippi, 654 F Supp 1168, 1181 (SD Miss 1987), *affd on other grounds,* 837 F2d 1398 (5th Cir 1988).

[207] Western Air Lines, Inc v Criswell, 472 US 400, 423 (1985).

[208] See **§5.08.**

[209] See **§5.10.** In Johnson v American Airlines, Inc, 745 F2d 988 (5th Cir 1984), *cert denied,* 472 US 1027 (1985), the court approved a unique rationale in upholding the defendant's BFOQ. In the standard case, the challenged policy is one that explicitly sets forth a certain age limit as a job requirement. *Johnson* was different. The case involved an up-or-out policy whereby flight officers who were ineligible (for whatever reason) to rise to the top position of pilot, or captain, were forced to retire. A federal regulation—not challenged in *Johnson*—requires the retirement of commercial pilots at age 60. 14 CFR §121.383(c) (1993). Consequently, the airline also forced the retirement of flight officers upon attainment of that age since, by virtue of the regulation, they were ineligible for promotion. It further barred 60-and-over captains from transferring to flight officer positions. It was the up-or-out policy—which on its face made no reference to age—that was challenged by the plaintiffs. The airline successfully defended its non-age-based policy by putting forth evidence that employing ex-captains would block the flight officer positions for use as training seats for future pilots. The policy was also justified with evidence that some ex-captains in flight officer position—although it could not be predicted which ones—would endanger the safety of flights by disrupting

It is clear, given the tenor of the decisions, that expert testimony plays a critically important role in BFOQ cases. Not surprisingly, BFOQ mandatory retirement cases do not readily lend themselves to disposition by way of summary judgment, since they are typically heavily geared to conflicting expert testimony.[210]

§5.12 Age Limits as BFOQs for Hiring

Age limits are most commonly thought of as generating concerns about discrimination when they are used as the bases for discharging or forcibly retiring employees. However, age restrictions can also come into play at the initial stage of the employment relationship, when a minimum or maximum age is set as a condition of eligibility for hiring. Age maxima are common, for example, with regard to eligibility for hiring as law enforcement officers.[211] The bona fide occupational qualification (BFOQ) defense set forth in §4(f)(1)[212] of the Age Discrimination in Employment Act (ADEA)[213] has been asserted in a number of cases in which challenges have been made to hiring restrictions.

---

crew coordination and reverting to captaincy behavior, i.e., back seat driving, so to speak, in times of emergencies.

210 *See* Childers v Morgan County Bd of Educ, 817 F2d 1556 (11th Cir 1987).

211 *See, e.g.*, Equal Employment Opportunity Commn v University of Tex Health Science Ctr, 710 F2d 1091 (5th Cir 1983); Equal Employment Opportunity Commn v Missouri State Highway Patrol, 748 F2d 447 (8th Cir 1984), *cert denied*, 474 US 828 (1985); Equal Employment Opportunity Commn v Mississippi, 654 F Supp 1168 (SD Miss 1987), *affd*, 837 F2d 1398 (5th Cir 1988); Equal Employment Opportunity Commn v City of Linton, 623 F Supp 724 (SD Ind 1985); Hahn v City of Buffalo, 596 F Supp 939 (WDNY 1984), *affd*, 770 F2d 12 (2d Cir 1985); Equal Employment Opportunity Commn v County of Allegheny, 705 F2d 679 (3d Cir 1983); Equal Employment Opportunity Commn v County of Los Angeles, 526 F Supp 1135 (CD Cal 1981), *affd*, 706 F2d 1039 (9th Cir 1983), *cert denied*, 464 US 1073 (1984).

212 29 USC §623(f)(1).

213 *Id* §§621-634.

(In 1986 the Act was amended to allow employers to impose age limitations, pursuant to §4(i),[214] for the hiring of firefighters and law enforcement officers without employers having to justify such requirements in terms of the BFOQ defense, provided certain conditions were met, i.e., that the age requirement was in effect pursuant to a state law or a local ordinance as of March 3, 1983, and that the exclusion based on age was made pursuant to a bona fide hiring plan that was not a subterfuge to avoid the purposes of the ADEA.[215] This provision expired on December 31, 1993.[216] Thus, while the development of BFOQ doctrine during the life of this provision was considerably diminished, the demise of §4(i) has opened the way for renewed litigation, and it also has restored to relevance the pre-1986 case law addressing the BFOQ defense in denial of hire situations).

In *Equal Employment Opportunity Commission v University of Texas Health Science Center*[217] the Court of Appeals for the Fifth Circuit upheld a maximum hiring age of 45 for campus police officers. The fact that employees hired prior to age 45 continued working after attaining that age arguably undercut the defendant's BFOQ defense. However, officers with even relatively few years of seniority generally were assigned to administrative work, and so the older officers did not have to perform the rigorous work performed by new hires.

Apart from the factors of physical strength, agility, and stamina that the Health Science Center maintained were necessary to the job, the defendant put forth another basis for its policy. Because the job involved interacting with students in a college setting, it was argued that younger officers were needed because they were better able to relate to youthful offenders. In accepting this argument, the court distinguished its own often-cited earlier ruling involving the comparable BFOQ defense provi-

---

[214] *Id* §623(i).

[215] See **ch 3.**

[216] *Id.*

[217] 710 F2d 1091 (5th Cir 1983).

sion contained in Title VII of the Civil Rights Act of 1964.[218] In that decision, *Diaz v Pan American World Airways, Inc,*[219] the Court of Appeals for the Fifth Circuit had held that an airline could not justify hiring only female flight attendants on the grounds that females better served the psychological needs of passengers and were overwhelmingly preferred by them. The court rejected the customer preference argument with the reasoning that the nonmechanical functions performed by flight attendants were tangential to the essence of the defendant's business, i.e., the safe transportation of passengers. In contrast, the *University of Texas* court reasoned as follows: "[T]he asserted ability of younger officers is in no way tangential to their primary task of insuring the safety and protection of the campus community and preserving order."[220]

Typically—at least in cases that concern employees who work in occupations related to public safety—the defendant will ground its BFOQ defense on medical evidence, contending generally that older employees are increasingly susceptible to the onset of sudden illnesses, i.e., strokes and heart attacks, that can create endangerment to the public if they occur while the employee is on the job. This evidence can generate conflicting results that may well be a function of the persuasiveness of the expert witnesses, rather than a reflection of differing basic medical data. For example, in *Equal Employment Opportunity Commission v Missouri State Highway Patrol*[221] the trial court, reviewing the medical evidence, upheld an age-32 hiring maximum which was imposed as to state troopers.[222] In contrast, in *Hahn v City of Buffalo*[223] an age-29 hiring maximum for police officers was struck down, the court rejecting the defendant's BFOQ defense. The *Hahn* court concluded, after an extensive review

---

[218] 42 USC §§2000e through 2000e-17.

[219] 442 F2d 385 (5th Cir), *cert denied,* 404 US 950 (1971).

[220] 710 F2d at 1096.

[221] 555 F Supp 97 (WD Mo 1982), *affd in part & revd in part,* 748 F2d 447 (8th Cir 1984), *cert denied,* 474 US 828 (1985).

[222] *See also* Poteet v Palestine, 620 SW2d 181 (Tex Civ App 1981).

[223] 596 F Supp 939 (WDNY 1984), *affd,* 770 F2d 12 (2d Cir 1985).

of the evidence, that the testimony of the defendant's experts had failed to establish that all or substantially all persons over age 40 are physically or emotionally unfit to perform as police officers. The court also heard much testimony as to whether persons over age 40 manifest susceptibilities to heart attacks that cannot be detected and which, because of this, justify a disqualification based on age alone. The court concluded that physically unqualified persons indeed can be identified with enough certainty so as to bar employers from simply using age as a proxy for individualized treatment.

Apart from reliance on medical data, employers in BFOQ cases involving hiring-age maxima often point to the operation of their seniority systems as bases for upholding their age-restrictive policies. For example, in *Missouri State Highway Patrol* the appellate court reversed the trial court on the question of an age-32 hiring maximum applied to police radio operators.[224] The court reasoned that these operators were engaged in a stressful activity, and that movement upwards to less rigorous supervisory positions required years of service. If no age maximum were set, older applicants would be hired who, because of lack of seniority, would not be able to move out of their stressful positions at a time in their lives when their ability to handle stress was declining because of increased age. In contrast, if the patrol only hired persons under age 32, the operators' waning abilities to handle stress would correlate with their enhanced abilities to rise to supervisory positions involving diminished stress.[225]

Usery v Tamiami Trail Tours, Inc, [226] and *Hodgson v Greyhound Lines, Inc,* [227] both involved bus companies that maintained age-35 eligibility caps for the hiring of new bus drivers. In both cases the companies argued that these caps were justified by virtue of the fact that older drivers, with years of seniority, chose

---

[224] Equal Employment Opportunity Commn v Missouri State Highway Patrol, 748 F2d 447 (8th Cir 1984), *cert denied,* 474 US 828 (1985).

[225] *Id* 457.

[226] 531 F2d 224 (5th Cir 1976).

[227] 499 F2d 859 (7th Cir 1974), *cert denied,* 419 US 1122 (1975).

the easy driving routes, leaving the more rigorous routes to the less senior employees. If the companies were forced to hire older new drivers, who by definition would have no seniority, these drivers would be assigned to the tough routes. Because there was a gradual decline in ability associated with age the result would be that the older new drivers would generate increased risks to passenger safety, whereas the older drivers with seniority would not, since, as their abilities declined, so too would the rigor of their activities. This argument was accepted by the court in *Greyhound.*[228] However, that decision is no longer viable because the court utilized a test for the BFOQ exception which was more defendant-generous than the formulation subsequently embraced by the Supreme Court in *Western Air Lines, Inc v Criswell.*[229] In *Tamiami,* on the other hand, the court rejected the defendant's argument. (However, it ultimately ruled for the defendant on the ground that it was not possible for the company to assess individually the physical abilities of older employees to perform the more rigorous assignments.)

The special nature of the job—and the training involved in it—were offered in *Smallwood v United Air Lines, Inc,*[230] as justifications for its ban on hiring new pilots over age 35. In the United system flight officers progressed during their careers from second officer to first officer to pilot. United argued that these three officers, who made up the complement of a given plane, had to work together effectively and that their joint efforts were made possible only by virtue of their having learned United's methods of flight operation exclusively. If older pilots were hired, they would certainly have had prior experience that would have been gained outside the United system, and this would be counterproductive. The court was unpersuaded by the defendant's argument. In contrast, the court deciding *Murnane v American Airlines,*

[228] The court also was persuaded by Greyhound's argument that the safest driver was one who was 55 years old and who had 16 years of driving experience—a combination that newly hired drivers who were older than 39 would never be able to put together. 499 F2d at 865.

[229] 472 US 400 (1985). See **§5.05.**

[230] 661 F2d 303 (4th Cir 1981), *cert denied,* 456 US 1007 (1982).

Inc,[231] approved a very similar argument and upheld as a BFOQ American's ban on the hiring of pilots over age 30. (However, the *Murnane* court utilized the now-discredited *Greyhound* test, and so its ruling is no longer viable.)

An employer may argue that the costs of training a new employee justify limiting hiring to persons under a certain age, so that—once trained—the employee will be on the job for a sufficient number of years to assure an adequate return to the employer of its training investment. This argument has some support in the ADEA's legislative history,[232] but it has been rejected by the courts.[233]

§5.13 The Jury's Role in BFOQ Cases

In *Western Air Lines, Inc v Criswell*[234] the Supreme Court espoused what it denominated an "objective" test[235] for determining the merits of a bona fide occupational qualification (BFOQ) defense[236] under the Age Discrimination in Employment Act (ADEA).[237] It enunciated a two-part inquiry that must be pursued.[238] The defendant in *Criswell*, contending that the trial court's jury instructions were deficient in guiding the jury in this inquiry, argued that juries were not competent to resolve complex medical disputes, such as existed by virtue of conflicting medical evidence concerning the detection of disease in older flight engineers. Because of juries' alleged failings, the defen-

---

[231] 667 F2d 98 (DC Cir 1981), *cert denied*, 456 US 915 (1982).

[232] See **§5.16.**

[233] *See, e.g.*, Smallwood v United Air Lines, Inc, 661 F2d 303, 307 (4th Cir 1981), *cert denied*, 456 US 1007 (1982); Hahn v City of Buffalo, 596 F Supp 939, 947 (WDNY 1984), *affd*, 770 F2d 12 (2d Cir 1985); Equal Employment Opportunity Commn v County of Los Angeles, 526 F Supp 1135, 1140-41 (CD Cal 1981), *affd*, 706 F2d 1039 (9th Cir 1983), *cert denied*, 464 US 1073 (1984).

[234] 472 US 400 (1985).

[235] *Id* 413.

[236] §4(f)(1), 29 USC §623(f)(1).

[237] 29 USC §§621-634.

[238] See **§5.05.**

dant argued, it should be sufficient that the invoker of the BFOQ defense simply prove that it had a rational basis in fact for believing that identification of those persons lacking suitable qualifications could not be done on an individualized basis. Rejecting this argument, the *Criswell* Court vigorously supported the role of juries in BFOQ cases:

> [The] "rational basis in fact" standard would have been tantamount to an instruction to return a verdict in the defendant's favor. Because that standard conveys a meaning that is significantly different from that conveyed by the statutory phrase "reasonably necessary," it was correctly rejected by the trial court.
>
> Western argues that a "rational basis" standard should be adopted because medical disputes can never be proved "to a certainty" and because juries should not be permitted "to resolve bona fide conflicts among medical experts respecting the adequacy of individualized testing. . . ." The jury, however, need not be convinced beyond all doubt that medical testing is impossible, but only that the proposition is true "on a preponderance of the evidence." Moreover, Western's attack on the wisdom of assigning the resolution of complex questions to 12 lay persons is inconsistent with the structure of the ADEA. Congress expressly decided that problems involving age discrimination in employment should be resolved on a "case-by-case basis" by proof to a jury.[239]

---

[239] 472 US at 421-22. The *Criswell* Court quoted the trial court's BFOQ instructions and upheld them against the defendant's challenges. Thus, the instructions set forth in the opinion can be used with confidence in subsequent BFOQ cases. The jury was instructed that the " 'BFOQ defense is available only if it is reasonably necessary to the normal operation or essence of defendant's business.' " *Id* 407. The jury was informed that " 'the essence of Western's business is the safe transportation of their passengers.' " *Id.* The jury was also instructed as follows:

> One method by which defendant Western may establish a BFOQ in this case is to prove:
>
> (1) That in 1978, when these plaintiffs were retired, it was highly impractical for Western to deal with each second officer over age 60 on

The Reasonable Factors Other Than Age Exception

§5.14 The Reasonable Factors Other Than Age Exception: Generally

Section 4(f)(1)[240] of the Age Discrimination in Employment Act (ADEA)[241] sets forth an exception for differentiations based on reasonable factors other than age (RFOA): "It shall not be unlawful for an employer, employment agency, or labor organization . . . (1) to take any action otherwise prohibited . . . where the differentiation is based on reasonable factors other than age[.]" There are two primary issues generated by this exception. First, there is the question of whether the RFOA language constitutes an affirmative defense. The courts are split on this issue, although clearly a majority endorses a negative answer. Second, there is the matter of determining what constitutes a reasonable factor other than age. These issues are addressed in the succeeding sections.

> an individualized basis to determine his particular ability to perform his job safely; and
>
> (2) That some second officers over age 60 possess traits of a physiological, psychological or other nature which preclude safe and efficient job performance that cannot be ascertained by means other than knowing their age.
>
> In evaluating the practicability to defendant Western of dealing with second officers over age 60 on an individualized basis, with respect to the medical testimony, you should consider the state of the medical art as it existed . . . [at the time the plaintiffs' alleged harm occurred].

Id 407-08.

240 29 USC §623(f)(1).

241 *Id* §§621-634.

§5.15 Case Law Concerning the RFOA Exception's Status as an Affirmative Defense

In *Western Air Lines, Inc v Criswell*[242] the Supreme Court deemed it unnecessary to decide one of the issues as to which it had granted certiorari, i.e., whether the reasonable factors other than age (RFOA) exception set forth in §4(f)(1)[243] of the Age Discrimination in Employment Act (ADEA)[244] constitutes an affirmative defense. In foregoing resolution of the RFOA provision's status, the Court looked to the posture of the case[245] as the basis for its position. The Court did not rely on the fact that earlier in the same term it arguably had already settled the matter when it referred, in passing, to the RFOA provision as an affirmative defense in *Trans World Airlines, Inc v Thurston.*[246] On the other hand, the *Criswell* Court's failure even to mention *Thurston* as the basis for its not addressing the issue in *Criswell* suggests that *Thurston* should not be read as having disposed of this question.

The Lower Courts' Positions

Insofar as lower court treatment is concerned, there is a split among the courts as to whether the RFOA exception constitutes an affirmative defense. The Courts of Appeals for the Third,[247]

---

242 472 US 400 (1985).

243 29 USC §623(f)(1).

244 *Id* §§621-634.

245 472 US at 408-09.

246 469 US 111, 122 (1985).

247 Equal Employment Opportunity Commn v Westinghouse Elec Corp, 725 F2d 211, 222-23 (3d Cir), *cert denied,* 469 US 820 (1984). As a result of this ruling, the validity of earlier decisions of district courts within the circuit to the contrary were negated. *See, e.g.*, Popko v City of Clairton, 570 F Supp 446 (WD Pa 1983); Equal Employment Opportunity Commn v City of New Castle, 32 FEP Cas (BNA) 1409 (WD Pa 1983), *affd without opinion,* 740 F2d 956 (3d Cir 1984).

Fifth,[248] Tenth,[249] and Eleventh[250] Circuits have ruled that the RFOA provision is not an affirmative defense. The result in these jurisdictions is that the defendant that invokes the provision only shoulders an easy burden of production, as opposed to the much more rigorous burden of persuasion that would apply were the RFOA an affirmative defense. A few district courts outside these circuits are in accord,[251] as well as are district courts within these circuits.[252]

In contrast, the Court of Appeals for the Ninth Circuit has subscribed to the view that the RFOA provision does constitute an affirmative defense.[253] The situation in the Eighth Circuit is

---

[248] Marshall v Westinghouse Elec Corp, 576 F2d 588 (5th Cir 1978). Other Fifth Circuit decisions both before and since *Marshall* have taken the same position. *See, e.g.*, Smith v Farah Mfg Co, Inc, 650 F2d 64, 67 (5th Cir 1981); Price v Maryland Casualty Co, 561 F2d 609, 613 (5th Cir 1977). It is only in the *Marshall* opinion, however, that the court offered any analysis. One earlier Fifth Circuit panel had ruled to the contrary. Hodgson v First Fed Sav & Loan Assn, 455 F2d 818 (5th Cir 1972).

[249] Schwager v Sun Oil Co, 591 F2d 58, 61 (10th Cir 1979).

[250] Iervolino v Delta Air Lines, Inc, 796 F2d 1408, 1415-16 (11th Cir 1986), *cert denied,* 479 US 1090 (1987). This, Cowen v Standards Brands, Inc, 572 F Supp 1576 (ND Ala 1983), a ruling to the contrary, was effectively negated.

[251] Jacobs v College of William & Mary, 517 F Supp 791 (ED Va 1980), *affd without opinion,* 661 F2d 922 (4th Cir), *cert denied,* 454 US 1033 (1981); Morgan v Goldschmidt, 33 FEP Cas (BNA) 797 (DDC 1980).

[252] *See, e.g.*, Walker v Mountain States Tel & Tel Co, 686 F Supp 269 (D Colo 1988); White v Bobbie Brooks, Inc, 30 Empl Prac Dec (CCH) ¶33,147 (Bankr ND Ohio 1982); Mizrany v Texas Rehabilitation Commn, 522 F Supp 611, 617 (SD Tex 1981), *affd without opinion,* 685 F2d 1384 (5th Cir 1982); Equal Employment Opportunity Commn v County of Allegheny, 519 F Supp 1328 (WD Pa 1981), *affd,* 705 F2d 679 (3d Cir 1983); Erwin v Bank of Miss, 512 F Supp 545 (ND Miss 1981); Carolan v Central Freight Lines, Inc, 489 F Supp 941, 944 (ED Tex 1980); Moore v Sears, Roebuck & Co, 464 F Supp 357, 363 (ND Ga 1979); Mastie v Great Lakes Steel Corp, 424 F Supp 1299 (ED Mich 1976); *see also* Bergeron v City of Goodlettsville, 705 F Supp 376, 381 (MD Tenn 1988).

[253] Criswell v Western Airlines, Inc, 709 F2d 544 (9th Cir 1983), *affd on other grounds,* 472 US 400 (1985); Equal Employment Opportunity Commn v County of Santa Barbara, 666 F2d 373, 375, 377 n6 (9th Cir 1982); *accord* Equal Employment Opportunity Commn v Northwest Airlines, Inc, 51 FEP Cas (BNA) 1317, 1322 (WD Wash 1989); *see also* Equal Employment Opportunity Commn v Local 350, Plumbers & Pipefitters, 998 F2d 641, 648 (9th Cir 1992);

unclear: *Cova v Coca-Bottling Co of St Louis*[254] seems to support reading the RFOA exception as an affirmative defense, but there is later case law casting some doubt on the circuit's position.[255] The case law in the First Circuit also is ambiguous: *Loeb v Textron, Inc,*[256] supports reading the RFOA language as not constituting an affirmative defense; *Equal Employment Opportunity Commission v Massachusetts*[257] provides support for a contrary reading. The situation in the Sixth Circuit also is unclear, with one decision, *Laugesen v Anaconda Co,*[258] supporting a reading of the RFOA exception as an affirmative defense—and a later ruling seemingly going in the other direction.[259] There are a few district court rulings from other jurisdictions that have identified the RFOA provision as an affirmative defense.[260]

Equal Employment Opportunity Commn v Northwest Airlines, Inc, 49 FEP Cas (BNA) 1433, 1435 (WD Wash 1987).

[254] 574 F2d 958, 959-60 (8th Cir 1978).

[255] The *Cova* decision is, at best, obscure. The rulings in Johnson v Perkins Restaurants, Inc, 815 F2d 1220 (8th Cir 1987), and Holley v Sanyo Mfg, Inc, 771 F2d 1161, 1168 (8th Cir 1985), while devoid of analysis regarding the correct characterization of the RFOA provision, would support moving this circuit out of the affirmative defense camp. On the other hand, Moore v McGraw Edison Co, 804 F2d 1026, 1030-31 (8th Cir 1986), neither lends support to the conclusion that the position of the Court of Appeals for the Eighth Circuit is that the RFOA exception is an affirmative defense nor does it lend support to reading the court's position being that the RFOA exception is not an affirmative defense.

[256] 600 F2d 1003 (1st Cir 1979).

[257] 987 F2d 64, 73 (1st Cir 1993).

[258] 510 F2d 307, 315 (6th Cir 1975); *accord* Marshall v Goodyear Tire & Rubber Co, 22 FEP Cas (BNA) 775, 778 (WD Tenn 1979).

[259] *See* Blackwell v Sun Elec Corp, 696 F2d 1176, 1180 & n5 (6th Cir 1983).

[260] Equal Employment Opportunity Commn v Babcock & Wilcox Co, 43 FEP Cas (BNA) 736, 741 (EDNC 1987); Equal Employment Opportunity Commn v Liggett & Meyers, Inc, 29 FEP Cas (BNA) 1611, 1643 (EDNC 1982) (dictum); Marshall v Baltimore & Ohio RR, 461 F Supp 362, 372 (D Md 1978), *affd in part & revd in part on other grounds,* 632 F2d 1107 (4th Cir 1980), *cert denied,* 454 US 825 (1981); *see also* Equal Employment Opportunity Commn v Westinghouse Elec Corp, 632 F Supp 343, 365 n11 (ED Pa 1986), *affd in part & vacated & remanded in part on other grounds,* 869 F2d 696 (3d Cir), *vacated,* 493 US 801 (1989); Grohs v Gold Bond Bldg Prods, 627 F Supp 1555, 1558 (ND Ill 1986); Equal Employment Opportunity Commn v Governor Mifflin School Dist, 623

Of course, a court may discuss the RFOA exception without characterizing it as being, or not being, an affirmative defense.[261]

The Lower Courts' Analyses

Judicial analysis rejecting the RFOA provision as constituting an affirmative defense is unpersuasive. The opinion of the Court of Appeals for the Third Circuit in *Equal Employment Opportunity Commission v Westinghouse Electric Corp*[262] is devoid of analysis. So, too, is the earlier-noted opinion of the Court of Appeals for the Tenth Circuit.[263]

The analyses put forth by the Court of Appeals for the First Circuit in *Loeb v Textron, Inc*[264] and by the Court of Appeals for the Fifth Circuit in *Marshall v Westinghouse Electric Corp*[265] are flawed. In *Loeb* the court reasoned that the similarities between the ADEA and Title VII of the Civil Rights Act of 1964[266] warranted reading Title VII analysis into the ADEA, and that under Title VII the defendant in a discriminatory treatment case only bears a burden of production. To the crucial point that the presence of exceptions in the ADEA—and their absence in Title VII—bars an uncritical equation of the two statutes, the court offered only a cryptic response.[267]

The *Marshall* court contrasted the bona fide occupational

F Supp 734, 740 (ED Pa 1985); Bishop v Jelleff Assocs, 398 F Supp 579 (DDC 1974).

[261] *See* Moore v McGraw Edison Co, 804 F2d 1026, 1030-31 (8th Cir 1986); Equal Employment Opportunity Commn v Community Unit Sch Dist No 9, 642 F Supp 902, 905 (SD Ill 1986). The court deciding Equal Employment Opportunity Commn v Pan Am World Airways, Inc, 52 FEP Cas (BNA) 920 (ND Cal 1987), noted, but did not resolve, the split among the courts. *Id* 924 n2.

[262] 725 F2d 211 (3d Cir 1983), *cert denied,* 469 US 820 (1984).

[263] Schwager v Sun Oil Co, 591 F2d 58 (10th Cir 1979).

[264] 600 F2d 1003 (1st Cir 1979).

[265] 576 F2d 588 (5th Cir 1978).

[266] 42 USC §§2000e through 2000e-17.

[267] 600 F2d at 1016.

qualification (BFOQ)[268] and RFOA exceptions. The former clearly embodies an affirmative defense that is applicable to general exclusionary employment policies and rules whereby "otherwise statutorily protected individuals [may be excluded] solely on the basis of class membership."[269] In contrast, the court reasoned, "[t]he good cause and differentiating factor [i.e. RFOA] exceptions . . . are denials of the plaintiff's prima facie case."[270] Accordingly, the court concluded—although without any clear explication—that the affirmative defense characterization associated with the BFOQ provision was inapplicable to the RFOA provision. In so reasoning, the court characterized the sequence of events involved in invocation of the RFOA exception:

> Plaintiff says that the employer fired him because of his age; employer replies, in effect, not so, plaintiff was fired for excessive absences, general inability, or some other nondiscriminatory reason. The natural tendency of the court to place the burden of proof upon the party desiring change and the special policy considerations disfavoring the statutory exceptions both justify the distinction between these defenses.[271]

This analysis by the *Marshall* court would seem to be misconceived. While the court deemed the RFOA provision to be applicable only to individual claims of discrimination by single plaintiffs (with the BFOQ defense applying in instances of general rules), the RFOA provision indeed has been applied to general rules.[272] In any event, the *Marshall* court's position is very much at odds with a well-accepted canon regarding construction of the ADEA. The *Marshall* court spoke, as just quoted, of the special policy considerations "disfavoring . . . statutory excep-

---

268 See **§5.02.**

269 576 F2d at 591.

270 *Id.* As to the good cause exception, see **§5.60.**

271 576 F2d at 591 (footnote omitted).

272 *See* Criswell v Western Airlines, Inc, 709 F2d 544 (9th Cir 1983), *affd on other grounds,* 472 US 400 (1985).

tions." Indeed, it is well established that civil rights statutes—and more particularly, the ADEA—are to be liberally construed and so exceptions to them are to be narrowly applied.[273] Yet, notwithstanding the *Marshall* court's rhetoric about exceptions being disfavored, what it actually did by rejecting a reading of the RFOA provision as an affirmative defense was to take the contrary interpretive tack.

While the foregoing decisions reveal lackluster analyses, the decisions by the courts that read the RFOA language as establishing an affirmative defense likewise are unimpressive exercises of legal cogency.The opinion of the Court of Appeals for the Eighth Circuit in *Cova v Coca-Cola Bottling Co*[274] is very obscure. What is more, the court's later ruling in *Holley v Sanyo Manufacturing, Inc,*[275] probably can be read—devoid though it is of direct analysis of the issue—as interpreting the RFOA provision as not constituting an affirmative defense. In the Sixth Circuit the appellate court's opinion in *Laugesen v Anaconda Co*[276] did not afford any particular insights. The court drew a distinction between policies having a discriminatory impact on older employees generally and single-plaintiff cases involving challenges to individualized decisions made by employers that harm particular individual plaintiffs. When the RFOA defense is invoked vis-a-vis allegedly discriminatory policies, the defendant—under the *Laugesen* court's formulation—must prove job relatedness,[277] as in disparate impact cases.[278] When an individual decision involving "a private single plaintiff" is all that is at issue,

---

[273] *See, e.g.,* Orzel v City of Wauwatosa Fire Dept, 697 F2d 743 (7th Cir 1983), *cert denied,* 464 US 992 (1984); Equal Employment Opportunity Commn v County of Santa Barbara, 666 F2d 373, 376 (9th Cir 1982); *cf* Dothard v Rawlinson, 433 US 321, 334 (1977) (construing the BFOQ exception contained in Title VII).

[274] 574 F2d 958 (8th Cir 1978).

[275] 771 F2d 1161, 1168 (8th Cir 1985).

[276] 510 F2d 307 (6th Cir 1975).

[277] *Id* 315.

[278] See **ch 7**.

however, the RFOA provision does not constitute an affirmative defense and so the burden of proof is on the plaintiff.[279]

The ruling of the Court of Appeals for the Ninth Circuit in *Criswell v Western Airlines, Inc,*[280] was abbreviated insofar as analysis regarding the RFOA provision was concerned. The court deemed significant the fact that "[t]he 'reasonable factors' defense appears alongside [sic] the BFOQ exception . . . [,]"[281] which clearly is an affirmative defense. It further cited to the position taken by the ADEA enforcement agencies, which has been that the burden of proof regarding the RFOA exception is on the defendant,[282] and it noted the deference due agency interpretations.[283] From these factors followed the conclusion that the RFOA exception constitutes an affirmative defense, although the court did not specify just what it was the defendant would have to prove.

In *Equal Employment Opportunity Commission v Massachusetts*[284] the Court of Appeals for the First Circuit referred to the RFOA exception as a "defense."[285] As to the merits, the court ruled that the requirement of submitting to a medical examination that was imposed on state and local employees upon their attaining age 70 did not constitute an RFOA. In so doing, the court stated that it could not "rationally conclude" that the statute requiring the medical examination was based on an RFOA.[286] This language would seem to suggest that if the reasonable factors other than age exception indeed constitutes an affirmative defense in the First Circuit, the defendant's burden in that circuit is simply to prove that there is a rational basis for the factor at issue—a relatively easy burden, indeed.

---

279 510 F2d at 315.

280 709 F2d 544 (9th Cir 1983), *affd on other grounds,* 472 US 400 (1985).

281 *Id* 552.

282 See **§5.18.**

283 709 F2d at 553 (citing Udall v Tallman, 380 US 1, 4-18 (1965)).

284 987 F2d 64 (1st Cir 1993).

285 *Id* 73.

286 *Id* 321.

Conclusion

While the judicial rulings both pro and con are short on persuasive analysis, the conclusion that the RFOA exception is an affirmative defense seems the correct one, in light of (1) the provision's placement in the ADEA contiguous to the BFOQ defense, (2) legislative history, and (3) analogical analysis.[287] These factors are discussed in the succeeding sections.

§5.16 Legislative History As to the RFOA Exception's Affirmative Defense Status

The reasonable factors other than age (RFOA) provision set forth in §4(f)(1)[288] of the Age Discrimination in Employment Act (ADEA)[289] has a fairly unilluminating history. Still, the limited insights afforded by this history support the argument that the RFOA provision should be read as an affirmative defense.

In January, 1967, President Johnson sent to Congress proposed legislation that in some modified form was enacted, later the same year as the ADEA. The Administration bill contained

---

[287] In 1990 the ADEA was amended in very significant ways by the Older Workers Benefit Protection Act (OWBPA), Pub L No 101-433, 104 Stat 987, *as amended by* Pub L No 101-521, 104 Stat 2287 (1990). See generally **§5.25.** The bill that eventually was passed by the Senate and House and enacted into law went through several modifications. The version that was reported out of the Senate Committee on Labor and Human Resources—which bill was succeeded by several variations—contained language imposing on employers, employment agencies, and labor organizations a burden of proof regarding the RFOA defense. However, the final version of the Senate bill, and its ultimate successor—the OWBPA itself—dropped that language. Little explanation was provided for this deletion. The final bill was a compromise fashioned by four senators—Senators Metzenbaum, Pryor, Heinz, and Hatch.While no committee report accompanied this compromise bill, the four did submit a document during the Senate debates entitled *Final Substitute: Statement of Managers,* 136 Cong Rec S13,596-97 (daily ed Sept 24, 1990), that, inter alia, addressed this matter of allocation of burdens. They therein "declare[d] that they are not disturbing or in any way affecting the allocation of the burden of proof for paragraph 4(f)(1) [29 USC §623(f)(1)]." 136 Cong Rec at S13,596.

[288] 29 USC §623(f)(1).

[289] *Id* §§621-634.

a subsection in which were joined—in the same language as that ultimately enacted—the bona fide occupational qualification (BFOQ)[290] and RFOA provisions. The hearings on the proposed legislation virtually ignored the RFOA exception. Secretary of Labor Wirtz made only fleeting, uninformative reference to the provision during the course of the Senate hearings.[291] The House hearings afforded no more guidance.[292]

---

290 See **§5.02.**

291 Secretary Wirtz asserted, in his prepared statement before the Senate, that it was only "arbitrary" age discrimination that the legislation aimed to eradicate. *Age Discrimination in Employment, Hearings on S. 830 Before the General Subcomm on Labor of the Senate Comm on Labor and Public Welfare,* 90th Cong, 1st Sess 39 (1967). He followed this with recitation of the defenses, and with the ensuing statement that these defenses were "obviously broad." *Id.*

The sole other attention directed during the course of the Senate hearings to the RFOA provision consisted of further commentary by Secretary Wirtz. He was asked by Senator Randolph to offer his view as to the refusal by an airline to train a 45-year-old man to be a pilot, given the facts that a Federal Aviation Administration (FAA) regulation required retirement at age 60, that the training period would be three years, and that the training would be very expensive. Responding in an admittedly tentative manner, Secretary Wirtz first quoted §4(f)(1), which of course contained—then and now—both the ADEA's BFOQ and RFOA defenses. Without identifying the one or the other defense as the source of his insights, Secretary Wirtz went on to state as follows:

> I would think that where there is that much training requirement, that that would be a legitimate factor; that you would weigh the period of the usefulness of that person against the period of the training that was required, taking full account of the cost factors and human factors. . . .
>
> I would not think it would be a violation of the provision to deny employment on those terms.

Id 49.

292 The closest to a direct discussion concerning the RFOA exception occurred during the course of a dialogue between Representative Burton and Secretary Wirtz. The congressman asked whether the provisions of the legislation would override a collective bargaining agreement with reference to seniority. The following colloquy then occurred:

> Secretary Wirtz. . . . If a seniority clause were so constructed or a retirement clause were so constructed that it unfairly attached significance to age, my answer would be "Yes" to your question.
> Mr. Burton. Who would judge that?
> Secretary Wirtz. The Secretary of Labor.
> Mr. Burton. By what standards?
> Secretary Wirtz. By the standards of whether there is differentiation on the basis of age which the facts do not warrant.

The ensuing committee reports and debates on the ADEA bills maintained the same opacity regarding the RFOA language. While the committee reports noted the existence of the provision, they did not explain it. The sole effort at substantive elucidation was made by Senator Yarborough, chairman of the Senate committee and Senate manager of the legislation. He stated as follows:

> The bill provides for four exceptions from the enforcement provisions:
>
> . . . .
>
> Second. Where differentiation is based on reasonable factors other than age. For example, if a test shows that a man cannot do certain things. He might fail to pass the test at 35; he might fail to pass the test at 55. Some men slow up sooner than others. If the job requires a certain speed and the differentiation is based upon factors other than age, the law would not apply.[293]

It seems safe to conclude that the RFOA provision was not deemed to be distinctive from, or different than, the BFOQ exception with which it shares placement in §4(f)(1). Secretary Wirtz, representing the Johnson administration's views as to the ADEA legislation, treated the provisions as coequal. He spoke of all of them—and here he was including as well the exceptions embodied in §4(f)(2),[294] which was subsequently modified, and in §4(f)(3)[295]—as being "broad."[296] Senator Yarborough also

---

Age Discrimination in Employment, Hearings before the General Subcomm on Labor, Comm on Education and Labor, US House of Rep, 90th Cong, 1st Sess 14 (1967).

[293] 113 Cong Rec 31253 (Nov 6, 1967).

[294] 29 USC §623(f)(2).

[295] *Id* §623(f)(3).

[296] *Age Discrimination in Employment, Hearings on S.830 Before the General Subcomm on Labor of the Senate Comm on Labor and Public Welfare,* 90th Cong, 1st Sess 39 (1967).

referred to these provisions without differentiation, describing them as the "four exceptions," as quoted earlier. Moreover, from the inception of the legislation the RFOA language has been situated contiguously to the BFOQ provision, which has consistently and without argument been recognized as an affirmative defense.[297] There is nothing in the history of the ADEA that justifies regarding this contiguity as being the product of hasty, last-minute drafting, to which could be attributed an inappropriate or unintended placement of the two provisions. In addition, there is nothing in the legislative history indicating that anyone envisioned the RFOA exception being in some manner different—insofar as burdens of proof are concerned—from the other exceptions contained in §4(f).[298]

In brief, while the legislative history offers little revelation, it supports the conclusion that an uphill battle confronts the party who would argue that the RFOA exception is to be read differently from the BFOQ in terms of burdens.

§5.17 The Equal Pay Act's Relevance to the RFOA Exception's Status as an Affirmative Defense

The Age Discrimination in Employment Act (ADEA)[299] is a hybrid—a mix of prohibitory language derived from Title VII of the Civil Rights Act of 1964[300] and enforcement mechanisms derived from the Fair Labor Standards Act (FLSA).[301] The prohibitions imposed by the ADEA do not exactly track those con-

---

297 See **§5.02.**

298 29 USC §623(f). As is the case regarding the BFOQ defense, it has been well established for most of its life that the bona fide employee benefit exception plan set forth in §(4)(f)(2), 29 USC §623(f)(2), constitutes an affirmative defense, with the burden of proof being on the defendant. See generally **§5.28.** As for the good cause exception contained in §4(f)(3), 29 USC §623(f)(3), there is very little case law. See **§5.60.**

299 29 USC §§621-634.

300 42 USC §§2000e through 2000e-17.

301 29 USC §§200-219.

tained in Title VII, however, inasmuch as the age statute contains exceptions not included in the other statute. Title VII, for example, contains no analogue to the ADEA's reasonable factors other than age (RFOA) provision.[302] But the Equal Pay Act (EPA)[303] does, and it is that analogue which is of special significance here.

The EPA outlaws wage differentials between men and women who perform equal work. There are, however, four exceptions to this prohibition, including one which provides as follows: "No employer . . . shall discriminate . . . except where such [different] payment is made pursuant to . . . a differential based on any other factor other than sex."[304] In 1967, when Congress received from the Johnson Administration, considered, modified, and eventually passed the bill that ultimately was signed into law as the ADEA, it was clear that these EPA exceptions constituted affirmative defenses as to which the employer bore the burden of proof.[305] Moreover, the EPA is a part of the FLSA, and it was likewise clear in 1967 that it was the general rule "that the application of an exemption under the Fair Labor Standards Act is a matter of affirmative defense on which the employer has the burden of proof."[306]

Given this construction of the FLSA generally, and of one of its component parts, i.e., the EPA, specifically, the observations of the Court in *Lorillard v Pons,*[307] in which the Court held that jury trials are available in private ADEA suits, are particularly apposite:

---

[302] *Id* §623(f)(1).

[303] *Id* §206(d).

[304] *Id* §206(d)(1)(iv).

[305] *See* Wirtz v Basic, Incorporated, 256 F Supp 786, 790 (D Nev 1966). This holding subsequently was iterated in Corning Glass Works v Brennan, 417 US 188, 196-97 (1974), as well as in numerous lower court decisions cited in *Corning Glass. Id* 196 n11.

[306] *See, e.g.,* Corning Glass Works v Brennan, 417 US 188, 197-98 (1974); Arnold v Ben Kanowsky, Inc, 361 US 388, 392 (1960); Walling v General Indus Co, 330 US 545, 547-48 (1947).

[307] 434 US 575 (1978).

> Congress is presumed to be aware of an administrative or judicial interpretation of a statute and to adopt that interpretation when it re-enacts a statute without change. . . . So too, where . . . Congress adopts a new law incorporating sections of a prior law, Congress normally can be presumed to have had knowledge of the interpretations given to the incorporated law, at least insofar as it affects the new statute.
>
> That presumption is particularly appropriate here since, in enacting the ADEA, Congress exhibited both a detailed knowledge of the FLSA provisions and their judicial interpretation and a willingness to depart from those provisions regarded as undesirable or inappropriate for incorporation. . . .
>
> This selectivity that Congress exhibited in incorporating provisions and in modifying certain FLSA practices strongly suggests that but for those changes Congress expressly made, it intended to incorporate fully the remedies and procedures of the FLSA.[308]

(The Court in *Lorillard* held that jury trials are available in private ADEA suits.) The conclusion to be drawn from this analysis is that just as the EPA's *factor other than sex* exception imposes upon the defendant the burden of proof, so does the ADEA's RFOA exception impose the same burden.

§5.18 Agency Interpretations As to the RFOA Exception's Status as an Affirmative Defense

Initially, the Age Discrimination in Employment Act (ADEA)[309] was administered by the Department of Labor.[310] In mid-1979 enforcement authority was taken over by the Equal

---

[308] *Id* 580-82.

[309] 29 USC §§621-634.

[310] See **ch 2.**

Employment Opportunity Commission (EEOC).[311] When it administered the Act the Labor Department viewed the reasonable factors other than age (RFOA) provision[312] as an exception to the Act's prohibitions which was to be interpreted narrowly, with the defendant bearing the burden of proof as to the applicability of the exception.[313] Subsequently, the EEOC issued interpretations regarding the Act for which it had assumed administrative and enforcement authority, and the section addressing the RFOA exception likewise places the burden of proof on the invoker of the provision.[314]

The EEOC interpretation draws a distinction, however, that turns on the nature of the challenged action. When an employment practice that ostensibly is age neutral is attacked because it has an adverse impact on age-defined groups, the EEOC's position is that the employer must prove that the challenged practice or policy constitutes a business necessity.[315] This tracks the analysis generally utilized in disparate impact cases.[316] In contrast, when the RFOA exception is invoked as a defense to an individual claim of discriminatory treatment, the employer, according to the EEOC, "bears the burden of showing that the 'reasonable factor other than age' exists factually."[317] The EEOC interpretation does not offer any explanation, however, as to what this latter task involves. There is case law which conflicts with the distinction drawn by the EEOC.[318] There is also case law

(*Text continued on page 5-71*)

---

311 *Id.*

312 §4(f)(1), 29 USC §623(f)(1).

313 29 CFR §860.103(e) (1986) (effectively rescinded, 46 Fed Reg 47724 (Sept 29, 1981), and ordered removed from the CFR, 52 Fed Reg 23812 (June 25, 1987)).

314 29 CFR §1625.7 (1993).

315 *Id* §1625.7(d); *accord* Laugesen v Anaconda Co, 510 F2d 307, 315 (6th Cir 1975).

316 See **ch 7.**

317 29 CFR §1625.7(e) (1993).

318 Bishop v Jelleff Assocs, 398 F Supp 579, 593 (DDC 1974); Donnelly v

Exxon Research & Engg Co, 12 FEP Cas (BNA) 417 (DNJ 1971), *affd without opinion,* 521 F2d 1398 (3d Cir 1975). *But see* Hays v Republic Steel Corp, 12 FEP Cas (BNA) 1640, 1645-46 (ND Ala 1974), *affd in part & revd in part,* 531 F2d 1307 (5th Cir 1976).

expressing approbation of the agency position.[319]

The distinction made by the EEOC between group-based claims and individual claims is not one that has been adopted by most courts, nor have the substantive burdens the interpretation imposes in group and individual claim situations been generally embraced in the judicial forum. It is at least clear, however, that the enforcement agencies consistently have been in disagreement with those decisions expressing the view that the RFOA exception is never to be read as an affirmative defense.[320]

§5.19 A Possible Resolution of the Issue of the RFOA Exception's Status as an Affirmative Defense

The foregoing discussion supports, although it certainly does not compel, the conclusion that the reasonable factors other than age (RFOA) exception set forth in §4(f)(1)[321] of the Age Discrimination in Employment Act (ADEA)[322] should be read as an affirmative defense. However, this conclusion generates difficulties that must be resolved; if they are not, reading the RFOA's exception as an affirmative defense proves to be a meaningless legal gesture. Some review of the case law developed outside of direct judicial consideration of the RFOA exception is necessary to understand this situation.

---

[319] *See* Popko v City of Clairton, 570 F Supp 446 (WD Pa 1983); Equal Employment Opportunity Commn v City of New Castle, 32 FEP Cas (BNA) 1409 (WD Pa 1983), *affd without opinion,* 740 F2d 956 (3d Cir 1984). In Laugesen v Anaconda Co, 510 F2d 307 (6th Cir 1975), one of the few appellate court rulings reading the RFOA exception as an affirmative defense, the court did draw a distinction between policies affecting older employees generally and employer decisions affecting only individual employees or job applicants. But that distinction led to a different conclusion than that arrived at by the EEOC, for in the instance of an individual claimant the *Laugesen* court would not read the RFOA exception as at all constituting an affirmative defense, and so the burden of proof would rest with the plaintiff in that situation.

[320] See **§5.15.**

[321] 29 USC §623(f)(1).

[322] *Id* §§621-634.

Impact of Other Doctrine

Both the Supreme Court in *Hazen Paper Co v Biggins*[323] as well as virtually every court of appeals,[324] have embraced in the ADEA context the paradigm for litigating individual grievances involving circumstantial evidence of discrimination that is set forth in *McDonnell Douglas Corp v Green*[325] and *Texas Department of Community Affairs v Burdine.*[326] Both of these decisions by the Supreme Court addressed Title VII of the Civil Rights Act of 1964,[327] on which the ADEA is in part modeled. In *McDonnell Douglas* the Court established the formula regarding the burden to be satisfied by the plaintiff in establishing a prima facie violation.[328] In *Burdine* the Court set forth the formula applicable to the defendant once the prima facie case has been established: the defendant need only articulate, by way of rebuttal, a legitimate, nondiscriminatory reason for the action that the plaintiff has challenged.[329] This burden is only one of production; the burden of persuasion remains at all times with the plaintiff.[330]

Given this legal framework, the ADEA defendant typically responds to a prima facie circumstantial case of discriminatory treatment by asserting justifications such as the following:

—the plaintiff's job application was rejected because she lacked the requisite skills; or

—the plaintiff was fired because he failed to perform his job adequately; or

—the plaintiff was demoted because he could not get along with his fellow workers.[331]

---

[323] 113 S Ct 1701, 1707 (1993).

[324] See **ch 7.**

[325] 411 US 792 (1973).

[326] 450 US 248 (1981).

[327] 42 USC §§2000e through 2000e-17.

[328] See **ch 7.**

[329] 450 US at 255. See **ch 7.**

[330] 450 US at 255. See **ch 7.**

[331] See **ch 7.**

In each of these archetypal instances the defendant will have articulated a legitimate, nondiscriminatory—i.e., non-age-based—reason for its action. In accordance with *McDonnell Douglas* and *Burdine,* and more recently *St Mary's Honor Center v Hicks,*[332] the plaintiff then must establish that the defendant's justification is pretextual.[333] Otherwise, the defendant will prevail.

The analytical sticking point here is that these classic examples of excuses put forth by ADEA defendants, in substance amount to reasonable factors other than age. In other words, a defendant that explains that it fired the plaintiff because he or she was an inadequate worker really is stating that it fired that employee because of a reasonable factor other than age, i.e., inadequate performance. Granted, usually defendants do not literally label their *Burdine*-mandated justifications as reasonable factors other than age, but they nonetheless are such in a generic sense. (Indeed, at least some courts, without directly citing to the RFOA provision contained in the ADEA, have equated the articulation of a legitimate, nondiscriminatory reason with the assertion of a reasonable factor other than age.)[334] The problem is, however, that if a defendant, following the course prescribed by *Burdine,* can rebut a plaintiff's prima facie claim by merely producing evidence that its decision was based on what amounts

---

[332] 113 S Ct 2742 (1993). See **ch 7.**

[333] 450 US at 259.

[334] *See, e.g.,* Cooper v Asplundh Tree Expert Co, 836 F2d 1544, 1548 (10th Cir 1988); Johnson v Perkins Restaurants, Inc, 815 F2d 1220, 1221 (8th Cir 1987); Equal Employment Opportunity Commn v Wyoming Retirement Sys, 771 F2d 1425, 1429 (10th Cir 1985); Holley v Sanyo Mfg, Inc, 771 F2d 1161, 1168 (8th Cir 1985); Krieg v Paul Revere Life Ins Co, 718 F2d 998 (11th Cir 1983), *cert denied,* 466 US 929 (1984); Schwager v Sun Oil Co, 591 F2d 58 (10th Cir 1979); Bittar v Air Canada, 512 F2d 582 (5th Cir 1975); Holdridge v Thornburgh, 804 F Supp 876, 882 (ND Tex 1992) (federal job applicant suit); Metz v Transit Mix, Inc, 646 F Supp 286, 291 (ND Ind 1986), *revd on other grounds,* 828 F2d 1202 (7th Cir 1987); White v Bobbie Brooks, Inc, 30 Empl Prac Dec (CCH) ¶33,147 (Bankr ND Ohio 1982); Morgan v Goldschmidt, 33 FEP Cas (BNA) 797, 799 (DC Cir 1980) (federal employee suit); Raggett v Foote Mineral Co, 16 FEP Cas (BNA) 1771 (MD Tenn 1975); *see also* Equal Employment Opportunity Commn v Great Atl & Pac Tea Co, 618 F Supp 115, 119 (ND Ohio 1985); Jacobs v William & Mary College, 517 F Supp 791 (ED Va 1980), *affd without opinion,* 661 F2d 922 (4th Cir), *cert denied,* 454 US 1033 (1981).

to a reasonable factor other than age, there is no reason for that defendant to ever invoke the RFOA defense. Indeed, it would be stupid for a defendant to do so, since the invoker of this defense bears, not the easy burden of production prescribed by *Burdine,* but rather a much more onerous burden of persuasion. (Of course, if it should turn out that the reasonable factor other than age is not persuasive when articulated as a response to a prima facie claim, in accordance with *Burdine,* it follows that it would not be persuasive if then articulated as an affirmative defense. Thus, there still would be no point in pressing the RFOA affirmative defense.)

The result, in light of *Burdine,* is that the RFOA provision appears to be devoid of any substantive significance. The *only* situations in which the RFOA affirmative defense comes into possible play are situations for which *Burdine* already has drawn a much more defendant-protective legal blueprint, with the consequence being that the RFOA provision simply never will be invoked. After all, why should a defendant maximize, rather than minimize, it's legal task? Yet it is a truism of statutory construction that "[i]t is a court's duty 'to give effect, if possible, to every clause and word of a statute,' . . . rather than to emasculate an entire section."[335] Accordingly, so the canons of statutory construction go, a statute is to be construed so that no part will be inoperative or superfluous, void or insignificant.[336] To allow *Burdine* to swallow the RFOA defense is to choose a course in conflict with these legal aphorisms.

The Proposed Solution

There are two potential solutions for this situation.

The first is to read the RFOA provision as not establishing an affirmative defense. The forgoing discussion in **§§5.15-5.18** presumably renders that solution of dubious merit, notwithstanding that the majority of courts that have addressed this issue have so construed the RFOA exception.

---

335 United States v Menasche, 348 US 528, 539-40 (1955) (quoting Montclair v Ramsdale, 107 US 147, 152 (1882)).

336 Indianapolis Power & Light Co v ICC, 687 F2d 1098, 1101 (7th Cir 1982).

The alternative solution is one that both allows for recognition of the RFOA exception as an affirmative defense and for the viability of *Burdine's* ADEA case law progeny. This solution entails reading the RFOA exception as a variable provision that is understood to constitute an affirmative defense in some settings, and to simply capture in statutory language the *Burdine* concept in other settings. Acceptance of this solution requires reference to the genesis of the ADEA, and to the Act's continuing thrust.

The 1965 report of the Secretary of Labor that called for adoption of a federal ban on age discrimination in employment,[337] the hearings on the bill that ultimately was enacted as the ADEA, and the debates on the bill all supported a conclusion that remains valid today: arbitrary reliance upon age is bad, but not all reliance upon age is arbitrary. Thus, as is stated in §2 of the ADEA,[338] "arbitrary" discrimination is that which the Act condemns. It is when an employer may be relying upon outmoded notions about the incapacities of older people, or upon outmoded myths about older workers not being able to do a decent day's work, that the ADEA's protection is most needed.[339] Here,

---

337 United States Dept of Labor, Report to the Congress Under Section 715 of the Civil Rights Act of 1964, *The Older American Worker: Age Discrimination in Employment* (1965).

338 29 USC §621(b).

339 Some courts have maintained that if age is at all overtly used as a differentiating criterion, the RFOA provision is not even applicable. *See, e.g.,* Equal Employment Opportunity Commn v Massachusetts, 987 F2d 64, 72-73 (1st Cir 1993); Equal Employment Opportunity Commn v City of New Castle, 32 FEP Cas (BNA) 1409 (WD Pa 1983), *affd without opinion,* 740 F2d 956 (3d Cir 1984); Popko v City of Clairton, 570 F Supp 446 (WD Pa 1983); Equal Opportunity Commn v County of Allegheny, 519 F Supp 1328 (WD Pa 1981), *affd,* 705 F2d 679 (3d Cir 1983); Marshall v Goodyear Tire & Rubber Co, 22 FEP Cas (BNA) 775 (WD Tenn 1979). The Equal Employment Opportunity Commission (EEOC) interpretation of the RFOA defense asserts the same position: "When an employment practice uses age as a limiting criterion, the defense that the practice is justified by a reasonable factor other than age is unavailable." 29 CFR §1625.7(c) (1993). On the other hand, in Criswell v Western Airlines, Inc, 709 F2d 544 (9th Cir 1983), *affd on other grounds,* 472 US 400 (1985), the court held that the RFOA language indeed constituted an affirmative defense, and in that case the airline maintained a policy that openly excluded pilots who reached age 60 from qualifying as flight engineers. *See*

the risks of arbitrariness are at their greatest. In such instances, the RFOA arguably should give the least possible leeway to employer abuse, and so it is in the context of reliance on misplaced stereotypes that the exception should be read as an affirmative defense, with the tough burden of persuasion thereby being imposed on the entity utilizing the meritless stereotype. In other situations, however, a more relaxed understanding of the defendant's burden arguably is appropriate.

Thus, rigorous application of the RFOA provision should apply whenever an employer, employment agency, or labor organization utilizes a policy that, even if not explicitly reliant upon age, has age-related consequences that affect more than one worker. This is because the utilization of a policy—whether formal or informal—likely means that the defendant has relied upon some generalization about older workers as a group, and this type of thinking carries with it all the potentials for abuse characteristic of stereotypical treatment of people in group, as opposed to individual, terms. This is not to say that all age-neutral policies with age-related consequences inevitably will run afoul of the ADEA.[340] But, given Congress's apprehension regarding the ageism embodied in canards about older workers' compromised competencies, the risks of unfair discrimination would seem to justify application of a rigorous reading of the RFOA language.[341] Thus, even if a policy does not have consequences for the protected group that are sufficiently statistically extreme to satisfy the demands of disparate impact doctrine, it

---

also Equal Employment Opportunity Commn v Pan Am World Airways, Inc, 52 FEP Cas (BNA) 920, 924 (ND Cal 1987).

340 *See, e.g.,* Equal Employment Opportunity Commn v Wyoming, 460 US 226 (1983).

341 This analysis comports with the EEOC's interpretation in 29 CFR §1625.7(d) (1993). Earlier, the analogy afforded by the Equal Pay Act (EPA), 29 USC §206(d), was pointed to as a basis for concluding that the RFOA exception constitutes an affirmative defense. See **§5.17.** The EPA analogy, once having been evoked, perhaps cannot be ignored here. Thus, it must be conceded that under the EPA the defendant does not bear as heavy a burden as is proposed in the text for ADEA defendants.

still will be subjected to special legal treatment by virtue of the defendant's having to prove the policy's legitimacy.[342]

If a defendant is charged with individual wrongdoing vis-a-vis a specific plaintiff, the standard *Burdine* formula still would come into play under this proposed resolution of the RFOA affirmative exception issue. Here, the danger of stereotypical thinking is diminished, since it is individual acts that are at issue.[343] A ruling for the defendant would not entail harm to group members who were not before the court. In brief, the stakes in cases involving individual acts are smaller, and so the guidance of *Burdine* can apply.[344] (This conclusion is in accord, as it so happens, with the cases in which courts have casually equated the *Burdine* rebuttal burden with the RFOA exception.)[345]

The Nature of the Defendant's Burden When the RFOA Exception Is Read as an Affirmative Defense

If one concludes that in certain circumstances the RFOA exception is to be read as constituting an affirmative defense, there remains the matter of determining the substantive nature of that burden. In *Laugesen v Anaconda Co*[346] the Court of Appeals for the Sixth Circuit took the position that in instances of policies having discriminatory impacts, the defendant would have to bear the rigorous burden of proving business necessity.[347] At the other end of the spectrum, the Court of Appeals for the First Circuit, while apparently reading the RFOA exception as an

---

342 In regard to discriminatory impact cases, see **ch 7.**

343 Of course, if these acts are part of a pattern or practice reflective of an ageist policy, this analysis would not pertain. As to claims based on alleged discriminatory patterns and practices, see **ch 7.**

344 This structure is subscribed to, in good measure, in Laugesen v Anaconda Co, 510 F2d 307, 315 (6th Cir 1975).

345 See note 334.

346 510 F2d 307 (6th Cir 1975).

347 *Id* 315. At the time *Laugesen* was decided, disparate impact doctrine, which was embraced bythe Supreme Court in Griggs v Duke Power Co, 401 US 424 (1971), had not yet been infused into the ADEA setting. That infusion has since occurred. See **ch 7.**

affirmative defense in *Equal Employment Opportunity Commission v Massachusetts,*[348] seemed to subscribe to the idea that the defendant only needed to prove that its policy was rational.[349]

Insofar as there is a policy at issue that has a disparate impact on the protected group which rises to the level of statistical disparity that would satisfy a court subscribing to standard disparate impact doctrine, the *Laugesen* court would seem to have the right solution. In other words, the defendant should have the burden of proving business necessity—a legal term of art that has been fleshed out, albeit not without considerable ambiguity, in cases arising under Title VII of the Civil Rights Act of 1964,[350] as well as in ADEA cases.[351]

While it might seem that this conclusion makes the RFOA exception redundant insofar as impact situations are concerned, the state of the law is such that that conclusion would be ill-advised. In *Wards Cove Packing Co v Atonio,*[352] a decision addressing Title VII, the Court rewrote disparate impact doctrine. One aspect of this revision involved removing from the defendant the burden of ever having to prove business necessity and imposing, for the entire course of a disparate impact case, the burden of proof on the plaintiff's shoulders. Since Title VII case law, particularly rulings by the Supreme Court, regularly are looked to as persuasive analogical guides by ADEA courts,[353] *Wards Cove*—not surprisingly—has been followed in the age discrimination setting.[354] While *Wards Cove* eventually was overturned statutorily by the Civil Rights Act of 1991 insofar as Title VII is concerned,[355] the decision appears to continue to play a persuasive analogical role for ADEA courts, inasmuch as the ADEA

---

[348] 987 F2d 64 (1st Cir 1993).

[349] *Id* 70.

[350] 42 USC §§2000e through 2000e-17.

[351] See **ch 7.**

[352] 490 US 642 (1989).

[353] See **ch 2.**

[354] See **ch 7.**

[355] Pub L No 102-166, 105 Stat 1071. See **ch 7.**

was not comparably amended.[356] Thus, the RFOA affirmative defense indeed is not redundant insofar as it is read as imposing upon the defendant, rather than the plaintiff, a burden of proving business necessity—a burden no longer applicable, as it turns out, in ADEA disparate impact cases. Moreover, not all jurisdictions have endorsed the applicability to the ADEA of disparate impact analysis, whatever its form, and in those jurisdictions the RFOA defense thus certainly cannot be deemed redundant.[357]

Where a policy has an effect on the protected group, but that effect does not rise to the level of statistical disparity that disparate impact case law requires,[358] the RFOA exception still could have a role to play as an affirmative defense, for the reasons dis-

---

[356] *See* Eglit, *The Age Discrimination in Employment Act, Title VII of the Civil Rights Act of 1964, and the Civil Rights Act of 1991: Three Acts and a Dog that Didn't Bark,* 39 Wayne L Rev 1093 (1993).

[357] Arguably, the RFOA exception, by its very existence, debunks the applicability of disparate impact analysis to the ADEA. In other words, the RFOA provision explicitly approves the use of reasonable factors other than age, and this approbation extends—it could be argued—to age-neutral factors, even if they have a disparate impact on age-defined groups. This role for the RFOA exception, i.e., as a legal Trojan Horse, so to speak, that militates against the applicability of another, judicially devised mode of analysis, was subscribed to by Justice Rehnquist in his lone dissent from the denial of certiorari in Markham v Geller, 451 US 945 (1981). The same argument was made unsuccessfully in Equal Employment Opportunity Commn v Governor Mifflin Sch Dist, 623 F Supp 734 (ED Pa 1985). A modified argument along these lines was made in Player, *Title VII Impact Analysis Applied to the Age Discrimination in Employment Act: Is a Transplant Appropriate?,* 14 U Tol L Rev 1261 (1983). Professor Player does not contend that disparate impact analysis is entirely foreclosed under the ADEA, but he does argue, in light of the RFOA exception, for a less rigorous form of such analysis than applies under the ADEA's analogue, Title VII. The contrary position is detailed in Eglit, *The Age Discrimination in Employment Act's Forgotten Affirmative Defense: The Reasonable Factors Other Than Age Exception,* 66 BU L Rev 155 (1986), which was written prior to the gutting of disparate impact case law by the Court in *Wards Cove.* The consequences of *Wards Cove* which prescribes, by way of analogy, a diminished (from the plaintiff's perspective) form of impact analysis, arguably make even more apt (and certainly more urgent, from the plaintiffs perspective), the argument for reading the RFOA exception as a distinct affirmative defense not merely duplicative of disparate impact analysis and not to be confused with such analysis.

[358] See **ch 7.**

cussed above. However, it would not be appropriate to impose on a defendant the same heavy burden, i.e., the burden of proving business necessity that exists where the statistics are more compelling. Rather, in a situation where there is some degree of general adverse consequences, albeit of a somewhat muted level, it should be sufficient for the defendant to prove that the policy or decision at issue is *substantially* reasonable. Thereby, there would be some degree of work that the defendant would have to undertake which would exceed the minimal task that would exist were only a mere rationality standard to be used.[359]

§5.20 What Constitutes a Reasonable Factor Other Than Age

Obviously, there is room for dispute as to whether the reasonable factors other than age (RFOA) provision[360] set forth in the Age Discrimination in Employment Act (ADEA)[361] constitutes an affirmative defense. In any event, there is considerable room for flexible interpretations by courts and litigants as to what constitute reasonable factors other than age, given that the language of the provision is opaque and the legislative history offers virtually no restrictive clarifications.[362] While the case law is instructive,[363] it must be approached with at least two cautionary notes.

---

[359] The mere rationality test is commonly employed in cases arising under the Equal Protection Clause of the Fourteenth Amendment. US Const amend XIV, §1. Its use virtually guarantees that plaintiffs, who must prove in such cases that the policies or decisions at issue are irrational, will lose. See **ch 10.**

[360] §4(f)(1), 29 USC §623(f)(1).

[361] 29 USC §§621-634.

[362] See **§5.16.**

[363] There are, however, a number of courts which, while addressing the RFOA exception, have not reached the merits of the question; that is, they never determined whether the defendant's action or decision indeed was justifiable on RFOA grounds. *See, e.g.,* Krieg v Paul Revere Life Ins Co, 718 F2d 998, 999 (11th Cir 1983), *cert denied,* 466 US 929 (1984); Marshall v Westinghouse Elec Corp, 576 F2d 588, 591-92 (5th Cir 1978); Laugesen v Anaconda Co, 510 F2d 307, 313 (6th Cir 1975); Moore v Sears, Roebuck & Co, 464 F Supp 357, 366 (ND Ga 1979); *see also* Marshall v Goodyear Tire & Rubber Co, 22 FEP Cas (BNA) 775, 778-79 (WD Tenn 1979). In Equal Employment Opportu-

First, generalizations are confounded by the cases being very much fact bound.[364] Second, accurate generalizations cannot be applied across the gamut of RFOA case law because determinations of reasonable factors other than age are at least in part a function of judicial understandings of the burden that must be satisfied by defendants, and on this latter issue the courts of course are split.

The most common type of ADEA case involves a discharge.[365] The defendant typically contends, by way of producing the legitimate, nondiscriminatory explanation for the discharge that is required by *Texas Department of Community Affairs v Burdine,*[366] that the inadequate job performance of the terminated plaintiff generated the employee's termination. This holds true both in cases specifically addressing the RFOA exception, as well as in those failing to do so.[367] Thus, for example, in *Bittar v Air Canada*[368]—in which the exception *was* addressed—the court concluded that the defendant had satisfied its burden of production[369] under the RFOA provision with evidence of "numerous instances of unsat-

---

nity Commn v Pan Am World Airways, Inc, 52 FEP Cas (BNA) 920 (ND Cal 1987), the argument was made—but was not resolved by the court—that the challenged practice was required by a collective bargaining agreement, which agreement, it was claimed, constituted a reasonable factor other than age. *Id* 924-25.

364 The Equal Employment Opportunity Commission has pointed out that "[w]hether such differentiations exist must be decided on the basis of all the particular facts and circumstances surrounding each individual situation." 29 CFR §1625.7(b) (1993).

365 See **ch 3.**

366 450 US 248 (1981). See **ch 7.**

367 *See, e.g.,* Moore v McGraw Edison Co, 804 F2d 1026, 1030 (8th Cir 1986); Elliott v Group Medical & Surgical Serv, 714 F2d 556, 566 (5th Cir 1983), *cert denied,* 467 US 1215 (1984); Scharnhorst v Independent Sch Dist No 710, 686 F2d 637, 640 (8th Cir 1982), *cert denied,* 462 US 1109 (1983); Chamberlain v Bissell, Inc, 547 F Supp 1067 (WD Mich 1982).

368 512 F2d 582 (5th Cir 1975).

369 Obviously, the court did not interpret the RFOA exception as constituting an affirmative defense.

isfactory job performance on the part of the plaintiff."[370] Similarly, a reduction in force may lead to termination of employees who, while they may have adequately carried out their former job functions, performed less well than their co-workers and so were the most expendable in a time of retrenchment.[371] A reduction in force also may result in the discharge of employees who, although adequate in their old jobs, lack the skills needed for the jobs remaining following the employer's shrinkage. Such lack of qualification will satisfy the RFOA provision in the discharge scenario,[372] as it will, as well, in a refusal-to-hire-or-promote case.[373] A reorganization or reduction in force may result in the abolition of the employee's former position, and the nonexistence of any replacement job also constitutes a reasonable factor other than age.[374]

It has been suggested that a uniformly applied educational

---

[370] 512 F2d at 582; *accord* Price v Maryland Casualty Co, 561 F2d 609, 612 (5th Cir 1977); Erwin v Bank of Miss, 512 F Supp 545, 551-52 (ND Miss 1981); Carolan v Central Freight Lines, Inc, 489 F Supp 941, 944 (ED Tex 1980); *see also* Cova v Coca-Cola Bottling Co, 574 F2d 958, 959-60 (8th Cir 1978); Magruder v Selling Areas Mktg, Inc, 439 F Supp 1155, 1164 (ND Ill 1974); Bishop v Jelleff Assoc, 398 F Supp 579, 593-94 (DDC 1974).

[371] *See, e.g.*, Schwager v Sun Oil Co, 591 F2d 58, 61 (10th Cir 1979); Raggett v Foote Mineral Co, 16 FEP Cas (BNA) 1771, 1777 (MD Tenn 1975); Gill v Union Carbide Corp, 368 F Supp 364, 368 (ED Tenn 1973); Stringfellow v Monsanto Co, 320 F Supp 1175, 1181-82 (WD Ark 1970); White v Bobbie Brooks, Inc, 30 Empl Prac Dec (CCH) ¶33,147 (Bankr ND Ohio 1982). As to reductions in force generally, see **ch 7.**

[372] *See* Moore v McGraw Edison Co, 804 F2d 1026, 1030 (8th Cir 1986); Smith v Farah Mfg, 650 F2d 64, 68-70 (5th Cir 1981).

[373] *See* Morgan v Goldschmidt, 33 FEP Cas (BNA) 797, 799 (DDC 1980). Actually, because this was a federal employee case, the court erred in referring to the RFOA exception, since §15, 29 USC §633a, of the ADEA, establishes a separate and distinct mechanism for addressing age discrimination allegedly perpetrated by the federal government. Pursuant to §15(f), 29 USC §633a(f), the provisions of the rest of the Act—including the RFOA exception—are inapplicable. See generally **ch 9.**

[374] *See* Moore v McGraw Edison Co, 804 F2d 1026, 1030 (8th Cir 1986); Mizrany v Texas Rehabilitation Commn, 522 F Supp 611, 616-17 (SD Tex 1981), *affd without opinion*, 685 F2d 1384 (5th Cir 1982).

requirement that is reasonably related to the job requirements may be permissible as an RFOA.[375]

These foregoing rulings all involved courts that construed the RFOA exception as imposing only a mild burden of production. Thus, the guidance afforded by these decisions only cautiously can be heeded in jurisdictions and in legal settings in which the defendant's burden is a heavier one.[376]

Of course, even if a court construes the RFOA exception as an affirmative defense, a defendant still may prevail. Thus, in one of the rare decisions both so construing the RFOA provision and reaching the merits of the defendant's argument, the court deciding *Equal Employment Opportunity Commission v Governor Mifflin School District*[377] upheld a pay scheme that treated older teachers less advantageously than younger ones. The court viewed this scheme as justified by a reasonable factor other than age, i.e., generally improving the lot of all teachers as a group. On the other hand, in *Equal Employment Opportunity Commission v Massachusetts*[378] the Court of Appeals for the First Circuit, which also appeared to view the RFOA exception as an affirmative defense, addressed a requirement imposed by state law that certain state and local employees submit to annual physical examinations once they attained age 70. Those who failed to pass the exam would be involuntarily retired. The Commonwealth argued that the requirement of passing the exam was a reasonable factor other than age. The court disagreed:

> [I]t is clear that an individual's fitness to work is based on a number of factors, of which age is only one. . . . [T]he record contains no evidence that any factor other than the employee's age was taken into account in requiring an annual medical examination. Thus, . . . we are forced to conclude that age is exactly what . . . [the statute] is based on.

---

375 Equal Employment Opportunity Commn v County of Allegheny, 519 F Supp 1328, 1335 (WD Pa 1981), *affd,* 705 F2d 679 (3d Cir 1983).

376 Common sense instructs that if a court using a mild test strikes down (rather than upholds) a policy or practice, that policy or practice will not survive a more rigorous test.

377 623 F Supp 734, 744-46 (ED Pa 1985).

378 987 F2d 64 (1st Cir 1993).

> The reasonable factor other than age defense is simply not applicable to . . . [the statute].[379]

An age-based statute that limits who may be hired or designates priorities for termination cannot qualify as an RFOA.[380] More generally, "reliance on a discriminatory statute is not considered a reasonable factor other than age."[381]

Insofar as tests measuring knowledge or intellectual capacity are concerned, the interpretations of the Department of Labor, which originally administered the Act, expressed particular concern about the potentials for abuse, but did not go so far as to entirely reject test results as an RFOA on which to base hiring and other employment decisions.[382] The Equal Employment Opportunity Commission (EEOC), which has administered the ADEA since mid-1979, likewise has registered sensitivity to the potential for abuse by the use of tests. It has been asserted that tests defended as reasonable factors other than age are to be scrutinized in accordance with the Uniform Guidelines on Employment Selection Procedures, the extensive multiagency standards issued in 1978 to provide guidance for acceptable testing methodologies.[383]

Factors Having a Correlation with Age and the Impact of *Hazen Paper Co v Biggins*

Prior to 1993 several policies and practices claimed to be legitimate reasonable factors other than age fared particularly poorly in the courts—even in jurisdictions in which the RFOA excep-

---

379 *Id* 70.

380 *See* Equal Employment Opportunity Commn v County of Allegheny, 705 F2d 679 (3d Cir 1983); Popko v City of Clairton, 570 F Supp 446 (WD Pa 1983). *But see* Brown v Goodyear Tire & Rubber Co, 3 Kan App 2d 648, 599 P2d 1031 (1979), *affd,* 227 Kan 645, 608 P2d 1356, *appeal dismissed,* 449 US 914 (1980).

381 Equal Employment Opportunity Commn v School Bd of Pinellas County, 742 F Supp 622, 624 (MD Fla 1990).

382 29 CFR §860.104(b) (1986) (effectively rescinded, 46 Fed Reg 47724 (Sept 29, 1981), and ordered removed from the CFR, 52 Fed Reg 23812 (June 25, 1987)).

383 29 CFR §1625.7(d) (1993).

tion is not viewed as an affirmative defense. Some justifications were virtually foreclosed as ever being reasonable factors other than age. The Courts of Appeals for both the Third[384] and Ninth[385] Circuits held that an employee's eligibility for early retirement, and thus for retirement benefits, could not constitute an RFOA justifying excluding the employee from other benefits available to workers ineligible for such retirement.[386] Similarly, the Court of Appeals for the Third Circuit rejected pension eligibility as a basis for differentiation among employees.[387] In these instances, the courts viewed the factor relied upon as being so closely linked to age as to constitute a virtual proxy for it. Thus, the courts rejected the defendants' arguments because their acceptance was seen as being tantamount to accepting age itself—as opposed to a factor *other* than age—as a legitimate basis for differentiation. Likewise, since seniority often is linked with age, efforts to justify job layoffs keyed to this factor also failed when the RFOA exception was evoked.[388]

---

[384] *See* Equal Employment Opportunity Commn v Westinghouse Elec Corp, 869 F2d 696, 706-07 (3d Cir), *vacated,* 493 US 801 (1989); Equal Employment Opportunity Commn v Westinghouse Elec Corp, 725 F2d 211, 222 (3d Cir 1983), *cert denied,* 469 US 820 (1984).

[385] *See* Equal Employment Opportunity Commn v Borden's, Inc, 724 F2d 1390, 1394 (9th Cir 1984).

[386] *Accord* Equal Employment Opportunity Commn v Great Atl & Pac Tea Co, 618 F Supp 115 (ND Ohio 1985).

[387] Equal Employment Opportunity Commn v City of Altoona, 723 F2d 4, 6 (3d Cir 1983), *cert denied,* 467 US 1204 (1984); *accord* White v Westinghouse Elec Co, 862 F2d 56, 62 (3d Cir 1988); Equal Employment Opportunity Commn v Babcock & Wilcox Co, 43 FEP Cases (BNA) 736 (EDNC 1987); Equal Employment Opportunity Commn v Great Atl & Pac Tea Co, 618 F Supp 115, 119 (ND Ohio 1985); Popko v City of Clairton, 570 F Supp 446, 451-52 (WD Pa 1983); Equal Employment Opportunity Commn v City of New Castle, 32 FEP Cas (BNA) 1409, 1413 (WD Pa 1983), *affd without opinion,* 740 F2d 956 (3d Cir 1984); Hays v Republic Steel Corp, 12 FEP Cas (BNA) 1637, 1645 (ND Ala 1974), *affd,* 531 F2d 1307 (5th Cir 1976). *Contra* Pickering v USX Corp, 758 F Supp 1460, 1462, 1463 (D Utah 1990).

[388] *See* Equal Employment Opportunity Commn v City of Altoona, 723 F2d 4 (3d Cir 1983), *cert denied,* 467 US 1204 (1984). *But see* Schultz v Piro, 40 Pa Commw 395, 397 A2d 484 (1979). As to the treatment of seniority in terms of disparate impact, see **ch 7.** Of course, an action taken pursuant to a seniority

Efforts to rely on the supposedly higher costs alleged to be associated with older job applicants having extensive experience or with older employees having long tenure generated particularly emphatic rejection in most instances.[389] In sum, where age (or its proxy) was used as the limiting criterion in an employment policy, the RFOA exception was understood as not being available to the employer.[390]

In this vein, the Court of Appeals for the Ninth Circuit, which regards the RFOA exception as an affirmative defense,[391] rejected the defendant's RFOA argument in deciding *Equal Employment Opportunity Commission v Local 350, Plumbers & Pipefitters.*[392] The defendant union operated a hiring hall, but in order to be eligible for job referrals retirees had to cease receiving their pensions. Since only employees ages 55 and over were eligible to retire, there "thus [was] a very close connection between age and the factor on which discrimination . . . [was] based."[393] The trial court reasoned that the policy was intended to help out-of-work employees obtain jobs, and that this aim was a legitimate reasonable factor other than age. The Court of Appeals disagreed:

> This proposed justification fails because it rests on pension receipt, a status closely related to age. "A retired member receiving a pension"—a member necessarily aged 55 or older—is treated differently from other members seeking employment, for example, from a member drawing unemployment benefits or a member employed in another trade.[394]

---

plan may be justified under the bona fide seniority plan affirmative defense. See **§§5.57-.59.**

[389] See **§5.20.**

[390] Equal Employment Opportunity Commn v Northwest Airlines, Inc, 49 FEP Cas (BNA) 1433, 1435 (WD Wash 1987).

[391] See **§5.15.**

[392] 998 F2d 641 (9th Cir 1992),

[393] *Id* 646.

[394] *Id* 647.

Other arguments as to the policy's constituting an RFOA also were rejected. The union argued that it needed to preserve work opportunities for its members and that if a large number of retirees returned to work, this would have detrimental consequences for its nonretired out-of-work members. The court deemed this excuse to be unpersuasive on several grounds.[395] The union's argument that retirees who returned to work would quit after 39 hours of employment in a month so as to preserve their pension benefits also was found wanting.[396] Finally, the union contended that it was unfair to allow one group of workers to collect a pension, which constituted a lifetime stipend, while other out-of-work individuals were unsubsidized. Again, the court responded negatively:

> [I]t is hard to see how the "lifetime" versus "temporary" subsidy distinction justifies Local 350's policy. First, it is once again an age-related distinction: generally, only older workers will have "lifetime" stipends. Moreover, if Local 350 believes it is unfair for "subsidized" workers to enjoy the benefits of its [hiring] list, it should refuse to allow unemployed workers on the list for as long as they can draw unemployment benefits.[397]

In *Equal Employment Opportunity Commission v Community Unit*

---

395 The court responded to the union's argument with the following reasoning:

> [I]t is hard to see why Local 350's management of employment opportunities should be carried out by requiring retirees to forego their pensions before being allowed to sign up for work. Once again, the proposed factor seems to embody the very discrimination that is the subject of this suit. If preventing retirees from reentering the working force is the rationale (which it could not be, under the ADEA), no retirees should be allowed to sign up. Moreover, as the EEOC noted, the Local had fewer than 130 retired members in 1990 and since 1981 only a handful have sought to return to work.

Id.

396 *Id.*

397 *Id.*

School District No 9[398] the plaintiffs—two former school administrators—had given their employer notice of their intended future retirement at the end of the 1983-84 school year. Subsequently, the two plaintiffs' classifications were changed from administrators to teachers for that school year. The employer argued that economic necessity required it to reduce its complement of administrators, that it wanted continuity in administration over time, that the retirement of the plaintiffs in the near future militated against this aim of continuity, and that therefore the plaintiffs were appropriate subjects for reclassification. In brief, all this put together meant that the employer had relied on a reasonable factor other than age. The court, however, held that "notification of an intent to retire is so inexorably linked with age that it cannot be viewed as a separate factor."[399]

The Supreme Court indirectly entered the fray with its ruling in *Hazen Paper Co v Biggins.*[400] Biggins had been discharged at age 62, just a few weeks prior to the date on which his pension would have vested. He sued and prevailed under both the ADEA and the Employees Retirement Income Security Act (ERISA).[401] At issue before the Supreme Court was Biggins' ADEA claim, but only insofar as it was argued that the defendant's practice constituted discriminatory treatment.[402] No claim of disparate impact was before the Court: this was a point emphasized both by the majority, in an opinion written by Justice O'Connor,[403] and in the concurrence of Justice Kennedy, which was joined by the Chief Justice and Justice Thomas.[404] Moreover, the RFOA exception was never referred to (although the case nonetheless is relevant to RFOA analysis). The Court reversed and remanded for a new determination as to whether the evidence, now to be considered in light of its opinion, supported a finding for Biggins.

---

398 642 F Supp 902 (SD Ill 1986).

399 *Id* 905.

400 113 S Ct 1701 (1993).

401 29 USC §1001 *et seq.*

402 See generally **ch 7.**

403 113 S Ct at 1706.

404 *Id* 1710.

The Court asserted that "there is no disparate treatment under the ADEA when the factor motivating the employer is some feature other than the employee's age."[405] Justice O'Connor then briefly outlined disparate, or discriminatory, treatment analysis:

> In a disparate treatment case, liability depends on whether the protected trait (under the ADEA, age) actually motivated the employer's decision. . . . The employer may have relied upon a formal, facially discriminatory policy requiring adverse treatment of employees with that trait. . . . Or the employer may have been motivated by the protected trait on an ad hoc, informal basis. . . . Whatever the employer's decisionmaking process, a disparate treatment claim cannot be used unless the employee's protected trait actually played a role in that process and had a determinative influence on the outcome.[406]

It follows that "[w]hen the employer's decision is wholly motivated by factors other than age, the problem of inaccurate and stigmatizing stereotypes disappears."[407] And with an assertion key to the discussion in this section, Justice O'Connor went on to add the following: "This is true even if the motivating factor is correlated with age, as pension status typically is."[408] In justifying this position, Justice O'Conner set forth the following reasoning:

> Pension plans typically provide that an employee's accrued benefits will become nonforfeitable, or "vested," once the employee completes a certain number of years of service with the employer. . . . On average, an older employee has had more years in the work force than a younger employee, and thus may well have accumulated more years of service

405 *Id* 1705.
406 *Id* 1706.
407 *Id.*
408 *Id.*

> with a particular employer. Yet an employee's age is analytically distinct from his years of service. An employee who is younger than 40, and therefore outside the class of older workers as defined by the ADEA . . ., may have worked for a particular employer his entire career, while an older worker may have been newly hired.[409]

In sum, "[b]ecause age and years of service are analytically distinct, an employer can take account of one while ignoring the other, and thus it is incorrect to say that a decision based on years of service is necessarily 'age-based.' "[410]

The Court, however, went on to offer a number of caveats, and these muddy the legal waters:

> We do not preclude the possibility that an employer who targets employees with a particular pension status on the assumption that these employees are likely to be older thereby engages in age discrimination. Pension status may be a proxy for age, not in the sense that the ADEA makes the two factors equivalent . . . but in the sense that the employer may suppose a correlation between the two factors and act accordingly. Nor do we rule out the possibility of dual liability under ERISA and the ADEA where the decision to fire the employee was motivated both by the employee's age and by his pension status. Finally, we do not consider the special case where an employee is about to vest in pension benefits as a result of his age, rather than years of service, . . . and the employer fires the employee in order to prevent vesting.[411]

The Court, in a seeming final effort to stress the limited nature of its ruling—a narrowness already highlighted by the foregoing caveats—essentially concluded its discussion with the assertion that its holding "is simply that an employer does not violate the

---

[409] *Id* 1706-07.

[410] *Id* 1707.

[411] *Id.*

ADEA just by interfering with an older employee's pension benefits that would have vested by virtue of the employee's years of service."[412]

Biggins appears to render no longer viable a number of the ADEA lower court decisions discussed *supra.* One can no longer reject the legitimacy of an employer policy, practice, or decision simply because it was based upon a non-age factor that might be thought to have a particular correlation with older age. However, the caveats set forth by the Court leave considerable room for plaintiffs to argue, on the facts, that their situations are sufficiently different from that in *Biggins* to justify rejecting an RFOA-based argument by an employer. (Of course, the Court failed to even note the RFOA exception, let alone denominate it either as an affirmative defense or something less than that.) What a plaintiff in a case grounded on discriminatory treatment theory will have to do in order to surmount the barrier posed by *Biggins* is to show some determinative age-based motivation accounting for the defendant's reliance upon an ostensibly non-age-based factor. In brief, the plaintiff will have to do what he or she in any event is ordinarily required to do in a discriminatory treatment case,[413] i.e., prove that discriminatory animus played a role (albeit not the exclusive role), rather than relying upon *ipse dixits,* i.e., "senior people are older people," or "pension-eligible people are older people," that even if true do not in and of themselves establish ageist animus.

Of course, the *Biggins* Court very clearly left for another day the relevance of disparate impact analysis, and so it may ultimately turn out that the victory that a plaintiff cannot obtain with a discriminatory treatment argument—which is all that was proffered in *Biggins*—will be possible to secure with a disparate impact argument.

---

[412] *Id* 1707-08.

[413] See **ch 7.**

§5.21 —Cost as a Reasonable Factor Other Than Age

There often will be a correlation between age, tenure, and salary, with older employees commonly having more years on the job and consequently higher salaries than their younger counterparts. For the employer intent upon reducing costs, termination of older workers may appear to be the most direct way to achieve this end, particularly when the quality of the work product has little or no correlation with experience and so the discharge of older, higher-paid employees will not result in diminution of output either in terms of quantity or quality. The employer's desire to minimize its costs of doing business seemingly comes into conflict, however, with the protection afforded to older workers by the Age Discrimination in Employment Act (ADEA).[414] The Court of Appeals for the Seventh Circuit set forth its view as to the resolution of this apparent conflict in *Graefenhain v Pabst Brewing Co*:[415]

> Congress enacted the ADEA precisely because many employers or younger business executives act as if they believe that there are good business reasons for discriminating against older employees. Retention of senior employees who can be replaced by younger, lower-paid persons frequently competes with other values, such as profits or conceptions of economic efficiency. The ADEA represents a choice [by Congress] among these competing values. It stands for the proposition that this is a better country for its willingness to pay the costs for treating older employees fairly.[416]

---

414 29 USC §§621-634.

415 827 F2d 13 (7th Cir 1987).

416 *Id* 21 n8.

Whether one deems such rhetoric persuasive or not, the Supreme Court's 1993 ruling, *Hazen Paper Co v Biggins*,[417] must be taken into account in assessing the case law concerning the cost/age equation. And the consequence of adding *Biggins*, which did not at all refer literally to the ADEA's reasonable factors other than age (RFOA) exception, to the legal mix is that the assessment voiced in *Graefenhain*—an assessment implicit in a number of rulings, discussed *infra*—now is at least questionable.

Agency Views

The tension between cost concerns and the antidiscrimination principle embodied in the ADEA has been apparent from the outset. The Department of Labor, which until mid-1979 administered and enforced the statute, issued a now-rescinded interpretation of the RFOA exception[418] that unmistakably rejected cost as a basis for making differentiations between older and younger workers.[419] The Equal Employment Opportunity Commission (EEOC), which took over enforcement of the ADEA from the Labor Department, takes a similar position: "A differentiation based on the average cost of employing older employees as a group is unlawful except with respect to employee

---

[417] 113 S Ct 1701 (1993).

[418] §4(f)(1), 29 USC §623(f)(1).

[419] 29 CFR §860.103(b) (1985) (effectively rescinded, 46 Fed Reg 47724 (Sept 9, 1981), and ordered removed from the CFR, 52 Fed Reg 23811 (June 25, 1987)), provided as follows:

> [A] general assertion that the average cost of employing older workers as a group is higher than the average cost of employing younger workers as a group will not be recognized as a differentiation under the terms and provisions of the Act, unless one of the other statutory exceptions applies. To classify or group employees solely on the basis of age for the purpose of comparing costs, or for any other purpose necessarily rests on the assumption that the age factor alone may be used to justify a differentiation—an assumption plainly contrary to the purpose of the Act and the purpose of Congress in enacting it. Differentials so based would serve only to perpetuate and promote the very discrimination at which the Act is directed.

benefit plans which qualify for the section 4(f)(2) exception [see **§5.22** *et seq*] to the Act."[420]

Legislative History

The legislative history of the ADEA affords some minimal basis for cost being a relevant factor both in determining what criteria will constitute reasonable factors other than age and what job requirements will constitute bona fide occupational qualifications (BFOQs).[421]

Lower Court Rulings

Notwithstanding the legislative history (which in any event is very limited on the cost issue), ADEA case law is in the main quite consistent in rejecting cost as a basis for terminating or otherwise disadvantaging older workers, except in the context of the §4(f)(2)[422] exception concerning employee benefit plans, where considerations of cost explicitly are allowed.[423] Several courts addressing the BFOQ exception[424] have rejected economic factors as valid bases for BFOQs.[425] In applying disparate impact analysis to challenged employer actions, the courts also have rejected employers' reliance on cost factors where that reliance, while age neutral on its face, has a disparate impact on persons within the ADEA-protected age group.[426]

There are several decisions—indeed, they generally are the most analytically rigorous of the rulings involving cost—that involve the ADEA's RFOA exception.[427] Some of these present a mix both of disparate impact analysis and references to the

---

420 29 CFR §1625.7(f) (1993).

421 See **§5.16,** note 291.

422 29 USC §623(f)(2).

423 See **§§5.32-.33.**

424 §4(f)(1), 29 USC §623(f)(1). See generally **§§5.02-5.13.**

425 See **§5.09.**

426 See **ch 7.**

427 In two rulings the Court of Appeals for the Ninth Circuit noted, but did not address on the merits, the issues discussed in this section. *See* Douglas v Anderson, 656 F2d 528, 534 n6 (9th Cir 1981); Haydon v Rand Corp, 605 F2d 453, 455 (9th Cir 1979).

RFOA exception—a merging of doctrine that also is seen in the EEOC's interpreting the RFOA exception as evoking, in some contexts, the requirement that defendants prove job relatedness.[428] (This is an analytic approach also suggested in this text.)[429] *Geller v Markham*[430] is one such decision. The plaintiff alleged that she was denied a teaching position in the West Hartford, Connecticut, school system because of a policy that teachers be recruited at salary levels below the sixth step of the salary schedule—a level reached by teachers with more than five years' experience. The court held as a matter of law that the plaintiff had established a prima facie case of disparate impact by showing that the rule disqualified 92.6 per cent of Connecticut teachers over 40, while disqualifying only 60 per cent of teachers under 40. The court rejected the school board's argument that the policy actually was justifiable as a cost-cutting measure. In so doing, it relied on the then-extant Department of Labor interpretation which provided that employees could not be classified solely on the basis of age for the purpose of cutting costs.[431]

The Court of Appeals for the Eighth Circuit mixed disparate impact analysis and the EEOC interpretation regarding the RFOA exception in *Leftwich v Harris-Stowe State College.*[432] This case involved a reorganization of the college at which the plaintiff was employed as a tenured associate professor, whereby the college was transferred from a city educational system to the state college system. In lieu of retaining the plaintiff, who was over 40, the new management selected a nontenured under-40 teacher. This decision was made pursuant to a plan specifically designed to allow for the retention of only a set number of tenured faculty and a set number of nontenured faculty, with the intended result being a reduction in costs. The plaintiff's statisti-

---

[428] 29 CFR §1625.7(d) (1993).

[429] See **§5.19.**

[430] 635 F2d 1027 (2d Cir 1980), *cert denied,* 451 US 945 (1981).

[431] This interpretation is quoted in note 419 *supra. See also* Equal Employment Opportunity Commn v City of Altoona, 723 F2d 4 (3d Cir 1983), *cert denied,* 467 US 1204 (1984).

[432] 702 F2d 686 (8th Cir 1983).

cal expert testified that there was a positive significant correlation between age and salary, such that use of salary would have an adverse impact on older faculty members. The court, citing the EEOC and Department of Labor RFOA interpretations rejecting cost as a reasonable factor other than age, spurned the defendant's cost justification. The court stated as follows:

> [B]ecause of the close relationship between tenure status and age, the plain intent and effect of the defendants' practice was to eliminate older workers who had built up, through years of satisfactory service, higher salaries than their younger counterparts. If the existence of such higher salaries can be used to justify discharging older employees, then the purpose of the ADEA will be defeated.[433]

Without any discussion implicating disparate impact analysis or explicitly invoking the RFOA exception, the Court of Appeals for the Eleventh Circuit approvingly reported in *Tullis v Lear, Inc,*[434] that the trial court—in addressing the claim of a school bus driver who was discharged at age 66 with the explanation that the high cost of liability insurance required his being let go—had "correctly concluded that increased insurance cost is not a factor that would exempt the school from compliance with the ADEA."[435] In support of this proposition the court cited the earlier-quoted EEOC interpretation.[436]

District courts also have asserted that budgetary considerations cannot constitute reasonable factors other than age justifying discharge.[437] Thus, for example, the Court deciding *Popko v*

---

[433] *Id* 691. "[U]nder *Leftwich,* an age discrimination claimant is entitled to a separate [jury] instruction reflecting . . . [the] decision in that case if such instruction is warranted by the evidence." Walker v St Anthony's Medical Ctr, 881 F2d 554, 561 (8th Cir 1989).

[434] 874 F2d 1489 (11th Cir 1989).

[435] *Id* 1490.

[436] 29 CFR §1625.7(f) (1993).

[437] *See* Popko v City of Clairton, 570 F Supp 446 (WD Pa 1983); Equal Employment Opportunity Commn v City of New Castle, 32 FEP Cas (BNA) 1409 (WD Pa 1983), *affd without opinion,* 740 F2d 956 (3d Cir 1984); *see also* Kaczor v City

City of Clairton[438] reasoned that budgetary considerations offered as the explanation for a reduction in force whereby older, pension-eligible employees were selected for termination could not constitute an RFOA since the actual process of selecting those to be discharged, e.g., older pension-eligible individuals violated the ADEA.

Both *Geller* and *Leftwich* totally foreclosed the possibility of cost factors constituting reasonable factors other than age. In *Equal Employment Opportunity Commission v Chrysler Corp*[439] the Court of Appeals for the Sixth Circuit did not go so far. At issue was a forced retirement plan that Chrysler attempted to justify as necessary to reduce costs in the face of the corporation's possible insolvency. Chrysler contended that this economic necessity constituted a reasonable factor other than age. The court did not totally reject the notion that economic necessity could come within the terms of the RFOA exception. Rather, it enunciated a two-part test that an employer would have to meet: "First, the necessity for drastic cost reductions obviously must be real. . . . Second, the forced early retirements must be the least-detrimental alternative means available to reduce costs."[440] On the facts, the court concluded that Chrysler had failed to satisfy the second part of this test.

In a major opinion discussing the cost factor, the Court of Appeals for the Seventh Circuit split two to one in *Metz v Transit Mix, Inc,*[441] on the issue of whether "the salary savings that can be realized by replacing a single employee in the ADEA age-protected range with a younger, lower-salaried employee constitutes a permissible, nondiscriminatory justification for the replacement."[442] The majority asserted a clearly negative position. Metz had worked for the defendant for 26 years and regu-

---

of Buffalo, 657 F Supp 441, 443-44 (WDNY 1987) (refusal to hire senior employee because of his higher salary).

438 570 F Supp 446 (WD Pa 1983).

439 733 F2d 1183 (6th Cir 1984).

440 *Id* 1186.

441 828 F2d 1202 (7th Cir 1987).

442 *Id* 1205.

larly had received annual salary increases. He was replaced by a 43-year-old earning about one-half of his salary. The majority reasoned as follows:

> The ADEA is aimed at protecting the individual employee. . . . Given the correlation between Metz's higher salary and his years of satisfactory service, allowing Transit Mix to replace Metz based on the higher cost of employing him would defeat the intent of the statute.[443]

The court did not adopt the *Chrysler* formulation, nor did it reject it. But it did observe that even if *Chrysler's* two-part test were satisfied, Transit Mix would lose.[444] In conclusion, the court stated:

> We are, of course, aware that employers must control costs if they are to remain competitive and that this imperative of survival will inevitably create tensions with the legal prohibitions against age discrimination. We think it would be unwise, however, to translate this imperative into a rule that an older employee can be fired and replaced by an equally proficient younger employee merely because the older employee happens to be earning more money at the moment. There are a number of less burdensome measures that can be introduced if necessary before "industrial capital punishment" is brought into play.[445]

Subsequently, in *Jardien v Winston Network, Inc,*[446] the Court of Appeals for the Seventh Circuit approved a trial court jury instruction embodying the *Metz* principle. The trial court had instructed the jury as follows: "The salary savings that can be realized by replacing a younger, lower-salaried employee does [sic] not constitute a permissible, non-discriminatory justifica-

---

[443] *Id* 1206-07 (footnote omitted).

[444] *Id* 1208.

[445] *Id* 1211; *see also* Thompson v Fieldcrest Mills, Inc, 51 Empl Prac Dec (CCH) ¶39,411 (SDNY 1989).

[446] 888 F2d 1151 (7th Cir 1989).

tion for the replacement."[447] This instruction was proper because there was "sufficient evidence in the record to suggest that . . . [the defendant] may have attempted to justify . . . [the plaintiff's] dismissal as a salary savings."[448]

In contrast to the unavailing efforts of the defendants in the foregoing cases to invoke a cost justification for their challenged decisions, the argument of the defendant in *Equal Employment Opportunity Commission v Atlantic Community School District*[449] was successful. The EEOC contended that the individual on whose behalf it sued, a 40-year-old woman with 10 years' teaching experience, had been rejected for a position with the defendant because teachers' salaries were determined by years of experience and thus she would have been a more expensive hire than the 23-year-old with only two years' experience who was in fact hired. The EEOC argued that there is a correlation between age and years of experience, such that those with more experience will necessarily be older. It follows, it was argued, that where salary increases with experience, it constitutes age discrimination to hire a less experienced person with the aim of saving money, because this is tantamount to preferring a young person over an older one.

The Court of Appeals for the Eighth Circuit, addressing the EEOC's argument that the trial court had erred in not giving the jury an instruction encapsulating the EEOC's experience-cost-age theory, rejected the EEOC's approach.[450] The court, seeing in the EEOC's theory untoward consequences, reasoned as follows:

---

447 *Id* 1157.

448 *Id* 1158.

449 879 F2d 434 (8th Cir 1989).

450 The proposed instruction provided as follows:

> It is illegal under federal law for an employer to discriminate against older workers because they are higher in the employer's pay scale as a result of their years of experience. If you find that the salary level Mrs. Parks would have been eligible for because of her years of experience was a determining factor in defendant's decision not to hire her, you should find for the plaintiff.

Id 435.

> Because . . . [the] instruction equates age 40 and over with experience, it would require a finding of age discrimination whenever an applicant 40 and over is not hired by an employer who has agreed to pay salaries based on experience. It would also impermissibly result in a distinction between applicants who have the same experience on the sole basis of whether they were over or under 40. Nowhere, for example, does [the] EEOC adequately refute the district court's recognition that acceptance of [the] EEOC's instruction as a statement of the law would, contrary to the ADEA, effectively require a preference in hiring of those 40 and over.[451]

The *Atlantic Community School District* ruling by the Court of Appeals for the Eighth Circuit represented a significant retreat from its earlier *Leftwich* decision. If one were to attempt to confine the later decision to the hiring context, to the end of endeavoring to maintain *Leftwich's* viability in nonhiring situations, that effort would founder on the fact that the ADEA itself does not incorporate differing standards of discrimination for hiring, as opposed to other employer, decisions: §4(a)[452] makes it unlawful "to fail or refuse to hire or to discharge any individual or otherwise discriminate against any individual . . . because of age." In brief, the *Atlantic Community School District* court's analysis, while set forth in a hiring dispute, does not lend itself to being confined just to hiring situations.[453]

---

451 *Id* 437 (footnote omitted).

452 29 USC §623(a).

453 Insofar as *Leftwich* and *Geller* were concerned, the *Atlantic Community School District* court attempted to distinguish them with the observation that they involved persons "who, unlike Parks, had an employment relationship with the employer before age-related salary discrimination occurred." 879 F2d at 437. The court stretched to describe *Geller,* which as a practical matter was a hiring case, as a case where age discrimination occurred as a result of the 55-year-old plaintiff having been replaced two weeks after she began work, when the employer realized the financial impact of her being hired. Apparently, the same distinction, i.e., an already existing employment relationship, justified distinguishing Dace v ACF Indus, Inc, 722 F2d 374 (8th Cir 1983), *supplemented*

An earlier lower federal court ruling also took a generous view of the economic needs of employers. In *Mastie v Great Lakes Steel Corp*[454] the court held that the higher cost associated with the employment of older workers was a valid reasonable factor other than age, at least so long as the consideration of such cost was predicated "upon an individual as opposed to a general assessment that the older worker's cost of employment is greater than for other workers."[455] *Mastie,* however, is both aberrational (save for *Atlantic Community School District*) and, in any event, does not appear to be viable in light of the later Chrysler ruling by the appellate court for the circuit in which the *Mastie* court sits.[456]

Hazen Paper Co v Biggins

The Supreme Court's ruling in *Hazen Paper Co v Biggins*[457] in effect supports the analysis of the court that decided the *Atlantic Community School District* case. It also leaves the other rulings discussed *supra* of uncertain viability[458]—at least insofar as they

---

on other grounds, 728 F2d 976 (8th Cir 1984), and Metz v Transit Mix, Inc, 828 F2d 1202 (7th Cir 1987), a discriminatory treatment case discussed in the text.

[454] 424 F Supp 1299 (ED Mich 1976).

[455] *Id* 1319; *see also* Adama v Doehler-Jarvis, 115 Mich App 82, 320 NW2d 298 (1982), *revd on other grounds,* 419 Mich 905, 353 NW2d 438 (1984) (construing state statute).

[456] *See also* Donnelly v Exxon Research & Engg Co, 12 FEP Cas (BNA) 417 (DNJ 1971), *affd without opinion,* 521 F2d 1398 (3d Cir 1975). A second court utilized the same analysis as that put forth in *Mastie,* only to be reversed on appeal. In Metz v Transit Mix, Inc, 646 F Supp 286 (ND Ind 1986), *revd,* 828 F2d 1202 (7th Cir 1987), the district court ruled that "the higher cost of the employee may be a permissible consideration [on which to base a discharge when addressing a single personnel decision], although it would be impermissible as a basis for a general policy governing personnel decisions." *Id* 294. On appeal, however, the Court of Appeals for the Seventh Circuit rejected this analysis. Metz v Transit Mix, Inc, 828 F2d 1202 (7th Cir 1987). The court quoted this text's characterization of *Mastie* as aberrational, and further noted this treatise's pointing out that *Mastie* likely was no longer good law in light of *Chrysler. Id* 1206 n7.

[457] 113 S Ct 1701 (1993).

[458] Indeed, the Court cited *Metz* as one of the cases in which "courts of appeals repeatedly have faced the question whether an employer violates the ADEA by acting on the basis of a factor . . . that is empirically correlated with age."

relied upon simplistic discriminatory treatment, rather than disparate impact, analysis.[459] However, as discussed in the preceding section, the *Biggins* majority itself framed its ruling in narrow terms, and it further offered a number of caveats to its basic holding, which was that "there is no disparate treatment under the ADEA when the factor motivating the employer is some feature other than the employee's age."[460]

Of course, decisions such as *Metz* and *Leftwich* should not have been read, even prior to *Biggins,* as totally barring employers from considering costs when making personnel decisions. For even under these rulings, cost could safely be taken into account, so long as the consideration of costs was unrelated to age.[461] This was pointed out in *Bay v Times Mirror Magazines, Inc:*[462]

> [T]here is nothing in the ADEA that prohibits an employer from making employment decisions that relate an employee's salary to contemporaneous market conditions and the responsibilities entailed in particular positions and concluding that a particular employee's salary is too high. To be sure, high salary and age may be related, but, so long as the employer's decisions view each employee individually on merit, do not impose a general rule that has a disparate impact on older workers, . . . and are based solely on financial considerations, its actions are not barred by the ADEA.[463]

Id 1705. It was this question that the Court answered in the negative, subject to a number of caveats. See **§5.20.**

459 As discussed in **§5.20,** both the majority and the concurring justices in *Biggins* stressed that the plaintiff had not made a disparate impact argument, and that they were not addressing disparate impact analysis.

460 113 S Ct at 1705.

461 *See, e.g.,* Sills v Fort Pitt Steel Casting Co, Inc, 24 FEP Cas (BNA) 927 (WD Pa 1979), *affd without opinion,* 633 F2d 311 (3d Cir 1980). The numerous decisions upholding reductions in force, see **ch 7,** amply demonstrate that employers certainly are not precluded from taking cost-cutting actions—even such severe ones as the discharging of employees—so long as they do so on grounds independent of age.

462 936 F2d 112, 117 (2d Cir 1991).

463 *Id* 117. For a discussion of disparate impact, see **ch 7.**

It is where cost is used as a disguise for making decisions that in fact are motivated by ageist animus that the ADEA's proscriptions certainly come into play. So *Biggins* instructs.[464] But so, too, perhaps, do *Metz* and the other decisions discussed *infra,* albeit perhaps not with as much force as that expressed in the Supreme Court's ruling. More than that, disparate impact analysis—which was not addressed in *Biggins*—still supports the proposition put forth by the Court of Appeals for the First Circuit in *Rivas v Federacion de Associanones Pecuaria de Puerto Rico:*[465] "[E]conomic savings from discharging older employees is not a legitimate business justification under the ADEA, 29 USC §623(f)(1)."[466]

Employee Benefits and Employee Benefit Plans

§5.22 Employee Benefits and Employee Benefit Plans: Introduction

The status and treatment of employee benefits and employee benefit plans under the Age Discrimination in Employment Act of 1967 (ADEA)[467] are matters of particular complexity. This is in part due to the fact that there have been major statutory and judicial changes—even reversals in direction—over the years regarding these facets of the employment relationship. In addition, there is a particularly important administrative interpretation regarding benefits and benefit plans that provides an extensive adjunct, albeit not a legally binding one,[468] to the statutory language. To this mix must be added a number of signifi-

---

464 See **§5.20.**

465 929 F2d 814 (1st Cir 1991).

466 *Id* 821-22.

467 29 USC §§621-634.

468 The interpretation, 29 CFR §1625.10 (1993), was not promulgated in accordance with the rule-making procedures of the Administrative Procedure Act (APA), 5 USC §553, and so is not legally binding. Nonetheless, it, like other agency interpretations, can command considerable judicial deference. See generally **ch 2.**

cant judicial rulings, ranging from *Public Employees Retirement System v Betts*[469] and *United Air Lines, Inc v McMann,*[470] decided by the Supreme Court in 1989 and 1977, respectively, through decisions by numerous courts of appeals and district courts.

§5.23 —The §4(f)(2) Benefit Plan Affirmative Defense in the 1980s

As originally enacted in 1967, the Age Discrimination in Employment Act (ADEA)[471] contained an exculpatory provision, §4(f)(2),[472] that allowed an employer, employment agency, or labor organization to make decisions and to take actions that otherwise would run afoul of the Act's prohibitions, provided the entity could prove that those decisions and/or actions were undertaken in observance of a bona fide employee benefit plan. In 1978 the section was amended so as to erect a caveat to this affirmative defense: a covered entity could not impose involuntary retirement based on a protected individual's age, even if the terms of a particular benefit plan purported to allow it to do so.[473]

Section 4(f)(2) remained unchanged for the next decade in terms of its language; thus, during the 1980s it read as follows:

> It shall not be unlawful for an employer, employment agency, or labor organization (2) to observe the terms of . . . any bona fide employee benefit plan such as a retirement, pension, or insurance plan, which is not a subterfuge to evade the purposes of the Act, except that no such employee benefit plan shall exclude the failure to hire any individual, and no such . . . employee benefit plan shall require or permit the involuntary retirement of any individ-

---

469 492 US 158 (1989).

470 434 US 192 (1977).

471 29 USC §§621-634.

472 *Id* §623(f)(2) (pre-1990 amendment).

473 Age Discrimination in Employment Act Amendments of 1978, Pub L No 95-256, §2(a), 92 Stat 189.

> ual specified by section . . . [12(a), 29 USC §631(a),] of this Act because of the age of such individual.

The legislative history of §4(f)(2), as originally enacted, supported reading this provision as a reflection of congressional concern about the economic burdens that it was feared employers would confront if they were forced (by virtue of the enactment of the ADEA absent such an exception) to bear the anticipated higher costs expected to result if older workers had to receive benefits equivalent to those provided to younger workers.[474] Thus, for example, the Senate manager of the 1967 legislation explained as follows:

> [A]n employer will not be compelled to afford older workers exactly the same pension retirement or insurance benefits as younger workers and thus employers will not, because of the often extremely high cost of providing certain benefits to older workers, actually be discouraged from hiring older workers.[475]

On the other hand, abuse was to be averted. Thus, at the core of §4(f)(2) was the focus on *subterfuge:* a differential in treatment between a younger and an older employee could not be justified by pointing to a benefit plan as the basis for that differing treatment if the plan was a "subterfuge to evade the purposes of the Act."[476]

Given the language of §4(f)(2) and given the foregoing legislative rationale, for 20 years the bona fide employee benefit plan exception was understood by the ADEA enforcement agencies—first the Department of Labor and, since mid-1979, the Equal

---

474 *See* House Comm on Educ & Labor, Age Discrimination in Employment Act of 1967, HR Rep No 805, 90th Cong, 1st Sess (1987); *see also* the debates on the legislation, at 113 Cong Rec 31254-55, 34745-46, 34747 (1967).

475 113 Cong Rec at 31254-55.

476 §4(f)(2), 29 USC §623(f)(2) (pre 1990-amendment). As to the case law concerning subterfuge, see **§§5.35-.36.**

Employment Opportunity Commission (EEOC)[477]—as allowing age-based differentials in benefits only if such differentials could be cost justified. The EEOC (and before it the Department of Labor) embraced an *equal cost or equal benefit* principle to express this focus:

> A benefit plan will be considered in compliance with the statute where the actual amount of payment made, or cost incurred, in behalf of an older worker is equal to that made or incurred in behalf of a younger worker, even though the older worker may thereby receive a lesser amount of benefits or insurance coverage.[478]

These agency interpretations, while not legally binding, typically commanded considerable judicial deference.[479]

Both agency interpretation[480] and case law[481] further established that §4(f)(2) constituted an affirmative defense, with the burden of proof therefore resting on the defendant that invoked §4(f)(2) in response to a grievant's claim.

---

[477] During its tenure as administrative and enforcement agency for the ADEA, the Department of Labor issued interpretations regarding §4(f)(2). 29 CFR §860.120 (effectively rescinded, 46 Fed Reg 47724 (Sept 29, 1981), and ordered removed from the CFR, 52 Fed Reg 23812 (June 25, 1987)). From the time the EEOC took over administrative and enforcement duties in 1979, until mid-1987, the EEOC simply adopted the Department of Labor's interpretations as its own. In 1987 the EEOC formally transferred these provisions into its own chapter in the Code of Federal Regulations. *See* 29 CFR §1625.10 (1993). Almost simultaneously the Labor Department formally ordered the removal of its own long-defunct interpretations from the CFR. 52 Fed Reg 23812 (June 25, 1987).

[478] 29 CFR §1625.10(a)(1) (1993). There was at one time an exception to this approval of differential benefits (conditioned on equality of expenditures) that concerned health insurance benefits. It was insufficient that expenditures for such benefits were equal if, in fact, coverage turned out to be unequal. See **§5.46.**

[479] As to the general deference accorded EEOC interpretations and guidelines, see **ch 2.**

[480] 29 CFR §1625.10(a)(1) (1993).

[481] See **§5.28.**

§5.24 —The *Betts* Decision and Its Impact on §4(f)(2)

The employee benefit plan defense embodied in the pre-1990 amendment version of §4(f)(2)[482] of the Age Discrimination in Employment Act (ADEA),[483] and the administrative interpretation construing the provision,[484] were gutted of their substantive rigor in 1989 by *Public Employees Retirement System v Betts.*[485] This ruling dramatically departed, in a number of ways, from numerous lower court decisions that had interpreted the provision.

The *Betts* Court pointed out that §4(a)(1)[486] of the ADEA bars employers from failing or refusing to hire, discharging, or otherwise discriminating against individuals with respect to "compensation, terms, conditions, or privileges of employment." Arguably, the Court reasoned, this prohibition could be read as encompassing employee benefit plans of the type covered by the then-extant version of §4(f)(2), which prohibited plan provisions that were subterfuges for violating the Act. Such a reading, however, would "render the [then-extant] §4(f)(2) exemption nugatory with respect to post-Act plans."[487] The Court explained why this was so:

> Any benefit plan that by its terms mandated discrimination against older workers would also be facially irreconcilable with the prohibitions in §4(a)(1) and, therefore, with the purpose of the Act itself. It is difficult to see how a plan provision that expressly mandates disparate treatment of older workers in a manner inconsistent with the purposes of the Act could be said not to be a subterfuge to evade those purposes, at least where the plan provision was adopted after enactment of the ADEA.[488]

---

[482] 29 USC §623(f)(2) (pre 1990-amendment).

[483] *Id* §§621-634.

[484] 29 CFR §1625.10 (1993).

[485] 492 US 158 (1989).

[486] 29 USC §623(a)(1).

[487] 492 US at 177.

[488] *Id.*

From this perception flowed a critical shift in focus from the past:

> [I]f §4(f)(2) is viewed as exempting the provisions of a bona fide benefit plan from the purview of the ADEA so long as the plan is not a method of discriminating in other, non-fringe-benefit aspects of the employment relationship, both statutory provisions can be given effect. This interpretation of the ADEA would reflect a congressional judgment that age-based restrictions in the employee benefit plans covered by §4(f)(2) do not constitute the "arbitrary discrimination in employment[,]" [§2(b), 29 USC §621(b),] that Congress sought to prohibit. . . . Instead, under this construction of the statute, Congress left the employee benefit battle for another day, and legislated only as to hiring and firing, wages and salaries, and other nonfringe-benefit terms and conditions of employment.[489]

Thus, after 20 years of contrary understanding, the Court recast the then-extant §4(f)(2) as a device insulating employee benefit plans from attack unless a plan was "used as a subterfuge for age discrimination in *other* aspects of the employment relation [that are already protected under the Act]."[490]

The Court could hardly do less than concede that its interpretation of §4(f)(2) permitted "employers wide latitude in structuring employee benefit plans."[491] Still, Justice Kennedy, author of the majority opinion, tried to maintain that this interpretation did "not render the 'not a subterfuge' proviso a dead letter."[492] He offered some examples of how the exception retained some substantive rigor:

> Any attempt to avoid the prohibitions of the Act by cloaking forbidden discrimination in the guise of age-based differen-

---

489 *Id.*

490 *Id* 180 (emphasis added). The Court relied on its reading of the legislative history to support this revisionist treatment of the §4(f)(2) exception. *Id* 178-80.

491 *Id* 180.

492 *Id.*

> tials in benefits will fall outside the §4(f)(2) exemption. Examples of possible violations of this kind can be given. Under §4(d) [,29 USC §623(d),] of the ADEA, for example, it is unlawful for an employer to discriminate against an employee who has "opposed any action made unlawful by" the Act or has participated in the filing of any age-discrimination complaints or litigation. Nothing in §4(f)(2) would insulate from liability an employer who adopted a plan provision formulated to retaliate against such an employee. See 29 CFR §1625.10(d)(5) (1988). Similarly, while §4(f)(2) generally protects age-based reductions in fringe benefits, an employer's decision to reduce salaries for all employees while substantially increasing benefits for younger workers might give rise to an inference that the employer was in fact utilizing its benefits plan as a subterfuge for age-based discrimination in wages, an activity forbidden by §4(a)(1).[493]

It was in light of the foregoing analysis that the majority turned to the specific plan at issue in *Betts* and upheld it. The plan that was the subject of attack provided two forms of monthly retirement benefits. Age-and-service retirement benefits were paid to employees who, at the time of retirement, had at least five years of service and were at least age 60; or had 30 years of service; or were age 55 and had at least 25 years of service. Disability retirement benefits were available to employees who were under age 60 at the time of retirement, had at least five years of service, and were permanently disabled. Betts, who had become disabled, was over 60 at the time of her retirement, and was therefore ineligible for disability benefits, which by virtue of the statutory formula were—at least in her situation—higher than age-and-service retirement benefits.

Since age was the critical criterion in determining eligibility for the financially more attractive disability benefits, Betts sued under the ADEA. She won at both the district court and court of appeals levels, but the Supreme Court reversed and

---

493 *Id.*

remanded. In explaining why the plan survived attack, Justice Kennedy wrote as follows:

> Because appellee has failed to meet her burden of proving that the reduction in benefits at age 60 was the result of an intent to discriminate in some nonfringe-benefit aspect of the employment relation, summary judgment for appellee was inappropriate.[494]

In other words, overt uses of age, designed to afford lesser benefits to older workers than to younger ones, were legal if they were nothing more than they purported to be—i.e., blatant age-based differentiations. It was only when a benefits differentiation could be established to be a ruse for discriminating in some context other than fringe benefits, and where that ruse could be proven to be motivated by an actual intent to discriminate, that an age-based benefits differentiation would violate the ADEA.

Justice Marshall dissented and wrote an opinion in which Justice Brennan joined. In their view, it was entirely appropriate—in light of the statutory language, prior case law, the agency interpretations, legislative history, policy concerns, and fairness—to read the §4(f)(2) exception as legitimizing only those benefit plans as to which the differentials in treatment made pursuant to them could be "justified by a plausible business purpose."[495]

Along with reading any significant meaning out of the then-extant §4(f)(2), the *Betts* Court delivered the coup de grace to the *equal cost or equal benefit* principle:[496]

> [W]e conclude that the phrase "any bona fide employee benefit plan such as a retirement, pension or insurance plan" cannot reasonably be limited to benefit plans in which all age-based reductions in benefits are justified by age-related cost considerations. Accordingly, the interpre-

---

494 *Id* 182.

495 *Id* 185 (Marshall, J., joined by Brennan, J., dissenting).

496 See **§5.23.**

> tive regulation construing §4(f)(2) to include a cost-justification requirement is contrary to the plain language of the statute and is invalid.[497]

The Court further reshaped the legal landscape by rejecting the accepted agency and judicial readings of §4(f)(2) as being an affirmative defense, to be proved by the employer.[498] The Court ruled as follows:

> [W]hen an employee seeks to challenge a benefit plan provision as a subterfuge to evade the purposes of the Act, the employee bears the burden of proving that the discriminatory plan provision actually was intended to serve . . . [a discriminatory end].[499]

As this quotation indicates, the Court further introduced into §4(f)(2) jurisprudence a requirement of "actual intent."[500] Hitherto, intent typically had not been a matter of concern: either an otherwise discriminatory plan could be justified under the terms of the exception or it could not be. Now, intent became integral to a plaintiff's claim of discrimination.[501]

In one respect *Betts* did preserve existing law. The Court held that plans adopted prior to the enactment of the ADEA could not, by definition, be subterfuges to evade the purposes of the Act, and so age-based differentials embodied in such plans were

---

497 492 US at 175.

498 See **§5.23.**

499 492 US at 181.

500 *Id.*

501 Prior to *Betts,* discriminatory intent typically would simply be presumed on the basis of the plaintiff's establishing a prima facie claim of injury—a claim often based on a plan provision that on its face made an age-based distinction. The burden of proof then would shift to the defendant to prove that its plan was not a subterfuge to evade the purposes of the ADEA. The question of whether the plaintiff had established the requisite discriminatory intent was not a matter of intense focus by the courts. Subsequent to *Betts,* the lower courts focused with more particularity on the intent issue. See **§5.36.** (As to the legality under the ADEA of actions and decisions having a disparate impact on an ADEA-protected individual, without there being any discriminatory intent, see **ch 7.**)

immune from attack under the statute. This holding reaffirmed the position taken earlier by the Court in *United Air Lines, Inc v McMann.*[502]

In 1990 the Older Workers Benefit Protection Act (OWBPA),[503] overturning *Betts,* was signed into law. However, inasmuch as the OWBPA by its terms did not apply retroactively,[504] *Betts* retained vitality for that period running from the time it was decided, June 23, 1989, until the effective date of the OWBPA,[505] which generally was April 14, 1991.[506] More than that, case law supported the conclusion, albeit not with complete uniformity, that *Betts* remained viable and controlling with regard to claims arising prior to the decision's being rendered.[507]

§5.25 The Older Workers Benefit Protection Act (OWBPA) and the Revised §4(f)(2)

Legislation to overturn *Public Employees Retirement System v Betts*[508] was introduced in the Senate on August 3, 1989.[509] An

---

[502] 434 US 192 (1977). See **§5.27.**

[503] Pub L No 101-433, 104 Stat 978 (1990), *as amended by* Pub L No 101-521, 104 Stat 2278 (1990).

[504] See **§5.25.**

[505] *Id.*

[506] *See* Equal Employment Opportunity Commn v Westinghouse Elec Corp, 925 F2d 619, 622 n2 (3d Cir 1991); Darchuk v Kellwood, 790 F Supp 1453 (ED Mo 1991); *see also* Equal Employment Opportunity Commn v Boeing Servs Intl, 968 F2d 549, 553 n3 (5th Cir 1992) (OWBPA applies prospectively and so does not apply to complaint filed in 1989 (although it was unclear whether the complaint was filed prior to, or after, the *Betts* ruling)).

[507] *See* Bell v Trustees of Purdue Univ, 975 F2d 422, 426 (7th Cir 1992); American Assn of Retired Persons v Farmers Group, Inc, 943 F2d 996, 1000 n6 (9th Cir 1991), *cert denied,* 112 S Ct 937 (1992); Tusting v Bay View Fed Savs & Loan Assn, 789 F Supp 1034 (ND Cal 1992); *see also* Cipriano v Board of Educ, 968 F2d 1502 (2d Cir 1992), *affg* 772 F Supp 1346 (WDNY 1991). *Contra* Mitchell v Mobil Oil Corp, 896 F2d 463, 471 n3 (10th Cir), *cert denied,* 498 US 898 (1990).

[508] 492 US 158 (1989).

[509] S 1511, 101st Cong, 1st Sess (1989).

identical bill was introduced the following day in the House.[510] Subsequent to approval by the Senate committee of the proposed legislation, S 1511, but prior to consideration by the full Senate, a committee substitute was introduced.[511] This in turn was superseded by a committee-authorized modification of the substitute.[512] Thus, the first version of S 1511 was supplanted by a second version, which was the one addressed in the Senate report on the legislation.[513] Two further versions ensued even before debate began in the Senate, and there was a final version devised by the proposed legislation's chief sponsors, Senators Metzenbaum, Pryor, and Heinz, and its chief critic, Senator Hatch.[514] While there was no committee report accompanying the final bill, there was a document submitted by the four senators, entitled "Final Substitute: Statement of Managers,"[515] which set forth explanatory material regarding it.

The Metzenbaum-Pryor-Heinz-Hatch compromise bill was adopted in the Senate by a 94 to 1 vote on September 24, 1990. Subsequently, the House took up the Senate-passed bill on October 2, 1990; it was adopted the following day by a vote of 406 to 17. President Bush signed the legislation—the Older Workers Benefit Protection Act (OWBPA)[516]—into law on October 16, 1990. Thereafter, technical changes were made that were incorporated into the text of the OWBPA.[517]

---

510 HR 3200, 101st Cong, 1st Sess (1989). During consideration of the Senate bill by the Senate Committee on Labor and Human Resources, and of the House bill by the House Committee on Education and Labor, amendments were made to the respective Senate and House bills whereby a title addressing releases, or waivers, of liability was added to each. See **§5.65.**

511 136 Cong Rec S13236-38 (daily ed Sept 17, 1990).

512 136 Cong Rec S13238-40 (daily ed Sept 17, 1990).

513 Senate Comm on Labor & Human Resources, The Older Workers Benefit Protection Act, S Rep No 263, 101st Cong, 2d Sess (1990).

514 136 Cong Rec S13594-96 (daily ed Sept 24, 1990).

515 *Id* 13,596-97.

516 Pub L No 101-433, 104 Stat 978 (1990).

517 The legislation making these technical changes was initially introduced as HR 5759, 101st Cong, 2d Sess (1990). The bill was passed in the House on October 2, 1990. 136 Cong Rec H8628 (daily ed Oct 2, 1990). Subsequently, an amended version of HR 5759 was passed by the Senate on

The OWBPA amended the Age Discrimination in Employment Act (ADEA)[518] in several significant respects that dealt both with §4(f)(2)[519] of the age statute and with new issues, as well.[520] These changes are discussed in succeeding sections.

October 16, 1990. *Id* S15,399 (daily ed Oct 16, 1990). The following day this amended version was adopted in the House. *Id* H10021 (daily ed Oct 17, 1990). The legislation provided as follows:

> *Be it enacted by the Senate and House of Representatives of the United States of America in Congress assembled,* That section 4(l)(2) of the Age Discrimination in Employment Act of 1967, as added by the Older Workers Benefit Protection Act, is amended—
>
> (1) in subparagraph (A)—
>
> (A) in clause (i) by striking "and" at the end,
>
> (B) in clause (ii) by striking the comma at the end and inserting ";or", and
>
> (C) by inserting after clause (ii) the following:
>
> "(iii) the values described in both clauses (i) and (ii);" and
>
> (2) in subparagraph (D)—
>
> (A) by inserting after "For purposes of this paragraph" the following: "and solely in order to make the deduction authorized under the paragraph",
>
> (B) by striking "and" at the end of clause (i),
>
> (C) by striking the period at the end of clause (ii) and inserting ";or", and
>
> (D) by adding at the end the following new clause:
>
> "(iii) the package of benefits provided by the employer is as described in clauses (i) and (ii)."

The legislation was signed by the President on November 5, 1990. This new law, amending the OWBPA, was directed simply at "the technical issue of what can be offset against an employee's severance payment under section 4(l)(2) of the ADEA, as added by S 1511. This technical amendment . . . [did] not affect the meaning of any other provisions of the . . . [ADEA]." 136 Cong Rec S15399 (daily ed Oct 16, 1990) (remarks of Senator Hatch).

518 29 USC §§621-634.

519 *Id* §623(f)(2).

520 On March 27, 1992, the Equal Employment Opportunity Commission (EEOC) issued a request for public comments, directed to the end of securing the public's views as to the interpretation and application of the OWBPA amendments. Equal Employment Opportunity Commn, 29 CFR Part 1625, Age Discrimination in Employment Act, 57 Fed Reg 10626-629 (Mar 27, 1992). The request set forth a series of specific questions as to which responses were solicited. The closing date for such comments was July 27, 1992. *Id* 10626. As of June 10, 1994, no final interpretations or regulations had been issued.

Coverage of Federal Employees by the OWBPA

Section 15[521] of the ADEA establishes a statutory scheme of regulation for federal government employees and job applicants that is completely separate from the legal framework constructed by the Act for the private sector and for state and local governmental employees and job applicants.[522] Inasmuch as the changes made in the ADEA by the OWBPA[523] were addressed to sections of the ADEA other than §15, it follows that these changes did not apply to federal employees and job applicants (although there is some ambiguity as to whether that part of the OWBPA that establishes a regulatory scheme regarding waivers, or releases, of liability is inapplicable in the federal sector).[524] The legislative history supports this conclusion as to the inapplicability of the OWBPA in the federal employment setting.[525]

---

521 29 USC §633a.

522 See **ch 9.**

523 Pub L No 101-433, 104 Stat 978, *as amended by* Pub L No 101-521, 104 Stat 2278 (1990).

524 See **§5.65.**

525 Senator Hatch, who opposed both the final Senate committee's version of S 1511, which—as discussed at the beginning of this section—ultimately was passed and enacted into law as the OWBPA, as well as this committee bill's first two successors, because of the costs that allegedly would be imposed on the states by virtue of state pension and benefit systems having to come into compliance with the amended ADEA, offered an amendment that provided that no benefit plan of a state, local governmental body, or private employer would be deemed in violation of the ADEA if a similar plan were in effect for the federal government. 136 Cong Rec S13254-55 (daily ed Sept 17, 1990). This was an indirect way of insulating these entities from having to comply with the changes wrought by the then-proposed OWBPA, since the requirements imposed by those changes—at the time of the proposed Hatch amendment—were not ones under which the federal government labored vis-a-vis its employees.

Senator Pryor then offered an amendment to Senator Hatch's proposed amendment, making S 1511 applicable to the federal government. 136 Cong Rec S13291 (daily ed Sept 18, 1990). The Pryor amendment was adopted by an 80 to 19 vote. 136 Cong Rec S13296 (daily ed Sept 18, 1990). Thereafter, the Hatch amendment, as amended, was adopted. 136 Cong Rec S13297 (daily ed Sept 18, 1990). The result at that point was that the OWBPA—if then adopted—would have applied to the federal government. Subsequently, however, in the course of a compromise bill (which was enacted into law as the OWBPA) being devised by Senators Metzenbaum, Pryor, Heinz, and Hatch, the pro-

Coverage of Retirees by the OWBPA

Some attention was focused on the status of retirees during consideration of the OWBPA.[526] In response to a query by Senator Bentsen regarding whether retirees were protected under the ADEA, Senator Pryor, one of the managers of the legislation, responded as follows during the Senate debate:

> The . . . Senator is correct [that the ADEA does not apply to retirees.] The ADEA applies only to employees and those individuals seeking employment. However, it does apply to an individual whose retirement benefits are discriminatorily structured prior to retirement.[527]

The same propositions were articulated by the manager of the legislation in the House, Representative Clay.[528]

Effective Date of the OWBPA Amendments to §4 of the ADEA

As a general matter, the provisions of the OWBPA that amended §4 of the ADEA[529] applied only to: (1) employee benefit plans established or modified on or after October 16, 1990; and (2) other conduct occurring more than 180 days after October 16, 1990, i.e., April 14, 1991.[530] Thus, employers, employment agencies, and labor organizations generally had 180 days to come into compliance with the amended ADEA. If employee benefits were provided pursuant to a collective bargaining agreement and the benefits established by such agreements did not satisfy the requirements of the amended ADEA,

---

posed coverage of federal workers was dropped, as was the Hatch proposal. 136 Cong Rec S13598 (daily ed Sept 24, 1990).

[526] Pub L No 101-433, 104 Stat 978, *as amended by* Pub L No 101-521, 104 Stat 2278 (1990).

[527] 136 Cong Rec S13609 (daily ed Sept 24, 1990).

[528] *Id* H8618 (daily ed Oct 2, 1990).

[529] 29 USC §623.

[530] OWBPA §105(a); *accord* Equal Employment Opportunity Commn v City Colleges of Chicago, 944 F2d 339, 341 n2 (7th Cir 1991).

the OWBPA provisions did not go into effect until the earlier of: (1) the date on which the contract expired; or (2) June 1, 1992.[531]

State and local governmental bodies were given until October 16, 1992 to come into compliance with the OWBPA-amended ADEA.[532] (Special provision was made regarding disability benefits.[533] A public employer could come into compliance with regard to such benefits simply by adopting a new plan satisfying the requirements of the amended ADEA. However, it also could, if it so chose, both create a new plan and retain its old plan, provided that employees covered under the old disability benefits plan were given 180 days to elect to move to the new plan. An employee could choose to remain with the old plan, even though the benefits provided under it did not comport with the amended ADEA.)[534]

---

531 OWBPA §105(b).

532 *Id* §105(c)(1).

533 As to such benefits, see **§§5.48-.49.**

534 OWBPA §105(c)(2). In the document entitled "Final Substitute: State of Managers," noted earlier in the text, the view was set forth that this election allowed to governmental employees was to be a one-time event to be used in the context of complying with the OWBPA. 136 Cong Rec S13597 (daily ed Sept 24, 1990). The four senators stated as follows: "The managers intend that once an employee either elects or does not elect to be covered by the new disability benefits under section 105(c)(2), the employee may not change his or her decision. Thus, an employee will not be permitted to opt in and out of two plans." *Id.* This view was reiterated in a colloquy between Senator Ford and Senator Pryor, one of the bill's managers. *Id* S13608-609 (daily ed Sept 24, 1990). During debate on S1511 Senator Ford inquired of Senator Pryor, who authored the statement as to the notice requirement set forth in the provision regarding a public employer's establishment of a new disability benefits plan, whereby "reasonable notice" had to be given to all employees before the employer implemented a new plan. OWBPA §105(c)(2)(A)(i). He asked whether this notice provision required employers "to give notice before they amend or 'establish' a new . . . plan, or to give notice before they implement the plan?" *Id* S13609 (daily ed Sept 24, 1990). Senator Pryor responded as follows:

> In this case "establish" means implement. Reasonable notice must be given to employees before the new disability benefits plan is implemented, and a 180-day consideration period must be provided after the election offer is made.

Id.

Section 105(e) of the OWBPA confirmed that ongoing benefit payments to individuals that began prior to October 16, 1990 were not affected by the OWBPA, although by the terms of §105(e) the fact that a plan was adopted prior to enactment of the ADEA no longer insulated that plan from the requirements of the statute.[535]

§5.26 —The OWBPA-Amended §4(f)(2)

The Older Workers Benefit Protection Act (OWBPA)[536] consigned *Public Employees Retirement System v Betts*[537] to history by overriding the *Betts* Court's various holdings. The 1990 Act rewrote §4(f)(2)[538] of the Age Discrimination in Employment Act (ADEA),[539] which of course was the focus of the *Betts* ruling. In so doing, the OWBPA scuttled the term *subterfuge*, which was contained in the text of the previous version of the section and had been central to it.[540] The OWBPA built directly into the new language of §4(f)(2) the *equal benefit or equal cost* principle,[541] and the 1990 enactment further established on the face of §4(f)(2) that that section constitutes an affirmative defense. The OWBPA also amended §11 of the ADEA to leave no room for doubt that "[t]he term 'compensation, terms, conditions, or privileges of employment' encompasses all employee benefits, including such benefits provided pursuant to a bona fide employee benefit plan."[542] The OWBPA also extended §4(f)(2) to plans adopted

---

[535] Pub L No 101-433, §105(e), 104 Stat 978, 982-83, *as amended by* Pub L No 101-521, 104 Stat 2287 (1990).

[536] Pub L No 101-433, 104 Stat 978, *as amended by* Pub L No 101-521, 104 Stat 2287 (1990).

[537] 492 US 158 (1989).

[538] 29 USC §623(f)(2).

[539] *Id* §§621-634.

[540] See **§§5.23, 5.34-.35.**

[541] See **§§5.32-.33.**

[542] §11(1), 29 USC §630(1). The Senate committee report on the legislation that ultimately was enacted as the OWBPA explained that "[t]he distinction made between employee benefits and employee benefit plans is designed to

prior to the ADEA's enactment.[543]

As a result of the OWBPA, §4(f)(2) now reads as follows:

> It shall not be unlawful for an employer, employment agency or labor organization—. . . .
>
> (2) to take any action otherwise prohibited under subsection (a), (b), (c), or (e) of this section—
>
> (A) to observe the terms of a bona fide seniority system that is not intended to evade the purposes of this Act, except that no such seniority system shall require or permit the involuntary retirement of any individual specified by section 12(a) [29 USC §631(a)] because of the age of such individual; or
>
> (B) to observe the terms of a bona fide employee benefit plan—
>
> (i) where, for each benefit or benefit package, the actual amount of payment made or cost incurred on behalf of an older worker is no less than that made or incurred on behalf of a younger worker, as permissible under Section 1625.10, title 29, Code of Federal Regulations (as in effect on June 22, 1989); or
>
> (ii) that is a voluntary early retirement incentive plan consistent with the relevant purpose or purposes of this Act[.] Notwithstanding clause (i) or (ii) of subparagraph (B), no such employee benefit plan or voluntary early retirement incentive plan shall excuse the failure to hire any individual, and no such employee benefit plan shall require or permit the involuntary retirement of any individual specified by section 12(a), because of the age of such individual. An employer, employment agency or labor organization acting under subparagraph (A), or under clause (i) or (ii) of sub-

---

ensure that each discreet [sic] benefit (whether provided pursuant to an employee benefit plan or not) is subject to the prohibitions of section 4(a)(1)." Senate Comm on Labor & Human Resources, The Older Workers Benefit Protection Act, S Rep No 263, 101st Cong, 2d Sess 17 (1990).

543 The OWBPA added a new subsection 4(k) to the ADEA: "A seniority system or employee benefit plan shall comply with this Act regardless of the date of adoption of such system or plan." §4(k), 29 USC §623(k).

paragraph (B), shall have the burden of proving that such actions are lawful in any civil enforcement proceeding brought under this Act[.]

By its terms the OWBPA by only applied prospectively.[544] Thus, *Betts* remained legally alive and relevant for events occurring, and for lawsuits and charges of discrimination filed, between the time *Betts* was decided and the time the OWBPA-amended ADEA became effective,[545] as well as for claims arising prior to *Betts.*[546]

§5.27 —The Relation of the Old and New §4(f)(2) to Pre-Act Plans

Prior to §4(f)(2)[547] of the Age Discrimination in Employment Act (ADEA)[548] being rewritten by the Older Workers Benefit Protection Act (OWBPA)[549] in 1990, the central focus of the provision was on the question of subterfuge.[550] In *United Air Lines, Inc v McMann*[551] the Supreme Court held that the plan at issue, which entailed the imposition of involuntary retirement on employees at age 60, could not be a subterfuge to evade the purposes of the ADEA since the plan had been adopted "in good faith" prior to the enactment of the ADEA.[552]

Subsequent to the *McMann* decision Congress amended the ADEA so as to bar employers, employment agencies, and labor

---

[544] See **§5.25.**

[545] *Id.*

[546] *Id.*

[547] 29 USC §623(f)(2) (pre 1990-amendment).

[548] *Id* §§621-634.

[549] Pub L No 101-433, 104 Stat 978, *as amended by* Pub L No 101-521, 104 Stat 2287 (1990).

[550] The original version of §4(f)(2) barred an employer, employment agency, or labor organization from being able to successfully invoke the affirmative defense if the plan on which it sought to rely was "a subterfuge to evade the purposes of the Act." See **§5.23.**

[551] 434 US 192 (1977).

[552] *Id* 203.

organizations from relying on employee benefit plans as bases for imposing retirement on employees who would otherwise be protected under the ADEA.[553] The legislative history of that 1978 amendment suggested that Congress not only condemned mandatory retirement imposed pursuant to a plan, but that it also rejected the *McMann* Court's position that a pre-ADEA plan could not be a subterfuge to evade the Act's purposes simply by virtue of its having been adopted prior to the enactment of the statute.[554] Nonetheless, most of the lower courts that subsequently addressed the question concluded that *McMann* was not undermined by these congressional statements.[555]

In *Public Employees Retirement System v Betts*[556] the Court revisited the issue and held that "an employee benefit plan adopted prior

---

553 At the time *McMann* was decided, the ADEA only extended protection to individuals ages 40 through 64. In 1978 the Act was amended to raise the ceiling for coverage of most employees and job applicants in the private sector to age 70, and in 1986 that age ceiling was removed for most individuals. See **ch 3**.

554 The report of the conference committee that harmonized the Senate and House bills' differences stated with regard to *McMann* as follows:

> The conferees specifically disagree with the Supreme Court's holding and reasoning in that case. Plan provisions in effect prior to the date of enactment are not exempt under section 4(f)(2) by virtue of the fact that they antedate the act or these amendments.

Conference Comm, Age Discrimination in Employment Act Amendments of 1978, HR Rep No 950, 95th Cong, 2d Sess 8 (1978). In addition, the Senate committee's earlier report on its version of the 1978 amendment rejected a pre-*McMann* decision of the Court of Appeals for the Fifth Circuit—Brennan v Taft Broadcasting Co, 500 F2d 212 (5th Cir 1974)—in which that court had asserted the position later set forth in *McMann.* Senate Comm on Labor & Human Resources, Amending the Age Discrimination in Employment Act Amendments of 1977, S Rep No 493, 95th Cong, 1st Sess 10 (1977).

555 *See, e.g.,* Equal Employment Opportunity Commn v Cargill, Inc, 855 F2d 682 (10th Cir 1988); Equal Employment Opportunity Commn v County of Orange, 837 F2d 420 (9th Cir 1988); Crosland v Charlotte Eye, Ear & Throat Hosp, 686 F2d 208, 213 (4th Cir 1982); Equal Employment Opportunity Commn v Maine, 644 F Supp 223 (D Me 1986), *affd without opinion,* 823 F2d 542 (1st Cir 1987). *But see* Michigan State Employees Assn v Civil Serv Commn, 177 Mich App 231, 441 NW2d 423 (1989).

556 492 US 158 (1989).

to enactment of the ADEA cannot be a subterfuge."[557] *Betts,* however, did not insulate every aspect of a plan which, in its initial form, was adopted prior to the ADEA's enactment. Prior to *Betts* the case law supported the proposition put forth in *Equal Employment Opportunity Commission v Home Insurance Co:*[558] "The mere fact that an employer had a pre-Act plan that arguably complied with the Act cannot validate the plan's post-Act modification to introduce new age-discriminatory terms."[559] The *Betts* Court confirmed the validity of this position.[560] The Court did not speak to the details, however. But it was asserted in *Equal Employment Opportunity Commission v County of Orange*[561] that for a postenactment modification to a pre-Act plan to be sufficient to warrant treating the plan as a subterfuge, the modification had to "be

---

[557] *Id* 168.

[558] 672 F2d 252 (2d Cir 1982).

[559] *Id* 259 n2; *accord* Equal Employment Opportunity Commn v Baltimore & Ohio RR Co, 632 F2d 1107 (4th Cir 1980), *cert denied,* 454 US 825 (1981); Smart v Porter Paint Co, 630 F2d 490, 495-96 (7th Cir 1980); Sikora v American Can Co, 622 F2d 1116, 1124 (3d Cir 1980); Equal Employment Opportunity Commn v Michigan, 51 FEP Cas (BNA) 294, 300 n7 (WD Mich 1988); Marshall v Eastern Airlines, Inc, 474 F Supp 364, 369 (SD Fla 1979), *affd,* 27 FEP Cas (BNA) 1686 (5th Cir), *cert denied,* 454 US 818 (1981); Marshall v Atlantic Container Line, GIE, 470 F Supp 71 (SDNY 1979).

[560] 492 US at 169. Post-*Betts* lower court decisions supported this position, as well. Equal Employment Opportunity Commn v Westinghouse Elec Corp, 925 F2d 619 (3d Cir 1991); Warren v Oil, Chem & Atomic Workers Union—Industry Pension Fund, 729 F Supp 563, 570 (ED Mich 1989); *see also* Equal Employment Opportunity Commn v Massachusetts, 54 FEP Cas (BNA) 436, 439 (D Mass 1990).

In deLoraine v MEBA Pension Trust, 499 F2d 49, 50 (2d Cir), *cert denied,* 419 US 1009 (1974), the court assumed arguendo that the ADEA would apply to, and proscribe, improper postenactment administration of a plan adopted prior to the ADEA's enactment. (Cowlishaw v Armstrong Rubber Co, 450 F Supp 148 (EDNY 1978), addressed the validity of a postenactment practice pursued in accordance with the terms of a pre-Act plan. In ruling for the plaintiff the *Cowlishaw* court relied heavily on another pro-plaintiff decision, Hannan v Chrysler Motors Corp, 443 F Supp 802 (ED Mich 1978), whose substance was later repudiated in Carpenter v Continental Trailways, 635 F2d 578 (6th Cir 1980), *cert denied,* 451 US 986 (1981), as well as by most other courts. Thus, *Cowlishaw* quickly became a ruling of dubious strength.)

[561] 837 F2d 420 (9th Cir 1988).

significant or at least relevant to the challenged discriminatory practice."[562]

The legal picture was not changed by the enactment in 1990 of the OWBPA. Subsection 4(k) was added to the ADEA to provide that "[a] seniority system or employee benefit plan shall comply with this Act regardless of the date of adoption of such system or plan."[563] However, §105(e)[564] of the OWBPA insulates pre-Act plans (but not post-Act modifications) from attack. It provides that the OWBPA amendments to the ADEA do not apply to benefit payments that were commenced prior to the OWBPA and that continued after the effective date pursuant to a plan in effect on the OWBPA's effective date, except that no substantial modification to such a plan can be made if the intent of the modifications is to evade the purposes of the OWBPA-amended ADEA.

---

[562] *Id* 423; *accord* Snair v City of Clearwater, 787 F Supp 1401, 1410 (MD Fla 1992).

[563] §4(k), 29 USC §623(k). During the Senate debates on the legislation, Senator Ford sought clarification from Senator Pryor, one of the managers of the legislation, as to how §4(k) meshed with §105 of the OWBPA, which section provides that the legislation only applies prospectively. See **§5.25.** A portion of their colloquy follows:

> Mr. Pryor: First let me state that I do not believe that a conflict exists. S.1511 [, the Senate bill which was enacted as the OWBPA,] applies only prospectively to benefits established or modified on or after the date of enactment of this legislation. This prospective application encompasses every change made in the ADEA by S 1511, including the change contained in subsection (k) to which you refer. The purpose of this new subsection 4(k) is to make clear the intent of Congress that the amendments included in this legislation apply to all benefit plans, including those which predate enactment of the ADEA.
>
> Mr. Ford: Is it correct to say, then, that subsection 4(k) will not cause the requirements of this legislation to apply retroactively to a seniority system or an early retirement incentive plan, even if it has been modified over the past 10 years?
>
> Mr. Pryor: That is correct.

136 Cong Rec S13,609 (daily ed Sept 24, 1990).

[564] Publ L No 101-433, §105(e), 104 Stat 978, 982-83, *as amended by* Pub L No 101-521, 104 Stat 2287 (1990).

§5.28 Burdens of Proof Under the New §4(f)(2)

Prior to the Supreme Court's decision in *Public Employees Retirement System v Betts,*[565] both agency interpretation[566] and the case law[567] firmly established that the exception contained in the then-extant version of §4(f)(2)[568] of the Age Discrimination in Employment Act (ADEA)[569] constituted an affirmative defense. Thus, an employer, employment agency, or labor organization that sought to rely upon a benefit plan as the basis for engaging in a practice or making a decision that ordinarily would violate the ADEA bore the burden of proving that the plan did not constitute a subterfuge to evade the purposes of the ADEA.[570] The *Betts* Court announced a 180-degree shift in legal direction:

> [W]hen an employee seeks to challenge a benefit plan provision as a subterfuge to evade the purposes of the Act, the employee bears the burden of proving that the discriminatory plan provision actually was intended to serve . . . [a discriminatory end].[571]

The Older Workers Benefit Protection Act (OWBPA)[572] amended the ADEA so as to return §4(f)(2) to it's pre-*Betts* status: the rewritten §4(f)(2) explicitly asserts that "[a]n employer, employment agency, or labor organization . . . [observing the

---

[565] 492 US 158 (1989).

[566] 29 CFR §1625.10(a)(1) (1993).

[567] *See, e.g.,* Equal Employment Opportunity Commn v City of Mt Lebanon, 842 F2d 1480, 1488 n6 (3d Cir 1988); Karlen v City Colleges, 837 F2d 314, 318 (7th Cir), *cert denied,* 486 US 1044 (1988); Crosland v Charlotte Eye, Ear & Throat Hosp, 686 F2d 208, 212 (4th Cir 1982); Equal Employment Opportunity Commn v Home Ins Co, 672 F2d 252 (2d Cir 1982); Equal Employment Opportunity Commn v Eastern Airlines, Inc, 27 FEP Cas (BNA) 1686, 1687 (5th Cir), *cert denied,* 454 US 818 (1981).

[568] 29 USC §623(f)(2) (pre-1990 amendment).

[569] *Id* §§621-634.

[570] Subterfuge was the key concept in the pre-OWBPA version of §4(f)(2). See **§§5.23, 5.34-.35.**

[571] 492 US at 181.

[572] Pub L No 101-433, 104 Stat 978, *as amended by* Pub L No 101-521, 104 Stat 2287 (1990).

terms of a bona fide employee benefit plan] shall have the burden of proving that such . . . [action is] lawful in any civil enforcement proceeding brought under this Act."

It should be noted that under §4(f)(2)(B)(ii)[573] an employer, employment agency, or labor organization may avoid liability by observing the terms of a bona fide plan "that is a voluntary early retirement incentive plan *consistent with the relevant purpose or purposes of this Act.*"[574]

In *Cipriano v Board of Education,*[575] a pre-OWBPA decision, the court asserted that the burden of proof regarding subterfuge, the then-operative legally significant element of §4(f)(2),[576] would be less when an employer was defending a voluntary early retirement plan, as opposed to a mandatory retirement plan. In such an instance the employer only would need to "come up with some evidence" establishing a "legitimate business reason."[577] No such reading of the OWBPA-rewritten §4(f)(2) is directly authorized by the language of the provision, or directly supported by the legislative history. However, it is correct to note that the language of §4(f)(B)(2)(ii) is broad enough to encompass the proposition that an employer's burden is the light one of adducing just "some" evidence. Moreover, inasmuch as §4(f)(2)(B)(ii) does not embrace the *equal benefit or equal cost* principle, in contrast to §4(f)(2)(B)(i),[578] but rather speaks to a plan "being consistent with the relevant purpose or purposes" of the ADEA, the *Cipriano* formulation of a defendant's burden—i.e., that of proving a "legitimate business justification"—is not negated by the OWBPA-rewritten §4(f)(2).[579] (Of course, even if Cipriano's "some evidence" and "legitimate business reason" standards have survived the rewriting of §4(f)(2)

---

573 29 USC §623(f)(2)(B)(ii).

574 *Id* (emphasis added).

575 785 F2d 51 (2d Cir 1986).

576 See **§5.23.**

577 785 F2d at 58.

578 29 USC §623(f)(2)(B)(i). In regard to the *equal benefit or equal cost* principle, see **§5.32.**

579 As to voluntary retirement plans generally, see **§§5.53-.56.**

and are deemed to be compatible with the "reasonable purpose or purposes" language of §4(f)(2)(B)(ii), as it seems they are, it does not follow that the *Cipriano* standards need be applied in jurisdictions other than the Second Circuit.) Nor, for that matter, need they be applied in the Second Circuit itself, inasmuch as the *Cipriano* court construed statutory language that subsequently was changed.

There is another issue here. As pointed out above, by the terms of §4(f)(2) the entity claiming to have observed the terms of a plan bears the burden of proving the plan's legitimacy under the terms of the ADEA. However, the individual who claims that his departure pursuant to a supposed voluntary early retirement incentive plan actually was involuntary bears the burden of proving the matter of involuntariness.[580]

§5.29 'Observing the Terms' Under the Old and New §4(f)(2)

Section 4(f)(2)[581] of the Age Discrimination in Employment Act (ADEA)[582] provides that an employee benefit plan can successfully be relied upon as an affirmative defense only if the employer, employment agency, or labor organization invoking the defense has "observe[d] the terms" of the plan. This language is the same as that contained in the version of §4(f)(2) which existed prior to its being rewritten by the Older Workers Benefit Protection Act (OWBPA)[583] in 1990.[584] Inasmuch as there

---

580 Final Substitute: Statement of Managers, 136 Cong Rec S 13596 (daily ed Sept 24, 1990). This Statement was jointly endorsed by the chief sponsors—Senators Metzenbaum, Pryor, and Heinz—as well as by the chief one-time critic, Senator Hatch, of the Senate bill that was passed by the Senate and ultimately enacted into law. It afforded some explanation as to various elements of the final version of the bill, which had gone through a number of modifications before assuming the form in which it was ultimately passed.

581 29 USC §623(f)(2).

582 *Id* §§621-634.

583 Pub L No 101-433, 104 Stat 478, *as amended by* Pub L No 101-521, 104 Stat 2287 (1990).

584 For the earlier version, see **§5.23.**

was no change effected as between the pre-OWBPA and OWBPA-created versions of §4(f)(2), the pre-OWBPA case law addressing the "observe the terms" requirement is of continuing relevance.

Explicit Authorization in the Plan

The case law establishes the general principle that an employer, employment agency, or labor organization will not be deemed to have observed the terms of a plan if in fact the plan does not explicitly authorize or direct the particular action or decision at issue. The particular rulings from which this generalization flows concerned challenges to involuntary age-based retirement, which could be imposed pursuant to a bona fide benefit plan prior to §4(f)(2)'s being amended in 1978 so as to bar reliance on a plan as a basis for this practice.[585] While these decisions concerned a practice no longer legal after enactment of the 1978 amendment, the cases nonetheless are apposite insofar as they address the legal requirements that must be satisfied regarding the "observe the terms" language, since this language exists independently of the particular practice or decision that a defendant seeks, or sought, to justify as being in observance of a plan's terms.

The cases establish that a decision or practice that ordinarily would be violative of the ADEA cannot be justified as being in observance of a plan if the plan is silent as to the decision maker's authority to make the decision or pursue the practice in question. In other words, the argument that a plan's silence constitutes an implicit, legally sufficient expression of approbation for the employer's engaging in such practice or making such decision as a means of observing the terms of the plan has proven to be bankrupt. There must be express authorization for the

---

[585] Age Discrimination in Employment Act Amendments of 1978, Pub L No 95-256, §2(a) 92 Stat 189.

challenged action or decision.[586] Thus, courts have rejected the argument—in the context of considering pre-1978 amendment forced retirement—that an employer's past practice regarding retirement could serve in lieu of an express provision in a benefit plan as a basis for justifying the involuntary retirement of individuals who fell within the protected age group under the statute.[587] Similarly, courts rejected the argument that because at common law employers traditionally were free under the employment-at-will doctrine[588] to terminate employees for any reason,[589] specific authorization in a plan for retirement was unnecessary.

There is no good reason why the proposition that a plan must expressly sanction the action or decision at issue—a proposition established by case law addressing the question of involuntary retirement in observance of plans at a time when such retirement legally could be imposed—should not hold true outside the retirement context.[590]

Employer Discretion

Sometimes the language of a plan may permit an action, but not require that that action actually be taken. There is some disagreement as to whether in such a situation an employer,

---

[586] *See, e.g.*, Sexton v Beatrice Foods Co, 630 F2d 478, 486 (7th Cir 1980); Allen v Colgate-Palmolive Co, 539 F Supp 57 (SDNY 1981).

[587] *See, e.g.*, Equal Employment Opportunity Commn v Baltimore & Ohio RR Co, 632 F2d 1107, 1110-11 (4th Cir 1980), *cert denied*, 454 US 825 (1981); Equal Employment Opportunity Commn v Baltimore & Ohio RR Co, 557 F Supp 1112, 1119 n5 (D Md 1983). The history of practices within a company may be useful, however, in giving meaning to unclear terms of a plan. For example, in United Airlines, Inc v McMann, 434 US 192 (1977), the Court considered a plan that established age 60 as the normal retirement age. The Court read this plan as requiring retirement at that age, rather than as simply affording the employer discretion; this reading was based on the employer's consistent practice of requiring retirement at that age.

[588] As to this doctrine, see **ch 10.**

[589] *See, e.g.*, Equal Employment Opportunity Commn v Baltimore & Ohio RR Co, 632 F2d 1107, 1110-11 (4th Cir 1980), *cert denied*, 454 US 825 (1981); Sexton v Beatrice Foods Co, 630 F2d 478, 485 (7th Cir 1980).

[590] *See* Germann v Levy, 553 F Supp 700 (ND Ill 1982).

employment agency, or labor organization may successfully claim that it has observed the terms of the plan if it in fact exercises the discretion afforded it by the plan. The ADEA enforcement agency, the Equal Employment Opportunity Commission (EEOC), takes a negative position; the case law in the main is to the contrary.

The EEOC's view is that "[w]here the employer, employment agency, or labor organization is not required by the express provisions of the plan to provide lesser benefits to older workers, section 4(f)(2) does not apply."[591] In other words, "individual, discretionary acts of discrimination"[592] do not fit within the §4(f)(2) defense, in contrast to differential treatment that results from the defendant decision maker being required by a plan to observe a particular term of the plan. The logic underlying this proposition is articulated in the EEOC interpretation addressing §4(f)(2):

> Where a discriminatory policy is an express term of a benefit plan, employees presumably have some opportunity to know of the plan and to plan (or protest) accordingly. Moreover, the requirement that the discrimination actually be prescribed by a plan assures that the particular plan provision will be equally applied to all employees of the same age.[593]

In *United Airlines, Inc v McMann*[594] the Court noted, but did not resolve, the question of the legality of early retirement at the employer's option. It neither endorsed nor rejected the foregoing agency position, which at the time of the *McMann* decision had been put forth by the agency then authorized to administer

---

[591] 29 CFR §1625.10(c) (1993).

[592] *Id.*

[593] *Id.* Such an interpretation, while not of binding legal force, typically will be accorded considerable deference by the courts. See **ch 2.**

[594] 434 US 192 (1977).

the ADEA, i.e., the Department of Labor.[595] A number of lower courts, however, have addressed the matter of employer discretion. Several courts of appeals, as well as district courts both within and outside these circuits, have held that an employer indeed will be deemed to have observed the terms of a plan, even if the plan only permits, and does not require, such retirement.[596] The proposition that the "observe the terms" requirement will be satisfied in contexts other than retirement when a plan only permits, rather than requires, a particular action or decision is supported by *United Independent Flight Officers, Inc v United Airlines, Inc.*[597]

Of course, even if an employer, labor organization, or employment agency is afforded discretion by a plan, that discretion must be exercised in a manner that does not violate the ADEA.[598]

---

595 The Department of Labor's position was noted by the Court in *McMann:*

> The Department [of Labor's] more recent position . . . is that pre-65 retirements "are unlawful unless the mandatory retirement provision . . . is required by the terms of the plan and is not optional. . . ." Having concluded . . . that the United plan calls for mandatory retirement at age 60, however, we need not consider this further.

Id 197 n4.

596 Equal Employment Opportunity Commn v United Air Lines, Inc, 755 F2d 94 (7th Cir 1985); Carpenter v Continental Trailways, 635 F2d 578 (6th Cir 1980), *cert denied,* 451 US 986 (1981); Smart v Porter Paint Co, 630 F2d 490 (7th Cir 1980); Renaudin v Gulf Oil Corp, 623 F2d 414 (5th Cir 1980); Karijolic v Illinois Bell Tel Co, 601 F2d 596 (7th Cir 1979), *cert denied,* 444 US 1045 (1980); Marshall v Hawaiian Tel Co, 575 F2d 763 (9th Cir 1978); Thompson v Chrysler Corp, 569 F2d 989 (6th Cir 1978); Zinger v Blanchette, 549 F2d 901 (3d Cir 1977), *cert denied,* 434 US 1008 (1978); Weidman v Western Elec Co, 527 F Supp 263 (MDNC 1981); Leece v Wisconsin Dept of Transp, 26 FEP Cas (BNA) 1117 (WD Wis 1981); Bisturis v Western Elec Co, 24 FEP Cas (BNA) 525 (ND Ill 1980), *affd without opinion,* 692 F2d 759 (1992); Martin v Western Elec Co, 20 FEP Cas (BNA) 1577 (ND Ill 1978), *affd without opinion,* 601 F2d 595 (7th Cir 1979); McKinley v Bendix Corp, 420 F Supp 1001 (WD Mo 1976); Dunlop v General Tel Co, 13 FEP Cas (BNA) 1210 (CD Cal 1976). *Contra* Langman v Western Elec Co, 488 F Supp 680 (SDNY 1980). Two district courts in the Sixth Circuit held to the contrary, but they are no longer good law in light of *Carpenter. See* Marshall v American Motors Corp, 475 F Supp 875 (ED Mich 1979); Hannan v Chrysler Motors Corp, 443 F Supp 802 (ED Mich 1978).

597 572 F Supp 1494, 1507 n10 (ND Ill 1983).

598 *See, e.g.,* Cowlishaw v Armstrong Rubber Co, 450 F Supp 148 (EDNY 1978).

Other Issues

Gabarczyk v Board of Education[599] concerned the claim of a teacher who, upon retirement, was ineligible to receive a retirement incentive benefit offered pursuant to the employer-union collective bargaining agreement because she was 61 years old, rather than the requisite 55. The plaintiff argued that the school district had failed to observe the terms of the retirement incentive plan because other teachers older than 55 in fact had received the benefit. However, while in fact there was one such teacher, this did not lead—according to the court—to the conclusion that the defendant had not observed the plan's terms. The court reasoned as follows:

> That defendants may have improperly granted the benefit to one teacher, while denying it to Gabarczyk and all others who were ineligible, does not suggest that defendants did not "observe" the terms of the . . . [collective bargaining] agreement, [which set forth the incentive program]. . . . Nor does it preclude summary judgment, for no reasonable jury could find, based on what was in all likelihood a single administrative error, that defendants did not observe the terms of the agreement.[600]

(In *Lynch v JP Stevens & Co, Inc,*[601] the court looked to *Gabarczyk,* which involved one person being treated advantageously due to an administrative error, and generalized far beyond that decision in asserting that "[a]n employee benefit plan does not fail to be bona . . . fide simply because an employer makes exceptions to the terms of the plan for certain employees."[602])

---

599 738 F Supp 118 (SDNY 1990).

600 *Id* 124.

601 758 F Supp 976 (DNJ 1991).

602 *Id* 1020. As to the bona fides of a plan, see **§5.31.**

§5.30 Defining Benefit and Determining the Bona Fides of a Benefit Plan Under the Old and New §4(f)(2)

Both in its originally enacted form[603] and as rewritten in 1990 by the Older Workers Benefit Protection Act (OWBPA),[604] §4(f)(2)[605] of the Age Discrimination in Employment Act (ADEA)[606] contained, and contains an affirmative defense that may be invoked by an employer, employment agency, or labor organization that claims to have observed the terms of a "bona fide employee benefit plan."

A *benefit plan* is a plan that provides benefits, often referred to as *fringe benefits,* in contrast to wages or salary.[607] "A nonfringe benefit immediately compensates an employee for current services—job performance—while a fringe benefit ordinarily rewards the employee for longevity."[608] In *Public Employees Retirement System v Betts*[609] the Court wrote: "[W]hatever the precise meaning of the phrase 'any . . . employee benefit plan such as a retirement, pension, or insurance plan,' [which was the language of §4(f)(2) prior to its being amended by the OWBPA,] . . . it is apparent that a disability retirement plan falls squarely within that category."[610] So, too, does severance pay.[611]

---

603 See **§5.23.**

604 Pub L No 101-433, 104 Stat 978, *as amended by* Pub L No 101-521, 104 Stat 2287 (1990).

605 29 USC §623(f)(2).

606 *Id* §§621-634.

607 *See* Equal Employment Opportunity Commn v Boeing Servs Intl, 968 F2d 549, 555 (5th Cir 1992): ("[T]he term 'employee benefit plan' simply means the fringe benefit aspects of the employment relationship"); *accord* 29 CFR §1625.10(b) (1993). An *employee-pay-all* benefit plan constitutes a term, condition, or privilege of employment, and in such a plan "benefits for older workers may be reduced only to the extent and according to the same principles as apply to other plans under section 4(f)(2)." *Id.*

608 Equal Employment Opportunity Commn v Boeing Servs Intl, 968 F2d 549, 556 (5th Cir 1992).

609 492 US 158 (1989).

610 *Id* 166. While the *Betts* Court's holdings were overturned by the OWBPA, see **§5.25,** *Betts* remained viable as to the matter of defining *bona fide employee*

Payments made by a university into a defined contribution pension plan for its employees were deemed as a matter of law to constitute fringe benefits by the court of appeals that decided *Bell v Purdue University.*[612] The Court of Appeals for the Ninth Circuit characterized a profit-sharing plan as a "hybrid" in *American Association of Retired Persons v Farmers Group, Inc.*[613] The plan functioned as a retirement plan, and so exhibited characteristics of a fringe benefit. But the plan also was designed to compensate employees for work actually performed, and so it constituted wages, as well, since it provided "immediate compensation once an employee ha[d] been with the company for five years."[614] (Ultimately, the court held that (1) the plan constituted an employee benefit plan and (2) that it violated the ADEA.)[615]

In *Finnegan v Trans World Airlines, Inc,*[616] the trial court—after first noting that the Supreme Court had yet to set forth definitively the scope of the "bona fide employee benefit plan" language—looked to a Supreme Court decision construing the Employee Retirement Income Security Act (ERISA)[617] for guidance:

> In *Massachusetts v Morash,* 490 U.S. 107 (1989), decided the same term [as *Betts,*] . . . the Court held that where vacation benefits are paid out of an employer's general assets rather than from a trust fund, those benefits constitute a "payroll practice," rather than an "employee benefit plan" as that

---

benefit plan; inasmuch as nothing in the OWBPA touched on redefining the phrase, or suggested that the *Betts* Court's observation regarding the phrase was undermined by the legislation.

611 Equal Employment Opportunity Commn v Westinghouse Elec Corp, 925 F2d 619 (3d Cir 1991). This decision rested on *Betts,* which remains valid for defining benefits and benefit plans.

612 975 F2d 422, 427-28 (7th Cir 1992).

613 943 F2d 996, 1003 (9th Cir 1991), *cert denied,* 112 S Ct 937 (1992).

614 *Id* 1003 (footnote omitted).

615 See **§5.36.**

616 767 F Supp 867 (ND Ill 1991), *affd,* 967 F2d 1161 (7th Cir 1992).

617 29 USC §1001 *et seq.*

> term is used in ERISA. . . . This court sees no reason for the term "employee benefit plan" to be construed differently in both ERISA and the ADEA.[618]

In contrast, in deciding *Equal Employment Opportunity Commission v Boeing Services International*[619] the Court of Appeals for the Fifth Circuit rejected reliance on *Massachusetts v Morash*[620] because it was a decision construing ERISA and there were policy concerns peculiar to that statute that were operative in fashioning the ruling. The court ruled that equivalent pay that was awarded to certain employees to replace lost paid holidays and lost contributions by the employer to a retirement plan constituted a fringe benefit. The court reasoned that payments to a retirement plan constituted a fringe benefit, and so payments made as a substitute should, as well. Insofar as the substitute pay to replace lost paid holidays was concerned, the court deemed this to be "more akin to health insurance—a fringe benefit ordinarily available on an immediate and equal basis to all employees—than vacation pay—compensation dependent on current job performance."[621] (The *Morash* Court had characterized vacation pay as a nonfringe benefit because it did not depend on any contingency beyond the control of the employee).[622]

Typically, courts have defined *bona fide* to mean that the plan exists and that it pays benefits.[623] There is some variation as to

---

[618] 767 F Supp at 873 n17.

[619] 968 F2d 549 (5th Cir 1992).

[620] 490 US 107 (1989).

[621] 968 F2d at 557.

[622] 490 US at 115.

[623] *See, e.g.,* Patterson v Independent Sch Dist No 709, 742 F2d 465 (8th Cir 1984); Carpenter v Continental Trailways, 635 F2d 578 (6th Cir 1980), *cert denied,* 451 US 986 (1981); Jensen v Gulf Oil Ref & Mktg Co, 623 F2d 406, 413 (5th Cir 1980); Marshall v Hawaiian Tel Co, 575 F2d 763 (9th Cir 1978); International Bhd of Elec Workers, Local 1439, AFL-CIO v McMahon, 585 F Supp 261, 264 (ED Mo 1984), *affd,* 761 F2d 1257 (8th Cir 1985); Allen v Colgate-Palmolive Co, 539 F Supp 57, 62 (SDNY 1981); McKinley v Bendix Corp, 420 F Supp 1001, 1003 (WD Mo 1976).

what, if anything, constitutes the requisite extent of benefits. Some courts have stated—without any particular emphasis—that the benefits must be substantial.[624] Other courts have imposed no such requirement; thus, for example, the court deciding *Smart v Porter Paint Co*[625] stated that a "plan is generally considered bona fide if it is 'genuine' or 'authentic,' *i.e.*, a plan which has truly existed and has actually paid benefits."[626]

The interpretation issued by the Equal Employment Opportunity Commission (EEOC) regarding the bona fides of a plan does not speak to the substantiality issue, although other requirements are set forth.[627] It provides that a "plan is considered 'bona fide' if its terms (including cessation of contributions or accruals in the case of retirement income plans) have been accurately described in writing to all employees and if it actually provides the benefits in accordance with the terms of the plan."[628] Furthermore, according to the EEOC, the plan must actually pro-

---

[624] *See* Gabarczyk v Board of Educ, 738 F Supp 118, 125 n2 (SDNY 1990); Equal Employment Opportunity Commn v Chrysler Corp, 729 F Supp 1002, 1008 n3 (SDNY 1990); Equal Employment Opportunity Commn v USX Corp, 50 Empl Prac Dec (CCH) ¶39,143, at p 58,249 (ED Pa 1989), *affd without opinion,* 909 F2d 1475 (3d Cir 1990); *see also* Bell v Purdue Univ, 975 F2d 422, 427 (7th Cir 1992). See also the decisions cited in note 623. Some courts have left the question of substantiality of benefits for resolution at trial. *See* Sikora v American Can Co, 622 F2d 1116, 1124 (3d Cir 1980); Raymond v Bendix Corp, 15 FEP Cas (BNA) 49 (ED Mich 1977).

[625] 630 F2d 490 (7th Cir 1980).

[626] *Id* 494; *accord* Crosland v Charlotte Eye, Ear & Throat Hosp, 686 F2d 208, 212 n3 (4th Cir 1982); United Indep Flight Officers, Inc v United Air Lines, Inc, 572 F Supp 1494, 1507 n10 (ND Ill 1983), *affd on other grounds,* 756 F2d 1274 (7th Cir 1985); Germann v Levy, 553 F Supp 700 (ND Ill 1982); Weidman v Western Elec Co, Inc, 527 F Supp 263, 268 (MDNC 1981). In United Air Lines, Inc v McMann, 434 US 192 (1977), the Court accepted the employee's concession that the plan at issue was bona fide "in the sense that it exists and pays benefits." *Id* 194. Citing this language, the court deciding Alford v City of Lubbock, 664 F2d 1263 (5th Cir), *cert denied,* 456 US 975 (1982), held a plan to be bona fide even though it paid no benefits at all to some (but not all) employees.

[627] 29 CFR §1625.10(b) (1993).

[628] *Id.*

vide the described benefits; otherwise, the notification regarding its provisions would be misleading. Prompt notification of changes in a plan is required.[629]

In one early ruling a court asserted a position somewhat at odds with that of the EEOC. In *Brennan v Taft Broadcasting Co*[630] the plaintiff argued that the plan at issue was not bona fide because adequate information regarding it had not been provided, the employee only having seen a summary, rather than a complete, version of the plan. (Such disclosure of course is required by the EEOC interpretation.) The court rejected the appellant's argument; it was sufficient that the defendant had "a plan, that it truly existed, and that . . . [the employee] was paid approximately $15,000 as a result of it."[631]

It does not necessarily follow that because a plan is bona fide it cannot, by definition, be violative of the ADEA.[632] For example, the pension plan at issue in *Snair v City of Clearwater*[633] existed, and it paid benefits. The legal flaw was that new hires over age 45 were excluded from eligibility for participation in the plan.[634]

§5.31 —Whether a Benefit Constitutes a Bona Fide Plan or Part of a Such Plan

Sometimes an effort to invoke the bona fide employee benefit plan exception set forth in §4(f)(2)[635] of the Age Discrimination in Employment Act (ADEA)[636] will fail because the benefit involved is not deemed to constitute, for the purposes of the

---

629 *Id.*

630 500 F2d 212 (5th Cir 1974).

631 *Id* 217.

632 *See* Equal Employment Opportunity Commn v Home Ins Co, 672 F2d 252, 260 (2d Cir 1982); Equal Employment Opportunity Commn v Home Ins Co, 553 F Supp 704 (SDNY 1982).

633 817 F Supp 108 (MD Fla 1993).

634 As to age-based exclusions from pension plans generally, see **§5.35.**

635 29 USC §623(f)(2).

636 *Id* §§621-634.

ADEA, a bona fide plan or a part of such a plan. The case law provides a number of examples of this scenario.

The Cost-Justification Factor

Equal Employment Opportunity Commission v Westinghouse Electric Corp[637] involved in the denial of layoff income and benefits to individuals who had been terminated when the plant in which they worked closed and who, because they were age 55 and older, were eligible, by the terms of their benefits plan, for early retirement. The contested layoff income and benefits were available, in contrast, to employees who had two or more years of service and who were ineligible for early retirement. Westinghouse argued that the layoff income and benefits plan qualified as a bona fide employee benefits plan, and thus the age-based differential treatment of workers was legal by virtue of §4(f)(2). The court rejected the argument. "The thread common to retirement, insurance and pension plans [, all of which qualify under the §4(f)(2) exception,] is the age-related cost factor."[638] Here, the plan at issue did not reflect this factor.[639] Rather, eligibility to receive benefits was based solely on an employee's length of service, i.e., at least two years, and the occurrence of a layoff.

The court deciding *Cipriano v Board of Education*[640] held that a plan offering retirement incentives to certain teachers, i.e., those between the ages of 55 and 60, with 20 or more years of experience, constituted a bona fide benefit plan. The argument that the plan did not reflect cost considerations—an argument that had been made successfully by the plaintiff in *Westinghouse*—failed here. Without holding that plans can be bona fide only if they do indeed reflect such considerations, the *Cipriano* court

---

637 725 F2d 211 (3d Cir 1983), *cert denied,* 469 US 820 (1984).

638 *Id* 224. *Westinghouse* was severely criticized in Comment, *Interpreting Section 4(f)(2) of the ADEA: Does Anyone Have a "Plan"?,* 135 U Pa L Rev 1055 (1987). Among other flaws, the author pointed to the fact that "many [legitimate] kinds of retirement and insurance plans do not have age-related costs." *Id* 1073.

639 725 F2d at 224.

640 785 F2d 51 (2d Cir 1986).

reasoned that cost factors in any event often are involved in voluntary retirement incentive plans, since by inducing older, higher-paid employees to retire, these plans achieve cost savings for employers.

While the *Cipriano* court skirted the question of whether a plan by definition could not be bona fide if it did not reflect cost considerations, in an early ADEA ruling, *Brennan v Taft Broadcasting Co,*[641] the Court of Appeals for the Fifth Circuit firmly rejected the notion that a plan could be bona fide only if it reflected cost factors. The court deciding *Gabarczyk v Board of Education*[642] also took the position that a plan did not have to be cost justified to be bona fide.

Brennan and *Gabarczyk* were invalidated by enactment of the Older Workers Benefit Protection Act (OWBPA)[643] in 1990. The OWBPA amended the employee benefit plan defense provision so as to expressly provide in §4(f)(2)(B)(i),[644] which addresses plans other than voluntary retirement incentive plans, that the §4(f)(2) defense only can be invoked successfully if the differential in treatment embodied in the plan at issue is cost justified, i.e., it satisfies the *equal benefit or equal cost* principle.[645] Inasmuch as *Public Employees Retirement System v Betts*[646] continued to apply to claims arising prior to the effective date of the OWBPA,[647] reasoning such as that employed in *Brennan* and *Gabarczyk* had continuing viability even after the statutory changes.

Cipriano was not undermined by the OWBPA insofar as the decision might be read as supporting the proposition that a plan can be bona fide even if the differentiations it imposes are not

---

641 500 F2d 212 (5th Cir 1974).

642 738 F Supp 118 (SDNY 1990).

643 Pub L No 101-433, 104 Stat 978, *as amended by* Pub L No 101-521, 104 Stat 2287 (1990).

644 29 USC §623(f)(2)(B)(i).

645 See **§§5.32-.33.**

646 492 US 158 (1989).

647 See **§5.24.**

cost justified. This is because §4(f)(2)(B)(ii)[648] of the OWBPA-amended ADEA speaks to voluntary retirement incentive plans, such as that at issue in *Cipriano,* and rather than embracing the cost-justification requirement, this subsection only requires that such plans "be consistent with the relevant purpose, or purposes, of the ADEA." This language leaves room for the survival of plans that do not satisfy the *equal benefit or equal cost* principle.

Other Factors

In deciding *Equal Employment Opportunity Commission v Westinghouse Electric Corp* the court, as discussed earlier, rejected the defendant's effort to invoke the §4(f)(2) defense because it was of the view that the plan at issue was not bona fide since it did not reflect cost factors. The *Westinghouse* court also rejected the argument that because the layoff income and benefits plan at issue was tied to Westinghouse's pension plan, it qualified under the ADEA exception. "[I]t [still] is more analogous to a 'fringe benefit' than to the types of employee benefit plans covered under 4(f)(2)."[649] In brief, the layoff income and benefits plan was "functionally independent" of a bona fide plan.[650]

---

648 29 USC §623(f)(2)(B)(ii).

649 725 F2d at 225.

650 *Id; see also* Equal Employment Opportunity Commn v Westinghouse Elec Corp, 869 F2d 696, 707 (3d Cir), *vacated,* 493 US 801 (1989).

A later panel of the Court of Appeals for the Third Circuit addressed the same severance plan in light of Public Employees Retirement Sys v Betts, 492 US 158 (1989)—a decision whose major holdings have since been overturned by the OWBPA. See **§5.25.** The later *Westinghouse* court rendered a decision that in effect overturned the earlier ruling. Equal Employment Opportunity Commn v Westinghouse Elec Corp, 907 F2d 1354 (3d Cir), *vacated without opinion,* 917 F2d 124 (3d Cir 1990). The latter *Westinghouse* court noted that the *Betts* Court had stated "that the inclusion of the terms 'retirement, pension, or insurance' suggests an enumeration rather than an exclusive listing of plans that qualify for the [§4(f)(2)] exemption." *Id* 1360 (quoting *Betts,* 492 US at 173). The *Westinghouse* court went on to reason that severance plans fit within the exemption:

> Unlike wages and salaries, which are contingent on job performance, severance pay is linked to an employee's length of service and the occurrence of a layoff. . . . In light of the broad definition of 'bona fide employee benefit plan' endorsed by the Court in *Betts,* we must conclude

The court deciding *Alford v City of Lubbock*[651] held that the state retirement plan involved in the case was bona fide, but it further held that the city's policy of denying accrued sick leave pay to city employees whose retirement was covered by the state retirement plan was not part of a bona fide employee benefit plan. In response to the argument that the sick leave payment policy was tied to length of service, the court said: "[The city] may not deny an entire class of older employees . . . any participation in a fringe benefit unrelated to a bona fide 'retirement, pension, or insurance' plan simply by artificially trying to tie the benefit to such a plan."[652]

Similarly, in *Equal Employment Opportunity Commission v Borden's, Inc,*[653] the court held that a severance pay policy that allegedly discriminated against older workers was not an integral part of the employer's retirement plan, and thus the employer could not successfully invoke the ADEA exception.[654] The contrary posi-

---

> that the plans may qualify for the §4(f)(2) exemption so long as they are not intended as a subterfuge to avoid the purpose of ADEA.

907 F2d at 1360; *accord* Kolman v Oscar Mayer Foods Corp, 53 FEP Cas (BNA) 1256, 1261-62 (ED Pa 1990). (The effective overturning of *Betts* turned on other issues, and so the *Betts* Court's inclusion of severance plans within the reach of §4(f)(2) would seem to remain a viable interpretation. However, the foregoing language from *Westinghouse* is no longer valid. At the time the 1990 *Westinghouse* decision was rendered, the concept of subterfuge was at the core of the §4(f)(2) exception. See **§§5.23, 5.34-.35.** The OWBPA rewrote §4(f)(2) so as to jettison this concept. See **§5.26.** Thus, a plan (other than a voluntary retirement incentive plan) will not qualify under the OWBPA unless it is cost justified, as discussed *supra* in this section).

651 664 F2d 1263 (5th Cir), *cert denied,* 456 US 975 (1982).

652 *Id* 1272 n12.

653 724 F2d 1390 (9th Cir 1984).

654 *Accord* Equal Employment Opportunity Commn v Westinghouse Elec Corp, 869 F2d 696, 707 (3d Cir), *vacated,* 493 US 801 (1989); Equal Employment Opportunity Commn v USX Corp, 50 Empl Prac Dec (CCH) ¶39,143 (ED Pa), *affd without opinion,* 909 F2d 1475 (3d Cir 1990) (relying on the subsequently vacated *Westinghouse* ruling); Equal Employment Opportunity Commn v Babcock & Wilcox, 43 FEP Cas (BNA) 736 (EDNC 1987); Equal Employment Opportunity Commn v Great Atl & Pac Tea Co, 618 F Supp 115 (ND Ohio 1985); Equal Employment Opportunity Commn v Curtiss-Wright Corp, 40 FEP Cas (BNA) 666 (DNJ 1982); *see also* Betts v Hamilton County

tion was taken, however, in *Equal Employment Opportunity Commission v Chrysler Corp.*[655] Likewise, in *Equal Employment Opportunity Commission v Firestone Tire & Rubber Co*[656] a severance award was deemed to be an integral part of a defendant's pension plan.[657]

In *Equal Employment Opportunity Commission v Fox-Point Bayside School District*[658] the court rejected the plaintiff's argument regarding the allegedly inadequate bona fides of a plan. The plan, which was the product of collective bargaining, was subject to the teacher retirement system created by state statute. The state law in turn clearly contemplated that certain aspects of the system were to be subject to collective bargaining. Thus, the state scheme and the school district/union agreement were significantly intertwined. Accordingly, the court rejected the argument that because the mandatory retirement provision of which the plaintiff complained, and which was authorized by the state statute, was separate from the collective bargaining agreement, it followed that §4(f)(2)—which, it was argued, applied to such agreements, but not to state statutes—was inapplicable. The court reasoned that there was no requirement that an employee benefit plan, in order to fit within §4(f)(2), had to be the product of collective bargaining. In any event, here the mandatory retirement requirement was contained in the collective bargaining agreement, as well as in the statutory scheme.

In *Karlen v City Colleges of Chicago*[659] retirees were entitled to lump-sum payments representing their unused accumulated leave, with the amount of the payment declining as the age of the individual retiree rose. The court held that these payments were a valid part of a bona fide retirement plan, rather than

---

Bd of Mental Retardation, 631 F Supp 1198 (SD Ohio 1986), *affd,* 848 F2d 692 (6th Cir 1988), *revd,* 492 US 158 (1989).

655 729 F Supp 1002 (SDNY 1990).

656 650 F Supp 1561 (WD Tenn 1987).

657 *Accord* Abenante v Fulflex, Inc, 701 F Supp 296 (DRI 1988).

658 772 F2d 1294 (7th Cir 1985).

659 No 84 C 2925 (ND Ill Dec 12, 1986) (unreported), *revd on other grounds,* 837 F2d 314 (7th Cir), *cert denied,* 486 US 1044 (1988).

being an unrelated fringe benefit. The court reasoned that such payments were a " 'wage substitute,' "[660] and explained as follows:

> The Board, in essence, gives its faculty the option of continuing to work or foregoing that entitlement. Those who give up years that they might have worked are compensated by means of the lump sum payments. This . . . [was] entirely different from the schemes in *Westinghouse* and *Borden's,* in which "no relationship exist[ed] between the value of the job given up and the value of the benefits."[661]

---

[660] Slip op at 7.

[661] *Id* (quoting Britt v EI duPont deNemours & Co, 768 F2d 593, 595 (4th Cir 1985)). The *Karlen* court held that a retirement incentive constitutes a bona fide plan for the purposes of §4(f)(2). So, too, did the court deciding Cipriano v Board of Educ, 785 F2d 51 (2d Cir 1986), as noted in the text. Arguably, a Supreme Court ruling handed down subsequent to both of these decisions called them into question. In Fort Halifax Packing Co v Coyne, 482 US 1 (1987), the Court addressed the intersection of a Maine statute dealing with severance pay and the Employee Retirement Income Security Act of 1974 (ERISA), 29 USC §1001 *et seq.* The state law required a one-time severance payment and the question was whether this statute was preempted by ERISA. In concluding that it was not, the Court ruled that the one-time payment did not constitute an employee benefit plan, and so did not fit within the language of the ERISA preemption provision, which speaks just to "employee benefit plan[s]." 29 USC §1144(a). Rather, the severance payment merely constituted an employee benefit. The court reasoned as follows:

> The requirement of a one-time, lump-sum payment triggered by a single event requires no administrative scheme whatsoever to meet the employer's obligation. The employer assumes no responsibility to pay benefits on a regular basis, and thus faces no periodic demands on its assets that create a need for financial coordination and control. Rather, the employer's obligation is predicated on the occurrence of a single contingency that may never materialize. . . . To do little more than write a check [if a severance payment is made at some point] hardly constitutes the operation of a benefit plan.

482 US at 12.

Inasmuch as §4(f)(2) of the ADEA speaks, as does ERISA, to employee benefit plans, *Fort Halifax* would seem to be of analogical relevance. Moreover, when Congress amended the ADEA in 1986, see **§5.41,** it also amended ERISA; in both instances the aim was to outlaw discriminatory aspects of pension and retirement plans. In adopting identical amendatory language regarding the ADEA and ERISA, Congress expressly stated that the definition of *employee benefit plan* contained in §3 of ERISA, 29 USC §1003(3), should apply to the

In *Lynch v JP Stevens & Co, Inc*[662] the court asserted that "[a]n employee benefit plan does not fail to be bona fide . . . simply because an employer makes exceptions to the terms of the plan for certain employees."[663]

§5.32 The Equal Benefit or Equal Cost Principle and the Old and New §4(f)(2)

Section 4(f)(2)[664] of the Age Discrimination in Employment Act (ADEA)[665] explicitly incorporates the *equal benefit or equal cost* principle that is articulated and elucidated in an interpretation—29 CFR §1625.10[666]—issued by the ADEA enforcement agency, the Equal Employment Opportunity Commission (EEOC). This interpretation originally was issued by the EEOC to explain and detail the contours of §4(f)(2) as that statutory provision read prior to its being rewritten by the Older Workers

---

ADEA. Omnibus Budget Reconciliation Act of 1986 (OBRA), Pub L No 99-509, §9201, 100 Stat 1874, 1975.

Notwithstanding the foregoing, in Cipriano v Board of Educ, 700 F Supp 1199, 1204-05 (WDNY 1988), *Fort Halifax* was held not to dispute the accuracy of deeming the early retirement incentive plan at issue to be a bona fide plan for the purpose of §4(f)(2). *Accord* Gabarczyk v Board of Educ, 738 F Supp 118, 124 (SDNY 1990). Additionally, *Fort Halifax* was rejected outright as being irrelevant in Equal Employment Opportunity Commn v Chrysler Corp, 729 F Supp 1002 (SDNY 1990).

(The earlier decisions discussed in the text—Equal Employment Opportunity Commn v Westinghouse Elec Corp, 725 F2d 211 (3d Cir 1983), *cert denied*, 469 US 820 (1984); Alford v City of Lubbock, 664 F2d 1263 (5th Cir), *cert denied*, 456 US 975 (1982); and Equal Employment Opportunity Commn v Borden's, Inc, 724 F2d 1390 (9th Cir 1984)—are consistent with *Fort Halifax*. In each of these cases there was a one-time payment of some sort, and in each instance the court held—albeit for reasons other than that articulated in *Fort Halifax*—that the payment did not constitute a part of a bona fide plan.)

662 758 F Supp 976 (DNJ 1991).

663 *Id* 1020.

664 29 USC §623(f)(2).

665 *Id* §§621-634.

666 29 CFR §1625.10 (1993).

Benefit Protection Act (OWBPA)[667] in 1990. At that time §4(f)(2) focused on the question of *subterfuge.*[668] The EEOC took the position that, "[i]n general, a plan or plan provision which . . . [prescribed] lower benefits for older employees on account of age . . . [was] not a 'subterfuge' within the meaning of section 4(f)(2), provided that the lower level of benefits . . . [was] justified by age-related cost considerations."[669] While the term *subterfuge* was jettisoned by the OWBPA in the rewritten version of §4(f)(2), the text of which is set out below, the *equal benefit or equal cost* principle not only remained, but was given statutory imprimatur by virtue of the incorporation of 29 CFR §1625.10. The EEOC has succinctly summarized this principle:

> A benefit plan will be considered in compliance with the statute where the actual amount of payment made, or cost incurred, in behalf of an older worker is equal to that made or incurred in behalf of a younger worker, even though the older worker may thereby receive a lesser amount of benefits or insurance coverage.[670]

Thus, for example, it is the EEOC's position that §4(f)(2) does "not apply . . . to paid vacations and uninsured sick leave, since reductions in these benefits would not be justified by significant cost considerations," inasmuch as the costs of vacation and sick leave do not vary with an employee's age.[671]

The receipt of lesser benefits by an older worker, as compared to those received by his or her younger fellow workers, can be justified as fitting within §4(f)(2)—thereby relieving the employer of liability—only if the employer spends an equal, or near-equal amount, on all of its employees, regardless of age. "[B]enefit levels for older workers can be reduced," according

---

667 Pub L No 101-433, 104 Stat 978, *as amended by* Pub L No 101-521, 104 Stat 2287 (1990).

668 See **§§5.23, 5.34-.35.**

669 29 CFR §1625.10(d) (1990).

670 *Id* §1625.10(a)(1) (1993).

671 *Id; accord* Senate Comm on Labor & Human Resources, The Older Workers Benefit Protection Act, S Rep No 263, 101st Cong, 2d Sess 18 (1990).

to the EEOC, "to the extent necessary to achieve approximate equivalency in cost of older and younger workers."[672]

The animating force generating the *equal benefit or equal cost* principle when it was first devised was the perception that benefits for older workers could be more expensive to purchase than would be benefits for younger workers.[673] For example, a disability plan that guarantees a monthly payment of $2,000 for any disabled employee would cost more to secure for a 55-year-old than for a 30-year-old, since the experience of insurers supports the conclusion that there is a greater risk of a claim being made by the former individual than by the latter, inasmuch as older workers are more likely to suffer disabling illnesses. Given this scenario (which may not necessarily be, or have been, empirically verifiable, but which is simply used here for the purpose of illustration), it was feared that an employer would be disinclined to hire the older job applicant, since the cost attributable to his or her employment would be greater than that associated with a younger employee. The answer was to allow the employer to satisfy the antidiscrimination demand of the ADEA by spending an equal amount, or a near-equal amount, on younger and older workers, even if that amount did not purchase the same level of benefits for both. Thereby, while there would not be equality in terms of benefits per se, at least there would be equality in terms of expenditures.

Public Employees Retirement System v Betts[674] spurned the *equal benefit or equal cost* principle. "[T]he requirement that employers show a cost-based justification for age-related reductions in benefits appears nowhere in the statute itself," the Court observed.[675] The OWBPA, however, resurrected the principle, insofar as bona fide employee benefit plans that are not voluntary retirement incentive plans are concerned. Section 4(f)(2) of the ADEA, as rewritten by the OWBPA, provides in relevant part as follows:

---

672 29 CFR §1625.10(a)(1) (1993).

673 See **§5.23.**

674 492 US 158 (1989).

675 *Id* 170.

> It shall not be unlawful . . .
> (B) to observe the terms of a bona fide employee benefit plan—
> (i) where, for each benefit or benefit package, the actual amount of payment made or incurred on behalf of an older worker is no less than that made or incurred on behalf of a younger worker, as permissible under Section 1625.10, title 29, Code of Federal Regulations (as in effect on June 22, 1989); or
> (ii) that is a voluntary early retirement incentive plan consistent with the relevant purpose or purposes of this Act[.]

§5.33 —The Equal Benefit or Equal Cost Principle: The EEOC Interpretation

An interpretation issued by the Equal Employment Opportunity Commission (EEOC), i.e., 29 CFR §1625.10,[676] sets forth and details the *equal cost or equal benefit* principle. This interpretation was explicitly incorporated into §4(f)(2)[677] of the Age Discrimination in Employment Act (ADEA)[678] by virtue of an amendment made to the ADEA by the Older Workers Benefit Protection Act (OWBPA)[679] in 1990.

The rewriting of §4(f)(2) by the OWBPA removed the term *subterfuge,* which until that change had been central to the concept of wrongdoing.[680] As of June 15, 1994, the EEOC had not yet issued a revision of §1625.10 reflecting this statutory change. However, the basis for harmonizing the notion of subterfuge, which is retained in the interpretation, and the new statutory language, was articulated in the Senate committee report on the bill which, in modified form, ultimately was enacted as the OWBPA. It was asserted in the report that "because the term

---

676 29 CFR §1625.10 (1993).

677 29 USC §623(f)(2).

678 *Id* §§621-634.

679 Pub L No 101-433, 104 Stat 978, *as amended by* Pub L No 101-521, 104 Stat 2287 (1990).

680 See **§§5.23, 5.34-.35.**

'subterfuge' has . . . been eliminated . . . from section 4(f)(2), discussion of the term . . . in the EEOC regulation is superfluous except as it is understood to mean the 'equal benefit or equal cost' principle."[681] The Senate report further explained that the *equal benefit or equal cost* principle applies "to governmental as well as private employee benefit plans,"[682] a proposition that had already been established by decisions rendered prior to its express statutory embrace in the amended ADEA.[683]

The EEOC interpretation is based on certain premises. For one, a plan will not be violative of the ADEA just because older workers are provided with lesser benefits than are younger workers.[684] Second, generally (but not always), as long as an employer expends the same, or nearly the same, amount on an older worker as it does on a younger worker, the employer will be acting legally—even if that expenditure for the older worker buys less, by way of benefits, than the same amount purchases for a younger worker.[685] Third, "[i]n general, a plan or plan provision which prescribes lower benefits for older employees on account of age is not a 'subterfuge' within the meaning of section 4(f)(2),

---

[681] Senate Comm on Labor & Human Resources, The Older Workers Benefit Protection Act, S Rep No 263, 101st Cong, 2d Sess 18 (1990) [hereinafter Senate Report]. It was further explained in the Senate report as follows:

> In clarifying section 4(f)(2), the Committee has purposely eliminated the word "subterfuge" from the new section. In so doing, the Committee intends to make clear that under this bill, and subject to the exceptions that are discussed below, the *only* justification for age discrimination in an employee benefit is the increased cost in providing the particular benefit to older individuals.

Id. (While this report addressed a version of the bill that was later changed, see **§5.25**, the foregoing explanation still has validity since, in fact, the final version of the legislation did delete the term *subterfuge.*)

[682] *Id.*

[683] *See, e.g.*, Equal Employment Opportunity Commn v Mt Lebanon, 842 F2d 1480, 1489 (3d Cir 1988).

[684] 29 CFR §1625.10(a)(1) (1993).

[685] *Id.*

provided that the lower level of benefits is justified by age-related cost considerations."[686]

The EEOC interpretation sets out with considerable specificity certain requirements that must be satisfied. As a general matter, cost data that are relied upon to justify the provision of lower benefits to older workers on account of age must "be valid and reasonable."[687] Data will be deemed to satisfy this standard when the employer has "cost data which show the actual cost of providing the particular benefit (or benefits) in question over a representative period of years."[688] If reliable cost information, either for the employer's own employees or for a larger group of similarly situated employees, is unavailable, "reasonable projections made from existing cost data" that are valid and reasonable are acceptable.[689]

Cost comparisons and adjustments must be made either on a benefit-by-benefit[690] or on a benefit package basis.[691] As to adjustments made on a benefit-by-benefit basis, they must "be made in the amount or level of a specific form of benefit for a specific event or contingency."[692] An example is provided in the EEOC interpretation: "[H]igher group term life insurance costs for older workers would justify a corresponding reduction in the amount of group term life insurance coverage for older workers,

---

686 *Id* §1625.10(d). Citing the just-quoted language in a pre-OWBPA ruling, the court deciding Karlen v City Colleges of Chicago, 837 F2d 314 (7th Cir), *cert denied,* 486 US 1044 (1988), stated: "[W]here . . . the employer uses age—not cost, or years of service, or salary—as the basis for varying retirement benefits, he had better be able to prove a close correlation between age and cost if he wants to shelter in the safe harbor of section 4(f)(2)." *Id* 319.

687 29 CFR §1625.10(d)(1) (1993).

688 *Id.* "An employer may rely on cost data for its own employees over such a period, or on cost data for a larger group of similarly situated employees." *Id.* If, however, an employer's costs are significantly different from those experienced for that group of similarly situated employees, the employer may not rely on the cost data regarding those employees "where such reliance would result in significantly lower benefits for its own older employees." *Id.*

689 *Id.*

690 As to the application of the benefit-by-benefit approach to plans involving life insurance and long-term disability, see **§§5.43** and **5.48** respectively.

691 29 CFR §1625.10(d)(2) (1993).

692 *Id* §1625.10(d)(2)(i).

on the basis of age."[693] While the benefit-by-benefit approach allows for cost-based reductions in benefits, it does not allow for the substitution of one form of benefit for another, even if both forms of benefit address the same contingency, such as death.[694]

Under the benefit package approach, an employer can aggregate cost comparisons and adjustments.

> This approach is generally recognized as providing greater flexibility to employers and has been useful when applied to "cafeteria" style benefit programs, *i.e.*, those in which the employer designates a specified dollar amount which can be used by each eligible employee to purchase the benefits most attractive to each individual.[695]

This approach, however, cannot be "used to reduce the cost to the employer or the favorability to the employees of overall employee benefits for older employees."[696] Nor may the benefit package approach be used for retirement or pension plans.[697] Under a benefit package approach, "[n]o employees may be deprived because of age of one benefit without an offsetting benefit being made available to them."[698]

The EEOC interpretation addresses the data necessary to justify benefit reductions under a benefit package approach:

> [E]mployers must be able to show that deviations from a benefit-by-benefit approach do not result in lesser cost to

---

693 *Id.* The Senate report on the bill that in modified form was enacted as the OWBPA purported to explain this further: "In other words, if a $100 contribution purchases $50,000 of coverage for an employee age 35 and only $25,000 for an employee age 60, that difference in coverage is lawful under these amendments, as it was under prior law." Senate Report, *supra,* note 681, at 19. As to application of the benefit-by-benefit approach to life insurance, see **§5.43.**

694 29 CFR §1625.10(d)(2)(i) (1993).

695 Senate Report, *supra* note 670, at 19.

696 29 CFR §1625.10(d)(2)(ii) (1993).

697 *Id* §1625.10(f)(2)(i).

698 *Id* §1625.10(f)(2)(iv).

> them or less favorable benefits to their employees. A general example consistent with these limitations may be given. Assume two employee benefit plans, providing Benefit "A" and Benefit "B." Both plans fall within section 4(f)(2), and neither is a retirement or pension plan subject to special rules. Both benefits are available to all employees. Age-based cost increases would justify a 10% decrease in both benefits on a benefit-by-benefit basis. The affected employees would, however, find it more favorable—that is, more consistent with meeting their needs—for no reduction to be made in Benefit "A" and a greater reduction to be made in Benefit "B." This "trade-off" would not result in a reduction in health benefits. The "trade-off" may therefore be made. The details of the "trade-off" depend on data on the relative cost to the employer of the two benefits. If the data show that Benefit "A" and Benefit "B" cost the same, Benefit "B" may be reduced up to 20% if Benefit "A" is unreduced. If the data show that Benefit "A" costs only half as much as Benefit "B", however, Benefit "B" may be reduced up to only 15% if Benefit "A" is unreduced, since a greater reduction in Benefit "B" would result in an impermissible reduction in total benefit costs.[699]

The cost comparisons and adjustments that legitimately can be made under §4(f)(2) can be done on the basis of age brackets of up to five years.[700] Thus, a particular benefit may be reduced for employees of any age within the protected group by an amount no greater than that which could be justified by the additional cost to provide them with the same level of the benefit

---

699 *Id* §1625.10(f)(2)(v).

700 *Id* §1625.10(d)(3). This process is known as *age banding.* It was specifically endorsed by the Senate Committee on Labor and Human Resources in its report addressing the bill that in modified form was enacted as the OWBPA. Senate Report, *supra* note 681, at 19.

as younger employees within a specified five-year age group immediately preceding theirs.[701]

The EEOC interpretation also addresses the issue of employee contributions. An older employee can be required as a condition of employment to make greater contributions in support of a benefit plan than a younger employee.[702] As a condition of participation in a voluntary plan, an older employee can be required to make greater contributions than a younger employee, but only if the older employee is "not thereby required to bear a greater proportion of the total premium cost (employer-paid and employee-paid) than the younger employee."[703] This prescription applies to three different contribution arrangements:

—in employee-pay-all plans older employees can be required to contribute up to the full premium cost;[704]

—in noncontributory, i.e., employer-pay-all plans, older workers cannot be required to make contributions if younger workers are not required to do so;[705]

—in contributory plans, i.e., plans in which employers and participants share premium costs, the "required contribution of participants may increase with age so long as

---

701 29 CFR §1625.10(d)(3) (1993).

For example, where an employer chooses to provide unreduced group term life insurance benefits until age 60, benefits for employees who are between 60 and 65 years of age may be reduced only to the extent necessary to achieve approximate equivalency in costs with employees who are 55 to 60 years old. Similarly, any reductions in benefit levels for 65 to 70 year old employees cannot exceed an amount which is proportional to the additional costs for their coverage over 60 to 65 year old employees.

Id.

702 *Id* §1625.10(d)(4)(i).

703 *Id* §1625.10(d)(4)(ii).

704 *Id* §1625.10(d)(4)(ii)(A).

705 *Id* §1625.10(d)(4)(ii)(B).

> the *proportion* of the total premium required to be paid by the participants does not increase with age."[706]

An older employee can be given the option to make additional contributions so as to achieve the same level of benefits as are available to younger employees (assuming that the differential that the older employee is seeking to ameliorate is otherwise legitimate under §4(f)(2)).[707]

§5.34 The Old §4(f)(2)'s Focus on Subrterfuge Prior to *Betts*

Prior to being rewritten by the Older Workers Benefit Protection Act (OWBPA)[708] in 1990, §4(f)(2)[709] of the Age Discrimination in Employment Act (ADEA)[710] had as its central focus the question of *subterfuge.* A practice or decision that ordinarily would violate the ADEA could only be justified as being in pursuance of a bona fide employee benefit plan if the plan was "not a subterfuge to evade the purposes of the" ADEA.[711] The §4(f)(2) provision was deemed to be an affirmative defense, to be proven by the entity invoking it, i.e., an employer, employment agency, or labor organization.[712]

Public Employees Retirement System v Betts[713] deprived §4(f)(2) of virtually all of its substantive rigor.[714] As a consequence, pre-*Betts* subterfuge case law was largely rendered irrelevant. While *Betts* was in turn overridden by the OWBPA, the 1990 Act, in rewriting §4(f)(2), discarded the term *subterfuge.* Instead, the amended provision condemns plans (other than voluntary retirement

---

706 *Id* §1625.10(d)(4)(ii)(C).

707 *Id* §1625.10(d)(4)(iii).

708 Pub L No 101-433, 104 Stat 978, *as amended by* Pub L No 101-521, 104 Stat 2287 (1990).

709 29 USC §623(f)(2) (pre-1990 amendment).

710 *Id* §§621-634.

711 §4(f)(2), 29 USC §623(f)(2) (pre-1990 amendment).

712 See **§5.23.**

713 492 US 158 (1989).

714 See **§5.24.**

incentive plans) that cannot be cost justified in terms of an *equal benefit or equal cost* principle.[715] However, since the *subterfuge* concept had been equated by a number of the pre-*Betts,* pre-OWBPA courts with this same cost-justification requirement, the *subterfuge* case law—consigned for a time to legal desuetude by *Betts*—was in some measure resurrected by the OWBPA-amended ADEA.

Moreover, the subterfuge case law retains some relevance for §4(f)(2)(B)(ii),[716] which speaks to voluntary retirement incentive plans. For while this particular subsection of §4(f)(2) does not embrace a cost-justification requirement as a predicate to such plans being successfully relied upon as affirmative defenses to charges of discrimination, the new OWBPA-crafted provision does require that such plans must be "consistent with the relevant purpose, or purposes, of" the ADEA. This broad language thus also leaves room for the continuing relevance of pre-*Betts* rulings that endorsed the *equal benefit or equal cost* principle, as well as decisions that addressed the legitimacy of plans in terms of other considerations.[717]

In *United Air Lines, Inc v McMann*[718] the Court "reject[ed] any *per se* rule requiring an employer to show an economic or business purpose in order to satisfy the subterfuge language of the Act."[719] This could not be read as meaning that the employer

---

715 See **§5.32**.

716 29 USC §623(f)(2)(B)(ii).

717 A pre-*Betts* ruling that addressed a nonretirement plan, and that further did not utilize cost-justification analysis, presumably is not very useful in terms of legal precedent since enactment of the OWBPA, inasmuch as such a plan (i.e. a non-retirement plan) can be relied upon by employers, employment agencies, labor organizations only if it can be justified, as pointed out *supra,* in terms of the *equal benefit or equal cost* principle. Nonetheless, because voluntary retirement incentive plans do not rise or fall based on cost-justification analysis, such a pre-*Betts* ruling could have some relevance for assessing such plans even after enactment of the OWBPA. Moreover, the fact that such a pre-*Betts* decision might have addressed a plan involving something other than retirement need not necessarily preclude the decision's affording some guidance.

718 434 US 192 (1977).

719 *Id* 203.

did not need to show any purpose,[720] but only that the employer was not confined to purposes of an economic or business nature. At the same time, however, the employer certainly was within its rights in offering a business or economic purpose, which typically it would do. Thus, for example, the court deciding *Crosland v Charlotte Eye, Ear & Throat Hospital*[721] held that a defendant could successfully invoke the defense "by proving that the [plan] provision [in question] was motivated by a legitimate business or economic purpose which, objectively assessed, reasonably justified it."[722]

On the other hand, and notwithstanding the *McMann* Court's assertion, the court deciding *Equal Employment Opportunity Commission v Home Insurance Co*[723] asserted that the pre-*Betts* burden of proof imposed upon the defendant was that of proving "valid business reasons for its action,"[724] and so if "the employer . . . [offered] no reasonable business explanations, . . . the court [was] compelled to draw the conclusion that the employer's action was subterfuge."[725] The same court enunciated a lesser burden vis-a-vis so-called voluntary retirement plans[726] in *Cipriano v Board of Education.*[727] *Cipriano* concerned a plan whereby incentives were offered to younger employees to retire. The plaintiffs were older workers, i.e., people over age 60, who by reason of their age were ineligible. The court stated that "[t]he evidence of business reasons required to show that a voluntary early retirement plan is not a subterfuge would

---

[720] In Smart v Porter Paint Co, 630 F2d 490 (7th Cir 1980), the court—confronting the defendant's motion for summary judgment—stated as follows: "[A]n employer's motion for summary judgment requires a prima facie showing that subterfuge is not present. This in turn requires some evidence of the purposes which the [plan] amendment in question is intended to serve." *Id* 495.

[721] 686 F2d 208 (4th Cir 1982).

[722] *Id* 215.

[723] 672 F2d 252 (2d Cir 1982).

[724] *Id* 260.

[725] *Id* 260 n11.

[726] See generally **§§5.53-.56.**

[727] 785 F2d 51 (2d Cir 1986).

almost necessarily be less than what was required to make such a showing in the case of a mandatory plan."[728] The pre-*Betts* court further asserted that "the employer . . . must come up with some evidence that the plan is not a subterfuge to evade the purposes of the ADEA by showing a legitimate business reason for structuring the plan as it did."[729]

The Court of Appeals for the Third Circuit held in *Equal Employment Opportunity Commission v City of Mt Lebanon*[730] that "to disprove subterfuge . . . [the defendant] must demonstrate why general age-related cost factors required it to reduce benefits for older workers to the extent and in the manner prescribed" in the challenged plan.[731] In amplifying this proposition the court rejected the notion (a notion that the trial court had read *Cipriano* as supporting) that the mere proffering of a business reason for differential benefits between older and younger employees would suffice. Cost justification was at the heart of the §4(f)(2) exception, and "[i]n order to 'cost justify' a reduced level of benefits for older employees . . . an employer . . . [had to] establish a connection or nexus showing how general cost savings data support[ed] the extent of reductions in its particular plan."[732] In explaining further, the *Mt Lebanon* court observed as follows:

> [M]erely proffering a business reason for reducing benefit levels, *e.g.*, it saves the employer money, does not necessarily mean an employer was not also using its benefit program

---

728 *Id* 59.

729 *Id* 58.

730 842 F2d 1480 (3d Cir 1988).

731 *Id* 1490.

732 *Id* 1492; *accord* Puckett v United Air Lines, Inc, 704 F Supp 145, 148 (ND Ill 1989); American Assn of Retired Persons v Farmers Group, Inc, 700 F Supp 1052, 1055 (CD Cal 1988), *affd on other grounds,* 943 F2d 996 (9th Cir 1991), *cert denied,* 112 S Ct 937 (1992); *see also* Equal Employment Opportunity Commn v Westinghouse Elec Corp, 869 F2d 696, 710 (3d Cir), *vacated,* 493 US 801 (1989) ("to qualify as exempt under §4(f)(2), a plan must involve age-related cost factors, i.e., the cost of providing benefits pursuant to the plan must increase with age"); Equal Employment Opportunity Commn v USX Corp, 50 Empl Prac Dec (CCH) ¶39143, at p 58250-251 (ED Pa 1989), *affd without opinion,* 909 F2d 1475 (3d Cir 1990).

> to evade the ADEA's purposes. Requiring an employer to cost justify its reduced benefit schedule to disprove subterfuge gives meaning to the "legitimate business purpose" showing [which *Cipriano* enunciated].[733]

The *Mt Lebanon* court also articulated the proposition that the bona fide employee benefit plan exception allowed for an employer to prevail by proving that it acted in good faith:

> [W]e do not believe Congress could have contemplated holding an employer liable for evading the ADEA when the employer made a good faith effort to implement a bona fide plan with no intention to evade the purposes of the ADEA, but its legal counsel or insurer erred or misrepresented the true extent of the needed reductions and thereby reduced benefits beyond the level necessary to compensate for the increased cost of insuring older employees.[734]

Expanding upon this good-faith defense, the court explained that an employer could not "close its eyes or ignore actions by its insurer or legal counsel that it . . . [knew would] result in the plan violating the ADEA."[735] Moreover, the employer had an obligation to inquire into the plan's lawfulness, which obligation

---

[733] 842 F2d at 1493. The *Mt Lebanon* court embraced the *approximate equality* principle put forth in the interpretation published by the Equal Employment Opportunity Commission (EEOC). *See* 29 CFR §1625.10(a)(1) (1993). The court, after articulating the factfinder's task as being that of assessing "whether the stated business or economic purpose reasonably justified the reduced benefits," 842 F2d at 1493, stated: "If the cost of a reduced duration of benefits for older workers . . . [was] approximately equal to the cost of providing the same type of benefits to younger workers, the employer's benefit plan . . . [was] not a subterfuge." *Id.* To meet the burden of proving cost justification, "employers . . . [had to] link the general data [, if that was what was offered,] allowing some type of reduction to the specific level of reductions set forth in their plan." *Id.* An employer would fail if the general data showed that it had to spend 50% more to provide the same benefits to older workers as were provided to younger employees, yet it reduced benefits to the former by 75%.

[734] *Id* 1494 (footnote omitted).

[735] *Id.*

was not relieved by this good-faith defense.[736] Accordingly, the employer could not successfully prove the defense by the mere production of a "conclusory certification" from the insurer that the plan was legal.[737] Rather, "[t]here . . . [had to] be cost data proving a correlation between age and cost, which . . . [allowed] an employer to assess the insurer's benefit schedule."[738] This good-faith defense did not otherwise appear in the pre-OWBPA case law, and it certainly is not set forth in the OWBPA-amended §4(f)(2).

§5.35 —Treatment of Specific Plans in Terms of Subterfuge Prior to *Betts*

As discussed in **§5.24,** *Public Employees Retirement System v Betts*[739] gutted §4(f)(2)[740] of the Age Discrimination in Employment Act (ADEA)[741] of virtually all substantive rigor. When *Betts* was decided, §4(f)(2) focused on the question of *subterfuge*. Subsequently, the Older Workers Benefit Protection Act (OWBPA)[742] negated the holdings of *Betts,* and as a result the pre-*Betts* case law—or at least some of it—resumed its relevance. Some of those decisions were addressed in the preceding section. Additional pre-*Betts* rulings are noted here.

Plan amendments were held illegal when adopted for the purpose of terminating older workers.[743] On the other hand, plans

---

[736] *Id.*

[737] *Id.*

[738] *Id.*

[739] 492 US 158 (1989).

[740] 29 USC §623(f)(2) (pre-1990 amendment).

[741] *Id* §§621-634.

[742] Pub L No 101-433, 104 Stat 978, *as amended by* Pub L No 101-521, 104 Stat 2287 (1990).

[743] *See, e.g.*, Equal Employment Opportunity Commn v Home Ins Co, 672 F2d 252 (2d Cir 1982); Equal Employment Opportunity Commn v Baltimore & Ohio RR Co, 632 F2d 1107, 1113 (4th Cir 1980), *cert denied,* 454 US 825 (1981); Equal Employment Opportunity Commn v Home Ins Co, 553 F Supp 704 (SDNY 1982); Marshall v Eastern Airlines, Inc, 474 F Supp 364 (SD Fla 1979), *affd,* 27 FEP Cas (BNA) 1686 (5th Cir), *cert denied,* 454 US 818 (1981).

and plan amendments were upheld when they were shown to be motivated by legitimate purposes.[744]

In *Potenze v New York Shipping Association*[745] the court rejected the argument that a plan whereby employees 65 and over were subjected to an offset against their Social Security benefits, whereas employees ages 62 to 64 were not, was a subterfuge to evade the ADEA's purpose simply because better alternatives could have been used by the employer. In *Abenante v Fulflex, Inc*,[746] the plaintiffs also failed in their effort to establish a violation. The case involved a collectively bargained separation pay agreement whereby the employer deducted from its employees, separation, or severance, payments an amount representing the present value of the employees' vested accrued pension benefits. The plaintiffs argued that because the present value of a vested pension payable upon attainment of age 65 is more valuable to an older person than it is to a younger person, the agreed-upon deduction reduced older employees' severance pay to a greater extent than it did the severance pay of younger employees with similar lengths of employment. The court accepted this analysis, explaining that the "present value of a future pension for an older employee is greater . . . because the older employee has a greater chance to attain the pension age."[747] The court rejected, however, the plaintiffs' claim that the deduction was discriminatory. Reasoning that the relevant inquiry was whether older employees really were treated less well in terms of the

---

[744] *See, e.g.*, Carpenter v Continental Trailways, 635 F2d 578 (6th Cir 1980), *cert denied*, 451 US 986 (1981); Weidman v Western Elec Co, 527 F Supp 263 (MDNC 1981); Marshall v Atlantic Container Line, GIE, 470 F Supp 71 (SDNY 1979). The court deciding Equal Employment Opportunity Commn v Baltimore & Ohio RR Co, 557 F Supp 1112 (D Md 1983), upheld the employers' amending of their pension plans to lower the compulsory retirement age from 65 to 62 (at a time when age-based mandatory retirement was still legal when imposed pursuant to a bona fide plan).

[745] 804 F2d 235 (2d Cir 1986), *cert denied*, 481 US 1029 (1987).

[746] 701 F Supp 296 (DRI 1988).

[747] *Id* 300.

"total benefits" they received or would receive,[748] the court concluded that the "evidence supports the finding that the value of the total benefits received by similarly situated older employees is at least equal to and in some instances exceeds the value of the total benefits received by similarly situated younger employees."[749] Thus, the plaintiffs failed to establish a prima facie case of discrimination. (Arguably the court erred, however: the relevant question is not whether the older plaintiffs fared no worse than their younger colleagues, but whether they would have fared better absent the age-related deduction. The court protected itself, however, by assuming arguendo that a prima facie violation had been established and then concluding that the plan would have passed muster under §4(f)(2).)[750]

Germann v Levy[751] involved an allegedly discriminatory reduction of insurance benefits. The court was unwilling to conclude that because of the Equal Employment Opportunity Commission (EEOC) *equal benefit or equal cost* interpretation,[752] it followed as a matter of law that a subterfuge existed if the plan did not meet this equal cost standard.[753] The court held that the challenged benefit plan was not discriminatory, even though it involved lesser expenditures by the employer than were made for younger employees. It justified this result with the observation that every one of the plans that had been available for purchase by the employer for its employees entailed a like benefit reduction.[754] More importantly, the court read *subterfuge* as requiring both knowledge on the part of the employer and an

---

748 *Id.*

749 *Id.*

750 By virtue of §4(l)(2), 29 USC §623(l)(2), which was added to the ADEA by the OWBPA, some offsets of previous benefits against severance pay are legal. See **§5.47.**

751 553 F Supp 700 (ND Ill 1982).

752 See **§5.33.**

753 553 F Supp at 703 n9.

754 *But see* Arizona Governing Commn for Tax Deferred Annuity & Deferred Compensation Plans v Norris, 463 US 1073, 1086-91 (1983) (suit arising under Title VII of the Civil Rights Act of 1964, 42 USC §§2000e through 2000e-17).

element of willfulness.[755] Here, the employer had been ignorant of the fact that the plan it had purchased was not wholly cost responsive to age differentials, the result being that it in fact was paying less for older employees than for younger employees. The court further expressed doubt that the defendant's failure to discuss this issue with the insurance company could satisfy the willfulness requirement.[756] In light of the express incorporation of the EEOC *equal benefit or equal cost* principle into §4(f)(2)(B)(i),[757] and in further light of the lack of any reference in the statute to a defendant's willfulness as being an element that, if absent, will prevent a plaintiff from prevailing, it is safe to conclude that *Germann* is no longer legally viable.

In contrast, a policy was held to be a subterfuge in *Johnson v Mayor & City Council of Baltimore.*[758] Pursuant to the policy at issue, the employer ceased to credit workers under the pension plan for work performed after they attained age 60. The court deemed this to be nothing more than an attempt to circumvent an earlier ruling in which it had held that the workers—who were firefighters—could not be retired at age 60.

Likewise, in *Equal Employment Opportunity Commission v New York*[759] a city administrative code provision was struck down because there was no age-related cost justification for the provision, which authorized city firefighters to borrow from their pension funds, save where a loan could not be repaid before the firefighter reached age 65. The plaintiff, who was 67, was ineligible for a loan because of his age. The court perceived "no added cost in lending pension funds to firefighters 65 and over, as compared to younger firefighters."[760]

---

[755] 553 F Supp at 704.

[756] *Id.*

[757] 29 USC §623(f)(2)(B)(i).

[758] 637 F Supp 903 (D Md), *later proceeding,* 41 Empl Prac Dec ¶36,557 (D Md 1986), *affd without opinion,* 829 F2d 35 (4th Cir 1987).

[759] 48 Empl Prac Dec (CCH) ¶38,443 (SDNY 1988).

[760] *Id* at p 54,515.

In *United Independent Flight Officers, Inc v United Air Lines, Inc*[761] the court granted summary judgment for the defendants in a case arising out of a change in the benefit plan whereby the defendants refused to credit as years of participation those years in which the plaintiffs did not voluntarily contribute to the plan. The challenged plan had been preceded by a voluntary plan, in which pilots employed by the airlines had been free to choose whether or not to contribute to a pension plan. In 1965 United undertook to fund the plan completely. Subsequently, in 1972 the benefit accrual formula was changed, with retirement benefits being based on a formula that took into account years of participation in the plan. For pilots hired prior to 1965 the amount of retirement income would vary according to their years of participation in the original plan. For post-1965 hires their years of participation would equal their years of service (minus one year, according to the plan). The plaintiffs sought credit for all years of pre-1965 service regardless of whether they had contributed in the pre-1965 years to the then-voluntary plan. The court rejected the argument that the plan had an unlawful disparate impact upon older pilots. It also concluded that there was no evidence to support a claim of intentional age discrimination.

Alford v City of Lubbock[762] involved a defined contribution plan that required a minimum of 15 years' service as a precondition to eligibility for benefits and that mandated retirement at age 65.[763] The plan excluded employees who were hired after their fiftieth birthdays. The court, relying in part on the ADEA's legislative history,[764] upheld the exclusion. In *Crosland v Charlotte Eye,*

---

761 572 F Supp 1494 (ND Ill 1983), *affd on other grounds,* 756 F2d 1274 (7th Cir 1985).

762 664 F2d 1263 (5th Cir), *cert denied,* 456 US 975 (1982).

763 Both involuntary retirement, and the cessation of protection under the Act at 65, are now no longer allowed. See **§5.52** concerning involuntary retirement, and **ch 3** concerning age limitations on coverage.

764

> Say an applicant for employment is 55, comes in and seeks employment, and the company has bargained for a plan with its labor union that provides that certain moneys will be put up for a pension plan for anyone who worked for the employer for twenty years so that a 55-year-old

Ear & Throat Hospital,[765] in contrast, the court held that an age-based exclusion from a plan did constitute a subterfuge. Actually, such exclusions were, and are, condemned by the EEOC in its interpretation.[766] More importantly (since the interpretation is not legally binding),[767] such exclusions (i.e., exclusions based on age) are forbidden as a result of 1986 amendments to the Employee Retirement Income Security Act[768] that took effect in most instances on January 1, 1988.[769]

§5.36 —Post-*Betts* Interpretations of Subterfuge

The Continuing Relevance of *Betts*

Following the Supreme Court's parsing of §4(f)(2)[770] of the Age Discrimination in Employment Act (ADEA)[771] in *Public Employees Retirement System v Betts,*[772] the employee benefit plan exception set forth in that section was construed and applied entirely differently than it had been before the *Betts* ruling. Eventually, *Betts* in large measure was consigned to the legal dust heap by the Older Workers Benefit Protection Act (OWBPA).[773] By

---

> employee [who] would not be employed past 10 years [because he will be retired at age 65]. This means he cannot be denied employment because he is 55, but he will not be able to participate in that pension plan because unlike a man hired at 44, he has no chance to earn 20 years retirement.

113 Cong Rec 31255 (1967) (remarks of Sen. Yarborough).

765 686 F2d 208 (4th Cir 1982); *accord* Snair v City of Clearwater, 817 F Supp 108 (MD Fla 1993).

766 29 CFR §1625.10(f)(1)(iv)(A) (1993).

767 See **ch 2.**

768 29 USC §1001 *et seq.*

769 Omnibus Budget Reconciliation Act of 1986 (OBRA), Pub L No 99-509, §§9203, 9204(b), 100 Stat 1874, 1980. See **§5.37.**

770 29 USC §623(f)(2) (pre-1990 amendment).

771 *Id* §§621-634.

772 492 US 158 (1989).

773 Pub L No 101-433, 104 Stat 978, *as amended by* Pub L No 101-521, 104 Stat 2287 (1990).

its terms, however, the OWBPA, did not apply retroactively.[774] Thus, while the *Betts* holdings were overturned insofar as post-OWBPA claims were concerned, the decision remained viable for claims arising after the 1989 decision, and before the OWBPA went into effect,[775] which for most situations was April 14, 1991.[776] In addition, given that the OWBPA applied only prospectively, *Betts* governed as to claims arising prior to the Supreme Court ruling.[777] Accordingly, *Betts* and its case law progeny remained of continuing relevance even after the enactment of the OWBPA, and so the decisions merit attention.

The Case Law

In *Robinson v County of Fresno*[778] the plaintiff challenged a pension plan provision utilizing a formula whereby workers who retired at a later age received "lesser benefits than workers with the same amount of service who retired at an earlier age."[779] The Court of Appeals for the Ninth Circuit observed that *Betts* had rejected the proposition "that a [plan] provision which has a discriminatory effect should be regarded as a 'subterfuge' unless justified by increased costs or other economic considerations."[780] Now, the *Robinson* court pointed out, the plaintiff had to prove that the "employer's intent in making the [plan] modification . . . [at issue in the case related] 'to hiring and firing, wages and salaries, [or] other non-fringe-benefit terms and conditions

---

774 See **§5.25.**

775 *See* Equal Employment Opportunity Commn v Westinghouse Elec Corp, 925 F2d 619, 622 n2 (3d Cir 1991); Darchuk v Kellwood, 790 F Supp 1453 (ED Mo 1991).

776 See **§5.26.**

777 Bell v Trustees of Purdue Univ, 975 F2d 422 (7th Cir 1992); American Assn of Retired Persons v Farmers Group, Inc, 943 F2d 996, 1000 n6 (9th Cir 1991), *cert denied,* 112 S Ct 937 (1992); *see also* Cipriano v Board of Educ, 968 F2d 1502 (2d Cir 1992), *affg* 772 F Supp 1346 (WDNY 1991). *Contra* Mitchell v Mobil Oil Corp, 896 F2d 463, 471 n3 (10th Cir), *cert denied,* 498 US 898 (1990).

778 882 F2d 444 (9th Cir 1989).

779 *Id* 445.

780 *Id* 446.

of employment.' "[781] Here, the plaintiff had failed to meet his burden: without any analysis, the court simply asserted that "Robinson has not shown that the change in benefits formula demonstrates an intent to discriminate in any non-fringe benefits area."[782]

The plaintiffs likewise were unsuccessful in *Bell v Trustees of Purdue University.*[783] They attacked as discriminatory the now-ended practice of the university of discontinuing contributions to the faculty pension plan when the faculty member attained normal retirement age, which was defined as age 65. This practice was pursued for a six-year period, commencing on July 1, 1982, the effective date of the ADEA amendment raising to age 70 the age cap for tenured faculty members.[784] and ending on January 1, 1988, the effective date of a 1986 amendment to the ADEA which ensured that employers could no longer refuse to make contributions to pension plans on behalf of persons above the normal retirement age.[785] The plaintiffs contended that Purdue wanted to get rid of older faculty members, and that the cessation of pension contributions was intended to achieve this end by discouraging employees over age 65 from continuing to work for the university. In other words, the university's practice either was a disguised form of forced retirement, or it at the least constituted discrimination in compensation. In either instance, the plaintiffs argued, Purdue was seeking to use the university pension plan, which during the period in question allowed it to cease making contributions, as a subterfuge for discrimination. The Court of Appeals for the Seventh Circuit rejected the plaintiffs' contentions, and ruled that the trial court should have granted the defendant's motion for summary judgment. The court justified its decision with the following explanation:

---

[781] *Id* (quoting *Betts,* 492 US at 177).

[782] 882 F2d at 447.

[783] 975 F2d 422 (7th Cir 1992).

[784] See **ch 3.**

[785] See **§5.41.**

> The plaintiffs maintain that ceasing contributions evaded either the prohibition against wage cuts or forced retirement based on age. The plaintiffs, however, misunderstand the nature of evasion. . . . The plaintiffs in this case have offered no evidence that the fringe benefit cut in this case is anything more than meets the eye—an age differential in fringe benefits which is permitted under the ADEA. . . .
>
> Similarly, Purdue has not evaded the prohibition against firing, refusing to hire, or forcing retirement of employees. . . . The defendants have not given the plaintiffs a Hobson's choice such as giving them an option of retiring at age 65 or losing their pension. Granted, Purdue's decision to cease contributions at age 65 gives employees less incentive to continue working past age 65 than they would have if Purdue continued making contributions. But taking away an incentive in the form of a fringe benefit is not the kind of evasion prohibited by *Betts'* interpretation of the ADEA.[786]

In *Equal Employment Opportunity Commission v Chrysler Corp*[787] the court likewise upheld a plan under which severance benefits were denied to terminated employees age 55 or older if they were eligible for and received early retirement benefits. This was not a subterfuge to evade the purposes of the ADEA because the employer lacked the requisite intent.[788] (The court's basis for this conclusion was a technical one with little significance beyond the facts of the case. It turned on the question of whether the defendant had acted willfully, for purposes of the three-year statute of limitations applicable to willful violations.[789] Since the court determined that the employer had not so acted, it followed that it was "impossible for plaintiff to state a claim arising out of an intentional subterfuge.")[790]

---

[786] 975 F2d at 429.

[787] 729 F Supp 1002 (SDNY 1990).

[788] As to the legality of offsets applied against severance payments, see **§5.47.**

[789] See **ch 3.**

[790] 729 F Supp at 1008-09.

Betts' emphasis on discriminatory intent on the part of the employer also was determinative of the result in *Equal Employment Opportunity Commission v Bethlehem Steel Corp.*[791] At issue was a plan which, similar to that in *Chrysler Corp,* denied severance payments to terminated employees who were eligible for pension benefits. No evidence of an intent to discriminate with regard to a nonfringe benefit was adduced in *Bethlehem Steel,* so the court granted the defendant's motion for summary judgment.[792] The same scenario was played out in *Tusting v Bay View Federal Savings & Loan Association,*[793] which involved a change in the health benefits that made up a part of the employer's retirement plan.

Gabarczyk v Board of Education[794] constituted another entry to the list of unsuccessful plaintiffs' efforts in the post-*Betts* era. Under the retirement incentive plan at issue, a benefit was available to teachers who retired at age 55 but not to older retirees, such as the 61-year-old plaintiff. The court upheld the plan because "the retirement incentive plan . . . [did] not discriminate in 'some nonfringe benefit aspect' of the employment relation[.]"[795]

In contrast to the foregoing group of decisions, in *Snair v City of Clearwater*[796] the plaintiff was able to adduce enough evidence of discriminatory intent to at least stave off the defendant's motion for summary judgment. And the plaintiffs prevailed in *American Association of Retired Persons v Farmers Group, Inc.*[797] This case concerned pension and profit-sharing plans that entailed the cessation of employer contributions upon the employee's attainment of age 65 and the cessation of accrual of service and

---

[791] 727 F Supp 952 (ED Pa 1990).

[792] *Accord* Berger v Edgewater Corp, 784 F Supp 263 (WD Pa 1991); Cipriano v Board of Educ, 772 F Supp 1346 (WDNY 1991), *affd on other grounds,* 968 F2d 1502 (2d Cir 1992); Kolman v Oscar Mayer Foods Corp, 53 FEP Cas (BNA) 1256, 1262 (ED Pa 1990).

[793] 789 F Supp 1034 (ND Cal 1992).

[794] 738 F Supp 118 (SDNY 1990).

[795] *Id* 122; *see also* Darchuk v Kellwood, 790 F Supp 1453 (ED Mo 1991).

[796] 787 F Supp 1401 (MD Fla 1992).

[797] 943 F2d 996 (9th Cir 1991), *cert denied,* 112 S Ct 937 (1992).

salary credits—which increased an employee's retirement benefits once he or she retired—upon attainment of that age. The court concluded that these provisions were discriminatory on their face. The employer, the court concluded, "wanted to get rid of older workers and . . . the pension plan . . . [provisions were] one way to help accomplish that goal."[798] The employer was held liable because it had failed to establish a legitimate, nondiscriminatory reason for the challenged provisions.

§5.37 Pension and Retirement Benefits Under §4(f)(2)

There never has been any question that retirement and pension benefits fall within the ambit of the bona fide employee benefit plan exception, set forth in §4(f)(2)[799] of the Age Discrimination in Employment Act (ADEA). Indeed, the language of this section, before it was rewritten in 1990 by[800] the Older Workers Benefit Protection Act (OWBPA),[801] expressly addressed benefit plans "such as . . . retirement, pension, or insurance plan[s]."[802]

Since the enactment of the ADEA a number of statutory changes have been made that concern these retirement and pension benefits. In addition, the Equal Employment Opportunity Commission (EEOC) interpretation that speaks to benefit plans,[803] while not legally binding,[804] provides direction and guidance that is applicable to retirement benefits, as well as to other types of benefits. Moreover, the interpretation to some

---

798 *Id* 1002.

799 29 USC §623(f)(2).

800 *Id* §§621-634.

801 Pub L No 101-433, 104 Stat 978, *as amended by* Pub L No 101-521, 104 Stat 2287 (1990).

802 29 USC §623(f)(2) (pre-1990 amendment).

803 29 CFR §1625.10 (1993).

804 See **ch 2**.

extent speaks specifically to pension plans,[805] including defined contribution[806] and defined benefit[807] plans. For example, a primary focus of the EEOC interpretation in the past was the matter of cessation of employer contributions and accruals of benefits at normal retirement age (an age that was not defined, but was often deemed in a plan to be age 65) when an employee continued working beyond that age.[808]

The EEOC interpretation also addresses the matter of participation. It provides that no employee hired prior to normal retirement age can be excluded from a defined contribution

---

805 *Pension plan* is defined in §1002(2) of the Employee Retirement Income Security Act of 1974 (ERISA), 29 USC §1002(2), as "any plan, fund, or program . . . maintained by an employer or by an employee organization, or by both . . . [which] (i) provides retirement income to employees or (ii) results in a deferral of income by employees for periods extending to the termination of covered employment or beyond."

806 *Defined contribution plan* is defined in §1002(34) of the Employee Retirement Income Security Act of 1974 (ERISA), 29 USC §1002(34):

> [A] pension plan which provides for an individual account for each participant and for benefits based solely upon the amount contributed to the participant's account, and any income, expenses, gains and losses, and any forfeitures of accounts of other participants which may be allocated to such participant's account.

807 *Defined benefit plan* is defined in §1002(35) of the Employee Retirement Income Security Act of 1974 (ERISA), 29 USC §1002(35):

> The term "defined benefit plan" means a pension plan other than an individual account plan; except that a pension plan which is not an individual account plan and which provides a benefit derived from employer contributions which is based partly on the balance of the separate account of a participant—
>
> (A) for the purposes of section 1052 of this title, shall be treated as an individual account plan, and
>
> (B) for the purposes of paragraph (23) of this section and section 1054 of this title, shall be treated as an individual account plan to the extent benefits are based upon the separate account of a participant and as a defined benefit plan with respect to the remaining portion of benefits under the plan.

(Section 1052, 29 USC §1052, deals with minimum participation standards; §1002(23), 29 USC §1002(23), defines *accrued benefit;* §1054, 29 USC §1054, deals with benefit accrual requirements. The term *individual account plan* is equated with "defined contribution plan," the definition of which is set forth in §1002(34), 29 USC §1002(34), which is quoted in note 806.)

808 See **§§5.40-.41.**

plan.[809] (In *Alford v City of Lubbock*[810] the court upheld a plan that excluded from participation employees hired after their 50th birthdays. However, 1986 statutory changes negated *Alford.*)[811] The interpretation also precludes application of the benefit package approach to retirement or pension plans.[812]

§5.38 —Attainment of a Minimum Age for Pension and Retirement Benefits: The §4(l)(1)(A) Affirmative Defense

Section 4(l)(1)[813] of the Age Discrimination in Employment Act[814] was added to the Act in 1990 by the Older Workers Benefit Protection Act (OWBPA).[815] This section provides that an employee pension plan can set the attainment of a minimum age as a condition of eligibility for normal or early retirement bene-

---

809 29 CFR §1625.10(f)(1)(iv)(A) (1993). The interpretation further provides as follows:

> With respect to defined benefit plans not subject to the Employee Retirement Income Security Act (ERISA), Pub. L. 93-406, 29 U.S.C. 1001, 1003(a) and (b), an employee hired at an age more than 5 years prior to normal retirement age may not be excluded from such a plan unless the exclusion is justifiable on the basis of cost considerations as set forth elsewhere in . . . [29 CFR §1625.10]. With respect to defined benefit plans subject to ERISA, such an exclusion would be unlawful in any case.

Id.

810 664 F2d 1263 (5th Cir), *cert denied,* 456 US 975 (1982).

811 While the EEOC interpretation allows the exclusion from a defined benefit plan of an employee hired less than five years prior to normal retirement age, see note 809, amendments to the Employee Retirement Income Security Act, 29 USC §1001 *et seq,* made by the Omnibus Budget Reconciliation Act of 1986 (OBRA), Pub L No 99-509, §9203, 100 Stat 1874, 1980, precluded the continuing viability of that interpretation once the OBRA amendments took effect on January 1, 1988 (or later in the case of certain plans maintained pursuant to a collective bargaining contract, as provided by §9204, 100 Stat 1980, of OBRA). See Snair v City of Clearwater, 817 F Supp 108 (MD Fla 1993).

812 29 CFR §1625.10(f)(2)(ii)(A) (1993).

813 29 USC §623(l)(1).

814 *Id* §§621-634.

815 Pub L No 101-433, 104 Stat 978, *as amended by* Pub L No 101-521, 104 Stat 2287 (1990).

fits. The Senate report on the bill which, in modified form, was enacted into law as the OWBPA, explained this provision:

> For example, a pension plan may provide that benefits are not payable until an individual reaches the age of 55, 60, or 65. The Committee intends to make clear that this practice, a universally accepted part of pension plan design and a practice lawful under ERISA, does not violate the ADEA prohibition against differential benefits based on age.[816]

The Senate report further identified §4(l)(1) as an affirmative defense, with the entity relying upon the provision having the burden of pleading and proving its applicability.[817]

Section 4(l)(1) confirms what the pre-§4(l)(1) case law already had established, i.e., that an age minimum for the receipt of benefits does not violate the ADEA.[818]

§5.39 —Pension Subsidies and Social Security Bridge Payments: The §4(l)(1)(B) Affirmative Defenses

Section 4(l)(1)(B)[819] of the Age Discrimination in Employment Act (ADEA)[820] was added to the Act in 1990 by the Older Work-

---

[816] Senate Comm on Labor & Human Resources, The Older Workers Benefit Protection Act, S Rep No 263, 101st Cong, 2d Sess 20-21 (1990) [hereinafter Senate Report]. In the version of the Senate bill reported out of committee, which was modified before being passed by the Senate, this approval of a minimum age requirement was confined to defined benefit pension plans. However, in the ultimately enacted OWBPA this limitation was dropped. Under §4(l)(1)(A), 29 USC §623(l)(1)(A), "an employee pension benefit plan (as defined in section 3(2) of the Employee Retirement Income Security Act of 1974 (29 U.S.C. 1002(2)) . . . [may provide] for the attainment of a minimum age."

[817] Senate Report, *supra*, note 816, at 22, 29.

[818] *See, e.g.*, Hamilton v Caterpiller, Inc, 966 F2d 1226 (7th Cir 1992). See also **§5.55.**

[819] 29 USC §623(l)(1)(B).

[820] *Id* §§621-634.

ers Benefit Protection Act (OWBPA).[821] This section provides, with regard to defined benefit plans (as defined in §3(35)[822] of the Employee Retirement Income Security Act (ERISA)),[823] that pension subsidies and Social Security bridge payments will not violate the ADEA's prohibitions, notwithstanding their use of age as a basis for eligibility for such benefits.[824] The section reads as follows:

> (l) It shall not be a violation of subsection (a), (b), (c), or (e) solely because . . .
>
> (B) a defined benefit plan . . . provides for—
>
> (i) payments that constitute the subsidized portion of an early retirement benefit; or
>
> (ii) social security supplements for plan participants that commence before the age and terminate at the age (specified by the plan) when participants are eligible to receive reduced or unreduced old-age insurance benefits under title II of the Social Security Act (42 U.S.C. 401 et seq.), and that do not exceed such old-age insurance benefits.

With regard to subsection (i), which addresses pension subsidies, the Senate report on the bill that eventually was enacted, in modified form, as the OWBPA offered the following rationale:

> Under many plans, benefits are payable at ages earlier than the normal retirement age specified in the plan. Actuarial funding assumptions utilized by defined benefit pension plans are based on longevity and other factors related to age. Earlier receipt of the benefit justifies an actuarial

---

[821] Pub L No 101-433, 104 Stat 978, *as amended by* Pub L No 101-521, 104 Stat 2287 (1990).

[822] 29 USC §1002(35).

[823] *Id* §1001 *et seq.*

[824] Senator Pryor, one of the managers of the Senate bill that ultimately was enacted into law as the OWBPA, pointed out that these are the two most common forms of exit incentives: "According to the General Accounting Office, as many as two-thirds of the early retirement incentives offered by employers take one of these two forms." 136 Cong Rec S13603 (daily ed Sept 24, 1990).

> reduction because the benefits presumably will be paid for a longer period of time. An actuarial reduction of .5% for each month prior to normal retirement is common. Thus, for example, an employee who retires at age 62 in a plan that has a normal retirement age of 65 may experience an 18% reduction in the benefit payable under the plan. Arithmetic reductions that are linked to actuarial determinations also are used by private and public pension plans.
>
> Some defined benefit pension plans, however, forego the imposition of part or all of the permissible actuarial reduction. Thus, for instance, some plans provide for the payment of normal retirement benefits to individuals who satisfy certain age and service requirements, even if those individuals have not yet attained the normal retirement age specified in the plan. The portion of the benefit that could be actuarially reduced, but is not, constitutes the subsidized portion of an early retirement benefit within the meaning of this bill.
>
> Even though such plans provide subsidies only for employees who retire prior to the normal retirement age, the Committee intends to approve these early retirement subsidies.[825]

Social Security bridge payments also were explained in the Senate report:

> Typically, a social security bridge payment is a fixed monthly payment intended to substitute for social security benefits that will become available to the plan participant either at age 62 (eligibility for reduced Social Security benefits) or age 65 (eligibility for unreduced Social Security benefits).
>
> The Committee concludes that the payment of such supplemental pension benefits . . . is lawful . . . so long as the

---

[825] Senate Comm on Labor & Human Resources, The Older Workers Benefit Protection Act, S Rep No 263, 101st Cong, 2d Sess 21 (1990) [hereinafter Senate Report].

supplement does not exceed the amount of the Social Security benefits.

The fact that younger retired workers may receive the benefits for a greater number of years and may therefore receive greater total benefits does not make these plans unlawful. *See Dorsch v. L.B. Foster Company,* 782 F.2d 1421 (7th Cir. 1986). If a plan provides these benefits, the benefits may not terminate at an age earlier than the first age of eligibility for reduced old-age insurance benefits.[826]

The Senate report identifies the authorizations of pension subsidies or Social Security bridge payments as erecting affirmative defenses.[827]

---

826 *Id.* Under §4(l)(1)(B)(ii), 29 USC §623(l)(1)(B)(ii), an employer may discontinue the payment of Social Security bridge payments once the recipient becomes eligible to receive Social Security old-age insurance benefits. A colloquy between two of the managers of the legislation—obviously intended to create binding legislative history—focused on a potential implication regarding disability benefits of this discontinuance of bridge payments:

> Mr. Heinz: . . . As I understand it, the reference to old age benefits [in §4(l)(1)(B)(ii)] is not intended to imply that it would be unlawful age discrimination for a pension plan to discontinue Social Security disability supplements upon the pensioner's attainment of eligibility for Social Security disability benefits.
>
> Mr. Metzenbaum: That is correct. Many pension plans offer retirement to certain participants suffering disability or permanent incapacity. Because Social Security disability benefits do not begin until completion of a waiting period, some pension plans offer, in addition to [a] basic disability pension benefit, a disability supplement intended to take the place of Social Security disability insurance benefits. However, as I understand it, such pension plans not infrequently discontinue payment of the disability pension supplement upon the participant's attaining eligibility for Social Security disability insurance benefits. Throughout the extended deliberation over the bill, there has been no suggestion that the receipt of Social Security disability benefits—for which there is no minimum age requirement—is so related to age as to be tantamount to an age related disqualification.

136 Cong Rec S13,601 (daily ed Sept 24, 1990).

827 Senate Report, *supra,* note 825, at 22, 29.

§5.40 —Freezing Employer Contributions and the Accrual of Benefits

In 1978 the Age Discrimination in Employment Act (ADEA)[828] was amended to raise the age ceiling for coverage under the statute from 65 to 70.[829] At the same time, §4(f)(2)[830] of the Act—the employee benefit plan exception—was amended to bar an employer from imposing involuntary retirement pursuant to such a plan.[831]

When Congress considered these changes, concern was expressed as to their consequences for the pension costs that would be incurred by employers. An official of the Department of Labor, which at the time had administrative and enforcement responsibility for the Act, expressed the view in a written analysis that employers would be able to freeze benefits at normal retirement age.[832] While Congress relied on this analysis, it was not literally incorporated into the statutory language. Subsequent to the enactment of the 1978 amendments, however, the Department of Labor issued its interpretations regarding the §4(f)(2) exception, and the Department took the position that an employer was free to terminate both its own contributions and the accrual of benefits for an employee as of the time the employee reached normal retirement age, even if the employee did not cease working at that time.[833] While *normal retirement age* was not defined, it was generally taken to mean age 65.

---

[828] 29 USC §§621-634.

[829] The Age Discrimination in Employment Act Amendments of 1978, Pub L No 95-256, §3, 92 Stat 189, 189 (amending §12 of the Act, codified at 29 USC §631). (The age-70 cap subsequently was removed for most individuals by a 1986 amendment. Age Discrimination in Employment Amendments of 1986, Pub L No 99-592, §2(c), 100 Stat 3342, 3342).

[830] 29 USC §623(f)(2) (pre-1990 amendment).

[831] Age Discrimination in Employment Act Amendments of 1978, Pub L No 95-256, §2(a), 92 Stat 189.

[832] *See* Senate Comm on Human Resources, Amending the Age Discrimination in Employment Act of 1967, S Rep No 493, 95th Cong, 1st Sess 14-16 (1977).

[833] 29 CFR §860.120(f)(1)(iv)(B)(1), (3)-(7) (1986) (ordered removed from the CFR, 52 Fed Reg 23812 (June 25, 1987)).

This approval of a freeze on employer contributions and on accrual of benefits generated much controversy and criticism.[834] Indeed, shortly after transfer of ADEA enforcement and administrative authority on July 1, 1979, to the Equal Employment Opportunity Commission (EEOC), the EEOC's general counsel advised the Commission that the Labor Department's interpretation—which was kept in effect following the transfer—was " 'incorrect.' "[835]

In June 1984, the EEOC commissioners voted to rescind the provisions allowing for the freezing of contributions and credits and to adopt rules requiring continued employer contributions and continued pension crediting as long as an employee remained on the job.[836] Subsequently, however, the commissioners reversed themselves: they voted to terminate the rulemaking and to not rescind the interpretations, after all.[837] Thus, they remained intact at the agency level.

Meanwhile, in the Courts, efforts also had been mounted to attack the interpretations. In *Von Aulock v Smith*[838] the Court of Appeals for the District of Columbia held that the plaintiffs did

---

[834] For example, in the Ninth Annual Report of the National Commission for Employment Policy, it was observed as follows: "In some cases, the ADEA regulations appear to contradict the purpose and intent of the Act or conflict with other legislation. For example, the regulations allow private plans to make distinctions in pension accruals after normal retirement age." National Commn for Employment Policy, Older Workers: Prospects, Problems and Policies 17 (1985).

[835] Memorandum from Leroy D. Clark to EEOC Commissioners, Aug 20, 1979, *quoted in* American Assn of Retired Persons v Equal Employment Opportunity Commn, 655 F Supp 228, 233 (DDC), *revd & remanded,* 823 F2d 600 (DC Cir 1987), *see also* remarks by EEOC Vice Chairman Daniel Leach, 1985-89 Empl Prac Guide (CCH) Transfer Binder for New Developments ¶5126 (Nov 15, 1979); *Stopping Pension Accruals at 65 May Become Illegal,* Legal Times of Wash, Apr 28, 1980, at 4.

[836] American Assn of Retired Persons v Equal Employment Opportunity Commn, 655 F Supp 228, 234 (DDC), *revd & remanded,* 823 F2d 600 (DC Cir 1987).

[837] *Id* 235.

[838] 720 F2d 176 (DC Cir 1983).

not have standing to attack the interpretations.[839] However, in a later ruling, *Bell v Trustees of Purdue University,*[840] the Court of Appeals for the Seventh Circuit reached the merits. It upheld the legitimacy of a plan that precluded the employer from contributing to the plan subsequent to the employee's attainment of the normal retirement age contained in the plan.

The plaintiffs in *American Association of Retired Persons v Equal Employment Opportunity Commission*[841] had more success. The district court held that the EEOC had unlawfully withheld or unreasonably delayed rescission of the interpretations, and had unlawfully withheld or delayed rulemaking on this issue. The court further ordered the EEOC to rescind the interpretations within 20 days, and to include with its notice of rescission a statement that employers could no longer use reliance on the interpretations as a good-faith defense to liability.[842] The court also ordered the EEOC to promptly publish for notice and comment the proposed rules it earlier had voted to adopt (or similar rules) requiring continued pension contributions, credits, and accruals for employees who worked beyond normal retirement age,

---

[839] The plaintiffs argued that but for the interpretations allowing employers to refuse to adjust pension benefits to take account of service past age 65, their employer would not maintain the pension plan at issue. While the court purported not to address the substantive issue of whether the differential treatment accorded to employees upon reaching age 65 ran afoul of the ADEA, it clearly asserted the view that the EEOC interpretations and the differential treatment they authorized jibed with the Act.In Monroe v United Air Lines, Inc, 569 F Supp 645 (ND Ill 1983), *revd on other grounds,* 736 F2d 394 (7th Cir 1984), *cert denied,* 470 US 1004 (1985), the court addressed, but did not rule on, the freezing of contributions and accruals. In Kadane v Hofstra Univ, 682 F Supp 166 (EDNY 1988), the court did not rule on the legitimacy under the ADEA of an employer ceasing contributions at age 65. The court did hold, however, that insofar as the ADEA requires notice of such termination of contributions, that requirement was satisfied in light of the fact that there was satisfactory notice under the Employee Retirement Income Security Act of 1974 (ERISA), 29 USC §1001 *et seq,* and "[t]he requirements of the ADEA are satisfied if the requirements of ERISA are satisfied." 682 F Supp at 171.

[840] 975 F2d 422 (7th Cir 1992).

[841] 655 F Supp 228 (DDC), *revd & remanded,* 823 F2d 600 (DC Cir 1987).

[842] *Id* 241. The rescission applied to all of 29 CFR §860.120(f)(1)(iv)(B) (1986) (ordered removed from the CFR, 52 Fed Reg 23811 (June 25, 1987)). As to the good-faith reliance defense, see **§5.62.**

which the court defined as age 70.[843] In reaching the conclusions supporting these orders, the court reasoned as follows:

> Within a "rule of reason" analysis of the facts of the case, what becomes perfectly clear is that for seven years the EEOC has let stand an interpretation of the ADEA that it has itself consistently considered to be erroneous. During that same seven-year period, the Commission piled delay upon delay. . . .
>
> As for the [Department of Labor's] Interpretative Bulletin, it still stands—although it is wrong—wrong according to the Commission's counsel, at least two of its chairpersons, and a number of votes by the Commission itself.[844]

In accordance with the order of the *American Association of Retired Persons* court, the EEOC rescinded the interpretations allowing employers to cease contributions to, and accruals in, pension and retirement plans.[845] The rescission stated that good-faith reliance on the rescinded provision no longer would constitute a defense to liability for failure to contribute to a plan.[846] The EEOC further issued proposed rules requiring employers to continue contributions and accruals for employees who worked beyond the normal retirement age.[847]

Subsequent to these regulatory activities, however, the trial court ruling was reversed in *American Association of Retired Persons v Equal Employment Opportunity Commission.*[848] The consequence was to free the EEOC of the court-imposed requirement of promulgating new rules.[849] The reversal did not, however,

---

843 655 F Supp at 241.

844 *Id* 238-39 (footnote omitted).

845 52 Fed Reg 8448 (Mar 18, 1987).

846 *Id.*

847 52 Fed Reg 10584-586 (Apr 2, 1987).

848 823 F2d 600 (DC Cir 1987).

849 Ultimately, the EEOC terminated the court-ordered rulemaking and it accordingly withdrew the notice of proposed rulemaking regarding contributions and accruals for persons working beyond the normal retirement age. 53 Fed Reg 27360-361 (July 20, 1988).

address the rescission of the agency interpretation that in the past had allowed the freezing of contributions and credits, since the EEOC had not appealed that portion of the district court's order requiring the rescission. Thus, the rescission remained in effect. The outcome, then, of the *American Association of Retired Persons* litigation was that the interpretive approval of a freeze on employer contributions and accruals as to employees working beyond the normal retirement age ceased to exist as of March 18, 1987, the date of the EEOC's rescission of the interpretation.[850]

In theory, employers could continue to cease contributing to plans and to cease accruals at normal retirement age, but they could no longer rely on a formal agency interpretation as the basis for so doing, which reliance could be used as a valid defense.[851] In practice, then, employers had to face the fact that—as detailed by the *American Association of Retired Persons* district court—on repeated occasions EEOC officials had asserted the position that such a freeze contravened the ADEA's ban on discrimination. Thus, the continued adherence by employers to prior practice—now unbuttressed by the approval previously expressed in the EEOC interpretation—exposed them to potential liability should suits be filed by disgruntled employees. And given the well-documented view that such prior practice could not be squared with the ADEA, these potential plaintiffs would seem to have had good prospects of prevailing.

Ultimately, this uncertain situation was resolved by statutory changes that went into effect in 1988, dealing with the question of pension crediting and accruals. These changes are addressed in the next section.

---

[850] 52 Fed Reg 8448 (Mar 18, 1987).

[851] See **§5.62.**

§5.41 —Freezing Employer Contributions and the Accrual of Benefits: The 1986 Amendments

In October 1986 the Omnibus Budget Reconciliation Act of 1986 (OBRA) was signed into law.[852] This Act included provisions dealing with pension contributions, credits, and accruals under the Age Discrimination in Employment Act (ADEA).[853] Specifically, the 1986 amendments, codified at §4(j)[854] of the ADEA, prohibit—with some exceptions—employers, employment agencies, and labor organizations from establishing or maintaining pension funds that either require or permit the following:

> (A) in the case of a defined benefit plan, the cessation of an employee's benefit accrual, or the reduction of the rate of an employee's benefit accrual, because of age, or
>
> (B) in the case of a defined contribution plan, the cessation of allocations to an employee's account, or the reduction of the rate at which amounts are allocated to an employee's account because of age.[855]

---

[852] Pub L No 99-509, 100 Stat 1874.

[853] 29 USC §§621-634.

[854] 29 USC §623(j). Originally, this provision was designated as §4(i). However, the Age Discrimination in Employment Amendments of 1986, Pub L No 99-592, §3(a), 100 Stat 3342, 3342 also added a new §4(i). Thus, for a time there were two such sections. This confusing situation eventually was corrected by a technical amendment made to the ADEA in 1990 by §103 of the Older Workers Benefit Protection Act (OWBPA), Pub L No 101-433, 104 Stat 978, 979, *as amended by* Pub L No 101-521, 104 Stat 2287 (1990). Under the amendment the subsection (i) added by OBRA was redesignated as §4(j) by §103(2) of the OWBPA. Pub L No 101-433, 104 Stat 978, 979, *as amended* by Pub L No 101-521, 104 Stat 2287 (1990). However, even after the redesignation of the section the provision was mistakenly referred to as §4(i). *See* Atkins v Northwestern Airlines, Inc, 967 F2d 1197 (8th Cir 1992). (Section 4(i), which afforded reduced protection to firefighters and law enforcement officers, was repealed on December 31, 1993. See **ch 3**).

[855] OBRA, Pub L No 99-509, §9201, 100 Stat 1874, 1973-74 (codified at §4(j)(1), 29 USC §623(j)(1)).

Section 4(j) further provides that an employer, employment agency, or labor organization may safely observe a plan provision to the extent that the provision imposes—without regard to age—a limit on the amount of benefits or a limit on the number of years of service or years of participation to be considered in determining benefits.[856]

The amendments enacted in 1986 applied only to plan years beginning on or after January 1, 1988, except that a later date could apply in the case of plans maintained pursuant to collective bargaining agreements.[857] Regulations were to be issued by the Department of the Treasury, the Department of Labor, and the Equal Employment Opportunity Commission (EEOC) to implement these and companion changes made in the Internal Revenue Code of 1986[858] and in the Employee Retirement Income Security Act of 1974 (ERISA).[859] These regulations were to be issued before February 1, 1988,[860] and were to be consistent with each other.[861]

Regulatory Activity

The EEOC issued proposed regulations implementing OBRA

---

[856] OBRA, Pub L No 99-509, §9201, 100 Stat 1874, 1974 (codified at §4(j)(2), 29 USC §623(j)(2)).

[857] OBRA, Pub L No 99-509, §9204(a), 100 Stat 1874, 1979-80. The report of the conference committee that harmonized the differing provisions of the bills passed by the House and the Senate had made clear that the 1986 amendments—which did not take effect until 1988, as noted above—had no impact prior to the effective date of the changes. Conf Comm, Omnibus Reconciliation Act of 1986, HR Rep No 1012, 99th Cong, 2d Sess 382 (1986):

> No inference is to be drawn by the addition of section 4(i) [subsequently redesignated as §4(j)] as to whether or to what extent employee benefit plans might have been required to provide benefit accruals, or allocations to employees' accounts for employees protected under ADEA prior to the effective date of section 4(i) [subsequently redesignated as §4(j)].

[858] 26 USC §1 *et seq; see id* §§410(a)(2), 411(b)(1)(H).

[859] 29 USC §1001 *et seq; see id* §§1052(a), 1054.

[860] OBRA, Pub L No 99-509, §9204(e), 100 Stat 1874, 1980.

[861] *Id* §9204(d), 100 Stat 1874, 1980.

in late 1987.[862] It was not until April, 1988, however, that the Internal Revenue Service (IRS) issued its proposed regulations.[863] The EEOC then determined not to finalize its rules until it reached agreement with the IRS on the question of retroactivity.

The proposed IRS regulations provided that effective for plan years beginning 1988 and thereafter, a defined benefit plan could not disregard any years of service with regard to a participant who had at least one hour of service for the plan sponsor in a plan year beginning in 1988 or thereafter. In contrast, the "proposed EEOC regulations provided that such years of service before 1988 could be disregarded, so long as such years of service occurred after the participant reached the plan's normal retirement age."[864]

Ultimately, the EEOC decided to defer to the IRS, and it so announced in a public notice published in January, 1989.[865] In that notice the EEOC stated as follows:

> [T]he final regulations to be issued will provide that the OBRA benefit accrual rules apply to all years of service (including years of service before January 1, 1988) completed by a participant in a noncontributory defined benefit plan who has at least 1 hour of service with the plan sponsor in a plan year beginning on or after January 1, 1988. . . .
>
> For purposes of this notice, a noncontributory defined benefit plan is a defined benefit plan that does not provide for mandatory employee contributions. No inference should be drawn as to the position that may be taken in final EEOC or IRS regulations regarding defined benefit plans that provide for mandatory employee contributions.[866]

---

[862] 52 Fed Reg 43560-63 (Nov 27, 1987).

[863] 53 Fed Reg 11876-86 (Apr 11, 1988).

[864] 54 Fed Reg 604 (Jan 9, 1989).

[865] EEOC, 29 CFR pt 1625, Employee Benefit Pension Plans, 54 Fed Reg 604 (Jan 9, 1989).

[866] *Id.*

The EEOC further advised as follows:

> With respect to defined contribution plans, the final regulations to be issued by the two agencies will provide that the OBRA benefit accrual rules do not require that retroactive allocations be made to the accounts of participants for plan years beginning before January 1, 1988. However, such final regulations will provide that if a defined contribution plan allocates amounts to the accounts of participants under a formula that takes prior service into account, no year of service (including years of service before January 1, 1988) may be disregarded because of age in determining allocations to the accounts of participants for plan years beginning on or after January 1, 1988.[867]

As a result of the proposed differing treatment of the retroactivity issue as between noncontributory defined benefit plans and defined contribution plans, an individual who became 65 prior to 1988 and who is covered under a defined contribution plan only accrues post-age-65 benefits from 1988 on, whereas if an individual covered by a defined benefit plan attained age 65 prior to 1988, he or she became entitled to accruals starting with his or her 65th birthday.

As of June 15, 1994 no final regulations had been issued. However, the IRS has asserted that its proposed regulations can be relied upon for guidance by taxpayers pending the issuance of final regulations.[868]

Case Law

Atkins v Northwest Airlines, Inc,[869] arose out of a benefit plan that allegedly gave greater benefits, on the basis of age, to some individuals than others. The plans provided for the continued accrual of pension benefits until an employee had worked for 25 years, at which point the benefits ceased accruing on the basis

---

[867] *Id.*

[868] 53 Fed Reg at 11878 (Apr 11, 1988).

[869] 967 F2d 1197 (8th Cir 1992).

of longevity but continued to increase based on a computation keyed to the participants' final average earnings. Another feature of the plan provided that if an employee retired before age 60, his or her monthly pension payments would be reduced, or discounted, to account for the longer projected payment period. Thus, an employee who retired at age 60 after 25 years of service would receive a higher monthly pension payment than would an employee with 25 years of service who retired at age 55, where both had the same final average earnings. However, as an actuarial matter they both would receive the same total benefits, since the reduced amount paid to a 55-year-old would be offset by the fact that the payments would be made for a longer period of time, on average, than they would be for a 60-year-old.

The plaintiffs, who had retired after age 60, argued that just as payments were lowered for those who retired at ages younger than 60 so as to reflect the actuarially predicted longer period of payments, payments should be increased for individuals who retired after age 60 since such individuals would receive payments for an actuarially predicted shorter period of time than would younger retirees. The court rejected their argument: "[T]he lifting of the early retirement discount at age sixty does not constitute a change or a reduction in an 'accrued benefit' under ADEA[.]"[870]

In *Puckett v United Air Lines, Inc,*[871] United argued with regard to contributions by it to the company fixed benefit retirement income plan that the OBRA amendments should not be read as requiring credit for time worked after the normal retirement date, but prior to the OBRA effective date. The IRS had taken the position, in its proposed regulations implementing the OBRA amendments, that it would maintain its pre-OBRA stance, to wit: " 'For a participant who has at least 1 hour of service for the plan sponsor in a plan year beginning in 1988 or thereafter, a defined benefit plan may not disregard any years of service, *including years of service before 1988,* because of age in

[870] *Id* 1201.

[871] 705 F Supp 422 (ND Ill 1989).

determining the participant's plan benefit.' "[872] The court rejected United's challenge to the IRS interpretation and held that "[w]hen an employee retires in a plan year beginning on or after January 1, 1988, the OBRA amendments shall govern the terms of his pension benefits."[873] Accordingly, the court held that "employees who retire after the effective date of OBRA must receive credit for all years of service, including those prior to the effective date, in determining their benefit" under the fixed benefit plan at issue in the case.[874]

The *Puckett* court also addressed the rule regarding the effective date of the OBRA vis-a-vis collectively bargained plans. Section 9204(a)(2)[875] of the amendments provided for a "special rule" for such plans. When applied to the defendant's benefit plans, this rule resulted in the effective date of the OBRA amendment being January 1, 1989, for one of United's benefit plans and December 1, 1988, for the other. The court held that the OBRA special rule indeed applied. The deferral of the effective date in the instances of collectively bargained plans also was addressed in *Atkins v Northwest Airlines, Inc,* in which the court rejected the argument that the contract had not been ratified by an early enough date to allow the defendant to rely on the deferred implementation provision.

The court deciding *Davidson v Cincinnati Milacron, Inc,*[876] rejected the plaintiff's argument that the defendant's cessation of pension contributions and of benefit accruals once the plaintiff had turned 65 was violative of the ADEA. Looking to *Public Employees Retirement System v Betts*[877] as the controlling decision, the *Davidson* court concluded that there was no subterfuge inso-

---

[872] *Id* 423 (quoting IRS Notice 88-126, 1988-52 IRB 6 (emphasis supplied by the court)).

[873] 705 F Supp at 423.

[874] *Id* 424.

[875] Pub L No 99-509, §9204(a)(2), 100 Stat 1874, 1979-80.

[876] 59 FEP Cas (BNA) 154 (SD Ohio 1991), *affd without opinion,* 966 F2d 1451 (6th Cir 1992).

[877] 492 US 158 (1989).

far as the cessation of contributions was concerned.[878] As for the argument by the plaintiff that the ADEA had been violated by virtue of the cessation of the accrual of benefits at age 65, the court pointed to the fact that the plaintiff had been receiving pension payments even as he continued working for the same employer after age 65, and it reasoned as follows:

> [The defendant] . . . satisfies its alleged obligation for the continued accrual of benefits because the actuarial equivalent of the in-service distribution of benefits to . . . [the plaintiff] ($32,025.74 annually) exceeded the amount of additional yearly benefit ($4,061.65) which . . . [the plaintiff's] continued service could have accrued after age 65.[879]

The court then invoked §4(j)(3)[880] to justify the cessation of benefit accrual; this subsection provides as follows:

> In the case of any employee who, as of the end of any plan year under a defined benefit plan, has attained normal retirement age under such plan—
>
> (A) if distribution of benefits under such plan with respect to such employee has commenced as of the end of such plan year, then any requirement of this subsection for continued accrual of benefits under such plan with respect to such employee during such plan year shall be treated as satisfied to the end of the actuarial equivalent of in-service distribution of benefits[.]

A state statutory scheme that conflicted with §4(j) was held to be preempted by the ADEA in *Equal Employment Opportunity Commission v Massachusetts.*[881]

---

878 The focus on subterfuge no longer exists, since this term was eradicated by the OWBPA's amendment of §4(f)(2), 29 USC 623(f)(2). See **§5.25.**

879 59 FEP Cas (BNA) at 161.

880 29 USC §623(j)(3).

881 54 FEP Cas (BNA) 436 (D Mass 1990).

§5.42 —Allocations in Defined Contribution Plans

The freezing of employee contributions and of accruals of benefits upon attainment of normal retirement age was authorized in the past by agency interpretations, which were rescinded as a result of a court order in March, 1987.[882] This court-ordered rescission included within its ambit a provision dealing with the issue of account allocations.[883] However, the Equal Employment Opportunity Commission (EEOC)—observing that the court order regarding this particular provision in fact was not based on any actual challenge to the positions taken in that provision—issued a policy statement in 1987 asserting its continuing agreement with the principles set forth in the provision.[884] Thus, even though the provision in question does not appear in the Code of Federal Regulations, the EEOC has spoken on the issue.

The now-rescinded provision stated as follows:

> In a defined contribution plan, investment gains and losses and employment termination forfeitures are typically allocated to individual accounts instead of being used to allocate employer contributions. Where this is done, the allocations shall not be made less favorably on the basis of age to older employees (including those continuing to work past normal retirement age) than to younger employees. This rule shall apply regardless of whether or not the defined contribution plan is "supplemental."[885]

In its 1987 policy statement expressing agreement with, and reaffirmation of, the principles set forth in the now-defunct for-

---

[882] See **§5.40.**

[883] 29 CFR §860.120(f)(1)(iv)(B) (1986) (ordered removed from the CFR, 52 Fed Reg 23812 (June 25, 1987)).

[884] EEOC Policy Statement N-915: Application of Section 4(f)(2) of the Age Discrimination in Employment Act of 1967 (ADEA), as amended, to Defined Contribution Plans 3 (Sept 4, 1987). (This policy statement is reproduced in the Appendix that appears at the end of the last volume.)

[885] 29 CFR §860.120(f)(iv)(B) (1986) (ordered removed from the CFR, 52 Fed Reg 23812 (June 25, 1987)).

mal agency interpretation the EEOC commented with specific references to the types of allocations as follows:

> (1) "Investment gains and losses" are always allocated to individual accounts in a defined contribution plan. The allocations are made according to the formula set forth in the plan documents, and are usually made proportionately, based upon account balances. The allocations to the accounts of older employees cannot be made in a manner that discriminates on the basis of age, even if the employee is working beyond the plan's normal retirement age.
> (2) "Employee termination forfeitures" occur when an employee terminates employment prior to becoming fully vested under the pension plan, and all or part of the employee's account balance attributable to employer contributions is forfeited by the employee. In some plans, such forfeited amounts are used to reduce the amount of the required annual employer contributions. In other plans, the forfeitures are divided among the accounts of the remaining plan participants according to the formula set forth in the plan. As was stated with respect to investment gains and losses, discrimination in such allocations on the basis of age is prohibited. Such gains and losses include interest and dividends, but can also include gains and losses on the purchase and sale of property.[886]

§5.43 The Application of §4(f)(2) to Life Insurance

Pursuant to §4(f)(2)[887] of the Age Discrimination in Employment Act (ADEA),[888] an employee benefit plan must satisfy the *equal benefit or equal cost* principle[889] in order to be successfully relied upon by an employer, employment agency, or labor orga-

886 EEOC Policy Statement N-915, *supra* note 884, at 3.

887 29 USC §623(f)(2).

888 *Id* §§621-634.

889 See **§§5.32-5.33.**

nization as a basis for making a decision or taking an action that otherwise would violate the ADEA. An interpretation issued by the Equal Employment Opportunity Commission (EEOC) fleshes out the meaning and scope of the bona fide employee benefit plan exception.[890] In so doing, it addresses, inter alia, the treatment of life insurance.

According to the EEOC interpretation, "[c]ost comparisons and adjustments under section 4(f)(2) must be made on a benefit-by-benefit basis or on a 'benefit package' basis[.]"[891] The interpretation goes on to discuss how a benefit-by-benefit approach would apply to a life insurance benefit plan. First observing that "[it] is not uncommon for life insurance coverage to remain constant until a specified age, frequently 65, and [to] then be reduced,"[892] the interpretation provides as follows:

> This practice will not violate the Act (even if reductions start before age 65), provided that the reduction for an employee of a particular age is no greater than is justified by the increased cost of coverage for that employee's specific age bracket encompassing no more than five years. It should be noted that a total denial of life insurance, on the basis of age, would not be justified under a benefit-by-benefit analysis. However, it is not unlawful for life insurance coverage to cease upon separation from service.[893]

The EEOC issued a policy statement in November, 1987, in which it provided an illustration of how the foregoing interpretation would operate:

> (a) Employer R provides $55,000 term life insurance for all of its employees in the 62-66 age bracket. (These figures are hypothetical and intended only to demonstrate the concept of 5-year bracketing). The cost of the same amount

---

[890] 29 CFR §1625.10 (1993).

[891] *Id* §1625.10(d)(2).

[892] *Id* §1625.10(f)(1)(i).

[893] *Id.*

of life insurance for employees in the 67-71 age bracket is 110% of the cost of such insurance for individuals in the 62-66 age bracket. The employer will be in compliance with 29 CFR §860.120(f)(1)(i) [, now codified as *id* §1625.10(f)(1)(i),] if it provides $50,000 term coverage for all individuals in the 67-71 age bracket, calculated as follows: 100%/110% × $55,000 = $50,000.

(b) In part (a) above, the employer would not be in compliance with the regulations if it provided less than $50,000 in coverage to the 67-71 age bracket, cut off benefits entirely at age 70, or based the reductions on the costs of providing coverage to persons within a bracket of more than five years, e.g., ages 67-73 compared to ages 60-66.[894]

In *International Brotherhood of Electric Workers, Local 1439, AFL-CIO v Union Electric Co*[895] the Court of Appeals for the Eighth Circuit upheld the defendant's invocation of the bona fide employee benefit plan exception with regard to a provision in the company's group life insurance policy that barred employees over age 40 from electing increased optional coverage. Under the plan there was, from the employee's perspective, a level premium throughout his or her tenure. But because the plan functioned on standard actuarial principles, the cost of insuring employees rose as they aged and accordingly the company's expenses, i.e., its share of the increasing premium, rose as a given employee grew older. Under the plan there was also an open enrollment period for any new employee during the first 60 days of his or her employment with the company. Thus, the newly hired 55-year-old employee was just as eligible for participation as was the newly hired 25-year-old. The problem would arise if a 55-year-old long-time employee sought to choose the

---

894 EEOC Policy Statement N-915: Application of Section 4(f)(2) of the Age Discrimination in Employment Act of 1967 (ADEA), as Amended, to Life Insurance and Long-Term Disability Plans (Nov 10, 1987). (This policy statement is reproduced in the Appendix which appears at the end of the last volume).

895 761 F2d 1257 (8th Cir 1985).

increased optional coverage; he or she would be barred, whereas the 35-year-old long-time employee would not be.

In upholding the legality of the plan, the court stated as follows:

> The forty-year-old age cutoff in the eligibility provisions simply reflects adherence to sound actuarial principles; without the age cutoffs, older employees could opt into the plan at an advanced age (with a higher risk of claim) without having contributed to the premium pool through their young low-risk years. We hasten to add, however, that the result of this appeal might well be different if the policy did not include the initial sixty-day open enrollment period for older employees or if the employees' share of the premium did not remain level for the life of the policy.[896]

In *Michigan State Employees Association v Civil Service Commission*[897] the court held a state employee life insurance plan violative of the Act where the plan provided that, starting at age 61, there would be an annual benefit reduction of 15 per cent, so that by age 65 an employee would have only 25 per cent of the benefit he or she had had at age 60.

§5.44 The Application of §4(f)(2) to Sickness and Vacation Benefits

The Equal Employment Opportunity Commission (EEOC) interpretation[898] addressing the contours and application of the bona fide employee benefit exception set forth in §4(f)(2)[899] of the Age Discrimination in Employment Act (ADEA)[900] does not approve reductions in paid vacations or paid sick leave on the

---

[896] *Id* 1258.

[897] 177 Mich App 231, 441 NW2d 423 (1989).

[898] 29 CFR §1625.10 (1993).

[899] 29 USC §623(f)(2).

[900] *Id* §§621-634.

basis of age.[901] This is because such reductions cannot be justified by significant cost considerations.[902] Reductions in sick leave are permitted, however, in instances where the employer insures against sick leave and the reductions imposed are cost justified.[903]

Employers sometimes set conditions on payment for accrued, but unused, sick leave and/or vacation time. If these conditions appear to discriminate against a protected age group, they may be subject to attack under the ADEA. Such attacks have met with mixed success.

In *Alford v City of Lubbock*[904] the employer refused to pay retiring employees for their accrued, but unused, sick leave unless they participated in the employer's pension plan. Employees who were 50 years old or older at the time of hire were excluded from the pension plan because they could not accumulate a sufficient period of service to qualify for benefits. The court held that the refusal to pay for accrued sick leave was based on age and not protected by §4(f)(2). It found the sick leave payment to be no different than any other fringe benefit paid to employees regardless of age. It was a single, easily calculated benefit and accordingly far different from the complicated pension plans which Congress indicated, by adoption of §4(f)(2), it did not want to disturb.

In *Equal Employment Opportunity Commission v Air Line Pilots Association*[905] older pilots challenged a change in the bidding procedures for scheduling vacation days. Pilots who were retiring had previously been permitted to schedule all of their vacation days for dates following their retirement date. Thereby, they in effect obtained a lump-sum payment for accrued vacation time. A new collective bargaining agreement required pilots retiring at age 60 (which they had to do by virtue of a Federal Aviation Adminis-

---

901 29 CFR §1625.10(a)(1) (1993).

902 *Id.*

903 44 Fed Reg 30649 (May 25, 1979).

904 664 F2d 1263 (5th Cir), *cert denied,* 456 US 975 (1982).

905 661 F2d 90 (8th Cir 1981).

tration regulation requiring retirement at that age)[906] to use a specified portion of their vacation days prior to their retirement dates. No such provision restricted the use of vacation days of pilots electing to retire early. Consequently, the district court held the restriction violative of the ADEA.[907] On appeal, the Court of Appeals for the Eighth Circuit reversed.[908] Because a pilot who elected to retire during the calendar year in which he turned 60, but prior to his 60th birthday, would be able to receive a lump-sum payment for all accrued vacation days, the policy did not—in the appellate court's view—discriminate on the basis of age, but rather on the basis of whether an employee chose early retirement. Moreover, the court found that because early retirement was rare, sporadic, and unpredictable at the time vacation bids were submitted, there was no ascertainable class of early retiring pilots, since it could not be determined at that time who would elect to retire early. The court concluded that the rule applied equally regardless of age because it required employees to bid for vacation leave in proportion to their anticipated period of service in the coming year.

At issue in *Finnegan v Trans World Airlines, Inc,*[909] was a reduction of employee's benefits, which reduction included the capping of paid vacations at four weeks a year. Previously, employees with more than 16 years of service had been entitled to longer periods of this benefit, ranging up to as much as seven weeks for workers with 30 years of service. Inasmuch as most workers with more than 16 years of service would be at least 40 years of age, and certainly those with 30 years or more of service would be over that age, it followed that the brunt of this cap on paid vacations fell on those within the ADEA-protected group. The

---

[906] 14 CFR §121.383(c) (1993).

[907] Equal Employment Opportunity Commn v Air Line Pilots Assn, Intl, 489 F Supp 1003 (D Minn 1980), *revd,* 661 F2d 90 (8th Cir 1981).

[908] Equal Employment Opportunity Commn v Air Line Pilots Assn, Intl, 661 F2d 90 (8th Cir 1981).

[909] 967 F2d 1161 (7th Cir 1992).

court pointed out that §4(f)(2) is directed to allowing employers to take account of the higher costs for older workers of certain fringe benefits. It went on to note that it did "not understand TWA to be arguing that a schedule of paid vacations can be regarded in that light."[910] Thus, if the cap on paid vacations was to pass muster, it could not do so within the safe harbor of §4(f)(2). However, the court still ruled for the defendant. While it recognized that the cap had a disparate impact on older workers,[911] it was unwilling to conclude that a prima facie claim thereby was established by virtue of this impact:

> Across-the-board cuts in wages and fringe benefits necessitated by business downturns or setbacks are a far cry from the situations that brought the [disparate impact] theory into being. These cuts are not a legacy of deliberate discrimination on grounds of age; they are not the product of inertia or insensitivity. They are an unavoidable response to adversity. Their adverse impact on older workers is unavoidable too, because it is impossible to reduce the costs of fringe benefits without making deeper cuts in the benefits of older workers, simply because, by virtue of being older, they have greater benefits. In this situation no inference of discrimination, whether deliberate or merely inadvertent (but avoidable), can be drawn from the greater impact of curtailing employees' benefits on older workers. Otherwise every time a company tried to reduce its labor costs the federal courts would be dragged in and asked to redesign the reduction so as to shift the burden to some unprotected class of workers.[912]

---

[910] *Id* 1163.

[911] As to disparate impact analysis, see **ch 7.**

[912] 967 F2d at 1164.

§5.45 The Application of §4(f)(2) to Health Insurance

Section 4(f)(2)[913] of the Age Discrimination in Employment Act (ADEA)[914] establishes that an employer, employment agency, or labor organization may take actions and make decisions that would otherwise violate the Act if the entity involved can successfully prove that in so doing it was observing the terms of a bona fide employee benefit plan. Pursuant to §4(f)(2)(B)(i),[915] a complained-of differential in treatment resulting from the observance of a plan's terms must be cost justified, i.e., the entity charged with discrimination must be able to establish that it was expending an amount on older workers equal to, or nearly equal to, the amount spent on younger individuals, even if that amount did not purchase equality in terms of benefits.[916]

While §4(f)(2) and the *equal benefit or equal cost* principle that §4(f)(2)(B)(i) embraces do not explicitly address health insurance plans, such plans clearly are covered by these provisions. In addition, there is another provision, §4(l)(2),[917] that addresses health insurance benefits, as well as another section—§4(g)[918]—concerning health benefits that also deserves attention, although it was repealed in 1989. This section will deal with the application of §4(f)(2) and the *equal benefit or equal cost* principle.

The general rules and guidelines already discussed regarding the *equal benefit or equal cost* principle apply here as well.[919] There is very little in the legislative history of the ADEA by way of particularized focus on health insurance benefits, save for a colloquy between Senators Bentsen and Pryor on the floor of the Senate during consideration of the Older Workers Benefit Protection

---

913 29 USC §623(f)(2).

914 *Id* §§621-634.

915 *Id* §623(f)(2)(B)(i).

916 See **§§5.32-5.33.**

917 29 USC §623(l), (2). See **§5.47.**

918 §4(g), 29 USC §623(g) (repealed). See **§5.46.**

919 See **§§5.32-5.33.**

Act (OWBPA),[920] which amended the ADEA so as to write explicitly into §4(f)(2) the *equal benefit or equal cost* principle. Their colloquy concerned a facet of the operation of the Texas teacher retirement system. This system entailed alternate packages of health care coverage being offered to prospective retirees, the particular package offered being based on whether the prospective retiree was eligible for Medicare Part B health insurance coverage, which eligibility arises upon attainment of age 65. For those who were 65 and older, the Texas system incorporated a Medicare Part B *carve out,* whereby the system's private coverage was not extended to those services which were covered under Medicare. For prospective retirees under 65, on the other hand, the state system provided coverage for the services for which Medicare would pay in the case of an older retiree. In other words, there was no *carve out* for those under age 65. The consequence was that the coverage provided by the state system for younger employees was greater than it was for those 65 and older.

Senator Bentsen's concern was whether this age-based distinction would run afoul of the proscription of age discrimination set forth in the ADEA, as it was proposed to be amended by the OWBPA. The particular question Senator Bentsen put to Senator Pryor (who was one of the floor managers of the legislation) was as follows: "If the system pays approximately the equivalent amount to purchase the private insurance for the prospective retiree under 65 as for the prospective retiree 65 or older, does [sic] the system's retiree health packages violate the ADEA as amended by . . . [the legislation which, in modified form, was ultimately enacted into law as the OWBPA]?"[921] Senator Pryor responded in the negative:

> The purpose of equal benefit or equal cost is to allow employers to take account of the fact that the cost of some benefits rises with the age of the employee. If your scenario

---

[920] Pub L No 101-433, 104 Stat 978, *as amended by* Pub L No 101-521, 104 Stat 2287 (1990).

[921] 136 Cong Rec S13,609 (daily ed Sept 24, 1990).

> is correct and the system spends the same amount in acquiring health coverage for all prospective retirees regardless of age, I would say that it has satisfied the equal benefit or equal cost principle.[922]

(In *Potenze v New York Shipping Association,*[923] a pre-OWBPA decision, the court rejected the argument that a plan was a subterfuge to evade the ADEA's purposes simply because better alternatives could have been used by the employer.[924] Under that plan, employees ages 65 and over were subjected to an offset against their Social Security benefits, whereas employees ages 62 to 64 were not).

§5.46 —Health Insurance: The Repealed §4(g)

From 1982 through 1989 the Age Discrimination in Employment Act (ADEA)[925] contained a provision, §4(g),[926] that applied to employers providing group health insurance coverage to their employees. Such employers had to provide, to their employees and their spouses who were age 65 and over, coverage under the same conditions that applied, pursuant to the employers' group plans, to under-65 employees and their spouses.[927] The

---

[922] *Id* S13, 610.

[923] 804 F2d 235 (2d Cir 1986), *cert denied,* 481 US 1029 (1987).

[924] As explained in **§5.23,** the OWBPA, in amending §4(f)(2), discarded the term *subterfuge.*

[925] 29 USC §§621-634.

[926] *Id* §623(g) (repealed). Section 4(g) was enacted in its original form in 1982, by virtue of §116(a) of the Tax Equity and Fiscal Responsibility Act of 1982, Pub L No 97-248, 96 Stat 324, 353. Changes were later made by the Deficit Reduction Act of 1984, Pub L No 98-369, §2301(b)(1), 98 Stat 494, 1063, and the Consolidated Omnibus Budget Reconciliation Act of 1985, Pub L No 99-272, §§9201(b)(1), (2), 100 Stat 82, 171. Subsequently, §4(g) was reenacted, with no additional changes, by the Age Discrimination in Employment Amendments of 1986, Pub L No 99-592, §2(a), 100 Stat 3342, at 3342. Ultimately, §4(g) was repealed by the Omnibus Budget Reconciliation Act of 1989, Pub L No 101-239, §6202(b)(3)(C)(i), 103 Stat 2106, 2233.

[927] *Group health* plan was defined in §4(g)(2), 29 USC §623(g)(2) (repealed), by reference to §162(i)(2) of the Internal Revenue Code, 26 USC §162(i)(2).

consequence of this provision was that employers could not point to differential costs for the coverage of older versus younger employees and rely upon that differential as the basis for extending different benefits.

In the instance of noncontributory plans, i.e., plans to which employees contribute no part of the premium, employees who were 65 and older had to receive the same benefits as were provided younger employees. This did not mean that no distinctions could be made between different employees. But it did mean—according to a policy statement issued by the Equal Employment Opportunity Commission (EEOC)[928]—that "the employer's coverage for employees aged 65 or older and their spouses . . . [had to] be under the same conditions as the most favorable health care benefits provided to younger employees or their spouses."[929] Contributory plans are those in which employees contribute some part of the premium. Section 4(g) precluded requiring employees who were 65 or over to contribute at a higher level than younger employees. While contribution levels

---

928 The interpretations issued initially by the Department of Labor, 29 CFR §860.120 (1986) (effectively rescinded, 46 Fed Reg 47724 (Sept 29, 1981), and ordered removed from the CFR, 52 Fed Reg 23812 (June 25, 1987)), were subsequently transferred into the Equal Employment Opportunity Commission's (EEOC's) section of the CFR, 52 Fed Reg 23811 (June 25, 1987), codified at 29 CFR §1625.10 (1993). These interpretations, however, did not reflect the equality of coverage mandated by §4(g). In June 1983, the EEOC published interim regulations implementing §4(g). 48 Fed Reg 26437-38 (June 7, 1983), promulgating 29 CFR §1625.20. However, in December 1985, the EEOC rescinded these interim provisions, while at the same time it declined to issue final regulations. 50 Fed Reg 50614-15 (Dec 11, 1985). The agency did assert that the extant agency interpretations regarding group health insurance coverage, contained in 29 CFR §1625.10(f)(1)(ii) (1987), were no longer valid. In 1988 the EEOC formally removed the provision that was not in accord with §4(g) from its interpretations. 53 Fed Reg 5971-74, at 5972 (Feb 29, 1988).

929 EEOC Policy Statement No N-915.026: Application of §4(g) of the Age Discrimination in Employment Act of 1967 (ADEA), *as amended* (Coverage of Older Workers Under Group Health Plans) 7 (May 12, 1988). Such policy statements do not have the force of law; they do, however, command some degree of judicial deference. See **ch 2**.

could be raised to reflect increased costs, the increases had to be distributed equally, even if the increased costs were the result of covering older workers.[930]

An employer did not fall outside the reach of §4(g) simply because its plan was maintained through a third party, such as an insurance agent or company.[931] On the other hand, an employer did not elude the reach of §4(g) just because it did not contribute to a group health plan: employee-pay-all plans that were made available through employers covered by the ADEA constituted plans within the ambit of §4(g).[932] However, an employer that was not covered by the ADEA because it did not satisfy the ADEA's definition of what constitutes an employer[933] would not come within the reach of the Act simply because it participated in a multi-employer trust, some members of which were covered employers within the meaning of the ADEA.[934]

The legislative history of §4(g) established Congress's intent that an employee did not have to participate in the plan offered by his or her employer. He or she was free to retain Medicare as his or her primary health care coverage.[935] The coverage pro-

---

930 *Id* 7-8.

931 *Id* 3.

932 *Id* 4.

933 *See* §11(b), 29 USC §630(b), discussed in **ch 3.**

934 EEOC Policy Statement No N-915.026, *supra* note 929, at 3-4.

935 Conference Comm, Tax Equity and Fiscal Responsibility Act of 1982, S Rep No 530, 97th Cong, 2d Sess 414 (1982). "[A]s to those employees or spouses who elect Medicare coverage, an employer may pay or contribute toward the Medicare Part B premium . . . and provide health insurance coverage for items and services *wholly* uncovered by Medicare." EEOC Policy Statement No N-915.026, *supra* note 929, at 8 (emphasis in original). Such payment would not be deemed to constitute an unlawful inducement to elect Medicare. *Id.*

> [E]mployees and their spouses age 65 or older . . . [were to] be provided with information regarding their rights under section 4(g) . . . and . . . the covered individual . . . [is to] continue to be covered by the employer's health plan unless and until he or she (1) notifies the employer, in writing, that he or she does not want such coverage to continue, or (2) otherwise ceases to be eligible for such coverage for a reason that would

vided by §4(g) to a spouse was an independent right belonging to that individual. Thus, when a 62-year-old employee's spouse turned age 65, it was the nonemployee spouse's prerogative to decide whether to continue in the employer group health plan or to elect to switch to Medicare for primary coverage.[936] When the employee turned 65, he or she could—as discussed above—choose Medicare for primary coverage and drop the employer plan. At that juncture, the employer could discontinue coverage for the spouse without violating §4(g) if dependent coverage likewise would be terminated under the plan for the spouse of an under-65 employee who chose not to be covered under the plan.[937] In other words, if spousal coverage under a plan was dependent upon the employee's being covered—and this was true for all employees and spouses, regardless of age—then spousal coverage could be discontinued when the employee elected to take Medicare as primary coverage.[938]

While *Karlen v City Colleges of Chicago*[939] concerned §4(g), it did not actually deal with the substance of the provision. The case involved a termination of insurance benefits for faculty members upon attainment of age 65. The plaintiffs were retirees who, after retiring early, filed suit challenging allegedly discriminatory aspects of the defendant's early retirement program. The district court reasoned that these individuals were not employees:

> [Section 4(g)] does not cover the insurance rights of retirees. . . . The plaintiffs assert that the term "employee" must

---

> make an employee under age 65 ineligible for coverage (e.g., failure to pay premiums.)

Id 5.

936 EEOC Policy Statement No N-915.026, *supra* note 929, at 5. Obviously, and consistent with the legislative history, coverage was applicable to the nonemployee spouse who was 65 even if the employee was under 65. (However, the employee had to be at least 40.) *Id* 6.

937 *Id* 5-6.

938 *Id* 6.

939 No 84 C 2925 (ND Ill Dec 12, 1986) (unreported), *revd,* 837 F2d 314 (7th Cir), *cert denied,* 486 US 1044 (1988).

> be construed to include retirees, but such an interpretation would prevent an employee from doing what [29 USC] §623(f)(2) permits—to make distinctions in benefits as part of a bona fide retirement plan. Employers may not deny older employees identical group health coverage, but they can deny it to those who have retired pursuant to a bona fide retirement plan.[940]

This reasoning seemed amiss.[941] In any event, the decision was reversed on appeal.[942] Since the appellate court held that the case should be remanded for a trial on the plaintiffs' claims, it was clear that the reviewing court rejected the trial court's analysis, even though it did not directly rebut that analysis by way of explicit discussion.

Section 4(g) was repealed by virtue of the enactment of the Omnibus Reconciliation Act of 1989 (OBRA),[943] in the course of Congress's restructuring of the Medicare program's role as a secondary payer. Older workers and their spouses did not thereby suffer a loss of any protection or rights, however. Rather, there is simply a different statutory locus for the assertion of those rights and protections. By virtue of the changes that were made, Medicare itself now provides that for items or services furnished to a person who is 65 or older and who is covered under a group health plan, either directly by virtue of being an employee or secondarily by virtue of being the spouse of an employee, the plan may not take into account the individual's

---

[940] Slip op at 15; *accord* Provident Life & Accident Ins Co v Leonard, 526 So 2d 721 (Fla Dist Ct App 1988), *review denied,* 563 So 2d 633 (1990).

[941] In theory, this reasoning would have barred every retiree from maintaining suit following retirement—a consequence that would have devastated much of the case law discussed in the preceding sections concerning the employee benefit plan exception. For that matter, the court's logic also could have been extended to bar suit by a former employee who claimed to be a victim of post-employment retaliation—another consequence not consistent with the extant case law. *See, e.g.*, Equal Employment Opportunity Commn v Cosmair, Inc, 821 F2d 1085, 1089 (5th Cir 1987). See generally **ch 4** as to retaliation.

[942] Karlen v City Colleges of Chicago, 837 F2d 314 (7th Cir), *cert denied,* 486 US 1044 (1988).

[943] Pub L No 101-239, §6202(b)(3)((C)(i), 103 Stat 2106, 2233.

entitlement to Medicare Part A coverage.[944] It is further required that group health plans must provide the same benefits, under the same conditions, for any employee who is 65 or older, as well as that employee's spouse if he or she is 65 or older, as are provided for employees and spouses under age 65.[945]

§5.47 Severance Pay and the §4(l)(2) Affirmative Defense

Prior to *Public Employees Retirement System v Betts*[946] being decided, lower courts had held that the Age Discrimination in Employment Act (ADEA)[947] was violated if an employer denied severance pay to an employee because he or she was eligible for a pension—a denial that typically would primarily adversely affect older employees, since they were the ones most likely to have sufficient seniority to be pension eligible.[948] After *Betts*, however, the Court of Appeals for the Third Circuit held to the contrary: "[T]he mere denial of severance pay, without more,

---

944 42 USC §1395y(b)(i)(I).

945 *Id* §1395y(b)(i)(II).

> [T]hese requirements do not apply to (i) group health plans sponsored by or contributed to by an employer with fewer than 20 employees for each working day in each of 20 or more calendar weeks in the current or preceding calendar year; (ii) individuals enrolled in a multiemployer or multiple employer group health plan sponsored or contributed to by an employer with fewer than 20 employees for each working day in each of 20 or more calendar weeks in the current or preceding calendar year, if the plan elects to be excepted; and (iii) items or services furnished in a month to an individual if for the month the individual is, or would upon application be, entitled to benefits . . . [for treatment of] (end stage renal disease).

House Conf Rep No 386, Omnibus Reconciliation Act of 1989, 101st Cong, 1st Sess 822 (1989), *reprinted at* 4 US Code Cong & Adm News, 101st Cong, 1st Sess 3018, 3245 (1989), referring to the provisions enacted by the 1989 Act that are codified at 42 USC §1395y(b)(ii).

946 492 US 158 (1989). As to the *Betts* decision generally, see **§5.24.**

947 29 USC §§621-634.

948 *See, e.g.*, Equal Employment Opportunity Commn v Borden's, Inc, 724 F2d 1390 (9th Cir 1984).

is not actionable under ADEA."[949] While the Older Workers Benefit Protection Act (OWBPA),[950] enacted in 1990, overturned *Betts,* the legislation did not return the law entirely to the status quo ante. Rather, under the ADEA, as amended by the OWBPA, this particular type of benefit packaging—i.e., offsetting severance payments by the amount of certain (albeit not all) other benefit payments—is now legitimate, a status it would not have had under pre-*Betts* case law. To be more specific, when a contingent event occurs unrelated to age, e.g., a plant shutdown or a large-scale reduction in force, the employer, under the amended ADEA, is allowed to reduce the severance benefits to which workers otherwise would be entitled by the value of their retiree health benefits. In addition, severance pay can be offset by the value of "shutdown sweeteners," i.e., additional pension benefits provided to workers solely because of a plant closing or because of layoffs.[951] Specifically, §4(l)(2)[952] provides as follows:

> (A) It shall not be a violation of subsection (a), (b), (c), or (e) [, 29 USC §623(a), (b), (c), or (e),] solely because following a contingent event unrelated to age—
>
> (i) the value of any retiree health benefits received by an individual eligible for an immediate pension; and
>
> (ii) the value of any additional pension benefits that are made available solely as a result of the contingent

---

[949] Equal Employment Opportunity Commn v Westinghouse Elec Corp, 930 F2d 329, 333 (3d Cir 1991).

[950] Pub L No 101-433, 104 Stat 978, *as amended by* Pub L No 101-521, 104 Stat 2287 (1990).

[951] There were several versions of the Senate bill, S1511, 101st Cong, 1st Sess (1990), that preceded the one that actually was passed by the Senate, and ultimately was enacted into law. See **§5.25.** Under the penultimate version of S1511, an employer was allowed to integrate so-called *shutdown,* or pension, *sweeteners* with severance pay, i.e., to offset the former against the latter, only if the employer also provided a package of retiree health benefits. This pro-employee limitation on the ability of an employer to engage in this offset was eliminated, however, in the final compromise bill, thereby allowing for the integration of shutdown sweeteners without strings attached.

[952] 29 USC §623(l)(2).

event unrelated to age and following which the individual is eligible for not less than an immediate and unreduced pension; or,

(iii) the values described in both clauses (i) and (ii); are deducted from severance pay made available as a result of the contingent event unrelated to age.

It is §4(l)(2)(A)(ii)[953] that addresses so-called *shutdown sweeteners.* The Senate report on the bill, S 1511,[954] which in modified form eventually was passed by the Senate and House and was enacted into law as the OWBPA addressed a version of the bill that conditioned an employer's ability to utilize a deduction for such sweeteners on its also offering retirees health benefits.[955] The OWBPA, however, did not maintain that condition precedent,[956] and so the Senate report's discussion of shutdown sweeteners was directed to what turned out to be a superseded provision. Even so, the language of the enacted §4(l)(2)(A)(ii) is the same as that in the committee version of S 1511 insofar as a deduction for shutdown sweeteners is approved only if the individual is eligible, following the plant shutdown, for "an immediate and unreduced pension," and so the Senate report retains relevance the term "unreduced pension" was explained in the Senate report as follows:

> [F]or example, if at the time of a plant closing an employee was entitled to 80% of a normal retirement pension and as a result of the shutdown that individual . . . became entitled to an amount equal to 100% of a normal retirement pension, the value of the additional 20% . . . may permissibly be offset against severance benefits.[957]

---

953 *Id* §623(l)(2)(A)(ii).

954 S 1511, 101st Cong, 1st Sess (1989).

955 Senate Comm on Labor & Human Resources, The Older Workers Benefit Protection Act, S Rep No 263, 101st Cong, 2d Sess (1990) [hereinafter Senate Report].

956 See note 951.

957 Senate Report, *supra* note 955, at 24.

By virtue of §4(l)(2)(B),[958] if pension benefits are actuarially reduced, the amount of the deduction, or offset, must be reduced by the same amount. "Thus, for example, if an individual receiving retiree health benefits received a pension that is actuarially reduced by 18%, the value of that individual's retiree health benefits (as calculated under this section) shall be reduced by 18% before any deduction is taken."[959]

By virtue of §4(l)(2)(D),[960] an employer cannot utilize the benefit packaging addressed in §4(l)(2)(A)[961]—i.e., the offsetting of severance pay with the value of retiree health benefits—unless these benefits are either at least as valuable as Medicare benefits, in the case of workers under age 65; at least as valuable as 25 per cent of the value of Medicare benefits, in the case of workers 65 and older; or both. According to the Senate Report, "[i]n calculating the value of employer-provided benefits for individuals 65 and older, benefits that duplicate those provided under Medicare must be disregarded."[962]

Section 4(l)(2)(E)[963] sets out formulae for calculating the value of retiree health benefits. If an employer's obligation "to provide benefits is of limited duration," §4(l)(2)(E)(i)[964] applies. An example illustrates the application of the formula prescribed under this subsection. Suppose an employer that is shutting down a plant promises to provide health benefits to retirees until they reach age 65. Suppose, further, that the employer is offering severance pay of $15,000. And finally, suppose that the plant shutdown occurs when the employee in question is 62. The employer, under these facts, can—according to the statutory formula—offset $9,000 against the severance pay (3 years × $3,000), and so the employee still would be entitled to $6,000 in severance pay, along with the health benefits.

---

958 29 USC §623(l)(2)(B).

959 Senate Report, *supra* note 955, at 24.

960 29 USC §623(l)(2)(D).

961 *Id* §623(l)(2)(A).

962 Senate Report, *supra* note 955, at 25.

963 29 USC §623(l)(2)(E).

964 *Id* §623(l)(2)(E)(i).

Suppose the employer's obligation to provide health benefits is of unlimited duration. In this instance, the formula set forth in §4(l)(2)(E)(ii)[965] applies. Continuing with the hypothetical 62-year-old, she would not be entitled to any severance since the value of her retiree health benefits, i.e., $48,000 according to the statutory formula set forth in the subsection, would exceed the severance payment of $15,000.[966]

Section 4(l)(2)(E)(iv)[967] provides that the value of premiums for retiree health benefits paid by the recipient is to be applied to reduce the value of the health benefits "by whatever percentage of the overall premium the individual is required to pay." "Thus, for example, if an employee under age 65 contributes $100 of the required monthly premium of $400, and is promised benefits for life at the time of separation, the employer may deduct from severance pay $36,000 (75% × $48,000)."[968]

In instances where an employer fails to fulfill its obligations regarding retiree health benefits, suits for specific performance are authorized by §4(l)(2)(F).[969] The Senate report provided some explication regarding the issue of the employer's obligations:

> Modification of benefits in such a manner as to increase significantly the cost to participants or beneficiaries for receipt of benefits or reduce significantly the benefits provided is not permitted by paragraph 4(l)(2)(E). But relatively minor or insignificant increases in cost or reductions in benefits provided shall not constitute a failure to fulfill the obligation described in the paragraph. In determining whether a cost increase (or benefit reduction) is significant, the

---

965 *Id* §623(l)(2)(E)(ii).

966 The foregoing formulae "were based on medical costs reported in a . . . study by the General Accounting Office, [i.e.,] *Employee Benefits: Companies' Retiree Health Liabilities Large, Advance Funding Costly,* GAO/HRD-89-51 (June 1989), with assumptions added for life expe[c]tancy and dependent content." Senate Report, *supra* note 955, at 25.

967 29 USC §623(l)(2)(E)(iv).

968 Senate Report, *supra* note 955, at 26.

969 29 USC §623(l)(2)(F).

> effects of any cumulative changes on the employees are relevant. Thus, for example, an increase in an employee's monthly premium contribution for dental coverage form [sic] $3 to $4 would be insignificant. By contrast, five consecutive changes, each one requiring an additional $5 monthly premium contribution from the employee[,] would be a significant increase in the cost of the benefits and would not, therefore, fall within the protection of Section 4(l)(2). Although the Committee recognizes the need for flexibility, it is loath [sic] to permit employers to "nickel and dime" their way to significant benefit reductions at the employees' expense.[970]

In a statement submitted during the Senate debates by the managers of the legislation[971] some attention was paid to the health benefits offset:

> Many employer-sponsored retiree medical plans provide medical coverage for retirees only until the retiree becomes eligible for Medicare. In many of these cases, where coverage is provided to retirees only until they attain Medicare eligibility, the value of the employer-provided retiree medical benefits exceeds the value of the retiree's Medicare benefits. Other employers provide medical coverage to retirees at a relatively high level until the retirees become eligible for Medicare and at a lower level thereafter. In many of these cases, the value of the medical benefits that the retiree received before becoming eligible for Medicare exceeds the total value of the retiree's Medicare benefits and the medical benefits that the employer provides after the retiree

---

[970] Senate Report, *supra* note 955, at 26.

[971] The ultimate version of S 1511 that was voted on by the Senate was a compromise fashioned by Senators Metzenbaum, Pryor, Heinz, and Hatch, the managers of the legislation. While there was no committee report accompanying this version of the bill, there was a document submitted by these four, entitled *Final Substitute: Statement of Managers,* 136 Cong Rec S13596-97 (daily ed Sept 24, 1990). This statement set forth explanatory material regarding the bill.

> attains Medicare eligibility. These practices are not prohibited. . . . Similarly, nothing in . . . [the OWBPA] should be construed as authorizing a claim on behalf of a retiree on the basis that the actuarial value of employer-provided health benefits available to that retiree not yet eligible for Medicare is less than the actuarial value of the same benefits available to a younger retiree.[972]

The Senate report identified §4(l)'s authorization of offsets against severance pay as an affirmative defense.[973]

§5.48 The Application of §4(f)(2) to Disability Benefits

The Equal Employment Opportunity Commission (EEOC) has issued an interpretation that provides guidance as to the applicability of the *equal benefit or equal cost* principle[974] to disability benefits. This interpretation originally was designed to flesh out the meaning and scope of the bona fide employee benefit plan defense set forth in §4(f)(2)[975] of the Age Discrimination in Employment Act (ADEA)[976] prior to its being rewritten in 1990 by the Older Workers Benefit Protection Act (OWBPA).[977] However, the OWBPA-amended ADEA expressly embraces the *equal benefit or equal cost* principle in §4(f)(2)(B)(i),[978] and so the EEOC interpretation remains of continuing relevance. (In addition, the OWBPA added a new affirmative defense, set forth in §4(l)(3),[979]

---

972 136 Cong Rec S13597 (daily ed Sept 24, 1990).

973 Senate Report, *supra* note 955, at 22, 29.

974 See **§§5.32-33.**

975 29 USC §623(f)(2) (pre-1990 amendment).

976 *Id* §§621-634.

977 Pub L No 101-433, 104 Stat 978, *as amended by* Pub L No 101-521, 104 Stat 2287 (1990).

978 29 USC §623(f)(2)(B)(i).

979 *Id* §623(l)(3).

that allows employers to reduce disability benefits to reflect the beneficiary's receipt of pension benefits.)[980]

The EEOC interpretation provides that under a benefit-by-benefit approach, "where employees who are disabled at younger ages are entitled to long-term disability benefits, there is no cost-based justification for denying such benefits altogether, on the basis of age, to employees who are disabled at older ages."[981] If benefit reductions—both in terms of the level of benefits and their duration—are at all justifiable, they only can be made on the basis of age-related cost considerations (save for reductions made to reflect pension benefits, in accordance with §4(l)(3)).[982] An employer may avoid cost increases associated with providing coverage to older workers by reducing the level of benefits available to them.[983] "An employer may also avoid such cost increases by reducing the duration of benefits available to employees who become disabled at older ages, without reducing the level of benefits."[984] In other words, an employer may act—provided it does

---

[980] See **§5.49.**

[981] 29 CFR §1625.10(f)(ii) (1993). When the interpretation was issued in 1979, the EEOC noted that in the past termination of benefits at age 65 had been common, but because the ceiling under the ADEA for coverage of individuals was raised in 1978 to age 70, see **ch 3,** a cutoff of benefits at age 65 no longer was justifiable. Termination at age 70 was legal, however. In 1986 the ADEA was amended again so as to remove an age ceiling altogether for most individuals. See **ch 3.** As a consequence of this amendment, termination of benefits at age 70 simply because of that chronological occurrence likewise no longer is justifiable, as confirmed by an EEOC policy statement issued in November 1987. EEOC Policy Statement N-915: Application of Section 4(f)(2) to the Age Discrimination in Employment Act of 1967 (ADEA), as amended, to Life Insurance and Long-Term Disability Plans (Nov 10, 1987). (This policy statement is reproduced in the Appendix which appears at the end of the last volume). In 1988 the EEOC issued a revised interpretation reflecting the removal of the age-70 cap from the ADEA. 53 Fed Reg 5971-74 (Feb 29, 1988). Now, termination of disability benefits because of age is barred at any age. However, the termination of benefits or coverage on the basis of nonage factors is not barred. *Id.*

[982] 29 USC §623(l)(l). See **§5.49.**

[983] 29 CFR §1625.10(f)(ii) (1993).

[984] The interpretation sets forth acceptable modes of reductions of benefits:

(A) With respect to disabilities which occur at age 60 or less, benefits cease at age 65.

so consistently with the *equal benefit or equal cost* principle.[985]

An EEOC policy statement provides examples both as to a legitimate reduction in the duration of benefits and a legitimate reduction in the level of benefits:

> . . . Employer S provides a long-term disability plan under which all employees suffering from a long-term disability that occurred before the age of 60 receive unreduced benefits until the age of 65 and employees disabled after age 60 receive unreduced benefits for five years.
>
> Employer T provides a long-term disability plan under which all employees suffering from a long-term disability receive benefits from the date of disability until the earlier of recovery from disability or retirement. The amount of

---

> (B) With respect to disabilities which occur after age 60 benefits cease 5 years after disablement.

Id. Cost data may support other modes of reduction, as well. *Id.*

985 During the Senate debate on the bill that ultimately was enacted into law as the OWBPA, two of the managers of the legislation addressed application of the principle to disability plans:

> Mr. Heinz: . . . I would like my distinguished colleague . . . to clarify the application of the equal benefit or equal cost principle to the benefits paid from long-term disability plans to older plan participants. I understand it is the intent of the legislation to permit long-term disability plans to link the amount or duration of benefit payments to the attainment of a specified age upon disability, so long as the amount or duration can be justified on an actuarial basis. For example, if the disability occurred at age 60, benefits might be payable for 5 years. At older ages, the duration of payment would be further reduced, so that if the disability occurred after age 60, the plan might not be required to pay benefits for more than 1 year.
>
> Mr. Pryor: . . . [I]f an employer could show that the age based reduction in the duration of long-term disability benefits that he outlined in his example can be justified because the cost of providing the shorter duration of benefits to the oldest worker is at least equal to the cost of providing the longer duration of benefits to the younger worker, then that employer's plan would comply with the equal . . . benefit for [sic] equal cost principle.

136 Cong Rec S13,608 (daily ed Sept 24, 1990).

> disability benefits, however, is reduced for older persons based upon increased age-related costs calculated within five year brackets.[986]

The EEOC went on to point out the following:

> [A]n employer would not be in compliance with the regulations if the employer reduced the duration or level (or both) of the benefits in excess of the reduction permitted by the "safe harbor" [afforded by 29 CFR §1625.10(f)(1)(ii)] or by bona fide cost data . . . [;] used age 70 as an arbitrary cut-off point for persons disabled after the age of 65 . . . [;] or based reductions upon cost comparisons of age brackets greater than five years.[987]

In *Equal Employment Opportunity Commission v City of Mt Lebanon*[988] the court addressed a plan that provided for the termination of disability benefits to city employees at ages 62 to 68. Under the schedule of duration of benefits prescribed by the plan, as the age at which an employee became disabled increased, the duration of benefit payments decreased, so that at age 69 benefits would be paid for just one year. The court first cited approvingly the EEOC interpretation's general endorsement of plans that, although paying different benefit amounts, involve an equal expenditure for each employee. The court then went on to hold that "an employer can prove an employee benefit plan is not a subterfuge [[989]] . . . [by] proving

---

[986] EEOC Policy Statement N-915, *supra* note 981, at 4.

[987] *Id.*

[988] 651 F Supp 1259 (WD Pa 1987) *vacated & remanded,* 842 F2d 1480 (3d Cir 1988).

[989] *Subterfuge* was the key concept set forth in §4(f)(2) prior to the section's being rewritten by the OWBPA. See **§5.23.** The term was deleted from the language of the ADEA by the OWBPA. Now, an employee benefit plan (that is not a voluntary retirement incentive plan, see **§5.53)** only can be successfully invoked as an affirmative defense if the plan satisfies the *equal benefit or equal cost* principle. See **§§5.32-.33**. To the extent that a pre-OWBPA decision addressed this principle, in the context of addressing the issue of subterfuge, that decision continued to be relevant even after the OWBPA amended the ADEA. See **§5.34.**

an economic or business purpose or valid reasons for the challenged terms even though every detail of the cost-justification regulations is not met."[990] The court proceeded to uphold the plan.[991]

The district court's ruling was vacated on appeal.[992] The Court of Appeals for the Third Circuit engaged in an extensive analysis of what constitutes subterfuge,[993] and sent the case back to the trial court so that it could apply the doctrinal criteria the higher court had enunciated. The appellate court clearly had no quarrel, however, with the general notion that disability benefits can differentiate between older and younger employees, as long as the differentiation can be justified adequately by an employer on the basis of cost concerns. Like the trial court, the court of appeals looked to the EEOC interpretation (which the court, like the district court, erroneously characterized as "regulations").[994]

§5.49 —Disability Benefits Reductions: The §4(l)(3) Affirmative Defense

Section 4(l)(3)[995] of the Age Discrimination in Employment Act (ADEA)[996] was added to the ADEA by the Older Workers Benefit Protection Act (OWBPA)[997] in 1990. This provision legitimizes the reduction of long-term disability benefits by pension benefits:

---

990 651 F Supp at 1263.

991 To the argument that the plan somehow forced involuntary retirement, the court responded as follows: "The EEOC cites no factual basis in the record to support this argument. The EEOC cites no legal authority to the effect that a similar schedule of duration of benefits forces involuntary retirement." *Id* 1264.

992 Equal Employment Opportunity Commn v City of Mt Lebanon, 842 F2d 1480 (3d Cir 1988).

993 See note 989.

994 842 F2d at 1489.

995 29 USC §623(1)(3).

996 *Id* §§621-634.

997 Pub L No 101-433, 104 Stat 978, *as amended by* Pub L No 101-521, 104 Stat 2287 (1990).

> It shall not be a violation of subsection (a), (b), (c), or (e) solely because an employer provides a bona fide employee plan or plans under which long-term disability benefits received by an individual are reduced by any pension benefits (other than those attributable to employee contributions)—
>
> (A) paid to the individual that the individual voluntarily elects to receive; or
>
> (B) for which an individual who has attained the later of age 62 or normal retirement age is eligible.[998]

S 1511,[999] the bill that ultimately was enacted into law as the OWBPA, went through several modifications before being passed by the Senate. The version of S 1511 that was reported out of the Senate Committee on Labor and Human Resources, and that was accompanied by a committee report,[1000] did not contain §4(l)(3). Rather, this section first appeared, albeit in a different form than that eventually enacted into law, in the second successor to the committee bill;[1001] it was retained, in modified form, in the final compromise version of S 1511—the version that was passed by the Senate and subsequently enacted into law.

---

[998] On its face, the provision only speaks to pension benefits offsetting disability benefits. Thus, it would appear from a literal reading of §4(l)(3) that an employer may not look to Social Security or workers' compensation benefits that are received by an employee and use these to offset the individual's disability benefits. (There is a pre-OWBPA decision allowing an employer to reduce an employee's health benefits by the amount of Medicare coverage that the employee had. Potenze v New York Shipping Assn, 804 F2d 235 (2d Cir 1986), *cert denied,* 481 US 1029 (1987). See **§5.50**).

[999] 101st Cong, 1st Sess (1989).

[1000] Senate Comm on Labor & Human Resources, The Older Workers Benefit Protection Act, S Rep No 263, 101st Cong, 2d Sess (1990).

[1001] This version provided as follows:

> It shall not be a violation of subsection (a), (b), (c), or (e) solely because an employer provides a bona fide employee benefit plan or plans under which long-term disability benefits received by an individual are reduced by any pension benefits paid to the individual that the individual voluntarily elects to receive.

136 Cong Rec S13,239 (daily ed Sept 17, 1990).

Senator Pryor, one of the managers of the legislation, explained the genesis and aim of §4(1)(3):

> Disability pension integration was an issue raised by many in the early stages of this legislation and its development. On the issue of long-term disability, the charge against this bill has been that it will require the employer to pay the employee disability and pension benefits at the same time. Since an employee who is on disability is considered to still be actively working, it makes sense that an employer should not be forced to duplicate disability and pension benefits. The compromise [bill] . . . allows complete integration of disability with pension benefits. The employer may offset against disability . . . [:] first, any pension benefit that the employee has voluntarily elected to receive, and second, any pension benefit for which an employee who is at least 62 or normal retirement age, whichever is greater, is eligible to receive. This effectively eliminates any duplicate payments.[1002]

Speaking to §4(1)(3), Senator Jeffords stated as follows during the debates on S 1511:

> It is my understanding that agreement has been reached that these two benefits can be integrated in such a way that the employee receives combined payments at the level of the greater of either pension or disability. Thus, the income stream to the employee is not decreased, only the source of the funds is shifted.[1003]

On its face, however, §4(1)(3) does not reflect Senator Jeffords' understanding; that does not seem to be the way the provision works out in application, either. For example, if an employee is receiving $400 per month in disability benefits, and an additional $400 in pension payments, for a total of $800, the

---

[1002] *Id* S13,604 (daily ed Sept 24, 1990).

[1003] *Id* S13,606.

employer can reduce the disability benefits by the pension benefits, so that the employee winds up receiving $400 monthly. In other words, each dollar of disability benefits is offset by a dollar of pension benefits, reducing the former down to $0, while leaving the employee still receiving his or her pension of $400. Thus, the employee's income stream in fact apparently can be reduced, by virtue of §4(1)(3), from $800 down to $400. For the employee who is eligible for a pension, but does not want to start receiving it, he or she will end up with an income stream of $0, since the disability benefits will be reduced down to $0, and he or she will not be receiving any pension benefits, either.

Representative Clay, manager of the legislation in the House, added some explanation of §4(1)(3) in a summary of S 1511 that he included in the Congressional Record during the course of House consideration of the bill:

> Although the bill authorizes a monetary offset to long-term disability benefits for certain pension benefits, it does not authorize an employer to abrogate any rights an employee may have that are associated with disability (e.g., recall rights, continued pension accruals under section 4(j) of the ADEA), if those rights are otherwise protected under the ADEA.[1004]

In addition, Representative Clay tried to respond to the scenario discussed above, i.e., the situation where an employee has his or her income reduced as a result of §4(1)(3), by asserting the position that §4(1)(3) could not be applied so as to lead to the forced retirement of an employee:

> The offset to long-term disability benefits . . . may not be made if it requires or permits involuntary retirement. For example, in some cases, the offset may not have the effect of requiring involuntary retirement. An individual with an independent source of income and no immediate short-term income needs may receive a reduced long-term dis-

---

[1004] *Id* H8618 (daily ed Oct 2, 1990).

> ability benefit and decide not to draw the pension benefit to which he or she may be entitled for several years, thus retaining the option to return to work and/or continuing pension accruals. On the other hand, to reduce the long-term disability benefit of an individual with critical short-term income needs and no other source of income except his or her pension may result in constructively forcing that individual to retire in order to meet those financial needs. Such involuntary retirement would be prohibited under these amendments, as it would be under the *Betts* decision itself.[1005]

Putting aside the fact that the statement of one member of the House, albeit a significant one given his role as manager of the legislation at issue, is not a very strong link in constructing the meaning of statutory language, there is the further fact that Representative Clay only provided a partial answer to the problem an employee may confront as a result of the application of §4(1)(3). He sketched out a scenario where the financial plight of the employee becomes so severe as a result of the offset of pension benefits against disability benefits that the employee is forced to resign. This, Representative Clay contended, would be illegal, since forced retirement is barred by the ADEA. While he was correct as far as he went, the fact is that an employee may suffer a diminution in income not so severe as to lead to involuntary retirement, yet nonetheless financially painful. While this may or may not be acceptable, depending upon one's perspective, there can be little dispute that this eventuality belies the optimistic view of Senator Jeffords that §4(1)(3) cannot be applied so as to cause financial distress to an employee.

[1005] *Id.*

§5.50 Government Benefits

The interpretation issued by the Equal Employment Opportunity Commission (EEOC) regarding the employee benefit plan exception set forth in §4(f)(2)[1006] of the Age Discrimination in Employment Act (ADEA)[1007] addresses, inter alia, government benefits. "An employer does not violate the Act by permitting certain benefits to be provided by the Government, even though the availability of such benefits may be based on age."[1008] An example that the interpretation provides concerns Medicare: "It is not necessary for an employer to provide health benefits which are otherwise provided to certain employees by Medicare."[1009] The interpretation imposes a limitation on employer freedom in this context:

> [T]he availability of benefits from the government will not justify a reduction in employer-provided benefits if the result is that, taking the employer-provided and Government-provided benefits together, an older employee is entitled to a lesser benefit of any type (including coverage for family and/or dependents) than a similarly situated younger employee.[1010]

Potenze v New York Shipping Association[1011] seems to be in accord with this interpretation. In *Potenze* the court rejected the argument that a plan whereby employees ages 65 and over were subjected to an offset against their Social Security benefits, whereas employees ages 62 to 64 were not, was a subterfuge to evade the ADEA's purposes simply because better alternatives could have been used by the employer.

[1006] 29 USC §623(f)(2).

[1007] *Id* §§621-634.

[1008] 29 CFR §1625.10(e) (1993).

[1009] *Id.*

[1010] *Id.*

[1011] 804 F2d 235 (2d Cir 1986), *cert denied,* 481 US 1029 (1987).

§5.51 §4(f)(2)'s Application to Hiring Decisions

Section 4(f)(2)[1012] of the Age Discrimination in Employment Act (ADEA)[1013] on its face prohibits invocation of the employee benefit plan exception as a basis for a refusal to hire. This prohibition was addressed in *Abbott v Federal Forge, Inc*,[1014] where the plaintiffs—who charged discrimination in hiring—claimed that the employer had violated §4(f)(2) by using a pension plan as an excuse not to hire.

The plaintiffs' argument proved to be a losing one. The district court reasoned that the language of §4(f)(2), i.e., "no such employee benefit plan shall excuse the failure to hire any individual," did "not directly proscribe failures to hire on the basis of a seniority system, but . . . only acts as a limitation on the defense that an employer was observing the terms of an employee benefit plan."[1015] Thus, according to the district court (as explained by the court of appeals), §4(f)(2) "would only come into play where the employer invokes §623(f)(2) as a defense"[1016]—something that the employer did not do here. Since the employer had not invoked the provision, §4(f)(2) was deemed by the district court to be inapplicable in assessing the legitimacy of the employer's hiring practices—which were otherwise nondiscriminatory in the district court's view. The court of appeals affirmed, agreeing with the district court's analysis.

In an opinion letter issued in 1983 the Equal Employment Opportunity Commission (EEOC) addressed the question of whether an employer is legally obligated to consider for rehire any of its former employees who retired under a bona fide employee benefit plan. The EEOC set forth three conclusions:

1012 29 USC §623(f)(2).

1013 *Id* §§621-634.

1014 912 F2d 867 (6th Cir 1990).

1015 *Id* 877.

1016 *Id*.

1. An employee who retires prior to age 70[[1017]] and who is still within the age group protected by the ADEA may not be denied consideration for rehire merely because he has retired.
2. An employee who retired pursuant to an early retirement incentive or special benefit may not be denied consideration for rehire merely because he has retired as long as he is within the age group protected by the ADEA.
3. An employee who is retired prior to age 70 pursuant to §12(c) [, 29 USC §631(c),] of the ADEA may be denied consideration for rehire by the employer for another bona fide executive or high policy-making position.[[1018]] Said individual may not be denied consideration for rehire by the employer for other positions as long as he is within the age group protected by the ADEA.[1019]

§5.52 §4(f)(2)'s Application to Involuntary Retirement

Section 4(f)(2)[1020] of the Age Discrimination in Employment Act (ADEA)[1021] explicitly prohibits employers, employment agencies, and labor organizations from relying on the terms of a bona fide employee benefit plan as the basis for requiring or permitting involuntary retirement.[1022] Given this bar on the

---

[1017] At the time of this letter's issuance, the ADEA's coverage of employees in the private sector ceased upon their attainment of age 70. Hence, the reference to age 70 in the letter.

[1018] As to the ADEA exception allowing the involuntary retirement of bona fide executives and high level policy makers once they attain age 65, see **ch 3.**

[1019] EEOC OL-1 (Dec 13, 1983). (This opinion letter is reproduced at the end of the last volume in the Appendix.)

[1020] 29 USC §623(f)(2).

[1021] *Id* §§621-634.

[1022] *Accord* 29 CFR §1625.10(d)(7) (1993). Prior to the Act's being amended by the Age Discrimination in Employment Act Amendments of 1978, Pub L No 95-256, 92 Stat 189, such retirement was allowed. Save for one situation,

imposition of involuntary retirement in accordance with the terms of an employee benefit plan, the Court of Appeals for the First Circuit ruled in *Equal Employment Opportunity Commission v Massachusetts*[1023] that an annual medical examination requirement imposed by state law upon state and local employees upon their attaining age 70, which exam led to involuntary retirement if it was not passed, ran afoul of §4(f)(2).

The court deciding *Betts v Hamilton County Board of Mental Retardation & Developmental Disabilities*[1024] held that the plaintiff had been involuntarily retired in violation of both §4(f)(2) and

---

the amendment became effective upon enactment. *But see* McDonnell v Gannett News Serv, Inc, 518 F Supp 1326 (D Del 1981). The one caveat concerned employees covered by collective bargaining agreements in effect on September 1, 1977. As to these individuals, the amendment could become effective on a later date. Case law developed concerning whether a collective bargaining agreement was or was not in effect on a particular date. *See* Equal Employment Opportunity Commn v Fox Point-Bayside Sch Dist, 772 F2d 1294 (7th Cir 1985); Graczyk v United Steelworkers of Am, 763 F2d 256 (7th Cir), *cert denied,* 474 US 970 (1985); Equal Employment Opportunity Commn v United Air Lines, Inc, 755 F2d 94 (7th Cir 1985); Anness v United Steelworkers of Am, 26 FEP Cas (BNA) 1340 (ND Ohio 1981), *revd,* 707 F2d 917 (6th Cir 1983); Retail Store Employees Union, Local 876 v Montgomery Ward & Co, 540 F Supp 301 (ED Mich 1982), *affd without opinion,* 714 F2d 142 (6th Cir 1983). Other issues concerning collective bargaining agreements and their relation to the 1978 amendment also were litigated. *See* Moon v Aeronca, Inc, 541 F Supp 747 (SD Ohio 1982); Knight v County of Dane, 30 FEP Cas (BNA) 1107 (WD Wis 1982); Stoner v Young, 533 F Supp 561 (ED Mich 1980).

In Harmon v UAW, 690 F Supp 585 (ED Mich 1988), the court dealt with the question of whether the collective bargaining agreement was in effect at the time of the plaintiff's involuntary retirement upon attainment of age 70.

These decisions are noted here, even though the 1978 amendment obviously is comparatively ancient history, because Congress on more than one occasion has allowed for a similar delay in the effective date of an amendment. For example, when the ADEA was amended in 1986 to remove the age-70 ceiling on ADEA coverage for most private sector employees, see **ch 3,** there was a delay provision as to employees covered by collective bargaining agreements. Age Discrimination in Employment Amendments of 1986, Pub L No 99-592, §7(a), 100 Stat 3342, 3344-45. Thus, the case law developed in response to the 1978 amendment may have analogical utility regarding amendments in the future.

[1023] 987 F2d 64 (1st Cir 1993).

[1024] 897 F2d 1380 (6th Cir), *cert denied,* 498 US 963 (1990).

§4(a)(1),[1025] which prohibits an employee from being discharged or otherwise discriminated against because of age. Betts, a 61-year-old county employee, had become permanently disabled and thus was no longer able to work. She was given two options under Ohio law: (1) an unpaid medical leave, which would have provided her with no benefits; or (2) length-of-service retirement, which would have afforded her a monthly benefit of $158.50. If she had been under 60, there would have been a third option available under Ohio law: she would have been eligible for disability benefits, which in her case would have amounted to $355.02 monthly, and she further would have been eligible to be recalled to work if her condition improved.

Having available to her only the first two options, Betts chose length-of-service retirement.

As the court saw the matter, the issue before it was whether "[w]hen an employer forces an employee to retire because of job performance or some other legitimate reason not based on age, and then forces the employee into a less desirable retirement plan because of age, does the employer's conduct constitute 'involuntary retirement . . . because of age' in violation of §4(f)(2)?"[1026] The court responded in the affirmative:

> [Betts] was denied the third option of disability benefits solely because of her age. . . . [S]imilarly situated people under 60 would have been entitled to disability benefits. If Betts had been 59 and had retired because of an illness, she would have been entitled to that third option. This after-retirement discrimination based on age . . . [makes] the §4(f)(2) exemption unavailable . . . here.[1027]

The Court of Appeals for the Ninth Circuit also ruled for the plaintiffs in *American Association for Retired Persons v Farmers Group,*

[1025] 29 USC §623(a)(1).

[1026] 897 F2d at 1382.

[1027] *Id* 1383.

Inc.[1028] Pursuant to the pension plan provision at issue, employees who continued to work after reaching age 65 did not receive additional salary or service credits, which credits were used to calculate monthly retirement benefits. Moreover, "no actuarial increase was provided for the period during which the employee continued to work"[1029] after attaining age 65. The court concluded that the defendant "wanted to get rid of older workers and that the pension plan . . . [provision] was one way to help accomplish this goal."[1030] Since §4(f)(2) thus could not protect the employer, and since the employer offered no legitimate, nondiscriminatory justification, it was held liable.

The plaintiffs in *Tusting v Bay View Federal Savings & Loan Association*[1031] originally had been promised that their health insurance coverage would continue after their retirement. In 1988, however, their employer unilaterally amended the benefits program, thereby affording the plaintiffs—who at that point still were working for the employer—a choice. They could continue working, but their employer henceforth would only pay for a portion of their health insurance premiums and would not pay for any future increases in premiums; or the plaintiffs could retain full postretirement health insurance coverage, provided they retired within the six-week period following the program change. The plaintiffs claimed that because of their ages and medical conditions they effectively were uninsurable, and so they had no choice but to resign, thereby assuring continuing employer-paid health insurance coverage. The court concluded that this benefit program did not fit within §4(f)(2). That section does not insulate from attack involuntary retirement brought about as a result of an employee benefit plan, and the court reasoned that the program here effectively did impose constructive discharge, or, in other words, involuntary retirement.[1032]

[1028] 943 F2d 996 (9th Cir 1991), *cert denied,* 112 S Ct 937 (1992).

[1029] *Id* 1002.

[1030] *Id.*

[1031] 54 FEP Cas (BNA) 403 (ND Cal 1990).

[1032] *Id* 405.

Ultimately, however, the *Tusting* court ruled for the defendants. It reasoned that the Supreme Court's decision in *Public Employees Retirement System v Betts*[1033] governed, and that the burden therefore was on the plaintiffs to prove, as a part of their prima facie case, that the changes were motivated by discriminatory intent.[1034] The court concluded that the plaintiffs had failed to adduce facts sufficient to establish such intent.[1035]

The plaintiffs likewise were unsuccessful in *Bell v Trustees of Purdue University*,[1036] in which they attacked as discriminatory the university's former practice of discontinuing contributions to the faculty pension plan when a faculty member attained normal retirement age, which was defined as age 65.[1037] This practice had been pursued for a six-year period, commencing on July 1, 1982—the date on which an amendment to the ADEA raising to age 70 the age cap for tenured faculty members went into effect[1038]—and ending on January 1, 1988, which was the effective date of a 1986 amendment to the ADEA which ensured that employees could no longer refuse to make contributions to pension plans on behalf of persons above the normal retirement age.[1039] The plaintiffs contended that the university wanted to get rid of older faculty members, and that the cessation of pension contributions was intended to achieve this end by discouraging employees who were over age 64 from continuing to work for the university. In other words, the university's practice either was a disguised form of forced retirement, or it at the least constituted discrimination in compensation. In either instance, the

---

[1033] 492 US 158 (1989). See **§5.24.**

[1034] The *Betts* decision entailed an enhanced focus on the issue of intent. See § **5.24.** However, the decision was overridden by the Older Workers Benefit Protection Act (OWBPA), Pub L No 101-433, 104 Stat 2287 *as amended by* Pub L No 101-521, 104 Stat 2278 (1990), and the OWBPA-amended ADEA does not maintain this emphasis on the matter of intent.

[1035] *See also* Renzenbrink v Metal Carbides Corp, 54 FEP Cas (BNA) 835, 842 (ND Ohio 1990).

[1036] 975 F2d 422 (7th Cir 1992).

[1037] As to the illegality today of ceasing such contributions, see **§5.41.**

[1038] See **ch 3.**

[1039] See **§5.41.**

university—so the plaintiffs' argument went—was seeking to use the pension plan, which during the period in question allowed it to cease making contributions, as a subterfuge for discrimination. The Court of Appeals for the Seventh Circuit rejected the plaintiffs' contentions and ruled that the trial court should have granted the defendants' motion for summary judgment. The court justified its ruling as follows:

> The plaintiffs maintain that ceasing contributions evaded either the prohibition against wage cuts or forced retirement based on age. The plaintiffs, however, misunderstand the nature of evasion. . . . The plaintiffs in this case have offered no evidence that the fringe benefit cut in this case is anything more than meets the eye—an age differential in fringe benefits which is permitted under the ADEA. . . .
>
> Similarly, Purdue has not evaded the prohibition against firing, refusing to hire, or forcing retirement of employees. . . . The defendants have not given the plaintiffs a Hobson's choice such as giving them an option of retiring at age 65 or losing their pension. Granted, Purdue's decision to cease contributions at age 65 gives employees less incentive to continue working past age 65 than they would have if Purdue continued making contributions. But taking away an incentive in the form of a fringe benefit is not the kind of evasion prohibited by [the Supreme Court's]. . . interpretation of the ADEA [in *Betts*.] [1040]

§5.53 §4(f)(2)'s Application to Voluntary Retirement Plans: Text, History, Burdens of Proof, Standing

Voluntary retirement programs, entailing employers offering employees the option—usually sweetened with various financial incentives—to retire early, became increasingly common during

---

[1040] 975 F2d at 429.

the 1980s.[1041] A number of legal issues arose during this time, focused particularly on questions regarding: (1) the voluntariness of the plan; (2) differentiations made as to who was eligible to participate in a given plan; and (3) differentiations made regarding the levels of participation of those who were deemed to be eligible to participate. Often, the bona fide employee benefit plan exception set forth in §4(f)(2)[1042] of the Age Discrimination in Employment Act (ADEA)[1043] would come into play—particularly regarding the latter two issues.[1044] Specific issues aside, the courts uniformly endorsed the legal proposition that voluntary retirement plans were legal—at least in the abstract—under the ADEA.[1045]

In 1990 §4(f)(2) was rewritten by the Older Workers Benefit Protection Act (OWBPA),[1046] the result being that the provision now does what the case law already had done: it expressly approves voluntary retirement plans. Specifically, under §4(f)(2)(B)(ii)[1047] it is legal for an employer, employment agency, or labor organization to take actions or make decisions that otherwise would violate the ADEA if in so doing it "observe[s] the terms of a bona fide employee benefit plan . . . that is a voluntary early retirement incentive plan consistent with the relevant purpose or purposes of" the ADEA.[1048] Obviously, given the explicit language of §4(f)(2)(B)(ii), the entity relying upon this affirmative defense will fail in its effort if it cannot prove that the plan at issue satisfies this standard. Moreover, in no event can such

---

1041 *See generally* E. Meier, Early Retirement Incentive Programs: Trends and Implications (1986).

1042 29 USC §623(f)(2).

1043 *Id* §§621-634.

1044 *See generally* McMorrow, *Retirement and Worker Choice: Incentives to Retire and the Age Discrimination in Employment Act,* 29 BC L Rev 347 (1988).

1045 See **ch 4.**

1046 Pub L No 101-433, 104 Stat 978, *as amended by* Pub L No 101-521, 104 Stat 2287 (1990).

1047 29 USC §623(f)(2)(B)(ii).

1048 As to the *observing the terms* requirement, see **§5.29.** As to the bona fides of a plan, see **§§5.30-5.31.**

a plan "excuse the failure to hire any individual,"[1049] nor can such a plan "require or permit the involuntary retirement of any individual" protected under the ADEA.[1050]

It is particularly important to understand that there is a key substantive difference between §4(f)(2)(B)(ii) and §4(f)(2)(B)(i),[1051] whose focus is on plans other than voluntary retirement incentive plans. Under the latter provision, a plan must be cost-justified if it is to be successfully invoked as an affirmative defense. This means it must satisfy the *equal benefit or equal cost* principle.[1052] In contrast, §4(f)(2)(B)(ii) utilizes a broader standard. True, under the "consistent with the relevant purpose or purposes" language of §4(f)(2)(B)(ii), there is nothing to preclude the offering of a cost-justification argument as the potentially legally sufficient explanation for the age differentiation of which a grievant complains. But, given the language of §4(f)(2)(B)(ii), there is nothing that limits the charged entity to offering a cost-justification argument as the *only* legally sufficient explanation for the age-differentiated treatment at issue.

The four senators who were the managers of the Senate bill, S 1511,[1053] that ultimately was enacted into law as the OWBPA, explained the "consistent with the relevant purpose or purposes" phrase in §4(f)(2)(B)(ii) in a statement which they submitted to accompany the bill during its consideration by the full Senate:

> This standard does not apply to early retirement incentive plans described in paragraph 4(l)(1).[1054] It also does not apply to such plans unless a prima facie case of age discrimi-

---

1049 29 USC §623(f)(2)(B)(ii). See **§5.51.**

1050 29 USC §623(f)(2)(B)(ii). See **§5.52.**

1051 29 USC §623(f)(2)(B)(i).

1052 See **§§5.32-5.33.**

1053 101st Cong, 1st Sess (1989).

1054 §4(l)(1), 29 USC §623(l)(1), provides that the ADEA will not be violated if a plan imposes a minimum age requirement as a prerequisite to eligibility for normal or early retirement benefits, see **§5.38,** or if a plan provides for pension subsidies and/or Social Security bridge payments. See **§5.39.**

nation has been established under section 4(a) [29 USC §623(a)].

. . . The phrase "purposes of the Act" has been used as a standard in the ADEA for over 20 years, and the common approach has been to consider only the purpose or purposes that are relevant to the issue at hand. We endorse that approach. An early retirement incentive plan need not be shown to be consistent with every purpose of the ADEA in order to be found lawful. That would be an impossible burden for an employer to meet. As a general matter, the purpose implicated in considering an early retirement incentive plan or any particular feature of such a plan is the purpose of prohibiting arbitrary age discrimination in employment.

Early retirement incentive plans that withhold benefits to older workers above a specific age while continuing to make them available to younger workers may conflict with the purpose of prohibiting arbitrary age discrimination in employment. The purpose of prohibiting arbitrary age discrimination in employment also is undermined by denying or reducing benefits to older workers based on age-related stereotypes. For example, it would be unlawful under this . . . [bill] to exclude older workers from an early retirement incentive plan based on stereotypical assumptions that "older workers would be retiring anyway."[1055]

The Senate managers also emphasized that a broad range of voluntary retirement incentive plans would pass muster under §4(f)(2)(B)(ii):

[1055] 136 Cong Rec S13,596 (daily ed Sept 24, 1990). The bill reported out of the Senate Committee on Labor and Human Resources, which bill was modified in a number of ways before being passed by the Senate, see **§5.25,** required that a legitimate voluntary retirement incentive plan be one that "*furthers* the purposes of the Act." Senate Comm on Labor & Human Resources, The Older Workers Benefit Protection Act, S Rep No 263, 101st Cong, 2d Sess 67 (1990) (emphasis added) [hereinafter Senate Report]. As the foregoing statement of the managers suggests, it was concluded that such a standard would have been too difficult to satisfy. *See also* 136 Cong Rec S13,606 (daily ed Sept 24, 1990) (statement of Sen. Jeffords).

It is . . . clear that a wide variety of voluntary early retirement incentive plans would be lawful under the ADEA. For example, early retirement incentives that provide a flat dollar amount (e.g., $20,000), service-based benefits (e.g., $1,000 multiplied by the number of years of service), or a percentage of salary to all employees above a certain age were permissible before the [*Public Employees Retirement System of Ohio v*] *Betts* [, 492 US 158 (1989),] decision and would remain lawful under this substitute. Similarly, early retirement incentives that provide flat dollar increases in pension benefits (e.g., $200 per month) or percentage increases (e.g. 20%), would continue to remain lawful. Finally, early retirement incentives that impute years of service and/or age would satisfy the ADEA. For example, a plan that gives employees who have attained age 55 and who retire during a specified window period credit for 5 additional years of service and/or age would be lawful.

We recognize that employees may welcome the opportunity to participate in such programs, and we do not intend to deprive employees of such opportunities or to deny employers the flexibility to offer such programs rather than resorting to involuntary layoffs.[1056]

[1056] 136 Cong Rec S13,596 (daily ed Sept 24, 1990). During consideration of the Senate bill, Senator Pryor, one of the managers of the legislation, was asked by Senator Ford as to the status of a voluntary retirement incentive program that "was not a permanent part of the benefit plan, but was offered only when necessary, such as to avoid involuntary layoffs or other reductions in force. . . [.]" *Id* S13,609. Senator Pryor responded: "[I]f these plans are truly voluntary and are consistent with the relevant purpose, or purposes, of the act, and do not result in arbitrary age discrimination, they need not be a permanent part of the employer's benefit plan." *Id.*

The manager of the legislation in the House of Representatives, Representative Clay, submitted an explanation of S 1511 when it was taken up in the House. While this explanation was for the most part similar to that put forth in the Senate managers' statement, there was some additional analysis offered. With regard to voluntary early retirement incentive plans, Representative Clay observed that the purpose of prohibiting arbitrary age discrimination may be undermined "by denying or reducing benefits to older workers based on . . . some . . . commonly recognized proxy for age (e.g., pension eligibility or receipt)." 136 Cong Rec H8618 (daily ed Oct 2, 1990). He further asserted

Burdens of Proof

Section 4(f)(2) expressly imposes upon the entity invoking §4(f)(2)(B)(ii) the burden of proving that its actions or decisions are lawful under the voluntary retirement incentive provision.[1057] The Senate managers of S 1511 asserted, however, that "[u]nder the ADEA, an employer does not have to prove that an early retirement incentive is voluntary."[1058] Rather, the "employee retains the burden of proof regarding the issue of voluntariness."[1059]

---

that "[i]n determining whether a program is consistent with the purpose of prohibiting arbitrary age discrimination in employment, non-age related cost to the employer is never an acceptable basis for providing lesser benefits for older workers. (*Metz v. Transit Mix Inc.,* 828 F.2d 1202, 1206 (7th Cir. 1987))." *Id.* As to cost as a basis for differential treatment, see generally **§§5.32-.33.** As to the *Betts* decision generally, see **§5.24.**

[1057] Section 4(f)(2) provides: "An employer, employment agency, or labor organization acting under . . . clause . . . (ii) of subparagraph (B), shall have the burden of proving that such actions are lawful in any civil enforcement proceeding brought under this Act[.]"

[1058] 136 Cong Rec S13,606 (daily ed Sept 24, 1990). In the Senate report on S 1511 it was stated, in the context of discussing early retirement incentive plans, that "[i]f subsequent layoffs or terminations are contemplated or discussed, employees should be advised of the criteria by which those decisions will be made." Senate Report, *supra* note 1055, at 27. The managers of S 1511, in the document that they submitted to accompany the compromise version of the bill which they had fashioned and that was passed by the Senate and thence eventually enacted into law, "expressly disavowed" this sentence. 136 Cong Rec at S13,597.

[1059] 136 Cong Rec at S13,596. This assertion conflicted with, and presumably overrode, the contrary position that earlier had been asserted in the Senate Report, *supra* note 1055, at 27.

The Court of Appeals for the Second Circuit addressed a voluntary retirement plan in Paolillo v Dresser Indus, Inc (*Paolillo I*), 43 FEP Cas (BNA) 338 (2d Cir), *withdrawn,* 821 F2d 81 (2d Cir 1987), and *Paolillo II*—Paolillo v Dresser Indus, Inc, 821 F2d 81 (2d Cir 1987). In the first—and subsequently withdrawn—opinion, the court had held that the standard discriminatory treatment prima facie case formulation set forth in McDonnell Douglas v Green, 411 US 792 (1973), see **ch 7,** should not apply to job terminations stemming from the use of early retirement plans. Rather, all that a plaintiff had to do was to establish that he or she was a member of the age group protected under the ADEA and that his or her employment had ended as a result of an early retirement plan. The burden then would shift to the employer "to show that . . . [the employee] voluntarily chose early retirement." 43 FEP Cas at 341. Thus, the

Standing

One need not actually retire pursuant to a plan to have standing to challenge its allegedly discriminatory aspects.[1060] However, there can be problems regarding the timeliness of a filing of a charge of unlawful discrimination if an individual waits to complain until the plan actually has a direct impact on him or her.[1061]

§5.54 —Voluntary Retirement Plans: The Voluntariness Issue

For the most part, the Age Discrimination in Employment Act (ADEA)[1062] outlaws age-based mandatory retirement.[1063] On the other hand, an employee's voluntary choice to retire of course is not prohibited by the Act. More than that, §4(f)(2)(B)(ii)[1064] of the Act—added to the ADEA by the Older Workers Benefit Protection Act (OWBPA)[1065] in 1990—expressly approves of voluntary retirement being offered as an option to employees. In so doing, this provision allows age-based distinctions that ordinarily would violate the ADEA, provided they are made in observance of the terms of a voluntary retirement incentive plan that is "consistent with the relevant purpose or purposes" of the Act.

---

defendant had to establish voluntariness; the plaintiff did not have to prove involuntariness. The later *Paolillo* opinion totally deleted discussion of this issue, and since the first opinion was withdrawn, the burden allocations made by the first ruling were rendered nugatory. In any event, the OWBPA's legislative history, as quoted in the text, rejects the *Paolillo I* formulation of burdens (although that decision was not specifically mentioned).

1060 *See* American Assn of Retired Persons v EI duPont de Nemours & Co, Inc, 677 F Supp 351, 354 (ED Pa 1987).

1061 See **ch 6.**

1062 29 USC §§621-634.

1063 In some rare situations mandatory retirement based on age still may be imposed. See **ch 3.**

1064 29 USC §623(f)(2)(B)(ii).

1065 Pub L No 101-433, 104 Stat 978, *as amended by* Pub L No 101-521, 104 Stat 2287 (1990).

The question of voluntariness generated several judicial rulings under the pre-OWBPA version of §4(f)(2),[1066] and that case law remained relevant even after the rewriting of the provision, inasmuch as the new §4(f)(2)(B)(ii) simply expressly states what the case law already had established, i.e., that voluntary retirement plans are, at least in the abstract, legal under the ADEA. What the OWBPA added to the legal mix, apart from the specific statutory language, was some relevant legislative history speaking to the question of voluntariness. In an explanatory document submitted by the Senate managers of the compromise bill that was passed in the Senate and ultimately enacted into law, the following was asserted as to this issue:

> Because, by definition, early retirement incentive plans are made available exclusively to olders [sic] workers, relevant circumstances must be carefully examined to ensure that older workers made a voluntary decision. In order to determine whether a voluntary decision has been made, among the factors that may be relevant are (1) whether the employee had sufficient time to consider his or her options; (2) whether accurate and complete information has been provided regarding the benefits available under the early retirement incentive plan; and (3) whether there have been threats, intimidation and/or coercion. . . .
>
> . . . Some observers have construed language in the Committee Report to mean that an early retirement incentive offer that was very generous, in other words, almost too good to refuse, might also be challenged on the basis of voluntariness. Nothing in these amendments should be construed to give rise to any challenge to an early retirement incentive plan on the basis that the attractiveness of the offer induces employees to retire. The attractiveness of an early retirement incentive does not call into question the voluntariness of an employee's decision to take advantage of that incentive.[1067]

1066 29 USC §623(f)(2). See **ch 4.**

1067 136 Cong Rec S13,596 (daily ed Sept 24, 1990).

A number of courts—both prior to the enactment of the OWBPA and since—have addressed the voluntariness issue and they reflect, to a greater or lesser extent, the concerns expressed in the foregoing quotation (which clearly does not impose any rigid requirements that must be met to establish the existence of voluntariness.) To some extent the decisions lend themselves to generalizations; on the other hand, to some extent they are fact-specific.

The Court of Appeals for the Second Circuit addressed the issue of voluntariness in the *Paolillo* litigation, which produced two decisions, the first of which—*Paolillo I*[1068]—was withdrawn and replaced by the second—*Paolillo II.*[1069] Two of the three plaintiffs in *Paolillo* had been afforded three days from the time they were given the full details of an ostensibly voluntary retirement option within which to decide whether to accept or reject it. The third employee had only one day. All three opted for retirement, and then later sued. The trial court granted the defendant's motion for summary judgment, reasoning that the plaintiffs had acted voluntarily and so had failed to establish that their departures in fact were tantamount to discharges in violation of the ADEA. In assessing whether their retirements indeed were voluntary, the *Paolillo II* appellate court ruled that "employees must be given a reasonable amount of time to reflect and to weigh their options in order to make a considered choice."[1070] "The amount of time reasonably required," the court continued, "will vary depending on the circumstances of each case."[1071]

Scrutinizing the facts, the court concluded that the trial court had erred in deciding that, as a matter of law, the plaintiffs had acted voluntarily. In reaching this conclusion the appellate court noted that "the shortness of time given to appellants to make

---

1068 43 FEP Cas (BNA) 338 (2d Cir), *withdrawn,* 821 F2d 81 (2d Cir 1987). (The first ruling was published in the advance sheets of the West reporter at 813 F2d 583, but because of its withdrawal prior to publication of the hardbound volume of 813 F2d, it does not appear in that volume.)

1069 821 F2d 81 (2d Cir 1987).

1070 *Id* 84.

1071 *Id.*

a decision, the reason for the compressed time period [i.e., the failing employer's need to have time to assess the effect of the retirement plan], the [extensive] length of service of . . . [the plaintiffs—i.e., 31 years, 16 years, and 15 years] with . . . [the company] and the apparent complexity of the options open to them certainly raise[d] a material issue as to whether . . . [the plaintiffs] were given sufficient time to make a considered choice."[1072]

Henn v National Geographic Society[1073] was decided after *Paolillo I* but prior to *Paolillo II.* Without completely rejecting the suspicion voiced in the Second Circuit ruling regarding a situation in which an employee is given only a brief period of time to decide whether to accept or reject an early retirement plan offer, the *Henn* court made clear that it did not find such suspicion to be very much on point: "[T]he need to make a decision in a short time, under pressure, is an unusual definition of 'involuntary.' "[1074] On the other hand, the *Henn* court was not willing to totally foreclose the relevance of this consideration—a consideration it listed along with several others as being appropriate under certain circumstances:

> The "voluntariness" question . . . turns on such things as: did the person receive information about what would happen in response to the choice? was the choice free from fraud or other misconduct? did the person have an opportunity to say no? A very short period to make a complex choice may show that the person could not digest the information necessary to the decision.[1075]

Neither *Paolillo II* nor *Henn* offers any very clear guidelines for readily resolving the question of voluntariness in a given case. They do, however, reveal somewhat different stances,

---

1072 *Id.*

1073 819 F2d 824 (7th Cir), *cert denied,* 484 US 964 (1987).

1074 *Id* 828.

1075 *Id* 828-29; *accord* Gray v York Newspapers, Inc, 957 F2d 1070, 1085 (3d Cir 1992).

although the difference is mainly one of degree and not substance. In *Henn* the court was willing to conclude that voluntariness existed—so long as the employees had adequate information and an adequate time to consider the offer, even if, as the court put it, the employees "felt pressure and perceived the choice to be excruciating."[1076] In the court's view, these latter circumstances were "not important."[1077] In *Paolillo II* the court seemed to be somewhat more sensitive to the trauma of the situation and so seemed to suggest that it would view pressure and the psychological pain of the choices confronting the employee to be relevant factors in arriving at the ultimate assessment of whether a retirement indeed was voluntary.

Ultimately, the *Henn* court's position was that a departure would be deemed to be involuntary only if it amounted to a constructive discharge.[1078] Moreover, that discharge had to be one improperly based on age.[1079] Thus, in the Seventh Circuit, unless the employee is able to establish (1) that the employer made his or her working conditions so intolerable that involuntary resig-

---

[1076] 819 F2d at 829.

[1077] *Id.*

[1078] A number of the involuntary retirement cases focus on the issue of whether there was a constructive discharge. Unlike *Henn,* however, they do not necessarily stand for the proposition that absent the plaintiff's ability to establish that he or she was constructively discharged, the involuntariness of the retirement will not be established. As to constructive discharge generally, see **ch 7.**

[1079] There is nothing unique about this focus on age. As a general matter, any discharge, or other action or decision in the workplace, must have been motivated, at least to determinative extent, by the employee's age in order for an intentional violation of the ADEA to be established. See **ch 7.**

In Rathemacher v IBM Corp, 57 FEP Cas (BNA) 460 (DNJ 1991), the court quoted from Spangle v Valley Forge Sewer Auth, 839 F2d 171 (3d Cir 1988), to the following effect:

> "In order to establish a constructive discharge [claim], the plaintiff must establish that the employer knowingly permitted *conditions of discrimination* so intolerable that a reasonable person would have felt compelled to resign."

57 FEP Cas (BNA) at 462 (quoting *Spangle,* 839 F2d at 173 (emphasis added)).

nation effectively was forced upon the employee,[1080] and (2) that the employer did so because of the employee's age, the employee will not be able to establish the involuntariness of his or her retirement.[1081]

In *Henn* the plaintiffs were unable to establish constructive discharge on the facts. In other cases, also, allegations of involuntary retirement have failed.[1082] In *Bodnar v Synpol, Inc,*[1083] for example, the plaintiffs unsuccessfully contended that they had not really been offered an opportunity to voluntarily retire, in light of three factors:

—they were only afforded 15 days to reach their decisions;

—there was what amounted to a 'threat' by their supervisors that if not enough employees retired and the offerees' jobs were consequently eliminated because of the company's need to cut costs, the offerees would be denied severance pay or nonpension benefits;

[1080] 819 F2d at 830.

[1081] In Monroe v United Air Lines, Inc, 569 F Supp 645 (ND Ill 1983), *revd,* 736 F2d 394 (7th Cir 1984), *cert denied,* 470 US 1004 (1985), the court reviewed the competing arguments as to how pension benefits should be adjusted for the prevailing plaintiffs. Under a revised plan prepared by the defendant and the plaintiffs' union (which was hostile to the plaintiffs' interests), age 60 was set as the normal retirement age. The court had no problem with this—at least given the facts before it; as it noted, the Act does not bar the establishment of a normal retirement age—"a concept that necessarily carries potential benefits that make pre-age-70 retirement more attractive." *Id* 649 n5. (At that time, the Act had not yet been amended to raise the age for coverage beyond age 70. See **ch 3.**) However, the court did add a cautionary note by way of dictum: "Obviously, some differences in treatment might make early retirement so attractive, or continued employment so onerous in comparison, as to generate the real world equivalent of mandatory retirement at that normal date." *Id* 649 n5. Presumably, in referring to an early retirement offer being "attractive," the court meant that the offer was attractive given the alternative, i.e., remaining in an intolerable situation. Given *Henn's* demand that the so-called voluntary retirement be tantamount to a constructive discharge, the first part of the quoted sentence, regarding the attractiveness of early retirement, no longer appears to be valid.

[1082] *See, e.g.,* Ackerman v Diamond Shamrock Corp, 670 F2d 66 (6th Cir 1982).

[1083] 843 F2d 190 (5th Cir), *cert denied,* 488 US 908 (1988).

—the tone and manner of the individuals who explained the plan.

The court concluded that these factors—both separately and cumulatively—did not establish an involuntariness situation. In offering some guidance as to what would constitute a constructive discharge in the context of a retirement plan offering, the court stated as follows:

> An employer's "offer" of early retirement may create a prima facie case of age discrimination by constructive discharge if it sufficiently alters the status quo that each choice facing the employee makes him worse off. Of course, no individual employee or employee group may claim constructive discharge where all employees are subject to the same working conditions.[1084]

Bodnar should not be read too broadly; the offer of early retirement that the court addressed left the employee with a choice between retirement or something worse than his or her current situation. As a general matter, the courts are agreed that the mere offer of an early retirement option, without any untoward consequences should that offer not be accepted, will not suffice to establish constructive discharge.[1085]

Relying on *Bodnar,* the court deciding *Lynch v JP Stevens & Co, Inc,*[1086] asserted that "a threat by an employer that terminations would take place if insufficient numbers of employees accepted the early retirement incentive does not constitute a *prima facie* case of age discrimination if the risk of job elimination is shared by all employees."[1087] An employer's encouraging an employee to elect to retire under a voluntary retirement plan, with the

---

[1084] *Id* 193.

[1085] *See, e.g.,* Hebert v Mohawk Rubber Co, 872 F2d 1104, 1111 (1st Cir 1989); Lasley v Veterans Admin, 789 F Supp 1468, 1475 (ED Mo 1992); Tusting v Bay View Fed Sav & Loan Assn, 789 F Supp 1034, 1039 (ND Cal 1992); Weihaupt v American Medical Assn, 46 FEP Cas (BNA) 377, 379 (ND Ill 1988), *affd & vacated in part & remanded on other grounds,* 874 F2d 419 (7th Cir 1989).

[1086] 758 F Supp 976 (DNJ 1991).

[1087] *Id* 1019; *see also* Austin v Champion Intl Corp, 57 FEP Cas (BNA) 1381 (SD Tex 1992).

alternative being an offer of what the employee deemed to be an insubstantial job but which, in fact, was a job at the same salary and in the same division in which he had been working, did not comprise a set of facts sufficient to constitute constructive discharge in *Schuler v Polaroid Corp.*[1088] And in *Equal Employment Opportunity Commission v Westinghouse Electric Corp*[1089] the court ruled that "[t]he choice between retirement and unpaid layoff with recall rights does not constitute involuntary retirement where . . . the employee's layoff was unrelated to age."[1090] The Court of Appeals for the Third Circuit likewise was unwilling to conclude that the plaintiff had been constructively discharged in *Gray v York Newspapers, Inc;*[1091] it stated as follows:

> The evidence demonstrates that . . . [the plaintiff] deliberated her options carefully, and elected an early retirement package which . . . [the defendant] had no obligation to offer in the first place. We recognize that . . . [the plaintiff] probably did perceive that the new management was less affable than that to which she had been accustomed, and we may assume that she *subjectively* believed that continued employment would have been uncomfortable and that she would have been demoted or terminated at some point in the future. However, as aptly stated by the Court of Appeals for the Fourth Circuit:
>
> > the law does not permit an employee's subjective perceptions to govern a claim of constructive discharge. . . .[1092]

[1088] 44 FEP Cas (BNA) 1415 (D Mass 1987), *affd on other grounds,* 848 F2d 276 (1st Cir 1988).

[1089] 925 F2d 619 (3d Cir 1991).

[1090] *Id* 634.

[1091] 957 F2d 1070 (3d Cir 1992).

[1092] *Id* 1082-83 (quoting Bristow v Daily Press, Inc, 770 F2d 1251, 1255 (4th Cir 1985), *cert denied,* 475 US 1082 (1986) (*Gray* court's emphasis)). There is a split in the courts between taking an objective approach or a subjective approach in assessing constructive discharge claims. See generally **ch 7.** Obviously, the *Gray* court subscribed to the objective approach, which is the majority position. See **ch 7.**

The court concluded that another of the plaintiffs also had not been constructively discharged. This plaintiff had been concerned as to whether the proposed change of her job from full time to part time would entail her loss of health insurance coverage. She inquired of her supervisor as to this, but received no response. She assumed, on the basis of that silence, that the answer was a negative one and accordingly she elected to retire, since as a retiree she would be covered by the company's health insurance plan. The court was unwilling to conclude that she had been constructively discharged:

> [T]he fact that . . . [the plaintiff] did not make any further inquiry [regarding the issue of health insurance coverage], in addition to the fact that she did not complain to anyone regarding her predicament [, i.e., her uncertainty as to the status of health insurance coverage vis-a-vis the part-time position and her supervisor's nonresponsiveness regarding the issue], indicates that her decision to retire was voluntary.[1093]

Of course, not all plaintiffs have been unsuccessful in establishing that they were involuntarily retired,[1094] even though the task of proving the occurrence of actions and/or decisions on the employer's part sufficient to establish the involuntariness of the retirement is a difficult one. In *Mitchell v Mobil Oil Corp*[1095] the court first quoted the first sentence excerpted above from *Bodnar.* It then went on to observe that "[a]n early retirement program which requires an employee to make the difficult choices between retirement with the receipt of previously unavailable incentives and continued work under the same conditions [as existed prior to the incentive plan's coming on the scene] . . . does not result in constructive discharge because the employee is no worse off whichever option the employee

---

[1093] 957 F2d at 1086.

[1094] *See, e.g.,* Anderson v Montgomery Ward, Inc, 650 F Supp 1480 (ND Ill 1987), *vacated in part on other grounds,* 704 F Supp 162 (ND Ill 1989); *see also* Downey v Southern Natural Gas Co, 649 F2d 302 (5th Cir 1981).

[1095] 896 F2d 463 (10th Cir), *cert denied,* 498 US 898 (1990).

chooses."[1096] But here the plaintiff succeeded, under this standard, in establishing that he indeed had been constructively discharged.

Mitchell's claim was prompted by a change in the retirement plan benefits offered by Mobil to its employees. Employees could elect, upon retirement, to receive a lump-sum payment in lieu of an annuity. In the case of such an election, the lump sum would have the same actuarial value as the annuity, discounted by 5 per cent. In the case of an employee choosing to retire early the lump-sum payment would be reduced by 5 per cent for each year of retirement prior to age 60. For an employee to be eligible for this lump-sum option, he or she had to be 56 or older and had to have, at the date of retirement, a net worth of at least $250,000 or an accumulated lump sum of more than that amount. In 1984 Mobil announced that the plan was to be amended six months hence, whereby the discount was to be increased to 9.5 per cent, and the eligibility threshold was to be raised from $250,000 to $450,000, with the latter amount thereafter rising in correlation with the consumer price index.

As a result of the announced change, Mitchell, who was 56, had to make a decision. He could continue working, but if he did he might never be eligible for the lump-sum option because of his inability to satisfy either the initial $450,000 threshold or the rising threshold coming into play thereafter. Or he could choose to retire. (At that point in time his lump sum, which was only discounted at 5 per cent, was worth approximately 140 per cent more than the annuity because at that point the market rate of interest was 9 per cent). Mitchell claimed that by his being forced to make the choice he made, i.e., to retire, Mobil had constructively discharged him. The appellate court agreed:

> The relevant question . . . is whether Mobil's amendment of the plan forced Mr. Mitchell . . . to choose between two options both of which would leave him worse off than the status quo.

[1096] *Id* 467.

> . . . Mobil's . . . program . . . did not give Mr. Mitchell a choice between the receipt of a previously unavailable early retirement incentive and the continuation of work under the status quo which preceded the offer of early retirement. Instead, Mobil created a choice between two options either of which would leave Mr. Mitchell worse off than he had been prior to the change. . . . Prior to Mobil's amending the plan . . . Mr. Mitchell could have worked until the age of sixty-five and still remain[ed] eligible for the lump-sum option under the old criteria. The other choice would permit Mr. Mitchell to continue working, but whereas prior to the Plan's amendment he could be certain to qualify for the lump-sum option, now, because Mobil had increased the threshold and linked it to the . . . [consumer price index], he would have to requalify for this benefit for which he had already become eligible at the age of fifty-five. Moreover, he would never be certain that he could achieve the potentially increasing threshold by retirement age.[1097]

The court further required, for establishment of a prima facie case of age discrimination, that the plaintiff prove that Mobil would have treated him less favorably, because of his age, had he remained on the job. That, too, was established by Mitchell:

> Although Mobil's employees who were under age fifty-five at the time Mobil amended the eligibility criteria might have expected to obtain the lump-sum benefit, none of them qualified for it at that time; consequently, only employees over the age of fifty-five who had already qualified to receive the lump-sum benefit, like Mr. Mitchell, would have to *requalify* for it under the new eligibility criteria if they decided to stay on the job.[1098]

[1097] *Id* 467-68.

[1098] *Id* 468 (emphasis in original). The *Mitchell* court went on to approve the trial court's instructions to the jury regarding the issue of constructive discharge. In so doing the court quoted the instruction in question. *Id.*

An offer of a retirement option, with the only alternative being an undesired relocation to another city, was deemed to effectuate a constructive discharge in *Walker v Mountain States Telephone & Telegraph Co.*[1099] (On the other hand, like facts—combined with the alternative job carrying with it a lower salary—did not suffice to establish constructive discharge in *Toussaint v Ford Motor Co).*[1100] Repeated inquiries about the employee's plans to retire, combined with a demotion, replacement by a younger person, threats of increased work demands in the new position, and the nonimposition of such demands on others, together combined to establish constructive discharge in *Calhoun v Acme Cleveland Corp.*[1101]

In *Hebert v Mohawk Rubber Co*[1102] the plaintiff initially failed in his effort to establish that he was constructively discharged. In part—perhaps a fatal part—this failure was due, from the court's perspective, to his failure to protest or complain. Hebert claimed that on the basis of his perception of a pattern of terminations in his company, the early retirement option offered him really could not have been rejected, since the alternative would have been—as he saw it—discharge. He was successful, however, in at least getting the employer to sweeten the retirement package in response to a counterproposal he made. In assessing all this, the trial court reasoned as follows:

> The plan offered to Hebert was not presented as a take-it-or-leave-it proposition. Instead, it was phrased in terms of an offer. . . . Hebert . . . merely accepted what he may have believed to be his fate, and tried—successfully—to strike the best bargain he could. . . . At no point did he make any complaint to his superiors, raise any objections other than those expressed in his letter stating his counter-offer, seek any solace nor present his allegations of discrimination to

---

1099 686 F Supp 269 (D Colo 1988).

1100 581 F2d 812 (10th Cir 1978).

1101 798 F2d 559 (1st Cir 1986).

1102 47 FEP Cas (BNA) 152 (D Mass 1988), *revd & remanded,* 872 F2d 1104 (1st Cir 1989).

> the . . . [company] hierarchy. In taking such an apparently stoic stance, Hebert may have served the goals of securing an attractive retirement plan, but may have forfeited his opportunity to make plain that he was being fired and thus expose any discrimination he subjectively felt.[1103]

On appeal the Court of Appeals for the First Circuit took a less benign view of the situation and accordingly reversed, stating as follows:

> [T]o accept the reasoning . . . that a person's acceptance of an early retirement package is voluntary when faced with a "choice" between the Scylla of forced retirement or the Charybdis of discharge . . . is to turn a blind eye on the "take-it-or-leave-it" nature of such an "offer." . . . [W]e hold that, absent the option to choose to keep working under lawful conditions, an employer's offer of a choice between early retirement with benefits or discharge without benefits is nothing other than a discharge.[1104]

Looking to the facts, the appellate court concluded: "The fact that Hebert, when confronted with the retire-or-be-fired choice, bargained for all that he could get in the way of benefits simply does not change the fact, based on the court's review of the facts, that this was, at bottom, a forced retirement, not a voluntary one."[1105]

In *Westfall v City of Cohoes*[1106] the court rejected the defendant's argument that the plaintiff had acceded to his ultimate retirement when, years earlier, he had voluntarily joined the benefit plan that contained the provision that was later relied upon to force his ouster. The court said: "[V]oluntary participation in an employee benefit plan does not make that employee's subse-

---

1103 *Id* 157.

1104 Hebert v Mohawk Rubber Co, 872 F2d 1104, 1113 (1st Cir 1989).

1105 *Id.*

1106 683 F Supp 888 (NDNY 1988).

quent forced retirement pursuant to the terms of that plan 'voluntary' so as to allow the employer to assert §4(f)(2) as a defense.''[1107]

§5.55 —Voluntary Retirement Plans: Exclusion of an Individual

Voluntary retirement plans faced increasing challenges under the Age Discrimination in Employment Act (ADEA)[1108] during the 1980s, as such plans proliferated and in turn generated claims of unfair treatment. The courts uniformly responded with the conclusion that these plans did not—at least in the abstract—run afoul of the ADEA.[1109] Thus, when §4(f)(2)[1110] of the ADEA was amended in 1990 by the Older Workers Benefit Protection Act (OWBPA)[1111] so as to explicitly approve voluntary retirement incentive plans (provided they meet the requirements of §4(f)(2)(B)(ii)),[1112] the ADEA simply was thereby brought into conformity with the existing case law.

1107 *Id* 897. Two attorneys who represented management interests in an amicus submission in Paolillo v Dresser Indus, Inc, 821 F2d 81 (2d Cir 1987), (Paolillo I), observed as follows:

> An express acknowledgment of voluntariness on the program's acceptance form remains a viable initial obstacle to a plaintiff's proof of constructive discharge. It is not likely, however, to be conclusive. Where an employee can marshal enough proof that he or she was coerced into accepting the plan, a document professing voluntariness, which was signed as a precondition to acceptance, has been held not to be dispositive.

Freund & Prager, *Is an Early Retirement Incentive a Benefit—Or a ''Gilded Shove?''*, 10 Natl LJ 29, 30 (Sept 14, 1987) (footnote omitted). In support of their last assertion, the authors cited *Paolillo,* 821 F2d at 84, and Anderson v Montgomery Ward & Co, Inc, 650 F Supp 1480, 1486 (ND Ill 1987), *vacated,* 704 F Supp 162 (CD Ill 1989).

1108 29 USC §§621-634.

1109 See **ch 4.**

1110 29 USC §623(f)(2).

1111 Pub L No 101-433, 104 Stat 978, *as amended by* Pub L No 101-521, 104 Stat 2287 (1990).

1112 29 USC §623(f)(2)(B)(ii). See **§5.53.**

Section 4(f)(2)(B)(ii) clearly does not extend approval to all voluntary retirement incentive plans. An employer, employment agency, or labor organization may rely upon a plan that utilizes or causes age-based differentiations that ordinarily would violate the Act only if those differentiations arise pursuant to a bona fide plan that is "consistent with the relevant purpose or purposes" of the Act. As explained by the managers of the bill that was enacted into law as the OWBPA, "[a]s a general matter, the *purpose* implicated in considering an early retirement incentive plan or any particular feature of such a plan is the purpose of prohibiting arbitrary age discrimination in employment."[1113] Inasmuch as early retirement incentive plans typically utilize age as a key predicate for distinguishing between those who are eligible to participate in the program and those who are excluded, the question arises whether such use of age to serve a gatekeeper function, so to speak, constitutes the arbitrary age discrimination that is condemned by the ADEA.

Pre-OWBPA case law is very much relevant as to what will constitute arbitrary age discrimination in the context of a voluntary retirement plan. The legislative history of the OWBPA also provides some direction.

Legislative History

The OWBPA's Senate managers stated as follows regarding the question of what constitutes a plan "consistent with the relevant purpose or purposes" of the ADEA, insofar as the exclusion of individuals on the basis of age is concerned:

> Early retirement incentive plans that withhold benefits to older workers above a specific age while continuing to make them available to younger workers may conflict with the purpose of prohibiting arbitrary age discrimination in employment. The purpose of prohibiting arbitrary age discrimination in employment also is undermined by denying or reducing benefits to older workers based on age-related

---

[1113] 136 Cong Rec S13,596 (daily ed Sept 24, 1990) (emphasis added).

> stereotypes. For example, it would be unlawful under this . . . [bill] to exclude older workers from an early retirement incentive plan based on stereotypical assumptions that "older workers would be retiring anyway." [1114]

In brief, the focus was on the exclusion of individuals on the basis of being too old, rather than on those excluded for being too young.

Pre-OWBPA Case Law

Voluntary early retirement programs were challenged prior to enactment of the OWBPA both by persons who were excluded from programs and by individuals whose participation was less advantageous than that of other persons.[1115]

Patterson v Independent School District No 709[1116] fits into the former category: the plaintiff was totally foreclosed from the program. (Actually, the plan at issue in *Patterson* could also have provided an example of the second situation had the plaintiff been somewhat younger, since she then could have participated, but at a less advantageous level than that of younger persons.) The case involved a state statute that had been enacted in 1980 and that provided financial incentives to younger teachers to retire by offering them $10,000 to leave their jobs at age 55. For each year over age 55 until age 60 the financial boon was reduced by $500, and for each year over 60 the annual reduction was $1,500. Patterson was 67 in 1981 when she retired and so was completely ineligible for the retirement plan's benefits. The court deemed this sliding scale of diminishing benefits to be "entirely compatible with [§4(f)(2), 29 USC] §623(f)(2)."[1117] In reaching this conclusion, the court did not offer any particularly independent analysis: rather, it relied heavily on *Mason v Lister.*[1118]

[1114] *Id.*

[1115] *See* **§5.56.**

[1116] 742 F2d 465 (8th Cir 1984).

[1117] *Id* 468.

[1118] 562 F2d 343 (5th Cir 1977).

The plaintiff in *Mason,* a 46-year-old federal employee with 21 years of government service, sought to retire with an annuity under the Federal Employees Early Retirement Act.[1119] He was denied the annuity, however, because that statute required employees under age 50 to have 25 years of service before they were eligible to receive it. Mason contended that the statute fatally conflicted with the ADEA, which in 1974 had been amended so as to apply to federal employees.[1120] The *Mason* court looked to the §4(f)(2) exception. While acknowledging that this provision did not, as a literal matter, apply to federal employees,[1121] the court nonetheless reasoned that the legislative history of the 1974 amendment made it clear that Congress intended the federal government to have the same flexibility as did private employers. This included "the right to administer legitimate retirement programs."[1122] In rejecting the argument that the ADEA superseded the other federal statute the court stated as follows:

> Thus [, applying the thrust of the exception, albeit not §4(f)(2) literally,] the ADEA itself exempts conduct by the government as an employer pursuant to a bona fide retirement plan unless the plan is designed as a subterfuge to evade the purposes of the Act. Here, the retirement scheme . . . could not be a subterfuge because it is strictly optional with the employee. It does not give the government the power to forcibly retire older workers.[1123]

Independent analysis on the *Patterson* court's part was largely absent. Thus, one must assess the aptness of its reliance on

---

[1119] 5 USC §8336.

[1120] See **ch 3.**

[1121] Section 15, 29 USC §633a, of the ADEA sets up a separate scheme of prohibitions and enforcement vis-a-vis federal employees and job applicants for federal employment. See **ch 9.**

[1122] 562 F2d at 345.

[1123] *Id* 346; *accord* Equal Employment Opportunity Commn v Westinghouse Elec Corp, 632 F Supp 343, 369 (ED Pa 1986), *affd in part & revd in part on other grounds,* 869 F2d 696 (3d Cir), *vacated,* 493 US 801 (1989).

Mason, and this reliance was questionable, given the difference in the individuals harmed. In *Patterson* the plaintiff was a woman who claimed that she was being treated less well than younger employees. In *Mason,* however, the plaintiff's problem was that he was too young and so was not eligible for the benefit available to older employees. This latter situation is, at least in the abstract, less troubling so far as the ADEA enforcement agency—the Equal Employment Opportunity Commission (EEOC)—is concerned. In one of its interpretations, the EEOC asserted as follows: "The extension of additional benefits, such as increased severance pay, to older employees within the protected age bracket may be lawful if an employer has a reasonable basis to conclude that those benefits will counteract problems related to age discrimination."[1124] Of course, this interpretation may, in a given situation, be totally irrelevant; indeed, in *Mason* there was nothing to suggest that the challenged statute was designed to compensate for past age discrimination. Nonetheless, the essential point is that the problem of older workers denied access to benefits that are made available to younger employees is one that the *Mason* court did not at all touch on, notwithstanding its invocation in *Patterson.* Thus, *Mason* was a weak precedent on which to hang the *Patterson* ruling. Moreover, it also should be noted that the legislative history of the OWBPA, quoted above, calls into question the legality of programs such as that upheld in *Patterson.*

The *Mason* court ruled against a plaintiff who complained of discrimination resulting from his youthfulness excluding him from a voluntary retirement program. Ten years later another court ruled similarly in *Wehrly v American Motors Sales Corp,*[1125] where the court reasoned as follows:

> Had . . . [the plaintiff] waited another year he would have been within the [retirement plan's] guidelines, in terms of

---

[1124] 29 CFR §1625.2 (1993); *see* Schuler v Polaroid Corp, 848 F2d 276, 278 (1st Cir 1988) (the ADEA "does not forbid treating older persons *more* generously than others" (court's emphasis)). As to preferential treatment of older persons, see generally **ch 4.**

[1125] 678 F Supp 1366 (ND Ind 1988).

> his age, and would have been eligible for special early retirement. So he was not excluded like the plaintiffs in *Cipriano* [*v Board of Education,* 785 F2d 51 (2d Cir 1986), discussed *infra*], but rather, was simply ineligible.[1126]

The court continued:

> If the plaintiff could establish a prima facie case because he was ineligible (too young) as opposed to excluded (too old), then every potential plaintiff could create a presumption of discrimination upon denial of special early retirement, requiring employers to show a sound business purpose for the structure of a plan, as well as the absence of "subterfuge," under §4(f)(2). . . . That would be a manifestly unreasonable burden to place upon employers.[1127]

The discussion in *Wehrly* was echoed in dictum in *Karlen v City Colleges of Chicago:*[1128]

> [An] early retirement plan that treats you better the older you are is not suspect under the . . . [ADEA]. . . . [T]he . . . [ADEA] does not protect the young as well as the old, or even, we think, the younger *against* the older. The protected zone begins at age 40, but if on that account workers 40 or older but younger than the age of eligibility for early

---

[1126] *Id* 1382.

[1127] *Id* 1382-83. Engaging in the assumption, for argument's sake, that the plaintiff had established a prima facie case by virtue of his ineligibility, the *Wehrly* court went on to reason that there was no question that the plan was supported by a sound business purpose. Moreover, there was nothing supporting the notion that the plan was a subterfuge.

While the term *subterfuge* was dropped from §4(f)(2) when the ADEA was amended in 1990 by the OWBPA, see **§5.25,** the new §4(f)(2)(B)(ii) still requires that a plan be "consistent with the purpose or purposes" of the ADEA. Thus, the reasoning of *Wehrly* is not undercut by the fact that the court referred to *subterfuge;* that simply was the predecessor term for what now is expressed by the just-quoted language of the rewritten §4(f)(2).

[1128] 837 F2d 314 (7th Cir), *cert denied,* 486 US 1044 (1988).

> retirement could complain—[i.e.,] workers 40 to 54 . . .—early retirement plans would effectively be outlawed, and that was not the intent of the framers of the . . . [ADEA].[1129]

In *Equal Employment Opportunity Commission v Westinghouse Electric Corp.*[1130] it was again older employees—as in *Patterson*—who complained. They argued that the ADEA was violated because, by virtue of being eligible for early retirement, they could not receive a benefit package that was made available to younger employees who were laid off and who were ineligible for early retirement. Westinghouse sought to justify the differential in treatment by invoking §4(f)(2). The court rejected this defense, reasoning that the package was not a bona fide plan because it did not reflect age-related cost factors.[1131] Thus, the *Westinghouse* decision did not reach the question of the legitimacy of early retirement incentive plans per se.[1132]

Cipriano v Board of Education[1133] involved a retirement incentive plan whereby teachers between the ages of 55 and 60 were offered added payments in addition to the benefits otherwise payable upon early retirement. The court never reached the merits of the plan, which was challenged by 61-year-old plaintiffs who, by virtue of their age, were ineligible for these payments. Nonetheless, the court did have several important things to say. The court held that the plan was bona fide, for the purpose of falling within the ambit of §4(f)(2). This did not necessarily insulate the defendant from liability, however. It still had the burden to "come up with some evidence" that the plan was not a subter-

---

[1129] *Id* 318 (emphasis in original); *see also* Cronin v ITT Corp, 737 F Supp 224, 229 n6 (SDNY), *affd without opinion,* 916 F2d 709 (2d Cir 1990).

[1130] 725 F2d 211 (3d Cir 1983), *cert denied,* 469 US 820 (1984).

[1131] Under the OWBPA-amended ADEA, a voluntary retirement incentive plan is not necessarily fatally flawed if it is not cost justified. §4(f)(2)(B)(ii), 29 USC §623(f)(2)(B)(ii). See **§5.53.**

[1132] *See also* Equal Employment Opportunity Commn v Borden's, Inc, 724 F2d 1390 (9th Cir 1984).

[1133] 785 F2d 51 (2d Cir 1986).

fuge to evade the purposes of the ADEA.[1134] This burden entailed the employer's "showing a legitimate business reason for structuring the plan as it did."[1135] The court declined to offer guidance on the precise contours of this showing, but it did assert that "[t]he evidence of business reasons required to show that a voluntary early retirement plan is not a subterfuge would almost necessarily be less than what was required to make such a showing in the case of a mandatory plan."[1136]

On remand the trial court ruled that evidence of economic savings was relevant to the defendant's attempt to show legitimate business reasons for the challenged plan.[1137] It went on to uphold the plan by virtue of its fitting within the protection of §4(f)(2). In other words, the plan was not discriminatory. The court reasoned as follows:

> [T]he reason the age 55-60 limitation was adopted "was a desire to have a real 'incentive,' as opposed to a bonus. The incentive was intended to encourage teachers within that age group to retire sooner than they might otherwise

---

1134 *Id* 58. The term *subterfuge* was dropped from §4(f)(2) when that section was rewritten by the OWBPA. See **§5.26.**

1135 785 F2d at 58.

1136 *Id* 59. In fact, there is nothing in the legislative history of the OWBPA, or in the language of §4(f)(2), which as rewritten by the OWBPA speaks directly to burden of proof allocations (albeit not to the quantum of proof required), see **§§5.28, 5.53,** to suggest that this formulation is a valid one outside the Second Circuit. Moreover, inasmuch as the legislative history of the rewritten §4(f)(2) could have spoken directly to this formulation had Congress deemed it a commendable one, an inference arguably can be drawn—albeit certainly not with complete assurance as to its accuracy—that *Cipriano* is no longer valid even within the Second Circuit, now that §4(f)(2) addresses the burden of proof issue (albeit, concededly, not the quantum of proof question). (Of course, drawing inferences from congressional silence is a very problematic venture. *Compare* Apex Hosiery Co v Leader, 310 US 469 (1940) with Helvering v Hallock, 309 US 106 (1940). *See generally* Eglit, *The Civil Rights Act of 1991, the Age Discrimination in Employment Act, and Title VII of the Civil Rights Act of 1964: Three Acts and A Dog That Didn't Bark,* 39 Wayne L Rev 1093 (1993).) On the other hand, the broad language of §4(f)(2)(B)(ii) concededly leaves room for the *Cipriano* formulation still to be viable. See **§5.28.**

1137 Cipriano v Board of Educ, 700 F Supp 1199 (WDNY 1988), *vacated in part,* 772 F Supp 1346 (WDNY 1991), *affd,* 968 F2d 1502 (2d Cir 1992).

> have done, allowing hiring and retention of younger personnel at cost savings." . . . The cost savings anticipated by the Board was the difference between the salary of an older, more senior teacher (approximately $25,000 per year at the time the plan was adopted) and the salary of a less experienced teacher at the entry level (approximately $10,000). . . . In other words, while paying the incentive to a 60 year-old teacher would cost the Board $10,000, it might have the immediate result of saving the Board $5,000 since it would reduce the payroll by $15,000 (the difference between a salary of $25,000 and a salary of $10,000), minus the cost of the incentive ($10,000). The savings would be even greater on a long-term basis as the cost of the incentive payment becomes factored into the payroll savings as time goes by. From the [defendant] Union's perspective, the incentive plan was agreed to as a means of retaining jobs by avoiding the layoff of younger, less senior teachers.[1138]

The *Cipriano* district court did firmly caution that "[t]here . . . [was] little doubt that such reasons would be insufficient under §4(f)(2) if the adoption of the plan resulted in the involuntary retirement or discriminatory hiring of any employee."[1139] Here, however, no claims of such forced retirements or wrongful refusals to hire had been made.

Notwithstanding that the *Cipriano* court concluded that the plan at issue was not discriminatory on the abstract, the court further concluded that it was discriminatory as applied. Because the plaintiffs were over age 60, they had never even been eligible to retire under the incentive program, which only was offered to teachers between the ages of 55 and 60. Accordingly, the court reasoned, the plan was not "truly voluntary."[1140] Moreover, since the "defendants neither provided any incentive benefits nor incurred any costs for such benefits on behalf of plaintiffs," it followed that "the only basis for denying plaintiffs' participa-

---

[1138] *Id* 1208-09.

[1139] *Id* 1209.

[1140] *Id* 1211.

tion in the incentive plan was the fact that the plaintiffs were over age 60, and 'would be retiring anyway.' "[1141] Thus, the court concluded as follows:

> Since the critical element of "voluntariness" was not satisfied, and since the fact that plaintiffs would eventually retire at some point in their careers is not . . . [a] legitimate business reason . . . , plaintiffs were thus arbitrarily discriminated against solely because of their age in violation of the ADEA, and none of the reasons given by defendants . . . are sufficient to establish a §4(f)(2) defense to that discrimination.[1142]

Subsequently, this ruling was vacated insofar as the court had ruled that the plan was discriminatory as applied.[1143] The court reasoned that the Supreme Court's decision in *Public Employees Retirement System v Betts,*[1144] which was handed down after the district court ruling, left it with no alternative. The *Cipriano* court reasoned that *Betts* required the plaintiffs to prove that the defendant Board's plan was intended to serve the purpose of discriminating with regard to some nonfringe benefit. This was a burden the plaintiffs clearly could not satisfy, inasmuch as the relevant incentive plan at issue clearly was a fringe benefit.

§5.56 —Voluntary Retirement Plans: Limitations on Participation by Individuals Short of Total Exclusion

In some instances, a voluntary retirement incentive plan will completely exclude certain individuals from participation in a

---

1141 *Id.*

1142 *Id.* This last point in the quoted passage is echoed by the legislative history of the OWBPA, quoted above in the text.

1143 Cipriano v Board of Educ, 772 F Supp 1346 (WDNY 1991), *affd,* 968 F2d 1502 (2d Cir 1992).

1144 492 US 158 (1989).

voluntary early retirement plan.[1145] In other situations, individuals will be allowed to participate, but there will be gradations, or limitations, such that some people can take greater advantage of the various aspects of a plan than can others. Where age is the basis for such differentiation between individuals, the Age Discrimination in Employment Act (ADEA)[1146] comes into the picture. And when that occurs, the employer that devised and administers the plan almost certainly will invoke §4(f)(2)(B)(ii)[1147] of the Act. This provision was added to the ADEA by the Older Workers Benefit Protection Act (OWBPA)[1148] in 1990. It legitimizes actions and decisions that ordinarily would violate the ADEA, provided the defendant can prove that the age differentiation at issue was made in observance of the terms of a bona fide plan that is a voluntary retirement incentive plan "consistent with the relevant purpose or purposes" of the ADEA.

While the pre-OWBPA version of the employee benefit plan exception did not expressly refer to voluntary retirement plans, as does §4(f)(2)(B)(ii), such plans were addressed on a number of occasions by the courts under the pre-OWBPA provision. That provision condemned employee benefit plans that were *subterfuges* to avoid the purposes of the ADEA. While the term *subterfuge* was dropped by the OWBPA,[1149] §4(f)(2)(B)(ii) condemnation of plans that are not "consistent with the relevant purpose or purposes" of the ADEA certainly allows the pre-OWBPA case law to retain continuing relevance. In other words, a plan that was a subterfuge under the old version would be one that is not today (and was not then) consistent with the ADEA's purposes.

1145 See **§5.55.**

1146 29 USC §§621-634.

1147 *Id* §623(f)(2)(B)(ii).

1148 Pub L No 101-433, 104 Stat 978, *as amended by* Pub L No 101-521, 104 Stat 2287 (1990).

1149 See **§5.25.**

Britt v EI duPont deNemours & Co, Inc,[1150] illustrates the situation in which there are varying levels of participation in a voluntary retirement program, and the complainant is an individual who, while not totally excluded, is allowed to participate at only a diminished level. The case involved a plan that offered severance pay based upon seniority as an inducement to voluntarily retire. This program in its initial phase was not offered at all to pension-eligible employees, i.e., employees over age 50 with 15 years on the job. The program was soon amended, however, so as to be available to pension-eligibles, but with the caveat that if an employee eligible for a pension accepted the offer, certain pension benefits that he or she otherwise would have received would be deferred. A group of pension-eligible employees filed suit, contending that the severance pay program was discriminatory because reliance upon pension eligibility by the employer as a condition of eligibility was equivalent to discriminatory reliance upon age. The trial court ruled against the plaintiffs, holding that the plan constituted a bona fide seniority system.[1151]

The appellate court affirmed, but on different grounds. It never reached the question of whether duPont had a valid statutory affirmative defense because it concluded that the plan was not, in the first instance, discriminatory. The appellate court characterized the severance pay as a wage substitute, rather than a fringe benefit. "Taking the severance pay option amounted in effect to additional wage earning necessitating the deferral of pension benefits in exactly the same way that continuing to work would necessitate [such] deferral."[1152] The court further explained as follows:

> duPont did not truly require pension-eligible employees to give up anything of value not also required of others in its operation of the . . . program. Giving pension-eligible

[1150] 768 F2d 593 (4th Cir 1985).

[1151] As to the seniority system defense, see **§§5.57-5.59.**

[1152] 768 F2d at 595.

employees the choice of participating in the . . . [program] gave them the . . . [same] option given to all other employees of giving up the right to work for severance pay.[1153]

The defendant in *Dorsch v LB Foster Co*[1154] did not invoke the pre-OWBPA §4(f)(2)[1155] bona fide benefit plan defense, and so the ruling is not, in strict terms, apposite here. Nonetheless, it is instructive. At issue was a retirement plan whereby an employee who retired, voluntarily or not, was entitled to payments of $600 each month until age 62, so long as his or her age at the time of retirement totaled, when combined with years on the job, 75 years or more. The plaintiff argued that this plan discriminated against older employees. For example, a 55-year-old with 20 years of service could retire and receive payments for seven years. In contrast, a retiring 61-year-old who also had 20 years on the job would be eligible for payments only for one year.

The court's actual rationale for upholding the plan's legitimacy was quite cryptic. The court observed that one of the purposes of the ADEA is to alleviate the difficulties experienced by older workers in obtaining new employment after losing their jobs. Here, "paying equal monthly benefits serves one of the remedial purposes of the Act—providing financial support to unemployed workers and their dependent families."[1156] The court did not explain, however, how this justified greater total payments to younger workers than to older workers.

In *Karlen v City Colleges of Chicago*[1157] a district court dealt with another voluntary retirement plan that provided benefits that declined as the retiree's age increased, and that further foreclosed a benefit for retirees who retired after age 65. More specifically, the plan authorized lump-sum payments for unused sick

---

[1153] *Id.*

[1154] 782 F2d 1421 (7th Cir 1986).

[1155] 29 USC §623(f)(2).

[1156] 782 F2d at 1429.

[1157] No 84 C 2925 (ND Ill Dec 12, 1986) (unreported), *revd,* 837 F2d 314 (7th Cir), *cert denied,* 486 US 1044 (1988).

leave, with the payments decreasing as the age of the retiree rose. There was a particularly sharp drop between ages 64 and 65: retirees aged 60 through 64 would receive payments equaling 80 per cent of their unused sick leave; retirees ages 65 and over would receive payments equaling only 45 per cent of their unused leave. In addition, pursuant to the plan group health insurance coverage would be provided to retirees up through age 65, but for faculty members who retired after age 65, no coverage would be paid for by the employer.

The court held that this plan was legitimate under the pre-OWBPA §4(f)(2) exception. It cited approvingly, without actually affirmatively adopting, the formulation of the defendant's burden articulated in *Cipriano v Board of Education*[1158]—i.e., that the defendant had to come up with some evidence of legitimate business reason, but this evidence would be less than is required in a case involving a mandatory plan. Here, the court concluded, the defendants had established ample cost justification for their program, which was designed to save costs by the device of inducing early retirement. In examining the greater lump-sum sick leave benefit granted to younger retirees, the court saw an "obvious reason" for the differential:[1159] "[T]he cost savings by the Board in not paying salary for 15 years for ages 55-70 ($818,074) is far greater than the savings in avoiding payment of salary for the five years between ages 65 and 70 ($193,256)."[1160] More had to be offered to younger employees, the court reasoned, since they were giving up more in potential salary. The court acknowledged that the total savings to the employer would have to take into account the cost of the retiree's replacement. However, the defendant was facing a problem of declining enrollment, and so apparently some retirees might not be replaced at all. In any event, even if each retiree were replaced, savings would be achieved. What is more, there was an inverse correlation between the amount of savings and the age of the retiree: the older the retiree, the less the savings.

[1158] 785 F2d 51 (2d Cir 1986).

[1159] Slip op at 9-10.

[1160] *Id.*

Finally, the court did not see the sharp drop at age 65—from 80 per cent to 45 per cent of accrued sick leave, combined with the loss of the insurance benefit at age 65—as damning: "[T]his is the linchpin of the program's effectiveness—unless the benefits of early retirement decline at a faster rate over time than the benefits of remaining on board, there is really no monetary incentive to retire early."[1161]

The plaintiffs argued that the program had to be defended with the justification that the cost of providing benefits to older workers was greater, rather than on the basis of the employer's saving money by inducing the early retirement of younger workers. Further, the plaintiffs argued that the defendants had to show that the cost of a given benefit bore a relation to the employee's age. Without expressing positions as to whether these assertions by the plaintiffs embodied valid general propositions, the court simply concluded that the defendants had satisfied the demands posed by the plaintiffs' arguments:

> [P]aying accumulated sick leave to older workers costs more than paying it to younger workers because they have had more time to accumulate sick leave. . . . The drop from 80% to 45% reflects that the older worker has accumulated more sick leave; it costs almost as much to pay age 70 retirees their 45% lump sum as it does to pay age 64 retirees their 80%."[1162]

Similarly, the cost of insurance benefits for older workers rises with age, the court asserted.

Karlen was reversed on appeal.[1163] For the appellate court it was clear that the plaintiffs were victims of discrimination, since while "[e]veryone between 55 and 69 is eligible for early retirement, . . . those between 64 and 69—an older age group—are disfavored relative to the younger employees in the eligible

---

[1161] *Id* 12.

[1162] *Id* 12-13.

[1163] Karlen v City Colleges of Chicago, 837 F2d 314 (7th Cir), *cert denied,* 486 US 1044 (1988).

group."[1164] This would not have necessarily led to liability, since at the time the §4(f)(2) employee benefit defense was available. In order to succeed with this defense, however, the defendants would have had to prove that the benefit plan was not a subterfuge. In order to do so here, where the employer was using "age—not cost, or years of service, or salary—as the basis for varying retirement benefits," the employer would have had to "be able to prove a close correlation between age and cost if he . . . [wanted] to shelter in the safe harbor of section 4(f)(2)."[1165] Examining the facts, the court concluded as follows:

> As far as the record discloses, the Colleges could achieve all of the lawful objectives of their . . . [program] by tying the sick-pay distribution to salary and years of service [rather than age] and the insurance coverage to the actual difference in premium costs that is due to the age of the employee. If so, this is further evidence that the actual program is a subterfuge, designed to get rid of faculty members when they reach 65.[1166]

Ultimately, the court held that the district court had erred in granting the defendants' motion for summary judgment, since the defendants' evidence did not establish that a reasonable jury could not have found the challenged plan to be a subterfuge.[1167]

In a decision that touched only briefly on the age discrimination issue, the pre-OWBPA court deciding *Trenton v Scott Paper Co*[1168] rejected the argument that a retirement plan had a discriminatory impact because the employees who were eligible for the plan were younger than those who were ineligible. The court

---

[1164] *Id* 318.

[1165] *Id* 319.

[1166] *Id* 320.

[1167] The *Karlen* appellate court ruling was distinguished in Cipriano v Board of Educ, 700 F Supp 1199, 1210-11 (WDNY 1988), *vacated in part,* 772 F Supp 1346 (WDNY 1991), *affd,* 968 F2d 1502 (2d Cir 1992).

[1168] 832 F2d 806 (3d Cir 1987), *cert denied,* 485 US 1022 (1988).

asserted that "[a]rguably, *any* early retirement incentive program gives more benefit to younger workers than to older ones."[1169]

The Bona Fide Seniority System Defense

§5.57 The Bona Fide Seniority System Defense: Introduction

Section 4(f)(2)[1170] of the Age Discrimination in Employment Act (ADEA)[1171] renders lawful employers, employment agencies, and labor organizations taking actions and making decisions that ordinarily would violate the Act, provided that in so doing the entity taking the action or making the decision "observe[s] the terms of a bona fide seniority system that is not intended to evade the purposes of the Act." In no event, however, may a seniority system "require or permit the involuntary retirement of any individual specified by section 12(a) [, 29 USC §631(a),] because of the age of such individual."[1172] This language is, save for one major change, virtually identical to that which existed prior to the amending of §4(f)(2) in 1990 by the Older Workers Benefit Protection Act (OWBPA).[1173] That change was the deletion of the word "subterfuge" from the section: in other words the pre-OWBPA §4(f)(2) barred reliance upon a seniority system that constituted a subterfuge to evade the purposes of the ADEA.[1174] Now, as quoted above, the provision speaks to a system "that is not intended to evade the purposes of the Act . . .," terminology that certainly is sufficiently broad in scope so as to

---

1169 *Id* 811 (emphasis in original).

1170 29 USC §623(f)(2).

1171 *Id* §§621-634.

1172 §4(f)(2), 29 USC §623(f)(2).

1173 Pub L No 101-433, 104 Stat 978, *as amended by* Pub L No 101-521, 104 Stat 2287 (1990).

1174 See **§5.58.**

condemn systems that are, in a generic sense, subterfuges to avoid the ADEA's purposes.

The rewritten §4(f)(2) was a response to *Public Employees Retirement System v Betts,*[1175] a decision that virtually gutted of its substantive rigor the other feature of the employment relationship to which §4(f)(2) then—and now—is addressed, i.e., bona fide employee benefit plans.[1176] While *Betts* was focused on benefit plans, its impact nonetheless was felt, as well, on §4(f)(2)'s coverage of seniority systems. For example, it had been widely held by the lower courts prior to *Betts* that §4(f)(2), in speaking to benefit plans, erected an affirmative defense. An employer, employment agency, or labor organization would bear the burden of proving that its challenged differential treatment of older, as compared to younger, individuals was justifiable pursuant to the terms of the plan.[1177] There was no reason to read §4(f)(2) differently insofar as it addressed seniority systems. Thus, while there was less case law speaking to the issue, it likewise was generally was accepted that the exception regarding seniority systems also created an affirmative defense to be proven by the entity relying upon the system to impose the challenged differential treatment.[1178] Because the *Betts* Court held that §4(f)(2), as applied to benefit plans, did not constitute an affirmative defense, it followed by analogy that §4(f)(2) likewise no longer could be read as constituting an affirmative defense in the case of seniority systems.[1179]

1175 492 US 158 (1989).

1176 See **§5.24.**

1177 See **§5.28.**

1178 *See, e.g.,* Lusardi v Xerox Corp, 118 FRD 351, 367 (DNJ 1987) (dictum); Cook v Pan Am World Airways, Inc, 647 F Supp 816, 824 (SDNY 1986), *affd,* 817 F2d 1030 (2d Cir), *cert denied,* 484 US 913 (1987); Equal Employment Opportunity Commn v Liggett & Meyers, Inc, 29 FEP Cas (BNA) 1611, 1643 (EDNC 1982) (dictum); *see also* Equal Employment Opportunity Commn v Pan Am World Airways, Inc, 52 FEP Cas (BNA) 920 (ND Cal 1987).

1179 *See* Renzenbrink v Metal Carbides Corp, 54 FEP Cas (BNA) 835, 840 (ND Ohio 1990).

The OWBPA overturned *Betts,* including it's treatment of that the burden of proof issue.[1180] Accordingly, since the OWBPA's amendments to the ADEA went into effect—which generally was on April 1, 1991, although not in all instances[1181]—the seniority system exception once again constitutes an affirmative defense.[1182] By the terms of the OWBPA, however, the OWBPA amendments did not apply retroactively.[1183] Thus, a claim growing out of a decision made or action taken between the date *Betts* was decided, i.e., June 23, 1989, and the time the OWBPA amendments took effect will entail the burden of proof being on the plaintiff to establish the inefficacy of the seniority system as a justification for the complained-of discrimination. Moreover, there is case law holding that *Betts* is to be applied retroactively, making it applicable to claims arising prior to that ruling.[1184]

While there was case law establishing that a seniority system adopted prior to enactment of the ADEA could not by definition constitute a subterfuge to evade the purposes of the ADEA,[1185] and therefore could not be attacked under the Act, the OWBPA added a section to the ADEA which provides that a "seniority system shall comply with this Act regardless of the date of adoption of such system[.]"[1186]

[1180] See **§5.25.**

[1181] *Id.*

[1182] Even though the bona fide seniority system exception was understood as embodying an affirmative defense that should only come into play once a prima facie case was established, the court deciding Colizza v United States Steel Corp, 49 FEP Cas (BNA) 779 (WD Pa 1989), reasoned that because the defendant could successfully invoke the defense, this precluded the plaintiff from being able to establish a prima facie case. *Id* 785.

[1183] See **§5.24.**

[1184] *See* Bell v Trustees of Purdue Univ, 975 F2d 422, 426 (7th Cir 1992); American Assn of Retired Persons v Farmers Group, Inc, 943 F2d 996, 1000 n6 (9th Cir 1991), *cert denied,* 112 S Ct 937 (1992); Cipriano v Board of Educ, 772 F Supp 1346 (WDNY 1991), *affd on other grounds,* 968 F2d 1502 (2d Cir 1992). *Contra* Mitchell v Mobil Oil Corp, 896 F2d 463, 471 n3 (10th Cir), *cert denied* 498 US 898 (1990).

[1185] Equal Employment Opportunity Commn v Pan Am World Airways, Inc, 52 FEP Cas (BNA) 920, 924 (ND Cal 1987).

[1186] §4(k), 29 USC §623(k).

§5.58 —Defining *Seniority System*

Section 4(f)(2)[1187] of the Age Discrimination in Employment Act (ADEA)[1188] allows employers, employment agencies, and labor organizations to engage in actions and to make decisions that ordinarily would violate the ADEA, so long as they are observing the terms of bona fide seniority systems that are not intended to evade the purposes of the ADEA.[1189] In an interpretation that, while not legally binding,[1190] is given considerable deference by the courts,[1191] the Equal Employment Opportunity Commission (EEOC) takes the position that a seniority system must use length of service as the primary criterion for allocating employment opportunities and prerogatives;[1192] that the terms of the system must be communicated to the employees;[1193] and that a system that gives junior employees greater rights than senior employees within the protected age group may be a sub-

---

[1187] 29 USC §623(f)(2).

[1188] *Id* §§621-634.

[1189] The statute reads as follows:

> (f) It shall not be unlawful for an employer, employment agency, or labor organization—
>
> . . . .
>
> (2) to take any action otherwise prohibited under subsection (a), (b), (c), or (e) of this section—
>
> (A) to observe the terms of a bona fide seniority system that is not intended to evade the purposes of this Act, except that no such seniority system shall require or permit the involuntary retirement of any individual specified by section 12(a) [, 29 USC §631(a),] because of the age of such individual;
>
> . . . .
>
> . . . An employer, employment agency, or labor organization acting under subparagraph (A) . . . shall have the burden of proving that such actions are lawful in any civil enforcement proceeding under this Act[.]

[1190] The interpretation was not issued pursuant to the rule-making procedures of the Administrative Procedure Act, 5 USC §553, and so is not legally binding.

[1191] See **ch 2**.

[1192] 29 CFR §1625.8(a) (1993); *accord* Cook v Pan Am World Airways, Inc, 771 F2d 635, 644 (2d Cir 1985), *cert denied,* 474 US 1109 (1986).

[1193] 29 CFR §1625.8(c) (1993).

terfuge to evade the purposes of the Act.[1194] The EEOC interpretation further provides that a system that discriminates on the basis of race, color, religion, sex, or national origin will be closely scrutinized to ensure that it is bona fide under the ADEA.[1195]

While the Supreme Court has not had occasion to address the meaning or scope of the ADEA exception, it has addressed on several occasions a similar seniority system exception set forth in Title VII of the Civil Rights Act of 1964,[1196] a statute whose case law ADEA courts often look to for analogical guidance.[1197] In *California Brewers Association v Bryant,*[1198] one of the Title VII rulings, the Court defined *seniority system* as a scheme which provides increasing rights and benefits to employees as their length of service increases.[1199] A later district court, addressing the ADEA exception, similarly explained: "[T]he 'principal feature of any seniority system is that preferential treatment is dispensed on the basis of some measure of time served in employment.' "[1200]

While the length of service factor is central, seniority systems can legitimately include rules that accomplish necessary functions, even if these rules are not themselves directly related to length of service.[1201] Thus, for example, the *Bryant* Court held that a rule dividing employees into permanent and temporary status based on whether they had worked 45 weeks or less in a calendar year, was a part of the seniority system and was therefore within the reach of the Title VII seniority system exception.

1194 *Id* §1625.8(b).

1195 *Id* §1625.8(d).

1196 42 USC §§2000e through 2000e-17.

1197 See **ch 2.**

1198 444 US 598 (1980).

1199 *Id* 605-06.

1200 Renzenbrink v Metal Carbides Corp, 54 FEP Cas (BNA) 835, 840 (ND Ohio 1990) (quoting NAACP v Detroit Police Officers Assn, 900 F2d 903, 907-08 n5 (6th Cir), *cert denied,* 498 US 983 (1990).

1201 *California Brewers Assn v Bryant,* 444 US at 607-08.

It has been held under Title VII that whether a seniority system is bona fide is an issue of fact.[1202] The bona fides of a seniority system are not defeated by the fact that the system perpetuates pre-Act discrimination. So ruled the Court, addressing a Title VII claim, in *International Brotherhood of Teamsters v United States.*[1203] In *American Tobacco Co v Patterson*[1204] the Court rejected the argument that an exception to the *Teamsters* rule should be devised for seniority systems that were created after Title VII became effective.

At issue in *Finnegan v Trans World Airlines, Inc,*[1205] was a change in the company vacation policy. The new policy based each employee's entitlement to vacation time on his or her continuous years with the company, and set the amount of vacation time each employee annually could accrue on the basis of the employee's seniority. The court held that this vacation policy constituted a seniority system. It reasoned as follows: "[A] seniority system need not have been the result of collective bargaining to fall within the scope of §4(f)(2)."[1206] As to the merits of the plaintiff's claim, the court asserted: "[N]othing in the ADEA prohibits employers from altering the terms of a benefit seniority system as long as the new system is not a subterfuge for engaging in arbitrary age discrimination."[1207]

[1202] Pullman-Standard v Swint, 456 US 273 (1982).

[1203] 431 US 324 (1977).

[1204] 456 US 63 (1982).

[1205] 767 F Supp 867 (ND Ill 1991), *affd,* 967 F2d 1161 (7th Cir 1992).

[1206] *Id* 873.

[1207] *Id* (footnote omitted). The court's reference to "subterfuge" stemmed from the fact that it was addressing the version of §4(f)(2) that existed prior to its being rewritten by the Older Workers Benefit Protection Act, Pub L No 101-433, 104 Stat 978, *as amended by* Pub L No 101-521, 104 Stat 2287 (1990). The rewritten version does not include that term. Nonetheless, the change in the wording of §4(f)(2)(A), 29 USC §623(f)(2)(A), does not undercut the continuing relevance of decisions addressing subterfuge. See **§§5.57, 5.59.**

§5.59 —Seniority Systems: The ADEA Case Law

The bona fide seniority system exception set forth in §4(f)(2)[1208] of the Age Discrimination in Employment Act (ADEA)[1209] has not been a prolific source of litigation, presumably because seniority systems typically benefit older workers and thus those who are the usual grievants under the Act ordinarily will not find in the operation of seniority plans bases for complaint. Still, there is some case law.

The decisions handed down prior to the amendment of §4(f)(2) in 1990 by the Older Workers Benefit Protection Act (OWBPA)[1210] spoke to statutory language that no longer exists. Prior to the OWBPA's rewriting of §4(f)(2), the statute allowed employers, employment agencies, and labor organizations to prove that an age differentiation that ordinarily would violate the ADEA could be justified as the product of the entity's observance of the terms of a bona fide seniority system that was not a "subterfuge" to avoid the purposes of the ADEA. The reformulated §4(f)(2) deletes the term *subterfuge;* now §4(f)(2)(A) provides that the employer, employment agency, or labor organization may avoid liability if it can prove that it "observe[d] the terms of a bona fide seniority system that is not intended to evade the purposes of" the ADEA.[1211]

It is important to appreciate that the subsection specifically speaks to the terms of a system that is not "intended" to evade the ADEA's purposes. But for this proviso, it would seem—given that seniority systems by definition accord preference based on seniority and given that seniority typically (although not always) correlates with age[1212]—that virtually every seniority system could be attacked as having an adverse disparate impact based on age. In other words, an ostensibly neutral system (neutral

---

[1208] 29 USC §623(f)(2).

[1209] *Id* §§621-634.

[1210] Pub L No 101-433, 104 Stat 978, *as amended by* Pub L No 101-521, 104 Stat 2287 (1990).

[1211] 29 USC §623(f)(2)(A).

[1212] See **ch 4.**

in the sense that it is tied to length of service rather than age) will redound negatively to the interests of younger persons. Many of these people, while younger, still will be in the ADEA-protected age group, i.e., individuals ages 40 and over. Thus, they will be able to invoke the ADEA. Because, however, seniority systems only can be attacked if discriminatory intent is involved, challenges based on disparate impact are foreclosed.[1213]

It is also important to note that the pre-OWBPA case law typically focused on the question of *subterfuge.* This is understandable, since that was the term explicitly set forth in phrasing the former language of §4(f)(2). While the term *subterfuge* is now gone, the case law remains relevant, since §4(f)(2)(A) speaks to seniority systems that are "intended to evade the purposes" of the Act. This is a concept that is broad enough to foreclose systems that are, in a generic sense, subterfuges for perpetuating discrimination.

Pre-OWBPA Case Law

The defendant in *Morelock v NCR Corp*[1214] utilized a system whereby employees accumulated seniority according to vocational classifications, but they retained their seniority when they moved from one classification to another. Two such classifications were *senior tech* and *junior tech.* Junior techs could, when qualified, advance to senior tech rank. The distinction was based on experience, ability, and skill. Prior to 1968 employees who were laid off in one vocational classification could bump junior employees in a vocation in which they had previously worked. In 1968 these bumping rights were eliminated, thereby precluding a laid-off senior tech from bumping back into a junior tech

---

[1213] See Finnegan v Trans World Airlines, Inc, 767 F Supp 867, 874 (ND Ill 1991), *affd on other grounds,* 967 F2d 1161 (7th Cir 1992). As to disparate impact analysis, see **ch 7.**

[1214] 586 F2d 1096 (6th Cir 1978), *cert denied,* 441 US 906 (1979). *But see* Stone v Western Air Lines, Inc, 544 F Supp 33 (CD Cal 1982) (bona fides of seniority system not an issue where the alleged age discrimination does not stem from the application of the seniority rules, but from a policy not related to the seniority rules).

position. The court held that the elimination of these bumping rights did not defeat the system's bona fides even though it forced the layoff of senior techs within the protected age group. The court relied on uncontradicted evidence that the junior tech classification was created to permit NCR to hire inexperienced technicians at lower wages, that the classifications were based on skill and ability, that the system was facially neutral, and that both classifications consisted of employees within and outside the protected age group. It further relied on the absence of evidence that age was a factor in changing employees' bumping rights. Finally, the court held that a stipulation that the reason for the plaintiffs' layoffs was lack of work precluded a finding that the seniority system was used as a subterfuge to evade the ADEA.

The defendant in *Colizza v United States Steel Corp*[1215] also successfully invoked the pre-OWBPA bona fide seniority system exception. The plaintiffs, who were laid off from one division, were not reemployed in another division because the collective bargaining agreement provided for separate seniority lines. *Dalton v Mercer County Board of Education*[1216] involved the claim of a 61-year-old who was rejected for a position for which a 41-year-old was hired. While the plaintiff had no seniority with the employer, the man who was hired had already worked for the employer for 17 years. The court noted that a state law left little discretion to the defendant board; that law required hiring to be done on the basis of seniority. Accordingly, inasmuch as the 41-year-old was otherwise qualified and that "he had a great deal of seniority, to comply with state law the Board was required to hire him over . . . [the plaintiff][.]"[1217] In holding this situation to be legal, the court relied on the bona fide seniority system provision: given the state law, the defendant "did no more than follow the seniority system required by state statute."[1218]

1215 49 FEP Cas (BNA) 779 (WD Pa 1989).

1216 887 F2d 490 (4th Cir 1989).

1217 *Id* 491.

1218 *Id* 492.

In *Hodgson v Greyhound Lines, Inc*[1219] the court upheld the employer's age limit for hiring as a bona fide occupational qualification (BFOQ), in part because the seniority system would force new hires to be given the most physically demanding assignments. This effective blanket immunity for the effects of the seniority system was rejected, however, in *Usery v Tamiami Trail Tour, Inc,*[1220] in which the court relied on other evidence in sustaining the BFOQ. In *Kentroti v Frontier Airlines, Inc,*[1221] the court rejected the plaintiff's argument that the ADEA requires layoffs to be based on company-wide seniority rather than on departmental seniority.

In *Johnson v American Airlines*[1222] the court rejected the defendant's invocation of the pre-OWBPA bona fide seniority system defense. The defendant contended that its refusal to allow pilots nearing age 60—the retirement age for their position—to downbid to the position of flight officer, which carried with it a then-legal age-70 retirement requirement,[1223] could be justified under the defense. The court suggested that the defendant's reliance upon the defense was misplaced because the defense was designed to allay employers' concerns that older employees would have to be accorded benefits disproportionate to their actual length of service. Thus, provisions in a seniority plan unrelated to benefits—as here—could not justify what, but for the defense, would be considered discriminatory treatment. *Air Lines Pilots Association, International v Trans World Airlines, Inc,*[1224] also involved an airline company's refusal to allow pilots and first officers to downbid to flight engineer positions. Here, too, the defendant was unsuccessful in invoking the bona fide seniority system defense.

[1219] 499 F2d 859 (7th Cir 1974), *cert denied,* 419 US 1122 (1975). See **ch 5.**

[1220] 531 F2d 224 (5th Cir 1976).

[1221] 585 F2d 967 (10th Cir 1978).

[1222] 32 FEP Cas (BNA) 1236 (ND Tex 1983).

[1223] The age cap of 70 was removed by a 1986 amendment to the ADEA. See **ch 3.**

[1224] 713 F2d 940 (2d Cir 1983), *affd in part & revd in part sub nom* Trans World Airlines, Inc v Thurston, 469 US 111 (1985).

The court deciding *Equal Employment Opportunity Commission v Westinghouse Electric Corp*[1225] concluded that while the seniority system at issue had a disparate impact on older workers in terms of determining who would be laid off,[1226] the bona fide seniority system provision constituted a valid defense.[1227]

In *Cook v Pan American World Airways, Inc,*[1228] the court asserted that, absent evidence that the employer acted "in bad faith or with an age-discriminatory motive," the "mere fact that plaintiffs would have fared better under a different scheme . . . [did] not show that the merged seniority list [was] a 'subterfuge' to evade the ADEA[.]"[1229] On remand, the district court reasoned as follows:

> While it is not an absolute requirement that . . . [the defendants] demonstrate a business or economic reason to justify a bona fide seniority system, . . . a showing of a "legitimate business reason" for accepting the plan is sufficient to demonstrate that the plan is not a "subterfuge."[1230]

The *Cook* case involved an integrated seniority system that was devised by an arbitrator who was called upon to arbitrate the disputes arising out of the merger of two pilot seniority lists, which merger in turn was occasioned by the merger of Pan American Airways with National Airlines. The merged seniority list was opposed by Pan Am's pilots. Pan Am, the surviving airline, was not a party to the arbitration, but it nonetheless accepted the award. Pan Am was aware when it adopted the merged list that pre-merger Pan Am pilots as a group were older

---

1225 632 F Supp 343 (ED Pa 1986), *vacated in part on other grounds,* 869 F2d 696 (3d Cir), *vacated,* 493 US 801 (1989).

1226 As to disparate impact analysis generally, see **ch 7.**

1227 As discussed above, the language of §4(f)(2)(A) would now not seem to allow room for application of disparate impact analysis.

1228 771 F2d 635 (2d Cir 1985), *cert denied,* 474 US 1109 (1986).

1229 *Id* 644.

1230 Cook v Pan Am World Airways, Inc, 647 F Supp 816, 823 (SDNY 1986), *affd,* 817 F2d 1030 (2d Cir), *cert denied,* 484 US 913 (1987) (quoting Cipriano v Board of Educ, 785 F2d 51, 58 (2d Cir 1986)).

than pre-merger National pilots. It was further aware that, as a consequence, any integrated seniority system that disadvantaged pre-merger Pan Am pilots would correlatively disadvantage older pilots. The airline justified its adoption of the plan with the explanation that it desired "to integrate the airlines as quickly as possible with a system that was 'operationally manageable.' "[1231]

The plaintiff unsuccessfully argued that the defendant's motion for summary judgment should be denied because Pan Am's actions were a subterfuge, in that Pan Am had adopted the seniority plan in reckless disregard of whether older workers would suffer. As the court saw it, the plaintiff was asking the court "to hold that Pan Am must make a good faith effort to learn and comply with the ADEA's requirements to obviate a finding of 'reckless disregard,' "[1232] which is a form of willfulness. The court rejected this effort to equate subterfuge with reckless disregard: all a defendant needed to do to establish that its plan was not a subterfuge was to show a legitimate business reason for the plan. A defendant did "not have to go further and demonstrate a lack of willfulness."[1233]

As discussed earlier, almost by definition seniority systems are going to have disproportionately adverse impacts on younger workers. In *Cook,* however, it was older workers who claimed that the new seniority plan disadvantaged them, while it benefited younger pilots. But even here the court was willing to find the bona fide seniority plan defense a winning one. In so doing, the court—aware of the plan's disparate impact, but unprepared or unwilling to discuss disparate impact case law—in effect articulated a lesser burden for an employer in this setting than applies in disparate impact situations. Rather than imposing on the defendant the standard burden that is imposed in disparate impact cases, to wit, the burden of proving business necessity, the court prescribed an easier task for the defendant:

[1231] 647 F Supp at 823.

[1232] *Id* 825.

[1233] *Id.*

> Pan Am concededly knew that the system created by the [arbitrator's] Award had a disproportionate impact on the seniority rights of Pan Am pilots, who were older as a group than the National pilots. Nonetheless, Pan Am was justified in relying on the arbitration process in which the age of the pilots was a major concern, and in relying on its own *legitimate business reason* for adopting the Award.[1234]

Post-OWBPA Case Law

At issue in *Equal Employment Opportunity Commission v Francis W Parker School*[1235] was a seniority system that allowed the school principal to exercise flexibility regarding the entry level salaries of new hires. The principal rejected the plaintiff, who had applied for a position with the school, because he believed that he could not hire the applicant at a salary level lower than his years of experience would dictate under the seniority scheme's salary chart, and the job opening at issue did not entail a salary as high as that to which the principal believed the plaintiff to be entitled according to the chart. Because the principal refused to exercise the discretion that he in fact had to hire the applicant at a lesser salary, he was deemed by the court to not have observed the terms of the system. Accordingly, the defendant could not rely on the seniority system as a defense for its rejection of the plaintiff.

1234 *Id* 826 (emphasis added). In a policy statement issued in 1987, the Equal Employment Opportunity Commission (EEOC) took the position that it has the authority to assert jurisdiction over matters of alleged age discrimination involving integrated seniority lists that result from the merger of airlines, even though it does not have the authority to approve or disapprove such mergers. EEOC Policy Statement N-915: The Issue of Whether the Commission Can Assert Jurisdiction Over Charges/Complaints Raising Issues of Discrimination Based on Age Arising from the Implementation of an Integrated Seniority List Developed Pursuant to an Airline Merger Approved under the Federal Aviation Act (FAA) by the Department of Transportation (DOT) (Aug 10, 1987). This policy statement is reproduced in the Appendix at the end of the last volume.

1235 61 FEP Cas (BNA) 967 (ND Ill 1993).

The Good Cause Exception

§5.60 The Good Cause Exception

The Age Discrimination in Employment Act (ADEA)[1236] sets forth in §4(f)(3)[1237] an exception providing that "[i]t shall not be unlawful for an employer, employment agency, or labor organization . . . to discharge or otherwise discipline an individual for good cause." The legislative history regarding the good cause exception is very abbreviated. What there is suggests that this provision should be deemed to be an affirmative defense,[1238] like the other exceptions set forth in §4(f) of the Act. If it is so read, it follows that the defendant that invokes the defense bears the burden of proof as to there having been good cause for the action at issue.

The scant legislative history notwithstanding, several courts have stated or indicated, without any analysis, that §4(f)(3) does not constitute an affirmative defense.[1239] A few courts have asserted the contrary.[1240] The basis for questioning the good

---

1236 29 USC §§621-634.

1237 *Id* §623(f)(3). This defense does not literally apply to federal employees, as to whom a separate scheme of prohibitions and exceptions is established by §15, 29 USC §633a. See **ch 9.**

1238 The same legislative history applicable to the reasonable factors other than age exception, which also is set forth in §4(f)(2), 29 USC §623(f)(2), of the Act, is applicable to the good cause provision. That legislative history is reviewed in **§5.16.**

1239 *See* Marshall v Westinghouse Elec Corp, 576 F2d 588, 591 (5th Cir 1978); Smith v Farah Mfg Co, Inc, 650 F2d 64, 67 (5th Cir 1981); Lusardi v Xerox Corp, 118 FRD 351, 364 (DNJ 1987); Mizrany v Texas Rehabilitation Commn, 522 F Supp 611, 617 (SD Tex 1981), *affd without opinion,* 685 F2d 1384 (5th Cir 1982); Carolan v Central Freight Lines, Inc, 489 F Supp 941, 944 (ED Tex 1980); Moore v Sears, Roebuck & Co, 464 F Supp 357, 363 (ND Ga 1979); *see also* Bell v Gas Serv Co, 778 F2d 512 (8th Cir 1985); Holley v Sanyo Mfg, Inc, 771 F2d 1161, 1168 (8th Cir 1985); Brennan v Reynolds & Co, 367 F Supp 440 (ND Ill 1973).

1240 *See* Havelick v Julius Wile Sons & Co, Inc, 445 F Supp 919 (SDNY 1978); Equal Employment Opportunity Commn v Liggett & Meyers, Inc, 29 FEP Cas (BNA) 1611, 1643 (EDNC 1982) (dictum). In Phipps v Gary Drilling Co, Inc, 722 F Supp 615 (ED Cal 1989), the court termed the good cause exception

cause exception's constituting an affirmative defense flows from the way in which an enormous number of ADEA courts have dealt with defendants' rebuttals to prima facie cases that involve the very same facts as would be put forth by way of good cause defenses.[1241] In addressing these rebuttals, which typically are not articulated under the rubric of §4(f)(3) per se, the courts have seen the defendants as only bearing a burden of production. These decisions, then, do not seem to square with good cause being deemed to be an affirmative defense. To understand this situation, brief reference to the case law that has developed devoid of any apparent consideration of the §4(f)(3) good cause exception is necessary.

Most ADEA cases involve circumstantial evidence that is adduced to address individual acts of alleged discrimination. In formulating the respective legal requirements imposed on plaintiffs and defendants in such cases, ADEA courts have followed the case law developed by the Supreme Court in construing Title VII of the Civil Rights Act of 1964.[1242] In *McDonnell Douglas Corp v Green*[1243] the Supreme Court set forth the formula to be satisfied by the plaintiff in establishing a prima facie violation of Title VII in an individual discriminatory treatment case. In *Texas Department of Community Affairs v Burdine*[1244] the Court clarified the defendant's burden, which is simply to articulate a legitimate, nondiscriminatory reason for its action. Throughout, the plaintiff bears the burden of persuasion; the defendant only must satisfy a mild burden of production.[1245] The *Burdine* formu-

---

a "statutory defense," *id* 620, but did not further describe or treat it as an affirmative defense as to which the defendant bore the burden of proof. *See also* Sutton v Atlantic Richfield Co, 646 F2d 407, 412 n6 (9th Cir 1981) (making reference to the district court's holding, but abjuring deciding the question at the appellate level).

1241 See **ch 7.**

1242 42 USC §§2000e through 2000e-17.

1243 411 US 792 (1973). See **ch 7.**

1244 450 US 248 (1981). See **ch 7.**

1245 Texas Dept of Community Affairs v Burdine, 450 US 248 (1981).

lation is subscribed to by many ADEA courts, and is rejected by none.[1246]

Typically, in circumstantial evidence cases involving discharges and demotions, the defendant in an ADEA case will produce evidence that the plaintiff was not performing adequately.[1247] This, in effect, is an assertion of good cause for the negative job action taken by the employer. Indeed, a court may even expressly invoke §4(f)(3) and use the phrase *good cause* in explaining why a plaintiff's age claim fails.[1248] Under the *McDonnell Douglas/Burdine* the defendant will prevail, once having produced such evidence, unless the plaintiff can establish that the defendant's excuse is pretextual.[1249] Inasmuch as a defendant can prevail—at least so long as it had a legitimate good cause for its action[1250]—simply by meeting a burden of production, it would be a misguided defendant who would seek to adduce the very same evidence under the rubric of §4(f)(3). If that section indeed sets forth an affirmative defense, the defendant would have to satisfy a burden of proof, and its chances of losing would be considerably increased.

Two possible conclusions follow from the many cases in which what looks exactly like a good cause justification by a defendant has not been treated, in fact, as the assertion of an affirmative defense. One is that the good cause exception indeed is not an affirmative defense, but rather is simply a statutory statement—adopted in 1967 when the ADEA was enacted—of what later would become ensconced in the case law by virtue of the *Burdine* decision: i.e., a defendant can satisfy its burden by articulating the fact that the plaintiff was terminated for good cause, not age. A second alternative is to conclude that *Burdine* is inapplicable to the ADEA, and that the many ADEA courts that have deemed

---

[1246] See **ch 7.**

[1247] *Id.*

[1248] *See* Stuart v Normandy Osteopathic Medical Ctr, 57 FEP Cas (BNA) 941, 942 (ED Mo 1991).

[1249] See **ch 7.**

[1250] *Id.*

it compellingly persuasive by way of analogy were decided wrongly.

The latter solution is not tenable. The case law is too voluminous for it all to be overturned just to afford the good cause exception some rigor by treating it as constituting an affirmative defense. Rather, the conclusion seems necessary that the good cause exception does not constitute an affirmative defense—at least in the typical circumstantial evidence case. Rather, in this situation, the standard *Burdine*-based rebuttal decisions—which, as noted already, sometimes even literally use the term *good cause* when addressing the defendant's articulated legitimate, nondiscriminatory justification[1251]—are valid.

This conclusion of *Burdine's* applicability in the ADEA does not necessarily lead, however, to the further conclusion that the good cause exception is a statutory cipher. The *Burdine* prescription does not apply in cases involving direct evidence of discrimination. In such cases, a defendant bears a much heavier burden if it is to evade liability: it must prove that it would have made the same decision anyway.[1252] Thus, in a discharge case where the plaintiff has adduced sufficient direct evidence of discrimination, the defendant will have to argue that it would have discharged the plaintiff even absent the discrimination. In other words, the defendant will have to prove that there was good cause for the challenged employment decision, i.e., the plaintiff was incompetent or dishonest or had some other negative quality. In this context, then, the statutory good cause exception makes sense as an affirmative defense. (Admittedly, in this scenario it becomes merged with the judicially devised *same decision* defense, and is thereby rendered redundant, since the defendant already is going to have to satisfy the *same decision* affirmative defense. When §4(f)(3) provision was crafted in 1967, however, it was not redundant, inasmuch as the *same deci-*

1251 *See, e.g.*, Halsell v Kimberly-Clark Corp, 683 F2d 285, 291-92 (8th Cir 1982), *cert denied*, 459 US 1205 (1983).

1252 See **ch 7**.

sion defense did not exist at that time and Congress understandably did not then anticipate the later-developed *same decision* defense.)[1253]

The Foreign Laws Defense

§5.61 The Foreign Laws Defense

Case law prior to 1984 rejected plaintiffs' arguments that the Age Discrimination in Employment Act (ADEA)[1254] applied extraterritorially.[1255] In that year the Act was amended to do by statute what the courts had refused to do judicially.[1256] Thus, some grievants who work abroad can claim the protection of the ADEA.[1257] However, there are limits to the extent of this protection.

For one, §4(h)(2)[1258]—which was added to the ADEA by the 1984 amendments—excepts from the Act's coverage an employer when it "is a foreign person not controlled by an American employer." (This provision applies both to domestic and extraterritorial acts of alleged, or actual, discrimination.)[1259]

1253 Even in this more rigorous setting, however, the inaccuracy of a defendant's business decision regarding the plaintiff should not deprive it of the defense unless, of course, the inaccuracy of its judgment regarding the defendant is so blatant or inexplicable that it supports the conclusion that the defendant would not have made the same decision had it been acting without discriminatory animus. *See* Cline v Roadway Express, Inc, 689 F2d 481, 487 n7 (4th Cir 1982); Havelick v Julius Wile Sons & Co, Inc, 445 F Supp 919, 926 (SDNY 1978). See generally **ch 7** as to the *same decision* defense.

1254 29 USC §§621-634.

1255 See **ch 3.**

1256 Older Americans Act Amendments of 1984, Pub L No 98-549, §802, 98 Stat 1767, 1792.

1257 See **ch 3.**

1258 29 USC §623(h)(2).

1259 See **ch 3.**

Second, §11(f)[1260] defines *employee* to include an individual "who is a citizen of the United States employed by an employer in a workplace in a foreign country." Thus, a foreign national working abroad is not protected by the ADEA. Finally, §4(f)(1)[1261] erects an explicit affirmative defense with regard to discrimination abroad:

> It shall not be unlawful for an employer, employment agency, or labor organization—
>
> (1) to take any action otherwise prohibited under subsections (a), (b), (c), or (e) of . . . [§4, 29 USC §623,] where such practices involve an employee in a workplace in a foreign country, and compliance with such subsections would cause such employer, or a corporation controlled by such employer, to violate the laws of the country in which such workplace is located.[1262]

By the terms of this defense, two elements must be satisfied by an entity seeking to invoke it.

First, the alleged discrimination must "involve an employee in a workplace in a foreign country." Second, the entity that invokes the §4(f)(1) defense must establish that compliance with the ADEA would "cause . . . [it] to violate the laws of the country in which . . . [the] workplace is located."

There is no statutory definition of *laws,* nor is there any enlightening legislative history regarding the term's meaning. The issue was addressed extensively, however, in *Mahoney v RFE/RLE, Inc,*[1263] a case involving the mandatory retirement at age 65 of the two plaintiffs pursuant to the union contract covering the defendant's employees in Germany. The defendant's expert testified that age-based mandatory retirement is a deeply embedded feature of German labor law, and that mandatory

---

1260 29 USC §630(f).

1261 *Id* §623(f)(1).

1262 This provision was added to the ADEA by §802(c)(1) of the Older Americans Act Amendments of 1984, Pub L No 98-459, 98 Stat 1767, 1792.

1263 818 F Supp 1 (DDC 1992).

retirement provisions are contained in the vast majority of German collective bargaining agreements and therefore they are considered in Germany to have legal force. The court responded by first asserting that the question of defining *laws* in §4(f)(1) is a matter of federal law, turning on congressional intent. Whatever the significance of mandatory retirement provisions in collective bargaining agreements in Germany, there were "two crucial facts"[1264] here:

> First, the provision is part of a contract between an employer and unions—both private entities—and has not in any way been mandated by the German government. Second, the provision does not have general application, as laws normally do, but binds only the parties to the contract.[1265]

The court accordingly concluded that the defendant's argument, based on the commonality of a practice in Germany, was unpersuasive: "Practices and policies, even when embodied in contracts, are not 'laws.' "[1266]

The defendant further argued that inasmuch as the incorporation into its collective bargaining agreement of a mandatory retirement requirement preceded the extension of the ADEA extraterritorially, the contractual provision should prevail. The court found this argument unpersuasive, as well. The defendant also pointed to the fact that after the ADEA had been amended to apply in foreign countries, the defendant had sought to accommodate the new provisions by signing individual employment contracts that allowed certain employees to continue working past age 65. However, the defendant's 'works council' (which was bound by German law to give effect to contractual provisions) had rejected that effort because of the abrogation of the mandatory retirement requirement effectuated by these individual contracts. The defendant had then appealed to the German

---

1264 *Id* 3.

1265 *Id.*

1266 *Id.*

labor courts, which ruled against it on five occasions. The defendant accordingly pointed to these decisions as constituting *laws* barring its compliance with the ADEA. Again, the court was unpersuaded:

> The labor court decisions . . . involved a narrower issue than that addressed here. Those decisions simply held that the *union contract* did not permit a retirement age higher than 65; they merely enforced the contract upon the parties to it. . . . They did not hold that anything in *German law* compelled the decisions reached. Plaintiffs in this action are challenging the application of the contract's discriminatory provision itself, not the lack of individual employment contracts. If overseas employers could avoid application of the ADEA simply by embedding an age-discriminatory provision in a contract, having a foreign court enforce the contract, and calling the court's decision "law," then the Act's extraterritorial provisions would be largely nullified, for employers could easily contract around the law.[1267]

The defendant argued that it had done all that it could by seeking to negotiate individual contracts abrogating the mandatory retirement provision, by going to the works council, and by appealing to the German labor courts. It further contended that any further effort would have been futile: even if it had terminated the contract by giving six months' notice of termination, that would have been to no avail, since under the contractual terms the contract remained in effect until a new one was negotiated and the union would not relent on the mandatory retirement issue. The court was unsympathetic:

> [T]o the extent that defendant has demonstrated a genuine issue of fact as to the "futility" of these various options, the futility arises from the policies of the German labor unions, and not from German *law.* The defendant is essentially arguing that the German unions simply will not allow it to

[1267] *Id* 5 (emphasis in original).

eliminate the mandatory retirement policy. But the United States Congress will not allow it to *retain* the policy. Of the two, only Congress makes law.[1268]

Finally, the defendant in *Mahoney* contended that application of the ADEA to its German operations violated international law. This, too, proved to be a losing argument:

> [D]efendant does not identify any principle of international law that would be violated by . . . an application of the law. Where there is a basis for the exercise of jurisdiction (such as nationality) and such exercise is reasonable, U.S. law may properly be applied overseas. . . . Here, there is no actual conflict with German law. Congress has expressed a strong interest in protecting U.S. nationals from age discrimination, and the exercise of jurisdiction is reasonable.[1269]

The Equal Employment Opportunity Commission (EEOC), in a policy guide issued to elucidate its views as to the employer's burden regarding the foreign laws defense, takes the unexceptionable position that "[a] 'law' . . . clearly does not include a corporation/business's rules, regulations or policies of employment."[1270]

Apart from the issue of defining *laws* for the purpose of the §4(f)(1) defense, the statutory language also entails focusing on the laws of the country that is the site of the workplace. Thus, for example, even if a corporation is incorporated in Country X, and compliance with the ADEA would cause it to violate Country X's laws, the corporation could not successfully invoke the §4(f)(1) defense with regard to its employment practices in its plant located in Country Y unless the corporation's compli-

---

[1268] *Id* 5-6 (emphasis in original).

[1269] *Id* 6.

[1270] EEOC Policy Guide No N-915.046, Analysis of the sec. 4(f)(1) "Foreign Laws" Defense of the Age Discrimination in Employment Act of 1967 3 (Dec 5, 1989). (This policy guide is reproduced in the Appendix at the end of the last volume.)

ance with the ADEA would violate the laws of Country Y—the site of the workplace.

The Good-Faith Reliance Defense

§5.62 The Defense of Good Faith—Conformity with, and Reliance on, Agency Pronouncements

Section 7(e)[1271] of the Age Discrimination in Employment Act (ADEA)[1272] incorporates §10 of the Portal-to-Portal Act,[1273] and a statutory defense to liability under the ADEA is thereby created. Section 10 provides, in relevant part, as follows:

> [N]o employer shall be subjected to any liability . . . if he pleads and proves that the act or omission complained of was in good faith in conformity with and in reliance on any written administrative regulation, order, ruling, approval, or interpretation, of the . . . [Equal Employment Opportunity Commission], or any administrative practice or enforcement policy of such agency with respect to the class of employers to which he belonged. Such a defense, if established, shall be a bar to the action or proceeding, notwithstanding that after such act or omission, such administrative regulation, order, ruling, approval, interpretation, practice, or enforcement policy is modified or rescinded or is determined by judicial authority to be invalid or of no legal effect.[1274]

[1271] 29 USC §626(e).

[1272] *Id* §§621-634.

[1273] *Id* §259.

[1274] *Id* §259(a). The court that decided Marshall v Baptist Hosp, Inc, 473 F Supp 465, 477 (MD Tenn 1979), *revd on other grounds,* 668 F2d 234 (6th Cir 1981), relied on the statutory language to hold that once a Portal-to-Portal Act defense is established, a court is deprived of jurisdiction to grant injunctive relief. Other courts, however, have granted injunctive relief. *See*

Inasmuch as §10 on its face refers only to employers, it is arguable that the provision does not apply to labor organizations or employment agencies, the practices of which also are regulated by the ADEA. The case law is confined to employer invocations of the defense, and so there is no authoritative pronouncement on this possible reading.

The Department of Labor has issued extensive interpretations construing §10.[1275] In early 1983 the Equal Employment Opportunity Commission (EEOC), the enforcement agency for the ADEA, issued regulations—much briefer than the Labor Department's interpretations—regarding §10.[1276] It is unclear whether these should be read as superseding the earlier Labor Department interpretations. The EEOC regulations do not address §10 with a depth in any way comparable to the DOL's interpretations, and do not even address issues that are considered in the interpretations. It thus would seem sensible to conclude that, to the extent that the EEOC regulations do not conflict with the Labor Department interpretations, those interpretations should continue to be of relevant guidance to courts.

The case law almost exclusively addresses claims for back pay. One district court, however, has observed that §10 does not create a defense to suits for injunctions to bar future violations of the ADEA.[1277] The same court declined to determine whether the statute likewise is inapplicable to an equitable claim for reinstatement.[1278] Another court, in a cryptic ruling, rejected a good faith defense invoked in a suit involving a discriminatory pension plan.[1279] In *Equal Employment Opportunity Commission v Northwest*

Northwestern-Hanna v McComb, 166 F2d 932 (8th Cir 1948); Spirt v Teachers Assurance & Annuity Assn, 93 FRD 627 (SDNY), *affd in part & revd in part on other grounds*, 691 F2d 1054 (2d Cir 1982), *vacated*, 463 US 1223 (1983).

1275 29 CFR §§790.13-.19 (1993).

1276 *Id* §1626.18.

1277 Marshall v Atlantic Container Line, 18 FEP Cas (BNA) 1167, 1176 n28 (SDNY 1978).

1278 *Id.*

1279 Equal Employment Opportunity Commn v Home Ins Co, 553 F Supp 704 (SDNY 1982) (ADEA case).

Airlines, Inc,[1280] the employer failed on the merits with its good faith defense, which it had invoked in response to claims arising out of its mandatory retirement policy and its downbid procedure for pilots.

Even where an employer relies in good faith on an agency pronouncement, there still may be a question as to whether the employer properly implemented the regulation, order, or other formal pronouncement on which it relied.[1281] There is authority for the proposition that the employer must not only rely in good faith on the pronouncement; it must also in good faith conform its actions to the pronouncement.[1282]

The definition of good faith has generated some dispute. There is authority for reading §10 as evoking an objective test, or a subjective test, or a combination of the two. The objective test was articulated in *Beebe v United States:*[1283] "[T]he test of an employer's good faith in relying upon an administrative order or regulation is 'whether he acted as a reasonably prudent man would have acted under similar circumstances.' "[1284] The subjective test seems to involve an assessment of the employer's state of mind in the particular situation.[1285]

The EEOC regulations do not address the issue at all, but the Department of Labor's interpretations set forth a standard combining the objective and subjective tests:

1280 49 FEP Cas (BNA) 1433 (WD Wash 1987) (ADEA case).

1281 *See, e.g.,* Ariens v Olin Mathieson Chem Corp, 382 F2d 192 (6th Cir 1967).

1282 *See, e.g.,* Equal Employment Opportunity Commn v Home Ins Co, 672 F2d 252, 265 (2d Cir 1982) (ADEA case); *see also* 29 CFR §790.14 (1993).

1283 640 F2d 1283 (Ct Cl 1981).

1284 *Id* 1293 (quoting Kam Koon Wan v EE Black, Ltd, 188 F2d 558, 562 (9th Cir), *cert denied,* 342 US 826 (1951)); *accord* Clifton D Mayhew, Inc v Wirtz, 413 F2d 658 (4th Cir 1969); Marshall v Baptist Hosp, Inc, 473 F Supp 465 (MD Tenn 1979), *revd on other grounds,* 668 F2d 234 (6th Cir 1981); Campbell v Jones & Laughlin Steel Corp, 96 F Supp 189, 194 (WD Pa 1951); Burke v Mesta Co, 79 F Supp 588, 611 (WD Pa 1948).

1285 *See, e.g.,* Addison v Huron Stevedoring Corp, 204 F2d 88, 93 (2d Cir), *cert denied,* 346 US 877 (1953); Van Aalten v Hurley, 176 F Supp 851, 856 (SDNY 1959).

> The legislative history of the Portal [sic] Act makes it clear that the employer's "good faith" is not to be determined merely from the actual state of his mind. Statements made in the House and Senate indicate that "good faith" also depends upon an objective test—whether the employer, in acting or omitting to act as he did, and in relying upon the regulation, order, ruling, approval, interpretation, administrative practice or enforcement policy, acted as a reasonably prudent man would have acted under the same or similar circumstances. "Good faith" requires that the employer have honesty of intention and no knowledge of circumstances which ought to put him upon inquiry.[1286]

In *Equal Employment Opportunity Commission v Home Insurance Co*,[1287] an ADEA case, the court seemingly applied this hybrid approach and on the facts found the defendant's contention wanting. The court first concluded that the district court had erred in ruling that "all that was required is that the employer have evinced an 'honest intention to ascertain what the . . . Act requires and to act in accordance with it.' "[1288] It then went on to state as follows, in the context of the facts before it, which involved an uninformative administrative interpretation susceptible to different readings by employers:

> In the circumstances here we believe that "honest intention to ascertain" is not sufficient to establish good faith within the meaning of the Portal [sic] Act. An employer may well make an honest effort to become informed as to the precise

---

[1286] 29 CFR §790.15(a) (1993); *accord* Beebe v United States, 640 F2d 1283 (Ct Cl 1981); Quinn v New York State Elec & Gas Corp, 621 F Supp 1086 (NDNY 1985) (ADEA case); Martinez v Phillips Petroleum Co, 283 F Supp 514 (D Idaho 1968), *affd*, 424 F2d 547 (9th Cir 1970). Without elucidation, the court in Equal Employment Opportunity Commn v Northwest Airlines, Inc, 49 FEP Cas (BNA) 1433 (WD Wash 1987) (ADEA case), asserted that "[t]he employer must prove its reliance by objective, as opposed to subjective evidence." *Id* 1435.

[1287] 672 F2d 252 (2d Cir 1982).

[1288] *Id* 266 (quoting Addison v Huron Stevedoring Corp, 204 F2d 88, 93 (2d Cir 1953)).

requirements of the Act; and even if the only information made available to it is a haec-verba repetition of the terms of the statute, its intention was no less honest. But where the administrative interpretation is uninformative and leaves the employer to make its own reading of the precise requirements of the statute, the employer's honest, but unsuccessful, intention to obtain information does not relieve it of liability.[1289]

Adequacy of the Document Relied Upon

A number of courts—almost none of them dealing with ADEA claims—have been called upon to determine whether an employer acted in good faith. This is a question of fact.[1290]

To successfully invoke the defense, the employer must establish that the document relied upon satisfies §10 of the Portal-to-Portal Act. The employer can rely only upon a ruling, order, or other pronouncement of the agency official vested with primary or final authority to administer the regulatory statute, and not minor agency employees.[1291] Thus, an employer was not entitled to rely upon a summary of unpaid wages given to it by a Department of Labor investigator with an indication that this summary represented an indication of the employer's total liability.[1292]

[1289] *Id.*

[1290] *See, e.g.*, Hodgson v Miller Brewing Co, 457 F2d 221, 228 (7th Cir 1972); Martinez v Phillips Petroleum Co, 283 F Supp 514, 527 (D Idaho 1968), *affd*, 424 F2d 547 (9th Cir 1970); Equal Employment Opportunity Commn v Baltimore & Ohio RR, 557 F Supp 1112, 1121 (D Md 1983) (ADEA case); *see also* James v Continental Ins Co, 424 F2d 1064 (3d Cir 1970) (court held that the trial court had not erred in receiving evidence outside of the jury's presence to determine the applicability of the good faith defense, where a jury had been empaneled to render a special verdict as to whether the plaintiff was an employee covered by the Fair Labor Standards Act, 29 USC §§200-219).

[1291] *See, e.g.*, Hodgson v Miller Brewing Co, 457 F2d 221, 228 (7th Cir 1972); United States v Stocks Lincoln-Mercury, Inc, 307 F2d 266, 271 (10th Cir 1962); Usery v Godwin Hardware, Inc, 426 F Supp 1243, 1268 (WD Mich 1976); Spring v Washington Glass Co, 153 F Supp 312 (WD Pa 1987); *accord* 29 CFR §790.17 (1993).

[1292] Murphy v Miller Brewing Co, 307 F Supp 829 (ED Wis 1969), *affd*, 457 F2d 221 (7th Cir 1972).

The EEOC regulations, quoted below, designate the appropriate officers on whom an employer may place reliance. In accordance with the statutory language, a regulation, order, ruling, approval, or interpretation must be in writing.[1293] While it has been held that an unwritten administrative practice or enforcement policy could be relied upon,[1294] the EEOC regulations are very clear in foreclosing such a possibility. They provide as follows:

> [O]nly (1) a written document, entitled "opinion letter," signed by the Legal Counsel on behalf of and as approved by the Commission, or (2) a written document issued in the conduct of litigation, entitled "opinion letter," signed by the General Counsel on behalf of and as approved by the Commission, or (3) matter published and specifically designated as such in the *Federal Register,* may be relied upon[.][1295]

Thus, oral discussions with an agency officer, combined with a memorandum written by an employer to himself, will not suffice as a written agency interpretation.[1296] Nor will reliance upon a pending constitutional attack in the courts suffice, since there is no written document.[1297] Likewise, an employer that is being sued by the EEOC may not rely upon the statements made by an EEOC attorney in another case.[1298]

1293 *See, e.g.,* Usery v Godwin Hardware, Inc, 426 F Supp 1243, 1268 (WD Mich 1976); Hodgson v Veterans Cleaning Serv, Inc, 351 F Supp 741, 746 (MD Fla 1972), *modified on other grounds,* 482 F2d 1362 (5th Cir 1973); Pilkenton v Appalachian Regional Hosps, Inc, 336 F Supp 334 (WD Va 1971); *accord* 29 CFR §790.13(a) (1993).

1294 *See, e.g.,* Marshall v Baptist Hosp, Inc, 473 F Supp 465, 479 (MD Tenn 1979), *revd on other grounds,* 668 F2d 234 (6th Cir 1981). *Contra* Anness v United Steelworkers of Am, 707 F2d 917, 921-22 (6th Cir 1983) (ADEA case).

1295 29 CFR §1626.18(a) (1993).

1296 Pilkenton v Appalachian Regional Hosps, Inc, 336 F Supp 334 (WD Va 1971).

1297 *See* King v Board of Educ, 435 F2d 295 (7th Cir 1970), *cert denied,* 402 US 908 (1971).

1298 Equal Employment Opportunity Commn v Westinghouse Elec Corp, 632 F Supp 343, 358 (ED Pa 1986), *affd in part & vacated & remanded in part on other grounds,* 869 F2d 696 (3d Cir), *vacated,* 493 US 801 (1989) (ADEA case).

An employer may not properly rely on a vague and ambiguous agency bulletin that explicitly characterizes the position taken therein as tentative.[1299] Nor may an employer successfully claim reliance where the documents relied upon in fact afford no guidance as to the employer's actions.[1300] Likewise, an employer only may rely upon a regulation so as to be in conformity with it, if it in fact applies to the employer's situation,[1301] and if it is issued by the agency vested with primary or final authority to administer the ADEA—i.e., the EEOC.[1302] An employer need not solicit an opinion from the enforcement agency when the regulation on which it relies is clear.[1303]

The EEOC regulations provide that an opinion letter, when addressed to the specific addressee, has no effect upon situations other than that of the specific addressee.[1304] If it is not so addressed, there are rulings establishing that an employer that invokes a §10 defense need not have directly received the ruling on which it relies, given §10's allowance of reliance upon documents applicable "to the class of employers to which . . . [the

---

1299 *Id.*

1300 Equal Employment Opportunity Commn v Home Ins Co, 672 F2d 252, 264-65 (2d Cir 1982) (ADEA case). An employer failed to establish that there was a formal document on which it could adequately rely where it pointed to a voluntary dismissal of an appeal by the Department of Labor in an earlier case involving substantially similar facts. Hodgson v Royal Crown Bottling Co, 465 F2d 473 (5th Cir 1972).

1301 Gathercole v Global Assocs, 560 F Supp 642, 646 (ND Cal 1983), *revd on other grounds,* 727 F2d 1485 (9th Cir), *amended,* 34 Empl Prac Dec (CCH) ¶34,563 (9th Cir), *cert denied,* 469 US 1087 (1984) (ADEA case). "[T]he bulletin allegedly relied upon and conformed with must be specific enough to cover the employment situation at issue." Equal Employment Opportunity Commn v Baltimore & Ohio RR, 557 F Supp 1112, 1121 (D Md 1983) (ADEA case).

1302 Gathercole v Global Assocs, 560 F Supp 642, 646 (ND Cal 1983), *revd on other grounds,* 727 F2d 1485 (9th Cir), *amended,* 34 Empl Prac Dec (CCH) ¶34,563 (9th Cir), *cert denied,* 469 US 1087 (1984) (ADEA case).

1303 Quinn v New York State Elec & Gas Corp, 621 F Supp 1086 (NDNY 1985) (ADEA case).

1304 29 CFR §1626.18(b) (1993).

employer raising the defense] belonged."[1305] However, where the agency pronouncement makes clear that a determination depends upon all the circumstances of each case, good faith reliance on less than direct communication is more difficult to establish.[1306]

If the regulation, order, or other pronouncement on which the employer relied does not apply to its situation, the §10 defense will not succeed.[1307] But if it was the agency that rendered an erroneous interpretation, the employer's defense will not be negated.[1308] If the agency changes its position to one that conflicts with its own regulations, but it does not rescind those regulations, the employer may rely upon them.[1309]

Instances in Which Good Faith Reliance Is Argued

Individual cases disclose the fact-based approach the courts must use, once they get past the question of the adequacy of the document on which the employer claims to have relied. Thus, for example, where an employer relied upon the advice of its own attorney that an agency ADEA regulation authorized what an agency official said it did not allow, the employer's knowledge

---

1305 29 USC §259(a); *see* Marshall v Baptist Hosp, Inc, 473 F Supp 465, 480 (MD Tenn 1979), *revd on other grounds,* 668 F2d 234 (6th Cir 1981); *see also* Martinez v Phillips Petroleum Co, 283 F Supp 514 (D Idaho 1968), *affd,* 424 F2d 547 (9th Cir 1970). *But see* 29 CFR §790.18(g) (1993), where the Department of Labor reads this language as only modifying §10's reference to practices and policies, and not the language concerning regulations, etc. The cases cited in this note do not seem to read the language so narrowly.

1306 *See, e.g.,* Marshall v Baptist Hosp, Inc, 473 F Supp 465, 480 (MD Tenn 1979), *revd,* 668 F2d 234 (6th Cir 1981).

1307 *See, e.g.,* Equal Employment Opportunity Commn v Baltimore & Ohio RR, 632 F2d 1107, 1112 (4th Cir 1980), *cert denied,* 454 US 825 (1981) (ADEA case); Gathercole v Global Assocs, 545 F Supp 1280, 1283 (ND Cal 1982), *later proceeding,* 560 F Supp 642 (ND Cal 1983), *revd on other grounds,* 727 F2d 1485 (9th Cir), *amended,* 34 Empl Prac Dec (CCH) ¶34,563 (9th Cir), *cert denied,* 469 US 1087 (1984) (ADEA case); Allen v Colgate-Palmolive Co, 539 F Supp 57, 66 (SDNY 1981) (ADEA case).

1308 *See, e.g.,* Dymond v United States Postal Serv, 515 F Supp 396, 398 (ED Mo 1981), *affd,* 670 F2d 93 (8th Cir 1982).

1309 *See, e.g.,* Marshall v Hawaiian Tel Co, 575 F2d 763, 767 n8 (9th Cir 1978) (ADEA case).

of the agency employee's opinion did not defeat its ability to successfully invoke the good faith defense.[1310] As it so happened, on the merits the court found the employer's alleged wrongful act to be lawful under the ADEA, and so it did not address what would have happened regarding the good-faith defense had the agency official's position been correct.

In *Clifton D. Mayhew, Inc v Wirtz*[1311] the Court of Appeals for the Fourth Circuit rejected a good faith defense because the defendant had knowledge, by virtue of correspondence and consultation with its attorney, of amendatory statutory language that conflicted with the Department of Labor interpretative bulletin on which the employer claimed to have relied. The court reasoned as follows:

> [W]here the two [readings] are obviously conflicting, we think . . . [the employer] does not objectively act in "good faith" when he chooses to "believe" the one exempting him from coverage. The law had been changed and the employer knew it. "If he did not know, it was because he did not look, or looking, did not see, or want to see what was so plainly there."[1312]

In a somewhat similar situation,[1313] the same court of appeals 10 years later remanded a case for determination of whether a defendant in good faith could have relied on a 1967 agency opinion letter, given arguably conflicting 1974 amendments to the Fair Labor Standards Act.[1314] It was not until 1977 that the type of plan that the defendant utilized was actually held by a court to be unlawful under the 1974 amendments. The question for the trial court was whether the opinion letter and amendments

---

[1310] Marshall v Atlantic Container Line, GIE, 470 F Supp 71, 74 (SDNY 1979) (ADEA case).

[1311] 413 F2d 658 (4th Cir 1969).

[1312] *Id* 663 (quoting Mitchell v Raines, 238 F2d 186, 188 (5th Cir 1956)).

[1313] Marshall v Emersons, Ltd, 598 F2d 1346, 1348 (4th Cir 1979).

[1314] 29 USC §§200-219.

were so obviously conflicting that the defendant "could not have been objectively acting in good faith when it chose to follow the opinion letter."[1315]

In *Equal Employment Opportunity Commission v Baltimore & Ohio Railroad*[1316] the same court addressed a good faith defense in the context of an ADEA suit that involved an amendment to railroad companies' pension plans. The amendment lowered the compulsory retirement age from 65 to 62. A company vice-president, apparently a lawyer, had read administrative interpretations of the Act prior to the adoption of the amendment to the plans, one of which interpretations was generally supportive of the companies' position that the amendment was not violative of the statute. The Department of Labor had initiated an investigation of the companies' retirement practices, however, and had advised the companies that they were in violation of the ADEA by forcing retirement prior to age 65. A few months later, the amendment was adopted. In the court's view, the good faith defense could not be invoked successfully: "In light of this sequence of events indicating the railroad companies' specific knowledge of the discriminatory character of their conduct, they . . . have not established, by objective evidence, . . . good faith reliance on an administrative interpretation[.]"[1317]

1315 Marshall v Emersons, Ltd, 598 F2d 1346, 1348 (4th Cir 1979). For other assessments of the substantive merits of §10 defenses, see Marshall v Baptist Hosp, Inc, 668 F2d 234 (6th Cir 1981); Beebe v United States, 640 F2d 1283 (Ct Cl 1981); Pilkenton v Appalachian Regional Hosps, Inc, 336 F Supp 334, 340 (WD Va 1971); Martinez v Phillips Petroleum Co, 283 F Supp 514 (D Idaho 1968), *affd,* 424 F2d 547 (9th Cir 1970). For hypothetical examples illustrating the scope of the good faith requirement, see 29 CFR §790.15 (1993).

1316 632 F2d 1107 (4th Cir 1980), *cert denied,* 454 US 825 (1981).

1317 *Id* 1113. Subsequently, the district court in this case reaffirmed its original position, i.e., that the defendants had established good faith reliance—a position as to which the court of appeals had reversed. Equal Employment Opportunity Commn v Baltimore & Ohio RR, 557 F Supp 1112 (D Md 1983). The district court reasoned in 1983 that the question of good faith reliance is a question of fact. It observed that following the court of appeals' ruling, the Supreme Court had decided Pullman-Standard v Swint, 456 US 273 (1982), in which it was held that findings of fact may not be set aside unless they are declared clearly erroneous. Given that the court of appeals, although it had reversed, had not held the earlier district court's finding to be clearly errone-

Releases from, or Waivers of, Liability

§5.63 Releases from Liability: Generally

Releases from liability are a common facet of the American workplace. In return for some benefit to which he or she is not otherwise entitled, an employee, job applicant, or former employee agrees to waive his or her right to pursue present and/or future legal claims which he or she has, or may have. In 1989 the United States General Accounting Office reported on the commonality of releases in one context—i.e., as the quid pro quo given by employees in return for enhanced early retirement packages offered by employers:

> About 80 percent of *Fortune* 100 companies sponsored an exit incentive program at least once during 1979 through 1988, according to company officials. About 30 percent of these companies required their employees to sign a waiver as a condition for receiving enhanced benefits. Overall, waiver usage increased during the years 1985-88 and was highest in 1987 and 1988, when 35 percent of companies with exit incentives used them.[1318]

Waivers of liability of course are not confined just to early retirement incentive plans. A waiver may be extracted from an individual as part of the settlement of a pending, or imminent, legal cause of action. Similarly, a release of liability may be part of a package devised to encourage the voluntary departure of a troublesome employee.

Increasingly, releases have generated litigation. The matter of releases also brought forth a regulatory effort in the late 1980s by the Equal Employment Opportunity Commission (EEOC),

---

ous, the district court in 1983 felt itself empowered to reaffirm its earlier decision.

[1318] United States General Accounting Office, Report to Congressional Requesters, Age Discrimination—Use of Waivers by Large Companies Offering Exit Incentives to Employees 2 (Apr 1989).

the agency charged with enforcing the Age Discrimination in Employment Act (ADEA).[1319] These developments, reflective of a growing concern about what standards, if any, should govern releases—particularly releases executed by individuals without their being approved, or even scrutinized, by the EEOC—culminated in 1990 with enactment of the Older Workers Benefit Protection Act (OWBPA).[1320] One portion of the OWBPA added to the ADEA §7(f),[1321] whose terms must be satisfied for a release executed without the approval of, or supervision by, the EEOC to be legally binding.

Section 7(f) became effective as of October 16, 1990, the date of the OWBPA's enactment.[1322] It is inapplicable to releases executed prior to that date.[1323] Accordingly, pre-OWBPA case law regarding releases remains relevant as to pre-OWBPA releases. The legislative history of the OWBPA also points to pre-OWBPA judicial rulings as still being valid as to the questions of releasors' knowledge and the voluntariness of their releasing employers from actual and possible claims.[1324] Thus, the pre-OWBPA case law is all the more of continuing relevance.

Section 7(f)(4)[1325] of the ADEA provides that a waiver may not affect the EEOC's "rights and responsibilities to enforce" the ADEA. Nor may a waiver "be used to justify interfering with the protected right of an employee to file a charge or participate in an investigation or proceeding by the" EEOC. This preclusion of a waiver being allowed to interfere with the EEOC's enforcement authority replicates the position enunciated in a pre-OWBPA decision—*Equal Employment Opportunity Commission v*

1319 29 USC §§621-634.

1320 Pub L No 101-433, 104 Stat 978, *as amended by* Pub L No 101-521, 104 Stat 2287 (1990).

1321 29 USC §626(f).

1322 Pub L No 101-433, §202(a), 104 Stat 978, 984, *as amended by* Pub L No 101-521, 104 Stat 2287 (1990).

1323 *Id; accord* Ulvin v Northwestern Natl Life Ins Co, 943 F2d 862, 866 (8th Cir 1991), *cert denied,* 112 S Ct 970 (1992).

1324 See **§§5.65, 5.67.**

1325 29 USC §626(f)(4).

Cosmair, Inc.[1326] The *Cosmair* court also held that, although the right to file a charge with the EEOC cannot be waived, an "employee can waive . . . the right to recover in a suit brought by the EEOC on the employee's behalf."[1327] While §7(f)(4) does not address this latter proposition, the Senate report accompanying the initial version of the bill that, in modified form, ultimately was enacted as the OWBPA, expressed approval of such waiver of the right to recover.[1328]

The following sections in this chapter address both the pre-OWBPA case law and the OWBPA-fashioned §7(f).

§5.64 Unsupervised Releases: The Pre-OWBPA Situation

The FLSA Backdrop

In the mid-1980s controversy developed as to whether releases of claims arising under the Age Discrimination in Employment Act (ADEA)[1329] were legally binding absent approval by the Equal Employment Opportunity Commission (EEOC). Dispute was generated in the first instance by the language of §16(b)[1330] of the Fair Labor Standards Act (FLSA),[1331] which is incorporated into the ADEA by §7(b)[1332] of the latter statute. Section 16(b) provides that the enforcement agency "is authorized to supervise the payment of unpaid, minimum wages or the overtime compensation owing to any employee."

In *Brooklyn Savings Bank v O'Neil*[1333] the Court held that a release of FLSA liability would not be valid and binding where,

---

1326 821 F2d 1085 (5th Cir 1987).

1327 *Id* 1091.

1328 Senate Comm on Labor & Human Resources, The Older Workers Benefit Protection Act, S Rep No 263, 101st Cong, 2d Sess 35 (1990).

1329 29 USC §§621-634.

1330 *Id* §216(b).

1331 *Id* §§200-219.

1332 *Id* §626(b).

1333 324 US 697 (1945).

although there was no dispute as to the amount of back pay and liquidated damages due and owing the employee, the employee received less than this amount by virtue of the settlement.[1334] In *Schulte Co v Gangi*[1335] the Court further held that even where there was a dispute as to whether an employee was covered by the FLSA (unlike *O'Neil,* in which no dispute as to coverage existed), a release likewise would not be valid and binding if it relieved the employer of liability for an amount less than would be due if liability were established.

From these two decisions flowed a distinction between settlements of bona fide disputes concerning legal issues and settlements of bona fide disputes regarding factual matters. The latter settlements could be entered into by employees and employers without government approval; the former, however, were precluded by the two Supreme Court rulings.[1336] Since the ADEA incorporates the FLSA's enforcement provisions, the argument could be made that the foregoing FLSA case law—whereby unsupervised waivers in some instances will not be deemed to bar subsequent lawsuits—should apply to disputes arising under the age discrimination statute.

There was, however, another line of cases—decided under the ADEA's analogue, Title VII of the Civil Rights Act of 1964[1337] —establishing the validity of waivers made by grievants with Title VII claims, so long as such waivers were made knowingly and voluntarily. Because of the kinship of Title VII and the ADEA, as well as the consequent frequent reliance of ADEA

1334 *See generally* D.R. Rimmer, Annotation, *Settlement of Back Wage Claims Under §16(b), (c) of Fair Labor Standards Act (29 USC §216(b), (c)),* 65 ALR Fed 698 (1983).

1335 328 US 108 (1946).

1336 This distinction is reflected in 29 USC §253, which was enacted subsequent to *O'Neil,* and which allows for the unsupervised settlement of factual disputes in FLSA cases so long as there is "a bona fide dispute as to the amount payable." *See* Stilwell v Hertz Drivurself Stations, 174 F2d 714 (3d Cir 1949).

1337 42 USC §§2000e through 2000e-17.

courts on Title VII precedents,[1338] the Title VII analogy was persuasive (albeit certainly not dispositive) in dealing with waivers of ADEA claims.

ADEA Case Law

Starting in the 1980s, a number of courts began addressing the validity of unsupervised waivers of ADEA claims. In almost every instance the courts ruled—directly or inferentially—that such waivers, or releases, were valid and binding so long as they were executed by the employees knowingly and voluntarily.

The first major decision was *Runyan v National Cash Register Corp.*[1339] The plaintiff was a lawyer who had worked for the National Cash Register Corporation (NCR) and who was described as having years of experience in the fields of labor law and fair employment practices law. Upon being informed, at age 59, that he was to be discharged, he expressed the view that he believed himself to be the victim of age discrimination. Eventually, a consulting agreement was negotiated whereby Runyan continued to receive income from NCR. This was conditioned on his signing a release of all his claims against NCR relating to his employment and discharge. The release did not specifically refer to the ADEA; rather, in typical language, it provided that the consulting agreement Runyan had entered into was "in full accord and satisfaction of any and all claims . . . [he] may have against NCR *arising out of the course of . . . [his] employment and/or the termination of any employment[.]*"[1340]

The en banc Court of Appeals for the Sixth Circuit viewed the case as involving a bona fide factual—rather than legal—dispute as to whether NCR discharged Runyan in violation of the ADEA.[1341] With a carefully limited framing of its position,

---

1338 See **ch 2**.

1339 787 F2d 1039 (6th Cir) (en banc), *cert denied,* 479 US 850 (1986).

1340 *Id* 1041 (emphasis in original).

1341 "The dispute is not over legal issues such as the ADEA's coverage or its applicability. Rather, the parties contest factual issues concerning the motivation and intent behind NCR's decision to discharge Runyan." *Id* 1044.

the court held that "an unsupervised release of a claim in a bona fide factual dispute of this type under these circumstances is not invalid."[1342] In fleshing out what it meant by "these circumstances," the court pointed out that Runyan was not "among the lowest paid segment of the nation's workers, who likely have little education and little understanding of their legal rights, a factor which the Court in *O'Neil* and *Gangi* deemed very important."[1343] Rather, Runyan was an experienced labor lawyer who "knowingly and deliberately" executed the release.[1344] Thus, the situation here was "very different from cases concerning releases of FLSA claims by lay persons seeking payment of minimum wages, in amounts ascertainable by uncomplicated methods, usually with little knowledge of their legal rights."[1345] (In a footnote the court emphasized the distinction between FLSA cases, where the factual issues regarding pay and hours are "amenable to determination with some precision," and ADEA cases, in which the factual issues "frequently concern determinations of motivation and intent, controversies that are more difficult to resolve.")[1346] The court further emphasized that a release should not be deemed valid where there was " 'overreaching or exploitation' " by the employer.[1347] In determining whether such existed, the court prescribed looking to "[o]rdinary contract

---

1342 *Id.*

1343 *Id.* Valenti v International Mill Servs, Inc, 610 F Supp 36 (ED Pa), *later proceeding,* 634 F Supp 57 (ED Pa 1985), *revd,* 45 FEP Cas (BNA) 1054 (3d Cir 1987) (unreported), *rehg en banc granted & opinion vacated,* __ F2d __ (3d Cir 1988), while decided before the en banc *Runyan* decision, illustrated one of the gaps left by that ruling, whereby there remained considerable room for attacking unsupervised releases. The *Valenti* court specifically contrasted the competence of the lawyer plaintiff in *Runyan* with the naivete of the engineer plaintiff here, who "never thought at the time he was being discharged that he may have been discriminated against because of his age or that he possibly had an age discrimination claim." *Id* 38.

1344 787 F2d at 1044.

1345 *Id.*

1346 *Id* 1044 n8.

1347 *Id* 1045 (quoting Schulte, Inc v Gangi, 328 US 108, 122 (1946) (Frankfurter, J., dissenting)).

principles."[1348] Thereby, questions of knowledge and voluntariness would be resolved. Using such principles, the court rejected Runyan's argument that the waiver did not apply to his ADEA claims because it did not specifically refer to the ADEA.[1349] In the court's view, Runyan—given his background—could hardly have maintained that he was ignorant of the Act and that the release's silence so signified.

Thus, *Runyan* established that unsupervised releases of ADEA claims could be valid and binding, given the right set of circumstances. (Of course, if the enforcement agency or a court had scrutinized and approved a proposed settlement, the release embodied in the settlement unquestionably would be binding.)[1350] By mid-1992 the legitimacy of unsupervised releases that were executed knowingly and voluntarily had been established—either directly or inferentially—not only in the Sixth Circuit, but in the Second,[1351] Third,[1352] Fourth,[1353] Fifth,[1354]

[1348] *Id* 1045.

[1349] *Id* 1044 n10. In Anderson v Montgomery Ward & Co, 650 F Supp 1480 (ND Ill 1987), *vacated in part on other grounds,* 704 F Supp 162 (ND Ill 1989), the court refused to rule for the defendant on its summary judgment motion, which was based on the claimed binding effect of the release signed by the plaintiffs. In so doing, the court distinguished *Runyan* by reasoning that (1) unlike the labor lawyer plaintiff in *Runyan,* the plaintiffs here were unsophisticated; (2) the plaintiffs had never actually negotiated with their employer, but rather were presented with a take-it-or-leave-it proposition; and (3) there was no evidence suggesting that the plaintiffs had attempted to take advantage of their employer by entering into an agreement they never intended to keep. *Id* 1486.

[1350] *See, e.g.,* Lynn's Food Stores, Inc v United States, 679 F2d 1350 (11th Cir 1982) (non-ADEA case).

[1351] Bormann v AT&T Communications, Inc, 875 F2d 399 (2d Cir), *cert denied,* 493 US 924 (1989).

[1352] Coventry v United States Steel Corp, 856 F2d 514 (3d Cir 1988).

[1353] Dorosiewicz v Kayser-Roth Hosiery, Inc, No 86-3163 (4th Cir June 24, 1987) (unreported).

[1354] O'Hare v Global Natural Resources, Inc, 898 F2d 1015 (5th Cir 1990); Equal Employment Opportunity Commn v Cosmair, Inc, 821 F2d 1085 (5th Cir 1987).

Eighth,[1355] Ninth,[1356] and Eleventh[1357] Circuits, as well.

The Abortive EEOC Regulation

The validity of unsupervised releases also was addressed by the EEOC, which issued a regulation in mid-1987 approving waivers and releases of private rights under the ADEA.[1358] However, Congress annually barred this regulation from taking effect.[1359] Eventually, the regulation was permanently negated by §202(b) of the Older Workers Benefit Protection Act,[1360] and it accordingly was removed from the Code of Federal Regulations by the EEOC.[1361]

§5.65 §7(f) of the OWBPA-Amended ADEA: The Statutory Language

Section 7(f)[1362] of the Age Discrimination in Employment Act

---

1355 Hillebrand v M-Tron Indus, Inc, 827 F2d 363 (8th Cir 1987), *cert denied,* 488 US 1004 (1989); Lancaster v Buerkle Buick Honda Co, 809 F2d 541 (8th Cir), *cert denied,* 482 US 928 (1987); Moore v McGraw Edison Co, 804 F2d 1026, 1033 (8th Cir 1986).

1356 Cassino v Reichhold Chems, Inc, 817 F2d 1338 (9th Cir 1987), *cert denied,* 484 US 1047 (1988) (the court, while not expressly discussing the issue of the legitimacy of unsupervised releases, by inference approved them).

1357 Gormin v Brown-Foreman Corp, 963 F2d 323 (11th Cir 1992).

1358 29 CFR §1627.16(c) (1991) (removed from the CFR, 57 Fed Reg 4158 (Feb 4, 1992)). The regulation required that for such waivers or releases to be valid they had to be "knowing and voluntary, . . . [had to] not provide for the release of prospective rights or claims, and . . . [could not be] in exchange for consideration that includes employment benefits to which the employee is already entitled." 29 CFR §1627.16(c)(1) (1991). The regulation set forth criteria to be utilized in assessing whether a waiver was made knowingly and voluntarily. The regulation barred waivers of employees' rights to file charges of unlawful discrimination and to participate in EEOC investigations. *Id* §1627.16(c)(3).

1359 See **§5.68.**

1360 Pub L No 101-433, 104 Stat 978, *as amended by* Pub L No 101-521, 104 Stat 2287 (1990).

1361 57 Fed Reg 4158 (Feb 4, 1992).

1362 29 USC §626(f).

(ADEA)[1363] was added to the ADEA by the Older Workers Benefit Protection Act (OWBPA).[1364] Section 7(f) sets forth a series of minimal threshold requirements that must exist for a release to be deemed to have been executed knowingly and voluntarily. These requirements vary, to some extent, depending upon whether the release was executed "in connection with an exit incentive program or other employment termination program offered to a group or class of employees."[1365] The requirements are modified further if the waiver is executed in settlement of a charge filed with the Equal Employment Opportunity Commission (EEOC) or of a lawsuit.[1366]

What must be understood is that no matter the context, the satisfaction of these threshold procedural requirements will not automatically lead to the conclusion that a given waiver was indeed entered into by an employee or former employee knowingly and voluntarily. Rather, a factfinder still may conclude that a particular waiver is not enforceable.

The threshold requirements are set forth in §7(f)(1) and (2):[1367]

> (1) . . . Except as provided in paragraph (2), a waiver may not be considered knowing and voluntary unless at a minimum
>
> (A) the waiver is part of an agreement between the individual and the employer that is written in a manner calculated to be understood by such individual, or by the average individual eligible to participate;
>
> (B) the waiver specifically refers to rights or claims arising under this Act;
>
> (C) the individual does not waive rights or claims that may arise after the date the waiver is executed;

1363 *Id* §§621-634.

1364 Pub L No 101-433, 104 Stat 978, *as amended by* Pub L No 101-521, 104 Stat 2287 (1990).

1365 §7(f)(1)(F)(ii), (H), 29 USC §626(f)(1)(F)(ii), (H).

1366 §7(f)(2), 29 USC §626(f)(2).

1367 29 USC §626(f)(1), (2).

(D) the individual waives rights or claims only in exchange for consideration in addition to anything of value to which the individual already is entitled;

(E) the individual is advised in writing to consult with an attorney prior to executing the agreement;

(F)(i) the individual is given a period of at least 21 days within which to consider the agreement; or

(ii) if a waiver is requested in connection with an exit incentive or other employment termination program offered to a group or class of employees, the individual is given a period of at least 45 days within which to consider the agreement;

(G) the agreement provides that for a period of at least 7 days following the execution of such agreement, the individual may revoke the agreement, and the agreement shall not become effective or enforceable until the revocation period has expired;

(H) if a waiver is requested in connection with an exit incentive or other employment termination program offered to a group or class of employees, the employer (at the commencement of the period specified in subparagraph (F)) informs the individual in writing in a manner calculated to be understood by the average individual eligible to participate, as to

(i) any class, unit, or group of individuals covered by such program, any eligibility factors for such program, and any time limits applicable to such program; and

(ii) the job titles and ages of all individuals eligible or selected for the program, and the ages of all individuals in the same job classification or organizational unit who are not eligible or selected for the program.

(2) A waiver in settlement of a charge filed with the Equal Employment Opportunity Commission, or an action filed in court by the individual or the individual's representative, alleging age discrimination of a kind prohibited under section 4 [29 USC §623] or 15 [29 USC §633a] may not be considered knowing and voluntary unless at a minimum

(A) subparagraphs (A) through (E) of paragraph (1) have been met; and

(B) the individual is given a reasonable period of time within which to consider the settlement agreement.

The Senate managers of the bill passed by the Senate and House and later signed into law as the OWBPA purported to leave intact pre-OWBPA case law insofar as those decisions concerned the substantive determination of whether, in a given situation, a waiver has been executed knowingly and voluntarily.[1368] In fact, however, the courts in some of the pre-OWBPA cases may have ignored or undervalued factors that §7(f) sets forth as procedural minima that first must be established as having been satisfied before one can move on to the substantive matters of knowledge and voluntariness. To the extent that a pre-OWBPA court might have held a waiver to be knowing and voluntary absent one of the now-statutorily prescribed threshold procedural requirements, such a ruling would no longer be valid. Apart from this caveat, however, the pre-OWBPA case law is still viable and affords, in the various courts' treatment of specific factual circumstances.[1369] relevant guidance.

Also of some utility is the Senate report accompanying the version of the bill initially reported out of the Senate Committee on Labor and Human Resources. Even though the provisions dealing with waivers were later somewhat modified, the modifications were very minor and so the explanations and directions in that report remain on point. In addressing the mode of inquiry to be used in determining whether a waiver was made knowingly and voluntarily—an inquiry that follows the establishment by the party asserting the validity of the waiver that the statutory threshold requirements have been satisfied—the Senate committee specifically expressed support for the *totality of the circum-*

1368 "With respect to the allocation of burdens of proof and production on the issue of whether a waiver was 'knowing and voluntary,' the managers do not intend to disturb the law as it existed prior to passage of this bill[.]" 136 Cong Rec S13,597 (daily ed Sept 24, 1990).

1369 See generally **§§5.68-5.69.**

stances approach employed in *Cirillo v Arco Chemical Co*[1370] and it disapproved, as did its counterpart in the House, the approach used in *Lancaster v Buerkle Buick Honda Co,*[1371] which entailed the application of ordinary contract principles.[1372] Some of the factors looked to under the *totality of the circumstances* approach in fact are replicated in the new §7(f).

In *Cirillo* the court asserted as follows:

> [R]elevant factors . . . include, but are not limited to, the following considerations: (1) the clarity and specificity of the release language; (2) the plaintiff's education and business experience; (3) the amount of time plaintiff had for deliberation about the release before signing it; (4) whether plaintiff knew or should have known his rights upon execution of the release; (5) whether plaintiff was encouraged to seek, or, in fact, received benefit of counsel; (6) whether there was an opportunity for negotiation of the terms of the agreement; and (7) whether the consideration given in exchange for the waiver and accepted by the employee exceeds the benefits to which the employee was already entitled by contract or law.[1373]

§7(f)'s Relevance to Federal Employees

There is some ambiguity as to the applicability of the waiver provisions to federal employees. Section 15 of the ADEA[1374] establishes a separate scheme of protection and enforcement for federal employees,[1375] and so the other provisions of the ADEA do not apply to these individuals. Since the waiver provisions

---

[1370] 862 F2d 448 (3d Cir 1988). See **§5.68.**

[1371] 809 F2d 539 (8th Cir), *cert denied,* 482 US 928 (1987). See **§5.68.**

[1372] Senate Comm on Labor & Human Resources, The Older Workers Benefit Protection Act, S Rep No 263, 101st Cong, 2d Sess 32 (1990); *accord* House Comm on Educ & Labor, Older Workers Benefit Protection Act, HR Rep No 664, 101st Cong, 2d Sess 51 (1990).

[1373] 862 F2d at 451.

[1374] 29 USC §633a.

[1375] See **ch 9.**

added to the ADEA by the OWBPA are placed in §7[1376] of the statute, it would follow that they are inapplicable to federal employees and job applicants. However, §7(f)(2),[1377] which addresses waivers executed in the context of settlements, provides that "a waiver of a charge filed with the Equal Employment Opportunity Commission, or an action filed in court . . . alleging age discrimination of a kind prohibited under sections 4 or 15 may not be considered knowing and voluntary unless it meets certain procedural threshold requirements."

This quoted language is a less than direct extension of protection to federal employees: the reference to discrimination of a "kind prohibited under section . . . 15" seems a little odd: if the drafters clearly wanted to protect federal employees, they could have said so in a straightforward manner. Moreover, there are some additional problems aside from inartful drafting. The language refers to "charges," whereas federal employees file complaints with employing agencies.[1378] This language difference argues against the applicability of the waiver provisions to federal employees. A similar conclusion follows from the fact that a federal employee in fact never files an original grievance, whether it is called a complaint or a charge, with the EEOC; rather, the grievance begins with a filing with the employing agency.

Still, there seems to be no good policy reason for excluding federal employees from the protection of the waiver provisions. Moreover, the legislative history does not foreclose such a reading. (Nor does it explicitly endorse such, however.) In sum, there is some basis for the waiver provisions being read as applicable to federal employees, but there are also bases for a contrary reading. The dispositive resolution of this problem presumably will only be achieved by virtue either of an amendment to the ADEA or a regulatory interpretation by the EEOC.

1376 29 USC §626.

1377 *Id* §626(f)(2).

1378 29 CFR §1614.106 (1993).

§5.66 §7(f)'s Requirements Concerning Group Termination and Reduction Programs

The waiver section of the Older Workers Benefit Protection Act (OWBPA),[1379] adding §7(f)[1380] to the Age Discrimination in Employment Act (ADEA),[1381] elicited very little attention in the course of the Senate and House debates on the legislation. However, the Senate report accompanying an earlier version of S 1511,[1382] the bill ultimately enacted into law in modified form, affords useful guidance regarding the intent of the committee majority which reported out the bill to the Senate for consideration. (Even though the bill adopted and signed into law differed from that reported out by the Senate committee, the changes regarding waivers that were made subsequent to the committee report being written were, but for one change discussed below regarding attorney's fees, simply grammatical in nature. Thus, the report's explanation of the substance of the waiver language remained valid.)[1383]

1379 Pub L No 101-433, 104 Stat 978, *as amended by* Pub L No 101-521, 104 Stat 2287 (1990).

1380 29 USC §626(f).

1381 *Id* §§621-634.

1382 101st Cong, 1st Sess (1989).

1383 The language of the bill reported out of the House Committee was close to that of the Senate-passed version. There was one notable difference, however: the House bill provided that a prerequisite to any waiver of ADEA rights was the assertion of a "bona fide claim." HR 3200, §201, 101st Cong, 1st Sess (1989). The House bill defined such a claim as a charge filed with the Equal Employment Opportunity Commission (EEOC), a court action, or "a specific allegation of age discrimination (including an identification of the nature of the discrimination and a statement of facts evidencing the discrimination) communicated . . . in good faith and in writing . . . to the employer . . . ; and . . . without the instigation or assistance of the employer . . . against which the allegation is made." *Id.* In the House report, some of this language was explained:

> The requirement that the written allegation be communicated in good faith goes to the intent of the individual making the allegation, and not to the merits of the claim itself. This distinction also applies when interpreting the concept of a "bona fide" claim. The Committee intends that both of the terms ("bona fide" and "good faith") refers [sic] to claims that are genuinely motivated and not spurious.

The requirements imposed as to group termination and reduction programs—requirements set forth in §7(f)(1)(F)(ii) and (H)[1384]—were explained in the Senate report. In the course of that explication, the committee's perceptions regarding the provisions applicable in a one-on-one, employer-employee negotiated release also were explained:

> Individual separation agreements are the result of actual or expected adverse action against an individual employee. The employee understands that action is being taken against him, and he may engage in arms-length negotiation to resolve any differences with the employer.
>
> Group termination and reduction programs stand in stark contrast to the individual separation. . . . The trademark of involuntary termination programs is a standardized formula or package of employee benefits that is available to more than one employee. The trademark of voluntary reduction programs is a standardized formula or package of benefits designed to induce employees voluntarily to sever their employment. In both cases, the terms of the programs generally are not subject to negotiation between the parties. In addition, employees affected by these programs have little or no basis to suspect that action is being taken based on their individual characteristics. Indeed, the employer generally advises them that the termination is not a function of their individual status. Under these circumstances, the need for adequate information and access to advice before waivers are signed is especially acute.[1385]

Because group termination and reduction programs "often involve large numbers of employees and complex financial

---

House Comm on Educ & Labor, Older Workers Benefit Protection Act, HR Rep No 664, 101st Cong, 2d Sess 50 (1990). No such language appeared in the version of S 1511 addressed in the Senate committee report on the legislation. Senate Comm on Labor & Human Resources, Older Workers Benefit Protection Act, S Rep No 263, 101st Cong, 2d Sess (1990) [hereinafter Senate Report], or in any succeeding version of the Senate bill.

1384 29 USC §626(f)(1)(F)(ii), (H). These provisions are reproduced in **§5.65.**

1385 Senate Report, *supra* note 1383, at 32.

arrangements, . . . individuals . . . [are] given at least 45 days within which to consider the agreement."[1386] The data required by §7(f)(1)(H) are designed to "permit older workers to make more informed decisions."[1387]

The special protections provided as to exit incentive and group termination programs "are not necessary," according to the Senate report, "where individuals already are engaged in an adversarial dispute[.]"[1388] Accordingly, the threshold requirements applicable to waivers arising out of settlements of EEOC charges and lawsuits are essentially the same as those applicable to waivers entered into in connection with individually negotiated settlement agreements executed by employees and employers.

(A provision in S 1511 obligating employers to pay 80 per cent of the fees and costs for services provided by an employee's attorney in connection with a waiver request, up to a maximum of 10 hours at the attorney's usual hourly rate, was deleted as a result of changes made by the Senate bill's managers in the course of modifying the bill between the time it emerged from committee and the time it was passed by the Senate.)

[1386] *Id* 33.

[1387] *Id* 34. The version of S 1511 reported out of the Senate Committee on Labor and Human Resources contained a requirement that an employer also provide information as to possible future demotions, terminations, or other adverse actions that might occur if an employee declined to participate in an incentive program, and the approximate date when such actions reasonably might occur. *Id* 69. This provision's ultimate deletion from the compromise bill enacted into law was cryptically explained by Senator Jeffords, who was involved in devising the compromise:

> This language was specifically deleted because of the potential impact such mandated disclosures might have on voluntary retirement issues in exit incentive programs given the language included at page 27 of the committee report.

136 Cong Rec S13,607 (daily ed Sept 24, 1990). (The language at page 27 of the Senate report iterated the disclosure requirement contained in the just-discussed deleted legislative language. This language was specifically negated in a document submitted by the chief sponsors of the compromise bill, "Final Substitute: Statement of Managers," which set forth explanatory material regarding the bill. 136 Cong Rec S13,595 (daily ed Sept 24, 1990).)

[1388] Senate Report, *supra* note 1383, at 34.

§5.67 §7(f) of the ADEA: Burdens of Proof

The claim that a release bars suit is an affirmative defense and so must be raised and proved by the defendant.[1389] (If that defense fails, and if the plaintiff ultimately prevails on his or her substantive discrimination claim, the consideration received from the defendant must be deducted from the prevailing plaintiff's award).[1390]

Section 7(f)(3)[1391] of the Age Discrimination in Employment Act (ADEA)[1392] provides that in disputes concerning the threshold procedural requirements set forth in §7(f)(1) and (2)[1393] the party asserting a waiver's validity has the burden of proving "that a waiver was knowing and voluntary pursuant to" subsections (f)(1) and (2). In a statement placed in the Congressional Record by the Senate managers of S 1511,[1394] the bill that—enacted as the Older Workers Benefit Protection Act (OWBPA)[1395]—added §7(f) to the ADEA, a distinction was drawn between the burden of proof regarding the threshold procedural requirements,[1396] and the burden of proof as to the ultimate issue of whether a waiver was knowingly and voluntarily executed:

> The managers intend that in any dispute over whether the requirements, conditions and circumstances set forth in paragraph 7(f)(1)(A)-(H) or 7(f)(2)(A)-(B) have been met, the party asserting the validity of the waiver shall have the burden of proving in a court of competent jurisdiction as an affirmative defense that the waiver process satisfied each of the factors in that paragraph. With respect to the alloca-

---

1389 Isaacs v Caterpillar, Inc, 765 F Supp 1359, 1365-71 (CD Ill 1991).

1390 *Id* 1372; *cf* Hogue v Southern RR Co, 390 US 516, 518 (1968) (case arising under the Federal Employers Liability Act, 45 USC §51 *et seq*).

1391 29 USC §626(f)(3).

1392 *Id* §§621-634.

1393 *Id* §626(f)(1), (2). These subsections are reproduced in **§5.65.**

1394 101st Cong, 1st Sess (1989).

1395 Pub L No 101-433, 104 Stat 978, *as amended by* Pub L No 101-521, 104 Stat 2287 (1990).

1396 These requirements are reproduced in full in **§5.65.**

tion of burdens of proof and production on the issue of whether a waiver was "knowing and voluntary," the managers do not intend to disturb the law as it existed prior to passage of this bill, including the law under Rule 12 and Rule 56 of the Federal Rules of Civil Procedure.[1397]

In light of this persuasive legislative history, pre-§7(f) decisions regarding the question of whether a waiver is knowing and voluntary remain viable.[1398] As it turns out, however, the specific question of burdens received no direct attention in the pre-§7(f) ADEA rulings. There are, however, non-ADEA decisions placing on employees the burden of establishing the invalidity of waivers, or releases, by showing that they were not entered into knowingly or voluntarily.[1399] These decisions conflict with the position set forth in the Senate committee report on the legislation, however.[1400] Thus, one is left with something of a legal quandary: the expectation expressed at one point in the legislative history was that the employer would bear the burden of

---

[1397] 136 Cong Rec S13,597 (daily ed Sept 24, 1990). (This statement is consistent with the position set forth in the Senate committee report on the bill that in modified form was enacted as the OWBPA. In the report the Committee on Labor and Human Resources stated as follows:

> [O]rdinarily, an employer asserting a waiver defense will be obligated to prove . . . that the relevant factors set forth in . . . [§]7(f)(1) or 7(f)(2) have been satisfied. Once that occurs, the employee may produce additional evidence to suggest that the waiver was not "knowing and voluntary." The employer's burden at that point is to prove that with respect to the issues raised by the employee, the waiver was both knowing and voluntary.

Senate Comm on Labor & Human Resources, The Older Workers Benefit Protection Act, S Rep No 263, 101st Cong, 2d Sess 35 (1990).

[1398] See **§§5.69-.70.**

[1399] *See, e.g.,* Anselmo v Manufacturers Life Ins Co, 771 F2d 417, 420 (action arising out of alleged breach of contract and fraudulent misrepresentation) 417, 420 (8th Cir 1985); Reed v SmithKline Beckman Corp, 569 F Supp 672, 674-75 (ED Pa 1983) (case arising under Title VII of the Civil Rights Act of 1964, 42 USC §§2000e through 2000c-17); Hohlweiler v Pennsylvania RR, 294 F Supp 1377, 1381 (ED Pa 1969), *affd,* 436 F2d 1382 (3d Cir), *cert denied,* 404 US 884 (1971) (action arising under Federal Employers' Liability Act, 45 USC §51 *et seq*).

[1400] See note 1397.

proving that a release was executed knowingly and voluntarily.[1401] Yet the legislative history also embraces the case law (without identifying in which direction that case law went), and it turns out that that case law, such as it is, places the burden of proof on the employees.

No clear answer regarding allocations of burdens of proof emerges. In some situations a defendant may have greater access than the plaintiff to the relevant information involved in a dispute and so it justifiably can be held accountable for bearing the burden of proof. Insofar as a release is concerned, however, the releasor is just as likely (or even more likely) to have the relevant information as to the issues of knowledge and voluntariness. Accordingly, if these matters are in dispute, it does not seem amiss for the releasor to bear the burden of proving lack of knowledge or involuntariness, even while the defendant shoulders the burden of proving that the initial statutory thresholds have been satisfied.

§5.68 Knowledge and Voluntariness: Pre-§7(f) Case Law and Regulations

If a release is not entered into knowingly and voluntarily, it will not be enforceable against the employee who signed it. This proposition was fundamental prior to the enactment of the Older Workers Benefit Protection Act (OWBPA)[1402] and it is at the core of §7(f)[1403] of the Age Discrimination in Employment Act (ADEA)[1404]—which section was added by the OWBPA to the age discrimination statute. Thus, if a release is the product of fraud, duress, lack of consideration, or mutual mistake of fact,

---

1401 See *id.*

1402 Pub L No 101-433, 104 Stat 978, *as amended by* Pub L No 101-521, 104 Stat 2287 (1990).

1403 29 USC §626(f).

1404 *Id* §§621-634.

House Comm on Educ & Labor, Older Workers Benefit Protection Act, HR

it will not bar subsequent suit by the releasor.[1405]

In determining questions of knowledge and voluntariness, some pre-OWBPA courts took the position that ordinary contract principles applied.[1406] "Under such principles, '[p]roperly executed waivers of possible employment-related discrimination claims knowingly and voluntarily made between an employee and his employer . . . [would] be enforced absent the typical exceptions for fraud, duress, lack of consideration or mutual mistake.' "[1407] Other courts applied a *totality of the circumstances* standard.[1408] This latter standard entailed looking at a number of factors:

> [R]elevant factors . . . include, but are not limited to, the following considerations: (1) the clarity and specificity of the release language; (2) the plaintiff's education and business experience; (3) the amount of time plaintiff had for deliberation about the release before signing it; (4) whether plaintiff knew or should have known his rights upon execution of the release; (5) whether plaintiff was encouraged to seek, or in fact received benefit of counsel; (6) whether there was an opportunity for negotiation of the

---

1405 *See* Ott v Midland-Ross Corp, 600 F2d 24 (6th Cir 1979). Where an employee who earlier entered into a settlement agreement attempted to rescind it because of alleged fraudulent inducement, the suit to rescind arose under federal law even prior to the enactment of §7(f). Consequently, federal standards applied in determining the validity of the employee's arguments. O'Hare v Global Natural Resources, Inc, 898 F2d 1015, 1017 (5th Cir 1990); Seredinski v Clifton Precision Prods Co, 776 F2d 56 (3d Cir 1985).

1406 *See, e.g.*, Lancaster v Buerkle Buick Honda Co, 809 F2d 539, 541 (8th Cir), *cert denied,* 482 US 928 (1987); Runyan v Natl Cash Register Corp, 787 F2d 1039, 1044 n10 (6th Cir), *cert denied,* 479 US 850 (1986) (en banc); Massi v Blue Cross & Blue Shield Mut, 765 F Supp 904 (ND Ohio 1991).

1407 Massi v Blue Cross & Blue Shield Mut, 765 F Supp 904, 908 (ND Ohio 1991) (quoting Shaheen v BF Goodrich Co, 873 F2d 105, 107 (6th Cir 1989)).

1408 *See, e.g.*, O'Hare v Global Natural Resources, Inc, 898 F2d 1015, 1017 (5th Cir 1990); Bormann v AT&T Communications, Inc, 875 F2d 399, 403 (2d Cir), *cert denied,* 493 US 924 (1989); Cirillo v Arco Chem Co, 862 F2d 448, 451 (3d Cir 1988); Coventry v United States Steel Corp, 856 F2d 514, 524 (3d Cir 1988); Chamberlin v Contel Customer Support, Inc, 54 FEP Cas (BNA) 1490, 1494 (ND Ga 1990); Mullen v New Jersey Steel Corp, 733 F Supp 1534 (DNJ 1990); George v Mobil Oil Corp, 739 F Supp 1577 (SDNY 1990).

> terms of the agreement; and (7) whether the consideration given in exchange for the waiver and accepted by the employee exceeds the benefits to which the employee was already entitled by contract or law.[1409]

The Court of Appeals for the Eleventh Circuit observed, in deciding *Gormin v Brown-Forman Corp,*[1410] that the *totality of the circumstances* and contract approaches as a practical matter essentially entailed examining the same factors. Rather than opting for a particular label, the court simply set forth a variety of issues, not intended to be exclusive, to be looked at; these paralleled those set forth in the just-quoted excerpt from *Cirillo v Arco Chemical Co.*[1411] Without endorsing any particular approach, the Court of Appeals for the Seventh Circuit ruled in *Fortino v Quasar Co*[1412] that "[u]nder any approach" the plaintiff had to lose.

The Abortive EEOC Regulation

In 1987 the Equal Employment Opportunity Commission (EEOC) promulgated a regulation authorizing waivers and releases of private rights under the ADEA, provided they were knowing and voluntary. In making a determination as to whether a release was knowing and voluntary, the agency was "likely to find supportive" several factors:

> (i) The agreement was in writing, in understandable language, and clearly waived the employee's rights or claims under the ADEA;
>
> (ii) A reasonable period of time was provided for employee deliberation;

[1409] Cirillo v Arco Chem Co, 862 F2d 448, 451 (3d Cir 1988); *see also* Bormann v AT&T Communications, Inc, 875 F2d 399, 403 (2d Cir), *cert denied,* 493 US 924 (1989); Coventry v United States Steel Corp. 856 F2d 514, 523 (3d Cir 1988); Equal Employment Opportunity Commn v American Express Publishing Co, 681 F Supp 216, 219 (SDNY 1988).

[1410] 963 F2d 323 (11th Cir 1992).

[1411] 862 F2d 448 (3d Cir 1988).

[1412] 950 F2d 389 (7th Cir 1991).

(iii) The employee was encouraged to consult with an attorney.[1413]

In the commentary accompanying the issuance of this regulation, the EEOC asserted that "[i]t . . . [was] the Commission's position that a release may be valid as to claims of which a signing party has actual knowledge and those that could have been discovered upon reasonable inquiry."[1414] The implementation of this provision was suspended for fiscal year 1988 (October 1, 1987-September 30, 1988) by an amendment to an appropriations bill passed by Congress and signed by the President on December 22, 1987.[1415] This suspension subsequently was made applicable to fiscal year 1989 by a rider attached to an appropriations bill for that fiscal year.[1416] The delay was later further extended to fiscal year 1990.[1417] Ultimately, the provision was consigned to history by the OWBPA, which provided for its permanent negation.[1418] Following the statutory destruction of the

---

[1413] 29 CFR §1627.16(c)(2) (1991) (removed from the CFR, 57 Fed Reg 4158 (Feb 4, 1992)). The provision continued as follows:

> These are not intended as exclusive nor must every factor necessarily be present in order for a waiver to be valid, except that a waiver must always be in writing. Moreover, even where these three factors are present, if a waiver is challenged, the Commission will look to the substance and circumstances to determine whether there was fraud or duress.

Id.

[1414] 52 Fed Reg 32295 (Aug 27, 1987).

[1415] Continuing Appropriations, Fiscal Year 1988, Pub L No 100-202, 101 Stat 1329, 1329-31 (1987).

[1416] Departments of Commerce, Justice & State, The Judiciary and Related Agencies Appropriations Act, 1989, Pub L No 100-459, 102 Stat 2186, 2216 (1988).

[1417] Department of Commerce, Justice, and State, the Judiciary, and Related Agencies Appropriations Act, 1990, Pub L No 101-162, 103 Stat 988, 1020 (1989). Notwithstanding that the EEOC regulation was held in suspended animation, so to speak, the court deciding Duke v Uniroyal, Inc, 719 F Supp 428 (EDNC 1989), used the "common sense framework" embodied in the regulation in determining that the plaintiff had knowingly and voluntarily waived his rights. *Id* 432.

[1418] Pub L No 101-433, §202(b), 104 Stat 978, 984, *as amended by* Pub L No 101-521, 104 Stat 2287 (1990).

regulation, it was removed from the Code of Federal Regulations by the EEOC.[1419]

§5.69 —Pre-§7(f) Particular Determinations as to Knowledge and Voluntariness

Section 7(f)[1420] was added to the Age Discrimination in Employment Act (ADEA)[1421] by the Older Workers Benefit Protection Act (OWBPA).[1422] This provision creates a set of standards that a release of an ADEA claim must satisfy if it is to be deemed legally binding. Notwithstanding the enactment of this statutory framework, pre-OWBPA case law remains relevant.[1423]

In *Equal Employment Opportunity Commission v United States Steel Corp*[1424] the court particularly focused on the issues of knowledge and voluntariness. The Equal Employment Opportunity Commission (EEOC) had filed suit against the steel company, charging it with violating the ADEA by requiring employees to sign a release of their rights under the statute as a precondition to obtaining a certain retirement pension. The EEOC claimed that because of these releases, which, inter alia, proscribed signatories from counseling or assisting in the prosecution of ADEA claims, it was having difficulty investigating the alleged wrongdoing.

The court initially issued a temporary restraining order barring the company from enforcing the release agreements, as well as from terminating the pensions of any individuals who assisted the agency.[1425] Subsequently, the court issued a preliminary

---

1419 57 Fed Reg 4158 (Feb 4, 1992).

1420 29 USC §626(f).

1421 *Id* §§621-634.

1422 Pub L No 101-433, §201, 104 Stat 978, 983-84, *as amended by* Pub L No 101-521, 104 Stat 2287 (1990).

1423 See **§§5.63, 5.67.**

1424 583 F Supp 1357 (WD Pa 1984).

1425 Equal Employment Opportunity Commn v United States Steel Corp, 34 FEP Cas (BNA) 697 (WD Pa 1984).

injunction to similar effect.[1426] In so doing, the court first reasoned that the releases, embodying waivers of ADEA claims and rights, were not part of a settlement or compromise of a legal claim. Assuming arguendo, however, that the releases were part of a settlement, the court concluded that the alleged settlements—of which the releases were a critical part—were not entered into knowingly and voluntarily. In reaching this conclusion the court looked to a number of factors: a lack of negotiations; an absence of counsel representing the employees; and a lack of explanation of the releases, combined with the fact that the language of the releases was somewhat ambiguous.

In another ruling by a trial court also located in the Third Circuit, the plaintiff once again prevailed. At issue in *Mashman v Universal Match Corp*[1427] was a release executed to resolve the plaintiff's claim to back commissions. Following execution of the release, Mashman was discharged; it was his termination that gave rise to his ADEA suit. At the outset, the court set forth the general proposition that the "release of rights under the ADEA is suspect where it is not part of the settlement of an age discrimination claim."[1428] The court then applied the *totality of the circumstances* approach dictated by *Cirillo v Arco Chemical Co*[1429] for courts in the Third Circuit. First, the court observed, the release did not address any discrimination claim. Second, the amount paid to Mashman pursuant to the agreement, whereby he released the defendant from liability for any and all future claims, was close to what he was claiming by way of back commissions. "Moreover," the court observed, "there is evidence that defendant would have paid the $4,500 for back commissions even if Mr. Mashman did not sign the Release."[1430] The court continued: "These . . . factors weigh very heavily in support of a conclusion that there was not a knowing and willful waiver of a [sic] age

---

[1426] Equal Employment Opportunity Commn v United States Steel Corp, 583 F Supp 1357, 1363 (WD Pa 1984).

[1427] 727 F Supp 941 (ED Pa 1989).

[1428] *Id* 944.

[1429] 862 F2d 448 (3d Cir 1988). See **§5.68.**

[1430] 727 F Supp at 945.

discrimination claim."[1431] Accordingly, the court held that the release did not bar the plaintiff's suit.[1432] In *Cook v Buxton, Inc*,[1433] also, the court ruled that the release was not binding. Applying the *totality of the circumstances* analysis, the court held that the 10 days given the plaintiff to consider whether to sign the release was not a "reasonable length of time in which to permit a terminated employee to deliberate."[1434] The court also looked to the fact that the plaintiff had not been encouraged by his employer to consult an attorney prior to signing the release—a factor also deemed of relevance by the Court of Appeals in *Coventry v United States Steel Corp*.[1435]

Insofar as the role of attorneys is concerned, case law supports the conclusion that if an individual signs a release knowingly and voluntarily, but believing an attorney's erroneous advice that the release is unenforceable, the release will be deemed binding.[1436]

[1431] *Id.*

[1432] Valenti v International Mill Servs, Inc, 610 F Supp 36 (ED Pa), *later proceeding*, 634 F Supp 57 (ED Pa 1985), *revd*, 45 FEP Cas (BNA) 1054 (3d Cir 1987), *rehg en banc granted & opinion vacated*, — F2d — (3d Cir 1988) (unreported), also turned on the issues of knowledge and voluntariness. (The history of the unreported appellate court treatment of the *Valenti* district court ruling is explained in Coventry v United States Steel Corp, 856 F2d 514, 517-18 n4 (3d Cir 1988).) The court refused to rule for the defendant, who claimed that a release signed by the plaintiff barred his subsequent suit. Adverting to the language of the release and to the circumstances surrounding it, as well as to the public policy embodied in the ADEA of protecting a civil right, the court stated as follows:

> The court here is dealing with plaintiff's civil rights. A broad release which does not mention the instant age discrimination claim coupled with the fact that the parties never discussed the general release and thus did not shed any light as to its meaning and the parties' intentions, cannot be construed as a waiver of the claim.

610 F Supp at 38.

[1433] 793 F Supp 622 (WD Pa 1992).

[1434] *Id* 625.

[1435] 856 F2d 514, 524 (3d Cir 1988).

[1436] *See* Fortino v Quasar Co, 950 F2d 389, 395 (7th Cir 1991); *see also* Warnebold v Union Pac RR, 963 F2d 222, 223 (8th Cir 1992); *cf* Pilon v University of Minn, 710 F2d 466, 468 (8th Cir 1983) (case arising under Title VII of the Civil Rights Act of 1964, 42 USC §§2000e through 2000e-17).

In *Arnold v Postmaster General*[1437] the defendant argued that because the plaintiffs knew of the complained-of transfer policy long before they actually were transferred, they had waived any complaint as to it. The court rejected the argument: "That plaintiffs might be transferred . . . is not a circumstance or fact which supports a factual or legal conclusion that it was a knowing and voluntary waiver of plaintiffs' prospective rights under the ADEA."[1438]

Assessing the facts under its *totality of the circumstances* standard, the Court of Appeals for the Second Circuit concluded in *Bormann v AT&T Communications, Inc*[1439] that the releases in question were signed knowingly and voluntarily.[1440] The same scenario transpired in *O'Hare v Global Natural Resources, Inc.*[1441] On the other hand, in *Goff v Kroger Co*[1442] the court refused to grant the defendant's summary judgment motion, reasoning that there was a genuine issue of material fact as to whether the release and covenant not to sue signed by the plaintiff had been executed knowingly.

The court deciding *Widener v Arco Oil & Gas Co*[1443] utilized both general contract principles as well as the *totality of the circumstances* approach in upholding the validity of a release. In *Pears v Spang*[1444] the court applied the seven factors set forth in *Cirillo*

[1437] 667 F Supp 6 (DDC 1987), *revd on other grounds,* 863 F2d 994 (DC Cir 1988), *cert denied,* 493 US 846 (1989).

[1438] *Id* 18. *But see* Khan v Grotnes Metalforming Sys, Inc, 679 F Supp 751, 763 n7 (ND Ill 1988). As to the general issue of the significance for statute of limitations purposes of a continuing policy or practice that is not to be applied to an employee until a long time after he or she is aware of the policy or practice, see **ch 6.**

[1439] 875 F2d 399 (2d Cir), *cert denied,* 493 US 924 (1989).

[1440] *See also* Murphy v IBM Corp, 810 F Supp 93 (SDNY 1992).

[1441] 898 F2d 1015 (5th Cir 1990); *accord* Chamberlin v Contel Customer Support, Inc, 54 FEP Cas (BNA) 1490, 1494-95 (ND Ga 1990); Fay v Peterson Publishing Co, 52 FEP Cas (BNA) 1531 (SDNY 1990).

[1442] 687 F Supp 1189 (SD Ohio 1988).

[1443] 717 F Supp 1211 (ND Tex 1989).

[1444] 718 F Supp 441, 445-47 (WD Pa 1989).

as making up the *totality of the circumstances* approach,[1445] and held that the plaintiff had released the defendant and so could not maintain a postrelease ADEA suit. The court deciding *Ponzoni v Kraft General Foods, Inc*,[1446] followed the same analytical path and came to the same conclusion. Without labeling its approach, the court also upheld the validity of the release in *Harrison v Arlington Independent School District.*[1447] In *Constant v Continental Telephone Co*[1448] the court, without explicitly embracing the *totality of the circumstances* approach, looked to the factors involved in applying it, and in particular focused on the question of whether the releasor had had a fair opportunity to consult an attorney. Assessing the facts, the court concluded in the affirmative.[1449]

There are conflicting judicial statements as to whether the existence of duress will be obviated by a terminated employee's acceptance of the benefits flowing from the agreement into which he or she had been forced to enter.[1450] Generally, this issue comes up in terms of the question of whether an allegedly invalid release has been ratified by the plaintiff by his or her retention of the benefits received pursuant to the agreement with the employer.[1451]

Financial Hardship

One particular aspect of the broader question of whether a release was entered into voluntarily arises in the context of the

---

[1445] See **§5.68.**

[1446] 774 F Supp 299 (DNJ 1991), *affd without opinion,* 968 F2d 14 (3d Cir 1992).

[1447] 717 F Supp 453 (ND Tex 1989), *affd without opinion,* 891 F2d 904 (5th Cir 1989).

[1448] 745 F Supp 1374 (CD Ill 1990).

[1449] *See also* Carroll v Primerica Financial Servs Ins Marketing, 811 F Supp 1558 (ND Ga 1992) (court concluded that plaintiffs were given sufficient time to consider release and to consult attorneys where they were allowed three or four days, but as to one plaintiff, who was afforded only one day, this amount of time was deemed insufficient).

[1450] *Compare* Pitts v Dayton Power & Light Co, 748 F Supp 527, 535 n6 (SD Ohio 1989) (taking negative position) *with* Constant v Continental Tel Co, 745 F Supp 1374, 1385 (CD Ill 1990) (taking affirmative position). As to the issue of ratification of an invalid release generally, see **§5.75.**

[1451] See **§5.75.**

claim that an individual gave up his or her rights because of economic hardship, duress, or coercion. Typically, a discharged employee will face difficult choices. Litigation can be both expensive and prolonged, and rarely will the candid plaintiff's attorney be able to offer any solid assurance of eventual success. Unless the plaintiff is totally free of financial concerns, these factors can be daunting. Often an individual, recently discharged and with poor prospects for securing a new or at least comparably remunerative job, will be in grim financial straits. Can an employee sign a release in return for securing some payment from the employer and then repudiate the release and file suit, arguing that the release is no bar because it was the product of economic hardship and therefore was not entered into voluntarily?

Typically, the answer is a negative one. It has been said that one challenging a release as invalid because of economic coercion or duress must establish three elements: "(1) that one side involuntarily accepted the terms of another; (2) that circumstances permitted no other alternative; and (3) that said circumstances were the result of coercive acts of the opposite party."[1452] Particularly important, "[t]he assertion of duress must be proven by evidence that the duress resulted from defendant's wrongful and oppressive conduct and not by plaintiff's necessities."[1453] In *Cirillo v Arco Chemical Co,*[1454] an ADEA case, the court stated the rule to be that "one asserting duress must establish a wrongful act or threat which prevented a party from exercising

---

[1452] WR Grimshaw Co v Nevil C Withrow Co, 248 F2d 896, 904 (8th Cir 1957), *cert denied,* 356 US 912 (1958); *accord* Undersea Engg & Constr Co, Inc v International Tel & Tel Corp, 429 F2d 543, 550 (9th Cir 1970); Lancaster v Buerkle Buick Honda Co, 39 FEP Cas (BNA) 721 (D Minn 1985), *affd on other grounds,* 809 F2d 539 (8th Cir), *cert denied,* 482 US 928 (1987). Essentially the same three factors were articulated in Frumkin v IBM Corp, 801 F Supp 1029, 1044 (SDNY 1992).

[1453] WR Grimshaw Co v Nevil C Withrow Co, 248 F2d 896, 904 (8th Cir 1957), *cert denied,* 356 US 912 (1958); *accord* Inland Empire Builders, Inc v United States, 424 F2d 1370, 1377 (Ct Cl 1970) (quoting Fruhauf Southwest Garment Co v United States, 111 F Supp 945, 951 (Ct Cl 1953)).

[1454] 862 F2d 448 (3d Cir 1988).

his free will and judgment."[1455] Additionally, "[w]here . . . the avenue of litigation is open to the challenging party but he chooses not to pursue it, it cannot be said that the subsequent settlement was a product of economic duress."[1456]

A few ADEA courts have touched on the economic duress argument. In *Cirillo* the court asserted that "economic pressure alone is insufficient to establish a claim of duress that would void an otherwise valid release."[1457] In *Equal Employment Opportunity Commission v American Express Publishing Corp*[1458] the court asserted that, even assuming that the defendant knew of the employee's overdue mortgage payment and family needs when it offered a severance payment conditioned on his signing a release, it could not "be held responsible for pressure put on . . . the employee by others."[1459]

Mogley v Chicago Title Insurance Co[1460] involved an employee who was informed by his employer that he was to be terminated as of July 31, 1981. He was given the option of accepting early retirement as of January 31, 1982, on which date he would become eligible for substantially increased benefits. This option, however, was conditioned on Mogley's signing a release as to the company's potential ADEA liability for having terminated him. The court's direct concern was the late filing by the employee of his charge of unlawful discrimination. Mogley claimed that the defendant should be estopped from raising the timeliness issue because of the choice it had required him to

---

[1455] *Id* 452 n2 (quoting Plechner v Widener College, Inc, 569 F2d 1250, 1261 (3d Cir 1977)); *accord* Pitts v Dayton Power & Light Co, 748 F Supp 527, 533 (SD Ohio 1989); *cf* Coral Gables Imported Motorcars, Inc v Fiat Motors, 673 F2d 1234 (11th Cir), *modified*, 680 F2d 105 (11th Cir 1982), *cert denied*, 459 US 1104 (1983) (construing New York law).

[1456] Undersea Engg & Constr Co, Inc, v International Tel & Tel Corp, 429 F2d 543, 550 (9th Cir 1970).

[1457] 862 F2d at 452 n2; *see also* Constant v Continental Tel Co, 745 F Supp 1374, 1384 (CD Ill 1990); McBriarty v AT&T, 52 FEP Cas (BNA) 58 (DNJ 1990).

[1458] 681 F Supp 216 (SDNY 1988).

[1459] *Id* 219.

[1460] 719 F2d 289 (8th Cir 1983).

make and because of the fact that had he timely filed he would have had to have done so before the early retirement date of January 31, and thereby he would have lost the increased benefits. In rejecting the plaintiff's argument, the court observed that Mogley was not "*entitled* to the additional retirement benefits as a matter of course[.]"[1461] Rather, they were the consideration given in return for the release. The court went on to state as follows:

> Mogley is correct in his assertion that had he filed his EEOC complaint prior to January 31, 1982, he risked losing the increased benefits. But this is only because he had agreed not to file a complaint in order to become entitled to those benefits. . . . Appellant cites no persuasive authority in the case law that an employer's holding out of alternatives to the employee—here termination or early retirement—and the employee's acceptance of the most favorable terms offered constitute a basis for tolling of the limitations period.[1462]

In *DiMartino v City of Hartford*[1463] the court ruled that economic duress sufficient to avoid a settlement agreement does not exist unless the settling party is in " 'such exiguous circumstances' that if he did not accept the settlement the defendant's cancellation of his disability pension, which the city allegedly threatened, 'would put him in want or prevent him from successfully collecting the pension.' "[1464] Since DiMartino had other sources of income, and since he had legal remedies available if his disability payments were terminated, he failed to establish economic

---

[1461] *Id* 291 (emphasis in original).

[1462] *Id; see also* Ackerman v Diamond Shamrock Corp, 670 F2d 66 (6th Cir 1982); Bodnar v Synpol, Inc, 633 F Supp 13 (ED Tex 1986), *affd,* 843 F2d 190 (5th Cir), *cert denied,* 488 US 908 (1988); Oglesby v Coca-Cola Bottling Co, 640 F Supp 1333 (ND Ill 1985); Lancaster v Buerkle Buick Honda Co, 39 FEP Cas (BNA) 721 (D Minn 1985), *affd on other grounds,* 809 F2d 539 (8th Cir), *cert denied,* 482 US 928 (1987).

[1463] 636 F Supp 1241 (D Conn 1986).

[1464] *Id* 1251 (quoting Vines v General Outdoor Advertising Co, 171 F2d 487, 490 (2d Cir 1948)).

duress. In *Pitts v Dayton Power & Light Co*[1465] the court, construing Ohio law, insisted that for a claim of duress to be established, the perpetrator of the duress had to have acted unlawfully.[1466]

In *Coventry v United States Steel Corp*[1467] the court concluded that there had not been a sufficient showing that the plaintiff had voluntarily and willingly signed the challenged release. Among the factors on which the court focused was the pressure put on the plaintiff. He was told that if he was eligible for a pension he would be ineligible, by the terms of the company's plan, for severance pay. This "placed unfair economic pressure upon him to sign the waiver to avoid having all of his income and benefits cease immediately."[1468]

§5.70 —Knowledge and Voluntariness Case Law in the Post-OWBPA, Pre-Effective Date of §7(f) Era

The legislative history of §7(f)[1469] of the Age Discrimination in Employment Act (ADEA),[1470] which was added to the statute by the Older Workers Benefit Protection Act (OWBPA)[1471] in 1990 and which became effective as to releases executed after the OWBPA's being signed into law on October 16, 1990,[1472] makes clear that Congress intended the pre-§7(f) case law concerning the issues of knowledge and voluntariness on the part of releasors to be of continuing relevance.[1473] Not surprisingly, then, the case law that has developed since the addition of §7(f) to the ADEA reflects the influence of pre-§7(f) decisions. In the

---

1465 748 F Supp 527 (SD Ohio 1989).

1466 *Id* 534.

1467 856 F2d 514 (3d Cir 1988).

1468 *Id* 524 n12.

1469 29 USC §626(f).

1470 *Id* §§621-634.

1471 Pub L No 101-433, 104 Stat 978, *as amended by* Pub L No 101-521, 104 Stat 2287 (1990).

1472 Id §202(a), 104 Stat 978, 984.

1473 See **§§5.63, 5.67.**

previous section, decisions rendered prior to the enactment of §7(f) were addressed. Here, decisions rendered after §7(f) was enacted, but which concerned claims arising before that provision (which does not apply retroactively) went into effect, are addressed.

The court deciding *Nicholas v Department of Health,*[1474] in assessing whether a release had been knowingly and voluntarily executed by the grievant, looked to the *totality of the circumstances* approach that had been enunciated in pre-OWBPA cases[1475] (and that had been endorsed by the Senate committee that produced the bill that ultimately was enacted into law as the OWBPA).[1476] In *Ross v Arcata Graphics Co*[1477] the court did the same and the court concluded that the plaintiff had not knowingly and voluntarily executed the release for several reasons, all of them keyed to the factors that typically are taken into account in *totality of the circumstances* cases:[1478]

> The release Ross signed supposedly released Arcata from "any claim" arising out of her termination. It does not specifically state that she was releasing her right to file an

---

1474 57 FEP Cas (BNA) 1453 (D Colo 1990), *affd without opinion,* 951 F2d 1259 (10th Cir 1991).

1475 See **§5.68.**

1476 Senate Commn on Labor & Human Resources, The Older Workers Benefit Protection Act, S Rep No 263, 101st Cong, 2d Sess 32 (1990); *accord* House Commn on Educ & Labor, Older Workers Benefit Protection Act, HR Rep No 664, 101st Cong, 2d Sess 51 (1990).

1477 788 F Supp 1298 (WDNY 1992).

1478 The Court of Appeals for the Second Circuit noted several relevant factors in Bormann v AT&T Communications, Inc, 875 F2d 399 (2d Cir), *cert denied,* 493 US 924 (1989):

> "1) the plaintiff's education and business experience, 2) the amount of time the plaintiff had possession of or access to the agreement before signing it, 3) the role of plaintiff in deciding the terms of the agreement, 4) the clarity of the agreement, 5) whether the plaintiff was represented by or consulted with an attorney, and 6) whether the consideration given in exchange for the waiver exceeds employee benefits to which the employee was already entitled by contract or law."

Id 403 (quoting Equal Employment Opportunity Commn v American Express Publishing Corp, 681 F Supp 216, 219 (SDNY 1988)).

> action under ADEA. This release was contained in a severance agreement Ross was handed shortly after she had been informed that she was terminated. She was asked to sign it on the spot. Ross did not have any input into the content of the severance agreement and was required to sign it in order to receive her severance benefits. She did not contact an attorney. Arcata did not recommend that she do so and she was not even given an opportunity to do so. While Ross is an educated and experienced businessperson who might have been able to intelligently waive her rights in a bargaining situation, there is no indication that there was any discussion about the severance agreement; either she would sign it and get her severance benefits or she would not sign and not receive such benefits. Given these circumstances, this Court finds that Ross did not voluntarily waive her right to file an action under ADEA.[1479]

In *Seward v BOC Division of General Motors Corp*[1480] the court looked to state law in rejecting the plaintiff's claim that he had signed a release under duress. The plaintiff also contended that the release he had signed was invalid because he had not been represented by counsel when he was given the proposed waiver or when he reviewed it, and because he had not been given an opportunity to negotiate the terms of the release.[1481] While the court recognized that some ADEA courts had taken into account the presence or absence of counsel in determining whether a waiver had been signed with sufficient understanding on the part

---

[1479] 788 F Supp at 1303.

[1480] 805 F Supp 623 (ND Ill 1992).

[1481] The plaintiff signed the release in May, 1989. While §7(f)(1)(E), 29 USC §626(f)(1)(E), of the ADEA provides that a waiver will not be considered to have been executed knowingly and voluntarily unless the individual was "advised in writing to consult with an attorney prior to executing the agreement," §7(f) did not become effective until October 16, 1990, and is not deemed to apply retroactively. See **5.63**.

of the releasor,[1482] the court found the plaintiff's contention wanting here:

> In light of Seward's education, his years of experience with GMC, and his knowledge of contract law [in light of his being a real-estate agent as well as his having studied contract law in connection with real estate], the absence of counsel and the lack of negotiation did not prevent Seward from understanding the legal significance of his decision to execute the Release.[1483]

The *Seward* court also rejected the plaintiff's claim that he had been fraudulently induced to sign the release.[1484]

§5.71 —Knowledge and Voluntariness Under §7(f)

The district court deciding *Collins v Outboard Marine Corp*[1485] addressed the validity of a release in light of §7(f)[1486] of the Age Discrimination in Employment Act (ADEA),[1487] which became effective on October 16, 1990.[1488] The court readily concluded that the release did not satisfy the statutory requirements that the release make mention of the employee's rights under the ADEA; that the employee be given at least 21 days within which to consider the agreement; and that the employee be advised in writing to seek legal counsel regarding his or her rights under

---

1482 *See, e.g.*, Coventry v United States Steel Corp, 856 F2d 514 (3d Cir 1988); Equal Employment Opportunity Commn v American Express Publishing Corp, 681 F Supp 216, 219 (SDNY 1988).

1483 805 F Supp at 623; *see also* Frumkin v IBM Corp, 801 F Supp 1029, 1043 (SDNY 1992).

1484 805 F Supp at 630-32.

1485 808 F Supp 590 (ND Ill 1992).

1486 29 USC §626(f).

1487 *Id* §§621-634.

1488 See **§5.63**.

the ADEA. In deciding *Carr v Armstrong Air Conditioning, Inc,*[1489] the court looked to the same deficiencies—as well as the release's failure to afford the releasor the seven days to revoke the agreement required by §7(f)—in concluding that the waiver at issue was invalid.

The defendants in *Oberg v Allied Van Lines, Inc,*[1490] conceded that waivers it had requested of the plaintiffs did not satisfy §7(f)(1)(F)(ii)[1491] or §7(f)(1)(H),[1492] both of which speak to waivers involving groups or classes of employees. The defendants maintained that they did not have to comply with these provisions because the waivers at issue did not involve such groups or classes. The court disagreed, asserting that "sixty plus employees terminated at one time satisfies OWBPA's definition of a group termination.[1493]

§5.72 The Requirement of Consideration

As a general matter, at common law a release was not binding if it was not supported by consideration. This was the accepted position in cases arising under the Age Discrimination in Employment Act (ADEA)[1494] prior to the enactment in 1990 of a specific provision, §7(f),[1495] which requires in §7(f)(1)(D)[1496] that for a release to be valid it must be supported by consideration.[1497] There is no reason to conclude that the pre-§7(f) case law is not relevant in determining what will constitute adequate consideration for the purposes of §7(f).

[1489] 817 F Supp 54 (ND Ohio 1993).

[1490] 11 F3d 679 (7th Cir 1993).

[1491] 29 USC §626(f)(1)(F)(ii).

[1492] *Id* §626(f)(1)(H).

[1493] 11 F3d at 682.

[1494] 29 USC §§621-634.

[1495] *Id* §626(f).

[1496] *Id* §626(f)(1)(D).

[1497] Lancaster v Buerkle Buick Honda Co, 39 FEP Cas (BNA) 721, 722 (D Minn 1985), *affd on other grounds,* 809 F2d 539 (8th Cir), *cert denied,* 482 US 928 (1987); Constant v Continental Tel Co, 745 F Supp 1374, 1384 (CD Ill 1990).

"The key factor in determining the validity of the release is not the amount of consideration the person giving the release receives, unless it is merely a token amount, but rather whether the person received something to which he was not previously entitled."[1498] This proposition, enunciated in the common-law context, is now set forth in statutory language: §7(f)(D)(1) provides that a waiver may not be considered knowing and voluntary—the basic prerequisites for a release to be binding—unless "the individual waives rights or claims only in exchange for consideration in addition to anything of value to which the individual already is entitled."

In *O'Hare v Global Natural Resources, Inc,*[1499] the plaintiff was entitled to certain benefits if he was discharged without cause, but he was entitled to a lesser package of benefits if he was fired for cause. After receiving notice that there was a basis for his being terminated for cause, O'Hare signed a settlement agreement by the terms of which he waived his right to sue, in return for the smaller package of benefits. In subsequently rejecting O'Hare's claim that the release was unsupported by consideration, the Court of Appeals for the Fifth Circuit asserted that O'Hare "gave up a disputed right to the benefits he would have received had he been discharged without cause for an undisputed right to a smaller package of benefits."[1500]

Nicholas v Department of Health[1501] involved a defendant that granted the plaintiff retroactive leave without pay for a two-month period, September 26 through November 30. The employer also rescinded its earlier discharge of the plaintiff, which discharge the plaintiff claimed was in violation of the

---

[1498] Schmitt-Norton Ford, Inc v Ford Motor Co, 524 F Supp 1099, 1103 (D Minn 1981), *affd without opinion,* 685 F2d 438 (8th Cir 1982), *quoted in* Runyan v NCR Corp, 573 F Supp 1454, 1460 (SD Ohio 1983), *revd on other grounds,* 759 F2d 1253 (6th Cir), *affd,* 787 F2d 1036 (6th Cir) (en banc), *cert denied,* 479 US 850 (1986); *accord* Chaput v Unisys Corp, 964 F2d 1299, 1301 (2d Cir 1992); DiMartino v City of Hartford, 636 F Supp 1241, 1250 (D Conn 1986).

[1499] 898 F2d 1015 (5th Cir 1990).

[1500] *Id* 1017.

[1501] 57 FEP Cas (BNA) 1453 (D Colo 1990), *affd without opinion,* 951 F2d 1259 (10th Cir 1991).

ADEA. As a result of the retroactive leave the plaintiff became eligible for disability retirement benefits—an eligibility that she would have not enjoyed had the discharge not been rescinded. In return, the plaintiff executed a release. The plaintiff argued that because she would have been entitled to these benefits had she not been illegally discharged, she had only received from the defendant that to which she was in any event legally entitled, and so the release was not supported by consideration. The court rejected her argument, reasoning that "[a]bsent the settlement agreement, in order to collect disability retirement benefits, the plaintiff would have had to pursue successfully her claim [of illegal discharge] against the defendant."[1502] In other words, the defendant's agreement to make the plaintiff eligible for the benefits relieved the plaintiff of the task of having to engage in litigation to obtain them. Consequently, the release was supported by consideration.

The plaintiff in *Warnebold v Union Pacific Railroad*[1503] also argued that the release he had executed was not supported by consideration. He reasoned that the railroad had a pre-existing obligation to pay him in any event, pursuant to a federal statute and an Interstate Commerce Commission order that provided protection to railroad employees who had been adversely affected by certain business transactions. The railroad contended that Warnebold in fact was not entitled to such benefits because he was a manager. The trial court had concluded that because the plaintiff's right to such benefits was a matter of dispute (which presumably would have to be resolved though litigation), the payment to him made by the employer pursuant to the release constituted consideration. The *Warnebold* appellate court affirmed.

[1502] *Id* 1455.

[1503] 963 F2d 222 (8th Cir 1992).

§5.73 Public Policy and Other Limitations on Releases

In *Equal Employment Opportunity Commission v Cosmair, Inc,*[1504] the Court of Appeals for the Fifth Circuit held that a waiver of the right to file a charge of unlawful discrimination with the Equal Employment Opportunity Commission was void as against public policy. The court reasoned that "[a]llowing the filing of charges to be obstructed by enforcing a waiver of the right to file a charge could impede EEOC enforcement of the civil rights laws."[1505] This was because the EEOC—the administrative and enforcement agency for the Age Discrimination in Employment Act (ADEA)[1506]—"depends on the filing of charges to notify it of possible discrimination."[1507]

The *Cosmair* court also ruled that, although the right to file a charge with the EEOC could not be waived, an "employee can waive not only the right to recover in his or her own lawsuit but also the right to recover in a suit brought by the EEOC on the employee's behalf."[1508] In addition, the court asserted that "the fact that a waiver of the right to file a charge is void does not invalidate a waiver of a cause of action with which it is conjoined."[1509] The legislative history of the Older Workers Benefit Protection Act (OWBPA)[1510] echoes the *Cosmair* court's positions, i.e., waivers of the right to file charges with the EEOC are invalid, but individuals can waive their rights to recover in their own suits and/or by way of EEOC suits.[1511]

1504 821 F2d 1085 (5th Cir 1987).

1505 *Id* 1090.

1506 29 USC §§621-634.

1507 *Id* 1090.

1508 *Id* 1091; *accord* Isaacs v Caterpillar, Inc, 765 F Supp 1359, 1371 (CD Ill 1991).

1509 821 F2d at 1091.

1510 Pub L No 101-433, 104 Stat 978, *as amended by* Pub L No 101-521, 104 Stat 2287 (1990).

1511 Senate Commn on Labor & Human Resources, The Older Workers Benefit Protection Act, S Rep No 263, 101st Cong, 2d Sess 35 (1990).

The Court of Appeals for the Sixth Circuit, however, made an apt observation in *Equal Employment Opportunity Commission v McLean Trucking Co,*[1512] a case arising under the ADEA's analogue, Title VII of the Civil Rights Act of 1964.[1513] The court pointed out that the fact that an individual has settled his or her claim should not be understood as precluding the EEOC from suing in its public interest role[1514] to seek elimination of the employer's discriminatory practices, and the settlor "should not and cannot practically be prevented from enjoying the benefits inuring generally to all . . . [of a defendant employer's] employees as the result of the eradication of any unlawful practices which may be proved to exist or the benefit of improvements in working conditions.")[1515]

While an individual may waive his or her cause of action as part of a voluntary, knowing settlement of a present claim, there can be no prospective waiver of the individual's rights under the ADEA. Decisions issued prior to enactment of the OWBPA set forth this proposition,[1516] and the ADEA, as amended by the OWBPA, confirms it with specific statutory language codified at §7(f)(1)(C).[1517]

There is another body of case law dealing with waivers of rights in the context of collective bargaining. In *Alexander v Gardner-Denver Co*[1518] the Court barred a union from waiving an individual member's cause of action under Title VII. The Court stated: "Of necessity, the rights conferred [by Title VII on individual employees] can form no part of the collective-bargaining

---

1512 525 F2d 1007 (6th Cir 1975).

1513 42 USC §§2000e through 2000e-17.

1514 See **ch 6.**

1515 525 F2d at 1011.

1516 Constant v Continental Tel Co, 745 F Supp 1374, 1379 (CD Ill 1990); Westfall v City of Cohoes, 683 F Supp 888, 897 n14 (NDNY 1988); Arnold v Postmaster Gen, 667 F Supp 6, 18 (DDC 1987), *revd on other grounds,* 863 F2d 994 (DC Cir 1988), *cert denied,* 493 US 846 (1989); *cf* Alexander v Gardner-Denver Co, 415 US 36, 51 (1974) Title VII case.

1517 29 USC §626(f)(1)(C).

1518 415 US 36 (1974).

process[.]''[1519] This holding was transposed into the ADEA setting in *Equal Employment Opportunity Commission v County of Calumet.*[1520]

There is a split in authority as to the enforceability of a release whereby an individual waives his or her right to seek redress in the courts under the ADEA, and instead agrees to arbitrate any future dispute.[1521] The Supreme Court ruling in *Gilmer v Interstate/Johnson Lane Corp*[1522] did not resolve the issue of the legitimacy of releases executed by employees, insofar as direct employee-employer contracts (as contrasted with employee agreements with third-party regulatory bodies to arbitrate disputes with employers) are concerned.[1523] The *Gilmer* Court did, however, offer strong signals that it would uphold employer-employee agreements to arbitrate if it were afforded the opportunity to rule on such agreements.[1524]

The EEOC takes the position that forfeiture clauses in employee benefit plans, whereby benefit rights are lost if an employee sues the employer or participates in any formal proceeding against the employer, are invalid.[1525] Thus, an employer presumably may not condition the extension of benefits to an employee on his or her waiving liability—at least so long as the employee is, as a matter of course or legal right, entitled to the

---

[1519] *Id* 51.

[1520] 686 F2d 1249 (7th Cir 1982); *accord* Equal Employment Opportunity Commn v Board of Governors of State Colleges & Univs, 665 F Supp 630 (ND Ill 1987).

[1521] *Compare* Nicholson v CPC Intl, Inc, 877 F2d 221 (3d Cir 1989) (unenforceable) *with* Gilmer v Interstate/Johnson Lane Corp, 895 F2d 195 (4th Cir 1990), *affd,* 500 US 20 (1991) (enforceable); Garfield v Thomson McKinnon Sec, Inc, 731 F Supp 841 (ND Ill 1988) (enforceable).

[1522] 500 US 20 (1990).

[1523] See **ch 7.**

[1524] *Id.*

[1525] 29 CFR §1625.10(d)(5) (1993); *see* Equal Employment Opportunity Commn v Maryland Natl Capital Park & Planning Commn, 673 F Supp 746 (D Md 1987) (plaintiff not estopped from challenging allegedly discriminatory disability plan, where defendant argues that the plan was a contract and that parties to that contract were estopped from contesting it).

benefits. If he or she is not so entitled, a different conclusion may follow.[1526]

§5.74 General Propositions Regarding Releases

Admissibility into Evidence of Employer's Effort to Secure Release from Employee

In response to the plaintiff's effort to establish, or buttress, his age discrimination claim by offering evidence that the employer had sought a post discharge release of claims in exchange for giving the plaintiff $25,000, the Court of Appeals for the Ninth Circuit has stated that "[t]he mere offer of money in exchange for a release of all claims does not by itself raise an inference that . . . [this employer's] articulated reasons for discharging . . . [this employee] are pretextual."[1527] However, the same court also has taken the rather unique position that evidence regarding a settlement offer made contemporaneously with a notice of termination is admissible.[1528]

Clarity of Release's Language

To be binding a release must be unambiguous.[1529] Obviously, then, if an employer intends to secure such a waiver, the document should be clear in its language.[1530] While the best course

---

1526 *See* O'Shea v Commercial Credit Corp, 930 F2d 358 (4th Cir), *cert denied,* 112 S Ct 177 (1991); Mogley v Chicago Title Ins Co, 719 F2d 289 (8th Cir 1983).

1527 Mundy v Household Finance Corp, 885 F2d 542, 547 (9th Cir 1989).

1528 Cassino v Reichhold Chems, Inc, 817 F2d 1338 (9th Cir 1987). See generally **ch 6.**

1529 Seward v BOC Div of Gen Motors Corp, 805 F Supp 623, 627 (ND Ill 1992).

1530 For cases in which the agreement generated ambiguity, rather than certainty, see Lee v Rapid City Area Sch Dist No 51-4, 981 F2d 316, 329 (8th Cir 1992); Gardstein v Kemp & Beatley, Inc, 42 Empl Prac Dec (CCH) ¶36,853 (SDNY 1987); Anderson v Montgomery Ward & Co, 650 F Supp 1480, 1486 (ND Ill 1987), *vacated in part on other grounds,* 704 F Supp 162 (ND Ill 1989); Bernstein v Consolidated Foods Corp, 622 F Supp 1096 (ND Ill 1984); Oglesby v Coca-Cola Bottling Co, 620 F Supp 1336 (ND Ill 1985).

would be to specifically refer to the Age Discrimination in Employment Act (ADEA)[1531] when setting forth what present and future claims are being waived,[1532] there is case law establishing that a release does not need to mention the ADEA specifically.[1533] Thus, a release will be deemed to be unambiguous where it recites that "all claims known and unknown" are barried.[1534] Accordingly, the document under scrutiny in *Constant v Continental Telephone Co*[1535] was deemed binding, inasmuch as it provided that the plaintiff released the employer from " '. . . all claims, actions, causes of action, and liabilities of whatsoever kind or nature, including but not limited to claims of discrimination. . . . ' "[1536]

On the other hand, the Court of Appeals for the Eighth Circuit concluded, in deciding *McElroy v Union Pacific Railroad Co,*[1537] that a release whereby the grievant agreed that "performance by . . . [the defendant] of the provisions contained herein constituted complete fulfillment . . . of all its obligations to him" did not suffice to foreclose his maintaining suit. The court reasoned that "the term 'obligations' includes only McElroy's rights to severance pay and benefits and not to other claims against the company such as his ADEA claim."[1538] And in *Cook v Buxton, Inc,*[1539] the court concluded "that the failure to include language [in the release] which specifically addresses ADEA or laws prohibiting

---

1531 29 USC §§621-634.

1532 *See* Ponzoni v Kraft Gen Foods, Inc, 774 F Supp 299, 310 (DNJ 1991), *affd without opinion,* 968 F2d 14 (3d Cir 1992); Pears v Spang, 718 F Supp 441, 445-46 (WD Pa 1989).

1533 Lancaster v Buerkle Buick Honda Co, 809 F2d 539, 540 (8th Cir), *cert denied,* 482 US 928 (1987); Constant v Continental Tel Co, 745 F Supp 1374, 1380 (CD Ill 1990).

1534 Constant v Continental Tel Co, 745 F Supp 1374, 1380 (CD Ill 1990).

1535 745 F Supp 1374 (CD Ill 1990).

1536 *Id* 1380. Similarly, the release at issue in Nicholas v Department of Health, 57 FEP Cas (BNA) 1453 (D Colo 1990), *affd without opinion,* 951 F2d 1259 (10th Cir 1991), was found to be sufficiently clear to justify the conclusion that the plaintiff had knowingly and voluntarily waived her ADEA claims.

1537 961 F2d 1397, 1398 (8th Cir 1992).

1538 *Id* 1399.

1539 793 F Supp 622 (WD Pa 1992).

employment discrimination significantly diminishes the weight of . . . defendant's position" in support of the validity of the release.[1540]

Rescission of a Release

The plaintiff in *Ponzoni v Kraft General Foods, Inc,*[1541] was unsuccessful in arguing that he had rescinded the release that he had signed. He contended that he had retrieved the signed release and that his subsequent return of it was the unintentional consequence of his turning it in with some other forms to the employer. The court did not believe him, however. The plaintiff in *Frumkin v IBM Corp*[1542] retained the severance pay he had received, but maintained that he nonetheless had adequately repudiated the release, which he claimed was the product of duress. The asserted repudiation was his filing of a charge of unlawful discrimination with the Equal Employment Opportunity Commission raising the claims that supposedly he had waived by executing the release. The court deemed this argument unpersausive.

§5.75 The Binding Force of Invalid Releases

From the perspective of an employer or other entity against whom an adverse claim might be made, the purpose of a release, or waiver, is to insulate it from suit. Sometimes, however, the releasee's goal will be thwarted: the individual who ostensibly waived his or her rights by executing the release will subsequently seek to pursue them.

As a predicate to his or her effort to surmount the barrier seemingly posed by the release he or she executed, the releasor will claim that the release is invalid. The releasee in turn will contend that (1) the release is valid, and/or (2) even if it is not, the releasor ratified it in some way, and/or (3) more specifically,

---

1540 *Id* 625.

1541 774 F Supp 299 (DNJ 1991), *affd without opinion,* 968 F2d 14 (3d Cir 1992).

1542 801 F Supp 1029 (SDNY 1992).

by failing to tender back the benefits received pursuant to the release, the releasor thereby is barred from evading the strictures of, the otherwise invalid document.

First Approach: The Release's Invalidity

The success of the releasee's first tack—i.e., arguing the validity of the release—is controlled by the terms of §7(f)[1543] of the Age Discrimination in Employment Act (ADEA),[1544] which was added to the ADEA by the Older Workers Benefit Protection Act (OWBPA).[1545] Section 7(f) prescribes the necessary features of a valid release.[1546]

Second Approach: Arguing Ratification

As for the releasee's second-line effort, i.e., arguing that the release, even if invalid initially, was ratified, there was pre-OWBPA judicial support for the proposition that an invalid release of an ADEA claim was subject to ratification by the releasor. Two leading decisions are *O'Shea v Commercial Credit Corp*[1547] and *Grillet v Sears, Roebuck & Co.*[1548] In both cases the issue of ratification was intertwined with the question of tendering back the benefits received by the releasor in accordance with the terms of the release. In other words, implicit in the decisions—which focussed on the tender-back issue—was acceptance of the proposition that an invalid release could be ratified. The specific form of ratification the courts addressed was the retention of benefits by the releasees.

In *O'Shea v Commercial Credit Corp* the Court of Appeals for the Fourth Circuit ruled that even if a release of a claim arising under the ADEA at some point could have been attacked as being invalid, the releasor's acceptance of a benefit promised by the

---

1543 29 USC §626(f).

1544 *Id* §§621-634.

1545 Pub L No 101-433, 104 Stat 978, *as amended by* Pub L No 101-521, 104 Stat 2287 (1991).

1546 See **§5.65.**

1547 930 F2d 358 (4th Cir), *cert denied,* 112 S Ct 177 (1991).

1548 927 F2d 217 (5th Cir 1991).

employer as an incentive for the employee's having signed the release can be deemed to have "demonstrated an intent to ratify the agreement."[1549] In support of this conclusion, the *O'Shea* court noted that "[i]t is a well-established proposition that the retention of the benefits of a voidable contract may constitute a ratification."[1550]

In deciding *Grillet* the Court of Appeals for the Fifth Circuit likewise subscribed to the rule that "[i]f a releasor . . . retains the consideration [paid to him or her in return for executing the release] after learning that the release is voidable, her continued retention of the benefits constitutes a ratification of the release."[1551] The plaintiff had received periodic payments over the course of several months totaling 50 weeks' worth of severance pay. She argued that she should not have been deemed to have ratified the release because she had tendered back the full amount paid, with accrued interest, at the time she opposed the defendant's motion for summary judgment. She had made this tender, however, on the condition that she be restored to her former position, with back pay running from the date she had signed the release—a date two years prior to her having tendered the return of the money. This condition set on the tender proved to be of significance to the court in determining whether the tender was effective in precluding the conclusion that she had ratified the release. Relevant, also, to the court's assessment was the timing of the offer made by the plaintiff. She had learned a week after executing the release that Sears had offered new job assignments to three younger employees in her former department. Nonetheless, she thereafter continued accepting the severance pay payments over a several-month period, and she did not sue until more than a year after she had been terminated.

[1549] 930 F2d at 362.

[1550] *Id*; *accord* Widener v Arco Oil & Gas Co, 717 F Supp 1211, 1217 (ND Tex 1989).

[1551] 927 F2d at 220; *accord* Ponzoni v Kraft Gen Foods, Inc, 774 F Supp 299, 317 (DNJ 1991), *affd without opinion*, 968 F2d 14 (3d Cir 1992).

The court concluded that the plaintiff had ratified the release she had signed, reasoning as follows:

> This offer is simply too little, too late. A party seeking rescission must attempt to restore the status quo ante—that is, to return the parties to the positions they held just before they entered into the agreement. Just before Grillet signed the release, she was entitled to receive ten weeks' severance pay and to sue Sears for the alleged age discrimination. . . .
>
> Grillet was not entitled to remain in her current position; she could secure that right only by suing Sears and proving that she had been wrongfully discharged. By offering to tender back the consideration only if Sears restored her position, Grillet has not made an adequate attempt to restore the *status quo ante.*[1552]

Apart from Grillet having imposed a condition on the tender which undermined the argument that the tender negated the release, the tender further was defective because it was untimely:

> The law of contracts "requires a party claiming wrongful inducement to seek rescission shortly after discovering the misrepresentation." . . . To avoid ratifying the release through her conduct, Grillet should have returned the consideration soon after she learned that some younger employees in her department had not been terminated.[1553]

The district court deciding *Seward v BOC Division of General Motors Corp*[1554] agreed with the foregoing rulings: "[T]o avoid ratifying the Release through his conduct, . . . [the plaintiff]

1552 927 F2d at 221.

1553 *Id* (citations omitted); *see also* Haslach v Security Pac Bank Or, 779 F Supp 489 (D Or 1991) (ratification existed where 10 months had elapsed between time plaintiff first questioned validity of release and the date when he tendered to employer the severance pay he had received pursuant to agreement with employer when release was executed).

1554 805 F Supp 623 (ND Ill 1992).

should have at least refused the additional retirement benefits once he learned of the alleged invalidity of the Release."[1555]

The Court of Appeals for the Seventh Circuit rejected *O'Shea* and *Grillet* in deciding *Oberg v Allied Van Lines, Inc.*[1556] The court understood the enactment of the OWBPA as supplanting common-law decisions. It reasoned that "[u]nder OWBPA, unless a waiver contract takes the form required by the statute, an employer and an employee cannot contract to waive the ADEA provisions [set forth in §7(f)]."[1557] Accordingly, "[n]o matter how many times parties may try to ratify . . . [an invalid ADEA] waiver, the language of the OWBPA, 'an individual may not waive [except pursuant to the dictates of §7(f)],' forbids any waiver."[1558]

Third Approach: Failure of the Plaintiff to Tender Back Consideration

The third, albeit not completely distinct from the second, tack that a releasee may pursue in seeking to stave off suit by a releasor is to argue that by virtue of the releasor not having tendered back the benefits received from the releasee, the releasor ratified the initial agreement. In *Hogue v Southern Railway Co*,[1559] which involved a suit under the Federal Employers' Liability Act (FELA),[1560] the Court asserted that "[t]he question whether a tender back of the consideration was prerequisite to the bringing of the suit is to be determined by federal rather than state law."[1561] While this ruling obviously involved a statute other than the ADEA, the Court of Appeals for the Eleventh Circuit wrote

---

[1555] *Id* 633.

[1556] 11 F3d 679 (7th Cir 1993).

[1557] *Id* 683.

[1558] *Id*; *accord* Collins v Outboard Marine Corp, 808 F Supp 590 (ND Ill 1992).

[1559] 390 US 516 (1968).

[1560] 45 USC §51 *et seq.*

[1561] 390 US at 517.

in *Forbus v Sears, Roebuck & Co,*[1562] which did arise under the age discrimination statute, that it found "*Hogue's* reasoning persuasive regarding the application of federal law to the ADEA claims presented in the instant case."[1563]

The *Forbus* court reasoned as follows in subscribing to the proposition that a tender of the benefits received pursuant to a release was not necessary as a predicate to the releasor's bringing suit:

> The Court in *Hogue* found that a tender requirement would deter meritorious challenges to releases in FELA [Federal Employers' Liability Act] lawsuits. The same deterrence factor applies to ADEA claims. Forcing older employees to tender back their severance benefits in order to attempt to regain their jobs would have a crippling effect on the ability of such employees to challenge releases obtained by misrepresentation or duress. Such a rule would, in our opinion, encourage egregious behavior on the part of employers in forcing certain employees into early retirement for the economic benefit of the company. . . .
>
> We conclude that, as a matter of federal law, ADEA plaintiffs are not required to tender the consideration received for releases as a condition prerequisite to challenge those releases in court, and that the Retirees' retention of their severance benefits during the pendency of this lawsuit does not constitute ratification of those releases.[1564]

The Court of Appeals for the Seventh Circuit also looked to *Hogue* for guidance. The *Oberg* court observed that in *Hogue* the Court had held that an employee who had previously executed a release did not have to, as a precondition to suing under FELA, tender back to his employer any of the consideration he had received for signing the release. Deeming this conclusion, as well

---

1562 958 F2d 1036 (11th Cir), *cert denied,* 113 S Ct 412 (1992).

1563 *Id* 1040.

1564 *Id* 1041.

as that in *Forbus,* persuasive, the *Oberg* court ruled that the plaintiffs before it "were not required to tender back their severance benefits before filing their ADEA claims[.]"[1565] Likewise, the court deciding *Carr v Armstrong Air Conditioning, Inc,*[1566] adhered to the *Forbus-Oberg* approach.

Subsequent to the *Oberg* ruling, the Court of Appeals for the Fifth Circuit, which earlier had decided *Grillet,* again addressed the ratification issue, in *Wamsley v Champlin Refining & Chemicals, Inc.*[1567] The court adhered to the analysis earlier set forth in *Grillet,* and it criticized *Oberg.* The *Wamsley* court observed that a promise that is void cannot be ratified, inasmuch as such a promise does not constitute a contract to begin with, and so there literally is nothing to ratify. However, the court reasoned that the failure of a waiver to satisfy the requirements of §7(f) does not render the waiver void, but only voidable. Accordingly, a waiver that is defective in terms of §7(f) can be ratified. Accordingly, if a releasor chooses to retain, and thereby to not tender back to the releasee, the consideration paid by the latter in return for the releasor's promise not to sue, such retention of the consideration constitutes ratification.

The district court that decided *Constant v Continental Telephone Co*[1568] took the position that "ratification does not prevent a court from examining whether or not the release was executed knowingly and voluntarily."[1569] Ratification does, however, "prevent a plaintiff from later raising allegations of duress."[1570]

(*Alphonse v Northern Telecom, Inc,*[1571] involved a release that had been executed prior to the effective date of §7(f). The court

---

[1565] 11 F3d at 684; *accord* Isaacs v Caterpillar, Inc, 765 F Supp 1359 (CD Ill 1991).

[1566] 817 F Supp 54 (ND Ohio 1993).

[1567] 11 F3d 634 (5th Cir 1993).

[1568] 745 F Supp 1374 (CD Ill 1990).

[1569] *Id* 1385.

[1570] *Id.*

[1571] 776 F Supp 1075 (EDNC 1991).

applied the contract law approach[1572] and looked to state law to analyze the plaintiffs' claims that they had been fraudulently induced to sign releases by the defendant's false statement that their jobs were being eliminated. Without resolving the issue, the court concluded that the plaintiffs had ratified their releases by retaining the pay and other benefits received pursuant to these releases for two years after they learned of the alleged fraud.)

If a tender of the benefits received is not considered a condition precedent to maintaining a suit, it follows that these benefits are to be deducted from the award secured by the plaintiff should he or she ultimately prevail on the merits of his or her ADEA claim.[1573]

§5.76 Breach of a Release Agreement

In *Equal Employment Opportunity Commission v Cosmair, Inc,*[1574] a discharged employee—Terry—had entered into an agreement whereby he released Cosmair 'from all actions, causes of actions, claims and demands[.]'[1575] Despite this release, the employee filed a charge of unlawful discrimination with the Equal Employment Opportunity Commission (EEOC). Cosmair consequently ceased to make the severance payments that it had agreed to pay in return for the release agreement. Terry filed suit, contending that the employer had retaliated against him in violation of the Age Discrimination in Employment Act (ADEA).[1576] Cosmair defended by arguing that Terry had breached his contract with the company, and the breach relieved it of its obligation to make payments.

1572 See **§5.68.**

1573 Forbus v Sears, Roebuck & Co, 958 F2d 1036, 1041 (11th Cir), *cert denied,* 113 S Ct 412 (1992) (citing Hogue v Southern RR, 390 US 516, 518 (1968)); *accord* Carr v Armstrong Air Conditioning, Inc, 817 F Supp 54, 58 (ND Ohio 1993); *see also* Oberg v Allied Van Lines, Inc, 11 F3d 679, 684 (7th Cir 1993).

1574 821 F2d 1085 (5th Cir 1987).

1575 *Id* 1087.

1576 29 USC §§621-634.

The court rejected this justification by reasoning that the release did not obligate the plaintiff not to file a charge, and so he had not breached the agreement. Accordingly, the employer "was not relieved of its obligation to perform: therefore, its discontinuing payments was unlawful retaliation."[1577] In so reasoning, the court observed that, by executing the release, Terry had waived all actions, claims, and demands—each of which entails the seeking of "one's own."[1578] The purpose of a charge, however, is not to seek recovery, but rather to inform the EEOC of a possible violation of the ADEA. (Indeed, the charge filed by Terry contained no demand for relief.) Ultimately, the court—conceding that there was some evidence indicating that the parties also had intended to bar the filing of charges—held that waivers of the right to file charges are void as against public policy.

In *Isaacs v Caterpillar, Inc,*[1579] the court rejected a counterclaim filed by the plaintiffs' former employer. The employer alleged that the releases signed by former employees had been contractually breached when these employees later filed an ADEA suit. The court asserted that the "filing of a good faith lawsuit does not constitute a breach of the agreement evidenced by that release."[1580] The court termed the releases before it *defensive releases,* and asserted that "unless a covenant not to sue expressly provides for damages in the event of breach, it will be presumed to be for *defensive* purposes only[.]"[1581] It went on to state that even if state law (which it applied here) did allow recovery of damages for breach of a defensive release, the ADEA preempted and barred such a claim.[1582] In deciding *Carroll v Primerica Finan-*

[1577] 821 F2d at 1089.

[1578] *Id.*

[1579] 702 F Supp 711 (CD Ill 1988).

[1580] *Id* 713.

[1581] *Id* (emphasis in original).

[1582] *Id* 715.

cial Services Insurance Marketing,[1583] the district court adhered to the *Isaacs* court's analysis. In contrast, it was established in *Widener v Arco Oil & Gas Co*[1584] that if the employee who releases the employer from liability breaches a valid release by bringing an action that he or she agreed not to bring by virtue of the release, the employer may recover the costs and attorney's fees expended in defending the action.[1585]

An agreement that is breached by any party to the agreement is legally enforceable in a cause of action based on a breach of contract theory.[1586] "[T]he great weight of binding precedent . . . holds that a district court has jurisdiction to enforce a settlement agreement, at least when a party refuses to comply with the agreement before the case has been dismissed."[1587] If a settlement is valid, it will preclude the grievant from subsequently litigating the claim that he or she had earlier settled.[1588]

Administrative Exemptions

§5.78 Administrative Exemptions: Apprenticeships and Other Programs

Section 9[1589] of the Age Discrimination in Employment Act (ADEA)[1590] originally authorized the Secretary of Labor to "establish such reasonable exemptions to and from any or all provisions of this Act as he may find necessary and proper in the

---

1583 811 F Supp 1558, 1567-68 (ND Ga 1992)

1584 717 F Supp 1211 (ND Tex 1989).

1585 *Id* 1217.

1586 *Cf* Brewer v Muscle Shoals Bd of Educ, 790 F2d 1515 (11th Cir 1986) (suit arising under Title VII of the Civil Rights Act of 1964, 42 USC §§2000e through 2000e-17); Ferguson v Flying Tiger, Inc, 688 F2d 1320 (9th Cir 1982) (*id*); Fulgence v J Ray McDermott & Co, 662 F2d 1207 (5th Cir 1981) (*id*).

1587 Kent v Baker, 815 F2d 1395, 1398 (11th Cir 1987). *But see* Londono v City of Gainesville, 768 F2d 1223 (11th Cir 1985) (disagreed with by *Kent*).

1588 Wilmes v United States Postal Serv, 810 F2d 130 (7th Cir 1987).

1589 29 USC §628.

1590 *Id* §§621-634.

public interest." Exercising this authority, the Secretary created an exemption for bona fide apprenticeship programs.[1591] On July 1, 1979, the Equal Employment Opportunity Commission (EEOC) took over administration and enforcement of the ADEA.[1592] It soon proposed rescinding the apprenticeship exemption,[1593] but subsequently it reversed its course and retained the provision in its interpretation of the ADEA. The EEOC interpretation provides as follows:

> Age limitations for entry into bona fide apprenticeship programs were not intended to be affected by the Act. Entry into most apprenticeship programs has traditionally been limited to youths under specified ages. This is in recognition of the fact that apprenticeship is an extension of the educational process to prepare young men and women for skilled employment. Accordingly, the prohibitions contained in the Act will not be applied to bona fide apprenticeship programs which meet the standards specified in [29 CFR] §§521.2 and 521.3[.][1594]

The exemption for apprenticeship programs was struck down in *Quinn v New York State Electric & Gas Corp*,[1595] the court concluding that it was unsupported by, and indeed in conflict with, the language of the ADEA. The court read the legislative history of the Act as precluding the exemption. Congress, the court reasoned, was aware that in seven of the twenty-three states that had age discrimination laws at the time the ADEA was adopted there were exemptions for apprenticeship programs. "The absence of an exemption for apprenticeship programs in the federal legislation, despite congressional awareness of such provisions in state laws, is indicative of an intent to not exempt such

---

[1591] 29 CFR §860.106 (1986) (effectively rescinded, 46 Fed Reg 47724 (Sept 29, 1981), and ordered removed from the CFR, 52 Fed Reg 23812 (June 25, 1987)).

[1592] See **ch 2.**

[1593] 45 Fed Reg 64212 (Sept 29, 1980).

[1594] 29 CFR §1625.13 (1993).

[1595] 569 F Supp 655 (NDNY 1983).

programs from" the ADEA.[1596] Moreover, tradition could not support such an exemption: "It was to remedy the unfairness, and to avoid the social and economic costs of such practices, however common, that prompted the enactment of the Act."[1597] Equally unavailing was the justification that apprenticeship is an extension of the educational process, a justification proffered by the EEOC in the body of the exemption.

Subsequent to the *Quinn* ruling the EEOC once again proposed to rescind the exemption.[1598] On July 30, 1987, however, the EEOC Commissioners voted 3 to 1 to drop the proposed change, thereby leaving the exception intact. The EEOC explained the vote by pointing out that apprenticeship programs are specifically addressed by Title VII of the Civil Rights Act of 1964,[1599] but they are not by the ADEA. This "clearly demonstrates that Congress made a deliberate decision not to include apprenticeship programs" within the reach of the age discrimination statute.[1600]

The EEOC also has exempted "all activities and programs under federal contracts or grants, or carried out by . . . [state] public employment services . . ., designed exclusively for, or to encourage the employment of, persons with special employment problems[.]"[1601] On January 20, 1988, the EEOC issued a policy statement indicating its position regarding the nature and scope of this exemption, and the processing of cases involving the exemption.[1602] In the statement the EEOC asserted the unsurprising proposition that the employer that invokes the exception

---

1596 *Id* 662.

1597 *Id* 663.

1598 50 Fed Reg 17857 (Apr 29, 1985).

1599 42 USC §§2000e through 2000e-17.

1600 Older Americans Report 2 (Aug 21, 1987). The formal reaffirmation of the apprenticeship exemption was issued on Sept 1, 1987. 52 Fed Reg 33809 (Sept 8, 1987).

1601 29 CFR §1627.16(a) (1993).

1602 EEOC Policy Statement N-915: Specific Exemptions from Coverage Pursuant to §9 of the Age Discrimination in Employment Act (ADEA) of 1967, as amended (Jan 20, 1988). (This policy statement is reproduced in the Appendix at the end of the last volume.)

bears the burden of showing that it comes within the exception.[1603] The statement further advised that the exemption only is available for specific activities or programs that aid employees who have been certified as individuals with special employment problems. Thus, an individual who applies for a job with an employer that has a federal job training contract will be covered by the ADEA if the job for which he or she applies is not one of those set aside under the contract for individuals with special employment problems.[1604]

Provisions regarding the obtaining of an administrative exemption, and the record-keeping requirements regarding exempt entities, are set forth in EEOC regulations.[1605]

[1603] *Id* 3.

[1604] *Id* 5.

[1605] 29 CFR §§1627.15, .16 (1993).

Enforcement of the Age Discrimination in Employment Act in the Nonfederal Sector

6

Enforcement by Nonfederal Private Grievants: Administrative and Procedural Issues Prior to Filing Suit

Private Enforcement by Nonfederal Grievants

§6.01 Overview of Issues Arising Prior to Filing Suit

The Age Discrimination in Employment Act (ADEA)[1] is a particularly complex statute. Its proscription of age bias in the workplace is constricted both by significant substantive requirements—such as the provision limiting the Act's coverage to employers having 20 or more employees for 20 or more weeks[2] —and by extensive exceptions, such as those allowing the use of (1) age as a bona fide occupational qualification[3] and of (2) age-related distinctions in benefit plans.[4]

---

[1] 29 USC §§621-634.

[2] See **ch 3.**

[3] See **ch 5.**

[4] *Id.*

In addition, difficulties in interpretation and application—both for grievants and those charged with violations of the Act—are generated by the procedural requirements of the ADEA, which are the focus of this chapter.

Whether because of grievants' missteps at the initial stages of pursuing their claims, or attorneys' ignorance or lack of care, or a combination of the two, the ADEA's procedural facets have given rise to an enormous number of reported cases. Sometimes, the errors made at the outset can be overcome. Often, however, they cannot be. Thus, both grievants and defendants must be cognizant of the procedural predicates to pursuing ADEA claims. These predicates create major hurdles for plaintiffs to clear if the merits of their claims are to be adjudicated. Correlatively, they potentially provide defendants with very significant bases for squelching claims of discrimination before the merits are ever reached. (A separate enforcement scheme exists for federal job applicants, employees, and former employees.[5] That system is not addressed in this chapter, whose focus is employment issues involving employers, employment agencies, and labor organizations in the private sector, as well as state and local governmental entities.)

The most significant procedural hurdle—as evidenced by a plethora of cases—concerns the requirement that an aggrieved individual resort to administrative remedies prior to filing suit. The nonfederal grievant must file a *charge of unlawful discrimination*[6] with the Equal Employment Opportunity Commission (EEOC), which since July 1, 1979 has had enforcement responsibility for the Act.[7] If the individual resides in a state that has a

---

[5] See **ch 9.**

[6] See **§6.02.**

[7] Prior to that date, the Department of Labor enforced the ADEA. Enforcement authority was transferred to the EEOC by President Carter's Reorganization Plan No 1 of 1978, 92 Stat 3781, 43 Fed Reg 19807 (May 9, 1979), *reprinted at* 5 USC app. The validity of this transfer of authority was called into serious question in a number of cases decided following the Supreme Court's ruling in Immigration & Naturalization Serv v Chadha, 462 US 919 (1983). In *Chadha*

statute prohibiting age discrimination in employment, and an agency empowered to grant or seek relief under the statute, the charging party has 300 days following the alleged discrimination within which to file his or her charge with the EEOC.[8] He or she must also file a complaint of discrimination with the state agency,[9] but the state complaint need not be pursued, or even timely filed under state law in order to satisfy the ADEA's requirement of a state filing.[10] (If, a grievant does pursue his or her state remedies in the state court system, that will foreclose his or her ability to pursue a claim later in federal court).[11]

If the aggrieved individual does not reside in a state with a statute prohibiting age discrimination in employment, and an agency empowered to grant or seek relief under such a statute, the time limit for filing the EEOC charge is reduced to 180 days.[12] But, no matter which time requirements apply for the EEOC filing, the time limits are subject to equitable tolling and equitable estoppel.[13]

After filing the administrative complaint, the aggrieved individual must wait at least 60 days before filing suit under the ADEA.[14] Until 1991 a two-year statute of limitations was applicable to the filing of suits involving nonwillful violations, and a

---

the Court held unconstitutional the legislative veto provision contained in the Immigration and Nationality Act, 8 USC §1254(c)(2). Since the transfer of enforcement authority to the EEOC was effected by an executive order issued pursuant to another federal statute containing a legislative veto provision, i.e., the Reorganization Act of 1977, 5 USC §§901-912, *Chadha* was looked to as the analogical basis for challenging the constitutionality of that transfer. See **ch 2**. Ultimately, the issue was resolved by the enactment of legislation specifically authorizing EEOC enforcement. Ratification of Reorganization Plans as a Matter of Law, Pub L No 98-532, 98 Stat 2705 (1984) (codified at 5 USC §901 *et seq*).

[8] See **§6.08.**

[9] See **§6.25.**

[10] See **§6.27.**

[11] See **§6.65.**

[12] See **§6.08.**

[13] See **§§6.17-6.21.**

[14] See **§6.37.**

three-year statute of limitations applied to willful violations.[15] The Civil Rights Act of 1991[16] abolished these requirements and supplanted them with a provision requiring the filing of suit within 90 days following the receipt by the grievant of a notice from the EEOC that the agency has dismissed the charge of unlawful discrimination or otherwise terminated its consideration of the charge.[17] (The 1991 amendment did not, however, address the statute of limitations applicable to suits filed by the EEOC).[18] Again, there is the possibility that equitable estoppel or equitable tolling can come into play so as to allow a plaintiff to sue even though he or she did not timely file.[19]

§6.02 Administrative Charges and Complaints

Section 7(d)[20] of the Age Discrimination in Employment Act (ADEA)[21] requires the filing of a charge of unlawful discrimination[22] with the ADEA enforcement agency, the Equal Employ-

---

[15] See **§6.30.**

[16] Pub L No 102-166, 105 Stat 1071.

[17] See **§6.30.**

[18] *Id.*

[19] See **§§6.33-.34.**

[20] 29 USC §626(d).

[21] *Id* **§§621-634.**

[22] As the Act originally read, it was a *notice of intent to sue* that had to be filed with the federal enforcement agency. Age Discrimination in Employment Act of 1967, Pub L No 90-202, §7(d), 81 Stat 602, 605. The Act was amended in 1978 to change the terminology to *charge of unlawful discrimination.* Age Discrimination in Employment Act Amendments of 1978, Pub L No 95-256, §4(b)(1), 92 Stat 189, 190. This change, however, was "not intended to alter the basic purpose of the notice requirement, [i.e., providing the agency] with sufficient information so that it may notify prospective defendants and to provide the . . . [agency] with an opportunity to eliminate the alleged unlawful practices through informal methods of conciliation." Conference Comm, Age Discrimination in Employment Act Amendments of 1978, HR Rep No 950, 95th Cong, 2d Sess 12 (1978).

The motivating force for the amendment apparently was concern about the narrow judicial interpretations that had been rendered regarding the notice requirement. This concern was particularly prompted by judicial treatment of the time limitations applicable to the filing of the notice: "Failure to timely

ment Opportunity Commission (EEOC), at least 60 days prior to suit being filed.[23] A complete failure to file, or a failure to file an adequate or timely charge, will lead to a dismissal or to summary judgment for the defendant.[24]

An EEOC regulation defines a charge as "a statement filed with the Commission by or on behalf of an aggrieved persons which alleges that the named prospective defendant has engaged in or is about to engage in actions in violation of the Act[.]"[25] Thus, it is clear that the charging party can be, but need not be, the grievant.[26] In many states the EEOC has entered into work-sharing agreements with state antidiscrimination agencies pursuant to which the state agency agrees to send to the EEOC a copy of each charge filed with it.[27] A state antidiscrimination

---

file the notice as required by section 7(d) [29 USC §626(d)] has been the most common basis for dismissal of ADEA lawsuits by private individuals. The 180-day [filing] requirement has been interpreted as jurisdictional by some courts, and consequently complaints are dismissed." Senate Comm on Labor & Human Resources, Amending the Age Discrimination in Employment Act Amendments of 1977, S Rep No 493, 95th Cong, 1st Sess 12 (1977).

[23] While a grievant must initiate the EEOC grievance process by filing a charge, there is no need under the ADEA for a grievant to exhaust his or her employer's internal grievance processes. Greene v Standard Register Co, 60 FEP Cas (BNA) 1151, 1161 (WD Mich 1992).

[24] *See, e.g.*, Barrow v New Orleans SS Assn, 932 F2d 473, 476-77 (5th Cir 1991); Michaelson v Exxon Research & Engg Co, 808 F2d 1005, 1009 (3d Cir 1987); Vaught v RR Donnelly & Sons Co, 745 F2d 407, 410 (7th Cir 1984); Redd v Fisher Controls, 814 F Supp 547 (WD Tex 1992); Kraemer v University of Minn, 752 F Supp 283, 285 (D Minn), *affd without opinion*, 915 F2d 1579 (8th Cir 1990), *cert denied*, 498 US 1028 (1991); Caudill v Farmland Indus, Inc, 698 F Supp 1476, 1478 (WD Mo 1988), *affd on other grounds*, 919 F2d 83 (8th Cir 1990); Jay v International Salt Co, 694 F Supp 207 (WD La 1988), *affd on other grounds*, 868 F2d 179 (5th Cir 1989).

[25] 29 CFR §1626.3 (1993).

[26] For an example of a case where a charge filed by one employee was made on behalf of others, but the charging party did not himself claim to be the victim of age discrimination, see Anderson v Phillips Petroleum Co, 722 F Supp 668 (D Kan 1989). For an example of a charge filed by a wife on behalf of her husband (actually, she read his written statement over the telephone to an agency employee), see Glass v IDS Fin Servs, Inc, 778 F Supp 1029 (D Minn 1991).

[27] *See, e.g.*, Stearns v Consolidated Mgmt, Inc, 747 F2d 1105 (7th Cir 1984).

agency that refers copies of charges filed with it to the EEOC can serve as an appropriate filing entity.[28]

> The requirement that plaintiff file a claim with the EEOC before initiating a federal lawsuit[[29]] serves two important purposes: 1) to provide the EEOC with an opportunity to conciliate the employee's claim with the employer, and 2) to notify the employer of the nature of the claim against it.[30]

As the foregoing quotation suggests, the filing of an individual charge implies that the charging party is prepared to make known his or her identity: "While the first notice to the respondent of the charge may not state who the charging party is, his or her identity will generally be made known to the respondent through the conciliation process."[31] Although it does not literally speak to the issue of identifying the charging party, §7(d)[32] of the Act does require that the charged party be promptly notified of the charge.[33] The EEOC regulation, however, provides

---

[28] *Id.* In Stember v Borough of Baldwin, 31 FEP Cas (BNA) 690 (WD Pa 1983), the court erroneously stated that a grievant did not have to file a charge with the EEOC if he or she pursued state administrative redress pursuant to §14(b), 29 USC §633(b), discussed in **§§6.25-6.27.** 31 FEP Cas (BNA) at 692. Rather, as noted in Turgeon v Rush-Presbyterian-St Luke's Medical Ctr, 51 FEP Cas (BNA) 933 (ND Ill 1989), "[w]here a claimant has commenced state proceedings but later chooses to sue in federal court, he is required to first file with the EEOC." *Id* 934. Of course, if a copy of his or her charge has been sent by the state agency to the EEOC in accordance with a work-sharing agreement between the two entities, the grievant need not file another charge.

[29] Notwithstanding the reference to "federal lawsuit[s]," the filing requirement applies not only to suits filed in federal court, but also to ADEA suits filed in state court. *See, e.g.,* Patrowich v Chemical Bank, 98 AD2d 318, 470 NYS2d 599, *affd on other grounds,* 63 NY2d 541, 473 NE2d 11, 483 NYS2d 659 (1984). As to the ability of grievants to pursue relief under the ADEA in state courts, see **§6.39.**

[30] Wheeldon v Monon Corp, 946 F2d 533, 535-36 (7th Cir 1991).

[31] 48 Fed Reg 138 (Jan 3, 1983).

[32] 29 USC §626(d).

[33] *Accord* 29 CFR §1626.11 (1993). The failure of an agency employee to send a copy of the charge to the alleged wrongdoer will not preclude the grievant from suing. Glass v Financial Servs, Inc, 778 F Supp 1029, 1042-43 (D Minn 1991). Regarding the effect of agency errors on the grievant's charge-

that if a charge is filed on behalf of a grievant, rather than by the grievant, the employee's identity is kept secret.[34] It is subject to disclosure only if he or she consents in writing, unless disclosure is necessary in a court proceeding.[35]

A charging party may request the withdrawal of his or her charge.[36] Even if the grievant withdraws his or her charge from the EEOC, however, suit still may be maintained so long as the charge was not withdrawn less than 60 days after it was filed with the EEOC.[37]

Complaints

Rather than filing a charge, a person may file a complaint with the EEOC—i.e., an allegation that a named prospective defendant has engaged in, or is about to engage in, an unlawful act. When a complaint discloses a possible violation, the EEOC is supposed to so advise the complainant and to assist him or her in filing a charge if the complainant so wishes.[38] By filing a complaint, the grievant secures the benefit of anonymity, since an EEOC regulation provides that the identity of a complainant ordinarily will not be disclosed without his or her prior written consent, unless necessary in a court proceeding.[39]

---

filing obligation, see generally **§6.21.** A similar provision contained in Title VII of the Civil Rights Act of 1964, 42 USC §§2000e through 2000e-17, has prompted some decisions, which the Supreme Court, in Equal Employment Opportunity Commn v Shell Oil Co, 466 US 54 (1984), characterized as demonstrating a "forgiving view." *Id* 66 n16 (citing Equal Employment Opportunity Commn v Burlington N, Inc, 644 F2d 717, 720-21 (8th Cir 1981); Smith v American President Lines, Ltd, 571 F2d 102, 107 n8 (2d Cir 1978); Equal Employment Opportunity Commn v Airguide Corp, 539 F2d 1038, 1042 (5th Cir 1976)).

[34] 29 CFR §§1626.4, 1626.15(b) (1993).

[35] *Id.*

[36] *Id* §1626.13.

[37] Ingram v Dallas County, 688 F Supp 1146, 1157-59 (ND Tex 1988). As to the 60-day waiting period that is a precondition to filing suit, see **§6.37.**

[38] 29 CFR §1626.4 (1993).

[39] *Id* §§1626.4, .15(b).

Because a complaint is not a charge, the filing of a complaint very likely will not satisfy the statutory charge-filing requirement.

§6.03 Elements of an Adequate Charge: Form

The Age Discrimination in Employment Act (ADEA)[40] does not set forth the requisite form for an adequate charge of unlawful discrimination, which charge is required by §7(d)[41] of the Act as a predicate to suit. The Equal Employment Opportunity Commission (EEOC) takes the position that an oral complaint is sufficient where it is transcribed by an EEOC official into a written charge.[42]

Decisions interpreting the *notice of intent to sue* requirement set forth in the pre-1978 version of §7(d)[43] had split on the issue of whether an oral notice was adequate.[44] Cases decided after the amendment changing the terminology of §7(d) from *notice of intent to sue* to *charge alleging unlawful discrimination* have required that the charge be in writing.[45] However, it is sufficient (and this is congruent with the EEOC's position) that a complaint be made

---

[40] 29 USC §§621-634.

[41] *Id* §626(d).

[42] 29 CFR §1626.8(b) (1993).

[43] See **§6.02.**

[44] *Compare* Reich v Dow Badische Co, 575 F2d 363 (2d Cir), *cert denied,* 439 US 1006 (1978); Hays v Republic Steel Corp, 531 F2d 1307 (5th Cir 1976); Enos v Kaiser Indus Corp, 443 F Supp 798 (DDC 1978); Burgett v Cudahy Co, 361 F Supp 617 (D Kan 1973) (oral notice insufficient) *with* Noto v JFD Elecs Corp, 446 F Supp 92 (EDNC 1978); Sutherland v SKF Indus, 419 F Supp 610 (ED Pa 1976); Woodford v Kinney Shoe Corp, 369 F Supp 911 (ND Ga 1973) (oral notice sufficient).

[45] *See* Greene v Whirlpool Corp, 708 F2d 128, 130 (4th Cir 1983), *cert denied,* 464 US 1042 (1984); Salazar v AT&T Co, 715 F Supp 351 (SD Fla 1989); Schroeder v Copley Newspaper, 691 F Supp 1127 (ND Ill 1988), *affd on other grounds,* 879 F2d 266 (7th Cir 1989); Fulton v NCR Corp, 472 F Supp 377 (WD Va 1979). In Woodard v Western Union Tel Co, 650 F2d 592 (5th Cir 1981), a suit filed prior to, but decided after, the amendment's enactment, the Court of Appeals for the Fifth Circuit held that an oral notice was not adequate to satisfy the pre-amendment notice of intent to sue requirement.

orally by the grievant if it is then set down in written form by an EEOC employee.[46] Oral statements that an EEOC employee fails to reduce to writing can be taken into account, at least when combined with other written matter provided by the grievant, in reaching the conclusion that an adequate charge was filed.[47]

A completed intake questionnaire can suffice as an adequate charge,[48] although at least the Court of Appeals for the Seventh Circuit is unwilling to subscribe to a general rule that all such questionnaires will be adequate. Rather, in this court's view, the equities of the situation must be examined.[49] The critical point is "to not let the title of the form triumph over substance."[50]

A grievant's written and signed statement filed with a state agency that has a work-sharing agreement with the EEOC,[51] as a result of which a filing with the agency will be deemed to be a filing with the EEOC, will be sufficient for EEOC purposes even if the statement is inadequate for state filing purposes.[52]

---

[46] *See* Michaelson v Exxon Research & Engg Co, 808 F2d 1005 (3d Cir 1987); Schroeder v Copley Newspaper, 879 F2d 266, 270 n2 (7th Cir 1989); Pirone v Home Ins Co, 507 F Supp 1281 (SDNY 1981), *affd without opinion,* 742 F2d 1430 (2d Cir 1983). In Dickerson v Deluxe Check Printers, Inc, 703 F2d 276 (8th Cir 1983), the court held adequate a charge which consisted of the written statement that the plaintiff signed at the end of her interview with an agency investigator.

[47] *See* Glass v IDS Fin Servs, Inc, 778 F Supp 1029, 1040 (D Minn 1991).

[48] *See* Clark v Coats & Clark, Inc, 865 F2d 1237 (11th Cir 1989); Steffen v Meridian Ins Co, 859 F2d 534 (7th Cir 1988), *cert denied,* 491 US 907 (1989); Downes v Volkswagen of Am, Inc, 59 FEP Cas (BNA) 440 (ND Ill 1992); Bidic v Prudential Ins Co, 42 FEP Cas (BNA) 1418 (DNJ 1987).

[49] Early v Bankers Life & Cas Co, 959 F2d 75 (7th Cir 1992); *see* Adams v Schuyler, Roche & Zwirner, PC, 803 F Supp 202 (ND Ill 1992).

[50] Steffen v Meridian Life Ins Co, 859 F2d 534, 543 (7th Cir 1988), *cert denied,* 491 US 907 (1989).

[51] As to such agreements, see **§6.02.**

[52] Cook v Lee College, 798 F Supp 417 (SD Tex 1992).

§6.04 Elements of an Adequate Charge: Substance

Some courts strictly interpreted the *notice of intent to sue*[53] language of the original version of §7(d)[54] of the Age Discrimination in Employment Act (ADEA),[55] which was supplanted in 1978 by the current language requiring the filing of a charge of unlawful discrimination.[56] They held that if a communication to the agency responsible at that time for enforcement of the ADEA, i.e., the Department of Labor, did not state clearly that a lawsuit was to be filed, such communication would not be sufficient to satisfy the notice requirement, even if age discrimination was alleged.[57] Since the 1978 amendment the courts generally have taken a much more plaintiff-solicitous posture. Generally, the filing with the ADEA enforcement agency—the Equal Employment Opportunity Commission (EEOC)—simply "must be of a kind that would convince a reasonable person that the grievant has manifested an intent to activate the Act's machinery."[58]

A regulation issued by the EEOC affords guidance by setting forth the information that a charge should include:

—the name, address and telephone number of the person making the charge

---

[53] See **§6.02.**

[54] 29 USC §626(d).

[55] *Id* §§621-634.

[56] See **§6.02.**

[57] *See, e.g.*, Woodard v Western Union Tel Co, 650 F2d 592 (5th Cir 1981); Hageman v Philips Roxane Labs, Inc, 623 F2d 1381 (9th Cir 1980); Dartt v Shell Oil Co, 539 F2d 1256 (10th Cir 1976), *affd by an equally divided Court*, 434 US 99 (1977); Hiscott v General Elec Co, 521 F2d 632 (6th Cir 1975). *Contra* Langman v Western Elec Co, 488 F Supp 680 (SDNY 1980); Woodford v Kinney Shoe Corp, 369 F Supp 911 (ND Ga 1973); Burgett v Cudahy Co, 361 F Supp 617 (D Kan 1973).

[58] Bihler v Singer, 710 F2d 96, 99 (3d Cir 1983); *accord* Steffen v Meridian Life Ins Co, 859 F2d 534, 543-44 (7th Cir 1988), *cert denied*, 491 US 907 (1989) (intake questionnaire submitted to EEOC satisfied charge-filing requirement, in context of facts of case).

—the name and address of the person against whom the charge is made
—a clear and concise statement of the facts, including pertinent dates, constituting the alleged unlawful employment practices
—if known, the approximate number of employees of the prospective respondent employer or members of the prospective respondent labor organization
—a statement regarding when proceedings were commenced before the state agency charged with enforcement of fair employment practice laws.[59]

Notwithstanding this directive regarding the information that should be set forth in a charge, the regulation at the same time also expresses a more relaxed view as to what will constitute an adequate charge: simply naming the prospective respondent and generally alleging the discriminatory act will be sufficient.[60]

The EEOC regulation does not require that the plaintiff's age or birth date be provided. Nor did the court deciding *Rodriguez Calderon v Banco Santander-Puerto Rico.*[61]

The courts today generally require little of a charging party.[62] Where the information given is sufficient, but the plaintiff has used the wrong form to supply that information, the filing can be deemed adequate.[63] The charge, whatever the format used, is not, and need not be, equivalent to the statement of a prima facie case, and so the charge need not meet the requirements

---

[59] 29 CFR §1626.8 (1993).

[60] *Id* §1626.6.

[61] 671 F Supp 898 (DPR 1987).

[62] It should be noted that even if the defendant does not raise the issue of a charge not sufficiently setting forth those claims that subsequently are alleged in the plaintiff's lawsuit, the court on its own initiative may do so, and may dismiss the suit (or portions of it) because of the administrative charge's deficiencies. *See* Jenks v Mountain States Tel & Tel Co, 53 FEP Cas (BNA) 1708, 1713-14 (D Utah 1989).

[63] Anness v United Steelworkers of Am, 707 F2d 917 (6th Cir 1983).

of the prima facie case.[64] In deciding *Stearns v Consolidated Management, Inc,*[65] the Court of Appeals for the Seventh Circuit deemed a charge adequate so long as it informed the EEOC that the aggrieved person was seeking redress for age discrimination and that he or she expected the agency to take action.[66] Likewise, in deciding *Rabzak v Berks County*[67] the Court of Appeals for the Third Circuit held that a letter written by the plaintiff to the EEOC was sufficient since it named the defendant and generally alleged that the plaintiff had been discharged because of his age.[68] Similarly, in *Holenka v Gold Circle*[69] a letter was deemed adequate to constitute a charge where it identified the potential defendant and the alleged discrimination, and went on to state that suit would be filed "if necessary."[70] In *Oglesby v Coca-Cola Bottling Co*[71] the court rejected the argument that the letter that the plaintiff had filed with the EEOC was inadmissible because it was unauthenticated.

The foregoing examples of relatively liberal (from the plaintiff's perspective) judicial rulings notwithstanding, not all communications with the EEOC will suffice for charge-filing purposes. For example, the plaintiff failed to establish that a valid charge had been filed in *Bihler v Singer Co.*[72] The plaintiff

---

[64] *See* Powers v Grinnell Corp, 915 F2d 34, 38-39 (1st Cir 1990); Pruet Prod Co v Ayles, 784 F2d 1275, 1279 (5th Cir 1986); Vaught v RR Donnelly & Sons Co, 745 F2d 407, 411-12 (7th Cir 1984). *But see* Weaver v Department of Agric, 54 FEP Cas (BNA) 937, 940 (D Kan 1990) (time for filing charge does not start to run until plaintiff has knowledge of facts rising to level of a prima facie case).

[65] 747 F2d 1105 (7th Cir 1984).

[66] *Id* 1113.

[67] 815 F2d 17 (3d Cir 1987).

[68] *Accord* Foster v National Bank, 857 F2d 1058 (5th Cir 1988). *But see* Vinson v Ford Motor Co, 806 F2d 686 (6th Cir 1986), *cert denied,* 482 US 906 (1987).

[69] 35 FEP Cas (BNA) 621 (ND Ohio 1983), *affd without opinion,* 745 F2d 56 (6th Cir 1984).

[70] *Id* 623; *see also* Best v St Clare's Hosp, 51 FEP Cas (BNA) 588 (SDNY 1989); Mulcahey v Hydro-Line Mfg Co, 707 F Supp 331 (ND Ill 1988).

[71] 620 F Supp 1336 (ND Ill 1985).

[72] 710 F2d 96 (3d Cir 1983).

had sent a demand letter to his former employer, and had also sent a copy to the EEOC, in which he stated that his discharge constituted unlawful age discrimination and that he intended to institute legal proceedings if he did not secure satisfaction. He argued that the copy of the letter sent to the EEOC constituted an adequate filing with the agency. The court disagreed, reasoning that the statement regarding intent to institute legal proceedings was to be read as a statement as to future action to be taken only if the grievant were not reinstated, and not as an assertion, at the present moment, of a formal charge to the EEOC. The court cautioned that its ruling was fact-bound; it did not mean to suggest that the filing requirement could never be satisfied by sending the EEOC a copy of a letter addressed to an alleged violator.[73] Nor did the court rule that a letter addressed to the EEOC, and stating that the complainant intended to institute legal proceedings if the employer did not afford redress, could never constitute an adequate filing.[74]

In *Comfort v Rensselaer Polytechnic Institute*[75] the court deemed inadequate a letter sent to the EEOC that enclosed a copy of the charges filed with the state human rights agency the enclosure being provided so that, in the words of the plaintiff, the EEOC would " 'have these documents on hand if the time should come in the immediate future when I find it necessary to file formally with the EEOC.' "[76] But in *Stearns v Consolidated Management, Inc,*[77] as discussed above, the court properly held that a copy of a charge filed with the state agency, which copy was sent by the agency to the EEOC, was adequate. The court acknowledged that "a truly 'informational only' copy of a [state]

[73] *Id* 100.

[74] *Id.* And indeed there is case law, including a decision of the same court, i.e., Rabzak v Berks County, 815 F2d 17 (3d Cir 1987), supporting construing a letter as constituting a valid charge. *See also* the cases cited in note 68.

[75] 575 F Supp 258 (NDNY 1983).

[76] *Id* 260.

[77] 747 F2d 1105 (7th Cir 1984).

charge may be inadequate under the ADEA,"[78] but found the letter to be a sufficient charge on the facts of that case. It adequately informed the EEOC, in the court's view, that the aggrieved person was seeking redress and that she expected the Commission eventually to take action.[79]

On the other hand, the charge-filing requirement was not satisfied by the plaintiff in *Vinson v Ford Motor Co.*[80] The court reasoned that the plaintiff's mention, in an interview with an EEOC employee, of a demotion—one of a series of events recounted by the plaintiff—was insufficient to constitute a charge of unlawful discrimination regarding demotion. As the court described the scenario, in the course of the interview the plaintiff had "complained about a series of events, the [1979] demotion being one of many, which culminated in plaintiff's belief he had been discriminated against based on age when he was denied a promotion in 1980."[81] Had the plaintiff instead specified the demotion as itself being a direct result of age discrimination, the court would have been satisfied.

There is support for the proposition that the grievant at the least must clearly indicate in his or her charge that he or she is complaining of age discrimination.[82] However, these rulings were handed down prior to the EEOC regulation discussed *infra,* and that regulation does not require an express reference to age discrimination per se.[83]

---

[78] *Id* 1112-13.

[79] For another liberal construction of the charge-filing requirements, see Oglesby v Coca-Cola Bottling Co, 620 F Supp 1336 (ND Ill 1985).

[80] 806 F2d 686 (6th Cir 1986), *cert denied,* 482 US 906 (1987).

[81] *Id* 688.

[82] *See* Pirone v Home Ins Co, 507 F Supp 1281, 1287 (SDNY 1981), *affd without opinion,* 742 F2d 1430 (2d Cir 1983); Tonka v American Tel & Tel Co, 22 Empl Prac Dec (CCH) ¶30,855, at p 15,596-97 n5 (ND Ga 1980), *affd without opinion,* 679 F2d 251 (11th Cir 1982).

[83] *See* 29 CFR §1626.8 (1993). Regulations are of legal force, see **ch 2,** and presumably a plaintiff relying on this particular provision could successfully defend against the argument that he or she had failed expressly to mention that he or she was complaining of age discrimination. Regarding the good-faith reliance defense, see **ch 5.**

§6.05 Pursuing in Court Claims Additional to Those Set Forth in the Charge

A large number of cases concern the situation where a valid charge of unlawful discrimination was filed in a timely manner, but the plaintiff seeks in the ensuing suit that follows to attack decisions and actions that were not mentioned in the charge. Most courts are of the view that the suit may be maintained, provided that it addresses only acts of discrimination that are like, or are reasonably related to, the allegations set forth in the charge. This judicial position allows, but is not limited to, claims encompassing acts that, while not referred to in the charge, occurred during the pendency of the charge before the Equal Employment Opportunity Commission (EEOC).[84] By way of

---

[84] *See, e.g.*, Boge v Ringland-Johnson-Crowley Co, 976 F2d 448, 451 (8th Cir 1992); Limongelli v Postmaster Gen, 707 F2d 368, 373 (9th Cir 1983); Herrmann v Whirlpool Corp, 60 FEP Cas (BNA) 1130, 1134 (WD Mich 1992); Chojar v Levitt, 773 F Supp 645, 650-51 (SDNY 1991); Patel v Lutheran Medical Ctr, Inc, 753 F Supp 1070, 1073 (EDNY 1990); Donahue v Pendleton Woolen Mills, Inc, 719 F Supp 149, 152-53 (SDNY 1988); Less v Nestle Co, Inc, 705 F Supp 110, 112 (WDNY 1988); Smith v Sentry Ins, 674 F Supp 1459, 1468 (ND Ga 1987); Ryman v Office & Professional Employees Intl Union Local No 66, 628 F Supp 421, 429 (ED Tex 1985); Singer v Uni-Marts, Inc, 37 FEP Cas (BNA) 1197 (WD Pa 1985); Curto v Sears, Roebuck & Co, 38 FEP Cas (BNA) 547 (ND Ill 1984); Equal Employment Opportunity Commn v Ford Motor Co, 573 F Supp 755 (D Colo 1983), *affd on other grounds*, 732 F2d 120 (10th Cir 1984); *see also* Powers v Grinnell Corp, 915 F2d 34 (1st Cir 1990); Steffens v Meridian Life Ins Co, 859 F2d 534, 544 (7th Cir 1988), *cert denied*, 491 US 907 (1989); Pilski v Prentice-Hall, Inc, 41 FEP Cas (BNA) 1204 (D Md), *affd without opinion*, 41 FEP Cas (BNA) 1888 (4th Cir 1985); Borumka v Rocky Mountain Hosp & Medical Serv, 599 F Supp 857 (D Colo 1984); Herman v National Broadcasting Co, 569 F Supp 282, 287 (ND Ill 1983), *affd in part & revd in part on other grounds*, 744 F2d 604 (7th Cir 1984), *cert denied*, 470 US 1028 (1985) (dictum); Jacobson v American Home Prods Corp, 36 FEP Cas (BNA) 559 (ND Ill 1982); Scaramuzzo v Glenmore Distilleries Co, 501 F Supp 727 (ND Ill 1980); *cf* Jenkins v Blue Cross Mut Hosp Ins, Inc, 538 F2d 164 (7th Cir), *cert denied*, 429 US 986 (1976) (suit arising under Title VII of the Civil Rights Act of 1964, 42 USC §§2000e through 2000e-17). (A charge filed under the Age Discrimination in Employment Act (ADEA), 29 USC §§621-634, can even support a suit under Title VII, 42 USC §§2000e through 2000e-17, where a reasonable investigation by the EEOC of the ADEA claim would lead to the facts supporting the Title VII claim. Pajic v Cigna Corp, 56 FEP Cas (BNA) 1628, 1633 (ED Pa 1990)).

example of this judicial stance, *Kent v AVCO Corp*[85] asserted, utilizing typical analysis, that "[a] federal complaint does not have to be a mirror image of the administrative complaint but may include allegations reasonably related to and growing out of the administrative charge filed."[86]

While most cases involve claims that arose while the charge was still pending before the EEOC, it does not matter—according to the Court of Appeals for the Second Circuit—whether these later claims arose prior to the EEOC's terminating its consideration of the grievant's charge, or after administrative proceedings were concluded.[87] Moreover, one district court has ruled that even claims that existed prior to the filing of the charge, but were not mentioned in the charge, may be addressed.[88] There also is support for the contrary position, however.[89]

A number of courts have used language that amounts to the same standard as the *like or reasonably related to* formulation: i.e., a plaintiff may address in his or her lawsuit any issue that could reasonably be expected to have grown out of the EEOC's investigation of the plaintiff's charge of discrimination.[90] Thus, the *Kent* court further stated that the claim asserted in court must have been " 'within the scope of the EEOC investigation reasonably expected to grow out of' the plaintiff's administrative filing."[91]

A small number of courts have taken a narrower view, rejecting the proposition that a suit may be maintained as to claims

---

85 815 F Supp 67 (D Conn 1992).

86 *Id* 69.

87 Malarkey v Texaco, Inc, 983 F2d 1204, 1209 (2d Cir 1993).

88 *See* Batiste v Jefferson Guar Bank, 59 FEP Cas (BNA) 317 (ED La 1992).

89 *See* Steffen v Meridian Life Ins Co, 859 F2d 534 (7th Cir 1988), *cert denied*, 491 US 907 (1989).

90 *See, e.g.*, Powers v Grinnell Corp, 915 F2d 34, 38 (1st Cir 1990); Barrow v General Longshore Workers Local Union No 300, 58 FEP Cas (BNA) 847, 848 (ED La 1992); Ghahramani v BASF Corp, 755 F Supp 708, 711 (MD La 1991); Watlington v University of PR, 751 F Supp 318, 324 (DPR 1990); Hawley v Dresser Indus, Inc, 737 F Supp 445 (SD Ohio 1990).

91 815 F Supp at 69 (quoting Miller v International Tel & Tel Corp, 755 F2d 20, 23-24 (2d Cir 1985)); *accord* Batiste v Jefferson Guar Bank, 59 FEP Cas (BNA) 317 (ED La 1992).

that were not set forth in the plaintiff's charge even if they are like or related to the claims that are identified in the administrative charge. For example, in *Foit v Suburban Bancorp*[92] the court ordered dismissal of allegations made in the complaint regarding a pattern and practice of discrimination, since those allegations had not been included in the original charge filed at the administrative level. The court stated: "It is simply not enough that the claims therein are 'like or related' to those asserted" at the agency level.[93]

Where the EEOC is at fault for not having allowed the grievant to amend his or her charge to include a later claim not set forth in the original charge, equitable considerations will enable the grievant to pursue that later claim in a subsequent suit—even if it is neither like, nor reasonably related to, the original charge. Thus, in *Albano v Schering-Plough Corp*[94] the court acknowledged that the plaintiff's claim of constructive discharge as set forth in his suit was not like or reasonably related to the denial of promotion of which he had complained in his charge filed with the EEOC. However, the facts were that Albano had had at least 14 conversations with the EEOC; furthermore, he had been assured three times that his charge encompassed the constructive discharge claim, and because of this agency personnel had denied him permission to amend his charge. "Under the facts," the court held "that equitable considerations excuse[d] Albano's

---

[92] 549 F Supp 264 (D Md 1982).

[93] *Id* 266; *accord* Algea v Schweiker, 529 F Supp 163, 166 (D Md 1981); Looney v Commercial Union Assurance Cos, 428 F Supp 533 (ED Mich 1977); *see also* Caldwell v National Assn of Home Builders, 771 F2d 1051 (7th Cir 1985); Nelson v Massey-Ferguson, Inc, 36 FEP Cas (BNA) 365 (ED Wis 1984); Wippel v Prudential Ins Co, 33 FEP Cas (BNA) 412 (D Md 1982); Golletti v Arco/Polymers, Inc, 32 FEP Cas (BNA) 1796 (WD Pa 1983); Vinson v Ford Motor Co, 806 F2d 686 (6th Cir 1986), *cert denied,* 482 US 906 (1987); Miller v International Tel & Tel Co, 755 F2d 20, 25 (2d Cir), *cert denied,* 474 US 851 (1985); *cf* Chisholm v United States Postal Serv, 665 F2d 482 (4th Cir 1981) (federal employee suit arising under the ADEA's analogue, Title VII of the Civil Rights Act of 1964, 42 USC §§2000e through 2000e-17).

[94] 912 F2d 384, 387-88 (9th Cir 1990), *cert denied,* 498 US 1085 (1991).

failure to exhaust administrative remedies" by not raising the constructive discharge claim in the charge.[95]

Judicial willingness to allow plaintiffs to go beyond the exact language of the administrative charges they have filed does not mean, of course, that every kind of issue may be brought into a suit. In *Ruth v Allis-Chalmers Corp*[96] the Court of Appeals for the Sixth Circuit—while subscribing to a plaintiff-generous position, i.e., that the complaint could encompass anything within the scope of the EEOC investigation that would reasonably be expected to grow out of the charge of discrimination—nonetheless deemed a claim of discriminatory refusal to hire to be barred because the charge had only alleged wrongful termination.[97] Similarly, in *James v Capital City Press*[98] the court deemed claims concerning a job denial and refusals to promote not to be sufficiently related to the claims raised in the EEOC charge, which concerned a wrongful suspension and discharge.[99] Likewise, in *Cheng v GAF Corp*[100] the court refused to allow the plaintiff to pursue a claim regarding an alleged unlawful refusal to promote, since the charge only complained of unlawful involuntary early retirement.[101] And in *Thomas v Brown & Root, Inc*,[102] the court apparently used the *like or reasonably related to* standard, but

---

[95] *Id* 388. As to the effect of agency errors on the grievant's charge-filing obligation, see generally **§6.21.**

[96] 43 Empl Prac Dec (CCH) ¶37,133 (6th Cir 1987).

[97] Using the same formulation, the court came to a contrary conclusion, i.e., it ruled for the plaintiff, in Hawley v Dresser Indus, Inc, 737 F Supp 445 (SD Ohio 1990).

[98] 742 F Supp 347 (MD La 1990).

[99] *See also* Cline v General Elec Credit Auto Lease, Inc, 748 F Supp 650 (ND Ill 1990) (no reasonable relationship between allegation of sexual harassment made in charge filed with EEOC and claim of age discrimination, which was not mentioned in charge).

[100] 566 F Supp 350 (SDNY 1982), *revd on other grounds,* 713 F2d 886 (2d Cir 1983).

[101] *See also* D'Aquino v Citicorp/Diner's Club, Inc, 750 F Supp 960 (ND Ill 1990).

[102] 745 F2d 279 (4th Cir 1984).

applied it rigorously so as to hold against the plaintiff, who sought to litigate a discharge that occurred two months subsequent to the filing of his administrative charge.[103]

Kent v AVCO Corp[104] also fits within this grouping of rulings adverse to plaintiffs. Kent had alleged in the charge he filed with the EEOC that he had been coerced into early retirement by AVCO's threat to reduce his earned retirement health and insurance benefits if he did not retire. In his complaint he not only pursued this involuntary retirement claim; he also contended that he had been compensated below the norm, that he had been provided inferior work accommodations, and that he had been wrongfully denied a promotion. The court ruled that these claims could not be pursued in Kent's lawsuit:

> [T]he EEOC investigation focused on whether AVCO coerced plaintiff into early retirement by threatening to reduce his insurance benefits if he did not retire. . . . Without other allegations pertaining to the constructive discharge, the EEOC could not have been expected to investigate other forms of discrimination or coercive behavior. Nowhere in the administrative complaint did plaintiff allege that his working conditions were made so difficult that a reasonable person in his position would have felt compelled to resign. There was no mention of low wages,

---

[103] The same formulation was used in Malarkey v Texaco, Inc, 55 FEP Cas (BNA) 411, 413 (SDNY 1991), and also was applied in a somewhat rigorous manner (from the plaintiff's perspective). The *Malarkey* court required that for an alleged act of discriminatory conduct, (i.e., a denial of promotion), to be deemed to be related to the denials complained of in the charge filed with the EEOC, the subsequent promotion decisions had to "be traced to the same decision-makers who made the decisions specifically described in . . . [the] EEOC complaint." *Id* 414. The court further restricted the leeway accorded the plaintiff by stating as follows:

> A promotion decision can be traced to one of those specific decision-makers only if that decision-maker exercised enough control or discretion over the [subsequent] promotion decision so that the same course of . . . age discrimination alleged in the EEOC charge can reasonably be inferred to have affected the subsequent promotion decision.

Id.

[104] 815 F Supp 67 (D Conn 1992).

> denied promotions, or inadequate secretarial services. Without these allegations, the EEOC could not have been expected to, and did not, inquire into the alleged acts of discrimination contained in . . . the federal complaint. Those allegations are not reasonably related to the scope of the administrative complaint.[105]

The Court of Appeals for the Second Circuit, addressing a case that had been in litigation for 10 years, refused to allow a plaintiff to pursue claims that had arisen after the filing of her charge with the EEOC. Those claims involved conduct that was significantly different from that which was the basis of her original charge. Moreover, the plaintiff had known about these three years prior to trial, yet she had done nothing during that period to bring them to the defendant's attention.[106]

In *Ritter v Mount St Mary's College*[107] the Court of Appeals for the Fourth Circuit addressed the claims of a plaintiff who had filed an EEOC charge alleging a discriminatory denial of tenure. The plaintiff argued that she had been improperly barred in court from litigating her claims involving alleged "systemic age discrimination and disparate treatment."[108] The appellate court responded in a cryptic and negative manner. "[A]ppellant's complaint to the . . . [EEOC] clearly alleged only a denial of tenure claim. Thus, Mrs. Ritter has not met the jurisdictional prerequisite to arguing these other theories in federal courts."[109] The *Ritter* ruling appears to limit a grievant not only to the facts stated—or not stated—in an administrative charge, but further limits a grievant (who may well have filed his or her charge pro se) just to the legal theories stated (or perhaps implied) in the charge. (Arguably, however, the *Ritter* court's assertion can be read more nallowly: a claim of systemic discrimination entails

---

105 *Id* 70.

106 Malarkey v Texaco, Inc, 983 F2d 1204, 1209-10 (2d Cir 1993).

107 814 F2d 986 (4th Cir), *cert denied,* 484 US 913 (1987).

108 *Id* 993.

109 *Id.*

a showing of numerous acts of wrongdoing,[110] and it was the grievant's failure to allege those acts in the EEOC charge that foreclosed raising the systemic, or pattern or practice, discrimination claim in court).

Retaliation Claims

The Age Discrimination in Employment Act (ADEA)[111] outlaws retaliation against individuals who participate in the enforcement of the Act, or who oppose actions they reasonably believe to be violative of the Act.[112] Clearly, the filing of a charge with the EEOC—whether the claim made therein is valid or not—constitutes protected participation.[113] Not uncommonly, a plaintiff will contend in his or her lawsuit that he or she was the victim of retaliation that occurred following the filing of a charge of discrimination, which charge addressed other allegedly unlawful acts. The question then arises as to whether a claim based on the alleged violation of the antiretaliation provision of the ADEA, which claim was not itself the subject of a charge, may be maintained as a part of the plaintiff's lawsuit.

The courts' answers generally have been in the affirmative.[114] However, in *Malarkey v Texaco, Inc,*[115] the court ruled somewhat differently. The charge filed with the EEOC had identified retaliation as one of the ways in which discrimination against the

---

[110] See **ch 7.**

[111] 29 USC §§621-634.

[112] §4(d), 29 USC §623(d). See generally **ch 4.**

[113] See **ch 4.**

[114] *See, e.g.,* Wentz v Maryland Cas Co, 869 F2d 1153 (8th Cir 1989); Patel v Lutheran Medical Ctr, Inc, 753 F Supp 1070, 1073 (EDNY 1990); Smith v Sentry Ins, 674 F Supp 1459, 1468 (ND Ga 1987); Scaramuzzo v Glenmore Distilleries Co, 501 F Supp 727 (ND Ill 1980); *cf* Gupta v East Tex State Univ, 654 F2d 411 (5th Cir 1981) (case arising under Title VII of the Civil Rights Act of 1964, 42 USC §§2000e through 2000e-17); Goza v Bolger, 538 F Supp 1012 (ND Ga 1982), *affd without opinion,* 741 F2d 1383 (11th Cir 1984) (federal employee suit arising under Title VII); *see also* Volk v Multi-Media Corp, 526 F Supp 157 (SD Ohio 1981). *But see* Meyers v Amerada Hess Corp, 647 F Supp 62 (SDNY 1986); Looney v Commercial Union Assurance Cos, 428 F Supp 533 (ED Mich 1977).

[115] 55 FEP Cas (BNA) 411, 415 (SDNY 1991).

plaintiff had been manifested. What was at issue was the plaintiff's ability to pursue in court subsequent claims of retaliation as to which no charge was filed with the EEOC. The court ruled that the later claims could not be litigated unless the later retaliation was perpetrated by the same persons allegedly involved in the earlier retaliation actually identified in the charge. A restrictive view, departing from the mainstream of the case law, also was expressed by the Court of Appeals for the Seventh Circuit in *O'Rourke v Continental Casualty Co.*[116] The court first observed that "an employee may present claims 'like or reasonably related to the allegations of the charge and growing out of such allegations.' "[117] It then asked the following rhetorical question: "Is retaliation related to age discrimination in this way?"[118] The court then answered its own question by stating simply: "We have held that it is not."[119]

The *O'Rourke* court cited as support for this last assertion its decision in *Steffen v Meridian Life Insurance Co.*[120] *Steffen,* however, actually involved a narrow factual situation; therefore, it really does not support the blanket assertion in *O'Rourke* that retaliation claims can never be related to earlier claims of discrimination. In *Steffen* the alleged retaliation had occurred prior even to the filing of a charge with the EEOC, and it was the failure to include in that charge any allegation or statement regarding that pre-charge retaliatory action that was fatal to the plaintiff's effort subsequently to pursue the retaliation claim in court.[121]

§6.06 Suing an Entity Not Named in a Charge

A charge of unlawful discrimination filed with the Equal Employment Opportunity Commission (EEOC) both affords the

---

116 983 F2d 94, 97 (7th Cir 1993).

117 *Id* 97 (quoting Jenkins v Blue Cross Mut Hosp Ins, Inc, 538 F2d 164, 167 (7th Cir 1976)).

118 983 F2d at 97.

119 *Id.*

120 859 F2d 534, 544-45 (7th Cir 1988), *cert denied,* 491 US 907 (1989).

121 *Id.*

agency the opportunity to attempt informal conciliation, and serves to apprise the alleged wrongdoer of the fact that someone has a grievance.[122] Understandably, a grievant's failure to name in the charge the entity allegedly responsible for the alleged wrongdoing disserves both these ends. The question thus can arise as to whether, in a later lawsuit brought under the Age Discrimination in Employment Act (ADEA),[123] a plaintiff will be able to pursue a claim against an entity or person not named in the charge, given that the EEOC in theory will not have had an opportunity to pursue its mandated conciliation efforts[124] and given further that the alleged wrongdoer may not have had an opportunity to mend its ways. The answer is *maybe,* the conclusion in any given case depending upon the facts.

A variety of factual scenarios have been addressed by the courts.

If a defendant was named in the administrative complaint that is required to be filed with the state antidiscrimination agency,[125] that can be sufficient to put it on notice of an allegation of wrongdoing. Accordingly, dismissal of any later ADEA lawsuit could be deemed to be unwarranted even though the alleged wrongdoer was not named in the EEOC charge.[126] References to the alleged misdeeds of the named alleged wrongdoer in the body of a charge will suffice, even though the name of the wrongdoer was not placed in the appropriate box on the charge form.[127] In like vein, even if a given person or entity is not expressly named as a wrongdoer, the inclusion of a person's or entity's name in a factual statement made to the EEOC can

---

[122] §7(d), 29 USC §626(d), requires the EEOC promptly to notify an entity named in a charge that a charge has been filed. *Accord* 29 CFR §1626.11 (1993).

[123] 29 USC §§621-634.

[124] See **§6.29.**

[125] See **§6.25.**

[126] *See* Small v Bethlehem Steel Corp, 33 FEP Cas (BNA) 414 (D Md 1983).

[127] *See* Lewis v Swindell Dressler Intl Co, 58 FEP Cas (BNA) 975 (WD Pa 1992).

be sufficient to permit his or her inclusion as a defendant in a subsequent judicial proceeding.[128]

The *Substantial Identity* Standard

A number of courts consider a charge to be sufficient to support a later suit against a person or entity not named in the charge if the charge identified an agent of that entity or named a person or entity sharing *substantial identity* with the party named in the charge—i.e., "the persons with whom the . . . [EEOC] would negotiate, or persons who should know of the named defendant's conduct."[129] Thus, the failure to name a parent corporation need not preclude the maintenance of a suit against it if the charge named its wholly owned subsidiary.[130] Indeed, it has been held that a wholly owned subsidiary of a parent corporation may be sued, even when the parent was not named and the only entity named in the charge was another wholly owned subsidiary of the parent company.[131] A successor corporation to the original defendant will also be deemed a proper defendant even though the successor entity was not named in the EEOC charge.[132] In contrast, it also has been held that a separate subsidiary of a company may not be sued where, even though the parent company was named in the charge, the subsidiary was not

---

[128] Wasilchuk v Harvey's Wagon Wheel, Inc, 610 F Supp 206, 208 (D Nev 1985); *see also* Rathke v HCA Mgmt Co, Inc, 744 F Supp 1037, 1039 (D Kan 1990) (defendant need not have been named in charge if it was "informally referred to in the charge"); Perera v Flexonics, Inc, 727 F Supp 406 (ND Ill 1989) (where individual defendant was mentioned by name in the EEOC charge and participated in the proceedings carried out pursuant to a like charge filed with the state antidiscrimination agency, this was sufficient to preclude summary judgment for defendant).

[129] Quinn v Bowmar Pub Co, 445 F Supp 780, 784 (D Md 1978); *accord* Barkley v Carraux, 533 F Supp 242 (SD Tex 1982).

[130] Watson v Fuller Brush Co, 570 F Supp 1299 (WD Mich 1983); Jacobson v American Home Prods Corp, 36 FEP Cas (BNA) 559 (ND Ill 1982). *Contra* Clouser v Copperweld Steel Co, 38 FEP Cas (BNA) 1807 (ND Ohio 1985).

[131] Jacobson v American Home Prods Corp, 36 FEP Cas (BNA) 559, 559 (ND Ill 1982).

[132] Bernstein v Consolidated Foods Corp, 622 F Supp 1096 (ND Ill 1984).

itself named in the charge or otherwise implicated in the administrative proceedings at the pre-suit stage of the dispute.[133]

The courts are split as to whether suit may be brought against a manager or officer of a company who was responsible for the decision of which the plaintiff complains, but who was not named in the charge.[134] A number of courts have ruled in the affirmative,[135] while a number of others have subscribed to the contrary position.[136]

In *Rio v Presbyterian Hospital*[137] the court imposed the requirement that not only must there be substantial identity between the unnamed defendant and the named defendant, but, further, the unnamed defendant also must be aware of the administrative proceedings. This is a position taken by other courts, as well.[138]

---

[133] *See, e.g.*, Osborne v United Technologies Corp, 18 FEP Cas (BNA) 766 (D Conn 1978); Woodford v Kinney Shoe Corp, 7 FEP Cas (BNA) 114, 115 n* (ND Ga 1972).

[134] Actually, there also can be question as to whether an individual employee, even if named in a charge, can be held liable under the ADEA. See **ch 3.**

[135] *See, e.g.*, Bapat v Connecticut Dept of Health Servs, 815 F Supp 525 (D Conn 1992); Haag v Board of Educ, 655 F Supp 1267, 1272-73 (ND Ill 1987); Elbe v Wausau Hosp Ctr, 606 F Supp 1491 (WD Wis 1985); Flaherty v Itek Corp, 500 F Supp 309 (D Mass 1980); Goodman v Board of Trustees, 498 F Supp 1329 (ND Ill 1980); Geller v Markham, 481 F Supp 835 (D Conn 1979), *affd in part & revd on other grounds*, 635 F2d 1027 (2d Cir 1980), *cert denied*, 451 US 945 (1981); Sartin v City of Columbus Utils Commn, 421 F Supp 393, 400-01 (ND Miss 1976), *affd without opinion*, 573 F2d 84 (5th Cir 1978); *see also* Borumka v Rocky Mountain Hosp & Medical Serv, 599 F Supp 857 (D Colo 1984); Maxey v Thompson, 680 F2d 524 (7th Cir 1982) (suit against head of state agency sufficient to put agency, itself, on notice).

[136] *See, e.g.*, Shestina v Cotter & Co, 32 FEP Cas (BNA) 674 (ND Ohio 1983); Stiessberger v Rockwell Intl Corp, 29 FEP Cas (BNA) 1273 (ED Wash 1982); Allen v Colgate-Palmolive Co, 539 F Supp 57, 69 (SDNY 1981); Quinn v Bowmar Pub Co, 445 F Supp 780, 784-85 (D Md 1978); Travers v Corning Glass Works, 76 FRD 431 (SDNY 1977).

[137] 561 F Supp 325 (SDNY 1983).

[138] *See* Agugliaro v Brooks Bros, Inc, 802 F Supp 956, 960-61 (SDNY 1992); Bumpers v International Mill Servs, Inc, 595 F Supp 166, 170 (ED Pa 1984); Lettich v Kenway, 590 F Supp 1225 (D Mass 1984). In Gunning v San Antonio Teachers Credit Union, 652 F Supp 697 (WD Tex 1987), the court articulated a slightly different formulation: there must be substantial identity, and the unnamed defendant must have had notice of the administrative proceeding. While *notice* can be a term of art, it is not likely that the court meant that the unnamed defendant must actually have received a formal notice, given that the court cited in support of its assertion *Bumpers* and *Lettich*. The same formu-

The court that decided *Agugliaro v Brooks Brothers, Inc,*[139] although endorsing this position, pointed out that while the named defendants argued that the unnamed defendant—the parent corporation—did not have actual notice of the plaintiff's EEOC charge, they did not argue further that the unnamed defendant was unaware of the charge. Venturing the opinion that the unnamed parent corporation most likely would have been informed of the EEOC charge and of any ensuing investigation, the court concluded that "[i]n any event, an inference to that effect is entirely reasonable."[140]

The Four-Part Test

A formulation more extensive than the *substantial identity* standard was enunciated initially in *Glus v GC Murphy Co*[141] and has since been put forth by several ADEA courts.[142] It was utilized, for example, by the court that decided *Pauls v Elaine Revell, Inc*[143] which relied upon *Eggleston v Chicago Jouneyman Plumbers' Local Union No 130, UA,*[144] a case decided under Title VII of the Civil Rights Act of 1964,[145] in which the court in turn relied upon *Glus.* The *Eggleston* court had set forth a four-pronged test:

---

lation was used in Equal Employment Opportunity Commn v Puerto Rico Job Corps, 729 F Supp 208, 213 (DPR 1990).

139 802 F Supp 956 (SDNY 1992).

140 *Id* 961.

141 562 F2d 880, 888 (3d Cir 1977).

142 *See* Bapat v Connecticut Dept of Health Servs, 815 F Supp 525, 530 (D Conn 1992); Ames v Whitman's Chocolates, 57 FEP Cas (BNA) 1301, 1307 (ED Pa 1991); Buffington v Phelps Dodge Corp, 800 F Supp 945, 947 (DNM 1990) (quoting Romero v Union Pac Ry, 615 F2d 1303, 1312 (10th Cir 1980) (which in turn was quoting Glus v GC Murphy Co, 562 F2d 880, 888 (3d Cir 1977))); Rathke v HCA Mgmt Co, Inc, 744 F Supp 1037 (D Kan 1990); Borecki v Eastern Intl Mgmt Corp, 694 F Supp 47, 53 (DNJ 1988); Harris v First Natl Bank, 680 F Supp 1489 (D Kan 1987); Weber v LDC/Milton Roy, 42 FEP Cas (BNA) 1507 (DNJ 1986).

143 571 F Supp 1018 (ND Ill 1983).

144 657 F2d 890 (7th Cir 1981), *cert denied,* 455 US 1017 (1982).

145 42 USC §§2000e through 2000e-17. ADEA courts often look to judicial constructions of Title VII for analogical guidance, given the similarity of language and purpose of the two statutes. See **ch 2.**

> "(1) Whether the role of the unnamed party could through reasonable effort by the complainant be ascertained at the time of the filing of the EEOC complaint.
> (2) Whether, under the circumstances, the interests of a named party are so similar to the unnamed parties that for the purpose of obtaining voluntary conciliation and compliance it would be unnecessary to include the unnamed party in the EEOC proceedings.
> (3) Whether its absence from the EEOC proceedings resulted in actual prejudice to the interests of the unnamed party.
> (4) Whether the unnamed party has in some way represented to the complainant that its relationship with the complainant is to be through the named party."[146]

Applying both the aforementioned four–part test and the *substantial identity* test,[147] the *Pauls* court concluded that the failure to name either the chairman or the president of the defendant corporation in the administrative charge did not warrant dismissal of the later lawsuit, given that the corporation itself had been named and that reference was made to those two individuals in the portion of the charge setting forth the factual allegations.

It has been stated that no one prong of this four-part test is determinative,[148] and that the four criteria amount to a balancing

---

[146] 657 F2d at 908 (quoting Glus v GC Murphy Co, 562 F2d 880, 888 (3d Cir 1977)). While in Goodman v Board of Trustees, 498 F Supp 1329 (ND Ill 1980), the court utilized a *substantially identical* test, the court deciding Holly v City of Naperville, 571 F Supp 668 (ND Ill 1983), suggested that that test had been supplanted within the Seventh Circuit by the *Eggleston* test.

[147] The *Pauls* court viewed the *substantial identity* standard as simply a specific application of the *Eggleston* formulation. 571 F Supp at 1023 n9. The court deciding Bapat v Connecticut Dept of Health Servs, 815 F Supp 525, 530 (D Conn 1992), also used both approaches.

[148] *See* Ames v Whitman's Chocolates, 57 FEP Cas (BNA) 1301, 1307 (ED Pa 1991); Borecki v Eastern Intl Mgmt Corp, 694 F Supp 47, 54 (DNJ 1988).

test.[149] In *Perera v Flexonics, Inc,*[150] the court interpreted this approach as entailing two crucial factors: whether the unnamed defendant had notice of the charges, and whether it had the opportunity to participate in voluntary conciliation.[151] In *Rathke v HCA Management Co, Inc,*[152] in which the fourth prong of the test was not satisfied, the court limited the applicability of the test to situations where a grievant files his or her charge without the benefit of legal counsel. In this circumstance, a plaintiff will be allowed to proceed against a party not named in the charge of unlawful discrimination, provided the foregoing elements (or most of them) are met.

In deciding *Borecki v Eastern International Management Corp,*[153] the court also invoked the four-part test in holding that the plaintiff could not maintain suit against the unnamed defendant. The court agreed with the argument made by the defendant that the requisite commonality of interest between him and the named defendants—two corporations and an officer of them—could not be established by his ownership interest in those corporations. The court stated as follows:

> While . . . [the unnamed defendant] undoubtedly has an interest in minimizing the corporations' potential losses, this may not be co-extensive with his interest in avoiding personal liability. Thus, even if he had notice of the EEOC charge, since it did not put him on notice of his amenability to suit we cannot find his interests to be so similar to the corporate defendant's [sic] that "it would be unnecessary to include [him] in the EEOC proceedings." Similarly, the corporations' interest in minimizing their losses are sufficiently distinct from . . . [the unnamed defendant's] interest in minimizing his personal losses that the corporations' par-

---

149 Ames v Whitman's Chocolates, 57 FEP Cas (BNA) 1301, 1307 (ED Pa 1991).

150 727 F Supp 406 (ND Ill 1989).

151 *Id* 411.

152 744 F Supp 1037 (D Kan 1990).

153 694 F Supp 47 (DNJ 1988).

ticipation in the EEOC proceedings cannot be deemed to have obviated the need to include . . . [the unnamed defendant] in the EEOC process.[154]

Other Approaches

In *Clouser v Copperweld Steel Co*[155] the court used a *clear identity of interest* test and held that a parent corporation could not be sued since only its subsidiary had been named in the charge. In *Wasilchuk v Harvey's Wagon Wheel, Inc,*[156] the court asserted, as to a defendant who was not named in the EEOC charge, that "it is necessary to ascertain whether . . . [he or she] participated in employment decisions, had actual notice of the EEOC charge and had an opportunity to participate in an attempted resolution of it."[157] In the absence of a factual record from which to make such an ascertainment, the defendant's motion to dismiss was denied.[158]

A particularly broad approach was endorsed by the court deciding *Koppman v South Central Bell Telephone Co.*[159] It stated that the ADEA does "not require that the individual defendant be named in the plaintiff's EEOC charge, but rather that the individual [need only] be within '[t]he reasonable limits of an investigation potentially triggered by an EEOC charge.' "[160]

Joinder of a Party Not Named in the Plaintiff's Charge

The court that decided *Boczon v Northwestern Elevator Co, Inc,*[161] reasoned that "[a]lthough the . . . prior charge requirement should apply to a plaintiff seeking to join a party defendant not

---

[154] *Id* 55.

[155] 38 FEP Cas (BNA) 1807 (ND Ohio 1985).

[156] 610 F Supp 206 (D Nev 1985).

[157] *Id* 209.

[158] *Id.*

[159] 59 FEP Cas (BNA) 345 (ED La 1992).

[160] *Id* 353 (quoting Terrell v United States Pipe & Foundry Co, 644 F2d 1112, 1123 (5th Cir 1981)).

[161] 652 F Supp 1482 (ED Wis 1987).

named in its . . . charge, the rule should not preclude a defendant who had no control over the . . . charging decision from seeking proper joinder of an additional defendant."[162]

§6.07 Filing a Charge or Complaint with the Correct Entity

Charges of discrimination and complaints may be submitted in person, by phone, or by mail to any district or area office of the Equal Employment Opportunity Commission (EEOC), or to its headquarters office in Washington, D.C.[163] There are several judicial rulings addressing the status of charges that were not filed at the right place. For example, in *Whiteman v Kroger Co*[164] the court refused to grant a motion to dismiss that was based on the plaintiff's having filed the charge with the Secretary of Labor, who has not had enforcement authority for the Age Discrimination in Employment Act (ADEA)[165] since July 1, 1979.[166] The court justified its position by looking to the literal language of §7(b)[167] of the Act, which at the time still named the Secretary as the enforcement official, and so did not reflect the 1979 transfer of enforcement authority to the EEOC.[168]

A charge that was erroneously filed with the wrong district office was deemed by the court deciding *Hague v Spencer Turbine Co*[169] to have been filed as of the date it was received by the forwarding office. It thus was considered to have been timely filed, even though it was received in the proper office only after the

---

162 *Id* 1486. As to joinder generally, see **§6.52.**

163 29 CFR §1626.5 (1993).

164 548 F Supp 563 (CD Ill 1982).

165 29 USC §§621-634.

166 See **ch 2.**

167 29 USC §626(b).

168 *See also* Scaramuzzo v Glenmore Distilleries Co, 501 F Supp 727 (ND Ill 1980) (plaintiff's charge was addressed to the Department of Labor; although the court did not discuss the misfiling, it did not reject the charge).

169 28 FEP Cas (BNA) 450 (MDNC 1982).

filing period had expired.[170] In *Stephens v Boise Cascade Corp*[171] the court devised an equitable exception to the requirement of filing with the EEOC where the plaintiff had timely filed her pro se charge with a local antidiscrimination agency that, unbeknownst to her, did not qualify as a referral agency.[172] However, a misfiling with a federal agency that has no jurisdiction regarding age claims whatsoever will not constitute a valid filing, and so will not thereby save the hapless complainant.[173]

In contrast to those foregoing rulings in which courts were willing to excuse complainants' misfilings, the court deciding *Moore v Astra Pharmaceutical Products, Inc*[174] ruled against the plaintiff. His charge of discrimination had been erroneously sent by his attorney to the Department of Labor rather than the EEOC, and did not arrive at the latter agency until after the charge-filing period had elapsed. The court reasoned that "the prescriptive period is not subject to equitable tolling where the plaintiff is represented by counsel, and is therefore charged with knowledge of the relevant ADEA provisions and the procedural requirements of filing an EEOC complaint."[175]

§6.08 Timely Filing of the Charge

The failure to file a charge of unlawful discrimination in a timely manner has been the downfall of a host of would-be plaintiffs desirous of seeking redress under the Age Discrimination in Employment Act (ADEA).[176] Such failure will constitute a determinative basis for a court's granting of a defendant's

---

[170] *See also* Pirone v Home Ins Co, 507 F Supp 1281 (SDNY 1981), *affd without opinion,* 742 F2d 1430 (2d Cir 1983); Erpelding v Thornhill, 18 FEP Cas (BNA) 1479 (ED Mich 1976).

[171] 50 FEP Cas (BNA) 362 (ND Ind 1988).

[172] As to referral agencies, see **§6.26.**

[173] Meckes v Reynolds Metals Co, 604 F Supp 598 (ND Ala), *affd without opinion,* 776 F2d 1055 (11th Cir 1985).

[174] 58 FEP Cas (BNA) 905 (ED La 1992).

[175] *Id* 908.

[176] 29 USC §§621-634.

motion to dismiss or motion for summary judgment.[177] Section 7(d)[178] of the Act requires a charge to be filed with the Equal Employment Opportunity Commission (EEOC) within one of the following time periods:

—180 days following the occurrence of the alleged discrimination, if the claim is being asserted in a state which has no state agency capable of seeking or providing relief for age discrimination under state law;[179] or

—within 300 days of the alleged discrimination if the claim is being asserted in a state that does meet the just-noted criteria, or within 30 days following receipt by the grievant of a notice of termination of state proceedings, whichever is earlier.[180]

The case law, albeit sparse, is divided on the question of whether a charge may be filed prior to the occurrence of the alleged wrong.[181]

In contrast to the statutory scheme set forth in the ADEA's analogue, Title VII of the Civil Rights Act of 1964,[182] which precludes the filing of a charge with the EEOC (which also enforces that Act) until state proceedings are terminated or until 60 days have elapsed since state proceedings were begun,[183] no waiting period for filing the administrative charge is imposed by the age

---

177 *See, e.g.,* Barrow v New Orleans SS Assn, 932 F2d 473, 476-77 (5th Cir 1991). See generally **§6.02.**

178 29 USC §626(d).

179 See **§6.26.**

180 *Id.*

181 In Anisgard v Exxon Corp, 409 F Supp 212 (ED La 1975), the court held that a notice of intent to sue—the statutory predecessor to the charge of unlawful discrimination, see **§6.02**—was timely even though it was filed before the employee was terminated. *But see* Thomas v Brown & Root, Inc, 745 F2d 279 (4th Cir 1984).

182 42 USC §§2000e through 2000e-17.

183 *Id* §2000e-5(c).

discrimination statute.[184] Rather, an ADEA claimant may file charges simultaneously with the state agency and the EEOC, or he or she may file with the state and 10, 15 or 20 days thereafter file his or her EEOC charge.[185] (Even if a complainant does not himself or herself file with both the state and federal agencies, the EEOC has so-called work-sharing agreements with most state agencies[186] and a typical facet of such agreements is a proviso establishing that a filing with a state agency will result in the agency's automatic referral by it of a copy of the charge to the EEOC. Thereby, a filing with the EEOC will be effectuated. More than that, it has been held that whether or not the state agency actually refers a copy of the complaint filed with it to the EEOC, the timely filing with the state entity in any event will be deemed to constitute a filing with the EEOC—at least so long as it satisfies the prerequisites for charges, that are filed with the EEOC).[187]

Pursuant to Federal Rule of Civil Procedure 6(a),[188] the day on which the discriminatory event occurs is not counted in com-

---

[184] Several ADEA courts, however, have mistakenly asserted the contrary. *See* Kaimowitz v Board of Trustees, 951 F2d 765, 766 (7th Cir 1991); Agosto Morales v El Mundo Corp, Inc, 790 F Supp 34, 35 (DPR 1992); Gay v AVCO Fin Servs, Inc, 769 F Supp 51, 53 (DPR 1991); Coleman v Clark Oil & Refining Co, 563 F Supp 1035 (ED Wis 1983); *see also* Dapelo v Banco Nacional de Mexico, 767 F Supp 49, 52 (SDNY 1991). Regarding the 60-day waiting period, which is applicable to the filing of ADEA lawsuits, rather than the filing of charges, see generally **§6.37.**

[185] *See* Oscar Mayer & Co v Evans, 441 US 750, 757 (1979); *accord* Curto v Sears, Roebuck & Co, 552 F Supp 891 (ND Ill 1982).

[186] These are entered into in accordance with 29 CFR §1626.10 (1993).

[187] *See* American Assn of Retired Persons v EI DuPont de Nemours & Co, Inc, 677 F Supp 351, 355 n10 (ED Pa 1987). What is more, in Weaver v Department of Agric, 54 FEP Cas (BNA) 937 (D Kan 1990), where there was no work-sharing agreement but as a matter of courtesy the state agency routinely sent a copy of each complaint filed with it to the EEOC, the court was willing to assume that this courtesy copy satisfied the charge-filing requirement. *Id* 940. As to the requisites for charges filed with the EEOC, see **§§6.03, 6.04.**

[188] Fed R Civ P 6(a).

puting the 180- or 300-day filing periods.[189] An EEOC regulation specifies when a charge shall be deemed to have been deemed filed:

> (1) Charges filed by mail: (i) Date of postmark, if legible, (ii) Date of letter, if postmark is illegible, (iii) Date of receipt by Commission, or its designated agent, if postmark and letter date are illegible and/or cannot be accurately affixed;
>
> (2) Written charges filed in person: Date of receipt;
>
> (3) Oral charges filed in person or by telephone, as reduced to writing: Date of oral communication received by Commission.[190]

The case law is split. Some courts have ruled that receipt of the charge, rather than the date of mailing, is the critical date;[191] others have deemed the date of mailing to be the date of filing.[192]

If a charge, once filed, is amended to allege additional acts that constitute unlawful employment practices related to or growing out of the subject matter of the original charge, the amendment will be deemed to relate back to the date the original charge was first received.[193] "An amendment does not relate back, however, where it adds an entirely new and distinct claim

---

189 *Accord* McConnell v Thomson Newspapers, Inc, 802 F Supp 1484, 1496 (ED Tex 1992); Treadwell v John Hancock Mut Life Ins Co, 666 F Supp 278 (D Mass 1987).

190 29 CFR §1626.7(c) (1993).

191 *See, e.g.,* Taylor v General Tel Co, 759 F2d 437 (5th Cir 1985); Wall v National Broadcasting Co, Inc, 768 F Supp 470, 472 n2 (SDNY 1991); Welty v SF&G, Inc, 605 F Supp 1548 (ND Ala 1985); Thompson v Spring Mills, Inc, 576 F Supp 651, 660 n2 (DSC 1982).

192 *See, e.g.,* Farr v Continental White Cap, Inc, 762 F Supp 814, 816 (ND Ill), *vacated in part on other grounds,* 774 F Supp 522 (ND Ill 1991); Duke v Uniroyal, Inc, 719 F Supp 428, 433 (EDNC 1989).

193 29 CFR §1626.8(c) (1993); *see* Lindsey v Baxter Healthcare Corp, 757 F Supp 888, 898-99 (ND Ill 1991), *affd in part & revd in part on other grounds,* 962 F2d 586 (7th Cir), *cert denied,* 113 S Ct 442 (1992); Kohn v GTE North, Inc, 754 F Supp 563 (SD Ohio 1990).

of discrimination."[194] In a somewhat related vein, there is one case supporting the notion that a suit based upon a timely charge will not be maintainable where that charge effectively constitutes an effort to resurrect claims set forth in an earlier untimely charge. More specifically, in *Redd v Fisher Controls*[195] the court dealt with a plaintiff who had filed an untimely charge based upon her allegedly having been denied promotions and having then been discharged based on her age. She subsequently sought to be rehired and, after being rejected, she filed a timely charge alleging a discriminatory refusal to rehire. The court granted the defendant's motion for summary judgment as to the count of her suit alleging the failure to rehire, reasoning as follows:

> Were the Court to hold otherwise, the limitations . . . [period] of . . . the . . . [ADEA] could be circumvented in discriminatory discharge cases by simply requesting to be rehired whenever one has failed to file a complaint of discriminatory discharge within the applicable time limit. Recognizing that, other courts have similarly held that failure to reinstate or rehire does not generally constitute an actionable new act of discrimination or continuing discrimination so as to allow the limitations period to begin at the time when the former employee requests reinstatement.[196]

There is contrary case law, however, whereby a plaintiff was allowed to proceed with that part of his or her suit that was based on a timely filed charge, while not being allowed to litigate claims that were related to the timely filed claim, but were not themselves the subjects of timely filed charges.[197]

---

[194] Conroy v Boston Edison Co, 758 F Supp 54, 58 (D Mass 1991).

[195] 814 F Supp 547 (WD Tex 1992).

[196] *Id* 550.

[197] Potter v Continental Trailways, Inc, 480 F Supp 287 (D Colo 1979). As to continuing violations, see generally **§§6.13-.14.**

30-Day Filing Period When State Agency Terminates Proceedings

Weaver v Department of Agriculture[198] is the very rare judicial ruling addressing the 30-day filing requirement, i.e., the requirement that a charge be filed with the EEOC within 30 days of notice of termination of state proceedings, if that date is earlier than 300 days after the occurrence of the alleged unlawful action. In *Weaver* the plaintiff did not file with the EEOC until the 39th day. While the court as a general matter apparently was willing to consider tolling this statute of limitations, the plaintiff offered no grounds for the court to do so.[199]

Equitable Relief from Onus of Untimely Filing of Charge

In the early days of the ADEA there was a conflict in the courts as to whether the timely filing of the statutory predecessor of a charge (i.e., a notice of intent to sue)[200] with the federal enforcement agency was a jurisdictional prerequisite to an ADEA action, or whether the Act's time limits for charge-filing were in the nature of statutes of limitations and thereby were subject to equitable tolling or equitable estoppel. This conflict no longer exists. The courts are now in accord that the latter position is the correct one,[201] with the retreat of those courts that

---

198 54 FEP Cas (BNA) 937 (D Kan 1990).

199 As to tolling generally, see **§§6.17-6.21.**

200 See **§6.02.**

201 *See* **First Circuit:** Kale v Combined Ins Co of Am, 861 F2d 746, 752 (1st Cir 1988); **Second Circuit:** Dillman v Combustion Engg, Inc, 784 F2d 57, 59 (2d Cir 1986); **Third Circuit:** Bonham v Dresser Indus, Inc, 569 F2d 187, 192-93 (3d Cir 1977), *cert denied,* 439 US 821 (1978); **Fourth Circuit:** Lawson v Burlington Indus, Inc, 683 F2d 862 (4th Cir), *cert denied,* 459 US 944 (1982); Slatin v Stanford Research Inst, 590 F2d 1292 (4th Cir 1979); **Fifth Circuit:** Coke v General Adjustment Bureau, Inc, 640 F2d 584 (5th Cir 1981) (en banc); **Sixth Circuit:** Wright v Tennessee, 628 F2d 949 (6th Cir 1980) (en banc); **Seventh Circuit:** Stearns v Consolidated Management, Inc, 747 F2d 1105 (7th Cir 1984); Kephart v Institute of Gas Technology, 581 F2d 1287 (7th Cir 1978); **Eighth Circuit:** Nielsen v Western Elec Co, 603 F2d 741 (8th Cir 1979); **Ninth Circuit:** Naton v Bank of Cal, 649 F2d 691 (9th Cir 1981); **Tenth Circuit:** Williams v Meese, 926 F2d 994, 996 n1 (10th Cir 1991); Dartt v Shell Oil Co,

previously had taken a negative position[202] being prompted at least in part by the legislative history of the 1978 amendment changing the filing requirement from a notice of intent to sue to a charge of unlawful discrimination.[203] The various equitable bases for relieving a plaintiff of his or her untimely filing are discussed *infra.*[204]

Defendant's Assertion or Waiver of Untimeliness Defense

The plaintiff's failure to timely file his or charge is to be raised as an affirmative defense by the defendant.[205] Whether or not an equitable basis exists for relieving a late filing plaintiff of the onus of having untimely filed, the defendant's failure to raise the timeliness issue will be deemed to constitute a waiver of the defense.[206] However, if the plaintiff fails to raise the defendant's

---

539 F2d 1256 (10th Cir 1976), *affd by an equally divided Court,* 434 US 99 (1977); **Eleventh Circuit:** Burnam v Amoco Container Corp, 755 F2d 893 (11th Cir 1985).

[202] *See* Hiscott v General Elec Co, 521 F2d 632 (6th Cir 1975); Powell v Southwestern Bell Tel Co, 494 F2d 485 (5th Cir 1974).

[203] The amendment reflected a compromise struck between the House of Representatives' version of the legislation, which did not at all change the then-extant filing requirement, and the Senate's version, which called for the complete elimination of the time limits. Conference Comm, Age Discrimination in Employment Act Amendments of 1978, HR Rep No 950, 95th Cong, 2d Sess 12 (1978). The conference committee that meshed the two versions kept the time limits, but purported to ease the burden of the filing by requiring that only a charge be filed, with the understanding that the time limits would not be jurisdictional. *Id* 12-13.

[204] See **§§6.17-6.21.**

[205] *Cf* Mondy v Secretary of the Army, 845 F2d 1051, 1058 n3 (DC Cir 1988) (case arising under Title VII of the Civil Rights Act of 1964, 42 USC §§2000e through 2000e-17).

[206] Stephens v CIT Group/Equipment Fin, Inc, 955 F2d 1023, 1026 (5th Cir 1992); Orzel v City of Wauwatosa Fire Dept, 697 F2d 743, 747 n8 (7th Cir), *cert denied,* 464 US 992 (1983). In a case arising under the ADEA's analogue, Title VII of the Civil Rights Act of 1964, 42 USC §§2000e through 2000e-17, it was reasoned that a failure to raise the issue of untimeliness with the EEOC at the administrative level does not constitute a waiver of the untimeliness defense in the courtroom. Janowiak v Corporate City of S Bend, 576

failure to plead the affirmative defense of untimeliness, the plaintiff's silence will be deemed to be a waiver of its objection to the defendant's lapse, and so the defendant may raise this defense at the appellate level.[207] A general denial by the defendant in its answer of the plaintiff's allegation that he or she " 'performed all conditions precedent to bringing . . . [the] action' " will be sufficient to preserve the untimeliness defense.[208]

A defendant's removal to federal court of a case filed in state court will not be deemed to constitute a waiver of the defendant's argument that the plaintiff did not timely file the charge of unlawful discrimination.[209] And the issuance by the EEOC of a notice or letter to the charging party informing it that he or she may sue will not be deemed to constitute a waiver of the individual defendant's lack of timeliness defense.[210] In other words, the EEOC cannot waive a charged party's right to raise the issue of untimeliness.[211]

EEOC Suit Where Individual Charge Is Untimely

Even if an individual is barred from suing because of his or her failure to file an administrative charge in a timely manner, his or her claim still may be asserted by the EEOC, which will not be barred notwithstanding the fact that the individual on whose behalf it is suing would be precluded from asserting the claim.[212] In a related vein, the Court of Appeals for the Fourth

---

F Supp 1461, 1465 (ND Ind 1983), *revd on other grounds,* 750 F2d 557 (7th Cir 1984), *judgment vacated on other grounds,* 481 US 1001 (1987).

[207] Hamilton v Komatsu Dresser Indus, Inc, 964 F2d 600, 603 n1 (7th Cir), *cert denied,* 113 S Ct 324 (1992).

[208] Roy v Amoco Oil Co, 747 F Supp 661, 666 (SD Fla 1990), *affd without opinion,* 925 F2d 1475 (11th Cir), *cert denied,* 112 S Ct 87 (1991).

[209] Fryman v ConAgra, Inc, 57 FEP Cas (BNA) 635, 639 (ED Ky 1991).

[210] *Id* 638-39.

[211] Allen v Diebold, Inc, 807 F Supp 1308, 1313 (ND Ohio 1992).

[212] *See* Equal Employment Opportunity Commn v Roadway Express, Inc, 33 Empl Prac Dec (CCH) ¶34,265 (EDNC 1981). As to suits by the EEOC, see generally **§6.60.**

Circuit ruled against an employer that refused to comply with an EEOC subpoena, the employer doing so with the argument that the EEOC's investigation was based on an untimely charge filed by an individual and so the agency had no authority to pursue the claim on the charging party's behalf. This court, in *Equal Employment Opportunity Commission v American & Efird Mills, Inc,*[213] held that the EEOC has independent investigatory authority that is not limited by the untimeliness of an employee charge.[214]

Timely Filing with State Agency as Condition Precedent to Securing 300-Day Grace Period for Filing

As noted above, a charging party has 300 days within which to file his or her charge if the charge is filed in a state that has a law banning discrimination in employment and a state agency empowered to grant or to seek relief for an alleged victim of such discrimination. Typically, state statutes will set time limits—just as does the ADEA, itself—for the filing of claims of discrimination with the state agencies. Not unexpectedly, then, the question arises as to whether an individual who seeks to avail himself or herself of the 300-day ADEA filing period must have timely filed with the state agency in order to obtain the benefit of the 300-day period for filing with the EEOC.

The ADEA does not on its face resolve this question. Nor was an answer provided by the Supreme Court's decision in *Oscar Mayer & Co v Evans,*[215] in which the Court held that ADEA grievants must seek state relief if the injury occurred in a state having a state antidiscrimination law and an adequately empowered

---

[213] 964 F2d 300 (4th Cir 1992).

[214] *See also* Equal Employment Opportunity Commn v Sears, Roebuck & Co, 55 FEP Cas (BNA) 482 (D Or 1991); Equal Employment Opportunity Commn v Ritenour Sch Dist, 692 F Supp 1068 (ED Mo 1988); Equal Employment Opportunity Commn v Gladieux Refinery, Inc, 631 F Supp 927 (ND Ind 1986).

[215] 441 US 750 (1979).

state agency.[216] A number of lower courts have addressed the issue, however, and they have responded in the negative: an ADEA grievant need not file in a timely manner under state law in order to secure the advantage of the 300-day ADEA filing period. This is the position taken by the Courts of Appeals for the First,[217] Second,[218] Third,[219] Seventh,[220] Ninth,[221] and Eleventh[222] Circuits,[223] as well as by a state court.[224] The EEOC is in agreement.[225] In addition, the Supreme Court has held the same

---

216 See **§6.25.**

217 The Court of Appeals for the First Circuit initially had required a grievant to file with the state within 180 days following the discriminatory act in order to qualify for the 300-day filing provision. Ciccone v Textron, Inc, 616 F2d 1216 (1st Cir), *vacated,* 449 US 914 (1980). This ruling was vacated by the Supreme Court and remanded for reconsideration in light of Mohasco Corp v Silver, 447 US 807 (1980), a ruling addressing Title VII of the Civil Rights Act of 1964. Ciccone v Textron, Inc, 449 US 913 (1980). On remand the court of appeals reversed its prior ruling, holding that a grievant would have the benefit of the 300-day period for filing with the EEOC whether or not he or she had timely filed with the state. Ciccone v Textron, Inc, 651 F2d 1 (1st Cir), *cert denied,* 452 US 917 (1981).

218 Goodman v Heublein, Inc, 645 F2d 127 (2d Cir 1981).

219 Davis v Calgon, 627 F2d 674 (3d Cir 1980), *cert denied,* 449 US 1101 (1981).

220 Anderson v Illinois Tool Works, Inc, 753 F2d 622 (7th Cir 1985).

221 Aronsen v Crown Zellerbach, 662 F2d 584 (9th Cir 1981), *cert denied,* 459 US 1200 (1983); Bean v Crocker Natl Bank, 600 F2d 754 (9th Cir 1979).

222 McKelvy v Metal Container Corp, 854 F2d 448, 451 n5 (11th Cir 1988).

223 Initially, like the First Circuit, see *supra* note 217, the Court of Appeals for the Sixth Circuit had required that for a grievant to gain the benefit of the 300-day filing period under the ADEA, he or she had to have filed a claim with the state agency within 180 days. Ewald v Great Atl & Pac Tea Co, 620 F2d 1183 (6th Cir), *vacated,* 449 US 914 (1980). The Supreme Court vacated and remanded for reconsideration in light of Mohasco v Silver, 447 US 807 (1980), a Title VII decision. Ewald v Great Atl & Pac Tea Co, 449 US 914 (1980). The court of appeals dealt with the remand in an unpublished opinion, which, according to a circuit rule, is without precedential significance. In the analogous Title VII setting the Court of Appeals for the Sixth Circuit has held the longer period to apply under a virtually identical statutory filing provision. Jones v Airco Carbide Chem Co, 691 F2d 1200 (6th Cir 1982).

224 Bousquet v Polyform Corp, 401 Mass 1002, 515 NE2d 1188 (1987).

225 46 Fed Reg 43037 (Aug 26, 1981).

with regard to a virtually identical provision in Title VII.[226] There are a few lower courts outside the jurisdiction of these appellate courts that have ruled to the contrary, however.[227]

Other Issues

While a charge of unlawful discrimination must be filed within the designated 180-day or 300-day period, the events and documentation that a plaintiff may adduce in support of his or her

---

[226] Equal Employment Opportunity Commn v Commercial Office Prods Co, 486 US 107 (1988).

[227] *See* DePriest v Seaway Food Town, Inc, 543 F Supp 1355 (ED Mich 1982). In Borowski v Vitro Corp, 634 F Supp 252 (D Md 1986), *revd without opinion*, 829 F2d 119 (4th Cir 1987), the court held that a timely state filing is indeed a prerequisite to the availability of the 300-day filing period, so long as the state filing period is at least 180 days.

In Coleman v Clark Oil & Refining Co, 568 F Supp 1035 (ED Wis 1983), the court drew an improper analogy between the ADEA and Title VII, and thence erroneously applied Mohasco Corp v Silver, 447 US 807 (1980). The plaintiff in *Coleman* had not filed his charge of discrimination with the EEOC until 297 days after the alleged discriminatory act had occurred. The EEOC then deferred to the state agency for processing by the latter. The court reasoned that *Mohasco* was applicable to the ADEA, 568 F Supp at 1039 n5; that *Mohasco* required that a state have 60 days to consider a charge; and that the charge would not be deemed to be filed with the EEOC until those 60 days had elapsed. Accordingly, notwithstanding the fact that Coleman had filed with the EEOC within the requisite 300-day filing period, the *Coleman* court held as a matter of law that his filing would not be deemed to have been made with the federal agency until 357 days (297 plus 60) after the alleged discriminatory act. Thus, he was deemed not to have timely filed with the EEOC.

In reaching this erroneous conclusion, the court interpreted §14(b), 29 USC §633(b), of the ADEA as providing that "state agencies [have] an exclusive right to process discrimination charges for 60 days, during which time federal charges may not be brought." 568 F Supp at 1039. In fact, while 42 USC §2000e-5(c) so provides as to Title VII charges, §14(b) of the ADEA does not. Rather, the latter provision only states that no "suit" may be brought before 60 days after state proceedings have been commenced.

The courts that decided Foutty v Equifax Servs, Inc, 762 F Supp 295, 296-97 (D Kan 1991), and Shockley v Vermont State Colleges, 38 FEP Cas (BNA) 1523 (D Vt 1984), also erroneously applied *Mohasco* to ADEA claims. In contrast, the courts deciding Aronson v Gressly, 961 F2d 907, 911-12 (10th Cir 1992), and Astacio-Sanchez v Fundacion Educativa Ana G Mendez, 724 F Supp 11 (DPR 1989), correctly pointed out the inapplicability of *Mohasco.*

claim are not similarly circumscribed and so evidence of events occurring outside that period need not be excluded.[228]

§6.09 Commencement of the Time Period for Filing a Charge

While it is clear that a grievant seeking redress under the Age Discrimination in Employment Act (ADEA)[229] must file a charge of unlawful discrimination with the Equal Employment Opportunity Commission (EEOC) within either 180 or 300 days of the alleged illegal action or decision (or within 30 days of a state agency's terminating its proceedings, if the 30th day occurs earlier than the conclusion of the 300-day period),[230] the determination of just when these time periods begin to run can be a very difficult enterprise. A general rule can be readily stated: the "limitations period begins to run on the date that the defendant takes some adverse personnel action against the plaintiff, and not when the full consequences of the action are felt."[231] The problems arise in the application of this rule, as the discussion in this and succeeding sections discloses. While much of this ensuing discussion involves case law developed in the context of discharge situations, there are some rulings dealing with wrongful denials of hiring[232] and promotion,[233] and with demotions.[234]

---

[228] Weeden v Minnesota Mining & Mfg Co, 781 F Supp 1576, 1583-84 (ND Ga 1991), *affd without opinion,* 998 F2d 1022 (11th Cir 1993).

[229] 29 USC §§621-634.

[230] See **§6.08.**

[231] Davidson v Indiana-Am Water Works, 953 F2d 1058, 1059 (7th Cir 1992).

[232] *See* Crutchfield v Pulaski County Special Sch Dist, 647 F Supp 884 (ED Ark 1986); Herman v National Broadcasting Co, 569 F Supp 282, 286 (ND Ill 1983), *affd in part & revd in part,* 744 F2d 604 (7th Cir 1984), *cert denied,* 470 US 1028 (1985).

[233] *See* Coleman v Clark Oil & Ref Co, 568 F Supp 1035 (ED Wis 1983).

[234] The date on which the violation occurred—or on which the grievant should have become aware of it—in the past was critical to the determination of whether a plaintiff had failed to satisfy the Act's statute of limitations for filing

§6.10 —Triggering of the Charge-Filing Period by an Identifiable, Albeit Ambiguous, Act or Decision

The key decision regarding the question of determining the date on which the period for filing a charge of unlawful discrimination begins to run is *Delaware State College v Ricks.*[235] This Supreme Court ruling addressed the Age Discrimination in Employment Act's (ADEA)[236] analogue, Title VII of the Civil Rights Act of 1964,[237] which—like the ADEA—also contains a requirement that a charge be filed with the Equal Employment Opportunity Commission (EEOC) within a set time period.[238]

The college professor plaintiff in *Ricks* alleged that he was the victim of a discriminatory denial of tenure by virtue of the university having illegally acted on the basis of his national origin. The plaintiff was informed of the tenure denial by a letter dated June 26, 1974. However, that letter extended to him an offer of a one-year teaching contract, at the expiration of which, June 30, 1975, his employment with the college would end. The *Ricks* Court held that the time period for the filing of the charge began to run from the date the tenure denial decision was communicated to the teacher, rather than the date on which his employment actually ended.

Following *Ricks* the Court, in another non-ADEA decision—*Chardon v Fernandez*[239]—made clear that its rejection of the last day of work as being the triggering event was not confined to the academic denial of tenure setting. Rather, the *Ricks* formulation applies generally to all terminations of employment.

---

suit, see **§§6.30-6.31,** and it remains so with respect to the determination of the accrual period for damages. See **ch 8.**

235 449 US 250 (1980).

236 29 USC §§621-634.

237 42 USC §§2000e through 2000e-17.

238 Judicial constructions of Title VII are commonly looked to by ADEA courts, given the commonality of terms of the two Acts and their common purpose: eradication of discrimination in the workplace. See generally **ch 2.**

239 454 US 6 (1981).

Since *Ricks* lower court ADEA decisions have left no doubt that this Supreme Court ruling applies, by way of analogy, in the age discrimination context.[240] The result is that the filing period begins to run when the ADEA grievant knows—or reasonably should know—that an unlawful action has occurred or that an unlawful decision has been made.[241] Sometimes, of

---

[240] *See, e.g.*, Wilson v Westinghouse Elec Corp, 838 F2d 286, 288 (8th Cir 1988); Janikowski v Bendix Corp, 823 F2d 945, 947 (6th Cir 1987); Mull v ARCO Durethene Plastics, Inc, 784 F2d 284 (7th Cir 1986); Price v Litton Business Sys, Inc, 694 F2d 963 (4th Cir 1982); Sharpe v Philadelphia Hous Auth, 693 F2d 24 (3d Cir 1982); Kinniry v Aetna Ins Co, 35 FEP Cas (BNA) 1474 (D Conn 1984); Zebedeo v Martin E Segal Co, Inc, 582 F Supp 1394 (D Conn 1984); Bratton v American Natl Ins Co, 32 FEP Cas (BNA) 953 (ND Ga 1983); Lutz v Association Films, Inc, 552 F Supp 985 (SDNY 1982). *Contra* Equal Employment Opportunity Commn v Home Ins Co, 553 F Supp 704 (SDNY 1982).

In Elliott v Group Medical & Surgical Serv, 714 F2d 556 (5th Cir 1983), *cert denied,* 467 US 1215 (1984), the court held that *Ricks* was not to be applied retroactively, and thus decided the question of timeliness on the basis of pre-*Ricks* case law. It proceeded to affirm the jury's conclusion that the filings of two of the plaintiffs were not untimely even though, had the filing period been computed as starting to run from the date the plaintiffs were informed of their termination, the 180-day period would have ended before they filed. The court looked to the date on which the plaintiffs actually ceased working. Other courts, however, applied *Ricks* to situations that occurred prior to that decision. *See* Mull v ARCO Durethene Plastics, Inc, 784 F2d 284 (7th Cir 1986); Miller v International Tel & Tel Co, 755 F2d 20 (2d Cir), *cert denied,* 474 US 851 (1985); Sprott v Avon Prods, Inc, 596 F Supp 178 (SDNY 1984); Kinniry v Aetna Ins Co, 35 FEP Cas (BNA) 1474, 1476-79, 1479 n5 (D Conn 1984).

[241] *See, e.g.*, Sawchik v EI duPont deNemours & Co, 783 F2d 635 (6th Cir 1986); Baer v R&F Coal Co, 782 F2d 600, 602 (6th Cir 1986); Heiar v Crawford County, 746 F2d 1190 (7th Cir 1984), *cert denied,* 472 US 1027 (1985); Price v Litton Business Sys, Inc, 694 F2d 963, 965 (4th Cir 1982); Aronsen v Crown Zellerbach, 662 F2d 584 (9th Cir 1981), *cert denied,* 459 US 1200 (1983); Smilan v United Airlines, Inc, 796 F Supp 723, 727 (EDNY 1992). Thus, the argument that the filing period does not begin until the adverse financial effects of the alleged discrimination begin to be felt, on a date subsequent to the actual discrimination, will fail. Zelewski v American Fed Sav Bank, 811 F Supp 456, 461 (D Minn 1993).

Where the last day of work coincides with the day the employee learns of his or her termination, but the employee continues to receive remuneration beyond that date, it still is the date of termination which controls. Gray v Phillips Petroleum Co, 638 F Supp 789 (D Kan 1986), *affd in part & revd in part on other grounds,* 858 F2d 610 (10th Cir 1988). In Goff v Eastern Associated Coal Corp, 29 FEP Cas (BNA) 1831 (SD W Va 1981), *affd without opinion,* 679

course, there can be considerable ambiguity as to whether the plaintiff knew, or reasonably should have known of such action or decision.[242] Even so, *Ricks* set the standard (albeit by way of analogy, rather than direct controlling precedential force) and so correlatively, pre-*Ricks* decisions that used different triggering dates or events—such as a discharged employee's official termination date as recorded by the employer,[243] or the last day a

---

F2d 881 (4th Cir 1982), the court, while asserting that "the requisite time within which notice must be given begins to run when the employee knows, or has reason to know, of the unlawful discriminatory practice," 29 FEP Cas (BNA) at 1834, reasoned that the time period did not begin to run when the plaintiff was first laid off, but only when he was informed later that the layoff was to be permanent. In Sharpe v Philadelphia Hous Auth, 693 F2d 24 (3d Cir 1982), the Court of Appeals for the Third Circuit also followed *Ricks.* However, in *Sharpe* the plaintiff was able to preserve one of his claims, since he alleged that the manner in which the defendant had dealt with his internal appeal of the allegedly discriminatory decision differed from the way it dealt with the appeal of a younger employee. The court cited *Ricks,* in which the Supreme Court had asserted as follows:

> In order for the limitations period to commence with the date of discharge [rather than the earlier date on which the decision to discharge was communicated to the employee], Ricks would have had to allege and prove that the *manner* in which his employment was terminated differed discriminatorily from the manner in which the College terminated other professors who had also been denied tenure.

693 F2d at 27 (quoting *Ricks,* 449 US at 258 (emphasis supplied by *Sharpe* court)).

242 See **§6.11.**

243 *See* Moses v Falstaff Brewing Corp, 525 F2d 92 (8th Cir 1975). Courts that used this approach relied on the termination date indicated in the defendant's records, even if the grievant actually stopped working for the employer at an earlier point in time. *See* Kephart v Institute of Gas Technology, 581 F2d 1287, 1288 n1 (7th Cir 1978); Flaherty v Itek Corp, 500 F Supp 309 (D Mass 1980); Forman v Block Drug Co, 16 FEP Cas (BNA) 414, 418 n4 (EDNY 1977). When the last day of work coincided with the date on which the employee was notified of his or her termination, most courts used this date—even if the employer's records reflected a later termination date or the former employee continued receiving benefits after that last day of work. *See, e.g.*, Naton v Bank of Cal, 649 F2d 691, 695 & 695 n3 (9th Cir 1981); Wilkerson v Siegfried Ins Agency, Inc, 621 F2d 1042 (10th Cir 1980); Coke v General Adjustment Bureau, Inc, 616 F2d 785 (5th Cir 1980); Downie v Electric Boat Div, 504 F Supp 1082 (D Conn 1980); Gray v Mortgage Bankers Assn of Am, 492 F Supp 914 (DDC 1980); Edwards v Western Elec Co, 21 FEP Cas (BNA) 592 (WDNC 1978); Parrish v Schlumberger, Ltd, 19 FEP Cas (BNA) 717 (SD Tex 1979);

discharged employee actually worked[244]—are invalid.

Ambiguities aside, another complication is a function of the judicially defined difference between allegedly discriminatory policies that are facially discriminatory and those that, while ostensibly not violative of the ADEA, have discriminatory consequences for older people. Where the employer has a facially discriminatory policy of which an employee is aware, but which will not directly affect the employee for some time, i.e., not until his or her attainment of age 65, let us say, the grievant need not contemplate filing suit until he or she actually reaches that age and is subjected to, or will imminently be subjected to, the injury imposed by the policy in question.[245] Accordingly, the pre-suit charge need not be filed until that time, even though the grievant is aware years before that date of the policy that, sometime in the future, will adversely affect him or her.[246] In contrast, if a policy is not overtly discriminatory, but the grievant perceives (or should perceive) that if and when it is applied to him or her in the future it will have adverse age-related consequences, the grievant may not wait for those consequences actually to occur.

Noto v JFD Elec Corp, 446 F Supp 92 (EDNC 1978); Johnston v Aerojet Gen Corp, 18 FEP Cas (BNA) 1107 (ED Cal 1978); Clark v Frito-Lay, Inc, 17 FEP Cas (BNA) 935 (ND Ohio 1978); Davis v RJR Foods, Inc, 420 F Supp 930 (SDNY 1976), *affd without opinion,* 556 F2d 555 (2d Cir 1977); *see also* Ott v Midland-Ross Corp, 523 F2d 1367 (6th Cir 1975) (reaching same result as to running of statute of limitations). One court distinguished the receipt of vacation pay from other benefits where, during the time between the plaintiff's last day of work and his last pay check, the plaintiff was taking his accrued vacation at the direction of the defendant. Davis v Boy Scouts of Am, 457 F Supp 665 (DNJ 1978).

[244] *See, e.g.,* Miller v International Tel & Tel Co, 755 F2d 20 (2d Cir), *cert denied,* 474 US 851 (1985); Elliott v Group Medical & Surgical Serv, 714 F2d 556 (5th Cir 1983), *cert denied,* 467 US 1215 (1984); Bonham v Dresser Indus, Inc, 569 F2d 187 (3d Cir 1977), *cert denied,* 439 US 821 (1978); Payne v Crane Co, 560 F2d 198 (5th Cir 1977); Clark v West Chem Prod, Inc, 557 F2d 1155 (5th Cir 1977); Jackson v Alcan Sheet & Plate, 462 F Supp 82 (NDNY 1978); Thomas v Blue Cross & Blue Shield, 449 F Supp 1021 (MDNC 1978); Cobb v Chevron USA, Inc, 15 FEP Cas (BNA) 408 (ND Ga 1977).

[245] See **§6.15.**

[246] *See* Cohn v AE Staley Mfg Co, 734 F Supp 832 (ND Ill 1990).

Rather, he or she must act now—that is, upon learning of the policy—to challenge it by filing a change of unlawful discrimination.[247]

§6.11 —Determining the Start of the Charge-Filing Period When the Triggering Act or Decision Is Ambiguous

It is easy enough to state, as an abstract proposition, that the time for filing a charge of unlawful discrimination under the Age Discrimination in Employment Act (ADEA)[248] begins to run when the grievant is informed of the allegedly adverse action or decision.[249] Specific instances reveal, however, how difficult the task sometimes can be to determine whether a given notice or event was sufficiently clear to trigger the running of the charge-filing period. Moreover, as discussed *infra,*[250] it can be even more difficult to fashion a correct solution when a grievant in fact actually did not know of the adverse action or decision, but arguably should have known of it.

Facts Sufficient to Start Accrual of Filing Period

As was stressed by the Court of Appeals for the Seventh Circuit in *Vaught v RR Donnelly & Sons Co,*[251] the facts deemed sufficient to initiate the running of the filing period need not be those which would establish a prima facie violation. Rather, they need only be enough to support the filing of a charge with the Equal Employment Opportunity Commission (EEOC). More than that, the fact that some relevant evidence was initially unknown to the grievant will not justify tolling the running of the charge-

---

[247] See **§6.15.**

[248] 29 USC §§621-634.

[249] In Aronsen v Crown Zellerbach, 662 F2d 584, 593 (9th Cir 1981), *cert denied,* 459 US 1200 (1983), it was suggested that if written notice is sent, the time period for filing a charge begins to run upon receipt of the notice. *Id* 594.

[250] See **§6.12.**

[251] 745 F2d 407, 411 (7th Cir 1984).

filing period, as long as the facts known to the grievant were sufficient to alert him or her to the possibility that wrongful discrimination existed.[252] Moreover, the possibility that the adverse decision might be reversed does not negate its being the trigger for starting the running of the filing period.[253]

Clarity of the Notice

The ambiguity of the employer's notice to the employee or job applicant may be sufficient to delay the accrual of the discrimination claim, and therefore the commencement of the charge-filing period.[254] There is no legal requirement, however, that formal notice of some sort be given, and so the filing period will begin to run once the individual is aware of sufficient facts to support a charge, whether or not formal notice was provided the grievant.[255] An oral notice—if it is clear—will suffice.[256] Conversely, an unclear oral statement will not be deemed to put the employee on notice.[257] (That a company generally utilizes written termination notices will not render an oral notice unreasonable, and no more than reasonable notice is required).[258]

Sometimes, there will be uncertainty as to the credence to be accorded communication. In *Linn v Andover Newton Theological School,*[259] for example, the plaintiff successfully argued that the initial notification of discharge given to him was inadequate

---

[252] *See* Christopher v Mobil Oil Corp, 950 F2d 1209 (5th Cir), *cert denied,* 113 S Ct 68 (1992).

[253] Miller v International Tel & Tel Co, 755 F2d 20, 24 (2d Cir), *cert denied,* 474 US 851 (1985).

[254] *See, e.g.,* Smallwood v United Air Lines, Inc, 661 F2d 303, 309 (4th Cir 1981), *cert denied,* 456 US 1007 (1982); Zebedeo v Martin E Segal Co, Inc, 582 F Supp 1394 (D Conn 1984).

[255] Vaught v RR Donnelly & Sons Co, 745 F2d 407 (7th Cir 1984).

[256] Mull v ARCO Durethene Plastics, Inc, 784 F2d 284 (7th Cir 1986); Miller v International Tel & Tel Co, 755 F2d 20, 24 (2d Cir), *cert denied,* 474 US 851 (1985).

[257] *See* Clark v Resistoflex Co, 854 F2d 762, 766-67 (5th Cir 1988).

[258] Mull v ARCO Durethene Plastics, Inc, 784 F2d 284 (7th Cir 1986).

[259] 642 F Supp 11 (D Mass 1985), *vacated on other grounds & remanded with instructions to reduce verdict,* 874 F2d 1 (1st Cir 1989).

because the person communicating it did not have dismissal power under the rules of the institution. A similar argument failed, however, in *Calhoun v Federal National Mortgage Association.*[260] In *Allen v American Home Products, Inc,*[261] there was a question of fact as to whether it was the date the plaintiffs learned of their layoffs, or the later date on which the defendant announced permanent closure of the plant, that triggered the running of the filing period. The *Allen* court asserted as follows: "An employee is terminated when his employer announces the final decision to discharge its workers, and not at a preannouncement time when the worker reasonably might know his job is in jeopardy."[262]

Similarly, in *Gross v Goldome*[263] the court stated that "it is the date upon which an employee receives a 'definite notice of termination,' not merely a notice of placement on some probationary status, that is significant."[264] Likewise, in *Farr v Continental White Cap, Inc,*[265] the court reasoned that the plaintiff's initial meeting with the defendant's managers and executives had not led to his being sufficiently informed of his options. It was not until a later meeting that the plaintiff learned that his transfer to the unidentified position of which he had been told at the first meeting would actually be a demotion. Accordingly, it was only on the date of the second meeting that he was deemed to have received notice of an adverse action, for purposes of the accrual of his discrimination claim and the commencement of the charge-filing period.

The Court of Appeals for the Seventh Circuit, in *Gustovich v*

---

[260] 823 F2d 451, 456 (11th Cir 1987), *cert denied,* 484 US 1078 (1988).

[261] 658 F Supp 451 (ND Ind 1987).

[262] *Id* 452; *accord* Watlington v University of PR, 751 F Supp 318 (DPR 1990); *see also* Leite v Kennecott Corp, 558 F Supp 1170 (D Mass), *affd without opinion,* 720 F2d 658 (1st Cir 1983); Speece v Leaseway Transp Corp, 721 F Supp 144, 146 (ND Ohio 1988).

[263] 47 FEP Cas (BNA) 1337 (WDNY 1988).

[264] *Id* 1377-78.

[265] 774 F Supp 522 (ND Ill 1991).

AT&T Communications, Inc,[266] responded to the argument that the plaintiffs' claim had accrued when they received negative performance ratings. The court stated that the charge-filing period began "to run . . . only if a sub-par evaluation . . . [was] an adverse employment decision, which it . . . [was] not."[267] The court continued:

> Most negative appraisals have nothing to do with age (or other discrimination) but instead reflect poor performance. There is nothing to complain about until a poor rating carries or directly portends a loss of job or pay. "*Ricks* does not hold that the statute of limitations begins to run as soon as the handwriting is on the wall." . . . The limitations period therefore did not start until . . . [the plaintiffs received definite notice of their terminations].[268]

Another decision addressing the ambiguities of notice is *Colgan v Fisher Scientific Co,*[269] where the employee received a performance evaluation containing a statement that his lackluster performance would be reevaluated in 60 to 90 days. The evaluation further stated that "[i]f a definite improvement is not shown in that time frame, additional action *will be taken.*"[270] Furthermore, there was a check mark beside the statement on that portion of the evaluation form which read as follows: " '[U]nless there is significant improvement in performance, demotion, reassignment or separation is indicated.' "[271] In the court's view, the "statement clearly signaled that Colgan had an opportunity to redeem himself by an improved performance over the next

---

[266] 972 F2d 845, 847 (7th Cir 1992).

[267] *Id* 847.

[268] *Id* 847 (quoting Cada v Baxter Healthcare Corp, 920 F2d 446, 449 (7th Cir 1990), *cert denied,* 111 S Ct 2916 (1991)).

[269] 935 F2d 1407 (3d Cir), *cert denied,* 112 S Ct 379 (1991).

[270] *Id* 1419 (emphasis in original).

[271] *Id.*

60 to 90 days."[272] Continuing in this vein, the court observed that "[t]he performance evaluation had no immediate consequence on Colgan's employment, such as a loss of seniority, nor did it alert Colgan to the possibility that consequences would flow from it without an opportunity for him to improve his performance."[273] Also relevant to the court's conclusion was the fact that a policy dictating that employees with prior negative evaluations would be those first selected for discharge in reduction-in-force situations was not adopted until months after the evaluation in question. "Therefore, when Colgan received his poor evaluation, it did not put him on formal notice that it would make him one of the first to be discharged when the company later decided on the reduction in force."[274] Thus, "considering the totality of the circumstances," the court concluded that the "allegedly discriminatory evaluation did not trigger the start of the limitations period."[275]

In *Miller v Beneficial Management Corp*[276] the issue involved when the plaintiff knew, or should have known, that the enhanced title (and correlative enhanced salary) that she wanted, and the denial of which led to her suit, would not be forthcoming. The defendant argued that she was on notice from the moment she assumed the position (devoid of the enhanced title and salary) in question, given that her predecessor had possessed the title in dispute. She contended that she did not know, and had no reason to know, that she would never become a vice president in the company until, four years later, her ongoing efforts to secure the advancement were finally formally rejected. The court agreed that a reasonable jury could have found the plaintiff's contention persuasive, and so it reversed the trial court's grant of the defendant's motion for summary judgment.

---

[272] *Id.*

[273] *Id* 1419-20.

[274] *Id* 1420.

[275] *Id.* The court did caution, however, that it was not going "so far as to hold that a performance evaluation can never trigger the limitations period." *Id* 1421.

[276] 977 F2d 834 (3d Cir 1992).

Poindexter v Northrop Corp[277] involved a letter sent by the defendant in response to the plaintiff's application for employment. Northrop advised the applicant in its letter of January 20, 1987, that while it did not presently have a position available, it would keep the application in its active file for a year, and if a position became available, the company would contact the plaintiff. The court, in denying the defendant's motion for summary judgment based on the claimed untimeliness of the plaintiff's filing, ruled that the date that triggered the filing period was January 27, 1988—the date on which Poindexter's application was removed from Northrop's files. The court reasoned that Northrop's letter to Poindexter did not constitute a rejection; rather, it held out hope that he might yet be hired. Thus, the filing of a charge by Poindexter, based on that letter, would have been premature. It was not until the removal of his letter from Northrop's files that Poindexter could "reasonably have been expected to be aware of the allegedly discriminatory conduct."[278] In a like vein, the court in *Monnig v Kennecott Corp*[279] stated that "[t]o constitute a notice of termination, a specific date on which employment will be discontinued must be stated."[280]

In *Farr v Continental White Cap, Inc,*[281] the court ruled that the plaintiff did not have clear knowledge that he was being demoted until his employer gave him full information as to the particular facets of the position that the plaintiff was told was in store for him. And because, in *Smilan v United Airlines, Inc,*[282] there was ambiguity as to whether the plaintiff had been adequately apprised that the allegedly discriminatory contractual provision

---

277 728 F Supp 1362 (ND Ill 1990).

278 *Id* 1367.

279 603 F Supp 1035 (D Conn 1985).

280 *Id* 1038; *see also* Trumbull v Health Care & Retirement Corp of Am, 756 F Supp 532, 535-36 (MD Fla), *affd without opinion,* 949 F2d 1162 (11th Cir 1991) (memorandum from employer to plaintiff that his "continued employment . . . will be based upon findings during . . . visits" to the facility run by plaintiff "did not convey conclusively that a decision had been made to discharge Plaintiff").

281 762 F Supp 814 (ND Ill 1991).

282 796 F Supp 723 (EDNY 1993).

was going to be applied to him, the defendant's motion for summary judgment was denied.

Relevance of Alleged Wrongdoer's Records and of Last Date of Work

Both the date contained in an employer's records and the date of the last day worked, while not determinative as to starting the running of the charge-filing period, can be relevant in assessing whether a grievant had sufficient knowledge for the period to begin running. (Of course, where the notice of discharge given the employee is unambiguous, the last date worked will be irrelevant.)[283] *Needham v Beecham, Inc,*[284] is illustrative. On November 15, 1979, the plaintiff received a phone call from his superior, who informed him that he was being fired and that he was to come to the superior's office the next day for a "final check out."[285] The plaintiff did not comply, however. Two additional, and equally unsuccessful, attempts to convince him to do so followed. Finally, the plaintiff met with the defendant's director of personnel on December 5, 1979; at that time the plaintiff completed a termination check list and it was agreed that he would be paid his regular salary through December 5.[286] The court concluded that November 15 was in fact the date of the plaintiff's termination; it relied both on the phone call made that day and on the fact that the plaintiff rendered no services to the defendant after that date.[287]

---

[283] *See, e.g.*, Pettit v Sears, Roebuck & Co, 32 FEP Cas (BNA) 1867 (ED Pa 1982); Pierce v Green Giant Co, 26 FEP Cas (BNA) 1683 (ND Tex 1981); *see also* Barber v Commercial Union Ins Co, 27 FEP Cas (BNA) 703 (ED Pa 1981); *cf* McDonnell v Gannett News Serv, Inc, 518 F Supp 1326 (D Del 1981) (issue of date of retirement for purposes of determining whether 1978 amendment regarding mandatory retirement applied).

[284] 515 F Supp 460 (D Me 1981).

[285] *Id* 463.

[286] *Id* 464.

[287] *Id* 466; *see also* Volk v Multi-Media, Inc, 516 F Supp 157, 161 (SD Ohio 1981).

§6.12 —Determining the Start of the Charge-Filing Period When the Grievant Lacks Knowledge of the Triggering Act or Decision

The Legal Standards

Clearly, the facts giving rise to a claim of age discrimination under the Age Discrimination in Employment Act (ADEA)[288] are not always going to be immediately apparent to a potential grievant. In such an instance, the task becomes that of determining when the plaintiff became aware, or will be deemed to have become aware constructively, of information sufficient to trigger the running of the charge-filing period.

Most courts take the position that the time for filing a charge of unlawful discrimination does not begin to run until the facts " 'which would support a cause of action are apparent or should be apparent to a person with a reasonably prudent regard for his rights.' "[289] This does not mean, however, that a grievant can wait until he or she has information rising to the level of what would be needed to constitute a prima facie violation of the ADEA.[290] The Court of Appeals for the Fifth Circuit made the following observation in *Blumberg v HCA Management Co:*[291]

---

[288] 29 USC §§621-634.

[289] Davis v Ceco Bldg Sys, 813 F Supp 1202, 1206 (ND Miss 1993) (quoting Reeb v Economic Opportunity Atlanta, Inc, 516 F2d 924, 930 (5th Cir 1985)); *accord* Vaught v RR Donnelly & Sons Co, 745 F2d 407, 410-11 (7th Cir 1984); Felty v Graves-Humphreys Co, 604 F Supp 730 (WD Va 1985), *revd on other grounds,* 785 F2d 516 (4th Cir 1986); Monnig v Kennecott Corp, 603 F Supp 1035, 1038 (D Conn 1985).

[290] Powers v Grinnell Corp, 915 F2d 34, 38-39 (1st Cir 1990); Pruet Prod Co v Ayles, 784 F2d 1275, 1279 (5th Cir 1986); Vaught v RR Donnelly & Sons Co, 745 F2d 407, 411-12 (7th Cir 1984). *But see* Weaver v Department of Agric, 54 FEP Cas (BNA) 937, 940 (D Kan 1990) (time for filing charge does not start to run until plaintiff had knowledge of facts rising to level of prima facie case); *see also* Belda v Morse-Diesel, Inc, 55 FEP Cas (BNA) 1245, 1246 (ND Ill 1990) ("[t]ypically, all that is required under . . . [*Vaught's* charge] standard is that the plaintiff have a prima facie case of discrimination against his employer").

[291] 848 F2d 642 (5th Cir 1988), *cert denied,* 488 US 1007 (1989).

> [I]t is not necessary for a claimant to know all of the evidence for her to file a claim or to begin the . . . [running of the charge-filing] period. . . . The time begins when facts that would support a cause of action are or should be apparent. . . . [A] plaintiff who is aware that she is being replaced in a position she believes she is able to handle by a person outside the protected age group knows enough to support filing a claim.[292]

In similar vein, the Court of Appeals for the Ninth Circuit has suggested that the time for filing a charge should begin to run from the date the plaintiff should have known of the discriminatory motive.[293]

The Ambiguity of Various Factual Scenarios

Obviously, there is much room for uncertainty. For example, it can be questioned whether notice of other discriminatory conduct, such as a possible transfer or demotion, will start the running of the filing period for a claim of unlawful discharge. The answer—at least in the Ninth Circuit—is no.[294] Similarly, in a case in which the defendant uses a two-step scheme and the potential discrimination does not become apparent until months after the first step in the scheme, the filing period will not start running until the second step—which for the first time reveals the discrimination—occurs.[295]

In a denial of hire situation there may well be no notice afforded to a job applicant; all he or she will know is that the employer to whom an application was submitted never

---

[292] *Id* 645; *see also* Burkholder v State Chem Mfg Co, 48 FEP Cas (BNA) 831, 833 (WD Pa 1988).

[293] Aronsen v Crown Zellerbach, 662 F2d 584, 594 (9th Cir 1981), *cert denied,* 459 US 1200 (1983); *see* Thomas v EI DuPont de Nemours & Co, Inc, 574 F2d 1324 (5th Cir 1978); Johnson v International Harvester Co, No 79 C 4141 (ND Ill Feb 5, 1982) (unreported).

[294] McConnell v General Tel Co of Cal, 814 F2d 1311, 1317 (9th Cir 1987), *cert denied,* 484 US 1059 (1988).

[295] Stover v Chairman, Equal Employment Opportunity Commn, 673 F Supp 522 (DDC 1987) (federal employee suit).

responded. In *Weaver v Department of Agriculture*[296] (in which the applicant in fact did receive a formal notice of rejection), the court asserted that "[i]n a failure to hire situation, . . . [the time for filing a charge starts to run on] the date the allegedly unlawful decision not to hire is made and communicated to the plaintiff (or, at the latest, the date the plaintiff reasonably would be aware of facts that would give rise to a *prima facie* case of illegal discrimination)."[297] In *Blacklock v Massachusetts,*[298] a denial of promotion case, the time for filing a charge was deemed not to start running until the plaintiff learned that a much younger and less qualified person was likely to be chosen for the position for which she had applied. Prior to this, she did not know enough to support the filing of a charge and so could not be held accountable for not having filed one.

The court that decided *Eubanks v Harvard Industries, Inc,*[299] was more resistant to the plaintiff's excuse for filing late, i.e., that she had not learned until about six months after being laid off that younger women had not also been laid off. The court stated: "A reasonably prudent person should have taken some action to determine who else was or was not laid off, rather than wait-[ing] over five months for a chance meeting at a grocery store [with someone who told her of the younger women being retained]"[300] In *Wimberg v University of Evansville*[301] the court ruled that the plaintiff, who was demoted on or about March 12, 1984, should have known that she was the victim of possible age discrimination about three weeks later, when she was replaced by a younger woman.

The facts supporting the plaintiff's position were more persuasive to the three-judge Fourth Circuit panel that decided

---

296 54 FEP Cas (BNA) 937 (D Kan 1990).

297 *Id* 940.

298 54 FEP Cas (BNA) 440 (D Mass 1990).

299 712 F Supp 146 (ED Ark), *affd without opinion,* 889 F2d 1092 (8th Cir 1989).

300 *Id* 148; *see also* Barnes v Hillhaven Rehabilitation & Convalescent Ctr, 686 F Supp 311, 314 (ND Ga 1988).

301 761 F Supp 587 (SD Ind 1989).

Hamilton v 1st Source Bank,[302] which concerned a discriminatory compensation claim. During the course of discovery as to his initial claim of wrongful discharge, the plaintiff learned of disparities between the salary he had been receiving and the salaries paid his younger former colleagues who were performing the same tasks. At that point, the plaintiff filed a new charge with the Equal Employment Opportunity Commission (EEOC), raising for the first time the pay issue. This charge was filed 17 months after he had ceased working for the defendant as a result of the discharge, and 16 months after his first EEOC charge had been filed. The court, in fashioning what it termed a "discovery" rule,[303] held that the plaintiff's pay discrimination charge had been timely filed. It distinguished *Delaware State College v Ricks*[304] and cases following it by reasoning that in those decisions, as well as in *Lorance v AT&T Technologies, Inc,*[305] a "key element . . . was the fact that the plaintiff had actual notice that she or he would be discharged or that the seniority system was being implemented."[306] The court contrasted that situation with one involving, as here, a discriminatory pay scheme: "there is no reason to suspect discrimination each time one is handed a paycheck."[307] At least this was so given the fact that the defendant observed the "normal and prudent American business practice . . . [of discouraging] sharing information about salaries."[308] The court then confirmed the applicability of the rule generally observed by the federal courts that a statute of limitations does "not begin to run until 'a reasonable plaintiff should have known facts that would support a charge of discrimination.' "[309] This rule, as the court further observed, "is circumscribed by the

---

302 895 F2d 159 (4th Cir), *vacated in part,* 928 F2d 86 (4th Cir 1990) (en banc).

303 *Id* 165.

304 449 US 250 (1980). See **§6.10.**

305 490 US 900 (1989). See **§6.15.**

306 895 F2d at 163.

307 *Id* 164.

308 *Id.*

309 *Id* (quoting Equal Employment Opportunity Commn v O'Grady, 857 F2d 383, 393-94 (7th Cir 1988)).

requirement that the claimant must have been reasonably prudent in exercising potential opportunities to discover putative discrimination."[310]

The foregoing analysis was overruled by the full Court of Appeals for the Fourth Circuit.[311] The en banc court in part relied upon the language of §7(d)[312] of the ADEA, which provides that a charge "shall be filed [with the EEOC] . . . within 180 days after the alleged unlawful practice *occurred.*"[313] The court asserted that Congress "meant what it plainly and unequivocally said," i.e., that a charge "shall be filed within 180 days of the *occurrence* of the alleged violation."[314] The court further reasoned that, apart from the fact that the discovery rule that the three-judge court of appeals panel had enunciated flew in the face of the statutory language, it also was unworkable. The court of appeals stated as follows:

> An "occurrence" is a discrete event, whereas a plaintiff's acquisition of knowledge is a continuing process. One can never be sure exactly when on that continuum of awareness a plaintiff knew or should have known that the limitations period should have begun. A discovery rule thus substitutes a vague and uncertain period for a definite one.[315]

Thus, the discovery rule previously embraced in the Fourth Circuit was rejected.[316]

---

[310] *Id.*

[311] Hamilton v 1st Source Bank, 928 F2d 86 (4th Cir 1990) (en banc).

[312] 29 USC §626(d).

[313] Emphasis added.

[314] 928 F2d at 87 (emphasis in original).

[315] *Id* 88.

[316] The plaintiff repeatedly asserted that he was not asserting any claim of equitable estoppel or tolling; thus, the court had no basis for determining if the plaintiff could in some way be relieved of the onus of having failed to file in a timely manner. As to equitable estoppel and equitable tolling, see **§§6.17-.21.**

In *Anderson v Touche Ross & Co*[317] the court was more responsive to the plaintiff's claim—at least at the preliminary motion to dismiss stage. The plaintiff alleged that his replacement was hired 10 months after his discharge and it was at that point that the statute of limitations for filing the charge should have begun to run. The court refused to grant the defendant's motion, reasoning that it was possible that a basis for equitable estoppel could be developed by the plaintiff.[318]

The matter of the plaintiff's knowledge often will generate dispute where the plaintiff claims that he or she reasonably relied on the defendant's representations that the decision at issue was made, or an action was taken, for legitimate reasons, and subsequently the plaintiff learns of information that suggests that age bias was the real reason for that decision or action. In such situations the principles of equitable estoppel and equitable tolling come to the fore.[319]

§6.13 —Extension of the Filing Time on the Basis of a Continuing Violation

On a number of occasions plaintiffs in Age Discrimination in Employment Act (ADEA)[320] suits have invoked continuing violation analysis in their efforts to counter claims that they did not file timely charges of unlawful discrimination with the Equal Employment Opportunity Commission (EEOC).[321] Pursuant to such analysis, "acts which occurred outside of the . . . limitations

---

[317] 52 FEP Cas (BNA) 8 (D Mass 1990).

[318] *But see* Wall v National Broadcasting Co, Inc, 768 F Supp 470 (SDNY 1991).

[319] See **§6.17, 6.19-.20.**

[320] 29 USC §621-634.

[321] A plaintiff's pleading need not "explicitly assert a 'continuing violation,' as long as sufficient facts are set forth to constitute a continuing violation; the court must look to the facts alleged, not the language used." McGrew v B&E Marine, Inc, 56 FEP Cas (BNA) 1546, 1554 (ND Ind 1991).

period are not time-barred if they are part of a continuing violation which extended into the limitations period," and "the limitations period does not begin to run until the time of the final act."[322] Thus, the plaintiff's argument is that an action—once commenced, or a policy—once adopted, or a decision—once made, was continuing in nature and so his or her charge did not have to be filed when the action was first taken or the decision was first made or the policy was first adopted, but rather its filing

---

[322] Cashie v Harris Corp, 742 F Supp 1133, 1137 (MD Fla 1990), *affd without opinion,* 930 F2d 923 (11th Cir 1991). The analysis in Furr v AT&T Technologies, Inc, 824 F2d 1537 (10th Cir 1987), seems to be anomalous. In that case there were seven plaintiffs, all complaining of discriminatory denials of promotions. Six of the seven first filed charges with the EEOC on August 20, 1981. Furr filed his charge on January 27, 1982, and his suit on June 9, 1982. The other six filed suit on March 25, 1983. Subsequently, the suits were consolidated. The jury found that Furr and two of the three other prevailing plaintiffs—Peterson and O'Connell—should have been promoted on August 15, 1978, and that the fourth prevailing plaintiff—Hunt—should have been promoted on May 1, 1981. AT&T argued that Furr, Peterson, and O'Connell had failed to timely file and to timely sue, since the discrimination had occurred in 1978, yet they had waited more than three years before filing charges, and even longer than that to sue. The court, however, rejected that argument, and did so by relying upon Hunt's timely filing. The court stated as follows:

> A claim of age discrimination . . . may be based on a continuing policy and practice of discrimination that began before the statutory filing period, as long as the employer continues to apply the discriminatory policy and practice to a point within the relevant filing period, and plaintiff is not merely complaining of the continuing effects of a discriminatory practice that existed only before the relevant filing period. There must be at least one instance of the discriminatory practice within the filing period for the continuing violation theory to apply.

Id 1543.

As an abstract statement the foregoing is unexceptionable; its application by the *Furr* court was problematic, however, because the instance of discrimination within the charge-filing and suit-filing periods to which the court looked involved only Hunt. So far as a ruling in favor of Hunt on the timeliness issue was concerned, *Furr* is unremarkable. However, the court's willingness to allow the other three plaintiffs to piggyback on Hunt's timely filing is a strange variation on continuing violation analysis. (In a representative action, other factors come into play, see **§6.23,** but the *Furr* ruling did not involve Hunt serving in the role of representative plaintiff on behalf of the others; indeed, each plaintiff filed on his or her own behalf, albeit six joined in one suit.)

could be delayed until (at the latest) 180 or 300 days after the violation ceased.[323]

The parameters of continuing violations are quite unclear. As one court noted, "[continuing violation analysis] it is a concept which apparently has grown with each court and litigant's repetition of its vaguely defined edges."[324] The motivating force for plaintiffs pursuing continuing violation arguments is clear, however: the "continuing violation doctrine allows a plaintiff to get relief for a time-barred act by linking it with an act that is within the limitations period."[325]

There are several scenarios that can give rise to a continuing violation argument.

Extended Decision-making Process

The first continuing violation scenario involves a situation where a decision-making process takes place over a period of time, the result being that it is difficult to identify a particular point in time when the alleged violation occurred. For example, a refusal to hire an individual may be the culmination of (1) several months of interviewing various candidates, (2) internal discussions by the individuals responsible for making a choice, (3) the extension of offers that are rejected, (4) the acceptance by a candidate of an offer, (5) and the ensuing rejection of the grievant. In this type of situation, the Supreme Court established in *Delaware State College v Ricks,*[326] the date on which the claim accrued is when the grievant knew, or reasonably should have known, of the adverse decision. Of course, there can be considerable ambiguity as to just when that knowledge was obtained, or reasonably should have been obtained.[327]

---

[323] *See* United Air Lines, Inc v Evans, 431 US 553, 561 (1977) (Marshall, J., dissenting). *See generally* Note, *The Continuing Violation Theory of Title VII After United Air Lines, Inc v Evans,* 31 Hastings LJ 929 (1980).

[324] Allen v Diebold, Inc, 807 F Supp 1308, 1320 (ND Ohio 1992).

[325] Selan v Kiley, 969 F2d 560, 564 (7th Cir 1992).

[326] 449 US 250 (1980). See **§6.10.**

[327] See **§§6.11-.12.**

Express Discriminatory Policy

The second continuing violation scenario involves situations in which there is an express policy that a grievant alleges to be discriminatory, and which is applied over time to various individuals, including—eventually—the grievant. The Supreme Court has addressed this situation in *Lorance v AT&T Technologies, Inc.*[328]

Present Effects of a Past Wrong

The third continuing violation scenario entails a situation where a plaintiff claims that she or he is suffering the present effects of an earlier discriminatory act. This scenario was addressed, and its persuasiveness as a legal construct debunked, in *United Air Lines, Inc v Evans,*[329] which arose under the ADEA's analogue, Title VII of the Civil Rights Act of 1964.[330] The plaintiff, a flight attendant from 1966 to 1968, had been forced to resign because of a United policy requiring female flight attendants to be unmarried. Although the plaintiff was rehired in 1972, she was denied seniority credit for her prior service. The Court, in rejecting her contention that the airline's refusal to give her credit for her prior service constituted a continuing violation, stated as follows: "United's seniority system does indeed have a continuing impact on her pay and fringe benefits. But the emphasis should not be placed on mere continuity; the critical question is whether any present violation exists."[331] In the Court's view, it was the plaintiff's forced ouster in 1968 that was the illegal act, rather than the subsequent refusal—after she was rehired—to give her credit for her prior service, inasmuch as this refusal was no different as to her than it was for any other individual who had previously left the airline's employ for legitimate reasons and who subsequently was rehired. And insofar as the

---

[328] 490 US 900 (1989). See **§§6.15-.16.**

[329] 431 US 553 (1977).

[330] 42 USC §§2000e through 2000e-17. As to ADEA courts' common reliance on judicial constructions of Title VII, see **ch 2.**

[331] 431 US at 558.

1968 ouster was concerned, the time had long passed to challenge that act.

Series of Covert Discriminatory Acts or Decisions

The final, and probably most commonly litigated, continuing violation situation involves disputes in which "the plaintiff charges that the employer has, for a period of time, followed a practice of discrimination, but has done so covertly, rather than by way of an open notorious policy."[332] In this situation "the challenged practice is evidenced only by a series of discrete, allegedly discriminatory acts."[333] The Court of Appeals for the Seventh Circuit explained what the plaintiff must do to succeed with this approach in *Young v Will County Department of Public Aid*:[334]

> To succeed under a continuing violation theory, [the plaintiffs] must demonstrate that the acts of alleged discrimination are part of an ongoing pattern of discrimination and that at least one of the alleged discrete acts of discrimination occurred within the relevant limitations period.[335]

Essentially the same was stated by the Court of Appeals for the Second Circuit, in deciding *Miller v International Telephone & Telegraph Co.*:[336]

> When employees are hired or refused employment pursuant to a continuous practice and policy of discrimination, the commencement of the statute of limitations period may be delayed until the last discriminatory act in furtherance of it, . . . provided such a continuing violation is clearly asserted both in the EEOC filing and in the complaint.

[332] Stewart v CPC Intl, Inc, 679 F2d 117, 121 (7th Cir 1982).

[333] *Id.*

[334] 882 F2d 290 (7th Cir 1989).

[335] *Id* 292.

[336] 755 F2d 20 (2d Cir), *cert denied*, 474 US 851 (1985).

However, a continuing violation may not be based on an employee's having suffered from the effects of an earlier discriminatory act.[337]

The Court of Appeals for the Sixth Circuit, in a non-ADEA decision (which was approvingly relied upon by a later ADEA district court)[338] described the situation where a longstanding policy can give rise to a continuing violation argument:

> Unrelated incidents of discrimination will not suffice . . .; rather, there must be a continuing "over-arching policy of discrimination." . . . Generally, "[r]epeated requests for further relief from a prior act of discrimination will not set the time limitations running anew." . . . However, where there has been a long-standing policy of discrimination, *repeated* attempts to gain employment or promotions may *each* trigger the running of a new limitations period. . . . [T]here must be a specific allegedly discriminatory act against the plaintiff within the relevant limitations period measured back from the time of the complaint.[339]

The key issue is determining whether the acts that are alleged to constitute a continuing violation may be treated as one, so that even those individual incidents that occurred more than 300 days prior to the filing of a charge of discrimination may be attacked by a plaintiff who filed a timely charge as to a later occurring act. A three-factor test addressed to this determination was articulated by the Court of Appeals for the Fifth Circuit in *Berry v Board of Supervisors of LSU*,[340] a non-ADEA decision that was approvingly cited and quoted by the Court of Appeals for the Seventh Circuit in *Selan v Kiley*,[341] an ADEA ruling:

---

337 *Id* 25; *accord* O'Malley v GTE Serv Corp, 758 F2d 818 (2d Cir 1985); *see also* Dixon v Anderson, 928 F2d 212, 216 (6th Cir 1991).

338 Allen v Diebold, Inc, 807 F Supp 1308, 1322 (ND Ohio 1992).

339 Dixon v Anderson, 928 F2d 212, 217 (6th Cir 1991) (quoting Janikowski v Bendix Corp, 823 F2d 945, 948, 949 (6th Cir 1987) (*Dixon* court's emphasis)).

340 715 F2d 971 (5th Cir 1983).

341 969 F2d 560 (7th Cir 1992).

"The first [factor] is subject matter. Do the alleged acts involve the same type of discrimination, tending to connect them in a continuing violation? The second is frequency. Are the alleged acts recurring (e.g. a biweekly paycheck) or more in the nature of an isolated work assignment or employment decision? The third factor, perhaps of most importance, is degree of permanence. Does the act have the degree of permanence which should trigger an employee's awareness of and duty to assert his or her rights, or which should indicate to the employee that the continued existence of the adverse consequence of the act is to be expected without being dependent on a continuing intent to discriminate?"[342]

The *Selan* court (which applied the three *Berry* factors and concluded that the plaintiff could not establish the existence of a continuing violation) explained that it is the third factor that is to be stressed, and it quoted from another ruling in support of this proposition:

"What justifies treating a series of separate violations as a continuing violation? Only that it would have been unreasonable to require the plaintiff to sue separately on each one. In a setting of alleged discrimination, ordinarily this will be because the plaintiff had no reason to believe he was a victim of discrimination until a series of adverse actions established a visible pattern of discriminatory treatment."[343]

---

[342] *Selan,* 969 F2d at 565 (quoting *Berry,* 715 F2d at 981); *accord* Caudill v Farmland Indus, Inc, 698 F Supp 1476, 1482 (WD Mo 1988), *affd on other grounds,* 919 F2d 83 (8th Cir 1990). In *Caudill* the court refused to find a continuing violation premised on an initial refusal to hire, followed some months later by alleged pressure exerted by the defendant on the plaintiff's employer to discharge him, followed several months later by the plaintiff's discharge by that employer.

[343] 969 F2d at 565-66 (quoting Malhotra v Cotter & Co, 885 F2d 1305, 1310 (7th Cir 1989)). The court deciding Wingfield v United Technologies Corp, 678 F Supp 973 (D Conn 1988), focused on the matter of the plaintiff's awareness of his potential claim. In the Second Circuit, the court concluded: "[T]he

§6.14 —Particular Examples of Continuing Violation Claims

Discharges and Refusals to Rehire Discharged or Laid-Off Employees

Plaintiffs in Age Discrimination in Employment Act (ADEA)[344] cases have invoked continuing violation arguments in numerous contexts, with varying success.[345] One scenario involves the discharge of a number of individuals. These discharges can estab-

---

continuing violation doctrine . . . is not predicated upon equitable considerations of whether the plaintiff knew or should have known that he had a claim of discrimination prior to the running of the limitations period." *Id* 978. This contrasts with the Fifth Circuit, where, as the *Wingfield* court understood the case law, the filing period would be triggered once the plaintiff became aware of the facts supportive of a discrimination claim. *Id.* At the same time, however, the *Wingfield* court acknowledged that even in the Second Circuit the matter of awareness on the plaintiff's part is a relevant factor to consider in deciding whether equitable tolling is appropriate. *Id* 978 n6.

The court deciding Gore v Pee Dee Farm Credit Serv, 60 FEP Cas (BNA) 240 (DSC 1992), *affd without opinion,* 1 F3d 1233 (4th Cir 1993), focused on the plaintiff's knowledge:

> A plaintiff who knows or should have known that he was being discriminated against when acts occurring outside the three hundred day filing period occurred can not invoke the continuing violation theory to reach back and litigate those time-barred claims. . . . The entire rationale behind the continuing violation theory is that the plaintiff "had no reason to believe he was a victim of discrimination until a series of adverse actions established a visible pattern of discriminatory mistreatment." *Malhotra v. Cotter and Co.,* 885 F.2d 1305, 1310 . . . (7th Cir 1989)."

Id 243.

[344] 29 USC §§621-634.

[345] The plaintiff in Woerner v Bell Helicopter, 16 FEP Cas (BNA) 480 (ND Tex 1977), contended that the defendant's policy of holding all employment applications open for 18 months, combined with the fact that 20 persons had been hired during that period for the position sought by the plaintiff, constituted a continuing refusal to hire. While the court indicated that it was inclined to reject the plaintiff's argument because he knew, before the 18 months expired, that he would not be hired, *id* 481, it ultimately resolved the timeliness issue on equitable tolling grounds. *Id* 482. As to equitable tolling, see **§§6.17, 6.19-.20.**

lish a continuing violation, provided the evidence shows a "pervasive series or pattern of events within the filing period."[346]

The continuing refusal of an employer to reinstate a terminated employee generally will not be deemed to constitute a continuing violation.[347] The fact that a former employee applies to be rehired and is rejected generally will not be read as a continuing violation scenario involving both the original discharge and the subsequent rejection of the applicant/former employee.[348] However, it is conceivable that in a situation involving a refusal to hire, a grievant who did not timely file a charge of unlawful discrimination as a result of an initial refusal could re-apply for the job and, being once again rejected, now could timely file as to the latter act, i.e., the rejection of his or application.[349]

---

[346] Equal Employment Opportunity Commn v Barrett, Haentjens & Co, 705 F Supp 1065, 1072 (MD Pa 1988).

[347] *See, e.g.,* Janikowski v Bendix Corp, 823 F2d 945, 948 (6th Cir 1987); Charlier v SC Johnson & Son, Inc, 556 F2d 761, 765-66 (5th Cir 1977); Woodburn v LTV Aerospace Corp, 531 F2d 750 (5th Cir 1976); Hiscott v General Elec Co, 521 F2d 632 (6th Cir 1975); Jones v Peabody Coal Co, 53 Empl Prac Dec (CCH) ¶40,029 (WD Ky 1989); Kinniry v Aetna Ins Co, 35 FEP Cas (BNA) 1474 (D Conn 1984); Edwards v Western Elec Co, 21 FEP Cas (BNA) 592, 593 (WDNC 1978); Mazzare v Burroughs Corp, 473 F Supp 234 (ED Pa 1979); Schroeder v Dayton-Hudson Corp, 448 F Supp 910 (ED Mich 1977); Kephart v Institute of Gas Technology, 17 FEP Cas (BNA) 274 (ND Ill 1977), *revd on other grounds,* 581 F2d 1287 (7th Cir 1978); Clark v Emerson Elec Mfg Co, 430 F Supp 216 (ND Miss 1977); Chant v United States Postal Serv, 14 FEP Cas (BNA) 839 (ND Tex 1976) (federal employee suit); *cf* Marshall v American Motors Corp, 475 F Supp 875, 884 (ED Mich 1979) (same result under statute of limitations for filing suit.

[348] *See, e.g.,* Caldwell v National Assn of Home Builders, 771 F2d 1051, 1055-56 (7th Cir 1985); Burnam v Amoco Container Co, 755 F2d 895 (11th Cir 1985); Herber v Boatmen's Bank, 781 F Supp 1255, 1263-64 (WD Tenn 1991); Equal Employment Opportunity Commn v Northwest Airlines, Inc, 51 FEP Cas (BNA) 1317, 1326-27 (WD Wash 1989); Brudne v Amalgamated Trust & Sav Bank, 627 F Supp 458 (ND Ill 1986); Benima v Smithsonian Inst, 471 F Supp 62, 65 (D Mass 1979); Brohl v Singer Co, 407 F Supp 936 (MD Fla 1976). *Contra* Kammer v National Broadcasting Co, Inc, 37 FEP Cas (BNA) 1293 (SDNY 1984).

[349] However, an employer's denial of a new application will not be deemed to constitute a separate act of discrimination if, at the time the plaintiff reapplies, the defendant is not hiring for the position. *See, e.g.,* Law v United Air Lines, Inc, 519 F2d 170 (10th Cir 1975); Powell v Southwestern Bell Tel Co, 494 F2d 485, 489 (5th Cir 1974).

Where the courts are somewhat split is on the issue of whether this second charge could support a later lawsuit, albeit one limited just to the issue addressed in the timely filed charge, i.e., the later refusal to hire. Two decisions illustrate sharply different responses to this scenario.

The plaintiff in *Redd v Fisher Controls*[350] failed to timely file a charge regarding both an alleged discriminatory termination and a failure to promote. She filed a separate timely charge based on her former employer's alleged discriminatory refusal to rehire her. The court, however, was unwilling to allow the plaintiff to proceed on the latter claim; it reasoned as follows:

> Were the Court to hold otherwise, the limitations . . . [period] of . . . the . . . [ADEA] could be circumvented easily in discriminatory discharge cases by simply requesting to be rehired whenever one has failed to file a complaint of discriminatory discharge within the applicable time limit. Recognizing that, other courts have similarly held that failure to reinstate or rehire does not generally constitute an actionable new act of discrimination or continuing discrimination so as to allow the limitations period to begin at the time when the former employee requests reinstatement.[351]

Thus, in the *Redd* court's view, the plaintiff could neither litigate the claims which were the subject of an untimely charge, nor could she even litigate the refusal to rehire, which ostensibly was the subject of a timely charge. In support of this view the court cited, among other rulings, *Collins v United Air Lines, Inc,*[352] for the proposition that a "[d]enial of [a] request for reinstatement does not constitute a new and separate discriminatory act or a continuing violation as '[a] discharged employee who seeks to be reinstated is really litigating the unfairness of his original discharge.' "[353]

---

[350] 814 F Supp 547 (WD Tex 1992).

[351] *Id* 550.

[352] 514 F2d 594 (9th Cir 1975).

[353] 814 F Supp at 550 (quoting *Collins*, 514 F2d at 596 (which in turn was quoting NLRB v Textile Mach Works, 214 F2d 929, 932 (3d Cir 1954))).

The court deciding *Potter v Continental Trailways, Inc,*[354] took a contrary tack. The plaintiff, who had applied for employment as a bus driver, initially was rejected on the basis of his age. He was told by the defendant's agent, however, that he could apply for a job as a part-time driver because there was no age limit for that position. By virtue of the collective bargaining agreement in force, a part-time driver who worked more than 20 days per month automatically qualified for becoming a full-time driver, and the plaintiff's aim was to secure a permanent job by this indirect route. The plaintiff was foiled, however, in his attempt to make an end run around his age-based preclusion by reason of the defendant's general manager instructing his supervisor to not assign the plaintiff more than 20 days' of work in any month. At that point, the plaintiff re-applied for a full-time position and he was again refused. This second refusal, the court ruled, constituted a separate act of discrimination, and so it held that the plaintiff's filing was timely regarding that refusal.[355]

Just as a discharge followed by a refusal or failure to rehire generally are deemed by the courts to be two distinct acts, a layoff followed by a refusal or failure to recall the laid off worker likewise have been deemed to be legally separate actions.[356]

---

[354] 480 F Supp 207 (D Colo 1979).

[355] *See also* Reich v New York Hosp, 513 F Supp 854 (SDNY 1981). The *Potter* court also allowed the plaintiff to proceed on the first refusal to hire, finding the defendant equitably estopped from asserting the timeliness issue. 480 F Supp at 211.

[356] *See* Lawson v Burlington Indus, Inc, 683 F2d 862 (4th Cir), *cert denied,* 459 US 944 (1982); Allen v Diebold, Inc, 807 F Supp 1308, 1320-22 (ND Ohio 1992); Belda v Morse-Diesel, Inc, 55 FEP Cas (BNA) 1245, 1247 (ND Ill 1990); Chamberlin v Contel Customer Support, Inc, 54 FEP Cas (BNA) 1490, 1493 (ND Ga 1990); Nogar v Henry F Teichmann, Inc, 640 F Supp 365, 369 (WD Pa 1985), *affd without opinion,* 44 FEP Cas (BNA) 448 (3d Cir 1986); Yokum v St Johnsburg Trucking Co, Inc, 595 F Supp 1532 (D Conn 1984); Morris v Frank IX & Sons, Inc, 486 F Supp 728, 733 (WD Va 1980); Cutright v General Motors Corp, 486 F Supp 590 (WD Pa 1980); Wagner v Sperry Univac, Div of Sperry Rand Corp, 458 F Supp 505 (ED Pa 1978), *affd without opinion,* 624 F2d 1092 (3d Cir 1980); *see also* Haupt v International Harvester Co, 571 F Supp 1043 (ND Ill 1983). *But see* Hiscott v General Elec Co, 521 F2d 632, 635 (6th Cir 1975).

In Allen v American Home Prods, Inc, 658 F Supp 451 (ND Ind 1987), the

Discriminatory Compensation

There is support for the proposition that where there is an allegedly discriminatory compensation scheme, each successive paycheck will be deemed to be another facet of a continuing violation.[357]

---

plaintiffs contended that the discriminatory act by the defendant consisted of its decision to close a plant because it was staffed predominantly by older workers. Some of the plaintiffs had been laid off prior to the date of closure. The court rejected the defendant's summary judgment motion, which was based on the argument that the date of layoff was the trigger date for starting the running of the filing period. The court reasoned that a genuine issue existed as to whether the plaintiffs' termination occurred at the time of the layoff or at the time of the closure. While it might be argued that the court was giving an expansive, plaintiff-protective interpretation to a layoff situation, the case really can be read more narrowly, and consistently with *United Air Lines:* all that the plaintiffs were complaining about, in terms of making a claim under the ADEA, was the closure. In other words, they were arguing that the closure was a separate and distinct act, foreclosing any possibility of recall. Thus, it really was the discriminatory foreclosure of recall rights that was at issue, rather than the question of whether a layoff—followed by a failure to recall—constituted one continuous act.

Equal Employment Opportunity Commn v City of Chicago, 51 FEP Cas (BNA) 503 (ND Ill 1989), was also a denial of hire case. It did not involve a late-filed charge, however; rather, the court's focus was on the lateness of the filing of suit. The dispute arose out of a city police department policy barring anyone over age 34 from taking an examination, passage of which was a precondition to being considered eligible for hiring. The names of those who passed the 1981 test were placed on a roster, from which people were selected from time to time over the course of the next few years. The court held that "any violation stemming from the City's 1981 exam continued for as long as the roster produced from that exam continued to be used." *Id* 513-14. In reaching that conclusion, the court distinguished *United Air Lines* and Delaware State College v Ricks, 449 US 250 (1980), discussed in **§6.10,** and harmonized its position with that set forth in Lorance v AT&T Technologies, 490 US 900 (1989), discussed in **§6.15.**

[357] *See* Miller v Beneficial Management Corp, 977 F2d 834, 843-44 (3d Cir 1992). (Actually *Miller* involved the statute of limitations for filing suit, rather than the charge-filing time limitations). *Cf* Gibbs v Pierce County Law Enforcement Support Agency, 785 F2d 1396, 1399-400 (9th Cir 1986) (non-ADEA case); Bartelt v Berlitz Sch of Languages, Inc, 698 F2d 1003, 1004 (9th Cir), *cert denied,* 464 US 915 (1983) (*id*); Hall v Ledex, Inc, 669 F2d 397, 398 (6th Cir 1982) (*id*); Hodgson v Behrens Drug Co, 475 F2d 1041, 1050 (5th Cir), *cert denied,* 414 US 822 (1973) (*id*). *Contra* Smilan v United Airlines, Inc, 796 F Supp 723, 728-29 (EDNY 1992); *cf* Hendrix v City of Yazoo City, 911 F2d 1102, 1103 (5th Cir 1990) (non-ADEA case).

Refusals to Promote and Demotions

Generally, the courts view refusals to promote[358] and demotions[359] as discrete acts by employers, rather than as continuing violations.[360] This position holds sway even where the demoted employee seeks restoration to his former position.[361] Typically, if a demotion leads to other consequences that simply are the

---

[358] *See, e.g.,* Kao v Scherl, 49 Empl Prac Dec (CCH) ¶38,889 (EDNY 1989); Less v Nestle Co, Inc, 705 F Supp 110, 115 (WDNY 1988); Williams v Bolger, 33 FEP Cas (BNA) 631 (DDC 1983) (federal employee suit); Golletti v Arco/Polymers, Inc, 32 FEP Cas (BNA) 1796 (WD Pa 1983), *vacated & remanded without opinion,* 762 F2d 993 (3d Cir 1985); Malarkey v Texaco, Inc, 559 F Supp 117 (SDNY 1982), *affd on other grounds,* 704 F2d 674 (2d Cir 1983); Donaldson v Cafritz Co, 30 FEP Cas (BNA) 436 (DDC 1981); Stout v Amoco Prod Co, 508 F Supp 30 (D Wyo 1980); Trammell v Southern Bell Tel & Tel Co, 19 FEP Cas (BNA) 962 (ND Ga 1979); Zalvis v Southern Bell Tel & Tel Co, 19 FEP Cas (BNA) 958 (ND Ga 1977). *But see* Buffington v General Time Corp, 677 F Supp 1186 (MD Ga 1988); Coleman v Clark Oil & Ref Co, 568 F Supp 1035 (ED Wis 1983); Collins v Manufacturers Hanover Trust Co, 542 F Supp 663, 670 (SDNY 1982).

[359] *See, e.g.,* Phillips v Southern Bell Tel & Tel Co, 650 F2d 655 (5th Cir 1981); Downey v Southern Natural Gas Co, 649 F2d 302 (5th Cir 1981); Macellaro v Goldman, 643 F2d 813 (DC Cir 1980); Thaklar v Provident Natl Bank, 58 FEP Cas (BNA) 1435 (ED Pa 1991); Malarkey v Texaco, Inc, 559 F Supp 117 (SDNY 1982), *affd on other grounds,* 704 F2d 674 (2d Cir 1983); Allen v Colgate-Palmolive Co, 539 F Supp 57 (SDNY 1981); Tobin v Trans Union Sys Corp, 488 F Supp 622 (ED Pa 1980); Mader v Control Data Corp, 19 FEP Cas (BNA) 1192 (D Md 1978).

[360] *See, e.g.,* Goldman v Sears, Roebuck & Co, 607 F2d 1014 (1st Cir 1979), *cert denied,* 445 US 929 (1980); Hawley v Dresser Indus, Inc, 737 F Supp 445 (SD Ohio 1990); Slevin v Safeguard Business Sys, 31 FEP Cas (BNA) 193 (ND Ill 1982); Malarkey v Texaco, Inc, 559 F Supp 117 (SDNY 1982), *affd on other grounds,* 704 F2d 674 (2d Cir 1983); Sanders v Duke Univ, 538 F Supp 1143, 1146-47 (MDNC 1982); *see also* Roy v Amoco Oil Co, 747 F Supp 661, 667 (SD Fla 1990), *affd without opinion,* 925 F2d 1475 (11th Cir), *cert denied,* 112 S Ct 87 (1991) (discharged employee's continuing requests to continue in Amoco's employ, which were met with rejection, not sufficient to establish continuing violation); Wippel v Prudential Ins Co, 33 FEP Cas (BNA) 412 (D Md 1982). *But see* Wulach v Bear, Stearns & Co, 48 FEP Cas (BNA) 727, 731 (SDNY 1988); Burroughs v Great Atl & Pac Tea Co, 462 So 2d 353 (Ala 1984) (change of status of employee from full time to part time, with weekly changes in hours of assignment, constitutes continuing violation).

[361] *See, e.g.,* Thomas v EI DuPont de Nemours & Co, 574 F2d 1324, 1327-28 (5th Cir 1978); *see also* Goldman v Sears, Roebuck & Co, 607 F2d 1014 (1st Cir 1979), *cert denied,* 445 US 929 (1980).

expectable fallout of the demotion, the fact that these consequences will not take effect until some time following the demotion itself will not convert the demotion into a continuing violation.[362] But, if the demotion is seen as being one aspect of a larger scheme culminating in the plaintiff's discharge, there may be a continuing violation.[363] Thus, if a series of demotions, or a demotion and denial of subsequent promotion, are part of a general plan to disadvantage older workers, a continuing violation may be found to exist.[364]

A series of failures to promote typically will not be seen as a series of connected events, but rather as individual, discrete acts.[365] The Court of Appeals for the Third Circuit, however, took a different view in deciding *Miller v Beneficial Management Corp*,[366] which actually concerned the statute of limitations for filing suit. *Miller* involved the unsuccessful efforts of the plaintiff over a three- or four-year period to obtain a promotion to the position of vice-president. The court drew a distinction between

---

[362] *See* Randlett v Owens-Ill, Inc, 419 F Supp 103 (ND Tex 1976); *see also* Allen v Colgate-Palmolive Co, 539 F Supp 57 (SDNY 1981) (factual issue remains concerning whether subsequent event was an independent act of discrimination or was based on demotion); Tobin v Trans Union Sys Corp, 488 F Supp 622, 629-30 (ED Pa 1980) (*id*). The court deciding Huffman v IGW Sys, Inc, 621 F Supp 658 (SD Ind 1985), rejected a continuing violation argument arising out of an alleged wrongful discharge, followed some years later by a rehiring, followed ultimately by the refusal of the employer to credit for retirement benefits purposes the years worked prior to the discharge. The plaintiff argued that her consequent reduced benefits were the result of the continuing violation perpetrated by the employer, i.e., the refusal to credit the earlier years in computing her seniority, which was the benchmark for computing benefits.

[363] *See* Labus v Navistar Intl Transp Corp, 740 F Supp 1053, 1058-60 (DNJ 1990); Robb v Chemetron Corp, 17 FEP Cas (BNA) 1535, 1544-45 (SD Tex 1978).

[364] *See* Taylor v Home Ins Co, 777 F2d 849 (4th Cir 1985), *cert denied*, 476 US 1142 (1986); Herrmann v Whirlpool Corp, 60 FEP Cas (BNA) 1130 (WD Mich 1992); Small v Bethlehem Steel Corp, 33 FEP Cas (BNA) 414 (D Md 1983).

[365] *See* Samuel v Merrill Lynch, Pierce, Fenner & Smith, 771 F Supp 47, 49 (SDNY 1991).

[366] 977 F2d 834 (3d Cir 1992); *see also* Ware v Howard Univ, Inc, 816 F Supp 737 (DDC 1993).

denials of promotions involving a series of separate, distinct jobs, and denials involving repeated refusals of the employer to elevate an employee into one specific position. As to the latter scenario, the court was satisfied that this should be characterized as a continuing violation.

Other Scenarios

In *Horn v United Air Lines, Inc,*[367] the court refused to find a continuing violation arising out of the plaintiff first being placed on probation, then being demoted, and then ultimately being discharged. Each action was a separate one, in the court's view.[368] Likewise, the court deciding *Morton v Associated Dry Goods Corp*[369] viewed the allegedly wrongful demotion and discharge as separate and distinct wrongs, each of which triggered its own filing period. A continuing violation, on the other hand, may be established by virtue of a series of acts undertaken by the employer that were intended to force the plaintiff to involuntarily retire.[370]

§6.15 —The Adoption of a Policy or Practice as Affecting the Time for Filing a Charge: The Effect of *Lorance*

An employer (or other covered entity) under the Age Discrim-

---

[367] 30 Empl Prac Dec (CCH) ¶33,314 (ND Ill 1983).

[368] A similar analysis was employed in Blomberg v Colgate-Palmolive Co, 33 FEP Cas (BNA) 1809 (D Minn 1983); *see also* Allen v Colgate-Palmolive Co, 539 F Supp 37, 39 (SDNY 1981).

[369] 792 F Supp 1136 (SD Ind 1992).

[370] *See* Bruno v Western Elec Co, 829 F2d 957 (10th Cir 1987); *see also* Blumenthal v G-K-G, Inc, 737 F Supp 493 (ND Ill 1990) ((1) maintenance by defendant of an allegedly discriminatory pension and profit sharing plan aimed at phasing out older employees as they approached age 70, plus (2) refusal by defendant to provide plaintiff with new accounts, result being to gradually reduce his work load and thereby to force him into retirement, sufficient to establish—at least for purposes of motion to dismiss—continuing violation).

ination in Employment Act (ADEA))[371] may pursue a continuing practice or policy which may not actually have a direct effect for some years as to a given individual. For example, an employer may adopt a mandatory retirement policy that appears to be obviously unlawful under the Act, but that will not impose its burden on a 45-year-old employee until, after 20 years, the employee reaches the critical age specified in the tainted policy. The question arises, given such a scenario, whether the employee must file a charge of unlawful discrimination either within 180 or 300 days (1) of the policy's adoption or (2), if it is already in place before he or she is hired, within 180 or 300 days of being hired, or (3) whether he or she can wait until the policy is invoked by the employer to oust the employee upon his or her turning 65 years of age.

The answer given by lower courts addressing such situations prior to the Supreme Court's 1989 decision, *Lorance v AT&T Technologies, Inc,*[372] was that the employee could wait until he or she suffered direct harm. Thus, for example, in *Heiar v Crawford County*[373] the Court of Appeals for the Seventh Circuit held that the filing time began to run when the plaintiffs received notice of their termination, rather than on the earlier adoption date of the mandatory retirement policy that ultimately led to their termination.[374] Similarly, in a case involving an allegedly discriminatory benefit plan of longstanding duration, the discrimination was not deemed to arise for purposes of filing a charge just at the time the plan was adopted—which was years before the charge was filed. Rather, the Court of Appeals for the Eighth Circuit reasoned that so long as the plan remained in effect, the alleged ADEA violation continued.[375] The same analysis was used by the Court of Appeals for the Second Circuit regarding an allegedly discriminatory seniority system in *Cook v Pan Ameri-*

[371] 29 USC §§621-634.

[372] 490 US 900 (1989).

[373] 746 F2d 1190 (7th Cir 1984), *cert denied,* 472 US 1027 (1985).

[374] *Accord* Colby v Graniteville Co, 635 F Supp 381 (SDNY 1986).

[375] International Bhd of Elec Workers, Local 1439 v Union Elec Co, 37 FEP Cas (BNA) 1346 (8th Cir 1985).

can World Airways, Inc.:[376] the claim of a grievant was deemed to arise when the system was applied to him or her, provided the charge of discrimination filed with the EEOC articulated a continuing violation.[377]

The continuing viability of these decisions now must be considered in light of *Lorance,* a decision addressing Title VII of the Civil Rights Act of 1964.[378] Because *Lorance* applies analogically in the ADEA context,[379] some—if not all—of the pre-*Lorance* rulings are no longer valid, as the following analysis reveals.

The plaintiffs in *Lorance* were three women whose claims arose out of a collectively bargained change in the company seniority system. Until 1979 all hourly wage earners had accrued seniority on the basis of years in the plant, and workers promoted to the job of tester retained this seniority following promotion. In that year the challenged change was adopted, resulting in testers' seniority being determined on the basis of time spent in that particular job, with plant-wide seniority only being subject to recapture after five years on the job as a tester. This change, the plaintiffs contended, was the product of gender-based discriminatory animus. It was prompted, they argued, by changing work patterns: the tester positions traditionally had been filled almost exclusively by men, but in the 1970s an increasing number of women began to secure these jobs. The alteration in the seniority system, it was claimed, reflected a " 'conspir[acy] to change

---

[376] 771 F2d 635, 646 (2d Cir 1985), *cert denied,* 474 US 1109 (1986).

[377] Like reasoning was used in cases involving the statute of limitations for filing suit during those years when suit had to be filed within two or three years of the act of discrimination. *See, e.g.,* Crosland v Charlotte Eye, Ear & Throat Hosp, 686 F2d 208 (4th Cir 1982); Morelock v NCR Corp, 586 F2d 1096 (6th Cir 1978), *cert denied,* 441 US 906 (1979); Equal Employment Opportunity Commn v Goodyear Tire & Rubber Co, 35 Empl Prac Dec (CCH) ¶34,596 (ND Ohio 1984); Equal Employment Opportunity Commn v Home Ins Co, 553 F Supp 704 (SDNY 1982). As to the statute of limitations for filing suit, see **§6.30.**

[378] 42 USC §§2000e through 2000e-17. It is to Title VII that courts construing the ADEA often look, given the similarities in prohibitory language of the two statutes and their common goal of eradicating discrimination in the workplace. See **ch 2.** Thus, *Lorance* clearly is apposite here.

[379] See discussion below.

the seniority rules, in order to protect incumbent male testers and to discourage women from promoting into the traditionally male-tester jobs,'[.]''[380]

While this allegedly discriminatory change was adopted during an economic slowdown in 1979, it was not until 1982 that the plaintiffs, whose seniority had been affected by the changed policy, were demoted. It was not until April, 1983, that they first filed charges of discrimination with the Equal Employment Opportunity Commission (EEOC) as a consequence of the direct harm, i.e., demotion, they experienced. The issue before the Court was whether the trial court had erred in granting the defendant's motion for summary judgment on the ground that the plaintiffs had not timely filed their charges.

The Court had to take into account the fact that by virtue of the particular language of the section of Title VII dealing with seniority plans,[381] only plans that are motivated by discriminatory intent can be successfully attacked under that statute. In other words, a facially neutral seniority plan that has a disproportionately adverse impact on members of a Title VII-protected group does not violate Title VII, absent the grievant being able to establish discriminatory intent.[382] The plaintiffs' argument was not that the seniority system at issue overtly treated women differently than men or that it was operated in a discriminatory manner, but rather that the amended plan had a discriminatory impact on the sexes and this impact was unlawful because the system had its genesis in purposeful gender discrimination—to wit, the 1979 alteration.

The Court concluded that that 1979 change had occurred well outside the limitations period for a complaint filed in 1983, and so the plaintiffs' claims were time-barred. In reaching this conclusion, the Court rejected the applicability of continuing viola-

---

[380] 490 US at 903.

[381] 42 USC §2000e-2(h).

[382] The ADEA seniority system defense is in accord: a seniority system will not be violative of the age statute just because it has an adverse impact on an age-defined group. See **ch 5**.

tion analysis.[383] In other words, the Court found wanting the argument that the employer could be regarded as guilty of a violation that occurred "not only when the contractual right was eliminated but also when each of the concrete effects of that elimination were felt."[384] The Court invoked *Delaware State College v Ricks,*[385] a Title VII decision which has been consistently followed by ADEA courts,[386] for the proposition that " '[t]he proper focus is upon the time of the *discriminatory acts,* not upon the time at which the *consequences* of the acts become most painful.' "[387] In relying upon *Ricks* the Court rejected the dissenters' effort to distinguish that ruling on the ground that in that earlier decision "[t]he allegedly discriminatory denial of tenure . . . served notice to the plaintiff that his termination a year later would come as a 'delayed, *but inevitable* consequence',"[388] whereas "[o]n the day AT & T's seniority system was adopted, there was no reason to believe that a woman who exercised her plantwide seniority to become a tester would ever be demoted as a result of the new system,"[389] and so any adverse consequence of the change was, in 1979, "speculative."[390] The majority, in debunking this argument, wrote as follows:

> Of course, the benefits of a seniority system, like those of an insurance policy payable upon the occurrence of a non-inevitable event, are by their nature speculative—if only because they depend upon the employee's continuing desire to work for the particular employer. But it makes no more sense to say that no "concrete harm" occurs when an employer provides a patently less desirable seniority

---

383 See **§6.13.**

384 490 US at 906.

385 449 US 250 (1980).

386 See **§6.10.**

387 490 US at 907 (quoting *Ricks,* 449 US at 258 (emphasis in original)).

388 490 US at 917 (quoting *Ricks,* 449 US at 257-58) (Marshall, J., joined by Blackmun, J., dissenting) (emphasis added by Marshall, J.).

389 490 US at 914.

390 *Id.*

> guarantee than what the law requires, than it does to say that no concrete harm occurs when an insurance company delivers an accident insurance policy with a face value of $10,000, when what has been paid for is a face value of $25,000. It is true that the injury to the employee becomes substantially *more* concrete when the less desirable seniority system causes his demotion, just as the injury to the policyholder becomes substantially more concrete when the accident occurs and the payment is $15,000 less than it should be. But that is irrelevant to whether there was *any* concrete injury at the outset. What the dissent means by "concrete harm" is what *Ricks* . . . referred to as the point at which the injury becomes "most painful"—and that case rejected it as the point of reference for liability.[391]

In sum, then, the limitations period began running on the date the system's discriminatory alteration was adopted.[392]

There was, however, a very important limit on the reach of *Lorance:* "There is no doubt . . . that a facially discriminatory seniority system (one that treats similarly situated employees differently) can be challenged at any time[.]"[393] Thus, whereas a facially neutral seniority system challenged under Title VII because it was adopted with discriminatory motive (which is a requisite, as discussed earlier, to a Title VII-based attack on such a system) must be attacked after its adoption within the statutorily prescribed charge-filing period, challenges to facially discriminatory systems are not so limited. The Court explained this distinction in a footnote:

> With a facially neutral system the discriminatory act occurs *only* at the time of adoption, for each application is nondiscriminatory (seniority accrues for men and women on an identical basis). But a facially discriminatory system (e.g., one that assigns men twice the seniority that women receive

---

391 *Id* 907 n3 (emphasis in original).

392 *Id* 909.

393 *Id* 912.

> for the same amount of time served) by definition discriminates each time it is applied. This is a material difference for purposes of the analysis we employed in [*United Air Lines, Inc v*] *Evans* [,431 US 553 (1977), see **§6.13**] and *Ricks*—which focuses on the timing of the *discriminatory* acts for purposes of the statute of limitations.[394]

The consequence of the *Lorance* decision was to require a grievant to file a charge (1) even if it was not clear at the time the rule or policy in question was adopted that it ultimately would be applied to him or her, or (2) even if the rule or policy were eventually to apply, would not do so until many years in the future. Thus, *Lorance* encouraged the filing of charges based on mere speculation. More than that, the decision required grievants to pursue legal actions and to thereby engender workplace animosities, when such might well be unnecessary because the complained-of rule or policy—if left unchallenged for the moment—might be changed before being applied to the grievant, or the grievant in any event might leave the firm's employ before the rule would ever come into play.

Another caveat to *Lorance,* apart from that concerning facially discriminatory policies, was articulated in another Title VII decision, albeit not one decided by the Supreme Court: *Chambers v Parco Foods, Inc.*[395] *Chambers,* like *Lorance,* involved a seniority system, the allegedly discriminatory facet of which had been adopted as part of a collectively bargained contract in 1979. The provision was retained without change as a component of later contracts, the most recent retention being in 1988. The plaintiff argued that each readoption of the provision triggered anew the running of the period for filing a charge of discrimination with the EEOC. While on the facts the plaintiff lost, the court did agree that the "maintenance" of an allegedly discriminatory contractual provision could be considered a distinct discriminatory act, "provided that the plaintiff can point to evidence of a discriminatory act or discriminatory intent in the provision's

---

394 *Id* 912 n5 (emphasis in original).

395 935 F2d 902 (7th Cir 1991).

reenactment.''[396] Accordingly, "if a plaintiff can point to evidence of discriminatory motive in the renegotiation or 'maintenance' of a seniority system, then that date provides the time at which the statute of limitations begins to run, for it is at that point that the 'discriminatory act' took place.''[397]

While the *Lorance* decision dealt with an allegedly discriminatory seniority rule, lower courts addressing Title VII claims, applied the ruling in other contexts. Moreover, *Lorance* has been deemed apposite regarding ADEA claims, as well.[398] Thus, it was applied to a mandatory retirement policy allegedly violative of the ADEA in *Equal Employment Opportunity Commission v City of Chicago,*[399] and to the modification of a seniority system in *Barrow v New Orleans Steamship Association.*[400] *Lorance* also was deemed applicable to a modification of a retirement benefit plan in *Thompson v Prudential Insurance Co of America.*[401] And in *Equal Employment Opportunity Commission v City Colleges*[402] the Court of Appeals for the Seventh Circuit asserted that it saw "no reason for confining *Lorance* to Title VII suits challenging seniority systems.''[403] This widening circle of *Lorance's* influence was somewhat curtailed, however, by the enactment of §112 of the Civil Rights Act of 1991 (CRA).[404]

---

[396] *Id* 906.

[397] *Id.*

[398] It is the EEOC's position that *Lorance* applies only to seniority systems. EEOC Notice No 915.002: Enforcement Guidance on the Effect of Section 112 of the Civil Rights Act of 1991 on the Supreme Court Decision in *Lorance v AT&T Technologies, Inc,* and Charges Involving Seniority Systems (Oct 20, 1993). (This issuance is reproduced in the Appendix at the end of the last volume.)

[399] 51 FEP Cas (BNA) 503 (ND Ill 1989); *see also* Priester v Amoco Corp, 60 FEP Cas (BNA) 1083 (ND Ill 1990).

[400] 932 F2d 473 (5th Cir 1991).

[401] 795 F Supp 1337 (DNJ 1992), *affd without opinion,* 993 F2d 226 (1993).

[402] 944 F2d 339 (7th Cir 1991).

[403] *Id* 343.

[404] Pub L No 102-166, §112, 105 Stat 1071, 1078-79.

The Civil Rights Act of 1991

Section 112 of the CRA amended Title VII by adding a subsection overriding *Lorance* insofar as seniority systems challenged under that statute are concerned:

> (2) For purposes of this section, an unlawful employment practice occurs, with respect to a seniority system that has been adopted for an intentionally discriminatory purpose in violation of this title (whether or not that discriminatory purpose is apparent on the face of the seniority provision), when the seniority system is adopted, when an individual becomes subject to the seniority system, or when a person aggrieved is injured by the application of the seniority system or provision of the system.[405]

In light of this narrowly drawn language, *Lorance* appears to retain its viability in nonseniority system situations, and so the ostensibly pro-plaintiff change made to Title VII seems to be of quite limited scope. What renders this conclusion—seemingly an eminently reasonable one, given the statutory language—somewhat dubious, is the legislative history. A document was inserted in the Congressional Record by Senator Danforth, who was the primary Senate participant in the fashioning of the compromise language incorporated by the Senate into the bill that, was ultimately enacted as the CRA. This document was represented as expressing the views of all of the original cosponsors of the legislation, both Democrats and Republicans. Entitled "Sponsors' Interpretative Memorandum on Issues Other than Wards Cove—Business Necessity/Cumulation/Alternative Business Practice," it was noted in the document that *Lorance* had been applied in contexts other than those involving seniority systems, as well as in a non-Title VII context, i.e., the ADEA. Introducing these observations with the word "[u]nfortunately," the document went on to assert that "[t]his legislation should be interpreted as disapproving the extension of . . . [*Lorance*] to

---

[405] §706(e)(2), 42 USC §2000e-5(e)(2).

contexts outside of seniority systems."[406] The committee reports on the House version of what was ultimately enacted, in different form, as the CRA also expressed concern about *Lorance* being extended to contexts other than seniority systems.[407]

It is difficult to know what to make of the statements in the Congressional Record, as well as those in the committee reports. They certainly evidence a desire on the part of those members of Congress who were extensively involved in the drafting and managing of the legislation to limit *Lorance.* But if that intent really was shared by a majority in both houses, it would seem that the language of the new subsection of Title VII would have reflected it, rather than speaking on its face only to seniority systems. Presumably, a court called upon to interpret the new Title VII provision could deem *Lorance* overturned in all contexts by following the tack the Court used in *United Steelworkers of America v Weber,*[408] where Justice Brennan, writing for the majority, invoked the *spirit* of Title VII to uphold a voluntary affirmative action plan that seemingly conflicted with the language of the statute.[409] However, the more legitimate approach would seem to be to read the language of the Title VII subsection to mean what is set forth on its face, i.e., that it is indeed applicable only to seniority systems, rather than to read it as proscribing what it in fact does not on its face proscribe.

Of more direct concern here is the significance for the ADEA of the amendment to Title VII. As already noted, *Lorance* has been read by ADEA courts as being applicable by way of analogy—a hardly surprising interpretation, given the long history of

---

[406] 137 Cong Rec S15485 (daily ed Oct 30, 1991); *accord* 137 Cong Rec H9530 (daily ed Nov 7, 1991) (statement of Representative Edwards, chair of the House Judiciary Committee subcommittee having jurisdiction over the CRA).

[407] *See* Committee on the Judiciary, US House of Representatives, Civil Rights Act of 1991, HR Rep No 40, pt 2 102d Cong, 1st Sess, at 23 (1991); Committee on Education and Labor, US House of Representatives, Civil Rights and Women's Equity in Employment Act of 1991, HR Rep No 40, pt 1 102d Cong, 1st Sess, at 62 (1991), ("Although the *Lorance* decision involved a seniority system, its reasoning is applicable to many other employment practices, causing equally harsh and inequitable results.")

[408] 443 US 193 (1979).

[409] 42 USC §2000e-2(j).

ADEA courts looking to judicial constructions of Title VII for guidance.[410] Moreover, *Lorance* has been applied by ADEA courts to employment issues other than seniority rules and systems. Nothing on the face of the Title VII subsection added by the CRA even addresses, let alone limits, *Lorance's* continuing applicability to ADEA claims.[411] Thus, *Lorance* remains viable in the age context.[412]

If, however, one were somehow to infuse into the ADEA the rejection of *Lorance* that was effectuated for Title VII purposes by the CRA, that reading of the CRA's consequences for the ADEA would have to be tempered by the question of whether the CRA applies retroactively, or only applies to charges and/or lawsuits pending when the CRA was signed into law on November 21, 1991. While the Supreme Court ruled in *Landgraf v USI Film Products Co*[413] that the CRA provisions concerning the availability of certain damages and of jury trials in the Title VII context only apply prospectively, the decision is obscure as to other changes made by the 1991 Act. The Court drew a distinction between substantive and procedural changes,

---

[410] See **ch 2**.

[411] The only hard data even partially disputing the proposition that *Lorance* remains alive and well in the ADEA setting are the just-discussed statements in the Congressional Record, wherein a number of members urged that *Lorance* not be extended to nonseniority system situations. As discussed, these statements are of problematic import. Moreover, even taking them as having some significance, they do not condemn the extension of *Lorance* to ADEA-based challenges to seniority systems, but only the extension of the decision to contexts involving claims other than those arising out of allegedly discriminatory seniority systems. Thus, even reading the statements in their broadest possible terms, *Lorance* at the very least would still appear to be viable when applied to ADEA-based challenges involving seniority systems. In any event, and at a less speculative level, since in fact there is no statutory language actually modifying *Lorance* insofar as it has been read as an analogical guide for the ADEA, the decision retains its full vigor for ADEA claims, being applicable both to challenges involving seniority systems and to other issues, as well.

[412] *See* Thompson v Prudential Ins Co of Am, 795 F Supp 1337, 1348-50 (DNJ 1992), *affd without opinion*, 993 F2d 226 (1993). For a full discussion of the import of the CRA for the ADEA, see Eglit, *The Civil Rights Act of 1991, Title VII, and the Age Discrimination in Employment Act: Three Acts and a Dog That Didn't Bark,* 39 Wayne L Rev 1093 (1993).

[413] 114 S Ct 1483 (1994).

such that "[c]hanges in procedural rules may often be applied in suits arising before their enactment without raising concerns about retroactivity."[414] The change made to override *Lorance* would seem to constitute a procedural change. However, it does not automatically follow that retroactive application is appropriate: *Landgraf* left room even for the conclusion that these kind of changes also only apply prospectively. On balance, it would seem that retroactive application is appropriate. The CRA's rejection of *Lorance,* after all, did not create any new rights. It simply allows individual to sue as to policies and practices that presumably would have been adopted whether or not an aggrieved individual would have to sue quickly, or could wait until the policy or practice directly affected him or her. The real sticking point in any event remains: the CRA's rejection of *Lorance* does not extend to the ADEA context.[415]

It should be emphasized, however, that the Equal Employment Opportunity Commission takes a contrary position. In its view §112 of the CRA is applicable to the ADEA.[416]

§6.16 —Applying *Lorance* to Charge-Filing Under the ADEA

The first point to be made in assessing the relevance of *Lorance v AT&T Technologies, Inc,*[417] to the filing of charges of unlawful discrimination under the Age Discrimination in

---

[414] *Id* 1502.

[415] In deciding Smilan v United Airlines, Inc, 796 F Supp 723 (EDNY 1992), the court, while applying *Lorance* to the facts before it, responded to the argument that the Supreme Court ruling was inapplicable because of the CRA with the assertion that "[t]o the extent that the Civil Rights Act of 1991 is applicable to the facts of this case, the Court holds that its provisions are to be given only prospective effect." *Id* 727 n6.

[416] EEOC Policy Guide No N-915.002, Enforcement Guidance on the Effect of Section 112 of the Civil Rights Act of 1991 on the Supreme Court Decision in Lorance v. AT&T Technologies, Inc. and Charges Involving Seniority Systems (Oct 20, 1993). This policy guide, which does not have the force of law, see **ch 2**, is reproduced in the Appendix at the end of the last volume.

[417] 490 US 900 (1989).

Employment Act (ADEA)[418] is that it would not seem to make a difference whether the claim at issue entails a seniority system or some other policy or practice.[419] Thus, for example, a mandatory retirement policy, even if not part of a seniority system per se, would fit within the *Lorance* analysis. This perception is confirmed by *Equal Employment Opportunity Commission v City Colleges of Chicago,*[420] a ruling of the Court of Appeals for the Seventh Circuit that involved an allegedly discriminatory early retirement plan. Likewise, *Lorance* was deemed applicable (but not fatal) in *Equal Employment Opportunity Commission v City of Chicago,*[421] which involved a challenge to a policy barring persons 35 and over from taking a test, the passage of which was a precondition to becoming eligible to be considered for hiring as a police officer.[422]

Second, the *Lorance* Court established that when a grievant attacks a facially neutral practice or policy as being discriminatorily motivated (in other words, when a grievant utilizes discriminatory treatment, rather than discriminatory impact, theory), the triggering event for starting the running of the filing period is the date of adoption of the discriminatory plan or policy, or of an amendment thereto.[423] Thus, in *Barrow v New Orleans Steamship Association*[424] the plaintiff's charge, according to the court, should have been filed when the allegedly discriminatory seniority system that he was attacking was adopted, "regardless of when the effects of such system . . . [were] actually felt."[425] And an allegedly discriminatory change in a benefit plan should have been attacked when it was adopted, according to the district

---

418 29 USC §§621-634.

419 *But see* Davidson v Board of Governors, 920 F2d 441, 443 (7th Cir 1990).

420 944 F2d 339 (7th Cir 1991).

421 51 FEP Cas (BNA) 503 (ND Ill 1989).

422 *See also* Colgan v Fisher Scientific Co, 935 F2d 1407 (3d Cir), *cert denied,* 112 S Ct 379 (1991).

423 Presumably, the equitable estoppel and equitable tolling cases regarding extensions of the time for filing charges, see **§§6.17-6.21,** continue to apply.

424 932 F2d 473 (5th Cir 1991).

425 *Id* 478.

court deciding *Thomson v Prudential Insurance Co of America.*[426] Likewise, the court deciding *Smilan v United Airlines, Inc,*[427] which in part involved an allegedly discriminatory policy concerning rates of pay, ruled that the policy, being neutral on its face, should have been attacked when the plaintiff first knew of the policy, rather than when it ultimately had an impact on him.

In *Priester v Amoco Corp*[428] the court strained to devise a more-or-less hybrid approach that encompassed both *Lorance* and continuing violation analysis. The court reasoned that the plaintiff's cause of action vis-a-vis a mandatory retirement policy accrued when he was informed that the policy was applicable to him. That date had long passed, and so the defendant argued that the plaintiff's charge of unlawful discrimination was untimely. But the court further reasoned that the policy constituted a continuing violation, and so the plaintiff's cause of action did not accrue until the date on which the plaintiff was terminated because of the policy. In unpersuasively distinguishing *Lorance,* the *Priester* court focused on the fact that a seniority system was at issue in the Supreme Court ruling and so the interests of third parties, i.e., other workers whose rights were keyed to their positions on the seniority list, could be impaired by challenges made only years after the system's adoption. In contrast, here there were "no third parties who would be deprived of rights by a somewhat late challenge to a retirement policy."[429] In other words, this case did not "implicate the third party reliance of concern to the *Lorance* Court."[430]

Third, and in contrast to the second lesson drawn from *Lorance,* when a grievant attacks a facially discriminatory practice or policy he or she need not pursue legal redress as soon as the practice or policy is adopted. Rather, the grievant may wait until he or she suffers direct, personal harm. This conclusion—a

---

[426] 795 F Supp 1337 (DNJ 1992), *affd without opinion,* 993 F2d 226 (3d Cir 1993).

[427] 796 F Supp 723 (EDNY 1992).

[428] 60 FEP Cas (BNA) 1083 (ND Ill 1990).

[429] *Id* 1087.

[430] *Id.*

direct application of the caveat asserted by the *Lorance* Court itself[431]—was applied in *Cohn v AE Staley Manufacturing Co.*[432] Likewise, in *Smilan* another allegedly discriminatory policy provision (other than the one addressed *supra*) was deemed to be discriminatory on its face, and so the triggering event for the accrual of the charge-filing period was the date on which the plaintiff knew or should have known that the provision was going to be applied to him, rather than the date of the provision's adoption.[433]

Of course, there can be, and often will be, dispute as to whether a given policy is facially discriminatory.[434] In *Tusting v Bay View Federal Savings & Loan Association,*[435] for example, it was argued that a benefits policy was facially discriminatory in that it was being amended to give the choice to employees of either retiring early and retaining full post-retirement medical benefits, or staying on the job with reduced health insurance benefits from then on. The plaintiffs contended that because of their advanced ages and various medical problems, they were essentially uninsurable and so they had to take early retirement in order to be able to retain full health insurance coverage. The court agreed with the plaintiffs: "Such an age discrimination policy is facially discriminatory."[436]

---

[431] See **§6.15.**

[432] 734 F Supp 832 (ND Ill 1990); *see also* Equal Employment Opportunity Commn v Hawaii, 764 F Supp 158, 161 (D Haw 1991); Tusting v Bay View Fed Sav & Loan Assn, 54 FEP Cas (BNA) 403 (ND Cal 1990) (dealing with filing of suit, rather than charge); Equal Employment Opportunity Commn v City of Chicago, 51 FEP Cas (BNA) 503 (ND Ill 1989).

[433] 796 F Supp at 727.

[434] *See* Herrmann v Whirlpool Corp, 60 FEP Cas (BNA) 1130 (WD Mich 1992), where the court rejected the defendant's attempt to invoke *Lorance* by reasoning that whereas in *Lorance* the policy at issue had been fully explained to the plaintiffs at the time of its adoption, the policy at issue here, if it existed, had not been explained to the plaintiff. *Id* 1132 n1. What this analysis really seemed to be about was the issue of whether the policy was discriminatory on its face, or at least would have appeared to be so had the plaintiff known of it.

[435] 54 FEP Cas (BNA) 403 (ND Cal 1990).

[436] *Id* 405.

Lorance's Relation to Disparate Impact Analysis

The *Lorance* Court asserted that "[w]ith a facially neutral system the discriminatory act occurs *only* at the time of adoption, for each application is nondiscriminatory (seniority accrues for men and women on an identical basis)."[437] The Court further asserted that "each application . . . [of the seniority system at issue was] nondiscriminatory" because there was no disparity in treatment, given that men and women were treated identically).[438]

This reasoning has been applied in the ADEA context, as well. The court deciding *Equal Employment Opportunity Commission v City Colleges of Chicago*[439] ruled that a new limitations period did not begin with each application of an employee benefit plan. And in *Barrow v New Orleans Steamship Association*[440] the court similarly held untimely a charge of discrimination leveled against a facially neutral seniority system, where the plaintiff did not file his charge until a year after he became aware of the adverse effect of the system.

A limited relaxation of the rigidity of the *Lorance* Court's analysis was devised in *Davidson v Board of Governors.*[441] The case involved a collective bargaining agreement providing that when faculty members were first hired their salaries would be determined by individual negotiations, but thereafter a faculty member could obtain an individualized salary increase only if he or she produced a bona fide written offer of employment from some other entity. If he or she did so, he or she then would be eligible for a raise equalling the enhanced salary that offer entailed. The plaintiff argued that this compensation scheme was discriminatory:

> [A] compensation scheme under which an existing employee to get a raise must come up with an offer from

---

[437] 490 US at 912 n5 (emphasis in original).

[438] *Id.*

[439] 944 F2d 339 (7th Cir 1991).

[440] 932 F2d 473 (5th Cir 1991).

[441] 920 F2d 441 (7th Cir 1990).

> another employer, while the starting salary of a new employee is not subject to any such limitation, discriminates against older workers because existing employees are likely to be, on average, older than new ones. As Davidson sees it, his university's compensation scheme set in motion a chain of events certain to result eventually in his receiving a lower salary than some younger faculty members of no greater experience or ability. He can get raises only by producing offers from other employers, while new and presumably younger employees can sign on at any salary that the university is generous enough to offer them.[442]

In sum, the salary scheme had a disparate impact on older faculty, according to the plaintiff. The problem, in terms of the question of charge-filing, was that of determining when the time for filing began to run: when the plan was adopted, or when it culminated, in actuality, in the disparity that the plaintiff predicted. The court reasoned as follows:

> There are two ways to handle this problem. The first is to hold that the claim of a plaintiff who wants to proceed on a disparate impact theory of liability does not arise ("accrue" is the common legalism) until the disparate impact occurs. The second is to hold that although the claim arises when the practice that he is challenging is first made applicable to him (when he is hired, if the practice was adopted earlier, or when the practice is adopted, if as here he had been hired before), provided only that he knows about the practice and its application to his situation, the statute of limitations will be tolled until he has had a reasonable opportunity to determine whether he had a claim.[443]

The court opted for the second approach:

> After all, it is the practice of which the plaintiff is complaining (here, the scheme of compensating new faculty differ-

---

[442] *Id* 444.

[443] *Id* 445.

> ently from existing faculty), rather than the disparity of its impact upon the class to which he belongs; that disparity is just evidence, albeit essential evidence, that the practice is discriminatory, and hence actionable. What prevents his suing right off is not that the practice of which he complains has not been adopted as yet or has not been applied to him as yet but that he does not have enough evidence to determine whether the practice is unlawful and he could not obtain that evidence with due diligence—it doesn't yet exist. For such cases, equitable tolling provides the tailored solution.[444]

Thus, the district court had erred in dismissing the plaintiff's suit as time-barred. Rather, it should have determined whether, "shortly after the collective bargaining agreement was signed, [the plaintiff] had in hand, or could with due diligence have obtained, the minimum evidence he needed in order to determine whether he had a claim under the . . . [ADEA.]"[445]

The court deciding *Finnegan v Trans World Airlines, Inc,*[446] also rejected the notion that the date on which a cause of action accrues as to an ostensibly age-neutral policy that has a disparate impact on older workers is the date on which actual injury is experienced by the plaintiff employee. Rather, the date on which the adoption of the policy at issue is communicated to the affected employee is the date on which the cause of action accrues, or, if there is no such communication, it is the date on which the policy goes into effect.[447]

---

[444] *Id.*

[445] *Id.*

[446] 767 F Supp 867 (ND Ill 1991), *affd on other grounds,* 967 F2d 1161 (7th Cir 1992).

[447] *Id* 872; *accord* Kolman v Oscar Mayer Foods Corp, 53 FEP Cas (BNA) 1256, 1258 n4 (ED Pa 1990).

§6.17 —Equitable Tolling and Equitable Estoppel Applied to Charge-Filing: Generally

The courts are agreed that the time limits set by §7(d)[448] of the Age Discrimination in Employment Act (ADEA)[449] for the filing of charges of unlawful discrimination—i.e., a filing must be made with the Equal Employment Opportunity Commission (EEOC) within 180 or 300 days of the alleged unlawful discriminatory event or decision, or within 30 days of the termination of state proceedings[450]—are not jurisdictional in nature and so are subject to equitable modification. Given the right facts, a late-filing plaintiff may secure either the benefit of equitable tolling of the time requirements or equitable estoppel of a defendant's successfully asserting the lateness of filing as a basis for dismissal of the suit. It should be noted, however, that tolling and estoppel will only operate to negate the onus of untimely filing; they will not excuse a total failure to file a charge.[451]

Distinguishing Between Equitable Tolling and Equitable Estoppel

The Court of Appeals for the Fourth Circuit pointed out the distinction between equitable tolling and equitable estoppel in *Felty v Graves-Humphreys Co:*[452] "Equitable tolling focuses on the plaintiff's excusable ignorance of the employer's discriminatory act. Equitable estoppel, in contrast, examines the defendant's conduct and the extent to which the plaintiff has been induced to refrain from exercising his rights."[453] This distinction has

---

[448] 29 USC §626(d).

[449] *Id* §§621-634.

[450] See **§6.08.**

[451] *See, e.g.,* Hageman v Philips Roxane Labs, Inc, 623 F2d 1381, 1385 (9th Cir 1980); White v University of Mass, 26 FEP Cas (BNA) 1672, 1681 (D Mass 1981); Bengochea v Norcross, Inc, 464 F Supp 709 (ED Pa 1979); McCrickard v Acme Visible Records, Inc, 409 F Supp 341 (WD Va 1976).

[452] 785 F2d 762 (5th Cir 1988).

[453] *Id* 769 n4 (footnotes omitted). The distinction between equitable estoppel and equitable tolling was made, with critically important consequences for the litigants, in Cocke v Merrill Lynch & Co, Inc, 817 F2d 1559 (11th Cir 1987);

been echoed by other courts of appeals.[454] However, a number of courts have not so nicely delineated the two legal constructs; the blurring of the distinction between estoppel and tolling was particularly delineated by the Court of Appeals for the Seventh Circuit in deciding *Cada v Baxter Healthcare Corp:*[455]

> Many cases, it is true, in the age discrimination field as in other areas, fuse the two doctrines, presumably inadvertently. The most recent example in this circuit is *Stark v Dynascan Corp.*, 902 F.2d 549, 551 (7th Cir. 1990), which quotes from an earlier case the erroneous statement that "to invoke equitable tolling, the plaintiff must therefore show that the defendant attempted to mislead him." In fact that is what the plaintiff must show if he is trying to invoke equitable estoppel. For equitable tolling all he need show is that he could not by the exercise of reasonable diligence have discovered essential information bearing on his claim.[456]

A different view, and one that the *Cada* court criticized, was set forth by the Court of Appeals for the Second Circuit in *Dillman v Combustion Engineering, Inc,*[457] which in turn was quoting from a non-ADEA ruling, *Cerbone v International Ladies' Garment Workers' Union:*[458]

> "Unlike equitable tolling, which is invoked in cases where the plaintiff is ignorant of his cause of action because of the defendant's fraudulent concealment, equitable estop-

---

see also Morse v Daily Press, Inc, 822 F2d 1351 (4th Cir), *cert denied,* 484 US 965 (1987).

454 *See, e.g.*, Mercado-Garcia v Ponce Fed Bank, 979 F2d 890, 895-96 (1st Cir 1992); Rhodes v Guiberson Oil Tools Div, 927 F2d 876, 878 (5th Cir), *cert denied,* 112 S Ct 198 (1991); Mull v ARCO Durethene Plastics, Inc, 784 F2d 284, 291 (7th Cir 1986).

455 920 F2d 446 (7th Cir 1990), *cert denied,* 111 S Ct 2916 (1991).

456 *Id* 452.

457 784 F2d 57 (2d Cir 1986).

458 768 F2d 45 (2d Cir 1985).

> pel is invoked in cases where the plaintiff knew of the existence of his cause of action but the defendant's conduct caused him to delay bringing his lawsuit."[459]

Thus, for the *Dillman* court, the defendant's misconduct was an element not only in equitable estoppel situations—a posture with which all courts would agree—but also in equitable tolling situations. It is this latter interpretation that departed from the positions articulated in *Felty, Cada,* and other decisions.[460] Indeed, the Court of Appeals for the Seventh Circuit, in deciding *Cada,* pointed out the error—in its view—of the *Cerbone* court's (and therefore the *Dillman* court's) reasoning:

> *Cerbone* . . . fuses the two tolling doctrines . . . by saying that equitable tolling differs from equitable estoppel only in that the plaintiff does not know he has a claim in the former case and does in the latter; in both cases the defendant has taken steps to prevent the plaintiff from suing. Plainly, the second part of this proposition is incorrect. . . . [E]quitable tolling does not require any conduct by the defendant.[461]

The arguable trenchancy of the *Cada* critique notwithstanding, other courts in addition to the *Dillman* court have not subscribed to the clear-cut distinction espoused in *Cada,* and instead have deemed a defendant's actions at least relevant to the tolling question.[462] Indeed, as the quotation from *Dillman* indicates, some courts even seem to require affirmative misconduct by the employer for equitable tolling to come into play.[463]

---

[459] *Id* 60-61 (quoting *Cerbone,* 768 F2d at 49-50).

[460] See cases cited in note 454.

[461] 920 F2d at 452.

[462] *See, e.g.,* Miller v Beneficial Mgmt Corp, 977 F2d 834, 845 (3d Cir 1992); Wilkerson v Siegfried Ins Agency, Inc, 621 F2d 1042, 1045 (10th Cir 1980). While Harris v WGN Continental Broadcasting Co, 650 F Supp 568, 574 n9 (ND Ill 1986), would fall into this camp, the later *Cada* decision by the Court of Appeals for the Seventh Circuit negated its viability.

[463] *See* Reyher v Champion Intl Corp, 975 F2d 483, 489 (8th Cir 1992); Foutty v Equifax Servs, Inc, 764 F Supp 621 (D Kan 1991); Foutty v Equifax Servs, Inc, 762 F Supp 295, 298 (D Kan 1991).

Whatever the judicial posture as to the significance of the defendant's words or actions, it should be noted that there need not be bad intent on the employer's part for estoppel to apply, so far as some courts are concerned.[464]

Factors Relevant to Determining Appropriateness of Halting the Running of the Charge-Filing Period

The Court of Appeals for the First Circuit set forth several factors relevant to determining whether the charge-filing time requirements should be tolled[465] in *Kale v Combined Insurance Co of America*:[466]

> Courts have often cited to five equitable factors that should be weighed when considering whether to allow equitable tolling in a given case. These factors are: "(1) lack of actual notice of filing requirement; (2) lack of constructive knowledge of the filing requirement; (3) diligence in pursuing one's rights; (4) absence of prejudice to the defendant; and (5) a plaintiff's reasonableness in remaining ignorant of the notice requirement."[467]

The *Kale* court further observed as follows:

---

[464] *See* Herrmann v Whirlpool Corp, 60 FEP Cas (BNA) 1130, 1134 (WD Mich 1992). See generally **§6.20.**

[465] The term "tolled" is used here in the generic sense to include both equitable tolling and equitable estoppel situations.

[466] 861 F2d 746 (1st Cir 1988).

[467] *Id* 752 (quoting Andrews v Orr, 851 F2d 146, 151 (6th Cir 1988)); *accord* Abbott v Moore Business Forms, Inc, 439 F Supp 643, 646 (DNH 1977) (citations omitted), *quoted with approval in* Wright v Tennessee, 628 F2d 949, 953 (6th Cir 1980) (*en banc*); Perazzo v Top Value Enters, Inc, 590 F Supp 428 (SD Ohio 1984); *see also* Boothe v New York Assn for the Blind, 524 F Supp 736, 738 (SDNY 1981) ("Among the specific considerations courts have weighed . . . are the extent of plaintiff's untimeliness, whether the employer was responsible for plaintiff's failure to act in time, and whether the employer was aware of plaintiff's intent to sue"). For a particularly harsh application of the diligence factor, see Meckes v Reynolds Metals Co, 604 F Supp 598 (ND Ala), *affd without opinion,* 776 F2d 1055 (11th Cir 1985).

> In the analogous area of equitable tolling under Title VII [of the Civil Rights Act of 1964, 42 USC §§2000e through 2000e-17], the Supreme Court has modified one aspect of this approach by holding that "absence of prejudice is a factor to be considered in determining whether the doctrine of equitable tolling should apply once a factor that might justify tolling is identified, [but] it is not an independent basis for invoking the doctrine."[468]

The lack of prejudice to the defendant was dispositive in *Petrelli v City of Mount Vernon,*[469] where the court recounted the plaintiff's "persistent efforts to convince Mount Vernon that it was misapplying the relevant law,"[470] the result being to "certainly put Mount Vernon on notice that litigation was a possibility."[471]

Without question, the plaintiff's knowledge is a relevant factor in the tolling determination. As a general matter, a grievant's ignorance of the ADEA, whether due to his or her own lack of knowledge or due to his or her failure to seek legal counsel, will not suffice to justify tolling; there must be something more for a grievant to be able to evoke judicial relief from the onus of his or her dilatoriness.[472] Thus, the Court of Appeals for the

---

[468] 861 F2d at 753 (quoting Baldwin County Welcome Ctr v Brown, 466 US 147, 152 (1984)).

[469] 796 F Supp 748 (SDNY 1992), *revd & remanded on other grounds,* 9 F3d 250 (2d Cir 1993).

[470] *Id* 753.

[471] *Id.*

[472] *See, e.g.*, Barrow v New Orleans SS Assn, 932 F2d 473, 478 (5th Cir 1991); Lasson v American Wheel & Brake, Inc, 610 F2d 506 (8th Cir 1979); Quina v Owens-Corning Fiberglass Corp, 575 F2d 1115 (5th Cir 1978); Begley v Howmet Turbine Components Corp, 47 FEP Cas (BNA) 1880 (ND Ind 1988); Mull v ARCO Durethene Plastics, Inc, 599 F Supp 158, 164 (ND Ill 1984), *affd on other grounds,* 784 F2d 284 (7th Cir 1986); Gray v Mortgage Bankers Assn of Am, 492 F Supp 914, 916 (DDC 1980); Wagner v Sperry Univac, Div of Sperry Rand Corp, 458 F Supp 505, 515 (ED Pa 1978), *affd without opinion,* 624 F2d 1092 (3d Cir 1980); Thomas v Blue Cross & Blue Shield, 449 F Supp 1021, 1025 (MDNC 1978); *see also* Pieckelun v Kimberly-Clark Corp, 493 F Supp 93 (ED Pa 1980); Morris v Frank IX & Sons, Inc, 486 F Supp 728, 734 (WD Va 1980); Cutright v General Motors Corp, 486 F Supp 590 (WD Pa 1980).

Eleventh Circuit stated in *McClinton v Alabama By-Products Corp*[473] as follows:

> When an employee is generally aware of his rights, ignorance of specific legal rights or failure to seek legal advice should not toll the [limitations] period. A contrary result would permit an aggrieved employee aware of his general rights to sit on those rights until he leisurely decided to take action. This would be inconsistent with and undermine the underlying ADEA policy of encouraging speedy, nonjudicial resolutions to age discrimination employment disputes.[474]

Judicial refusals to toll the running of the filing period have involved looking both to the plaintiff's specific knowledge of the filing requirements,[475] and to his or her general knowledge[476] of the ADEA. Insofar as the latter type of knowledge is concerned, the *Kale* court stated that tolling is not warranted where the plaintiff had actual knowledge of his or her rights, and that "[a]ctual knowledge occurs where an employee either learns or is told of his ADEA rights, even if he becomes only generally aware of the fact that there is a statute outlawing age discrimina-

---

[473] 743 F2d 1483 (11th Cir 1984).

[474] *Id* 1486; *accord* Jackson v Richards Medical Co, 961 F2d 575, 580 (6th Cir 1992); *see also* Callan v Pepsi-Cola Bottling Co, Inc, 801 F Supp 448, 455 n7 (D Kan 1992).

[475] *See, e.g.*, Greene v Whirlpool Corp, 708 F2d 128 (4th Cir 1983), *cert denied*, 464 US 1042 (1984); Hageman v Philips Roxane Labs, Inc, 623 F2d 1381, 1386 (9th Cir 1980); Templeton v Western Union Tel Co, 607 F2d 89, 91 (5th Cir 1979); Powell v Southwestern Bell Tel Co, 494 F2d 485, 490 (5th Cir 1974); Moon v Aeronca, Inc, 541 F Supp 747 (SD Ohio 1982); Tobin v Trans Union Sys Corp, 488 F Supp 622 (ED Pa 1980); Parrish v Schlumberger, Ltd, 19 FEP Cas (BNA) 717, 720 (SD Tex 1979); *see also* Perazzo v Top Value Enters, Inc, 590 F Supp 428 (SD Ohio 1984).

[476] *See, e.g.*, Nielsen v Western Elec Co, 603 F2d 741, 744 (8th Cir 1979); Barnes v Hillhaven Rehabilitation & Convalescent Ctr, 686 F Supp 311, 314 (ND Ga 1988); Welty v SF&G, Inc, 605 F Supp 1548, 1564 (ND Ala 1985); Chambers v European Am Bank & Trust Co, 601 F Supp 630 (EDNY 1985); Draeger v Jockey Intl, Inc, 583 F Supp 570 (SDNY), *affd without opinion*, 751 F2d 368 (2d Cir 1984).

tion and providing relief therefor."[477] In deciding *Mercado-Garcia v Ponce Federal Bank*[478] the same court, in concluding that the plaintiff had actual knowledge of his rights under the ADEA, noted that in his position as human resources manager the plaintiff had himself counseled the defendant regarding age discrimination matters.

In considering this knowledge factor, the courts have taken into account the plaintiff's general level of intelligence.[479] It has been held that the filing period may be tolled for that period of time during which the claimant was adjudicated mentally incompetent or institutionalized pursuant to a diagnosis of mental incompetence.[480] In contrast to these cases demonstrating particular solicitude for plaintiffs, in cases where grievants have been assisted by attorneys, the courts have been particularly reluctant to relieve them of the onus of late filings by tolling the charge-filing time requirements.[481] If, however, the attorney pro-

---

[477] 861 F2d at 753.

[478] 979 F2d 896 (1st Cir 1992).

[479] *See, e.g.*, Draeger v Jockey Intl, Inc, 583 F Supp 570 (SDNY), *affd without opinion*, 751 F2d 368 (2d Cir 1984); Gray v Mortgage Bankers Assn of Am, 492 F Supp 914, 916 (DDC 1980).

[480] Bassett v Sterling Drug, Inc, 578 F Supp 1244 (SD Ohio 1984), *appeal dismissed without opinion*, 770 F2d 165 (6th Cir 1985). *But see* Kerver v Exxon Prod Research Co, 40 FEP Cas (BNA) 1567 (SD Tex 1986) (plaintiff's depression is insufficient justification for tolling where plaintiff not rendered non compos mentis).

[481] *See, e.g.*, Kale v Combined Ins Co of Am, 861 F2d 746, 753 (1st Cir 1988) ("[c]onstructive knowledge . . . is attributed to an employee in situations where he has retained an attorney"); Morse v Daily Press, Inc, 826 F2d 1251 (4th Cir), *cert denied*, 484 US 965 (1987); Kephart v Institute of Gas Technology, 581 F2d 1287 (7th Cir 1978); Burkley v Martin's Super Markets, Inc, 741 F Supp 161 (ND Ind 1990); Williams v Whirlpool Corp, 41 FEP Cas (BNA) 383 (WD Ark 1986); Cole v CBS, Inc, 634 F Supp 1558 (SDNY 1986); Jacobson v Pitman-Moore, Inc, 624 F Supp 937 (D Minn 1985), *affd without opinion*, 786 F2d 1172 (8th Cir 1986); Downey v Firestone Tire & Rubber Co, 35 FEP Cas (BNA) 30 (DDC 1984), *revd & remanded without opinion*, 762 F2d 137 (DC Cir 1985); Hay v Wells Cargo, Inc, 596 F Supp 635 (D Nev 1984), *affd without opinion*, 796 F2d 478 (9th Cir 1986); Sprott v Avon Prods, Inc, 596 F Supp 178 (SDNY 1984); Leite v Kennecott Copper Corp, 558 F Supp 1170 (D Mass), *affd without opinion*, 720 F2d 658 (1st Cir 1983); Knight v County of Dane, 30 FEP Cas (BNA) 1107 (WD Wis 1982); Sanders v Duke Univ, 538 F Supp 1143, 1146 n2 (MDNC 1982); Needham v Beecham, Inc, 515 F Supp 460, 467 (D

vides the plaintiff with erroneous information, tolling may be justified.[482] Moreover, the fact that the plaintiff is an attorney need not necessarily preclude the application of equitable tolling.[483]

Length of Time For Which the Running of the Charge-Filing Period Will be Tolled

The question of how long the statute of limitations should be tolled elicited particular attention in *Cada v Baxter Healthcare Corp*,[484] a case in which the court concluded that equitable estoppel could not be invoked and so only equitable tolling came into play. The plaintiff initially was told of his termination on May 5, 1987, but he argued that a later date, May 22, was the date on which he actually learned—from the proper supervising official—of his discharge. On July 7, while Cada was still on the job, his replacement—a young woman—took over. Cada claimed that it was not until he learned who was replacing him that he had a basis for believing he was a victim of age discrimination. Ultimately, Cada filed a charge of unlawful discrimination with the EEOC on March 4, 1988. If the statute of limitations was tolled during the period running from May 5 to July 7, 1987, Cada's charge would have been timely.

Me 1981); Downie v Electric Boat Div, 504 F Supp 1082, 1086 (D Conn 1980); Tobin v Trans Union Sys Corp, 488 F Supp 622, 628 (ED Pa 1980); Noto v JFD Elecs Corp, 446 F Supp 92, 94 (EDNC 1978); Abbott v Moore Business Forms, Inc, 439 F Supp 643, 646 (DNH 1977); Wagner v Sperry Univac, Div of Sperry Rand Corp, 458 F Supp 505, 514 (ED Pa 1978), *affd without opinion*, 624 F2d 1092 (3d Cir 1980). *But see* Meyer v Riegel Prod Corp, 720 F2d 303 (3d Cir 1983), *cert dismissed*, 465 US 1091 (1984); Quina v Owens-Corning Fiberglass Corp, 575 F2d 1115, 1118 (5th Cir 1978); Dartt v Shell Oil Co, 539 F2d 1256, 1261 n4 (10th Cir 1976), *affd by an equally divided Court*, 434 US 99 (1977); Quicker v American V Mueller, 712 F Supp 824, 829 (D Colo 1989); Slenkamp v Borough of Brentwood, 603 F Supp 1298 (WD Pa 1985), *affd without opinion*, 826 F2d 1057 (3d Cir 1987); Jacobson v Pitman-Moore, Inc, 573 F Supp 565 (D Minn 1983); Volk v Multi-Media, Inc, 516 F Supp 157, 162 (SD Ohio 1981).

482 *See, e.g.*, Quina v Owens-Corning Fiberglass Corp, 575 F2d 1115, 1118 (5th Cir 1978); Fulton v NCR Corp, 472 F Supp 377 (WD Va 1979).

483 Miller v Beneficial Management Corp, 977 F2d 834, 845 n6 (3d Cir 1992).

484 920 F2d 446 (7th Cir 1990), *cert denied*, 111 S Ct 2916 (1991).

The court asserted that "if fraudulent concealment [by the employer] is shown the court must subtract from the period of limitations the entire period in which the tolling condition is in effect, . . . for otherwise the defendant would obtain a benefit from his inequitable conduct."[485] However, the court took a different view regarding accounting for time in an equitable tolling (as opposed to estoppel) situation, given that in this situation both parties are "innocent."[486] The court explained its position:

> When Cada discovered on July 7 that he had been replaced by a young and (as it seemed to him) inexperienced employee, he still had eight months in which to file his claim. . . . He offered no excuse for the delay. . . .
>
> We do not think equitable tolling should bring about an automatic extension of the statute of limitations by the length of the tolling period or any other definite term.[487]

The court went on to enunciate an applicable legal presumption:

> When the necessary information is gathered after the claim arose but before the statute of limitations has run, the presumption should be that the plaintiff could bring suit within the statutory period and should have done so. The presumption will be more easily rebuttable the nearer the date of obtaining the information is to the date at which the statutory period runs out.[488]

Here, the interval was eight months between the plaintiff's acquisition of information sufficient to raise a suspicion that he was a victim of age discrimination and the filing of his charge. Reasoning that "a plaintiff who invokes equitable tolling to suspend the statute of limitations must bring suit within a reason-

[485] *Id* 452.

[486] *Id.*

[487] *Id.*

[488] *Id* 453.

able time after he has obtained, or by due diligence could have obtained, the necessary information,''[489] the court held Cada's charge to have been untimely filed.[490]

In brief, once a grievant learns of facts that suggest that he or she is the victim of age discrimination, the tolling ends and the grievant then must act diligently to protect his or her rights.[491]

Burdens of Proof

It is the plaintiff who bears the burden either of "proving that. . . . [that defendant] is estopped from relying on the EEOC filing period,''[492] according to one panel of the Court of Appeals for the Fifth Circuit, or of "demonstrating a factual basis" for tolling, according to other panels of the same court.[493] Similarly, the district court deciding *Gore v Pee Dee Farm Credit Service*[494]

---

[489] *Id; accord* Allen v Diebold, Inc, 807 F Supp 1308, 1318-19 (ND Ohio 1992).

[490] In Young v SCM Corp, 45 FEP Cas (BNA) 393 (ND Ill 1988), the court stated that tolling would be appropriate until such time as the facts that would support a charge of discrimination were apparent or should have been apparent to a reasonable person. To the extent that this formulation conflicts with *Cada,* if it does, it of course is invalid.

[491] *See* Stafford v Sierra Vista Fry Fire Dist, 61 FEP Cas (BNA) 1097, 1099-1100 (Ariz 1993). For a particularly harsh application of this proposition, see Meckes v Reynolds Metals Co, 604 F Supp 598 (ND Ala), *affd without opinion,* 776 F2d 1055 (11th Cir 1985). For a much more generous willingness to find sufficient ambiguity in the situation to justify the plaintiff's delaying filing, see Shockley v Vermont State Colleges, 38 FEP Cas (BNA) 1523 (D Vt 1984). Subsequently, however, a different district court judge held that the plaintiff's delay was not justified, and this ruling was affirmed. Shockley v Vermont State Colleges, 793 F2d 478 (1st Cir 1986); *see also* Kerver v Exxon Prod Research Co, 40 FEP Cas (BNA) 1567 (SD Tex 1986).

[492] Rhodes v Guiberson Oil Tools Div, 927 F2d 876, 879 (5th Cir), *cert denied,* 112 S Ct 198 (1991).

[493] Conaway v Control Data Corp, 955 F2d 358, 362 (5th Cir), *cert denied,* 113 S Ct 186 (1992); Blumberg v HCA Management Co, Inc, 848 F2d 642 (5th Cir 1988), *cert denied,* 488 US 1007 (1989).

[494] 60 FEP Cas (BNA) 240 (DSC 1992), *affd without opinion,* 1 F3d 1233 (4th Cir 1993).

stated that "[t]he burden of establishing equitable tolling rests with the plaintiff."[495]

If the plaintiff satisfies his or her burden, the defendant will then bear the burden of proof in overcoming the claimed basis for tolling—at least when that basis is the failure of the employer to have posted the requisite workplace notice regarding the ADEA.[496]

The Roles of Juries and Courts

It has been held that the determination of whether sufficient grounds exist for equitable tolling is properly a jury question.[497] More specifically, it has been held, or asserted, in cases in which the plaintiff's lack of knowledge of the ADEA was the basis for late filing that the question of when the employee acquired actual knowledge of his or ADEA rights is a fact question, and thus for the jury to decide.[498] Accordingly, in *Beshears v Asbill*[499] it was deemed to be a jury question as to whether an employee manual setting forth a condemnation of age discrimination, but not identifying the ADEA as a basis for that condemnation, constituted a means for employees to obtain knowledge that age discrimination is illegal.

In *Rhodes v Guiberson Oil Tools Division*[500] the court dealt with a situation where the parties agreed that the issues of equitable estoppel and tolling would be decided by the magistrate; on

---

[495] *Id* 243.

[496] See **§6.18.**

[497] Pruet Prod Co v Ayles, 573 F Supp 895 (SD Miss 1983), *affd on other grounds,* 784 F2d 1275 (5th Cir 1986); *see also* Dillman v Combustion Engg, Inc, 784 F2d 57, 61 (2d Cir 1986); Equal Employment Opportunity Commn v Ford Motor Co, 573 F Supp 755, 757 (D Colo 1983), *affd on other grounds,* 732 F2d 120 (10th Cir 1984).

[498] Vance v Whirlpool Corp, 716 F2d 1010, 1013 (4th Cir 1983), *cert denied,* 465 US 1102 (1984); Elliott v Group Medical & Surgical Serv, 714 F2d 556, 563-64 (5th Cir 1983), *cert denied,* 467 US 1215 (1984); Galvin v Vermont, 598 F Supp 144, 148-49 (D Vt 1984).

[499] 930 F2d 1348, 1352-53 (8th Cir 1991).

[500] 927 F2d 876, 881 (5th Cir), *cert denied,* 112 S Ct 198 (1991).

appeal the court "review[ed] the applicability of equitable estoppel to the facts of . . . [the] case de novo as a question of law."[501]

§6.18 —Equitable Tolling and Estoppel Due to the Covered Entity's Failure to Post Notices

Section 8[502] of the Age Discrimination in Employment Act (ADEA)[503] requires each entity covered by the Act, i.e., employers, employment agencies, and labor organizations, to post in "conspicuous places upon its premises a notice prepared or approved by the Equal Employment Opportunity Commission (EEOC) setting forth information as the Commission deems appropriate to effectuate the purposes of" the ADEA.

In deciding *Kale v Combined Insurance Co of America*[504] the Court of Appeals for the First Circuit made the following observation as to the content of the required notice:

> Congress has delegated [by virtue of §8] the responsibility for the make-up of the notices to the EEOC. . . . Absent a notice that is so inadequate as to not allow employees a "meaningful opportunity" to become aware of their rights under the ADEA, the EEOC's judgment of what is a proper notice will not be disturbed.[505]

The court proceeded to reject the argument that the notices posted by the defendant were insufficient because they failed to specifically detail the filing periods for charges of unlawful discrimination.

Failure to Post Notice as Basis for Tolling

According to the Court of Appeals for the Seventh Circuit, the posting of the required notice "creates a presumption that

---

[501] *Id* 881.

[502] 29 USC §627.

[503] *Id* §§621-634.

[504] 861 F2d 746 (1st Cir 1988).

[505] *Id* 754.

the employee could have learned of the EEOC requirements."[506] Correlatively, there is a very considerable body of judicial rulings holding that the failure of a covered entity to post the required notice will justify tolling the running of the charge-filing period.[507] The Court of Appeals for the Seventh Circuit explained the justification for tolling in deciding *Kephart v Institute of Gas Technology:*[508]

> It is quite apparent that Congress imposed this requirement on employers to insure that protected employees would be fully informed of their rights under the ADEA. And it is equally apparent that this end would not be realized if employers were free to breach the posting requirement without penalty.[509]

In *Wilkerson v Siegfried Insurance Agency, Inc,*[510] the Court of Appeals for the Tenth Circuit stated that "the simple failure to post notices, without intent to actively mislead the plaintiff . . . , does not extend the time" for filing a discrimination charge.[511] Typically, however, the cases do not require bad intent on the defendant's part as a condition precedent to a court's tolling the

---

506 Wheeldon v Monon Corp, 946 F2d 533, 537 (7th Cir 1991).

507 *See, e.g.,* Vance v Whirlpool Corp, 716 F2d 1010 (4th Cir 1983), *cert denied,* 465 US 1102 (1984); Elliott v Group Medical & Surgical Serv, 714 F2d 556, 563-64 (5th Cir 1983), *cert denied,* 467 US 1215 (1984); Kephart v Institute of Gas Technology, 581 F2d 1287 (7th Cir 1978); Bonham v Dresser Indus, Inc, 569 F2d 187, 193 (3d Cir 1977), *cert denied,* 439 US 821 (1978); Klausing v Whirlpool Corp, 623 F Supp 156 (SD Ohio 1985), *appeal dismissed without opinion,* 785 F2d 309 (6th Cir 1986); Pirone v Home Ins Co, 507 F Supp 1281, 1287 (SDNY 1981), *affd without opinion,* 742 F2d 1430 (2d Cir 1983); Kazanzas v Walt Disney World Co, 518 F Supp 292 (MD Fla 1981), *revd on other grounds,* 704 F2d 1527 (11th Cir), *cert denied,* 464 US 982 (1983); Weiler v National Multiple Sclerosis Socy, 27 FEP Cas (BNA) 1460 (SDNY 1980); Franci v AVCO Corp, 460 F Supp 389, 397-98 (D Conn 1978); Bishop v Jelleff Assocs, 398 F Supp 579, 592-93 (DDC 1974); *see also* Comfort v Rensselaer Polytechnic Inst, 575 F Supp 258 (NDNY 1983) (dictum).

508 581 F2d 1287 (7th Cir 1978).

509 *Id* 1289.

510 683 F2d 344 (10th Cir 1982).

511 *Id* 347.

charge-filing deadlines, and so the *Wilkerson* court's position is an unusual one. Still, the mere failure of a covered entity to post the requisite notice need not automatically lead to tolling:

> [A] number of courts have held that . . . [the failure to post a notice] will support equitable tolling without going any further. . . .
>
> We do not think, however, that the inquiry should end there. The court should also assess any countervailing equities against the plaintiff. For example, did he diligently pursue his claim, . . . was his ignorance of his rights unreasonable under the circumstances, . . . and would allowing equitable tolling still fulfill the basic purposes behind the limited filing period—namely, providing the government an opportunity to conciliate while the complaint is fresh and giving early notice to the employer of possible litigation. . . . Finally, even if the court finds that the above factors call for equitable tolling, it must then take account of the degree to which delay prejudices the defendant.[512]

Knowledge on Grievant's Part as Precluding Tolling Even Where Notice Was Not Posted

A plaintiff who is aware of his or her ADEA rights cannot rely on the employer's failure to post the notice as a justification for having not filed a timely charge of unlawful discrimination.[513] Accordingly, a person whose job entails having particular exper-

---

[512] Kale v Combined Ins Co of Am, 861 F2d 746, 753 (1st Cir 1988) (citations and footnote omitted).

[513] *See, e.g.,* Callowhill v Allen-Sherman-Hoff, Inc, 832 F2d 269, 272 n3 (3d Cir 1987), *cert denied,* 485 US 962 (1988); Greene v Whirlpool Corp, 708 F2d 128 (4th Cir 1983), *cert denied,* 464 US 1042 (1984); Templeton v Western Union Tel Co, 607 F2d 89 (5th Cir 1979); Draeger v Jockey Intl, Inc, 583 F Supp 570 (SDNY), *affd without opinion,* 751 F2d 368 (2d Cir 1984); Butz v Hertz Corp, 554 F Supp 1178 (WD Pa 1983); Knight v County of Dane, 30 FEP Cas (BNA) 1107 (WD Wis 1982); Parrish v Schlumberger, Ltd, 19 FEP Cas (BNA) 717 (SD Tex 1979); Malinowski v State Farm Ins Co, 18 FEP Cas (BNA) 693, 695 (WD Pa 1978).

tise regarding personnel matters,[514] or who is himself or herself responsible for posting the notice at issue, cannot point to his or her employer's failure to post that notice as an equitable basis for being relieved of the onus of an untimely filing.[515]

Even if an employee only had general knowledge of his or her rights, the fact that he or she did not have specific knowledge of his or her rights under the ADEA[516] or of the ADEA's timing requirements will not, according to some courts, justify tolling.[517] Similarly, awareness by a grievant of a right not to be discriminated against on the basis of age can preclude equitable estoppel, even if the employee was not specifically aware of the ADEA.[518] More than that, in the Eighth Circuit, if the employee had the means of obtaining knowledge of his or her rights under the ADEA by virtue of his or her particular job function, equitable tolling will not be justified even if the employee did not in fact obtain such knowledge.[519] Thus, plaintiffs who "by virtue of their education, training and experience as personnel managers . . . [possess] a general awareness of their ADEA rights or . . . [have] the means to obtain such knowledge . . . are not

---

514 *See* Pruet Prod Co v Ayles, 784 F2d 1275, 1280 (5th Cir 1986) (plaintiff had been responsible for personnel matters); Fressell v AT&T Technologies, Inc, 35 FEP Cas (BNA) 658 (ND Ga 1984) (employees could not claim ignorance when their job duties included being acquainted with employer's affirmative action program, which included nondiscrimination on basis of age).

515 *See, e.g.*, Wilkerson v Siegfried Ins Agency, Inc, 683 F2d 344, 347 (10th Cir 1982); Adams v Federal Signal Corp, 559 F2d 433 (5th Cir 1977); Malinowski v State Farm Ins Co, 18 FEP Cas (BNA) 693 (WD Pa 1978).

516 McBrayer v City of Marietta, 967 F2d 546, 548 (11th Cir 1992).

517 *See, e.g.*, Schroeder v Copley Newspaper, 879 F2d 266, 271-72 (7th Cir 1989); Clark v Resistoflex Co, a Div of Unidynamics Corp, 854 F2d 762, 768 (5th Cir 1988); DeBrunner v Midway Equip Co, 803 F2d 950 (8th Cir 1986); McClinton v Alabama By-Products Corp, 743 F2d 1483, 1486 (11th Cir 1984); Glass v IDS Fin Servs, Inc, 778 F Supp 1029, 1047 (D Minn 1991).

518 *See, e.g.*, McClinton v Alabama By-Products Corp, 743 F2d 1483 (11th Cir 1984); Chambers v European Am Bank & Trust Co, 601 F Supp 630 (EDNY 1985). Equitable estoppel and equitable tolling, while different, often are confused. See **§6.17.**

519 Beshears v Asbill, 930 F2d 1348, 1351-52 (8th Cir 1991); DeBrunner v Midway Equip Co, 803 F2d 950, 952 (8th Cir 1986).

entitled to invoke equitable tolling on the basis of . . . [an employer's] failure to post ADEA notices."[520]

There is case law supporting the proposition that once an individual who is unfamiliar with the ADEA learns of his or her rights under the Act, the filing period will then begin to run.[521] In particular, if an individual unaware of his or her rights retains an attorney, that action will begin the running of the filing period.[522] This is so even if the attorney is ignorant of the ADEA and/or

---

[520] Glass v IDS Fin Servs, Inc, 778 F Supp 1029, 1047 (D Minn 1991). The court noted that while four of the plaintiffs claimed that they did not know that age discrimination was illegal during the time they were division managers, they "all admitted that they had access to information about their ADEA rights as a result of home office sales bulletins, . . . bulletins, the marketing manager's EEOC handbook or the division office policy and procedure manual." *Id* 1047 n24. Thus, they "had the means to obtain information concerning their ADEA rights, and . . . [therefore they were] not entitled to equitable tolling[.]" *Id.*

[521] *See, e.g.*, Kephart v Institute of Gas Technology, 581 F2d 1287, 1289 (7th Cir 1978); Bonham v Dresser Indus, Inc, 569 F2d 187 (3d Cir 1977), *cert denied,* 439 US 821 (1978); Edwards v Kaiser Aluminum & Chem Sales, Inc, 515 F2d 1195, 1200 (5th Cir 1975); Less v Nestle Co, Inc, 705 F Supp 110, 115 (WDNY 1988); McCrickard v Acme Visible Records, Inc, 409 F Supp 341 (WD Va 1976). In Holly v City of Naperville, 571 F Supp 668 (ND Ill 1983), the court acknowledged that the failure to post the notice would toll the running of the filing period. However, it then went on to reason that (1) the plaintiff's filing of his suit on November 15, 1982, made obvious that he at least had knowledge of his rights under the ADEA by that date; (2) he thus should have filed his EEOC charge within 180 (or 300) days after that date; (3) he had not done so; and (4) therefore the defendant's argument that the plaintiff had failed to file a timely administrative charge was a winning one when addressed by the court some seven months after suit was filed. In brief, the lesson confirmed by *Holly* is that while a failure of the employer to post the requisite ADEA notice will toll the running of the filing period, the employee may not rely upon that failure to entirely forego filing an administrative charge once he or she has knowledge of the Act, and instead simply proceed to court.

[522] *See, e.g.*, Daugherity v Traylor Bros, Inc, 970 F2d 348, 353 n8 (7th Cir 1992); Kale v Combined Ins Co of Am, 861 F2d 746, 753 (1st Cir 1988); Bonham v Dresser Indus, Inc, 569 F2d 187 (3d Cir 1977), *cert denied,* 439 US 821 (1978); Edwards v Kaiser Aluminum & Chem Sales, Inc, 515 F2d 1195, 1198 (5th Cir 1975); Less v Nestle Co, Inc, 705 F Supp 110, 115 (WDNY 1988); *see also* Vance v Whirlpool Corp, 716 F2d 1010, 1012 (4th Cir 1983), *cert denied,* 465 US 1102 (1984); Abbott v Moore Business Forms, 439 F Supp 643 (DNH 1977).

its filing requirements.[523] If the grievant is an attorney, he or she generally will be charged with knowledge of the ADEA, notwithstanding not having had any experience with it.[524] On the other hand, if an inquiry simply is made of an attorney in a situation where the grievant has not entered into an attorney-client relationship, the information (and/or misinformation) given by the attorney may not constitute a bar to tolling.[525] Contact between an individual and a lawyer solely for the purpose of the employee's determining whether to retain the attorney will not commence the running of the time period.[526] Advice given to the grievant by the defendant's attorney also will not suffice for commencement of the running of the time period.[527] And consultation with an attorney regarding pension rights will not commence the running of the time period if the attorney and the plaintiff never discussed the issue of age discrimination.[528]

All the foregoing variations concerning communications with attorneys aside, the failure of a grievant to consult an attorney will not justify tolling.[529]

---

[523] *See, e.g.,* Kephart v Institute of Gas Technology, 581 F2d 1287 (7th Cir 1978); Downey v Firestone Tire & Rubber Co, 35 FEP Cas (BNA) 30 (DDC 1984), *revd & remanded without opinion,* 762 F2d 137 (DC Cir 1985); Knight v County of Dane, 30 FEP Cas (BNA) 1107 (WD Wis 1982). *But see* Quina v Owens-Corning Fiberglass Corp, 575 F2d 1115, 1118 (5th Cir 1978); Jacobson v Pitman-Moore, Inc, 573 F Supp 565 (D Minn 1983); Fulton v NCR Corp, 472 F Supp 377 (WD Va 1979).

[524] Pruet Prod Co v Ayles, 784 F2d 1275, 1280 (5th Cir 1986).

[525] *See, e.g.,* Quicker v American V Mueller, 712 F Supp 824, 829 (D Colo 1989); Slenkamp v Borough of Brentwood, 603 F Supp 1298 (WD Pa 1985), *affd without opinion,* 826 F2d 1027 (3d Cir 1987).

[526] Bass v Burleigh, 727 F Supp 1030 (MD La 1989), *appeal dismissed without opinion,* 918 F2d 176 (5th Cir 1990); Linn v Andover Newton Theological Sch, 642 F Supp 11 (D Mass 1985), *vacated on other grounds & remanded,* 874 F2d 1 (1st Cir 1989).

[527] Linn v Andover Newton Technological Sch, 642 F Supp 11, 14 (D Mass 1985), *vacated on other grounds & remanded,* 874 F2d 1 (1st Cir 1989).

[528] Nogar v Henry F Teichmann, Inc, 640 F Supp 365, 370-71 (WD Pa 1985), *affd without opinion,* 800 F2d 1137 (3d Cir 1986).

[529] McBrayer v City of Marietta, 967 F2d 546, 548 (11th Cir 1992).

Burden of Proof

As a general matter, the plaintiff bears the burden of proving his or her entitlement to equitable tolling or that the defendant should be estopped from relying on the plaintiff's late filing.[530] The defendant (which typically is an employer, rather than an employment agency or a labor organization, which entities also are covered by the ADEA) bears the burden of proving that the employee was generally aware of his or her rights.[531] There is support, however, for the proposition that for a plaintiff to avoid the entry of summary judgment in favor of the defendant, the plaintiff must do more than simply aver that no notice was posted.[532]

Number and Placement of Postings

Notwithstanding that the language of §8 of the ADEA refers in the plural to the posting of the notice in conspicuous *places,* a single posting of the notice will suffice if it is posted "in a centrally located area where employees are likely to see it."[533] Moreover, "[n]otice is sufficient if it is posted conspicuously so that employees have a meaningful opportunity for becoming aware of their . . . rights."[534] The failure of an individual to see a notice will not justify tolling unless the posting was inadequate.[535] If,

---

530 See **§6.17.**

531 Beshears v Asbill, 930 F2d 1348, 1352 (8th Cir 1991); DeBrunner v Midway Equip Co, 803 F2d 950, 952 (8th Cir 1986); McClinton v Alabama By-Products Corp, 743 F2d 1483, 1486 (11th Cir 1984); Nogar v Henry F Teichmann, Inc, 640 F Supp 365, 370 (WD Pa 1985), *affd without opinion,* 800 F2d 1137 (3d Cir 1986).

532 Soderlund v Ben Franklin, 41 FEP Cas (BNA) 1709 (ND Ill 1986).

533 Morse v Daily Press, Inc, 826 F2d 1351, 1353 (4th Cir), *cert denied,* 484 US 965 (1987), *accord* Dunham v McLaughlin Body Co, 812 F Supp 867, 871 (CD Ill 1992).

534 *Morse,* note 532 *supra,* at 1353.

535 *See, e.g.,* Posey v Skyline Corp, 702 F2d 102 (7th Cir), *cert denied,* 464 US 960 (1983); Hrzenak v White-Westinghouse Appliance Co, 682 F2d 714 (8th Cir 1982); Bonham v Dresser Indus, Inc, 569 F2d 187, 193 n7 (3d Cir 1977), *cert denied,* 439 US 821 (1978); Berry v Joseph E Seagram & Sons, Inc, 744 F Supp 214 (CD Cal 1990); Bomberger v Consolidated Coal Co, 623 F Supp 89 (WD Pa 1985); Kraus v Canteen Serv Co, 39 FEP Cas (BNA) 1377 (ED Mich

however, the notice was posted in a manner insufficient to alert a reasonable person to his or her rights, the filing period will be tolled.[536]

The mere statement by the plaintiff that he or she did not see the notice is not enough, standing alone, to preclude summary judgment for the defendant,[537] particularly when the defendant submits an affidavit by the person responsible for posting the notice in which that person asserts that the notice indeed was posted.[538] Similarly, a mere conclusory allegation by a plaintiff that a notice was not posted will not suffice to avoid summary judgment.[539]

The requirement imposed by §8 that a notice be posted in a conspicuous place does not mean that it must be posted at the place where a particular individual, i.e., the plaintiff, works. The posting need only be in a place where an employee is " 'likely' " to see the notice.[540] Thus, the fact that a given individual did not

---

1985); Fressell v AT&T Technologies, Inc, 35 FEP Cas (BNA) 658 (ND Ga 1984); Perazzo v Top Value Enters, Inc, 590 F Supp 428 (SD Ohio 1984); Lewis v General Elec Co, 34 FEP Cas (BNA) 1756 (WD Ky 1983); Keitz v Lever Bros Co, 563 F Supp 230 (ND Ind 1983); Smith v Flesh Co, 512 F Supp 46, 54 (ED Mo 1981); Downie v Electric Boat Div, 504 F Supp 1082 (D Conn 1980); Fulton v NCR Corp, 472 F Supp 377, 384 (WD Va 1979); Gebhard v GAF Corp, 59 FRD 504, 507 (DDC 1973); *see also* Byers v Follmer Trucking Co, 763 F2d 599 (3d Cir 1985); Parrish v Schlumberger, Ltd, 19 FEP Cas (BNA) 717, 720 (SD Tex 1979). In Davis v CV Mosby Co, 34 FEP Cas (BNA) 1092 (WD Mo 1983), the court refused to excuse the executor of the former employee's estate from the timely filing requirement where the executor argued that, while the decedent had seen the prominently posted ADEA notice, he, i.e., the executor, had not.

536 *See* Snow v Government Employees Fin Corp, 25 FEP Cas (BNA) 844, 845 (D Colo 1981).

537 Daugherity v Traylor Bros, Inc, 970 F2d 348, 353 n8 (7th Cir 1992).

538 Vaught v RR Donnelly & Sons Co, 745 F2d 407, 412 (7th Cir 1984); Heideman v PFL, Inc, 710 F Supp 711, 718 (WD Mo 1989), *affd,* 904 F2d 1262 (8th Cir 1990), *cert denied,* 498 US 1026 (1991); English v Pabst Brewing Co, 645 F Supp 186 (WDNC 1986), *affd,* 828 F2d 1047 (4th Cir 1987), *cert denied,* 486 US 1044 (1988).

539 Peffley v Durakool, Inc, 669 F Supp 1453, 1459 (ND Ind 1987); Soderlund v Ben Franklin, 41 FEP Cas (BNA) 1709, 1710 (ND Ill 1986).

540 Dunham v McLaughlin Body Co, 812 F Supp 867, 872 (CD Ill 1992) (quoting Morse v Daily Press, Inc, 826 F2d 1351, 1353 (4th Cir 1987)).

work in the building where the notice is posted will not be fatal to the defendant's assertion that it complied with §8; the posting need only be at a site where the plaintiff would have had a "meaningful opportunity" to see the notice.[541]

In instances where an individual is not regularly employed at the office where the notice is posted, the frequency of the grievant's visits to the office can be relevant in determining whether equitable relief from the onus of having filed an untimely charge is warranted.[542] The district court deciding *Dunham v McLaughlin Body Co*[543] utilized an analysis focusing on the employer's expectations: "[T]he actual number of times an employee visited the site has been less important that [sic] an employer's legitimate expectation that the employee would, in fact, visit the site as a function or a privilege of employment."[544] Thus, where an employer could legitimately expect an employee to visit the office at which the notice was posted, the fact that the employee did not actually visit that office will not work to the detriment of the employer. In such a situation, the employee will be deemed to have had a meaningful opportunity to see the notice.[545] Taking a position even more solicitous of the defendant, the Court of Appeals for the Fourth Circuit, in deciding *English v Pabst Brewing Co,*[546] ruled that the frequency of visitation by the employee was irrelevant to the question of whether tolling was appropriate. The employer's only obligation, in the court's view, was to post a notice in conspicuous places, and so the fact

---

541 *Id.*

542 *See, e.g.,* Charlier v SC Johnson & Son, Inc, 556 F2d 761 (5th Cir 1977); Hrzenak v White-Westinghouse Appliance Co, 510 F Supp 1086 (WD Mo 1981), *affd,* 682 F2d 714 (8th Cir 1982); *see also* Quicker v American V Mueller, 712 F Supp 824 (D Colo 1989); Edgeworth v Fort Howard Paper Co, 673 F Supp 922 (ND Ill 1987); Shields v Grocers Supply Co, 568 F Supp 61 (SD Tex 1983); Malinowski v State Farm Ins Co, 18 FEP Cas (BNA) 693, 694-95 (WD Pa 1978).

543 812 F Supp 867 (CD Ill 1992).

544 *Id* 873.

545 *Id.*

546 828 F2d 1047 (4th Cir 1987), *cert denied,* 486 US 1044 (1988).

that an employee might only rarely visit the office where the notice was posted would not justify tolling.

Some courts, however, have suggested that where an employee does not work in the office, special effort may be required of the employer. For example, in *Kale v Combined Insurance Co of America*[547] the court stated that "[i]n such a case, the employer might be required to take steps other than posting in order to ensure that his employees have a meaningful opportunity to learn of their ADEA rights."[548]

§6.19 —Fraud, Deception, and Other Misconduct as Bases for Tolling or Estoppel

Affirmative misconduct by an entity required to comply with the Age Discrimination in Employment Act (ADEA),[549] i.e., an employer, employment agency, or labor organization, can lead to a plaintiff securing equitable relief from the onus of his or her failure to file a timely charge of unlawful discrimination with the Equal Employment Opportunity Commission (EEOC).[550] Typically, such situations will be treated in terms of the defendant being equitably estopped from asserting the untimeliness of the plaintiff's charge as a basis either for dismissing the plaintiff's suit or for granting the defendant's motion for summary judgment. Sometimes, however, equitable tolling will be the tack followed by a court.[551]

---

[547] 861 F2d 746 (1st Cir 1988).

[548] *Id* 755 n10; *see also* Charlier v SC Johnson & Son, Inc, 556 F2d 761, 765 (5th Cir 1977).

[549] 29 USC §§621-634.

[550] See also cases involving defendants' conduct, and such conduct's relation to tolling and estoppel, in the context of statute of limitations issues, discussed in **§6.34.**

[551] Of course, the line separating equitable estoppel from equitable tolling is not an altogether clear one. See **§6.17.**

Intentional Misrepresentations and Other Employer Misconduct

The clearest case for equitable estoppel exists where an employer engages in intentionally misleading actions or intentionally makes misrepresentations, with the result being the lulling of a grievant into delaying filing his or her charge of discrimination.[552] (Even if the employee consults an attorney, estoppel will be warranted if the deception misleads not only the employee, but the attorney as well.[553]) Other employer conduct also can justify estoppel. For example, the Court of Appeals

---

[552] *See, e.g.,* Gray v Phillips Petroleum Co, 858 F2d 610, 615 (10th Cir 1988); Lawson v Burlington Indus, Inc, 683 F2d 862 (4th Cir), *cert denied,* 459 US 944 (1982); Aronsen v Crown Zellerbach, 662 F2d 584 (9th Cir 1981), *cert denied,* 459 US 1200 (1983); Coke v General Adjustment Bureau, Inc, 640 F2d 584 (5th Cir 1981), *affg* 616 F2d 785 (5th Cir 1980); Wilkerson v Siegfried Ins Agency, Inc, 621 F2d 1042 (10th Cir 1980); Harris v WGN Continental Broadcasting Co, 650 F Supp 568 (ND Ill 1986); Jones v Premier Indus Corp, 611 F Supp 142 (ND Ga 1985); Golletti v Arco/Polymers, Inc, 35 FEP Cas (BNA) 1325 (WD Pa 1984); Baruah v Young, 536 F Supp 356 (D Md 1982); Sanders v Duke Univ, 538 F Supp 1143 (MDNC 1982); Barber v Commercial Union Ins Co, 27 FEP Cas (BNA) 703 (ED Pa 1981); Fulton v NCR Corp, 472 F Supp 377 (WD Va 1979); Potter v Continental Trailways, Inc, 480 F Supp 207 (D Colo 1979); Wagner v Sperry Univac, Div of Sperry Rand Corp, 458 F Supp 505 (ED Pa 1978), *affd without opinion,* 624 F2d 1092 (3d Cir 1980); Griffin v First Pa Bank, 443 F Supp 563, 567 (ED Pa 1977); Davis v RJR Foods, Inc, 420 F Supp 930, 934 (SDNY 1976), *affd without opinion,* 556 F2d 555 (2d Cir 1977); *see also* Callan v Pepsi-Cola Bottling Co, Inc, 801 F Supp 448, 453-54 (D Kan 1992); Allotta v Chase Manhattan Bank, 547 F Supp 198, 200 (SDNY 1982).

The court deciding Quicker v American V Mueller, 712 F Supp 824 (D Colo 1989), stated as follows:

> By actively concealing the manner in which they hired Plaintiff's replacement, by concealing the fact that there were other sales positions open in Colorado, and by leading Plaintiff to believe that he would have to physically travel the newly expanded territory, [which travel his physical disability prevented,] Defendants made Plaintiff's discharge appear less wrongful than it actually was, making it less likely that Plaintiff would seek legal redress.

Id 828-29.

[553] Meyer v Riegel Prods Corp, 720 F2d 303, 309 (3d Cir 1983), *cert dismissed,* 465 US 1091 (1984).

for the Seventh Circuit ruled in *Wheeldon v Monon Corp*[554] that the employer's delay in responding to the inquiry of the Office of Federal Contract Compliance (OFCCP) regarding the plaintiff's complaint filed with it, which delay in turn led to the plaintiff's untimely filing with the EEOC when it was finally determined that the OFCCP did not have jurisdiction, justified estopping the employer from raising the statute of limitations.

Denying an employer any gain from its wrongdoing in such a situation comports with the familiar equitable maxim that "no man may take advantage of his own wrong."[555] Beyond one's trotting out this hoary legal chestnut, however, it is very difficult to isolate any consistent threads of analysis or to make any useful generalizations, for the cases are exceedingly fact-bound.

There is support for the position that estoppel is not confined just to situations where the employer's acts of deception were egregious.[556] Clearly, however, not all courts would conclude that misleading conduct or statements will—without more—justify estoppel, even where such conduct or statements have lulled a grievant into not filing a charge of discrimination. Caution regarding estoppel was expressed, for example, by the Court of Appeals for the First Circuit in *Kale v Combined Insurance Co of America:*[557]

> [A] number of courts have held that . . . [misleading conduct by the defendant] will support equitable tolling without going any further. . . .
>
> We do not think, however, that the inquiry should end there. The court should also assess any countervailing equities against the plaintiff. For example, did he diligently pursue his claim, . . . was his ignorance of his rights unreasonable under the circumstances, . . . and would allowing equitable tolling still fulfill the basic purposes

---

[554] 946 F2d 533 (7th Cir 1991).

[555] Glus v Brooklyn E Dist Terminal, 359 US 231, 232 (1959).

[556] Meyer v Riegel Prods Corp, 720 F2d 303, 307 (3d Cir 1983), *cert dismissed,* 465 US 1091 (1984).

[557] 861 F2d 746 (1st Cir 1988).

behind the limited filing period—namely, providing the government an opportunity to conciliate while the complaint is fresh and giving early notice to the employer of possible litigation. . . . Finally, even if the court finds that the above factors call for equitable tolling, it must then take account of the degree to which delay prejudices the defendant.[558]

The Significance of an Employer's Nondisclosure of Its Wrongdoing

There seems to be agreement that an employer's denial of wrongdoing and/or its refusal to admit that it has acted on the basis of an individual's age will not constitute the type of misrepresentation sufficient to support equitable estoppel when that employer later contends that the plaintiff's suit should be dismissed, or summary judgment for the defendant should be granted, because the plaintiff had failed to file a timely charge of unlawful discrimination. In other words, "the failure to tell plaintiff that he was demoted because of his age is not the type of deception or fraud that operates to toll the limitations periods."[559] This position is emphatically illustrated by *Moore v Astra Pharmaceutical Products, Inc,*[560] a case involving a situation where the employer was expressly asked by the plaintiff's attorney, at the time they met to discuss the terms of the plaintiff's termination, whether the employee was being terminated because of his age and whether a younger person was going to replace him. The employer answered in the negative in both respects. As things turned out, a younger individual subsequently was alleg-

---

[558] *Id* 753 (citations and footnote omitted).

[559] Klausing v Whirlpool Corp, 623 F Supp 156, 162 (SD Ohio 1985), *appeal dismissed without opinion,* 785 F2d 309 (6th Cir 1986); *accord* Cada v Baxter Healthcare Corp, 920 F2d 446, 451 (7th Cir 1990), *cert denied,* 111 S Ct 2916 (1991); Heideman v PFL, Inc, 904 F2d 1262, 1266 (8th Cir 1990), *cert denied,* 498 US 1026 (1991); Allen v Diebold, Inc, 807 F Supp 1308, 1314-15 (ND Ohio 1992); Morton v Associated Dry Goods Corp, 792 F Supp 1136, 1141 (SD Ind 1992); Glass v IDS Fin Servs, Inc, 778 F Supp 1029, 1047 (D Minn 1991).

[560] 58 FEP Cas (BNA) 905 (ED La 1992).

edly hired as the plaintiff's replacement. The court, rejecting the argument that this scenario justified estopping the defendant from arguing that the plaintiff's charge had not been timely filed, stated as follows:

> [A]n employer is not estopped from invoking the complainant's failure to timely file a charge because it does not expressly declare that an employee is being terminated because of his age. . . . Therefore, the mere fact that . . . [the employer] represented to plaintiff and his counsel that plaintiff was not being terminated due to his age, and that he did not know if plaintiff was to be replaced by a younger individual did not estop the defendant from invoking the limitation period.[561]

Reliance and Knowledge on the Plaintiff's Part

As the Court of Appeals for the Seventh Circuit has opined, there must not only be improper conduct by the covered entity; there must also be "actual and reasonable reliance on such conduct" by the plaintiff.[562] Thus, where a plaintiff has not been misled by an employer's misrepresentation, the plaintiff will have no basis for invoking equitable estoppel principles.[563] Similarly, for a plaintiff to be able to claim legitimate reliance on the defendant's conduct, he or she must have a reasonable basis for so doing.[564]

In a related vein, there is ample support for the proposition that a plaintiff will not be able to obtain equitable relief from the late filing of his or her charge of unlawful discrimination when—notwithstanding the defendant's misrepresentations as to why the adverse action had been taken or the adverse decision

---

[561] *Id* 908.

[562] Hamilton v Komatsu Dresser Indus, Inc, 964 F2d 600, 605 (7th Cir), *cert denied*, 113 S Ct 324 (1992).

[563] *See* Gore v Pee Dee Farm Credit Serv, 60 FEP Cas (BNA) 240, 244-45 (DSC 1992), *affd without opinion*, 1 F3d 1233 (4th Cir 1993).

[564] *See, e.g.*, Aronsen v Crown Zellerbach, 662 F2d 584, 595 (9th Cir 1981), *cert denied*, 459 US 1200 (1983); *see also* Needham v Beecham, 515 F Supp 460, 467 (D Me 1981).

had been made—the plaintiff believed or suspected that the real motive for the defendant's conduct was age discrimination.[565] Alleged concealment by the defendant of the facts will not be legally significant when the plaintiff "was aware of virtually all of the evidence of discrimination upon which he" or she later relies.[566] Moreover, even if the plaintiff did not have a suspicion that age discrimination was involved in the adverse decision, if he or she was aware of facts sufficient to have alerted him or her, as a reasonable person, to the possibility of such discrimination, equitable relief may be inappropriate.[567] Accordingly, so long as the grievant had sufficient facts to suggest the existence of discriminatory treatment, the fact that he or she was not aware of all of the evidence in support of the claim, and the further fact that the defendant had not disclosed that evidence, will not justify equitable estoppel.[568] What is more, even if the plaintiff had no reason initially to suspect discrimination on the employer's part, and only later acquired information suggesting such wrongdoing, that scenario will not in and of itself justify tolling, according to the court deciding *Burkholder v State Chemical Manufacturing Co.*[569]

---

565 *See, e.g.*, Caldwell v National Assn of Home Builders, 771 F2d 1051, 1056 n1 (7th Cir 1985); Tobin v Trans Union Sys Corp, 488 F Supp 622, 628 (ED Pa 1980); Benima v Smithsonian Inst, 471 F Supp 62, 66 (D Mass 1979); Mazzare v Burroughs Corp, 473 F Supp 234, 239 (ED Pa 1979); Woerner v Bell Helicopter, 16 FEP Cas (BNA) 480, 481 (ND Tex 1977); *see also* Allen v Diebold, Inc, 807 F Supp 1308, 1317 (ND Ohio 1992); Bratton v American Natl Ins Co, 32 FEP Cas (BNA) 953 (ND Ga 1983), *affd without opinion*, 740 F2d 978 (11th Cir 1984). In Miller v State Chem Mfg Co, 706 F Supp 1166 (WD Pa 1988), the court did not deem tolling to be justified on the basis of newly discovered evidence that consisted of the plaintiff's former supervisor telling the plaintiff—two years after his discharge—that the plaintiff had been discharged because of his age. Earlier, at the actual time of discharge, the plaintiff had been advised that he was "too old for the job." *Id* 1168.

566 Olson v Mobil Oil Corp, 904 F2d 198, 201 (4th Cir 1990).

567 *See, e.g.*, Conaway v Control Data Corp, 955 F2d 358 (5th Cir), *cert denied*, 113 S Ct 186 (1992); Olson v Mobil Oil Corp, 904 F2d 198 (4th Cir 1990).

568 *See* Christopher v Mobil Oil Corp, 950 F2d 1209 (5th Cir), *cert denied*, 113 S Ct 68 (1992).

569 48 FEP Cas (BNA) 831, 833 (WD Pa 1988).

Reviewing some of the case law, the court deciding *Perazzo v Top Value Enterprises, Inc,*[570] concluded that not only must there be misleading conduct, but there must also be a "close nexus between the employer's lulling assurances and the claimant's failure to timely file."[571] Thus, even though in the court's view the defendant's officers acted unfairly and in bad faith by ignoring Perazzo's inquiries regarding the actions that ultimately formed the basis for the suit, silence was not deemed to constitute misleading conduct. There was no nexus, inasmuch as the silence "signaled, rather than obscured, discrimination."[572]

Davis v CECO Building Systems[573] is illustrative of these themes. The plaintiff, who suffered from a work-related disability, had been fired after he refused to accept a position that he claimed was too strenuous for him. There were no lighter duty positions available, according to the employer. Several months later, so the plaintiff contended, he learned that the employer had in fact hired two younger persons to do light duty work, and he soon thereafter filed a charge of unlawful discrimination. This charge, however, was not filed within 180 days of the date of termination. In rejecting the plaintiff's argument that the running of the charge-filing period should be deemed to have been tolled, the court reasoned that at the time of his discharge the plaintiff had in fact known, as his deposition revealed, that there were other jobs available besides the one he had rejected, and so when he was told that there were no other jobs he "should have suspected at that point that Ceco was possibly misleading him or concealing its true reasons for terminating his employment."[574] And the court continued as follows:

---

[570] 590 F Supp 428 (SD Ohio 1984).

[571] *Id* 434.

[572] *Id* 435.

[573] 813 F Supp 1202 (ND Miss 1993).

[574] *Id* 1207; *see also* Streadwick v Hygenic Corp, 61 FEP Cas (BNA) 933, 934 (ND Ill 1993) (in response to plaintiff's argument that she had been given inconsistent reasons for her discharge and so she did not know why she was fired, and that therefore equitable tolling should apply to relieve her of the onus of her late filing, the court responded: "Those arguments were expressly rejected in *Stark v. Dynascan Corp.*, 902 F.2d 549 (7th Cir. 1990), where the

> Although Mr. Davis may not have known the exact contours of his age claim at the time of his termination, *see Blumberg [v HCA Management Co*[575]], . . . he, like any "person similarly situated with a prudent regard for his rights," . . . was certainly in a position "to evaluate the propriety of the reasons for [his] dismissal immediately." *Blumberg,* 848 F.2d at 645. . . . The court therefore finds that Mr. Davis's charge of discrimination . . . was untimely and not subject to any equitable modification.[576]

It has even been held that equitable relief from the negative consequence of the late filing of a charge, the claim for such relief being based on the grievant's claim that he or she was misled by the employer, will not be in order where the discharged employee suspected that his or her termination was in some way questionable even though the employee's misgivings did not focus on suspected age discrimination. So reasoned the district court that decided *Heideman v PFL, Inc,*[577] which involved a situation where it was not until six years after discharge that the plaintiff gained possession of a devastatingly inculpatory memorandum prepared by a senior officer of the defendant which, in retrospect, seemed to explain the plaintiff's mistreatment. The court noted that at the time he was fired the plaintiff had thought there was something " 'fishy' " about the situation, although he had not suspected age bias as being a factor at the time.[578] Accordingly, he could not now argue successfully for tolling because, "[g]iven the . . . facts and circumstances surrounding . . . [his] termination, . . . a reasonably diligent employee would

---

court held that conflicting reasons for termination not only do not excuse a[n] [un]timely EEOC filing but actually should have alerted the plaintiff to probable discrimination.")

[575] 848 F2d 642 (5th Cir 1988), *cert denied,* 488 US 1007 (1989).

[576] 813 F Supp at 1207 (citation omitted).

[577] 710 F Supp 711 (WD Mo 1989), *affd,* 904 F2d 1262 (8th Cir 1990), *cert denied,* 498 US 1026 (1991).

[578] *Id* 719.

have been put on notice of his cause of action."[579] (The appellate court, in affirming the order granting the defendant's motion for summary judgment, pointed to several factors, in addition to the plaintiff's initial suspicion, justifying the affirmance. First, the defendant had posted the requisite ADEA notice.[580] Second, the plaintiff had initially contacted an attorney but had chosen to forego pursuing his suspicions because of the costliness of legal representation; thus, "Heideman had the means to get the truth he sought [i.e., the real reason for his supposedly nondiscriminatory discharge], but chose not to take advantage of the opportunity because of the cost . . . [, which] cost does not justify equitable tolling.")[581]

Somewhat in contrast to the foregoing decisions, the Court of Appeals for the Third Circuit has asserted that the filing period will be tolled until the employee becomes aware of facts sufficient to support a plausible claim of discrimination.[582] In this court's view, a mere suspicion on the employee's part of wrongdoing would not bar application of the equitable tolling doctrine.[583] (However, according to the Court of Appeals for the Seventh Circuit, if the facts are such that "a reasonable person in . . . [the plaintiff's] position should have been aware that he possessed a colorable claim of age discrimination," tolling will not be in order.)[584] *Rhodes v Guiberson Oil Tools Division*[585] also illustrates a somewhat solicitous view regarding the matter of plaintiffs' knowledge—a view taking into account a variety of facts in reaching a conclusion as to how the equities balance out:

---

[579] *Id* 720 (footnotes omitted).

[580] See **§6.18.**

[581] Heideman v PFL, Inc, 904 F2d 1262, 1267 (8th Cir 1990), *cert denied,* 498 US 1026 (1991); *see also* Barnes v Hillhaven Rehabilitation & Convalescent Ctr, 686 F Supp 311, 314 (ND Ga 1988).

[582] Meyer v Riegel Prods Corp, 720 F2d 303, 308 (3d Cir 1983), *cert dismissed,* 465 US 1091 (1984).

[583] *Id* 308-309.

[584] Stark v Dynascan Corp, 902 F2d 549, 552 (7th Cir 1990).

[585] 927 F2d 876 (5th Cir), *cert denied,* 112 S Ct 198 (1991).

> Here the defendant was told on his severance report that he might be reinstated . . . and that he was being laid off because of a reduction in work force . . . [due to an economic downturn]. These [were] misrepresentations, [and] combined with the economic downturn in the oil industry [, which downturn made the employer's explanation for the plaintiff's discharge seem plausible, they] should have been found . . . to have misled Rhodes from thinking that he was being discharged because of his age. . . .
>
> Until [Rhodes] . . . learned he was replaced by a younger man, he could not be expected to evaluate the "propriety of the reasons" for his dismissal because until then the excuse of reduction in work force seemed highly reasonable and because he did not have sufficient facts to approach the EEOC. Further, Guiberson Oil had told Rhodes that he was an employee worthy of being considered for re-hire. Rhodes had no reason, until discovery of Guiberson Oil's hiring of a [younger] replacement, to suspect that Guiberson Oil was guilty of age discrimination.[586]

§6.20 —The Relevance to Tolling and Estoppel of the Absence of Intentional Misconduct by the Employer

In some cases arising under the Age Discrimination in Employment Act (ADEA)[587] courts have been willing to countenance estoppel even when the employer did not utter any intentionally misleading statement or engage in any intentionally deceptive act (or failure to act). In *Connor v Hodel,*[588] for example, the court tolled the filing period despite there being no intent to deceive on the part of the employer. The situation there involved the employer failing to identify the person who had received the promotion that the plaintiff had sought, the result

---

[586] *Id* 881.

[587] 29 USC §§621-634.

[588] 36 FEP Cas (BNA) 362 (DDC 1984) (federal employee suit).

being that the plaintiff had no basis for suspecting that age was a factor in the promotion process.

In deciding *Bonham v Dresser Industries, Inc,*[589] the Court of Appeals for the Third Circuit reasoned that the filing period could be tolled in light of the defendant's president having written a letter that was optimistic as to the possibility of the plaintiff securing alternative employment with the company. The court reasoned that tolling or estoppel was appropriate "while Bonham was actively pursuing this attempt amicably to resolve his employment situation and while the company was sending positive signals."[590]

The Court of Appeals for the Eleventh Circuit has taken a position similar to that of the *Bonham* court. In *Cocke v Merrill Lynch & Co, Inc,*[591] the court ruled that "while the employer is actively trying to find a position within the company for the employee, the . . . filing period . . . is equitably tolled until such time as it is or should be apparent to an employee with a reasonably prudent regard for his rights that the employer has ceased to actively pursue such a position."[592] The court in part justified this analysis by reasoning that, whereas an employer's attempt to mitigate the harshness of a decision does not give rise to equitable estoppel absent employer fraud or misrepresentation, equitable tolling does not require employer misconduct.[593]

The Court of Appeals for the Ninth Circuit also seemed to take a position sympathetic to the plaintiff in *McConnell v General Telephone Co.*[594] Rather than requiring intentional deception on the defendant's part, the court asserted as follows: "Representations of possible alternative employment within the company may toll the statute of limitations under the doctrine of equitable

---

[589] 569 F2d 187 (3d Cir 1977), *cert denied,* 439 US 821 (1978).

[590] *Id* 193; *accord* Monnig v Kennecott Corp, 603 F Supp 1035 (D Conn 1985); Franci v Avco Corp, 460 F Supp 389 (D Conn 1978); *see also* Golletti v ARCO Polymers, Inc, 648 F Supp 287 (WD Pa 1986).

[591] 817 F2d 1559 (11th Cir 1987).

[592] *Id* 1561.

[593] *See also* Amburgey v Corhart Refractories Corp, Inc, 936 F2d 805 (5th Cir 1991).

[594] 814 F2d 1311 (9th Cir 1987), *cert denied,* 484 US 1059 (1988).

estoppel when the representations lull the employee into an untimely filing."[595] Protracted settlement negotiations, even if they do not involve reinstating the discharged grievant, also may justify tolling.[596]

Contrasting with these benign views of the equities (insofar as plaintiffs are concerned) is *Price v Litton Business Systems, Inc,*[597] in which the court stressed the intent element regarding the employer's actions and statements. The defendant in *Price,* after demoting the plaintiff, subsequently made repeated representations that it would come forward with alternative jobs. While it in fact did so, the offers were for lesser positions. The court reasoned as follows:

> [T]he attempt to mitigate the harshness of a decision terminating an employee, without more, cannot give rise to an equitable estoppel. . . . [T]he employee's failure to file in timely fashion . . . [must be] the consequence either of a deliberate design by the employer or of actions that the employer should unmistakably have understood would cause the employee to delay filing his charge.[598]

This posture has considerable support from other courts.[599]

---

[595] *Id* 1317. (However, the court's approving citation of Aronsen v Crown Zellerbach, 662 F2d 584 (9th Cir 1981), *cert denied,* 459 US 1200 (1983), as support arguably undercut this reading, since in *Aronsen* the court seemed to require some affirmative aim on the employer's part to lull the employee into inaction.) *See also* Labus v Navistar Intl Transp Corp, 740 F Supp 1053 (DNJ 1990).

[596] Foutty v Equifax Servs, Inc, 764 F Supp 621 (D Kan), *supplanting* 762 F Supp 295 (D Kan 1991).

[597] 694 F2d 963 (4th Cir 1982).

[598] *Id* 965 (footnote and citation omitted).

[599] *See, e.g.,* Aungst v Westinghouse Elec Corp, 937 F2d 1216, 1225-26 (7th Cir 1991); Mull v ARCO Durethene Plastics, Inc, 784 F2d 284, 292 (7th Cir 1986); Dillman v Combustion Engg, Inc, 784 F2d 57 (2d Cir 1986); Kriegesmann v Barry-Wehmiller Co, 739 F2d 357 (8th Cir), *cert denied,* 469 US 1036 (1984); Glass v IDS Fin Servs, Inc, 778 F Supp 1029, 1047-48 (D Minn 1991); Soderlund v Ben Franklin, 41 FEP Cas (BNA) 1709, 1711 (ND Ill 1986); Quinn v Amoco Fabrics Co, 35 FEP Cas (BNA) 1791 (SD Ga 1984); *see also* Cerbone v International Ladies' Garment Workers' Union, 768 F2d 45

Without repudiating its analysis set forth in *Price,* the Court of Appeals for the Fourth Circuit in articulated a significantly more pro-plaintiff analysis regarding estoppel in *Felty v Graves-Humphreys Co.*[600] In the course of discharging the plaintiff, the employer warned Felty that if he discussed his termination with anyone he would be subject to immediate dismissal. He thereby would be precluded from what was offered as an alternative—i.e., the opportunity to stay on for a period of time, with a continuation of salary and other benefits. There was no question, in the court's view, that Felty indeed was well aware of his discharge, and that he had reason to believe that it was based on his being deemed too old. On its face, then, the situation seemed to offer little basis for estoppel. The court reasoned otherwise, however. It regarded the severance arrangement's being conditioned on silence as constituting a form of coercion: "The older employee facing an uncertain financial future with reduced chances of employment would be particularly vulnerable to such a 'carrot and stick' approach."[601] This coercion, as the court saw it, caused Felty to delay filing a charge of discrimination with the Equal Employment Opportunity Commission (EEOC), and therefore estoppel was justified.[602]

(2d Cir 1985); Lawson v Burlington Indus, Inc, 683 F2d 862, 864 (4th Cir), *cert denied,* 459 US 844 (1982); Williams v Whirlpool Corp, 41 FEP Cas (BNA) 383 (WD Ark 1986); Brudne v Amalgamated Trust & Sav Bank, 627 F Supp 458, 464 n12 (ND Ill 1986); Shipper v Avon Prods, Inc, 605 F Supp 701 (SDNY 1985); Fressell v AT&T Technologies, Inc, 35 FEP Cas (BNA) 658 (ND Ga 1984); Clark v Resistoflex Co, Div of Unidynamics Corp, 854 F2d 762, 768-69 (5th Cir 1988).

[600] 785 F2d 516 (4th Cir 1986).

[601] *Id* 520.

[602] According to the court, "[t]he length of time that an employer's coercion is effective is a question of fact." *Id.* In offering some guidance, the court observed: "Any affirmative act by the employee to enforce his rights would indicate that the employer's improper influence has ended. We note, however, that private conversations with friends in the work force would not qualify as an affirmative act." *Id.* Subsequently, the Court of Appeals for the Fourth Circuit again addressed the issue of estoppel vis-a-vis Felty, and concluded that the plaintiff's failure timely to file could not be excused. Felty v Graves-Humphreys Co, 818 F2d 1126 (4th Cir 1987).

As in *Felty*, the plaintiff in *Mogley v Chicago Title Insurance Co*[603] was presented with a choice, albeit not one seen by the court as being coercive. Here, estoppel was deemed not to be warranted. The employer extended to employees the choice of terminating on one date with certain benefits, or of retiring on a later date with enhanced benefits, provided—as to this latter option—that the employee signed a release relieving the employer of all liability. Because the trigger date for the running of the filing period started to run on the first date, and because the filing period had expired by the time of the second date—for which the employee had opted—the employee's filing with the EEOC was untimely. In the court's view, there "was no persuasive authority in the case law that an employer's holding out of alternatives to the employee—here termination or early retirement—and the employee's acceptance of the most favorable terms offered constitute a basis for tolling of the limitations period."[604]

Other courts have articulated the more rigorous (from the plaintiff's perspective) type of analysis seen in *Price v Litton Business Systems, Inc*, and *Mogley*, as contrasted with rulings like *Bonham, Cocke*, and *McConnell*.[605] For example, the court deciding *Wagner v Sperry Univac, Division of Sperry Rand*[606] stated that "[a] litigant may not . . . avoid the statute of limitations simply because the decision it forces him to make—whether to pursue legal remedies before all avenues of informal settlement are exhausted—is a difficult one."[607]

---

603 719 F2d 289 (8th Cir 1983).

604 *Id* 291; *see also* Kriegesmann v Barry-Wehmiller Co, 739 F2d 357 (8th Cir), *cert denied*, 469 US 1036 (1984); Kazanzas v Walt Disney World Co, 704 F2d 1527, 1532 (11th Cir), *cert denied*, 464 US 982 (1983). *Kazanzas* was narrowed in Cocke v Merrill Lynch & Co, Inc, 817 F2d 1559 (11th Cir 1987).

605 See cases cited in note 599.

606 458 F Supp 505 (ED Pa 1978), *affd without opinion*, 624 F2d 1092 (3d Cir 1980).

607 *Id* 516; *see also* Lawson v Burlington Indus, Inc, 683 F2d 562 (4th Cir), *cert denied*, 459 US 944 (1982); Caldwell v National Assn of Home Builders, 598 F Supp 371, 377 (ND Ind 1984), *revd on other grounds*, 771 F2d 1051 (7th Cir 1985) (dictum); Mayor v Western Elec Co, 487 F Supp 84, 86-87 (WD Mo

There are convincing arguments both for rigor and for the contrary posture. To allow a grievant to obtain added time for filing, simply by asserting that there was some hope of reconciling differences, could extend the filing period for unspecified days, months, possibly even years. Moreover, such a possibility would dissuade employers from sincerely seeking to work out alternative arrangements, lest by so doing they would lay themselves open to legal claims for extended periods.[608] Finally, strict adherence to the filing requirements averts confusion for employees, who may be uncertain as to whether, upon ultimately filing after negotiations break down, a court will deem those negotiations sufficiently substantive as to have justified a reasonable person in relying upon them and delaying filing. On the other hand, the rigor of the *Wagner* court's position—echoed by other courts[609]—does not really take into account the real possibility of some improvement in the grievant's situation being engendered by the filing of a charge with the EEOC. Thus, the posture of the *Bonham, Cocke,* and *McConnell* courts also merits commendation.

Other situations have generated less by way of conflicting case law. An employee's claimed belief that an in-house grievance procedure would take care of his complaint will not justify tolling.[610] Nor will the employee's fears that filing a charge of unlaw-

---

1980); Platt v Burroughs Corp, 424 F Supp 1329, 1333 (ED Pa 1976). *Contra* Snow v Government Employees Fin Corp, 25 FEP Cas (BNA) 844 (D Colo 1981); *see also* Welty v SF&G, Inc, 605 F Supp 1548, 1559 (ND Ala 1985). Settlement discussions between the attorneys for the grievant and the employer were not deemed to toll the running of the filing period where (1) the employer's attorney never told the plaintiff's lawyer that it was not necessary for the plaintiff to file a charge, and (2) the employer's attorney never told his counterpart that the employer definitely would settle the claim. Salazar v AT&T Co, 715 F Supp 351 (SD Fla 1989).

608 *Wagner,* 458 F Supp at 515-16. Likewise, where an employee is allowed to stay on the payroll for a while, "it would be a unique distortion of equitable principles . . . to penalize defendant." Cole v CBS, Inc, 634 F Supp 1558, 1565 (SDNY 1986).

609 See cases cited in notes 597 and 599.

610 *See, e.g.,* Vaught v RR Donnelly & Sons Co, 745 F2d 407 (7th Cir 1984); Sanders v Duke Univ, 538 F Supp 1143 (MDNC 1982).

ful discrimination will somehow jeopardize future job opportunities.[611] It also has been stated, or strongly suggested, that there is no merit to the argument that a plaintiff's reliance on grievance procedures under a collective bargaining agreement would toll the ADEA's limitations period.[612] Likewise, a grievant cannot justify tolling by arguing that filing with the EEOC was delayed while he or she awaited the outcome of an arbitration proceeding.[613]

An employer's representation that it will review the grievant's discharge will not justify tolling.[614] The employee's fear that if he or she pursues legal redress a loss of benefits will ensue is no justification for delay.[615] Nor, it has been held, will tolling be justified on the basis of the grievant's fear that the employer will retaliate against the grievant's spouse, where the spouse also works for the employer.[616]

§6.21 —Relation of Government Agency's Conduct to Flaws in Charge-Filing

Tolling the time period for the filing of a charge of unlawful discrimination with the Equal Employment Opportunity Commission (EEOC), which filing is required by §7(d)[617] of the Age

---

[611] *See, e.g.*, Frank v Capital Cities Communications, Inc, 48 FEP Cas (BNA) 1381, 1384 (SDNY 1984); Allotta v Chase Manhattan Bank, 547 F Supp 198 (SDNY 1982).

[612] *See* Barrow v New Orleans SS Assn, 932 F2d 473, 478 (5th Cir 1991); Fisher v CPC Intl, Inc, 591 F Supp 228, 233 (WD Mo 1984).

[613] Shockley v Vermont State Colleges, 793 F2d 478 (1st Cir 1986).

[614] Conaway v Control Data Corp, 955 F2d 358, 363 (5th Cir), *cert denied*, 113 S Ct 186 (1992).

[615] O'Malley v GTE Serv Corp, 758 F2d 818 (2d Cir 1985); Chambers v European Am Bank & Trust Co, 601 F Supp 630 (EDNY 1985).

[616] Crandall v Prudential Ins Co, 691 F Supp 814, 826-27 (DNJ 1988), *vacated without opinion*, 870 F2d 650 (3d Cir 1989).

[617] 29 USC §626(d).

Discrimination in Employment Act (ADEA),[618] generally will be deemed appropriate if the EEOC misleads the grievant into not filing a charge at all, or not filing a timely one.[619] In deciding *Early v Bankers Life & Casualty Co*[620] the Court of Appeals for the Seventh Circuit emphasized that ordinarily it will be equitable tolling, rather than equitable estoppel, that will come into play vis-á-vis lapses by the EEOC:

> Misleading conduct by the EEOC can be a basis for tolling the administrative statute of limitations. Objection to such tolling cannot be based on the policy against estopping government agencies. That policy comes into play only when it is a suit against the agency[.][621]

Tolling is particularly justified where the defendant in any event was aware of the plaintiff's complaining of age discrimination and so was not prejudiced by any lack of notice regarding the matter.[622]

Reliance by a plaintiff on the EEOC's misrepresentation that the limitations period is " 'no problem' " and would be " 'extend[ed]' " while the EEOC pursued conciliation efforts will justify tolling, unless the plaintiff is represented by an attorney; if he or she is, counsel will be deemed to be presumptively aware of the Act's requirements.[623] Whether the plaintiff is represented by counsel or not, the EEOC's repeated assurances that an agency suit will be filed, with the result being that the plaintiff

---

[618] *Id* §§621-634.

[619] *See* Gray v Phillips Petroleum Co, 858 F2d 610 (10th Cir 1988); Vance v Whirlpool Corp, 716 F2d 1010 (4th Cir 1983), *cert denied,* 465 US 1102 (1984); *cf* Dickerson v Deluxe Check Printers, Inc, 703 F2d 276 (8th Cir 1983) (court suggested, in dictum, that even had plaintiff's written charge been technically deficient, the assurance of the then-enforcement agency, the Department of Labor, that she had complied with the charge requirement would preclude a holding that the charge was deficient).

[620] 959 F2d 75 (7th Cir 1992).

[621] *Id* 81.

[622] *See* Galvan v Bexar County, 785 F2d 1298 (5th Cir 1986).

[623] Leite v Kennecott Copper Corp, 558 F Supp 1170, 1172 (D Mass), *affd without opinion,* 720 F2d 658 (1st Cir 1983).

delays in filing a charge, also will justify tolling the limitations period.[624]

It has been held that the failure of the EEOC or its predecessor, the Department of Labor, to inform grievants of the need to submit proper filings justifies tolling of the filing period.[625] And where a grievant was given the impression by the enforcement agency that there was nothing to be done about the alleged acts of discrimination, tolling was deemed to be in order.[626] In a similar vein, an EEOC employee's erroneous representation that the intake questionnaire filled out by the plaintiff was all that was necessary for the grievant to file, tolled the running of the charge-filing period.[627] When an agency district office transferred a timely filed charge to another district office, but the transferred charge was ignored because the wrong form had been used, tolling was deemed justified.[628]

Tolling was deemed to be justified where the state agency's employees, who failed to refer the complaint to the EEOC, lulled the plaintiff—who was not represented by an attorney—into believing it has been referred.[629] Likewise, tolling was allowed by the court deciding *Williams v Warehouse Markets, Inc*,[630] where

---

[624] *Id.*

[625] *See, e.g.*, Dartt v Shell Oil Co, 539 F2d 1256 (10th Cir 1976), *affd by an equally divided Court*, 434 US 99 (1977); Snow v Government Employees Fin Corp, 25 FEP Cas (BNA) 844 (D Colo 1981); Russell v Curtin Matheson Scientific, Inc, 17 FEP Cas (BNA) 845 (SD Tex), *as amended*, 18 FEP Cas (BNA) 179 (SD Tex), *leave to appeal denied*, 18 FEP Cas (BNA) 866 (5th Cir), *cert denied*, 439 US 972 (1978); Woerner v Bell Helicopter, 16 FEP Cas (BNA) 480 (ND Tex 1977); Abbott v Moore Business Forms, Inc, 439 F Supp 643 (DNH 1977); *see also* O'Connor v Pan Am, 53 FEP Cas (BNA) 419 (SDNY 1990). *But see* Reich v Dow Badische Co, 575 F2d 363, 369 (2d Cir), *cert denied*, 439 US 1006 (1978); Mitchell v United States Steel Corp, 54 FEP Cas (BNA) 1050 (ND Ala 1984); Frasco v Joseph Schlitz Brewing Co, 532 F Supp 1020 (MDNC 1982).

[626] Catlett v Owens-Illinois, Inc, 454 F Supp 358 (WD Mo 1978).

[627] Early v Bankers Life & Casualty Co, 959 F2d 75 (7th Cir 1992).

[628] Anness v United Steelworkers of Am, 26 FEP Cas (BNA) 1340 (ND Ohio 1981), *revd & remanded on other grounds*, 707 F2d 917 (6th Cir 1983).

[629] James v Miller-Wohl Co, 35 FEP Cas (BNA) 1846 (WDNY 1994).

[630] 637 F Supp 724 (D Nev 1986).

the state agency either never received, or lost, the charge mailed to it and so did not refer it to the EEOC.

Tolling aside, when an agency employee fails properly to record the plaintiff's oral charge of alleged age discrimination, the plaintiff will not be barred from filing suit.[631] And when an agency employee fails to send a copy of the charge to the charged party, that, too, will not preclude the grievant from suing.[632] In a similar vein, the failure of the EEOC to refer a charge to a state antidiscrimination agency will not support dismissing an ADEA suit on the ground that the complaint was not timely filed with that state agency.[633] In these instances, in other words, the absence of the predicate charge will not bar the plaintiff from suing.

Antitolling Decisions

It certainly does not invariably follow that every alleged agency lapse will justify tolling the charge filing time requirements. For one, a plaintiff who is familiar with the ADEA may not rely on the agency's failure to advise him or her of the need to file a charge as an excuse for an untimely filing.[634] Thus, where an individual, already knowing of the ADEA and its time requirements for filing, spoke to EEOC employees on the telephone, and got a 'run-around,' but was not misled, tolling was not justi-

---

[631] Holly v City of Naperville, 571 F Supp 668 (ND Ill 1983); *see also* Glass v IDS Fin Servs, Inc, 778 F Supp 1029, 1040 (D Minn 1991).

[632] Glass v IDS Fin Servs, Inc, 778 F Supp 1029, 1042-43 (D Minn 1991).

[633] Gabrielle v Barrett, Haentjens & Co, 663 F Supp 1187 (MD Pa 1986); Agostine v Iowa Beef Processors, 35 FEP Cas (BNA) 328 (D Neb 1984); *see also* Sarsha v Sears, Roebuck & Co, 747 F Supp 454 (ND Ill 1990) (under work-sharing agreement between EEOC and state human rights agency, the latter designated an EEOC employee as state's agent for reviewing charges received by EEOC, and the designated EEOC employee concluded that charge had been filed after the state filing period had run; in such a situation, it was the shared interpretation of the EEOC and the state agency that there was no need to file with the state, and accordingly the EEOC employee properly did not refer the charge to the state agency).

[634] *See, e.g.*, Woodard v Western Union Tel Co, 650 F2d 592, 595 (5th Cir 1981).

fied.[635] When an individual's contact with the enforcement agency first occurs only after the time for filing a charge has elapsed, it would not matter how the agency might have erred in responding, since the dilatoriness of the grievant would preclude the agency's action being prejudicial.[636]

According to one district court, the mere failure of an agency employee to inform a grievant of the timing requirements for filing need not necessarily justify tolling.[637] Other courts have taken a more emphatically negative position. The district court deciding *Sitarski v IBM Corp*[638] asserted that "[timing] information omitted in a telephone conversation . . . does not rise to the level of conduct . . . [justifying tolling]".[639] Likewise, the Court of Appeals for the Fifth Circuit held, in *Conaway v Control Data Corp*,[640] that "the alleged incomplete oral statements [regarding the need to file a charge of discrimination within 300 days of the alleged discrimination] made by the EEOC to . . . [the plaintiff] during a telephone conversation will not support equitable tolling."[641]

In *Schroeder v Copley Newspaper*[642] the district court took an unusually harsh, even aberrational, position as to the task confronting a grievant pointing to agency action (or inaction) as a basis for tolling. The court, relying upon case law dealing with instances where grievants have sought equitable estoppel based on an employer's actions,[643] asserted as follows: " 'Equitable estoppel is available only if the employee's otherwise untimely

---

635 Moon v Aeronca, Inc, 541 F Supp 747 (SD Ohio 1982).

636 *See, e.g.*, Ewald v Great Atl & Pac Tea Co, 620 F2d 1183, 1188 (6th Cir), *vacated on other grounds*, 449 US 914 (1980); Fulton v NCR Corp, 472 F Supp 377, 384 (WD Va 1979).

637 *See* Mitchell v United States Steel Corp, 54 FEP Cas (BNA) 1050 (ND Ala 1984).

638 708 F Supp 889 (ND Ill 1989).

639 *Id* 891.

640 955 F2d 358 (5th Cir), *cert denied*, 113 S Ct 186 (1992).

641 *Id* 363. *But see* Downes v Volkswagen of Am, Inc, 59 FEP Cas (BNA) 440, 443 (ND Ill 1992).

642 691 F Supp 1127 (ND Ill 1988), *affd*, 879 F2d 266 (7th Cir 1989).

643 See **§6.19.**

filing was the result either of a deliberate design by the employer or of actions that the employer should unmistakably have understood would cause the employee to delay filing his charge.' "[644] On appeal, the Court of Appeals for the Seventh Circuit, while utilizing a somewhat different standard, still demonstrated hostility to tolling the charge-filing period for the plaintiff: for agency action to justify tolling of the statute of limitations, the agency would have to have " 'affirmatively induced' " or " 'lulled' " the plaintiff into inaction.[645] The court concluded that these standards were not met by virtue of an EEOC employee having told the plaintiff, when he visited the EEOC office, that "there 'wasn't much' that the EEOC 'could do for him.' "[646] The court further noted that "while Schroeder may not have been 'familiar' with the ADEA when he . . . [went to] the EEOC, he nevertheless understood he had rights under the ADEA . . . ; and that is enough."[647]

The failure of a state agency to refer a filed complaint with it to the EEOC will not justify tolling—at least where the complainant was represented by counsel and where the work-sharing agreement between the state and the EEOC provided for such a referral only when the complainant specifically requested it, and no such request was made.[648]

§6.22 Reliance on a Charge Filed by Another Grievant: The Single Filing Rule

Section 7(d)[649] of the Age Discrimination in Employment Act

---

[644] 691 F Supp at 1130 (quoting Mull v ARCO Durethene Plastics, Inc, 784 F2d 284, 292 (7th Cir 1986)).

[645] Schroeder v Copley Newspaper, 879 F2d 266, 271 (7th Cir 1989) (quoting Woodard v Western Union Tel Co, 650 F2d 592, 595 (5th Cir 1981)).

[646] *Id.*

[647] *Id.*

[648] Kinniry v Aetna Ins Co, 35 FEP Cas (BNA) 1474 (D Conn 1984).

[649] 29 USC §626(d).

(ADEA)[650] requires that before a person may file suit, a charge of unlawful discrimination must be filed with the Equal Employment Opportunity Commission (EEOC). Prior to a 1978 amendment to the Act, the language of the statute provided that "[n]o civil action may be commenced by any individual . . . until the individual has given . . . not less than sixty days' notice of an intent to file such action."[651] Thus, the pre-amendment language spoke of a "notice of intent" to sue and, further, it spoke of an "individual" giving such notice.[652] In 1978 §7(d) of the Act was amended so as to provide that an action may not be commenced "until 60 days after a *charge alleging unlawful discrimination* has been filed."[653] Thus, "notice of an 'intent' to sue" was supplanted by "charge alleging unlawful discrimination" and, more importantly here, the reference to "individual" was eliminated. These changes were only meant, however, to be "clarification-s[s] and not . . . substantive changes[s]," and so "pre-alteration precedent . . . [remained] viable."[654] This change's particular relevance is discussed *infra.*

A number of courts have been called upon to address the question of whether an individual who did not himself or herself file a charge at all—or, if he or she did so, the charge was not timely—may opt into a representative action filed by a named plaintiff who did file a timely charge. (The typical class action maintained pursuant to Federal Rule of Civil Procedure 23 is not available in the ADEA context. Rather, any individual who wants to participate in a representative action, i.e., an action in which a named plaintiff represents his or her own interests, as well as those of other individuals, must affirmatively opt into the

---

650 *Id* §§621-634.

651 §7(d), 29 USC §626(d) (pre-1978 amendment version).

652 *Id.*

653 (Emphasis added).

654 Anson v University of Tex Health Science Ctr, 962 F2d 539, 541 n2 (5th Cir 1992); *see also* Franci v AVCO Corp, AVCO Lycoming Div, 538 F Supp 250, 253 (D Conn 1982).

lawsuit).[655] The courts today are largely in agreement in subscribing to the *single filing* rule, i.e., under some circumstances a grievant who did not file a charge may opt into a representative action by 'piggybacking' on the named plaintiff's charge. It is on the question of what circumstances are sufficient to justify allowing a non-charge-filing or late-filing individual to opt in that the decisions diverge.

Most Restrictive Position: All Opt-In Plaintiffs Must Have Filed Timely Charges

In an older ruling the Court of Appeals for the Eleventh Circuit took the position that each class member must have timely filed a what was then styled a notice of an intent to sue with the enforcement agency.[656]

Middle Position: The Charge Must Disclose that More Claims Than Just Those of the Charging Party Are Involved

The large majority of courts embrace the single filing rule: an individual who did not file a charge may opt into a representative action, so long as the charge filed gave notice to the EEOC and to the defendant that the discrimination of which the charging party complained involved more individuals than just himself or herself. It is the conveyance of information regarding the multiplicity of individuals that is critical here. Thus, for example, the Court of Appeals for the Eighth Circuit asserted in *Kloos v Carter-Day Co*[657] that because the purpose of a charge is to afford the EEOC an opportunity to resolve the dispute short of litigation and because, further, the charge serves to apprise the

---

[655] As to representative actions generally, see **§§6.45-.51.**

[656] *See, e.g.,* Allison v Western Union, 680 F2d 1318 (11th Cir 1982); *accord* Price v Maryland Casualty Co, 561 F2d 609 (5th Cir 1977). *Contra* Russell v Curtis Matheson Scientific, Inc, 17 FEP Cas (BNA) 845 (SD Tex), *as amended,* 18 FEP Cas (BNA) 179 (SD Tex), *leave to appeal denied,* 18 FEP Cas (BNA) 866 (5th Cir), *cert denied,* 439 US 972 (1978). *Price* is of dubious continuing validity in light of Anson v University of Tex Health Science Ctr, 962 F2d 539 (5th Cir 1992).

[657] 799 F2d 397 (8th Cir 1986).

employer of its alleged wrongdoing, "[a]n allegation of class-wide discrimination or claim of class representation"[658] is necessary. Otherwise, the "[f]ailure to require some notice of class claims in the charge would [unfairly] require employers to treat all individual charges as potential class actions."[659] The Court of Appeals for the Third Circuit echoed this assertion in *Lusardi v Lechner.*[660]

Other courts also echo these views. The Court of Appeals for the Ninth Circuit stated, in *Naton v Bank of California,*[661] that to allow a nonfiling party to opt into a representative suit, the notice or charge on which that party seeks to rely must provide adequate notice that the claim involved is not an individual one, but rather involves a course of alleged unlawful conduct of larger scope.[662] And in deciding *Anderson v Montgomery Ward & Co*[663] the Court of Appeals for the Seventh Circuit stated as follows:

> [T]he charge must, at the very least, contain an allegation of class-wide discrimination. This notification is necessary in order to satisfy Congress' express desire that the defendant understand, during the conciliation stage, the magnitude of his potential liability.[664]

The Court of Appeals for the Second Circuit took a similar, albeit somewhat more tempered, position in *Tolliver v Xerox Corp,*[665] where it drew a distinction based on the size of the workplace:

---

[658] *Id* 400.

[659] *Id.*

[660] 855 F2d 1062, 1077-78 (3d Cir 1988).

[661] 649 F2d 691 (9th Cir 1981).

[662] *Accord* Church v Consolidated Freightways, Inc, 137 FRD 294, 302 (ND Cal 1991); Hopper v Timex Corp, 595 F Supp 668 (MD Ark 1984); Frank v Capital Communications, Inc, 33 Empl Prac Dec (CCH) ¶34,285 (SDNY 1983); *see also* Sussman v Vornado, Inc, 90 FRD 680 (DNJ 1981).

[663] 852 F2d 1008 (7th Cir 1988).

[664] *Id* 1016 (citations omitted).

[665] 918 F2d 1052 (2d Cir 1990), *cert denied,* 499 US 983 (1991).

> Where the grievance arises in a work unit of modest size, . . . mere similarity of the grievances within the same general time frame suffices to permit the "single filing rule." . . . However, where the grievances are alleged to arise throughout a large group, the lack of conciliation of one individual grievance does not necessarily mean that conciliation efforts would be unavailing if the EEOC and the employer were alerted to the broad scope of the claim. Though we do not think the administrative claim in such circumstances need specify that the claimant purports to represent a class or others similarly situated, there must be some indication that the grievance affects a group of individuals defined broadly enough to include those who seek to piggyback on the claim. Such a claim alerts the EEOC that more is alleged than an isolated act of discrimination and affords sufficient notice to the employer to explore conciliation with the affected group.[666]

Other courts, as well, have taken the position that as long as the named plaintiff has timely filed with the agency, there is no need for the additional opt-in plaintiffs to have done so.[667] Still accord-

---

[666] *Id* 1058 (footnote omitted). In Pirone v Home Ins Co, 507 F Supp 1281 (SDNY 1981), a district court expressed the view that because the purpose of the charge is to initiate the conciliation process, the enforcement agency must be informed by that charge that an individual named in it—but who is not the actual charging party—believes himself or herself to be a victim of age discrimination and that he or she is contemplating a lawsuit or is desirous of pursuing informal conciliation. The agency can only be so informed when the nonfiling party authorizes the filing party to file a charge on his or her behalf. *Pirone* is no longer viable, in light of *Tolliver.* Likewise, Pandis v Sikorsky Aircraft Div of United Tech Corp, 431 F Supp 793 (D Conn 1977), in which a more liberal position vis-a-vis opt-in plaintiffs was asserted, no longer is valid, given *Tolliver.*

[667] *See, e.g.*, Russell v Curtis Matheson Scientific, Inc, 17 FEP Cas (BNA) 845 (SD Tex), *as amended,* 18 FEP Cas (BNA) 179 (SD Tex), *leave to appeal denied,* 18 FEP Cas (BNA) 866 (5th Cir), *cert denied,* 439 US 972 (1978); Cavanaugh v Texas Instruments, Inc, 440 F Supp 1124 (SD Tex 1977); Mistretta v Sandia Corp, 12 FEP Cas (BNA) 1225 (DNM 1975); Hays v Republic Steel Corp, 12 FEP Cas (BNA) 1637 (ND Ala 1974); Burgett v Cudahy Co, 361 F Supp 617 (D Kan 1973); *see also* Mistretta v Sandia Corp, 639 F2d 588 (10th Cir 1980); Shuster v Federated Dept Stores, Inc, 508 F Supp 118 (ND Ga 1980) (nonclass action suit). This rule also has been embraced by a number of courts in cases

ing to the Court of Appeals for the Third Circuit, deciding *Lusardi v Lechner,*[668] while the original complainant's charge does not have to state specifically that it is being brought on behalf of "others similarly situated," it must "notif[y] [the employer] that it allegedly discriminates against persons over 40 years old as a class."[669]

While there is some suggestion that some courts require that a grievant who files a charge have intended to represent a class,[670] there is precedent rejecting such an intent requirement.[671]

In deciding *Church v Consolidated Freightways, Inc,*[672] a district court took the position that the mechanism for putting the EEOC on notice of the class nature of a claim was not limited just to a charge of unlawful discrimination filed with the agency: "The method from which the EEOC received notice should not serve to defeat a classwide claim of discrimination; rather, it should suffice that the EEOC has notice from the charge or notice in fact, however received, so that it can begin the concilia-

---

arising under Title VII of the Civil Rights Act of 1964, 42 USC §§2000e through 2000e-17, the statutory analogue of the ADEA to which, as discussed in **ch 2,** ADEA courts often look for guidance. *See* Walker v Jim Dandy Co, 747 F2d 1360, 1366 (11th Cir 1984); Lilly v Harris-Teeter Supermarket, 720 F2d 326, 335 (4th Cir 1983), *cert denied,* 466 US 951 (1984); Foster v Gueory, 655 F2d 1319, 1321-23 (DC Cir 1981); Allen v United States Steel Corp, 665 F2d 689, 695 (5th Cir 1982); Allen v Amalgamated Transit Union Local 788, 554 F2d 876, 882-83 (8th Cir), *cert denied,* 434 US 891 (1977).

668 855 F2d 1062 (3d Cir 1988). In light of *Lusardi,* the more liberal position vis-a-vis opt-in plaintiffs asserted in Coventry v United States Steel Corp, 34 FEP Cas (BNA) 97 (WD Pa 1984), no longer is valid.

669 855 F2d at 1078; *accord* Lockhart v Westinghouse Credit Corp, 879 F2d 43, 52-53 (3d Cir 1989); Church v Consolidated Freightways, Inc, 137 FRD 294, 302 (ND Cal 1991).

670 *See* Naton v Bank of Cal, 649 F2d 691, 697 (9th Cir 1981).

671 *See* Anderson v Montgomery Ward & Co, 852 F2d 1008, 1017 (7th Cir 1988); Kloos v Carter-Day Co, 799 F2d 397, 400 (8th Cir 1986); Glass v IDS Fin Servs, Inc, 778 F Supp 1029, 1045-46 (D Min 1991).

672 137 FRD 294 (ND Cal 1991).

tion process."[673] The court concluded that the charges, along with the affidavits accompanying them, afforded adequate notice.

The court deciding *Glass v IDS Financial Services, Inc*,[674] also addressed the issue of whether the communications made to the EEOC had provided fair notice of the existence of class claims. Noting that the courts generally "have . . . found general allegations of class-wide age discrimination sufficient to permit plaintiffs to assert class-wide claims,"[675] the court deemed sufficient a phone call by the plaintiff's wife to the state antidiscrimination agency, during which she read a statement written by her husband to the listener, in which statement reference was made to discrimination vis-á-vis both her husband and other persons. The court also deemed persuasive the intake questionnaire submitted to the state agency by the named plaintiff, notwithstanding that a copy of this questionnaire had not been provided to the charged party. In that questionnaire the plaintiff specifically named four people younger than himself who had been promoted and five men older than himself who had been demoted.

Least Restrictive Position: The Charge Need not Disclose The Group Nature of The Grievance

Some courts have taken a position more generous to opt-in plaintiffs. They have allowed individuals to be included as parties in lawsuits even though the representative plaintiff's charge made no mention of the opt-in plaintiffs, nor indicated in any way that the alleged violation was by its nature one involving more individuals than the charging party.[676] (In *Gormin v Brown-*

---

[673] *Id* 302.

[674] 778 F Supp 1029 (D Minn 1991).

[675] *Id* 1041.

[676] *See, e.g.*, Johnson v American Airlines, Inc, 531 F Supp 957 (ND Tex 1982), *affd on other grounds*, 745 F2d 988 (5th Cir 1984), *cert denied*, 472 US 1027 (1985); Shuster v Federated Dept Stores, Inc, 508 F Supp 118 (ND Ga 1980); *see also* Snair v City of Clearwater, 787 F Supp 1401, 1408-09 (MD Fla 1992); Gray v Phillips Petroleum Co, 638 F Supp 789 (D Kan 1986), *affd in part & revd in part on other grounds*, 858 F2d 610 (10th Cir 1988).

Forman Corp[677] the court left open the possibility that it would deem permissible the opting in of an individual even where the named plaintiff had not, in his or her charge, indicated the class nature of the claim).

Limiting of Issues to Those Addressed in the Charge

Over and above the requirement imposed by most courts as to noncharge-filing opt-in plaintiffs that the charge filed by the representative plaintiff must indicate that more than just his or her grievance is at issue, a number of courts have imposed another limitation: the opt-in plaintiffs will be limited to the issues raised by the representative plaintiff in his or her timely filed charge.[678] In fact, of course, this position can afford considerable room for judicial flexibility, as is revealed by the liberal formulation devised by the Court of Appeals for the Eighth Circuit in *Ulvin v Northwestern National Life Insurance Co.*[679] In that case the court fleshed out the contours of the *single filing* rule that it had embraced in *Kloos:* "[W]hen the filed charge is quite specific as to the scope of the class claim it raises, opt-in plaintiff should not be permitted to raise claims that are *far outside* of that scope."[680]

Timeliness of Claims of Non-Charge-Filing Plaintiffs

Another caveat imposed by some courts is that the representative plaintiff will not be allowed to represent persons who could not have timely complied with the charge-filing requirement as of the date of the representative plaintiff's filing with the agen-

---

[677] 744 F Supp 1100 (MD Fla 1990).

[678] *See, e.g.*, Walker v Mountain States Tel & Tel Co, 112 FRD 44, 46 (D Colo 1986); Russell v Curtis Matheson Scientific, Inc, 17 FEP Cas (BNA) 845 (SD Tex), *as amended,* 18 FEP Cas (BNA) 179 (SD Tex), *leave to appeal denied,* 18 FEP Cas (BNA) 866 (5th Cir), *cert denied,* 439 US 972 (1978); Cavanaugh v Texas Instruments, Inc, 440 F Supp 1124 (SD Tex 1977); Pandis v Sikorsky Aircraft, Div of United Technologies Corp, 431 F Supp 793 (D Conn 1977); Burgett v Cudahy Co, 361 F Supp 617 (D Kan 1973).

[679] 943 F2d 862 (8th Cir 1991), *cert denied,* 112 S Ct 970 (1992).

[680] *Id* 865 (emphasis added). *Ulvin* was distinguished on its facts by the court deciding Glass v IDS Fin Servs, Inc, 778 F Supp 1029, 1043-44 (D Minn 1991).

cy.[681] In *Anderson v Montgomery Ward & Co, Inc,*[682] however, the Court of Appeals for the Seventh Circuit allowed individuals to opt in even though they could not themselves have timely filed charges at the time the representative plaintiff had filed his charge (provided that the plaintiff into whose suit they were opting had filed a charge in which he alleged class-based age dis-

---

[681] *See, e.g.*, Walker v Mountain States Tel & Tel Co, 112 FRD 44, 47 (D Colo 1986); Sussman v Vornado, Inc, 90 FRD 680 (DNJ 1981); Geller v Markham, 481 F Supp 835 (D Conn 1979), *affd in part & revd in part on other grounds,* 635 F2d 1027 (2d Cir 1980), *cert denied,* 451 US 945 (1981); Russell v Curtis Matheson Scientific, Inc, 17 FEP Cas (BNA) 845 (SD Tex), *as amended,* 18 FEP Cas (BNA) 179 (SD Tex), *leave to appeal denied,* 18 FEP Cas (BNA) 866 (5th Cir), *cert denied,* 439 US 972 (1978); Cavanaugh v Texas Instruments, Inc, 440 F Supp 1124 (SD Tex 1977); Pandis v Sikorsky Aircraft, Div of United Tech Corp, 431 F Supp 793 (D Conn 1977); Forman v Block Drug Co, 16 FEP Cas (BNA) 414 (EDNY 1977) (dictum); Erpelding v Thornhill, 18 FEP Cas (BNA) 1479 (ED Mich 1976); *see also* Behr v Drake Hotel, 586 F Supp 427 (ND Ill 1984); Frank v Capital Cities Communications, Inc, 88 FRD 674 (SDNY 1981).

Under §7(d)(2), 29 USC §626(d)(2), a grievant has 300 days within which to file a charge of unlawful discrimination when the claim arises in a state having a state law banning age discrimination in employment and an entity authorized to grant or to seek relief for victims of such discrimination. If there is no such state law and state agency, a 180-day filing period applies. §7(d)(1), 29 USC §626(d)(1). See generally **§6.08.** Section 14(b), 29 USC §633(b), requires that if there is such a state law and such a state agency, a grievant must seek redress at the state level as a predicate to seeking relief under the ADEA. See **§6.25.** Suppose a named plaintiff in a representative action complied with §14(b) and indeed did file a claim at the state level under state law within the 300-day period. Should all other members of the class likewise have the benefit of this time period, even though they in fact did not file any claim at the state level? Or, because they did not so file, should they be limited to 180 days, so that they may not consent to entering a class suit on the 181st day after the alleged wrong occurred? This question was left open in *Pandis.* In *Geller* the district court stated that the 300-day period would be available to all members of the class if it was available to the representative plaintiff. In Walker v Mountain States Tel & Tel Co, 112 FRD 44, 47 (D Colo 1986), however, the court ruled that the 300-day filing period that was available to the representative plaintiff would not be available to opt-in plaintiffs who resided in states in which the 180-day filing period applied. In Frank v Capital Cities Communications, Inc, 509 F Supp 1352 (SDNY 1981), the court addressed, but did not resolve, this issue.

[682] 852 F2d 1008 (7th Cir 1988).

crimination or in which he claimed to represent a class.) Other courts are in accord with this stance.[683]

The court that decided *Church v Consolidated Freightways, Inc,*[684] ruled that notice of the representative suit could issue to potential opt-in plaintiffs who had not filed charges with the EEOC,[685] as long as the alleged acts of discrimination of which they complained had occurred within 180 or 300 days (depending upon whether the jurisdiction had a nondiscrimination law and an agency authorized to seek relief) prior to the earliest filing by a named plaintiff of his or her EEOC charge. Thus, the date of the EEOC charge that had been filed by a representative plaintiff, rather than the date of the alleged discrimination itself, was established as the key date for timing computations. The court further ruled that there was no closure date as to such opt-in plaintiffs where "acts of ongoing discrimination in furtherance of an earlier implemented plan are alleged."[686]

In *Burke v Merrill Lynch & Co*[687] the court ruled that only individuals who had timely filed with the EEOC could serve as named plaintiffs, whereas individuals who had not timely filed could participate as opt-in, or unnamed, plaintiffs. (These opt-in,

---

683 *See* Durant v Maher Chevrolet, Inc, 759 F Supp 787 (MD Fla 1991); Heagney v European Bank, 122 FRD 125, 129 (EDNY 1988); Levine v Lane Bryant, 700 F Supp 949 (ND Ill 1988); Gray v Phillips Petroleum Co, 49 FEP Cas (BNA) 65 (D Kan 1986), *affd in part & revd & remanded in part on other grounds,* 858 F2d 610 (10th Cir 1988); *see also* Burt v Manville Sales Corp, 116 FRD 276 (D Colo 1987); Walker v Mountain States Tel & Tel Co, 112 FRD 44 (D Colo 1986). The district court deciding Allen v Marshall Field & Co, 29 FEP Cas (BNA) 314 (ND Ill 1982), which in an earlier ruling—Allen v Marshall Field & Co, 93 FRD 438 (ND Ill 1982)—had avoided deciding the question, held that even though some of the opt-in plaintiffs could not have timely filed with the enforcement agency at the time the representative plaintiffs filed their charges with the EEOC, they still could opt in because the defendant's failure to post the statutorily required notice regarding the ADEA equitably estopped its raising the timeliness issue. See **§6.18.** In light of *Anderson,* this cautious position vis-a-vis untimely opt-in plaintiffs—whereby the court relied on the failure of the employer to post the requisite notice as the basis for its ruling—would not be necessary.

684 137 FRD 294 (ND Cal 1991).

685 As to the issuance of notice to potential opt-in plaintiffs, see **§§6.46-.50.**

686 137 FRD at 310.

687 52 FEP Cas (BNA) 244 (DNJ 1989).

untimely plaintiffs could not, however, maintain individual claims; "[o]nly claims asserted by the class . . . [could] be asserted.")[688]

In contrast to the foregoing rulings, there are some decisions, in which courts have been unwilling to relieve untimely opt-in plaintiffs of the onus of their dilatoriness. In *Mitchell v United States Steel Corp*[689] the court rejected the argument that the earlier noted 1978 amendment to the ADEA opened the door to opt-in plaintiffs who had not timely filed their charges of discrimination. It held that only those individuals who had timely filed with the EEOC could opt into the federal court suit. Likewise, in *Fressell v AT&T Technologies, Inc,*[690] the court ruled against the opt-in plaintiffs. The court made two points. First, there were several discrete acts of alleged wrongdoing, each of which affected only one of the plaintiffs. Second, neither the timely filed charges of the representative plaintiffs, nor the subsequent conciliation efforts by the EEOC, made any mention of other, similarly situated individuals.[691]

The Court of Appeals for the Fifth Circuit has held that a grievant whose claim did not arise until *after* the charge was filed by the representative plaintiff could not opt into the suit filed by that plaintiff.[692]

Significance of the 1978 Amendment

One of the language changes made by the 1978 amendment has been pointed to as supportive, in the charge-filing context, of the position that not all plaintiffs need file with the enforcement agency. More specifically, several courts have pointed to the fact that the pre-1978 language provided that a private lawsuit could not be commenced "until the individual has given" 60 days' notice of intent to sue, while the amendment changed

---

688 *Id* 245.

689 33 Empl Prac Dec (CCH) ¶34,103 (ND Ala 1984).

690 35 FEP Cas (BNA) 658 (ND Ga 1984).

691 *Id* 660.

692 Anson v University of Tex Health Science Ctr, 962 F2d 539 (5th Cir 1992); *see also* Oshiro v Pan Am World Airways, Inc, 378 F Supp 80 (D Haw 1974).

§7(d) to provide that no private action may be commenced "until 60 days after a charge . . . has been filed." This change, it has been reasoned, eliminated the literal requirement that each grievant file with the EEOC, and so allows a plaintiff to rely on a charge filed by another individual.[693]

An EEOC regulation unmistakably contemplates charges being filed "on behalf" of grievants.[694] While the regulation's language suggests some sort of fiduciary relationship between the filing party and the person on whose behalf the charge is filed, the EEOC commentary accompanying the issuance of the regulation does not suggest that there need be any relationship between the two individuals. Pointing to the 1978 language change, the EEOC has asserted that "[t]he change from the active to the passive mode [sic] lifts the burden from the individual aggrieved to personally file the charge, and allows any charge . . . which gives sufficient notice to the Commission to conciliate to satisfy the [§]7(d) requirement."[695] Further EEOC commentary reinforces the conclusions (1) that a party who has not filed a charge may rely upon another person's charge, so long as the matter complained of is within the scope of the previously filed charge, and (2) that there need be no special relationship between the two parties:

> The [earlier proposed] regulation . . . may have created the impression that [§]7(d) requires that the individual who wishes to file suit, must file a charge. The statute and Commission regulations provide that a properly filed charge may be filed on behalf of the individual, or that an aggrieved person may bring suit so long as the matter complained of

---

[693] *See, e.g.*, Anderson v Montgomery Ward & Co, Inc, 852 F2d 1008, 1015-16 & n10 (7th Cir 1988); Johnson v American Airlines, Inc, 531 F Supp 957, 963 (ND Tex 1982), *affd on other grounds*, 745 F2d 988 (5th Cir 1984), *cert denied*, 472 US 1027 (1985); Shuster v Federated Dept Stores, Inc, 508 F Supp 118 (ND Ga 1980); Pirone v Home Ins Co, 507 F Supp 1281, 1286 (SDNY 1981), *affd without opinion*, 742 F2d 1430 (2d Cir 1983).

[694] 29 CFR §1626.3 (1993).

[695] 48 Fed Reg 138-39 (Jan 3, 1983).

> was within the scope of the previously filed charge, regardless of who filed it.[696]

Thus, for example a charge may be filed with the EEOC on behalf of a grievant by the state agency with which the grievant initially filed a complaint of discrimination.[697]

Status of an Opt-In Plaintiff

The court deciding *Nowicki v USX Corp*[698] allowed a party to opt in, given that the filing plaintiff had identified him in the administrative charge as a similarly situated victim of the defendant's alleged discrimination. (There was no issue regarding the opt-in plaintiff being untimely.) However, the court stated that while the opt-in plaintiff could participate in the lawsuit, he could not do so in the role of co-plaintiff.[699] In so doing the court said it was adopting a rule set forth in *Bean v Crocker National Bank.*[700] A reading of *Bean* reveals no such rule, however. Apart from that obscurity, there also is no explanation in *Nowicki* as to what the court envisioned as being the role of an individual who could participate, but could not be a co-plaintiff.

Filing with the State Agency

In *Lusardi v Xerox Corp*[701] the court noted that it generally has been held that unnamed plaintiffs who subsequently opt in to representative actions need not have filed with their state enforcement agency if the named plaintiff had done so.[702] In both decisions that the *Lusardi* district court cited—*Mistretta v*

---

[696] *Id.*

[697] Stearns v Consolidated Mgmt, Inc, 747 F2d 1105 (7th Cir 1984).

[698] 672 F Supp 854 (WD Pa 1987).

[699] *Id* 857.

[700] 600 F2d 754 (9th Cir 1979), relied upon in *Nowicki,* 672 F Supp at 857.

[701] 99 FRD 89 (DNJ 1983), *appeal dismissed on other grounds,* 747 F2d 147 (3d Cir 1984).

[702] *Id* 91 n5.

Sandia Corp[703] and *Bean v Crocker National Bank*—the filing party had indicated that he was filing on behalf of others similarly situated. Likewise, in *Frank v Capital Cities Communications, Inc*,[704] the court did not require that each opt-in plaintiff have filed with the state agency "[s]o long as the named plaintiffs comply by filing a charge which makes clear the class nature of their complaint[.]"[705]

§6.23 —Individual Suit by a Non-Charge-Filing Plaintiff Who Relies on Another Individual's Charge

If a representative action is disallowed, question can arise as to the legal posture of opt-in plaintiffs who failed to file timely charges of unlawful discrimination with the Equal Employment Opportunity Commission (EEOC) but who, had the representative action gone forward, would have been allowed to remain in court by virtue of their 'piggybacking' on the claim of a representative plaintiff who had timely filed with the agency.[706] Several district courts have ruled that in such a situation the late-filing opt-in plaintiff's suit should be dismissed.[707]

In deciding *Tolliver v Xerox Corp*[708] the Court of Appeals for the Second Circuit took a major step beyond both these rulings

---

[703] 639 F2d 588 (10th Cir 1980). In *Mistretta* it was held that the notice of intent to sue filed with the federal enforcement agency by two representative plaintiffs, with a copy sent to the state antidiscrimination agency, was sufficient to satisfy the state's filing requirements as to the represented plaintiffs, who never filed with the state. *Id* 594-95. As to state filing requirements generally, see **§6.27.**

[704] 48 FEP Cas (BNA) 551 (SDNY 1983).

[705] *Id* 552; *see also* Foster v CBS Records, Div of CBS, Inc, 109 FRD 168 (SDNY 1986).

[706] See generally **§6.22.**

[707] *See* Allen v Xerox Corp, 58 FEP Cas (BNA) 1054 (D Conn 1990); Aleszcyk v Xerox Corp, 54 FEP Cas (BNA) 622 (WDNY), *revd & remanded,* 918 F2d 1052 (2d Cir 1990), *cert denied,* 499 US 983 (1991); Benedict v Xerox Corp, 144 Misc 2d 490, 544 NYS2d 418 (1989).

[708] 918 F2d 1052 (2d Cir 1990), *cert denied,* 499 US 983 (1991).

involving opt-in plaintiffs and those decisions addressing more generally the *single filing* rule.[709] The court upheld the right of 18 former employees of Xerox to maintain their own individual suits, all on the basis of a charge filed by another former employee, Lusardi. Lusardi had timely filed a charge of unlawful discrimination with the EEOC; this charge alleged that Xerox "had discriminated 'against persons such as myself over forty as a class particularly with respect to the implementation of a reduction in salaried work force.' "[710] Subsequently, some 1,300 individuals—including the 18 individuals here—filed written consents opting into the suit filed by Lusardi. The group represented by Lusardi ultimately was decertified, however. The notice of decertification advised members of the decertified class that the statute of limitations for the only potential means of redress now available, i.e., individual lawsuits, would be tolled from the date each had opted into the *Lusardi* case until December 23, 1988.

None of the 18 individuals who were the subject of the *Tolliver* appellate court ruling had filed timely charges of unlawful discrimination with the EEOC. Because of this the district court dismissed their suits. The court of appeals reversed. The appellate court embraced the *single filing* rule, which provides that the timely filing of an administrative charge with the EEOC by one individual will enable other grievants to join in that individual's suit so long as the claims of these individuals " 'aris[e] out of similar discriminatory treatment in the same time frame.' "[711] The facts in *Tolliver,* however, presented a significant variation on the *single filing* rule, because the *Tolliver* plaintiffs were not seeking to join in another preexisting suit, the representative plaintiff in which had timely filed a charge of unlawful discrimination. Rather, they were seeking to pursue their own separate suits.

---

[709] See **§6.22.**

[710] 918 F2d at 1058.

[711] Snell v Suffolk County, 782 F2d 1094, 1100 (2d Cir 1986) (quoting Ezell v Mobile Hous Bd, 709 F2d 1376, 1381 (11th Cir 1983)).

The court held that these plaintiffs indeed could maintain their separate causes of action, although it offered very little by way of justification. The court simply stated that because under the ADEA there is no requirement that a plaintiff obtain a right-to-sue letter from the EEOC as a precondition to filing suit,[712] there is "therefore no reason to require ADEA plaintiffs seeking to benefit from the single filing rule to join pre-existing individual suits."[713] The court concluded that the charge filed by Lusardi sufficed to allow the 18 plaintiffs to proceed.[714] "In assessing the adequacy of a charge for purposes of the single filing rule, the question is whether 'it can fairly be said that no conciliatory purpose [i.e., the conciliation of charges which the EEOC is required to pursue[715]] would be served by filing separate EEOC charges.' "[716] Here, in the court's view, inasmuch as the Lusardi charge put Xerox and the EEOC on notice that discrimination had occurred throughout the company, there was "no reason to think that conciliation would have been more likely if these 18 appellants had filed individual claims."[717]

Finally, the court rejected the argument that the *single filing* rule would be inapplicable if the individual plaintiffs were not

---

[712] Such agency permission is required under §706(f)(1), 42 USC §2000e-5(f)(1), of Title VII of the Civil Rights Act of 1964, *id* §§2000e through 2000e-17. As the *Tolliver* court correctly pointed out, no such notice of right must issue before a grievant may sue in the ADEA context. Rather, a claimant seeking redress under the ADEA need only wait 60 days after filing a charge of unlawful discrimination with the EEOC, and he or she then may file suit. As to the 60-day waiting period, see **§6.37.** (A notice does issue by the EEOC when it has completed its internal agency efforts, and this notice starts the running of the statute of limitations for filing suit. See **§6.30.** However, the grievant need not wait for this notice as a precondition to suing).

[713] 918 F2d at 1057.

[714] The court pointed out that since Lusardi's charge had been filed within 300 days of the date of the earliest discharge of any of the *Tolliver* plaintiffs, it did not "consider whether the single filing rule would be available to revive the claim of a plaintiff discharged more than 300 days prior to the filing of the administrative claim on which he seeks to piggyback." *Id* 1058 n3.

[715] See **§6.29.**

[716] 918 F2d at 1058 (quoting Foster v Geary, 655 F2d 1319, 1322 (DC Cir 1981)).

[717] *Id.*

similarly situated for purposes of a representative action being pursued.[718] "Though a class action may not be suitable, the claims of these 18 appellants are nonetheless sufficiently similar to those of the original named plaintiffs to satisfy the purposes of the notice filing requirement."[719]

Michnuk v GO Carlson, Inc,[720] also involved a suit filed by an individual who had not filed a timely charge with the EEOC and who sought to rely on a charge filed by another grievant. This case involved claims filed by five plaintiffs who jointly filed suit. One of the five—Coogan—had not timely filed with the EEOC. In an effort to stave off the defendant's attempt to dismiss the late filer, it was argued that the suit should be converted into a representative action, with Coogan then being permitted to opt into this action. The court, however, saw no need to pursue this tack. So long as the charge filed with the EEOC by one of the five joint plaintiffs was "explicitly representative," i.e., it "place[d] the defendant on notice as to which employees were affected by the allegedly discriminatory act or acts," the late-filing plaintiff could maintain his claim on his own behalf, rather than just as a plaintiff relying on representation by a named plaintiff in a representative action.[721] Here, the charges of the other plaintiffs had identified Coogan as an injured party, thereby satisfying the standard set by the court.

§6.24 Reliance on Another Cause of Action as a Basis for Excusing the Failure to File a Charge

Federal Rule of Civil Procedure 15(c) provides as follows: "Whenever the claim . . . asserted in the amended pleading arose out of the conduct, transaction, or occurrence set forth . . . in the original pleading, the amendment relates back to the date

---

[718] See **§6.50.**

[719] 918 F2d at 1059.

[720] 52 Empl Prac Dec (CCH) ¶39,560 (ED Pa 1989).

[721] *Id* ¶60,628.

of the original pleading." In *Tusting v Bay View Federal Savings & Loan Association*[722] Rule 15(c) served as the linchpin for a decision in favor of the plaintiff. Tusting and his fellow plaintiffs had filed a suit under the Employee Retirement Income Security Act of 1974 (ERISA),[723] complaining of a change in their health insurance benefit plan whereby employees who retired after a specified date would no longer be entitled to full employer-paid health insurance premiums. More than 300 days after this change was announced, the plaintiffs filed a charge of unlawful discrimination with the Equal Employment Opportunity Commission (EEOC), claiming that the benefit plan modification violated the Age Discrimination in Employment Act (ADEA).[724] The plaintiffs then sought leave to amend their federal court complaint to add an ADEA claim. The defendant moved for summary judgment, arguing that this claim was time barred because the plaintiff had failed to timely file with the EEOC.

The court, looking to Rule 15(c), allowed the plaintiffs to go forward with their ADEA claim, reasoning as follows:

> [I]t is undisputed that the new ADEA claim arises out of the same event as the prior, timely ERISA claim—Bay View's change to its health benefit plan. The ERISA claim and the ADEA claim share a common core of operative facts; the only difference is the legal theories upon which plaintiffs rely. Bay View had ample notice that its conduct surrounding the change of its health benefit plans is alleged to be wrongful. . . . Bay View has known of the lawsuit, known of the parties, and known of the events that allegedly entitle plaintiffs to relief. On these facts, the Court perceives no basis for allowing Bay View to take advantage of a nonjurisdictional procedural bar to a decision on the merits of the ADEA claim.[725]

---

[722] 762 F Supp 1381 (ND Cal 1991).

[723] 29 USC §1001 *et seq.*

[724] *Id* USC §§621-634.

[725] 762 F Supp at 1383.

Thus, a new legal theory, based on a statute not at all invoked when suit was originally filed, was allowed to be introduced into the litigation, the absence of the filing of a charge of discrimination notwithstanding.

The *Tusting* decision is at least somewhat problematic.[726] It is not entirely without precedential support, however.[727]

§6.25 Resort to State Relief

Section 14(b)[728] of the Age Discrimination in Employment Act (ADEA)[729] requires a grievant to seek relief at the state level if certain requisites regarding the availability of state relief are met:

> In the case of an unlawful practice occurring in a State which has a law prohibiting discrimination in employment because of age and establishing or authorizing a State authority to grant or seek relief from such discriminatory practice, no suit may be brought . . . before the expiration of sixty days after proceedings have been commenced under the State law.

At one time there was a split in the lower courts as to whether a grievant was required to first seek state relief before suing under the ADEA. Some courts took an affirmative position,[730] while others were of the view that the seeking of redress at the state level was optional.[731] The Supreme Court resolved the con-

---

726 *See, e.g.*, Wallace v Town of Stratford Bd of Educ, 674 F Supp 67, 70 (D Conn 1986); Campbell v AC Petersen Farms, Inc, 69 FRD 457 (D Conn 1975).

727 *See generally* 6A C. Wright & A. Miller, Federal Practice and Procedure §1497 (1971 & Supp 1990).

728 29 USC §633(b).

729 *Id* §§621-634.

730 *See* Reich v Dow Badische Co, 575 F2d 362 (2d Cir), *cert denied,* 439 US 1006 (1978); Curry v Continental Airlines, 513 F2d 691, 693 (9th Cir 1975).

731 *See* Holliday v Ketchum, MacLeod & Grove, Inc, 584 F2d 1221 (3d Cir 1978) (en banc); Oscar Mayer & Co v Evans, 580 F2d 298 (8th Cir 1978) (en banc), *revd,* 441 US 750 (1979); Smith v Joseph Schlitz Brewing Co, 419 F Supp

flict in 1979, holding in *Oscar Mayer & Co v Evans*[732] that resort to available state administrative remedies is mandatory. The Court reasoned that the purpose of § 14(b) is to divert from the federal courts those claims that might be settled by state agencies.[733] This goal would be compromised, in the Court's view, if resort to state remedies were optional, because state agencies obviously would be unable to address, not to mention resolve, complaints if they were not even brought to their attention.[734]

There was one caveat, however, to the *Oscar Mayer* Court's requiring resort to state remedies as a predicate to seeking relief under the ADEA: this requirement was applicable only to claims for individual relief. In other words, grievants who are represented by a named plaintiff in an ADEA representative action do not each have to pursue state remedies.[735]

As a result of *Oscar Mayer* the state of the law is that, absent some equitable basis for excusing a grievant from his or her failure to file with a state agency, that failure generally will preclude going forward with a federal suit.[736] However, § 14(b) does not

---

770 (DNJ 1976), *revd,* 584 F2d 1231 (3d Cir 1978) (en banc), *vacated,* 442 US 908 (1979). The ADEA was amended in some respects in 1978. See **ch 2.** While the amendments did not address the state filing issue, in the Senate report that accompanied the amendments, Senate Comm on Human Resources, Amending the Age Discrimination in Employment Act Amendments of 1977, S Rep No 493, 95th Cong, 1st Sess 6-7 (1977) there was a passage that was subsequently approved by the House-Senate conference committee that worked out the differences between the House and Senate versions of the legislation, in which the conflicting judicial interpretations were noted and support was expressed for those decisions deeming resort to state administrative remedies as being optional Conference Comm, Age Discrimination in Employment Act Amendments of 1978, HR Rep No 950, 95th Cong, 2d Sess 12 (1978).

732 441 US 750 (1979).

733 *Id* 756.

734 The Court was unpersuaded that the ability of an ADEA claimant to file suit 60 days after the administrative filing and to thereby effectively terminate state proceedings precluded concluding that the commencement, at least, of state proceedings should be required. *Id* 757.

735 *Id* 758 n6.

736 Echard v Devine, 726 F Supp 1045 (ND W Va 1989). *But see* Thaklar v Provident Natl Bank, 58 FEP Cas (BNA) 1435 (ED Pa 1991), where the court reasoned (1) that a dismissal was not required by reason of the plaintiff's failure to have at all filed a charge with the state agency, and (2) that a stay of the

incorporate all requirements of state law into the ADEA. Indeed, §14(b) expressly makes it unnecessary for an ADEA grievant to do any more than file with the state agency a written and signed statement setting forth the facts.[737] In other words, a filing may be defective for state purposes because the grievant fails to comply with some or all of the state requirements, yet that filing nonetheless may be adequate for the purpose of satisfying the requirement set by §14(b).[738]

In accordance with §7(d)(2),[739] a grievant is afforded at the most 300 days within which to file his or her federal charge of discrimination with the Equal Employment Opportunity Commission (EEOC).[740] In *Drez v ER Squibb & Sons, Inc,*[741] the defendant argued that the filing with the state agency also had to be perfected within that 300-day period. In other words, the state filing—it was argued—had to satisfy a filing requirement that is set, not by state law, but by the ADEA and, what is more, a filing requirement that is set regarding filings with the federal, not a state, agency. The *Drez* court disagreed.

If a grievant has filed with the appropriate state agency, a second filing need not be made with such agency when a second claim arises after the first filing, if the second claim is "reason-

---

federal court proceeding was, at least in the abstract, an appropriate alternative, but (3) inasmuch as there had been "a substantial opportunity for administrative review of the . . . [plaintiff's] claims of alleged discrimination [since the federal lawsuit was filed], a stay of court proceedings in this case would appear to serve no practical purpose." *Id* 1438.

737 See **§6.27.** Actually, in states that have work-sharing agreements with the Equal Employment Opportunity Commission (EEOC), entered into in accordance with 29 CFR §1626.10 (1993), a filing with the Commission will result, if the terms of the agreement so provide (as they do in Illinois, for example), in automatic referral by the EEOC of a copy of a complaint to the state agency. *See* Wanamaker v Columbian Rope Co, 713 F Supp 533, 540 (NDNY 1989); Agostine v Iowa Beef Processors, 35 FEP Cas (BNA) 328 (D Neb 1984). Thereby, the requirement of filing with the state will be satisfied, Peters v Fansteel, 736 F Supp 198 (ND Ill 1990), and so a grievant will not have to file personally with the state.

738 See **§6.27.**

739 29 USC §626(d)(2).

740 See **§6.08.**

741 674 F Supp 1432 (D Kan 1987).

ably related" to the initial claim.[742] Thus, in *Patel v Lutheran Medical Center, Inc,*[743] the court held that a claim of retaliation—as to which the plaintiff had not filed an administrative complaint with the state agency—was reasonably related to his prior state filing, and so a second state filing was not required as a precondition to the plaintiff's pursuing the retaliation claim in his federal ADEA suit.

§6.26 —Determining which State Laws and Agencies Satisfy §14(b)

The amount of time available to a person who believes that he or she is the victim of age discrimination violative of the Age Discrimination in Employment Act (ADEA),[744] and who is desirous of filing the charge of unlawful discrimination with the Equal Employment Opportunity Commission (EEOC) that is required by §7(d)[745] of the Act, depends on state law. Section 7(d) provides that the charge must be filed within 180 days of the alleged unlawful practice, but it immediately expands the window of opportunity for grievants by providing that "in a case to which section 633(b) [§14(b)] applies, [the charge shall be filed] within 300 days after the alleged unlawful practice occurred, or within 30 days after receipt by the individual of notice of termination of proceedings under State law, whichever is earlier."[746]

---

742 Goodman v Hublein, Inc, 645 F2d 127, 131 (2d Cir 1981). The problem of charges that are filed with the EEOC but do not address all the issues that subsequently are raised in the grievant's lawsuit has generated a large number of rulings. See **§6.05.**

743 753 F Supp 1070 (EDNY 1990).

744 29 USC §§621-634.

745 *Id* §626(d).

746 *Id.* Some ADEA courts speak of states that have such agencies as being "deferral" states. *See, e.g.,* Hamilton v Komatsu Dresser Indus, Inc, 964 F2d 600, 603 (7th Cir), *cert denied,* 113 S Ct 324 (1992); Aronson v Gressly, 961 F2d 907, 910 (10th Cir 1992); Jackson v Richards Medical Co, 961 F2d 575, 578 (6th Cir 1992); Astacio-Sanchez v Fundacion Educativa Ana G Mendez, 724 F Supp 11, 14 (DPR 1989); Clark v Burroughs Corp, 621 F Supp 660, 661 (ED Ark 1985). This characterization derives from case law construing

By the terms of §14(b), as interpreted by the Court in *Oscar Mayer & Co v Evans,*[747] a plaintiff—in order to pursue redress under the ADEA—must both seek state relief if there is an adequate state agency and an adequate state law,[748] and must timely file an administrative charge of discrimination with the EEOC. And the time available for the EEOC filing is a function of whether there is such an adequate state agency and an adequate state law.[749] True, a grievant who erroneously believes that there is no adequate state agency or state law, and who therefore files only with the EEOC, will not thereby have fatally erred.[750] But a plaintiff who mistakenly believes that the requisite §14(b) state agency and state law do exist can end up with his or her ADEA action being dismissed if his or her filing with the EEOC was

---

Title VII of the Civil Rights Act of 1964, 42 USC §§2000e through 2000e-17. While the substantive prohibitions of Title VII are in some respects analogous to those of the ADEA, the term *deferral state* has been improperly infused into the ADEA. Under Title VII there is a requirement that a complainant in a deferral state cannot even file a charge with the EEOC until he or she first files with the state agency and then waits 60 days. §706(c), 42 USC §2000e-5(c). In a very literal sense, then, the litigant and the EEOC must defer to the state, allowing it a 60-day period within which to address (or not address) a claim without any involvement of any kind by the federal agency. In contrast, an ADEA grievant may file simultaneously with the EEOC and the state agency. What is more, an ADEA claimant need not even timely file with the state; indeed, he or she can fulfill the state filing requirement even after the ADEA suit has been filed. See **§6.27.**

After waiting 60 days from the date of filing with the state agency, the ADEA complainant then may file suit in federal court. See **§6.37.** In contrast, a Title VII grievant cannot file suit without first receiving a notice of right to sue from the EEOC, 42 USC §§2000e-5(f)(1) and, as noted above, the EEOC cannot even receive a charge until 60 days after the state agency filing. In sum, as observed in Proffit v Keycom Elec Publishing, 625 F Supp 400 (ND Ill 1985): "Title VII reflects a far more meaningful policy of deferral to state agencies than the purely token state-filing provision of ADEA." *Id* 406. Thus, the term *deferral state* is a misnomer in the ADEA context. A more correct term would be *referral state,* because it is true that the state agency is at least supposed to have an opportunity to address a claimant's age discrimination claim.

[747] 441 US 750 (1979).

[748] See **§6.25.**

[749] *Id.*

[750] *See* **§6.27.**

not made until some time after the expiration of the 180-day filing period that is applicable in states not having qualifying agencies and/or laws.[751] (A complainant will not be penalized, however, for mistakenly believing that the type of age discrimination of which he or she complains actually is covered by the state law. Rather, even if it turns out that in fact the law does not apply, the complainant still may avail himself or herself of the 300-day filing period).[752]

Section 14(b) sets two conditions regarding state law for the state-filing requirement to come into play and, correlatively, for the 300-day, rather than the 180-day, period for filing a charge with the EEOC to apply. First, there must be a state law prohibiting age discrimination in employment; second, there must be a state entity authorized to grant relief from or seek relief for; the discriminatory practices involved.[753] Those states that the EEOC has designated as qualified referral states are listed in 29 CFR §1626.9.[754]

What Constitutes a State Law Satisfying §14(b)

A state law that does nothing more than declare age discrimination to be contrary to public policy will not satisfy §14(b)'s first requirement.[755] A local ordinance does not qualify as a state law.[756] If the grievant's claim fits within some exception to a state law or for some other reason the claim is not covered, he or she

---

[751] *See* Eklund v Lubrizol Corp, 529 F2d 247 (6th Cir 1976); Kincaid v Roadway Express, Inc, 481 F Supp 720 (EDNC 1979).

[752] *See* Heiar v Crawford County, 746 F2d 1190 (7th Cir 1984), *cert denied,* 472 US 1027 (1985).

[753] *See* Simpson v Whirlpool Corp, 604 F2d 997 (6th Cir 1979); Goodman v Board of Trustees, 498 F Supp 1329 (ND Ill 1980).

[754] 29 CFR §1626.9 (1993).

[755] *See, e.g.,* Dixon v Stephenson, Inc, 614 F Supp 60 (DDC 1985); Spagnuolo v Whirlpool Corp, 467 F Supp 364 (WDNC 1979), *affd in part & revd in part on other grounds,* 641 F2d 1109 (4th Cir), *cert denied,* 454 US 860 (1981).

[756] Dixon v Stephenson, Inc, 614 F Supp 60 (DDC 1985).

will not run afoul of §14(b) by failing to seek state recourse.[757] An amendment to a state law that expands its reach will not be applied retroactively to defeat a plaintiff's ADEA claim where the alleged discriminatory action took place prior to the amendment.[758]

Section 14(b) speaks to "an unlawful practice occurring in a State which has a law prohibiting discrimination[.]" An unusual factual scenario brought into focus the *occurring in a State* language in *Kovalic v DEC International, Inc.*[759] The plaintiff had been employed in Great Britain by a British subsidiary of a Wisconsin company, i.e., DEC. Having been discharged by DEC pursuant to a decision made at a board of directors meeting held in Madison, Wisconsin, Kovalic filed a charge of unlawful discrimination with the Wisconsin office of the EEOC 298 days after his termination. DEC argued that since the alleged discrimination had occurred, if at all, in Great Britain, Kovalic could not avail himself of the 300-day filing period. Rather, he had to have filed within 180 days of the discharge, and because he had not done so his suit—DEC argued—should have been dismissed as untimely.

---

[757] *See, e.g.*, Sturgeon v Avon Prods, Inc, 571 F2d 5 (7th Cir 1978); Husch v Szabo Food Serv, Inc, 662 F Supp 1291, 1296 n10 (ND Ill 1987), *revd on other grounds*, 851 F2d 999 (7th Cir 1988); Galvin v Vermont, 598 F Supp 144 (D Vt 1984); Farkas v New York State Dept of Health, 554 F Supp 24, 26 n6 (NDNY 1982), *affd without opinion*, 767 F2d 907 (2d Cir), *cert denied*, 474 US 1033 (1985). *But see* Heiar v Crawford County, 746 F2d 1190 (7th Cir 1984), *cert denied*, 472 US 1027 (1985).

[758] *See, e.g.*, Willis v Berger Transfer & Storage, Inc, 529 F Supp 279 (ND Ill 1981); *see also* Curry v Continental Airlines, 513 F2d 691, 694 (9th Cir 1975); Davis v Boy Scouts of Am, 457 F Supp 665, 670 (DNJ 1978). In Schultz v Dempster Sys, Inc, 561 F Supp 1230 (ED Tenn 1983), it was held that the plaintiff could not avail himself of the 300-day filing period because the state antidiscrimination agency empowered to address age discrimination in employment had not come into existence until after his claim arose. The court was unwilling to construe the statute creating the agency as applying retroactively, and so the alleged wrong—when it transpired—was not an event "occurring," in the words of §14(b), "in a state . . . [having] a law prohibiting discrimination in employment because of age[.]"

[759] 161 Wis 2d 863, 469 NW2d 224 (Ct App 1991).

The Wisconsin appellate court rejected DEC's argument. The court first relied on *Heiar v Crawford County*,[760] where it was argued that the 300-day filing period did not apply because the state nondiscrimination statute excepted from its coverage law enforcement personnel, and the plaintiff was a law enforcement officer. The *Heiar* court, while acknowledging that it was "pretty clear that the state agency cannot help the claimant,"[761] had nonetheless ruled that the 300-day filing period applied, reasoning that "it should be enough that there is a law at least potentially applicable to the employer . . . and an agency charge with enforcing it."[762] Here, the *Kovalic* court reasoned, the potential applicability of Wisconsin law was even greater than in *Heiar:* "Kovalic was employed by DEC, a Wisconsin company, to manage one of its subsidiaries. He was hired and trained by DEC, reported to DEC, was paid by DEC and ultimately, was fired by DEC (pursuant to a) decision . . . made by the company's board of directors meeting in Madison."[763]

What Constitutes a State Agency Satisfying §14(b)

There is support for the proposition that a general delegation of authority to a state agency to enforce a class of laws, such as a labor code, that includes a ban on age discrimination will not suffice to qualify the state agency for the purposes of §14(b).[764] In any event, even if an agency is specifically charged with dealing with age discrimination, §14(b) will not be satisfied if the agency can only investigate and conciliate and cannot grant or seek relief.[765]

---

760 746 F2d 1190 (7th Cir 1984), *cert denied,* 472 US 1027 (1985).

761 *Id* 1195.

762 *Id* (citations omitted).

763 469 NW2d at 228-29.

764 *See, e.g.*, Eklund v Lubrizol Corp, 529 F2d 247 (6th Cir 1976); Curry v Continental Airlines, 513 F2d 691 (9th Cir 1973); Bertrand v Orkin Exterminating Co, 419 F Supp 1123 (ND Ill 1976), *affd on rehearing,* 432 F Supp 952 (ND Ill 1977).

765 *See, e.g.*, Spagnuolo v Whirlpool Corp, 467 F Supp 364 (WDNC 1979), *affd in part & revd in part on other grounds,* 641 F2d 1109 (4th Cir), *cert denied,*

§6.27 —Satisfying State Procedural Requirements

If there is an adequate state law and an adequate state agency, in terms of the standards set by §14(b)[766] of the Age Discrimination in Employment Act (ADEA),[767] grievants who believe themselves to be the victims of unlawful age discrimination must, in accordance with the terms of the ADEA as interpreted by the Supreme Court in *Oscar Mayer & Co v Evans,*[768] make some gesture of pursuing state redress if they are ultimately to be able to seek relief under the federal statute.[769] Not surprisingly, the various state statutes[770]—like the ADEA, itself—set forth proce-

---

454 US 860 (1981); Usery v Indiana & Mich Elec Co, 13 Empl Prac Dec (CCH) ¶11,334 (SD Ind 1976); *see also* Brownlow v Edgecomb Metals Co, 573 F Supp 679 (ND Ohio 1983), *revd on other grounds,* 867 F2d 966 (6th Cir 1989).

In Lugo Garces v Sagner Intl, Inc, 534 F2d 987 (1st Cir 1976), the court addressed Puerto Rico's prohibition of age discrimination in employment. While the statute at issue authorized the Commonwealth Secretary of Labor to "order the payment of any sum owing to [victims of discrimination]," the *Lugo Garces* court doubted whether the statute conferred on the Secretary investigatory and conciliatory authority. The court concluded that §14(b) did not apply to Puerto Rico. Subsequently, in Hadfield v Mitre Corp, 562 F2d 84 (1st Cir 1977), the same appellate court addressed a district court ruling whereby the trial court had ruled that the plaintiff did not have to initially file a charge with the Massachusetts Commission Against Discrimination (MCAD) because here, as under the statute addressed in *Lugo Garces,* the state law allowed a grievant to in any event bypass the agency and sue in state court. While the Court of Appeals for the First Circuit acknowledged that *Lugo Garces* could be read to support the district court's holding, the appellate court reversed, reasoning that inasmuch as MCAD had authority to investigate and conciliate the dispute, a grievant's initial resort to state proceedings would serve the §14(b) aim of diverting disputes from the federal courts. *Accord* Forman v Block Drug Co, 16 FEP Cas (BNA) 414 (EDNY 1977). (Some years later it was held that the Puerto Rico statutory scheme in fact did satisfy §14(b)'s requirements. Astacio-Sanchez v Fundacion Educativa Ana G Mendez, 724 F Supp 11 (DPR 1989); *see also* Calderon-Trujillo v Ready-Mix Concrete, Inc, 635 F Supp 95 (DPR 1986)).

[766] 29 USC §633(b).

[767] *Id* §§621-634.

[768] 441 US 750 (1979).

[769] See **§6.25.**

[770] Most states have antidiscrimination statutes that include within their reach age discrimination in employment. See **ch 11.**

dural requirements that must be satisfied by claimants seeking redress. Also not surprisingly, question can arise as to how to treat for ADEA purposes a claimant who fails to satisfy these procedural predicates for state relief and, because of this failure, thereby arguably fails to pursue the state relief that is a predicate for seeking redress under the ADEA.

State Substantive Requirements Re Filings

Section 14(b) provides some direction with regard to some aspects of the state scenario:

> If any requirement for the commencement of such proceedings is imposed by a State authority other than a requirement of the filing of a written and signed statement of the facts upon which the proceeding is based, the proceeding shall be deemed to have been commenced for the purposes of this subsection at the time such statement is sent by registered mail to the appropriate State authority.[771]

An ADEA suit will not be dismissed simply because the administrative complaint filed with the state agency did not satisfy state requirements. All that is required is observance of the requirements set forth in §14(b).[772] Moreover, the grievant has no obligation to exhaust state remedies; all he or she must do is file with the state agency.[773]

State Time Limits

In deciding *Oscar Mayer* the Court expressly asserted that insofar as satisfying §14(b) is concerned, state proceedings need not be commenced within the time limits set by state law. Requiring

---

771 Although the grievant's statement was not sent by registered mail, the court deciding Punch v Singer Co, 463 F Supp 450, 453 (SDNY 1978), deemed the actual receipt by the state agency and the agency's treatment of the statement as a sufficient attempt to institute proceedings.

772 Ackerman v Ohio Knife Co, 589 F Supp 768 (SD Ohio 1984).

773 *See, e.g.*, Oscar Mayer & Co v Evans, 441 US 750, 776 (1979); Mizrany v Texas Rehabilitation Commn, 522 F Supp 611, 616 (SD Tex 1981), *affd without opinion*, 685 F2d 1384 (5th Cir 1982).

the contrary, i.e., that grievants satisfy state limits, could lead to onerous local filing standards controlling the legal fates of ADEA claimants—an unacceptable state of affairs: "Congress could not have intended to consign federal lawsuits to the 'vagaries of diverse state limitations statutes.' "[774]

As a result of *Oscar Mayer,* an ADEA plaintiff in a state that has an adequate state antidiscrimination law and an adequate state agency, as required by §14(b), need not commence state proceedings in compliance with the timing requirements of the state law at issue.[775] (Nor need the plaintiff file his or her state complaint within the time period—i.e., 300 days—set for the filing of the charge of unlawful discrimination with the federal enforcement agency, the Equal Employment Opportunity Commission (EEOC).)[776] Indeed, the *Oscar Mayer* Court's view was that a plaintiff may even file with the state agency *after* he or she has filed his or her federal ADEA lawsuit.[777]

---

[774] 441 US at 763 (quoting Occidental Life Ins Co v Equal Employment Opportunity Commn, 432 US 355, 371 (1977)).

[775] *See* Husch v Szabo Food Serv Co, 851 F2d 899, 1002 n6 (7th Cir 1988); Reinhard v Fairfield Maxwell, Ltd, 707 F2d 697 (2d Cir 1983); Callan v Pepsi-Cola Bottling Co, Inc, 801 F Supp 448, 455 (D Kan 1992); Glass v IDS Fin Servs, Inc, 798 F Supp 1411, 1417 n11 (D Minn 1992); Donahue v Pendleton Woolen Mills, Inc, 719 F Supp 149, 152 (SDNY 1988); Clark v Burroughs Corp, 621 F Supp 660 (ED Ark 1985); Bumpers v International Mill Servs, Inc, 595 F Supp 166 (ED Pa 1984); Perazzo v Top Value Enters, Inc, 590 F Supp 428, 432 (SD Ohio 1984); Schlosser v Firestone Tire Co, 33 FEP Cas (BNA) 1403 (ND Ohio 1983); Lang v International Harvester Co, 33 FEP Cas (BNA) 603 (D Md 1983); Krenning v Darling, 572 F Supp 923 (SD Ohio 1983); Van Atta v Kal-Aero, Inc, 555 F Supp 912 (WD Mich 1983).

[776] *See, e.g.,* Reinhard v Fairfield Maxwell, Ltd, 707 F2d 697 (2d Cir 1983); Drez v ER Squibb & Sons, Inc, 674 F Supp 1432 (D Kan 1987). In Jones v Baskin, Flaherty, Elliot & Mannino, 738 F Supp 937 (WD Pa 1989), *affd without opinion,* 897 F2d 522 (3d Cir), *cert denied,* 498 US 811 (1990), the court erroneously stated that the plaintiff had to "file both the EEOC charge and the state charge within 300 days in order to preserve his federal cause of action, regardless of any state statute of limitations." *Id* 938.

[777] 441 US at 765; *see also* Overgard v Cambridge Book Co, 858 F2d 371 (7th Cir 1988); Simpson v Whirlpool Corp, 604 F2d 997 (6th Cir 1979); Smith v Joseph Schlitz Brewing Co, 604 F2d 220 (3d Cir 1979); Perazzo v Top Value Enters, Inc, 590 F Supp 428, 432 (SD Ohio 1984); Horn v United Air Lines, Inc, 30 Empl Prac Dec (CCH) ¶33,314 (ND Ill 1983). *But see* Curto v Sears, Roebuck & Co, 552 F Supp 891 (ND Ill 1982) (held that while the state

The Court further established that where a plaintiff asserting an ADEA claim has failed to file with the state agency, the correct approach to be followed by the federal trial court in which an ADEA suit has been filed is to stay the federal action, rather than to dismiss it.[778] The majority of lower courts that have since ruled on the issue are in accord with this position.[779] In deciding *Cornett v Avco Financial Services,*[780] however, the Court of Appeals for the Fourth Circuit ruled that *Oscar Mayer* did not establish that a stay was to be imposed as a matter of course. Rather, it

---

filing did not have to be timely in the sense of complying with the state statute's filing deadline, the state filing did have to be made prior to the filing of an ADEA suit); *accord* Fugate v Allied Corp, 582 F Supp 780 (ND Ill 1984). The court's position in *Curto* seems strange, because the court itself later noted that in *Oscar Mayer* the Supreme Court had approved the filing of a state charge even after initiation of the ADEA lawsuit. 552 F Supp at 896 n12.

In Edmunds v Ryder/P*I*E* Nationwide, Inc, 659 F Supp 341 (SD Fla 1987), the court erroneously stated that a charge may not be filed with the EEOC until after a filing has been made with the state agency. *Id* 342. Other courts have erroneously stated that an EEOC charge may not be filed until 60 days have elapsed since the state filing. See **§6.37.**

778 441 US at 765 n13.

779 *See, e.g.,* Piecuch v Gulf & W Mfg Co, 626 F Supp 65 (ND Ohio 1985); Perazzo v Top Value Enters, Inc, 590 F Supp 428 (SD Ohio 1984); Mason v Midwestern Fidelity Corp, 589 F Supp 751 (SD Ohio 1984); Stoecklein v Illinois Tool Works, Inc, 589 F Supp 139 (ND Ill 1984); Horn v United Air Lines, Inc, 30 Empl Prac Dec (CCH) ¶33,314 (ND Ill 1983); *see also* Clark v American Home Foods Div, 34 FEP Cas (BNA) 813 (D Mass 1982), *affd,* 35 FEP Cas (BNA) 1401 (1st Cir 1984). In deciding Riggle v CSX Transp, Inc, 755 F Supp 676 (D Md 1991), the court rejected the argument that the suit should be dismissed in light of the plaintiff's failure to have filed an administrative complaint with the state agency, but instead of staying the suit pending a state filing, the court proceeded to the merits. The court reasoned that the peculiar language of the state statute arguably allowed it to exercise its jurisdiction, and, moreover, judicial economy dictated addressing the plaintiff's claims, "rather than subjecting both parties to needless and expensive delay." *Id* 679.

The court that decided DePriest v Seaway Food Town, Inc, 543 F Supp 1355 (ED Mich 1982), appeared to be of the mistaken view that inasmuch as the plaintiff had not filed with the state agency, the court was without jurisdiction to entertain her ADEA suit. *Id* 1360. Actually, the court had jurisdiction, but in accordance with *Oscar Mayer,* it should not have exercised it until the plaintiff filed with the agency.

780 792 F2d 447 (4th Cir 1986).

read *Oscar Mayer* as enunciating only a rule of discretion, and then refused to exercise its discretion to relieve the plaintiff of his failure to timely file with the state agency. In *Smith v General Scanning, Inc,*[781] the Court of Appeals for the Seventh Circuit also directed a dismissal of the plaintiff's suit for failure to satisfy the state filing requirement.[782]

Filing with the EEOC as Satisfying the Requirement to File with the State

Prior to the ADEA's requiring the filing of a charge of unlawful discrimination with the EEOC as a precursor to suit, the Act called for what really was the same filing, but was titled in the Act a *notice of intent to sue.*[783] The Court of Appeals for the Tenth Circuit held, in *Mistretta v Sandia Corp,*[784] that a notice that was filed by representative plaintiffs with the federal enforcement agency, with a copy sent to the state agency, was sufficient to satisfy the state filing requirement as to individuals who were opt-in plaintiffs in the ADEA suit and who had not filed at all with the state.[785] The same result has been reached now that it is a charge, rather than a notice of intent to sue, that is filed with the EEOC: an adequate charge filed with the EEOC that is referred by the Commission to the state agency can suffice to commence the state proceeding.[786]

In states that have work-sharing agreements with the EEOC,[787] a filing with the federal agency will result in a simultaneous filing of the complaint with the state agency.[788] This generally will con-

---

[781] 832 F2d 96 (7th Cir 1987).

[782] *Accord* Vesey v Vitro Corp, 55 FEP Cas (BNA) 1100 (D Md 1990); *see also* Overgard v Cambridge Book Co, 858 F2d 371 (7th Cir 1988).

[783] See **§6.03.**

[784] 639 F2d 588, 594-95 (10th Cir 1980).

[785] As to opt-in plaintiffs and representative actions generally, see **§§6.45-.50.**

[786] McKelvy v Metal Container Corp, 854 F2d 448, 451 (11th Cir 1988); *see also* Anderson v Illinois Tool Works, Inc, 753 F2d 622, 624 n2 (7th Cir 1985).

[787] These are entered into in accordance with 29 CFR §1626.10 (1993).

[788] *See* Peters v Fansteel, Inc, 736 F Supp 198 (ND Ill 1990); Agostine v Iowa Beef Processors, 35 FEP Cas (BNA) 328 (D Neb 1984); *see also* Marsh v

stitute a filing with the state agency for the purposes both of (1) satisfying the requirement of resort to state remedies[789] and (2) starting the running of the 60-day period[790] that must elapse before suit may be commenced.[791] (However, this will not inevitably be the case: the terms of a work-sharing agreement may require more than just a filing with the EEOC as a predicate for the effectuation of a state filing.)[792] By the terms of a work-sharing agreement, or by a mutually shared interpretation of the terms, the EEOC and the state agency may establish that a charge filed with the EEOC need not be referred to the state agency if the period for filing with the state has elapsed by the time the grievant files with the EEOC.[793] Actually, a charge filed with the EEOC may be regarded as constituting a filing with the state agency as well, even if there is no work-sharing agreement with the state agency and even if there is no evidence that the charge in fact was referred by the EEOC to the state agency.[794]

In *Petrelle v Weirton Steel Corp*[795] the Court of Appeals for the Fourth Circuit was confronted with a situation where the work-sharing agreement required the referral of charges filed by the EEOC to the state agency, but there was no record of the plaintiff's charge actually having been received by the latter agency. The court, recognizing "that public officials are accredited with a presumption of regularity,"[796] reasoned that "[t]he presumption is 'sufficient to sustain the inference' that the . . . [EEOC]

WMAT-TV, Inc, 32 FEP Cas (BNA) 806 (D Md 1982); *accord* 29 CFR §1626.10(c) (1993).

789 *See* Kaimowitz v Board of Trustees, 951 F2d 765, 766-67 (7th Cir 1991).

790 See **§6.37.**

791 *See, e.g.*, Wanamaker v Columbian Rope Co, 713 F Supp 533, 540-42 (NDNY 1989); Stoecklein v Illinois Tool Works, Inc, 589 F Supp 139, 144-45 n7 (ND Ill 1984).

792 *See* Petrelle v Weirton Steel Corp, 953 F2d 148 (6th Cir 1991).

793 *See* Sarsha v Sears, Roebuck & Co, 747 F Supp 454 (ND Ill 1990).

794 Colgan v Fisher Scientific Co, 935 F2d 1407, 1414-15 (3d Cir), *cert denied,* 112 S Ct 379 (1991).

795 953 F2d 148 (4th Cir 1991).

796 *Id* 153.

did 'whatever was appropriate' to effectuate the procedure."[797] Accordingly, the presumption led to the conclusion that the charge had been referred by the EEOC to the state agency, and "[o]nce the presumption . . . [arose and the inference based on it was drawn], the burden shift[ed] to Weirton Steel to show that the charge was not referred."[798]

Mistakes in Filing

A filing in the wrong state will not satisfy the filing requirement; thus, a filing with state A's agency will be of no avail if the charge of unlawful discrimination should have been made with state B's agency.[799] However, there may be equitable grounds that justify allowing a grievant who erred by filing with the wrong state agency to file with the correct state agency.[800] An equitable basis for relieving the grievant of the need to file with a state agency can exist if an employee of the state agency advised the grievant not to file with the state because the time for filing had elapsed.[801]

§6.28 EEOC Records and Files and Access to Them Prior to Suit

Investigatory Files

Once a suit is filed by a grievant seeking redress under the Age Discrimination in Employment Act (ADEA),[802] the federal rules of procedure afford ample discovery tools to both parties

---

[797] *Id* 153-54 (quoting RH Stearns Co v United States, 291 US 54, 63 (1934)); *see also* Seredinksi v Clifton Precision Prods Co, 776 F2d 56, 63 n11 (3d Cir 1985).

[798] 953 F2d at 154.

[799] Smith v General Scanning, Inc, 832 F2d 96 (7th Cir 1987); DePriest v Seaway Food Town, Inc, 543 F Supp 1355, 1359-60 (ED Mich 1982).

[800] Husch v Szabo Food Serv Co, 851 F2d 999 (7th Cir 1988).

[801] Sarsha v Sears, Roebuck & Co, 747 F Supp 454 (ND Ill 1990).

[802] 29 USC §§621-634.

for the securing of information relevant to the case.[803] Even before litigation commences, however, both the grievant and the charged party may be able to secure access to the file developed by the Equal Employment Opportunity Commission (EEOC) in the course of its investigating the charge of unlawful discrimination.[804]

In theory, at least, there should be a variety of types of information in the file: "[I]f properly prepared, [it] will . . . include the charge, any jurisdictional notations, statements of the employer and other witnesses, employment documents, the employer's position statement, and the investigator's recommendation."[805] In actuality, the file is likely to contain a far more limited collection of information, reflective of the typically cursory attention accorded to charges by agency investigators.[806] In any event, whether comprehensive or limited, sometimes the data sometimes will be useful. This is particularly so for the grievant, who may be able to glean information concerning the charged party's explanation for the adverse action or decision; the names of relevant individuals to contact or depose; admissions; and other material relevant to deciding whether to proceed with litigation in the first instance, and how to conduct the litigation if suit is filed. The possible securing of information useful in pursuing the claim should be reason enough for a grievant to seek to secure this data. The fact that a plaintiff's attorney's failure to examine this file may be taken into account in considering whether sanctions should be imposed for filing a meritless suit affords further reason for reviewing the EEOC investigatory file.[807] The basic information supplied by the grievant to the EEOC—and there is likely to be little beyond that—is

---

[803] See **§§6.69-.70** as to discovery.

[804] As to EEOC investigatory authority, see **§6.56.**

[805] Fretz, *Using the EEOC Investigative File in Employment Discrimination Cases,* 26 Clearinghouse Rev 422, 423 (Aug 1992).

[806] *See* United States Gen Accounting Office, EEOC and State Agencies Did Not Fully Investigate Discrimination Charges (GAO/HRD 89-11 Oct 1988).

[807] *See* D'Aquino v Citicorp/Diner's Club, Inc, 139 FRD 357, 361 (ND Ill 1991).

transmitted to the charged party, since both the statute[808] and an EEOC regulation[809] require that the charged party be notified of the charge. This means that typically the charged party will be informed of the charging party's identity;[810] certainly the charged party will be apprised of the nature of the alleged wrong. Thus, it is unlikely that the file will be particularly useful to the charged party as a source of additional information.

Access to an investigatory file may be useful to other persons, in addition to the individual whose charge initiated the development of that particular file. For example, grievant C may have an interest in seeing what is in the files of grievants A and B, since those grievants filed charges against the same respondent as did grievant C. However, it is reported that "the EEOC refuses to divulge such information pursuant to the 'personal privacy' exception under Exemption 7(C)"[811] of the Freedom of Information Act.[812]

EEOC Records Systems

The EEOC has in place various records systems. The system dealing with age discrimination claims, named "Age and Equal Pay Act Discrimination Case Files," is designated "EEOC-1."[813] By regulation,[814] the files in this system have been designated by the EEOC as being exempt from various provisions of the

---

[808] §7(d), 29 USC §626(d) ("Upon receiving . . . a charge, the Commission shall promptly notify all persons named in such charge as prospective defendants in the action[.]").

[809] 29 CFR §1626.11 (1993) ("Upon receipt of a charge, the Commission shall promptly notify the respondent that a charge has been filed").

[810] The identity of a complainant (in contrast to a charging party), a confidential witness, or an aggrieved person on whose behalf a charge was filed may be kept confidential by the EEOC. *Id* §1626.4 (1993). As to the distinction between a charge and a complaint, see **§6.02.**

[811] Fretz, *supra* note 805.

[812] 5 USC §552(b)((7). The text of the exemption is set forth in note 827 *infra.*

[813] This system was published at 56 Fed Reg 10889-90 (Mar 14, 1991), and went into effect on May 13, 1991.

[814] 29 CFR pt 1611 (1993).

Privacy Act,[815] in part because, in the Commission's view, "[s]ubject individuals of the files in . . . [this system] have been provided a means of access to their records by the Freedom of Information Act."[816] A description of the system details the following aspects:

> **SYSTEM LOCATION:**
>
> Field offices where the charge or complaint of discrimination was filed. . . .
>
> CATEGORIES OF INDIVIDUALS COVERED BY THE SYSTEM:
>
> Persons other than federal employees and applicants who file charges or complaints with EEOC. . . .
>
> **CATEGORIES OF RECORDS IN THE SYSTEM:**
>
> This system contains the records compiled during the investigation of age . . . discrimination cases. These cases include:
>
> a. Documents submitted by charging party or complainant such as charge of discrimination, and personal interview statement, and correspondence.
>
> b. Documents submitted by employer such as statement of position, correspondence, statements of witnesses, documentary evidence such as personnel files, records of earnings, employee benefit plans, seniority list, job titles and descriptions, applicant data, organizational charts, collective bargaining agreements, petition to revoke or modify subpoena.
>
> c. Records gathered and generated by EEOC in the course of its investigation such as letters of referral to state fair employment practice agencies, correspondence with state fair employment practices agencies, witness statements, investigator's notes, investigative plan, report of initial and exit interview, investigator's analyses of evidence

---

[815] 5 USC §552a.

[816] 29 CFR §1611.3(c) (1993). The Freedom of Information Act, 5 USC §552, is discussed *infra.*

and charge, subpoenas, decisions and letters of determination, conciliation agreements, correspondence and any additional evidence gathered during the course of the investigation. . . .

ROUTINE USES OF RECORDS MAINTAINED IN THE SYSTEM, INCLUDING CATEGORIES OF USERS AND THE PURPOSES OF SUCH USES:

These records and information in these records may be used:

a. To disclose pertinent information to a federal, state, or local agency or third party as may be appropriate or necessary to perform the Commission's functions under the Age Discrimination in Employment Act. . . .

b. To disclose information contained in these records to state and local agencies administering state or local fair employment practices laws.

c. To disclose non-confidential and non-privileged information from closed ADEA . . . case files (a file is closed when the Commission has terminated its investigation and has decided not to sue) to the employer where a lawsuit has been filed against the employer involving that information, to other employees of the same employer who have been notified by the Commission of their right under 29 U.S.C. 216 to file a lawsuit on their own behalf, and their represen[t]atives.

d. To provide information to a congressional office from the record of an individual in response to an inquiry from the congressional office made at the request of a party to the charge.

e. To disclose pertinent information to the appropriate federal, state or local agency responsible for investigating, prosecuting, enforcing or implementing a statute, rule, regulation or order, where the EEOC becomes aware of an indication of a violation or potential violation of civil or criminal law or regulation.

f. To disclose information to another federal agency, to a court or a party in litigation before a court or in an administrative proceeding being conducted by a Federal agency either when the Government is a party to a judicial proceeding or in order to comply with the issuance of a subpoena.

POLICIES AND PRACTICES FOR STORING, RETRIEVING, ACCESSING, RETAINING, AND DISPOSING OF RECORDS IN THE SYSTEM:

STORAGE:

These records are maintained in file folders and in computer processable storage media.

RETRIEVABILITY:

These records are cross-indexed by charging party name, employer name and charge number. The records may be retrieved by any of the above three indexes.

SAFEGUARDS:

Paper records are maintained in a secured area to which only authorized personnel have access. Access to and use of these records is limited to those persons whose official duties require such access. The premises are locked when authorized personnel are not on duty. Access to computerized records is limited, through use of access codes and entry logs, to those whose official duties require access.[817]

---

[817] 56 Fed Reg 10889-890 (Mar 14, 1991). A modification of routine use "f" was scheduled to go into effect on May 9, 1994, unless comments from the public dictated otherwise. 59 Fed Reg 11056, 11058 (Mar 9, 1994). By the terms of this modification, the response of a system manager to a subpoena was changed. The EEOC explained this change:

> As presently written, this routine use allows the system manager to provide information when served with a subpoena, even if the Government is not a party to the litigation or to the administrative proceeding. In light of *Doe v. Stephens,* 851 F.2d 1457 (D.C. Cir. 1988), and *Doe v. DeGenova,* 779 F.2d 74 (D.C. Cir. 1985), the Commission has decided that the issuance of a subpoena by itself no longer qualifies as a valid routine use under subsection (b) of the Privacy Act. Therefore, the Commission will no longer make disclosures in response to a subpoena unless the Government is a party to the judicial or administrative proceeding. In those situations where the Government is not a party to the proceeding, records may be disclosed if a judge has actually signed the subpoena.

There are further aspects of the system description that address retention and disposal of the files in the system.[818]

Access to Files Pursuant to Freedom of Information Act

There is no EEOC regulation that expressly establishes a process for securing information in EEOC investigatory files. Thus, the formal mechanism for obtaining such files is to make a written request under the Freedom of Information Act (FOIA).[819]

> In those cases, the disclosure will be made in accordance with subsection (b)(11) of the Privacy Act.

Id 11057. The modified routine use "f" was to read as follows:

> f. To disclose information to another federal agency, to a court, or to a party in litigation before a court or in an administrative proceeding being conducted by a federal agency when the government is a party to the judicial or administrative proceeding.
> *Id* 11058.

[818] **RETENTION AND DISPOSAL:**

Cases that are dismissed or closed for other than no cause are destroyed six months following the date of dismissal or closure. No cause files that are of value in the development of future class action or pattern and practice cases are retired to the Federal Records Center one year after the date of the last action and destroyed after three additional years. All other no cause files are destroyed one year after the date of the last action. Negotiated settlement files are destroyed one year after the calendar year in which the settlement agreement is signed or after all obligations under the agreement are satisfied, whichever occurs later. Where monetary benefits are realized in concurrent Age, Equal Pay, and Title VII cases, the file is destroyed three years after the date of the last action. Other files are retired to the Federal Records Center one year after the date of the last action, including action in the federal courts or the last compliance review (the final report submitted by the respondent after conciliation to indicate compliance) and destroyed after three additional years, except landmark cases. Landmark cases are transferred to the nearest Federal Records Center two years after final court action and offered to the National Archives ten years after final court action.

SYSTEM MANAGERS AND ADDRESS:

Director of the field office where the charge was filed.

SYSTEM EXEMPTED FROM CERTAIN PROVISIONS OF THE ACT:

This system is exempt under 5 U.S.C. 552a(k)(2) from subsections (c)(3), (d), (e)(1), (e)(4)(G), (e)(4)(H), (e)(4)(I) and (f) of the Act.

56 Fed Reg 10890 (Mar 14, 1991).

[819] 5 USC §552.

There is an EEOC regulation implementing the FOIA.[820] An FOIA request, which is to be submitted to the regional attorney for the district office investigating a charge,[821] should reasonably describe the records sought.[822] The EEOC is supposed to respond within 10 days after receipt of the request, unless there is a need to search for or to collect documents from other EEOC offices, or to consult with other agencies having an interest in the request, or unless the material requested requires a voluminous search.[823]

The sticking point is that another EEOC regulatory provision provides that requests for information from open case files[824] normally will be denied pursuant to exemption (7) of the FOIA.[825] This exemption permits—but does not require[826]—an agency to withhold records or information to the extent that they fit within one or more of several concerns relating to law

---

[820] 29 CFR pt 1610 (1993).

[821] *Id* §1610.7(a)(4).

[822] *Id* §1610.5. The request "must be clearly and prominently defined as a request for information under the" FOIA. *Id* §1610.7(c). Likewise, the cover or envelope in which it is submitted should be similarly identified. *Id.*

[823] *Id* §1610.9.

[824] NLRB v Robbins Tire & Rubber Co, 437 US 214 (1978), involved access to open files of the National Labor Relations Board (NLRB), and affords some analogical insight regarding access to open files. At issue was the disclosure to a respondent of witnesses' statements related to a pending unfair labor practice proceeding. The Court, in holding that the FOIA did not require their disclosure, deemed the statements to be exempt as investigatory records whose disclosure would interfere with enforcement proceedings. The company seeking access to the statements argued that the NLRB had to establish that some sort of actual interference with witnesses by the company would result if the statements were disclosed, but the Court rejected this argument. Rather, it was willing to allow general determinations of likely interference to be made, based on the nature of the records involved. Both long-standing NLRB practice, and concern about witnesses being intimidated and therefore being reluctant to cooperate with agency investigators, justified the agency's refusal to disclose the statements at issue.

[825] 29 CFR §1610.17(g) (1993).

[826] *See, e.g.*, Chrysler Corp v Brown, 441 US 281 (1979).

enforcement.[827] Access to closed files under the FOIA is supposedly not limited; at least there is no EEOC regulation to that effect. Still, the agency may invoke one of the FOIA exemptions, including that focusing on law enforcement concerns, as well as exemption 5, which provides for the withholding by an agency of "inter-agency or intra-agency memorandums or letters which would not be available by law to a party other than an agency in litigation with the agency."[828]

While a party denied access to an ADEA investigatory file may challenge that denial in court, the one judicial ruling addressing the issue is unsupportive of such an effort. In the only reported FOIA case dealing with an ADEA grievance, *Forrester v United*

---

[827] 5 USC §552(b) exempts from disclosure the following:

> (7) records or information compiled for law enforcement purposes . . . to the extent that the production of such law enforcement records or information (A) could reasonably be expected to interfere with enforcement proceedings, (B) would deprive a person of a right to a fair trial or an impartial adjudication, (C) could reasonably be expected to constitute an unwarranted invasion of a personal privacy, (D) could reasonably be expected to disclose the identity of a confidential source, including a State, local, or foreign agency or authority or any private institution which furnished information on a confidential basis, and, in the case of a record or information compiled by criminal law enforcement authority in the course of a criminal investigation or by an agency conducting a lawful national security intelligence investigation, information furnished by a confidential source, (E) would disclose techniques and procedures for law enforcement investigations or prosecutions, or would disclose guidelines for law enforcement investigations or prosecutions if such disclosure could reasonably be expected to risk circumvention of the law, or (F) could reasonably be expected to endanger the life or physical safety of any individual.

[828] 5 USC §552(b)(5). One expert in ADEA analysis has observed as follows:

> Although routinely invoked by the EEOC in response to FOIA requests, this exemption should not pose a serious problem in gaining access to relevant documents in the investigatory file. The deliberative privilege applies only to *opinion* or recommendatory parts of documents, not to *factual* information contained therein. If the complainant's attorney seeks the agency's "opinion" in order to ensure a full assessment of the complainant's case, the agency's final decision in [sic] not covered by the exemption. Moreover, EEOC staff opinions can be obtained through informal conversations, independent of an FOIA request.

Fretz, *supra*, note 805, at 425.

States Department of Labor,[829] the plaintiff had sought unsuccessfully to obtain an investigatory report that was the basis for an administrative determination adverse to the plaintiff and that had been prepared by a compliance officer in the Labor Department, the agency which at the time was responsible for enforcing the ADEA.[830] The denial of the request was upheld, the court reasoning that the report was exempt under the FOIA because disclosure of the report would constitute an unwarranted invasion of personal privacy, an eventuality that fits within the list of bases for nondisclosure set forth in the FOIA's law enforcement exemption.[831] In the court's view, persons cooperating with compliance officers must feel free to do so without fear of reprisals (although there was in fact no evidence that there would be any reprisal in this particular instance).

Whether a file is open or closed, the EEOC generally takes the position, as previously noted, that third parties may not obtain access to investigatory files under the FOIA.

Title VII Analogy

In contrast to the ADEA, Title VII of the Civil Rights Act of 1964,[832] the judicial constructions of which often are looked to by ADEA courts for analogical guidance,[833] contains specific provisions barring the EEOC from disclosing to the public information obtained in the course of investigating or seeking to conciliate charges.[834] The agency, however, deems it proper to disclose to the grievant the investigatory file relating to his or her charge.[835] In deciding *Equal Employment Opportunity*

---

829 433 F Supp 987 (SDNY 1977), *affd without opinion*, 591 F2d 1330 (2d Cir 1978).

830 See **ch 2** as to the transfer of authority from the Labor Department to the EEOC.

831 See note 827.

832 42 USC §§2000e through 2000e-17.

833 See **ch 2.**

834 42 USC §§2000e-5(b), -8(e).

835 29 CFR §1610.17(d) (1993).

Commission v Associated Dry Goods Corp[836] the Supreme Court agreed with this distinction, i.e., a charging party is not a member of the public and so the EEOC can disclose to a grievant his or her Title VII open investigatory file.[837]

Information contained in a closed file was at issue in *Olitsky v Spencer Gifts, Inc*,[838] in which the Court of Appeals for the Fifth Circuit applied one of the aforementioned Title VII nondisclosure provisions, §706(b),[839] to an ADEA case. The court acknowledged "that there may exist some doubt as to whether §706(b) . . . has any application."[840] Since, however, the party who would have been expected to argue the provision's inapplicability in fact had not done so, the court considered itself free to import that provision into the age discrimination context. At issue was the admission into evidence of a file that had been prepared by the EEOC investigator, in which file were notes recording the investigator's conversation with the defendant's in-house

(*Text continued on page 6-177*)

---

836 449 US 590 (1981).

837 The Court, however, did not agree with the EEOC that the agency could disclose to a charging party files that had been compiled in investigating other, related charges. *Id* 603-04.

838 842 F2d 123 (5th Cir), *cert denied*, 488 US 925 (1988).

839 42 USC §2000e-5(b).

840 842 F2d at 126.

counsel. On appeal the defendant successfully argued that the admission of this file violated §706(b), which provides as follows:

> If the Commission determines . . . that there is reasonable cause to believe that the charge is true, . . . [it] shall endeavor to eliminate any such alleged unlawful employment practice by informal methods of conference, conciliation, and persuasion. Nothing said or done during and as a part of such informal endeavors may be made public by the Commission . . . or used as evidence in a subsequent proceeding without the written consent of the person concerned.

The *Olitsky* court ruled that "Section 706(b) clearly prohibits any use of EEOC conciliation material in subsequent litigation, even by the parties to the agency proceedings."[841] Accordingly, the trial court—although it was in fact dealing with an ADEA claim, to which §706(b) clearly does not, by its literal terms, apply—had erred in allowing admission of the EEOC file.

In also addressing a claim of access to a closed file, the Court of Appeals for the Second Circuit applied a different analysis, and arrived at a different result, when it decided *Binder v Long Island Lighting Co.*[842] The court asserted that Title VII's §706(b) is not relevant to the ADEA, even by way of analogy: "Congress enacted the ADEA in the wake of Title VII, and we believe that any omission in the text of the ADEA of a provision found in Title VII [, i.e., §706(b),] is likely to reflect a deliberate decision on Congress' part."[843] Moreover, the court saw no particular harm—and some good—in allowing the admission at trial of statements made by the employer to the EEOC during the course of the EEOC's investigation:

> Factual statements regarding past events are distinguishable from offers of compromise, and, if the principal objec-

---

841 *Id* 126.

842 933 F2d 187 (2d Cir 1991).

843 *Id* 193.

> tive of an EEOC proceeding is to ascertain what has occurred and, wherever possible, to resolve disputes without litigation, a rule that allows employers to give off-the-record accounts of relevant events will not necessarily advance that objective.[844]

Thus, the court embraced "a rule allowing the admission in subsequent litigation of factual statements made during the course of EEOC proceedings."[845] The court declined, however, to express any "view as to whether . . . [it] would reach the same conclusion had the statement [at issue here] been made during settlement negotiations between the parties."[846] Here, it was only addressing the defendant's "written explanation of the reasons for and timing of the challenged employment decision."[847]

The other Title VII provision concerning disclosure, i.e., 42 USC §2000e-8(c), bars the fruits of an EEOC Title VII investigation from being made public "prior to the institution of any proceeding" by the EEOC.[848] It, too, is unique to Title VII, but a court called upon to enforce this provision vis-a-vis Title VII issues may take into account the inhibiting effect of such enforcement on an allied EEOC investigation of ADEA issues.[849]

Privilege and Confidentiality

In *Equal Employment Opportunity Commission v G-K-G Inc*[850] the EEOC invoked a " 'government deliberative process' privilege."[851] This "protects documents which reflect 'advisory opinions, recommendations and deliberations comprising part of a process by which governmental decisions and policies are

---

[844] *Id.*

[845] *Id* 194.

[846] *Id* 194 n3.

[847] *Id.*

[848] *Accord* 29 CFR §1601.22 (1993).

[849] *See* Equal Employment Opportunity Commn v Recruit USA, 939 F2d 746, 754 n8 (9th Cir 1991).

[850] 131 FRD 553 (ND Ill 1990).

[851] *Id* 555.

formulated.' "[852] The court explained that "the privilege . . . only covers expressions of opinion, recommendations, or consultations; factual matter is not within the scope of the privilege."[853] It proceeded to uphold the EEOC's claim of privilege.

An EEOC regulation, 29 CFR §1626.4,[854] embraces a confidentiality requirement, providing generally that the identity of a complainant, confidential witness, or aggrieved person on whose behalf a charge was filed ordinarily will not be disclosed without prior written consent of the party whose identity is to be disclosed, unless disclosure is necessary in a court proceeding. The use of the word "ordinarily" in this section vests discretion in the EEOC, so that even absent consent it may disclose the party's identity. Indeed, in the commentary accompanying the issuance of the regulation, the Commission made clear that disclosure was within its discretion.[855]

Arguably, however, a limitation on this discretion is articulated in 29 CFR §1626.15(b).[856] This subsection provides that "[i]n the process of conducting any investigation or conciliation under this Act, the identity of persons who have provided information in confidence shall not be disclosed except in accordance with §1626.4." Here, the word "shall" suggests that the Commission must maintain the secrecy of the individual's identity, if that person has provided information with a caveat that his or her identity not be disclosed. While the cross-reference to §1626.4 might suggest a contrary reading, the use of the word "shall" in the one section and of the word "ordinarily" in the other would suggest that the cross-reference is only applicable for purposes of the procedures involved in disclosure—i.e., absent the EEOC's exercising its discretion to unilaterally disclose information, the person's identity cannot be disclosed unless, as provided in §1626.4, he or she first gives written con-

---

852 *Id* 556 (quoting McClelland v Andrus, 606 F2d 1278, 1287 (DC Cir 1979)).

853 131 FRD at 556.

854 29 CFR §1626.4 (1993).

855 48 Fed Reg 139 (Jan 3, 1983).

856 29 CFR §1626.15 (1993).

sent. In other words, the retention of EEOC discretion in §1626.4 is not compromised by the language of §1626.15(b).

The regulatory provision regarding confidentiality has its counterpart in judicial rulings in which courts have recognized a so-called informer's privilege.[857] This privilege's basis was explained in *Equal Employment Opportunity Commission v Consolidated Edison Co*:[858]

> The informer's privilege serves to protect the identities of those who complain to and assist the Government in its enforcement of . . . the antidiscrimination laws. The applicability of the privilege is determined by a balancing test, weighing the Government's interest in protecting the identities of its informants against the defendant's need for the materials in question. The rationale behind such a privilege is that the Government relies on private complainants and cooperators in order to enforce the antidiscrimination laws and must be able to protect their identities in order to secure their assistance. Were their identities revealed, they would be vulnerable to reprisal from their employer or former employer.[859]

In *Consolidated Edison* the court carefully balanced the company's need for information against the EEOC's desire to maintain confidentiality.[860]

EEOC Regulations

There is another EEOC regulation that in part is relevant to the question of obtaining information from the agency. The regulation provides that a person who submits data or evidence to the Commission may obtain a copy or transcript of it, on pay-

---

[857] *See, e.g.*, Equal Employment Opportunity Commn v G-K-G, Inc, 131 FRD 553 (ND Ill 1990).

[858] 37 FEP Cas (BNA) 1660 (SDNY 1981).

[859] *Id* 1661-62.

[860] *See also* Equal Employment Opportunity Commn v G-K-G Inc, 131 FRD 553 (ND Ill 1990).

ment of lawfully prescribed costs, subject to the caveat that a witness may for good cause be limited to inspection of the official transcript of his or her testimony.[861] Obviously, this provision does not address the ability of an individual or entity to obtain information in EEOC files provided by other individuals or entities.

§6.29 EEOC Conciliation and Its Effect on Private Suits

On receipt of a charge of unlawful discrimination, the Equal Employment Opportunity Commission, the enforcement agency for the Age Discrimination in Employment Act (ADEA),[862] is supposed to promptly seek to eliminate any alleged unlawful practice by informal methods of conciliation, conference, and persuasion.[863] There are only a few decisions concerning the consequences of the agency's failure to conciliate, or to conciliate adequately, in a private suit.[864]

The failure of the EEOC to conciliate was not deemed to bar the private plaintiff's suing in *Lundgren v Continental Industries, Inc.*[865] A like position was asserted by the court deciding *Horne v New England Patriots Football Club*:[866] "This requirement only extends to suits brought by the . . . [agency], not private litigants."[867] In contrast, the district court ruled in *Schuster v Feder-*

---

[861] 29 CFR §1626.14 (1993).

[862] 29 USC §§621-634.

[863] §7(d), 29 USC §626(d); *accord* 29 CFR §1626.12 (1993).

[864] There also is a conciliation requirement imposed as a predicate to the EEOC itself filing suit, and there is case law concerning the failure of the agency to conciliate in that context. See **§6.57.**

[865] 14 FEP Cas (BNA) 58 (ND Okla 1976); *cf* Oglesby v Coca-Cola Bottling Co, 620 F Supp 1336 (ND Ill 1985) (failure of the EEOC to investigate claim does not bar claimant from suing).

[866] 489 F Supp 465 (D Mass 1980).

[867] *Id* 470-71 n4; *accord* Donaldson v Cafritz, 30 FEP Cas (BNA) 436 (DDC 1981).

ated Department Stores, Inc,[868] that a stay was appropriate, but since the parties had not opposed the stay the court was not really called upon to address the merits of the matter.

§6.30 Statute of Limitations for Filing Suit: Generally

The statutory scheme regarding the statute of limitations for filing suit under the Age Discrimination in Employment Act (ADEA)[869] was radically changed by an amendment to the Act set forth in §115 of the Civil Rights Act of 1991 (CRA),[870] which was signed into law on November 21, 1991. This section of *Age Discrimination* addresses the ADEA statutory language in its pre- and post-amendment forms. The immediately succeeding sections address cases that, although construing the statute as it read prior to the 1991 change, remain relevant.

Prior to the 1991 amendment, §7(e)[871] of the ADEA incorporated §6(a) of the Portal-to-Portal Act,[872] which establishes a two-year statute of limitations for the bringing of suit, except for claims involving willful violations, in which instance a three-year statute of limitations applies. Section 7(e) further provided, prior to its being amended by the CRA, that the statute of limitations for the filing of a suit under the ADEA would be tolled for up to one year while the Equal Employment Opportunity Commission (EEOC) attempted to conciliate the grievance. Section 115 of the CRA amended §7[873] to strike the incorporation of the statutes of limitations contained in §6 of the Portal-to-Portal Act. It also removed the provision directing the tolling of the running of the statute of limitations during the time the EEOC was engaged in conciliation efforts.

---

[868] 508 F Supp 118 (ND Ga 1980).

[869] 29 USC §§621-634.

[870] Pub L No 102-166, §115, 105 Stat 1071, 1079.

[871] 29 USC §626(e).

[872] *Id* §255(a).

[873] *Id* §626.

Section §7(e), in its post-CRA form, provides that the EEOC is to give notice to a complainant when it has completed its internal agency efforts, i.e., investigation and attempted conciliation.[874] Pursuant to §7(e), the complainant then has 90 days from receipt of the notice within which to file suit. There is no requirement that the EEOC act within any particular time period. Thus, an EEOC notice issued any number of years after the alleged discrimination will, on its receipt, start the 90-day filing period running. As long as the plaintiff files within that 90 days, the action will be timely.

A claimant need not wait, however, for such notice; the ADEA provides, as it did before enactment of the CRA, that once a grievant has filed a charge of unlawful discrimination with the EEOC, he or she need only wait 60 days before filing suit.[875] This contrasts with the scheme set forth in the ADEA's analogue, Title VII of the Civil Rights Act of 1964.[876] Like the ADEA, Title VII sets a 90-day period for filing suit following the receipt of notice from the EEOC, but—unlike the ADEA—Title VII bars a claimant from suing until that notice of right to sue is received.[877]

The consequence of the changes made by the CRA is that ADEA plaintiffs no longer have to worry about suing within two or three years following the alleged wrongful act or decision.[878] On the other hand, a grievant must take care to file no later than 90 days following receipt of the EEOC notice. Presumably, the same equity-based arguments that applied to the former statutes of limitations, whereby a plaintiff might be relieved of the consequences of his or her filing late, will continue to apply, and there-

---

[874] See **§§6.56-.57.**

[875] See **§6.37.**

[876] 42 USC §§2000e through 2000e-17.

[877] *Id* §2000e-5(f)(1).

[878] The changes made by the CRA have nothing to do, however, with the timing requirements that apply to the filing of charges of unlawful discrimination with the EEOC. See **§6.08.**

fore the case law concerning equitable estoppel and equitable tolling remains relevant.[879]

Retroactive Application of the 1991 Amendment

Only one section of the CRA directly amended the ADEA; the other provisions, several of them of much greater substantive significance than the ADEA modifications, made changes in Title VII, 42 USC §1981, and the Americans with Disabilities Act.[880] The issue that quickly generated an enormous body of decisions was whether these changes to statutes other than the ADEA should be applied retroactively.

In contrast to the plethora of rulings concerning these latter changes, only two lower courts addressed the merits of the retroactivity issue vis-á-vis the ADEA modifications. In deciding *Callan v Pepsi-Cola Bottling Co, Inc,*[881] the court reasoned that inasmuch as the EEOC had notified the plaintiff of the termination of its investigation more than a year prior to the CRA amendment's effective date, that amendment was inapplicable.[882] The district court deciding *McConnell v Thomson Newspapers, Inc,*[883] ruled that while the substantive changes made by the CRA were not to be applied retroactively, procedural changes would be so applied. The court reasoned that there is a distinction between procedural and substantive statutes of limitations:

> A statute of limitations may be procedural or substantive, and its characterization may vary depending on the context of the issue before a court. . . . Whether a given statute of limitations is procedural or substantive depends on several factors, including whether the right of action existed at common law, and whether the statute of limitations appears in the same act as the statutorily created right. . . . The proper characterization of the statute of limitations for ADEA claims is settled law. Every Circuit which has consid-

---

879 See **§§6.33-.34.**

880 42 USC §12101 *et seq.*

881 801 F Supp 448 (D Kan 1992).

882 *Id* 452-53 n6.

883 802 F Supp 1484 (ED Tex 1992).

ered the issue has ruled that 29 U.S.C. §255, incorporated by reference into the ADEA, 29 U.S.C. §626(e), is merely a limitation on the remedy available, not on the right to bring the action, and is, thus, a procedural statute of limitations. . . . Because the statute of limitations for ADEA claims is procedural, there is no injustice in applying new §626(e) to plaintiff McConnell's ADEA claim.[884]

Accordingly, the court held that "section 115 of the Civil Rights Act of 1991 should be applied to claims that accrued prior to November 21, 1991, provided that such claims were viable on that date."[885] The court further pointed out, however, that its holding applied only to claims filed on or after that date: "Claims that were barred prior to that date cannot be revived," and "[c]laims timely filed [as of] November 21, 1991, will not need to resort to the new statute of limitations."[886]

In 1994 the Supreme Court addressed the question of the retroactive application of the CRA provisions concerning the availability of certain damages and of jury trials in Title VII actions.[887] The Court held that these provisions were not to be applied retroactively. The Court, however, pointed out there "there is no special reason to think that all the diverse provisions of the Act must be treated uniformly for . . . purposes [of retroactivity.]"[888] While the Court did not expressly address the changes made to the ADEA, it did cabin its ruling with some observations that mildly buttress the *McConnell* court's analysis. The Court drew a distinction between substantive changes made by the CRA and procedural changes. As to the latter, the Court observed that "[c]hanges in procedural rules may often be applied in suits arising before their enactment without raising concerns about retroactivity."[889] The Court also, however,

---

[884] *Id* 1495-96.

[885] *Id* 1495 (footnote omitted).

[886] *Id* 1495 n14.

[887] Landgraf v USI Film Prods Co, 114 S Ct 1483 (1994).

[888] *Id* 1505.

[889] *Id* 1502.

pointed out that it did not mean to "suggest that concerns about retroactivity have no application to procedural rules."[890]

Landgraf really affords no particular guidance as to how to deal with §115. One could reason that the abolition of the two- and three-year statutes of limitations applies to any case that had been filed, but not decided, prior to November 21, 1991. Or one could argue that while the former statutes of limitations apply to pending suits, they do not apply to pending administrative charges of discrimination that had not yet ripened into lawsuits as of November 21, 1991. Or one could argue for prospective effect: only plaintiffs whose claims arose after November 21, 1991, are relieved of the need to comply with the two- and three-year statutes of limitations negated by the §115.

No obvious answer emerges. On balance, the *McConnell* court's analysis seems a legitimate approach. More than that, it comports with the vague suggestion of approval offered by the Supreme Court as to the retroactive application of procedural changes.

Pre-Amendment, Still Valid Case Law as to General Propositions

Some of the case law that was devised prior to the 1991 amending of the ADEA retained its validity even after the changes in the statutory language regarding the statute of limitations for filing suit. For example, the proposition that an untimely suit will be dismissed continues to be valid, no matter the particular terms of the statute.[891] Moreover, the uncertainty

---

[890] *Id* 1502-03 n29.

[891] *See, e.g.*, Vuksta v Bethlehem Steel Corp, 540 F Supp 1276 (ED Pa 1982), *affd without opinion*, 707 F2d 1405 (3d Cir), *cert denied*, 464 US 835 (1983); Kentroti v Frontier Airlines, 16 FEP Cas (BNA) 1519, 1522 (D Colo 1976), *affd on other grounds*, 585 F2d 967 (10th Cir 1978); Conklin v RCA Corp, 16 FEP Cas (BNA) 950 (ED Pa 1976). In Mitchell v Los Angeles Community College Dist, 861 F2d 198 (9th Cir 1988), *cert denied*, 490 US 1081 (1989), a race, sex, and age discrimination case, the court erroneously ruled that the plaintiff's age discrimination suit was barred because he had failed to file it within 90 days after receiving a right to sue letter from the EEOC. The court, in so ruling, inappropriately applied the statutory 90-day filing requirement contained in Title VII of the Civil Rights Act of 1964, 42 USC §§2000e through 2000e-17.

as to whether the 1991 changes will be applied retroactively affords another basis for the pre-amendment case law's remaining relevant. Accordingly, it is relevant to note that the filing times set forth in §6(a) of the Portal-to-Portal Act, which prior to the 1991 amendment were, as discussed *supra,* incorporated into the pre-amendment §7(e) of the ADEA, speak explicitly only to claims for back pay and liquidated damages, and thus there has been some divergence in the courts as to whether they apply as well to suits for other kinds of equitable relief.[892] Other issues also can arise, as discussed below and in the next section.

Burden of Proof and Waiver of Defense

The usual view is that statutes of limitations must be pleaded and proved as affirmative defenses.[893] The Court of Appeals for the Sixth Circuit, however, has taken a contrary position, stating that the plaintiff bears "the burden of proof . . . to establish by

---

[892] *Compare* Wirtz v Chase, 400 F2d 665 (6th Cir 1968) (non-ADEA case); Marshall v American Motors Corp, 475 F Supp 875 (ED Mich 1979) (equitable claims are covered by §6(a)) *with* Reeves v International Tel & Tel Corp, 616 F2d 1342 (5th Cir 1980), *cert denied,* 449 US 1077 (1981) (non-ADEA case; equitable claims not covered by §6(a)); Equal Employment Opportunity Commn v City of Chicago, 51 FEP Cas (BNA) 503, 507-08 (ND Ill 1989) (equitable action not covered by §6(a) in suit by government enforcement agency). In Equal Employment Opportunity Commn v Westinghouse Elec Corp, 725 F2d 211 (3d Cir 1983), *cert denied,* 469 US 820 (1984), an ADEA case, the court obviously assumed that the limitations statute applied to claims for equitable relief.

[893] *See, e.g.,* Mumblower v Callicott, 526 F2d 1183 (8th Cir 1975) (non-ADEA case); Equal Employment Opportunity Commn v Liggett & Meyers, Inc, 29 FEP Cas (BNA) 1611, 1644 (EDNC 1982); Marshall v American Motors Corp, 475 F Supp 875, 884 (ED Mich 1979); Dunlop v Westinghouse Elec Corp, 17 FEP Cas (BNA) 1285 (SD Fla 1976). The issue was left unresolved in Equal Employment Opportunity Commn v Westinghouse Elec Corp, 632 F Supp 343, 372 n22 (ED Pa 1986), *affd in part & vacated & remanded in part on other grounds,* 869 F2d 696 (3d Cir), *vacated,* 493 US 801 (1989); *see also* Herman v National Broadcasting Co, Inc, 569 F Supp 282, 287-88 (ND Ill 1983), *affd in part & revd in part on other grounds,* 744 F2d 604 (7th Cir 1984), *cert denied,* 470 US 1028 (1985).

a preponderance of evidence those facts which are necessary to avoid the statute of limitations."[894] For those jurisdictions that do not follow this aberrational Sixth Circuit tack, the generally accepted view is that if the defendant fails to raise the defense it will be deemed waived.[895] "However, the courts do not apply such waiver strictly, but consider factors, such as the length of time that has passed and any prejudice to the other parties."[896]

Other Issues

If there is a disputed factual issue as to whether a suit was timely filed, the plaintiff must be allowed to present evidence on the issue, thereby precluding the grant of a motion for summary judgment.[897] There is limited case law as to whether the matter of equitable modification of the statute of limitations is a jury issue, with a few courts taking an affirmative position.[898]

The ADEA's statute of limitations presumably applies to ADEA suits filed in state courts, as well as those filed in federal courts.[899]

By virtue of Federal Rule of Civil Procedure 6(a), the day on which the triggering act occurred is excluded from the computation of time.[900]

---

[894] Ott v Midland-Ross Corp, 600 F2d 24, 34 (6th Cir 1979).

[895] *See* Bell v Purdue Univ, 975 F2d 422, 425 n4 (7th Cir 1992); Heiar v Crawford County, 746 F2d 1190 (7th Cir 1984), *cert denied*, 472 US 1027 (1985); Sharpe v Philadelphia Hous Auth, 693 F2d 24, 25-26 n1 (3d Cir 1982).

[896] Butler v Portland Gen Elec Co, 748 F Supp 783, 788 (D Or 1990), *affd without opinion*, 958 F2d 377 (9th Cir 1992).

[897] *See, e.g.*, Marshall v Kimberly-Clark Corp, 625 F2d 1300 (5th Cir 1980); Marshall v American Motors Corp, 475 F Supp 875, 883 (ED Mich 1979).

[898] See **§6.34.**

[899] *See* O'Neill v New York Bd of Fire Underwriters, 191 Misc 2d 485, 78 NYS2d 709 (Sup Ct 1948), *appeal dismissed*, 276 AD 1069, 97 NYS2d 200 (1950) (non-ADEA case).

[900] *See* McConnell v Thomson Newspapers, Inc, 802 F Supp 1484, 1496 (ED Tex 1992).

§6.31 —When a Cause of Action Accrues

Section 7(e), as Amended by the Civil Rights Act of 1991

By virtue of the amending of the Age Discrimination in Employment Act (ADEA)[901] in 1991,[902] ascertainment of the date on which the period for the filing of suit begins to run should in most instances be relatively easy. Suit must be filed within 90 days of receipt of notice from the Equal Employment Opportunity Commission (EEOC), according to §7(e).[903] There is some room for dispute here, however, since reliance upon receipt as the triggering event leaves room for arguments in situations where the notice is completely misdirected, or, even if sent to the right place, is received by someone other than the plaintiff, and so on. Moreover, if the 1991 changes are not applied retroactively, there are going to continue to be—at least for a while—issues arising out of the pre-amendment statutes of limitations.

Pre-1991 Amendment Statutory Language and Case Law

Section 6(a) of the Portal-to-Portal Act,[904] which remains valid in non-ADEA contexts and which formerly set the filing periods for ADEA suits,[905] provides that the limitations period begins to run when the cause of action accrues. Thus, it is error to deem the running of the limitations period as beginning at the time the charge of unlawful discrimination is filed with the EEOC—a filing that almost invariably will occur at some point subsequent to the alleged discrimination.[906]

---

[901] 29 USC §§621-634.

[902] See **§6.30.**

[903] 29 USC §626(e).

[904] *Id* §255(a).

[905] See **§6.30.**

[906] *See, e.g.,* Kazanzas v Walt Disney World Co, 704 F2d 1527 (11th Cir), *cert denied,* 464 US 982 (1983); Marshall v Kimberly-Clark Corp, 625 F2d 1300, 1301 (5th Cir 1980). *But see* Downey v Southern Natural Gas Co, 649 F2d 302, 304 (5th Cir 1981); Johnson v Al Tech Specialty Steel Corp, 33 FEP Cas (BNA) 1684 (NDNY 1983), *affd on other grounds,* 731 F2d 143 (2d Cir 1984).

At one time, there was a lack of uniformity among the courts as to the determination of when an ADEA violation occurred. Possible choices included the date on which the plaintiff became aware of the wrongdoing, the last date on which the plaintiff—in a discharge case—worked for the defendant, and the last date on which the plaintiff—again in a discharge case—received any remuneration or benefits from the defendant, if that occurred after the actual last day of work for the employer.[907] In 1980 the Supreme Court rendered a decision which, while construing neither the ADEA nor a statute of limitations for the filing of suit, effectively established the date for accrual of the limitations period. In *Delaware State College v Ricks*[908] the Court addressed a statutory requirement that an administrative complaint be filed under Title VII of the Civil Rights Act of 1964[909] within 180 days of the alleged violation. The Court held that an alleged violation occurs for the purposes of triggering this 180-day period when the grievant learns of the alleged wrong, rather than when the consequences of the discriminatory decision or action later become painful (assuming those consequences are not temporally congruent with the date on which the individual learns of the allegedly discriminatory decision or action).[910] Therefore, a Title VII grievant may not wait to file an administrative charge until he or she actually experiences tangible harm, such as termination of salary, if he or she was, or—as the concept has been embellished—should have been, aware prior to that time that the harm was in the offing some time in the future.

The ADEA is modeled on Title VII, and accordingly courts construing the ADEA regularly look to Title VII decisions for

---

[907] Regarding the like issue of when the 180-day or 300-day period for the filing of charges with the EEOC begins to run, see generally **§6.09.**

[908] 449 US 250 (1980).

[909] 42 USC §§2000e through 2000e-17.

[910] *Cf* Chardon v Fernandez, 454 US 6, 8 (1981) (case arising under Title VII) ("[T]he proper focus . . . is on the point of the *discriminatory act,* not the point at which the *consequences* of the act become painful." (emphasis in original)).

guidance.[911] Courts thus have looked to *Ricks* when confronted with the similar question under the ADEA, which also has a 180-day (as well as a 300-day) filing requirement regarding charges filed with the EEOC.[912] While statutes of limitations questions concerning the filing of suit under §7(e), as it read prior to its being amended in 1991, arose under a different provision of the ADEA than did questions concerning the filing of charges, the basic inquiry was the same in both instances: when did the alleged violation occur? Accordingly, the *Ricks* decision was applied.[913] This did not mean, of course, that there was no ambiguity as to when the grievant learned, or reasonably should have learned, of the facts suggesting that the Act had been violated. Again, ADEA case law—based often on Title VII decisions—concerning the beginning of the time period for filing charges with the EEOC[914] was deemed apposite in dealing with this problem.

There are a number of cases. In *Michaels v Jones & Laughlin Steel Corp,*[915] for example, there was a question as to when the plaintiff received notice of his termination. A notice that he was laid off, but that recall was likely, was deemed not to trigger the

---

[911] *See, e.g.,* Oscar Mayer & Co v Evans, 441 US 750, 756 (1979); Purtill v Harris, 658 F2d 134, 137 (3d Cir 1981), *cert denied,* 462 US 1131 (1983); Coke v General Adjustment Bureau, Inc, 640 F2d 584, 587 (5th Cir 1981). See generally **ch 2.**

[912] *See, e.g.,* Aronsen v Crown Zellerbach, 662 F2d 584 (9th Cir 1981), *cert denied,* 459 US 1200 (1983). See generally **§6.08.**

[913] *See, e.g.,* Chapman v Homco, Inc, 886 F2d 756 (5th Cir 1989), *cert denied,* 494 US 1067 (1990); O'Connell v Champion Intl Corp, 812 F2d 393 (8th Cir 1987); Jett v Drummond Co, 51 FEP Cas (BNA) 221, 225 (MD Ala 1989); Herman v National Broadcasting Co, Inc, 569 F Supp 282 (ND Ill 1983), *affd in part & revd in part on other grounds,* 744 F2d 604 (7th Cir 1984), *cert denied,* 470 US 1028 (1985); Equal Employment Opportunity Commn v Trans World Airlines, Inc, 544 F Supp 1187, 1191 n1 (SDNY 1982); Pfister v Allied Corp, 539 F Supp 224 (SDNY 1982); Equal Employment Opportunity Commn v Kimberly-Clark Corp, 531 F Supp 58 (ND Ga 1981); *see also* Equal Employment Opportunity Commn v Home Ins Co, 553 F Supp 704 (SDNY 1982) (nonprivate enforcement ADEA case).

[914] See **§§6.09-.21.**

[915] 628 F Supp 48 (WD Pa 1985).

statute of limitations for the plaintiff's discharge claim, since it did not notify him that he was being discharged.[916]

Continuing Violation Arguments

Some pre-CRA plaintiffs endeavored to elude a time cutoff for filing suit by arguing that they were the victims of continuing violations, that is, a series of discriminatory acts or decisions that persisted over time, with the last act or decision occurring sufficiently recently so as to fall within the two- or three-year suit-filing periods set by §6(a) of the Portal-to-Portal Act.[917] As a general matter, " '[t]o prevail on a continuing violation theory . . . the plaintiff must show more than the occurrence of isolated or sporadic acts of intentional discrimination.' "[918] It was not sufficient that a grievant presently was suffering the consequences of a past act of discrimination, if that act occurred so long ago that suit was not now timely. Rather, there must have been a discriminatory act or decision within the pre-CRA mandated two-year period (or three-year period in the case of willful violations) prior to the filing of suit.[919]

Some courts rejected plaintiffs' efforts to rely on continuing violation arguments.[920] Other courts accepted them.[921] (These

[916] *See also* Equal Employment Opportunity Commn v Home Ins Co, 553 F Supp 704 (SDNY 1982).

[917] 29 USC §255(a).

[918] Miller v Beneficial Management Corp, 977 F2d 834, 844 (3d Cir 1992) (quoting Jewett v International Tel & Tel Corp, 653 F2d 89, 91-92 (3d Cir), *cert denied,* 454 US 969 (1981)).

[919] *Cf* United Air Lines, Inc v Evans, 431 US 553 (1977) (case arising under Title VII). See generally **§6.13.**

[920] *See, e.g.,* Herman v National Broadcasting Co, Inc, 569 F Supp 282 (ND Ill 1983), *affd in part & revd in part on other grounds,* 744 F2d 604 (7th Cir 1984), *cert denied,* 470 US 1028 (1985); Allen v Colgate-Palmolive Co, 539 F Supp 57 (SDNY 1981); Brennan v Sun Oil Co of Pa, 17 FEP Cas (BNA) 1577 (ND Okla 1976), *revd & remanded on other grounds,* 592 F2d 563 (10th Cir), *cert denied,* 444 US 826 (1979); *see also* Nelson v Williams, 25 FEP Cas (BNA) 1214 (DDC 1980) (federal employee suit).

[921] The analysis in one of these latter decisions probably was rendered nonviable by United Air Lines v Evans, 431 US 553 (1977), discussed in **§6.13.** *See, e.g.,* Stanley v General Motors Corp, 71 FRD 99 (ED Wis 1976).

latter rulings must be re-examined, however, in light of *Lorance v AT&T Technologies, Inc,*[922] which is discussed in the next section.)

One of the decisions expressing a favorable response to a continuing violation claim is *Miller v Beneficial Management Corp.*[923] The Court of Appeals for the Third Circuit approved the application of continuing violation analysis to the plaintiff's claim that she was the victim of a discriminatory pay scheme, whereby she was receiving a lesser salary. The court, relying on cases construing the Equal Pay Act (EPA),[924] observed that "[m]ost courts appear to treat pay discrimination claims as continuing violations."[925] In other words, each paycheck constitutes another in a series of violations, extending back to the inception of the discriminatory pay scheme.[926]

In *Morelock v NCR Corp*[927] the theory was successfully applied to an allegedly discriminatory seniority system. The Court of Appeals for the Sixth Circuit stated as follows:

> An employee's cause of action for an alleged act of age discrimination caused by a discriminatory seniority system, does not accrue until his employment opportunities are adversely affected by the application to him of the provisions of that seniority system.[928]

---

922 490 US 900 (1989). See **§6.32.**

923 977 F2d 834 (3d Cir 1992).

924 29 USC §206(d). The opinion is somewhat unclear as to whether the court was addressing the pay claim under both the ADEA and the EPA, or only under the latter. The district court opinion likewise was somewhat unclear. Miller v Beneficial Management Corp, 776 F Supp 936 (DNJ 1991), *revd,* 977 F2d 834 (3d Cir 1992).

925 977 F2d at 843.

926 *See also* Gibbs v Pierce County Law Enforcement Support Agency, 785 F2d 1396, 1399-40 (9th Cir 1986) (non-ADEA case); Bartelt v Berlitz Sch of Languages, Inc, 698 F2d 1003, 1004 (9th Cir), *cert denied,* 464 US 915 (1983) (*id*); Hall v Ledex, Inc, 669 F2d 397, 398 (6th Cir 1982) (Equal Pay Act case); Hodgson v Behrens Drug Co, 475 F2d 1041, 1050 (5th Cir), *cert denied,* 414 US 822 (1973) (*id*).

927 586 F2d 1096 (6th Cir 1978), *cert denied,* 441 US 906 (1979).

928 *Id* 1103; *accord* Equal Employment Opportunity Commn v Home Ins Co, 553 F Supp 704 (SDNY 1982).

Thus, the cause of action did not arise when the system was adopted, but only when the plaintiffs were laid off pursuant to it. A similar analysis was used in the context of an alleged unlawful exclusion from a pension plan.[929] So, too, was like analysis utilized regarding long standing retirement policies: the cause of action did not arise until the employee reached retirement age and thence was terminated.[930]

The court deciding *Equal Employment Opportunity Commission v Elrod*[931] addressed a different continuing violation argument made by the plaintiffs. The individual claimants argued that they had timely claims because they received lower pension benefit payments after their unlawful mandatory retirement than they would have received but for their unlawful ousters. The court rejected this argument, however, stating that "a claim predicated upon a past discriminatory act will not survive the lapsed limitations period merely because an employee's pay or . . . pension benefits continues to be [adversely] affected by that past act."[932]

In *Equal Employment Opportunity Commission v Home Insurance Co*[933] the court concluded that a continuing violation existed as a result of an allegedly discriminatory pension plan. It went on to consider whether *Ricks* applied, asking whether the applicable statute of limitations should begin to run on the date the employee was terminated pursuant to the plan or on the date

---

[929] *See* Crosland v Charlotte Eye, Ear & Throat Hosp, 686 F2d 208 (4th Cir 1982).

[930] *See* Equal Employment Opportunity Commn v Elrod, 47 FEP Cas (BNA) 1651, 1655 (ND Ill 1986), *affd in part & revd in part on other grounds sub nom* Equal Employment Opportunity Commn v O'Grady, 857 F2d 383 (7th Cir 1988); Equal Employment Opportunity Commn v Goodyear Tire & Rubber Co, 35 Empl Prac Dec (CCH) ¶34,596 (ND Ohio 1984); *see also* Blumenthal v G-K-G, Inc, 737 F Supp 493 (ND Ill 1990) ((1) maintenance by defendant of an allegedly discriminatory pension and profit sharing plan aimed at phasing out older employees, plus (2) refusal by defendant over time to reduce plaintiff's share of new sales accounts, was sufficient to establish, at least for purposes of motion to dismiss, a continuing violation).

[931] 47 FEP Cas (BNA) 1651 (ND Ill 1986), *affd in part & revd in part on other grounds sub nom* Equal Employment Opportunity Commn v O'Grady, 857 F2d 383 (7th Cir 1988).

[932] *Id* 1656.

[933] 553 F Supp 704 (SDNY 1982).

on which he or she was made aware of the impending termination. The court concluded that *Ricks* did not apply, reasoning that the policy justifications supporting the *Ricks* rule were inapplicable in continuing violation situations.[934] Thus, the court held as follows:

> [W]here an employer maintains a discriminatory mandatory retirement provision, the timeliness of a claim asserting unlawful termination thereunder should be determined with reference to the earlier of the last day of employment, or, if applicable, the date on which the employer eliminates the unlawful provision.[935]

The EEOC, in *Equal Employment Opportunity Commission v Japan Air Lines Co*,[936] unsuccessfully invoked *Home Insurance.* The court refused to recognize the existence of continuing unlawful policy. Rather, the court concluded as follows: "The most that EEOC has proven is that JAL engaged in a number of discriminatory terminations or forced retirements and resignations in the course of a force reduction. This is not enough to constitute an on-going discriminatory employment system."[937]

The Court of Appeals for the Third Circuit addressed, in *Equal Employment Opportunity Commission v Westinghouse Electric Corp*,[938] a claim involving employees who had been counseled by the defendant regarding the options available under its policies vis-a-vis benefits should their plant be closed. Some years later the plant was closed, certain benefits were denied, and the EEOC filed suit on behalf of 65 employees. The court rejected the application of *Ricks* insofar as it was argued by Westinghouse that the date of counseling was the date on which the cause of

---

[934] *Id* 712-13.

[935] *Id* 713; *accord* Snair v City of Clearwater, 787 F Supp 1401, 1408 (MD Fla 1992).

[936] 39 Empl Prac Dec (CCH) ¶35,946 (SDNY 1985).

[937] *Id* p 41,469.

[938] 725 F2d 211 (3d Cir 1983), *cert denied*, 469 US 820 (1984).

action accrued. It viewed the situation as one involving a continuing violation and accordingly viewed the relevant accrual date as being that on which the plant actually closed.[939]

The analysis in *Furr v AT&T Technologies, Inc*,[940] seems to be anomalous. There were seven plaintiffs, all complaining of discriminatory denials of promotions. Six of the seven first filed charges with the EEOC on August 20, 1981. Furr filed his charge on January 27, 1982, and his suit on June 9, 1982. The other six filed suit on March 25, 1983. Subsequently, the suits were consolidated. The jury found that Furr and two of the three other prevailing plaintiffs—Peterson and O'Connell—should have been promoted on August 15, 1978, and that the fourth prevailing plaintiff—Hunt—should have been promoted on May 1, 1981. AT&T argued that Furr, Peterson, and O'Connell had failed to timely file and to timely sue, since the discrimination occurred in 1978, and they had waited more than three years before filing charges, and longer than that to sue. The court, however, rejected that argument, and did so by relying upon Hunt's timely filing. The court stated as follows:

> A claim of age discrimination . . . may be based on a continuing policy and practice of discrimination that began before the statutory filing period, as long as the employer continues to apply the discriminatory policy and practice to a point within the relevant filing period, and plaintiff is not

[939] On remand, the trial court noted that at the time of the appellate court's determination the record was unclear as to whether the plaintiffs had been aware prior to the plant closing of their ineligibility for the benefits which they now sought by way of their lawsuit. The record had since been clarified, and it was now established that they did know prior to the date of closure. Accordingly, it was the date of knowledge, rather than closure, that triggered the running of the limitations period. Equal Employment Opportunity Commn v Westinghouse Elec Corp, 646 F Supp 555, 564-65 (DNJ 1986); *accord* Equal Employment Opportunity Commn v Westinghouse Elec Corp, 651 F Supp 1172 (DNJ 1987), *affd on other grounds*, 907 F2d 1365 (3d Cir 1990). (Of course, it is possible in a given case that the two events—plant closure and employee knowledge—may coincide.) *Cf* Heiar v Crawford County, 746 F2d 1190 (7th Cir 1984), *cert denied*, 472 US 1027 (1985) (similar analysis in context of considering timeliness of filing of charge of unlawful discrimination).

[940] 824 F2d 1537 (10th Cir 1987).

> merely complaining of the continuing effects of a discriminatory practice that existed only before the relevant filing period. There must be at least one instance of the discriminatory practice within the filing period for the continuing violation theory to apply.[941]

While, as an abstract statement, the foregoing is unexceptionable, its application by the *Furr* court was problematic because the instance of discrimination within the charge-filing and suit-filing periods to which it looked involved only Hunt. So far as a ruling in favor of Hunt on the timeliness issue was concerned, *Furr* is unremarkable. However, the court's willingness to allow the other three plaintiffs to piggyback on Hunt's timely filing is an unusual variation on continuing violation analysis.[942]

§6.32 —The Impact of *Lorance*

The viability of continuing violation case law must be evaluated in light of *Lorance v AT&T Technologies, Inc,*[943] which involved the question of when a charge of discrimination must be filed under Title VII of the Civil Rights Act of 1964.[944] The *Lorance* Court held that the charge had to be filed, unless there was a facially discriminatory policy at issue,[945] when the grievant

---

[941] *Id* 1543.

[942] In a representative action, other factors come into play, see **§6.22,** but the *Furr* ruling did not involve Hunt serving in the role of representative plaintiff on behalf of the others; each plaintiff had filed on his or her own behalf, although six had joined in one suit.

[943] 490 US 900 (1989). See **§6.15.** For a discussion of continuing violation case law, see **§6.31.** Of course, continuing violation analysis is only relevant if the new statute of limitations established by the Civil Rights Act of 1991 (CRA), Pub L No 102-166, 105 Stat 1071, is not applied retroactively. See **§6.30.** Once the 90-day filing requirement set by the CRA-amended ADEA takes hold, see **§6.30,** continuing violation analysis becomes irrelevant since there will be a fixed date that will trigger the filing period.

[944] 42 USC §§2000e through 2000e-17.

[945] *Cf* Equal Employment Opportunity Commn v City of Chicago, 51 FEP Cas (BNA) 503 (ND Ill 1989) (charge-filing, rather than suit-filing, case). The court took *Lorance* into account in assessing the timeliness of the claims of some

learned of the policy, rather than when it had an impact—sometimes only years after its adoption or after the grievant became aware of it—on the individual.

The court deciding *Equal Employment Opportunity Commission v City Colleges of Chicago,*[946] which involved an allegedly discriminatory early retirement program, applied *Lorance* in determining whether suit had been timely filed. The court reasoned that the *Lorance* Court's caveat regarding facially discriminatory policies being subject to challenge at any time was inapplicable, even though the plan's offer of incentives to those who retired early was keyed to age: "[a]n early retirement plan is not facially discriminatory, and subject to challenge at any time, merely because it makes age-related distinctions in benefits available to eligible employees."[947]

Of course, there can be room for dispute as to whether a policy is facially discriminatory. *Tusting v Bay View Federal Savings & Loan Assn*[948] arose out of a change in a benefits policy whereby following the amendment employees would receive coverage of only part of the cost of their health insurance premiums. Employees who chose to retire early, however, were guaranteed full post-

---

of the individual plaintiffs. The suit arose out of a city policy barring anyone age 35 or over from taking an exam, passage of which was a precondition to being considered for hiring as a police officer. In the court's view, a "roster [of people eligible to be hired] created from a discriminatory exam, and used for purposes of hiring, constitutes a continuing violation over the entire period of its use." *Id* 510. Turning to *Lorance,* which dealt with a seniority system, the court noted that the Supreme Court had drawn a distinction between systems that were facially neutral but had a discriminatory impact, and systems that were facially discriminatory. As to the latter, the *Lorance* Court had asserted that a facially discriminatory seniority system could be challenged at any time.

The *City of Chicago* court reasoned that the exclusionary testing policy at issue was facially discriminatory, and so could be challenged years after its adoption, so long as there was an alleged violation of the ADEA by its use within 300 days of the time a charge of unlawful discrimination was filed.

946 740 F Supp 508 (ND Ill 1990), *affd,* 944 F2d 339 (7th Cir 1991).

947 *Id* 516. In reaching this conclusion the court looked to the now defunct Public Employees Retirement Sys v Betts, 492 US 158 (1989), which has been overridden by subsequent amendments to the ADEA, for instruction as to the nature of such plans. See **ch 5.**

948 54 FEP Cas (BNA) 403 (ND Cal 1990).

retirement coverage. The plaintiffs argued that because they were older and had various medical problems, they were uninsurable. The court ruled that "[s]uch an age discrimination policy is facially discriminatory."[949]

While the Civil Rights Act of 1991 (CRA)[950] amended Title VII so as to render *Lorance* no longer viable, to some extent, for Title VII purposes,[951] the decision retains its analogical strength insofar as the ADEA is concerned[952] for claims arising before the same 1991 Act set a new formula for filing ADEA suits, i.e., within 90 days of receipt of a notice from the EEOC.[953] This is because the Congress, in passing the CRA, did not amend the ADEA. Thus, *Lorance,* which prior to the CRA had powerful analogical force for the ADEA, retained its relevance for the age discrimination statute, notwithstanding its being effectively overturned for Title VII purposes.[954] Moreover, even if one were inclined to read into the ADEA an implicit rejection of *Lorance,* based on *Lorance's* seeming demise in the Title VII context, the fact is that the extent of *Lorance's* curtailment—even for Title VII purposes—was limited.[955] Thus, *Lorance* retains strength in both statutory settings. The final basis for continuing to heed *Lorance* in the ADEA context is the possibility that the CRA's overriding of *Lorance* only applies prospectively, the result being that *Lorance*

---

949 *Id* 405.

950 Pub L No 102-166, 105 Stat 1071.

951 See **§6.15.**

952 *Id. See generally* Eglit, *The Civil Rights Act of 1991, the Age Discrimination in Employment Act, and Title VII: Three Acts and a Dog That Didn't Bark,* 39 Wayne L Rev 1093 (1993).

953 See **§6.30.**

954 See Eglit, *supra* note 952. The EEOC's position is that *Lorance* only applied to seniority systems, and so its application in other contexts would be improper. EEOC Notice No 915.002: Enforcement Guidance on the Effect of Section 112 of the Civil Rights Act of 1991 on the Supreme Court Decision in Lorance v AT&T Technologies, Inc and Charges Involving Seniority Systems. (Oct 20, 1993). (This EEOC issuance is reproduced in the Appendix at the end of the last volume.)

955 See **§6.15.**

continues to apply to causes of action arising prior to the CRA's date of enactment, which was November 21, 1991.[956]

Given *Lorance's* continuing relevance for the ADEA, post-*Lorance* ADEA rulings in which courts followed the direction, albeit not the dictate, of *Lorance* remain viable. The consequence is that a grievant (1) as to whom the amended ADEA's notice issuance procedure does not apply because the cause of action arose prior to the CRA amendment, and (2) who wishes to challenge a policy or practice which is not facially discriminatory and which he or she believes will at some point adversely affect him or her, (3) must do so within two or three (in the instance of an alleged willful violation) years of that policy or practice's adoption or, if it was in place prior to his or her being hired, within two or three years of being hired or of becoming aware of the policy or practice.[957]

§6.33 —Tolling the Statute of Limitations

The Age Discrimination in Employment Act's (ADEA)[958] statute of limitations was changed in 1991 by an amendment to the Act made by the Civil Rights Act of 1991.[959] Whether that change applies retroactively or only prospectively, case law developed prior to the amendment continues to be relevant, and so requires attention.

Representative Actions

Typically, a statute of limitations is tolled by the commencement of the action. While §7 of the Portal-to-Portal Act—i.e., 29 USC §256—is not explicitly incorporated into the ADEA, it is arguably relevant to this issue, given that the enforcement

---

956 See **§6.15.**

957 Inasmuch as the CRA was signed into law on November 21, 1991, it will be too late, as of November 22, 1994, for dilatory plaintiffs to rely on the pre-CRA three-year statute of limitations.

958 29 USC §§621-634.

959 Pub L No 102-166, §115, 105 Stat 1071, 1079. See **§6.30.**

structure of the Fair Labor Standards Act,[960] to which the Portal-to-Portal Act applies, is incorporated into the age discrimination statute.[961] Private individual actions, according to §256, are deemed commenced on the day of filing.[962] Representative suits[963] and suits brought by the Equal Employment Opportunity Commission (EEOC) on behalf of grievants,[964] however, are deemed commenced as to individual claimants on one of two dates:

> (a) on the date when the complaint is filed, if [the individual] is specifically named as a party plaintiff in the complaint and his written consent to becoming a plaintiff is filed on such date in the court in which the action is brought, or (b) if the written consent was not so filed or if . . . [the individual's] name did not so appear—on the subsequent date on which such written consent is filed in the court in which the action was commenced.[965]

As the language makes clear, consents that fall within the subsection (b) situation do not relate back to the date on which the original complaint was filed.[966]

ADEA courts are split as to the import of §256. Some have taken the position that this statutory provision is inapplicable to the age discrimination statute. For these Courts the filing of a representative action will toll the statute of limitations for opt-in plaintiffs.[967] For example, the court deciding *Levine v Lane*

---

[960] 29 USC §§200-219.

[961] *But see* Levine v Lane Bryant, 700 F Supp 949 (ND Ill 1988).

[962] *Id.*

[963] As to such suits, see **§§6.45-.51.**

[964] See **§6.60.**

[965] *Id.* As to the statute of limitations as applied to individuals involved in suits filed by the EEOC, see **§6.59.**

[966] Owens v Bethlehem Mines Corp, 630 F Supp 309 (SD W Va 1986).

[967] *See, e.g.,* Sperling v Hoffman-La Roche, Inc, 145 FRD 357 (DNJ 1992); Mooney v Aramco Servs Co, 764 F Supp 461, 462-63 (SD Tex 1991); Mershon v Elastic Stop Nut Div of Harvard Indus, No 87-1319 (DNJ Mar 23, 1990) (unreported); Levine v Bryant, 700 F Supp 949, 953 (ND Ill 1988);

Bryant[968] allowed late filing opt-in plaintiffs to remain in the suit. The court rejected the argument that §256 was applicable to the ADEA and ruled that the statute of limitations should be deemed to be tolled when the named plaintiff brings the suit.[969] In other words, the court embraced the rule applicable to class actions brought pursuant to Federal Rule of Civil Procedure 23 that was established in *American Pipe & Construction Co v Utah.*[970]

In *Frank v Capital Cities Communications, Inc,*[971] the court, without at all adverting to §256, asserted that the claims of opt-in plaintiffs were not barred, even though their consents were not filed until more than three years after the dates of their discharges. The court stated that "the filing of the named plaintiffs' complaint [which did not name the opt-in plaintiffs] served to commence the action for all similarly situated class plaintiffs."[972] Since the named plaintiffs had filed within the limitations period, "the date of filing of individual consents . . . [was] irrelevant."[973]

Other courts have deemed §256 applicable, and have rejected the notion that the filing of the representative suit tolls the statute of limitations.[974]

Other Situations Involving Tolling

The statute of limitations is not tolled during the 60-day waiting period that must be observed before suit may be filed.[975] Nor,

---

Vivone v Acme Mkts, Inc, 687 F Supp 168, 169 (ED Pa 1988); *see also* Morelock v NCR Corp, 586 F2d 1096, 1103 (6th Cir 1978).

968 700 F Supp 949 (ND Ill 1988).

969 *Cf* Tolliver v Xerox Corp, 918 F2d 1052 (2d Cir 1990), *cert denied,* 499 US 983 (1991) (case addressing timeliness of charge filing), discussed in **§6.23.**

970 414 US 538 (1974); *accord* Mooney v Aramco Servs Co, 764 F Supp 461 (SD Tex 1991); Vivone v Acme Mkts, Inc, 687 F Supp 168 (ED Pa 1988).

971 48 FEP Cas (BNA) 551 (SDNY 1983).

972 *Id* 553.

973 *Id.*

974 *See, e.g.,* O'Connell v Champion Intl Corp, 812 F2d 393 (7th Cir 1987); Owens v Bethlehem Mines Corp, 630 F Supp 309 (SD W Va 1986).

975 *See, e.g.,* Ott v Midland-Ross Corp, 523 F2d 1367, 1369 (6th Cir 1975). As to the waiting period, see **§6.37.**

it has been held, is the statute of limitations tolled while the claim is pending before a state antidiscrimination agency.[976]

While §7(e)(2)[977] of the ADEA, as it read prior to its being amended in 1991,[978] provided for tolling of up to one year for suits filed by the EEOC in instances where the agency sought to conciliate the dispute,[979] some courts held or asserted that this tolling provision did not apply to private ADEA actions.[980] However, in 1989 the EEOC issued a regulation establishing that the tolling period pursuant to §7(e)(2) was applicable to private party litigation.[981] Thus, the running of the statute of limitations would be tolled, under the pre-1991 version of §7(e), during the time the EEOC's attempt to conciliate a private claim of discrimination.[982]

The pendency of a federal court ADEA action that is voluntarily dismissed, and then followed by the same plaintiff filing the identical suit in another jurisdiction, will not toll the running of the statute of limitations.[983] Accordingly, in *O'Connell v Champion International Corp*[984] the Court of Appeals for the Eighth Cir-

---

976 *See* Nurse v City of New York, 735 F Supp 69, 72 (SDNY 1990).

977 29 USC §626(e)(2).

978 See **§6.30.**

979 The questions of just when the conciliation process began, and, correlatively, the statute of limitations began to be tolled, could occasion dispute. *See* Equal Employment Opportunity Commn v Francis W Parker Sch, 61 FEP Cas (BNA) 967, 971 n5 (ND Ill 1993).

980 *See, e.g.*, Heiar v Crawford County, 746 F2d 1190 (7th Cir 1984), *cert denied*, 472 US 1027 (1985); Buffington v Phelps Dodge Corp, 800 F Supp 945, 948 n3 (DNM 1990); Leite v Kennecott Copper Corp, 558 F Supp 1170, 1172-73 (D Mass), *affd without opinion*, 720 F2d 658 (1st Cir 1983); Hovey v Lutheran Medical Ctr, 516 F Supp 554, 556 (EDNY 1981); *accord* Conference Comm, Age Discrimination in Employment Act Amendments of 1978, HR Rep No 950, 95th Cong, 2d Sess 13 (1978). *Contra* Vuksta v Bethlehem Steel Corp, 540 F Supp 1276, 1280 n13 (ED Pa 1982), *affd without opinion*, 707 F2d 1405 (3d Cir), *cert denied*, 464 US 835 (1983).

981 29 CFR §1626.15(b) (1993).

982 Of course, a court could choose to disagree with the EEOC regulation. See **Ch 2** as to the legal force of such regulations.

983 *See, e.g.*, Enos v Kaiser Indus Corp, 443 F Supp 798 (DDC 1978).

984 812 F2d 393 (8th Cir 1987).

cuit rejected the late-filing plaintiffs' argument that their complaints should relate back to the time of the filing of an earlier action. "[T]he relation-back doctrine must yield in ADEA cases to the specific provision of 29 USC §256 that an action may be commenced only by the filing of a complaint by a named individual, or by his affirmatively opting into a previously commenced class action."[985] The earlier discussion shows, however, that not all courts agree that §256 is applicable to ADEA claims. For such courts, "[t]he claims of . . . unnamed plaintiffs who later opted into . . . [a] case relate back to the date of the original complaint."[986]

In *Kazanzas v Walt Disney World Co*[987] the defendant had failed to post the notice of ADEA rights required by 29 USC §627.[988] While this was deemed sufficient to justify tolling the period for filing a charge of unlawful discrimination with the EEOC,[989] it failed as justification for tolling the statute of limitations for filing suit, for two reasons. First, the notice in any event would not have mentioned the then-applicable two-year statute of limitations; thus, the notice's presence would not have changed the situation. Second, the plaintiff knew of his rights under the ADEA.[990]

In *Equal Employment Opportunity Commission v American Express Centurion Bank*[991] the court held that the bank's refusal to comply with the agency's subpoena, which was issued in the course of an investigation of an aggrieved former employee's charge of unlawful discrimination, tolled the running of the statute of limitations for the period of noncompliance.[992]

---

[985] *Id* 394.

[986] Mooney v Aramco Servs Co, 764 F Supp 461, 464 (SD Tex 1991).

[987] 704 F2d 1527 (11th Cir), *cert denied,* 464 US 982 (1983).

[988] See **ch 3.**

[989] See **§6.18.**

[990] *See also* DeBrunner v Midway Equip Co, 803 F2d 950, 952 n5 (8th Cir 1986); McClinton v Alabama By-Prods Corp, 743 F2d 1483, 1486 n5 (11th Cir 1984); Klausing v Whirlpool Corp, 623 F Supp 156 (SD Ohio 1985), *appeal dismissed without opinion,* 785 F2d 309 (6th Cir 1986).

[991] 758 F Supp 217 (D Del 1991).

[992] *Id* 226.

§6.34 —Equitable Tolling and Equitable Estoppel

Equitable Tolling

Equitable tolling of the statute of limitations applicable to suits filed under the Age Discrimination in Employment Act (ADEA)[993] is dependent on the plaintiff establishing some excuse independent of the defendant's conduct for his or her late filing. Equitable estoppel, in contrast, focuses on the defendant's conduct. This distinction notwithstanding, the courts often confuse equitable tolling and equitable estoppel.[994] In deciding *Cada v Baxter Healthcare Corp*[995] the Court of Appeals for the Seventh Circuit highlighted this judicial confusion:

> Many cases, it is true, in the age discrimination field as in other areas, fuse the two doctrines, presumably inadvertently. The most recent example in this circuit is *Stark v. Dynascan Corp.*, 902 F.2d 549, 551 (7th Cir. 1990), which quotes from an earlier case the erroneous statement that "to invoke equitable tolling, the plaintiff must therefore show that the defendant attempted to mislead him." In fact that is what the plaintiff must show if he is trying to invoke equitable estoppel. For equitable tolling all he need show is that he could not by the exercise of reasonable diligence have discovered essential information bearing on his claim.[996]

Most equitable tolling cases involve late-filed administrative charges of discrimination.[997] The issue also can arise, however, in the suit-filing context. For example, in *Chapman v Homco, Inc,*[998] the plaintiff argued that it was not until two weeks after he was discharged that he learned he had been replaced by a younger

---

[993] 29 USC §§621-634.

[994] See generally **§6.17,** addressing this issue in the context of charge filing.

[995] 920 F2d 446 (7th Cir 1990), *cert denied,* 111 S Ct 2916 (1991).

[996] *Id* 452.

[997] See **§§6.17-6.21.**

[998] 886 F2d 756 (5th Cir 1989), *cert denied,* 494 US 1067 (1990).

man, so the filing period should not have begun to accrue until he discovered this. The court rejected the argument. A similar contention by a plaintiff was likewise unavailing in *Scheller v Hydrotherm, Inc.*[999] The plaintiff, who had been notified of his discharge on December 15, 1986, argued that the statute of limitations should not have begun running until February, 1987, when he learned that a younger man had been hired to fill his job slot, which he had been told was being abolished. The court asserted as follows:

> "A plaintiff's lack of knowledge of the discriminatory nature of an employment decision and the reasons for that lack of knowledge are relevant to an analysis of equitable tolling but play no part in determining the beginning of the statutory limitation period."[1000]

Looking to the facts, the court concluded that there was an insufficient basis for tolling the statute of limitations or estopping the defendant's invoking the dilatory filing as a defense.

In *Owens v Bethlehem Mines Corp*[1001] the court excused the late filing of two opt-in plaintiffs who had consented to participate in the named plaintiffs' action.[1002] The court attributed their delay to its own delay in ruling on the defendant's motion to deny class certification, and it accordingly deemed the statute of limitations to have been tolled during the period it was considering the motion.[1003]

The court deciding *Scheller* reasoned that even if the plaintiff was successful in establishing that the statute of limitations should be tolled on equitable grounds—i.e., his discovery that he had in fact been replaced by a younger man, which replacement cast doubt on the explanation given to him when he was

---

[999] 728 F Supp 377 (D Md 1989).

[1000] *Id* 381 (quoting Felty v Graves-Humphreys Co, 785 F2d 516, 518-19 (4th Cir 1986)).

[1001] 630 F Supp 309 (SD W Va 1986).

[1002] Regarding the filing of administrative charges by opt-in plaintiffs, see **§6.22**.

[1003] *See also* Dempsey v Pacific Bell Co, 789 F2d 1451 (9th Cir 1986).

terminated that his job was being abolished—the tolling would only defer the running of the statute of limitations until that discovery. Here, the plaintiff had 18 months in which to file after he discovered grounds for believing that he was the victim of age discrimination; since his failure to timely file at some point within that 18-month period could not be blamed on the defendant, it could not be excused.[1004] (The court distinguished the contrary conclusion reached in *Ott v Midland-Ross Corp,*[1005] discussed below in the text, by identifying *Ott* as a case involving equitable estoppel, rather than equitable tolling.)[1006]

Equitable Estoppel

It is a well-established equitable principle that "no man may take advantage of his own wrong,"[1007] Thus, a defendant whose actions have induced a plaintiff to delay filing suit until after the limitations period has run will be estopped from asserting the statute of limitations as a defense.[1008] The most extensive early discussion of equitable estoppel in the context of claims arising under the ADEA was provided by the Court of Appeals for the Sixth Circuit in two decisions, both denominated *Ott v Midland-Ross Corp.*[1009] The plaintiff alleged that he had been fraudulently

---

1004 *See also* Buffington v Phelps Dodge Corp, 800 F Supp 945 (DNM 1990) (while tolling was appropriate because of erroneous information given to plaintiff by the Equal Employment Opportunity Commission (EEOC), plaintiff's unduly long delay in obtaining counsel—which the EEOC had advised him to do and who might have led plaintiff to sooner file suit—led to ultimate conclusion that plaintiff's suit was untimely, given that the delay prejudiced the defendant by exposing it to increased damages should suit proceed and should it be held liable for liquidated damages, which are computed on basis of back pay due prevailing plaintiff). As to liquidated damages, see **ch 8.**

1005 600 F2d 24 (6th Cir 1979).

1006 *Id* 383.

1007 Glus v Brooklyn E Dist Terminal, 359 US 231, 232 (1959).

1008 *See, e.g.,* Vance v Whirlpool Corp, 707 F2d 483 (4th Cir), *affd,* 716 F2d 1010 (4th Cir 1983), *cert denied,* 465 US 1102 (1984); Ott v Midland-Ross Corp, 523 F2d 1367, 1370 (6th Cir 1975); Marshall v American Motors Corp, 475 F Supp 875, 884 (ED Mich 1979).

1009 600 F2d 24 (6th Cir 1979) (*Ott II*); 523 F2d 1367 (6th Cir 1975) (*Ott I*).

induced by the employer not to assert his rights. He claimed that: (1) he had been discharged; (2) he was later advised that the defendant was willing to reinstate him; (3) while he was awaiting a job assignment the defendant represented that if he would forgo his rights under the ADEA it would hire him as a consultant; and, (4) relying on this representation, he accepted early retirement and entered into a consulting agreement with the defendant, which agreement later was not honored.

The trial court dismissed the suit as untimely, but the appellate court reversed; it held that the plaintiff's allegations were adequate to bar a dismissal.[1010] On remand the trial court again held that the statute of limitations barred the suit and it granted the defendant's motion for summary judgment. Again, the court of appeals reversed.[1011] It explained as follows:

> A wrongful inducement . . . is not confined solely to fraud in the traditional sense, . . . and has even been held to exist where the perpetrator had made misrepresentations in good faith. . . . [T]he law does not require a person who seeks an estoppel to prove bad faith. . . . If the defendant made a misrepresentation for the purpose of inducing a plaintiff to delay suit . . . , it is estopped to plead the statute of limitations . . . , provided the plaintiff has acted in justifiable reliance upon the misrepresentation. It is unnecessary for the misrepresentation to have been made negligently or fraudulently.[1012]

In brief, the *Ott II* court did not require fraud, or even bad intent on the part of the defendant, as a predicate for equitable estoppel coming into play.

Other courts, however, have not taken such a sympathetic view regarding late-filing plaintiffs' interests. In *Pfister v Allied Corp*,[1013] for example, the plaintiff unsuccessfully argued that the defen-

---

1010 523 F2d 1367 (6th Cir 1975) (*Ott I*).

1011 600 F2d 24 (6th Cir 1979) (*Ott II*).

1012 *Id* 31-32 (citations omitted).

1013 539 F Supp 224 (SDNY 1982).

dant should be estopped from invoking the statute of limitations. Following the plaintiff's discharge, the defendant—at the plaintiff's request—had made an offer of monetary settlement, which was rejected. The plaintiff pointed to this offer, along with the defendant's alleged willingness to discuss an amicable resolution, as the bases for tolling or estoppel. The court disagreed: "There is no allegation that the defendant acted in bad faith or deceitfully lured the plaintiff into settlement discussions, or that it attempted in any way to cause the plaintiff to miss the appropriate filing date."[1014] A like standard, i.e., the requirement of fraud or misrepresentation on the defendant's part, was articulated by the Court of Appeals for the Eleventh Circuit in *Kazanzas v Walt Disney World Co.*[1015]

If the plaintiff has been wrongfully induced to forsake asserting his or her claim, he or she has a reasonable time to bring suit once the misrepresentation is discovered, or reasonably should have been discovered. As to what would be deemed to be reasonably discoverable, the second *Ott* appellate court asserted the following:

> The plaintiff . . . was obligated to exercise such diligence for the protection of his own rights as a reasonable and prudent person would have exercised under the same or similar circumstances. . . . [T]he jury should take into account the full relationship between the parties and the conduct of the defendant itself in determining whether the reassurances of the defendant, if made, would have induced a reasonable employee to have relied upon those assurances in expectation of a good faith performance. Ott was not obligated to assume that the assurances of the defendant were misrepresentations of fact or fraudulent, at least until such time as it would have so appeared to a reasonable person

---

1014 *Id* 227.

1015 704 F2d 1527, 1531-32 (11th Cir), *cert denied,* 464 US 982 (1983); *see also* Klausing v Whirlpool Corp, 623 F Supp 156 (SD Ohio 1985), *appeal dismissed without opinion,* 785 F2d 309 (6th Cir 1986).

> in the same situation as the plaintiff given his age, experience and intelligence.[1016]

As to what would constitute a reasonable time within which to bring suit once the plaintiff discovered, or reasonably should have discovered, the misrepresentation, the *Ott II* court said that the period of time during which the plaintiff was deceived should not be counted at all and that the plaintiff should have the full statutory period. Thus, if he or she was deceived for 18 months, there should have been a total of four and one-half years from the time of the alleged violation to sue, i.e., the three years then available in instances of willful violations, plus the 18 months.[1017] The court further went on to state that "in a proper case, a plaintiff may be permitted to prove that the remaining unexpired time was not a 'reasonable time' in which to bring suit," and it suggested that "[s]uch a circumstance may arise in the context of eleventh hour inducements on the eve of the expiration of the limitations period."[1018]

The plaintiffs in *Callowhill v Allen-Sherman-Hoff Co, Inc,*[1019] did not file their administrative charges of discrimination with the EEOC until almost two years after the alleged discrimination occurred. Their lateness in filing these charges was excused, however, because the defendant had failed to post the requisite notice of ADEA rights at the work site.[1020] While the plaintiffs promptly filed their charges upon learning of their rights, they

---

[1016] 600 F2d at 34 n13.

[1017] *Id* 33. A different rule was applied in Scheller v Hydrotherm, Inc, 728 F Supp 377 (D Md 1989). The *Scheller* court distinguished *Ott* by identifying its reasoning as being applicable to equitable estoppel situations, whereas the fact situation in *Scheller* concerned equitable tolling. *Id* 383. In Cada v Baxter Healthcare Corp, 920 F2d 446 (7th Cir 1990), *cert denied,* 111 S Ct 2916 (1991), the court also rejected *Ott. Cada* concerned equitable tolling. It also involved a late administrative charge, rather than an untimely lawsuit.

[1018] 600 F2d at 34 n12 (quoting *Ott I,* 523 F2d at 1370).

[1019] 832 F2d 269 (3d Cir 1987), *cert denied,* 485 US 962 (1988).

[1020] See **§6.18.**

then had to wait 60 days to file suit.[1021] By the time the 60-day period had run, the then-extant two-year period for filing suit had passed. Consequently, the defendant argued that the suits were untimely filed. The court held for the plaintiffs, but cautioned that its ruling was limited to the particular factual situation before it.

Jackson v Alcan Sheet & Plate Co[1022] also affords some guidance regarding equitable estoppel. The plaintiff in a timely manner had contacted the defendant's corporate office seeking a review of his discharge. This was followed by a letter reply asking him to allow time for the company to investigate. Some 20 days thereafter he was informed that the company had determined that he had been laid off properly. Subsequently he filed a timely complaint with the state antidiscrimination agency under state law. It was dismissed; the plaintiff appealed; and a final decision ultimately was returned almost two years later affirming the dismissal. At this point, the plaintiff did not seek state judicial review. Rather, after waiting about six months, he filed a federal ADEA suit. The court found no equitable basis for relieving him of the limitations bar to his suit. The court found there was "no evidence of intent on the part of Alcan to induce delay by means of its investigation into the circumstance surrounding plaintiff's discharge."[1023] Nor were there any allegations by the plaintiff that "the defendant in any way prevented plaintiff from learning of his ADEA rights or acted in any way to prejudice plaintiff's case so as to justify being estopped from asserting the statute of limitations."[1024] While the defendant had been required to prepare its case for the state proceedings, and thus it could not be said that it would be prejudiced if the plaintiff were allowed to maintain his federal suit, "this in itself does not justify denying defendant the protection afforded by the statute of limitations,

---

1021 See **§6.37.**

1022 462 F Supp 82 (NDNY 1978).

1023 *Id* 87.

1024 *Id; see also* Marshall v American Motors Corp, 475 F Supp 875, 884 (ED Mich 1979).

absent prejudicial behavior on its part."[1025] Finally, the fact that the plaintiff claimed to have waited to file suit until the state proceedings were completed did not warrant tolling the statute of limitations. "Waiting due to faith in the adequacy of one of two independent remedies is no excuse to justify tolling the statute of limitations of the other."[1026]

The court upheld the tolling of the running of the statute of limitations in *Equal Employment Opportunity Commission v Deutz-Allis Corp,*[1027] where the suit was filed late as a result of the defendant's recalcitrance in responding to the plaintiff's subpoena.[1028]

Role of the Jury

Notwithstanding the equitable nature of the issue, the court in *Ott v Midland-Ross Corp*[1029] deemed it appropriate for a jury to decide when and whether the defendant's acts effected a tolling or suspension of the statute of limitations and when and whether the plaintiff discovered, or in the exercise of reasonable diligence should have discovered, that he had been wrongfully induced. The court, however, confined its holdings to the facts of the case, where, as the court assessed the case, the equitable issues were tied up with the predominant legal issue, which was whether the termination was violative of the ADEA.[1030]

[1025] 426 F Supp at 87.

[1026] *Id.*

[1027] 49 FEP Cas (BNA) 97 (WD Mo 1989).

[1028] There is comparable case law dealing with the situation where the EEOC is the plaintiff. See **§6.59.**

[1029] 600 F2d 24 (6th Cir 1979).

[1030] *See also* Dillman v Combustion Engg, Inc, 784 F2d 57, 61 (2d Cir 1986); Vasconcellos v EG&G, Inc, 131 FRD 371 (D Mass 1990); *cf* Dillman v Combustion Engg, Inc, 784 F2d 57, 61 (2d Cir 1986) (dealing with untimely filing of charge of unlawful discrimination with EEOC); Pruet Prod Co v Ayles, 573 F Supp 895 (SD Miss 1983), *affd on other grounds,* 784 F2d 1275 (5th Cir 1986) (*id*).

§6.35 —Willfulness on the Part of the Defendant

The provisions of the Age Discrimination in Employment Act (ADEA)[1031] dealing with the time for filing suit were amended in 1991 by the Civil Rights Act of 1991 (CRA).[1032] As a consequence, identifying the time for filing suit has become a relatively straightforward exercise: suit must be filed within 90 days following receipt of notice from the Equal Employment Opportunity Commission (EEOC) that it has completed its consideration of the claimant's charge of unlawful discrimination.[1033] Because, however, the Supreme Court did not resolve the question, in deciding *Landgraf v USI Film Products Co,*[1034] of whether the new statute of limitations provision applies retroactively, the pre-CRA statutory language and the cases construing it remain relevant. Thus, the special rule applicable to willful violations of the ADEA under the pre-CRA statute of limitations requires attention.

Section 6(a) of the Portal-to-Portal Act,[1035] which was, until 1991, incorporated into the ADEA by §7(e)[1036] of the latter statute, provides that the statute of limitations will be extended from the normal two years to three in cases of "willful" violations by defendants.[1037] It is sufficient for the plaintiff to either allege in the pleadings that the defendant had acted willfully or to allege facts establishing willfulness.[1038] Such allegations will suffice to

---

[1031] 29 USC §§621-634.

[1032] Pub L No 102-166, §115, 105 Stat 1071, 1079. See **§6.30.**

[1033] §7(e), 29 USC §626(e).

[1034] 114 S Ct 1483 (1994).

[1035] 29 USC §255(a).

[1036] *Id* §626(e).

[1037] *Id* §255(a). While the Portal-to-Portal Act now does not apply to the ADEA, it remains applicable to the Fair Labor Standards Act, 29 USC §§200-219.

[1038] *See* Fed R Civ P 9(b); Pfister v Allied Corp, 539 F Supp 224 (SDNY 1982); *cf* Ayres v Federated Dept Stores, 24 FEP Cas (BNA) 528 (SDNY 1980); Rechsteiner v Madison Fund, Inc, 75 FRD 449 (D Del 1977) (both cases address willfulness in the context of liquidated damages claims; as to such claims, see **ch 8**).

overcome a defendant's motion to dismiss on the grounds that the suit was filed more than two years after the alleged violation.[1039] Conversely, the plaintiff's failure to allege either willfulness or facts establishing such will result in his or her being unable to invoke the willfulness caveat of §6(a).[1040] Moreover, in the view of one court, "a general conclusory assertion of willful discrimination supported [merely] by a suggested inference" drawn from the replacement of the plaintiff by a younger man would not be enough to survive a motion for summary judgment.[1041]

It has been held, or at least asserted, that because the question of willfulness necessarily implicates issues as to the defendant's mental state, knowledge, and intent, summary judgment is inappropriate.[1042] There also is considerable case law to the contrary, however.[1043] It also has been held that the issue of willfulness is a jury question.[1044]

Several courts have stated that the burden is on the defendant to prove the absence of willful conduct on its part.[1045] This posi-

---

[1039] *See, e.g.,* Collins v Manufacturers Hanover Trust Co, 542 F Supp 663, 671 (SDNY 1982); Kennedy v Mountain States Tel & Tel Co, 449 F Supp 1008, 1009 (D Colo 1978); Jackson v Illinois Cent Gulf RR, 15 FEP Cas (BNA) 400 (SD Ala 1977).

[1040] *See, e.g.,* Schroeder v Dayton-Hudson Corp, 448 F Supp 910, 914 (ED Mich 1977).

[1041] Scheller v Hydrotherm, Inc, 728 F Supp 377, 383 (D Md 1989).

[1042] *See* Spear v Dayton's, 33 FEP Cas (BNA) 267, 269 (D Minn 1983), *revd on other grounds,* 733 F2d 554 (8th Cir 1984); Allen v Colgate-Palmolive Co, 539 F Supp 57, 66 (SDNY 1981); *see also* Equal Employment Opportunity Commn v City of Mt Lebanon, 842 F2d 1480 (3d Cir 1988).

[1043] *See, e.g.,* Scheller v Hydrotherm, Inc, 728 F Supp 377 (D Md 1989); Parker v Federal Natl Mortgage Assn, 567 F Supp 265 (ND Ill 1983), *affd,* 741 F2d 975 (7th Cir 1984); Nash v Jacqueline Cochran, Inc, 548 F Supp 676 (SDNY 1982). As to the appropriateness, generally, of summary judgment dispositions where intent is an issue, see **ch 7.**

[1044] Agostine v Iowa Beef Processors, 35 FEP Cas (BNA) 328 (D Neb 1984).

[1045] *See, e.g.,* Equal Employment Opportunity Commn v Liggett & Meyers, Inc, 29 FEP Cas (BNA) 1611, 1645 (EDNC 1982); Marshall v Eastern Airlines, Inc, 474 F Supp 364, 370 (SD Fla 1979), *affd,* 27 FEP Cas (BNA) 1686 (5th Cir), *cert denied,* 454 US 818 (1981); Marshall v Goodyear Tire & Rubber Co, 22 FEP Cas (BNA) 775, 786 (WD Tenn 1979); Dunlop v Westinghouse Elec Corp, 17 FEP Cas (BNA) 1285, 1286 (SD Fla 1975).

tion arguably accords with the standard view that the applicability of a statute of limitations—in this instance the two-year statute of limitations that would apply absent willfulness on the defendant's part—is an affirmative defense, to be pleaded and proved by the defendant.[1046] This view of burdens was negated, however, by *McLaughlin v Richland Shoe Co.*[1047] This case arose under the Fair Labor Standards Act (FLSA),[1048] which was amended in 1947 by §6(a) of the Portal-to-Portal Act to allow a three-year filing period in the instance of a willful violation by an employer. Although the *McLaughlin* Court's attention was focused on establishing the correct reading of the word "willful," in the course of fixing on an interpretation the Court stated as follows: "To obtain the benefit of the 3-year exception, the Secretary [of Labor, i.e. the enforcement entity under the FLSA in the *McLaughlin* case,] must *prove* that the employer's conduct was willful[.]"[1049] While it is true that the Court was addressing an FLSA action by the Secretary of Labor, there is nothing to suggest that any different statement of the plaintiff's burden would be warranted in the ADEA setting, given the fact that the statutory provision at issue in *McLaughlin* was that which also applies to the ADEA insofar as pre-CRA cases are concerned.

Defining "Willful"

Neither §6 of the Portal-to-Portal Act nor its legislative history defines the word "willful." Accordingly, the courts were pressed to devise definitions, and they produced two prominent judicial constructions. One read "willful" as requiring nothing more than knowledge on the part of the defendant as to the possible applicability of the governing statute to its conduct. As the Court of Appeals for the Fifth Circuit asserted in *Coleman v Jiffy June*

[1046] See **§6.30.**

[1047] 486 US 128 (1988).

[1048] 29 USC §§201-219.

[1049] 486 US at 135 (emphasis added).

Farms, Inc:[1050] "Stated most simply, we think the test should be: Did the employer know the [statute] was in the picture."[1051] A number of courts, including several addressing ADEA claims, subscribed to this formulation, or variations very close to it.[1052] The other approach held that "willful" required that violations be "intentional, knowing or voluntary as distinguished from accidental," although this could include "careless disregard whether or not one has the right to act."[1053] ADEA courts, as well as others, also adopted this formula.[1054] Finally, some courts, while addressing willfulness allegations, avoided adopting any standard.[1055]

Whatever the standard utilized, the case law concerning willfulness generally was not particularly elucidating regarding application of the standards to the facts. In *Olsen v Southern Pacific Transportation Co*[1056] the court, after embracing the *Jiffy June Farms* test, simply stated that it assumed that if the defendant engaged in discriminatory acts, it did so with knowledge or with reason to know that it might violate the Act, and therefore willfulness was established. Likewise, in *Mistretta v Sandia Corp*[1057] the court, also citing the *Jiffy June Farms* line of cases, observed that the

---

[1050] 458 F2d 1139 (5th Cir 1971), *cert denied*, 409 US 948 (1972).

[1051] *Id* 1142. Actual awareness of the law was unnecessary. "Knowledge is imputed; 'everyone is charged with knowledge of the United States Statutes at Large, and their enactment gives legal notice of their contents'." Marshall v A&M Consolidated Indep Sch Dist, 605 F2d 186, 191 (5th Cir 1979) (quoting Cole v Railroad Retirement Bd, 289 F2d 65, 68 (8th Cir 1961)).

[1052] *See, e.g.*, Equal Employment Opportunity Commn v Governor Mifflin Sch Dist, 623 F Supp 734 (ED Pa 1985); Equal Employment Opportunity Commn v Liggett & Meyers, Inc, 29 FEP Cas (BNA) 1611, 1645 (EDNC 1982).

[1053] *See, e.g.*, Hodgson v Hyatt, 318 F Supp 390, 392-93 (ND Fla 1970).

[1054] *See, e.g.*, Herman v National Broadcasting Co, 744 F2d 604, 607 (7th Cir 1984), *cert denied*, 470 US 1028 (1985).

[1055] *See, e.g.*, Equal Employment Opportunity Commn v Great Atl & Pac Tea Co, 618 F Supp 115 (ND Ohio 1985); Collins v Manufacturers Hanover Trust Co, 542 F Supp 663, 671 (SDNY 1982).

[1056] 480 F Supp 773 (ND Cal 1979), *affd without opinion*, 654 F2d 733 (9th Cir 1981).

[1057] 15 FEP Cas (BNA) 1690 (DNM 1977), *affd on other grounds*, 639 F2d 600 (10th Cir 1980).

defendant knew that its conduct was subject to the ADEA, yet it continued to use a salary increase guide in which age was a criterion for deciding who received a salary increase. Consequently, the violation was deemed to be willful. Other courts offered even more perfunctory analyses.[1058]

A few courts did articulate somewhat more extensive analyses. In *Hicks v Communications Counselors Network, Inc*,[1059] for example, the court applied the *Jiffy June Farms* formulation and concluded that willfulness was established. It reasoned as follows:

> [T]he president of defendant . . . [company] and the individual who fired plaintiff, testified at his deposition that there was a federal act dealing with discrimination on the basis of age. As he must also have known that plaintiff was over 50 at the time of his termination, and as it appears reasonable to the court to impute . . . [the president's] knowledge to the defendants, the conclusion which of necessity follows is that the employer knew, or had reason to know, that any action taken with respect to plaintiff must comply with the . . . [ADEA]. That being so, regardless of which has the burden on this point, the . . . [willfulness] standard . . . has been met[.][1060]

In *Raggett v Foote Mineral Co*[1061] the court rejected the *Jiffy June Farms* formulation and endorsed the more stringent formula. It then applied this to the facts and concluded that there was no willful violation. While the defendant admitted being aware of the ADEA, it asserted that in good faith it believed that it was in compliance with the statute. Moreover, it had posted notices in the workplace regarding the ADEA, as required by the Act.[1062] Furthermore, the testimony of the employees and former employees involved in the termination decision indicated clearly

---

1058 *See, e.g.*, Bishop v Jelleff Assocs, 398 F Supp 579, 593 (DDC 1974).

1059 451 F Supp 575 (ND Ga 1978).

1060 *Id* 576.

1061 16 FEP Cas (BNA) 1771 (MD Tenn 1975).

1062 See **ch 3.**

that age was not a consideration in the determinations, much less a determining factor. Accordingly, the two-year limitations period applied, rather than the three-year period that followed willful violations.

Thurston and *McLaughlin*

In *Trans World Airlines, Inc v Thurston*[1063] the Supreme Court construed the willfulness requirement that is imposed as a predicate to the recovery of liquidated damages.[1064] It held that an employer would be liable for liquidated damages if it " 'knew or showed reckless disregard for the matter of whether its conduct was prohibited by the ADEA.' "[1065] Following the *Thurston* ruling, lower courts soon began to address the question of whether the definition set forth therein should apply to the willfulness requirement contained in the Portal-to-Portal Act regarding extension of the normal two-year statute of limitations for filing suit to three years.

Several ADEA courts held that *Thurston* was applicable.[1066] Ultimately, the Court settled the matter in *McLaughlin v Richland Shoe Co*,[1067] in which it held that the *Thurston* standard indeed applied in the statute of limitations context. While *McLaughlin* was an FLSA case, there is no reason for thinking that a different interpretation would apply in ADEA cases, given that in both instances it was the same statutory provision at issue.

The *McLaughlin* court focused on the issue of the correct reading of "willful" as a matter of law; it never developed any factual analysis. The Court, however, did give some general direction as to the application of the *Thurston* standard in a footnote. Noting first that there was language in *Thurston* which could be read

---

[1063] 469 US 111 (1985).

[1064] See generally **ch 8.**

[1065] 469 US at 126 (quoting Trans World Airlines, Inc v Thurston, 713 F2d 940, 956 (2d Cir 1983), *affd in part & revd in part,* 469 US 111 (1985)).

[1066] *See, e.g.,* Russo v Trifari, Krussman & Fishel, Inc, 837 F2d 40 (2d Cir 1988); Taylor v Battelle Labs, 680 F Supp 1165 (SD Ohio 1988).

[1067] 486 US 128 (1988).

as allowing a finding of willfulness to be premised on a finding of unreasonableness, the Court stated as follows:

> Our decision today should clarify this point: If an employer acts reasonably in determining its legal obligations, its action cannot be deemed willful. . . . If an employer acts unreasonably, but not recklessly, in determining its legal obligation, then . . . it should not be . . . considered [willful] under . . . the standard we approve today.[1068]

Applying the *Thurston/McLaughlin* Standard

In its effort to apply *Thurston,* the Court of Appeals for the Third Circuit devised the requirement, for purposes of defining willfulness in the context of considering entitlement to liquidated damages, that the plaintiff in an individualized discriminatory treatment case would have to establish that the defendant's conduct was outrageous.[1069] In *Crandall v Prudential Insurance Co*[1070] the court seemed to suggest that that interpretation carried over to the issue of willfulness in the statute of limitations context.[1071] In *Equal Employment Opportunity Commission v Britrail Travel International Corp*[1072] the applicability of the *Dreyer* outrageousness formulation to statute of limitations issues was confirmed. The court listed several factors "particularly relevant to the [willfulness] inquiry:"[1073]

> . . . (1) [w]hether discharging the employee denied him imminent pension benefits, (2) whether there have been previous violations of the ADEA, (3) whether there was a systematic purging of older employees. . . . Comments by

---

[1068] *Id* 135 n13.

[1069] Dreyer v Arco Chem Co, 801 F2d 651 (3d Cir 1986), *cert denied,* 480 US 906 (1987). See **ch 8.**

[1070] 691 F Supp 814 (DNJ 1988).

[1071] *Id* 828.

[1072] 733 F Supp 855 (DNJ), *affd without opinion,* 919 F2d 134 (3d Cir 1990).

[1073] *Id* 863.

> the employer and other employees are also useful in the analysis but not necessarily dispositive.[1074]

The court then assessed the facts and concluded that they did not support, either facially or by inference, the conclusion that the conduct complained of was outrageous. Ultimately, however, the Supreme Court rejected the outrageousness standard when it reaffirmed the *Thurston* formulation regarding willfulness for liquidated damages purposes in *Hazen Paper Co v Biggins.*[1075] Consequently, *Crandall and Britrail Travel* are no longer viable rulings.

The EEOC in 1989 issued a policy guide on the matter of defining willfulness, wherein it stated as follows:

> In planning or implementing a company wide job policy, the employer's obtaining and acting upon the advice of counsel will ordinarily be a factor in determining whether a violation was willful. Where an individualized claim of age discrimination is at issue, willfulness will not generally be found except in those instances where the evidence plainly demonstrates that an employee was terminated solely or predominately because of his or her age.[1076]

The EEOC's insistence that age have been the sole or predominant basis for an employer's action if willfulness is to be established is, like the *Dreyer* outrageousness standard, no longer viable. The *Hazen Paper* Court's reaffirmation of *Thurston,* plus its express rejection, as a matter of fact, of the predominant factor standard that some other lower courts had been articulating,[1077] leave no doubt on this score.

[1074] *Id.*

[1075] 113 S Ct 1701 (1993). See **ch 8.**

[1076] EEOC Policy Guide No N-915.042: Cases Involving the Definition of Willful Violation under the Age Discrimination in Employment Act (ADEA) for Purposes of Liquidated Damages and the Statute of Limitations 6 (May 1989). This policy guide is reproduced in the Appendix at the end of the last volume. (Such policy issuances are not of legally binding effect. See **ch 2**).

[1077] 113 S Ct at 1710.

Some courts, rather than adding embellishments to the *Thurston* standard, have applied it. For example, in deciding *Equal Employment Opportunity Commission v Westinghouse Electric Corp*[1078] the court concluded that Westinghouse had not acted recklessly when it adopted a severance policy that ultimately was held to be violative of the ADEA. At the time of the policy's adoption the state of the law was unclear; moreover, Westinghouse's lawyers had examined the legality of the policy. The court rejected the arguments that recklessness was established by virtue of: (1) Westinghouse's failure to seek an opinion letter from the EEOC regarding the policy's conformance with the ADEA; and (2) Westinghouse's refusal to enter into negotiation or conciliation efforts with the EEOC.[1079] The Court of Appeals for the Seventh Circuit took the position that "[a]n employer's conduct is not 'willful' when the employee acts reasonably, or even when it acts unreasonably, so long as its conduct is not reckless."[1080]

In *Zieger v Manhattan Coffee Co*[1081] the court considered testimony that the discharge decision was made by the defendant's chief operating officer and that the defendant was in contact with an employment discrimination compliance officer from its parent company. This evidence was sufficient to support submitting to the jury the issue of willfulness. The facts were clearer in *Equal Employment Opportunity Commission v Northwest Airlines, Inc;*[1082] they did not support a finding by the court of willfulness.

The foregoing cases make clear that the willfulness inquiry is a difficult one. Some courts, in undertaking this task, which ostensibly is just concerned with the technical matter of whether a suit was timely filed, have openly expressed the need to look to the merits of the plaintiff's claim. The district court deciding

---

1078 646 F Supp 555 (DNJ 1986).

1079 *See also* Equal Employment Opportunity Commn v USX Corp, 50 Empl Prac Dec (CCH) ¶39,143, at p 58,253 (ED Pa 1989), *affd without opinion*, 909 F2d 1475 (3d Cir 1990).

1080 Aungst v Westinghouse Elec Corp, 937 F2d 1216, 1223 (7th Cir 1991) (quoting Coston v Plitt Theaters, Inc, 860 F2d 834, 836 (7th Cir 1988) (quoting McLaughlin, 486 US at 128)).

1081 112 Ill App 3d 518, 68 Ill Dec 200, 445 NE2d 844 (1983).

1082 51 FEP Cas (BNA) 1317, 1328-29 (WD Wash 1989).

Frumkin v IBM Corp[1083] evaluated a motion for summary judgment based on the contention that the complaint was time-barred because it was not filed within two years of the alleged violation. If there had been a willful violation, the three-year statute of limitations would apply, and the complaint would have been timely. In deciding whether to grant the motion, the court reasoned that it had to look to the merits of the cause of action to determine whether the plaintiff had alleged facts sufficient to take to the jury the substantive issue of whether a willful violation existed. Concluding in the negative, the court accordingly ruled that the two-year statute of limitations applied. The *Frumkin* court took its cue from *Russo v Trifari, Krussman & Fishel, Inc.*[1084] There, the Court of Appeals for the Second Circuit likewise addressed the merits of the plaintiff's claim as a necessary first step in resolving the statute of limitations issue.

§6.36 —Extension of the Time for Filing Suit by Virtue of the Age Discrimination Claims Assistance Act

In 1988 Congress passed, and the President signed into law, the Age Discrimination Claims Assistance Act (ADCAA).[1085] The statute was a response to the admission by the Equal Employment Opportunity Commission (EEOC) that it had failed to act on approximately 900 charges filed under the Age Discrimination in Employment Act (ADEA),[1086] with the result that the then-applicable two-year statute of limitations had run while the innocent charging parties had awaited agency action. The 1988 legislation provided that for a period of 540 days following the date of enactment, which was April 7, 1988, individuals who had filed timely charges with the EEOC on January 1, 1984, or there-

[1083] 801 F Supp 1029 (SDNY 1992).

[1084] 837 F2d 40 (2d Cir 1988).

[1085] Pub L No 100-283, 102 Stat 78 (1988).

[1086] 29 USC §§621-634.

after could bring suit. Thus, these individuals were given until September 30, 1989 to file suit in federal court.[1087]

Subsequently, and pursuant to a study done by the United States General Accounting Office,[1088] it was determined that there was another large group of charges that had not been timely addressed:

> [From] April 8, 1988, to June 30, 1990, [there were] 2,801 age discrimination charges under ADEA [that] involved persons who lost their opportunity to file suit in federal court because EEOC district or state FEPA [fair employment practices act] officers failed to resolve the charges before the 2-year statute of limitations expired and the affected individuals did not initiate court action.[1089]

In response to this identification of a new group of grievants as to whom the statute of limitations had run through no fault of their own, Congress passed, and the President signed into law, the Age Discrimination Claims Assistance Amendments of 1990.[1090] This Act provided to claimants whose suits otherwise would be untimely an additional 15 months, i.e., through January 27, 1992, from the date of enactment, i.e., November 3, 1990, to sue in federal court, provided that: (1) these individuals had filed timely charges of unlawful discrimination with the EEOC after April 6, 1985; and (2) the statute of limitations had run after April 6, 1988, but within 180 days of the date of enactment, i.e., May 2, 1991. The legislation also required that, within 60 days after enactment, the EEOC had to provide notice to

---

1087 In amending the ADCAA, the Age Discrimination Claims Assistance Amendments of 1990, Pub L No 101-504, 104 Stat 1298, discussed in the text, reduced the extension of time to sue from 540 days to 450 days, i.e., through June 30, 1989. However, this change was apparently a clerical error, in the EEOC's view, and the EEOC ignored it. *See* United States Gen Accounting Office, *Age Employment Discrimination—EEOC's Investigation of Charges Under 1967 Law* 14 n1 (Sept 4, 1992).

1088 The results of this study are set out at 136 Cong Rec H9475 (daily ed Oct 11, 1990).

1089 *Id.*

1090 Pub L No 101-504, 104 Stat 1298.

those persons whose claims had lapsed informing them: (1) of their rights and of the benefits to which they were entitled under the ADEA; (2) of the date on which the statute of limitations on their claims had run; and (3) that they now had an additional period of time within which to file suit. This notice also had to be given to those persons whose claims lapsed, or would lapse, within 180 days after enactment. In this latter instance, the notice had to be given no later than 60 days after that 180-day period.

The ADCAA was available to save an otherwise untimely suit if the EEOC either failed to notify the claimant of his or her charge's disposition and the right to sue, or it failed to resolve the dispute through informal methods of conciliation, conference, and persuasion.[1091] Thus, one question that arose a number of times was whether the EEOC had provided adequate notice of the charge's disposition and the grievant's right to sue.

In *Turgeon v Rush-Presbyterian-St Luke's Medical Center*[1092] the court ruled that a letter from the EEOC to the plaintiff constituted adequate notice, given its content. Accordingly, the plaintiff's suit was dismissed as untimely. In contrast, in *Schleiniger v Des Moines Water Works*[1093] the court ruled that a letter sent by the EEOC to the plaintiff did not foreclose her from invoking the ADCAA because the letter did not set forth the agency's disposition of the plaintiff's claim. Likewise, in *Zabielski v Montgomery Ward & Co, Inc,*[1094] the Court of Appeals for the Seventh Circuit held that a letter from the EEOC to the plaintiffs which told them of their right to sue, but did not inform them of the EEOC's disposition of their charges, was not sufficient to remove the protection of the ADCAA. This view was seconded by the Courts

---

[1091] The ADCAA was applicable only to delays by the EEOC; thus, it was inapplicable to delays where the claimant never even filed with the agency. Gay v AVCO Fin Servs, Inc, 769 F Supp 51, 53-54 (DPR 1991).

[1092] 51 FEP Cas (BNA) 933 (ND Ill 1989).

[1093] 925 F2d 1100 (8th Cir 1991).

[1094] 919 F2d 1276 (7th Cir 1990).

of Appeals for the First Circuit in *Ruggieri v Warner & Swasey*[1095] and the Third Circuit in *Harter v GAF Corp.*[1096] In *Buffington v Phelps Dodge Corp,*[1097] also, the EEOC notice was held to be deficient.

The court deciding *Conkwright v Westinghouse Electric Corp*[1098] rejected the argument that a grievant knowledgeable regarding his rights under the ADEA was barred from invoking the ADCAA—an argument in part constructed on the *Turgeon* precedent.[1099] For additional applications of the ADCAA to save otherwise untimely suits, see *Albano v Schering-Plough Corp;*[1100] *Equal Employment Opportunity Commission v Puerto Rico Job Corp;*[1101] *Aleszczyk v Xerox Corp;*[1102] and *Equal Employment Opportunity Commission v Holiday Inn.*[1103]

In several cases the applicability of the ADCAA to claims of willful violations was addressed. The ordinary statute of limitations for ADEA claims was two years, until the ADEA was amended in 1991,[1104] but claimants alleging willful violations had three years under the pre-amended Act in which to file suit.[1105] Question regarding application of the ADCAA arose in situa-

---

1095 938 F2d 322 (1st Cir 1991).

1096 967 F2d 846 (3d Cir 1992).

1097 54 FEP Cas (BNA) 612 (DNM 1990).

1098 739 F Supp 1006 (D Md 1990), *affd on other grounds,* 933 F2d 231 (4th Cir 1991).

1099 *But see* Czaplicki v Sears, Roebuck & Co, 53 FEP Cas (BNA) 1058, 1061 (ND Ill 1990) (summary judgment for defendant where plaintiff: (1) had been informed by a letter from the EEOC of the ADEA's statute of limitations, and (2) plaintiff had been represented by an attorney from the start of the filing process; given the foregoing, "[n]o reasonable jury could fail to find that plaintiff understood she had an independent right to sue and that she had to file her . . . lawsuit within the applicable limitations period").

1100 912 F2d 384 (9th Cir 1990), *cert denied,* 498 US 1085 (1991).

1101 729 F Supp 208, 215-16 (DPR 1990).

1102 54 FEP Cas (BNA) 622 (WDNY), *affd in part & revd in part on other grounds sub nom* Tolliver v Xerox Corp, 918 F2d 1052 (2d Cir 1990), *cert denied,* 499 US 983 (1991).

1103 49 FEP Cas (BNA) 95 (WD Pa 1989).

1104 See **§6.30.**

1105 *Id.*

tions where the two-year period had run prior to the plaintiff's filing his or her suit, but the three-year period had not. The question concerning the ADCAA arose from one of the conditions precedent set by the ADCAA, as amended: for successful invocation of its extension of the time for filing, the statute of limitations had to have run prior to the date of the ADCAA's enactment, i.e., April 7, 1988, or the date of enactment of the 1990 amendments, i.e., November 3, 1990. In *Equal Employment Opportunity Commission v Holiday Inn* the court took the position "that all actions . . . will be considered as having a two year statute of limitations whether willful or not."[1106] In the earlier noted *Zabielski v Montgomery Ward & Co, Inc,* however, the court concluded that in cases involving willful violations the three-year period applied.

As a practical matter, the *Zabielski* approach did not necessarily bar plaintiffs from being able to rely on the ADCAA to revive their otherwise untimely suits that were filed more than two years after the alleged violation, but could have been filed before the three-year period had run. This was because plaintiffs, realizing that their efforts to prove willfulness would, if successful, have the perverse result of their suits being dismissed on untimeliness grounds, could simply not attempt to prove willfulness. The court explained this scenario:

> The choice between two and three years [as the appropriate statute of limitations to apply] depends not on what . . . [a plaintiff] alleges, but on what he proves. . . .
>
> [T]he Assistance Acts make it desirable for plaintiffs to fail to show willfulness—to make the period of limitations shorter. . . . [T]he length of the period . . . is a matter of proof rather than pleading. The upshot is that cases come out as if the "applicable" period were two years. Knowing that success in establishing an employer's willful discrimination will lead to victory for the employer, the employee

[1106] 49 FEP Cas at 96.

> will not even try to show willfulness. Failure of proof will mean that the period is two years, and the suit will proceed to the merits.[1107]

Of course, the consequence of this reasoning was to force plaintiffs to forego their claims of willful violations, which, if proved, would result in liquidated damages for the prevailing plaintiff.[1108] Thus, the *Zabielski* court's approach was not merely a mechanical ploy with no adverse consequence for the plaintiff. Deciding *Harter v GAF Corp*,[1109] the Court of Appeals for the Third Circuit deemed this consequence unacceptable. It took the position, in a case in which the plaintiff, in the court's view, effectively had pleaded his case in the alternative so as to allege both nonwillful and willful violations of the ADEA, that "[t]o make . . . [the plaintiff] forfeit his right to bring a willful violation claim in order to gain the benefit of the Claims Assistance Act would be contrary to the remedial claim-reviving purpose of that act."[1110] Accordingly, the court "view[ed] his complaint as though he had pleaded the willful-violation and ordinary-violation claims separately."[1111] Since the two-year statute of limitations had run as to the latter claim, the ADCAA, as amended, applied so as to preserve that claim.

One court held that the failure of the EEOC to notify the plaintiff of his or her rights under the ADEA within 60 days of April 7,

---

[1107] 919 F2d at 1280.

[1108] In Equal Employment Opportunity Commn v Chrysler Corp, 729 F Supp 1002 (SDNY 1990), the court held that the plaintiff's willfulness claim had to be dismissed, since on April 7, 1988—the date of enactment of the ADCAA—the statute of limitations as to that claim had not run. The court, however, was willing to allow the plaintiff EEOC to proceed with its cause of action arising out of alleged non-willful violations of the ADEA, which cause of action the court deemed to be "[s]ubsumed within the complaint," inasmuch as the complainant sought "equitable relief, . . . for which a showing of willfulness is not necessary." *Id* 1005. (The court noted in a footnote that the "proper way to resolve this issue procedurally would be to grant plaintiff leave to file an amended complaint . . . that does not allege a willful violation and therefore satisfies the statute of limitations provisions of ADCAA." *Id* 1005 n1.)

[1109] 967 F2d 846 (3d Cir 1992).

[1110] *Id* 851.

[1111] *Id.*

1988—a requirement imposed by the 1988 legislation (and one which was paralleled by a like provision in the 1990 Act)—would not bar the plaintiff from utilizing the protection afforded by the 1988 Act.[1112] Another court held, in light of the 1988 Act's language limiting its reach to charges filed after December 31, 1983, that an untimely filed suit could not be saved with the argument that the charge was pending at the administrative level after that date, if the charge actually was filed before January, 1984.[1113]

§6.37 The 60-Day Waiting Period for Filing Suit

Pursuant to §7(d)[1114] of the Age Discrimination in Employment Act (ADEA),[1115] an individual who wants to pursue remedies in court must wait for 60 days to elapse after the filing of a charge with the Equal Employment Opportunity Commission (EEOC) before filing suit.[1116] This waiting period applies not only to suits in federal court, but also to ADEA litigation pursued in state court.[1117]

In those instances in which the alleged discrimination occurred in a state having a law prohibiting discrimination and a state authority empowered to grant or seek relief, §14(b)[1118] also provides that the grievant must wait for 60 days to elapse

---

[1112] Rotterman v CBS, Inc, 726 F Supp 484, 493 (SDNY 1989).

[1113] Kyllo v Farmers Coop, 723 F Supp 1332 (D Minn 1989).

[1114] 29 USC §626(d).

[1115] *Id* §§621-634.

[1116] Even if the grievant withdraws a charge from the EEOC, suit still may be maintained, so long as the charge was not withdrawn less than 60 days after it was filed with the EEOC. Ingram v Dallas County, 688 F Supp 1146, 1157-59 (ND Tex 1988). But if the charge is withdrawn before the 60 days have elapsed and the EEOC did not have an opportunity within that shortened period of time to attempt conciliation, see **§6.29,** the 60-day waiting period will not be deemed to have been satisfied, even if the plaintiff waits more than 60 days after filing the charge before he or she files suit. Duke v Uniroyal, Inc, 719 F Supp 428, 433-34 (EDNC 1989).

[1117] Whitfield v City of Knoxville, 756 F2d 455 (6th Cir 1985).

[1118] 29 USC §633(b).

following the commencement of proceedings under the state law, unless these proceedings are earlier terminated.[1119] Congress's aim in imposing these 60-day waiting periods was to afford the EEOC or a state agency the opportunity to informally conciliate disputes and thereby divert them from the courts.[1120]

Even if an aggrieved individual files an administrative complaint with a state agency before he or she files with the EEOC, the individual still cannot file suit until 60 days have elapsed from the filing with the federal agency. (As a practical matter, in those states that have work-sharing agreements with the EEOC[1121] a charge filed with either the EEOC or a state agency will be deemed to have been simultaneously filed with the other agency, even if the complainant actually filed with just one of them).[1122] The contrary factual scenario may exist, i.e., there is no work-sharing agreement providing for simultaneous dual filing, and the administrative complaint is not filed with the state

---

[1119] Commencement of a state proceeding occurs when the grievant files with the state agency a written and signed statement of the facts upon which the state proceeding is based. *Id.* Furthermore, the proceeding shall be deemed to be commenced at the time the statement is sent by registered mail to the state agency. *Id.* See generally **§6.27.** In Coleman v Clark Oil & Ref Co, 568 F Supp 1035 (ED Wis 1983), the court misread §14(b). It interpreted the provision as barring the filing of a charge of discrimination with the EEOC, and from that erroneous reading drew the conclusion that a grievant had to wait 60 days after filing a charge with the state agency before it could file with the federal agency. The same error has been made by other courts. *See* Kaimowitz v Board of Trustees, 951 F2d 765, 766 (7th Cir 1991); Agosto Morales v El Mundo Corp, Inc, 790 F Supp 34, 35 (DPR 1992); Gay v AVCO Fin Servs, Inc, 769 F Supp 51, 53 (DPR 1991); *see also* Dapelo v Banco Nacional de Mexico, 61 FEP Cas (BNA) 284, 286 (SDNY 1991). In fact, §14(b) speaks only to a 60-day waiting period before *suit* may be filed.

[1120] Conference Comm, Age Discrimination in Employment Act Amendments of 1978, HR Rep No 950, 95th Cong, 2d Sess 12 (1978). In fact, however, there is no obligation on the complainant to exhaust state remedies, see **§6.27,** or even to cooperate with the state agency. *See, e.g.,* MacGill v Johns Hopkins Univ, 33 FEP Cas (BNA) 1254 (D Md 1983); Curto v Sears, Roebuck & Co, 552 F Supp 891 (ND Ill 1982).

[1121] Such agreements are authorized by 29 CFR §1626.10 (1993).

[1122] *See* McConnell v General Tel Co, 814 F2d 1311, 1315-16 (9th Cir 1987), *cert denied,* 484 US 1059 (1988); Stearns v Consolidated Mgmt, Inc, 747 F2d 1105, 1112-14 (7th Cir 1984); Stoecklein v Illinois Tool Works, Inc, 589 F Supp 139, 144-45 n7 (ND Ill 1984); *accord* 29 CFR §1626.10(c) (1993).

agency until some time after a charge of unlawful discrimination was filed with the EEOC. In this instance, if a grievant—having waited for 60 days after the EEOC filing—then files suit, the federal suit typically will not be dismissed; rather, it will be stayed until a state administrative complaint is filed and 60 days elapse.[1123]

While under Title VII of the Civil Rights Act of 1964[1124] an aggrieved individual must await receipt of notice of a right to sue from the EEOC before filing suit,[1125] no comparable requirement applies in the ADEA context. Thus, the district court deciding *Kohn v GTE North, Inc*,[1126] erred in thinking that a right to sue letter was a predicate to filing suit under the age discrimination statute. Section 7(e)[1127] of the ADEA was amended by the Civil Rights Act of 1991 (CRA)[1128] so as to create a 90-day statute of limitations for filing suit. The 90-day period begins with the receipt by the grievant of a notice from the EEOC stating its conclusions as to the administrative charge of unlawful discrimination that earlier had been filed by the grievant.[1129] Clearly this notice is not a required predicate to filing an ADEA suit, however, and so a grievant may file suit whether or not he or she has received the EEOC notice, provided 60 days have elapsed since the filing of the charge.[1130]

[1123] Oscar Mayer & Co v Evans, 441 US 750, 765 n13 (1979); *see* Curto v Sears, Roebuck & Co, 552 F Supp 891 (ND Ill 1982). See generally **§6.27.**

[1124] 42 USC §§2000e through 2000e-17.

[1125] *Id* §2000e-5(f).

[1126] 754 F Supp 563, 569-70 (SD Ohio 1990).

[1127] 29 USC §626(e).

[1128] Pub L No 102-166, §115, 105 Stat 1071, 1079.

[1129] See **§6.30.**

[1130] The originally proposed House version of the legislation that ultimately was enacted into law as the CRA was modified in a number of respects before being passed in the House, and the House-passed version was then supplanted by a version drafted and passed in the Senate. Even in its first incarnation, however, the CRA contained a provision amending the ADEA with regard to the question of the statute of limitations for filing suit. While that provision was changed in the course of consideration, it is not entirely irrelevant to note that in the reports of both House committees that had jurisdiction over the legislation, it was made clear that a claimant would be able to file suit without

A failure by the EEOC to undertake conciliation efforts will not prevent the plaintiff from filing suit once the 60-day waiting period has expired.[1131]

Stay vs Dismissal for Early-Filed Suits

There is case law standing for the proposition that the proper course for a court to follow is to dismiss the suit of a plaintiff who files before the 60-day waiting period following filing with the EEOC has elapsed.[1132] There also is case law expressing the view that rather than a dismissal, a stay until the 60-day period has passed is the proper course to follow.[1133] The reasoning supporting the former view is premised on the perception that the 60-day waiting requirement is jurisdictional and thus not subject to equitable modification.[1134] Other courts have taken a contrary

---

having to wait for receipt of the EEOC notice. See Committee on Education & Labor, US House of Representatives, Civil Rights and Women's Equity in Employment Act of 1991, HR Rep No 40, p 1 102d Cong, 1st Sess 96-97 (1991); Committee on the Judiciary, US House of Representatives, Civil Rights Act of 1991, HR Rep No 40, p 2 102d Cong, 1st Sess, 41 (1991).

[1131] *See, e.g.* Horne v New England Patriots Football Club, 489 F Supp 465, 470 n4 (D Mass 1980); Woerner v Bell Helicopter, 16 FEP Cas (BNA) 480, 482 (ND Tex 1977); Lundgren v Continental Indus, Inc, 14 FEP Cas (BNA) 58 (ND Okla 1976). *But see* Ryman v Office & Professional Employees Intl Union Local No 66, 628 F Supp 421, 429 (ED Tex 1985). As to conciliation by the EEOC, see **§6.29.**

[1132] *See, e.g.*, Vance v Whirlpool Corp, 707 F2d 483 (4th Cir), *affd,* 716 F2d 1010 (4th Cir 1983), *cert denied,* 465 US 1102 (1984); Wright v Tennessee, 628 F2d 949, 953 (6th Cir 1980); Reich v Dow Badische Co, 575 F2d 363, 367-68 (2d Cir 1978); Cannon v University of Chicago, 559 F2d 1063 (7th Cir 1976), *revd on other grounds,* 441 US 677 (1979); Rucker v Great Scott Supermarkets, 528 F2d 393, 395 (6th Cir 1976); Settino v City of Chicago, 642 F Supp 755 (ND Ill 1986); Hannon v Continental Natl Bank, 427 F Supp 215 (D Colo 1977); Berry v Crocker Natl Bank, 13 FEP Cas (BNA) 673, 678 (ND Cal 1976), *revd on other grounds sub nom* Bean v Crocker Natl Bank, 600 F2d 754 (9th Cir 1979); Mizuguchi v Molokai Elec Co, 411 F Supp 590, 592-93 (D Haw 1976).

[1133] *See* Dalessandro v Monk, 864 F2d 6 (2d Cir 1988); Gabriele v Chrysler Corp, 573 F2d 949, 956 n18 (6th Cir 1978), *vacated on other grounds,* 442 US 908 (1979) (dictum); Bertrand v Orkin Exterminating Co, 419 F Supp 1123, 1130 (ND Ill 1976).

[1134] *See* Vance v Whirlpool Corp, 707 F2d 483 (4th Cir), *affd,* 716 F2d 1010 (4th Cir 1983), *cert denied,* 465 US 1102 (1984); Wright v Tennessee, 623 F2d 949, 953 (6th Cir 1980); Reich v Dow Badische Co, 575 F2d 363, 367-68 (2d

view, deeming the 60-day waiting period to be subject to equitable modification after all.[1135]

In support of the latter position, and in refutation of the former, one might look to *Oscar Mayer & Co v Evans.*[1136] Inasmuch as a plaintiff who does not wait 60 days to file federal suit after commencing a state proceeding only will be subject, according to *Oscar Mayer,* to a stay pending the elapse of the 60-day period rather than a dismissal,[1137] arguably the same tack should be taken as to plaintiffs who fail to wait 60 days after filing their EEOC charges.[1138] The counterargument is that the ADEA

Cir 1978); Cannon v University of Chicago, 559 F2d 1063, 1077 (7th Cir 1976), *revd on other grounds,* 441 US 677 (1979); Rucker v Great Scott Supermarkets, 528 F2d 393 (6th Cir 1976); Duke v Uniroyal, Inc, 719 F Supp 428 (EDNC 1989); Van Heest v Case Hoyt Packaging Corp, 36 FEP Cas (BNA) 562 (DNJ 1984); Hannon v Continental Natl Bank, 427 F Supp 215 (D Colo 1977); Berry v Crocker Natl Bank, 13 FEP Cas (BNA) 673 (ND Cal 1976), *revd on other grounds sub nom* Bean v Crocker Natl Bank, 600 F2d 754 (9th Cir 1979); Mizuguchi v Molokai Elec Co, 411 F Supp 590 (D Hawaii 1976); *see also* Holenka v Gold Circle, 35 FEP Cas (BNA) 621 (ND Ohio 1983), *affd without opinion,* 745 F2d 56 (6th Cir 1984). (In Mason v Midwestern Fidelity Corp, 589 F Supp 751 (SD Ohio 1984), the court—while supposedly adhering to the view that the 60-day waiting requirement is jurisdictional—arguably stretched far to read the problematic factual situation as establishing that the waiting requirement was satisfied.) Several of the cases in which it was held that the 60-day filing period is jurisdictional, i.e., *Hannon, Rucker, Mizuguchi,* and *Berry,* relied upon case law holding that the ADEA's charge-filing requirement also is jurisdictional. Since those decisions regarding the filing of a charge are no longer valid, see **§6.08,** the reasoning of these decisions is at the least suspect.

[1135] *See* Dempsey v Pacific Bell Co, 789 F2d 1451 (9th Cir 1986) (holding that while 60-day waiting requirement is jurisdictional, it is subject to equitable modification); *accord* Chapman v City of Detroit, 808 F2d 459, 462 (6th Cir 1986). In deciding Brenimer v Great W Sugar Co, 567 F Supp 218 (D Colo 1983), the court expressed the view that the 60-day waiting period is not jurisdictional and therefore is subject to equitable modification. *Accord* Van Amerongen v Chief Indus, Inc, 635 F Supp 1200 (ND Ill 1986); Bertrand v Orkin Exterminating Co, 419 F Supp 1123, 1130 (ND Ill 1976), *affd on rehg,* 432 F Supp 952 (ND Ill 1977); *see also* Lopez v Bulova Watch Co, 582 F Supp 755 (DRI 1984).

[1136] 441 US 750 (1979).

[1137] See **§6.27.**

[1138] *See* Wilson v Westinghouse Elec Corp, 838 F2d 286, 290 (8th Cir 1988) (*Oscar Mayer* cited in subscribing to proposition that "suspension of proceedings . . . is preferable to dismissal with leave to refile, . . .").

expresses a much stronger commitment to EEOC conciliation than it does to pursuit of state agency relief.[1139] This cuts against treating equally as lightly a plaintiff's failure to accord the EEOC an opportunity to conciliate by not waiting the 60 days. The court deciding *Settino v City of Chicago*[1140] relied on this counter-argument.

Another basis for questioning the view that the 60-day filing period is jurisdictional is the fact that the case law regarding the nature of the time periods for filing of charges with the EEOC clearly establishes that those requirements, contained in the same section of the ADEA as is the 60-day waiting period—i.e., §7(d)[1141]—are subject to equitable modification.[1142]

Questions have arisen regarding the effect of the 60-day waiting period requirement where a plaintiff has filed a timely charge of discrimination with the EEOC as to some defendants and either later amends his or her charge so as to name additional defendants, or never amends the charge but names additional defendants in the suit ultimately filed. The consequence is that, while the 60-day period was observed as to the originally named defendants, it was not insofar as the later added parties are concerned. In *Hannon v Continental National Bank*[1143] the court held that the suit had to be dismissed as to the later-named defendant because the 60-day waiting period is jurisdictional and is thus a mandatory prerequisite to the court's hearing the suit.

Factual Scenarios Justifying Not Requiring the Plaintiff's Compliance with the 60-Day Waiting Period

Even in a jurisdiction in which the view is held that dismissal is ordinarily the appropriate response to a suit filed prior to the

---

1139 Indeed, in *Oscar Mayer* the Court characterized §14(b), 29 USC §633(b), as "intended only to give state agencies a limited opportunity to settle the grievances of ADEA claimants in a voluntary and localized manner." 441 US at 761.

1140 642 F Supp 755, 758 (ND Ill 1986).

1141 29 USC §626(d).

1142 See **§6.08**.

1143 427 F Supp 215 (D Colo 1977).

elapse of the 60-day waiting period, there will be situations where dismissal will not be warranted.[1144] For example, in *Popkins v Zagel*[1145] the court did not hold the plaintiff to the 60-day waiting requirement inasmuch as the defendants, in forcing the plaintiff's retirement, had acted pursuant to a state mandatory retirement statute and thus efforts at conciliation—which the 60-day hiatus is designed to facilitate—would have been meaningless. In a similar vein, if the EEOC apprises a grievant prior to the expiration of 60 days after the charge of unlawful discrimination was filed that conciliation efforts have failed and that the EEOC will not try further to resolve the matter, the plaintiff need not wait for the full 60 days to elapse.[1146] Likewise, the suit filed by a plaintiff who had waited 53 or 58 days after the charge-filing was not dismissed since conciliation had been attempted and thus the aim of the 60-day waiting period had been satisfied.[1147]

In *Sharpe v Philadelphia Housing Authority*[1148] the plaintiff had not waited the required 60 days. The defendant did not challenge the untimely filing, however, and thus the defense was deemed waived.[1149] As a seemingly independent ground, however, for resolving the issue of the plaintiff's failure to wait the 60 days, the Court of Appeals for the Third Circuit further reasoned that since the district court had not ruled on the defendant's motion to dismiss until more than 60 days after the administrative charge (which was referred by the EEOC to the state

---

[1144] *See, e.g.,* McLaurin v Fischer, 595 F Supp 318 (SD Ohio 1983); Lopez v Bulova Watch Co, 582 F Supp 755 (DRI 1984).

[1145] 611 F Supp 809 (CD Ill 1985).

[1146] *See, e.g.,* Nickel v Shatterproof Glass Corp, 424 F Supp 884, 887 (ED Mich 1976), *affd without opinion,* 599 F2d 1055 (6th Cir 1979). Pursuant to 29 CFR §1626.12 (1993), the EEOC is required to notify the charging party that conciliation has failed. Such notification enables the charging party "or any person aggrieved by the subject matter of the charge to commence suit without waiting for the elapse of 60 days." *Id.*

[1147] Dow v American Motors Corp, 440 F Supp 1389 (ED Wis 1977); *see also* Kazanzas v Walt Disney World Co, 518 F Supp 292 (MD Fla 1981), *revd on other grounds,* 704 F2d 1527 (11th Cir), *cert denied,* 464 US 982 (1983); Seider v Canada Dry Corp, 18 FEP Cas (BNA) 1786 (SDNY 1978).

[1148] 693 F2d 24 (3d Cir 1982).

[1149] *Id* 25-26 n1.

antidiscrimination agency) had been filed, the state agency in any event had had sufficient time to deal with the charge.[1150] In *Mason v Midwestern Fidelity Corp*[1151] the court reasoned that summary judgment for a defendant who argued that the 60-day waiting period was not observed was inappropriate. The issue was not raised by the defendant until after the time period had passed, and by that point, the court reasoned, the 60-day hiatus between the filing of the charge and the filing of the lawsuit would have been established, notwithstanding the plaintiff's initial failure to observe the waiting requirement. To the same effect is *Morris v Russell, Burdsall & Ward Corp,*[1152] where the court refused to dismiss the suit because by the time it addressed the plaintiff's summary judgment motion, based on the plaintiff's failure to wait, the 60 days had elapsed. The court deciding *Van Amerongen v Chief Industries, Inc,*[1153] reasoned similarly regarding the defendant's motion to dismiss.[1154]

In deciding *Wilson v Westinghouse Electric Corp,*[1155] the Court of Appeals for the Eighth Circuit rejected dismissal as the proper course to follow and suspended the proceeding pending the elapse of the 60 days, with the plaintiff being allowed to file a supplemental complaint after the 60 days had elapsed. Similarly, in *Goulding v Institute of Electrical & Electronics Engineers*[1156] the court, even while designating the 60-day waiting period as jurisdictional, ruled that the plaintiff's claims should be suspended until the period had run. (The court, unlike the *Wilson* court, said nothing about filing a supplemental complaint.)

[1150] *Id; see also* Morris v Russell, Burdsall & Ward Corp, 577 F Supp 147 (ND Ohio 1983).

[1151] 589 F Supp 751 (SD Ohio 1984).

[1152] 577 F Supp 147 (ND Ohio 1983).

[1153] 635 F Supp 1200 (ND Ill 1986).

[1154] *See also* Caudill v Farmland Indus, Inc, 698 F Supp 1476, 1486 (WD Mo 1988), *affd on other grounds,* 919 F2d 83 (8th Cir 1990) (motion to dismiss denied as to plaintiff who filed suit prior to elapse of 60 days; plaintiff instead was allowed to file supplemental pleading alleging that 60 days had now elapsed).

[1155] 838 F2d 286 (8th Cir 1988).

[1156] 739 F Supp 934 (SDNY 1990).

In *Stember v Borough of Baldwin*[1157] the plaintiff filed his charge with the EEOC, which then referred it to the state antidiscrimination agency. Both filings occurred less than 60 days prior to filing suit. The court held that it was appropriate to hold the suit in abeyance until the 60-day period expired. Had the court dismissed the suit, the plaintiff would have been barred from filing suit once the 60-day period ran by virtue of the Act's then-extant two-year statute of limitations.

The court deciding *Smilan v United Airlines, Inc,*[1158] while nodding in the direction of the proposition that a stay was the proper response to a suit that had been filed on the same day that the EEOC charge had been filed, nonetheless proceeded to address the merits of the defendant's motion. It ruled that the charge had not been timely filed and so the plaintiff's suit was in any event time-barred.

Insofar as representative actions are concerned,[1159] one court has asserted that individuals who had not waited the full 60 days still could opt into a lawsuit where the representative had waited for 60 days before filing suit.[1160]

Enforcement by Private Nonfederal Grievants: Procedural Issues Associated with the Judicial Forum

§6.38 The Initial Pleadings

The Age Discrimination in Employment Act (ADEA)[1161] clearly contemplates private enforcement in the courts. Section

---

1157 31 FEP Cas (BNA) 690 (WD Pa 1983).

1158 796 F Supp 723 (EDNY 1992).

1159 See generally **§§6.45-.51** as to such actions.

1160 Sussman v Vornado, Inc, 90 FRD 680, 688-89 (DNJ 1981).

1161 29 USC §§621-634.

7(c)[1162] authorizes "[a]ny person aggrieved . . . [to] bring a civil action in any court of competent jurisdiction for such legal or equitable relief as will effectuate the purpose of this chapter." Section 7(b)[1163] incorporates §16(b)[1164] of the Fair Labor Standards Act (FLSA),[1165] which likewise authorizes private suits.

The Complaint

The plaintiff's task of drafting an ADEA complaint is no different than that involved in other federal litigation. The plaintiff should take care to include all the requisite and relevant allegations. Pleading rules in the federal courts are hardly rigorous. Moreover, the courts generally will be particularly liberal regarding pro se pleadings.[1166] Still, there are some aspects of pleading that are better observed than ignored.

Ordinarily, one should plead the basis for the cause of action, i.e., §7(b) or §7(c) of the ADEA. The failure to mention the ADEA need not be fatal, however.[1167] The authority for the court to exercise jurisdiction also should be pleaded.[1168] There should be an allegation setting forth the relationship of the plaintiff to the defendant; i.e., employee-employer, union member-union,

---

[1162] *Id* §626(c). A separate enforcement scheme applies to federal job applicants, employees, and former employees. See **ch 9**.

[1163] 29 USC §626(b).

[1164] *Id* §216(b).

[1165] *Id* §§200-219.

[1166] *See, e.g.*, Cash v Jefferson Assocs, Inc, 978 F2d 217 (5th Cir 1992); Wolber v Service Corp Intl, 612 F Supp 235 (D Nev 1985).

[1167] Doss v South Cent Bell Tel Co, 834 F2d 421 (5th Cir 1987); McQuay v Yonkers Gen Hosp, 47 FEP Cas (BNA) 335 (SDNY 1987); Santos v Rush-Presbyterian-St Luke's Medical Ctr, 641 F Supp 353, 353 n1 (ND Ill 1986).

[1168] See **§6.39** as to the various jurisdictional statutes. Even if a complaint fails to cite the statute conferring jurisdiction, that omission will not defeat jurisdiction if the facts alleged in the complaint satisfy the jurisdictional requirements of the statute. *See, e.g.*, Hildebrand v Honeywell, Inc, 622 F2d 179 (5th Cir 1980); Knight v County of Dane, 30 FEP Cas (BNA) 1107 (WD Wis 1982); *see also* Schlesinger v Councilman, 420 US 738, 744 n9 (1975); Southpark Square, Ltd v City of Jackson, 565 F2d 338, 341 n2 (5th Cir 1977), *cert denied*, 436 US 946 (1978).

etc.[1169] The plaintiff also should set forth that he or she is within the protected age group.[1170] The complaint should further allege that the defendant meets the statute's requirements, e.g., that the defendant employer had 20 or more employees for each working day in each of 20 or more weeks of the current or preceding calendar year[1171] or that the defendant employment agency performed services for a covered employer,[1172] and so on. And there should be an allegation sufficient to establish that the defendant employer or labor organization is "engaged in an industry affecting commerce," the language of §11(b) and 11(d).[1173]

The plaintiff should allege that he or she has satisfied the Act's procedural requirements, i.e., the filing of a timely charge with the Equal Employment Opportunity Commission (EEOC),[1174] the filing of an administrative complaint with the state antidiscrimination agency,[1175] and the elapse of 60 days since these filings.[1176] In addition, the plaintiff should allege that the unlawful conduct occurred within 180 or 300 days prior to the filing of the EEOC charge, the relevant time period turning on the existence of a state antidiscrimination law and a state enforcement authority empowered to grant relief.[1177] If the

---

1169 Kuck v Bensen, 647 F Supp 743 (D Me), *vacated,* 649 F Supp 68 (D Me 1986).

1170 See **ch 3.**

1171 *Id.*

1172 *Id.*

1173 29 USC §630(b), (d). See **ch 3.**

1174 See **§6.08.** In Aponte v National Steel Serv Ctr, 500 F Supp 198 (ND Ill 1980), the court dismissed a count as a result of the plaintiff's failure to allege the filing of a charge; *see also* Sivell v Conwed Corp, 605 F Supp 1265 (D Conn 1985). *But see* Brooks v Monroe Sys for Business, Inc, 873 F2d 202 (8th Cir), *cert denied,* 493 US 853 (1989).

1175 See **§6.25.**

1176 See **§6.37.** In Vaughn v Chrysler Corp, 382 F Supp 143 (ED Mich 1974), the court required that the exhaustion of federal administrative remedies be specifically alleged in the complaint. *See also* Platt v Burroughs Corp, 424 F Supp 1329, 1333-34 (ED Pa 1976).

1177 See **§6.08.**

charge was not timely filed with the EEOC, sufficient facts should be alleged to justify tolling of the filing period.[1178]

Notwithstanding the foregoing discussion regarding the specificity of pleading compliance with the procedural prerequisites of the ADEA, it has been held to be sufficient for the plaintiff simply to make a general allegation that all conditions precedent have been fulfilled.[1179] Clearly, however, extreme brevity can be very troubling to a court.[1180]

The facts giving rise to the complaint should be set out, although the amount of detail may depend on the circumstances.[1181] At the least, the complaint must generally inform the court and the defendant of the reasons why the plaintiff believes age discrimination has occurred.[1182] Other allegations also may be appropriate. For example, if the plaintiff is relying on a continuing violation theory, the facts supporting such a theory should be pleaded.[1183] However, it should be noted that in deciding *Stamey v Southern Bell Telephone & Telegraph Co*[1184] the Court of Appeals for the Eleventh Circuit rejected the defendant's argument that the plaintiff's case, whereby she established her unlawful forced retirement, was fatally flawed because she had failed to specifically plead constructive discharge.[1185]

The better tack, if a plaintiff desires to recover liquidated damages, is to expressly allege the requisite willfulness on the part of the defendant, since this is a factor critical to the recovery

---

1178 See **§§6.17-.21.**

1179 Stearns v Consolidated Mgmt, Inc, 747 F2d 1105 (7th Cir 1984); Curtiss v Key Bank, 50 FEP Cas (BNA) 1208, 1210 (WDNY 1989).

1180 *See* Elbe v Wausau Hosp Ctr, 606 F Supp 1491, 1498 (WD Wis 1985).

1181 *See* Serwer, *Elements of a Claim,* in Age Discrimination Litigation A-14, A-15 (Federal Publications Inc 1982).

1182 Dugan v Martin Marietta Aerospace, 760 F2d 397 (2d Cir 1985).

1183 McGrew v B&E Marine, Inc, 56 FEP Cas (BNA) 1546, 1554 (ND Ind 1991).

1184 859 F2d 855 (11th Cir 1988), *cert denied,* 490 US 1116 (1989).

1185 *Id* 860 n12.

of such damages.[1186] However, the fact is that courts have been willing to allow plaintiffs to proceed as to their claims for such damages even absent any reference to willfulness per se.[1187]

A problem may arise if the plaintiff seeks to file a complaint that alleges wrongful acts not alluded to in the earlier filed charge of unlawful discrimination. Clearly, the majority view sides with the plaintiff; he or she will be able to pursue claims not mentioned in the charge if those claims are like, or reasonably related to the claim[s] that were set forth in the charge, or if the unmentioned claims could have been reasonably expected to have grown out of the EEOC's investigation of the charge.[1188]

The plaintiff need not allege that he or she does not fit within one of the statute's exemptions circumscribing the Act's coverage, such as, for example, that which allows individuals 65 and over to be retired if they are bona fide executives or high, policy-making officials.[1189] Rather, it is the defendant's burden to show

---

[1186] See **ch 8.** In Rechsteiner v Madison Fund, Inc, 75 FRD 499 (D Del 1977), the court held that a claim for liquidated damages was adequate where the plaintiff alleged that the defendant acted willfully, since Fed R Civ P 9(b) allows the pleading of states of mind in general form. *Accord* Pfister v Allied Corp, 539 F Supp 224 (SDNY 1982); *see also* Ayres v Federated Dept Stores, 24 FEP Cas (BNA) 528 (SDNY 1980). But there must at least be a conclusory allegation of willfulness, according to the court in Nelson v Massey-Ferguson, Inc, 36 FEP Cas (BNA) 365 (ED Wis 1984); *accord* Zeiter v Joy Mfg Co, 732 F Supp 943, 944 n2 (ND Ind 1989). *But see* Elbe v Wausau Hosp Ctr, 606 F Supp 1491, 1499 (WD Wis 1985), articulating a more plaintiff-generous standard that requires no mention of willfulness. As to liquidated damages generally, see **ch 8.**

There was a time when an alleged willful violation of the act also would allow a plaintiff to have the benefit of a longer period within which to file suit. See **§6.35.** Here, too, then, willfulness should have been alleged. However, the statute was amended in 1991 to negate the willfulness issue in the statute of limitations context. See **§6.30.**

[1187] *See* Cash v Jefferson Assocs, Inc, 978 F2d 217 (5th Cir 1992); Wanamaker v Columbian Rope Co, 713 F Supp 533, 539-40 (NDNY 1989); *see also* Pfister v Allied Corp, 539 F Supp 224, 228 (SDNY 1982).

[1188] See **§6.05.**

[1189] See **ch 5.**

that a particular employee fits within an exemption.[1190] In other words, a plaintiff need not plead that a defendant's affirmative defense is inapplicable—a hardly surprising proposition.

The prayer for relief should embody all those elements of relief that the plaintiff seeks.[1191]

The Answer

No particular insights are afforded by the case law as to a defendant's answer in an ADEA suit. A standard risk that all defendants, rather than just ADEA defendants, confront is the unintended waiver of an affirmative defense due to the failure to plead the defense. The simple and obvious direction set forth by Federal Rule of Civil Procedure 8(c) is that an affirmative defense must be pleaded as such. Whether an answer can be amended to correct the failure to plead a defense, or for other purposes, is a function of the application of Federal Rule of Civil Procedure 15(a), which provides that a party may amend its pleading by leave of court and such "leave shall be freely given when justice so requires."[1192] Leave may be " 'inappropriate where there is undue delay, bad faith, dilatory motive on the part of the movant, repeated failure to cure deficiencies by amendments previously allowed, undue prejudice to the opposing party by virtue of allowance of the amendment, or futility of the amendment.' "[1193] As to the relevance of undue delay to an ADEA defendant's effort to amend its answer to raise an affirmative defense, see *Daugherity v Traylor Bros, Inc.*[1194]

1190 Passer v American Chem Socy, 701 F Supp 1 (DDC 1988), *affd in part & revd in part on other grounds,* 935 F2d 322 (DC Cir 1991).

1191 As to relief, see **ch 8.**

1192 Fed R Civ P 15(a).

1193 Perrian v O'Grady, 958 F2d 192, 194 (7th Cir 1992) (quoting Villa v City of Chicago, 924 F2d 629, 632 (7th Cir 1991)).

1194 970 F2d 348 (7th Cir 1992).

§6.39 Federal and State Court Jurisdiction; Removal; Venue

Jurisdiction

Section 7(b)[1195] of the Age Discrimination in Employment Act (ADEA)[1196] incorporates the enforcement scheme embodied in §16(b)[1197] of the Fair Labor Standards Act (FLSA),[1198] which authorizes suit in "any court of competent jurisdiction." Likewise, §7(c)[1199] of the ADEA directly authorizes private suits (by nonfederal employees) with like language. It is well established that §16(b)'s language contemplates FLSA suits being brought not only in federal district courts, but also in state courts of competent jurisdiction.[1200] Similarly, the ADEA's own language has been construed as authorizing suit in either forum.[1201]

While both statutory provisions authorize suit by plaintiffs, they do not necessarily confer jurisdiction on the federal district courts to entertain such suits. Rather, for a federal court to be able to exercise jurisdiction over a matter, there typically must be a statute specifically vesting it with jurisdiction. Depending on the nature of the case, jurisdiction in an ADEA matter may

---

1195 29 USC §626(b).

1196 *Id* §§621-634.

1197 *Id* §216(b).

1198 *Id* §§200-219.

1199 *Id* §626(c).

1200 *See, e.g.*, Freudenberg v Harvey, 364 F Supp 1087, 1090 (ED Pa 1973) (non-ADEA case).

1201 *See, e.g.*, Chapman v City of Detroit, 808 F2d 459, 463 (6th Cir 1986); Jacobi v High Point Label, Inc, 442 F Supp 518, 520 (MDNC 1977); Patrovich v Chemical Bank, 63 NY2d 541, 473 NE2d 11, 483 NYS2d 659 (1984); Eagleburger v City of Springfield, 677 SW2d 914 (Mo Ct App 1984); Parker v Fort Sanders Regional Medical Ctr, 37 FEP Cas (BNA) 359 (Tenn Ct App 1983). However, in Cahoon v Alton Packaging Corp, 148 Ill App 3d 480, 499 NE2d 522 (1986), *appeal dismissed,* 482 US 922 (1987), the court ruled that an ADEA action could not be maintained in state court unless the plaintiff first exhausted state administrative remedies established by the state's own antidiscrimination statute. That statute provided that no court had jurisdiction over an alleged civil rights violation save in accordance with the statute, and it prescribed the administrative procedures to be pursued prior to suit.

be based on 28 USC §§1331,[1202] 1337,[1203] 1343(3), 1343(4),[1204] 29 USC §626(b),[1205] or 29 USC §626(c).[1206] Jurisdiction also has been based on §17[1207] of the FLSA.[1208] In a suit against the instrumentality of a foreign state, jurisdiction is grounded on 28 USC §1330.[1209] (28 USC §§2201 and 2202 empower the federal district courts to issue declaratory judgments and subsequent relief, but they are not jurisdictional statutes.)

[1202] *See, e.g.,* Miller v Beneficial Management Corp, 977 F2d 834, 841 (3d Cir 1992). Section 1331 confers on the district courts jurisdiction "of all civil actions arising under the Constitution, laws, or treaties of the United States." *See* Kenny v Board of Trustees, 563 F Supp 95 (D Mont 1983), *affd without opinion,* 770 F2d 170 (9th Cir 1985). When jurisdiction lies under §1337, §1331 is inapplicable. Smith v Sentry Ins, 41 FEP Cas (BNA) 1569, 1570 (ND Ga 1986).

[1203] 28 USC §1337 confers jurisdiction on the district courts over "any civil action or proceeding arising under any Act of Congress regulating commerce."

[1204] 28 USC §1343(3) and (4) are jurisdictional statutes applicable to state and local governmental defendants, private parties cloaked with the authority of state and local bodies, and private parties engaged in a conspiracy with state or local officials. These statutes vest courts with jurisdiction to hear suits commenced:

> (3) To redress the deprivation, under color of any State law, statute, ordinance, regulation, custom or usage, of any right, privilege or immunity secured by the Constitution of the United States or by any Act of Congress providing for equal rights of all citizens or of all persons within the jurisdiction of the United States;
>
> (4) To recover damages or to secure equitable or other relief under any Act of Congress providing for the protection of civil rights[.]

[1205] *See* DePriest v Seaway Food Town, Inc, 543 F Supp 1355, 1358 (ED Mich 1982). *See also* Whitfield v City of Knoxville, 567 F Supp 1344, 1346 (ED Tenn 1983), *affd on other grounds,* 756 F2d 455 (6th Cir 1985); Smith v Meijer, Inc, 566 F Supp 113 (SD Ohio 1983); Curto v Sears, Roebuck & Co, 552 F Supp 891, 892 n3 (ND Ill 1982).

[1206] *See, e.g.,* Bobbitt v PBA, Inc, 31 FEP Cas (BNA) 366 (D Minn 1983); Bilotti v Franklin Mint, 27 FEP Cas (BNA) 1031 (ED Pa 1981).

[1207] 29 USC §217.

[1208] Whitfield v City of Knoxville, 567 F Supp 1344, 1346 (ED Tenn 1983), *affd on other grounds,* 756 F2d 455 (6th Cir 1985).

[1209] *See* Gazder v Air India, 574 F Supp 134, 135 n4 (SDNY 1983).

While in most instances 28 USC §1337 would suffice as a basis for jurisdiction,[1210] 28 USC §§1331 and 1343(3) and (4) come into play because of a particular body of cases dealing with the extension of the ADEA to states as employers. In several cases courts have been called on to decide whether Congress exceeded its authority under the Commerce Clause[1211] in subjecting states to the strictures of the ADEA. Most courts[1212] have held that Congress, in extending the act's coverage to states, was exercising its enforcement power under §5 of the Fourteenth Amendment.[1213] Usually, they have also confirmed that Congress did not exceed its commerce power.[1214] Inasmuch as 28 USC §1337 only confers jurisdiction on the federal courts to deal with cases arising under Commerce-Clause-based legislation, this jurisdictional statute would not suffice in a case where the ADEA is upheld only as an exercise of Fourteenth Amendment power as to states. In this situation, 28 USC §§1331 and 1334(3) and (4) pertain, conferring jurisdiction on the courts because of the facts that the ADEA is a federal statute, jurisdiction as to which is provided by §1331, and that the ADEA is a civil rights statute providing for equal rights, which is relevant to the applicability of §1334(3) and (4).

Removal

If an ADEA suit is filed in state court, it may be removed to federal court by the defendant pursuant to a timely[1215] removal petition filed in accordance with 28 USC §1441(a).[1216] If an

---

1210 *See* Massarsky v General Motors Corp, 706 F2d 111, 114 n1 (3d Cir), *cert denied,* 464 US 937 (1983).

1211 US Const art 1, §8.

1212 See generally **ch 3.**

1213 US Const amend XIV, §5.

1214 See generally **ch 3.**

1215 *See* Cedillo v Valcar Enters & Darling Del Co, Inc, 773 F Supp 932, 933-34 (ND Tex 1991).

1216 Section 1441(a) provides, in part, that "[e]xcept as otherwise expressly provided by Act of Congress, any civil action brought in a State court of which the district courts of the United States have original jurisdiction, may be removed by the defendant or defendants[.]" *See* Baldwin v Sears, Roebuck & Co, 667 F2d 458 (5th Cir 1982). In Jacobi v High Point Label, Inc, 442 F Supp

ADEA claim is joined with state claims, removal may be had pursuant to 28 USC §1441(e)[1217] or §1441(b).[1218] But where the claim filed in state court only invokes a state law prohibiting age discrimination and does not rely on the ADEA, removal may not be had by arguing that the state law claim is in effect a federal ADEA claim by virtue of the similarity of the state and federal statutes.[1219]

Venue

The federal venue statute, 28 USC §1391(b), governs where a federal suit may be brought. This statute provides that an action not founded solely on diversity may be pursued in the judicial district in which any defendant resides or in which "a substantial part of the events or omission giving rise to the claim occurred[.]" 28 USC §1391(c) provides that a corporation resides in any judicial district in which it is subject to personal jurisdiction at the time the action commenced. The proposition that §7(c)(1) of the ADEA,[1220] which provides that aggrieved persons may bring civil actions under the age discrimination statute in any court of competent jurisdiction, constitutes a separate venue provision has been rejected.[1221]

---

518 (MDNC 1977), the court pointed out that the FLSA case law on removal is in disarray, but distinguished much of the case law holding that removal was not obtainable by noting that the decisions predated the 1948 amendment to 28 USC §1441(a) whereby Congress added the phrase "[e]xcept as expressly provided by Act of Congress" to the statute. The court stated: "In contrast to the pre-1948 cases denying removal, the growing majority of cases have not found any express bar to the removal of FLSA actions to federal court and, therefore, have concluded that removal is permissible under section 1441(a)." 442 F Supp at 520-21.

[1217] *See, e.g.*, Shanahan v WITI-TV, Inc, 565 F Supp 219, 221 (ED Wis 1982).

[1218] Boyle v Carnegie-Mellon Univ, 648 F Supp 1318, 1320 (WD Pa 1986).

[1219] *See* Pointer v Crown Cork & Seal Co, Inc, 791 F Supp 164 (SD Tex 1992); Nolan v Otis Elevator Co, 560 F Supp 119 (DNJ 1982).

[1220] 29 USC §626(c)(1).

[1221] Kretz v Harsco Corp, 60 FEP Cas (BNA) 211, 212 (ND Ind 1992).

The general law of venue is beyond the scope of this chapter.[1222] Thus, it is worth noting only for historical purposes (particularly in light of the fact that the venue provisions were amended in 1990), and not because these cases represent the present state of the law, that a couple of ADEA courts have addressed the matter. In *Quinn v Bowmar Publishing Co*[1223] a district court observed that some courts have utilized a *weight of the contacts test* in antitrust cases. According to this test, venue is proper, in a situation where the injury is widespread geographically, if significant sales causing substantial injury were made in the district in which venue is asserted or if some other overt act constituting a significant and substantial element of the offense occurred there.[1224] The application of this test, the *Quinn* court further observed, is problematic outside the antitrust area. The *Quinn* court thought it might be appropriate to employ as to the ADEA, however.[1225] In *Weil v New York State Department of Transportation*[1226] another district court utilized this test, albeit without explicitly discussing whether the test was an appropriate one for ADEA litigation.

In *Dolan v United States*[1227] the plaintiff, a resident of New York state, sued his superior, a federal official, in his individual capacity in the District of Columbia federal district court. In holding that the case should be transferred to the federal district court for the Western District of New York, the *Dolan* court reasoned that despite the plaintiff's assertions that the alleged acts of age discrimination were initiated in the District of Columbia, these acts actually were initiated and took effect where Dolan was working, i.e., in New York. The court further stated that it was "clear that the acts in New York that were taken with respect

[1222] *See generally* 15 C.A. Wright, A.R. Miller, & E.H. Cooper, Federal Practice and Procedure §3801 *et seq* (1986).

[1223] 445 F Supp 780 (D Md 1978).

[1224] *See, e.g.*, Philadelphia Hous Auth v American Radiator & Standard Sanitary Corp, 291 F Supp 252 (ED Pa 1968).

[1225] 445 F Supp at 783.

[1226] 400 F Supp 1364 (SDNY 1975).

[1227] 31 FEP Cas (BNA) 548 (DDC 1983).

to Dr. Dolan outweigh[ed] both in number and extent any acts that were taken with respect to him on a higher administrative level in the District of Columbia."[1228]

Often, there will be contractual language specifying the forum in which a claim arising out of an alleged breach is to be litigated. While a court may refuse to enforce such a forum clause, that contractual provision is entitled to "substantial consideration."[1229] In deciding *Weiss v Columbia Pictures Television, Inc,*[1230] the court concluded that enforcement of such a clause, over the objection of the plaintiff, was not inconsistent with the purposes of the ADEA.

§6.40 Federal Court Supplemental Jurisdiction: Generally

Often, a plaintiff will contend that the same facts that have given rise to his or her claim under the Age Discrimination in Employment Act (ADEA)[1231] also constitute the bases for a claim arising under either a state antidiscrimination statute or state common law doctrine concerning employees' rights. Consequently, it is not unusual that a plaintiff will seek to litigate both state and federal claims in the context of one lawsuit filed in federal court. In response to such situations—which range across a wide range of claims—the federal courts fashioned a body of law, initially in non-ADEA cases, approving the exercise of what was known as pendent jurisdiction.

The leading Supreme Court ruling was *United Mine Workers v Gibbs,*[1232] in which the Supreme Court held that, as a matter of constitutional power, a federal court could entertain jurisdiction

---

[1228] *Id* 550; *see also* Bane v Netlink, Inc, 925 F2d 637 (3d Cir 1991).

[1229] Weiss v Columbia Pictures Television, Inc, 801 F Supp 1276, 1278 (SDNY 1992).

[1230] 801 F Supp 1276 (SDNY 1992).

[1231] 29 USC §§621-634.

[1232] 383 US 715 (1966).

over non-diversity-based state law issues[1233] as to which it otherwise would lack subject matter jurisdiction, provided: (1) it already had a federal question before it, (2) the state and federal claims "derive[d] from a common nucleus of operative fact,"[1234] and (3) these claims were such that a plaintiff "would ordinarily be expected to try them all in one judicial proceeding."[1235] The Court further held that the exercise of pendent jurisdiction was discretionary and that the trial court, in exercising its discretion, should look to "considerations of judicial economy, convenience and fairness to litigants"[1236] and should avoid needless decisions of state law.

In 1990 Congress codified, in 28 USC §1367, this judicially created doctrine of pendent jurisdiction (as well as the judicially created doctrine of ancillary jurisdiction) under the designation *supplemental jurisdiction.*[1237] Pursuant to §1367(a) federal courts are authorized to exercise supplemental jurisdiction "over all other claims that are so related to claims in the action [that are] within . . . [the court's] original jurisdiction that they form part of the same case or controversy under Article III of the United States Constitution."[1238] A court may decline to exercise this jurisdiction in accordance with §1367(c), which provides as follows:

> The district courts may decline to exercise supplemental jurisdiction over a claim under subsection (a) if—
>
> (1) the claim raises a novel or complex issue of State law,

---

[1233] Under US Const art III, §2, the federal courts have jurisdiction to hear state law issues that arise in the context of disputes between citizens of different states. This is known as diversity jurisdiction.

[1234] 383 US at 725.

[1235] *Id.*

[1236] *Id* 726.

[1237] Judicial Improvements Act of 1990, Pub L No 101-650, §310(a), 104 Stat 5089, 5113. *See generally* Siegel, *Practice Commentary,* printed following the text of 28 USC §1367 in the United States Code.

[1238] 28 USC §1367(a).

(2) the claim substantially predominates over the claim or claims over which the district court has original jurisdiction,

(3) the district court has dismissed all claims over which it has original jurisdiction, or

(4) in exceptional circumstances, there are other compelling reasons for declining jurisdiction.[1239]

Inasmuch as the doctrine of pendent jurisdiction was not eradicated by the 1990 statute, but rather was codified by it, the pre-1990 case law remains relevant and so provides guidance for courts addressing the issue of supplemental jurisdiction.[1240] The codification of the pendent jurisdiction doctrine is not without its own significance, however. For one, the circumstances under which a court may decline to hear a claim within its supplemental jurisdiction are now carefully delineated. Moreover, whereas the Supreme Court asserted in *Gibbs* that the state law claim should be dismissed if the federal claim was dismissed before trial,[1241] under 28 USC §1367(c) a court can dismiss the state claims in such circumstance, but it is not required to do so. Similarly, in *Gibbs* the Court asserted that the state law claim should be dis-

---

1239 *Id* §1367(c). Section 310(c) of the Judicial Improvements Act of 1990, Pub L No 101-650, 104 Stat 5089, 5114 provides, that the amendments made by the Act applied only to civil actions commenced on or after the date of the Act's enactment, i.e., December 1, 1990. If a case was commenced prior to that date, but not removed to federal court until after that date, then the new provision would be deemed to be applicable "because the pertinent time for determining federal jurisdiction is the date on which such jurisdiction is invoked," i.e., the date of removal. Cedillo v Valcar Enters & Darling Del Co, Inc, 773 F Supp 932, 939 (ND Tex 1991).

1240 The court deciding James v Sun Glass Hut, Inc, 799 F Supp 1083 (D Colo 1992), observed as follows:

> "Because it is a codification of the old pendent jurisdiction doctrine, courts applying §1367 have continued to rely on . . . *Gibbs* . . . in assessing whether a state law claim is "so related" to a federal claim as to constitute the same case or controversy."

Id 1084.

1241 383 US at 726.

missed if state issues substantially predominated,[1242] but §1367(c), while allowing for dismissal in such a situation, does not require that a court so respond. In addition, the *Gibbs* Court asserted that the state law claim should be dismissed if the possibility of jury confusion would justify separating the state and federal claims for trial.[1243] Section 1367(c)(4) allows for, but does not require, dismissal.

ADEA case law supports the proposition that "where the proper resolution of the state law question is unclear, a federal court may properly decline to address the pendent issue."[1244] Section 1367(c)(4) would seem to be in accord.

A pendent party claim also may be at issue. Pendent party jurisdiction, the Supreme Court explained in *Finley v United States,*[1245] involves claims by "parties not named in any claim that is independently cognizable by the federal court."[1246] Pursuant to *Finley,* it is necessary that the jurisdictional statute under which a claim is maintained establishes a basis for jurisdiction as to the pendent party. *Finley* has been supplanted by 28 USC §1367(a), which provides, inter alia, that "supplemental jurisdiction shall include claims that involve the joinder or intervention of additional parties."

It should be noted that if the pendent claim is directed against a state official who is being charged with having violated state law, the Eleventh Amendment[1247] will bar a federal court's exercise of jurisdiction as to the claim.[1248]

1242 *Id* 726-27.

1243 *Id* 727.

1244 Sanders v Duke Univ, 538 F Supp 1143, 1148 (MDNC 1982) (quoting WA Krueger Co v Kirkpatrick, Pettis, Smith, Polian, Inc, 466 F Supp 800, 804 (D Neb 1979)); *accord* Mazzare v Burroughs Corp, 473 F Supp 234 (ED Pa 1979); Wagner v Sperry Univac, Div of Sperry Rand Corp, 458 F Supp 505 (ED Pa 1978), *affd without opinion,* 624 F2d 1092 (3d Cir 1980).

1245 490 US 545 (1989).

1246 *Id* 549.

1247 US Const, amend XI.

1248 Pennhurst State Sch & Hosp v Halderman, 465 US 89 (1984). See generally **Ch 3** as to the impact of the Eleventh Amendment.

§6.41 —Supplemental Jurisdiction in ADEA Cases: Claims Arising under State Antidiscrimination Statutes

A number of courts hearing Age Discrimination in Employment Act (ADEA)[1249] cases were called upon to address pendent state claims, now known as supplemental jurisdiction claims,[1250] in the years preceding the codification of pendent jurisdiction doctrine by virtue of the enactment of 28 USC §1367.[1251] Since the enactment of this provision, the case law has continued to develop. A small number of the rulings concern state claims grounded in state antidiscrimination statutes; the others involve state common law contract and tort claims.[1252]

The virtually unanimous judicial view is that a federal court may exercise supplemental jurisdiction as to state claims that are grounded in state antidiscrimination statutes. In the early days of the ADEA, however, there was a contrary position articulated in a couple of rulings—a position most prominently expressed by the district court that decided *Pandis v Sikorsky Aircraft Division of United Technologies Corp.*[1253]

The *Pandis* court subscribed to a general rule that it is inappropriate for a federal court to exercise pendent, or supplemental, jurisdiction over such claims.[1254] In so doing, the court looked to the language of §14(a)[1255] of the ADEA, which initially states that the ADEA does not affect the jurisdiction of state antidiscrimination agencies but then goes on to provide that "upon commencement of action under . . . [the ADEA] such action shall supersede any State action."[1256] The court looked to legislative history for an explanation of Congressional intent

---

1249 29 USC §§621-634.

1250 See **§6.40.**

1251 *Id.*

1252 See **§6.42** for a discussion of common law claims.

1253 431 F Supp 793 (D Conn 1977).

1254 *Accord* Deutsch v Carl Zeiss, Inc, 529 F Supp 15 (SDNY 1981).

1255 29 USC §633(a).

1256 See **ch 2** for a discussion of this provision.

as to the meaning of "supersede" and noted that in the 1967 report of the House Committee on Education and Labor on the ADEA, the Committee had stated that "commencement of an action under this act shall be a stay on any State action previously commenced."[1257] While acknowledging that it was arguable that the words "supersede" and "stay" applied only to state court actions and not to suits founded on state law but brought in federal court, the *Pandis* court chose to give the word "supersede" a broader reading:

> The fact that the filing of a federal ADEA lawsuit supersedes and stays any action pending in a state forum is a persuasive indication that it would be inappropriate for a federal court considering a federal ADEA claim to assume pendent jurisdiction over a cause of action grounded in state law. Congress clearly did not intend that state and federal actions would proceed simultaneously after the conciliation period, and to allow a state cause of action, whether based on diversity or pendent jurisdiction, to proceed in federal court would be inconsistent with the congressional intention that the federal remedy should take precedence.[1258]

(As an alternative ground for its ruling, the court went on to reason that there was serious doubt, in any event, as to whether the particular state statute before it afforded the plaintiff a right to any judicial action, given the posture of the state claim.)

Almost all other courts addressing state statutory claims that have been appended to federal ADEA suits have explicitly or implicitly rejected the absolutist position exemplified by *Pandis.* Indeed, *Pandis* itself is of very dubious present viability: the Court of Appeals for the Second Circuit, the *Pandis* court's circuit, seriously undercut, if not completely destroyed, the lower court ruling in deciding *Promisel v First American Artificial Flowers,*

[1257] House Comm on Educ & Labor, Age Discrimination in Employment Act of 1967, HR Rep No 805, 90th Cong, 1st Sess 6 (1967).

[1258] 431 F Supp at 796.

Inc.[1259] The court asserted that the *Pandis* court was "mistaken in assuming that [29 USC] §633(a)'s stay provision applies to actions pending in any and all state forums."[1260] Rather, it is only state administrative proceedings that are subject to the stay provision, the *Promisel* court reasoned, and so the logic of the *Pandis* court was flawed insofar as it read §633(a) as leading to the conclusion that the exercise of pendent jurisdiction was improper.

The district court that decided *Wagner v Sperry Univac, Division of Sperry Rand Corp*[1261] directly rejected *Pandis.* The plaintiff had set out a claim under a state statute. While the court ruled against exercising pendent jurisdiction, it was willing to assume that the plaintiff's claims under both the ADEA and the state law derived from a common nucleus of operative fact and that it therefore had the power to hear the state law claim if it chose. On the facts, however, the exercise of pendent jurisdiction was deemed inappropriate because there was an undecided state law procedural question that was viewed as more appropriately handled at the state level.[1262] Rather than endorsing the *Pandis* court's absolutist rule, the court embraced a case-by-case approach that allowed for the exercise of supplemental jurisdiction given facts warranting such:

> In my view, section 14(a) may quite plausibly be read as applying only to actions brought in state court, rather than as applying to all actions based on state law. This ambiguity in the statutory language is not resolved by the legislative history of either the original Act or the 1978 amendments. Under the circumstances, I believe it is preferable to treat each case on its own merits, rather than to hold that pendent jurisdiction over state-law age discrimination claims is generally inappropriate.[1263]

[1259] 943 F2d 251 (2d Cir 1991), *cert denied,* 112 S Ct 939 (1992).

[1260] *Id* 255.

[1261] 458 F Supp 505 (ED Pa 1978), *affd without opinion,* 624 F2d 1092 (3d Cir 1980).

[1262] *See also* Malarkey v Texaco, Inc, 559 F Supp 117, 123 (SDNY 1982), *affd on other grounds,* 704 F2d 674 (2d Cir 1983).

[1263] 458 F Supp at 519 n6.

In *Sussman v Vornado*[1264] another district court subscribed to the *Wagner* position and rejected *Pandis.* It then went on to hold that it properly should exercise pendent jurisdiction over a claim grounded in New Jersey statutes, reasoning that to do so would serve the interests of justice since no state court litigation had commenced, the case involved difficult factual issues, and therefore it would be more economical, convenient, and fair to resolve all claims in a single proceeding.[1265] And in deciding *James v KID Broadcasting Corp*[1266] the court, without adopting any per se rule, concluded that it would be appropriate to dismiss the pendent state statutory claims.[1267]

The Court of Appeals for the First Circuit ruled, in *Wildman v Lerner Stores Corp,*[1268] that the exercise of pendent jurisdiction below was proper even though the burden of proof under the local statute differed from that under the ADEA.[1269] In *Schlosser v Firestone Tire Co*[1270] and *Brenimer v Great Western Sugar Co*[1271] the courts exercised pendent jurisdiction without comment as to the substantive merits or demerits of such exercise.

Damages Issues

The Court of Appeals for the Ninth Circuit implicitly rejected the *Pandis* position, i.e., that pendent, or supplemental, jurisdiction should not (or could not) be exercised by an ADEA court as to a state claim arising under a state antidiscrimination statute,

---

[1264] 90 FRD 680 (DNJ 1981); *accord* Nestor v Quaker State Coca-Cola Bottling Co, 579 F Supp 289 (WD Pa 1984); Shanahan v WITI-TV, Inc, 565 F Supp 219 (ED Wis 1982).

[1265] *Accord* Van Atta v Kal-Aero, Inc, 555 F Supp 912 (WD Mich 1983).

[1266] 559 F Supp 1153 (D Idaho 1983).

[1267] *Accord* Goff v Kroger Co, 647 F Supp 87 (SD Ohio 1986).

[1268] 771 F2d 605 (1st Cir 1985).

[1269] *Contra* Flores Cruz v Avon Prods, Inc, 56 FEP Cas (BNA) 1299 (DPR 1987); Sward v San Juan PR Convention Bureau, 679 F Supp 148 (DPR 1987).

[1270] 33 FEP Cas (BNA) 1403 (ND Ohio 1983).

[1271] 567 F Supp 218, 222-23 (D Colo 1983).

in deciding *Kelly v American Standard, Inc.*[1272] The court affirmed a jury award for emotional distress made as to the plaintiff's pendent claim brought under a state antidiscrimination statute, while avoiding determining whether damages for pain and suffering were recoverable under the ADEA itself.[1273] The Court of Appeals for the Eighth Circuit is in accord in taking this tack.[1274] A number of other courts have clearly seen no problem in exercising pendent, or supplemental, jurisdiction regarding state statute-based claims that entail the potential recovery of damages not recoverable under the ADEA itself.[1275] Other courts have taken a different view, however.[1276]

In deciding *Freeman v Package Machinery Co*[1277] the Court of Appeals for the First Circuit affirmed a trial court ruling[1278] that involved the court's allowing the plaintiff to recover the same damages, dollar for dollar, on his state statutory count as he recovered under the ADEA. However, the trial court had further ruled that although the plaintiff was entitled to such damages,

---

[1272] 640 F2d 974 (9th Cir 1981). *See also* Hrzenak v White-Westinghouse Appliance Co, 682 F2d 714 (8th Cir 1982).

[1273] *See also* Berry v General Elec Co, 541 F Supp 800 (WD Ky 1982).

[1274] Ridenour v Montgomery Ward & Co, 786 F2d 867 (8th Cir 1986).

[1275] *See, e.g.*, Robertson v South College, 60 FEP Cas (BNA) 8 (ED Tenn 1992); Patel v Lutheran Medical Ctr, Inc, 753 F Supp 1070, 1075-77 (EDNY 1990); Cripps v United Biscuit of Great Britain, 732 F Supp 844, 847-48 (ED Tenn 1989); Tasaka v DDB Needham Worldwide, Inc, 729 F Supp 1014, 1017 n8 (SDNY 1990); Buscemi v Pepsico, Inc, 726 F Supp 99 (SDNY 1989); Wildman v Lerner Stores Corp, 582 F Supp 80 (DPR 1984), *affd,* 771 F2d 605 (1st Cir 1985); Nestor v Quaker State Coca-Cola Bottling Co, 579 F Supp 289 (WD Pa 1984); *see also* Anastasio v Schering Corp, 838 F2d 701, 705 n7 (3d Cir 1988); Marquez Velez v David M PR Graphic Supplies, Inc, 622 F Supp 568 (DPR 1985).

See **§6.42** concerning the treatment of this issue in the context of state common law pendent claims.

[1276] *See, e.g.,* Dapelo v Banco Nacional de Mexico, 767 F Supp 49 (SDNY 1991); Watlington v University of PR, Rio Pedras Campus, 722 F Supp 910 (DPR 1989); Goss v Pan Am World Airways, Inc, 654 F Supp 1306, 1309 (SDNY 1987); DiRito v Ideal Basic Indus, Inc, 617 F Supp 79 (D Colo 1985); Shirley v Brown & Williamson Tobacco Co, 608 F Supp 78 (ED Tenn 1984).

[1277] 865 F2d 1331 (1st Cir 1988).

[1278] Freeman v Package Mach Co, 49 FEP Cas (BNA) 1100 (D Mass 1987), *affd,* 865 F2d 1331 (1st Cir 1988).

he could collect them only once. The appellate court agreed: "a plaintiff is entitled to only one full recovery, no matter how many different legal grounds may support the verdict[.]"[1279] (In cases involving pendent state common law claims,[1280] courts have taken the like position that a prevailing plaintiff cannot obtain dual recoveries under the ADEA and state law.)[1281]

In a series of decisions the district court for the Southern District of Ohio exercised pendent jurisdiction as to claims based on Ohio's antidiscrimination statute, while taking care to avert the possibility of a dual recovery by the prevailing plaintiffs.[1282] In *Merkel v Scovill, Inc,*[1283] the court, holding that the exercise of pendent jurisdiction was proper, reasoned that liquidated damages under the ADEA embodied what would be considered to be punitive and compensatory damages under state law and that a double recovery would be improper.[1284] It was of the view that the possibility of a double recovery could be averted through a combination of carefully drafted jury instructions and special interrogatories to the jury.[1285] Similarly, in other rulings the same

---

[1279] 865 F2d at 1345.

[1280] See **§6.42.**

[1281] *See, e.g.,* Washburn v Kansas City Life Ins Co, 831 F2d 1404, 1410-11 (8th Cir 1987); Lettich v Kenway, 590 F Supp 1225 (D Mass 1984).

[1282] The peculiarities of the Ohio statutory scheme also have generated issues other than damages questions. *See, e.g.,* Carr v French Oil Mill Mach Co, 746 F Supp 700 (SD Ohio 1989).

[1283] 570 F Supp 133 (SD Ohio 1983).

[1284] *Accord* Garry v TRW, Inc, 603 F Supp 157 (ND Ohio 1985).

[1285] Subsequently, the court reduced the amount of compensatory damages awarded under the state claim by subtracting the amount awarded as liquidated damages under the federal Act. Merkel v Scovill, Inc, 570 F Supp 141, 150 (SD Ohio 1983); *accord* Merkel v Scovill, Inc, 573 F Supp 1055 (SD Ohio 1983), *affd in part & revd in part on other grounds,* 787 F2d 174 (6th Cir), *cert denied,* 479 US 990 (1986). In this last decision the court, responding to, and rejecting, the defendant's argument that it was error to have admitted testimony as to the state claim for damages for loss of reputation, humiliation, embarrassment, and/or loss of self-esteem, stated:

> [T]he proper approach is not to bar all pendent state claims where plaintiff also asserts a claim under the ADEA . . . but rather to look at the facts of a particular case and determine whether the admission of the

court saw no particular problem with entertaining pendent state statutory claims involving damages not available under the ADEA.[1286]

In contrast, the court deciding *Balmer v Community House Association*[1287] apparently conceded that a plaintiff could recover both liquidated damages under the ADEA and exemplary damages under a state statute, but it concluded that, because of the overlap of the two and because of the prejudicial nature of the testimony that would be offered in support of the state claim, the exercise of pendent jurisdiction was inappropriate.[1288] In *Equal Employment Opportunity Commission v City of Highland Park*[1289] the court exercised pendent jurisdiction over a state statutory claim and approved a settlement whereby damages for pain and suffering, which are not recoverable under the ADEA,[1290] were paid to settle the state claim. Without endorsing or criticizing any of the lower court cases, all of which were decided by district courts within the Sixth Circuit, the Court of Appeals for the Sixth Circuit, in deciding *Mitroff v Xomox Corp*,[1291] affirmed the trial court's decision not to hear pendent claims with the assertion that the trial court's ruling was supportable because testimony as to

---

> challenged testimony resulted in a substantial injustice to the moving party.

Id 1065. Here, there was no such injustice.

1286 *See* Bailey v Container Corp of Am, 594 F Supp 629 (SD Ohio 1984); Venezia v Scovill, Inc, 592 F Supp 3 (SD Ohio 1983); Mason v Midwestern Fidelity Corp, 589 F Supp 751 (SD Ohio 1984). In Bailey v Container Corp of Am, 660 F Supp 1048 (SD Ohio 1986), the court reduced the jury's punitive damages award made under state law by an amount equal to the liquidated damages award made under the ADEA, reasoning that the latter damages are punitive in nature and thus the plaintiff would secure an inappropriate dual recovery if no set-off were ordered.

1287 572 F Supp 1048 (ED Mich 1983).

1288 *See also* Borumka v Rocky Mountain Hosp & Medical Serv, 599 F Supp 857 (D Colo 1984).

1289 32 Empl Prac Dec (CCH) ¶33,947 (ED Mich 1983).

1290 See **ch 8**.

1291 797 F2d 271 (6th Cir 1986).

punitive and full compensatory damages under the state statute could have a "possible prejudicial effect . . . as to the ADEA claim."[1292]

Class Action Issues

The question has arisen in a couple of cases as to whether pendent jurisdiction may be exercised regarding a claim based on state law as to which the plaintiffs seek class certification under Federal Rule of Civil Procedure 23. The sticking point is that Rule 23 class actions may not be maintained by ADEA litigants[1293] The two courts to address this problem have allowed the state claim to go forward, subject to the limitation that the Rule 23 class be limited to those individuals who had opted into the ADEA action in accordance with the procedures applicable to ADEA opt-in representative actions.[1294]

Other Issues

Sometimes, the peculiarities of the state statutory and administrative scheme may generate special complexities when a federal court is called upon to exercise pendent jurisdiction over a claim arising under that scheme. Such is the scenario that has developed as a result of the New York statutory scheme, which arguably forecloses federal court review of state-based claims. As a matter of fact, a number of courts have managed their way around the ostensible state statutory bar to their exercising pendent jurisdiction.[1295] The Ohio statutory scheme also creates a possible bar to the federal courts exercising pendent jurisdiction regarding claims based on that state's statutory scheme. This

---

[1292] *Id* 279. *Accord* Realmuto v Yellow Freight Sys, Inc, 712 F Supp 287 (EDNY 1989).

[1293] See **§6.45.**

[1294] *See* Robinson v Sizes Unlimited, Inc, 685 F Supp 442 (DNJ 1988); Sperling v Hoffman-LaRoche, Inc, 118 FRD 392 (DNJ), *affd on other grounds,* 862 F2d 439 (3d Cir 1988), *affd,* 493 US 165 (1989). See generally **§§6.45-.51.**

[1295] *See, e.g.,* Promisel v First Am Artificial Flowers, Inc, 943 F2d 251 (2d Cir 1991), *cert denied,* 112 S Ct 939 (1992); Martel v Dean Witter Reynolds, Inc, 738 F Supp 53 (EDNY 1990), and the case law reviewed therein. *See also* Curtiss v Key Bank, 53 FEP Cas (BNA) 1576, 1578 (WDNY 1990).

potential bar under Ohio law also has been blocked from having effect.[1296]

While the bulk of the case law concerns state statutory or common law claims, pendent jurisdiction also may be exercised with regard to state constitutional claims.[1297]

In *Marshall v Southwestern Bell Telephone Co*[1298] the court rejected the efforts of the ADEA plaintiff's husband to maintain a state law claim for loss of consortium, and of the plaintiff's sons and mother to pursue state law claims for mental and emotional injuries. It reasoned that while §7(c)[1299] of the ADEA confers such jurisdiction on federal courts "as will effectuate the purposes of th[e] Act," the statute is "not to be read broadly, and [it] thus limit[s] the jurisdiction of this court to those causes of action which are actual violations of the respective acts themselves."[1300]

§6.42 —Supplemental Jurisdiction in ADEA Cases: State Common-Law Claims

Most Age Discrimination in Employment Act (ADEA)[1301] courts that have addressed what was formerly termed pendent jurisdiction and is now denominated as supplemental jurisdiction[1302] have done so in the context of considering the assertion of state common-law claims grounded in tort and/or contract law. Because the exercise of such jurisdiction is discretionary with the courts, and because the determination as to whether

---

1296 *See, e.g.*, Alan Lafferty v Coopers & Lybrand, 841 F2d 1126 (6th Cir 1988), *quoted in* Carr v French Oil Mill Mach Co, 746 F Supp 700, 704 (SD Ohio 1989).

1297 *See* Galvin v Vermont, 598 F Supp 144 (D Vt 1984).

1298 760 F Supp 113 (ED Tex 1991).

1299 29 USC §626(c).

1300 760 F Supp at 114.

1301 29 USC §§621-634.

1302 See **§6.40.**

jurisdiction should be exercised is invariably a fact-oriented one, generalizations cannot readily be drawn.[1303]

There is a split as to whether the unavailability of damages for pain and suffering and/or punitive damages under the ADEA[1304] should preclude the exercise of pendent, or supplemental, jurisdiction as to state common law claims that, if proven, would result in such damages. Some courts take a negative position regarding the exercise of such jurisdiction, while others do not.[1305]

An illustrative decision regarding the negative view as to the exercise of pendent jurisdiction over state common law claims entailing damages other than those recoverable under the ADEA is that of the Court of Appeals for the Sixth Circuit in *McLaurin v Fischer.*[1306] The court was less concerned with basic policy issues than it was with the possibility of jury confusion being occasioned by the standards regarding a state law claim for punitive damages differing from the standards applicable to recovering liquidated damages under the ADEA.[1307]

Another, more policy oriented, ruling hostile to the exercise of pendent jurisdiction was *Hannon v Continental National Bank.*[1308] The district court, after holding that damages for pain and suffering and punitive damages could not be obtained under the ADEA,[1309] went on to refuse to exercise pendent jurisdiction as to a tort claim for damages due to intentional infliction of emotional distress or loss of reputation, stating that its "adjudication of such state claims would circumvent the scope of the remedies

---

[1303] There is, however, at least one generalization that can be asserted: if the pendent claim is directed against a state official who is being charged with having violated state law, the Eleventh Amendment, US Const, amend XI, will bar a federal court's exercising jurisdiction as to this claim. Pennhurst State Sch & Hosp v Halderman, 465 US 89 (1984).

[1304] See **ch 8.**

[1305] Regarding the same problem in the context of pendent claims based on state statutes, see **§6.41.**

[1306] 768 F2d 98 (6th Cir 1985).

[1307] *Accord* Arnell v Pan Am World Airways, Inc, 611 F Supp 908 (SDNY 1985).

[1308] 427 F Supp 215 (D Colo 1977).

[1309] *Id* 218.

available under the federal cause of action, and subvert the policies of excluding damages for emotional distress under the ADEA."[1310]

The court that decided *Marchetti v Atlas Powder Co*[1311] invoked concerns paralleling those expressed both in *McLaurin* and in *Hannon.* The court dismissed the plaintiffs' state tort claims for damages for severe emotional distress. It was of the view that: (1) proof of intentional infliction of emotional distress would involve different legal and factual issues than those presented in an ADEA claim,[1312] for which damages for pain and suffering

---

1310 *Id; see also* Koehler v Chesebrough-Ponds, Inc, 705 F Supp 721 (D Conn 1988); Kelley v United Mine Workers of Am, 42 FEP Cas (BNA) 769 (SD Ohio 1986); Real v Continental Group, Inc, 627 F Supp 434 (ND Cal 1986); DiRito v Ideal Basic Indus, Inc, 617 F Supp 79 (D Colo 1985); Pascoe v Hoyle Lowdermilk, Inc, 614 F Supp 546 (D Colo 1985); Kempe v Prince Gardner, Inc, 569 F Supp 779 (ED Mo 1983); Smith v Meijer, Inc, 566 F Supp 113 (SD Ohio 1983); Shestina v Cotter & Co, 32 FEP Cas (BNA) 674 (ND Ohio 1983); James v KID Broadcasting Corp, 559 F Supp 1153 (D Idaho 1983); Douglas v American Cyanamid Co, 472 F Supp 298 (D Conn 1979) (pendent state defamation claim, which would give rise to damages not obtainable under the ADEA, dismissed). (The *Douglas* court also relied on there being different factual issues involved in the two claims.)

In Kennedy v Mountain States Tel & Tel Co, 449 F Supp 1008 (D Colo 1978), a judge sitting on the same court as the judge in *Hannon* reached the same result, dismissal of the pendent claim, by more or less turning the *Hannon* ruling on its head. The *Kennedy* court held, in contrast to *Hannon,* that punitive damages were recoverable under the ADEA. (This is no longer a viable position. See **ch 8**). It accordingly refused to exercise pendent jurisdiction as to the plaintiffs' tort claims for intentional infliction of emotional distress because "the plaintiffs' claims of mental distress can be remedied . . . [under the ADEA] without resort to the state cause of action." *Id* 1011. As for the plaintiffs' breach of contract claims, the court was of the view that there was an insufficient relationship between them and the ADEA cause of action.

1311 520 F Supp 271 (ED Pa 1981).

1312 *See also* Mazzare v Burroughs Corp, 473 F Supp 234 (ED Pa 1979), in which the court refused to exercise pendent jurisdiction as to a state claim for intentional infliction of emotional distress, reasoning that to establish such a claim the plaintiff would have to prove that the conduct complained of was of an extreme or outrageous type and that it caused physical harm, and that this proof would involve legal and factual issues different from those involved in the ADEA claim. Because medical testimony and reports would be required, the entire scope of the trial would be enlarged. Thus, judicial economy, convenience, and fairness would not be served, while the possibility of jury confusion would be increased. *See also* Kelly v Western Air Lines, 33 FEP Cas (BNA) 1082

were not recoverable; and (2) to allow the state claim to go forward would confuse the jury. The court further reasoned that the exercise of pendent jurisdiction would thwart the ADEA conciliation process by dissuading grievants from compromising claims at the administrative stage because they would be looking down the road to securing enhanced recoveries in the judicial forum.[1313]

The Court of Appeals for the Ninth Circuit asserted a contrasting, affirmative view regarding the exercise of pendent, or supplemental, jurisdiction in *Cancellier v Federated Department Stores.*[1314] The plaintiffs had included in their suit pendent claims for breach of a state-recognized covenant of good faith and fair dealing. The jury awarded damages for violations of both the ADEA and the covenant. The appellate court sustained the awards, reasoning as follows:

> Punitive and emotional distress damages for this [state] violation, unavailable under the ADEA, do not duplicate the ADEA award for back pay, lost benefits, and liquidated damages. While the wisdom of allowing open-ended state claims for breach of the implied covenant to coexist with ADEA claims whose financial redress Congress has carefully limited to specific damage elements . . . is arguable, it is for Congress, not us, to decide whether state common law remedies trench too closely on the federal scheme.[1315]

(D Utah 1983); Sanders v Duke Univ, 538 F Supp 1143, 1148 (MDNC 1982). Moreover, state law regarding such claims was sparse and this unsettled posture of state law further counseled against exercising pendent jurisdiction, the *Mazzare* court reasoned.

[1313] In Horne v New England Patriots Football Club, 489 F Supp 465 (D Mass 1980), the court refused to exercise pendent jurisdiction as to breach of contract claims because these were referable to arbitration, whereas the ADEA claims were not.

[1314] 672 F2d 1312 (9th Cir), *cert denied,* 459 US 859 (1982); *accord* Pettibon v Pennzoil Prods Co, 649 F Supp 759 (WD Pa 1986) (emotional distress claim); Savage v Holiday Inn Corp, Inc, 603 F Supp 311, 315 (D Nev 1985).

[1315] 672 F2d at 1318 (footnote and citations omitted). The court suggested that a separate verdict on each claim would be the preferable procedure, although it sustained the award despite the trial court's not having followed

The response of the court deciding *Buscemi v Pepsico, Inc,*[1316] to the possibility of jury confusion, a concern that animated the courts' analyses in *McLaurin* and *Marchetti,* discussed above, was not to dismiss the state claim but, rather, to bifurcate the trial and thereby conduct separate proceedings as to liability and damages.

Other courts have ruled on pendent (now supplemental) jurisdiction claims without addressing the damages question. In deciding *Ott v Midland-Ross Corp,*[1317] for example, the Court of Appeals for the Sixth Circuit confirmed the feasibility of a plaintiff's maintaining a pendent state claim. And in *Hovey v Lutheran Medical Center*[1318] the court exercised pendent jurisdiction over a state common law tort claim of abusive discharge.[1319] In *Rechsteiner v Madison Fund, Inc,*[1320] the plaintiff stated a claim under state law for breach of contract along with his ADEA claim. The court denied the defendant's motion to dismiss the pendent state claim, concluding that there existed a sufficient

---

this procedure. *Id* 1317. *See also* Zinaman v USTS New York, Inc, 798 F Supp 128, 132-33 (SDNY 1992); LeBlanc v City of Stamford, 51 FEP Cas (BNA) 1221 (D Conn 1988); New York v Holiday Inns, 656 F Supp 675 (WDNY 1984); Deen v Great Atl & Pac Tea Co, Inc, 608 F Supp 783 (WDNC 1985); Keenan v Foley Co, 35 FEP Cas (BNA) 937 (ED Wis 1984); Shanahan v WITI-TV, Inc, 565 F Supp 219, 225 (ED Wis 1982); Placos v Cosmair, Inc, 517 F Supp 1287 (SDNY 1981). In Real v Continental Group, Inc, 627 F Supp 434 (ND Cal 1986), the court took the view that punitive damages under the state common law claim could be recovered, but only to the extent that such an award exceeded, rather than duplicated, the liquidated damages award. *See also* Linn v Andover Newton Theological Sch, Inc, 874 F2d 1 (1st Cir 1989) (foreclosing double recovery on ADEA and breach of contract claims arising out of same transaction); Washburn v Kansas City Life Ins Co, 831 F2d 1404 (8th Cir 1987) (same). As to the issue of duplicative damages recoveries under state statutes and the ADEA, see **§6.41.**

[1316] 736 F Supp 1267 (SDNY 1990).

[1317] 600 F2d 24, 34-35 (6th Cir 1979).

[1318] 516 F Supp 554 (EDNY 1981).

[1319] *See also* Romero v Lone Star Co, 637 F Supp 1 (WD Tex 1984); Studint v LaSalle Ice Cream Co, Inc, 623 F Supp 232 (EDNY 1985); Ritter v Colorado Interstate Gas Co, 593 F Supp 1279 (D Colo 1984); Rio v Presbyterian Hosp, 561 F Supp 325 (SDNY 1983).

[1320] 75 FRD 499 (D Del 1977).

common nucleus of operative facts.[1321] In *Wagner v Sperry Univac, Division of Sperry Rand Corp*[1322] the court also addressed a pendent claim grounded in state contract law. Here, however, the defendant did not dispute the propriety of the court's exercising jurisdiction over the claim.[1323] Both in *Cory v SmithKline Beckman*

[1321] *Accord* Linn v Andover Newton Theological Sch, 642 F Supp 11 (D Mass 1985), *vacated on other grounds & remanded with instructions to reduce verdict,* 874 F2d 1 (1st Cir 1989); Bumpers v International Mill Servs, Inc, 595 F Supp 166 (ED Pa 1984); Van Atta v Kal-Aero, Inc, 555 F Supp 912 (WD Mich 1983); Goodman v Board of Trustees, 511 F Supp 602 (ND Ill 1981); Studint v LaSalle Ice Cream Co, Inc, 623 F Supp 232 (EDNY 1985) (breach of contract; wrongful termination; intentional/negligent infliction of emotional distress; fraud in the inducement). *See also* Vuksta v Bethlehem Steel Corp, 540 F Supp 1276 (ED Pa 1982), *affd without opinion,* 707 F2d 1405 (3d Cir), *cert denied,* 464 US 835 (1983), in which the court exercised pendent jurisdiction over a claim for intentional and improper interference with a contract. *Contra* Snyder v Washington Hosp Ctr, 35 Empl Prac Dec (CCH) ¶34,717 (DDC 1984).

[1322] 458 F Supp 505 (ED Pa 1978), *affd without opinion,* 624 F2d 1092 (3d Cir 1980); *see also* Halsell v Kimberly-Clark Corp, 683 F2d 285 (8th Cir 1982), *cert denied,* 459 US 1205 (1983); Goodman v Board of Trustees of Community College Dist 524, 498 F Supp 1329 (ND Ill 1980); Wehr v Burroughs Corp, 438 F Supp 1052 (ED Pa 1977).

[1323] In Cemer v Marathon Oil Co, 583 F2d 830 (6th Cir 1978), the plaintiff's ADEA suit had been dismissed because it was barred by the statute of limitations. Subsequently, the plaintiff filed a breach of contract suit in state court. The defendant, invoking diversity jurisdiction, removed the case to federal court and then moved for its dismissal on res judicata grounds. The district court granted the motion and the court of appeals affirmed, relying on the fact that a dismissal under Fed R Civ P 41(b) is, by the terms of the rule, deemed to be an adjudication on the merits. The court stated as follows:

> Where two successive suits seek recovery for the same injury, a judgment on the merits operates as a bar to the later suit, even though a different legal theory of recovery is advanced in the second suit. . . . Both the first and second suits seek to remedy a single alleged wrong—the discharge of Cemer by Marathon. In view of the diversity of the parties, both the contract claim and the ADEA claim were within the original jurisdiction of the district court in the first action and should have been brought together.

583 F2d at 832 (citations and footnote omitted). In a footnote the court stated that the district court would have been obligated to accept jurisdiction over the contract claim had it been joined in the first suit (citing Thermtron Prods, Inc v Hermansdorfer, 423 US 336, 352-53 (1976)). 583 F2d at 832 n1. It declined to reach the question of whether a party must assert a separate claim arising from a single injury where the claim is merely one within the court's pendent jurisdiction, as well as the question of the res judicata implications

Corp[1324] and *Smith v Montgomery Ward & Co, Inc,*[1325] the courts exercised pendent jurisdiction without comment, apparently because the defendants had not questioned the courts doing so.

In the past, the exercise of pendent jurisdiction would be deemed to be improper if the federal and state law claims did not derive from a common nucleus of operative facts.[1326] Now, under the codification of pendent jurisdiction doctrine, the state claim must be so related to the federal claim "that they form part of the same case or controversy,"[1327] a formulation paralleling the *common nucleus of operative facts* standard judicially devised in *United Mine Workers v Gibbs.*[1328] But even if there is a common nucleus of operative facts, i.e., the state and federal claims form part of the same case or controversy, a court may refuse to exercise supplemental jurisdiction pursuant to 28 USC §1367(c)(2) or (c)(4)[1329] if the scope of the issues raised in the state claim is broader than the scope of the issues involved in the ADEA claim.[1330] Similarly, if the state claims involve issues that have not generally been resolved by the state courts, a court may feel it

---

in such a situation. It did acknowledge "that unlike a claim within the court's original [diversity] jurisdiction, the adjudication of a pendent claim is committed to the district court's discretion and is not mandatory." *Id.*

1324 585 F Supp 871 (ED Pa 1984).

1325 567 F Supp 1331 (D Colo 1983).

1326 *See* Sanders v Duke Univ, 538 F Supp 1143 (MDNC 1982); *accord* Mason v Richmond Motor Co, Inc, 625 F Supp 883, 886 (ED Va 1986), *affd without opinion,* 825 F2d 407 (4th Cir 1987) (rejecting reformulation of pendent jurisdiction standards to require only a " 'loose factual connection' " between the federal and state claims).

1327 28 USC §1367(a). See **§6.40.**

1328 383 US 715, 725 (1966).

1329 See **§6.40.**

1330 *See, e.g.,* James v Sun Glass Hut, Inc, 799 F Supp 1083 (D Colo 1992); Brokke v Stauffer Chem Co, 703 F Supp 215 (D Conn 1988); Kelley v United Mine Workers of Am, 42 FEP Cas (BNA) 769 (SD Ohio 1986); DiRito v Ideal Basic Indus, Inc, 617 F Supp 79 (D Colo 1985); Pascoe v Hoyle Lowdermilk, Inc, 614 F Supp 546 (D Colo 1985); Lettich v Kenway, 590 F Supp 1225 (D Mass 1984); Smith v Meijer, Inc, 566 F Supp 113 (SD Ohio 1983); Kelly v Western Air Lines, 33 FEP Cas (BNA) 1082 (D Utah 1983). (The *Lettich* court, in so ruling, mistakenly reasoned that a plaintiff could not pursue claims under the ADEA and state law if those claims arose out of the same incident.)

appropriate to decline to exercise supplemental jurisdiction[1331] in accordance with 28 USC §1367(c)(4).

§6.43 Court-Appointed Counsel

There is no authorization for court-appointed counsel in the Age Discrimination in Employment Act (ADEA).[1332] The silence of the statute notwithstanding, there are several reported instances of counsel being appointed for pro se plaintiffs. In *Salmon v Corpus Christi Independent School District*[1333] the Court of Appeals for the Fifth Circuit looked for guidance to case law devised under Title VII of the Civil Rights Act of 1964,[1334] which does contain a provision authorizing the appointment of free counsel for a plaintiff "in such circumstances as the court may deem just."[1335] The *Salmon* court wrote that "the proper considerations include the probable success of the claims, the efforts by the plaintiff to retain counsel, and the plaintiff's financial ability."[1336] The court also looked to *Ulmer v Chancellor,*[1337] a decision addressing the issue of appointed counsel in a case brought pursuant to 42 USC §1983. *Ulmer,* the *Salmon* court said, established four factors to take into account:

> (1) the type and complexity of the case; (2) whether petitioner is capable of presenting his case adequately; (3) whether petitioner is in a position to investigate the case adequately; and (4) whether the evidence will consist in large part of conflicting testimony, so as to require skill in the presentation of evidence and in cross examination.[1338]

[1331] *See* Ritter v Colorado Interstate Gas Co, 593 F Supp 1279 (D Colo 1984).

[1332] 29 USC §§621-634.

[1333] 911 F2d 1165 (5th Cir 1990).

[1334] 42 USC §§2000e through 2000e-17.

[1335] §706(f)(1), 42 USC §2000e-5(f)(1).

[1336] 911 F2d at 1166.

[1337] 691 F2d 209 (5th Cir 1982).

[1338] 911 F2d at 1166.

Other courts have appointed counsel for pro se plaintiffs in ADEA suits,[1339] as well as in suits brought under both the ADEA and Title VII.[1340]

Although the foregoing cases did not mention it, there is a federal statute that is applicable to civil actions generally and that can serve as the basis for the appointment of counsel. 28 USC §1915(d) provides that "the court may request an attorney to represent . . . [an indigent] person unable to employ counsel. . . ." In deciding *Mallard v United States District Court*[1341] the Supreme Court held that §1915(d) does not authorize a federal court to require an unwilling attorney to represent an indigent in a civil case. It is this statute that is the basis for counsel being appointed to represent indigent ADEA litigants from time to time.

As pointed out in *DiAngelo v Illinois Department of Public Aid,*[1342] judges do not routinely make requests of attorneys under §1915(d); "they recruit lawyers for the parties only when the cases are colorable, the facts may be difficult to assemble, and the law is complex."[1343] In *Cooper v A Sargenti Co*[1344] the court denied the plaintiff-appellant's motion for the appointment of counsel pursuant to §1915(d) because of the lack of a showing of likely merit, a predicate that it had enunciated in an earlier ruling as necessary to such a motion being granted.

In *DiAngelo* the court held that an attorney who has honored a district court judge's request and assented to represent an indigent in the trial court is not thereby required to continue his or her role in the court of appeals. Moreover, the attorney who does not choose to continue at the appellate level need not file

---

1339 Such appointments were made, without any discussion or explanation, in Genoar v Clorox Co, 51 FEP Cas (BNA) 240 (ND Ill 1989), and Becker v Dunkin' Donuts of Am, Inc, 665 F Supp 211 (SDNY 1987).

1340 Perry v Kunz, 672 F Supp 1205, 1206 (ED Mo 1987), *revd on other grounds,* 878 F2d 1056 (8th Cir 1989); Santos v Rush-Presbyterian-St Luke's Medical Ctr, 641 F Supp 353 (ND Ill 1986).

1341 490 US 296 (1989).

1342 891 F2d 1260 (7th Cir 1989).

1343 *Id* 1262; *see also* Williams v Meese, 926 F2d 994, 996 (10th Cir 1991).

1344 877 F2d 170 (2d Cir 1989).

an *Anders* brief as a condition precedent to terminating his or her role. "Such submissions are not necessary, because civil appointments in the district courts do not carry over on appeal."[1345]

§6.44 Availability of Jury Trials

As originally enacted, there was no express authorization in the Age Discrimination in Employment Act (ADEA)[1346] for jury trials. Some early ADEA courts that were called upon to parse the act's silence looked—as ADEA courts often do[1347]—to Title VII of the Civil Rights Act of 1964,[1348] under which jury trials generally were not available,[1349] and rejected the notion that jury trials could be had in the ADEA context. Other courts, however, found contrary guidance in the fact that jury trials generally were allowed under the Fair Labor Standards Act,[1350] whose enforcement provisions are incorporated into the ADEA.[1351] Ultimately, the Supreme Court held in *Lorillard v Pons*[1352] that the parties to a private ADEA suit had a right to a jury trial on claims for back wages.

Shortly after the *Lorillard* ruling, the Act was amended[1353] to

---

[1345] 891 F2d at 1261.

[1346] 29 USC §§621-634.

[1347] See **ch 2.**

[1348] 42 USC §§2000e through 2000e-17.

[1349] Jury trials now are available in Title VII cases, as a result of an amendment made by the Civil Rights Act of 1991, Pub L No 102-166, §102, 105 Stat 1071, 1073, whereby 42 USC §1977a(c) was added to the United States Code. *Id* USC §1977a(c) provides for a jury trial at the demand of either a plaintiff or a defendant in a Title VII case in which the plantiff seeks compensatory or punitive damages.

[1350] 29 USC §§200-219.

[1351] *Compare* Morelock v NCR Corp, 546 F2d 682 (6th Cir 1976), *vacated,* 435 US 911 (1978) (no jury trial) *with* Rogers v Exxon Research & Engg Co, 550 F2d 834 (3d Cir 1977), *cert denied,* 434 US 1022 (1978) (jury trial).

[1352] 434 US 575 (1978).

[1353] Age Discrimination in Employment Act Amendments of 1978, Pub L No 95-256, §4(a)(2), 92 Stat 189, 190.

expressly provide that jury trials are available at the request of both plaintiffs and defendants in nonfederal employee cases. Accordingly, §7(c)(2)[1354] provides as follows:

> In an action brought under paragraph (1) [which establishes a private cause of action], a person shall be entitled to a trial by jury of any issue of fact in any such action for recovery of amounts owing as a result of a violation of this chapter, regardless of whether equitable relief is sought by any party in such action.[1355]

If the plaintiff has sustained no pecuniary loss, there is no role for a jury, in light of the statute's only authorizing juries in actions "for recovery of amounts owed."[1356] Thus, if only equitable claims are at issue, no jury trial may be had.[1357] Moreover, a jury trial may not be had when the defendant is an agent or instrumentality of a foreign state.[1358]

[1354] 29 USC §626(c)(2).

[1355] There has been considerable support registered by employers for the barring of jury trials in ADEA cases. The premise underlying this position is their perception that federal court juries are inclined to be disproportionately sympathetic to plaintiffs. *See Prohibition of Mandatory Retirement and Employment Rights Act of 1982, Hearing before the Subcomm on Labor, Comm on Labor and Human Resources,* 97th Cong, 2d Sess 83 (1982) (testimony of Charles Bakaly). Actually, empirical data on the issue are scanty. *See* McConnell, *Age Discrimination in Employment, in* Policy Issues in Work & Retirement 186-87 (H.S. Parnes ed 1983). Moreover, one researcher who conducted an empirical study, albeit one of limited dimension, concluded that the jury trial system does not discriminate against defendants. Fosberg, *A Comparison of Jury Trials & Bench Trials in Age Discrimination Cases,* 5 BIFOCAL 4 (Fall 1984); *see also* Clermont & Eisenberg, *Trial by Jury or Judge: Transcending Empiricism,* 77 Cornell L Rev 1124 (1992) (reporting, albeit not as to the specific matter of ADEA cases, that empirical data support the conclusion that there generally is a high degree of agreement between judges and juries as to the disposition of lawsuits).

[1356] McLaren v Emory Univ, 705 F Supp 563, 568 (ND Ga 1988).

[1357] Equal Employment Opportunity Commn v Emory Univ, 47 FEP Cas (BNA) 1770 (ND Ga 1988).

[1358] Kraikeman v Sabena Belgian World Airlines, 674 F Supp 136 (SDNY 1987); Carponcy v Air France, 38 FEP Cas (BNA) 1518 (SDNY 1985).

Bifurcation of Claims Involving Both Legal and Equitable Relief

An issue that commonly will arise in ADEA cases is the propriety of a jury's addressing the claims of a plaintiff who seeks both legal relief and equitable relief, such as an order directing his or her reinstatement to the position from which he or she was discharged. While §7(c)(2)'s terms make clear that a plaintiff's equitable claims will not preclude the right to a jury trial as to the legal claims in the case, the provision does not specify how the equitable issues are to be dealt with (nor did *Lorillard,* for that matter.)

The usual approach is to bifurcate the case, leaving for the jury the resolution of the legal issues and reposing authority for determination of the equitable claims in the court,[1359] with the jury trial being conducted first.[1360] However, in deciding *Ott v Midland-Ross Co*[1361] the Court of Appeals for the Sixth Circuit rejected the bifurcation approach, albeit not in the context of mixed legal and equitable claims for relief, but rather with regard to determining whether there was an equitable basis for tolling the statute of limitations. The court reasoned as follows:

1359 *See, e.g.,* Ventura v Federal Life Ins Co, 571 F Supp 48 (ND Ill 1983); Cleverly v Western Elec Co, 450 F Supp 507 (WD Mo 1978), *affd,* 594 F2d 638, 640 (8th Cir 1979); Quinn v Bowmar Pub Co, 445 F Supp 780 (D Md 1978); Chilton v National Cash Register Co, 370 F Supp 660 (SD Ohio 1974); Cleverly v Western Elec Co, 69 FRD 348 (WD Mo 1975).

1360 *See* Duke v Uniroyal, Inc, 928 F2d 1413, 1422 (4th Cir), *cert denied,* 112 S Ct 429 (1991); Locascio v Teletype Corp, 74 FRD 108, 112 (ND Ill 1977). *Cf* Lytle v Household Mfg, Inc, 494 US 545 (1990) (Title VII case); Dairy Queen, Inc v Wood, 369 US 469 (1962) (non-ADEA case). In Lindsey v American Cast Iron Pipe Co, 810 F2d 1094 (11th Cir 1987), the court did not insist that the legal issues be addressed first. Rather, the court took a more equivocal position: "When some issues are tried to the jury and some to the court, the jury issues generally should be heard first." *Id* 1097.

1361 600 F2d 24 (6th Cir 1979); *see also* Brenimer v Great W Sugar Co, 567 F Supp 218, 224 (D Colo 1983).

> Where the predominant issues in a suit are triable to a jury, as in an ADEA action, federal law looks with disfavor upon fragmenting a portion of the case for trial to the court. . . .
>
> In the context of the instant case, submission of the entire case to the jury is particularly appropriate. On the merits of the ADEA claim the jury must determine the defendant's motives for terminating Ott. On the issue of wrongful inducement, the good faith of Midland-Ross in offering the consultation agreement [and thereby forestalling Ott's seeking relief under the ADEA] is in question. Both factual disputes call for a resolution of credibility and are pieces of the larger mosaic of defendant's treatment of Ott.[1362]

There are varying views as to the binding nature of a jury's determination vis-a-vis the equitable issues in a given case. According to the Court of Appeals for the Ninth Circuit, the jury's determination "ordinarily" is deemed to be res judicata as to the equitable issues.[1363] A somewhat more rigorous view was expressed in *Cleverly v Western Electric Co;*[1364] the court reasoned that "*in the absence of exceptional circumstances* . . ., the jury's verdict in favor of plaintiff on the issue of age discrimination is *res judicata* for the purposes of the equitable claim for reinstatement."[1365] This view has been echoed by the Court of Appeals for the Second Circuit.[1366] An even more stringent position has been espoused by the Court of Appeals for the Eighth Circuit,

---

1362 *Id* 31 (citations omitted).

1363 Cancellier v Federated Dept Stores, 672 F2d 1312, 1319 (9th Cir), *cert denied,* 459 US 859 (1982); *accord* Burger v Health Ins Plan, 684 F Supp 46, 50 n5 (SDNY 1988).

1364 450 F Supp 507 (WD Mo), *affd on other grounds,* 594 F2d 638 (8th Cir 1978).

1365 450 F Supp at 511 (emphasis added); *see also* Criswell v Western Air Lines, Inc, 514 F Supp 384, 393 (CD Cal 1981), *affd,* 709 F2d 544 (9th Cir 1983), *affd on other grounds,* 472 US 400 (1985).

1366 Geller v Markham, 635 F2d 1027, 1036 (2d Cir 1980), *cert denied,* 451 US 945 (1981).

which, in deciding *Gibson v Mohawk Rubber Co,*[1367] approvingly quoted the foregoing assertion in *Cleverly,* but then went on to assert that rather than a jury's verdict just ordinarily being binding, as the Court of Appeals for the Ninth Circuit had observed, that verdict is without exception res judicata as to the court's equitable determinations.[1368]

Ritter v Mount St Mary's College[1369] involved the converse situation. Here, the question was whether a court's determination as to an equitable issue would preclude jury consideration of that issue. The court addressed the claims of a plaintiff who initially had filed suit under Title VII, the Equal Pay Act (EPA),[1370] and the ADEA. The trial court dismissed the EPA and ADEA claims and proceeded to decide the merits of the Title VII claim. Subsequently, the trial court ruling was reversed as to the ADEA and EPA claims, and the case was remanded. The trial court judge then ruled that the factual findings made in the Title VII suit collaterally estopped the plaintiff from establishing a prima facie ADEA claim because the two causes of action contained an identical element, i.e., the requirement that the plaintiff establish her qualifications.

On appeal, the plaintiff argued that she should not have been collaterally estopped, given that had she been allowed to proceed with her ADEA claim a jury, rather than a judge, would have made the relevant factual determinations. The appellate court ruled against her. Relying on *Parklane Hosiery Co, Inc v Shore,*[1371] the court stated as follows:

1367 695 F2d 1093 (8th Cir 1982).

1368 *Id* 1101; *see also* Equal Employment Opportunity Commn v Indian River Transp Co, 33 FEP Cas (BNA) 862, 862 (MD Fla 1982) (decision on the equitable issues would be "guided" by the jury's award); Monroe v United Air Lines, Inc, 32 FEP Cas (BNA) 1259, 1261 (ND Ill 1983), *revd on other grounds,* 736 F2d 394 (7th Cir 1984), *cert denied,* 470 US 1004 (1985) ("Court's findings may not conflict" with the jury's).

1369 814 F2d 986 (4th Cir), *cert denied,* 484 US 913 (1987).

1370 29 USC §206(d).

1371 439 US 322 (1979).

> *Parklane* decided that the judicial interest in the economical resolution of cases, which interest underlies the doctrine of collateral estoppel, does override the interest of the plaintiff in retrying before a jury the facts of a case determined by a court sitting in equity.[1372]

Bifurcation of liability and damages issues can create problems if the jury does not identify which specific acts were discriminatory, and such identification is relevant to the subsequent determination of damages.[1373]

Determining Whether Claims are Legal or Equitable

Some claims can be clearly categorized. For example, requests for judicial orders directing hiring, reinstatement, and promotion are equitable.[1374] Claims for attorney's fees and costs also regularly have been denominated as being equitable.[1375] There sometimes can be disagreement, however, as to whether a given claim should properly be characterized as equitable or legal. For example, if a claim for lost pension benefits[1376] is for a liquidated amount representing the present value of those benefits, there is mixed case law as to whether the relief sought is legal damages.[1377] If a plaintiff seeks restoration to his or her former pen-

---

[1372] 814 F2d 986, 991; *accord* Dickerson v Deluxe Check Printers, Inc, 703 F2d 276, 280 (8th Cir 1983).

[1373] *See* Griener v Allstate Ins Co, 43 FEP Cas (BNA) 79 (ED La 1987).

[1374] Lorillard v Pons, 434 US 575, 583 n11 (1978).

[1375] *See, e.g.,* Quinn v Bowmar Pub Co, 445 F Supp 780, 788 (D Md 1978); Lee v Sears, Roebuck & Co, 17 FEP Cas (BNA) 23 (WD Tenn 1978); Rechsteiner v Madison Fund, Inc, 75 FRD 499 (D Del 1977); Fellows v Medford Corp, 431 F Supp 199 (D Or 1977); Locascio v Teletype Corp, 74 FRD 108, 113 (ND Ill 1977); Cleverly v Western Elec Co, 69 FRD 348 (WD Mo 1975); Chilton v National Cash Register Co, 370 F Supp 660 (SD Ohio 1974).

[1376] See generally **ch 8.**

[1377] *See, e.g.,* Fellows v Medford Corp, 431 F Supp 199 (D Or 1977) (affirmative view); Combes v Griffin Television, Inc, 421 F Supp 841 (WD Okla 1976) *(id);* Chilton v National Cash Register Co, 370 F Supp 660 (SD Ohio 1974) *(id). Contra* Dickerson v Deluxe Check Printers, Inc, 703 F2d 276, 279 n2 (8th Cir 1983). *See also* Ventura v Federal Life Ins Co, 571 F Supp 48 (ND Ill 1983),

sion status by means of an order directing the employer to pay funds into the pension plan, there is case law support for deeming such relief to be equitable.[1378] The pension issue arguably was resolved in favor of treating pension claims as legal in 1978 when the jury trial provision was added to the ADEA. In its report accompanying the amendment the House-Senate conference committee looked to §7(b) of the Act,[1379] which authorizes the recovery of "amounts owing," and it defined these words as including "items of pecuniary or economic loss such as wages, fringe, and other job-related benefits."[1380]

The proper characterization of front pay, also known as damages in lieu of reinstatement,[1381] and the correlative role of juries in determining the propriety of, and amounts of, front pay awards are questions that have generated disagreement.[1382] As for liquidated damages, in *Lorillard,* discussed above, the Supreme Court only addressed the availability of jury trials as to claims for back pay.[1383] But in the report on the 1978 amend-

---

in which a claim for pension benefits to be lost in the future by virtue of the alleged wrongful discharge was deemed to be equitable in nature.

[1378] *See, e.g.*, Gibson v Mohawk Rubber Co, 695 F2d 1093 (8th Cir 1982); Geller v Markham, 635 F2d 1027, 1036 (2d Cir 1980), *cert denied,* 451 US 945 (1981); Cleverly v Western Elec Co, 450 F Supp 507 (WD Mo 1978), *affd,* 594 F2d 638 (8th Cir 1979); Quinn v Bowmar Pub Co, 445 F Supp 780 (D Md 1978). Engaging in an unsophisticated analysis which failed to recognize that the plaintiff may be seeking a liquidated amount, the *Geller* court stated as follows:

> Despite some case law that supports viewing lost pension rights as an aspect of damages, . . . the better view is that these rights fall within the category of equitable relief. . . . As distinguished from damage awards, which are payable to the plaintiff, pension benefits are paid into pension annuity funds. . . .

635 F2d at 1036 (citations omitted).

[1379] 29 USC §626(b).

[1380] Conference Comm, Age Discrimination in Employment Act Amendments of 1978, HR Rep No 950, 95th Cong, 2d Sess 13 (1978).

[1381] See generally **ch 8.**

[1382] See **ch 8.**

[1383] As to such claims, see **ch 8.**

ment the conference committee asserted that the private plaintiff's right to a jury trial also extends to claims for liquidated damages.[1384]

Waiver of Right to Jury

Federal Rule of Civil Procedure 38(b) provides that a party seeking to have his or her claim resolved by a jury must make a written demand for a jury "not later than 10 days after the service of the last pleading directed to such issue."[1385] The failure of a party to request a jury trial, or to make a timely demand, will result in his or her being deemed to have waived the right to such, and relief from this waiver will be available only at the court's discretion.[1386] The fact that a plaintiff sues pro se does not, according to one court, warrant any special leniency,[1387] while another has expressed a contrary view.[1388]

[1384] In the report of the House-Senate conference committee that harmonized the differences between the bills passed by the two chambers it was stated that "[b]ecause liquidated damages are in the nature of legal relief, it is manifest that a party is entitled to have the factual issues underlying such a claim decided by a jury." Conference Comm, HR Rep No 950, *supra* note 1380, at 14. As to such claims generally, see **ch 8.**

[1385] The court deciding Bentler v Bank of Am, 959 F2d 138, 141 (9th Cir 1992), stated that "when defendants are jointly liable on a cause of action . . ., a jury demand . . . is timely if served within 10 days after service of the last defendant's answer."

[1386] *See, e.g.,* Moody v Pepsi-Cola Metro Bottling Co, Inc, 915 F2d 201, 207-08 (6th Cir 1990); Washington v New York City Bd of Estimate, 709 F2d 792 (2d Cir), *cert denied,* 464 US 1013 (1983); Scharnhorst v Independent Sch Dist No 710, 686 F2d 637 (8th Cir 1982), *cert denied,* 462 US 1109 (1983); Sutton v Atlantic Richfield Co, 646 F2d 407, 409 n3 (9th Cir 1981); Hoffman v Alside, Inc, 596 F2d 822 (8th Cir 1979); Simon v Wiremold Co, 35 FEP Cas (BNA) 1819 (WD Pa 1984); Abbe v Allen's Store for Men, Inc, 94 FRD 295 (ND Ill 1982); Plummer v General Elec Co, 93 FRD 311 (ED Pa 1982); *see also* Equal Employment Opportunity Commn v El Paso Natural Gas Co, 36 FEP Cas (BNA) 1210 (WD Tex 1985) (involving suit by ADEA enforcement agency, as opposed to private plaintiff).

[1387] *See* Spear v Dayton's, 771 F2d 1140 (8th Cir 1985).

[1388] *See* Kopala v Pepsi-Cola Bottling Co, 55 FEP Cas (BNA) 1535 (ND Ind 1991).

Other Issues

The Court of Appeals for the First Circuit has asserted that the matter of whether a defendant has satisfied its burden of production in responding to the plaintiff's prima facie case[1389] is for the court, not a jury, to decide.[1390] In *Lockhart v Westinghouse Credit Corp*[1391] the court rejected the losing defendant's two-part argument: to wit, that in multiplaintiff litigation juries have a natural tendency to reach compromise verdicts entailing finding partially in favor of both the plaintiff and the defendant, and so the inclusion in a trial of improperly joined plaintiffs would unduly prejudice the defendant.[1392]

§6.45 Representative Actions: Generally

The Age Discrimination in Employment Act (ADEA)[1393] provides, in §7(b),[1394] that enforcement of claims by nonfederal grievants, i.e., grievants who are neither present or former federal employees nor applicants for federal employment, is to be in accordance with, inter alia, §16[1395] of the Fair Labor Standards Act (FLSA).[1396] This latter provision contains language directly relevant to the question of whether class or, more properly, representative, actions may be maintained under that Act[1397] and—by virtue of §16(b)'s incorporation into the ADEA—under

---

1389 See **ch 7**.

1390 Dea v Look, 810 F2d 12, 16 (1st Cir 1987); Loeb v Textron, Inc, 600 F2d 1003, 1016 n16 (1st Cir 1979). See generally specific sections of **chs 7** and **8** for discussion of the jury's role in specific contexts.

1391 879 F2d 43 (3d Cir 1989).

1392 *Id* 54.

1393 29 USC §§621-634.

1394 *Id* §626(b).

1395 *Id* §216.

1396 *Id* §§200-219.

1397 *See generally* Note, *The Class Action Suit Under the Age Discrimination in Employment Act: Current Status, Controversies, and Suggested Clarifications,* 32 Hastings LJ 1377 (1981).

the age discrimination statute as well. More specifically, §16(b) provides as follows:

> [An a]ction to recover such liability may be maintained in any court of competent jurisdiction by one or more employees for and in behalf of himself or themselves and other employees similarly situated. No employee shall be a party plaintiff to any such action unless he gives his consent in writing to become such a party and such consent is filed in the court in which such action is brought.[1398]

The second sentence articulates an opt-in concept, whereby a representative action may be maintained only if those who are represented affirmatively choose to join in the action.[1399] Correlatively, insofar as an individual grievant who is not a named plaintiff is concerned, "the commencement of a private opt-in type class action . . . does not extinguish. . . . [his or her] right . . . to bring a subsequent private action unless that employee has affirmatively opted into the litigation."[1400]

The opt-in approach is fundamentally different from that which applies in class actions maintained pursuant to Federal Rule of Civil Procedure 23. Under the latter provision an individual may file a class suit and each person who fits within the

---

[1398] The second sentence was added to the FLSA by the Portal-to-Portal Act of 1947, Pub L No 49, ch 52, §5(a), 61 Stat 84, 87, in order to curtail available remedies in the face of the potential enormous liabilities to which both private industry and government were exposed as a result of the decision in Anderson v Mt Clemens Pottery Co, 328 US 680 (1946). The Court in *Anderson* held that employees were owed compensation for in-plant activities performed before, and subsequent to, actual work. In the six months following the decision, 1,913 suits were filed, seeking in excess of $5.7 billion. Naton v Bank of Cal, 72 FRD 550, 552 n6 (ND Cal 1976), *affd,* 649 F2d 691 (9th Cir 1981). For a review of the history of §16(b), see Sussan & Scher, *Class Actions Under the Fair Labor Standards Act,* 11 Clearinghouse Rev 713 (Dec 1977).

[1399] Consents need not be filed as to suits brought by the Equal Employment Opportunity Commission. See **§6.60.**

[1400] Equal Employment Opportunity Commn v Pan Am World Airways, Inc, 897 F2d 1499, 1508 n11 (9th Cir), *cert denied,* 498 US 815 (1990).

description of the class is a class member and will automatically be bound by a favorable or unfavorable judgment (if the class is certified by a court) unless he or she opts out of the suit.[1401]

Given the language of §16(b), it follows that Rule 23 class actions may not be maintained under the FLSA.[1402] And given the incorporation of §16(b) into the ADEA, the same holds true vis-a-vis the age discrimination statute insofar as grievants who are neither present or former federal employees nor applicants for federal employment are concerned.[1403] (Inasmuch as a sepa-

---

[1401] *See generally* H. Newberg, Newberg on Class Actions (Shepard's/McGraw-Hill 1992). Actually, class members only have a statutory right to opt out of Rule 23(b)(3) class actions. Fed R Civ P 23(b)(3). They may not do so (at least absent judicial acquiescence) if the suit is maintained pursuant to subsections (b)(1) or (b)(2) of Rule 23. Fed R Civ P 23(b)(1), (b)(2). *See* LaChapelle v Owens-Illinois, Inc, 513 F2d 286, 288 n7 (5th Cir 1975).

[1402] *See, e.g.*, Kinney Shoe Corp v Vorhes, 564 F2d 859 (9th Cir 1977); Schmidt v Fuller Brush Co, 527 F2d 532 (8th Cir 1975); Sims v Parke Davis & Co, 334 F Supp 774 (ED Mich), *affd*, 453 F2d 1259 (6th Cir 1971), *cert denied*, 405 US 978 (1972). *See generally* McDaniel, Annotation, *Effect of "Opt-Out" Class Action Provision of Rule 23(c) of Federal Rules of Civil Procedure on §16(b) of Fair Labor Standards Act (29 USCS §216(b)) Regulating Class Actions Under Fair Labor Standards Act*, 44 ALR Fed 118 (1979); *see also* E. K. Spahn, *Resurrecting the Spurious Class: Opting-in to the Age Discrimination in Employment Act and the Equal Pay Act Through the Fair Labor Standards Act*, 71 Geo LJ 119 (1982).

[1403] *See, e.g.*, Price v Maryland Casualty Co, 561 F2d 609 (5th Cir 1977); LaChapelle v Owens-Illinois, Inc, 513 F2d 286 (5th Cir 1975); Silver v St Luke's Hosp, 38 FEP Cas (BNA) 1528 (D Colo 1985); Owens v Bethlehem Mines Corp, 108 FRD 207 (SD W Va 1985); Watkins v Milliken & Co, 613 F Supp 408 (WDNC 1984); Held v National RR Passenger Corp, 101 FRD 420 (DDC 1984); Lusardi v Xerox Corp, 99 FRD 88 (DNJ 1983), *appeal dismissed on other grounds*, 747 F2d 174 (3d Cir 1984); United Indep Flight Officers, Inc v United Air Lines, Inc, 572 F Supp 1494, 1498 (ND Ill 1983), *affd*, 756 F2d 1274 (7th Cir 1985); Allen v Marshall Field & Co, 93 FRD 438 (ND Ill 1982); Equal Employment Opportunity Commn v Chrysler Corp, 546 F Supp 54 (ED Mich 1982), *affd*, 733 F2d 1183 (6th Cir 1984); Sanders v National Cash Register Corp, 21 FEP Cas (BNA) 1643 (ND Ala 1979); Wagner v Loew's Theatres, Inc, 76 FRD 23 (MDNC 1977); Locascio v Teletype Corp, 74 FRD 108 (ND Ill 1977); Hill v Western Elec Co, 76 FRD 4 (MDNC 1976); Naton v Bank of Cal, 72 FRD 550 (ND Cal 1976), *affd*, 649 F2d 691 (9th Cir 1981); McGinley v Burroughs Corp, 407 F Supp 903 (ED Pa 1975); Cooke v Reynolds Metals Co, 65 FRD 539 (ED Va 1975); Burgett v Cudahy Co, 361 F Supp 617 (D Kan 1973); Hull v Continental Oil Co, 58 FRD 636 (SD Tex 1973); *see also* Bean v Crocker Natl Bank, 600 F2d 754 (9th Cir 1979); Montalto v Morgan Guar Trust

rate statutory scheme is established by the ADEA for federal employees,[1404] these individuals can, and do, maintain Rule 23 class action suits.[1405] As stated by the Court of Appeals for the Fifth Circuit in *LaChapelle v Owens Illinois, Inc*:[1406] Rule 23 and §16(b) actions are "mutually exclusive and irreconcilable."[1407]

Co, 83 FRD 150 (SDNY 1979); Mistretta v Sandia Corp, 12 FEP Cas (BNA) 1223 (DNM 1975).

In Rodriguez v Taylor, 428 F Supp 1118 (ED Pa 1976), *vacated in part & remanded,* 569 F2d 1231 (3d Cir 1977), *cert denied,* 436 US 913 (1978), the district court certified a class pursuant to Fed R Civ P 23(b)(2) without comment. The court of appeals pretermitted consideration of the issue of whether a Rule 23 class action could be maintained. Rodriguez v Taylor, 569 F2d 1231, 1235 n6 (3d Cir 1977), *cert denied,* 436 US 913 (1978). In Gebhard v GAF Corp, 59 FRD 504 (DDC 1973), the court denied a motion for class certification under Rule 23 because the plaintiffs had failed to meet Rule 23's requirements; i.e., numerosity, the impracticability of joinder, the presence of common questions of law and fact, and adequacy of representation. The court did not discuss the availability of Rule 23 class actions in the first instance, but given its disposition, it would seem that the court assumed that they could be maintained under the ADEA. Bishop v Jelleff Assocs, 4 FEP Cas (BNA) 1262 (DDC 1972), is confusing. The court required class members to file consents—a requirement embodied in §16(b) of the FLSA—yet it also held that the requirements of Rule 23 were satisfied and thus allowed a class action to proceed. In Watson v Fuller Brush Co, 570 F Supp 1299 (WD Mich 1983), the court erroneously allowed a class action to proceed. (Actually, the opinion is not clear in affirmatively stating that the court was addressing a Rule 23 class suit, although it likely was inasmuch as the plaintiffs were pursuing claims both under the ADEA and under Title VII of the Civil Rights Act of 1964, 42 USC §§2000e through 2000e-17, and under the latter Act Rule 23 class actions may be maintained).

For a commentator's argument that Rule 23 class actions should be allowed, see Comment, *Class Actions under the Age Discrimination in Employment Act: The Question is "Why Not?"*, 23 Emory LJ 831 (1974).

1404 See **ch 9.**

1405 *See* Danielson v Fletcher, 132 FRD 489 (ND Ohio 1990). See generally **ch 9.**

1406 513 F2d 286 (5th Cir 1975).

1407 *Id* 289. This is one of those instances when the ADEA clearly departs from the statute on which it is generally modeled, Title VII of the Civil Rights Act of 1964. 42 USC §§2000e through 2000e-17. The argument has been made and rejected that because of the similitude of the two statutes, the fact that Rule 23 class actions may be pursued under Title VII should lead to a like conclusion as to the ADEA. Naton v Bank of Cal, 72 FRD 550 (ND Cal 1976), *affd,* 649 F2d 691 (9th Cir 1979). While, in contrast, the court deciding Blankenship v Ralston Purina Co, 62 FRD 35 (ND Ga 1973), supported this argument, it was effectively overruled by decisions of the Court of Appeals

It follows that in §16(b) representative actions there is no need for plaintiffs to comply with the requirements of Rule 23.[1408] There may be complications, however, where there is a pendent state claim brought as a Rule 23 class action; Rule 23 issues thereby come into play insofar as the federal cause of action is concerned.[1409]

Just as an ADEA plaintiff (who is not a present or former federal employee or an applicant for federal employment) may not bring a class action under Rule 23, a defendant also is barred from securing an order directing that a group of individual plaintiffs who raise like questions of law and fact be treated as a Rule 23 class.[1410]

The Case for Applying Federal Rule of Civil Procedure 23 in the ADEA Context

A persuasive case has been made for requiring the named plaintiff in an ADEA representative action to satisfy the require-

---

for the Fifth Circuit holding that Rule 23 class actions are not available. *See, e.g.*, Price v Maryland Casualty Co, 561 F2d 609 (5th Cir 1977); LaChapelle v Owens-Illinois, Inc, 513 F2d 286 (5th Cir 1975). The *La Chapelle* trial court, which sat in the same district as the earlier *Blankenship* court, explicitly rejected *Blankenship.* LaChapelle v Owens-Illinois, Inc, 64 FRD 96, 97 (ND Ga 1974), *affd,* 513 F2d 286 (5th Cir 1975).

1408 *See, e.g.*, Kinney Shoe Corp v Vorhes, 564 F2d 859 (9th Cir 1977) (non-ADEA suit); Locascio v Teletype Corp, 74 FRD 108, 111 (ND Ill 1977); Roshto v Chrysler Corp, 67 FRD 28, 29 (ED La 1975); Cooke v Reynolds Metals Co, 65 FRD 539 (ED Va 1975); Burgett v Cudahy Co, 361 F Supp 617 (D Kan 1973). Of course, there must be compliance with §16(b) of the FLSA; accordingly, in the absence of a consent filed by an opt-in plaintiff, the putative representative plaintiff may not maintain a representative action. *See, e.g.*, Osborne v United Tech Corp, 16 FEP Cas (BNA) 586 (D Conn 1977). As to the matter of consent, see **§6.51.**

1409 In Sperling v Hoffman-LaRoche, Inc, 118 FRD 392, 411-12 (DNJ), *affd on other grounds,* 862 F2d 439 (3d Cir 1988), *affd,* 493 US 165 (1989), the plaintiffs themselves limited membership in the class pursuing the state claim to just those people who were members of the ADEA representative action. In Robinson v Sizes Unlimited, Inc, 685 F Supp 442 (DNJ 1988), it was the court that limited the Rule 23 class, confining it to those individuals who had opted into the ADEA representative action.

1410 Gray v Continental Airlines, Inc, 29 Empl Prac Dec (CCH) ¶32,865 (CD Cal 1982).

ments of Rule 23 insofar as those requirements are consistent with §16 of the FLSA. The district court that decided *Shushan v University of Colorado at Boulder*[1411] reasoned in part as follows as to §16:

> While the "opt-in" feature of Section . . . [16] is manifestly "irreconcilable" . . . with the "opt-out" feature of rule 23, it does not necessarily follow that every other feature of rule 23 is similarly irreconcilable with Section . . . [16]. . . . If rule 23 were wholly inapplicable, then an ADEA class under Section . . . [16] would be practically formless: the only requirement in the statute itself is embodied in the vague provision that the representative and the class members must be similarly situated.[1412]

The court interpreted the legislative history as not standing in the way of its reliance on Rule 23 for guidance. And it went on to debunk the argument that Rule 23 should be inapplicable because it serves to protect class members who are not before the court, yet who are bound by court judgments, whereas under the ADEA only people who affirmatively have opted in are involved in any given lawsuit:

> First, the procedures embodied in rule 23 are designed not only to protect the rights of class members, but also to allow effective disposition and management of the litigation. For example, the requirement[s] [of Rule 23] that the class be "numerous" . . ., the requirement that there be "questions of law or fact common to the class" . . ., or the requirement that, in one type of action, common questions of law or fact "predominate over any questions affecting only individual members" have . . . little to do with protection of class rights and much to do with handling the lawsuit effectively. Second, the fact that a person must file his written consent

---

1411 132 FRD 263, 265 (D Colo 1990); *see also* Church v Consolidated Freightways, Inc, 137 FRD 294, 306 (ND Cal 1991).

1412 132 FRD at 266.

> before he is bound by any judgment should not significantly lessen the court's responsibility to protect his rights by employing the procedures provided in rule 23. For example, in contrast to a person who actually intervenes in the action, either in person or through counsel, the person who merely files his written consent should not be expected fully to appreciate actual or potential conflicts between himself and the class representatives or counsel for the class representatives. The court should protect him by insuring that the representatives will fully and adequately protect his interest. Fed. R. Civ. P. 23(a)(4).[1413]

What makes the *Shushan* court's analysis more relevant and thus more deserving of recounting than the analyses of earlier courts that looked to Rule 23 is the fact that *Shushan* was decided after *Hoffman-LaRoche Inc v Sperling,*[1414] and the *Shushan* court found in that Supreme Court ruling support for its position. The court pointed out that the *Sperling* Court, as discussed in **§6.46**, "confirmed that district courts have broad authority to control class actions and to prevent potential misuse of such actions."[1415] And the *Shushan* court went on from there with its analysis of *Sperling's* import:

> The ADEA class action after *Sperling* is more like the familiar class action under rule 23 than a permissive joinder device in which the passive role of the court is "to administer and monitor the litigation process. . . ." A predictable effect of *Sperling* is that district courts will be confronted with more motions . . . which seek to define a potential class in broad terms, to obtain discovery identifying all members of the class, and to notify all such persons so that they can decide whether to "opt-in" to the action. In dealing with such motions, I cannot see why the district courts should fail to

---

[1413] *Id* 267.

[1414] 493 US 165 (1989).

[1415] 132 FRD at 268.

> utilize existing procedures, embodied in rule 23, which are designed to promote effective management, prevent potential abuse, and protect the rights of all parties.[1416]

In *Woodall v Drake Hotel, Inc,*[1417] the Court of Appeals for the Seventh Circuit addressed the situation of two opt-in plaintiffs as to whom class counsel had withdrawn, with leave of court, from representation; who had not been able to retain replacement counsel; and whose claims were dismissed for want of prosecution following class counsel's having negotiated a settlement on behalf of the other 88 named and opt-in plaintiffs. The court was sympathetic to the plaintiffs' contention that even though Rule 23 is inapplicable to ADEA representative actions, in reality unnamed plaintiffs both in Rule 23 class actions and ADEA representative actions are similarly situated in terms of their need for court protection. In both instances, class members typically are not involved in settlement negotiations. In both instances they "must rely on class representatives and class counsel to protect their interests."[1418] In both instances "the interests of the class and class representatives or counsel . . . [sometimes] diverge: the individual interests of the class representative may be antagonistic to the class, or class counsel may be tempted to bargain-away class rights as part of fee arrangement negotiations."[1419] Thus, the *Woodall* court recognized some of the same concerns addressed in *Shushan.*

The court of appeals went on to hold that the district court had erred in dismissing the two plaintiffs' causes of action, doing so in terms limiting its holding to the particular facts presented to it:

> [The two plaintiffs], like the "absent" class members [in a Rule 23 class action, i.e., those individuals who are represented by a Rule 23 class representative and who thus are

---

1416 *Id.*

1417 913 F2d 447 (7th Cir 1990).

1418 *Id* 451.

1419 *Id.*

absent from involvement in the litigating of the case], must rely on the district court as a backstop to insure that the settlement was fair and reasonable. . . . Also, like "absent" [Rule 23] class members, . . . [the plaintiffs here] needed notice that their rights were in jeopardy. . . . Even though the settlement did not bind . . . [the plaintiffs here], it adversely affected their ability to achieve redress. A class of ninety yields much greater bargaining power than a class of two. . . .

Thus, although we stop short of holding that Rule 23(e) should be applied generally to all ADEA class actions, it is clear in this case that because . . . [the two opt-in plaintiffs] did not receive notice of the proposed settlement, the district court abused its discretion by dismissing the class cause of action by reason of settlement.[1420]

§6.46 —Issuance of Notice

Suits brought under the Age Discrimination in Employment Act (ADEA)[1421] are not maintainable as class actions under Federal Rule of Civil Procedure 23.[1422] Rather, §16(b)[1423] of the Fair Labor Standards Act (FLSA)[1424] sets forth the exclusive means for pursuing class, or representative, actions by ADEA claimants. A key issue regarding such actions that has generated a number of judicial rulings is whether notice may be issued to prospective opt-in class members, whereby they are informed of the existence of the suit filed by the notice issuer and their opportunity to join it as plaintiffs.[1425] Ultimately, the question

---

[1420] *Id* 451-52.

[1421] 29 USC §§621-634.

[1422] Fed R Civ P 23. See **§6.45.**

[1423] 29 USC §216(b).

[1424] *Id* §§200-219.

[1425] As discussed in **§6.45**, an individual must affirmatively opt into an ADEA representative action; he or she does not automatically become a member of a plaintiff class simply by virtue of the plaintiff's seeking to represent a class, as is the situation in a Rule 23 class action.

of whether notice could issue was resolved in the affirmative by the Supreme Court in 1989 in *Hoffman-LaRoche Inc v Sperling.*[1426]

Pre-*Hoffman-LaRoche* Case Law

One position taken by some of the courts in rulings handed down prior to *Hoffman-La Roche* was that notice could not issue.[1427] *Kinney Shop Corp v Vorhes,*[1428] a non-ADEA decision, was the leading case. The court articulated two bases for its stance. First, it reasoned that permitting notice to be sent to potential plaintiffs would constitute solicitation of claims and could stir up litigation. Second, the court was of the view that the due process considerations that apply in Federal Rule of Civil Procedure 23 class actions did not pertain in §16(b) class actions. Under Rule 23 class members are bound by the determination in the case; thus, because they have rights and interests at stake, due process requires that they be afforded the opportunity to opt out of the litigation, thereby avoiding being bound. In contrast, a litigant is not bound in a §16(b) action unless he or she affirmatively opts in; thus, notice as a protective device required by due process is not needed.

A third basis for reading §16(b) as not authorizing the issuance of notice to prospective class members was grounded in the language and legislative history of the provision: in *Roshto v Chrysler Corp,*[1429] an ADEA suit, the court concluded that the "failure to provide for notice to the class can not [sic] be attributed to mere [legislative] oversight."[1430]

1426 493 US 165 (1989).

1427 *See* McKenna v Champion Intl Corp, 747 F2d 1211 (8th Cir 1984); Kinney Shoe Corp v Vorhes, 564 F2d 859 (9th Cir 1977); Watkins v Milliken & Co, 613 F Supp 408 (WDNC 1984); Mahoney v Crocker Natl Bank, 571 F Supp 287 (ND Cal 1983); Baker v Michie Co, 93 FRD 494 (WD Va 1982); Montalto v Morgan Guar Trust Co, 83 FRD 150 (SDNY 1979); Wagner v Loew's Theaters, Inc, 76 FRD 23 (MDNC 1977); McGinley v Burroughs Corp, 402 F Supp 903 (ED Pa 1975). *See also* Madrigal v Green Giant Co, 92 Lab Cas (CCH) ¶34,068 (ED Wash 1981); Joyce v Sandia Labs, 22 FEP Cas (BNA) 1727 (ND Cal 1980).

1428 564 F2d 859 (9th Cir 1977).

1429 67 FRD 28 (ED La 1975).

1430 *Id* 29.

In light of *Hoffman-La Roche, Kinney Shoe* and like rulings are no longer viable. Not all pre-*Hoffman-La Roche* case law was necessarily rendered defunct by the Supreme Court ruling, however. A far less absolute position, and one consistent with *Hoffman-La Roche,* was asserted in a number of other lower court decisions, most of them not arising under the ADEA, handed down prior to the 1989 Supreme Court ruling: they read §16(b) as permitting, although not requiring, the issuance of notice in "appropriate cases."[1431]

The leading decision espousing this approach was *Braunstein v Eastern Photographic Laboratories,*[1432] a non-ADEA case. In a per curiam opinion the Court of Appeals for the Second Circuit justified allowing notice by invoking "the broad remedial purpose of the . . . [FLSA], . . . as well as . . . the interest of the courts in avoiding multiplicity of suits."[1433] While the *Braunstein* court acknowledged concerns about the stirring up of litigation and

---

[1431] *See* Braunstein v Eastern Photographic Labs, 600 F2d 335, 336 (2d Cir 1978), *cert denied,* 441 US 944 (1979); Palmer v Reader's Digest Assn, Inc, 42 FEP Cas (BNA) 212 (SDNY 1986); Palmer v Reader's Digest Assn, Inc, 42 FEP Cas (BNA) 209 (SDNY 1986); Libront v Columbus McKinnon Corp, 36 FEP Cas (BNA) 878 (WDNY 1984); Lusardi v Xerox Corp, 99 FRD 89 (DNJ 1983), *appeal dismissed on other grounds,* 747 F2d 174 (3d Cir 1984); Neizil v Williams, 96 Lab Cas (CCH) ¶34,328 (MD Fla 1983); Kempton v Southland Corp, 90 Lab Cas (CCH) ¶33,984 (WD Tex 1981); Dicky v Wendy's Intl, 24 Wage & Hour Cas (CCH) 1026 (ND Ga 1980); Hubbard v Rubbermaid, Inc, 87 Lab Cas (CCH) ¶33,852 (D Md 1979); *see also In re* National Airlines, 14 FEP Cas (BNA) 1795 (SD Fla 1976). In both Heagney v European Am Bank, 122 FRD 125 (EDNY 1988), and Lilligren v Midwest Communications, Inc, 51 FEP Cas (BNA) 592, 594-95 (D Minn 1989), the courts neither directed nor prohibited the issuance of notice, thereby allowing the plaintiffs to proceed with their planned notices.

[1432] 600 F2d 335 (2d Cir 1978), *cert denied,* 441 US 944 (1979).

[1433] *Id* 336. ADEA courts have echoed this "broad remedial purpose" notion. *See* Equal Employment Opportunity Commn v Chrysler Corp, 546 F Supp 54 (ED Mich 1982), *affd on other grounds,* 733 F2d 1183 (6th Cir 1984); Allen v Marshall Field & Co, 93 FRD 438 (ND Ill 1982); Johnson v American Airlines, Inc, 531 F Supp 957 (ND Tex 1982), *affd on other grounds,* 745 F2d 988 (5th Cir 1984), *cert denied,* 472 US 1027 (1985); Frank v Capital Cities Communications, Inc, 88 FRD 674 (SDNY 1981).

solicitation of claims, it discounted them,[1434] reasoning that the trend in the case law increasingly extending First Amendment protection to lawyer advertising[1435] diminished the weight of such concerns.

Courts addressing ADEA claims prior to *Hoffman-La Roche* likewise took a pro-issuance stance.[1436] For example, in 1982 the Court of Appeals for the Seventh Circuit reasoned that, while there was no legislative history on the matter, it was "unlikely that Congress, having created a procedure for representative actions, would have wanted to prevent the class representative from notifying other members of the class that they had a champion."[1437] And the Court of Appeals for the Third Circuit approved a trial court's discretionary authority to issue notice.[1438]

In the Tenth Circuit the Court of Appeals, in *Dolan v Project Construction Corp,*[1439] ruled that district courts did not have authority to issue notice to potential plaintiffs. At the same time, however, the court was not willing to hold that the representative plaintiff's attorney was barred from sending out notice. The court stated that judges "should be particularly hesitant to restrict written communication between parties and potential

---

1434 *See also* Allen v Marshall Field & Co, 93 FRD 438 (ND Ill 1982); Monroe v United Airlines, Inc, 90 FRD 638 (ND Ill 1981); Frank v Capital Cities Communications, Inc, 88 FRD 674 (SDNY 1981); Soler v G&U, Inc, 86 FRD 524 (SDNY 1980).

1435 The court specifically cited Bates v State Bar, 433 US 350 (1977). Subsequent to *Bates* several additional decisions were rendered by the Court, including Shapero v Kentucky Bar Assn, 486 US 446 (1988).

1436 See cases cited in note 1433.

1437 Woods v New York Life Ins Co, 686 F2d 578, 581 (7th Cir 1982); *accord* Vivone v Acme Mkts, Inc, 105 FRD 65 (ED Pa 1985). (*Woods* was preceded by district court rulings in the Seventh Circuit holding that notice could issue. *See* Allen v Marshall Field & Co, 93 FRD 438 (ND Ill 1982); Monroe v United Airlines, Inc, 90 FRD 638 (ND Ill 1981). *Woods* of course controlled subsequent district court determinations in the Seventh Circuit. *See* Behr v Drake Hotel, 586 F Supp 427 (ND Ill 1984)).

1438 Sperling v Hoffman-La Roche Inc, 862 F2d 439 (3d Cir 1988), *affd,* 493 US 165 (1989).

1439 725 F2d 1263 (10th Cir 1984).

opt-in plaintiffs."[1440] *Dolan*, then, did not foreclose all communication between a representative plaintiff and potential opt-in individuals; it only rejected the issuance of notice by, or with the approval of, the courts,[1441] which is a restrictive position regarding the judicial role that is no longer viable in light of *Hoffman-La Roche.*

The Court of Appeals for the Eleventh Circuit, in deciding *Haynes v Singer Co, Inc,*[1442] declined to choose between a rule barring notice and one allowing it. The Court of Appeals for the District of Columbia, while also recognizing the split in authority, likewise offered no resolution for it.[1443]

Hoffman-La Roche

In *Hoffman-La Roche Inc v Sperling*[1444] the Supreme Court enthusiastically supported the proposition that notice could issue in ADEA representative suits. More than that, the Court emphatically supported judicial involvement, albeit of a limited and barely defined nature, in the notice issuance process.[1445] The Court based its stances on the underlying policy goal of efficient judicial administration:

> A collective action allows age discrimination plaintiffs the advantage of lower individual costs to vindicate rights by the pooling of resources. The judicial system benefits by efficient resolution in one proceeding of common issues of law and fact arising from the same alleged discriminatory activity.

1440 *Id* 1268.

1441 *Accord* Burt v Manville Sales Corp, 116 FRD 276 (D Colo 1987); Walker v Mountain States Tel & Tel Co, 112 FRD 44, 47 (D Colo 1986); Owens v Bethlehem Mines Corp, 108 FRD 207 (SD W Va 1985); *see also* Hallas v Western Elec Co, Inc, 26 Empl Prac Dec (CCH) ¶31,958 (SD Ohio 1981).

1442 696 F2d 884 (11th Cir 1983).

1443 Thompson v Sawyer, 678 F2d 257, 270 n8 (DC Cir 1982). At least one district court in the jurisdiction did subscribe to the pro-notice position. *See* Held v National RR Passenger Corp, 101 FRD 420 (DDC 1984).

1444 493 US 165 (1989).

1445 See **§§6.47-.50.**

> These benefits, however, depend on employees receiving accurate and timely notice concerning the pendency of the collective action, so that they can make informed decisions about whether or not to participate.[1446]

The Court did not offer much by way of specifics as to judicial involvement in the notice process. Clearly, the Court saw the trial court's role as one involving the exercise of discretion insofar as the content and distribution of notices is concerned.[1447] The Court did not say, however, whether notice could issue without judicial permission. As already discussed, some of the pre-*Hoffman-La Roche* courts took the position that they would neither bar nor approve notices, but rather would simply stand aside. Whether that posture is still tenable is unclear. The Court's enthusiastic endorsement of the benefits derived from judicial "monitoring [of the] preparation and distribution of . . . notice[s]"[1448] certainly suggests, however, the Court's strong preference for judicial involvement, even if the Court did not actually preclude the issuance of notices without such involvement.

§6.47 —Circumstances under which Notice Should Issue

In *Hoffman-La Roche Inc v Sperling*[1449] the Supreme Court endorsed the proposition that notice could issue to potential opt-in plaintiffs in suits litigated under the Age Discrimination in Employment Act.[1450] The Court clearly envisioned an active

---

1446 493 US at 486.

1447 "By monitoring preparation and distribution of the notice, a court can ensure that it is timely, accurate, and informative." *Id* 487.

1448 *Id.*

1449 493 US 165 (1989).

1450 29 USC §§621-634.

role for district courts in the notice issuance process.[1451] It did not, however, offer much by way of specifics.[1452] In particular, the Court, while recognizing that judicial authorization of notice lay in the trial court's discretion, did not specify when that discretion should be affirmatively exercised and when a court should veto the issuance of notices. Indeed, as discussed in **§6.46**, the Court even left undecided the question of whether notice could issue at all without judicial approbation.

Pre-*Hoffman-La Roche* case law presumably continues to afford useful guidance.[1453]

Unrestricted Issuance of Notice

One position would be that notice can always issue when a plaintiff seeks to pursue a representative action, as long as the formal requisites[1454] are satisfied. Arguably, *Woods v New York Life Insurance Co*[1455] supports this position: the Court of Appeals for the Seventh Circuit approved the issuance of notice in representative actions without hedging its approval with caveats limiting notice issuance just to certain situations. *Hoffman-La Roche* neither rejects nor unmistakably supports this absolutist position arguably attributable to *Woods*. Still, in *Hoffman-La Roche* the Court explicitly put forth the notion that an appropriate judicial role is to monitor, indeed, quite actively supervise, the "preparation and distribution of the notice[.]"[1456] Thus, a notice issuance process entailing notice always being issuable (if not actually issued), with or without judicial involvement, does not seem to square with the Supreme Court ruling.

[1451] See **§6.46.**

[1452] Indeed, the Court stated: "[W]e decline to examine the terms of the notice used here, or its concluding statement indicating court authorization. We confirm the existence of the trial court's discretion, not the details of its exercise." 493 US at 170.

[1453] *See generally* Note, *Notice to Class Members under the Fair Labor Standards Act Representative Action Provision,* 17 U Mich JL Ref 25 (1983).

[1454] See **§6.48.**

[1455] 686 F2d 578 (7th Cir 1982).

[1456] 493 US at 172.

Issuance of Notice in Appropriate Cases

In *Braunstein v Eastern Photographic Laboratories, Inc,*[1457] a non-ADEA decision to which numerous ADEA courts have looked for guidance, the court approved the proposition that notice could issue in "appropriate cases."[1458] The court did not, however, explain the basis for the district court's unreported order, which authorized notice and which the appellate court affirmed. Later cases do offer illustration, if not illumination, as to factual settings in which the issuance of notice has been either deemed appropriate or inappropriate.

The court deciding *Severtson v Phillips Beverage Co*[1459] took the position that "[t]o obtain court authorization to send . . . notice, [ADEA] plaintiffs must submit evidence establishing at least a colorable basis for their claim that a class of 'similarly situated' plaintiffs exist[s]."[1460] In *Johnson v American Airlines, Inc,*[1461] the plaintiffs were flight deck crew members involuntarily retired at age 60 because they were not allowed the option by the defendant of working in the position of flight engineer on reaching that age. They moved the court to allow the issuance of notice to persons similarly situated. In granting the motion the court compared the case before it to two Fair Labor Standards Act[1462] cases in which notice was authorized to issue to migrant farm workers, many of whom were indigent and were illiterate or non-English speaking, and who, in addition, were difficult to locate because of their peripatetic life styles.[1463] The court rejected the

---

1457 600 F2d 335 (2d Cir 1978), *cert denied,* 441 US 944 (1979).

1458 *Id* 336.

1459 137 FRD 264 (D Minn 1991).

1460 *Id* 267. The "similarly situated" terminology derives from §16(b) of the Fair Labor Standards Act, 29 USC §216(b), which is incorporated into the ADEA by §7(b) of the ADEA, 29 USC §626(b). As to determining when individuals are similarly situated, see **§6.50.**

1461 531 F Supp 957 (ND Tex 1982), *affd on other grounds,* 745 F2d 988 (5th Cir 1984), *cert denied,* 472 US 1027 (1985).

1462 29 USC §§200-219.

1463 Soler v G&U, Inc, 86 FRD 524 (SDNY 1980); Riojas v Seal Produce, Inc, 82 FRD 613 (SD Tex 1979).

airline crew members' high educational levels and incomes as justifications for denying notice. It viewed notice in the case before it as particularly appropriate because potential plaintiffs were scattered throughout the country and not likely to learn of the lawsuit through other means. Although the named plaintiffs had delayed two years in requesting the notice, the court concluded as follows: "[A]uthorization of class notice is appropriate in the instant action, for such notice will promote both the Court's interest in judicial economies as well as the broad remedial purposes of the ADEA by affording potential plaintiffs the maximum opportunity to vindicate their statutory rights."[1464]

If one emphasizes the factual characteristics of *Johnson,* the import of the case can be narrowed to a situation where the potential plaintiffs are geographically dispersed. On the other hand, the court's underlying thrust seems a broader one, aimed at "affording potential plaintiffs the maximum opportunity to vindicate their . . . rights."[1465]

In *Allen v Marshall Field & Co*[1466] the intended recipients of the notice were managerial employees of a large department store company that was charged with violating the ADEA. The defendant argued that newspaper articles and television reports about the case had adequately apprised potential claimants of the suit. The court rejected this contention, viewing such articles and reports as constituting "at best a hit-or-miss form of notice."[1467] The court justified notice as being appropriate on two grounds. First, the employer had publicly denied any discrimination against the named plaintiffs. Second, there was an uncontradicted allegation that the defendant had failed to post any notice, or otherwise inform its employees of information, regarding their rights under the ADEA, and it had thereby failed to comply

---

[1464] 531 F Supp at 961.

[1465] *Id.*

[1466] 93 FRD 438 (ND Ill 1982).

[1467] *Id* 443; *see also* Frank v Capital Cities Communications, Inc, 88 FRD 674, 677 (SDNY 1981).

with §8[1468] of the statute.[1469] Thus, by both action and omission the defendant employer had made formal notice of the suit necessary.[1470] In contrast, in *Kempton v Southland Corp*[1471] the court found no factual justification for allowing notice to issue. It relied on the fact that written notices published by the Department of Labor regarding employees' statutory rights were posted in all the defendant's stores.

§6.48 —Terms and Timing of the Notice

The Terms of the Notice

While the Supreme Court, in deciding *Hoffman-LaRoche Inc v Sperling*,[1472] enthusiastically endorsed judicial involvement in the notice issuance process, it offered little by way of specific guidance as to what this entailed. The Court asserted that "[b]ecause trial court involvement in the notice process is inevitable in cases with numerous plaintiffs where written consent is required by statute, it lies within the discretion of a district court to begin its involvement early, at the point of the initial notice, rather than at some later time."[1473] The Court amplified this pronouncement to some extent:

> The [district] court is not limited to waiting passively for objections about the manner in which the consents were obtained. By monitoring preparation and distribution of the notice, a [district] court can ensure that it is timely, accu-

---

[1468] 29 USC §627.

[1469] See **ch 3.**

[1470] Perhaps the import of the decision may be narrowed by virtue of the fact that the defendant in *Allen* was a particularly large company, and thus a suit filed against it—and the defendant's correlative denial in the media of wrongdoing—would garner more publicity than would suits in many other instances.

[1471] 90 Lab Cas (CCH) ¶33,984 (WD Tex 1981).

[1472] 493 US 165 (1989).

[1473] *Id* 171.

> rate, and informative. Both the parties and the court benefit from settling disputes about the content of the notice before it is distributed.[1474]

Apart from these abstractions, little else emerged. The Court apparently recognized that it might be argued in some cases that the language of a given notice raised ethical problems, but it declined to deal with the issue: "We do not address any conflicts between court-authorized notice and communications with potential plaintiffs by counsel, see *Shapero v Kentucky Bar Assn.,* 486 U.S. 466 . . . (1988), as these issues are not implicated in the case before us."[1475] On one point, however, the Court did offer an emphatic, albeit somewhat vague, admonition: "In exercising the discretionary authority to oversee the notice-giving process, courts must be scrupulous to respect judicial neutrality. To that end, trial courts must take care to avoid even the appearance of judicial endorsement of the merits of the action."[1476] However, that which might constitute the "appearance of judicial endorsement" was not delineated in the decision.

Some guidance as to both (1) ethical concerns arising out of the appearance (or actuality) of solicitation, and (2) maintaining the appearance (and actuality) of judicial neutrality, is provided by lower court decisions. For example, while there is neither statutory nor regulatory prescription regarding the content of the notice to be sent to potential representative action members, in some cases court-approved notices have been reprinted.[1477]

(*Text continued on page 6-296*)

[1474] *Id* 172.

[1475] *Id* 171 n2.

[1476] *Id* 174.

[1477] *See, e.g.,* Mahoney v RFE/RL, Inc, 58 FEP Cas (BNA) 718 (DDC 1992); Sperling v Hoffman-LaRoche, Inc, 118 FRD 392, 415-17 (DNJ), *affd,* 862 F2d 439 (3d Cir 1988), *affd,* 493 US 165 (1989); Allen v Marshall Field & Co, 93 FRD 438 (ND Ill 1982); Johnson v American Airlines, Inc, 531 F Supp 957 (ND Tex 1982), *affd on other grounds,* 745 F2d 988 (5th Cir 1984), *cert denied,* 472 US 1027 (1985); Monroe v United Airlines, Inc, 90 FRD 638 (ND Ill 1981); Geller v Markham, 481 F Supp 835 (D Conn 1979), *affd in part & revd in part on other grounds,* 635 F2d 1027 (2d Cir 1980), *cert denied,* 451 US 945 (1981).

The notice in *Johnson,* printed at 531 F Supp 966-67, provided as follows:

TO: PERSONS EMPLOYED BY AMERICAN AIRLINES, INC., AS FIRST PILOTS (CAPTAINS), COPILOTS, OR FLIGHT OFFICERS, AND WHOSE SIXTIETH BIRTHDAYS ARE BETWEEN APRIL 6, 1978, AND DECEMBER 31, 1984.

RE: Age Discrimination in Employment Act (ADEA) action against American Airlines, Inc.

These cases were filed in 1979 by American flight deck crewmembers who allege they were involuntarily retired shortly after their sixtieth birthdays. Plaintiffs claim that American violated the ADEA, 29 U.S.C. §621 et seq., by refusing to permit them to transfer to the position of Flight Officer (flight engineer) on or after their sixtieth birthdays. They seek principally (1) to retain their employment and seniority at age 60 and beyond and (2) to obtain back pay and other amounts allegedly owing.

If you are among the persons to whom this notice is addressed and you wish to have your right to employment and seniority with American beyond your sixtieth birthday litigated in this case, you should file your consent to be made a party plaintiff with the Clerk of the Court. It is entirely your own decision whether or not to do so and, if you do elect to become a party plaintiff, whether you prefer to be represented by the present plaintiff's attorneys[1] or by an attorney of your choosing. If you file a consent through a separate attorney, your Notice of Consent should be under the caption of the cases as listed above, should contain your name, address, telephone number, date of birth, date of signing and signature, and should state: "I hereby consent to be a party plaintiff in this case."

As already stated, you are not required to join in this case by filing your consent or to take any action unless you want to. It is completely voluntary. However, your determination whether or not to take action should be made promptly. Unless a Notice of Consent is actually filed with the Court on or before ________, 1982, you will not be permitted to join this case.

If you do not file a consent form and join in this case, you will not receive any back wages or other relief from the case if the plaintiffs prevail here. Any such relief would be obtainable by you only if you proceeded by bringing an independent action within the time provided by law.

This notice is for the sole purpose of determining the identity of those persons who wish to be involved in this case. Although the Court has authorized the sending of this notice, there is no assurance at this time that the Court will grant any relief in this case.

The ADEA prohibits anyone from discriminating or retaliating against you if you choose to take part in this case.

C.R. Johnson, Fred G. Johnson, *et al.*

By: ______________________________

One of their Attorneys

By including within the notice direction to recipients that they may choose their own counsel and are not limited to the counsel sending the notice, judicial concerns about such notices constituting unethical solicitation should be alleviated.[1478]

In *Walker v Mountain States Telephone & Telegraph Co*[1479] the court found several deficiencies in the notice the plaintiffs had sent out. For one, the plaintiffs had captioned the consent forms included with the notice as pleadings. In addition, the notice failed to explain the right of each recipient to obtain independent counsel. Third, the consent forms had been sent out without notice to opposing counsel. The court required that new notice be issued and that the form of the notice be agreed to by all parties.

The Court of Appeals for the Seventh Circuit, in *Woods v New York Life Insurance Co,*[1480] took the position that notice should not be issued under the letterhead of the court itself, lest this imprint be misunderstood as a representation by the court that the suit probably had merit. To the argument by the plaintiff's attorney that this imprimatur was needed in order to shield him from a possible complaint under state law that he was trying to stir up

---

> This notice has been authorized by the Honorable Robert M. Hill, the Judge to whom the case is assigned.
>
> 1. Plaintiffs' attorneys are:
>
> . . .
>
> If you wish them to represent you, you should contact them directly. You will have the opportunity to discuss with them in detail the nature of this case, including attorney's fees, together with other obligations you may incur.

1478 *See, e.g.,* Libront v Columbus McKinnon Corp, 36 FEP Cas (BNA) 878 (WDNY 1984); Johnson v American Airlines, Inc, 531 F Supp 957, 961 (ND Tex 1982), *affd on other grounds,* 745 F2d 988 (5th Cir 1984), *cert denied,* 472 US 1027 (1985). Where the legal representation is provided by a not-for-profit public interest organization whose primary task is the provision of free legal services, such as a government-funded legal aid office, the consent form may specifically designate that organization to be the consenting plaintiff's legal representative. *See, e.g.,* Riojas v Seal Produce, Inc, 82 FRD 613 (SD Tex 1979) (non-ADEA case).

1479 112 FRD 44 (D Colo 1986).

1480 686 F2d 578 (7th Cir 1982); *accord* Behr v Drake Hotel, 586 F Supp 427 (ND Ill 1984).

litigation, the court responded that approval of the notice by the court would bar state disciplining, which, if attempted, would violate the Supremacy Clause of the United States Constitution.[1481]

The *Woods* court also addressed the obligations of plaintiff's counsel vis-a-vis opposing counsel:

> [W]e do not think it would have been proper for Woods or his counsel to have sent out . . . [notices] without first communicating to the defendant's counsel his intention to do so, so that the defendant's counsel would have an opportunity to verify the accuracy of the notice and, if he wished, to move for an order amending the notice or limiting its distribution in an appropriate manner.[1482]

As authority for this limitation placed on plaintiff's counsel, the court drew an inference from §16(b)[1483] of the Fair Labor Standards Act,[1484] the provision authorizing representative suits that is incorporated into the ADEA by §7(b) of the latter Act,[1485] and from Federal Rule of Civil Procedure 83, which provides that "in all cases not provided for by rule, the district courts may regulate their practice in any manner not inconsistent with" the Federal Rules of Civil Procedure.

In *Sperling v Hoffman-La Roche, Inc,*[1486] the six original plaintiffs had sent a letter and consent form to potential opt-in individuals. The defendant unsuccessfully argued that the letter and consent form were deficient in several ways, including the following: (1) they failed to indicate that a person opting in had to believe that he or she was a victim of age discrimination; (2) they failed to explain that one of the theories on which the suit was based was disparate impact; (3) they failed to advise that

---

[1481] US Const, art VI.

[1482] 686 F2d at 580.

[1483] 29 USC §216(b).

[1484] *Id* §§200-219.

[1485] *Id* §626(b).

[1486] 118 FRD 392 (DNJ), *affd on other grounds,* 862 F2d 439 (3d Cir 1988), *affd,* 493 US 165 (1989).

the defendant had denied the charges; (4) they failed to identify plaintiffs' counsel; (5) they failed to advise recipients that they could select their own counsel; and (6) they failed to disclose that a person who opted in might be required to participate in discovery. The court further found no problem with the fact that the involvement of the original plaintiffs' counsel in drafting the solicitation letter was not disclosed in the letter. Indeed, the court saw some advantages in this: "A letter from a lawyer inviting one to join an action may create false hopes of success, or dissuade one from engaging a disinterested professional for a second opinion. A letter from another non-lawyer, however, does neither."[1487]

Timing of the Notice

Notice need not be issued just at the time the initial complaint is filed.[1488]

§6.49 —Recipients of the Notice

By its terms, §16(b) of the Fair Labor Standards Act,[1489] which provision is incorporated into the Age Discrimination in Employment Act (ADEA) by §7(b) of the latter statute,[1490] only allows representative suits on behalf of persons similarly situated to the named plaintiff. It follows that such persons, and only such persons, are the proper recipients of notice of the pending suit.

The question of who is similarly situated for notice purposes is essentially one answered on the basis of the specific facts involved in a given case.[1491] The court deciding *Frank v Capital*

1487 *Id* 409.

1488 Heagney v European Am Bank, 122 FRD 125, 130 n5 (EDNY 1988).

1489 29 USC §216(b).

1490 *Id* §626(b).

1491 *See, e.g.*, Lusardi v Xerox Corp, 99 FRD 89, 93 n8 (DNJ 1983), *appeal dismissed on other grounds*, 747 F2d 174 (3d Cir 1984); Sussman v Vornado, Inc, 90 FRD 680 (DNJ 1981); Burgett v Cudahy Co, 361 F Supp 617, 622 (D Kan 1973).

Cities Communications, Inc,[1492] held that the burden of persuasion as to the question of who should receive notice was on the plaintiff, where there was disagreement as to whether certain employees were similarly situated to the named plaintiffs. The court also held that notice should not be sent to persons whose claims were time barred.[1493]

The requirements of Federal Rule of Civil Procedure 23 have been looked to as guideposts for determining whether a representative action should be allowed to proceed on the basis of the parties being similarly situated,[1494] and these requirements are also available for helping to make the separate, earlier determination as to whether the parties are similarly situated for notice purposes.[1495] However, failure to satisfy the complicated prerequisites of Rule 23 regarding numerosity, commonality, typicality, and adequacy of representation[1496] should not preclude a finding as to the parties being similarly situated for the purposes of §16(b). In other words, ADEA plaintiffs clearly do not have to satisfy the demands of Rule 23.[1497]

1492 88 FRD 674 (SDNY 1981).

1493 *Accord* Foster v CBS Records, Div of CBS, Inc, 109 FRD 168 (SDNY 1986). The *Frank* court later amended its ruling to authorize notice to individuals who only possibly were time barred. The amended ruling did not change the court's position, however, concerning individuals who unquestionably were time barred. Frank v Capital Cities Communications, Inc, 509 F Supp 1352 (SDNY 1981). As to the ability of time-barred individuals to consent to join in a representative suit, see **§6.22.**

1494 *See, e.g.,* Hays v Republic Steel Corp, 12 FEP Cas (BNA) 1637 (ND Ala 1974). See generally **§6.50.**

1495 *See* Geller v Markham, 481 F Supp 835 (D Conn 1979), *affd in part & revd in part on other grounds,* 635 F2d 1027 (2d Cir 1980), *cert denied,* 451 US 945 (1981). It does not follow automatically that all persons deemed similarly situated for notice purposes will ultimately be deemed similarly situated for class certification purposes. See **§6.50.**

1496 *See generally* H. Newberg, Newberg on Class Actions (Shepard's/McGraw-Hill 1992).

1497 *See, e.g.,* Kinney Shoe Corp v Vorhes, 564 F2d 859 (9th Cir 1977) (non-ADEA suit); Locascio v Teletype Corp, 74 FRD 108, 111 (ND Ill 1977); Roshto v Chrysler Corp, 67 FRD 28, 29 (ED La 1975); Cooke v Reynolds Metals Co, 65 FRD 539 (ED Va 1975); Burgett v Cudahy Co, 361 F Supp 617 (D Kan 1973). *But see* Shushan v University of Colo at Boulder, 132 FRD 263 (D Colo

In *Allen v Marshall Field & Co*[1498] the defendant argued that notice was not appropriate because the named plaintiffs occupied varying positions in the corporate hierarchy, worked in different stores in various geographic locations, and alleged discriminatory actions on varying dates. Opt-in claimants, it was argued, would further broaden these diverse characteristics of the class. Additionally, the defendant argued that notification of potential claimants would produce a class composed of both present and former employees, with possibly conflicting interests. The court, however, reasoned that the named plaintiffs had alleged a campaign of discrimination transcending differences in status, geography, and dates, and thus there was sufficient similarity among the named plaintiffs and potential opt-in claimants to warrant the issuance of notice.[1499]

Similarly, in deciding *Church v Consolidated Freightways, Inc,*[1500] the court concluded, at the early stage of the litigation that it was addressing, that the "fact that individuals in the class . . . [were] located in different areas, had different jobs, and left [their jobs] for different reasons should not preclude court facilitation of the notice process."[1501] The court, in assessing the contours of the notice to issue to potential opt-in plaintiffs, amplified on this reasoning by ruling that those deemed to be similarly situated to the named plaintiffs need not have claims which even were mentioned in the charges of unlawful discrimination filed with the Equal Employment Opportunity Commission (EEOC). It would be sufficient that "the claims in the [federal court] complaint and discriminatory policies alleged [vis-a-vis the opt-in plaintiffs] are reasonably related to the claims alleged in . . . [the named plaintiffs'] EEOC charge."[1502]

1990). *See also* Church v Consolidated Freightways, Inc, 137 FRD 294 (ND Cal 1991). See generally **§6.50.**

1498 93 FRD 438 (ND Ill 1982).

1499 *See also* Johnson v American Airlines, Inc, 531 F Supp 957 (ND Tex 1982), *affd on other grounds,* 745 F2d 988 (5th Cir 1984), *cert denied,* 472 US 1027 (1985).

1500 137 FRD 294 (ND Cal 1991).

1501 *Id* 308.

1502 *Id* 309.

Taking its guidance from *Allen,* the court deciding *Behr v Drake Hotel*[1503] reasoned that "differences among employees with respect to employment responsibilities or discriminatory injuries suffered does not mean they are . . . dissimilarly situated[.]"[1504] Accordingly, the court held that it was appropriate to send notice to a number of individuals.

In *Palmer v Reader's Digest Association, Inc,*[1505] the court asserted that, while the plaintiffs need not be identically situated to potential opt-in plaintiffs, there has to be "some identifiable factual nexus which binds the named plaintiffs and the potential class members together as victims of a particular, alleged discrimination."[1506] The district court that decided *Sperling v Hoffman-LaRoche, Inc*[1507] asserted "that notice to absent class members need not await a conclusive finding of 'similar situations.' "[1508] Turning to the facts before it, the court concluded that there was sufficient information regarding the similarly situated issue to allow class notice. The court stated as follows:

> Plaintiffs have made detailed allegations in their pleadings, and have supported those allegations with affidavits which successfully engage defendant's affidavits to the contrary. Plaintiffs' allegations, as supported, describe a single decision, policy, or plan of defendant's, infected by a discriminatory aspect which led to the termination or demotion of every member of the class plaintiffs wish to represent, and the reallocation of responsibilities among the remaining, generally younger workers.[1509]

1503 586 F Supp 427 (ND Ill 1984).

1504 *Id* 432.

1505 42 FEP Cas (BNA) 212 (SDNY 1986).

1506 *Id* 213.

1507 118 FRD 392 (DNJ), *affd on other grounds,* 862 F2d 439 (3d Cir 1988), *affd,* 493 US 165 (1989).

1508 *Id* 406.

1509 *Id.*

In *Yates v Reliance Electric Co*[1510] the court denied authorization for the issuance of notice because the plaintiff had failed to present any facts supporting his claim that there indeed were other, similarly situated people who were potential plaintiffs. The court cited two unreported decisions that took contrasting approaches to the notice issuance question. In one of these, i.e., *Klegerman v FG Apparel, Inc,*[1511] the plaintiff had alleged that others in addition to himself had been fired, but the court denied the plaintiff's request to distribute notice until such time as he demonstrated the propriety of an order authorizing notice. On the other hand, in the other unreported ruling relied upon by the *Yates* court, i.e., *Santaro v Illinois Bell Telephone,*[1512] the court held that the mere allegation that an employer had engaged in a discriminatory course of conduct indeed was sufficient to permit notification. The *Santaro* court reasoned that should it later appear that individuals who opted in as a result of the notice indeed only had individual claims, rather than claims arising out of an orchestrated plan of discrimination, the suit then could be restructured.

Defendant Assistance in Identifying and Contacting Notice Recipients

The defendant can be required to furnish the representative plaintiff with the names and addresses of its employees.[1513] It

---

1510 40 Empl Prac Dec (CCH) ¶36,266 (CD Ill 1986).

1511 1986 WL 2531 (ND Ill 1986).

1512 1984 WL 1411 (ND Ill 1984).

1513 *See, e.g.,* Hoffman-LaRoche Inc v Sperling, 493 US 165, 170 (1989); Woods v New York Life Ins Co, 686 F2d 578, 580 (7th Cir 1982); Pines v State Farm Gen Ins Co, 58 FEP Cas (BNA) 387, 396 (CD Cal 1992); Church v Consolidated Freightways, Inc, 137 FRD 294, 310 (ND Cal 1991); Palmer v Reader's Digest Assn, Inc, 42 FEP Cas (BNA) 209 (SDNY 1986); Vivone v Acme Markets, Inc, 105 FRD 65 (ED Pa 1985); Held v National RR Passenger Corp, 101 FRD 420, 425 (DDC 1984); Monroe v United Airlines, Inc, 90 FRD 638 (ND Ill 1981); Frank v Capital Cities Communications, Inc, 88 FRD 674 (SDNY 1981); Geller v Markham, 481 F Supp 835 (D Conn 1979), *affd in part & revd*

does not follow, however, that because the defendant is required to provide to the named plaintiff a list of the names and addresses of potential notice recipients, the plaintiff is precluded from sending notice to persons not on that list.[1514] The defendant also can be required to allow the posting of notices on public bulletin boards in its offices.[1515] However, a court also may refuse a request for such posting,[1516] and it further may refuse to order the defendant to mail the notice to its agency directors and managers where the mailing "would not increase measurably plaintiffs' audience, and would enable plaintiffs to gain some increased exposure at defendants' cost instead of their own."[1517] Notice also may be authorized for publication in the newspapers.[1518]

---

in part on other grounds, 635 F2d 1027 (2d Cir 1980), *cert denied,* 451 US 945 (1981). (A court order so requiring is not appealable. Lusardi v Xerox Corp, 747 F2d 174 (3d Cir 1984).) *See also* Severtson v Phillips Beverage Co, 137 FRD 264, 267 (D Mass 1991) ("names and addresses of all persons who fall within plaintiff's proposed class definition.")

In Dolan v Project Constr Corp, 725 F2d 1263 (10th Cir 1984), the court ruled that courts do not have the authority to order the production of names of potential plaintiffs "for the *sole* purpose of establishing or notifying the class." *Id* 1267; *accord* Watkins v Milliken & Co, 613 F Supp 408 (WDNC 1984). However, *Dolan* and *Watkins* are no longer viable, given Hoffman-LaRoche, Inc v Sperling, 493 US 165 (1989).

1514 Pines v State Farm Gen Ins Co, 58 FEP Cas (BNA) 387, 397 (CD Cal 1992).

1515 *See, e.g.,* Frank v Capital Cities Communications, Inc, 88 FRD 674 (SDNY 1981); *see also* Sperling v Hoffman-LaRoche, Inc, 118 FRD 392, 404-05 (DNJ), *affd on other grounds,* 862 F2d 439 (3d Cir 1988), *affd on other grounds,* 493 US 165 (1989), in which the court indicated that it would look favorably on ordering such posting, given the right facts and their adequate presentation to the court by the plaintiffs.

1516 Pines v State Farm Gen Ins Co, 58 FEP Cas (BNA) 387, 397 (CD Cal 1992).

1517 *Id.*

1518 *See* Geller v Markham, 481 F Supp 835 (D Conn 1979), *affd in part & revd in part on other grounds,* 635 F2d 1027 (2d Cir 1980), *cert denied,* 451 US 945 (1981).

§6.50 —Determination of Those Similarly Situated

Section 16(b)[1519] of the Fair Labor Standards Act (FLSA)[1520] only allows representative suits when the parties are "similarly situated." A like standard is utilized in determining whether class actions may be maintained under Federal Rule of Civil Procedure 23. That rule sets forth with particularity requirements for the maintenance of such class actions, and these requirements can be looked to as guideposts for determining whether the "similarly situated" requirement of §16(b) is satisfied.[1521] However, the requirements for satisfying Rule 23 are considerably more involved than is the unitary "similarly situated" requirement of §16(b),[1522] and thus it should be clear that a §16(b) representative action can be maintained notwithstanding that the requisites of Rule 23 are not met. Indeed, the courts are clear in rejecting the notion that, as a general matter, Rule 23 requirements must be satisfied in §16(b) representative actions.[1523]

The question of who is similarly situated to whom sufficiently to allow a representative action to proceed is determined on the basis of the specific facts involved in the dispute.[1524] A general

---

[1519] 29 USC §216(b).

[1520] *Id* §§200-219.

[1521] *See, e.g.*, Lusardi v Xerox Corp, 118 FRD 351, 358 n18 (DNJ 1987), *mandamus granted with direction to modify order on other grounds*, 855 F2d 1062 (3d Cir 1988); Hays v Republic Steel Corp, 12 FEP Cas (BNA) 1637 (ND Ala 1974); *see also* Heagney v European Am Bank, 122 FRD 125, 127 n2 (EDNY 1988); Frank v Capital Cities Communications, Inc, 33 Empl Prac Dec (CCH) ¶34,285, at p 33, 087 n1 (SDNY 1983).

[1522] *See generally* H. Newberg, Newberg on Class Actions (Shepard's/McGraw-Hill 1992). Without any enlightening explanation, two parties who were deemed to be situated similarly to the named plaintiffs were allowed to consent to opt in in Coffin v South Carolina Dept of Social Servs, 562 F Supp 579, 592 (DSC 1983).

[1523] *See, e.g.*, Kinney Shoe Corp v Vorhes, 564 F2d 859 (9th Cir 1977) (non-ADEA suit); Locascio v Teletype Corp, 74 FRD 108, 111 (ND Ill 1977); Roshto v Chrysler Corp, 67 FRD 28, 29 (ED La 1975); Cooke v Reynolds Metals Co, 65 FRD 539 (ED Va 1975); Burgett v Cudahy Co, 361 F Supp 617 (D Kan 1973).

[1524] *See, e.g.*, Sussman v Vornado, Inc, 90 FRD 680 (DNJ 1981); Erpelding v Thornhill, 18 FEP Cas (BNA) 1479 (ED Mich 1976); Burgett v Cudahy Co,

theme that can be identified, however, is that in order for claimants to be seen as being similarly situated, they must be able to point to having been victimized by the same policy of, or decision by, the defendant. Thus, for example, the court deciding *Church v Consolidated Freightways, Inc,*[1525] wrote as follows:

> [I]n general, the standards governing a conclusive finding of 'similar situations' 'appear to require nothing more than substantial allegations that the putative class members were together the victims of a single decision, policy, or plan infected by age discrimination.'[1526]

The plaintiffs need not show that their positions are identical, but rather only that they are similar.[1527] The Court of Appeals for the Third Circuit pointed to several factors in deciding *Lockhart v Westinghouse Credit Corp:*[1528]

> The opt-in plaintiffs in the present action were all former employees within the Financial Services Division of . . . [the defendant], albeit in different branch locations. They all claimed that they were terminated from their employment positions as a result of a pattern, plan or practice of willful

361 F Supp 617, 622 (D Kan 1973). For an unduly restrictive assessment of the facts, see Hays v Republic Steel Corp, 12 FEP Cas (BNA) 1637 (ND Ala 1974). The *Hays* court reasoned that since the Secretary of Labor had tried conciliation efforts as to the representative plaintiffs, but had not had an opportunity to do so as to the potential class members who sought to consent to enter the suit but who had not filed notices with the Labor Department, the representative plaintiffs and the potential class members were not similarly situated and therefore class action status should be denied.

[1525] 137 FRD 294 (ND Cal 1991); *see also* Pines v State Farm Gen Ins Co, 58 FEP Cas (BNA) 387, 394-95 (CD Cal 1992).

[1526] 137 FRD at 303 (quoting Sperling v Hoffman-LaRoche, Inc, 118 FRD 392, 407 (DNJ), *affd on other grounds,* 862 F2d 439 (3d Cir 1988), *affd,* 493 US 165 (1989)); *see also* Glass v IDS Fin Servs, Inc, 778 F Supp 1029, 1079-80 (D Minn 1991).

[1527] *See, e.g.,* Burt v Manville Sales Corp, 116 FRD 276 (D Colo 1987); Frank v Capital Cities Communications, Inc, 33 Empl Prac Dec (CCH) ¶34,285 (SDNY 1983); Allen v Marshall Field & Co, 93 FRD 438, 443 (ND Ill 1982); Riojas v Seal Produce, Inc, 82 FRD 613, 616 (SD Tex 1979) (non-ADEA case).

[1528] 879 F2d 43, 51-52 (3d Cir 1989).

> age discrimination that was conducted by . . . [the defendant]. Moreover, they all claimed the same relief[.][1529]

The court deciding *Plummer v General Electric Co*[1530] utilized the same factors (in fact, the later *Lockhart* court quoted them approvingly)[1531] in concluding that while five plaintiffs should be deemed to be similarly situated, four plaintiffs should not be:

> The record indicates that they are employed in various Departments and Divisions of General Electric . . . and therefore it is difficult to see how Plummer can be relied upon to represent them adequately. Moreover, the defenses raised by General Electric will turn to a significant degree on the particular individual's employment situation and the decisions of particular managers about these employees.[1532]

In *Allen v Marshall Field & Co*[1533] a district court held, over the defendant's objection that the opt-in parties' claims were dissimilar to those of the representative plaintiffs, that the latter plaintiffs' allegation that the defendant had conducted a campaign of company-wide age discrimination created a rebuttable presumption that the individual claimants were similarly situated.[1534]

While in fact the court deciding *Behr v Drake Hotel*[1535] only had before it the question of to whom notice could be sent, the court also addressed the issue of class determination. The court reasoned that "differences among employees with respect to employment responsibilities or discriminatory injuries does not

---

[1529] *Id* 52; *accord* Plummer v General Elec Co, 93 FRD 311, 312 (ED Pa 1982).

[1530] 93 FRD 311 (ED Pa 1982).

[1531] 879 F2d at 51.

[1532] 93 FRD at 312.

[1533] 29 FEP Cas (BNA) 314, 317 (ND Ill 1982).

[1534] *See also* Larson v Hartford Ins Co, 53 FEP Cas (BNA) 1023 (ND Ill 1990); Yates v Reliance Elec Co, 40 Empl Prac Dec (CCH) ¶36,266 (CD Ill 1986); Frank v Capital Cities Communications, Inc, 48 FEP Cas (BNA) 551 (SDNY 1983). *But see* Ulvin v Northwestern Natl Life Ins Co, 141 FRD 130 (D Minn 1991).

[1535] 586 F Supp 427 (ND Ill 1984).

mean that they are so dissimilarly situated as to render inappropriate opting into this case."[1536]

In *Owens v Bethlehem Mines Corp*[1537] the court was satisfied that there was sufficient similarity between the named plaintiff and the opt-in plaintiffs where, even though they worked in different divisions, they all were subjected to the same allegedly discriminatory reduction in force. In the court's view, "a systematic reduction of the work force" involves "a decision obviously . . . made at a high level in the organization" and it is this special nature of a reduction in force "which makes the broader class definition appropriate."[1538]

The court deciding *Walker v Mountain States Telephone & Telegraph Co*[1539] dealt with a defendant that ranked managers on a five-level scale. The representative plaintiffs had referred just to first and second level managers in the administrative charges of unlawful discrimination that they had filed with the Equal Employment Opportunity Commission (EEOC), and so the court limited the class of those similarly situated just to managers in these two levels.[1540] The charging parties also had alleged that persons under age 40 continued to perform the functions that prior to the representative plaintiffs' departures had been performed by those plaintiffs. Accordingly, the class further was limited by the court to those persons whose former job functions continued to be performed by employees under age 40.

In deciding *Glass v IDS Financial Services, Inc,*[1541] the district court espoused the proposition that inasmuch as the "similarly situated" requirement is inapplicable in suits filed by the EEOC because the statutory predicates for EEOC suits[1542] do not contain such a requirement, it follows that plaintiffs need not be sim-

---

[1536] *Id* 432.

[1537] 108 FRD 207 (SD W Va 1985).

[1538] *Id* 212; *see also* Heagney v European Am Bank, 122 FRD 125, 127-28 (EDNY 1988).

[1539] 112 FRD 44 (D Colo 1986).

[1540] As to the naming of alleged wrongdoers in charges, see **§§6.03, 6.06.**

[1541] 778 F Supp 1029 (D Minn 1991).

[1542] 29 USC §§216(c), 217. See **§6.60.**

ilarly situated in a representative action that is filed by a private litigant and in which the EEOC intervenes.[1543] On a different tack, the same court—in assessing whether the plaintiffs were similarly situated—took into account the financial burden on the plaintiffs if they were required to sue individually rather than allowed to join in a representative action:

> The court . . . determines that a class action will effectuate the remedial purpose of the ADEA because it will permit plaintiffs to lower their individual costs by pooling their resources to prosecute their age discrimination claims. . . . The individual plaintiffs are less able to bear the cost of separate trials because they have fewer resources than . . . [the defendant] and a class action will give them a fair and full opportunity to adjudicate their claims.[1544]

Several issues concerning framing the correct group of similarly situated individuals were addressed in *Pines v State Farm General Insurance Co.*[1545] One consideration was the temporal scope of the class. The plaintiff argued that the allegedly similarly situated individuals had been subjected to a longstanding continuing violation, i.e., the allegedly discriminatory hiring policies of the defendant, and therefore the temporal boundary of the class should go all the way back to June 12, 1968—the date on which the Age Discrimination in Employment Act (ADEA)[1546] went into effect. The court rejected the argument, pointing to the lack of evidence that the defendant's pre-ADEA manuals that embodied the allegedly discriminatory policies had been acted on during that long period. Accordingly, the court used a different temporal guideline, which the plaintiffs conceded would be the correct one to employ if their continuing violation argument were to be rejected:

[1543] 778 F Supp at 1081.

[1544] *Id.*

[1545] 58 FEP Cas (BNA) 387 (CD Cal 1992).

[1546] 29 USC §§621-634.

> [T]he opt-in plaintiffs should consist of those similarly situated who either filed a timely EEOC charge or who could have filed a timely charge on the same date as the named plaintiff (in other words, those who suffered from incidents which occurred 180 or 300 days before . . . [the representative plaintiff's] EEOC charge was filed, depending on the state where it occurred[.][1547]

The *Pines* defendant further argued that those persons who were deterred from seeking employment with it should not be deemed to be similarly situated to the named plaintiff, who in fact had applied and had been rejected. The court agreed:

> Those who were entirely dissuaded from applying for the . . . trainee agent position . . . suffered the indirect residual effects of . . . [the defendant's] selection process policy, whereas . . . [the named plaintiff] suffered directly and tangibly from her actual encounters with . . . [the defendant's] allegedly age-based questions and age discrimination policy.[1548]

The earlier conditional certification of a class of 1,300-plus plaintiffs was found to be unjustified by the district court that decided *Lusardi v Xerox Corp.*[1549] While the plaintiffs claimed they were all victimized by the same discriminatory reduction in force (RIF), the court—in light of data obtained through discovery following the conditional certification—concluded that the plaintiffs were not similarly situated because they presented numerous individualized defenses:

> The action taken by Xerox cannot be referred to as a single RIF [reduction in force]. There were more than sixty RIFs occurring over a four year period which were conducted and implemented by thousands of local supervisors pursu-

---

1547 58 FEP Cas (BNA) at 395.

1548 *Id* 396.

1549 118 FRD 351 (DNJ 1987), *mandamus granted with direction to modify order on other grounds,* 855 F2d 1062 (3d Cir 1988).

> ant to varying procedures. The facts of the RIFs together with the fact that Xerox will defend plaintiffs' claims on an individual basis, asserting any or more of many defenses in a method consistent with the ADEA, foreclose the possibility of the proposed class claimants going forward as similarly situated.[1550]

The Court of Appeals for the Third Circuit subsequently addressed the merits of the trial court's decertification ruling in the context of a mandamus action brought by the plaintiff. The argument was made that there was statistical proof offered by the plaintiff as to the disparate impact of the defendant's reduction in force, and that the presence of this proof constituted a common issue of fact making all the opt-in claimants similarly situated. The appellate court did not dispositively accept or reject this argument. Rather, assuming arguendo that statistical evidence could create a prima facie case of discrimination (an assumption in fact confirmed as correct by other courts),[1551] the court asserted as follows:

> [T]he law is not clear . . . that the presence of statistical evidence of a disparate impact or a pattern of discrimination deprives a district court of its discretion to decide whether to certify, or continue to certify, an opt-in class under FLSA §16(b). To say a district court has no discretion to refuse or revoke class certification in a §16(b) systemic discrimination case whenever there is statistical impact, for example, is equivalent to saying that all individuals in a protected class are "similarly situated" under FLSA §16(b) when statistical evidence indicates a personnel policy has a disparate impact on the protected class as a whole. We do not think that legal proposition is as yet established, and is certainly not yet established as a matter of clear law.[1552]

1550 *Id* 372.

1551 See **ch 7.**

1552 Lusardi v Lechner, 855 F2d 1062, 1073 (3d Cir 1988).

Ultimately, the court remanded on the issue of error in the notice of decertification that had been issued by the trial court. Subsequently, the lower court reconfirmed its position that class certification was unwarranted:

> The members of the proposed class come from different departments, groups, organizations, suborganizations, units and local offices within the Xerox organization. The opt-in plaintiffs performed different jobs at different geographic locations and were subject to different job actions concerning reductions in work force which occurred at various times as a result of various decisions by different supervisors made on a decentralized employee-by-employee basis.[1553]

Unlike Federal Rule of Civil Procedure 23(c)(1), which imposes a requirement that a class determination (commonly known as certification) be made by the court, §16(b) makes no provision for certification. Even so, the notion of certification has been used, as one of the foregoing quotations from the *Lusardi* ruling shows, and as is further seen in *Sussman v Vornado, Inc,*[1554] in which the district court stated that "[i]n order to certify the ADEA class the proper inquiry for this court is whether the plaintiff is 'similarly situated' to the other terminated employees. . . ."[1555] It should be clear, however, that the certifying to which the *Vornado* court referred is somewhat of a misnomer or is, at the least, misleading. Class certification is a Rule 23 enterprise; it is an important and complicated judicial function. Under §16(b) of the FLSA, compliance with Rule 23 by the plaintiffs is neither required nor appropriate. All that is needed is the filing of a consent—subject, if the court so orders, to the consent

---

1553 Lusardi v Xerox Corp, 122 FRD 463, 465 (DNJ 1988); *see also* Ulvin v Northwestern Natl Life Ins Co, 141 FRD 130, 131 (D Minn 1991).

1554 90 FRD 680 (DNJ 1981).

1555 *Id* 684; *see also* Lusardi v Xerox Corp, 747 F2d 174 (3d Cir 1984); Ulvin v Northwestern Natl Life Ins Co, 141 FRD 130, 131 (D Minn 1991); Owens v Bethlehem Mines Corp, 630 F Supp 309 (SD W Va 1986); Franci v Avco Corp, 460 F Supp 389 (D Conn 1978).

being filed within some set time[1556]—by a party who is similarly situated to the representative plaintiff. Obviously, the court is not totally passive; it can assure that the parties are indeed similarly situated. That determination, however, should not be confused with Rule 23 class certification, which involves a number of considerations that need not be addressed under §16(b). In brief, the notion of class action certification that is common in Rule 23 class actions is not appropriate for FLSA class actions.[1557]

A class 'certification' under the ADEA is not appealable, at least as long as the 'certification' is conditional in nature, because it is not a final judgment terminating the litigation.[1558]

§6.51 —Form and Timing of Consent

Form of Consent

Section 16(b)[1559] of the Fair Labor Standards Act,[1560] which provision is incorporated into the Age Discrimination in Employment Act (ADEA)[1561] by §7(b)[1562] of the latter statute, does not set out any particular format that must be followed by a person consenting to join in a representative action. The statute simply provides that the consent is to be in writing and that it is to be filed in the court in which the suit is brought. Of course, if an individual is a named plaintiff in the original complaint, he or she need not file a consent to join in the representative action. In brief, " 'parties named in a suit, who have hired a lawyer to file a complaint on their behalf, have clearly indicated their

---

1556 See **§6.51.**

1557 Hallas v Western Elec Co, Inc, 26 Empl Prac Dec (CCH) ¶31,958, at p21,320 (SD Ohio 1981). *But see* Church v Consolidated Freightways, Inc, 137 FRD 294, 306 (ND Cal 1991); Shushan v University of Colo at Boulder, 132 FRD 263 (D Colo 1990).

1558 Lusardi v Xerox Corp, 747 F2d 174 (3d Cir 1984).

1559 29 USC §216(b).

1560 *Id* §§200-219.

1561 *Id* §§621-634.

1562 *Id* §626(b).

consent to suit.' "[1563] Moreover, where a complaint states a separate cause of action for each named plaintiff, individual relief is sought as to each, and no plaintiff purports to represent anyone other than himself or herself, there is no representative suit and therefore no consents are needed.[1564] (A common question that has arisen is whether individuals who did not file charges of discrimination with the enforcement agency may consent to joining in a representative action. This issue is addressed in **§6.22**).

A few decisions afford some guidance as to the matter of the consent's format. A typewritten list of the names of allegedly consenting plaintiffs has been held to be inadequate.[1565] On the other hand, a photocopy of signatures was deemed sufficient by another court to establish written consent.[1566] Signatures appended to a typewritten statement requesting that "legal action be taken to secure my claim for me due me under the Fair Labor Standards Act" also was deemed adequate by the same court.[1567] Similarly, signatures on handwritten consent forms which were not prepared by the signatories, themselves, have survived challenge.[1568] At least one court has ruled that a consent need not be notarized.[1569]

An example of an adequate consent is set forth in *Pandis v Sikorsky Aircraft Division of United Technologies Corp:*[1570]

1563 Anderson v Montgomery Ward & Co, Inc, 852 F2d 1008, 1018 (7th Cir 1988) (quoting Allen v Atlantic Richfield Co, 724 F2d 1131, 1135 (5th Cir 1984)); *accord* Durant v Maher Chevrolet, Inc, 759 F Supp 787, 790 (MD Fla 1991).

1564 Morelock v NCR Corp, 586 F2d 1096, 1103 (6th Cir 1978), *cert denied,* 441 US 906 (1979); *see also* Franci v Avco Corp, 460 F Supp 389 (D Conn 1978).

1565 Kulick v Superior Pipe Specialties Co, 203 F Supp 938 (ND Ill 1962) (non-ADEA suit).

1566 Montalvo v Tower Life Bldg, 426 F2d 1135, 1148-49 (5th Cir 1970) (non-ADEA suit).

1567 *Id.*

1568 Riojas v Seal Produce, Inc, 82 FRD 613 (SD Tex 1979) (non-ADEA suit).

1569 Kuhn v Philadelphia Elec Co, 475 F Supp 324 (ED Pa 1979) (non-ADEA case).

1570 431 F Supp 793 (D Conn 1977).

> Class member-Plaintiff VOOS hereby consents to the maintenance of a suit on his behalf by Plaintiff NICHOLAS PANDIS as representative of the class to which both NICHOLAS PANDIS and CARLETON E. VOOS belong, and further consents to be bound by any judgment in that suit.[1571]

An opt-in plaintiff ordinarily would not be served with papers filed after he or she filed the written consent.[1572] Whether he or she is or is not served, a person who joins a suit simply by filing a consent "should not be expected fully to appreciate actual or potential conflicts between himself and the class representative or counsel for the class representative."[1573] Accordingly, "[t]he court should protect him [or her] by insuring that the representative will fully and adequately protect his [or her] interest."[1574] (This assertion was made by a court that took the rare—and largely rejected—view[1575] that the standards set forth in Federal Rule of Civil Procedure 23 should apply as long as they were not inconsistent with the requirements of §16(b) of the FLSA).

An opt-in plaintiff need not notify the attorney for the representative plaintiff of having opted in.[1576] For litigation purposes, however, such notification usually will be of benefit to the opt-in plaintiff.[1577]

The Timing of Consent

The consent to join in a representative action need not be filed

---

1571 *Id* 797.

1572 Shushan v University of Colo at Boulder, 132 FRD 263, 264 (D Colo 1990).

1573 *Id* 267.

1574 *Id.*

1575 See **§6.50.**

1576 Monroe v United Air Lines, Inc, 565 F Supp 271 (ND Ill 1983), *revd on other grounds,* 736 F2d 394 (7th Cir 1984), *cert denied,* 470 US 1004 (1985).

1577 *Id.*

at the same time the suit itself is filed.[1578] Indeed, in many instances consenting parties will not even know of the suit until some time after it has been commenced, and thus the "opportunity to 'opt-in' continues at least until a reasonable time prior to the trial of the case."[1579] However, it would be unfair to the defendant to keep it in ignorance as to the full roster of plaintiffs. Accordingly, courts have often set cutoff dates for the appearance of additional plaintiffs, based on the premise that the defendant should have sufficient time before trial adequately to prepare a defense against each plaintiff.[1580]

If there is no prejudice to the defendant, a court may allow plaintiffs to opt in even after the cutoff date.[1581] In *Owens v Bethle-*

[1578] *See, e.g.,* Wagner v Loew's Theatres, Inc, 76 FRD 23, 24 (MDNC 1977).

[1579] *Id.*

[1580] *See, e.g.,* Pines v State Farm Gen Ins Co, 58 FEP Cas (BNA) 387, 397 (120 days after defendant supplies to plaintiffs names and addresses of people to whom notices will be sent regarding their opportunity to opt into suit); Mahoney v Crocker Natl Bank, 571 F Supp 287 (ND Cal 1983) (90 days before trial date); Johnson v American Airlines, Inc, 531 F Supp 957 (ND Tex 1982), *affd on other grounds,* 745 F2d 988 (5th Cir 1984), *cert denied,* 472 US 1027 (1985) (21 days after receipt of notice of option to opt into suit); Joyce v Sandia Labs, 22 FEP Cas (BNA) 1727 (ND Cal 1980) (within 60 days); Locascio v Teletype Corp, 74 FRD 108, 112 (ND Ill 1977) ("Defendant is entitled, at some point before trial, to a final list of the plaintiffs"); Naton v Bank of Cal, 72 FRD 550, 556 (ND Cal 1976), *affd on other grounds,* 649 F2d 691 (9th Cir 1981); Roshto v Chrysler Corp, 67 FRD 28 (ED La 1975) (consents must be filed at least 30 days prior to trial); Bishop v Jelleff Assocs, 4 FEP Cas (BNA) 1262, 1262 (DDC 1972) ("reasonable time," i.e., 45 days from date of court order); Wright v United States Rubber Co, 69 F Supp 621 (SD Iowa 1946) (non-ADEA suit); Wilson v FJ Egner & Sons, 53 F Supp 847 (ND Ohio 1944) (non-ADEA suit; consents must be filed at least 30 days prior to trial).

Without gearing its setting of a cutoff date to the question of fairness for the defendant, the court deciding Watkins v Milliken & Co, 613 F Supp 408 (WDNC 1984), allowed 30 days for opting in.

[1581] *See* Monroe v United Air Lines, Inc, 94 FRD 304 (ND Ill 1982). In Carter v Marshall, 457 F Supp 38, 41 (DDC 1978), the court was confronted with a motion to dismiss a plaintiff who had not filed a consent to opt in, allowed the plaintiff five days to file her consent. *Carter* involved a federal employee; today, in light of a 1978 amendment to §15 of the ADEA, 29 USC §633a(f), adding subsection (f), the consent requirement would not apply since opt-out class actions conducted pursuant to Fed R Civ P 23, are maintainable by federal employees, rather than opt-in representative actions. See **ch 9.**

hem Mines Corp[1582] the court had reason to excuse the late filing of two opt-in plaintiffs who had consented to participating in the named plaintiffs' action. The court attributed their delay to its own delay in ruling on the defendant's motion to deny class certification, and it accordingly deemed the statute of limitations to have been tolled during the period it was considering the motion.[1583]

The foregoing discussion has focused on the issue of a plaintiff's opting into a representative suit at too late a date in the litigation. The problem also can arise of a plaintiff arguably opting in too early. The ADEA provides that a complainant may not file suit until 60 days after having filed a charge of unlawful discrimination with the Equal Employment Opportunity Commission.[1584] Yet a plaintiff who has filed such a charge may seek to opt into a representative suit before that period has run. In *Sussman v Vornado, Inc*,[1585] a district court held that the plaintiff's doing so would not run afoul of the 60-day waiting period, the nonobservance of which in other circumstances could result in dismissal of the suit.[1586] This was because the purpose of the waiting period, i.e., to give the agency an opportunity to try to settle the dispute informally, had already been served by virtue of the period having run as to the representative plaintiff's charge.

§6.52 Joinder

Rules 18, 19, 20, and 21 of the Federal Rules of Civil Procedure deal with joinder. The Supreme Court has stated that "the impulse is toward entertaining the broadest possible scope of action consistent with fairness to the parties; joinder of claims, parties and remedies is strongly encouraged."[1587]

[1582] 630 F Supp 309 (SD W Va 1986).

[1583] As to the statute of limitations, see **§6.30.**

[1584] 29 USC §626(d). See **§6.37.**

[1585] 90 FRD 680 (DNJ 1981).

[1586] *See, e.g.*, Rucker v Great Scott Supermarkets, 528 F2d 393 (6th Cir 1976). See generally **§6.37.**

[1587] United Mine Workers v Gibbs, 383 US 715, 724 (1966).

In *King v Ralston Purina Co*[1588] the three plaintiffs, all suing the same defendant company but employed in different places and in different divisions of the company, sought to litigate their suit jointly. Their basis for so doing was that each alleged that he was discriminated against as part of a pattern and practice of unlawful age discrimination carried on by the defendant nationwide.[1589] This pattern and practice allegedly constituted the series of transactions or occurrences from which all their claims arose, and each claim allegedly raised the common question of whether the pattern and practice in fact had occurred.

The court held for the plaintiffs over the defendant's argument that joinder was improper, stating as follows:

> Common sense says that claims alleged to be part of a "pattern and practice" satisfy both the "transaction" and the "common question" requisites of Rule 20(a). In addition, the policy behind the rule will be served by joinder in this case. . . . If the claims were severed, the same evidence, including, perhaps, the testimony of all three plaintiffs, would have to be presented in three separate trials. It is far more convenient and economical for this evidence to be heard in one trial.[1590]

Joinder of the two plaintiffs also was deemed proper by the

1588 97 FRD 477 (WDNC 1983).

1589 As to pattern and practice lawsuits generally, see **ch 7**.

1590 97 FRD at 480. (Subsequently the defendant unsuccessfully sought, by way of a petition for a writ of mandamus, to have the three plaintiffs' claims severed and to have their separate actions transferred to the judicial districts in which their claims arose. *In re* Ralston Purina Co, 726 F2d 1022 (4th Cir 1984).)

In deciding Coffin v South Carolina Dept of Social Servs, 562 F Supp 579 (DSC 1983), the court denied the defendants' motion to sever the plaintiffs' claims. The defendants argued that the plaintiffs really were complaining of two discrete allegedly wrongful acts, but, in the court's view, it was not yet clear—given the early stage of the proceedings—that the plaintiffs' claims did not relate to or arise out of the same series of transactions or occurrences.

Court of Appeals for the Fourth Circuit in *Duke v Uniroyal, Inc,*[1591] with the court offering the following explanation:

> Both Duke and Fox were terminated on August 15, 1985, as part of the same reduction in force which was implemented by Uniroyal under a uniform policy adopted for selecting employees for discharge. The reduction was implemented by direction of Uniroyal's national sales manager . . . in consultations with its manager of employee relations. . . . Moreover, the decisions with respect to both Duke and Fox were the product of coordinated efforts in the selection of persons for discharge and in making transfers necessitated by restructuring. . . . Plaintiffs' claims arose out of the same transaction, a simple reduction in force, raising common questions of law and fact.[1592]

According to the Court of Appeals for the Third Circuit, permissive joinder of a potential plaintiff is barred if he or she failed first to file a timely charge of unlawful discrimination[1593] with the Equal Employment Opportunity Commission.[1594] Generally, but not always, a party who is not named in the grievant's administrative charge of discrimination cannot later be named as a defendant in an ADEA lawsuit.[1595] However, the court deciding *Boczon v Northwestern Elevator Co, Inc,*[1596] reasoned that "[a]lthough the prior charge requirement should apply to a plaintiff seeking to join a party defendant not named in its . . . charge, the rule should not preclude a defendant who had no

---

[1591] 928 F2d 1413 (4th Cir), *cert denied,* 112 S Ct 429 (1991).

[1592] *Id* 1420-21. There is non-ADEA case law arising under Rule 20(a) both supporting the proposition that an allegation of a company-wide policy of employment cannot justify joinder, *see, e.g.,* Martinez v Safeway Stores, Inc, 66 FRD 446 (ND Cal 1975); Smith v North Am Rockwell Corp, 50 FRD 515 (ND Okla 1970), and that it can. *See, e.g.,* Mosley v General Motors Corp, 497 F2d 1330 (8th Cir 1974); King v Pepsi Cola Metro Bottling Co, 86 FRD 4 (ED Pa 1979).

[1593] See **§6.08.**

[1594] Lockhart v Westinghouse Credit Corp, 879 F2d 43, 53 n11 (3d Cir 1989).

[1595] See **§6.06.**

[1596] 652 F Supp 482 (ED Wis 1987).

control over the . . . charging decision, from seeking proper joinder of an additional defendant."[1597]

Joinder may also be an issue where a plaintiff only names one defendant and that defendant contends that another entity—the subsidiary of the named defendant corporation, for example—is an indispensable party to the litigation.[1598]

§6.53 Survival of a Private Action Following a Party's Death

A suit brought under the Age Discrimination in Employment Act (ADEA)[1599] will survive the death of the plaintiff. An ADEA action can also survive the death of the defendant.[1600]

The court deciding *Ricca v United Press International, Inc,*[1601] was the first to so hold regarding a deceased plaintiff. Subsequent to the plaintiff's death his widow sought to be substituted as a plaintiff under Federal Rule of Civil Procedure 25(a)(1). This rule sets two preconditions for the substitution of a party: the death of a prior party and the survival of the underlying claim. The court deemed its resolution of the second condition a matter of federal, rather than state, law. The ADEA affords no explicit guidance, however; it is silent on the matter.

In resolving the question of survival, the *Ricca* court looked to a decision by the Court of Appeals for the Fifth Circuit involving another statute in which a distinction was drawn, on the basis of precedent, between penal and remedial claims:

> "Traditionally, the rule has been that actions for penalties do not survive the death of the plaintiff. . . . [Therefore, three criteria should be taken into consideration in order to determine] whether a particular statutory provision [is]

1597 *Id* 486.

1598 *See* Gay v AVCO Fin Servs, Inc, 769 F Supp 51 (DPR 1991).

1599 29 USC §§621-634.

1600 Khan v Grotnes Metalforming Sys, Inc, 679 F Supp 751 (ND Ill 1988).

1601 28 FEP Cas (BNA) 1816 (SDNY 1982).

> penal . . .: (a) whether the purpose of the action was to redress individual wrongs to the public; (b) whether the recovery ran to the individual or the public; (c) whether the recovery was disproportionate to the harm suffered."[1602]

The *Ricca* court applied these criteria and concluded that substitution was appropriate. Other courts, including several courts of appeals, also have confirmed, either expressly or implicitly, that a cause of action under the ADEA will survive the plaintiff's death.[1603]

Smith v Department of Human Services[1604] involved the question of whether a claim for liquidated damages survived the claimant's death. Observing that the "general rule under the federal common law is that an action for a penalty does not survive the death of the plaintiff,"[1605] the court held that since liquidated damages are punitive,[1606] the claim did not survive the decedent's death.

§6.54 Effect of an EEOC Suit on a Private Suit

Private Suit Filed Subsequent to EEOC Suit

Section 7(c)(1)[1607] of the Age Discrimination in Employment

---

[1602] *Id* 1817 (quoting James v Home Constr, Inc, 621 F2d 727, 730 (5th Cir 1980)).

[1603] *See* Fariss v Lynchburg Foundry, 769 F2d 958 (4th Cir 1985); Worsowicz v Nashua Corp, 612 F Supp 310 (DNH 1985); Asklar v Honeywell, Inc, 95 FRD 419 (D Conn 1982). In Rogers v Exxon Research & Engg Co, 550 F2d 834 (3d Cir 1977), *cert denied,* 434 US 1022 (1978), an executrix brought an ADEA action. Neither the district court nor the court of appeals addressed the question of whether the original plaintiff's ADEA claim survived his death. *See also* Sweat v Miller Brewing Co, 708 F2d 655, 656 (11th Cir 1983).

[1604] 876 F2d 832 (10th Cir 1989).

[1605] *Id* 834-35.

[1606] As to liquidated damages generally, see **ch 8.**

[1607] 29 USC §626(c)(1).

Act (ADEA)[1608] limits the ability of private individuals to sue by providing that "the right of any person to bring such action shall terminate upon the commencement of an action by the Equal Employment Opportunity Commission [EEOC] to enforce the right of such employee under this chapter." In addition, §7(b)[1609] incorporates §16(b)[1610] of the Fair Labor Standards Act (FLSA),[1611] which also contains a cutoff provision whereby private suits for back pay and liquidated damages are precluded once the enforcement agency files suit for injunctive relief under §17 of the FLSA.[1612]

A number of courts have held or indicated that a private individual may not commence an ADEA for back pay and other relief action following a comparable action being filed on his or her behalf by the EEOC.[1613] In *Equal Employment Opportunity Commission v United States Steel Corp*[1614] the court asserted as follows:

> [T]he provision of the ADEA prohibiting private suits once the EEOC files its complaint . . . [is] essentially a codification of the doctrine of representative claim preclusion with respect to those instances in which the EEOC litigates first: litigation by the representative party (the EEOC) seeking private relief for an individual precludes subsequent litiga-

---

1608 *Id* §§621-634.

1609 *Id* §626(b).

1610 *Id* §216(b).

1611 *Id* §§200-219.

1612 *Id* §217. As to the pursuit of such litigation by the EEOC, see **§6.60**.

1613 *See, e.g.*, Equal Employment Opportunity Commn v Pan Am World Airways, Inc, 897 F2d 1499, 1505 (9th Cir), *cert denied*, 498 US 815 (1990); Burns v Equitable Life Assurance Socy, 696 F2d 21 (2d Cir 1982), *cert denied*, 464 US 933 (1983); Dean v American Sec Ins Co, 559 F2d 1036 (5th Cir 1977), *cert denied*, 434 US 1066 (1978); Castle v Sangamo Weston, Inc, 31 FEP Cas (BNA) 324 (MD Fla 1983), *revd on other grounds*, 744 F2d 1464 (11th Cir 1984); Jones v City of Janesville, 488 F Supp 795 (WD Wis 1980); Lundgren v Continental Indus, Inc, 14 FEP Cas (BNA) 58 (ND Okla 1976); Bishop v Jelleff Assocs, 398 F Supp 579 (DDC 1974). See generally **§6.60** as to EEOC suits.

1614 921 F2d 489 (3d Cir 1990).

tion of the same claim by an individual for whom the representative sought relief.[1615]

Given this preclusion, the attorney for an individual who already is being represented by the EEOC may not even file an appearance.[1616] The fact that the EEOC suit is being pursued in a state court does not matter; it still will foreclose a later-filed private suit in federal court.[1617]

If the EEOC suit specifies time parameters in its allegations of wrongdoing, an individual who claims to have suffered unlawful discrimination on a date outside those parameters will not be precluded from filing his or her own suit for back pay and other relief subsequent to the filing of the EEOC suit.[1618] But an individual may be barred by the filing of an EEOC action from joining an existing representative action.[1619]

In addition to suing on behalf of specific allegedly injured parties, the EEOC may sue for injunctive relief pursuant to §17 of the FLSA. In this latter instance, the agency need not name the specific individuals on whose behalf it is suing or whose grievances gave rise to the suit. This agency authority leads to the question of whether an individual's ability subsequently to pursue his or her own suit is terminated by a §17 EEOC action.[1620] The Court of Appeals for the Ninth Circuit has answered in the negative, at least insofar as plaintiffs joining in an earlier-filed

---

[1615] *Id* 495.

[1616] Equal Employment Opportunity Commission v Fox Point-Bayside Sch Dist, 31 Empl Prac Dec (CCH) ¶33,609 (ED Wis 1983), *revd on other grounds,* 772 F2d 1294 (7th Cir 1985).

[1617] Chapman v City of Detroit, 808 F2d 459 (6th Cir 1986).

[1618] Verschuuren v Equitable Life, 554 F Supp 1188 (SDNY 1983).

[1619] *See* Mistretta v Sandia Corp, 12 FEP Cas (BNA) 1225, 1228 (DNM 1975).

[1620] *See, e.g.,* Equal Employment Opportunity Commission v Gilbarco, 615 F2d 985, 990 (4th Cir 1980). *But see* Monroe v United Air Lines, Inc, 565 F Supp 274 (ND Ill 1983), *revd on other grounds,* 736 F2d 394 (7th Cir 1984), *cert denied,* 470 US 1004 (1985), involving the award of attorney's fees, in which the court noted that the EEOC had intervened in a private suit. In this suit, a number of individuals had opted in after the initial private plaintiff filed the action, and after the EEOC had intervened. *Id* 281. As to §17 EEOC suits generally, see **§6.60.**

suit are concerned: in *American Association of Retired Persons v Farmers Group, Inc,*[1621] the court held that the "EEOC, by filing an action seeking only injunctive relief, did not foreclose injured employees from joining in an ongoing [earlier filed] lawsuit which sought relief that the EEOC chose not to pursue [i.e., damages for lost benefits]."[1622] And the district court deciding *Equal Employment Opportunity Commission v Chrysler Corp*[1623] suggested that the grievant's right should not be barred. But in contrast to the *Farmers Group* decision, another panel of the same court, in deciding *Equal Employment Opportunity Commission v Pan American World Airways, Inc,*[1624] ruled that "for purposes of extinguishing a claimant's private ADEA rights, the EEOC need only specify with reasonable certainty on the face of the complaint that its action has been filed on behalf of the employee . . . to foreclose subsequent private litigation."[1625]

Private Suit Filed Prior to EEOC Suit

While the foregoing discussion is addressed to private suits being filed after an EEOC suit has been filed, another issue raised by the ADEA provisions barring private suits concerns the effect of an EEOC action on an already filed private action. Most courts now take the position that the EEOC suit will not supersede the private suit. In other words, the filing of an EEOC action does not require the dismissal of the earlier filed private

---

1621 943 F2d 996 (9th Cir 1991), *cert denied,* 112 S Ct 937 (1992).

1622 *Id* 1006.

1623 546 F Supp 54, 65 (ED Mich 1982), *affd on other grounds,* 733 F2d 1183 (6th Cir 1984).

1624 897 F2d 1499 (9th Cir), *cert denied,* 498 US 815 (1990).

1625 *Id* 1507 n6. In Equal Employment Opportunity Commission v Consolidated Edison Co, 557 F Supp 468 (SDNY 1983), there was one individual who was not specifically named in the EEOC's suit, which alleged discrimination against the defendant's employees. However, the individual subsequently was identified by the EEOC in response to an interrogatory propounded by the defendant, and this identification occurred prior to the individual's attempt to pursue his own cause of action. *Id* 470 n2.

lawsuit, according to the Courts of Appeals for the Second,[1626] Fifth,[1627] and Eleventh Circuits,[1628] as well as some district courts.[1629] In addition, the ruling of the Court of Appeals for the Second Circuit arguably was cited approvingly by the Court of Appeals for the Ninth Circuit.[1630] Support for this position also arguably can be drawn from the ruling of the Court of Appeals for the Eighth Circuit in *Brennan v McDonnell Douglas Corp,*[1631] where the court authorized the ADEA enforcement agency to intervene in a private suit that had been filed prior to the agency suit and by so doing implicitly rejected dismissal of the private suit as the proper approach.

[1626] Burns v Equitable Life Assurance Socy, 696 F2d 21 (2d Cir 1982), *cert denied,* 464 US 933 (1983). *Burns* in effect overruled the earlier decided Reich v Dow Badische Co, 575 F2d 363 (2d Cir), *cert denied,* 439 US 1006 (1978), in which the Court of Appeals for the Second Circuit had stated in dictum that an EEOC suit would supersede a private suit. 575 F2d at 368.

[1627] Equal Employment Opportunity Commn v Wackenhut Corp, 939 F2d 241 (5th Cir 1991). In Dean v American Sec Ins Co, 559 F2d 1036 (5th Cir 1977), *cert denied,* 434 US 1066 (1978), the court said that if the Secretary of Labor, who at that time had enforcement authority regarding the ADEA, filed a suit within the 60-day period following a complainant's filing with the agency of his or her notice of intent to sue, that suit terminated the individual's right to maintain a private suit. *Id* 1038. The inference to be drawn was that a government suit filed subsequent to the private suit would not terminate the latter.

[1628] Castle v Sangamo Weston, Inc, 744 F2d 1464 (11th Cir 1984); Equal Employment Opportunity Commn v Eastern Airlines, Inc, 736 F2d 635 (11th Cir 1984).

[1629] *See, e.g.,* Blumenthal v G-K-G Inc, 737 F Supp 493 (ND Ill 1990); Howard v Daiichiya-Love's Bakery, Inc, 714 F Supp 1108, 1111 (D Haw 1989); Equal Employment Opportunity Commn v Chrysler Corp, 546 F Supp 54, 65 (ED Mich 1982), *affd,* 733 F2d 1183 (6th Cir 1984); *see also* Equal Employment Opportunity Commn v Commonwealth of Pa, 768 F2d 514, 516 (3d Cir 1985); Mistretta v Sandia Corp, 12 FEP Cas (BNA) 1225, 1228 (DNM 1975) (court barred individuals from opting into a representative action because a suit had been filed by the Department of Labor, but it did not dismiss the existing private suit.) *Contra* Jones v City of Janesville, 488 F Supp 795 (WD Wis 1980); Lundgren v Continental Indus, Inc, 14 FEP Cas (BNA) 58 (ND Okla 1976); Bishop v Jelleff Assocs, 398 F Supp 579, 592 (DDC 1974).

[1630] *See* Dempsey v Pacific Bell Co, 789 F2d 1451, 1452 (9th Cir 1986) (citing Burns v Equitable Life Assurance Socy, 696 F2d 21 (2d Cir), *cert denied,* 464 US 933 (1983)).

[1631] 519 F2d 718 (8th Cir 1975).

In *Equal Employment Opportunity Commission v United States Steel Corp*[1632] the Court of Appeals for the Third Circuit declined to determine "whether the filing of an EEOC action requires dismissal of a pending private action or merely bars the subsequent commencement of a private suit."[1633]

§6.55 Intervention by the EEOC in Private Suits

While not expressly authorized by the Age Discrimination in Employment Act (ADEA),[1634] intervention by the Equal Employment Opportunity Commission (EEOC) in private suits has been approved by a number of courts.[1635] For example, *Brennan v McDonnell Douglas Corp,*[1636] a ruling of the Court of Appeals for the Eighth Circuit, involved a suit by the Secretary of Labor, who at that time had enforcement authority regarding the ADEA.[1637] The agency suit had been filed after a private action had been commenced and the Secretary sought to have the two cases consolidated. The judge presiding over the private suit denied the motion to consolidate but indicated that he would entertain a motion to intervene. The Secretary's action was dismissed by a different judge on the assumption that the Secretary would intervene in the private suit. However, the Secretary's motion to intervene was denied as untimely. The appellate court reversed and ordered that the Secretary be permitted to inter-

---

[1632] 921 F2d 489 (3d Cir 1990).

[1633] *Id* 494 n4.

[1634] 29 USC §§621-634.

[1635] The ADEA is modeled, in part, on Title VII of the Civil Rights Act of 1964, 42 USC §§2000e through 2000e-17. Whereas 42 USC §2000e-5(f)(1) specifically authorizes intervention by the EEOC in private Title VII suits, there is no comparable ADEA provision.

[1636] 519 F2d 718 (8th Cir 1975). As to the effect of EEOC suits on private suits generally, see **§6.54.**

[1637] As to the transfer of enforcement authority to the EEOC, see **§6.56.**

vene, characterizing intervention as "a sensible approach to unraveling the procedural snarl."[1638]

In *Equal Employment Opportunity Commission v Wackenhut Corp*[1639] the court, discussing *Brennan,* observed as follows:

> We do not dispute that intervention by the EEOC in a private action may be *permissible* under the ADEA, provided the EEOC opts to intervene and chooses not to pursue an independent suit. We do not agree, however, that intervention is mandated as the only permissible route for the EEOC when a private plaintiff has filed suit first. . . . [It is not] barred from bringing enforcement actions on behalf of employees who have already filed individual actions under the ADEA.[1640]

Enforcement by the Equal Employment Opportunity Commission

§6.56 EEOC Investigative Authority

Section 7(a)[1641] of the Age Discrimination in Employment Act (ADEA)[1642] authorizes investigations by the Equal Employment Opportunity Commission (EEOC),[1643] as does an EEOC regula-

---

[1638] 519 F2d at 720. *See also* Air Line Pilots Assn, Intl v Trans World Airlines, Inc, 713 F2d 940 (2d Cir 1983), *affd in part & revd in part on other grounds sub nom* Trans World Airlines, Inc v Thurston, 469 US 111 (1985); Bauman v Jacobs Suchard, Inc, 52 FEP Cas (BNA) 1013 (ND Ill 1990); Monroe v United Air Lines, Inc, 565 F Supp 274 (ND Ill 1983), *revd on other grounds,* 736 F2d 394 (7th Cir 1984), *cert denied,* 470 US 1004 (1985). Attempted conciliation by the EEOC is not a condition precedent to its being permitted to intervene. Glass v IDS Fin Servs, Inc, 778 F Supp 1029, 1048-50 (D Minn 1991); Bauman v Jacobs Suchard, Inc, 52 FEP Cas (BNA) 1013 (ND Ill 1990).

[1639] 939 F2d 241 (5th Cir 1991).

[1640] *Id* 244.

[1641] 29 USC §626(a).

[1642] *Id* §§621-634.

[1643] President Carter's Reorganization Plan No 1, 92 Stat 3781, 43 Fed Reg 19807 (May 9, 1978), *reprinted at* 5 USC app, transferred enforcement authority regarding the ADEA to the EEOC as of July 1, 1979, from the Department

tion,[1644] as well. The Commission may initiate its own investigations.[1645] It further may investigate as a consequence of receiving a complaint, which is defined in an EEOC regulation as "information received from any source, that is not a charge, which alleges that a named prospective defendant has engaged in or is about to engage in actions in violation of the Act[.]"[1646] The Commission also may commence investigations on the basis of charges,[1647] including even charges that were not timely filed insofar as the charging party's own ability to seek private redress is concerned.[1648]

Even if a charging party withdraws a charge, the Commission may continue to investigate pursuant to its own independent investigative authority.[1649] The EEOC also may "enlarge upon the scope of a charge filed by an individual if in the course of

---

of Labor, which originally had been designated by the Act as to enforce the ADEA. The validity of the transfer of enforcement authority to the EEOC was called into serious question in a number of cases decided following the Supreme Court's ruling in Immigration & Naturalization Serv v Chadha, 462 US 919 (1983). In *Chadha* the Court held unconstitutional the legislative veto provision contained in the Immigration and Nationality Act, 8 USC §1254(c)(2). Since the transfer of enforcement authority to the EEOC was effectuated by an executive order that was issued pursuant to a federal statute also containing a legislative veto provision, i.e., the Reorganization Act of 1977, 5 USC §§901-912, *Chadha* was looked to as the basis for disputing the constitutionality of that transfer. See **ch 2.** Ultimately, the issue was resolved by the enactment of Ratification of Reorganization Plans as a Matter of Law, Pub L No 98-532, 98 Stat 2705 (1984) (codified at 5 USC §901 *et seq*), which expressly authorizes EEOC enforcement.

1644 29 CFR §1626.15(a) (1993).

1645 Equal Employment Opportunity Commn v Ritenour Sch Dist, 692 F Supp 1068, 1069 (ED Mo 1988).

1646 29 CFR §1626.3 (1993). See **§6.02.**

1647 See **§6.02** *et seq.*

1648 *See, e.g.*, Equal Employment Opportunity Commn v American & Efird Mills, Inc, 964 F2d 300 (4th Cir 1992); Equal Employment Opportunity Commn v Sears, Roebuck & Co, 55 FEP Cas (BNA) 482 (D Or 1991); Equal Employment Opportunity Commn v Ritenour Sch Dist, 692 F Supp 1068 (ED Mo 1988); Equal Employment Opportunity Commn v Gladieux Refinery, Inc, 631 F Supp 927 (ND Ind 1986). The EEOC has asserted the same position in a nonlitigation context. 48 Fed Reg 139 (Jan 3, 1983).

1649 29 CFR §1626.13 (1993).

its investigation it uncovers additional violations."[1650] The agency's ability in this regard is not unlimited, however. It is confined insofar as investigating a charging party's charge is concerned " 'to the investigation reasonably expected to grow out of the initial charge of discrimination.' "[1651] In the instance of a charging party, the respondent will have been informed of the charge and, generally, of the identity of the party;[1652] however, information provided in confidence by other parties may not be disclosed without the informant's prior written consent.[1653]

Subpoena Power

By virtue of §7(a) of the Act, §§9[1654] and §11[1655] of the Fair Labor Standards Act (FLSA)[1656] are incorporated into the ADEA. The EEOC thus has subpoena power to compel the attendance of witnesses and the production of documents, by virtue of §9 of the FLSA.[1657] This power is broad in scope.[1658] Moreover, the

---

[1650] Equal Employment Opportunity Commn v Rhone-Poulenc, Inc, 677 F Supp 264, 265 (DNJ 1988), *affd on other grounds,* 876 F2d 16 (3d Cir 1989).

[1651] *Id* (quoting Equal Employment Opportunity Commn v Westinghouse Elec Corp, 632 F Supp 343, 362 (ED Pa 1986), *affd in part & vacated & remanded in part on other grounds,* 869 F2d 696 (3d Cir), *vacated on other grounds,* 493 US 801 (1989)).

[1652] See **§6.28.**

[1653] 29 CFR §1626.4 (1993).

[1654] 29 USC §209. Section 9 incorporates 15 USC §§49, 50. Section 49 establishes agency access to documents and the right to copy them; the power to subpoena testimony and documents; and the authority of courts to compel testimony and production. Section 50 sets forth penalties for refusing to testify or produce documents and for providing false testimony.

[1655] 29 USC §211.

[1656] *Id* §§200-219.

[1657] *Accord* Equal Employment Opportunity Commn v Allstate Ins Co, 30 FEP Cas (BNA) 573 (ND Ill 1981). The EEOC's regulation confirms this subpoena power; it sets out the scope of the agency's subpoena power, specifies the form of the subpoena, and addresses the matter of enforcement. 29 CFR §1626.16 (1993).

[1658] *See, e.g.,* Equal Employment Opportunity Commn v Peat, Marwick, Mitchell & Co, 775 F2d 928 (8th Cir 1985), *cert denied,* 475 US 1046 (1986); Equal Employment Opportunity Commn v Township of Howell, 57 FEP Cas (BNA) 1027 (DNJ 1991); Shoe Works v Equal Employment Opportunity Commn, 685

subpoena power has been delegated by the Commission to certain designees, whose issuance of subpoenas is not subject to review by, or appeal to, the Commission.[1659]

As a general matter, and independent of the ADEA per se, a subpoenaed employer may question the reasonableness of a subpoena without suffering any penalties for noncompliance by raising objections in an action in federal district court.[1660] The employer, however, may not insist upon a judicial warrant as a condition precedent to a valid administrative subpoena.[1661] The question of whether an action under the ADEA actually can be maintained is not to be litigated in the context of a subpoena enforcement proceeding.[1662]

The EEOC's investigative efforts are not limited by the charge-filing requirements applicable to private suits.[1663] Thus, a subpoena directed to an employer cannot be quashed simply

---

F Supp 168 (SD Ohio 1987); Equal Employment Opportunity Commn v Quadrant Club, 35 FEP Cas (BNA) 195 (ND Tex 1984); Equal Employment Opportunity Commn v Allstate Ins Co, 30 FEP Cas (BNA) 573 (ND Ill 1981); *see also* Equal Employment Opportunity Commn v Deer Valley Unified Sch Dist, 968 F2d 904 (9th Cir 1992), an ADEA case in which the court, after looking to the EEOC's subpoena authority under Title VII of the Civil Rights Act of 1964, 42 USC §§2000e through 2000e-17, spoke more broadly to general agency authority (whether pursuant to statutes or otherwise was unclear):

> The Supreme Court stated in *United States v. Morton Salt Co.*, 338 U.S. 632 . . . (1950), that an agency "has a power of inquisition . . . which is not derived from the judicial function. It is more analogous to the Grand Jury, which does not depend on a case or controversy for power to get evidence but can investigate merely on suspicion that the law is being violated, or even just because it wants assurance that it is not." *Id* at 642-43. . . .

968 F2d at 906; *cf* University of Pa v Equal Employment Opportunity Commn, 493 US 182 (1990) (Title VII case in which Court confirmed EEOC's authority to subpoena information regarding faculty tenure decisions).

1659 29 CFR §1626.16(c) (1993). The EEOC offered an explanation of this provision at 48 Fed Reg 139-40 (Jan 3, 1983).

1660 *See* See v City of Seattle, 387 US 541 (1967) (non-ADEA case).

1661 Donovan v Lone Steer, Inc, 464 US 408 (1984) (non-ADEA case).

1662 Equal Employment Opportunity Commn v Ritenour Sch Dist, 692 F Supp 1068 (ED Mo 1988).

1663 See **§§6.02-.08**.

because the individual whose charge instigated the investigation did not timely file with the EEOC.[1664] In addition, a party may not successfully oppose a subpoena by raising what could be a defense if the agency subsequently decides to sue. For example, a party cannot succeed with the argument that the information sought by the agency need not be supplied because it relates to activities that, if the subject of suit, would be barred from attack on statute of limitations grounds.[1665]

Access to Records and Other Data

The EEOC has issued a regulation regarding the obligations of employers to maintain records.[1666] Generally, under Title VII of the Civil Rights Act of 1964,[1667] the EEOC has been deemed to have wide-ranging access to employer records,[1668] and no

[1664] *See, e.g.,* Equal Employment Opportunity Commn v American & Efird Mills, Inc, 964 F2d 300 (4th Cir 1992); Equal Employment Opportunity Commn v Sears, Roebuck & Co, 55 FEP Cas (BNA) 482 (D Or 1991); Equal Employment Opportunity Commn v Ritenour Sch Dist, 692 F Supp 1068 (ED Mo 1988); Equal Employment Opportunity Commn v Gladieux Refinery, Inc, 631 F Supp 927 (ND Ind 1986). The EEOC has asserted the same position in a nonlitigation context. 48 Fed Reg 139 (Jan 3, 1983).

[1665] Equal Employment Opportunity Commn v Delaware State Police, 618 F Supp 451 (D Del 1985). *But see* Equal Employment Opportunity Commn v Ocean City Police Dept, 820 F2d 1378 (4th Cir 1987), *judgment vacated on other grounds,* 486 US 1019 (1988) (case arising under Title VII of the Civil Rights Act of 1964, 42 USC §§2000e through 2000e-17). *Ocean City* was distinguished in Equal Employment Opportunity Commn v American Express Centurion Bank, 758 F Supp 217 (D Del 1991). The court, after articulating the general proposition that "a party may not defeat an agency's authority to investigate by raising what could be a defense if the agency subsequently decided to bring an action against the party," *id* 222, held that "the mere existence of a purported waiver of ADEA claims [executed by the charge-filing grievant] does not render a charge of age discrimination invalid for purposes of enforcing a subpoena issued by the EEOC." *Id* 225.

[1666] 29 CFR pt 1627 (1993). See **ch 3.**

[1667] 42 USC §§2000e through 2000e-17.

[1668] *See, e.g.,* University of Pa v Equal Employment Opportunity Commn, 493 US 182 (1990) (subpoena upheld as to confidential peer review material relating to faculty tenure review process); Equal Employment Opportunity Commn v Childrens Hosp Medical Ctr, 719 F2d 1426 (9th Cir 1983); *In re* Equal Employment Opportunity Commn, 709 F2d 392 (5th Cir 1983); Equal Employment Opportunity Commn v Cambridge Tile Mfg Co, 590 F2d 205

lesser scope of accessibility applies under the ADEA.[1669] In fact, the EEOC's investigative authority as to ADEA violations is even broader than its authority regarding Title VII. Under Title VII, the EEOC is entitled only to evidence "relevant to the charge under investigation."[1670] In contrast, there is no relevancy limitation imposed by the FLSA provisions regarding investigatory authority that are incorporated, as noted above, into the ADEA.[1671]

§6.57 Conciliation By the EEOC

Pursuant to §7(b)[1672] of the Age Discrimination in Employment Act (ADEA),[1673] the Equal Employment Opportunity Commission (EEOC) is required, before initiating a lawsuit, to "attempt to eliminate the discriminatory practice or practices alleged, and to effect voluntary compliance . . . through informal methods of conciliation, conference and persuasion." This conciliation obligation is not without limit, of course: both EEOC regulatory language and case law address its contours.

(6th Cir 1979); New Orleans Pub Serv, Inc v Brown, 507 F2d 160 (5th Cir 1975).

[1669] *See, e.g.*, United States Equal Employment Opportunity Commn v Recruit USA, 939 F2d 746 (9th Cir 1991); Equal Employment Opportunity Commn v Elrod, 674 F2d 601 (7th Cir 1982); *see also* United States Equal Employment Opportunity Commn v Massachusetts, 760 F Supp 685 (ND Ill 1990); Equal Employment Opportunity Commn v Delaware State Police, 618 F Supp 451 (D Del 1985); Equal Employment Opportunity Commn v Quadrant Club, 35 FEP Cas (BNA) 195 (ND Tex 1984). The EEOC can obtain compilations of documents under Title VII, as well as under the ADEA. Equal Employment Opportunity Commn v ADM Co, 39 FEP Cas (BNA) 80 (SD Iowa 1984). It may be deemed unduly burdensome, however, for an employer to be required to prepare numerous documents and explanations that are not in existence. Equal Employment Opportunity Commn v Gladieux Refinery, Inc, 631 F Supp 927 (ND Ind 1986).

[1670] 42 USC §2000e-8(a).

[1671] *See* Equal Employment Opportunity Commn v Shell Oil Co, 466 US 54, 64-65 (1984). As a practical matter, however, the courts have been very liberal in construing the relevancy requirement of the Title VII provisions. *Id* 69 n20.

[1672] 29 USC §626(b).

[1673] *Id* §§621-634.

EEOC Regulatory Language

Insofar as the EEOC has expressed its view, the agency's obligation to conciliate is confined to those situations where the Commission has a "reasonable basis to conclude that a violation of the Act has occurred or will occur."[1674] The identity of persons who have provided information in confidence ordinarily is not to be disclosed, except with the prior written consent of the informant, according to the EEOC's regulation.[1675]

Case Law

A number of courts have been in general agreement that the EEOC has the burden of initially informing a charged party of the alleged violation, affording it an opportunity to explain its potential liability[1676] and apprising it that suit will be filed if voluntary compliance is not achieved.[1677] In this vein, the court deciding *Equal Employment Opportunity Commission v Rhone-Poulenc,*

[1674] 29 CFR §1625.15(b) (1993). The regulation adverts to written notice being issued to the respondent of the EEOC's intent to begin or continue conciliation, such notice ordinarily to be issued in the form of a letter of violation. *Id.* The regulation cautions that failure to issue a written violation notice shall not be construed as a finding of no violation. *Id.*

[1675] *Id* §1626.4(b). See **§6.28.**

[1676] It has been held that the EEOC fails to fulfill its conciliation obligation if it does not tell the charged party of its intent to seek back pay. *See* Brennan v Ace Hardware Corp, 495 F2d 368 (8th Cir 1974). But the agency, according to another court, does not have to disclose how much back pay it will seek, at least long as it sets out the methodology it will use for computing back pay, thereby enabling the charged party to itself figure out the amount. *See* Marshall v Hartford Fire Ins Co, 78 FRD 97, 104 (D Conn 1978).

[1677] *See, e.g.,* Marshall v Sun Oil Co, 605 F2d 1331 (5th Cir 1979); Marshall v Western Elec Co, 20 Empl Prac Dec (CCH) ¶30,190 (WDNC 1979); Marshall v Tecumseh Prods Co, 19 FEP Cas (BNA) 1400 (WD Tenn 1978); Marshall v Hartford Fire Ins Co, 78 FRD 97 (D Conn 1978); Dunlop v Resource Sciences Corp, 410 F Supp 836 (ND Okla 1976); Usery v Goodyear Tire & Rubber Co, 16 FEP Cas (BNA) 566 (WD Tenn 1976); *see also* Brennan v Ace Hardware Corp, 495 F2d 368 (8th Cir 1974); Equal Employment Opportunity Commn v Westinghouse Elec Corp, 632 F Supp 343, 360 (ED Pa 1986), *affd in part & vacated & remanded in part on other grounds,* 869 F2d 696 (3d Cir), *vacated,* 493 US 801 (1989).

Inc,[1678] defined adequate conciliation as including four elements:

> "(1) informing the violator of ways in which he can bring himself into compliance with the Act;
> (2) telling him that terminated employees may recover back pay;
> (3) notifying him that the . . . [EEOC] may institute legal action; and
> (4) assuring him that he may respond to the violations, in light of the possible remedy."[1679]

The foregoing general and specific statements notwithstanding, not all courts agree that the EEOC must apprise the employer that suit will be filed. For example, in deciding *Equal Employment Opportunity Commission v Colgate-Palmolive Co*[1680] the court stated as follows:

> The E.E.O.C.'s duty to attempt conciliation is fulfilled if it 1) outines for the employer the reasonable cause for its belief that the employer is in violation of the Act, 2) offers an opportunity for voluntary compliance, and 3) responds in a reasonable and flexible manner to the reasonable attitude of the employer.[1681]

In pursuing the effort to achieve compliance, the agency—according to some courts—must undertake exhaustive conciliation efforts.[1682] This rigorous position contrasts with more mod-

---

[1678] 677 F Supp 264 (DNJ 1987), *affd on other grounds,* 876 F2d 16 (3d Cir 1989).

[1679] *Id* 266 (quoting Equal Employment Opportunity Commn v Chrysler Corp, 546 F Supp 54, 62 (ED Mich 1982), *affd,* 733 F2d 1183 (6th Cir 1984) (quoting Marshall v Sun Oil Co, 605 F2d 1331, 1334 (5th Cir 1979)).

[1680] 34 FEP Cas (BNA) 1551 (SDNY 1983).

[1681] *Id* 1555; *accord* Equal Employment Opportunity Commn v City of Chicago, 51 FEP Cas (BNA) 499, 501 (ND Ill 1987); Equal Employment Opportunity Commn v KDM Sch Bus Co, 612 F Supp 369, 374 n17 (SDNY 1985).

[1682] *See, e.g.,* Marshall v Sun Oil Co, 592 F2d 563, 566 (10th Cir), *cert denied,* 444 US 826 (1979); Brennan v Ace Hardware Corp, 495 F2d 368, 374 (8th Cir 1974); Barrett v Suffolk Transp Servs, Inc, 600 F Supp 81 (EDNY 1984);

erate formulations asserted by other courts, such as the requirement of "good faith conciliation efforts" called for by the court deciding *Equal Employment Opportunity Commission v Elrod,*[1683] or the formulation articulated in *Equal Employment Opportunity Commission v Cabot Corp:*[1684] "We will find the EEOC in compliance with the conciliation requirement if it has made a sincere and reasonable effort to resolve the dispute by providing the defendant with an adequate opportunity to respond to the charges and negotiate possible settlements."[1685] Ultimately, " 'the funda-

---

Equal Employment Opportunity Commn v Colgate-Palmolive Co, 34 FEP Cas (BNA) 1551, 1555 (SDNY 1983); Marshall v Newburg R-2 Sch Dist, 469 F Supp 1030, 1032 (ED Mo 1979); Marshall v Arlene Knitwear, Inc, 454 F Supp 715, 723 (EDNY 1978), *affd in part & revd in part without opinion,* 608 F2d 1369 (2d Cir 1979). Support for this position is found in the House committee report on the legislation that was ultimately enacted into law as the ADEA: "It is intended that responsibility for enforcement vested in the Secretary by Section 7 be initially and exhaustively directed through informal methods of conciliation, conference, and persuasion and formal methods applied only in the ultimate sense." House Comm on Educ & Labor, Age Discrimination in Employment Act of 1967, HR Rep No 805, 90th Cong, 1st Sess 5 (1967). (The reference to *Secretary* is due to the fact that until July 1, 1979, the ADEA was enforced by the Department of Labor. See **§6.56**).

[1683] 47 FEP Cas (BNA) 1663, 1664 (ND Ill 1986), *affd in part & revd in part on other grounds sub nom* Equal Employment Opportunity Commn v O'Grady, 857 F2d 383 (7th Cir 1988).

[1684] 48 FEP Cas (BNA) 1136 (ED Pa 1988).

[1685] *Id* 1137; *see also* Equal Employment Opportunity Commn v Westinghouse Elec Corp, 632 F Supp 343, 361 (ED Pa 1986), *affd in part & vacated & remanded on other grounds,* 869 F2d 696 (3d Cir), *vacated on other grounds,* 493 US 801 (1989); Marshall v Western Elec Co, 20 Empl Prac Dec (CCH) ¶30,190, at p11,997 (WDNC 1979); Marshall v Hartford Fire Ins Co, 78 FRD 97, 104 (D Conn 1978); Usery v Goodyear Tire & Rubber Co, 16 FEP Cas (BNA) 566 (WD Tenn 1976); *see also* Equal Employment Opportunity Commn v Prudential Fed Sav & Loan Assn, 763 F2d 1166 (10th Cir), *cert denied,* 474 US 946 (1985); Equal Employment Opportunity Commn v KDM Sch Bus Co, 612 F Supp 369, 374 (SDNY 1985); Marshall v Baltimore & ORR, 461 F Supp 362, 369 (D Md 1978), *revd on other grounds,* 632 F2d 1107 (4th Cir 1980), *cert denied,* 454 US 825 (1981) (refusing to require exhaustive efforts); Usery v Gilbarco, Inc, 21 FEP Cas (BNA) 1037, 1038 (MDNC 1977) ("affirmative effort toward informal settlement"); Dunlop v Resource Sciences Corp, 410 F Supp 836, 842 (ND Okla 1976).

mental question is the reasonableness and responsiveness of the EEOC's conduct under all the circumstances.' "[1686]

In any event, however one characterizes the EEOC's conciliation obligation, more is required of the agency than its just bringing the disputants together to state their positions.[1687] The agency may not impose undue conditions on one or both of the parties, however.[1688] On the other hand, there is no requirement that the agency continue in its attempts to work with charged parties that are completely resistant[1689] or that act in bad faith.[1690] If a charged party insists that it did not violate the ADEA, the

---

[1686] Equal Employment Opportunity Commn v KDM Sch Bus Co, 612 F Supp 369, 374 (SDNY 1985) (quoting EEOC v Klinger Elec Corp, 636 F2d 104, 107 (5th Cir 1981)).

[1687] In assessing the adequacy of the agency's conciliation efforts, the number of meetings and contacts with the parties may be relevant. *See* Equal Employment Opportunity Commn v Prudential Fed Sav & Loan Assn, 763 F2d 1166, 1169 (10th Cir), *cert denied,* 474 US 817 (1985); Hodgson v Approved Personnel Serv, Inc, 529 F2d 760, 764 (4th Cir 1975); Equal Employment Opportunity Commn v School Bd of Pinellas County, 742 F Supp 622, 624 (MD Fla 1990); Equal Employment Opportunity Commn v Franklin Square Sch Dist, 24 FEP Cas (BNA) 594, 595-97 (EDNY 1980); Marshall v Western Elec Co, 20 Empl Prac Dec (CCH) ¶30,190 (WDNC 1979); Marshall v Vagabond Hotels, Inc, 19 Empl Prac Dec (CCH) ¶9,212 (SD Cal 1977); Marshall v Roberts Dairy Co, 15 FEP Cas (BNA) 633 (D Neb 1977), *affd,* 572 F2d 1271 (8th Cir 1978).

[1688] For example, the EEOC cannot require a charged entity to waive the statute of limitations where there is still a considerable amount of time before the limitations period will expire. *See* Marshall v Sun Oil Co, 592 F2d 563 (10th Cir), *cert denied,* 444 US 826 (1979); Marshall v Newburg R-2 Sch Dist, 469 F Supp 1030 (ED Mo 1979).

[1689] *See, e.g.,* Marshall v Sun Oil Co, 605 F2d 1331 (5th Cir 1979); Glass v IDS Fin Servs, Inc, 778 F Supp 1029, 1050 (D Minn 1991); Equal Employment Opportunity Commn v American Express Publishing Corp, 681 F Supp 216, 221 n11 (SDNY 1988); Marshall v Western Elec Co, 20 Empl Prac Dec (CCH) ¶30,190 (WDNC 1979); Marshall v Hartford Fire Ins Co, 78 FRD 97, 107 (D Conn 1978); Marshall v Tecumseh Prods Co, 19 FEP Cas (BNA) 1400 (WD Tenn 1978). "However, an employer's refusal to conciliate an individual claim cannot be construed to indicate a refusal to conciliate a class claim." Equal Employment Opportunity Commn v American Express Publishing Corp, *supra,* 681 F Supp at 221 n11.

[1690] *See, e.g.,* Marshall v Arlene Knitwear, Inc, 454 F Supp 715 (EDNY 1978), *affd in part & revd in part without opinion,* 608 F2d 1369 (2d Cir 1979); Brennan v Weis Markets, 5 FEP Cas (BNA) 850 (MD Pa 1973).

EEOC may terminate its conciliation effort.[1691] It has been stated, however, that the "[f]ailure [of the charged party] to cooperate in an investigation does not relieve the . . . [agency of its] obligation to [at least] attempt conciliation."[1692]

According to the *Cabot Corp* court, "conciliation efforts must address specific allegations before those issues may be litigated."[1693] The court continued: "For example, it is insufficient for a plaintiff to allege simply 'nationwide discrimination'; more specificity is required."[1694] While the court deciding *Equal Employment Opportunity Commission v Arizona*[1695] was of the view that "[g]eneralized conciliation is acceptable for prospective relief, . . . there must be evidence of conciliation on the merits of the individual case to award back pay."[1696]

In suits pursued by the EEOC, the agency may include allegations of wrongdoing not raised in the original conciliation efforts.[1697]

1691 *See, e.g.,* Equal Employment Opportunity Commn v Sears, Roebuck & Co, 50 FEP Cas (BNA) 1123, 1125 (ND Cal 1989); Equal Employment Opportunity Commn v Chrysler Corp, 546 F Supp 54, 63 (ED Mich 1981), *affd on other grounds,* 733 F2d 1183 (6th Cir 1984); *see also* Equal Employment Opportunity Commn v School Bd of Pinellas County, 742 F Supp 622, 624 (MD Fla 1990); Equal Employment Opportunity Commn v KDM Sch Bus Co, 612 F Supp 369 (SDNY 1985).

1692 Dunlop v Resource Sciences Corp, 410 F Supp 836, 842-43 (ND Okla 1976).

1693 Equal Employment Commn v Cabot Corp, 48 FEP Cas (BNA) 1136, 1136 (ED Pa 1988).

1694 *Id* (quoting Equal Employment Opportunity Commn v Sears, Roebuck & Co, 650 F2d 14, 18-19 (2d Cir 1981)).

1695 824 F Supp 898 (D Ariz 1991).

1696 *Id* 901. As to the specificity with which the back pay issue must be addressed, see notes 1669, 1679 and accompanying text.

1697 Equal Employment Opportunity Commn v Sears, Roebuck & Co, 50 FEP Cas (BNA) 1123, 1125 (ND Cal 1989); Equal Employment Opportunity Commn v Westinghouse Elec Corp, 632 F Supp 343, 361-62 (ED Pa 1986), *affd in part & vacated & remanded in part on other grounds,* 869 F2d 696 (3d Cir), *vacated,* 493 US 801 (1989).

Conciliation Where There Are Multiple Grievants

In deciding *Equal Employment Opportunity Commission v American Express Publishing Corp*[1698] the court dismissed the claims asserted on behalf of unnamed employees of the defendant because the Equal Employment Opportunity Commission (EEOC) had failed to adequately put the defendant on notice during the course of the conciliation process that the EEOC had any interest broader than vindicating the claims of just the one named employee who the Commission had expressly identified. The court deciding *Equal Employment Opportunity Commission v Rhone-Poulenc, Inc,*[1699] held to the contrary, as did the court deciding *Equal Employment Opportunity Commission v Hugin Sweda, Inc.*[1700] The latter court, however, like others,[1701] including *American Express Publishing* for that matter—did impose a limited obligation on the agency: "While the EEOC is not obligated to conduct conciliation with respect to each member or potential member of a class, . . . it should at least put defendant on notice that a class action may be brought."[1702] Thus, if the EEOC's focus is on a general pattern or practice of discrimination, each alleged victim need not be identified, so long as the class of victims is adequately described.[1703] In *Equal Employment Opportunity Commission v Arizona*[1704] the court asserted that "when the allega-

---

1698 681 F Supp 216 (SDNY 1988).

1699 677 F Supp 264 (DNJ 1987), *affd on other grounds,* 876 F2d 16 (3d Cir 1989).

1700 750 F Supp 165 (DNJ 1990).

1701 *See, e.g.,* Marshall v Sun Oil Co, 605 F2d 1331 (5th Cir 1979); Equal Employment Opportunity Commn v Cabot Corp, 48 FEP Cas (BNA) 1136, 1137 (ED Pa 1988); Equal Employment Opportunity Commn v Chrysler Corp, 546 F Supp 54 (ED Mich 1982), *affd on other grounds,* 733 F2d 1183 (6th Cir 1984); Marshall v Western Elec Co, 20 Empl Prac Dec (CCH) ¶30,190 (WDNC 1979).

1702 750 F Supp at 165 (citation omitted).

1703 *See* Marshall v Sun Oil Co, 605 F2d 1331 (5th Cir 1979); Equal Employment Opportunity Commn v Chrysler Corp, 546 F Supp 54 (ED Mich 1982); Marshall v Western Elec Co, 20 Empl Prac Dec (CCH) ¶30,190 (WDNC 1979).

1704 824 F Supp 898 (D Ariz 1991).

tion charges large scale discrimination . . . , it does not require proof of conciliation on each individual case of discrimination."[1705]

On the other hand, there is some support for the proposition that if the EEOC seeks relief for more than one plaintiff, it must have done more than merely put the defendant on notice of the multiplicity of complainants; it must have engaged in conciliation efforts on behalf of each of them.[1706]

Consequence of EEOC's Failure to Conciliate or Its Failure to Conciliate Adequately

Most courts have taken the position that they have discretion to issue a stay of a lawsuit pending further conciliation.[1707] Generally, stays have been granted when there was partial, but inade-

---

[1705] *Id* 901.

[1706] *See, e.g.*, Equal Employment Opportunity Commn v Fox Point-Bayside Sch Dist, 24 FEP Cas (BNA) 668 (ED Wis 1980); Brennan v Texas Instruments, Inc, 12 FEP Cas (BNA) 1724 (ED Ky 1976); *see also* Marshall v Hills Bros, 432 F Supp 1320 (ND Ga 1977).

[1707] *See, e.g.*, Equal Employment Opportunity Commn v Prudential Fed Sav & Loan Assn, 763 F2d 1166 (10th Cir), *cert denied*, 474 US 946 (1985); Marshall v Sun Oil Co, 605 F2d 1331, 1337-38 n8 (5th Cir 1979); Brennan v Ace Hardware Corp, 495 F2d 368, 376 (8th Cir 1974); Equal Employment Opportunity Commn v Hugin Sweda, Inc, 750 F Supp 165, 167-68 (DNJ 1990); Equal Employment Opportunity Commn v City of Chicago, 51 FEP Cas (BNA) 499, 501 (ND Ill 1987); Equal Employment Opportunity Commn v Fox Point-Bayside Sch Dist, 24 FEP Cas (BNA) 668 (ED Wis 1980); Marshall v Hartford Fire Ins Co, 78 FRD 97, 107 (D Conn 1978); Marshall v Tecumseh Prods Co, 19 FEP Cas (BNA) 1400 (WD Tenn 1978); Marshall v Vagabond Hotels, Inc, 19 Empl Prac Dec (CCH) ¶9,212 (SD Cal 1977); Brennan v Texas Instruments, Inc, 12 FEP Cas (BNA) 1724 (ED Ky 1976); *see also* Marshall v Baltimore & ORR, 461 F Supp 362, 370 (D Md 1978), *revd on other grounds*, 632 F2d 1107 (4th Cir 1980), *cert denied*, 454 US 825 (1981) (inadequate conciliation cured by conciliation efforts after lawsuit was filed). This view is endorsed in the conference report on the 1978 amendments to the ADEA. Conference Comm, Age Discrimination in Employment Act Amendments of 1978, HR Rep No 950, 95th Cong, 2d Sess 13 (1978). *But see* Marshall v Tecumseh Prods Co, 19 FEP Cas (BNA) 1400 (WD Tenn 1978); Usery v Gilbarco, Inc, 21 FEP Cas (BNA) 1037 (MDNC 1977).

quate, conciliation.[1708] If, however, there was substantial failure on the EEOC's part to undertake meaningful conciliation, dismissal can be in order.[1709]

In *Equal Employment Opportunity Commission v Board of Governors*[1710] the court acknowledged the soundness of the general rule, which it stated as being that "when the EEOC has failed to conciliate an ADEA claim before bringing suit, the proceedings may be stayed so that conciliation may be attempted."[1711] Here, however, the magistrate to whom the court earlier had referred the case had been unsuccessful, despite numerous efforts on his part, to bring about a settlement. Thus, application of the general rule was deemed unwarranted. The court stated that "even if the EEOC failed to conciliate the claim[,] staying the litigation at this late date would appear to be fruitless[.]"[1712]

Other Issues

The agency may file suit prior to the completion of conciliation.[1713] Notwithstanding the obligation of the EEOC to seek to conciliate, a court may allow the EEOC to intervene in a pending private suit without its undertaking conciliation, so long as the

---

1708 *See, e.g.,* Equal Employment Opportunity Commn v Prudential Fed Sav & Loan Assn, 763 F2d 1166, 1169 (10th Cir), *cert denied,* 474 US 946 (1985); Equal Employment Opportunity Commn v Fox Point-Bayside Sch Dist, 24 FEP Cas (BNA) 668 (ED Wis 1980); Marshall v Newburg R-2 Sch Dist, 469 F Supp 1030 (ED Mo 1979); Marshall v Hartford Fire Ins Co, 78 FRD 97, 107 (D Conn 1978); Brennan v Texas Instruments, Inc, 12 FEP Cas (BNA) 1724 (ED Ky 1976). The court deciding Lundgren v Continental Indus, Inc, 14 FEP Cas (BNA) 58 (ND Okla 1976), denied the defendant's motion to dismiss, but did not then stay the proceeding in order to afford the enforcement agency an opportunity to conciliate.

1709 *See, e.g.,* Brennan v Ace Hardware Corp, 495 F2d 368, 376 (8th Cir 1974); Marshall v Vagabond Hotels, Inc, 19 Empl Prac Dec (CCH) ¶9,212 (SD Cal 1977); *see also* Marshall v Hills Bros, 432 F Supp 1320 (ND Cal 1977); Dunlop v Resource Sciences Corp, 410 F Supp 836, 843 (ND Okla 1976).

1710 706 F Supp 1377 (ND Ill 1989).

1711 *Id* 1381.

1712 *Id* 1382.

1713 Equal Employment Opportunity Commn v Westinghouse Elec Corp, 632 F Supp 343, 361-62 (ED Pa 1986), *affd in part & vacated & remanded in part on other grounds,* 869 F2d 696 (3d Cir), *vacated,* 493 US 801 (1989).

scope of the existing suit is not broadened by the Commission.[1714]

Product of Conciliation

If conciliation is successful in producing an agreement, the respondent is to be required, so far as is practicable, to eliminate its unlawful practices and to provide appropriate affirmative relief.[1715] Such agreement is to be reduced to writing and ordinarily will be signed by the EEOC's representative, the respondent, and the charging party, if any.[1716]

§6.58 Resort by the EEOC to State Remedies Prior to Filing Suit

Pursuant to §14(b)[1717] of the Age Discrimination in Employment Act (ADEA),[1718] an individual who wants to seek redress under the Act must first pursue remedies at the state level, provided there is: (1) a state law prohibiting age discrimination and (2) a state antidiscrimination agency that is empowered to grant relief to, or seek relief on behalf of, the victims of such discrimination.[1719] Section 14(b) further provides that after waiting 60 days—or less if the state agency terminates proceedings before that time period has elapsed—the grievant may file suit under the ADEA (provided that he or she also has filed a charge of unlawful discrimination with the Equal Employment Opportunity Commission (EEOC) and waited the requisite 60 days as to that filing).[1720]

The question can arise, not surprisingly, as to whether the EEOC similarly must first resort to state remedies in §14(b)

1714 Bauman v Jacobs Suchard, Inc, 52 FEP Cas (BNA) 1013 (ND Ill 1990).

1715 29 CFR §1626.15(c) (1993).

1716 *Id.* As to relief in the instance of the breach of a settlement agreement, see **ch 8.**

1717 29 USC §633(b).

1718 *Id* §§621-634.

1719 See **§§6.25-6.27.**

1720 See **§6.37.**

jurisdictions when it undertakes to sue under the ADEA. The Court of Appeals for the Second Circuit has responded, by way of dictum, in the negative.[1721] The Court of Appeals for the Third Circuit has embraced the same position in deciding *Marshall v Chamberlain Manufacturing Corp,*[1722] in which the court addressed the Act at a time when it was still being enforced by the Secretary of Labor.[1723] (The fact that enforcement authority was transferred to the EEOC as of July 1, 1979, does not undercut its reasoning.)[1724] In the *Marshall* court's view, the suit actually was being brought under the Fair Labor Standards Act (FLSA)[1725] provisions that are incorporated into the ADEA through §7(b)[1726] of the age statute,[1727] and the case law clearly supported the proposition that the FLSA did not require preliminary resort by the enforcement agency to state remedies.

The *Marshall* court took another tack as well, engaging in the assumption that the Labor Department's ADEA suit could be brought under §7[1728] of the age discrimination statute. In accordance with this legal scenario, the analogical guidance afforded by Title VII of the Civil Rights Act of 1964,[1729] which has a provision very similar to §14(b), came to the fore. That guidance led to the same negative conclusion regarding the need for the EEOC to seek redress first at the state level, inasmuch as there is no such requirement in Title VII as to EEOC suits.

1721 Reich v Dow Badische Co, 575 F2d 363, 368 (2d Cir), *cert denied,* 439 US 1006 (1978).

1722 601 F2d 100 (3d Cir 1979); *see also* Marshall v West Essex Gen Hosp, 575 F2d 1079 (3d Cir 1978) (Secretary's enforcement action conditioned on private individual's initial resort to state remedies).

1723 *Accord* Holliday v Ketchum, MacLeod & Grove, Inc, 584 F2d 1221, 1230 n38 (3d Cir 1978) (dictum); *see also* Marshall v West Essex Gen Hosp, 575 F2d 1079 (3d Cir 1978).

1724 As to the transfer of enforcement authority from the Department of Labor to the EEOC, see **ch 2.**

1725 29 USC §§200-219.

1726 *Id* §626(b).

1727 See **§6.60** regarding these provisions as they apply to EEOC suits.

1728 29 USC §626.

1729 42 USC §§2000e through 2000e-17.

A number of district courts in jurisdictions outside the Second and Third Circuits have echoed the conclusions of these two appellate courts.[1730]

§6.59 The Statute of Limitations for EEOC Suits

Statutes of Limitations Prior to the 1991 Amending of the ADEA

Until the Age Discrimination in Employment Act (ADEA)[1731] was amended by the Civil Rights Act of 1991 (CRA),[1732] a suit by the Equal Employment Opportunity Commission (EEOC) had to be filed either within two or three years of the alleged violation. This followed from the incorporation into the age discrimination statute of the Portal-to-Portal Act[1733] by the ADEA's §7(e).[1734] These were the same statutes of limitations that were applicable to suits by private litigants, with two years being the standard time period and three years being applicable in the instance of an alleged willful violation of the Act.[1735]

While the ADEA was amended by the CRA, it still is necessary to understand the formerly applicable statutes of limitations.

1730 *See* Equal Employment Opportunity Commn v Sperry-Univac Corp, 36 Empl Prac Dec (CCH) ¶35,019 (D Utah 1982); Equal Employment Opportunity Commn v Chrysler Corp, 546 F Supp 54, 64 (ED Mich 1982), *affd on other grounds,* 733 F2d 1183 (6th Cir 1984); Equal Employment Opportunity Commn v Blue Star Foods, Inc, 33 FEP Cas (BNA) 859 (SD Iowa 1979); Marshall v American Motors Corp, 475 F Supp 875, 881-83 (ED Mich 1979); Dunlop v Crown Cork & Seal Co, 405 F Supp 774 (D Md 1976); Usery v Norden Labs, Inc, 17 Empl Prac Dec (CCH) ¶8569 (D Neb 1976); *see also* Equal Employment Opportunity Commn v Kansas, 28 FEP Cas (BNA) 1036 (D Kan 1982) (EEOC action was not conditioned on private individual's filing of a timely charge). *Usery* should be discounted, given that it also stated what later proved to be an erroneous proposition in light of Oscar Mayer & Co v Evans, 441 US 750 (1979), i.e., that individuals in private actions did not have to resort to state remedies. See generally **§6.25.**

1731 29 USC §§621-634.

1732 Pub L No 102-166, 105 Stat 1071.

1733 29 USC §255.

1734 *Id* §626(e).

1735 See **§6.30.**

First, these provisions still apply to pre-amendment disputes. Second, some of the issues that arose, such as the availability of equitable relief for late-filing plaintiffs, arise under the amended statute. Thus, pre-amendment case law continues to be pertinent as well, the changes in statutory language notwithstanding.

Caveats to the Pre-Amendment Statutes of Limitations

There were two caveats to the two- and three-year statutes of limitations set forth in the ADEA as it read prior to its being amended in 1991. The first, involving the applicability of the statute of limitations to claims for equitable relief, entailed a small number of court decisions, which were in disagreement. One district court held that no time limitation applied to claims for such relief, even claims made by "those seeking hiring, which would involve the possibility of new employees and accordingly, new wages to pay."[1736] This holding flowed from the language of the statute of limitations provision incorporated by §7(b)[1737] of the age statute into the ADEA, i.e., 29 USC §255, which by its terms applies only to actions for "unpaid minimum wages, unpaid overtime compensation, or liquidated damages." On the other hand, in deciding *Equal Employment Opportunity Commission v Westinghouse Electric Corp*[1738] the Court of Appeals for the Third Circuit obviously assumed, although it did not directly discuss the proposition, that §255 applied to equitable claims.

The second caveat was much more clearly established, since it was set forth on the face of the pre-1991 ADEA: when the EEOC was engaged in the mandatory conciliation efforts that had to precede its filing suit,[1739] the statute of limitations was to

---

[1736] United States Equal Employment Opportunity Commn v City of Chicago, 51 FEP Cas (BNA) 503, 507 (ND Ill 1989).

[1737] 29 USC §626(b).

[1738] 725 F2d 211 (3d Cir 1983), *cert denied,* 469 US 820 (1984).

[1739] See **§6.57**.

be tolled for a period not in excess of one year.[1740] In the conference report on the 1978 amendment[1741] that created this proviso, it was stated that tolling began when the EEOC asserted, in a letter to the prospective defendant, that it was prepared to commence conciliation.[1742] This tolling was not triggered by an investigation by the EEOC; rather an EEOC effort to conciliate was the relevant event.[1743] The tolling period terminated when the EEOC ceased its attempts at conciliation; thus, if these efforts ended prior to the one-year maximum authorized for tolling, the tolling ended at that point, rather than continuing until the full year had run.[1744] There was room for argument, however, as to just when conciliation ended.[1745]

There was support for the view that tolling did not apply to conciliation efforts undertaken as the result of private complainants' charges being filed with the EEOC, inasmuch as the tolling

---

1740 29 USC §626(e)(2) (prior to its being amended by the CRA). The tolling provision did not apply to conciliation carried on prior to the 1978 amendment, i.e., prior to April 6, 1978. Equal Employment Opportunity Commn v Japan Air Lines Co, 39 Empl Prac Dec (CCH) ¶35,946 (SDNY 1985).

1741 Age Discrimination in Employment Act Amendments of 1978, Pub L No 95-256, §4(c), 92 Stat 189, 191.

1742 Conference Comm, Age Discrimination in Employment Act Amendments of 1978, HR Rep No 950, 95th Cong, 2d Sess 13 (1978). An EEOC regulatory provision provided that the date of issuance of written notice to the respondent of the Commission's intent to begin or continue conciliation determined when the statute of limitations was tolled. 29 CFR §1626.15(b) (1993).

1743 Taylor v Kansas, 52 FEP Cas (BNA) 1183 (D Kan 1989).

1744 Equal Employment Opportunity Commn v Britrail Travel Intl Corp, 733 F Supp 855 (DNJ), *affd without opinion,* 919 F2d 134 (3d Cir 1990); Equal Employment Opportunity Commn v Barrett, Haentjens & Co, 705 F Supp 1065, 1067-68 (MD Pa 1988); Equal Employment Opportunity Commn v Colgate-Palmolive Co, 586 F Supp 1341 (SDNY 1984).

1745 *See* McConnell v Thomson Newspapers, Inc, 802 F Supp 1484, 1500-01 (ED Tex 1992); Equal Employment Opportunity Commn v Britrail Travel Intl Corp, 733 F Supp 855 (DNJ), *affd without opinion,* 919 F2d 134 (3d Cir 1990); Equal Employment Opportunity Commn v Pan Am World Airways, Inc, 52 FEP Cas (BNA) 929, 939-40 (ND Cal 1988), *affd on other grounds,* 897 F2d 1499 (9th Cir), *cert denied,* 498 US 815 (1990); Equal Employment Opportunity Commn v Barrett, Haentjens & Co, 705 F Supp 1065 (MD Pa 1988); Equal Employment Opportunity Commn v Rhone-Poulenc, Inc, 677 F Supp 264, 266-67 (DNJ 1987), *affd,* 876 F2d 16 (3d Cir 1989).

provision only spoke to conciliation undertaken pursuant to §7(b)[1746] of the Act, which is the ADEA provision addressing agency, rather than private, enforcement.[1747] The EEOC's regulation, however, provided that once §7(b) conciliation was commenced, the period of tolling applied regardless of whether it was the EEOC or a private party that was the litigant.[1748]

Other Issues

The same standards that determined the accrual of the period in private suits[1749] applied to the statute of limitations issue considered in the context of EEOC suits.

Statutes of limitations questions can arise both as to suits for injunctive relief filed pursuant to §17[1750] of the Fair Labor Standards Act (FLSA),[1751] which is incorporated into the ADEA by §7(b)[1752] of the age statute, and as to suits filed to recover sums due employees filed pursuant to §16(c)[1753] of the FLSA, which also is incorporated into the ADEA by §7(b).[1754] Section 17 provides that injunctive relief may be sought, except as to "sums which employees are barred from recovering, at the time of the *commencement of the action* to restrain the violations, by virtue of [the applicable statute of limitations]."[1755] Thus, it may be neces-

---

1746 29 USC §626(b).

1747 *See* McConnell v Thomson Newspapers, Inc, 802 F Supp 1484, 1499 n20 (ED Tex 1992); Equal Employment Opportunity Commn v Japan Air Lines Co, 39 Empl Prac Dec (CCH) ¶35,946 (SDNY 1985); Leite v Kennecott Copper Corp, 558 F Supp 1170, 1173 n1 (D Mass), *affd without opinion,* 720 F2d 658 (1st Cir 1983); *accord* HR Rep No 950, *supra* note 1742, at 13.

1748 29 CFR §1626.15(b) (1993).

1749 See **§6.31**.

1750 29 USC §217.

1751 *Id* §§200-219.

1752 *Id* §626(b).

1753 *Id* §216(c).

1754 *See* Equal Employment Opportunity Commn v O'Grady, 857 F2d 383 (7th Cir 1988). See **§6.60** regarding the two different causes of action that the EEOC can pursue.

1755 (emphasis added).

sary to determine whether, on the date on which the EEOC filed suit, the claims of the individuals on whose behalf monetary relief was sought were time barred.[1756]

It has been held that the EEOC can seek relief under §16(c) on behalf of an individual who failed to file a timely charge of unlawful discrimination with the agency and who thus is barred from suing on his or her behalf.[1757] It also has been stated that the EEOC may maintain a suit under §17 for injunctive relief even if the individual grievants themselves are barred from filing suit because the statute of limitations for their filing their own suits has expired.[1758]

(The EEOC need not obtain the consent of individuals on whose behalf it files §16(c) suits.[1759] Nor is consent needed for the filing of §17 suits by the EEOC.[1760])

The 1991 Amendment

Section 115 of the CRA[1761] amended §7(e) of the ADEA so as to eliminate the two- and three-year statutes of limitations then applicable to private plaintiffs. Section 115 also eliminated the provision authorizing the tolling for up to a year of the running of the statute of limitations for suits filed by the EEOC while

---

[1756] Equal Employment Opportunity Commn v Home Ins Co, 553 F Supp 704 (SDNY 1982).

[1757] *See, e.g.*, Equal Employment Opportunity Commn v Sperry-Univac Corp, 36 Empl Prac Dec (CCH) ¶35,019 (D Utah 1982); Equal Employment Opportunity Commn v Roadway Express, Inc, 33 Empl Prac Dec (CCH) ¶34,265 (EDNC 1981). As to timely charge filing generally, see **§6.08** *et seq.*

[1758] Equal Opportunity Commn v Massachusetts, 54 FEP Cas (BNA) 436, 437-38 (D Mass 1990).

[1759] Equal Employment Opportunity Commn v Chrysler Corp, 546 F Supp 54, 75 (ED Mich 1982), *affd on other grounds,* 733 F2d 1183 (6th Cir 1984); Equal Employment Opportunity Commn v Wyoming Retirement Sys, 27 FEP Cas (BNA) 1291, 1292-93 (D Wyo 1981); *see also* Equal Employment Opportunity Commn v Blue Star Foods, Inc, 22 FEP Cas (BNA) 504, 506 (SD Iowa 1980). See **§6.60.**

[1760] *See, e.g.*, Equal Employment Opportunity Commn v Wyoming Retirement Sys, 27 FEP Cas (BNA) 1291, 1292-93 (D Wyo 1981); *see also* Equal Employment Opportunity Commn v Blue Star Foods, Inc, 22 FEP Cas (BNA) 504, 506 (SD Iowa 1980). See **§6.60.**

[1761] Pub L No 102-166, §115, 105 Stat 1071, 1079.

the agency pursued conciliation efforts. As a result of the amendment, a "*person* aggrieved"[1762] now receives a notice from the EEOC of the EEOC's dismissal of the plaintiff's charge or termination of its proceedings; a "civil action [then] may be brought . . . by a person defined in section 11(a) [29 USC §630(a)]" within 90 days of receipt of the notice.[1763]

The amendment did not directly address what statute of limitations would be applicable to suits filed by the EEOC. That omission in itself created much potential for uncertainty. This uncertainty was heightened by the fact that *person* is defined in §11(a) to include a variety of entities, but not the EEOC.

In deciding *McConnell v Thomson Newspapers, Inc,*[1764] the court concluded that "the EEOC is a 'legal representative' for the purposes of . . . [§11(a)] when it files a civil action on behalf of an individual to enforce the ADEA."[1765] The court then further reasoned as follows:

> New section 626(e) starts the limitations period when "the person aggrieved" receives notice of the dismissal of a charge or the termination of EEOC proceedings. Section 626(b) provides that the EEOC must attempt to eliminate the discriminatory practices alleged and to effect voluntary compliance with the requirements of the ADEA through informal methods of conciliation, conference, and persuasion, before filing a civil action. Reading 626(b) and 626(e) together, it is concluded that the EEOC must notify the person aggrieved by the purportedly discriminatory conduct when its informal methods of resolution fail, and that it has ninety days from the date of receipt of that notice by the person aggrieved to file a civil action.[1766]

1762 §7(e), 29 USC §626(e) (emphasis added).

1763 *Id.*

1764 802 F Supp 1484 (ED Tex 1992).

1765 *Id* 1499.

1766 *Id.*

There is good reason to question the *McConnell* court's imposition on the EEOC of a procedural formula, i.e., the giving of notice to a grievant followed by a 90-day window of opportunity for filing suit, that in fact is applied by the literal language of the statute only to private individuals. One can well question why the agency should be required, just because of the statutory scenario for private litigation, to send a notice to individuals to formally trigger the running of a 90-day period for filing its own suits.[1767] Granted, there is a legitimate concern about allowing defendants to be disadvantaged by stale suits being filed, and so there is justification for encouraging prompt filings, whether by private litigant, or the EEOC. But if the agency is intent on delay, it can in any event simply forego sending out the notice until it is imminently ready to sue, for there is nothing in the amended statute barring such an exercise of bureaucratic logrolling. Thus, the notice-sending requirement is not going to solve the problem of a dilatory agency effort. Moreover, in other contexts the courts have resisted requiring the EEOC to satisfy procedural requirements confronting private litigants[1768] and thus the court's approach here is without analogical support.

[1767] The court reasoned as follows:

> The superseded law tolled the statute for the EEOC, but not private parties, during the time the EEOC was attempting to effect voluntary compliance [pursuant to §7(b), 29 USC §626(b)], for a period up to one year. . . . If the EEOC does not dismiss a complainant's charge, new §626(e) ties the limitations on civil suits by private parties to the receipt of notice of the end of EEOC administrative proceedings. The limitations statute likewise should be read to link the timeliness of EEOC civil suits to notice of the end of voluntary compliance measures, since such measures differ only in that they are pursued in accordance with 29 U.S.C. §626(b), rather than §626(d) [,which prescribes EEOC conciliation and other informal methods of dispute resolution when a private charge of unlawful discrimination is filed with the agency].

Id 1499-1500.

[1768] The EEOC need not, when it sues under §17, 29 USC §217, of the Fair Labor Standards Act, *id* §§200-219, provide the names of the individuals on whose behalf it sues. This is in contrast to the requirement that in a private suit the names of all plaintiffs be set forth, either in the complaint or by means of consents filed by opt-in plaintiffs. *See* Equal Employment Opportunity Commn v Gilbarco, Inc, 615 F2d 985 (4th Cir 1980). See **§6.60** as to such suits.

In any event, even accepting for the moment the *McConnell* court's approach, the fact is that §7(b) of the ADEA authorizes suits by the EEOC pursuant to two sections of the Fair Labor Standards Act:[1769] §§16[1770] and 17.[1771] In a §16 suit the EEOC is suing on behalf of an individual, which is the scenario envisioned by the *McConnell* court. But in suits litigated pursuant to §17, the EEOC is seeking injunctive relief that will aid specific injured individuals but that also serves a broader mission: satisfaction of the agency's public interest function of assuring compliance with the law.[1772] Indeed, in a §17 suit the EEOC need not name an aggrieved individual on whose behalf it is suing.[1773] The *McConnell* court, however, did not address the different nature of the two suits that may be pursued by the EEOC. Accordingly, even if the court's analysis has some merit regarding §16 suits, it is deficient regarding §17 suits. For in the latter type of action the EEOC is not acting just in a representative capacity; thus, there is no apparent point in requiring the EEOC to wait for 90 days after sending notice to aggrieved individuals, since such people are not, or at least may not be, named in the suit.

What solution is there for the absence of a statute of limitations applicable to ADEA suits brought by the EEOC?

The courts have long held that the United States is not bound

---

Moreover, while a private grievant may not sue without having first resorted to state remedies, see **§§6.25-.27** the EEOC is not required to do so. *See* Marshall v Chamberlain Mfg Corp, 601 F2d 100, 101 (3d Cir 1979). See **§6.58.** In addition, while a private individual must first file a charge of unlawful discrimination with the EEOC before filing suit, the EEOC need not do so. *See* Glass v IDS Fin Servs, Inc, 778 F Supp 1029, 1051 (D Minn 1991); *cf* General Tel Co v Equal Employment Opportunity Commn, 446 US 318 (1980) (suit arising under Title VII of the Civil Rights Act of 1964, 42 USC §§2000e through 2000e-17, in which Court held that the EEOC was not required, when the EEOC itself was suing, to comply with the class action procedures imposed by Fed R Civ P 23).

1769 29 USC §§200-219.

1770 *Id* §216. See **§6.60.**

1771 29 USC §217. See **§6.60.**

1772 See **§6.60.**

1773 See **§6.60.**

by any limitations period unless Congress directs otherwise.[1774] Given that the Congress expressly dropped any reference to the statute that previously had been incorporated into the ADEA and had set the times for filing ADEA suits, i.e., the Portal-to-Portal Act,[1775] it would be difficult to persuasively argue that that provision, nonetheless, should be infused by judicial interpretation back into the ADEA.[1776] The solution devised by the *McConnell* court is strained, at best, and certainly unworkable for §17 suits. What is left, then, is a gap. There is simply no time limitation applicable to EEOC suits.

Concededly, there is nothing to suggest that when it amended the ADEA in 1991 Congress affirmatively entertained the intent to extend the time for the filing of EEOC suits beyond the then-applicable two- and three-year statutes of limitations. On the other hand, the fact is that Congress did not offer an alternative when it severed the ADEA's connection with the Portal-to-Portal

---

[1774] *See, e.g.,* Guaranty Trust Co v United States, 304 US 126 (1938).

[1775] 29 USC §255.

[1776] This argument nonetheless was successfully made by the defendant in Equal Employment Opportunity Commn v ITT Avionics Div, ITT Corp, Civ Action No 92-793 (JCL) (DNJ July 7, 1993) (unreported). The court, while expressing doubts as to the *McConnell* court's analysis, accepted for the moment the proposition that the EEOC could be treated as a grievant's legal representative. The court then pointed to the fact that the individual on whose behalf the EEOC was suing had failed to file a timely charge of unlawful discrimination with the EEOC. See **§6.08.** The court reasoned that "as representative, the EEOC can claim no greater rights than those possessed by the individual grievant." Slip op at 31. Accordingly, the agency could not "commence suit as . . . [the grievant's] legal representative where . . . [the grievant] himself would have been unable to do so" because of his late-filed charge. *Id.*

The *Avionics* court then went on to assert the much broader position that *McConnell* was wrongly decided and that the Portal-to-Portal Act's limitations periods indeed still did apply to EEOC actions. The court reasoned that the procedures imposed by the FLSA had to be applied to actions that, although concerning vindication of ADEA rights, actually involved the implementation of FLSA statutory provisions. Thus, the court concluded as follows:

> Based upon the statutory scheme as it now exists, the court concludes that the 1991 amendments to the ADEA left EEOC actions under 29 U.S.C. §§216(c) and 217 subject to the limitations period set forth in 29 U.S.C. §255(a) of the Fair Labor Standards Act.

Slip op at 32.

Act. Of course, it is true that reading the ADEA as containing no statute of limitations applicable to EEOC suits may result in defendants winding up opposing suits the facts of which extend relatively far back in time. While this is hardly a satisfactory response from the defense perspective, at least it can be reasoned that this extension of time for the EEOC to sue is consistent with the general public interest role of the agency, inasmuch as affording the Commission additional time to sue provides it with greater opportunity to vindicate that public interest.

There is, however, one caveat to the conclusion that the EEOC is not bound to satisfy any statute of limitations when it sues: the old statutes of limitations may still apply to causes of action commenced prior to November 21, 1991, the date of the CRA's enactment. This is because the Supreme Court has held that at least some of the amendments made by the CRA only apply prospectively.[1777] What makes for uncertainty here is the fact that the Court drew a distinction between the substantive changes made by the CRA involving the availability of jury trials and certain damages under Title VII of the Civil Rights Act of 1964,[1778] and procedural changes. As to the latter, the Court observed that "[ch]anges in procedural rules may often be applied in suits arising before their enactment without raising concerns about retroactivity."[1779] Whether the change in the statute of limitations effectuated by the amending of the ADEA should be deemed to be a procedural modification that can be applied retroactively to untimely suits filed by the EEOC prior to the CRA's enactment just does not appear to be determinable from the Supreme Court's decision.

1777 Landgraf v USI Film Prods Co, 114 S Ct 1483 (1994). While the decision did not address the changes made to the ADEA, but rather focused on much more significant changes made to Title VII of the Civil Rights Act of 1964, 42 USC §§2000e through 2000e-17, by the CRA, the decision still should apply to the ADEA modifications.

1778 42 USC §§2000e through 2000e-17.

1779 114 S Ct at 1502 n29.

Tolling Generally

There have been occasions when arguments have been made, sometimes convincingly, that the statute of limitations for the filing of suit by the EEOC under the ADEA should be tolled. Such arguments will continue to be persuasive, or will fail, independent of the particular filing deadline that applies assuming some statute of limitations is applicable (a legal scenario which is not, as just discussed, the view taken here, but which, as discussed, has garnered some judicial support.)

According to the Court of Appeals for the Seventh Circuit, in deciding *Equal Employment Opportunity Commission v O'Grady,*[1780] when an employer refuses to comply with an EEOC subpoena, tolling may be in order for the period during which there was noncompliance.[1781] On the other hand, the same court upheld the trial court's refusal to toll the running of the statute as to the claim of a woman whose identity as a potential claimant was not disclosed to the EEOC by the defendant as a result of poor record keeping by the defendant. The trial court characterized this lapse as "regrettable negligence."[1782]

Tolling as to Unnamed Individuals

Even though the EEOC is the named plaintiff when it sues, the argument could be made that the individuals on whose behalf it sues may not be represented, so to speak, by the agency because their individual claims are stale. This issue can arise in the context of an EEOC suit brought under §17 of the FLSA, in which suit specific individuals are not named. The few courts to address the question of whether a §17 EEOC suit tolls the

---

[1780] 857 F2d 383, 392-94 (7th Cir 1988).

[1781] *See also* Equal Employment Opportunity Commn v Gladieux Refinery, Inc, 631 F Supp 927 (ND Ind 1986); Equal Employment Opportunity Commn v City of Memphis, 581 F Supp 179, 182 (WD Tenn 1983).

[1782] 857 F2d at 393 (quoting, without citation, trial court ruling). The appropriateness of tolling may depend on whether the EEOC is maintaining a suit under §16, 29 USC §216, of the Fair Labor Standards Act (FLSA), *id* §§200-219, which is incorporated into the ADEA by §7(b) of the latter Act, *id* §626(b), or under §17 of the FLSA, *id* §217, which also is incorporated into the ADEA by §7(b). As to §16 and §17 suits generally, see **§6.60.**

statute of limitations for the injured individuals whose claims triggered the agency suit have given an affirmative answer: "an age discrimination action brought . . . under the authority of FLSA §17 is effectively commenced for all purposes with the filing of the complaint, regardless of whether the complaint names the aggrieved individuals."[1783] Even if the individuals were named only months after suit was filed through an amendment to the complaint or otherwise, their claims will not be time-barred as long as those claims were alive at the time the EEOC filed suit.

Section 16(c), however, sets forth a special definition of *commencement of an action* that precludes the same reading as is accorded to §17:

> In determining when an action is commenced by the . . . [EEOC] under this subsection for the purposes of the statutes of limitations . . ., it shall be considered to be commenced in the case of any individual claimant on the date when the complaint is filed if he is specifically named as a party plaintiff in the complaint, or if his name did not so appear, on the subsequent date on which his name is added as a party plaintiff in such action.

Thus, while the EEOC can file suit under §16(c) without naming specific individuals, a statute of limitations, if it applies, will not be tolled by the EEOC suit but will continue to run until the individuals are named.[1784]

[1783] Equal Employment Opportunity Commn v Gilbarco, Inc, 615 F2d 985, 990 (4th Cir 1980); *accord* Equal Employment Opportunity Commn v Pan Am World Airways, Inc, 897 F2d 1499, 1506-07 & n6 (9th Cir), *cert denied,* 498 US 815 (1990); Equal Employment Opportunity Commn v Westinghouse Elec Corp, 725 F2d 211 (3d Cir 1983), *cert denied,* 469 US 820 (1984); Equal Employment Opportunity Commn v Elrod, 47 FEP Cas (BNA) 1651, 1654 (ND Ill 1986), *affd in part & revd in part on other grounds sub nom* Equal Employment Opportunity Commn v O'Grady, 857 F2d 383 (7th Cir 1988); Equal Employment Opportunity Commn v Chrysler Corp, 546 F Supp 54, 61 (ED Mich 1982), *affd on other grounds,* 733 F2d 1183 (6th Cir 1984).

[1784] Equal Employment Opportunity Commn v Gilbarco, Inc, 615 F2d 985, 990 n5 (4th Cir 1980); Equal Employment Opportunity Commn v Elrod, 47

§6.60 EEOC Lawsuits

Section 7(b)[1785] of the Age Discrimination in Employment Act (ADEA)[1786] incorporates §11(b)[1787] of the Fair Labor Standards Act (FLSA).[1788] Thereby, the Equal Employment Opportunity Commission (EEOC) is authorized to sue for injunctive relief under §17[1789] of the FLSA, which also is incorporated into the ADEA by §7(b) of the latter Act. Section 7(b) also incorporates §16(c)[1790] of the FLSA, pursuant to which the EEOC may sue to recover back pay and other benefits due a grievant. However, as pointed out by the district court deciding *Equal Employment Opportunity Commission v Pan American World Airways, Inc*,[1791] "Nothing in the ADEA (or, via incorporation, the FLSA) requires the EEOC to bring an enforcement action on behalf of a particular grievant[.]"[1792]

It has been stated that in an EEOC enforcement action the individuals on whose behalf the EEOC seeks relief are not them-

---

FEP Cas (BNA) 1651, 1655 (ND Ill 1986), *affd in part & revd in part sub nom* Equal Employment Opportunity Commn v O'Grady, 857 F2d 383 (7th Cir 1988); Equal Employment Opportunity Commn v Chrysler Corp, 546 F Supp 54, 61 (ED Mich 1982), *affd on other grounds,* 733 F2d 1183 (6th Cir 1984).

In Donovan v Crisostomo, 689 F2d 869 (9th Cir 1982), an FLSA suit, the court held that even if the Department of Labor's suit for back pay were barred as to certain employees under §16(c), the Department still could seek to recover back pay under §17. *See also* Equal Employment Opportunity Commn v Westinghouse Elec Corp, 725 F2d 211 (3d Cir 1983), *cert denied,* 469 US 820 (1984).

1785 29 USC §626(b).

1786 *Id* §§621-634.

1787 *Id* §211.

1788 *Id* §§200-219.

1789 *Id* §217.

1790 *Id* §216(c).

1791 52 FEP Cas (BNA) 929 (ND Cal 1988), *affd on other grounds,* 897 F2d 1499 (9th Cir), *cert denied,* 498 US 815 (1990).

1792 *Id* 937.

selves plaintiffs.[1793] Over the years the EEOC has filed numerous suits, although the annual totals have only constituted small fractions of the numbers of private suits annually filed.[1794]

Pursuant to the terms of §16(c), the EEOC's authority under this provision is conditioned on two prerequisites: (1) an individual grievant must request the EEOC to act on his or her behalf, and (2) suit may not be filed if there is a novel question of law involved. The limitations embodied in §16(c) do not apply to §17.[1795]

It should be noted that in *Equal Employment Opportunity Commission v Chrysler Corp*[1796] the court held that, even as to a §16(c) suit, the EEOC may pursue litigation without securing the consents of the individuals on whose behalf suit is filed.[1797] This necessarily would seem to suggest that the ostensible request requirement need not actually be satisfied, since the EEOC can file suit, according to the *Chrysler* court, even on behalf of someone who has not evinced a desire to be represented. Indeed, even the unwilling individual has no recourse under the *Chrysler* approach: "[i]t is not logical to assume that an individual could thwart the . . . [enforcement agency's] authority by exercising a veto over the [enforcement] decision."[1798]

In suits maintained pursuant to §17 the EEOC has a broader mission than under §16(c). Under the latter, the concern is in vindicating the rights of a particular individual or individuals: in a §17 injunctive action the EEOC is exercising its public inter-

---

1793 *See, e.g.*, Equal Employment Opportunity Commn v Chrysler Corp, 49 FEP Cas (BNA) 1439, 1440 (ED Mich 1989); Equal Employment Opportunity Commn v Northwest Orient Airlines, 49 FEP Cas (BNA) 1430, 1431 (WD Wash 1987).

1794 See **ch 2**.

1795 *See, e.g.*, Equal Employment Opportunity Commn v Gilbarco, 615 F2d 985, 989 n3 (4th Cir 1980).

1796 546 F Supp 54 (ED Mich 1982), *affd on other grounds*, 733 F2d 1183 (6th Cir 1984).

1797 *Id* 75.

1798 *Id.*

est function of assuring compliance with the law.[1799] Accordingly, in §17 actions the question of whether the relief sought and awarded can or should exceed the needs of a particular grievant may arise.[1800]

The individual on whose behalf a §17 suit is filed need not have filed a charge of unlawful discrimination with the EEOC.[1801] Neither a §17 suit, or, for that matter, a §16 suit, will be barred by virtue of an individual grievant's having filed an untimely charge, whether the EEOC is filing its own suit initially or intervening in an earlier filed suit by a private litigant.[1802] Thus, even though individuals would be barred from suing because of their procedural lapses, the EEOC may assert the very claims they would have asserted had they not been time-barred.[1803]

Obtaining the consents of individual claimants is unnecessary.[1804] In §17 suits the EEOC need not even name any aggrieved individuals.[1805] This can generate problems concern-

---

[1799] *See, e.g.*, Equal Employment Opportunity Commn v Kansas, 28 FEP Cas (BNA) 1036, 1038 (D Kan 1982); *cf* Wirtz v Malthor, Inc, 254 F Supp 475 (D Nev 1966), *revd on other grounds*, 391 F2d 1 (9th Cir 1968) (FLSA suit). *But see* Equal Employment Opportunity Commn v Gilbarco, 615 F2d 985, 1010-11 (4th Cir 1980) (Murnaghan, J, concurring in part and dissenting in part).

[1800] See **ch 8.**

[1801] Reich v Dow Badische Co, 575 F2d 363, 367-68 (2d Cir), *cert denied*, 439 US 1006 (1978) (dictum); Equal Employment Opportunity Commn v Home Ins Co, 553 F Supp 704, 714 (SDNY 1982). As to charge-filing generally, see **§6.02.**

[1802] Glass v IDS Fin Servs, Inc, 778 F Supp 1029, 1050-51 (D Minn 1991).

[1803] *See* Equal Employment Opportunity Commn v Sperry-Univac Corp, 36 Empl Prac Dec (CCH) ¶35,019 (D Utah 1982); Equal Employment Opportunity Commn v Roadway Express, Inc, 33 Empl Prac Dec (CCH) ¶34,265 (EDNC 1981).

[1804] *See, e.g.*, Equal Employment Opportunity Commn v Sperry-Univac Corp, 36 Empl Prac Dec (CCH) ¶35,019 (D Utah 1982); Equal Employment Opportunity Commn v Home Ins Co, 553 F Supp 704, 714-15 (SDNY 1982).

[1805] *See, e.g.*, Equal Employment Opportunity Commn v Gilbarco, 615 F2d 985, 990 (4th Cir 1980); Equal Employment Opportunity Commn v Sperry-Univac Corp, 36 Empl Prac Dec (CCH) ¶35,019 (D Utah 1982); Equal Employment Opportunity Commn v Home Ins Co, 553 F Supp 704, 715 (SDNY 1982).

ing the statute of limitations[1806] and the question of whether a private individual's right to bring a suit is terminated.[1807]

In an FLSA suit the Court of Appeals for the Fifth Circuit held that there is no due process requirement that notice be given by the plaintiff agency to the individual or individuals on whose behalf it sues under §17.[1808] In *Equal Employment Opportunity Commission v Pan American World Airways, Inc,*[1809] an ADEA ruling, the court did not have to decide the notice issue, since the EEOC in fact had given notice that "disclosed to potential claimants the existence of the lawsuit and advised them that failure to contact the EEOC could lead to exclusion from any recovery resulting from the Commission's efforts."[1810] The district court in the *Pan Am* litigation had observed, however, that "[n]othing in the ADEA (or, via incorporation, the FLSA) requires the EEOC to bring an enforcement action on behalf of a particular grievant or to provide notice to victimized employees of their right to share in the damages."[1811]

The EEOC may sue on claims not contained in the original charge filed by an individual grievant, even if those claims bear no relationship to the allegations set forth in the charge.[1812] Thus, the EEOC has broader authority to sue than would a private claimant who seeks to litigate a claim not first set forth in his or her administrative charge.[1813] Without specifying whether the EEOC was suing under §17 or §16(c), the court deciding *United States Equal Employment Opportunity Commission v United Air Lines, Inc,*[1814] asserted that the EEOC's "authority to bring suit should not be dependent upon the identification of specific indi-

---

1806 See **§6.59.**

1807 See **§6.54.**

1808 Donovan v University of Tex at El Paso, 643 F2d 1201 (5th Cir 1981).

1809 897 F2d 1499 (9th Cir), *cert denied,* 498 US 815 (1990).

1810 *Id* 1508.

1811 Equal Employment Opportunity Commn v Pan Am World Airways, Inc, 52 FEP Cas (BNA) 929, 937 (ND Cal 1988), *affd on other grounds,* 897 F2d 1499 (9th Cir), *cert denied,* 498 US 815 (1990).

1812 Equal Employment Opportunity Commn v Sears, Roebuck & Co, 50 FEP Cas (BNA) 1123, 1124 (ND Cal 1989).

1813 See **§6.05.**

1814 132 FRD 198 (ND Ill 1990).

viduals who have suffered past injury, so long as the EEOC has a reasonable basis for concluding that a given policy is likely to have a discriminatory effect" in the future on unnamed individuals.[1815]

Relation of EEOC to Aggrieved Persons

One ruling, by a magistrate, has addressed the question of whether an attorney-client relationship exists between the EEOC and the individuals on whose behalf it sues. In *Gormin v Brown-Forman Corp*[1816] the magistrate held in the negative: "[W]ith regard to individuals named in the complaint [filed by the EEOC], the EEOC is not in an attorney-client relationship with the aggrieved employee[s]."[1817] (In so ruling, the magistrate noted that, of the 61 individuals named in the EEOC complaint, only one had initiated contact with the agency by filing a charge of unlawful discrimination.[1818]) The magistrate, having invoked cases decided under Title VII of the Civil Rights Act of 1964,[1819] explained as follows:

> The courts reason that when the EEOC sues in its own name, "albeit at the behest of and for the benefit of specific individuals, it acts also to vindicate the public interest in preventing employment discrimination," Williams [v United States, 665 F Supp 1466, 1470 (D Or 1987)] . . . quoting from General Telephone Co. v. EEOC, 446 U.S. 318, 326 . . . (1980). In EEOC enforcement actions, as distinguished from individual suits for relief, the EEOC acts for the benefit of a large group of aggrieved individuals who may have competing and conflicting interests. Thus, it is not undertaking class representation under Rule 23, Fed. R. Civ. P. because the EEOC is not bringing a representative action as is contemplated by that rule. Ibid.[1820]

[1815] *Id* 199.

[1816] 133 FRD 50 (MD Fla 1990).

[1817] *Id* 52.

[1818] *Id.*

[1819] 42 USC §§2000e through 2000e-17.

[1820] 133 FRD at 52-53.

The magistrate did express a caveat to its rejection of an attorney-client relationship between the EEOC and individuals on whose behalf it sues:

> [I]f a particular individual . . . has expressly asserted his desire to have EEOC counsel render him confidential legal advice, and that desire is demonstrable through affidavits or other documentation . . ., then the . . . [decisionmaker] may conclude that EEOC counsel has an attorney-client relationship with that individual.[1821]

The question of legal relationships also was at issue in *Equal Employment Opportunity Commission v United States Steel Corp.*[1822] The EEOC successfully sued on behalf of a number of USX employees, challenging the company's requirement that an employee execute a release as a condition of receiving a mutually satisfactory pension. Prior to the EEOC suit, several individuals had filed their own suits and had lost. USX claimed that res judicata precluded retroactive relief for these individuals. The court held for USX, although it did put forth one cautionary note (albeit not one of any avail to the particular individuals before the court):

> While it is true that the Commission has the responsibility to protect a vital public interest that transcends the interests of any or all aggrieved individuals, we have concluded . . . that the Commission's responsibilities include the representation of these grievants when it seeks individual relief on their behalf. Thus, when the Commission seeks individualized benefits under the ADEA for particular grievants, as it did in this case, the Commission functions to that extent as their representative, and the doctrine of representative claim preclusion applies. We recognize that the Commission's role differs when it attempts to protect a broader interest by seeking to enjoin discrimination affecting an

---

[1821] *Id* 53.

[1822] 921 F2d 489 (3d Cir 1990).

> entire class, and we express no view regarding the question whether the doctrine of representative claim preclusion could bar individuals from sharing in the protection of an injunction that serves broader public interests.[1823]

The court made clear that "[p]rivate litigation in which the EEOC is not a party cannot preclude the EEOC from maintaining its own action because private litigants are not vested with the authority to represent the EEOC."[1824] However, to summarize the foregoing discussion, "when the EEOC seeks to represent grievants [as in the *USX* case] by attempting to obtain private benefits on their behalf, the doctrine of representative claim preclusion must be applied."[1825]

Other Issues

While remedies are discussed in Chapter 8, it should be noted here that the EEOC cannot recover liquidated damages in §17 actions.[1826] There is a split in the courts as to the securing of liquidated damages under §16(c).[1827]

The court deciding *Equal Employment Opportunity Commission v Cosmair, Inc,*[1828] asserted, by way of dictum, that "an . . . employee can waive . . . his or her . . . right to recover in a suit brought by the EEOC on the employee's behalf."[1829] Thus, "where an employee has reached a valid settlement of his claims, the EEOC

[1823] *Id* 496.

[1824] *Id.*

[1825] *Id.*

[1826] *See, e.g.,* Equal Employment Opportunity Commn v O'Grady, 857 F2d 383, 386 (7th Cir 1988); Equal Employment Opportunity Commn v Gilbarco, 615 F2d 985, 991 (4th Cir 1980); Equal Employment Opportunity Commn v Home Ins Co, 553 F Supp 704, 715 (SDNY 1982).

[1827] *Compare* Equal Employment Opportunity Commn v Gilbarco, 615 F2d 985 (4th Cir 1980) (liquidated damages recoverable); Equal Employment Opportunity Commn v Home Ins Co, 553 F Supp 704, 715 (SDNY 1982) (*id*) *with* Hodgson v Wheaton Glass Co, 446 F2d 527, 534 (3d Cir 1971) (liquidated damages not recoverable).

[1828] 821 F2d 1085 (5th Cir 1987).

[1829] *Id* 1091.

cannot seek back pay on his behalf."[1830] However, this does not preclude the EEOC from suing in its public interest role to seek elimination of the employer's discriminatory practices.[1831]

A suit may not be maintained against the head of the EEOC by a federal employee who works for another agency and who is aggrieved by the alleged failings of the EEOC in dealing with the employee's case.[1832] Nor may suit be maintained by a private sector complainant aggrieved by the agency's handling or disposition of the charge of discrimination filed with the agency.[1833]

In *Equal Employment Opportunity Commission v McLean Trucking Co*[1834] the court held that the automatic stay which comes into play when an entity files a bankruptcy petition does not apply in the instance of a suit by the EEOC.

§6.61 Jurisdiction as to EEOC Suits

Pursuant to 28 USC §§1331 and 1337 the federal courts have jurisdiction to entertain Equal Employment Opportunity Commission suits under the Age Discrimination in Employment Act (ADEA).[1835] In addition, 29 USC §217, which is incorporated into the age statute by §7(b)[1836] of the ADEA, grants the federal courts jurisdiction with regard to suits for injunctive relief. Still another source of jurisdiction is 28 USC §1345, which grants original jurisdiction to federal courts regarding civil actions brought by federal agencies.[1837]

1830 Isaacs v Caterpillar, Inc, 765 F Supp 1359, 1371 (CD Ill 1991).

1831 Equal Employment Opportunity Commn v McLean Trucking Co, 525 F2d 1007, 1010 (6th Cir 1975).

1832 Svenson v Thomas, 607 F Supp 1004 (DDC 1985).

1833 Becker v Sherwin Williams, 717 F Supp 288, 294 (DNJ 1989).

1834 834 F2d 398 (4th Cir 1987).

1835 29 USC §§621-634.

1836 *Id* §626(b).

1837 *See, e.g.*, Equal Employment Opportunity Commn v County of Allegheny, 34 Empl Prac Dec (CCH) ¶34,549 (WD Pa 1984), *affd without opinion*, 36 Empl Prac Dec (CCH) ¶35,151 (3d Cir 1985); *cf* Equal Employment Opportunity Commn v Hernando Bank, 724 F2d 1188 (5th Cir 1984) (case arising under the Equal Pay Act, 29 USC §206(d)).

§6.62 Jury Trials in EEOC Suits

The right of either party to request a jury trial in Equal Employment Opportunity Commission (EEOC) enforcement actions under the Age Discrimination in Employment Act (ADEA)[1838] is well-established, although for a time there was some uncertainty concerning the availability of jury trial in EEOC suits.[1839] Section 7(c)(1)[1840] of the Act, added to the ADEA in 1978,[1841] provides as follows:

> Any person aggrieved may bring a civil action in any court of competent jurisdiction for such legal or equitable relief as will effectuate the purposes of this chapter: *Provided,* that the right of any person to bring such action shall terminate upon the commencement of an action by the Equal Employment Opportunity Commission to enforce the right of such employee under this chapter.
>
> (2) In an action brought under paragraph (1), a person shall be entitled to a trial by jury of any issue of fact in any such action for recovery of amounts owing as a result of a violation of this chapter, regardless of whether equitable relief is sought by any party in such action.

[1838] 29 USC §§621-634.

[1839] The EEOC's enforcement authority is set forth in §7(b) of the ADEA, 29 USC §626(b), which incorporates the enforcement provisions of the Fair Labor Standards Act (FLSA). *Id* §§200-219. Under the FLSA, enforcement may be by private action or by the Secretary of Labor. There is generally no right of jury trial in actions brought by the Secretary under the FLSA. *See, e.g.,* Paradise Valley Investigation & Patrol Serv, Inc v Dunlop, 521 F2d 1342 (9th Cir 1975) (suit under 29 USC §217); Sullivan v Wirtz, 359 F2d 426 (5th Cir), *cert denied,* 385 US 852 (1966) (*id*); Wirtz v Jones, 340 F2d 901 (5th Cir 1965) (*id*). *But see* Mitchell v City Ice Co, 273 F2d 560 (5th Cir 1960) (suit pursuant to 29 USC §216(c)); United States Equal Employment Opportunity Commn v Chicago Hous Auth, 725 F Supp 392 (ND Ill 1989) (*id*). Consequently, two early district court decisions held that no right to a jury trial existed in comparable enforcement actions under the ADEA. Brennan v International Harvester Co, 7 Empl Prac Dec (CCH) ¶9171 (ND Ill 1974); Hodgson v Bowman, 4 FEP Cas (BNA) 165 (ED Tenn 1971).

[1840] 29 USC §626(c)(1).

[1841] Age Discrimination in Employment Act Amendments of 1978, Pub L No 95-256, §4(a)(2), 92 Stat 189, 190.

By the terms of §7(c)(1), a jury trial is available to a "person aggrieved." In deciding *Equal Employment Opportunity Commission v Corry Jamestown Corp*[1842] the Court of Appeals for the Third Circuit held that the EEOC is a person for the purposes of the jury trial provision. As a policy basis for this conclusion, the court observed as follows:

> By allowing the Commission to bring suit on behalf of an individual, Congress could not have intended a result which would disadvantage the individual for whose benefit the statute was enacted. [Since a private plaintiff is entitled to a jury trial and] . . . since the Commission is . . . [the complainant's] sole representative, the Commission's right to a jury trial of a legal claim . . . should be no different from that of [the complainant].[1843]

The view that jury trials are available in EEOC actions has been echoed by several other courts of appeals, as well as by a number of district courts outside these appellate courts' jurisdictions.[1844]

1842 719 F2d 1219 (3d Cir 1983).

1843 *Id* 1215.

1844 *See* Equal Employment Opportunity Commn v Chrysler Corp, 759 F2d 1523 (11th Cir 1985); Equal Employment Opportunity Commn v Ford Motor Co, 732 F2d 120 (10th Cir 1984); Equal Employment Opportunity Commn v Brown & Root, Inc, 725 F2d 348 (5th Cir 1984); Equal Employment Opportunity Commn v Colgate-Palmolive Co, 586 F Supp 1341 (SDNY 1984); Equal Employment Opportunity Commn v Cudahy Foods Co, 588 F Supp 13 (WD Wash 1983); Equal Employment Opportunity Commn v American Bakeries Co, 33 FEP Cas (BNA) 862 (ED Mo 1982); Equal Employment Opportunity Commn v Consolidated Edison Co, 33 FEP Cas (BNA) 861 (SDNY 1981); Equal Employment Opportunity Commn v Western Elec Co, 33 FEP Cas (BNA) 860 (ED Mich 1981); Equal Employment Opportunity Commn v Blue Star Foods, Inc, 22 FEP Cas (BNA) 504 (SD Iowa 1980); *see also* Equal Employment Opportunity Commn v United Air Lines, Inc, 575 F Supp 309 (ND Ill 1983), *revd on other grounds,* 755 F2d 94 (7th Cir 1985). For a dissenting view, see Norton, *EEOC's Right to a Jury Trial and Liquidated Damages in Actions Under the Age Discrimination in Employment Act: A Dissenting View,* 3 Lab Law 819 (1987).

Marshall v Holland Hitch Co, 16 Empl Prac Dec (CCH) ¶8322 (WD Mich 1978), was decided a month after the 1978 amendment was enacted. The court relied on FLSA precedents to deny a jury trial, but it did not discuss the effect of the amendment.

Generally, joinder of legal and equitable claims does not result in the waiver of the right to a jury trial as to the legal claims.[1845] Given the language of §7(c) of the ADEA, it is clear that whether legal or equitable relief is sought by the EEOC, a jury trial is available regarding any issue of fact. In *Equal Employment Opportunity Commission v Indian River Transport Co*[1846] the court held that, in an ADEA suit brought by the EEOC under both §16(c)[1847] and §17[1848] of the Federal Labor Standards Act (FLSA), a jury trial was appropriate concerning the claims under the former section. As for §17 suits, the court stated that "[c]ases brought under 29 U.S.C. §217 do not require a jury trial."[1849] As discussed more extensively in **§6.44,** the jury trial generally will be conducted first. The jury verdict will be accorded varying degrees of force, depending on the jurisdiction, by the court when it addresses the equitable issues. For example, the court stated in *Indian River Transport* that "[t]he legal issues will be put to the jury first with the Court's decision on equitable issues to be guided by the jury's award."[1850]

Failure to file a timely jury demand can be rectified by a subsequent motion, but the granting of a motion for a jury trial is within the trial court's discretion to grant or deny, and unjustifiable delay may result in a negative ruling.[1851] In exercising its discretion, the court should "look favorably toward a . . . motion unless persuasive reasons exist to deny it," according to the

---

1845 Equal Employment Opportunity Commn v Brown & Root Co, Inc, 725 F2d 348, 349 n1 (5th Cir 1984) (citing Dairy Queen, Inc v Wood, 369 US 469 (1962)); *accord* Equal Employment Opportunity Commn v Ford Motor Co, 732 F2d 120 (10th Cir 1984).

1846 33 FEP Cas (BNA) 862 (MD Fla 1982).

1847 29 USC §216(c). See generally **§6.60.**

1848 29 USC §217. See generally **§6.60.**

1849 33 FEP at 862.

1850 *Id.*

1851 *See* Equal Employment Opportunity Commn v El Paso Natural Gas Co, 36 FEP Cas (BNA) 1210 (WD Tex 1985).

court deciding *Equal Employment Opportunity Commission v Britrail Travel International Corp.*[1852]

§6.63 Intervention by Private Grievants in EEOC Suits: Generally

As discussed in **§6.54,** initiation by the Equal Employment Opportunity Commission (EEOC) of a suit under the Age Discrimination in Employment Act (ADEA)[1853] generally will bar subsequent suits by individual grievants arising out of the same facts. A few courts even have held that a private suit filed prior to the EEOC action will be terminated by virtue of the later EEOC suit.[1854]

The bar on private suits has two statutory sources. Section 7(c)(1) of the ADEA[1855] specifically provides that "the right of any person to bring . . . [an] action [for legal or equitable relief] shall terminate upon the commencement of an action by the Equal Employment Opportunity Commission to enforce the right of such employee[.] " In addition, §7(b)[1856] of the ADEA incorporates §16(b) of the Fair Labor Standards Act (FLSA),[1857] and this provision authorizes grievants, as well as the enforcement agency, to sue for back pay and liquidated damages. Section 16(b) also contains a provision cutting off the ability of a grievant to sue when an agency action is commenced: "The right provided by this subsection to bring an action by or on behalf of any employee, and the right of any employee to become a party plaintiff to any such action, shall terminate upon the filing

---

1852 129 FRD 116, 117 (DNJ 1989), *affd without opinion,* 919 F2d 134 (3d Cir 1990).

1853 29 USC §§621-634.

1854 See **§6.54.**

1855 29 USC §626(c)(1).

1856 *Id* §626(b).

1857 *Id* §216(b).

of a complaint by the . . . [enforcement agency] in an action under section . . . [17, 29 USC] §217[.]"[1858]

The primary purpose of these bars on private litigation is to avert multiple suits. Obviously, a premise on which they are grounded is that the enforcement agency will adequately represent the interests of aggrieved employees or job applicants. Whether the agency in fact does so in a given case may be a matter of dispute, however, for the litigation priorities and/or strategies of the EEOC may diverge from those of the individuals whose interests it is ostensibly protecting. One can be cynical and conjecture that this divergence might stem from political pressures or from an administrative bias tilting toward the protection of employers from liability, rather than vigorous vindication of employee rights. From a more positive view, the potential for a split between an individual grievant's goals and those of the enforcement agency may be attributable to the fact that the EEOC, while charged with protecting individual employees' rights, also has a public interest role that legitimately can conflict with, or at least detract from, this charge.

This public interest role has been specifically referred to in cases involving enforcement by the Secretary of Labor under §17 of the FLSA, a provision enforced by the EEOC in the ADEA context. For example, in *Wirtz v Jones*[1859] the court observed that "the purpose of the injunction . . . [under §17] is not to collect a debt owed by an employer to his employee but to correct a

[1858] Actually, the cutoff provision in §16(b) is of more limited reach than the ADEA provision. The §16(b) cutoff only comes into play if the government files suit under §17; if suit is filed only under §16, the §16(b) cutoff does not apply. (Section 17 of the FLSA authorizes suits by the enforcement agency for injunctive relief).

Accordingly, if a settlement were to be negotiated in a §16(c) government FLSA enforcement action, it would not bind parties who had not opted into the suit and they could file their own suits, even if the settlement was nationwide in scope. *See, e.g.*, Dickey v Wendy's Intl, 24 Wage & Hour Cas (BNA) 1026 (ND Ga 1980). However, because of §7(c)(1) of the ADEA, even a government suit under §16(c) would operate to bar a private action.

[1859] 340 F2d 901 (5th Cir 1965).

continuing offense against the public interest."[1860] And in an ADEA ruling, *Equal Employment Opportunity Commission v Pan American World Airways, Inc,*[1861] the court asserted that "the government represents the interests of all groups, and not just those on whose behalf the government originally filed suit."[1862]

While put forth in the context of a suit arising under Title VII of the Civil Rights Act of 1964,[1863] the characterization of the EEOC's public interest role in *General Telephone Co v Equal Employment Opportunity Commission*[1864] is apposite here. This is because the ADEA's substantive prohibitions are modeled on those contained in Title VII, and because the EEOC enforces Title VII as well as the ADEA. The *General Telephone* Court stated as follows:

> Although the EEOC can secure specific relief, such as hiring or reinstatement, constructive seniority, or damages for backpay or benefits denied, on behalf of discrimination victims, the agency is guided by "the overriding public interest in equal employment opportunity . . . asserted through direct Federal enforcement." 118 Cong. Rec. 4941 (1972). When the EEOC acts, albeit at the behest of and for the benefit of specific individuals, it acts also to vindicate the public interest in preventing employment discrimination.[1865]

Given the foreclosure of subsequent private litigation when the EEOC sues, it arguably follows that private grievants should

---

[1860] *Id* 904.

[1861] 622 F Supp 633 (ND Cal 1985), *appeal dismissed,* 796 F2d 314 (9th Cir 1986), *cert denied,* 479 US 1030 (1987).

[1862] *Id* 640; *accord* Donovan v University of Tex, 643 F2d 1201, 1208 (5th Cir 1981); Equal Employment Opportunity Commn v AT&T Co, 365 F Supp 1105, 1122 (ED Pa 1973), *affd,* 506 F2d 735 (3d Cir 1974).

[1863] 42 USC §§2000e through 2000e-17.

[1864] 446 US 318 (1980).

[1865] *Id* 326 (footnote omitted); *see also* Equal Employment Opportunity Commn v United States Steel Corp, 921 F2d 489, 496 (3d Cir 1990) (ADEA case).

be able to intervene in EEOC suits to protect their interests in situations where they feel, for one reason or another, that the EEOC is not adequately safeguarding them. In fact, however, the meager body of case law is mixed: there is support both for concluding that intervention is barred in ADEA cases and that it is possible, at least in some circumstances.

The premises for making the argument for intervention are Federal Rule of Civil Procedure 24, and a non-ADEA, non-FLSA decision: *Trbovich v United Mine Workers of America.*[1866] Federal Rule 24 sets forth two bases for intervention as of right, and a further basis for permissive intervention:

> (a) Intervention of Right. Upon timely application anyone shall be permitted to intervene in an action (1) when a statute of the United States confers an unconditional right to intervene; or (2) when the applicant claims an interest relating to the property or transaction which is the subject of the action and he is so situated that the disposition of the action may as a practical matter impair or impede his ability to protect that interest, unless the applicant's interest is adequately represented by existing parties.
> (b) Permissive Intervention. Upon timely application anyone may be permitted to intervene in an action: (1) when a statute of the United States confers a conditional right to intervene; or (2) when an applicant's claim or defense and the main action have a question of law or fact in common. When a party to an action relies for ground of claim or defense upon any statute or executive order administered by a federal or state governmental officer or agency or upon any regulation, order, requirement, or agreement issued or made pursuant to the statute or executive order, the officer or agency upon timely application may be permitted to intervene in the action. In exercising its discretion the court shall consider whether the intervention will unduly delay or prejudice the adjudication of the rights of the original parties.

[1866] 404 US 528 (1972).

In the Title VII context, intervention as of right is clearly authorized by the statute.[1867] Of course, this authorization of an unconditional right to intervene does not mean that anyone may intervene at any time for any reason whatsoever. The intervention must be "timely"[1868] and the person seeking intervention must be "aggrieved."[1869] In determining the issue of timeliness, Title VII courts look to a number of factors.[1870] The question of who is aggrieved also has generated litigation.[1871]

The ADEA stands in sharp contrast to Title VII. The ADEA contains no affirmative authorization for intervention and so intervention is not available pursuant to Rule 24(a)(1).[1872] This fact does not necessarily preclude the possibility of intervention, however, since, arguably, a party still could intervene as of right under Rule 24(a)(2) or seek permission to intervene under Rule 24(b). It is at this juncture that the *Trbovich* decision becomes relevant, although certainly not dispositive.

Trbovich involved an action instituted by the Secretary of Labor under the Labor-Management Reporting and Disclosure Act of 1959 (LMRDA)[1873] to set aside an election of officers of the United Mine Workers. The petitioner was an individual member of the union who sought to intervene. The Court held that he could do so, subject to some limitations. The Secretary of Labor argued that intervention was barred because one provision of the LMRDA makes suit by the Secretary the "exclusive" post-

---

[1867] 42 USC §2000e-5(f)(1).

[1868] Fed R Civ P 24(a)

[1869] 42 USC §2000e-5(f)(1).

[1870] *See, e.g.,* Equal Employment Opportunity Commn v Westinghouse Elec Corp, 675 F2d 164 (8th Cir 1982); Stallworth v Monsanto, 558 F2d 257 (5th Cir 1977).

[1871] *See, e.g.,* Equal Employment Opportunity Commn v AT&T Co, 365 F Supp 1105 (ED Pa 1973), *affd on other grounds,* 506 F2d 735 (3d Cir 1974); United States v Allegheny-Ludlum Indus, Inc, 63 FRD 3 (ND Ala 1974), *affd,* 517 F2d 826 (5th Cir), *cert denied,* 425 US 944 (1975).

[1872] *Accord* Mitchell v McCorstin, 728 F2d 1422 (11th Cir 1984).

[1873] 29 USC §481 *et seq.*

election remedy.[1874] While the Court had held earlier that this provision barred union members from initiating private suits to set aside union elections,[1875] here the Court reasoned that the petitioner was simply seeking to participate in a pending suit that was plainly authorized by the statute and thus it could not be said that the exclusivity section defeated his claim. Reviewing the legislative history, the Court concluded that intervention was not per se barred:

> [T]he legislative history supports the conclusion that Congress intended to prevent members [of unions] from pressing claims not thought meritorious by the Secretary, and from litigating in forums or at times different from those chosen by the Secretary. Only if intervention would frustrate either of those objectives can the statute fairly be read to prohibit intervention[.][1876]

In line with this reasoning, the Court held that Trbovich could not intervene in the Secretary's suit to add two additional grounds for setting aside the union election, since these were claims that the Secretary presumably had determined to be without merit. But the Court further held that Trbovich could intervene as to the claims of illegality already presented by the Secretary's complaint.

The Court then turned to the question of whether Trbovich satisfied the requirement of Rule 24(a)(2), i.e., that his interests were not being adequately represented by the Secretary. In a footnote the Court observed that "[t]he requirement of the Rule is satisfied if the applicant shows that representation of his interest 'may be' inadequate; and the burden of making that showing should be treated as minimal."[1877] In reaching the conclusion that the burden indeed had been met by Trbovich, the Court focused on the dual role played by the Secretary of Labor under

---

[1874] *Id* §483.

[1875] Calhoon v Harvey, 379 US 134, 140 (1964).

[1876] 404 US at 536.

[1877] *Id* 538 n10; *see also* Usery v Brandel, 87 FRD 670 (WD Mich 1980).

the LMRDA—a duality arguably likewise present in the context of the EEOC's enforcement of the ADEA. The Court stated as follows:

> The statute plainly imposes on the Secretary the duty to serve two distinct interests, which are related, but not identical. First, the statute gives the individual union members certain rights against their unions, and "the Secretary of Labor in effect becomes the union member's lawyer" for purposes of enforcing those rights. . . . And second, the Secretary has an obligation to protect the "vital public interest in assuring free and democratic union elections that transcends the narrower interest of the complaining union member. . . . " Both functions are important, and they may not always dictate precisely the same approach to the conduct of the litigation. Even if the Secretary is performing his duties, broadly conceived, as well as can be expected, the union member may have a valid complaint about the performance of "his lawyer." Such a complaint, filed by the member who initiated the entire enforcement proceeding, would be regarded as sufficient to warrant relief in the form of intervention under Rule 24(a)(2).[1878]

§6.64 —Intervention by Private Grievants in EEOC Suits: Case Law

On its face, the Age Discrimination in Employment Act (ADEA)[1879] does not authorize intervention as of right in suits filed by the Equal Employment Opportunity Commission (EEOC).[1880] Arguably, however, intervention still may be successfully sought pursuant to Federal Rule of Civil Procedure 24(a)(2) or (b). There are very few ADEA decisions dealing with

---

[1878] 404 US at 539 (citations omitted).

[1879] 29 USC §§621-634.

[1880] *Accord* Mitchell v McCorstin, 728 F2d 1422 (11th Cir 1984).

the issue of intervention in EEOC suits, and they diverge in their dispositions.[1881]

Equal Employment Opportunity Commission v Pan American World Airways, Inc,[1882] concerned the EEOC's efforts to vindicate the claims of former Pan Am pilots who had lost their positions on attainment of age 60 and were then barred by Pan Am from moving over to flight engineer positions. There were 514 individuals who had been, or possibly had been, so harmed. Two of them ultimately objected to the settlement negotiated by the EEOC and one of them, an individual who had been allowed to intervene for the limited purpose of challenging the settlement agreement, argued on appeal that the trial court had improperly denied his motion to intervene as a full party plaintiff.

The appellate court ruled that the denial of the motion had been proper. In its view, the objector lacked the requisite interest in the litigation that is required by Rule 24(a).[1883] This was because, pursuant to §7(c)[1884] of the ADEA, an individual's own private suit is foreclosed after the EEOC files suit on his or her behalf:[1885] "King's [i.e., the objector's] rights under the ADEA terminated upon the commencement of the EEOC's action. . . . Thus, King . . . [had] no interest with which to support his intervention as a party plaintiff under Rule 24(a),"[1886] which provides for an unconditional right to intervene when "the applicant claims an interest relating to the property or transaction which is the subject of the [legal] action and the applicant is so situated that the disposition of the action may as a practical matter impair

---

[1881] The issue of intervention also may arise in cases involving private plaintiffs. *See, e.g.,* Cook v Pan Am World Airways, Inc, 52 FEP Cas (BNA) 903 (SDNY 1986). Typically, the legal analysis in these cases will not raise any particular ADEA concerns, but rather will be grounded in the case law construing Fed R Civ P 24.

[1882] 897 F2d 1499 (9th Cir), *cert denied,* 498 US 815 (1990).

[1883] Fed R Civ P 24(a).

[1884] 29 USC §626(c).

[1885] See **§6.54.**

[1886] 897 F2d at 1509.

or impede the applicant's ability to protect that interest.''[1887] The same rationale took care of King's request for permissive intervention under Rule 24(b): "Because the EEOC's commencement of its enforcement action terminated any rights King may have had against Pan Am, King can claim no substantive rights over which the district court would have had jurisdiction.''[1888]

While the would-be intervenors elicited extensive judicial analysis, they met with no better response in *Equal Employment Opportunity Commission v Consolidated Edison Co,*[1889] which involved an EEOC enforcement action under §16(c)[1890] and §17[1891] of the Fair Labor Standards Act (FLSA),[1892] both of which are incorporated into the ADEA by virtue of §7(b) of that Act.[1893] The EEOC suit had been filed prior to any suits being filed by individual employees. After more than two years of extensive discovery and pretrial preparation, the EEOC and the defendant entered into a negotiated settlement on the eve of trial, along with a stipulation to dismiss the case with prejudice. A number of the defendant's employees, whose rights the EEOC claimed to be protecting, objected to the terms of the settlement. Accordingly, they filed their own suit and moved: for an order pursuant to Federal Rule of Civil Procedure 60(b)(6); (1) dismissing the EEOC action without prejudice as to them and allowing them to litigate their claims in their newly filed suit; or (2) allowing them to opt out of the settlement and directing the EEOC to prosecute their claims; or (3) for an order pursuant to Rule 24(a)(2) allowing them to intervene in the EEOC suit, to opt out of the settlement, and to pursue their claims; or (4) for an order to hold a hearing as to the fairness of the settlement. The court responded negatively in all respects.

[1887] Fed R Civ P 24(a).

[1888] 897 F2d at 1510.

[1889] 557 F Supp 468 (SDNY 1983).

[1890] 29 USC §216(c).

[1891] *Id* §217.

[1892] *Id* §§200-219.

[1893] *Id* §626(b).

The court asserted that "once the EEOC commences an enforcement suit, an employee who has failed to file his own action and on whose behalf relief is sought is not permitted to intervene as a party pursuant to Fed R Civ P 24(a) in the ongoing suit."[1894] It cited a number of FLSA decisions in support of this position.[1895] (Subsequently, the court deciding *Equal Employment Opportunity Commission v Boeing Co*[1896] also held that once the EEOC files an ADEA action, the right of a person on whose behalf the suit is filed is terminated, and this being so, the individual has no legal interest to protect and so intervention pursuant to Rule 24(a)(2) is foreclosed.)

The *Consolidated Edison* court further stated that an individual nonparty claimant is not permitted to opt out of an EEOC-initiated suit and then commence his or her own suit.[1897] Moreover, if the EEOC files suit prior to a filing by an aggrieved employee on whose behalf it seeks relief, the disposition with prejudice of the claims asserted by the EEOC has preclusive effect on the employee's ADEA claims.[1898] The *Consolidated Edison* court summarized by stating the following:

> [A]n employee who fails to file a law suit seeking redress of his ADEA-recognized rights prior to the EEOC's commencement of a suit on such employee's behalf lacks any power to assert such rights, regardless whether the asser-

---

[1894] 557 F Supp at 472.

[1895] *See, e.g.*, Donovan v University of Tex, 643 F2d 1201, 1208 (5th Cir 1981); Marshall v United States Postal Serv, 481 F Supp 179, 180, 181 (DDC 1979); Usery v Board of Pub Educ, 418 F Supp 1037 (WD Pa 1976); Equal Employment Opportunity Commn v AT&T Co, 365 F Supp 1105, 1121 (ED Pa 1973), *affd on other grounds*, 506 F2d 735 (3d Cir 1974). (*Marshall* concerned intervention in the context of a suit brought pursuant to §16(c) of the FLSA. *Donovan, Usery*, and *American Telephone & Telegraph* addressed intervention in suits brought pursuant to §17 of the FLSA.)

[1896] 109 FRD 6 (WD Wash 1985).

[1897] 557 F Supp at 472.

[1898] *Id* 472; *accord* Equal Employment Opportunity Commn v Pan Am World Airways, Inc, 897 F2d 1499 (9th Cir), *cert denied*, 498 US 815 (1990); *see also* Dunlop v Pan Am World Airways, Inc, 672 F2d 1044, 1072 n6 (2d Cir 1982).

> tion is attempted within or without the EEOC suit, or before or after judgment is entered.[1899]

The *Consolidated Edison* court rejected the claimants' fairness argument, which was tied to §16(c), which provides: "The right . . . to bring an action by or on behalf of any employee . . . and of any employee to become a party plaintiff . . . shall terminate upon the filing of a complaint by the . . . [EEOC], . . . unless such action is dismissed without prejudice on motion of the . . . [EEOC]." The claimants argued that, in situations where the EEOC has moved for and obtained a dismissal with prejudice, the agency must meet the standards of an adequate class representative (notwithstanding that class actions under Federal Rule of Civil Procedure 23 may not be maintained under the ADEA or the FLSA.)[1900] In addition, they argued that if an individual claimant is adjudged by the court to have been inadequately represented by the EEOC, due process requires that the dismissal of his or her claim with prejudice should not be binding and that he or she should be allowed to proceed. The court, however, asserted that "the EEOC must be given the broad discretion accorded any plaintiff in the conduct and discontinuance of its suit."[1901]

Thus, the court closed the door to the intervenors and embraced a position holding that intervention is unavailable in ADEA suits. It left only one small loophole, grounded in equity: it was conceivable that there might arise instances of EEOC conduct relating to an enforcement proceeding that would require the application of the court's inherent equitable powers.[1902] Here, however, the facts did not warrant such judicial response.

The court did not speak in terms of equity (which is understandable, perhaps, because it was unreceptive to the intervenor's arguments and so had no occasion to invoke equitable

---

[1899] 557 F Supp at 472; *accord* Equal Employment Opportunity Commn v Chrysler Corp, 49 FEP (BNA) 1439 (ED Mich 1989).

[1900] See **§6.45.**

[1901] 557 F Supp at 474.

[1902] *Id.*

principles) in *Equal Employment Opportunity Commission v Chrysler Corp.*[1903] Even so, the facts arguably supported a different tack. The individual attempting to intervene originally had been named by the EEOC as one of 1,600 party plaintiffs in a suit it had filed in 1981 on their behalf. During the course of the litigation the EEOC voluntarily dismissed approximately 1,400 of these individuals. One of these was an individual, Soter, who was voluntarily dismissed by the agency on January 5, 1989. The suit, of which he was now no longer a part, was resolved by a partial consent decree dated December 23, 1988, and a final consent decree dated January 11, 1989. Neither decree named Soter as an individual entitled to relief.

The court first reasoned that Soter was never himself a plaintiff, notwithstanding his designation as such by the EEOC. Rather, he was merely a statutory beneficiary of the EEOC's suit.[1904] Rejecting his effort to intervene pursuant to Rule 24(a) by invoking *Equal Employment Opportunity Commission v Consolidated Edison,* the court also found wanting his effort to satisfy the requirements of Rule 24(b) for permissive intervention. It reasoned that: (1) Soter had never filed a charge of unlawful discrimination with the EEOC; (2) that such a charge is a prerequisite to filing an ADEA suit; (3) that a court therefore would not have had jurisdiction as to his suit had he filed it independently; and (4) a party seeking permissive intervention must, as Soter could not, "establish a basis for federal subject matter jurisdiction independent of the court's jurisdiction over the underlying action."[1905] The court did not discuss whether Soter's failure to file a charge was due to the EEOC's having originally undertaken to represent his interests in the suit filed in 1981 and whether, if that indeed was the reason he did not file a charge, it would be a basis for according him equitable relief from the charge-filing requirement so as to allow him then to surmount the jurisdictional barrier to granting his motion for permissive intervention.

1903 49 FEP Cas (BNA) 1439 (ED Mich 1989).

1904 *Id* 1440.

1905 *Id* 1441.

The lesson for a grievant is that even when the EEOC undertakes to sue on one's behalf, he or she had best still file a timely charge of discrimination with the EEOC to protect the possible option of later intervening. (Of course, for the courts in the cases discussed earlier, i.e., *Pan American World Airways* and *Consolidated Edison,* a timely filed charge would not have altered their positions that intervention was unavailable.)

Equal Employment Opportunity Commission v Eastern Air Lines, Inc,[1906] stands in contrast to the foregoing decisions, for the court operated on the assumption that intervention under Rule 24(a)(2) was not barred as a matter of law.[1907] Even so, the *Eastern Airlines* court, in dictum, did express particular deference to the EEOC's public interest role:

> It is noteworthy, and not insignificant, that when Congress saw fit to limit an individual discriminatee's private right to bring an action [by barring private suit once the EEOC filed suit] it did not expand the individual's right to enter the litigation by granting an unconditional right to intervene as Rule 24(a)(1) allows. While not the dispositive element in this question of intervention, the statutory scheme at least superficially justifies the conclusion that Congress had high regard for the agency authorized to promote age discriminatees' rights and did not wish to dilute the agency's power to litigate, even at the expense of a particular discriminatee's private action. Evidently, regardless how substantial the interest of any single litigant, that interest must yield to the larger interest served by EEOC when it proceeds on behalf of that litigant.[1908]

The thrust of the intervenors' argument of course was that the EEOC had failed to adequately protect their interests. Indeed, while the facts were only sketchily set forth by the court,

---

1906 97 FRD 646 (SD Fla 1983), *appeal dismissed,* 736 F2d 635 (11th Cir 1984).

1907 Similarly, in Mitchell v McCorstin, 728 F2d 1422 (11th Cir 1984), the court adhered to this assumption. *McCorstin,* however, involved intervention in a private suit, rather than in one brought by the EEOC.

1908 97 FRD at 649.

it would appear that the intervenors' view of things was not entirely baseless. When the case first arose, there were 23 charging parties. After two and a half years of pretrial activity, the dispute was settled. The 15 proposed intervenors objected. By the terms of the settlement all claims to back pay and liquidated damages were forfeited, and reinstatement was provided for only half of the charging parties. Thus, the sole relief obtained consisted of $30,000 in cash and $35,000 in travel credits, and the money and credits had to be divided equally among the charging parties. In brief, the charging parties wound up with little, particularly those who were not awarded reinstatement. Notwithstanding the paltry recovery, the court was unpersuaded by the intervenors' argument, based on *Trbovich v United Mine Workers of America,*[1909] that their representation by the EEOC was inadequate. In the court's view, "[t]he fairness of the consent decree . . . justifies the conclusion that representation was adequate."[1910] Because liability was not clear-cut, the relief secured, while limited, was fair under the circumstances, the court reasoned.

Even though *Eastern Air Lines* certainly is more employee-protective than are *Pan American World Airways* and *Consolidated Edison,* given that the *Eastern Air Lines* court at least was willing to accept the proposition that intervention was possible under Rule 24(a), the fact is that the decision hardly demonstrated an enthusiastic concern for employee rights. The deference accorded to the EEOC's decision to settle the case, if applied generally by other courts in other cases, sets a model affording applicants for intervention little chance of succeeding.[1911]

[1909] 404 US 528 (1972). See **§6.63.**

[1910] 97 FRD at 652 (footnote omitted).

[1911] While judicial deference to consent decrees is typical, and thus the *Eastern Air Lines* court cannot be charged with having abdicated its proper role, the degree of deference perhaps was more pronounced than either the facts, as disclosed in the opinion, or the law warranted. Indeed, the court's deference would seem to conflict with the minor burden imposed in *Trbovich* upon an intervenor claiming inadequate representation, as discussed in **§6.63.**

A much more employee-protective approach was adopted in *Equal Employment Opportunity Commission v Boeing Co.*[1912] The court, after first rejecting a claim to intervention as of right under Rule 24(a)(2), went on to deny permissive intervention under Rule 24(b). It reasoned that such intervention requires that there be an independent basis for federal subject matter jurisdiction over the claims. In an ADEA action commenced by the EEOC prior to any individual suit, there is no such basis. Indeed, the ADEA cuts off the possibility of a private suit subsequent to an EEOC action.[1913] Notwithstanding these negative responses to the would-be intervenors, the court went on to exercise its equity powers to allow the claimants to participate in various aspects of discovery and trial. The court set forth more specifically the role allowed the intervenors and their counsel:

1. They would be deemed to be parties of record for the purpose of receiving service of pleadings and scheduling of hearings and depositions;
2. the EEOC would be required to consult with the claimants' counsel before finalizing any proposed settlement and, while the claimants could not bar the EEOC from settling, the claimants could argue the fairness of the settlement prior to the entry of any final settlement;
3. the EEOC had to consult with the claimants' attorneys concerning case progress, motions, and discovery;
4. the claimants' attorneys were allowed to be present at all depositions and to inquire of each deponent; and
5. the claimants' attorneys were allowed to file separate briefs on all motions, and to participate in the trial (although the exact extent of such participation was left for later determination).

[1912] 109 FRD 6 (WD Wash 1985).

[1913] See **§6.54.**

Subsequent to *Boeing, Equal Employment Opportunity Commission v Pan American World Airways, Inc,*[1914] was decided. A group of individuals objected to the consent decree into which the named litigants had entered. Without engaging in detailed analysis, the court, largely relying on *Boeing,* allowed the claimants to intervene for the limited purpose of objecting to the decree. Subsequently, the district court addressed the efforts of 57 individuals to intervene in the suit following the district court's disapproval of a proposed consent decree. This time, the court denied their motion. It recognized that there was good reason to believe that the EEOC had inadequately represented these individuals, since the Commission on two occasions in the course of the litigation had approved proposed settlements rejected by the court because they were not sufficiently favorable to the individuals whose interests the EEOC purported to represent. And the court was willing to envision permissive intervention as being appropriate if, but only if, "the EEOC's representation is positively inadequate."[1915] But here there was "no indication that the EEOC . . . [would] fail to adequately represent the claimants at trial."[1916] Moreover, the court reasoned that "denying intervention as full party plaintiffs here . . . [would] not preclude permitting limited intervention in order to oppose any future consent decrees."[1917]

While the foregoing analysis would appear to preclude reading the court's position as being one completely antipathetic to intervention, the court went on to express a seemingly contrary position regarding permissive intervention. It invoked the rationale used in the anti-intervention decisions discussed earlier in this section, i.e., that the EEOC's filing of suit divests private

---

[1914] 622 F Supp 633 (ND Cal 1985), *appeal dismissed,* 796 F2d 314 (9th Cir 1986), *cert denied,* 479 US 1030 (1987).

[1915] Equal Employment Opportunity Commn v Pan Am World Airways, Inc, 52 FEP Cas (BNA) 926, 928 (ND Cal 1987).

[1916] *Id.*

[1917] *Id.*

parties of the right to sue and thus they have no independent jurisdictional basis on which to ground intervention. Because of this, "no showing that the EEOC's representation was inadequate, however compelling, could justify intervention under Rule 24(b)."[1918] Moreover, the court used this same logic to bar intervention here under Rule 24(a). Thus, it is surely problematic to read the 1987 district court opinion in *Pan American* as supportive of intervention, notwithstanding some language seemingly favorable to intervention in the abstract, because, once uttered, that language was immediately, and without a convincing explanation for the sudden shift in position, effectively negated.

Having whipsawed the movants seeking intervention with contrary positions, the court ultimately allowed for a "hybrid participation"[1919] by the claimants by allowing them to participate at trial as amici. In exercising its "inherent equitable powers,"[1920] the court justified this unusual tack on three grounds:

> First, the claimants have succeeded in raising some doubts about the effectiveness of EEOC representation. Second, the court is convinced that the claimants will provide a needed perspective and expertise to the proceedings.
>
> Finally, and perhaps most significantly, the EEOC welcomes such participation.[1921]

1918 *Id.*

1919 52 FEP at 928.

1920 *Id.*

1921 *Id.* The same type of participation was allowed in Equal Employment Opportunity Commn v Boeing Co, 109 FRD 6 (WD Wash 1985). The nature of the amici's involvement in *Pan American* was addressed by the court, 622 F Supp at 648, as it also was in *Boeing.* 109 FRD at 11. In a later ruling in the *Pan Am* litigation, the appellate court held that it was proper for the trial court to have denied intervention both under Rule 24(a) and Rule 24(b) to two claimants who had not been involved in the litigation when the two district court decisions discussed in the text were rendered. Equal Employment Opportunity Commn v Pan Am World Airways, Inc, 897 F2d 1499 (9th Cir), *cert denied,* 498 US 815 (1990).

General Issues for Both Private Claimants and the EEOC in Pursuing ADEA Claims

§6.65 The Res Judicata and Collateral Estoppel Effects of State and Federal Court Decisions

Pursuant to §14(b)[1922] of the Age Discrimination in Employment Act (ADEA),[1923] an individual who believes himself or herself to be the victim of age discrimination and intends to pursue an ADEA claim first must pursue a state remedy if the state has (1) a law prohibiting discrimination in employment because of age and (2) there is a state authority that can grant or seek relief from such discrimination.[1924] *Oscar Mayer & Co v Evans,*[1925] a Supreme Court decision, confirms that resort to the state remedy is mandatory.[1926] If a suit under the ADEA is filed while the state action is pending, the state proceeding typically will be stayed.[1927] If, however, a state determination is made before any such stay, the question arises as to the legal effect of that determination.

Title VII Precedents

Initially, ADEA case law did not directly address the consequences of a state court determination for an ADEA action. Title VII of the Civil Rights Act of 1964[1928] however, contains a very similar provision,[1929] which was the source of the ADEA's §14(b). Accordingly, and as expressed by the *Oscar Mayer* Court, inter-

---

[1922] 29 USC §633(b).

[1923] *Id* §§621-634.

[1924] See **§6.25.**

[1925] 441 US 750 (1979).

[1926] See **§6.25.**

[1927] See **§6.27.**

[1928] 42 USC §§2000e through 2000e-17.

[1929] *Id* §2000e-5(c).

pretations of Title VII's provision very strongly guide the construction of §14(b):

> Since the ADEA and Title VII share a common purpose, the elimination of discrimination in the workplace, since the language of §14(b) is almost *in haec verba* with [Title VII's] §706(c), and since the legislative history of §14(b) indicates that its source was §706(c), we may properly conclude that Congress intended that the construction of §14(b) should follow that of §706(c).[1930]

It follows, then, that the Supreme Court's 1982 decision in *Kremer v Chemical Construction Corp,*[1931] while addressed to the Title VII provision, bears very heavily on the ADEA's §14(b).

The *Kremer* Court addressed the res judicata[1932] and collateral estoppel[1933] significance for a Title VII federal suit of a state appellate court decision affirming the dismissal by the state agency of a religious discrimination claim. The Court looked to 28 USC §1738, which requires federal courts to give the same preclusive effect to state court judgments that those judgments would be given in the courts of the state from which the judgment emerged.[1934] An exception will not be recognized to §1738 "unless a later statute contains an express or implied partial repeal."[1935] Clearly, Title VII contains no express repeal; thus, the question for the *Kremer* court was whether a partial repeal as to Title VII cases could be implied. The Court answered in

---

1930 441 US at 756.

1931 456 US 461 (1982).

1932 "Under res judicata, a final judgment on the merits of an action precludes the parties or their privies from relitigating issues that were or could have been raised in that action." *Id* 466-67 n6.

1933 "Under collateral estoppel, once a court decides an issue of fact or law necessary to its judgment, that decision precludes relitigation of the same issue on [sic] a different cause of action between the same parties." *Id.*

1934 28 USC §1738 provides: "The . . . judicial proceedings of any court of any State . . . shall have the same full faith and credit in every court within the United States and its Territories and Possessions as they have by law or usage in the courts of such State[.]"

1935 456 US at 468.

the negative, reciting the two well-settled situations in which a repeal could be implied:

> "(1) [W]here provisions in the two acts are in irreconcilable conflict, the later act to the extent of the conflict constitutes an implied repeal of the earlier one; and (2) if the later act covers the whole subject of the earlier one and is clearly intended as a substitute, it will operate similarly as a repeal of the earlier act. But, in either case, the intention of the legislature to repeal must be clear and manifest. . . ."[1936]

Title VII fit neither category, according to the Court, given that state antidiscrimination laws play an integral role in the Title VII enforcement scheme. Apart from Title VII's statutory language, which specifically directs grievants to seek state relief, the Court looked to legislative history and found no basis there for concluding that Title VII constituted a partial repeal of §1738. Thus, the Court concluded that the state court's ruling on Kremer's claim was binding for res judicata and collateral estoppel purposes, and accordingly the district court's dismissal of his suit was affirmed.[1937]

There were two caveats put forth in the case. First, only state court rulings have a preclusive effect on ADEA actions: "[I]t is clear that unreviewed administrative determinations by state agencies . . . should not preclude . . . [federal court] review even if such a decision were to be afforded a preclusive effect in a state's own courts."[1938] Second, for state court proceedings to be preclusive, they "need do no more than satisfy the minimum procedural requirements of the Fourteenth Amendment's Due

---

1936 *Id* (quoting Radzanower v Touche Ross & Co, 426 US 148, 154 (1976), which in turn was quoting from Posadas v National City Bank, 296 US 497, 503 (1936)).

1937 *Accord* Unger v Consolidated Foods Corp, 693 F2d 703 (7th Cir 1982), *cert denied,* 460 US 1102 (1983). The *Unger* court held that *Kremer* applied retrospectively.

1938 456 US at 470 n7.

Process Clause."[1939] The Court examined the state administrative proceedings (later reviewed by the state court) which resulted in the dismissal of Kremer's claim and concluded that the Due Process Clause was satisfied.

Subsequently in *University of Tennessee v Elliott*[1940] the Court refused to create a federal common law rule of preclusion barring Title VII plaintiffs from litigating in federal court claims already addressed in state administrative proceedings.[1941]

Applicability of *Kremer* and *Elliott* to the ADEA

The only apparent bases for arguing against the application of *Kremer* and *Elliott* to the ADEA are the differences between the structure and interpretation of Title VII and the age discrimination statute. First, Title VII bars the filing of a charge with the Equal Employment Opportunity Commission (EEOC) until 60 days after the grievant has invoked the state remedy, unless the state proceedings have terminated earlier.[1942] In contrast, the ADEA allows for simultaneous filing and processing of the state complaint and the EEOC charge. The *Kremer* Court noted the 60-day delay requirement contained in Title VII in the course of supporting its conclusion that, rather than Title VII impliedly repealing 28 USC §1738, Title VII in fact envisioned state antidiscrimination laws as playing an integral role in the federal scheme.[1943] The Court's reliance on this factor, however, does not suggest that the ADEA, because it allows simultaneous treatment of the state and federal claims, is anything other than a statute that likewise envisions state antidiscrimination laws as playing an integral, albeit perhaps lesser, role.[1944] Certainly, this distinction would not seem to suffice to establish a "clear and

---

1939 *Id* 491.

1940 478 US 788 (1986).

1941 See **§6.66.**

1942 42 USC §2000e-5(c).

1943 456 US at 468.

1944 Section 14(a), 29 USC §633(a), of the ADEA provides that a federal ADEA suit supersedes a pending state action. There is no comparable provision in Title VII. See **§6.68.**

manifest" intention, insofar as the ADEA is concerned, to repeal 28 USC §1738. Indeed, in *Oscar Mayer & Co v Evans* the Court rejected the argument that, because the ADEA allows simultaneous filing while Title VII does not, different readings should be given the two statutes as to the matter of requiring resort to state agencies.[1945]

Second, the Court in *Alexander v Gardner-Denver Co*[1946] held that Title VII requires the EEOC to "accord substantial weight to final findings and orders made by State or local law," although the agency is not bound by such findings.[1947] While no like statement has emanated from the Supreme Court regarding the ADEA, the *Gardner-Denver* assertion hardly creates a distinction sufficient to warrant reading the ADEA as impliedly repealing 28 USC §1738.

In sum, a state court ruling that satisfies minimal due process standards and that addresses the merits under state law of an age discrimination claim, which claim likewise could be made under the ADEA, will be deemed to be res judicata, and will collaterally estop litigation of decided issues of law and fact necessary to the state court ruling.[1948]

On the other hand, the Court of Appeals for the Second Circuit, in deciding *Owens v New York City Housing Authority,*[1949] took a different position as to the collateral estoppel issue. A finding of misconduct arising out of a proceeding under the state civil service law dealing with Owens' discharge on disciplinary grounds was deemed not to preclude Owens from establishing a prima facie ADEA claim. A portion of that claim which entailed the plaintiff establishing that she was qualified for the position from which she was discharged. The court reasoned that "[a]n

---

[1945] 441 US at 756-57.

[1946] 415 US 36 (1974).

[1947] *Id* 48 n8.

[1948] *See, e.g.*, DiAngelo v Illinois, 51 FEP Cas (BNA) 1107 (ND Ill 1987), *appeal dismissed,* 891 F2d 1260 (7th Cir 1989); Rotert v Jefferson Fed Sav & Loan Assn, 623 F Supp 1114 (D Conn 1985). It is the Equal Employment Opportunity Commission's view that *Kremer* applies to the ADEA. EEOC Policy Statement No N-915: *Kremer v Chemical Constr Corp,* (May 6, 1986).

[1949] 934 F2d 405 (2d Cir), *cert denied,* 112 S Ct 431 (1991).

individual may well have the ability to perform job duties, even if her conduct on the job is inappropriate or offensive."[1950] With regard to the question of whether the state court proceeding erected a res judicata barrier to the plaintiff's ADEA claim, the court reasoned that the state court "was not empowered to address Owens' claims of discrimination or retaliation . . . [and so those] claims . . . [were] not barred."[1951] The court deciding *Glass v IDS Financial Services, Inc,*[1952] ruled that an individual state law claim of age discrimination litigated in state court did not preclude pursuit in federal court of an ADEA representative action alleging a pattern and practice of age discrimination over an extended period of time based on a wide range of allegedly discriminatory actions toward numerous individuals.[1953]

Preclusion can apply even if the ADEA claim was not actually made in the state court.[1954] If, however, the ADEA claim—or a particular aspect of it—could not have been made in state court, res judicata will not bar its being raised in federal court.[1955] And if the merits of the plaintiff's age discrimination claim were not addressed in the state proceeding, collateral estoppel may not pose a bar to the plaintiff's seeking relief in federal court.[1956]

1950 *Id* 409.

1951 *Id* 410.

1952 798 F Supp 1411 (D Minn 1992).

1953 As to the preclusive effect of arbitrators' determinations, see **ch 7.** As to the res judicata effect on an ADEA action of a state common-law breach of contract suit, see *Shaver v FW Woolworth Co,* 840 F2d 1361 (7th Cir), *cert denied,* 488 US 856 (1988). (The facts are so unique as to render the case of little general import.)

1954 *See* Hogue v Royse City, 939 F2d 1249 (5th Cir 1991); Langston v Insurance Co of N Am, 827 F2d 1044 (5th Cir 1987); Capraro v Gammino, Inc, 751 F2d 56 (1st Cir 1985); Bost v Metropolitan Dade County, 58 FEP Cas (BNA) 139 (SD Fla), *affd without opinion,* 951 F2d 1264 (11th Cir 1991); Maira v Stamm, 110 AD2d 1057, 488 NYS2d 914 (1985).

1955 Whitfield v City of Knoxville, 756 F2d 455 (6th Cir 1985); *accord* EEOC Policy Statement No N-915: *Kremer v Chemical Constr Corp,* (April 2, 1986).

1956 *See* Dolence v United States Natl Bank, 797 F Supp 423, 424 (WD Pa), *affd without opinion,* 975 F2d 1549 (3d Cir 1992); Equal Employment Opportunity Commn v Fox Point-Bayside Sch Dist, 31 Empl Prac Dec (CCH) ¶33,609 (ED Wis 1983), *revd on other grounds,* 772 F2d 1294 (7th Cir 1985); Rawson v Sears, Roebuck & Co, 554 F Supp 327 (D Colo 1983). *But see* Bost v Metropoli-

Normal res judicata rules can be overcome by the parties. Thus, if the parties agree, in terms or in effect, that the plaintiff can split his or her claims between federal and state courts, or if the defendant acquiesces to such claim splitting, the federal suit will not be barred by an earlier state court judgment.[1957]

Federal Court Decisions

In *Ritter v Mount St Mary's College*[1958] the Court of Appeals for the Fourth Circuit addressed the claims of a plaintiff who initially filed suit under Title VII, the Equal Pay Act (EPA),[1959] and the ADEA. The trial judge dismissed the EPA and ADEA claims and proceeded to decide the merits of the Title VII claim. Subsequently, the trial court ruling was reversed as to the ADEA and EPA claims, and the case was remanded. The trial court judge then ruled that the factual findings made in the Title VII suit collaterally estopped the plaintiff from establishing a prima facie ADEA claim because the two causes of action contained the identical element: the requirement that the plaintiff establish her qualifications.

On appeal, the plaintiff argued that she should not have been collaterally estopped, because if she had been allowed to proceed with her ADEA claim a jury, rather than a judge, would have made the relevant factual determinations.[1960] The appellate court ruled against her. Relying on *Parklane Hosiery Co, Inc v Shore,*[1961] the court stated as follows:

> *Parklane* decided that the judicial interest in the economical resolution of cases, which interest underlies the doctrine of collateral estoppel, does override the interest of the

---

tan Dade County, 58 FEP Cas (BNA) 139 (SD Fla), *affd without opinion,* 951 F2d 1264 (11th Cir 1991).

[1957] Calderon Rosado v General Elec Circuit Breakers, Inc, 805 F2d 1085 (1st Cir 1986).

[1958] 814 F2d 986 (4th Cir), *cert denied,* 484 US 913 (1987).

[1959] 29 USC §206(d).

[1960] At the time, jury trials, while available under the ADEA, see **§6.44,** were not available under Title VII.

[1961] 439 US 322 (1979).

plaintiff in retrying before a jury the facts of a case determined by a court sitting in equity.[1962]

Somewhat similar to *Ritter* is *Bryan v Chemical Bank,*[1963] in which the trial court earlier had ruled against the plaintiff on his Title VII claim. The court reasoned that in the Title VII part of the proceeding the judge, in order to have held that the plaintiff had been terminated for good cause, necessarily had to have found that no discrimination was involved. This finding collaterally estopped the plaintiff from now contending that age discrimination was the basis for his discharge. Similarly, in *Nichols v City of St Louis*[1964] the Court of Appeals for the Eighth Circuit reasoned that the conclusions of the city civil service commission and of the reviewing state court that Nichols had been discharged for good cause necessarily constituted a finding adverse to her age discrimination claim and therefore precluded her from litigating her discrimination claim in the context of an ADEA suit in federal court.

§6.66 The Res Judicata and Collateral Estoppel Effects of State Administrative Determinations

In *Kremer v Chemical Construction Corp*[1965] the Court, in holding that a state court ruling would be res judicata as to a subsequent suit under Title VII of the Civil Rights Act of 1964,[1966] expressed a very significant cautionary note: "[U]nreviewed administrative determinations by state agencies . . . should not preclude . . . [federal court] review[.]"[1967] In other words, the Court disclaimed the applicability of administrative res judicata in the Title VII context.

1962 814 F2d at 991.

1963 655 F Supp 322 (SDNY 1987).

1964 837 F2d 833 (8th Cir 1988).

1965 456 US 461 (1982). See **§6.65.**

1966 42 USC §§2000e through 2000e-17.

1967 456 US at 470 n7.

In *University of Tennessee v Elliott,*[1968] a subsequent Title VII ruling, the issue directly before the Court was whether a state administrative agency's determination should preclude subsequent suit in federal court. The Court rejected the argument. It reaffirmed what had been earlier asserted in *Kremer:* unreviewed state administrative determinations will not have preclusive effect vis-á-vis Title VII suits.[1969] Ultimately, in *Astoria Federal Savings & Loan Association v Solimino*[1970] the Court addressed the preclusive effect of nonjudicially reviewed state agencies' determinations on claims litigated in federal court under the Age Discrimination in Employment Act (ADEA).[1971]

Pre-*Solimino* Case Law

Prior to *Solimino* several lower courts had dealt with this issue and had arrived at differing conclusions. In *Duggan v Board of Education*[1972] the Court of Appeals for the Seventh Circuit held that unreviewed findings of fact made during a state administrative proceeding should not be given preclusive effect in a subsequent ADEA suit in federal court. The *Duggan* court took what amounted to an absolutist position on the matter: administrative res judicata was inapplicable under the ADEA. The Court of Appeals for the Second Circuit subsequently endorsed and followed *Duggan* in *Solimino v Astoria Federal Savings & Loan Association.*[1973] In *Delgado v Lockheed Georgia Co*[1974] the Court of Appeals for the Eleventh Circuit, while declining to take any ultimate position as to the general applicability of administrative res judi-

---

[1968] 478 US 788 (1986).

[1969] Given the similarities between the ADEA and Title VII, ADEA courts regularly look to Title VII case law for guidance. See **ch 2.**

[1970] 111 S Ct 2166 (1991).

[1971] 29 USC §§621-634.

[1972] 818 F2d 1291 (7th Cir 1987).

[1973] 901 F2d 1148 (2d Cir 1990), *affd,* 111 S Ct 2166 (1991); *accord* Ibrahim v New York State Dept of Health, 692 F Supp 1471 (EDNY 1988); *see also* Ledford v Rapid-Am Corp, 47 FEP Cas (BNA) 312 (SDNY 1988).

[1974] 815 F2d 641 (11th Cir 1987).

cata in ADEA cases, observed that the foregoing reasoning was "persuasive."[1975]

Somewhat in contrast to the foregoing rulings, the Court of Appeals for the Ninth Circuit left open the possibility that a judicially unreviewed state administrative determination could have preclusive effect in *Mack v South Bay Beer Distributors, Inc.*[1976] The Court of Appeals for the Seventh Circuit, in deciding *Buckhalter v Pepsi-Cola General Bottlers, Inc,*[1977] utilized the reasoning employed by the *Mack* court, but that decision ultimately was repudiated in a later ruling.[1978] In *Stillians v Iowa*[1979] the Court of Appeals for the Eighth Circuit, taking a much more assertive stance than did the court in *Mack,* ruled that an unreviewed state administrative decision should be given preclusive effect, as long as the claimant received a full and fair hearing before the administrative body.

The *Solimino* Ruling

The Supreme Court's *Solimino* decision laid to rest the lower courts' differences. The Court held that a judicially unreviewed state administrative finding regarding an individual's age discrimination claim has no preclusive effect vis-á-vis a federal lawsuit under the ADEA. In so doing, the Court in effect overruled *Stillians, Mack,* and any other decisions in the preclusion camp. Justice Souter, writing for a unanimous Court, offered several justifications for the ruling.

First, Justice Souter noted that while §14(b)[1980] of the ADEA requires a grievant first to pursue his or her state remedies,[1981] §14(b) also envisions a federal suit being filed at some point after such effort is made at the state level. He further noted that

---

[1975] *Id* 646.

[1976] 798 F2d 1279 (9th Cir 1986).

[1977] 768 F2d 847 (7th Cir 1985), *vacated & remanded,* 478 US 1017 (1986).

[1978] Buckhalter v Pepsi-Cola Gen Bottlers, Inc, 820 F2d 892 (7th Cir 1987).

[1979] 843 F2d 276 (8th Cir 1988).

[1980] 29 USC §633(b).

[1981] See **§6.25.**

§7(d)(2)[1982] also contemplates resort to federal court following the termination of state proceedings. He then went on to opine that "such federal proceedings would be strictly pro forma if state administrative findings were given preclusive effect."[1983]

Justice Souter also observed that ordinarily a complainant would only turn to federal court if he or she had lost in a state administrative proceeding. "In such a case, however, the employer would likely enjoy an airtight defense of collateral estoppel if a state agency determination on the merits were given preclusive effect."[1984] Justice Souter buttressed the Court's position by observing that administrative findings regarding federal employees are not deemed to preclude subsequent federal lawsuits,[1985] and "since there is no reason to believe federal enforcement agencies [are] any less competent than their state counterparts, it would be anomalous to afford more deference to one than the other."[1986]

Other adverse consequences would also follow from according state administrative determinations preclusive effect. For example, there would be disparities from state to state regarding ADEA claimants, "depending on whether a given jurisdiction had an age-discrimination statute of its own."[1987] Justice Souter also saw the refusal to accord preclusive effect to judicially unreviewed state administrative decisions as having the beneficial result of avoiding generating issues that otherwise could arise. For example, the rule adopted by the Court denying preclusive effect would foreclose disputes as to whether a particular state agency had "in fact 'act[ed] in a judicial capacity,' and afforded the parties "an adequate opportunity to litigate,' [*United States v*]

[1982] 29 USC §626(d)(2).

[1983] 111 S Ct at 2166.

[1984] *Id.*

[1985] As to federal employees' claims, see **ch 9.**

[1986] 111 S Ct at 2172.

[1987] *Id.*

Utah Constr. & Mining Co., 384 U.S. 394, 422 [1966], . . . so as to justify application of a normal rule in favor of estoppel."[1988]

Issues Unresolved by *Solimino*

While the *Solimino* decision resolved the general issue of whether preclusion flows from a judicially unreviewed state administrative ruling, the Court did not expressly address the treatment to be accorded any and every type of state administrative determination. The complainant in *Solimino* had first put forth a claim of age discrimination before a state antidiscrimination agency charged with enforcing a state law directly outlawing age discrimination in employment. The court deciding *Johnson v University of Wisconsin—Milwaukee*[1989] confronted an issue that the *Solimino* ruling did not address, i.e., whether preclusion will apply where an age discrimination claim was not expressly made, or addressed, in the state administrative forum. At issue in *Johnson* was the preclusive effect of determinations by a state workers' compensation examiner and administrative appellate tribunal, both of which had ruled that the plaintiff had been wrongfully discharged. It was argued that these determinations had preclusive effect on the plaintiff's subsequent ADEA federal court suit. The court, however, rejected the preclusion argument, asserting that both the issues and the substantive standards in the administrative proceedings differed from those in the ADEA suit.[1990] Similarly, in *Frank v Capital Cities Communications, Inc*,[1991] the court ruled that the state administrative proceeding did not preclude the federal suit because the state proceeding did not involve, or address, the same issue as was before the court in the federal ADEA suit.[1992]

[1988] 111 S Ct at 2173. In fact, it was on such questions that the court deciding Mack v South Bay Beer Distrib, Inc, 798 F2d 1279 (9th Cir 1986), had focused.

[1989] 783 F2d 59 (7th Cir 1986).

[1990] *Accord* Kendall v CF Indus, Inc, 624 F Supp 1102 (ND Ill 1982).

[1991] 689 F Supp 334 (SDNY 1988).

[1992] *See generally* Committee on Benefits to Unemployed Persons, *The Preclusive Effect of Unemployment Compensation Decisions on Subsequent Litigation*, 4 Lab Law 69 (1988).

While the type of situation addressed in *Johnson* was not before the Court in *Solimino,* it seems legitimate to conclude, given the Court's unhesitating rejection of preclusion in cases where grievants have had the clearest opportunities to vindicate their age discrimination claims in state administrative forums, that preclusion cannot be condoned in situations such as that addressed in *Johnson,* where the opportunities of claimants to vindicate their claims are more attenuated.[1993]

§6.67 The Res Judicata and Collateral Estoppel Effects of Federal Administrative Determinations

The situation may arise where a determination made by a federal agency is identified by a litigant as foreclosing pursuit of a claim under the Age Discrimination in Employment Act (ADEA)[1994] in a lawsuit in federal court. In *Cook v Pan American World Airways, Inc,*[1995] a determination of the Civil Aeronautics Board (CAB) was the basis for such an argument made by the defendants vis-a-vis the plaintiffs' ADEA suit. The court, rejecting the argument, relied on the ADEA's statutory commitment to de novo review and on the CAB's lack of authority to adjudicate the age discrimination issue involved in the case.

In *Rosenfeld v Department of Army*[1996] the plaintiff had been found by the federal Civil Service Commission to be suffering from a mental disability and so he was involuntarily retired. He later filed an ADEA action contending that age was the basis for his forced retirement. The defendant contended that the disability finding, which by virtue of a federal statute was not judicially reviewable, should have had preclusive effect as to his ADEA claim. The court rejected the defendant's argument.

[1993] As to the preclusive effect of arbitrators' rulings, see **ch 7.**

[1994] 29 USC §§621-634.

[1995] 771 F2d 735 (2d Cir 1985), *cert denied,* 474 US 1109 (1986).

[1996] 769 F2d 237 (4th Cir 1985).

In *Banks v Rockwell International Corp*[1997] the court held that by virtue of the plaintiff having litigated a suit under Title VII of the Civil Rights Act of 1964[1998] which involved the same alleged wrong as that at issue in the plaintiff's ADEA suit, the plaintiff was barred by res judicata from pursuing the age claim.

§6.68 Effect of an ADEA Action on State Administrative Claims

Section 14(a)[1999] of the Age Discrimination in Employment Act (ADEA)[2000] provides as follows:

> Nothing in this chapter shall affect the jurisdiction of any agency of any State performing like functions with regard to discriminatory employment practices on account of age except that upon commencement of action under this chapter such action shall supersede any state action.

As a result of this provision, an ADEA action, whether brought in federal or state court, will cause state agency action pursuant to a state antidiscrimination statute to be stayed.

The legislative history, both of the ADEA when it was first being considered in 1967[2001] and of amendments made in 1978 to the statute (although §14(a) was not itself amended),[2002] support reading §14(a) as prescribing stays, rather than dismissals, of state proceedings. The sparse case law is mixed as to whether

---

1997 57 FEP Cas (BNA) 529 (SD Ohio), *affd without opinion,* 941 F2d 1209 (6th Cir 1991).

1998 42 USC §§2000e through 2000e-17.

1999 29 USC §633(a).

2000 *Id* §§621-634.

2001 House Comm on Educ & Labor, Age Discrimination in Employment Act of 1967, HR Rep No 805, 90th Cong, 1st Sess, *reprinted in* 1967 US Code Cong & Admin News 2213, 2219.

2002 Senate Comm on Human Resources, Amending the Age Discrimination in Employment Act Amendments of 1977, S Rep No 493, 95th Cong, 1st Sess 6 (1977).

this is the correct reading.[2003] It has been held that a state administrative proceeding conducted by the state antidiscrimination agency with which the plaintiff filed a complaint (in addition to his ADEA suit filed in federal court), will be stayed pending resolution of the federal lawsuit.[2004]

The Court of Appeals for the Second Circuit, in deciding *Promisel v First American Artificial Flowers, Inc,*[2005] drew a distinction between state agency action, which is to be stayed, and state judicial proceedings, which (according to the *Promisel* court) are not.[2006] In so concluding, the court relied on the fact that "[t]he 'supersede' language comes at the end of a sentence which deals exclusively with the jurisdiction of state *agencies* performing 'like' functions in handling age discrimination claims[.]"[2007] In a related vein, it has been held that in a state that has no agency with jurisdiction over age discrimination, but does allow a private cause of action for age discrimination, §14(a) is inapplicable.[2008]

Whether the *Promisel* court was correct in the distinction it made, it is clearly correct to observe that in some states it may be possible to maintain a common-law action arising out of an allegedly discriminatory age-based employment practice.[2009] And given that the language of §14(a) speaks only to the "jurisdiction of any agency of any State," it follows that common-law judicial proceedings would not fit within this terminology, because, in contrast to the typical state statutory regulatory

---

[2003] *Compare* Dunlop v Pan Am World Airways, Inc, 672 F2d 1044, 1049 n7 (2d Cir 1982) (stay, and not dismissal, is appropriate) *with* Mares v Santa Fe Pub Sch, 106 NM 354, 743 P2d 110 (1987). In Fiorenza v First City Bank-Cent, 710 F Supp 1104 (ED Tex 1988), the court did not address the question of whether dismissal was a viable alternative; it simply stayed consideration of the state-based claim.

[2004] Wells v Cimarron Ins Co, Inc, 55 FEP Cas (BNA) 112 (D Kan 1991).

[2005] 943 F2d 251 (2d Cir 1991), *cert denied,* 112 S Ct 939 (1992).

[2006] It has been held that the stay requirement does not apply to a pending state appeal. National Cash Register v Riner, 413 A2d 890 (Del Super Ct 1979).

[2007] 943 F2d at 255 (emphasis in original).

[2008] *See, e.g.,* Shanahan v WITI-TV, Inc, 565 F Supp 219, 224 (ED Wis 1982).

[2009] See **ch 11.**

scheme, they do not entail the involvement of administrative agencies. Thus, §14(a), it would seem, does not result in the superseding of common-law actions. But, in a related (albeit not in the same) vein, it has been held that a federal court determination can collaterally estop a state court action based on a wrongful discharge theory.[2010]

A plaintiff cannot (1) waive the stay of a state proceeding caused by his or her filing of an ADEA suit, and (2) request the state agency to continue on with its processes.[2011]

In *Hunnewell v Manufacturers Hanover Trust Co*[2012] it was held that because of the peculiarities of the New York state statutory scheme, a plaintiff who brought an ADEA claim in federal court could not also bring a state-based claim either in state or federal court. The complexities of the interrelation of the ADEA and the New York scheme have been addressed by a number of courts.[2013]

§6.69 Discovery

The Federal Rules of Civil Procedure provide for liberal discovery by both plaintiffs and defendants in federal litigation. In the Age Discrimination in Employment Act (ADEA)[2014] context one generally looks to these rules, and to the case law construing them, rather than to any special jurisprudence of discovery specially devised to deal with ADEA claims. Not surprisingly, of course, there are ADEA decisions that address discovery issues. But, again, they do not set forth rules that are in any way unique to the ADEA setting. The extraction of special ADEA discovery

---

2010 Trepanier v Getting Organized, Inc, 155 Vt 259, 583 A2d 583 (1990).

2011 Corrente v St Joseph's Hosp & Health Ctr, 730 F Supp 493 (NDNY 1990).

2012 628 F Supp 759 (SDNY 1986).

2013 *See, e.g.,* Promisel v First Am Artificial Flowers, Inc, 943 F2d 251 (2d Cir 1991), *cert denied,* 112 S Ct 939 (1992). See generally **§6.42** regarding statutory claims.

2014 29 USC §§621-634.

rules aside, the decisions are very much fact oriented, the propriety of the discovery request turning on the particular facts of the case.[2015]

There is authority for the proposition that discovery by a plaintiff may be limited to the work unit in which he or she was employed. There is also contrary authority. *Marshall v Westinghouse Electric Corp,*[2016] supports the first position. A decision of the Court of Appeals for the Fifth Circuit, the court addressed a suit brought by the Department of Labor on behalf of a specific individual at a time when that agency still was responsible for enforcement of the ADEA.[2017] Several interrogatories were propounded to the defendant whereby information was sought about all persons whose employment had been terminated between 1972 and the present. The district court ruled that these interrogatories were unduly burdensome, and the appellate court affirmed. While the court of appeals recognized that the type of statistical evidence being sought was relevant to the individual employee's case, it observed that the discovery request encompassed some 7,500 employees in 32 districts and three plants. "[I]n the context of investigating an individual complaint the most natural focus is upon the source of the complained of discrimination—the employing unit or work unit."[2018] Consequently, "[t]o move beyond that focus the plaintiff and the

---

[2015] *See* Russell v Curtin Matheson Scientific, 493 F Supp 456 (SD Tex 1980); Davis v Boy Scouts of Am, 457 F Supp 665 (DNJ 1978).

[2016] 576 F2d 588 (5th Cir 1978); *accord* Heward v Western Elec Co, 35 FEP Cas (BNA) 807 (10th Cir 1984).

[2017] Enforcement authority for the ADEA, originally lodged in the Department of Labor, was transferred to the EEOC as of July 1, 1979. See **ch 2.**

[2018] 576 F2d at 592; *accord* Equal Employment Opportunity Commn v Ford Motor Co, 573 F Supp 755, 758-59 (D Colo 1983), *affd on other grounds,* 732 F2d 120 (10th Cir 1984); *see also* Equal Employment Opportunity Commn v Deutz-Allis Corp, 49 FEP Cas (BNA) 97 (WD Mo 1989). *Cf* Scales v JC Bradford & Co, 925 F2d 901, 906-07 (6th Cir 1991) (case arising under Title VII of the Civil Rights Act of 1964, 42 USC §§2000e through 2000e-17).

EEOC . . . [had to] show a more particularized need and relevance,"[2019] which they had failed to do.

In like vein, the Court of Appeals for the Eleventh Circuit denied the plaintiffs' request for corporation-wide discovery as to the implementation of a reduction in force throughout the various corporate employing units.[2020] If the plaintiffs were to obtain such discovery, they would have to show a "particularized need and likely relevance" as justification for conducting discovery reaching beyond the local units in which the decisions to discharge the plaintiffs had been made.[2021]

In contrast to the foregoing rulings, the Court of Appeals for the Second Circuit held in *Hollander v American Cyanamid Co*[2022] that the trial court had erred in denying discovery by the plaintiff regarding the nationwide practices of his employer. The appellate court reasoned that, although the discovery request went "beyond the narrow confines of the . . . [Connecticut] facility in which Hollander worked," the information sought was relevant and therefore properly discoverable.[2023] In deciding *Wehr v Burroughs Corp*[2024] the district court held for the plaintiff in a dispute regarding the plaintiff's requests for information relating to jobs or positions for which he was not qualified, stating as follows: "Plaintiff is entitled to discover whether the division or facility as a whole was plagued by age discrimination since such a finding might support an inference that plaintiff's discharge was motivated by a similar animus."[2025] And in *Catherman v Reyn-*

[2019] 576 F2d at 592; *accord* Heward v Western Elec Co, 35 FEP Cas (BNA) 807 (10th Cir 1984); Prouty v National RR Passenger Corp, 99 FRD 545, 547 (DDC 1983).

[2020] Earley v Champion Intl Corp, 907 F2d 1077 (11th Cir 1990).

[2021] *Id* 1085; *accord In re* Western Dist Xerox Litig, 140 FRD 264, 269 (WDNY 1991).

[2022] 895 F2d 80 (2d Cir 1990).

[2023] *Id* 84; *see also* Maresco v Evans Chemetics, 964 F2d 106, 114 (2d Cir 1992); Guruwaya v Montgomery Ward, Inc, 119 FRD 36 (ND Cal 1988), *affd without opinion,* 879 F2d 865 (9th Cir 1989).

[2024] 20 FEP Cas (BNA) 531 (ED Pa 1977).

[2025] *Id* 532; *see also* Goff v Kroger Co, 121 FRD 61 (SD Ohio 1988); Owens v Bethlehem Mines Corp, 108 FRD 207 (SD W Va 1985); Diminnie v General Elec Co, 35 Empl Prac Dec (CCH) ¶34,742 (WD Ky 1984); Jackson v Alterman Foods, 37 FEP Cas (BNA) 837 (ND Ga 1984).

olds Metals Co[2026] a district court refused to limit the plaintiff's request for documents to the defendant's region of the division in which the plaintiff had worked, but allowed discovery nationwide as to that division.

In *Allen v Colgate-Palmolive Co*[2027] the defendant disputed the plaintiff's demand for documents regarding 57 of the defendant's former and present employees. The plaintiff offered two justifications: he needed the information in order to determine whether a pattern and practice of discrimination on the basis of age existed, and he needed the data in order to determine whether preferential treatment had been given to any younger employees at his expense. The court ruled that some of the information sought was not sufficiently relevant to justify its production, given that some of the individuals were not similarly situated to the plaintiff. In *Catherman,* however, the district court concluded that a request for documents should be granted regarding six other persons within the ADEA-protected age group who had been terminated by the same division in which the plaintiff had been employed and in whose discharge decisions the company official who had discharged the plaintiff had participated.[2028] In *Equal Employment Opportunity Commission v Chrysler Corp*[2029] the court upheld a discovery request for statistical data that went to a showing that past practices and policies were age discriminatory, the logic being that such data would be relevant for establishing the existence and accuracy of the perceptions of present grievants as to their allegedly coerced, albeit ostensibly voluntary, retirements.[2030]

The question addressed by the court deciding *Kenney v Shaw*

[2026] 28 FEP Cas (BNA) 668 (ND Ga 1980).

[2027] 539 F Supp 57 (SDNY 1981).

[2028] *See also* Held v National RR Passenger Corp, 101 FRD 420 (DDC 1984).

[2029] 35 Empl Prac Dec (CCH) ¶34,683 (ED Mich 1984).

[2030] *Accord* Jackson v Alterman Foods, 37 FEP Cas (BNA) 837 (ND Ga 1984); *see also* Aspgren v Montgomery Ward & Co, Inc, 42 FEP Cas (BNA) 1425 (ND Ill 1983) (re discovery of defendant's career development manuals).

Industries, Inc,[2031] was whether discovery could be had by the plaintiff regarding employment decisions made by the defendant at times before and after the several-week period surrounding the acquisition by Shaw Industries of the company for which the plaintiffs had worked until the acquisition by the defendant. The court ruled in the affirmative, reasoning that the information sought was relevant to the plaintiff's proving a prima facie claim, and that "[f]urther, statistical evidence of a pattern or practice of discrimination is admissible to prove individual claims."[2032]

The court deciding *Foit v Suburban Bancorp*[2033] observed that a sole plaintiff would be entitled to discover business records of the defendant that contained or would lead to a proper statistical analysis of the defendant's past termination and transfer practices on an age basis.[2034] In *Willis v Golden Rule Insurance Co*[2035] the court ordered the defendant to answer interrogatories concerning (1) the names, ages, and other information regarding all persons occupying the position held by the plaintiff, and (2) age discrimination complaints filed against the defendant within a 5-year period.

In *Wehr,* discussed above, an interrogatory asking the defendant to identify all documents that supported the defendant's contention that the plaintiff's discharge was not attributable to age discrimination was held valid over the defendant's objection that the request required the defendant to prove a negative, i.e., that the plaintiff's discharge was not motivated by age discrimination. In the court's view, the interrogatory simply required that if such documents existed the defendant was to identify them, but it did not require the defendant to prove anything.

It has been held that records regarding ADEA suits and charges filed by grievants other than the plaintiff are discover-

---

2031 764 F Supp 1501 (ND Ga 1991).

2032 *Id* 1503.

2033 549 F Supp 264 (D Md 1982).

2034 *Id* 266 n5.

2035 56 FEP Cas (BNA) 1451 (ED Tenn 1991).

able.[2036] In contrast, in *Guruwaya v Montgomery Ward, Inc,*[2037] the court denied the discovery request directed to the defendant employer for the names, telephone numbers, and addresses of other employees who had filed complaints with the Equal Employment Opportunity Commission (EEOC). In *Equal Employment Opportunity Commission v Consolidated Edison Co*[2038] the court allowed discovery of the medical records of individuals on whose behalf the EEOC had sued Con Ed. The discovery request by Con Ed was limited to those employees as to whom there already was a contemporaneous entry asserting the existence of medical conditions affecting job performance.

The defendant in *Palmer v Reader's Digest Association, Inc,*[2039] contended that it was not age, but a restructuring necessitated by declining profits, that had caused the discharge of the plaintiffs. Given that excuse, the plaintiffs sought discovery of the defendant's financial statements to secure any existing data which could establish the pretextual nature of the defendant's excuse. The court ordered the defendant to produce such statements.

§6.70 —Privileges and Confidentiality in the Discovery Context

In *Equal Employment Opportunity Commission v G-K-G Inc*[2040] the court held that an informer's privilege shielded the identities of certain witnesses. In so doing, the court pointed out that "[i]f the two confidential witnesses were the only two witnesses involved in this case, GKG's argument would be more compelling."[2041] The facts were, however, that "the EEOC's [Equal Employment Opportunity Commission's] investigation did not rest solely upon the statements of the two witnesses; the investi-

---

2036 Jackson v Alterman Foods, 37 FEP Cas (BNA) 837 (ND Ga 1984).

2037 119 FRD 36 (ND Cal 1988), *affd without opinion,* 879 F2d 865 (9th Cir 1989).

2038 37 FEP Cas (BNA) 1664 (SDNY 1982).

2039 122 FRD 445 (SDNY 1988).

2040 131 FRD 553 (ND Ill 1990).

2041 *Id* 555.

gation was built upon the cooperation of numerous other witnesses—and GKG . . . [had] been given access to the identities of those witnesses and the substance of their knowledge."[2042]

The *GKG* court also recognized a "government deliberative process" privilege, which protects documents that reflect "advisory opinions, recommendations and deliberations comprising part of a process by which governmental decisions and policies are formulated."[2043] The court further added: "The privilege . . . only covers expressions of opinion, recommendations, or consultations; factual matter is not within the scope of the privilege."[2044]

Another issue of privilege was involved in a magistrate's ruling rendered in *Equal Employment Opportunity Commission v Fox Point-Bayside School District.*[2045] In order to secure liquidated damages, a plaintiff must prove that the defendant acted willfully.[2046] In *Fox Point-Bayside* the plaintiff sought to depose the defendant's board members in order to meet its burden on the willfulness issue. The defendant objected, invoking the attorney-client privilege with regard to board executive session discussions involving the board's attorney. As a consequence, neither the board members' denial that they knowingly violated the law nor their assertion that they relied on the advice of their attorney could be adequately assessed by the plaintiff. The magistrate granted the plaintiff's motion to compel discovery, given that "the record . . . demonstrates that individual board members sought out, listened to and considered the advice of their attorneys before acting."[2047]

Privilege, although of a different sort, also was at issue in

---

[2042] *Id.*

[2043] *Id* 556 (citation omitted).

[2044] *Id.*

[2045] 31 Empl Prac Dec (CCH) ¶33,609 (ED Wis 1983), *revd on other grounds,* 772 F2d 1294 (7th Cir 1985).

[2046] See **ch 8.**

[2047] 31 Empl Prac Dec at p 29,865.

Rollins v Farris,[2048] which involved a challenged denial of tenure decision. The defendants invoked what they termed a qualified academic peer review privilege as the basis for nondisclosure of confidential peer review materials. This issue most commonly has arisen in cases arising under Title VII of the Civil Rights Act of 1964.[2049] It was in addressing the enforcement of a subpoena issued pursuant to the EEOC's authority under that statute that the Supreme Court rejected the claim that tenure decisions merit some special protection. In deciding *University of Pennsylvania v Equal Employment Opportunity Commission*[2050] the Court spurned the university's invitation to create a peer review privilege; rather it established that the standard to be utilized in assessing the legitimacy of the EEOC's efforts to secure information regarding tenure decisions is that of mere relevancy.[2051] In so doing the Court relied on the express extensive investigatory authority vested in the EEOC by Title VII. Under the ADEA, the Commission has like—indeed, arguably even broader—authority,[2052] and thus there is no reason to read the *University of Pennsylvania* ruling as not having persuasive analogical force in the ADEA context.

On the other hand, discovery undertaken by a private litigant arguably might elicit a lesser judicial deference to the plaintiff's requests, since that express statutory agency investigative authority does not apply. This argument, however, would seem to cut against the general support for broad disclosure expressed by the federal discovery rules, and so the same wide-ranging access to information that the EEOC enjoys also should pertain for private litigants.[2053]

2048 109 FRD 714 (ED Ark 1985).

2049 42 USC §§2000e through 2000e-17.

2050 493 US 182 (1990).

2051 *Id* 584,

2052 See **§6.56.**

2053 This same conclusion applies to the other cases in this section in which discovery claims of the EEOC have been the direct focus of the courts.

At issue in *Hansen v Allen Memorial Hospital*[2054] was the question of whether investigatory material that had been developed by a state civil rights agency, and which was privileged under state law, was discoverable in the plaintiff's federal ADEA suit, which also involved pendent state claims. The court ruled that the federal law of privileges should govern and went on to conclude that the state agency's "asserted governmental interest in the integrity of its investigative process and in its need for confidentiality . . . [were] far too attenuated to uphold the assertion of the state law limited confidential privilege at issue."[2055]

The EEOC has issued a procedural regulation that addresses, among other things, the question of confidentiality. "The identity of a complainant, confidential witness, or aggrieved person on whose behalf a charge was filed will ordinarily not be disclosed without prior written consent, unless necessary in a court proceeding."[2056] This language gives the EEOC the discretion to disclose, a reading confirmed by the comments accompanying the issuance of the regulations.[2057]

The EEOC regulation also provides that a person who submits data or evidence to the Commission may, on payment of a prescribed cost, procure a copy or transcript thereof. However, a witness for good cause may be limited to inspection of the official transcript of his or her testimony.[2058]

§6.71 Issues Concerning the Admissibility of Evidence

In large measure, rulings regarding the admission of evidence in Age Discrimination in Employment Act (ADEA)[2059] cases are not going to afford any particular insights vis-á-vis the Act. Evi-

[2054] 141 FRD 115 (SD Iowa 1992).

[2055] *Id* 124.

[2056] 29 CFR §1626.4 (1993).

[2057] 48 Fed Reg 139 (Jan 3, 1983).

[2058] 29 CFR §1626.14 (1993).

[2059] 29 USC §§621-634.

dence law generally is universal, rather than being specialized for particular causes of action. Still, there are a number of issues that have been addressed by ADEA courts[2060] concerning the admissibility of various types of evidence and because these, for the most part, are issues that recur in ADEA litigation, they merit attention.[2061]

§6.72 —Evidence Regarding Discrimination Against People Other Than the Plaintiff

The issue of the admissibility of evidence regarding instances of discrimination (alleged or otherwise) perpetrated against persons other than the plaintiff has been addressed in a number of cases. The courts have split on the matter.

A negative position has been expressed by a number of courts.[2062] *Moorhouse v Boeing Co*[2063] is a relatively early example. The plaintiff, who first was demoted and later laid off, sought to introduce the testimony of other employees of Boeing, each of whom had filed his own Age Discrimination in Employment

---

[2060] As a general matter, appellate courts play a deferential role in reviewing lower courts' evidentiary rulings: "Evidentiary rulings made by the trial judge are ordinarily overturned only when found to be manifestly erroneous." Malarkey v Texaco, Inc, 983 F2d 1204, 1210 (2d Cir 1993). Thus, a district court's evidentiary rulings will be reversed only on a finding of abuse. Olitsky v Spencer Gifts, Inc, 964 F2d 1471, 1474 (5th Cir 1992), *cert denied,* 113 S Ct 1253 (1993).

[2061] Questions of a substantive nature, i.e.: (1) what constitutes circumstantial and direct evidence; (2) the adequacy and uses of statistical evidence; and (3) the significance of various types of evidence for the allocation of burdens of proof and for the establishment of violations, are addressed in **ch 7.** The sections in this chapter focus on issues concerning the admissibility of evidence.

[2062] *See, e.g.,* Lowe v Commack Union Free Sch Dist, 886 F2d 1364, 1376-77 (2d Cir 1989), *cert denied,* 494 US 1026 (1990); Schrand v Federal Pac Elec Co, 851 F2d 152 (6th Cir 1988); Haskell v Kaman Corp, 743 F2d 113 (2d Cir 1984); Eudy v BWD Automotive Corp, 51 FEP Cas (BNA) 724 (ND Ga 1988); Shamley v International Tel & Tel Corp, 44 FEP Cas (BNA) 1238 (SDNY 1987); Steinberg v St Regis/Sheraton Hotel, 583 F Supp 421 (SDNY 1984).

[2063] 501 F Supp 390 (ED Pa), *affd without opinion,* 639 F2d 774 (3d Cir 1980).

Act (ADEA)[2064] suit against Boeing. With respect to some of these individuals, Moorhouse sought to adduce their testimony regarding: (1) the adequacy of his work performance; (2) the deficiencies of Moorhouse's supervisor; (3) derogatory comments about older employees generally, and Moorhouse in particular; and (4) Boeing's departure from its normal procedures. These witnesses were also expected to testify that employees who had been downgraded in job level performed the same work after their downgradings as they had before, and that "many" older employees had been laid off.[2065]

As the court viewed the situation, with the exception of testimony concerning comments about age generally, the adequacy of Moorhouse's performance, and Boeing's departure from normal practices, the testimony of the proposed witnesses would have been drawn from each witness' knowledge of his own layoff. The court, which refused to admit this testimony regarding the witness' own layoffs, looked to Rule 403 of the Federal Rules of Evidence,[2066] which provides as follows:

> Although relevant, evidence may be excluded if its probative value is substantially outweighed by the danger of unfair prejudice, confusion of the issues, or misleading the jury, or by considerations of undue delay, waste of time, or needless presentation of cumulative evidence.

As the court assessed the situation, "having the . . . witnesses recount the isolated actions taken against them individually would be of limited probative value to show the existence of a pattern or practice[.]"[2067]

In *Weir v Litton Bionetics, Inc,*[2068] the court's exclusion of testimony was based on potential jury confusion and prejudice, two

---

2064 29 USC §§621-634.

2065 501 F Supp at 392.

2066 Fed R Evid 403.

2067 501 F Supp at 394. *Moorhouse* was distinguished in Lockhart v Westinghouse Credit Corp, 879 F2d 43, 54-55 (3d Cir 1989).

2068 43 FEP Cas (BNA) 663 (D Md 1987).

factors addressed in Rule 403. The court deciding *Sorba v Pennsylvania Drilling Co, Inc,*[2069] also refused to allow the admission of evidence—in this instance, evidence regarding the treatment of two other former employees of the defendant. However, the court's ruling was a narrow one by virtue of the court specifically noting that the plaintiff had failed to show a statistical pattern of discrimination.[2070] Arguably, the court would have ruled otherwise if such a pattern first had been established by the plaintiff.[2071]

Moorhouse and like cases clearly should not be read as precluding any evidence of employer practices against persons other than the plaintiff. Rather, the *Moorhouse* court's ruling turned on the court's view that the probative value of the evidence, in the context of that case, was outweighed by other factors. Numerous other courts have reached contrary conclusions, in the context of the facts before them. This is so in cases that, like *Moorhouse,* have involved juries.[2072] And courts in nonjury cases also regu-

---

[2069] 648 F Supp 292 (WD Pa 1986), *revd on other grounds,* 821 F2d 200 (3d Cir 1987), *cert denied,* 484 US 1019 (1988).

[2070] "[I]in the absence of any pattern, the evidence regarding the termination of . . . [the other employees] will be excluded." *Id* 294.

[2071] *See also* Haskell v Kaman, 743 F2d 113, 121 (2d Cir 1984) (evidence offered to show that fellow employees were subjected to like discrimination admissible only if it involves a sample "large enough to permit an inference that age was a determinative factor in the employer's decision").

[2072] *See, e.g.,* Bingman v Natkin & Co, 937 F2d 553, 557 (10th Cir 1991); Holzman v Jaymar-Ruby, Inc, 916 F2d 1298, 1303-04 (7th Cir 1990); Spulak v K Mart Corp, 894 F2d 1150, 1156 (10th Cir 1990); Uffelman v Lone Star Steel Co, 863 F2d 404, 408 (5th Cir), *cert denied,* 490 US 1098 (1989); Rengers v WCLR Radio Station, 825 F2d 160, 161-62 (7th Cir 1987), *vacated on other grounds,* 486 US 1020 (1988); Mathewson v National Automatic Tool Co, Inc, 807 F2d 87 (7th Cir 1986); Kneisley v Hercules, Inc, 577 F Supp 726 (D Del 1983); *see also* Clements v General Accident Ins Co of Am, 821 F2d 489, 492 (8th Cir 1987) (court approvingly adverted to plaintiff's introduction of evidence at trial regarding other workers). In deciding Schrand v Federal Pac Elec Co, 851 F2d 152 (6th Cir 1988), the court held that it was reversible error for the trial court to have admitted testimony by a former employee of the defendant as to what was said to him regarding his discharge. However, it was not error, the court further concluded, for this former employee to have testified as to company policies regarding older employees.

larly have approved the notion that evidence regarding the treatment of employees other than the plaintiff is relevant and admissible.[2073]

Thus, cases such as *Moorhouse* notwithstanding, evidence regarding the treatment of individuals other than the plaintiff is often admitted at the behest of plaintiffs for the purposes of establishing prima facie violations[2074] and establishing that defendants' rebuttals are pretextual[2075] and at the behest of defendants seeking to rebut claims of discrimination.[2076] Other cases confirm that circumstantial evidence regarding the treatment of other older employees is often admitted.[2077] For example, in *Allen v Park-Ohio Industries, Inc,*[2078] the plaintiff was allowed

---

2073 *See, e.g.,* Harpring v Continental Oil Co, 628 F2d 406 (5th Cir 1980), *cert denied,* 454 US 819 (1981); Butler v Portland Elec Co, 748 F Supp 783 (D Or 1990), *affd without opinion sub nom* Flynn v Portland Gen Elec Co, 958 F2d 377 (9th Cir 1992) (summary judgment stage of litigation); Nobler v Beth Israel Medical Ctr, 735 F Supp 65, 67 (SDNY 1990); Grecco v Spang & Co, 527 F Supp 978, 981 (WD Pa 1981); Caravetta v Goulding, 33 FEP Cas (BNA) 1220 (DDC 1980) (federal employee suit); Schulz v Hickok Mfg Co, 358 F Supp 1208, 1212 (ND Ga 1973).

2074 As to prima facie cases, see **ch 7.**

2075 *See, e.g.,* Sweat v Miller Brewing Co, 708 F2d 655, 656 (11th Cir 1983). *Cf* Hollander v American Cyanamid Co, 895 F2d 80, 84 (2d Cir 1990) (plaintiff's discovery request re defendant's nationwide practices vis-a-vis other over-40 employees was improperly denied by trial court, since "[e]vidence relating to company-wide practices may reveal patterns of discrimination against a group of employees, increasing the likelihood that an employer's offered explanation for an employment decision regarding a particular individual masks a discriminatory motive."). As to pretext generally, see **ch 7.**

2076 See **ch 7.**

2077 *See, e.g.,* Herman v National Broadcasting Co, 744 F2d 604 (7th Cir 1984), *cert denied,* 470 US 1028 (1985); Harpring v Continental Oil Co, 628 F2d 406 (5th Cir 1980), *cert denied,* 454 US 819 (1981); Massie v Indiana Gas Co, 752 F Supp 261, 267 (SD Ind 1990); Abrams v Lightolier, Inc, 702 F Supp 509, 511 (DNJ 1988); Endres v Helms, 617 F Supp 1260, 1267 n15 (DDC 1985); LaDolce v Bank Admin Inst, 585 F Supp 975 (ND Ill 1984); Bernstein v Consolidated Foods Corp, 622 F Supp 1096 (ND Ill 1984); Robb v Chemetron Corp, 17 FEP Cas (BNA) 1535 (SD Tex 1978). *But see* Steinberg v St Regis/Sheraton Hotel, 583 F Supp 421 (SDNY 1984), excluding evidence as to alleged discrimination perpetrated against employees outside the ADEA-protected age group. *See also* Jardien v Winston Network, Inc, 888 F2d 1151, 1156 (7th Cir 1989).

2078 60 FEP Cas (BNA) 111 (ND Ohio 1992).

to call as witnesses five former employees of the defendant to testify as to their treatment; the court deemed this testimony relevant to the plaintiff's contention that he had been discharged pursuant to a corporation-wide pattern and practice of discrimination. And the Court of Appeals for the Tenth Circuit even deemed evidence regarding the termination of employees occurring subsequent to the plaintiff's discharge as being "relevant to the question of defendant's policies and practices," where the terminations were not "too remote in time" following the plaintiff's own firing.[2079]

Statistical evidence—which reflects employer actions vis-á-vis persons who may not themselves be plaintiffs—regularly is deemed relevant in ADEA cases, as long as it is methodically sound.[2080] Of course, if it is flawed, it may be barred.[2081]

§6.73 —Evidence Regarding Past Actions Involving the Plaintiff and the Plaintiff's Past Performance

An issue that often may arise is the admissibility of evidence of past actions taken as to a plaintiff, even though those actions themselves are beyond the scope of direct redress because they are stale for purposes of the Age Discrimination in Employment Act's (ADEA's)[2082] time limitations regarding the filing of charges with the Equal Employment Opportunity Commission.[2083] In the context of a continuing violation claim,[2084] evidence of acts that—standing alone—would be stale, may be

---

[2079] Bingman v Natkin & Co, 937 F2d 553, 557 (10th Cir 1991).

[2080] See **ch 7.** *Cf* Equal Employment Opportunity Commn v Chrysler Corp, 35 Empl Prac Dec (CCH) ¶34,683 (ED Mich 1984) (regarding discovery concerning past practices).

[2081] *See* Weir v Litton Bionetics, Inc, 43 FEP Cas (BNA) 663 (D Md 1987).

[2082] 29 USC §§621-634.

[2083] See **§6.08.**

[2084] As to continuing violations, see **§§6.13-.14**

admitted.[2085] In *Malarkey v Texaco, Inc,*[2086] the court refused to accept the plaintiff's continuing violation theory, and thereby it precluded her from seeking relief as to certain past allegedly wrongful, but stale, actions. Nonetheless, the court deemed those prior acts relevant to her timely claim and so it stated: "These actions will . . . be allowed as evidence whether plaintiff was subsequently discriminated against[.]"[2087] Other courts have ruled similarly.[2088]

In a later appellate court ruling in the *Malarkey* litigation, the Court of Appeals for the Second Circuit ruled that evidence regarding the plaintiff's performance as an employee of the defendant during the period prior to the alleged acts of age and retaliatory discrimination was properly admitted:

> At the early point in her career, when she was considered a valued and highly competent secretary—before she lodged charges of discrimination against her employer—

2085 *See, e.g.,* Johnson v Wisconsin Pub Serv Corp, 708 F Supp 969 (ED Wis 1987). *Cf* Stewart v CPC Intl, Inc, 679 F2d 117, 121 (7th Cir 1982) (case arising under Title VII of the Civil Rights Act of 1964, 42 USC §§2000e through 2000e-17).

2086 559 F Supp 117 (SDNY 1982), *affd on other grounds,* 704 F2d 674 (2d Cir 1983).

2087 *Id* 121. A different judge presided at the trial; his refusal to admit this evidence was affirmed on appeal. Malarkey v Texaco, Inc, 794 F Supp 1237 (SDNY 1992), *affd,* 983 F2d 1204, 1211 (2d Cir 1993).

2088 *See, e.g.,* Furr v AT&T Technologies, Inc, 824 F2d 1537, 1543 (10th Cir 1987); Mathewson v National Automatic Tool Co, Inc, 807 F2d 87 (7th Cir 1986); Caldwell v National Assn of Home Builders, 771 F2d 1051, 1057 (7th Cir 1985); Morton v Associated Dry Goods Corp, 792 F Supp 1136, 1142 n4 (SD Ind 1992); Leffingwell v Sears, Roebuck & Co, 717 F Supp 620, 622 (ND Ill 1989); Thames v Maurice Sporting Goods, Inc, 686 F Supp 208, 213 n11 (ND Ill 1988); Cory v SmithKline Beckman Corp, 585 F Supp 871 (ED Pa 1974); James v KID Broadcasting Corp, 559 F Supp 1153 (D Idaho 1983); Marshall v American Motors Corp, 475 F Supp 875 (ED Mich 1979); *see also* Blomberg v Colgate-Palmolive Co, 33 FEP Cas (BNA) 1809, 1811 (D Minn 1983). *Cf* United Airlines, Inc v Evans, 431 US 553 (1977) (case arising under Title VII of the Civil Rights Act of 1964, 42 USC §§2000e through 2000e-17). *But see* Golletti v Arco/Polymers, Inc, 32 FEP Cas (BNA) 1796 (WD Pa 1983), *vacated & remanded without opinion,* 762 F2d 993 (3d Cir 1985) (dismissing portion of complaint addressing postcharge/precomplaint filing events).

> she had moved up the professional ladder very rapidly. A jury should be allowed to decide whether, absent any discrimination, she would have continued on the same upward trajectory.[2089]

Evidence offered by plaintiffs as to their performance is admissible for the purpose of rebutting employers' contentions that challenged discharges were based on plaintiffs' poor performance.[2090]

Even if a prima facie case has not been established as to a prior alleged wrong, evidence regarding that wrong may be admitted to support a claim as to another alleged wrong.[2091]

§6.74 —Testimony by Individuals Other Than the Plaintiff Regarding the Plaintiff

A number of courts of appeals are in accord that the testimony of co-workers is admissible when it is introduced to buttress the plaintiff's claim that the alleged basis for the allegedly wrongful act—typically, poor performance—is not factually supportable.[2092] Of course, such testimony will not always be admissible, but it will be the particular factual matrix, rather than any general

---

[2089] Malarkey v Texaco, Inc, 983 F2d 1204, 1210 (2d Cir 1993).

[2090] *See, e.g.*, Colgan v Fisher Scientific Co, 935 F2d 1407, 1422 (3d Cir), *cert denied,* 112 S Ct 379 (1991); Conkwright v Westinghouse Elec Corp, 933 F2d 231, 234 n3 (4t Cir 1991); Brown v M&M Mars, Inc, 883 F2d 505, 509 (7th Cir 1989); Uffelman v Lone Star Steel Co, 863 F2d 404, 407 (5th Cir), *cert denied,* 490 US 1098 (1989); O'Donnell v Georgia Osteopathic Hosp, Inc, 748 F2d 1543 (11th Cir 1984); Sweat v Miller Brewing Co, 708 F2d 655, 657 (11th Cir 1983); Sorba v Pennsylvania Drilling Co, Inc, 648 F Supp 292 (WD Pa 1986), *revd on other grounds,* 821 F2d 200 (3d Cir 1987), *cert denied,* 484 US 1019 (1988).

[2091] Abrams v Lightolier, Inc, 702 F Supp 509, 511 (DNJ 1988).

[2092] *See* Colgan v Fisher Scientific Co, 935 F2d 1407, 1422 (3d Cir), *cert denied,* 112 S Ct 379 (1991); Conkwright v Westinghouse Elec Corp, 933 F2d 231, 234 n3 (4th Cir 1991); Brown v M&M/Mars, 883 F2d 505, 509 (7th Cir 1989); Uffelman v Lone Star Steel Co, 863 F2d 404, 407 (5th Cir), *cert denied,* 490 US 1098 (1989); O'Donnell v Georgia Osteopathic Hosp, Inc, 748 F2d 1543 (11th Cir 1984); Sweat v Miller Brewing Co, 708 F2d 655, 657 (11th Cir 1983).

exclusionary rule excluding such testimony, that will bar its introduction.

For example, while the Court of Appeals for the Sixth Circuit ruled in *Hill v Spiegel,*[2093] a jury case, that the trial court had erred in admitting testimony by a fellow employee as to the reasons for the plaintiff's discharge, it was the nature of the particular testimony in this particular case that led the court to that conclusion. *Hill* concerned the testimony of a former manager who had been employed under the plaintiff's supervision, and who testified regarding his conversations with several other Spiegel employees concerning Hill's termination. The essence of his testimony was that he had been told by three co-workers that Hill had been discharged because of age. The court examined the functions performed by these three individuals and concluded that none of them had any involvement in the discharge decision. Thus, there was no basis for finding that their statements concerned, to use the standard set forth in Federal Rule of Evidence 801(d)(2)(D), "a matter within the scope of [their] agency."[2094]

The court deciding *Meschino v International Telephone & Telegraph Corp*[2095] rejected the argument that the testimony of the plaintiff's superior regarding his conversations with his supervisor, at whose behest the superior had fired the plaintiffs, constituted inadmissible hearsay, since the out-of-court statements "would be offered to show the defendant's state of mind, . . . [see Federal Rule of Evidence 803(3)] and would be offered against a party. See . . . [Federal Rule of Evidence 801(d)(2)]."[2096]

A lay witness may be allowed to express his or her opinion as to the motivation or intent of the employer's officers in their dealings with the plaintiff if the witness bases his or her testi-

---

[2093] 708 F2d 233 (6th Cir 1983).

[2094] 708 F2d at 237; *accord* Eudy v BWD Automotive Corp, 51 FEP Cas (BNA) 724 (ND Ga 1988); Taylor v Battelle Columbus Labs, 680 F Supp 1165, 1171 (SD Ohio 1988) ("Statements by co-workers [regarding the reasons for termination] are . . . generally inadmissible hearsay because those individuals were not involved in the termination decision"). *But see* Drake v CBS, Inc, 49 FEP Cas (BNA) 72, 75 n1 (ND Ill 1989).

[2095] 563 F Supp 1066 (SDNY 1983).

[2096] 563 F Supp at 1072.

mony on his own experience with the employer.[2097] And the court deciding *Butler v Portland General Electric Co*[2098] admitted, at the summary judgment stage, testimony of "any witness about his or her general beliefs regarding the . . . [defendant's] actions or their perceived effects, both in regard to age discrimination and to the permanence of employment at . . . [the defendant employer]."[2099]

In deciding *Haddad v Lockheed California Corp*[2100] the Court of Appeals for the Ninth Circuit addressed a plaintiff's argument that testimony adduced by the defendant should not have been admitted. The testimony was that of the defendant's management personnel regarding third parties' complaints about working with the plaintiff. The court held that the testimony was not hearsay. "[I]t was not offered to prove the truth of the complaints. . . . Instead, [it] . . . was offered to show that Lockheed management had received complaints regarding Haddad . . . [and it] was relevant in demonstrating Lockheed's nondiscriminatory intent[.]"[2101] The en banc Court of Appeals for the Eighth Circuit, in deciding *Lee v Rapid City Area School District No 51-4*,[2102] rejected testimony recounting the complaints that had been leveled by parents and students against the plaintiff, a teacher whose contract had not been renewed. It did so because of the "extremely general information" that the defendant provided by way of an offer of proof.[2103] The court, however, emphasized that it had in other cases "admitted com-

---

[2097] Hansard v Pepsi-Cola Metro Bottling Co, 865 F2d 1461, 1466-67 (5th Cir), *cert denied*, 493 US 842 (1989) (affirmative view). *But see* Visser v Packer Engg Assocs, Inc, 924 F2d 655, 659-60 (7th Cir 1991) (en banc); Mitroff v Xomox Corp, 797 F2d 271, 275-76 (6th Cir 1986).

[2098] 748 F Supp 783 (D Or 1990), *affd without opinion sub nom* Flynn v Portland Gen Elec Co, 958 F2d 377 (9th Cir 1992).

[2099] *Id* 787.

[2100] 720 F2d 1454 (9th Cir 1983).

[2101] *Id* 1456.

[2102] 981 F2d 316 (8th Cir 1992) (en banc).

[2103] *Id* 321-22 n2.

plaints about an employee and . . . [had] held them to be determinative."[2104]

In assessing the significance of supervisors' statements, the courts commonly will assert that the views or comments of people not in the chain of command as to the complained-of decision are not relevant to establishing discriminatory animus. Thus, for example, in deciding *Fortino v Quasar*[2105] the Court of Appeals for the Seventh Circuit upheld the trial court's refusal to admit evidence of a comment made by a management level employee regarding the average age of the company's employees. In so doing, the court reasoned as follows:

> None of the plaintiffs was in the . . . [division headed by the manager who had made the comment in question]. Nor had . . . [the manager] any role in their discharge or, indeed, in that of any other employees. . . . In these circumstances his comment about the average age of employees . . . had no probative value and, being prejudicial, was inadmissible. . . . "[A]ctions and comments by employees not involved in a discharge decision cannot provide a basis for charging other employees with discrimination."[2106]

The *Fortino* court was willing to concede, however, that "[t]here may be cases where an employee who is outside the chain of decision nevertheless has valuable information bearing on the charge of discrimination."[2107] And, indeed, in deciding *Malarkey v Texaco, Inc,*[2108] the Court of Appeals for the Second Circuit ruled that the trial court had properly "admitted into evidence statements about . . . [the plaintiff] made by various supervisors and managers who were not the decisionmakers on the

---

2104 *Id.*

2105 950 F2d 389 (7th Cir 1991).

2106 *Id* 395 (quoting Jardien v Winston Network, Inc, 888 F2d 1151, 1155 (7th Cir 1989)); *see also* Normand v Research Inst of Am, Inc, 927 F2d 857, 864 n3 (5th Cir 1991).

2107 950 F2d at 396.

2108 983 F2d 1204 (2d Cir 1993).

positions she alleges she was discriminatorily denied."[2109] The court explained that "[t]hese statements were received because they showed the pervasive corporate hostility towards . . . [the plaintiff] and supported her claim that she did not receive a promotion due to her employer's retaliatory animus."[2110]

§6.75 —Evidence Regarding Agency and Arbitrator Determinations and Communications to and from Agencies

Agency Determinations

The question of whether the plaintiff is entitled to inform the jury that the Equal Employment Opportunity Commission (EEOC) has made an administrative determination regarding the existence or nonexistence of an apparent violation of the Age Discrimination in Employment Act (ADEA)[2111] has evoked conflicting answers. An affirmative answer regarding an EEOC formal determination of lack of culpability on the employer's part was asserted in *Smilan v United Airlines, Inc.*[2112] And an EEOC letter asserting the agency's belief that the ADEA had been violated was held to be admissible in *Strickland v American Can Co.*[2113] The Court of Appeals for the Ninth Circuit, in deciding *Gilchrist v Jim Slemons Imports, Inc,*[2114] expressed some uncertainty, ruling only that a trial court judge may, in his or her discretion, admit or exclude such a letter.[2115] Similarly, the district court deciding

---

2109 *Id* 1210.

2110 *Id.*

2111 29 USC §§621-634.

2112 796 F Supp 723, 729 n7 (EDNY 1992).

2113 575 F Supp 1111 (ND Ga 1983).

2114 803 F2d 1488 (9th Cir 1986).

2115 *Accord* Abrams v Lightolier, Inc, 702 F Supp 509 (DNJ 1988). In *Abrams* the court stated that it would instruct the jury not to deem the letter dispositive. *Id* 512.

Roche v City of Normandy[2116] took the position that the question of whether a letter may or may not be admissible will depend on the circumstances.

In *LaDolce v Bank Administration Institute*[2117] the court ruled that EEOC investigative findings are admissible, but went on to state that "[t]he decision to admit into evidence results of an agency's determination of an employment discrimination claim is discretionary."[2118] Likewise, in *Smith v MIT*[2119] the Court of Appeals for the First Circuit held that it is within the trial court's discretion whether to admit into evidence the EEOC's investigative files.

The Court of Appeals for the Fifth Circuit addressed the question of the admissibility of the EEOC investigative file in *Olitsky v Spencer Gifts, Inc* (*Olitsky I*).[2120] In ruling that the trial court had erred in allowing the file's admission, the court relied on §706(b)[2121] of Title VII of the Civil Rights Act of 1964.[2122] While it is true that §706(b) indeed bars the admission of such files in Title VII cases, that provision on its face has no relevance to ADEA cases. All the court offered by way of explanation for its reliance on the Title VII provision was that the party who normally would have been expected to object to the statutory provision's relevance had not done so. In a later ruling in the same litigation, *Olitsky II*,[2123] the appellate court claimed that it had not decided in the earlier decision whether §706(b) applied in the ADEA context, and it continued to refrain from doing so now.[2124] It then went on to hold that the district court in the post-*Olitsky I* trial had properly admitted a letter that was in the EEOC file,

---

2116 566 F Supp 37, 40-41 (ED Mo 1983).

2117 36 FEP Cas (BNA) 1820 (ND Ill 1984).

2118 *Id* 1821.

2119 877 F2d 1106 (1st Cir), *cert denied*, 493 US 965 (1989).

2120 842 F2d 123 (5th Cir), *cert denied*, 488 US 925 (1988).

2121 42 USC §2000e-5(b).

2122 *Id* §§2000e through 2000e-17.

2123 Olitsky v Spencer Gifts, Inc, 964 F2d 1471 (5th Cir 1992), *cert denied*, 113 S Ct 1253 (1993).

2124 *Id* 1477.

reasoning that the letter concerned purely factual material relevant to the merits of the plaintiff's claim, as opposed to its constituting inadmissible information concerning proposals and counter-proposals made during the course of conciliation efforts.

The Court of Appeals for the Second Circuit also addressed §706(b) in deciding *Binder v Long Island Lighting Co*,[2125] but a different analysis was employed, and a different result was reached. This result was subsequently echoed by the Court of Appeals for the Tenth Circuit in *Equal Employment Opportunity Commission v Gear Petroleum, Inc.*[2126] The *Binder* court asserted that §706(b) is not relevant to the ADEA, even analogically: "Congress enacted the ADEA in the wake of Title VII, and we believe that any omission in the text of the ADEA of a provision found in Title VII [i.e., §706(b),] is likely to reflect a deliberate decision on Congress' part."[2127] Moreover, the court saw no particular harm, and some good, in allowing the admission at trial of statements made by the employer to the EEOC during the course of the EEOC's investigation:

> Factual statements regarding past events are distinguishable from offers of compromise, and, if the principal objective of an EEOC proceeding is to ascertain what has occurred and, wherever possible, to resolve disputes without litigation, a rule that allows employers to give off-the-record accounts of relevant events will not necessarily advance that objective.[2128]

Thus, the court embraced "a rule allowing the admission in subsequent litigation of factual statements made during the course of EEOC proceedings."[2129] The court, however, chose not to express any "view as to whether . . . [it] would reach the same

---

2125 933 F2d 187 (2d Cir 1991).

2126 948 F2d 1542 (10th Cir 1991).

2127 933 F2d at 193.

2128 *Id.*

2129 *Id* 194.

conclusion had the statement [at issue here] been made during settlement negotiations between the parties."[2130] Here, it was only addressing the defendant's "written explanation of the reasons for and timing of the challenged decision."[2131]

The Court of Appeals for the Tenth Circuit ruled in *Hall v Western Production Co*[2132] that the decision whether to admit a report prepared by the state fair employment practices agency was within the discretion of the trial court, and it upheld the exclusion of the report. The trial court had refused to admit the report, in which the agency set forth its conclusion that the defendant was innocent of wrongdoing, because it determined that all the evidentiary matter before the state agency could be presented to the federal court jury and thus the only purpose that would be served by admitting the report "would be to suggest to the jury that it should reach the same conclusion"[2133] as had the state agency, thereby causing unfair prejudice to the plaintiff.[2134]

The court deciding *Conkwright v Westinghouse Electric Corp*[2135] held that the findings of fact of the state antidiscrimination agency were inadmissible.[2136] The court acknowledged that the admission of the findings was discretionary with the trial court; here, the exercise of that discretion was justified by the court's view that the agency's report was untrustworthy.[2137] Other case

---

2130 *Id* 194 n3.

2131 *Id.*

2132 988 F2d 1050 (10th Cir 1993).

2133 *Id* 1058.

2134 *See also* Kesselring v United Technologies Corp, 753 F Supp 1359 (SD Ohio 1991).

2135 739 F Supp 1006 (D Md 1990), *affd on other grounds,* 933 F2d 231 (4th Cir 1991).

2136 *Id* 1014; *accord* Lucas v Wheeler Mach Co, 53 FEP Cas (BNA) 1729 (D Utah 1989).

2137 739 F Supp at 1014-15 n7.

law supports motions to strike allegations in complaints addressing such state rulings.[2138]

Arbitrators' Determinations

Evidence as to the determination of an arbitrator arising out of a grievance made pursuant to a collective bargaining agreement is admissible.[2139]

§6.76 —Evidence Regarding Settlements and Termination Agreements

Evidence of compromises or settlements, or offers of such, generally are inadmissible in federal court trials. This bar extends so far as to even preclude evidence of an earlier settlement with an employee other than the plaintiff.[2140] Federal Rule of Evidence 408[2141] sets forth the contours of this evidentiary bar:

> Evidence of (1) furnishing or offering or promising to furnish, or (2) accepting or offering or promising to accept, a valuable consideration in compromising or attempting to compromise a claim which was disputed as to either validity or amount, is not admissible to prove liability for or invalidity of the claim or its amount. Evidence of conduct or statements made in compromise negotiations is likewise not admissible. This rule does not require the exclusion of any evidence otherwise discoverable merely because it is pre-

---

[2138] *See, e.g.,* Ledford v Rapid-Am Corp, 47 FEP Cas (BNA) 312, 313 (SDNY 1988); Coffin v South Carolina Dept of Social Servs, 562 F Supp 579, 590-91 (DSC 1983). *Cf* Mitchell v Bendix Corp, 603 F Supp 920, 922 (ND Ind 1985) (case arising under Title VII of the Civil Rights Act of 1964, 42 USC §§2000e through 2000e-17).

[2139] *See* Criswell v Western Airlines, Inc, 709 F2d 544 (9th Cir 1983), *affd on other grounds,* 472 US 400 (1985).

[2140] Massie v Indiana Gas Co, 752 F Supp 261, 267 (SD Ind 1990) (settlement of charge of discrimination filed with the Equal Employment Opportunity Commission); LaDolce v Bank Admin Inst, 36 FEP Cas (BNA) 1820 (ND Ill 1984); Scaramuzzo v Glenmore Distilleries Co, 501 F Supp 727, 733 (ND Ill 1980).

[2141] Fed R Evid 408.

> sented in the course of compromise negotiations. This rule also does not require exclusion when the evidence is offered for another purpose, such as proving bias or prejudice of a witness, negativing a contention of undue delay, or proving an effort to obstruct a criminal investigation or prosecution.

It is not always clear, of course, whether an offer was made in an effort to compromise a claim.[2142] In deciding *Pierce v FR Tripler & Co*[2143] the Court of Appeals for the Second Circuit, attempting to devise a rule useful in dealing with this ambiguity, set forth the following position:

> [W]here a party is represented by counsel, threatens litigation and has initiated the first administrative steps in that litigation, any offer made between attorneys will be presumed to be an offer within the scope of Rule 408. The party seeking admission of an offer under those circumstances must demonstrate convincingly that the offer was not an attempt to compromise the claim.[2144]

The typical situation involves an offeree's seeking to introduce evidence of an offer in order to thereby generate the inference that the defendant had, by making the offer, acknowledged its culpability. In contrast, it was the defendant in *Pierce* who sought to introduce evidence as to the offer of employment that had been made to the plaintiff. It sought thereby: (1) to show that the plaintiff, who had rejected the offer, had failed to adequately mitigate damages; and (2) to establish the defendant's state of mind. Despite the offeror's being the moving party, the court ruled that no matter who seeks to introduce evidence of offers, such evidence is inadmissible. As for the company's argument that evidence of the offer was admissible pursuant to the "another purpose" language of Rule 408, the purpose here being

---

2142 *See* Equal Employment Opportunity Commn v Gear Petroleum, Inc, 948 F2d 1542 (10th Cir 1991).

2143 955 F2d 820 (2d Cir 1992).

2144 *Id* 827.

to establish the defendant's state of mind, the court likewise ruled against the defendant, reasoning as follows:

> In a disparate treatment discrimination case the determinative question is whether, at the time of the adverse employment action, the defendant was motivated by impermissible factors. This is precisely the issue on which . . . [the defendant] seeks to introduce the evidence of the job offer. Such evidence on the merits of the case goes to "liability for or invalidity of the claim" and thus does not fall within the "other purpose" exception to excludability under Rule 408.[2145]

In *Gilchrist v Jim Slemons Imports, Inc,*[2146] the Court of Appeals for the Ninth Circuit also adverted to the question of admitting evidence of a settlement offer for "another purpose."

The Court of Appeals for the Tenth Circuit abjured devising any per se rule in deciding *Equal Employment Opportunity Commission v Gear Petroleum, Inc.*[2147] Rather, it reasoned that each case in which the question of whether a communication constituted an excludable offer must be decided on its own facts. The court rejected the argument that two letters in the EEOC file from the defendant's attorney should have been admitted because they impeached later testimony of company executives and so they were being offered for a purpose other than establishing the existence of an offer of settlement. In so doing, the court noted that " '[t]he clear import of the Conference Report [on Rule 408] as well as the general understanding among lawyers is that [inconsistent] conduct or statements [made in connection with compromise negotiations] may *not* be admitted for impeachment purposes.' "[2148]

[2145] *Id* 829. For further discussion of *Pierce,* see Kandel, *Is Evidence of Ford Motor Offers Admissible?*, 18 Employee Relations LJ 287 (1992).

[2146] 803 F2d 1488, 1501 (9th Cir 1986).

[2147] 948 F2d 1542 (10th Cir 1991).

[2148] *Id* 1545 (quoting M. Graham, Federal Rules of Evidence 116 (2d ed 1987)).

The court deciding *Hisaw v Unisys Corp*[2149] refused to acquiesce to the defendant's request to admit statements made by the individual plaintiff, whose suit had been consolidated with an action filed by the Equal Employment Opportunity Commission (EEOC). These statements had been made by Hisaw in the course of discussions with the defendant's attorney. The court reasoned that the statements made by Hisaw, whose settlement with the defendant had left the EEOC suit unresolved, "were made pursuant to settlement negotiations which may have heavily swayed . . . [him] to change his view of matters in order to improve the terms of his [settlement] agreement with Unisys."[2150] In addition, the court noted that the EEOC had not been present when the statements in question had been made.

In deciding *Cassino v Reichhold Chemicals, Inc,*[2151] the Court of Appeals for the Ninth Circuit drew a distinction between settlement agreements, or releases, on the one hand, and termination agreements, on the other. The former type of agreement arises in connection with the negotiation and settlement of a dispute involving an aggrieved individual who has asserted that he or she is the victim of illegal wrongdoing and who, by the agreement, relinquishes the right to a judicial determination of the legal claim in return for valuable consideration. Termination agreements, proposed and/or actual, come into the picture at a different juncture in the employee-employer relationship, according to the *Cassino* court's analysis: ". . . when an employment relationship is terminated and the employer offers a contemporaneous severance pay package in exchange for a release of all potential claims, including claims for discriminatory acts that may have occurred at or before the termination."[2152]

Termination agreements, the *Cassino* court observed, "are generally made a part of the record . . . and are considered rele-

---

2149 57 FEP Cas (BNA) 296 (WD La 1991).

2150 *Id* 299.

2151 817 F2d 1338 (9th Cir 1987), *cert denied,* 484 US 1047 (1988).

2152 817 F2d at 1342; *see also* Moore v McGraw Edison Co, 804 F2d 1026, 1029 (8th Cir 1986). As to such releases, or waivers of liability, generally, see **ch 5.**

vant to the circumstances surrounding the alleged discharge itself."[2153] In brief, such agreements are "probative on the issue of discrimination."[2154] The *Cassino* court justified this analysis on policy grounds, with the reasoning that the goal of Rule 408 is to encourage the compromise and settlement of existing disputes, and this end is not at issue if an employer tries to condition severance pay on the release of potential claims.

In deciding *Mundy v Household Finance Corp*[2155] another panel of the Court of Appeals for the Ninth Circuit, mindful of the earlier *Cassino* decision, ruled that while settlement offers made after termination are inadmissible, "[s]everance pay packages contingent upon a release of claims which are offered contemporaneously with the notice of termination are not covered by . . . [Rule 408] and are admissible evidence on the issue of discrimination."[2156]

Notwithstanding the *Cassino* and *Mundy* courts' conclusions that proposed termination agreements are admissible into evidence, the fact is that the introduction into evidence of such agreements indeed may have adverse consequences that rise to the level of a policy concern. Employers may be deterred from proposing such releases, or waivers of liability, since adverse inferences may be drawn by a jury regarding the employer's discriminatory intent. What is more, this potential effect of the *Cassino* ruling was exacerbated by the court's later treatment of the issue of liquidated damages. Willfulness on the part of the employer is a necessary predicate to the award of such damages.[2157] *Willfulness* has been defined as entailing knowledge or reckless disregard on the part of the defendant as to whether its action was prohibited by the ADEA.[2158] The *Cassino* court: (1) looked to the termination agreement before it; (2) observed that it specifically required Cassino to waive his right to sue in

---

[2153] 817 F2d at 1342.

[2154] *Id; accord* Madden v Independence Bank, 771 F Supp 1510 (CD Cal 1991).

[2155] 885 F2d 542 (9th Cir 1989).

[2156] *Id* 546.

[2157] See **ch 8.**

[2158] *Id.*

return for his receipt of severance pay; and (3) concluded that "[f]rom this evidence, the jury could infer that Reichhold knew or showed reckless disregard for whether firing Cassino violated the ADEA."[2159]

Given this negative use, from the employer's perspective, to which a termination agreement might be put by a plaintiff, there would seem to be considerable incentive for employers to forego proposing them. Of course, that tack will leave the employer without the shield that such an agreement would otherwise afford regarding later litigation by an employee. But given the downside aspects of such an agreement, a careful employer may deem that shield not worth the risk. This, in turn, can have a negative consequence for the employee: once the employer can no longer obtain the benefit of a waiver of claims, the likelihood of its offering a severance pay package is necessarily diminished, if not completely destroyed.

§6.77 —Evidence Regarding Damages and Other Issues

Inasmuch as damages for pain and suffering are not recoverable[2160] under the Age Discrimination in Employment Act (ADEA),[2161] testimony as to pain and suffering is inadmissible.[2162] However, if there is a pendent state claim for such damages, such testimony is admissible as long as no substantial injustice is done to the defendant.[2163] Moreover, such state claims aside, evidence

---

[2159] 817 F2d at 1348.

[2160] See **ch 8.**

[2161] 29 USC §§621-634.

[2162] *See, e.g.,* Haskell v Kaman Corp, 743 F2d 113 (2d Cir 1984); Hill v Speigel, Inc, 708 F2d 233, 236 (6th Cir 1983); Walker v Pettit Constr Co, 605 F2d 128, 131 (4th Cir 1979), *modified sub nom* Frith v Eastern Air Lines, Inc, 611 F2d 950 (4th Cir 1979).

[2163] *See* Guthrie v JC Penney Co, Inc, 803 F2d 202, 208-09 (5th Cir 1986); Merkel v Scovill, Inc, 573 F Supp 1055, 1065 (SD Ohio 1983), *affd in part & revd in part on other grounds,* 787 F2d 174 (6th Cir), *cert denied,* 479 US 990 (1986). *But see* Balmer v Community House Assn, 572 F Supp 1048 (ED Mich 1983). As to pendent, or supplemental, jurisdiction generally, see **§§6.40-.42.**

of emotional distress may be relevant to issues other than the question of damages.[2164]

Miscellaneous Issues

The question of admissibility of evidence regarding the performance of the discharged plaintiff's successor has generated a few rulings, not all in agreement.[2165]

While a memorandum merely constituting a study of changes in the ADEA could well be subject to being excluded,[2166] a memorandum going beyond this to include editorializing about the changes' adverse impacts on the employer can be properly admissible.[2167]

As discussed in **§6.08,** a grievant must file a charge of unlawful discrimination with the Equal Employment Opportunity Commission within 180 or 300 days of the alleged wrongful act or decision. It has been held, in response to a convoluted argument made by a defendant in support of a motion for summary judgment, that the plaintiff is not limited to pointing just to allegedly discriminatory actions that occurred within the 180- or 300-day period preceding the filing of the charge.[2168] Thus, the plaintiff in that case, who claimed that he was unlawfully demoted when younger colleagues in comparable situations were not, was not precluded from identifying instances of better treatment

---

[2164] *See* Taylor v Home Ins Co, 777 F2d 849 (4th Cir 1985), *cert denied,* 476 US 1142 (1986).

[2165] *See, e.g.,* Douglas v Anderson, 656 F2d 528 (9th Cir 1981); Bruno v WB Saunders Co, 48 FEP Cas (BNA) 1613, 1621 (ED Pa 1988), *affd on other grounds,* 882 F2d 760 (3d Cir 1989), *cert denied,* 493 US 1062 (1990); Durso v Wanamaker, 38 FEP Cas (BNA) 1127 (ED Pa 1985); Golletti v Arco/Polymers, Inc, 32 FEP Cas (BNA) 1796 (WD Pa 1983), *vacated & remanded without opinion,* 762 F2d 993 (3d Cir 1985).

[2166] *See* Linn v Andover Newton Theological Sch, Inc, 874 F2d 1, 4 (1st Cir 1989); Stanojev v Ebasco Servs, Inc, 643 F2d 914, 922 (2d Cir 1981).

[2167] Linn v Andover Newton Theological Sch, Inc, 874 F2d 1, 3-4 (1st Cir 1989).

[2168] Wood v Southern Tel & Tel Co, 725 F Supp 1244, 1250-51 (ND Ga 1989).

accorded younger employees that occurred either subsequent to the filing of his charge or more than 180 days prior to the filing.[2169]

2169 The plaintiff was in a jurisdiction where the 300-day filing period was not available, so the defendant focused on the 180-day period as setting the argued-for boundary line.

AGE DISCRIMINATION

SECOND EDITION

July 1995 Supplement to Volume 1
Current to May 23, 1995

Howard C. Eglit
Professor
Chicago-Kent College of Law
Illinois Institute of Technology

This supplement prepared by John F. Buckley
National Legal Research Group
Charlottsville, Virginia

SHEPARD'S/McGRAW-HILL, INC.
P.O. Box 35300
Colorado Springs, Colorado 80935-3530

July, 1995

New sections appearing in this supplement:

§6.54A —Effect of an EEOC Suit on a Representative Action

Age in American Society and in the American Workplace

1

§1.01 The Roles of Age in Structuring Society

Page 1-6, note 22, delete citation and substitute:

Ward v Hickey, 996 F2d 448, 453 (1st Cir 1993).

The Age Discrimination in Employment Act—Introduction

2

§2.04 Exclusivity of the ADEA as a Remedy for Age Discrimination in Employment

Page 2-20, add to text at end of carryover paragraph:

In *Mummelthie v City of Mason City*, 873 F Supp 1293 (ND Iowa 1995), the court held that the ADEA is not the exclusive federal remedy for age discrimination claims. If facts giving rise to an ADEA violation also give rise to an independent federal right secured by statute or the Constitution, a §1983 action may be based on such facts. An employee cannot use §1983, however, to redress violations based directly on the ADEA itself rather than an independent federal constitutional right; the ADEA is the exclusive remedy for claims based on a violation of its own provisions. If a plaintiff could base her age discrimination claim on due process and equal protection, then she could maintain her claim under §1983.

The Age Discrimination in Employment Act—Who is Protected and Which Entities Must Comply with Its Requirements

3

§3.06 —Independent Contractors

Page 3-28, add to note 129:

McFadden-Peel v Staten Island Cable, 873 F Supp 757 (EDNY 1994) (independent contractor status is determined by reference to common law agency principles; although the plaintiff was not paid a salary and no taxes were paid on her behalf, the court found the quality of the plaintiff's responsibilities to be determinative; the plaintiff's five years of service, the plaintiff's oversight responsibility for several of the employer's departments, and the employer's right to control the means and manner of her work were highlighted by the court).

§3.13 —Determining the $44,000 Minimum Retirement Benefit

Page 3-66, add to note 330:

Morrissey v Boston Five Ctrs Sav Bank, 866 F Supp 643 (D Mass 1994) (holding that bank employee fit within the ADEA's exemption from the ban on mandatory age-based retirement for high policy makers who are entitled to a nonforfeitable pension of $44,000, even though one day before the employee's scheduled retirement, the bank transformed several thousands of dollars of the employee's forfeitable pension to nonforfeitable status in order to satisfy the $44,000 threshold).

§3.20 State and Local Governments

Page 3-96, add to note 492:

affd, 29 F3d 564 (10th Cir 1994).

Page 3-97, add after first sentence in first full paragraph:

The doctrine has also been applied in the district courts. *See, e.g., Burtnick v McLean*, 874 F Supp 698 (D Md 1995) (mayor and city council enjoy legislative immunity from ADEA claim arising out of elimination of plaintiff's position under a budget ordinance).

Page 3-100, add to text of carryover paragraph:

The Second Circuit held, in *Johnson v New York*, 49 F3d 75 (2d Cir 1995), that there was a violation of the ADEA where the state terminated a civilian air base security guard at age 60 because he could not fulfill the job condition of membership in the Air National Guard, which mandates retirement at age 60. The court noted that the Air National Guard was not subject to the ADEA but the state was, and its age-based firing of the employee was a violation of the Act.

§3.22 Religious Institutions

Page 3-107, add to text following last full paragraph:

The Court of Appeals for the Eighth Circuit, in *Weissman v Congregation of Shaare Emeth*, 38 F3d 1038, 1044 (8th Cir 1994), followed the decisions of the Second and Third Circuits, adopting a case-by-case approach where a lay employee accuses his religious employer of age discrimination. The court recognized that there may be cases involving lay employees in which the relationship between the employee and the employer is so pervasively religious that any age discrimination inquiry runs the risk of offending the First Amendment. However, due to the minimal intrusion of the ADEA and the limited scope of the inquiry, the court held that the determination of whether the ADEA poses a significant risk of infringement upon the First Amendment must be determined on a case-by-case basis.

If the employee is not a member of the clergy, and if none of the reasons asserted by the religious employer for the adverse employment action rests on religious grounds, the application of the ADEA to a religious employer is not, as a matter of law, sufficient to pose a significant risk of infringement upon the First Amendment.

The employee's position in *Weissman* had some religious components: he was required to have a positive attitude toward Judaism, a Jewish background, and knowledge about the Temple. The overwhelming majority of his responsibilities were secular, however. Moreover, the religious employer did not assert any of the religious duties or other religious reasons for the employee's termination. A general dissatisfaction with his performance cannot be said to be a religious reason for his termination. Accordingly, the ADEA could be applied without the risk of infringing First Amendment rights.

§3.27 Agents of the Employer

Page 3-120, add to text after first full paragraph:

Note also that in *EEOC v Watergate at Landmark Condominium*, 24 F3d 635 (4th Cir 1994), the Court of Appeals for the Fourth Circuit determined that a volunteer may be considered an agent of the employer. The court allowed testimony that two volunteer members of a condominium recreation committee were heard to make remarks concerning the age of the tennis club manager as a factor in her continued employment. The statements were nonhearsay admissions of a party-opponent, and although classified as volunteers, the two persons were nonetheless agents of the employer for purposes of the employee's ADEA claim.

Page 3-122, add to note 647 after Kauffman citation:

affd, 21 F3d 428 (6th Cir 1994) (table).

Page 3-128, add to text following first block quotation:

In *Birbeck v Marvel Lightening Corp*, 30 F3d 507 (4th Cir 1994), the Court of Appeals for the Fourth Circuit also rejected the idea of individual liability for agents of an employer. The court held that an employer's vice president is not a proper defendant under the ADEA, although the statute defined the term *employer* as the employer's *agent*. The word "agent" serves the function of imposing respondeat superior liability on the employer for a supervisor's conduct, not imposing individual liability. This holding rejected a decision by the Federal District Court for the Middle District of North Carolina to the contrary. *House v Cannon Mills, Inc*, 713 F Supp 159 (MDNC 1988).

Page 3-129, add to note 673:

Matthews v Rollins Hudig Hall Co, 874 F Supp 192 (ND Ill 1995) (supervisors may be individually and personally liable under the ADEA, as reflected in the interpretation of other anti-discrimination statutes, such as Title VII, and in the ADEA's incorporation of *agent* in the definition of employer); Hamilton v New York State Dept of Mental Hygiene, 876 F Supp 470 (WDNY 1994) (persons responsible for making and/or contributing to employment decisions for defendant employer may be liable as its agents). Note that House v Cannon Mills, 713 F Supp 159 (MDNC 1988), was overruled by Birbeck v Marvel Lightening Corp, 30 F3d 507 (4th Cir 1994).

The Age Discrimination in Employment Act—Prohibitions and Requirements

4

§4.06 —Transfers and Refusals to Transfer

Page 4-21, add to note 93:

affd, 21 F3d 428 (6th Cir 1994) (table).

Page 4-22, add to note 96:

affd, 25 F3d 635 (8th Cir 1994).

§4.07 —Practices Involving Promotions

Page 4-26, add to note 116:

affd, 21 F3d 428 (6th Cir 1994) (table).

§4.14 Preferences for Older Individuals by Covered Entities

Page 4-52, add to note 252:

affd, 20 F3d 1174 (11th Cir 1994) (table).

§4.18 —Protected Conduct: Opposition

Page 4-69, add to note 345:

affd, 21 F3d 428 (6th Cir 1994) (table).

The Age Discrimination in Employment Act—Statutory Affirmative Defenses, Regulatory Exemptions, and Waivers of Liability

5

§5.47 Severance Pay and the §4(1)(2) Affirmative Defense

Page 5-205, add to text following first full paragraph:

In *McCambridge v Bethlehem Steel Corp*, 873 F Supp 919 (ED Pa 1994), the court held that it does not matter whether or not the employee actually enrolls in the plan or receives the health benefits offered. The employer may reduce severance payments by the value of retiree health benefits so long as the employee is eligible to receive those benefits.

§5.61 The Foreign Laws Defense

Page 5-276, add to text in last paragraph after second sentence:

The district court's decision in *Mahoney v RFE/RLE, Inc*, 818 F Supp 1 (DDC 1992), discussed on pages 5-276 through 5-279, was reversed by the Court of Appeals for the District of Columbia. *Mahoney v RFE/RLE, Inc*, 47 F3d 447 (DC Cir 1995). The material in the text discussing the district court's decision should therefore be consulted for the background of the case only.

The court of appeals in *Mahoney* held that the district court's reasoning was in conflict with the Supreme Court's decision in *Norfolk & Western Railway v American Train Dispatcher's Assn*, 499 US 117 (1991). In *Norfolk & Western*, the Supreme Court held that a rail carrier's exemption from all other laws under 49 USC §11341(a) included a "carrier's legal obligations under a collective-bargaining agreement," 499 US at 127, and that a contract is without "legal force apart from the law that acknowledges its binding character." *Id* 130.

Explaining the import of the Supreme Court's ruling, the court of appeals stated as follows:

> The point of Norfolk & Western is that when a company fails to comply with a labor contract it violates "law," which is why the statutory exemption from "law" relieved carriers of their contractual obligations. Section 623(f)(1) of the Age Discrimination in Employment Act is indistinguishable. If RFE/RL had not complied with the collective bargaining agreement in this case; if it had retained plaintiffs despite the mandatory

> retirement provision, the company would have violated the German laws standing behind such contracts, as well as the decisions of the Munich Labor Court.

Mahoney v RFE/RL, Inc, 47 F3d at 449-50.

The court of appeals recognized that such an issue would never arise for a domestic employer because of the Supremacy Clause of the Constitution, but that for an overseas employer, the laws of the foreign country cannot, of course, be set aside by congressional legislation. *Id* 450.

The court dismissed the plaintiffs' argument that RFE/RL could have bargained harder for a change in the labor contract. Such agreements, the court noted, are common throughout the Federal Republic of Germany. Moreover, the court pointed to the fact that the company entered into the agreement prior to the extension of the ADEA, and that the plaintiffs could not argue that RFE/RL entered into the agreement in order to evade the ADEA. *Id* 451.

§5.75 The Binding Force of Invalid Releases

Page 5-338, delete citation in note 1567 and substitute:

11 F3d 534 (5th Cir 1993).

Enforcement of the Age Discrimination in Employment Act in the Nonfederal Sector

6

§6.05 Pursuing in Court Claims Additional to Those Set Forth in the Charge

Page 6-19, add to note 90:

Minetos v City Univ of NY, 875 F Supp 1046 (SDNY 1995) (under the "loose pleading" exception, claims not alleged in the EEOC charge will not be dismissed where the claims are sufficiently related to the allegations in the charge that it would be unfair to bar such a claim in a civil action; plaintiff's 12-page statement accompanying her charge that employer labeled her "too old for the job" should have sufficiently alerted the EEOC investigator to her age discrimination claim).

§6.17 —Equitable Tolling and Equitable Estoppel Applied to Charge-Filing: Generally

Page 6-98, add to note 472:

Anderson v Unisys Corp, 47 F3d 302 (8th Cir 1995) (300-day deadline for filing charge with the EEOC would be tolled for employee who was not assisted by counsel, and was misled by letter from Minnesota Department of Human Rights stating that Minnesota law imposed a one-year statute of limitations and that the state agency would assist with filing a claim with the EEOC).

§6.21 —Relation of Government Agency's Conduct to Flaws in Charge-Filing

Page 6-131, add to note 629:

Anderson v Unisys Corp, 47 F3d 302 (8th Cir 1995) (300-day deadline for filing charge with the EEOC would be tolled for employee who was not assisted by counsel, and was misled by letter from Minnesota Department of Human Rights stating that Minnesota law imposed a one-year statute of limitations and that the state agency would assist with filing a claim with the EEOC).

§6.30 Statute of Limitations for Filing Suit: Generally

Page 6-184, add to text at end of first carryover paragraph:

In *McCray v Corry Manufacturing Co*, 872 F Supp 209 (WD Pa 1994), the court held that the plain language of §626(e) specifies that a plaintiff's action is untimely unless filed within 90 days after receipt of notice from the EEOC that it has dismissed the charge or otherwise completed its consideration of the matter. The court stated that the 90-day requirement is mandatory, not permissive, and that the two-year statute of limitations incorporated into former §626(e)(1) did not survive the 1991 amendments.

Page 6-186, add to text following second full paragraph:

The Second Circuit Court of Appeals in *Vernon v Cassadaga Valley Central School District*, 49 F3d 886 (2d Cir 1995), agreed with the decisions cited in the text which held that the limitations change would apply retroactively. The court held that the requirement that the plaintiff file suit within 90 days after receipt of an EEOC right-to-sue letter is a "procedural rule" that applies to suits filed after its effective date, even though the underlying conduct preceded its effective date.

§6.31 —When a Cause of Action Accrues

Page 6-189, add to note 903:

See also Grady v Bunzl Packaging Supply Co, 874 F Supp 387 (ND Ga 1994) (Civil Rights Act of 1991 imposes 90-day time-to-sue limitation, which begins as soon as claimant receives notice that EEOC has dismissed or terminated administrative proceedings).

§6.33 —Tolling the Statute of Limitations

Page 6-201, add to note 967:

Sperling v Hoffman-La Rouche, Inc, 145 FRD 357 (DNJ 1992), *affd*, 24 F3d 463 (3d Cir 1994).

Page 6-202, add to text at end of carryover paragraph:

The Court of Appeals for the Eighth Circuit has held that employees who failed to file within 90 days of receiving right-to-sue letters from the EEOC were precluded from later joining a fellow employee's suit that was timely filed. *Anderson v Unisys Corp*, 47 F3d 302 (8th Cir 1995). The court found that *American Pipe & Construction Co v Utah*, 414 US 538 (1974), was not applicable because the 90-day statute of limitations had run before the principal plaintiff had attempted to amend the complaint to include other employees. 47 F3d at 308. The employer, therefore, did not know it was facing multiple litigants until after the statute of limitations had run. *Id.* The court went on to hold that employees who never filed an administrative charge, and thus never received a right-to-sue letter, may "piggyback" on a timely filed claim of a fellow employee. Once the employee files separate administrative charges, however, they must timely file a suit following receipt of the 90-day letter. *Id* 308-09.

Page 6-203, add to text at end of carryover paragraph:

Similarly, the 90-day statute of limitations is not tolled by filing a request for reconsideration of the EEOC decision. *McCray v Corry Manufacturing Co,* 872 F Supp 209 (WD Pa 1994).

§6.39 Federal and State Court Jurisdiction; Removal; Venue

Page 6-245, add to note 1219:

Warner v Ford Motor Co, 46 F3d 531 (6th Cir 1995) (a state law age discrimination claim challenging the validity of an early retirement agreement is not removable under 28 USC §1441, pursuant to the "complete preemption" exception to the well-pleaded complaint rule, even though ultimately the claim may be preempted by ERISA because it relates to a pension plan).

§6.50 —Determination of Those Similarly Situated

Page 6-308, add to note 1543:

Cf Flavel v Svedala Indus, Inc, 875 F Supp 550 (ED Wis 1994) (if employers were found at either summary judgment phase or in liability phase of trial not to have engaged in a pattern or practice of age discrimination, then the linchpin of the plaintiffs' claim that they were "similarly situated" as a single group would disappear and the plaintiffs would be required to pursue individual actions with separate juries, despite EEOC's remaining representative action).

§6.54A —Effect of an EEOC Suit on a Representative Action (New)

When a court is considering a representative action, it is less clear which claims will be cut off by an EEOC suit. This question was addressed by a district court in *Wilkerson v Martin Marietta Corp,* 875 F Supp 1456, 1462-64 (D Colo

1995). The court's task was complicated by the EEOC's filing suit while the determination of collective status was still pending.

In this case, a group of plaintiffs filed a motion to proceed collectively, months before the EEOC filed its own action. During the pendency of the decision to grant the collective action, many other employees filed notices of intent to opt-in. The court recognized that pursuant to 29 USC §626(c), the right of any person to bring a civil action terminates upon the commencement of an action by the EEOC to enforce the rights of such employee under the ADEA. 875 F Supp at 1463. The question for the court, then, was which of the opt-in candidates could be included in the collective action?

The court followed the majority of other courts that have narrowly construed the term *to bring* in §626(c) "to mean 'to commence,' and not a broader construction which might mean 'to commence or maintain.' " *Id* (citing *EEOC v Eastern Airlines*, 736 F2d 635, 639 (11th Cir 1984), and citing *Burns v Equitable Life Assurance Society*, 696 F2d 21 (2d Cir 1982), *cert denied*, 464 US 933, 104 S Ct 336 (1983)). Given this construction, the court held that the filing of an opt-in notice after a representative action is filed, but before the EEOC files an enforcement action, is permissible and appropriate. *Wilkerson v Martin Marietta Corp*, 875 F Supp at 1463-64. With regard to any opt-in plaintiffs who file after the date on which the EEOC files its complaint, the §626(c) cutoff provision would apply, and these late plaintiffs would be prevented from joining the representative action. *Id* 1464.

The employer argued that as to the plaintiffs who filed opt-in notices before the court ruled to approve the action to proceed as a representative action, the opt-in notice would be a legal nullity. *Id* 1463. The court disagreed, stating that it would be inappropriate to penalize the opt-in plaintiffs because the court did not rule on representative status prior to the EEOC filing, and, further, the defendant could assert no prejudice comparable to the opt-in plaintiffs' forfeiture. *Id* 1463-64. *See also Flavel v Svedala Industries, Inc*, 875 F Supp 550 (ED Wis 1994) (assuming that statutory authority on behalf of the EEOC to bring suit on behalf of aggrieved parties preempts class action procedure and joinder requirements of permissive joinder rule, EEOC may proceed in ADEA matter on behalf of plaintiffs whether or not they are similarly situated, common questions of law or fact predominate, or claims arise out of the same action or occurrence).

§6.55 Intervention by the EEOC in Private Suits

Page 6-326, add to note 1640:

EEOC v G-K-G, Inc, 39 F3d 740 (7th Cir 1994) (the EEOC has an unequivocal right to bring a suit against an employer to enforce the ADEA, and the previous filing of a substantially identical suit by the individual employee does not diminish the agency's clear statutory right to sue).

§6.59 The Statute of Limitations for EEOC Suits

Page 6-348, add at text following first paragraph:

Many of these points were raised in *Wilkerson v Martin Marietta Corp*, 875 F Supp 1456, 1459-60 (D Colo 1995), in which the court held that there is no applicable statute of limitations in age discrimination claims brought by the EEOC. The court cited legislative history indicating the existence of pervasive problems which the EEOC experienced in both processing and prosecuting age discrimination claims. In disagreeing with the logic of the *McConnell* court, the court noted that it refused to read the silence in the 1991 Civil Rights Act as an indication that Congress intended to substantially alter the status quo for EEOC limitations purposes. 875 F Supp at 1460.

§6.69 Discovery

Page 6-402, text, add at end of section:

In *Sempier v Johnson & Higgins*, 45 F3d 724 (3d Cir 1995), the court of appeals ruled that the federal district court abused its discretion in directing an employer in an ADEA suit to answer a "bill of particulars" instead of compelling answers to interrogatories or using other proper means under the Federal Rules of Civil Procedure.